Frommer's®

Northern Italy
with Venice, Milan & the Lakes

6th Edition

by Eric Sylvers

WILEY

John Wiley & Sons, Inc.

Published by:
John Wiley & Sons, Inc.
111 River St.
Hoboken, NJ 07030-5774

ISBN 978-1-118-07468-8 (paper); ISBN 978-1-118-26139-2 (ebk); ISBN 978-1-118-22255-3 (ebk); ISBN 978-1-118-23647-5 (ebk)

Editors: Emil J. Ross with Billy Fox
Production Editor: Heather Wilcox
Cartographer: Elizabeth Puhl
Photo Editor: Cherie Cincilla
Cover Photo Editor: Richard Fox

Design and Layout by Vertigo Design NYC

Graphics and Prepress by Wiley Indianapolis Composition Services
Front cover photo: Lago di Braies, in South Tyrol, with a view of the Dolomites ©Imagebroker / Alamy Images
Back cover photos: *Left:* The canals of Camogli, in Liguria ©Joana Kruse / Alamy Images; *Middle:* Venice's Campanile bell tower flanked by the Column of San Teodoro, in the Piazza San Marco ©Paul Seheult / Eye Ubiquitous / Alamy Images; *Right:* Venetian glass bottles ©Cosmo Condina Western Europe / Alamy Images

CONTENTS

LIST OF MAPS

ABOUT THE AUTHOR

Eric Sylvers has worked as a journalist and writer for more than a decade in Italy, where he has written about everything from the country's economic woes to bike racing. The California native, outdoor enthusiast, and avid biker has traveled up and down the peninsula many times, including once on foot from the Swiss border to the far southeastern coast (the heel of the boot). *Northern Italy with Venice, Milan & the Lakes* is his first Frommer's guide. Eric blogs about Italian food, wine, and culture at www.foodieinitaly.com.

HOW TO CONTACT US

In researching this book, we discovered many wonderful places—hotels, restaurants, shops, and more. We're sure you'll find others. Please tell us about them, so we can share the information with your fellow travelers in upcoming editions. If you were disappointed with a recommendation, we'd love to know that, too. Please write to:

Frommer's Northern Italy, 6th Edition
John Wiley & Sons, Inc. • 111 River St. • Hoboken, NJ 07030-5774
frommersfeedback@wiley.com

ADVISORY & DISCLAIMER

Travel information can change quickly and unexpectedly, and we strongly advise you to confirm important details locally before traveling, including information on visas, health and safety, traffic and transport, accommodations, shopping, and eating out. We also encourage you to stay alert while traveling and to remain aware of your surroundings. Avoid civil disturbances, and keep a close eye on cameras, purses, wallets, and other valuables.

While we have endeavored to ensure that the information contained within this guide is accurate and up-to-date at the time of publication, we make no representations or warranties with respect to the accuracy or completeness of the contents of this work and specifically disclaim all warranties, including without limitation warranties of fitness for a particular purpose. We accept no responsibility or liability for any inaccuracy or errors or omissions, or for any inconvenience, loss, damage, costs, or expenses of any nature whatsoever incurred or suffered by anyone as a result of any advice or information contained in this guide.

The inclusion of a company, organization, or website in this guide as a service provider and/or potential source of further information does not mean that we endorse them or the information they provide. Be aware that information provided through some websites may be unreliable and can change without notice. Neither the publisher nor author shall be liable for any damages arising herefrom.

FROMMER'S STAR RATINGS, ICONS & ABBREVIATIONS

Every hotel, restaurant, and attraction listing in this guide has been ranked for quality, value, service, amenities, and special features using a star-rating system. In country, state, and regional guides, we also rate towns and regions to help you narrow down your choices and budget your time accordingly. Hotels and restaurants are rated on a scale of zero (recommended) to three stars (exceptional). Attractions, shopping, nightlife, towns, and regions are rated according to the following scale: zero stars (recommended), one star (highly recommended), two stars (very highly recommended), and three stars (must-see).

In addition to the star-rating system, we also use seven feature icons that point you to the great deals, in-the-know advice, and unique experiences that separate travelers from tourists. Throughout the book, look for:

special finds—those places only insiders know about

fun facts—details that make travelers more informed and their trips more fun

kids—best bets for kids and advice for the whole family

special moments—those experiences that memories are made of

overrated—places or experiences not worth your time or money

insider tips—great ways to save time and money

great values—where to get the best deals

The following abbreviations are used for credit cards:

AE	American Express	**DISC**	Discover	**V**	Visa
DC	Diners Club	**MC**	MasterCard		

TRAVEL RESOURCES AT FROMMERS.COM

Frommer's travel resources don't end with this guide. Frommer's website, **www.frommers.com,** has travel information on more than 4,000 destinations. We update features regularly, giving you access to the most current trip-planning information and the best airfare, lodging, and car-rental bargains. You can also listen to podcasts, connect with other Frommers.com members through our active-reader forums, share your travel photos, read blogs from guidebook editors and fellow travelers, and much more.

THE BEST OF NORTHERN ITALY

Northern Italy's riches are vast, varied, and yours to discover, from art-packed museums and mosaic-filled cathedrals to Roman ruins and hill towns amid vineyards that produce some of Europe's best wines. You can dine at refined restaurants that casually flaunt their Michelin star ratings, or chow down with the town priest and police chief at osterie (small local eateries) that have spent generations perfecting traditional recipes. You can spend the night in a sumptuous Renaissance villa on Lake Como in the Alpine foothills where Napoleon once stayed, or in a converted 17th-century Venetian palazzo where your room opens directly onto the Grand Canal. Here's a short list of the best of what northern Italy has to offer.

THE best TRAVEL EXPERIENCES

o **Taking a Gondola Ride in Venice:** Yes, it looks hokey. Yes, it's way overpriced. But when it comes down to it, there's nothing quite so romantic after a long Venetian dinner as a ride on one of these long black skiffs. Settle back into the plush seats with that special someone and a bottle of wine, and slide through the waters of Venice's back canals guided by the expert oar of a gondolier. See p. 100.

o **Spending a Day Among the Islands of the Venetian Lagoon:** Venice's ferry system extends outside the city proper to a series of other inhabited islands in the lagoon. First stop, Murano, a village where the famed local glass-blowing industry began and where its largest factories and best artisans still reside. Not only can you tour a glass factory (complete with a hard sell in the display room at the end), but you'll discover a pair of lovely churches, one hung with paintings by Giovanni Bellini, Veronese, and Tintoretto, the other a Byzantine-Romanesque masterpiece of decoration. The isle of Burano is a colorful fishing village with an ancient lace-making tradition and houses painted a variety of

The multicolored village of Murano; PREVIOUS PAGE: The romantic, narrow alleyways of Bellagio.

The grounds of the palatial Villa Pisani.

supersaturated hues. Nearby, lonely Torcello may have been one of the first lagoon islands settled, but it's long been almost abandoned, home to a straggly vineyard, reed-banked canals, the fine Cipriani restaurant, and a stunning Byzantine cathedral swathed in mosaics (see "The Best Churches," below). Time it right, and you'll be riding the last ferry back from Torcello into Venice proper as the sun sets and lights up the lagoon waters. See p. 175.

○ **Cruising the Brenta Canal:** The lazy Brenta Canal, lacing its way into Veneto from Venice's lagoon, has long been the Hamptons of Venice, where the city's nobility and merchant princes have kept summer villas. From the massive, palatial Villa Pisani, with its elaborate gardens, to the Villa Foscari, designed by Palladio himself, most of these villas span the 16th to 19th centuries and are open to visitors. In the past few years, a few have even been opened as elegant hotels. There are two ways to tour the Brenta: on a leisurely full-day cruise between Padua and Venice, stopping to tour several villas along the way with an optional fish lunch; or by driving yourself along the banks, which allows you to pop into the villas you are most interested in—plus you can pull over at any grassy embankment for a picnic lunch on the canal. See p. 192.

○ **Driving the Great Dolomite Road:** From the Adige Valley outside Bolzano (Bozen in German) across to the ski resort of Cortina d'Ampezzo runs 110km (68 miles) of twisting, winding, switch-backed highway, called the Great Dolomite Road, which wends its way around some of the most dramatic mountain scenery in Italy. The Dolomites are craggier and sheerer than the rest of the Alps, and as this road crawls around the peaks and climbs over the passes, one breathtaking panorama after another opens before you, undulating to the distant Po plains to the south and the mighty Swiss Alps to the north. See p. 258.

○ **Riding the Cable Cars over Mont Blanc:** There are not many more dramatic trips in Europe than this one, where a series of cable cars and gondolas rise from Courmayeur in Valle d'Aosta to the 3,300m (10,800-ft.) Punta Helbronner, from which the icy vistas spread over Mont Blanc's flank in one direction and across to Monte Cervino (the Matterhorn) in the other. It is here that the true thrill ride begins as you clamber into a four-seat enclosed gondola that dangles from a trio of stout cables some 2.4km (1½miles) above the deep fissures of the Vallée Blanche glacier. It takes half an hour to cross to Aiguille du

Midi on French soil—the longest cable car ride in the world not supported by pylons. From here, you can take a jaunt down into France's charming resort town Chamonix, or turn around to head back into Italian territory, perhaps stopping at the Alpine Garden two-thirds of the way back to Courmayeur to sun yourself and admire the wildflowers. See p. 405.

o **Hiking the Cinque Terre:** At the southern end of the Italian Riviera lies a string of former pirate coves called the Cinque Terre. These five fishing villages are linked by a train line and a meandering trail

Courmayeur's cable car.

that clambers over headlands, plunges amid olive groves and vineyards, and skirts cliff edges above the glittering Ligurian Sea and hidden scraps of beach. Though tourists have discovered this magical corner of Italy, there are as yet no big resort hotels or overdevelopment, just *trattorie* on the tiny harbors and houses and apartments converted into small family hotels and short-term rental units. It takes a full, long day to hike from one end to the other, or you can simply walk the stretches you prefer (conveniently, the trails get progressively easier from north to south) and use the train to connect to the other towns. Pause as you like in the *osterie* and bars of each town to sample the dry Cinque Terre white wine and refresh yourself for the next stretch. See p. 446.

o **A Day on Lake Como:** Sure, you wish you had a week to explore every nook of Lake Como, but the reality is that all you can manage is a day trip from Milan. No worries—you can still visit three of the most beautiful spots on the lake and have a memorable day that just might be one of the highlights of your trip to northern Italy. See p. 349.

THE best MUSEUMS

o **Galleria dell'Accademia** (Venice): Founded in 1750 and gorgeously installed in a trio of Renaissance buildings by Napoleon in 1807, this is the most important gallery of Venetian painting and one of Italy's top museums. (Napoleon swelled the collections with altarpieces confiscated from churches and monasteries he suppressed.) The works, spanning the 13th through 18th centuries, include masterpieces by all the local northern Italian greats—the Bellini clan, Paolo Veneziano, Carpaccio, Giorgione, Mantegna, Piero della Francesca, Lorenzo Lotto, Palma il Vecchio, Paolo Veronese, Titian, Tintoretto, Tiepolo, and Canaletto. See p. 150.

o **Collezione Peggy Guggenheim** (Venice): The Guggenheim family was among the 20th century's greatest art patrons. Peggy followed the family tradition, amassing a stunning collection of modern art, but she went a step further by marrying the painter Max Ernst. Her half-finished 18th-century *palazzo* on the Grand Canal is now installed with her collections, including works by Picasso, Pollock (an artist Peggy "discovered"), Magritte, Dalí, Miró, Brancusi, Kandinsky, and Marini. See p. 149.

o **South Tyrol Museum of Archaeology** (Bolzano): Bolzano's major sight is a high-tech, modern museum crafted around one of the most important archaeological finds of the

Dan Graham's *Triangular Solid with Circular Inserts,* at the Collezione Peggy Guggenheim.

past 50 years. When hikers first discovered the body of Ötzi high in the Alps at the Austrian border, everyone thought he was a mountaineer who had succumbed to the elements. He turned out to be a 5,300-year-old hunter whose body, clothing, and tools had been preserved intact by the ice in which he was frozen. The Ice Man has done more to give us glimpses into daily life in the Stone Age than any other find, and the museum excels at relaying all that scientists are continually learning from him. See p. 243.

o **Pinacoteca di Brera** (Milan): One of Italy's finest collections of art, from medieval to modern, is housed in a 17th-century Milanese *palazzo.* While Venice's Accademia has a richer collection of Venetian art, the Brera has a broader collection of masterpieces from across northern and central Italy. As with the Accademia, the Brera started as a warehouse for artworks Napoleon looted from churches, monasteries, and private collections. There are masterpieces from Mantegna, Raphael, Piero della Francesca, the Bellinis,

The colonnaded *palazzo* of the Pinacoteca di Brera.

5

Signorelli, Titian, Tintoretto, Reni, Caravaggio, Tiepolo, and Canaletto. See p. 297.

o **Museo Egizio & Galleria Sabauda** (Turin): The world's first real museum of Egyptian artifacts remains one of the most important outside Cairo and London's British Museum. The history between Italy and Egypt dates back to Julius Caesar and Cleopatra, though this collection of 30,000 pieces was largely amassed by the Piedmont Savoy kings. The exhibits range

Neatly stacked sarcophagi at Turin's Museo Egizio.

from a papyrus *Book of the Dead* to a full 15th-century-B.C. temple to fascinating objects from everyday life. But Egypt isn't all; upstairs the Galleria Sabauda displays the Savoys' amazing collection of Flemish and Dutch paintings by Van Dyck, van Eyck, Rembrandt, Hans Memling, and Van der Weyden. See p. 377.

THE best CHURCHES

o **Basilica di San Marco** (Venice): No church in Europe is more lavishly decorated, more exquisitely mosaic-covered, more glittering with gold than Venice's San Marco. Built in the 11th century, the church has as its guiding architectural and decorative principles Byzantine style, but more than 7 centuries of expansion and decoration have left behind Romanesque and Gothic touches as well. The interior is encrusted with more than 3,700 sq. m (40,000 sq. ft.) of gold-backed mosaics crafted between the 12th and 17th centuries, some based on cartoons by Tintoretto, Veronese, and Titian. The uneven floor is a mosaic of marble chips in swirling patterns, and the Pala d'Oro altarpiece a gem-studded golden trophy from Constantinople. Stairs lead up to a view over the piazza from atop the atrium, where visitors get to see up close both the mosaics and the original *Triumphal Quadriga,* four massive bronze horses probably cast in the 2nd century A.D. See p. 139.

o **Santa Maria Gloriosa dei Frari** (Venice): "I Frari" is named for the Franciscan "brothers" who founded this Gothic giant in 1250. It was rebuilt between 1330 and 1453, which made it one of the most art-bedecked churches in Venice, filled with works of art by Donatello, Titian, Giovanni Bellini, and Canova. See p. 158.

o **Cattedrale di Torcello** (Torcello, Venice): Venice's oldest church is pretty much all that remains of one of the lagoon's earliest settlements on the almost-abandoned island of Torcello, north of what is now the city of Venice. Santa Maria Assunta, as the cathedral is known, was begun in the 7th century, its interior slathered with glittering gold-backed Byzantine mosaics in the 11th and 12th centuries (precursors to those that would later decorate Venice's San Marco). The inside of the entrance wall is filled with a massive *Last Judgment.* This was a common device in medieval churches: placing above the door from which parishioners would exit a scene depicting both the heavenly rewards that await the faithful and the horribly inventive, gruesome punishments for the damned in hell—sort of a final sermon at the end of the service to remind everyone what was at stake and to keep them holy until the following Sunday. The bell tower offers a pretty panorama over the sparsely populated island and surrounding lagoon. See p. 177.

o **Basilica di Sant'Antonio** (Padua): Think of all the people of Italian descent you know, or have heard of, named Tony. You're starting to get an idea of how popular the 13th-century, Portuguese-born St. Anthony is among Italians. The patron of lost articles (as well as Portugal, Brazil, fisherman, the elderly, and pregnant woman, to name just a few of his flock) lived in Padua, and when he died in 1231, the citizenry quickly canonized him and—in a remarkably short 76 years—built this huge church to honor his remains. The style in 13th-century Veneto was still largely Byzantine, so the brick basilica is topped by an octet of domes and twin minaret-style bell towers. Donatello, whose *Gattamelata* (the first large equestrian bronze cast after ancient Roman times) sits out front, crafted the high altar, but that is virtually ignored by the mass of faithful in favor of a chapel off the left aisle. This is where a constant stream of supplicants files past the saint's tomb to press their palms against it and leave flowers, small gifts, pic-

tures, and written prayers either thanking him or asking him to help them find everything from lost health to lost love to lost children (some even pray for lost material objects). Il Santo's robes are also preserved here, as are the silver-tongued preacher's miraculously preserved jawbone, vocal chords, and tongue, all kept in a chapel behind the high altar. See p. 184.

FROM TOP: Basilica di San Marco's dazzling mosaic work; the Cattedrale di Torcello dates to the 7th century.

o **Basilica San Zeno Maggiore** (Verona): Verona is home to perhaps the greatest Romanesque basilica in all of northern Italy, a stunning example of the early medieval sculptor's art. Between the 9th and 12th centuries, architects raised the church, created the massive rose window in the facade, and hired artists who revived the ancient art of casting in bronze to create magnificent doors set with 48 wonderfully minimalist panels telling stories from the Bible as well as the life of St. Zeno. The stone reliefs flanking them date to the 12th century. The 12th- to 14th-century frescoes inside lead up to Andrea Mantegna's 15th-century altarpiece. See p. 223.

o **Basilica** (Aquileia): Tiny Aquileia was a major town in Roman times and built a church in 313 just as soon as Constantine the Great declared the religion legal in the empire. The town was a hotbed of early Christianity, hosting a theological conference in 381 attended by the likes of Jerome and Ambrose. Though the church was rebuilt and frescoed in the 11th and 12th centuries, the original flooring has been uncovered and is now on display, a marvelous and precious mosaic of complicated paleo-Christian and pagan iconography. A crypt retains more mosaics from the 4th century, plus even earlier ones from a pagan house dating to the early 1st century See p. 276.

o **Tempietto Longobardo** (Cividale, near Udine): This fantastic 8th-century church hollowed out of the cliff face over Cividale's mighty gorge gives us a precious glimpse into true Lombard style, before the High Middle Ages began to mix and mingle the cultural groups of northern Italy. Flanking the entryway are statues and decorations carved directly out of the native limestone in an early Lombard Romanesque style. See p. 282.

o **Duomo** (Milan): The greatest Gothic cathedral south of the Alps, a massive pile of pinnacles and buttresses, was begun in the 14th century and took 500 years to complete—but it remained true to its original, Gothic styling. It's the fourth-largest church in the world, its cavernous interior peppered with statues and monuments. The highlight, though, is the chance to weave your way through the statue-peaked buttresses and clamber up onto the rooftop to gaze

Milan's Duomo flanked by a guardian lion from the Piazza del Duomo.

out across the city; on a clear day you can see to the Alps, rising from the lakes north of the Lombard plain. See p. 295.

o **Certosa** (Pavia, outside Milan): Though Milan's Sforza family completed this Carthusian monastery, it's really the late-14th-century brainchild of the Visconti clan. The massive building, rich with Lombardesque decorations and sculptures, was commissioned by Duke of Milan Gian Galeazzo Visconti in 1396 as a family mausoleum; it later became the repository of funerary monuments to Milan's greatest rulers and despots. Though Ludovico il Moro and his wife, Beatrice d'Este, boast the finest monument, neither is buried here. Indeed, the repository was never meant to be in Pavia in the first place; cash-poor Santa Maria della Grazie in Milan—the one with Leonardo's *The Last Supper* and the home of Beatrice's remains—sold it to the Certosa. This is still a working monastery, now hosting a Cistercian community, and you can tour an example of the little houses they occupy (a far cry from the cramped cells one pictures monks enduring) and purchase their own beauty products and liqueurs. See p. 322.

o **Cappella Colleoni** (Bergamo): The mercenary commander Bartolomeo Colleoni, a Bergamo native, fought so gloriously on behalf of Venice that the city gave him the generalship over the entire Venetian army. They commissioned Verrocchio to erect a statue in his honor in Venice and gave Colleoni control of his hometown. He commissioned his own tomb, which was created in the late 15th century as a separate chapel in Bergamo's cathedral. Colleoni invited one of the great sculptors decorating the magnificent Certosa at Pavia to carve on his tomb a complex series of panels and statues whose symbolisms interweave in medieval style grafted onto Renaissance architecture. In the 18th century, Tiepolo was brought in to fresco the ceiling. See p. 330.

o **Basilica di Superga** (Turin): Turin got a taste of the extravagant southern Italian baroque in the early 18th century when Sicilian architect Juvarra set up shop in town. After the Virgin saved the city from French troops, the

The ornately baroque Basilica di Superga.

Savoys dutifully erected a church in her honor and hired Juvarra for the job. He married early neoclassical ideals of proportion with the theatricality of the baroque to build this magnificent structure in the hills above Turin overlooking the Alps. Vittorio Amadeo II liked his results so much he decided to turn it into the Royal Tomb, wedging monuments to various Savoys into the chapels and the underground Crypt of Kings. See p. 380.

o **Sacra di San Michele** (outside Turin): Its stony bulk, elaborate carvings, and endless staircases, all towering over the valley from a Monte Pirchiriano perch, give this abbey a movie-set air more appropriate to a Tibetan monastery than a Christian abbey. The gravity-defying way it hangs halfway off the cliff face is all the more astonishing when you consider that the engineering is purely medieval—started in 983 and rebuilt in the 1100s. Before the Savoys were the bigwig kings they became, their early members were buried here, in rock-carved chapels under the partly frescoed main church interior; today free concerts are held here, with a range of offerings from Gregorian chants and Celtic music to classical pieces and gospel hymns. See p. 387.

THE best ARTISTIC MASTERPIECES

o **Tintoretto's Scuola Grande di San Rocco** (Venice): When the Scuola di San Rocco (a sort of gentlemen's club/lay fraternity) held an art competition in 1564, the Renaissance master Tintoretto pulled a fast one on his rivals. Instead of preparing a sketch for the judges like everyone else, he went ahead and finished a painting, secretly installing it in the ceiling of the Sala dell'Albergo off the second-floor hall. The judges were suitably impressed, and Tintoretto got the job. Over the next 23 years, the artist filled the *scuola's* two floors with dozens of works. The *Rest on the Flight into Egypt* on the ground floor is superb, but his masterpiece hangs in that tiny Sala dell'Albergo, a huge *Crucifixion* that wraps around the walls and ranks among the greatest and most moving works in the history of Venetian art. The San Rocco baroque orchestra holds excellent regular chamber concerts in this fantastic setting; for info, contact ℂ **348-190-8939** or visit **www.musicinvenice.com**. See p. 150.

o **Veronese's *Feast in the House of Levi,* Accademia** (Venice): Paolo Veronese was a master of human detail, often peopling his large canvases with a rogues' gallery of characters. When Veronese unveiled his *Last Supper,* puritanical church bigwigs nearly had a conniption. They threatened him with charges of blasphemy for portraying this holiest of moments as a rousing, drunken banquet that more resembled paintings of Roman orgies than the Last Supper. Veronese quickly renamed the work *Feast in the House of Levi,* a less holy subject at which Jesus and the Apostles were also present, and the mollified censors let it pass. See p. 150.

o **Giotto's Scrovegni Chapel** (Padua): Padua's biggest sight by far is one of the two towering fresco cycles created by Giotto (the other one is in Assisi), the artist who did more than any other to lift painting from its static Byzantine stupor and set it on the naturalistic, expressive, dynamic Gothic road toward the Renaissance. From 1303 to 1306, Giotto covered the walls of this private chapel with a range of emotion, using foreshortening, modeled figures, and saturated colors, revolutionizing the concept of art and kicking off the modern

Every surface is covered with murals at the Scuola Grande di San Rocco.

era in painting. The chapel, as a whole, is breathtaking, depicting scenes from the life of Mary and Jesus in 38 panels. See p. 186.

o **Leonardo da Vinci's *The Last Supper,* Santa Maria delle Grazie** (Milan): This tempera fresco looks somehow more like a snapshot of a real dinner table than the staged holy event that Last Suppers usually appear to be—instead of a hovering halo, Jesus' holy nimbus is suggested by the window behind his head. Leonardo was as much a scientist and inventor as he was painter, and unfortunately for us, he was wont to try new painting techniques directly on his major commissions rather than testing them fully first. When painting one fresco in Florence, he used wax in the pigments, but when it was drying too slowly, he put heaters along the wall, and the whole thing simply melted. Whatever chemistry he was experimenting with in Milan when Ludovico il Moro hired him to decorate the refectory (dining hall) of Santa Maria della Grazie with a Last Supper, it didn't work properly. The fresco began deteriorating almost as soon as he finished painting it, and it had to be touched up and painted over several times in the succeeding centuries. It also didn't help when Napoleon's troops moved in and used the wall for target practice, or when Allied World War II bombs tore the roof off the building, miraculously not damaging the fresco but still leaving it open to the elements for 3 years. A lengthy restoration stripped away the centuries of grime and overpainting, so what we see now is more or less pure Leonardo, even if the result is extremely patchy and looks rather faded. See p. 298.

o **Michelangelo's *Pietà Rondanini,* Castello Sforzesco** (Milan): During a lifetime in which he became the foremost artist of his age, acknowledged as a genius in painting, fresco, architecture, and engineering, Michelangelo never lost his love for marble and chisel. At age 89, he picked up his tools for the final time and continued work on this *Pietà* that he had begun a few years earlier. It may be unfinished—in fact, Michelangelo was in the midst of changing

The Galleria dell'Accademia.

it wholesale, reordering the figures and twisting the composition around—but this tall, languid representation of Mary bearing the body of Christ remains one of the sculptor's most remarkable works. At the end of his life, Michelangelo had grown so advanced in his thinking and artistic aesthetics that this minimalist work (the sculptor had early on developed a rough style dubbed *non finito,* or "unfinished") looks eerily as if it were chiseled in the 1950s rather than the 1560s. Michelangelo was in his Roman studio chiseling away on the statue when, on February 12, 1564, a fever struck him and he took to bed. He died 6 days later. See p. 294.

o **Mantegna's *Dead Christ,* Pinacoteca di Brera** (Milan): This masterpiece of the Brera's collection displays not only Mantegna's skill at modeling and keen eye for texture and tone, but also his utter mastery of perspective and how he used it to create the illusion of depth. In this case, we look at Jesus laid out on a slab from his feet end, the entire body foreshortened to squeeze into a relatively narrow strip of canvas. Like many great geniuses in the arts, Mantegna actually warped reality and used his tools (in this case, perspective and foreshortening) in an odd way to create his image. Most art teachers would tell you that the rules of perspective would call for the bits at the "near end" (in this case, the feet) to be large and those at the far end (that is to say, the head) to be small to achieve the proper effect, but Mantegna turned it around. At first glance, the work seems wonderfully wrought and perfectly foreshortened. But after staring a few moments, especially from up close, you realize the head is grotesquely large and the feet are tiny. Mantegna has given us perfect foreshortening by turning perspective on its end. See p. 297.

THE best CASTLES

o **Museo Castelvecchio** (Verona): Most people do the Romeo-and-Juliet trail, peak at the ancient Arena, and then call it a day in Verona. Unfortunately, few make it to the stunning castle on the river. This 14th-century stronghold, complete with its own fortified bridge across the river, was built by "Big Dog"

Cangrande II Scaligeri. It was so mighty that it survived the centuries intact until the Nazis bombed it in World War II. Though there are collections of local wood sculptures and canvases by Tintoretto, Tiepolo, Veronese, Bellini, and local boy Pisanello, the true treat here is just wandering the maze of halls, passageways, stony staircases, and ramparts to relive the bad old days of the Middle Ages. See p. 221.

o **Castello Sabbionara** (Avio, Trentino–Alto Adige): This bellicose castle was a true fortress and makes no bones about it. Built in the 11th century and enlarged in the 13th century, it helped define and hold the line between the constantly warring neighboring powers of Venice and Austria. It switched hands several times, and in the 13th century the Guard's Room was frescoed with marvelous scenes of battles fought here. See p. 239.

o **Castello del Buonconsiglio** (Trent): Serious history went down in Trent's Castle of Good Council. The name might not be apt, however, because the famous Council of Trent (p. 234)—many sessions of which were held here—effectively put up the wall between the Vatican and the burgeoning Protestant movement, which ended up being the cause (or at least excuse) for many European wars and numerous unjust politico-social systems, from the 16th century all the way to today. Much later, leaders of the *Irrendentisti* (a World War I–era movement that advocated giving the then-Austrian South Tyrol region to Italy) were imprisoned here, including the popular Cesare Battisti, who was executed in the yard. The castle is vast, built around the core 13th-century Castelvecchio and 15th-century palace of Trent's bishop-prince. The highlight is the *Cycle of the Months* fresco painted around 1400 and laden with late medieval symbolism. See p. 235.

o **Castel Roncolo** (Bolzano): This 13th-century castle sits atop a small cliff upriver from the town and looks like the most livable medieval castle you can imagine: cozy, with views of the vineyards. The central courtyard is hung with staircases and open wood balconies running along the upper stories, while

A rampart of Castello Sabbionara.

many rooms retain all sorts of wonderfully crude medieval frescoes, including a lovely set that tells the story of Tristan and Isolde, a popular romantic tale from the Middle Ages. See p. 244.

o **Castel Tirolo** (outside Merano): The entire Tyrol, covering northeastern Italy and much of western Austria, was once ruled from this medieval fortress perched dramatically on an outcropping 5km (3 miles) outside Merano. You must walk a long and narrow path to get here, where there's a gorgeously frescoed Romanesque chapel and a museum dedicated to Tyrolean history and culture. See p. 251.

Bolzano's quaint Castel Roncolo.

o **Castello di San Giusto** (Trieste): Built between 1470 and 1630, this gem has mighty ramparts to walk for city vistas, modest collections of armor and furnishings to peruse, and outdoor concerts and films presented in the huge courtyard in summer. See p. 271.

o **Castello di Miramare** (near Trieste): The "Castle Looking at the Sea" rises in gleaming white fairy-tale splendor along the coastline just a few miles from the center of Trieste. Built in the 1850s, it has been doomed to host ill-fated potentates ever since. Its original owner, Austrian Archduke Maximilian, was sent to Mexico to be emperor and ended up shot. Archduke Ferdinand spent the night here before going off to Sarajevo to be shot (which kicked off World

Castello di Miramare overlooks the Gulf of Trieste.

War I). Other dukes and ladies have met bitter ends after sojourning here, which is perhaps why it is now public property and no longer a royal guest-house. They do concerts here, plus sound-and-light shows telling the sad tale of the castle's builder, Maximilian. See p. 272.

o **Castello Scaligero** (Sirmione): This mighty midget is not spectacular as far as castles go, but—if you can apply this phrase to a fortress—it's cute as a button. Unimportant in most respects, it *is* picturesque, guarding the entrance to town with somber 13th-century stone turrets and surrounded by a moat complete with drawbridges. See p. 341.

o **Castello di Fenis** (Fenis, outside Aosta): The Challant viscounts controlled the Aosta Valley from this stronghold throughout the Middle Ages. The fres-coed figures strolling about the balconies of its central courtyard spout cartoon balloonlike scrolls of speech that are a treasure-trove for linguists unlocking the origins of the local dialect, which is founded largely in a medieval variant on French. The furnishings, though all genuine castle antiques, were culled from sources throughout this area, Switzerland, and France to give the place that medieval lived-in look. See p. 400.

THE best VILLAS & *PALAZZI*

o **Palazzo Ducale** (Venice): The Gothic *palazzo* from which the doges ruled the Venetian Republic for centuries offers two incredible experiences. One is simply to wander the gorgeous rooms and halls, which are decorated with frescoes and paintings (including the world's largest oil canvas) by all the Ve-netian School greats, from Titian, Tintoretto, and Veronese on down. The placards in each room are marvelously informative, not only about the art but also about the function of each room and its role in government or daily Ve-netian life. But to discover what really made the Byzantine Venetian political machine tick, take the **Secret Itineraries tour,** which lets you slip behind the camouflaged doors and enter the hidden world of the palace-within-the-palace, the chambers in which the real governing took place, all wedged into the massive space between the inner and outer walls of the *palazzo*. See the chamber where the powerful Council of Ten met, the tiny office where the doge's secretary kept track of all the machinations going on in high society, the tribunal where three judges condemned the guilty and hanged them from the rafters, and the cramped "leads" cells under the roof from which Casanova famously escaped. Then saunter across the storied Bridge of Sighs to explore the dank, dungeonlike prisons across the canal where lesser criminals served out their miserable terms—lagoon floods and all. See p. 146.

o **Ca' d'Oro** (Venice): Though no longer graced with the decorative facade that earned Venice's most beautiful *palazzo* its name ("House of Gold"), the 15th-century Ca d'Oro remains one of the most gorgeous palaces in Venice, out-side (see the main facade from the Grand Canal) and in. The gallery of art, donated—along with the palace—to the state by Baron Giorgio Franchetti in 1916, includes paintings by Van Dyck, Giorgione, Titian, and Mantegna. There's also a small ceramics museum and fantastic canal views. See p. 158.

o **Ca' Rezzonico** (Venice): Even though Venice was well past its heyday in the 18th century and inching closer to the fall of the Republic, this is nonetheless the era in which the city best expressed its own unique character, the age of

Casanova and costume balls, all the things we picture when we think of Venice. The Rezzonico, built in 1667 by the same architect who crafted the baroque Santa Maria della Salute, today re-creates that decadence of 18th-century Venice: The gracious *palazzo* has been outfitted, with period pieces culled from across the city, as an actual house from the era. Adding to the 200-year time warp are a series of scenes from daily Venetian life painted by Pietro Longhi, plus several carnival frescoes that Giandomenico Tiepolo (son of the more famous Giovanni Battista Tiepolo)

FROM TOP: **Ca' d'Oro abuts the Grand Canal; Palladio's Villa Barbaro.**

originally painted for his own house. See p. 154.

○ **Villa Pisani** (Stra, on the Brenta Canal): Tiepolo frescoed the ballroom for this massive 18th-century villa built for the family of a Venetian doge. Napoleon bought it in 1807 and its most notorious moment came in 1934 when two European leaders met here for their very first summit: Benito Mussolini and Adolf Hitler. The rooms are lavish and the extensive gardens include a quirky hedge maze. See p. 192.

○ **Villa Barbaro** (outside Asolo): Though the villas right around Vicenza get more sightseers, this 1560 Palladio-designed masterpiece outside Asolo is perhaps the most gorgeous. That's because it matches perfect Palladian architecture with stunning frescoes by Veronese, which carpet almost every inch of wall and ceiling inside. And to think it's still actually in private hands (though the inside can be visited). See p. 201.

o **Villa Rotonda** (outside Vicenza): If you've seen Monticello, the architecture of Washington, D.C., or Inigo Jones's buildings in England, you'll be prepared for La Rotonda—it influenced them all. UNESCO has placed this pinnacle of Palladio's architectural theories, a towering monument of human achievement and ingenuity, on the same World Heritage List as the Pyramids. This is Palladio's strict neoclassical take on the Renaissance in all its textbook glory, an ancient temple rewritten as a home and softened by Renaissance geometry of line. It was also one of his last, started in 1567, but largely executed by a faithful follower after the master's death. See p. 211.

o **Villa Valmarana** (outside Vicenza): This 17th-century Palladian-style villa is nicknamed *ai Nani*, or "of the dwarves," because its walls are patrolled by an army of stone dwarves. The architecture isn't all that incredible, but the 18th-century frescoes inside by Giambattista and Giandomenico Tiepolo certainly are. See p. 211.

o **Palazzo Patriarcale** (Udine): Until 1734, it was the bishops who ruled Udine as patriarchs. The final patriarch had the foresight to invite Tiepolo to decorate his palace with scenes from the Old Testament that double as early-18th-century fashion shows. There's also a fine collection of locally carved wood sculptures spanning the 13th to 18th centuries. See p. 279.

o **Palazzo Te** (Mantua): Raphael's protégé Giulio Romano, hounded from Rome over a scandalous series of erotic engravings, was let loose to fill libidinous Federico Gonzaga's Mannerist pleasure palace with racy frescoes. The place was built to look as if it were crumbling, from arch keystones to the illusionist frescoes in the Room of Giants. See p. 336.

o **Il Vittoriale** (Gardone, Lake Garda): Gabriele D'Annunzio was an Italian Hemingway-meets-Shelley, an adventurer, soldier, and poet who napped on a funeral bier covered in leopard skins; who carried on a torrid affair with the greatest actress of his age, Eleonora Duse; and who crafted every iota of his villa in meticulous Victorian detail. The "victory" after which the villa is named refers to an incident from the end of World War I: When the Adriatic town of Fiume, previously promised to Italy, seemed destined to end up in Yugoslav hands, D'Annunzio led his own army to occupy the town and claim it—much to the chagrin of the Italian commanders, who proceeded to bomb the city until he gave up and came home. The sheer volume of bric-a-brac here is enough to drive a maid with a feather duster nuts, but is redeemed by the fantastic anecdote or quirky explanation behind each one (hope for a chatty guide with a good command of English). Nestled in the extravagant gardens are a structure built as a ship, the actual boat D'Annunzio commanded during the Great War; his biplane; and his heroic hilltop tomb. See p. 343.

Il Vittoriale's eclectic decor.

o **Palazzo Reale** (Turin): This was where 17th- and 18th-century Savoy kings hung their crowns—in all their extravagant, overwrought,

The sweeping Palazzina di Caccia di Stupinigi.

gilded glory. From Gobelin tapestries to Oriental vases, from the royal armory to the elegant gardens laid out by master landscape architect Le Nôtre (who did the Versailles gardens and those of the Tuileries in Paris), this palace drips with royal frippery. See p. 379.

o **Palazzina di Caccia di Stupinigi** (outside Turin): Sicilian baroque genius Juvarra laid out this extravagant and palatial hunting lodge for the Savoys in 1729. (And Napoleon liked it so much that he set up housekeeping here for a time when he first conquered the region before pressing on.) To fill the numerous frescoed rooms and vast halls of its giant, sinuous X-shape, local authorities have collected furnishings, paintings, and other decorative elements from dozens of Savoy palaces to create a sort of museum of 18th- and 19th-century interior decor. See p. 381.

o **Galleria Nazionale di Palazzo Spinola** (Genoa): The collection of canvases here (by Antonello da Messina, Guido Reni, Luca Giordano, Van Dyck, and Bernardo Strozzi) are set against the stellar backdrop of a Genovese palace frescoed and decorated by the merchant-banking Spinola family. See p. 418.

THE best FESTIVALS

o **Carnevale** (Venice): In most Catholic countries, the week before Lent has long been a time to let down your hair and party. It all culminates in Shrove Tuesday, the day of feasting before Ash Wednesday kicks off the sober Lenten period. This bash has earned the day the nickname Fat Tuesday—called *Martedì Grasso* in Italian, but better known by its French name, Mardi Gras. Venice ranks with Rio and New Orleans as host of one of the most elaborate and famous Carnival celebrations anywhere. Every spring, the city brings back the 18th century in all its silk and brocade, pouf-sleeved, men-wearing-colored-hose, Casanova, ballroom-dancing glory. But rather than a Bacchanalian bash, Venice goes the genteel route, with concerts and masked costume balls filling performance spaces, churches, and frescoed palaces. Ten days leading up to Shrove Tuesday. See p. 164 and 166.

- **Venice International Film Festival:** This is one of the movie business's premier festivals, ranking just below Cannes in importance. The best films made over the past year from around the world are screened for audiences and judges at the Palazzo del Cinema, other movie houses, and sometimes even open-air *piazze*. Unlike, say, the Oscars, which celebrates highly promoted Hollywood products, this is a chance for all movies—from would-be blockbusters to low-budget, unknown indies—to catch the attention of critics and distributors. Late August/early September. See p. 164.

- **Biennale d'Arte** (Venice): One of the most important art festivals in the world is hosted every 2 years by Venice. Contemporary artists (both celebrated modern masters and talented unknowns), critics, and art aficionados from around the world fill the hotels to attend shows and peruse the works displayed in the gardens and Arsenale warehouses at the far end of the Castello district. June to early November, odd years. See p. 164.

- **Regata Storica** (Venice): Every Venetian must have an 18th-century outfit mothballed in a closet to break out for yearly fetes such as Carnevale and, of course, this "historical regatta"—less of a race than a day-long Grand Canal parade of gorgeously bedecked gondolas and other boats laden with costumed gentry. First Sunday in September. See p. 164.

- **Partita a Scacchi** (Marostica): This pretty little medieval hamlet, which barely fills the bottom third of the ring made by its ancient wall clambering up the hillside, would probably be overlooked if it weren't for the biennial festival that turns the checkerboard main piazza in front of the castle into a weird piece of yesteryear. After a parade of costumed gentlefolk and medieval-style entertainers (jugglers, fire-eaters, clowns), people dressed as chess pieces fill the piazza's board, the players sit atop a stage ready to call out their moves, and the match begins. Marostica has only a handful of hotels, so book a few months in advance. Second weekend in September, even years. See p. 206.

Elaborate Carnevale masks are a rite of passage in Venice.

o **Concerti in Villa** (Vicenza): The Veneto region around Vicenza opens up its villas or their grounds for a series of summertime concerts and performances. From famous masterpieces like Palladio's La Rotonda to little-known Renaissance villas, the settings are memorable and the music is sweet. June and July. See p. 207.

o **Opera in Arena** (Verona): La Scala and La Fenice may be more famous, but few opera stages in Italy have a more natural dramatic setting than Verona's ancient Roman amphitheater. Every season they put on *Aïda* as they have since 1913, along with other operatic masterpieces by Giuseppe Verdi. For a huge 2,000-year-old sports stadium open to the sky, the Arena enjoys surprisingly good acoustics. Late June through August. See p. 220.

o **Festival Shakespeariano** (Verona): Verona mixes its two powerhouse attractions—ancient Roman heritage and Shakespearean fame—in a theater festival of Shakespeare's plays (along with ballets and concerts, from classical to jazz) put on in the garden-set ruins of the ancient Teatro Romano. June through August. See p. 216.

o **Palio** (Asti): Medieval pageantry precedes this breakneck horse race on Asti's piazza. The 2 weeks leading up to it are known as the

FROM TOP: Verona's Roman arena hosts opera in summer; Asti's Palio festival culminates in a frantic horse race.

Douja d'Or, a grape-and-wine festival and trade fair. Rival town Alba spoofs the event with a race of their own—riding asses—in their **Palio degli Asini** on the first Sunday in October. Third Sunday in September. See p. 199.

o **Sanremo Festival** (San Remo): Since 1950, Sanremo has been Italy's beloved festival of pop music, where faded Italian stars get to strut their stuff, major international rock stars and artists are invited to perform, and scruffy teenage musicians from across Italy get the chance to play that carefully crafted song they just know would be a number-one hit if only they could sign a record contract (and many do). If you want to hear what will be belting out of Fiat speakers and pumping in the dance clubs, listen to the winning performances here. (The festival is amply covered on television, so you can get an idea from the inside of your hotel room if you don't make it for the real thing.) Late February or early March. See p. 428.

o **Sagra del Pesce** (Camogli): Take the world's largest frying pan (3.6m/12 ft. across) and place it on the wide, waterfront promenade of this tiny Riviera fishing town. Fill the pan with sizzling sardines and the town with hungry folks ready to party. There you have a *sagra*, or celebration of food—in this case, seafood, the town's traditional economic lynchpin. Second Sunday in May. See p. 432.

THE best LUXURY HOTELS

o **Hotel Gritti Palace** (Venice): The grandest hotel on the Grand Canal has hosted the crème de la crème of whoever visits Venice since Doge Andrea Gritti built the palace in the 16th century. Charles de Gaulle, Winston Churchill, Truman Capote, Mick Jagger, Giorgio Armani, Robert De Niro, Charlie Chaplin . . . the list goes on. This place is luxury everything: hand-painted and inlaid antiques, 18th-century stuccoed ceilings, cutting-edge designer entertainment centers, and, of course, balconies overlooking the Grand Canal (well, from the top-notch rooms, at least—everyone else gets to enjoy the view from the restaurant or piano bar). See p. 110.

o **Hotel Danieli** (Venice): Venice's *bacino* (the bay into which the Grand Canal spills) is lined with luxury hotels, but none beats the Danieli, a 14th-century doge's palace of pink plaster and elaborate marble windowsills that's been a hotel since 1822. The centerpiece is a four-story, sky-lit, enclosed courtyard of Byzantine-Gothic arches, open stairwells, balustrades, and verdant potted plants, off of which sit luxurious salons. It's worth popping your head in just to see it, even if you don't stay here. Insist upon a lagoon view

The Hotel Danieli's dazzling enclosed courtyard.

and try to stay in the original wing or, failing that, the larger rooms of the 19th-century *palazzo* next door. (Avoid the bland 1940s wing.) See p. 114.

○ **Hotel Cipriani** (Venice): This is quite possibly the best luxury hotel in Venice. It sits in splendid isolation at the tip of Giudecca, the only large island of central Venice not connected by a bridge (rather, it's a 10-min. boat ride to Piazza San Marco). Giuseppe Cipriani, the Venetian impresario behind Harry's Bar and the Locanda Cipriani on Torcello, where Ernest Hemingway loved to hang out (Cipriani even made it into a Papa story), crafted this retreat out of several Renaissance *palazzi* in 1959, offering stylish accommodations, discreet service, and modern comfort. See p. 123.

○ **Hotel Excelsior** (Venice): The Lido might never have been developed as a bathing resort if not for the prescience of Nicolò Spada, who created the Excelsior's Moorish-style central structure in 1907. As one of Venice's only custom-built luxury hotels, it didn't have to abide by all the historical considerations converted *palazzi* now have to take into account, so its architectural plans allowed for more spacious accommodations than those found in most Venetian hotels. Rooms overlook either the Adriatic (there's a private beach across the road) or the small, lush, Moorish garden. It also sports all the resort-type amenities: pool, fitness center, golf and tennis, and sauna. See p. 124.

○ **Villa Margherita** (Mira Porte, Brenta): This villa's role as a guesthouse hasn't changed much since it was built in the 17th century by Venice's Contarini family. It still looks much like a country-villa home (if your family happened to be Venetian and fabulously wealthy), with rooms overlooking the gardens, a restaurant across the street along the canal, and a similar sister property nearby with a swimming pool. See p. 193.

○ **Hotel Villa Cipriani** (Asolo): In 1962, Giuseppe Cipriani branched out from his premium-grade Venice mini-empire to turn this 16th-century villa into a well-appointed hotel. Once the home of poets Robert and Elizabeth Barrett Browning, it enjoys a dreamlike setting: the medieval hill town of Asolo, famed for its vistas over Veneto. See p. 200.

○ **Hotel Greif** (Bolzano): The Staffler family has owned this 500-year-old hotel on the main square of Bolzano—the Dolomiti's liveliest town—since 1796. In 1999 and 2000, they decided to overhaul it completely; the minimalist, modern vein of burnished steel and original contemporary art (with Internet-equipped laptops in every room) mixes with 19th-century antiques. See p. 245.

○ **Four Seasons Hotel Milano** (Milan): In 1993, the Four Seasons opened and rewrote the rules on deluxe hotels in Milan. Seven years were spent restructuring and transforming a 1476 convent, a process that brought many of its Renaissance elements back to light, including a lovely cloister. The rooms are huge by Italian city standards and flush with amenities and small luxuries such as CD stereos and king-size beds. The bilevel suites with frescoed vaulting are particularly nice. See p. 308.

○ **Grand Hotel et de Milan** (Milan): How do you define superior service? While resident guest Giuseppe Verdi, who lived for 30 years in the suite now named for him, lay dying in his bed, the hotel spread straw over the streets under his window every day to muffle the sounds of carriage wheels so as not to disturb the maestro's rest. They're constantly upping the luxury quotient here to keep the 1863 hotel looking and feeling its best. This means marble surfaces and lush upholstery, thick curtains, and antique furnishings. Okay, so the opera music trickling lightly from hidden speakers may be overdoing it, but what did you expect from a hotel 3 blocks from La Scala that has played host to divas and tenors for decades? See p. 309.

o **Villa d'Este** (Cernobbio, Lake Como): On short lists of the world's greatest hotels, the Villa d'Este always ranks near the top. There's nothing reproduction or faux about this place. The villa is true Renaissance, the marble precious, the guest book A-list, and the Empire furnishings so genuine they actually date back to when Napoleon's former aide-de-camp owned the property. Add to all that several pools (one floating on the lake), a vast park that hides tennis courts, a fitness center that includes squash courts and a virtual driving range, and a trio of restaurants. See p. 353.

o **Grand Hôtel et des Iles Borromées** (Stresa, Lake Maggiore): Ernest Hemingway loved this retreat by the lake so much he set part of *A Farewell to Arms* at the hotel. Shell out 3,200€ and you can stay in the suite named after him (which includes two bedrooms with king-size beds and huge marble bathrooms in each, frescoed ceilings, and a lake-view terrace). This ranks among Europe's most exclusive hotels. Rooms are appointed in a variety of styles, from 19th-century inlaid wood to Empire style to opulent Italianate rooms of lacquered furnishings and Murano chandeliers. See p. 364.

o **Hotel Splendido/Splendido Mare** (Portofino): Portofino is the fishing village chosen by the world's jet-set elite as their own little bit of Italy, its tiny harbor overshadowed by yachts; it's not surprising then that the hillside Splendido hotel is booked by the top names from Hollywood, European nobility registers, and CEO boardrooms. The villa itself is 19th century—though its foundation is a 16th-century monastery—set amid olive groves a 10-minute walk above the town. Suites come with antique furnishings and cutting-edge

The gardens of Villa d'Este.

entertainment centers. The sister hotel, Splendido Mare, sits right at the harborfront, stays open year-round, and offers dining with a view of the boats. See p. 442.

- **Royal Hotel** (San Remo): With such a small town and such a major pop festival, once a year you'll find a concentration of rock stars here rarely seen outside of a major benefit concert. The rest of the year, almost all of us can enjoy its private beach across the road, its cushy accommodations, its stuccoed bar, and the wonderful pool styled as if it were carved out of rock. See p. 430.

THE best MODERATELY PRICED HOTELS

- **Pensione Accademia** (Venice): If you ever wanted to live like Katharine Hepburn, here's your chance. Well, not exactly, though her character did live in this 16th-century Villa Maravege in the 1955 film *Summertime*. It sits in an enviable position, a flower-filled garden at the confluence of two canals emptying into the Grand Canal, and the rooms are done in a tasteful antique style that makes you feel as if you're staying in the home of your wealthy Venetian relative rather than in a hotel. See p. 122.

- **Hotel San Cassiano Ca' Favretto** (Venice): Straddling the line between moderate and expensive, this is actually one of the cheapest hotels on the Grand Canal. The rooms and bar terrace overlook the prettiest stretch of the canal, with the Ca' d'Oro directly across the waters. Even most non–Grand Canal rooms overlook a side canal. See p. 120.

- **Ca' Angeli** (Venice): It is hard not to be impressed with this 7-room hotel tucked away on a little street that deadends at the Grand Canal. Finding a room free can be a challenge unless you reserve well in advance, but that early planning will be well repaid, partly with an excellent organic breakfast served in a room overlooking the Grand Canal. The apartment sleeps five and is an attractive option for families with a few kids. See p. 119.

- **Hotel Majestic Toscanelli** (Padua): The management of the Toscanelli is always reinvesting in this gem of a hotel, three quiet shop- and *osteria*-lined blocks from the central Piazza delle Erbe. The reception is warm and helpful, and the location excellent. See p. 190.

- **Hotel Aurora** (Verona): Situated right on the scenic Piazza delle Erbe, the Aurora enjoys a combination of prime location, low prices, and perfect, simple comfort that keeps guests coming back. See p. 226.

- **Antica Locanda Solferino** (Milan): This hotel, which is perhaps a tad more costly than "moderate," has as much character as the fashionable Brera neighborhood where it resides. Its quirky amalgam of furnishings are fitted into generally spacious rooms. Sig. Gerardo Vitolo leads one of the friendliest managements in town; it's no wonder this delightful place stays booked by regulars, who enjoy its creaky, homey atmosphere. See p. 310.

- **Agnello d'Oro** (Bergamo): Bergamo may not quite be the Alps, but you're high up enough in their foothills that this tall, narrow ocher building with its flower-box windows, patio fountain, and sloping roof looks perfectly appropriate, offering a bit of Italianate Alpine charm smack-dab in the center of the

The charming Agnello d'Oro.

pedestrian medieval quarter. Furnishings are simple and serviceable, but the price and location can't be beat. See p. 423.

- o **Du Lac** (Bellagio, Lake Como): Of all the hotels lining Bellagio's little lakefront piazza, the Du Lac is the friendliest by a long shot. For over a century and a half, it has offered comfort and genuine hospitality, from the panoramic dining room and rooftop sun terrace to the simple but fully stocked rooms and the bar tables tucked under the arcades of the sidewalk. See p. 357.

- o **Verbano** (Stresa, Lake Maggiore): Why shell out a few hundred dollars for a hotel by the lake when you can pay the same price to have one *on* the lake? The Verbano sits at the tip of Isola dei Pescatori, an island of colorful fishermen's houses in the midst of Lake Maggiore, and has views from most rooms (as well as from the gravelly terrace where they serve excellent meals) over the landscaped Isola Bella, the lake, and the Alps beyond. See p. 365.

THE best BUDGET HOTELS

- o **Foresteria Valdese** (Palazzo Cavagnis; Venice): Eighteenth-century frescos decorate the ceilings in several rooms of this 16th-century *palazzo* run as a sort of hostel by the Waldesian and Methodist Church. You will feel very welcome, regardless of your religious beliefs or lack thereof, and most rooms have balconies over a lovely small side canal. The drawbacks are that many, but not all, of the accommodations are in shared rooms, and all the rooms lack amenities such as telephones and air-conditioning. See p. 116.

- o **Giardino dei Melograni** (Venice): The peaceful atmosphere of Campo del Ghetto Nuovo extends into this building and accompanying garden run by Venice's Jewish community. The accommodations are simple yet clean, and all rooms have a private bathroom. Everybody is welcome here and though this gem is not yet heavily trafficked, it is sure soon to be. Reserve early—and rather than just coming here to sleep, make sure you budget some time for discovering this wonderful corner of Venice. See p. 117.

25

o **Hotel Galleria** (Venice): This place is extraordinary: a 17th-century *palazzo* with double rooms costing about 100€, a half-dozen of which open directly onto the Grand Canal, all next door to one of Venice's top sights, the Accademia. Plus you get breakfast (including freshly baked bread) in bed. See p. 122.

o **Pensione Guerrato** (Venice): This charming *pensione* is run by a pair of brothers-in-law in a converted 13th-century convent near the daily Rialto market. The furnishings are mismatched but lovely—a mix of antiques culled from markets over the years—and the breakfast is excellent. They also rent two great apartments at excellent prices near Piazza San Marco. See p. 120.

Foresteria Valdese is run from a 16th-century *palazzo*.

o **Hotel Bernardi-Semenzato** (Venice): The friendly Pepoli family runs this well-maintained *palazzo* hidden a block off the main drag about halfway between the train station and San Marco. It's surrounded by *osterie* and good restaurants patronized by locals, and the modernized rooms retain rough wood-beam ceilings and antique-style furnishings. They also rent simple but spacious rooms in two annexes nearby that make you feel as if you're staying in your own Venetian apartment; one room has a fireplace, another overlooks a pair of side canals. See p. 118.

o **Due Mori** (Vicenza): Just off the central Piazza dei Signori lies this simple, no-frills but comfortable hotel, the oldest in Vicenza, packed with genuine 19th-century antiques and a friendly reception. See p. 212.

o **Hotel Aurora** (Milan): It would be a challenge to find a place in Milan on the low-end of the price range with a better price-to-quality ratio than this small hotel on one of the city's busiest shopping streets. What you save on the room, you can spend in the stores downstairs. See p. 312.

o **Grifone** (Sirmione, Lake Garda): Would you believe a vine-covered hotel where the simple rooms enjoy views of the lake and access to a small beach would cost less than 100€ for a double? Well, that's on offer at this gem of an inn around the corner from the little medieval castle. Book early. See p. 342.

THE best COUNTRYSIDE RETREATS

o **Cavallino d'Oro/Goldenes Rössl** (Kastelruth/Castelrotto, near Bozen): This rambling hotel has sat at the cobblestone center of a full-bore Tyrolean mountain hamlet since the 1400s, its swinging shingle emblazoned with its Golden

Horse moniker. The hotel includes a corner bar where the locals hang out for lunch and a genuine 18th-century *stuben* (beer nook) in the restaurant at the back. The lounge has expansive views of the Alps while the rooms offer modern comforts amid hand-painted wood furnishings and four-poster beds. The Urthaler family couldn't be more welcoming, and they happen to be Frommer's fans. See p. 247.

o **Hotel Castello Labers** (outside Merano): The road from town wends its way through vine-clad hills to the Stapf-Neubert family's 11th-century, countryside castle—a hotel since 1885. The cozy hunting salons cluster around a magnificent central staircase that leads up to the eclectic collection of abodes tucked into towers, eaves, and high-ceilinged rooms. A statue-studded garden out back offers views across the valley to the surrounding peaks, and they also have a heated pool, tennis courts, and a Tyrolean restaurant. See p. 253.

o **Villa Fiordaliso** (Gardone Riviera, Lake Garda): This Liberty-style villa was built in 1903 and immediately started attracting formidable owners, including poet Gabriele d'Annunzio and Claretta Petacci, Mussolini's mistress, who lived here in 1944 towards the end of World War II. The villa transformed in 1990 into one of the most popular high-end restaurants in the lake region (it has a Michelin star), with seven elegant guest rooms upstairs. See p. 345.

o **La Cascina del Monastero** (outside La Morra): The di Grasso family runs this *agriturismo* (a working farm that offers hospitality to guests), which has a vineyard and fruit orchard, as well as large guest rooms and apartments filled with comfortable rustic furnishings and exposed wood beams. This place would be worth staying at just for the fantastic breakfast spread—the only

The wine cellar at La Cascina del Monastero.

The rustic Milleluci.

drawback being that you may have to cancel lunch plans and return to your room for a nap. See p. 396.

○ **Milleluci** (outside Aosta): Four matrilineal generations of hoteliers have turned this family farm into one of the coziest, friendliest hotels in the whole of Valle d'Aosta. A fire crackles in the large lounge downstairs, and the rooms are done in woodsy Alpine style with canopy beds in suites, traditional wood furnishings, and hand-hewn ceilings. In true country tradition, the breakfast here is overwhelming, with freshly baked pies, cakes, and breads every morning accompanied by farm-fresh cheese, milk, and preserves. Unlike most countryside retreats, the Milleluci sports plenty of facilities a four-star hotel would be jealous of: a heated outdoor pool, tennis courts, exercise facilities, hot tub, and sauna. See p. 402.

○ **La Grange** (Courmayeur-Entrèves): Entrèves may not properly be country-side, but this tiny collection of Alpine chalets below the Mont Blanc cable-car station is so small it barely qualifies as a village, and the atmosphere is fully rustic. The Berthold family converted this hotel from a barn by fitting the rooms with a mix of antiques and sturdy country furnishings. It makes a refreshing (and far less expensive) alternative to the resort hotels of Courmayeur just down the road. See p. 406.

THE best RESTAURANTS

○ **La Cusina** (Venice): One of the few hotel dining rooms (in the Westin Hotel Europa & Regina) worth singling out. In warm weather, this becomes one of the most romantic dinner settings in town, the tables set on terraces that hang over the Grand Canal. The location alone makes it worth booking ahead, but happily the cooking is as delicious as the view is stunning, offering an inventive take on Italian cuisine based on Venetian and Veneto traditions and using the freshest ingredients. See p. 129.

A Carnevale mask overlooks diners at Le Bistrot de Venise.

o **Le Bistrot de Venise** (Venice): The menu at this upscale bistro is split three ways to satisfy your appetite (or at least, make your choice harder): Venetian/Italian, French, and ancient local recipes culled from historic cookbooks and documents. They attract hip artistic types by turning the back room into a coffeehouse-style performance space that hosts poets, acoustic musicians, art exhibits, and cabarets. See p. 129.

o **Al Covo** (Venice): Texan Diane Rankin makes the pastries and chats with guests while husband-chef Cesare Benelli watches over the kitchen at this always-popular restaurant. The warm welcome is compounded by excellent fresh seafood dishes with relatively reasonable prices (especially on the quality wine list). See p. 132.

o **A Beccafico** (Venice): If your trip to Italy this time around does not include a jaunt down to wonderful Sicily, you should first promise yourself you will rectify that on your next vacation; then as an added incentive to make sure you meet that promise, eat here one night to see how tasty the island's cuisine can be. See p. 130.

o **Trattoria Milanese** (Milan): In a city with many fine restaurants whose stars rise and fall almost as soon as they make it onto the map, this is a stalwart survivor, a traditional trattoria that has never stopped offering typical Milanese dishes, smart service, and moderate prices, a formula that has kept it successful for more than 70 years. See p. 314.

o **Antica Hosteria del Vino Buono** (Bergamo): This cozy restaurant is spread over two floors of a corner *palazzo* on the market square. The food is mountain-style, rib-sticking good, heavy on the game meats and thick polenta accompanied by hearty red wines. See p. 331.

o **Ochina Bianca** (Mantua): Mantuan cooking is somewhat more complex than most northern Italian cuisines, and the Venturinis put their own innovative spin on it at the "White Goose," marrying local ingredients with game and fresh fish from the Mincio. See p. 337.

o **C'era Una Volta** (Turin): That you have to ring the bell and climb to the first floor gives this place a clubby air, but owner Piero Prete will instantly make you feel like a longtime member as he greets you warmly and comes back around to help you select your wine. The cooking is traditional Torinese, excellently prepared. See p. 383.

o **La Libera** (Alba): Franco and Manuele reign over this stylish dining room on an alley off a pedestrian shopping street, with Marco in the kitchen crafting excellent variants on Piemontese cuisine by using only the freshest of ingredients, all locally produced, from the cheese to the fruit to the meats. See p. 394.

Simple yet elegant: La Libera.

THE best COUNTRYSIDE EATERIES

o **Al Camin** (outside Cortina d'Ampezzo): This barnlike structure lies along the rushing Brigantine mountain stream, 10 minutes outside town, and serves up hearty Alpine food in a woodsy dining room around a stone fireplace. Some regional specialties that are hard to find elsewhere these days are staples on Al Camin's seasonal menus. See p. 263.

o **La Maison de Filippo** (Entrèves): This is the never-ending meal to beat all feasts. Bring your calculator, or abacus, if you want to keep track of the courses. But it's not just quantity (two words: pace yourself): The food actually manages to be fantastic as well, and it's served in an archetypal rustic-countryside dining room of low wood ceilings and open kitchens. Sometimes there's even a dog under the table. Book here for the end of a day that will hold lots of skiing and hiking, and then plan to spend much of the following day digesting. See p. 406.

THE best DOWN-HOME
TRATTORIE & OSTERIE

o **Vino Vino** (Venice): Antico Martini is a pricey but good restaurant near La Fenice opera house; Vino Vino is its worst-kept secret, an inexpensive *osteria* branch that serves simple but tasty dishes from the same kitchen. You choose from the daily chalkboard menu, stake out a table, and then pick up your meal from the counter, along with a wine from their excellent and extensive shared wine cellar. See p. 131.

o **Ai Tre Spiedi** (Venice): Although this place changed ownership in 2006 and isn't the hidden gem it once was, you'll still find a great Venetian meal at reasonably low prices—not the cheapest in town, but some of the best value for your money. The owners are jolly, and the food is excellent, including the fish (which is sometimes dicey at the more inexpensive places in Venice). See p. 134.

o **Cantina do Mori** (Venice): This is one of Venice's best *bacari*, a wine bar that serves exquisite *cicchetti* (tapaslike snacks) to a crowd of regulars nightly under low-beam ceilings that seem unchanged since the joint opened in 1462. Casanova supposedly came to tipple here between affairs. See p. 135.

o **Toni del Spin** (Treviso): Seventy-five years of satisfying diners in Treviso has imparted a patina of reliability to this down-home trattoria of crisscrossing beams, swirling fans, and chalkboard menus. The choices are limited, but each dish is excellent, mixing local traditions with experimental cooking and some international dishes. The wine list is stellar—they also run the wine shop across the street. See p. 198.

o **La Taverna di Via Stella** (Verona): The Vantini brothers and their buddies run this newish, laid-back *osteria* that feels as if it's been around for centuries. Here the local volunteer fire squad shows up to hang out in uniform and hit on girls, and office workers troop in to unwind over traditional Veronese dishes and wine. (Of their some 180 bottles, 10 varieties are opened nightly so that you can sample by the glass.) See p. 228.

o **Osteria del Duca** (Verona): The ladies bustling around this old fave of a trattoria know to double-check with foreign visitors who have inadvertently ordered one of the many traditional Veronese dishes made of horse or donkey meat. The setting is romantic in true Verona style: It's on the ground floor of a medieval *palazzo* that most likely belonged to the historical Montecchi family, immortalized by Shakespeare as the Montagues, whose son Romeo fell in love with Juliet of the enemy Capulet clan. See p. 228.

Wine casks behind the bar at Cantina do Mori.

2

NORTHERN ITALY IN DEPTH

S‍ki in the Alps in the morning and sunbathe that same afternoon on the Riviera: check. Drink the world's finest wines in the vineyards that produced the grapes, while enjoying culinary diversity that runs the gamut from the eye-poppingly expensive to the down-homey: check. Appreciate true artistic genius in front of Leonardo Da Vinci's Last Supper and other masterpieces of western art: check. Shop until you drop in Milan, heaven on earth for any self-respecting fashionista: check.

And that's only the first half of the northern Italy highlight reel. There is also Tyrolean upper Adige, where castles outnumber towns and where your high-school German will be more useful than an Italian phrase book. There is Verona's beautiful historic center where Shakespeare's presence and Juliet's (fake) balcony can be felt and touched. There is the charming university town of Padua, where a Giotto masterpiece marks the epic shift in the history of art from the Middle Ages to the emotions, beauty, and movement of the Renaissance. There is the Ligurian coast dotted with the Cinque Terre and dozens of other fishing villages as well Portofino and a host of other chic resorts.

Oh yeah, and then there is Venice.

Northern Italy seduces with its grand old port cities of Genoa and Trieste as well as with the graceful, art-rich cities of Veneto. But the region is also where you will find the sleek, modern Italy that is associated with A-list names like Armani, Alfa Romeo, and Alessio. A mastery of design and fashion are only a logical outgrowth of an efficient culture that once used state-of-the-art canals—sketched out by Leonardo—to transport marble to construction projects like the Duomo in Milan, which is the fourth-largest cathedral in Christendom.

From the iconic architecture of Andrea Palladio to Milan's elegant fashion designs, the history of northern Italy is the story of the visibly irresistible. This chapter will help make sense of the events behind it all, and shed some light on the northern Italian persona that made this legacy possible.

NORTHERN ITALY TODAY

While the instinct is to begin this chapter with a look at northern Italy's most important city, that is not possible because there is no such place, and any attempt to coin one of the cities as the region's "capital" would be to ignore centuries of vastly different histories. Genoa is the principal port and has been a leading maritime power since the beginning of the second millennium. Turin was home to the royal family that ruled Italy for more than 80 years until the country became a republic at the end of World War II and was also briefly the capital of the newly unified Italy in the 1860s. Milan is Italy's financial capital, home to most of the nation's media, and it has a stronghold on its design and fashion. Venice is

FACING PAGE: *Brazen Serpent,* by Tintoretto, in the Scuola di San Rocco.

LEARN YOUR STRIPES: NORTHERN ITALIAN soccer TEAMS

Milan and nearby Turin are the meccas of Italian soccer (known here, as in the rest of Europe, as football) so before your arrival in northern Italy it's all but obligatory to memorize the colors of the big three teams—A. C. Milan, Inter, and Juventus—so you'll know who is celebrating when you see the people in the square or running down the street waving a colorful flag. This is especially key if you will be visiting during the soccer season (Sept–May).

A. C. Milan (aka Milan): A. C. Milan launched its owner, Silvio Berlusconi, to fame on a national level and eventually into the prime minister's chair as well. Founded in 1899 by English expats as a "football and cricket club" (hence "Milan," not *"Milano"*), the *Rossoneri,* as the team is nicknamed, reached its apex just after Berlusconi bought the club in 1986 and signed Dutch superstars Ruud Gullit, Frank Rijkaard, and Marco Van Basten. The club, which wears red-and-black jerseys—*rossoneri* in Italian—won the Serie A Italian Football Championship in 2011 after a 6-year drought, their longest since before Berlusconi's arrival.

Internazionale (aka Inter): The national champions from 2006 to 2010, Inter wears black-and-blue stripes—the *Nerazzurri.* The Milanese club split off from city rivals A. C. Milan in 1908 because of the latter's preference for granting playing time only to Italians. As it had a number of players from nearby Switzerland on its roster, it deemed itself an "international" club, and the name was born. It is the only club to have spent its entire history in the top league, Serie A. The two most hard-fought games of the year are the "derbies" that pit the two Milan clubs against each other. A bad season can be saved by a victory in the derby, especially if that keeps Milan's other team from taking the title.

Juventus (aka Juve): The fan base for the Agnelli family's personal soccer team, founded in 1897, is hardly confined to its hometown Turin. The *Bianconeri,* so called for their black-and-white jerseys—which might lead the novice observer to think a team of 11 referees is patrolling the field—have long been popular in Sicily and the rest of the south, home to the Agnelli's Fiat auto-making factories and laborers. Something akin to the New York Yankees, the fellows in black-and-white stripes have won more national championships (27) than any other club and are either unconditionally loved or passionately hated across the country. Also known by fans affectionately as *La Vecchia Signora,* the old woman.

unarguably one-of-a-kind in the world and the mecca for tourists. They could all have a claim to be the first mentioned in any discussion of northern Italy.

Northern Italians have always been an efficient and innovative people when it comes to industry, designing canals and locks to bring marble to construction projects, perfecting manufacturing methods, and inventing various machines— not to mention Alessandro Volta's creation of the first electric battery.

This ingenuity has led Italy—and northern Italy, in particular—to economic success. Today Italy ranks as the world's tenth-largest economy, and northern Italy's GDP per capita is about 25% higher than the European Union average (while in southern Italy it is 30% lower). This industrial base includes manufacturing giants such as Turin-based **Fiat** (the world's 6th-largest carmaker after its 2009 acquisition of Chrysler) and Trieste-based insurer **Assicurazioni Generali** (the 32nd-largest company in the world) to midsize family businesses that make up the lion's share of Italian productivity, to small locally owned businesses with less than 50 employees. These last two groups are the motor of the economy and northern Italy is dotted with medium and small manufacturers making everything from bicycle frames used by the world's best cyclists to high-pressure rubber hoses, furniture, and silk blouses.

Being home to so many entrepreneurs, northern Italy has an unsurprising appetite for politicians who offer hope for laissez-faire capitalism. In the 1990s, one of their own, a cruise ship crooner turned real estate investor turned media mogul, came to the forefront of Italian politics. **Silvio Berlusconi,** who hails from just outside Milan, is, according to *Forbes,* worth about $8 billion and was prime minister on and off for almost 2 decades. (Berlusconi has been Italy's prime minister three separate times: from 1994–95, from 2001–06, and from 2008–11.) He presided over *Il Popolo della Libertà* (The People of Freedom), the biggest party in the right-wing coalition that has its roots in northern populism. The second-biggest party in Berlusconi's People of Freedom coalition is the anti-immigration Northern League. Cracks began to emerge in the center-right coalition and Berlusconi's popularity dropped in elections in May 2011 that brought a center-left mayor to Milan for the first time since Berlusconi entered politics in 1994.

Berlusconi's time as the country's top elected official has been riddled with accusations of corruption and gaffes. The allegations surrounding the 75-year-old's business dealings and conflicts of interest have been accompanied by scandals linked to his private life—in particular, a penchant for partying with young women (sometimes not yet 18) at his villas near Milan and in Sardinia. He is currently on trial accused of paying an underage prostitute for sex and then abusing his power to try and cover it up.

Berlusconi has managed so far to avoid a final conviction with several convictions being overturned on appeal and other trials being dropped mid-course when new laws passed by the parliament he controls reduced the statute of limitations for crimes he was accused of. He has also attracted attention with his public gaffes, like calling U.S. President Barack Obama "tanned."

The center-left's victory in Milan in 2011 finally marked the turning point towards a decline in Berlusconi's popularity, and the septuagenarian's party lost a majority in Parliament after the country underwent a debt crisis. He resigned as prime minister on November 16, 2011 (see "Democracy at Last," p. 46).

LOOKING BACK: NORTHERN ITALIAN HISTORY

Prehistory & Early Settlers

Findings in caves around Isneria in the Abruzzi suggest that humans settled in Italy about a million years ago. Neanderthal man made a brief appearance, and Cro-Magnon, who knew how to fish and domesticate animals, showed up about 28,000 years ago.

Though prehistoric early cultural groups such as the Ligurians (Neolithic rulers of northwestern Italy—not just Liguria, but Piedmont and Lombardy as well—in 2400–1800 B.C.), Remedello (Copper Age folks centered on Brescia in 1800–1600 B.C.), Veneti (Bronze Age Illyrians settling the Veneto region around 1000 B.C.), and Villanovans (an influential Iron Age people of 1000–800 B.C. from the area around Bologna) inhabited parts of northern Italy, most of the peninsula's early action took place in central and southern Italy. Magna Graecia (Greater Greece) controlled Sicily and southern Italy all the way up to Naples. The Etruscans, probably a people who emigrated from Asia Minor between the 12th and 8th centuries B.C., settled into central Italy, ruling Tuscany, Umbria, and, as the Tarquin dynasty, acting as kings of a small Latin village, atop hills at a bend in the Tiber River, called Rome.

The Rise of Rome

Leaving aside the famous legend of a she-wolf nursing the abandoned twins Romulus and Remus (the former kills his brother and founds a village called Rome) and Virgil's *Aeneid* (Aeneas of Troy flees the burning city at the end of the Trojan War, makes his way to Romulus's little village, and turns it into an ancient superpower), Rome probably began as a collection of Latin and Sabine villages in the Tiber Valley. It was originally a kingdom ruled by the Etruscan Tarquin dynasty. In 509 B.C., the last Tarquin king raped the daughter of a powerful Roman.

DATELINE

Prehistory Neanderthal humans roam Italy; Cro-Magnon shows up.	**509 B.C.** Republic of Rome is founded; power is shared by two consuls.
1200 B.C. Etruscans begin to emigrate from Asia Minor, settling in Tuscany.	**494–450 B.C.** Office of the Tribune is established to defend plebeian rights. The Twelve Tablets stating basic rights are carved, the foundation of Roman law.
800 B.C. Greeks colonize Sicily and the peninsula's boot (collectively "Magna Graecia").	
753 B.C. Romulus, says legend, founds Rome. In fact, Rome grows out of a strategically located shepherd village.	**279 B.C.** Romans now rule the entire Italian peninsula.
700 B.C. Etruscans rise in power, peaking in the 6th century B.C.	**146 B.C.** Rome defeats Carthage; the Republic now controls Sicily, North Africa, Spain, Sardinia, Greece, and Macedonia.

After the girl committed suicide, infuriated Romans ejected the king and established a republic ruled by two consuls (chosen from among the patrician elite) whose power was balanced by tribunes elected from among the plebian masses.

The young Roman Republic sent its military throughout the peninsula and, by 279 B.C., ruled all of Italy. Rome's armies trampled Grecian colonies throughout the Mediterranean and, after a series of brutal wars, defeated Carthage (present-day Tunisia), a rival sea power and once Rome's archenemy. By 146 B.C., Rome controlled not only all of the Italian peninsula and Sicily, but also North Africa, Spain, Sardinia, Greece, and Macedonia.

Still, Rome wanted more. It invaded Gaulish lands to the north and added what we now call France and Belgium to its realm. Rome even crossed the English Channel and conquered Britain all the way up to the Scottish Lowlands (Hadrian's Wall still stands as a testament to how far north the Roman army got). However, so much military success so distant from Rome itself resulted in a severely weakened home front. With war booty filling the coffers, Rome ended taxation on its citizens. So much grain poured in from North Africa that the Roman farmer couldn't find a market for his wheat and simply stopped growing it. The booty had an additional price tag: corruption. Senators advanced their own lots rather than the provinces ostensibly under their care. Plebeians (ordinary citizens) clamored for a bigger share, and the slaves revolted repeatedly. More reforms appeased the plebes, while the slaves were put down with horrific barbarity (one famous slave revolt, led by Spartacus, was stopped by capturing the slave army and crucifying it on crosses that lined both sides of the Via Appia from Rome and stretched for miles upon miles).

Hail Caesar!

At the end of the 2nd century B.C., the Republic, sped along by a corrupt Senate, was corroding into near-collapse. Julius Caesar—successful general, skilled orator, and shrewd politician—stepped in to help maintain control over Rome's vast territories, but from the day Caesar declared himself "dictator for life," Rome, as

100 B.C.	Julius Caesar is born.
60 B.C.	Caesar, Pompey, and Crassus share power in the First Triumvirate.
51 B.C.	Caesar triumphs over Gaul (France).
44 B.C.	March 15, Caesar is assassinated, leaving all to his nephew and heir, Octavian.
27 B.C.	Octavian, now Augustus, is declared emperor, beginning the Roman Empire and 200 years of peace and prosperity.
B.C. 29 (or 33)	Jesus is crucified in the Roman province of Judea.

64–100	Nero persecutes Christians; a succession of military commanders restores order; Trajan expands the empire.
200	Goths invade from the north; the empire begins to decline.
313	With the Edict of Milan, Emperor Constantine I grants Christians freedom of religion. By 324, it is declared the official religion. Constantine also establishes Constantinople as the eastern capital, splitting the empire in half.

continues

a republic, was finished. After sharing governmental power with others in a series of Triumvirates, Caesar became the sole consul in 44 B.C.

Caesar rose in popular influence partly by endearing himself to the lower classes through a lifelong fight against the corrupt Senate. As his power crested, he forced many immoral senators to flee Rome, introduced social reforms, inaugurated the first of many new public building programs in the center of Rome (still visible as the Forum of Caesar), and added Gaul (France) to the dying Republic. But Caesar's emphasis on the plebeians and their concerns (as well as his own thirst for power) did little to endear him to the old guard of patricians and senators. On March 15, 44 B.C., Caesar strolled out of the Baths of Pompeii to meet

Reliefs from the 1st century B.C. at Verona's Roman theater.

Brutus, Cassius, and other "friends" who lay in wait with daggers hidden beneath their togas.

Caesar left everything to his nephew and heir, the 18-year-old Octavian. From the increasingly irrelevant Senate, Octavian eventually received the title Augustus, and from the people, lifetime tribuneship. And so Octavian became Emperor Augustus, sole ruler of Rome and most of the Western world.

The Empire

Augustus's long reign ushered in Pax Romana, 200 years of peace under Roman rule. The new emperor, who preferred to be called "First Citizen," reorganized the military and the provincial governments and reinstituted constitutional rule.

DATELINE *continued*

410–76 Waves of northern barbarian tribes continue to overrun Italy and sack Rome itself, eventually setting up their own puppet "emperors."

476 Last emperor deposed; the empire falls; the Dark Ages begin.

590–604 Church asserts political control as Pope Gregory I "the Great" brings some stability to the peninsula.

774–800 Frankish king Charlemagne invades Italy and is crowned emperor by Pope Leo

III. Upon his death, Italy dissolves into a series of small warring kingdoms.

962 Holy Roman Empire founded under Otto I, king of Saxony.

11th c. Normans conquer southern Italy and introduce feudalism. The first Crusades are launched.

1309–7 Papacy abandons Rome for Avignon, France.

1350–18th c. The Black Death decimates Europe, reducing Italy's population by a third.

continues

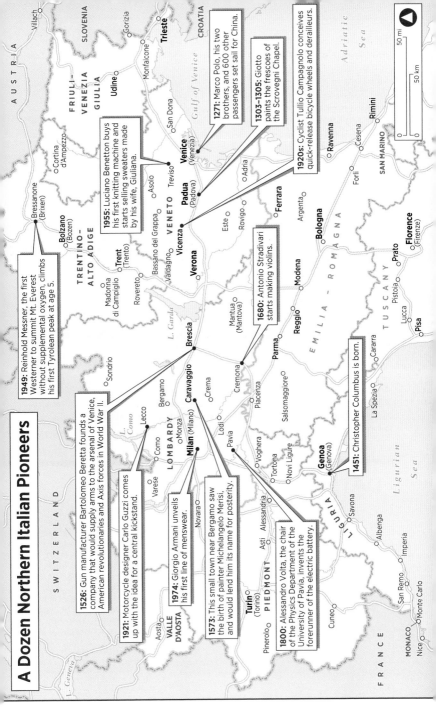

A Dozen Northern Italian Pioneers

1949: Reinhold Messner, the first Westerner to summit Mt. Everest without supplemental oxygen, climbs his first Tyrolean peak at age 5.

1955: Luciano Benetton buys his first knitting machine and starts selling sweaters made by his wife, Giuliana.

1271: Marco Polo, his two brothers, and 600 other passengers set sail for China.

1303–1305: Giotto paints the frescoes of the Scrovegni Chapel.

1920s: Cyclist Tullio Campagnolo conceives quick-release bicycle wheels and derailleurs.

1526: Gun manufacturer Bartolomeo Beretta founds a company that would supply arms to the arsenal of Venice, American revolutionaries and Axis forces in World War II.

1921: Motorcycle designer Carlo Guzzi comes up with the idea for a central kickstand.

1680: Antonio Stradivari starts making violins.

1974: Giorgio Armani unveils his first line of menswear.

1451: Christopher Columbus is born.

1573: This small town near Bergamo saw the birth of painter Michelangelo Merisi, and would lend him its name for posterity.

1800: Alessandro Volta, the chair of the Physics Department of the University of Pavia, invents the forerunner of the electric battery.

Succeeding emperors weren't so virtuous: deranged Tiberius and Caligula; hen-pecked Claudius I; and Nero, who in A.D. 64 persecuted the Christians of Rome with a viciousness easily equal to the earlier slave repressions. Several of the military commanders who became emperors were exceptions to the tyrant mold. Late in the 1st century, Trajan expanded the empire's eastern boundaries and constructed great public works, including a vast series of markets.

At this peak, Rome knew amenities not to be enjoyed again in Europe until the 18th century. Citizens were privileged to have police protection, fire fight-ing, libraries, sanitation, huge public baths (such as the Caracalla by the Appian Way), and even central heating and running water—if they could afford them.

The empire's decline began around A.D. 200. After sacking the city several times, Goths and other Germanic tribes set up their own leaders as emperors and were more interested in the spoils of an empire than in actually running one. And while Gibbon's famous opus *The Decline and Fall of the Roman Empire* takes up an entire bookshelf to explain Rome's downfall, in the end it all boils down to the fact that the empire had become just too big to manage.

After embracing Christianity in his famous 313 Edict of Milan, Emperor Constantine I tried to resolve the problem by moving the capital of the empire from Rome to the city of Byzantium (later renamed Constantinople and today known as Istanbul). The Roman Empire was irrevocably split in half: a western Roman Empire comprising most of Europe and North Africa, and an eastern Roman Empire filling southeast Europe and the Near East.

Curtain Going Down: The Dark Ages

In 476, the last emperor (ironically, named Romulus) fell from power and the Roman Empire collapsed. It would be 1,500 years before Italy was once again united as a single nation. As the 6th century opened, Italy was in chaos. Waves of barbarians from the north poured in while provincial nobles engaged in petty bickering, and Rome became the personal fiefdom of the papacy. The Goths con-tinued to rule the "Western Roman Empire" nominally from Ravenna but were

DATELINE *continued*

1450 City-states hold power; Venice controls much of the eastern Mediterranean. The Humanist movement rediscovers the art and philosophy of ancient Greece and gives rise to the artistic Renaissance.

ca. 1500 Peak of the High Renaissance; Italian artists working at the turn of the 15th century include Leonardo Da Vinci, Michelangelo, Raphael, Botticelli, Giovanni Bellini, Mantegna, and Titian.

1519–27 Carlos I Habsburg of Spain is crowned Holy Roman Emperor as Charles V in 1519. He wages war against the French, and the pope scurries back and forth in support of one side then the next as their wars are played out largely in Italy. In 1527, Charles V marches into Rome and sacks the city, while Pope Clement VII escapes. Charles occupies nearly all of northern Italy, divvying it up among his followers.

1535 Francesco II Sforza of Milan dies, leaving the Duchy in Spanish Habsburg hands.

soon driven out by Constantinople. It was the Roman Catholic Church, beginning with Pope Gregory I "the Great" late in the 6th century, which finally provided some stability. In 731, Pope Gregory II renounced Rome's nominal dependence on Constantinople and reoriented the Roman Catholic Church firmly toward Europe—in the process, finalizing the empire's division into east and west.

During the Dark Ages, some inhabitants of the Veneto flatlands, seeking some degree of safety from the barbarian hordes, slowly moved out onto the islets of the north Adriatic's wide, marshy lagoon. The villages they founded eventually grew into the fairy-tale city of Venice. In 564, another Germanic tribe, called the Lombards, clambered over the Alps and swept through much of Italy, conquering a good two-thirds of the peninsula ruled from their base at Pavia. By 599, Pope Gregory I "the Great" had begun flexing the secular power of the papacy (beginning a policy that would eventually set the pope at the head of Europe's power structure), negotiating a peace between Constantinople and Italy's new Lombard rulers.

The Lombards weren't satisfied, though, and by 752 had conquered Ravenna itself. The pope cast around for a new ally against the Lombards and settled on the powerful king of another Barbarian tribe, Pepin the Short of the Franks. In 754, Pepin invaded Italy and thrashed the Lombards; 20 years later, his famous son, Charlemagne, followed suit. Not satisfied with merely the Lombard crown, the French king continued to Rome and convinced the pope to crown him as a new emperor, the so-called Holy Roman Emperor, on Christmas Day in the year 800. This new imperial office would become the plum of western European monarchies for nearly a millennium and further helped cement the relationship between the papacy and the secular titular head of western Europe.

During the Middle Ages, northern Italy fragmented into a collection of city-states. The Lombards had to be content with a reduced duchy filling the Po Valley south of the Alps and Italy's large lakes, wedged between the eastern territory of the Republic of Venice and the western Duchy of Savoy in Piedmont, as well as the coastal territory ruled by the maritime Republic of Genoa. Plenty

1545–63 Council of Trent takes a hard line against the reformist Protestant movements sweeping Europe north of the Alps, launching the Counter-Reformation and, as an unexpected consequence, ultimately reducing the pope's power as a secular ruler of Europe to merely a prince of central Italy.

17th–19th c. Brigands control the countryside, the Austrians and Spanish everything else. By the mid–18th century, wealthy northern Europeans begin taking the Grand Tour, journeying to Italy to study ancient architecture and Italian old masters (as well as taking advantage of the sunny clime and low-cost living). Italy's tourism industry has begun.

1784 The French Revolution sparks Italian nationalism.

1796–1814 Napoleon sweeps through Italy, installing friends and relatives as rulers.

1814 Napoleon is defeated at Waterloo.

continues

of principalities, duchies, republics, and smaller city-states filled in the cracks, with Austrian Habsburg rulers snaking their influence down the Adige River valley into the Dolomites, as well as across the eastern Alps to the coastline curving around the Northern Adriatic, founding the port of Trieste. This put them in constant conflict with the territories of Venice, and the line dividing the realms of Venice's Republican doges and Austria's Habsburg emperors continued to shift, expand, and retreat well into the 20th century.

Meanwhile, the papacy's temporal power—the Papal States—slowly but inexorably shrank, eventually encompassing only Rome and portions of central Italy's provinces. Its political concerns turned to arguing with the German and Austrian emperors over the office of Holy Roman Emperor, which became increasingly irrelevant to daily affairs as the Renaissance dawned.

In the mid–14th century, the Black Death ravaged Europe, killing a third of Italy's population. Despite such setbacks, northern Italian cities grew wealthy from Crusade booty, trade with one another and with the Middle East, and banking. These wealthy principalities and pseudo-republics ruled by the merchant elite flexed their muscles in the absence of a strong central authority.

Curtain Going Up: The Renaissance

The Renaissance peaked in the 15th century as northern cities bullied their way to city-state status. Even while warring constantly with one another to extend their territories, such ruling families as the Medicis in Florence, the Estes in Ferrara, and the Sforzas and Gonzagas in Milan grew incredibly rich and powerful.

The princes, popes, and merchant princes who ruled Italy's city-states, spurred on by the Humanist philosophical movement, collectively bankrolled the explosion of poetic and artistic expression we now call the Renaissance (see "Art & Architecture," p. 47). But with no clear political authority or unified military, Italy was easy pickings, and by the mid–16th century, Spain, courtesy of Charles V, occupied nearly all of the country.

DATELINE *continued*

1830 Beginning of the Risorgimento political movement in Turin and Genoa, which will culminate in Italian nationalism, accompanied by a new Renaissance of literature and music.

1861 Kingdom of Italy is created under Victor Emanuel II, Savoy king of Piedmont (Piemonte), and united through the military campaign of General Garibaldi. Turin serves briefly as interim capital.

1870 Rome, last papal stronghold, falls to Garibaldi. Italy becomes a country with Rome as its capital.

Late 19th C. Mass emigration to America and other foreign shores, mostly from the impoverished, rural south.

1915 Italy enters World War I on Allied side.

1922 Mussolini and his Fascist supporters march on Rome and the king declares him prime minister.

The Second Fall

From the mid–16th century until the end of the 18th century, Italy suffered economic depression and foreign domination. As emphasis on world trade shifted away from the Mediterranean, Italy's influence diminished. Within Italy itself, Spanish Bourbons controlled the kingdoms of the south, the pope the center, and Austria and France fought over rule of the north, using Italy's realms—from the large Lombard duchy of Milan to tiny principalities like Mantua—as pawns in their power struggles. The only notable free state was the mighty Republic of Venice. These foreign overlords kept raising taxes, farming declined, the birthrate sank, and bandits proliferated. The 18th century is viewed as Italy's nadir. In fact, only Europe's eager ear for Italian music and eye for art and architecture kept the Italian profile haughty and its cultural patrimony resplendent.

It was the late-18th-century French Revolution and the arrival of Napoleon that lit Italy's nationalistic fire, although it would be the mid–19th century before the Risorgimento movement and a new king could spread the flame.

The Second Rise: The 19th Century

Italians initially gave Napoleon an exultant *benvenuto!* when he swept through the peninsula and swept out Italy's 18th-century political disasters (along with the Austrian army). But Napoleon, in the end, neither united Italy nor provided it with self-government—he merely set up his friends and relatives as new princes and dukes. Many Italians, however, were fired up by the Napoleonic revolutionary rhetoric. The Risorgimento (resurgence) nationalist movement—an odd amalgam of radicals, moderate liberals, and Roman Catholic conservatives—struggled for 30 years to create a single, united Italy under a constitutional monarchy.

You'll find Risorgimento heroes' names recalled in streets and *piazze* throughout Italy: Giuseppe Mazzini provided the intellectual rigor for the movement, the political genius of noble-born Camillo Cavour engineered the underpinnings of the new nation (he served as its second prime minister), and General Giuseppe Garibaldi and his "Red Shirt" soldiers did the legwork by conquering reluctant or

1935 Italy defeats and annexes Ethiopia.

1939 Italy, an ally of Nazi Germany, remains neutral as World War II breaks out and enters the war in June of the following year by invading France.

1943 Italy switches sides as Allied troops push Nazis north up the peninsula.

1945 In April, as the war is winding down, Mussolini and his mistress are caught trying to flee to Switzerland and are executed by partisans who hang them upside down in Milan's Piazzale Loreto, the same spot were the previous year the Germans had hung the bodies of 15 political prisoners.

1946 In a national referendum, Italians narrowly vote to end the monarchy and establish the Republic of Italy.

1950–93 Fifty changes of government were seen, along with the "economic miracle" that has made Italy the world's eighth-biggest economy.

continues

foreign-controlled territories. In 1861, Victor Emanuel II of the southern French House of Savoy, previously king only of Piedmont and Liguria, became the first king of Italy. By 1871, Garibaldi finally defeated the papal holdout of Rome, and the great city once again became capital of a unified Italy.

Finally, a Nation United

A united nation? On paper, yes, but the old sectional differences remained. While there was rapid industrialization in the north, the south labored under the repressive neo-feudal agricultural ways of the late 19th century, creating a north-south division and mutual mistrust that still pervades Italian society. The north views the south as indolent, a welfare state sucking dry the money made in the industrial north; the south sees the north as elitist and arrogant, constantly proposing or enacting laws to keep the south economically depressed. Many southerners escaped economic hardship and political powerlessness by emigrating to the industrialized north, or to greener pastures abroad in the U.S., South America, or northern Europe.

Italy entered World War I on the Allied side in exchange for territorial demands, and to vanquish that old foe Austria. In the end, the Austro-Hungarian Empire was defeated, but at the Paris Peace Conference, Italy was granted much less territory than had been promised (though it did receive Trento and Trieste), which compounded the country's problems. As southerners abandoned the country in droves, the economy stagnated, and what remained of Italy's world importance seemed to be fading rapidly, along came Benito Mussolini, promising to restore national pride and bring order out of the chaos.

Fascism Reigns

Mussolini marched on Rome in 1922, forced the king to make him premier, nicknamed himself Il Duce (the Duke), and quickly repressed all other political factions. He put his Fascist "Blackshirts" in charge of the entire country: schools,

DATELINE *continued*

1993–97 Series of disasters rocks Italy's cultural roots: 1993 Mafia bombing of Florence's Uffizi Galleries; January 1996 fire at Venice's La Fenice opera house; April 1997 conflagration in Turin's cathedral; and September 1997 earthquakes in Umbria, which destroyed priceless frescoes in Assisi.

1993–2000 Italy's Christian Democrat–controlled government dissolves amid corruption allegations. Silvio Berlusconi's right-wing coalition holds power for a few months, followed by center–left wing coalitions that introduce the most stable governments in decades under prime ministers Romano Prodi, Massimo d'Alema, and Giuliano Amato.

2001 Media magnate (and the world's 118th-richest man) Silvio Berlusconi—briefly prime minister in 1993—gains control again of the Italian government as the leader of the center-right coalition.

the press, industry, and labor. Seeking, as Italian despot-hopefuls throughout history have done, to endear himself to the general populace, Mussolini instituted a vast public-works program, most of which eventually failed. Mussolini fancied himself a second Caesar and spent some time excavating the archaeological remains of ancient Rome—not always with the most stringent scientific methods—to help glorify his reign and lend it authority. The Great Depression of the 1930s made life considerably more difficult for Italians, and, to divert attention from his shortcomings as a ruler, Mussolini turned to foreign adventures, defeating and annexing Ethiopia in 1935.

Mussolini entered Italy into World War II in 1940 as an Axis ally of the Nazis, but the Italian heart was not really in the war, and most Italians had little wish to pursue Hitler's anti-

Dictator Benito Mussolini.

Semitic policies. Italy had little success on the battlefield, and in 1943 with the country reeling, the king signed a peace treaty with the Allies and had Mussolini arrested. The German army immediately occupied two-thirds of Italy and with a daring raid managed to free Mussolini, who they set up as the head of a puppet government based out of Salò on Lake Garda. Two more years of war followed, with the partisan resistance and the Allies on one side and the remnants of the Fascist army and the Germans on the other.

2002 Italy, along with most of western Europe, begins using the euro as its currency.

2006 Italy's highest appeals court confirms Romano Prodi's razor-thin victory over Berlusconi in national elections, sending the one-time professor and European Commission President back to head the Italian government.

2008 The People of Freedom (*Il Popolo della Libertà*, PdL) party is founded when Forza Italia merges with Alleanza Nazionale. As the leader of this center-right political party, Berlusconi is once again elected Prime Minister in the general elections.

2010 Alleanza Nazionale leader Gianfranco Fini feuds with Berlusconi and breaks away from the PdL, weakening the prime minister's grip on power.

2011 Berlusconi's party loses majority in Parliamnet, and he resigns as Prime Minister.

The war ended in April 1945 with the partisans liberating many of northern Italy's largest cities, including Milan, ahead of the arrival of the Allied armies. Mussolini and his mistress were caught trying to flee to Switzerland and executed by partisans, who hung them upside down in Milan's Piazzale Loreto, the same spot where the previous year the Germans had hung the bodies of 15 political prisoners.

Democracy at Last

The monarchy had collaborated with the Fascists during the previous 2 decades so, perhaps unsurprisingly, after the war the Italians voted (narrowly) to become a republic, and in 1946 a new republican constitution went into effect. The south voted heavily in favor of the monarchy while the center and the majority of northern Italy voted for the republic.

Various permutations of the center-right Christian Democrat party ruled in a succession of more than 50 governments until 1993, when the entire government dissolved in a flurry of corruption and graft. The country's leaders were prosecuted (and many jailed) by what became known as the "Clean Hands" judges of Milan. The two main parties, the Christian Democrats and the Communists, both splintered in the aftermath, giving rise to some 16 major political parties and countless minor ones.

The parties formed various coalitions, leading to strange political bedfellows such as Forza Italia, headed by media mogul Silvio Berlusconi, which filled the post–Clean Hands national power vacuum in 1994 with a coalition that included both the nationalist Alleanza Nazionale party (formerly an openly fascist party) and the Lega Nord, the separatist "Northern League," which molded regionalism with populism. (In its early years, the Lega Nord preached splitting Italy in half, making Milan capital of a new country in the north called "Padania" and leaving Rome to govern the poor south.) In 2000, though, the Lega changed its tune to become more palatable and began calling for a decentralized government with more power going to individual regions.

The Lega Nord broke with Berlusconi after the two had ruled for less than a year; a nonpartisan government then ruled until a national election in 1996 brought the center-left Olive Tree coalition to power, bringing with it a novelty for Italy: 3 years of relatively stable rule under prime ministers Romano Prodi and then Massimo D'Alema. Interestingly, given the stereotype among fellow Europeans of Italy as a nation prone to graft and political chaos, Prodi—an economist before becoming prime minister and the man who reined in Italy's yearly deficits to qualify the country for the euro—was later named to head the European Commission to restore its status after a humiliating scandal.

By 2001, Berlusconi had fought off the dozens of legal charges of corruption (though courts in Spain, trying him for corporate crimes relating to his business relations in Iberia, found him guilty), and in April of that year, he and his right-wing partners came back into power, just in time to shepherd Italy through the switch from the lira to the euro in 2002. Berlusconi continued to consolidate power through 2002 and 2003, introducing ever more legislation to protect himself and his interests from criminal investigations, as well as laws that would allow his private media company to control even more of the country's communications industry. (Through the trio of state-run RAI channels and his own Mediaset network, he already controls the six most popular of Italy's seven free-to-air broadcast channels.) It is hard to say whether it was Berlusconi's legal troubles or his unpopular decision to support the United States' invasion and occupation of Iraq that turned the tide against him. Whatever the cause, the result in the 2006 elections was a loss to Romano Prodi by a slim margin of votes, though the triumphant return of the "Professor" was short-lived. Berlusconi came galloping back to power in the elections of 2008. But it would be his final turn, after a debt crisis in Europe finally forced his party out of power; he resigned as prime minister in late 2011.

Politically, some things never change in Italy. The same mistrust among factions continues: Cities are still paranoid about their individuality and their rights, and the division between north and south is as sharp as ever. The Mafia, which operates in Sicily, and similar organized crime groups including the Camorra in the region around Naples, have controlled aspects of life and politics in the south since at least the late 19th century. Now there are indications that organized crime has infiltrated northern Italian cities as well.

The outsider looks and wonders how the country keeps going amid the political chaos, Byzantine bureaucracy, and deep regional differences. The Italian just shrugs and rolls his eyes. Italians have always excelled at getting by under difficult circumstances and making the most of any situation. If nothing else, they're masters at survival.

ART & ARCHITECTURE

Art

When you mention art in Italy, thoughts fly first to the Renaissance—to Donatello, Michelangelo, Raphael, and Leonardo. But Italy's artistic heritage actually goes back at least 2,500 years.

CLASSICAL ART: GREEKS, ETRUSCANS & ROMANS (5TH C. B.C.–5TH C. A.D.)

Today all, or almost all, design roads lead to Milan. In the beginning, though, all roads led from Athens. What the **Greeks** identified early on that captured the hearts and minds of so many was the classical rendering of form. To the ancients, *classic* or *classical* simply meant perfection—of proportion, balance, harmony, and form. To the Greeks, man was the measure of perfection, an attitude lost in the Middle Ages and not rediscovered until the dawn of the Renaissance.

Although those early tourists to the Italian peninsula, the **Etruscans,** arrived with their own styles, by the 6th century B.C., they were borrowing heavily from the Greeks in their sculpture (and importing thousands of Attic painted vases). The **Romans,** in turn, copied heavily from the Greeks, often ad nauseam as they cranked out countless facsimiles of Greek sculptures to decorate Roman patrician homes and gardens. Bronze portraiture, a technique with Greek and Etruscan roots, was polished to photographic perfection.

Although painting got rather short shrift in ancient Rome (it was used primarily for decorative purposes), bucolic frescoes, the technique of painting on wet plaster, adorned the walls of the wealthy in Rome, though nothing significant survives in the north of Italy. Mosaics were rather better done and survived the ages more intact; you can see some of the best Roman mosaic flooring at the excavations of Aquileia in the Friuli.

BYZANTINE & ROMANESQUE (5TH–13TH C.)

Artistic expression in the Dark Ages and early medieval Italy was largely church related. Mass was recited in Latin, so to help explain the most important lessons to the illiterate masses, biblical bas-reliefs around the churches' main doors, as well as wall paintings and altarpieces inside, told key tales to inspire faith in God and fear of sin (Last Judgments were favorites). Otherwise, decoration was spare, and what little existed was often destroyed, replaced, or covered over the centuries as tastes changed and cathedrals were remodeled.

The Byzantine style of painting and mosaic was very stylized and static, an iconographic tradition imported from the remnant eastern half of the Roman Empire centered at Byzantium (its major political outposts in Italy were Ravenna and Venice). Faces (and eyes) were almond-shaped with pointy little chins, noses long, and folds in robes (always Virgin Mary blue over red) represented by stylized cross-hatching in gold leaf.

Romanesque sculpture was somewhat more fluid, but still far from naturalistic. Usually idiosyncratic and often wonderfully childlike in its narrative simplicity, it frequently freely mixed biblical scenes with the myths and motifs from local pagan traditions that were being slowly incorporated into early medieval Christianity.

Romanesque art was seen as crude by most later periods and was replaced or destroyed over the centuries; it survives mostly in scraps, innumerable column capitals, and tympanums (carvings set above church doors) all across Italy. Some of the best major examples of this era in northern Italy include the astounding mosaics decorating **San Marco Cathedral in Venice,** a late Byzantine church of domes and a glittering array of mosaics. (However, while the overall effect is indeed Byzantine, many of the mosaics are from various later dates.) **Verona's San Zeno Maggiore** sports 48 relief panels on the bronze doors, one of the most important pieces of Romanesque sculpture in Italy, cast between the 9th and 11th centuries and flanked by strips of 12th-century stone reliefs. **Aosta's Collegiata dei Santi Pietro e Orso,** on the edge of town, preserves part of an 11th-century fresco cycle and 40 remarkable 12th-century carved column capitals in the cloisters.

INTERNATIONAL GOTHIC (LATE 13TH TO EARLY 15TH C.)

Late medieval Italian art continued to be largely ecclesiastical. Church facades and pulpits were festooned with statues and carvings. In both Gothic painting and sculpture, figures tended to be more natural than in the Romanesque (and the colors in painting more varied and rich), but highly stylized and rhythmic, the figures' features and gestures exaggerated for symbolic or emotional emphasis. In painting especially, late Gothic artists such as Giotto started introducing greater realism, a sense of depth, and more realistic emotion into their art, sowing the seeds of the Renaissance.

Without a doubt, **Giotto** (1266–1337) was the greatest Gothic artist, the man who lifted painting from its Byzantine funk and set it on the road to the realism and perspective of the Renaissance. His most renowned work is the fresco cycle of Assisi's Basilica di San Francesco, but arguably better (and more certain of its authorship) is Padua's (Padova's) outstanding **Scrovegni (Arena) Chapel.** The bulk of great Gothic art resides in Tuscany and Umbria, but Verona was blessed to have **Antonio Pisanello** (1395–1455), whose frescoes survive in Sant'Anastasia and San Fermo, and in Mantua (Mantova) at the Palazzo Ducale.

RENAISSANCE & MANNERISM (EARLY 15TH TO MID–17TH C.)

From the 14th to 16th centuries, the popularity of the Humanist movement in philosophy prompted princes and powerful prelates to patronize a generation of innovative young artists. These painters, sculptors, and architects were experimenting with new modes in art and breaking with static medieval traditions to pursue a greater degree of expressiveness and naturalism, using such techniques as linear perspective (actually pioneered by architect Brunelleschi and sculptors Donatello and Ghiberti). The term *Renaissance,* or "rebirth," was only later applied to this period in Florence, from which the movement spread to the rest of Italy and Europe.

Eventually, the High Renaissance began to stagnate, producing vapid works of technical perfection but little substance. Several artists sought ways out of the downward spiral. Mannerism was the most interesting attempt, a movement that found its muse in the extreme torsion of Michelangelo's figures—in sculpture and painting—and his unusual use of oranges, greens, and other nontraditional colors, most especially in the Sistine Chapel ceiling. In sculpture, Mannerism produced twisting figures in exaggerated *contrapposto* positioning.

This list of Renaissance giants merely scratches the surface of the masters Italy gave rise to in the 15th and 16th centuries.

Donatello (Donato Bardi; ca. 1386–1466) was the first full-fledged Renaissance sculptor, with a patented *schiacciato* technique of warping low relief surfaces and etching backgrounds in perspective to create a sense of deep space. His bronze and marble figures are some of the most expressive and psychologically probing of the Renaissance. Among his many innovations, this unassuming artist cast the first equestrian bronze since antiquity, the *Gattamelata* in Padua.

Leonardo Da Vinci (1452–1519) was the original "Renaissance Man," dabbling his genius in a bit of everything, from art to philosophy to science. (On paper, he even designed machine guns and rudimentary helicopters.) Little of his remarkable painting survives, however, as he often experimented with new pigment mixes that proved to lack the staying power of traditional materials. Leonardo invented such painterly effects as the fine haze of *sfumato,* "a moisture-laden atmosphere that delicately veils . . . forms." Unfortunately, the best example of this effect, his fresco of *The Last Supper* in Milan (1495–97), is extremely deteriorated, though the 21-year restoration completed in 1999 has restored some of its former glory. See his *Portrait of a Musician* in Milan's Pinacoteca Ambrosiana for a less spectacular but better-preserved example.

Michelangelo Buonarotti (1475–1564), heavyweight contender for world's greatest artist ever, was a genius in sculpture, painting, architecture, and poetry. He marked the apogee of the Renaissance. Intensely jealous, probably manic-depressive, and certainly homosexual, Michelangelo was a complex and difficult man who enjoyed great fame in a life marked by a series of never-ending projects commissioned by Pope Julius II. Michelangelo worshiped the male nude as the ultimate form and twisted the bodies of his figures in different, often contradictory directions *(contrapposto)* to bring out their musculature. When forced against his will to paint the Sistine Chapel, he broke almost all the rules and sent painting headlong in an entirely new direction—the Mannerist movement—marked by nonprimary colors, impressionistic shapes of light, and twisting muscular figures. While you'll have to go to Florence and Rome to see his greatest creations, including the *David,* you can admire his final work in Milan, an oddly modern, elongated *Pietà* he was still working on when he died at age 89.

Raphael (Raffaello Sanzio; 1483–1520) is rightfully considered one of Western art's greatest draftsmen. Raphael produced a body of work in his 37 short years that ignited European painters for generations to come. So it's only fitting that his only significant work in northern Italy, kept in Milan's Pinacoteca Ambrosiana, is a sketch for the *School of Athens,* the fresco of which graces the papal apartments of the Vatican.

All of the above artists hailed from central Italy. Now we get to some home-grown northern Italian talents. Though his father, **Jacopo** (1400–71), and brother, **Gentile** (1429–1507), were also fine practitioners of the family business, it was **Giovanni Bellini** (1430–1516) who towered above them all with his painterly talent, limpid colors, sculptured forms, and complex compositions. Both he and his brother are best represented by works in Venice's Accademia and Palazzo Ducale, as well as Milan's Pinacoteca di Brera. Giovanni Bellini's style and talent reverberated through Venetian art for generations; he himself taught the likes of Titian, Giorgione, Sebastiano del Piombo, and Palma il Vecchio.

Gentile and Giovanni had a sister, too, and, as it happened, she married a young painter named **Andrea Mantegna** (1431–1506). Mantegna excelled at three of the main tenets of Renaissance art: He was an early master of perspective (which he could warp masterfully), he was a keen observer of anatomy (which he modeled with sculptural exactitude), and he made careful studies of ancient architecture (the proportions and details of which he incorporated into his paintings). You'll find Mantegna's paintings throughout the region, from his early *Madonna and Child with Saints* altarpiece for Verona's San Zeno, to his work as court painter to the Gonzagas in Mantua (the Palazzo Ducale's *Camera degli Sposi*), to his unparalleled *Dead Christ,* considered the masterpiece of Milan's Pinacoteca di Brera (no small honor, considering the heavyweights inhabiting the premier art gallery in northern Italy).

Titian (Tiziano Vecellio; 1485–1576) was the father of the Venetian High Renaissance, who imparted to the school his love of color and tonality and exploration of the effects of light on darkened scenes. In Venice, you'll find his works everywhere, from canvases in the Accademia collections to altarpieces decorating churches, such as the Frari, to his early and famous *Battle* scene (1513) in the Palazzo Ducale's Sala del Maggior Consiglio.

After Titian, 16th-century Venetian art was dominated by two powerful talents, Tintoretto and Paolo Veronese. **Tintoretto** (Jacopo Robusti; 1518–94) was something of a Venetian Mannerist, using a rapid, loose brushwork and a slightly somber, shadow-filled take on the tones of Titian's palette that together imparted a realism and vitality to his painting. Venice's Accademia has some works, of course, but his crowning glory is the Scuola Grande di San Rocco in Venice, for which he painted well over a dozen large-scale canvases. He also holds the honor of

What's in a Name?

Many Italian artists came to be known by nicknames—usually based on the town from which they came. "Tintoretto" was called that because of his love of color (*tinto* in Italian means colored). Leonardo had no official last name (he was the bastard son of a serving wench and her boss, a minor noble and landowner in the small town of Vinci), so everyone just called him "Leonardo from Vinci." Some also had silly nicknames, like Sandro Filipepi, better known to his buds as "Little Barrels"—or, in Italian, Botticelli.

having produced (with the help of son Domenico) the largest oil painting in the world (6.9×24m/23×79 ft.), the *Paradise,* decorating the end wall of the Sala del Maggior Consiglio in the Palazzo Ducale in Mantua.

Verona-born **Paolo Veronese** (Paolo Caliari; 1528–88) had a much brighter, tighter style, and he loved crowding his canvases with hordes of extras straight out of 16th-century central casting. In fact, his broad inclusion of earthy details ran him afoul of the Counter-Reformation spirit of the times, and he avoided incurring the church's wrath over the crowd of serving wenches and slave boys populating a *Last Supper* he painted only by hastily retitling it *Feast in the House of Levi* (now in Venice's Accademia). The church of San Sebastiano boasts his ceiling frescoes, but it's Venice's Palazzo Ducale that bookends the career of Veronese (containing both his earliest paintings and one of his final ones). His earliest Venetian commissions (1553) were for paintings in the chambers where two groups in the highest echelons of Venice's ruling body met, the Sala del Consiglio dei Dieci and the Sala dei Tre Capi del Consiglio. One of his final works (finished by his studio) was the huge *Apotheosis of Venice* decorating the ceiling of the Sala del Maggior Consiglio. Veronese would be the main artist to inspire Tiepolo and others in Venice's next generation of baroque artists.

BAROQUE & ROCOCO (LATE 16TH TO 18TH C.)

The baroque is a more theatrical and decorative take on the Renaissance, mixing a kind of super-realism based on the peasant models and chiaroscuro (harsh light and exaggeratedly dark shadows) of Caravaggio with compositional complexity and explosions of dynamic fury, movement, color, and figures. The baroque period produced many fine artists, but only a few true geniuses, and most of them, including Caravaggio and Bernini, created their best work in Rome and the south. **Caravaggio** (Michelangelo Merisi da Caravaggio; 1571–1610) may or may not have been born in Milan—that is still being debated—but what is certain is that the city where he worked as a young man holds two of his early works: *Basket of Fruit* in the Pinacoteca Ambrosiana and *Supper in Emmaus* in the Pinacoteca di Brera.

Rococo is this later baroque art gone awry, frothy, and chaotic. **Giovanni Battista Tiepolo** (1696–1770) was, by a long shot, the best rococo artist, influenced by not only his Venetian late-Renaissance predecessors but also the Roman and Neapolitan baroque. His specialty was painting ceiling frescoes (and canvases meant to be placed on ceilings) that opened up the space into cloud-filled heavens of light, angels, and pale, sunrise colors. Though he painted many works for Veneto villas, including the sumptuous Villa Valmarana and Villa Pisani, he also spent much of his time traveling throughout Europe on long commissions. (His work in Würzburg, Germany, enjoys distinction as the largest ceiling fresco in the world.) His son, **Giovanni Domenico Tiepolo** (1727–1804), carried on the family tradition in a Venice increasingly ruled by genre masters like **Antonio Canaletto** (1697–1738), whose ultrarealistic scenes of Venetian canals and palaces were snapped up by the collectors from across the Alps who began sniffing around Italy on their Grand Tour.

LATE 18TH CENTURY TO TODAY

After carrying the artistic church of innovation for over a millennium, Italy ran out of steam with the baroque, leaving countries such as France to develop the heights of neoclassicism (though Italy produced a few fine neoclassical sculptures) and late-19th-century Impressionism (Italians had their own version, called the **Macchiaioli**). Italy has not played an important role in late-19th/20th-century art, though it has produced a few great artists, whose works grace Milan's Pinacoteca di Brera, Palazzo Reale, and new Museo del Novecento, which opened in 2010.

Antonio Canova (1757–1822) was Italy's top neoclassical sculptor, popular for his mythological figures and Bonaparte portraits (he even did both Napoleon and his sister Pauline as nudes); in addition to the Brera in Milan, you'll find his work in Venice's Museo Correr. **Giovanni Fattori** (1825–1908), perhaps the best of the Macchiaioli, was fond of battle scenes and landscapes populated by long-horned white cattle.

A sickly boy and only moderately successful in his short lifetime, **Amadeo Modigliani** (1884–1920) helped reinvent the portrait in painting and sculpture after he moved to Paris in 1906. He is famed for his elongated, mysterious heads and rapidly painted nudes. Check them out at Milan's Pinacoteca di Brera and Museo del Novecento. **Giorgio de Chirico** (1888–1978) was the founder of freaky *metafisica,* "metaphysical painting," a forerunner of surrealism wherein figures and objects are stripped of their usual meaning through odd juxtapositions, warped perspective and reality, unnatural shadows, and other bizarre effects, as well as a general spatial emptiness. **Giorgio Morandi** (1890–1964) was influenced by *metafisica* in his eerily minimalist, highly modeled, quasi-monochrome still lifes. His paintings decorate Turin's Galleria d'Arte Moderna.

Italian artists living in 1909 Paris made a spirited attempt to take the artistic initiative back into Italian hands, but what the **Futurist** movement's **Umberto Boccioni** (1882–1916) came up with was largely cubism with an element of movement added in. **Gino Severini** (1883–1966) contributed a sophisticated take on color, which rubbed off on the core cubists as well. Both are represented at Milan's Pinacoteca di Brera and Museo del Novecento.

Architecture

While each architectural era has its distinctive features, there are some elements, general floor plans, and terms common to many. Also, some features may appear near the end of one era and continue through several later ones.

From the Romanesque period on, most churches consisted of either a single, wide aisle or a wide central nave flanked by two narrow aisles. The aisles are separated from the nave by a row of columns, or by square stacks of masonry called piers, usually connected by arches.

This main nave/aisle assemblage is usually crossed by a perpendicular corridor called a transept near the far, east end of the church so that the floor plan looks like a Latin Cross (shaped like a crucifix). The shorter, east arm of the nave is the holiest area, called the chancel; it often houses the stalls of the choir and the altar. If the far end of the chancel is rounded off, it is called an apse. An ambulatory is a curving corridor outside the altar and choir area, separating it from the ring of smaller chapels radiating off the chancel and apse.

Some churches, especially after the Renaissance, when mathematical proportion became important, were built on a Greek cross plan, each axis the same length. By the baroque period, funky shapes became popular, with churches built in the round, or as ellipses, and so forth.

It's worth pointing out that very few buildings (especially churches) were built in only one particular style. These massive, expensive structures often took centuries to complete, during which time tastes would change and plans would be altered.

ANCIENT ROME (1ST C. B.C.–4TH C. A.D.)

The Romans made use of certain Greek innovations, particularly architectural ideas. The first to be adopted was post-and-lintel construction—essentially, a weight-bearing frame, like a door. Later came adaptation of Greek columns for supporting buildings, following the classical orders of Doric column capitals (the plain ones) on the ground floor, Ionic capitals (with the scrolls on either end) on the next level, and Corinthian capitals (flowering with acanthus leaves) on the top.

Romans thrived on huge complex problems for which they could produce organized, well-crafted solutions. Roman builders became inventive engineers, developing hoisting mechanisms and a specially trained workforce. They designed towns, built civic centers, raised grand temples and public baths, and developed the basilica, a rectangle supported by arches atop columns along both sides of the interior and with an apse at one or both ends. Basilicas were used for courts of justice, banking, and other commercial structures. The design was repeated all over the Roman world, beginning around the 1st century A.D. Later, early Christians adapted the architectural style for the first grand churches, still called basilicas.

Roman urban planning still stamps the street layouts of cities from **Aosta** (which preserves a gate and theater stage) to **Brescia** (with an ancient temple and theater remaining in the city center) to **Verona** (which preserves a magnificent ancient amphitheater still used for performances). Roman ruins can be found all over the rest of northern Italy including the impressive Porta Palatina in **Turin.**

ROMANESQUE (A.D. 800–1300)

The Romanesque took its inspiration and rounded arches from ancient Rome (hence the name). Romanesque architects concentrated on building large churches with wide aisles to fit the ranks of people who came not only to hear the priests say Mass but mainly to worship at the altars of various saints. To support the weight of all that masonry, though, the walls had to be thick and solid (meaning they could be pierced only by few and rather small windows) resting on huge piers, giving Romanesque churches a dark, somber, mysterious, and often oppressive feeling.

The most identifiable Romanesque feature is its rounded arches. These load-bearing architectural devices allowed the architects to open up wide naves and spaces, channeling all the weight of the stone walls and ceiling across the curve of the arch and down into the ground via the columns or pilasters. The style also made use of blind arcades, decorative bands of "filled-in" arches, the columns engaged in the wall and the arches' curves on top protruding mere inches. Set into each arch's curve is often a lozenge, a diamond-shaped decoration, typically inlaid with marble of different colors.

The **Basilica of Sant'Ambrogio in Milan** (11th–12th c.) is festooned with the tiered loggias and arcades that would become hallmarks of the Lombard Romanesque.

GOTHIC (LATE 12TH TO EARLY 15TH C.)

By the late 12th century, engineering developments—most significantly the pointed arch, which could bear a much heavier load than a rounded one—freed architects from the heavy, thick walls of Romanesque structures and allowed ceilings to soar, walls to thin, and windows to proliferate.

Instead of dark, somber, relatively unadorned Romanesque interiors that forced the eyes of the faithful toward the altar and its priest droning on in unintelligible Latin, the Gothic churchgoer's gaze was drawn up to high ceilings filled with light, a window unto heaven. The priests still gibbered in a language few could understand, but now peasants could "read" the Gothic comic books of colorful frescoes lining the walls and panels in stained-glass windows.

The Gothic and stark Santa Maria dei Frari.

In addition to those pointy arches, another Gothic innovation was the famous flying buttress. These free-standing exterior pillars connected by graceful, thin arms of stone help channel the weight of the building and its roof out and down into the ground. To help counter the cross-forces involved in this engineering sleight of hand, the piers of buttresses were often topped by heavy pinnacles or statues. Inside, the general pointiness continued with cross-vaults. The square patch of ceiling between four columns, instead of being flat, would arch up to a point in the center, creating four sail shapes, sort of like the underside of a pyramid with bulging faces. The X separating these four "sails" was often reinforced with ridges called ribbing. As the Gothic style progressed, four-sided cross-vaults became six-, eight-, or multisided as architects played with the angles they could make. In addition, tracery—delicate, lacy spider webs of carved-stone curlicues—graced the pointy end of windows and just about any acute angle throughout the architecture.

The true, French-style Gothic flourished only in northern Italy, and the best example is **Milan's massive cathedral, the Duomo,** a festival of pinnacles, buttresses, and pointy arches begun in the late 14th century. **Venice's Santa Maria dei Frari** is a bit airier and boxier; **Padua's Basilica di Sant'Antonio** is largely Gothic, though its Romanesque facade and Byzantine domes may throw you off. In palace architecture, the Venetians developed a distinctive style of insetting lacy, lithe, pointed marble windows with an Eastern flair into pale pastel plaster walls. This is seen in countless palaces across **Venice,** especially in its most lavish: **Ca' d'Oro, Ca' Foscari,** and the model against which all were measured, the **Palazzo Ducale** itself.

RENAISSANCE (15TH–17TH C.)

As in painting, Renaissance architectural rules stressed proportion, order, classical inspiration, and mathematical precision to create unified, balanced structures. It was probably a Florentine architect, Filippo Brunelleschi, in the early

1400s, who first truly grasped the concept of "perspective" and provided artists with ground rules for creating the illusion of three dimensions on a flat surface.

The early Renaissance was truly codified by central Italian architects working in Florence and Rome, though influential early Florentine theorist **Leon Battista Alberti** (1404–72) built structures across Italy, including Sant'Andrea in Mantua. Urbino-born **Donato Bramante** (1444–1514), who would find fame in Rome building St. Peter's, got his start in Milan by converting the older church of San Satiro and rebuilding the altar end of Santa Maria delle Grazie.

The undisputed master of the High Renaissance was **Andrea Palladio** (1508–80), from Veneto, who worked in a much more strictly classical mode of columns, porticoes, pediments, and other ancient temple–inspired features (see the "Andrea Palladio—Father of Neoclassicism" box, below). In Venice, **Jacopo Sansovino** (1486–1570) reigned supreme, his loggia and Libreria Sansoviniana lining St. Mark's Square becoming a cornerstone of the High Renaissance, to be copied and repeated in such far-flung architectural endeavors as the cast-iron facades in New York's SoHo district.

Raphael protégé **Giulio Romano** (1492–1546) designed Mantua's impressive **Palazzo Te; Galeazzo Alessi** (1512–72) was the premier architect of Genoa's famed palaces, many of which are now museums.

BAROQUE & ROCOCO (17TH–18TH C.)

More than any other movement, the **baroque** aimed toward a seamless meshing of architecture and art. The stuccoes, sculptures, and paintings were all carefully designed to complement each other—and the space itself—to create a unified whole. This whole was both aesthetic and narrative, the various art forms all working together to tell a single, usually biblical, story (or often to subtly relate the deeds of the commissioning patron to great historic or biblical events).

In the baroque, classical architecture exchanges its crisp angles and ruler-straight lines for curves of complex geometry and an interplay of concave and convex. The overall effect is to lighten the appearance of structures and add movement of line and vibrancy to the static look of the classical Renaissance.

Unlike the sometimes severe and austere designs of the Renaissance, the baroque was playful. Architects festooned structures and encrusted interiors with an excess of decorations intended to liven things up—lots of ornate stuccowork, pouting cherubs, airy frescoes, heavy gilding, twisting columns, multicolored marbles, and general frippery.

The baroque was also a movement of multiplying forms. The baroque asked, "Why make do with one column when you can stack a half-dozen partial columns on top of each other, slightly offset, until the effect is like looking at a single column though a fractured kaleidoscope?" The baroque loved to pile up its forms and elements to create a rich, busy effect, breaking a pediment curve into segments so each would protrude farther out than the last, or building up an architectural feature by stacking short sections of concave walls, each one curving to a different arc.

The baroque flourished across Italy, but little of it was truly inspired architecture. You'll find good examples in Venice's Santa Maria della Salute, and especially in Turin, from the Castellamonte-designed Piazza San Carlo to the great works of Guarino Guarini (San Lorenzo, Palazzo Carignano, the chapel for the Holy Shroud in the cathedral) and Filippo Juvarra (Basilica di Superga, Palazzina di Stupinigi).

Rococo is the baroque gone awry into the grotesque, excessively complex and dripping with decorative tidbits.

ANDREA PALLADIO—FATHER OF
neoclassicism

Order, balance, elegance, harmony with the landscape, and a human scale are all apparent in the creations of architect **Andrea Palladio** (1508–80). Palladio was working as a stonemason and sculptor when, at age 30, inspired by the design of ancient buildings he studied on trips to Rome, he turned his hand to architecture and applied the principles of classical proportion to Renaissance ideals of grace, symmetry, and functionality. **Vicenza,** the little city near Venice where Palladio lived as a boy and where he returned in his prime, is graced with many Palladian *palazzo,* a church, and his Teatro Olimpico. In **Venice,** he designed the churches of San Giorgio Maggiore and Redentore.

Palladio is best known, though, for the villas he built on the flat plains of Veneto for Venetian nobles yearning to escape the cramped city. Nineteen of these villas still stand, including what may be his finest, **La Rotunda,** outside Vicenza. The design of this and

Palladio's other villas—square, perfectly proportioned, elegant yet functional—may strike a note of familiarity with American and British visitors: Palladio influenced generations of architects who followed his lead when they designed neoclassical plantation houses in the American South and country estates in England, his "Palladian" style informing everything from British architecture to Thomas Jefferson's Monticello.

NEOCLASSICAL TO MODERN (18TH–21ST C.)

By the middle of the 18th century, as a backlash against the excesses of the baroque and rococo, architects, inspired by the rediscovery of Pompeii and other ancient sites, began turning to the austere simplicity and grandeur of the classical age and inaugurated a **neoclassical** style. The classical ideals of mathematical proportion and symmetry, first rediscovered during the Renaissance, are the hallmark of every classically styled era—a reinterpretation of ancient temples into buildings and massive colonnaded porticos. Northern Italy's two famed opera houses, Milan's La Scala and Venice's La Fenice, are both excellent neoclassical exercises. To see perhaps the best example of the chilliness the neoclassical style often entailed, pop into Padua's Caffè Pedrocchi for a cappuccino.

Italy's take on the early-20th-century Art Nouveau movements was called **Liberty.** Like all Art Nouveau, Liberty decorators were rebelling against the era of mass production and stressed uniqueness. They created asymmetrical, curvaceous designs based on organic inspiration (plants and flowers) and used wrought iron, stained glass, tile, and hand-painted wallpaper. Turin and Milan have many fine examples of Liberty architecture.

The dome of the Mole Antonelliana.

The **Industrial Age** of the late 19th and early 20th centuries brought with it the first genteel shopping malls of glass and steel girders, such as the famed Galleria in Milan. Mussolini made a spirited attempt to bring back ancient Rome in what can only be called **Fascist** architecture: Deco meets Caesar. Monumentally imposing and chillingly stark white marble structures are surrounded by classical-style statues. Fascist architecture still infests all corners of Italy, though most of the right-wing reliefs and the repeated engravings of "DVCE"—Mussolini's nickname for himself—have long since been chipped out. One of the best, easily accessible, oft-overlooked examples is Milan's massive train station (so if you're stuck with a long wait, wander outside to squint up at the weird Deco gargoyles and call your layover sightseeing).

Fitting into no style is Turin's truly odd **Mole Antonelliana** (1863–97), designed as a synagogue but later put to various uses (currently, it is the national film museum). Its squat brick base is topped by a steep cone supporting several layers of Greek temples piled one atop the other at right angles, capped off in turn by a needlelike spire at 166m (544 ft.).

Since then, Italy has mostly poured concrete and glass skyscrapers like the rest of us, though a few architects in the medium have stood out. The mid–20th century was dominated by **Pier Luigi Nervi** (1891–1979) and his reinforced concrete buildings, including Turin's Exposition Hall (1949). Italy's greatest living architect, Pritzker Prize–winning **Renzo Piano** (b. 1937), lives in Paris, and most of his great commissions, including the Pompidou, are outside of Italy.

NORTHERN ITALY IN POPULAR CULTURE

Literature

NONFICTION

The best way to understand Italy's recent history is to read **Paul Ginsborg**'s seminal work, *A History of Contemporary Italy: Society and Politics, 1943–1988* (2003). Don't be put off by the academic sound of the title. It is extremely readable, comical at times, and probably the most oft-quoted history of modern Italy in the English-speaking world. A lot of ink has been spilled on modern Italian culture; none of it affords the same insight as Ginsborg's history.

Giacomo Casanova was a native Venetian and a renowned writer and adventurer famous for his romantic exploits. Although he wrote mostly in French and the most entertaining chapters of his life as a philanderer generally took place in faraway cities, he did dedicate some space to Venice in his memoirs, *History of My Life,* written in several volumes; a read through his exploits gives you a good idea of what life was like—or, at least, life among the very wealthy—in 18th-century Venice.

Few other countries have experienced such a volume of foreign examination of its national character and culture. The letters and poems of Romantic writers **Percy Bysshe Shelly** and **John Keats,** and the travel writings of **D. H. Lawrence** and **H. V. Morton,** include notable observations of northern Italy, which are almost universally flattering. In recent years, that torch has been passed to **Tim Parks,** a British expatriate who has lived near Verona with his Italian wife since 1981. His observations through the 1990s are documented in *Italian Neighbours* (1992) and *An Italian Education* (1996), which, mercifully, lacks the wide-eyed romantic view taken by so many others.

Of course, the best way to avoid that naïveté is to read the Italians themselves—when their texts are available in English. **Luigi Barzini**'s *The Italians* (1996) is a great place to start, but for an insider's view on today's Italy, check out **Alexander Stille**'s *The Sack of Rome: How a Beautiful Country with a Fabled History and a Storied Culture was Taken Over by a Man Named Silvio Berlusconi* (2006). **Gian Antonio Stella** and **Sergio Rizzo** wrote a definitive work on modern Italian politics, *The Caste: How Italian Politicians Have Become Untouchable* (2007).

FICTION

Northern Italy is the birthplace of many of the country's novelists and poets, from **Alessandro Manzoni, Italo Calvino, Carlo Levi,** and **Primo Levi** to the modern minds of **Dario Fo** and **Umberto Eco,** even if few of them wrote about their home.

The one great exception is Manzoni, who often wrote of northern Italy. His novel *The Betrothed (I Promessi Sposi,* in Italian), first published in 1827, is the quintessential northern Italian novel and is still considered the greatest work of fiction in modern Italian history. It is a love story about a young couple whom the local priest refused to marry, and their respective trials. It is a vivid account of the years of famine and plague in Milan, and the days when the Spanish nobility

Thomas Mann's *Death in Venice* took place partly in the cabanas of the Lido.

terrorized the northern tier. Wandering around Lake Como, especially, you'll miss the significance of the names of hotels, boats, and more without having read this masterpiece.

Perhaps the most famous work of fiction to be set in northern Italy is **William Shakespeare**'s iconic play *Romeo and Juliet,* which takes place in Verona. Shakespeare had a penchant for northern Italy and depicted the northern Italian bourgeoisie in several other plays that were set in the region: *The Merchant of Venice* naturally takes place in Venice, and *Othello* takes place partly in Venice.

Beyond Shakespeare, perhaps the most famous Venetian scenery is found in **Thomas Mann**'s novella *Death in Venice* (1912), which portrays a tourist on the Lido and his obsession with a young Polish boy. The story describes Venice's beaches and canals in detail; Mann said he came up with the idea for the plot while on vacation there. **Ernest Hemingway,** by contrast, was driving an ambulance through war zones and convalescing from an injury in a Milan hospital when he pictured the backdrop for *A Farewell to Arms* (1929), his semi-autobiographical novel about an American ambulance driver serving in Italy during World War I.

Film

It's hard to find a more impressive movie backdrop than Venice, which is why it pops up in everything from Shakespeare to James Bond.

Michael Radford's 2004 take on *The Merchant of Venice* brings 16th-century Venice into vivid color. There are also several silver-screen productions of *Othello;* the best-known version is probably Orson Welles's 1955 production in which he plays the title role.

There are a number of James Bond films that feature Venice and northern Italy. The very best Bond scene in Venice is a toss-up between the boat chase in *Moonraker* (1979) and a scene from *Casino Royale* (2006) in which an entire Venetian palazzo sinks into the lagoon. A more recent James Bond film, *Quantum of Solace* (2008), also features northern Italy, with a car chase scene set against the dramatic backdrop of Lake Garda.

George Lucas stole a page out of the Bond handbook with the spectacular boat chase scene in *Indiana Jones and the Last Crusade* (1989). A significant piece of the movie is set in Venice—not only on the canals, but also in the churches and palazzi—making it an ideal movie to see (again) before your trip.

One of the most famous films set in Venice is Luchino Visconti's 1971 adaptation of Thomas Mann's *Death in Venice,* called *Morte a Venezia* in Italian. Perhaps the most haunting scene in that film takes place on the sandy beaches of the Lido, when the main character, played by Dirk Bogarde, dies while sitting in a white suit on a beach chair. The characters in that story were not Italian, and the film has little to do with Italy other than that the tourists were vacationing there, but the northern Italian scenery is still breathtaking.

Visconti also directed the 1960 classic film *Rocco and His Brothers* (*Rocco e I Suoi Fratelli,* in Italian). Unlike *Death in Venice,* this film is a true northern Italian tale that depicts a family from the south trying to set down roots in job-rich Milan. This film stands out among several perfunctory films on that touchy subject. Similarly, a film that portrays the economic differences between northern and southern Italy is *Bread and Chocolate* (1973), which presents a comical take on a southern Italian immigrant's attempt to become a member of Swiss society. (While this story technically unfolds in Switzerland just over the border from Lombardy, it has come to symbolize the plight of the southern immigrant moving from Puglia and Naples to Milan, Turin, and the Italian-speaking Swiss canton of Ticino.)

One of the best modern films featuring northern Italy is Silvio Soldini's *Bread and Tulips* (*Pane e Tulipani,* in Italian; 2000), about the spiritual rebirth in Venice of a middle-aged woman named Rosalba. The familiar sound of that title is not accidental—like the character in *Bread and Chocolate,* Rosalba finds opportunity in the north. The beginning of the movie is set in the most recognizable of modern Italian landmarks: an Autogrill service station. When the tour bus carrying Rosalba's chauvinistic husband pulls out of the parking lot without her, she embarks on a trip that, instead of taking her home to her native Ancona, brings her north to Venice, where she finds a job as an assistant florist and a respite from her unbearable life.

Music

In the 14th century, Italy's music swept Europe. The country was an innovator in medieval music—**St. Ambrose,** bishop of Milan in the 4th century, introduced to the church the custom of singing liturgical chants. In the 12th century, **Guido d'Arezzo** developed the basis of the musical notation that we use today. Blind **Francesco Landini** introduced sophisticated, varied rhythms. And in the mid–16th century, the first violin appeared. Cremona artisans became the international standard-bearers of fine instrument craftsmanship, and local son **Stradivari,** who learned his craft under the great master **Amati,** achieved a standard in violin design never improved upon.

Poets, who wanted a closer relationship between word and music, got their wish by the late 16th century. Until then, music had been but an incidental element in various entertainments, but a group in Florence wanted to adapt Greek drama, which they believed had been sung throughout, to a new kind of "musical drama." It came to be called "opera," a new form that caught on fast. **Monteverdi** of *Orfeo* fame, the first great composer of opera, opened the way for succeeding generations of Italian composers and is himself enjoying new popularity today.

Since opening the first public opera house in 1637, Venice has continued to promote both operatic composers and productions. Venice's preeminent composer in the early 18th century was **Antonio Vivaldi,** who is most famous today for *The Four Seasons,* but who also wrote more than 500 other concertos and 40 operas. The prolific **Scarlatti** (known mainly for his instrumental music) was also a composer of opera, turning out more than 100 in an exuberant rococo style. It's also possible that Scarlatti played some of his music on **Bartolomeo Cristofori**'s 1709 invention, the *pianoforte,* forerunner of the modern piano.

Italy has produced many fine composers, but **Giuseppe Verdi** was the unquestioned operatic master of the 19th century. Verdi, son of an innkeeper, understood dramatic form and wrote exquisite melodies, and his musicianship was unsurpassed. He achieved success early on with his third opera, *Nabucco,* a huge hit, and then turned out *Rigoletto, Il Trovatore, Un Ballo in Maschera,* and *Aïda*—works that remain popular today. His powers continued unchecked as he grew older, maturing musically with such works as *Don Carlo* and his great *Otello* (written when the master was 73). At 80, he astonished the musical world with *Falstaff,* a masterpiece in *opera buffa* form, unlike anything he'd composed before.

Venice's La Fenice opera house premiered some of Italy's greatest composers, including Rossini and Verdi.

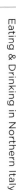

Opera buffa was Italy's most popular operatic form in the early 19th century, works of comedy with more surface than depth in which, unlike grand opera, individual musical numbers alternate with spoken dialogue. Opera buffa had its origins in the wisecracking comedians who had long entertained at fairs. **Rossini**'s charming *The Barber of Seville* and **Donizetti**'s *Daughter of the Regiment* are examples of the form.

Rossini and Donizetti were also significant contributors to grand opera in the early and mid–19th century. **Puccini** came along a bit later, and his lyrical *La Bohème, Tosca,* and *Madama Butterfly* continue to please crowds. Well known to today's international audiences is American-born (with Italian parentage) **Gian-Carlo Menotti,** who died in 2007. He spent much of his life in Italy, composed *Amahl and the Night Visitors,* and created the huge Festival of Two Worlds music extravaganza in Spoleto, one of the world's top festivals for classical and instrumental music.

EATING & DRINKING IN NORTHERN ITALY

For Italians, eating is not just something to do for sustenance three times a day. Food is an essential ingredient of the Italian spirit, practically an art form in a culture that knows a lot about art. Even when Italy was a poor nation, it was said that poor Italians ate better than rich Germans, English, or Americans.

Italians pay careful attention to the basics in both shopping and preparation. They know, for instance, which region produces the best onions or choicest peppers and when is the prime time of year to order porcini mushrooms, asparagus, truffles, or wild boar. If they're dining out, Italians expect the same care and pride they put into home cooking—and they get it. There are a lot of wonderful places to eat in Italy, from the fancy *ristorante* to the more humble, homey trattoria and the neighborhood joint called *osteria*.

Meals

Prima colazione (breakfast) is treated lightly—an espresso or cappuccino and *cornetto* (croissant with a light sugar glaze) at the corner bar. There are exceptions: Many hotels, tired of hearing foreign guests grouse about the paltry morning offerings of this *"prima colazione continentale,"* have taken to serving sumptuous buffets like those offered in the United States and north of the Alps, complete with ham, cheese, and sometimes eggs.

At the big meal of the day—be it *pranzo* (lunch) or *cena* (dinner)—portions on a plate may be smaller than visitors are accustomed to, but a traditional meal will have three courses: *antipasto, primo,* and *secondo.*

The *antipasto* (appetizer) is often a platter of *salumi* (cold cuts), *bruschette* or *crostini* (toasted or grilled bread topped with pâté or tomatoes), and/or vegetables prepared in oil or vinegar, or perhaps prosciutto and melon. Next is the **primo** (first course), which may be a *zuppa* or *minestra* (soup), pasta, *risotto* (Arborio rice boiled to be thick and sticky, usually studded with some vegetables). The **secondo** (second course) is usually meat, fish, seafood, chicken, or game and is often served with *polenta* (a cornmeal mush). To accompany the secondo, you order a **contorno** (side dish) of vegetables or a salad.

Traditionally, you won't find a pile of veggies next to your meat on the plate as in most American restaurants; however, a recent trend in Italian restaurants (especially ones that indulge in a more creative menu) is to include a side dish carefully chosen to complement your main course. At the end of the meal, dig into a **dolce** (dessert), which can include fruit, gelato (ice cream), various cakes or tiramisu (sweetened, creamy mascarpone cheese atop espresso-soaked lady fingers). Some restaurants in northern Italy will offer you *formaggio* (cheese) at the end of the meal, though this is much less common than in France.

Meals are usually accompanied by **wine** and a bottle of mineral water (*frizzante* or *non-frizzante*—fizzy or still), and followed by an espresso. (A common faux pas is to order cappuccino after dinner; Italians only drink it in the morning.) Espresso can be followed by **grappa,** a fiery *digestivo* liqueur made from what's left over after the winemaking process.

Restaurants

Traditionally, a **ristorante** (restaurant) is a bit more formal and expensive than a family-run **trattoria** or **osteria,** but the names are used almost interchangeably these days. (Trendy, expensive eateries often call themselves *osteria,* and little local joints may aggrandize themselves with the term *ristorante.*)

To save money and grab a meal with Italians on their lunch break, pop in to a **tavola calda** (literally "hot table"), a kind of tiny cafeteria where a selection of prepared hot dishes is served. A **rosticceria** is a *tavola calda* specializing in roasted meat and vegetables. Increasingly, there has been the appearance of the trendy **enoteca** (wine bar), which usually offers ample platters of cheese and mixed *salumi* such as salami, prosciutto (salt-cured ham hock), *lardo* (salt-cured pork fat aged on marble slabs), and *mortadella* (bologna); most also offer a hot dish or two.

Bruschette and *salumi* on an antipasto platter.

Any **bar** (a combo bar and cafe, where you go for your morning cappuccino, after-school ice cream, and evening aperitif) will also sell *panini* (sandwiches on a roll), *tramezzini* (giant tea sandwiches on sliced white bread with the crusts cut off), and *piadine* (flatbread sandwiches).

Pasta

Aside from pizza, pasta is probably Italy's best-known export. Most pasta is industrially produced, though keep in mind that within this category the quality varies immensely (in an Italian supermarket you'll find 1-lb. packages of pasta ranging in price between .25€ and 2€). And then there is **pasta fatta a mano** (handmade), the kind you should be on the lookout for every time you sit down at a restaurant in Italy. It's not as easy to find as you might think, and when it pops up on a menu your eyes should light up as it becomes a no-brainer what you are getting for your primo. Most high-end restaurants serve handmade pasta as do many family-run trattorie, but for everything in between it's a bit random. You can have excellent pasta dishes in a restaurant made with (good) industrially produced pasta, but when it's *fatta a mano* even the pasta neophyte can taste the difference.

Pasta (handmade or otherwise) comes in long strands, including spaghetti, linguine, and *trenette;* and in tubular *maccheroni* (macaroni) forms such as *penne* (pointed pasta quills) or *rigatoni* (fluted tubes), to name only a few. There are more than 600 pasta shapes in Italy and every sauce has a shape that it is most suited for.

Italy's Regional Cuisines

Each Italian region has had thousands of years to develop its own culinary practices—and its own distinctive wines—and each still proudly sticks by its native dishes. What most Americans think of as Italian dishes is what Italian immigrants brought with them to the U.S., but the majority of those came from southern Italy, which is why when we think "Italian," we think of olive oil, pasta with tomato sauce, garlic, and pizza. Generally, though, northern Italian cooking uses a lot more cream and butter in sauces, in addition to tomatoes. Also, pasta is not necessarily the first course of choice up north, often substituted by risotto.

VENICE & VENETO Venice gained fame and fortune as the spice market of the world beginning in the 12th century (when Marco Polo visited the Orient), which may help account for the amazing ways local chefs dress up the scampi, crab, squid, and other creatures they pluck from the Adriatic. The Venetians also have raised *fegato alla veneziana,* that humble combination of liver and onions, to an irresistible level of haute cuisine, and have done the same with *risi e bisi* (rice and peas).

Veneto's food products are as diverse as its geography. From the mountains and their foothills come a proliferation of mushrooms and game. The northerly reaches around Treviso produce wild white asparagus and cherries in the spring and, in the late fall, radicchio, a red chicory that was renowned in ancient Roman times. Much of the cuisine is based on the rice and corn grown here; on most menus here you'll find polenta, which is served with a hearty game stew with hints of Austrian influence. Risotto is often served as a first course along with the season's vegetables or, more characteristically, offerings from the Adriatic on the east.

Unlike in Tuscany, olive oil is used sparingly here—it is not unusual to see butter instead, which is so commonly associated with Emilian food. But above all, it is the Adriatic that dictates even the landlocked cuisines of Veneto.

The proliferation of desserts is a throwback to when Veneto was ceded to Austria—sweet reminders are evident in many pastry shops. Tiramisu (lady fingers soaked in espresso and liqueur, layered with sweetened mascarpone cheese and dusted with cacao), is said to have originated in Veneto and remains a favorite at Italian restaurants the world over.

Veneto—and Verona especially—plays an all-important role in the production and exportation of wines: Soave, Bardolino, Valpolicella, and Amarone are world-recognized varieties that originate in these acclaimed vineyards. No other region in Italy produces as many DOC (Denominazione di Origine Controllata, zones of controlled name and origin) red wines as Veneto. The rich volcanic earth of the Colli Euganei produces a good number of these, while a light and fizzy prosecco hails from the hills around Asolo. Wine is an integral element in any meal, and it's no compromise to limit yourself to the local regional wines that are some of Europe's finest.

THE DOLOMITES Dolomiti food is mountain food: rib-sticking and hearty, largely influenced by Austrian cuisine, with a few Italian touches. *Canederli* (bread dumplings) often replace pasta or polenta and are found floating in rich broths infused with liver; *speck* (smoked ham) replaces prosciutto; and Wiener schnitzel *Grostl* (a combination of potatoes, onions, and veal—the local version of corned beef hash, sometimes topped with a fried egg) and pork roasts are among preferred *secondi* (second courses).

FRIULI Friuli sits at the crossroads of many cultures, and consequently its cuisine is a mélange. It ranges from the firmly Alpine mountain fare of the borderland Tyrol to some exotic and hard-to-pronounce variations reflecting the region's mixed cultural heritage, coastal region, and Slovenian slant. Among these are *cevapcici,* Croatia's signature meatball-sausage dish. The Friulani also toss sauerkraut in their minestrone and call it *jota,* and throw sausage, turnips, and grape skins together to get *brovada,* a side dish that often accompanies roast or boiled meat—a farmer's supper if ever there was one. Friuli is also home to the town of San Daniele, which produces what is widely acknowledged as the best prosciutto in all of Italy—no small claim. It's the most delicate of Italy's raw hams.

Friuli wines range from local varieties such as the regal *tocai,* sweeter *verduzzo, malvasia,* and beefier *collio* to more international grapes such as merlot, cabernet

Osso buco with a side of risotto.

coffee **ALL DAY LONG**

Italians drink **caffè** (coffee) throughout the day, but only a little at a time and often while standing in a bar—remember that a "bar" in Italy is the place to go for your daily caffeine buzz. There's usually liquor available too, but it's the caffè that draws the customers.

Five types of coffee are popular in Italy. Plain old **caffè** is straight espresso in a demitasse, usually downed in one gulp. Espresso from a machine (as opposed to that made in the stove-top kettles most Italians use at home) is prepared by forcing steam through the tightly packed grounds, and despite popular perception, it actually contains less caffeine than typical American drip coffee; it's the rich taste that makes espresso seem so strong. **Cappuccino** is espresso mixed with hot milk and an overlay of foamy steamed milk, usually sipped for breakfast with a pastry and never as an after-dinner drink. "Stained" **caffè macchiato** is espresso with a wee drop of steamed milk, while **latte macchiato** is the reverse, a glass of hot milk "stained" with a shot of espresso. **Caffè corretto** is espresso "corrected" with a shot of liquor. **Caffè hag** is decaf. If you want a big mug of the murky watered-down coffee that percolates in offices and kitchens across America you'll have to order **caffè Americano,** which is disdained by most Italians.

sauvignon and cabernet franc, all the pinots, and chardonnay. For a list of vineyards and itineraries along Friuli's wine road, visit www.mtvfriulivg.it.

LOMBARDY Like most other northern regions, Lombardy favors butter over olive oil and seems not to be overly concerned with cholesterol. A specialty is *osso buco,* sliced veal sautéed with the bone and marrow. A fine starter for any meal is the region's vegetable soup with rice and bacon, *minestrone alla milanese,* or a risotto made from Arborio rice that grows on the region's low-lying plains and is often served in place of pasta. *Panettone,* a Christmas specialty that is the region's most popular dessert, is a local version of fruit cake that arrived from Vienna courtesy of Lombardy's 19th-century Austrian rulers. Austria also exported to Lombardy the breaded veal scallop of Wiener schnitzel, in Italy called *cotoletta alla Milanese.* Remember, too, that Lombardy is blessed with the Italian lakes, and trout and perch find their way into ravioli and other pasta dishes or can be simply sautéed as a secondo. Lombardy is also home to Gorgonzola cheese.

PIEDMONT & VALLE D'AOSTA Given such vast geographic diversity, it's not surprising that this region's cuisine varies according to the topography. In the southern stretches of Piedmont, the palate turns primarily to those magnificent red wines from the wine villages around Asti and Alba. Barbaresco, Barbera, Barolo, Dolcetto, Nebbiolo—the names are legendary, and they often appear on the table to accompany meat dishes stewed in red wine; one of the most favored of these is *brasato al Barolo* (beef or veal braised in Barolo).

The way to begin a meal here is with *bagna cauda,* literally, "hot bath," a plate of raw vegetables that are dipped into a steaming sauce of olive oil, garlic, and anchovies. The Piemontesi pasta is *tajarin,* and it is often topped with sauces made with walnuts or, for a special occasion, what is perhaps the region's greatest contribution to Italian cuisine, white truffles. Order *fritto misto* in the rest of Italy and you'll get a plate of mixed fried fish; order a *fritto misto piemontese* and you'll be presented with a plate of fried beef, pork or lamb innards, not for the faint of heart.

As the land climbs higher toward Valle d'Aosta, local mountain fare (a rib-sticking variant on Piemontese), called Valdostana, takes over—polenta is popular as are thick stews made with beef and red wine (*carbonada* is the most common stew like this), while the rich-flavored fontina is the preferred cheese.

Piedmont is also blessed with white truffles (the lovely town of Alba is Italy's truffle center), and they're used in a favorite local dish, *fonduta* (fondue). During the few months towards the end of the year that they are in season, white truffles can also be found shaved over scrambled eggs or egg pasta.

LIGURIA Anywhere you travel in this region, you will never be far from the sea: This is the homeland of the seafarers of Genoa, who brought back from the New World many cooking ingredients now taken for granted. Still, seafood is not as plentiful as you might assume here in the heavily fished north. But what is omnipresent are *acciughe* (anchovies), and once you try them fresh and *marinate* (marinated in lemon) as part of an antipasto, you will never underestimate the culinary merits of this little fish again. The sea-skirted region is also famous for its shellfish soup called *zuppa di datteri.*

More noticeable than fish are the many fresh vegetables that grow in patches clinging to the hillsides. They find their way into tarts (the *torta pasqualina* is one of the most elaborate, with umpteen layers of pastry; some restaurants serve it year-round) and sauces, none more typical of Liguria

Barolo's specialty.

than pesto—a simple and simply delicious concoction of basil, olive oil, pine nuts, *parmigiano,* and *pecorino* cheese ground together in a *pestello,* or mortar and pestle. (Ligurian cuisine breaks from the northern Italian mold and tends to favor olive oil over butter.) It's often used atop *trenette,* a short, hand-rolled twist of pasta sort of like an extra-thick spaghetti.

Ligurians are also adept at making fast food, and there's no better light lunch or snack than a piece of focaccia (flatbread that's often topped with herbs or olives or, when eaten as a snack, with cheese and vegetables) or *farinata* (a chickpea crepe that's served in wedges). Both are sold in bakeries and at small stands, making it easy to grab a bite before heading out to enjoy the other delights of the region.

Wine

Italy, with the right kind of terrain and the perfect amounts of sun and rainfall, happens to be ideal for growing grapes. Centuries ago, the Etruscans had a hearty wine industry, and the ancient Greeks bolstered it by transplanting their vine cuttings to Italy's southlands. And it was Italy, under the Romans, that first introduced the vine and its possibilities to France and Germany. Today Italy produces more than 2,000 wines and exports more to the rest of the world than any other country.

Each region has different growing conditions, and so each has its own special wines. **Piedmont** is the north's premier wine region, known for its heavy reds, including Barolo, Barbaresco, Barbera, and Grignolino, as well as sparkling white Asti Spumanti. Coastal **Liguria** hasn't developed many notable wines of its own, save the white Cinque Terre and Sciachetrà, a sweet dessert wine. **Veneto** produces Amarone, a rich red that should be tried on any trip to the region, provided you order the stewed meat or aged cheese that can stand up to it. The region specializes in more prosaic reds such as Valpolicella and Bardolino and, among whites, pinot grigio and Soave. The **Trentino** excels in whites, both sparkling and still. The **Friuli** masters the pinot grapes and cabernets, and also produces the traditional Verduzzo and Malvasia. **Lombardy** is not particularly known for its wines, though the area around Bergamo produces perfectly fine merlot, cabernet, pinot bianco, and pinto grigio, in addition to local Valcalepio; west of Brescia, they bottle an excellent sparkling dry white wine called Franciacorta that has the same production process as French champagne; and in the northeastern reaches of the region there is Valtellina Superiore, one of the few wines outside of Piedmont that squeezes the best out of the Nebbiolo grape.

Grappa, made from the skins, seeds, vines, and other remnants at the bottom of the pressing barrel, is a fiery *digestivo* drunk at the end of a meal to help you "digest" those large Italian repasts.

An *amaro* is a bitter liqueur usually drunk after a meal.

WHEN TO GO

The best time to visit northern Italy really depends on what you're planning to do. Skiers will find the best snow in the Dolomites from early January to mid-March, whereas sun worshippers will find the best sun and people-watching on the Riviera in the height of summer. Wine enthusiasts will find grapes on the vine in late summer and early fall, and might even take part in a harvest in late September or late October.

In a general sense, **April** to **June** and **September** and **October** are the most pleasant months for touring Italy—temperatures are usually mild and the hordes of tourists not so intense. But starting in mid-June, the summer rush really picks up, and from July to mid-September, the country teems with visitors. (It should also be noted that the post-summer cooling rains come to northern Italy almost like clockwork on Sept 1 and can last a week or two.)

August (with July a close runner-up) is the worst month to visit any Italian city. Not only does it get uncomfortably hot, muggy, and crowded with foreigners, but the entire country goes on vacation for at least the 2 middle weeks of the

ITALIAN wine CLASSIFICATIONS

In 1963, Italy's wine was codified into two classifications: table wine and DOC. **DOC (Denominazione di Origine Controllata)** wines are those a government board guarantees have come from an official wine-producing area and meet the standard for carrying a certain name on the label. A **vino di tavola (table wine)** classification merely means a bottle doesn't fit the preestablished standards and is no reflection of the wine's quality (see below).

In 1980, a new category was added. **DOCG** (the G stands for Garantita— guaranteed) is granted to wines with a certain subjective high quality. Traditionally, DOCG labels were merely the highest-profile wines that lobbied for the status. (Getting DOC and especially DOCG vastly improves reputations and, therefore, sales, though the costs of annually putting the wine up for testing are high.)

When the appellation was introduced, only five prestigious wines qualified as DOCG: Brunello, Barolo, Barbaresco, Chianti, and Vino Nobile di Montepulciano. Today, there are more than 60.

The wines have a few extra hoops to jump through to retain their Garantita status. The vineyards need to practice specific growing methods and cannot exceed a certain yield of fruit every year. The wines are subject to chemical analysis by government agencies. And to qualify in the first place, a wine must have held DOC status for at least 5 years.

Though **vino di tavola** usually connotes a humble, simple, quaffable house wine from some indeterminate local producer (perhaps a local farmer's cooperative or even the restaurant owner's brother-in-law), in the 1980s and 1990s, this "table wine" classification was also co-opted by wine estates that wanted to experiment with grape mixtures and tinker with foreign varietals to create nontraditional but mighty wines. The problem is that these could never be called DOC or DOCG, which by law must follow strict formula guidelines. When many respectable producers started mixing varietals with French grapes, such as merlot, cabernet, and chardonnay, to produce wines that, though complex and of high quality, don't fall into the conservative DOC/DOCG system, such a wine could then, by law, only be called a "lowly" vino di tavola.

In 1992, a new classification called **IGT (Indicazione Geografica Tipica)** was established, indicating that the wine is "typical of a geographic place." This class has been used to cover regional wines that are often, though by no means always, quite good yet are not famous enough (or lack a PR budget that's big enough) to go for DOC/ DOCG status.

month—and a good percentage take off the entire month, leaving the urban centers to the tourists. Venice in July and August is a swarming and sweltering Disneyland. Elsewhere, many hotels, restaurants, and shops are closed in mid-August—except along the coast and on the islands, which is where most Italians head.

From **late October to Easter,** most tourist sites have shorter winter hours or close for renovation periods, many hotels and restaurants take a month or two off between November and February, beach destinations become padlocked ghost towns, and it can get much colder than you'd expect (it may even snow). The crowds thin remarkably, especially in Venice, the exception being when the city teems with people around carnival.

In **mountain towns and ski resorts,** high season is from mid-December through mid-March and August; low season is April to May and October to November, when many hotels close for anywhere from a few weeks up to a month or two (spring can be a great time for excellent hiking in the mountains and, if you aren't too unlucky, mild weather to accompany the long days).

High season on most airlines' routes to Milan usually stretches from June to late September, plus Christmas/New Year's week. This is the most expensive and most crowded time to travel. **Shoulder season** is from the Easter season to May, late September to October, and December 15 to 24. **Low season** is generally January 6 to mid-March, November 1 to December 14, and January 1 to March 31.

Weather

It's hot all over Italy in **summer,** especially inland. The high temperatures often begin in May (sometimes later for the Alps), and can last sometimes into late September. July and August can be impossible, which explains why life in the cities slows down considerably (and life in the coastline resorts comes alive). Few budget hotels have air-conditioning (and just a handful of hotels in all of Italy have discovered mosquito screens, so when you open the windows for some respite from the heat, you tend to invite dozens of tiny bloodsuckers in as well). In Venice, the November rains kick off *acqua alta,* when the lagoon backs up a few times each month, flooding the central city with .6 to 1.8m (2–6 ft.) of water (no joke). That may sound like an invitation to stay away, but it's actually one of the most remarkable times to be there. Bring rubber boots.

Winters in the north of Italy are cold with rain and snow, and December through February can often be unpleasant unless you're skiing in Cortina or enjoy a snow-sprinkled city. Nights can be cold, and hotels' heating systems can be frustrating sometimes. Purpose-built, modernized hotels in their own buildings often have independent heating/cooling systems you (or they) can control, but in older hotels and in small ones that take up only part of a building, the heat can often be turned on for the winter only on a pre-established date dictated by the local government (usually Oct 15), and left on only during certain hours of the day (just one of the many lovely laws still hanging on from the Fascist era).

For the most part, it's drier in Italy than in North America. Because the humidity is lower, high temperatures don't seem as bad; exceptions are cities known for their humidity factor, such as Venice. It's important to remember that this is not a country as smitten by the notion of air-conditioning and central heating as the United States. And remember that the inexpensive hotels listed in this book are often the very places that will remind you of the pros and cons of ancient stone palazzi built with 1m-thick (3-ft.) walls. Don't expect the comfort of the Ritz at cheaper inns.

Holidays

Offices and shops in Italy are closed on the following dates: **January 1** (New Year's Day), **January 6** (Epiphany, usually called *La Befana*, after Italy's Christmas Witch, who used to bring the presents until Hollywood's version of Santa Claus moved the gift giving to Dec 25, though a few presents are always held over for *La Befana*), **Easter Sunday, Easter Monday, April 25** (Liberation Day), **May 1** (Labor Day), **June 2** (Republic Day), **August 15** (Assumption of the Virgin), **November 1** (All Saints' Day), **December 8** (Feast of the Immaculate Conception), **December 25** (Christmas Day), and **December 26** (Santo Stefano).

Closings are also observed in the following cities on feast days honoring patron saints: Venice, **April 25** (St. Mark); Genoa and Turin, **June 24** (St. John the Baptist); Trieste, **November 3** (San Giusto); and Milan, **December 7** (St. Ambrose).

Calendar of Events

For more details on each event below, contact the **tourist office** of the city or town where the festival is held (see the individual chapters).

For an exhaustive list of events beyond those listed here, check **http://events.frommers.com**, where you'll find a searchable, up-to-the-minute roster of what's happening in cities all over the world.

JANUARY

Epiphany celebrations, nationwide. All cities, towns, and villages in Italy stage Roman Catholic Epiphany observances and Christmas fairs. From Christmas to January 6.

Festival of Italian Popular Song, San Remo (Italian Riviera). A 3-day festival where major artists and up-and-comers perform the latest Italian pop songs and launch the newest hits. Late January.

Foire de Saint Ours, Aosta, Valle d'Aosta. Observing a tradition that has existed for 10 centuries, artisans from the mountain valleys come together to display their wares—often made of wood, lace, wool, or wrought iron—created during the long winter months. Late January.

FEBRUARY

Carnevale (Carnival), Venice. Venice's Carnival evokes the final theatrical 18th-century days of the Venetian Republic. Historical presentations, elaborate costumes, and music of all types in every piazza cap the festivities. The balls are by invitation, but the cultural events, piazza performances, and fireworks (on Fat Tuesday) are open to everyone. See p. 166 for more information. From 2 Fridays before Fat Tuesday to Fat Tuesday.

APRIL

Good Friday and Easter Week observances, nationwide. Processions and age-old ceremonies—some from pagan days, some from the Middle Ages—are staged. Beginning on the Thursday or Friday before Easter Sunday, usually in April.

MAY

Vogalonga, Venice. This 30km (20-mile) rowing "race" from San Marco to Burano and back again has been enthusiastically embraced since its inception in 1975, following the city's effort to keep alive the centuries-old heritage of the regatta. The event is colorful, and every local seems to have a relative or next-door neighbor competing. For details, call ✆ **041-521-0544** or visit **www.vogalonga.com**. A Sunday in mid-May.

JUNE

Regatta of the Great Maritime Republics. Every year, the four medieval maritime republics of Italy celebrate their glorious past with a boat race that rotates among Venice, Amalfi, Genoa, and Pisa. Call the tourist offices for details. Mid-June.

Biennale d'Arte, Venice. This is Europe's most prestigious International Exposition of Modern Art, taking place in odd-numbered years only. More than 50 nations take part, with art displayed in permanent pavilions in the Public Gardens and elsewhere about town. Many great modern artists have been discovered at this world-famous show. Contact the board at ✆ **041-521-8711,** or visit **www.labiennale.org** for more information. June to October.

Shakespearean Festival, Verona. Ballet, drama, and jazz performances are included in this festival of the Bard, with a few performances in English. June to September.

JULY

Opera at the Arena di Verona. Culture buffs flock to the open-air, 20,000-seat Roman amphitheater—one of the world's best preserved—for awesome productions of *Aïda* and others. Mid-June to early September.

Festa del Redentore (Feast of the Redeemer), Venice. This celebration marking the July 1576 lifting of a plague that had gripped the city is centered around the Palladio-designed Chiesa del Redentore on the island of Giudecca. A bridge of boats across the Giudecca Canal links the church with the banks of Le Zattere in Dorsoduro, and hundreds of boats of all shapes and sizes fill the Giudecca. It's one big floating *festa* until night descends and an awesome half-hour *spettacolo* of fireworks fills the sky. Third Saturday and Sunday in July.

AUGUST

Venice International Film Festival. Ranking after Cannes, this film festival brings together stars, directors, producers, and filmmakers from all over the world. Films are shown day and night to an international jury and to the public, at the Palazzo del Cinema, on the Lido, and other venues. Contact the tourist office or the Venice Film Festival at ✆ **041-521-8711,** or visit **www.labiennale.org**. Two weeks in late August to early September.

SEPTEMBER

Regata Storica, Grand Canal, Venice. Just about every seaworthy gondola, richly decorated for the occasion and piloted by *gondolieri* in colorful livery, participates in the opening cavalcade. The aquatic parade is followed by three regattas that proceed along the Grand Canal. You can buy grandstand tickets through the tourist office or arrive early and pull up along a piece of embankment near the Rialto Bridge for the best seats in town. First Sunday in September.

Partita a Scacchi con Personaggi Viventi, Marostica. This chess game is played in the town square by living pawns in period costume. The second Saturday and Sunday of September during even-numbered years.

OCTOBER

Sagra del Tartufo, Alba, Piedmont. The truffle is the honoree of this festival in Alba, the truffle capital of Italy, with contests, truffle-hound competitions, and tastings of this ugly but precious and delectable (and expensive) fungus. Two weeks in mid-October.

Maratona (Marathon), Venice. The marathon starts at Villa Pisani on the mainland, runs alongside the Brenta Canal, and ends along the Zattere for a finish at the Basilica di Santa Maria della Salute on the tip of Dorsoduro. For details, call ✆ **041-950-644.** Usually a Sunday in late October.

NOVEMBER

Festa della Salute, Venice. For this festival, a pontoon bridge is erected across the Grand Canal to connect the churches of La Salute and Santa Maria del Giglio, commemorating another delivery from a plague in 1630 that wiped out a third of the lagoon's population; it's the only day La Salute opens its massive front doors (a secondary entrance is otherwise used). November 21.

DECEMBER

Opera at La Scala, Teatro alla Scala, Milan. At the most famous opera house of them all, the season opens on December 7, the feast day of Milan's patron St. Ambrose, and runs into July. Though it's close to impossible to get opening-night tickets, it's worth a try and for most other performances you can get tickets if you reserve at least a week in advance. Call © **02-860-775** to book and 02-7200-3744 for general information on the program and availability. For a complete listing of performances and to book online, visit **www. teatroallascala.org**.

RESPONSIBLE TRAVEL

Environmentalism in Italy has always been an area of stark contrasts. Italians conserve fuel and energy like most Europeans do, they go to great lengths to limit air pollution, and their shopping habits of consuming locally grown vegetables and bringing a bag to the store would put a smile on just about any environmentalist's face. Meanwhile, local entities' recycling efforts have been called into question (for example, investigative journalism has revealed in the past that for a time most of the recyclables and trash in Rome were ending up in the same place), and, incredibly, sewage treatment plants have only begun to spring up around Milan in the past decade or so. Previously, it simply was flushed into the rivers.

That aside, the tourism industry here leads the charge in protecting the resources of a country where visitor-spending accounts for a whole lot of the nation's income. Northern Italy has taken several measures to ensure sustainable tourism. Many hotels in Milan and other northern Italian cities, as well as higher-end *agriturismi* in the countryside, have implemented green practices, like encouraging patrons to reuse towels rather than have them changed every day. Organic agriculture is widespread, especially on smaller farms around northern Italy that host visitors, so when you eat in a restaurant in this region, chances are that the food didn't travel very far to get to your table. (The national obsession with bottled water, however, is a blemish on an otherwise good record.)

Towns and provinces push for more intercity cycling paths to connect tourist sites, and many cities, like Milan, have implemented a bike-sharing program, which, for a nominal fee, allows people to ride bicycles around town for short increments of time (usually 30 min.). You pick up a bike in one of the many racks around town and leave it at another. Milan has also managed to cut down on traffic by instituting a fee for cars to enter the city center during the day from Monday to Friday. Venice, on the other hand, has no car traffic, as the only means of transportation in the city is by boat. This water traffic—as well as a history of poor sewage systems that fed right into the canals—has contributed to high levels of pollution in the city's water. However, Venice has recently taken measures to improve its water quality by installing more septic tanks and controlling sewage flow, and by improving standards of water treatment.

Public transportation is generally reliable, and trains provide an excellent way of getting around northern Italy. Buses can also take you around the countryside. However, there is no escaping the fact that most often a family with luggage will need a car to get around the remote areas of the northern Italian countryside.

Overall, as a nation that needs to import the great majority of its energy from far away, and with 60 million people living in relative proximity, Italians have always been a culture to live and consume at a sustainable rate and a very human scale.

You can do your part by reusing towels, taking public transportation whenever possible, discarding trash and recyclables in the appropriate bins, and eating locally grown produce. And don't shy away from Italy's tap water; it's very good.

SPECIAL-INTEREST TRIPS & ESCORTED GENERAL-INTEREST TOURS

Special-Interest Trips

ACADEMIC TRIPS & LANGUAGE CLASSES

A number of organizations offer intensive Italian language courses for adults in northern Italy, especially in Venice and Milan. A good budget option that attracts a variety of ages is the **Venice Institute** (www.istitutovenezia.com), which holds courses ranging from 1 to 24 weeks in Venice and Trieste starting at 160€ for 1 week. (One of the other great values of the experience is staying at the secluded Palladian cloisters on the Giudecca for about 230€ per week for a single with private bathroom.) There are language courses for every ability level, and the instructors are certified in Italian as a second language.

Milan is a venue for Italian classes, because many employees of foreign countries relocate here without much of a background in the language. **The International House of Milan** (www.ihmilano.com) is well known in these circles, as it specializes in key sectors; for example, there is a 2-week program devoted to the language of the fashion and design industry, which costs 530€. A slightly more affordable option is the **Scuola Leonardo da Vinci** (www.scuolaleonardo.com), where a general 2-week course is available for 340€ (plus a 70€ enrollment fee). It also has more specialized courses for food and gastronomy, and other subjects; prices and required fluency levels increase with specialization.

BIKE TOURS

Northern Italy is home to many of the biggest names in the cycling industry. Bianchi, Campagnolo, De Rosa, and Pinarello are all headquartered in Lombardy or Veneto.

Several operators specialize in setting up itineraries and making some of the arrangements for you or in leading fully guided bike tours. **Ciclismo Classico ★★** (*© **800/866-7314** in the U.S., or 781/646-3377; fax 781/641-1512; www.ciclismoclassico.com) is one of the best operators and has been leading bike and walking tours in Italy since 1988. A week-long tour of Piedmont runs about $4,300 per person, staying at premier accommodations. April through November, the outfit runs several guided tours through the Alps, Dolomites, and Friuli, and several trips out of Venice. Six- to fifteen-day trips usually include Italian-language and cooking lessons, along with wine tasting and cultural itineraries. Groups average 10 to 18 people, with all ages and ability levels welcome.

Experience Plus (© 800/685-4565 in the U.S., or 970/484-8489; www. experienceplus.com) offers both guided and self-guided biking and walking tours through northern Italy lasting 8 to 12 days.

WALKING TOURS

If you don't feel the need to cover so much territory, you can appreciate even more of the countryside by walking or hiking (called *trekking* in Italian). Italy's resource for everything from countryside ambles to serious mountain trekking is the **Club Alpino Italiano,** 19 Via Petrella, Milan 20124 (© 02-205-7231; fax 02-2057-23201; www.cai.it).

Many outfits run walking tours in northern Italy. Besides **Ciclismo Classico** (see above), you might want to try **Butterfield & Robinson,** 70 Bond St., Ste. 300, Toronto, ON M5B 1X3 (© 800/678-1147 or 416/864-1354 the U.S.; fax 416/864-0541; www.butterfield.com), which also does bike tours; or **Country Walkers** ★ (© 800/464-9255 in the U.S., or 802/244-1387; www.country walkers.com), which has a rather refined, romantic outlook on Italy and offers several northern Italy tours, including tours in Cinque Terre, the Dolomites, and the lakes region.

For walking tours in Venice, one of the better resources is **Context Travel** (© 215/240-4347 in the U.S. or © 06-9762-5204; www.contexttravel.com), which offers tours and seminars led by graduate students and other experts in their respective fields on everything from Renaissance art to ceramics to cuisine.

FOOD & WINE TRIPS

Just as it's not hard to find a cooking class in Italy (most top-flight hotels will show you how to make a classic northern Italian dish and pair it with the right wine for some extra money), nearly every organized tour will have a strong culinary component. **Discover Friuli** (www.discoverfriuli.com), for example, combines language courses, cooking classes, and wine tours in a single program.

There are also tour companies that concentrate solely on wine. **Cellar Tours** (www.cellartours.com), one of the better-known, high-end wine tour operators, will chauffer you in a Mercedes to the most prestigious vineyards in Piedmont, Friuli, and Veneto, and put you up in five-star accommodations; their tours cost 500€ to 1,000€ per person, per day, depending on the trip.

Sara Cossiga is an art historian, tour guide, and sommelier who offers tours of Venice and Veneto focused on food and wine (www.veniceveneto gourmet.com). Most tourist boards will also have a selection of guided tours of the vineyards in their province (mentioned in the individual chapters).

COOKING SCHOOLS

While most of Italy's best-known cooking schools are in Tuscany, the north has its share of cooking classes. In Milan, **Congusto** (© 02-6347-1266; www. congusto.it) has a rich offering of cooking courses, including one that teaches how to prepare a variety of dishes inspired by the futuristic ideas of celebrated Milanese architect and designer Gio Ponti. Three-hour classes, which are suspended in August, start at 70€ (p. 305). **LINGUA IT** (© 045-597-975; www. linguait.it) is an Italian-language school in Verona that offers a course on the food and wine of the region.

Some hotels also offer cooking classes. The **Four Seasons** in Milan (© 02-77088; www.fourseasons.com/milan) has half-day classes, held on Saturday mornings, that cost 100€ and start with a discussion of the daily menu with the hotel chefs and conclude in style with a four-course lunch. There are no courses in July and August.

Guided Tours

From the priciest pampered tours to the most inexpensive bare-bones trips, you'll find no shortage of tour operators who offer tours to northern Italy. Many travelers opt for escorted tours because they let you sit back and enjoy the trip without having to drive or worry about details. They take you to the maximum number of sights in the minimum amount of time with the least amount of hassle. They're particularly convenient for people with limited mobility, and they can be a great way to make new friends. On the downside, you'll have little opportunity for serendipitous interactions with locals. While these escorted trips are hassle-free and often cost-efficient, there really is no substitute for exploring the back roads of northern Italy in small numbers, making spur-of-the-moment decisions and finding unexpected gems.

Tour operators offering relatively cheap deals to northern Italy include **Globus Escorted Tours** (© 866/755-8581 in the U.S.; www.globusjourneys. com), **Insight Vacations** (© 353-1-276-3000; www.insightvacations.com), and **Trafalgar Tours** (© 866/544-4434 in the U.S.; www.trafalgar.com). It's hard to book your own hotels, transportation, and food for anything near the prices offered by these companies, but you likely won't stay or eat at top-notch establishments.

One higher-quality—and more expensive—tour operator is **Go Ahead Tours** (© 800/590-1170 the U.S.; www.goaheadtours.com). They offer refined trips that focus heavily on food and wine rather than just the standard tourist sites. For example, they offer an 11-day tour called "A Taste of Northern Italy & the Italian Riviera."

For more information on guided general-interest tours, including questions to ask before booking your trip, see **www.frommers.com/planning**.

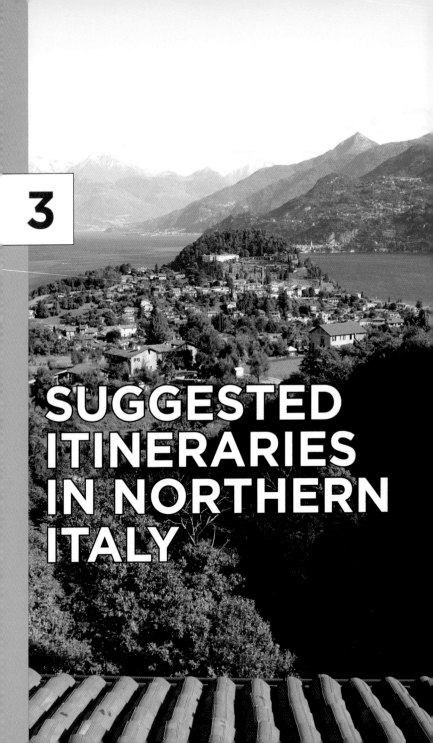

3

SUGGESTED ITINERARIES IN NORTHERN ITALY

N orthern Italy is an ideal getaway for people with varied interests, or for those who simply can't make up their minds. There is something for everyone here: sun and sea for beach lovers, Alpine peaks for adventurers, exquisite restaurants and art collections for the urbanite, rustic vineyard living for the farmer-at-heart. Romeo and Juliet's Verona is second only to the canals of Venice in amorous appeal, though smitten couples will find romantic settings at every turn.

Two of the following itineraries are designed around the most popular themes of any northern Italian vacation. All the routes begin in Milan, as Malpensa airport is the most common gateway to northern Italy, though tours could just as easily start at any of the area's many smaller airports that cater to European budget carriers. Remember that traveling from one end of the region to the other can be done in a single afternoon, if you follow the Po River plain. For train riders, this means becoming very familiar with the Milan-Venice high-speed link (and the spurs to Genoa and Turin), and for drivers, the Autostrada A4. While it's tempting to try alternate local roads, the A4 is Italy's most traveled highway for good reason—it saves a huge amount of time and goes almost everywhere you want to be.

THE REGIONS IN BRIEF
Venice & Veneto
The Po River created the vast flood plain of **Veneto** at the base of the **Dolomites,** a mountain chain that is part of the Alps and distinguishes itself with sharp pinnacles straight out of a fairy tale. What draws visitors to these agricultural flatlands are the art treasures of **Padua (Padova),** the Renaissance villas of Palladio in **Vicenza,** the ancient Roman and pseudo-Shakespearean sights of **Verona,** and—rising on pilings from a lagoon on the Adriatic coast—that most serene city of canals and year-round carnival, **Venice (Venezia).**

Friuli–Venezia Giulia
This forgotten northeast corner of Italy marks the border with Slovenia, a region of tame Alps, rolling hills, and Adriatic beaches. Its culture lies at the crossroads of Italy, Yugoslavia, and Austria—the Adriatic city of **Trieste** was once the main port for Vienna and the Habsburgs, and has the coffeehouses to prove it. The influence of the old, neighboring sea power Venice is still strong in its staunch ally of **Udine,** while nearby **Cividale dei Friuli** preserves remnants of cultures from the Celts through the Lombards, with coastal **Aquileia** weighing in with Roman ruins and mosaics.

FACING PAGE: **Bellagio, with Lake Como in the background.**

Trentino–Alto Adige

The **Dolomites,** bordering Austria, cap the eastern stretches of the **Trentino– Alto Adige** region while the peaks of the Alps crown the west. This region comprises legendary resorts such as **Cortina d'Ampezzo** and **Merano,** as well as the beautiful cities of **Trent (Trento)** and **Bolzano**—home to a fascinating international scientific treasure, the prehistoric Ice Man—that lie at the crossroads of the German and Italian worlds.

Milan & Lombardy

Lombardy (Lombardia) is Italy's wealthiest province, an industrial, financial, and agricultural powerhouse named for the Lombards, a Germanic people who migrated south over the Alps in the early Dark Ages (they were part of the barbarian hordes that overran the Roman Empire). The scenic diversity of this prosperous region ranges from legendary lakes, such as **Como, Garda,** and **Maggiore,** backed by Alpine peaks, to the flat, fertile plains of the Po River that are home to Lombardy's important cities. The region's capital, **Milan (Milano)**—hotbed of high fashion, high finance, and avant-garde design—is a city of great art and architecture (Leonardo's *The Last Supper* is but the beginning), and the region's Renaissance past is still much in evidence in **Bergamo, Mantua (Mantova),** musical **Cremona** (where Stradivarius once crafted his violins), and the other cities of the Lombard plains.

Piedmont & Valle d'Aosta

Piedmont (Piemonte) is loosely translated as "foot of the mountains," and the Alps are in sight from almost every parcel of this northwestern region, which

The tram leads to Milan's La Scala.

borders Switzerland and France. The flat plains of the Po River rise into rolling hills clad with orchards and vineyards. North of **Turin (Torino)**—the historic baroque capital of the region and, with its wealth of auto factories, a cornerstone of Italy's "economic miracle" of the 1960s—the plains meet the Alps head-on in **Valle d'Aosta,** with its craggy mountains, rugged mountain folk, and year-round skiing at resorts such as **Courmayeur** in the shadow of **Mont Blanc** (Monte Bianco).

Liguria & the Italian Riviera

The Italian Riviera follows the Ligurian Sea along a narrow coastal band backed by mountains. At the center of the rocky coast of **Liguria** is **Genoa (Genova),** the country's first port and still its most important—a fascinating city that greets visitors with a remarkable assemblage of Renaissance art and architecture. Some of Italy's most famous seaside retreats flank Genoa on either side, from the tony resort of **San Remo** on France's doorstep all the way down to the picturesque string of fishing villages known as the **Cinque Terre** that line the coast just above Tuscany.

NORTHERN ITALY IN 1 WEEK

This brief, 1-week loop brings you to northern Italy's must-see destinations, starting in Milan, northern Italy's major gateway, and winding up in Venice, before a 3-hour train ride back to the Lombard capital. It follows a very simple route that can easily be followed by train.

DAY 1: Milan ★

Most of this large city's major sites are confined to the area around the **Duomo,** in the epicenter, a good place to start any tour. The two top attractions, however—seeing a performance at **La Scala** opera house (p. 320) and viewing Leonardo da Vinci's *The Last Supper* (p. 298)—almost always require advance reservations. This is one of the few cities in the entire country with a reputation for nightlife, so if you are looking for chic bars and active nights past 11pm, best to get it done here. Also, if you're here during Fashion Week or another major trade fair, in particular the Salone del Mobile in mid-April, be sure to reserve your hotel in advance and be ready to pay at the very upper end of the listed prices.

DAY 2: Lake Como ★★

With a daylong boat pass, crisscross the lake, from **Como** (p. 349) and nearby **Cernobbio,** home of the famed **Villa d'Este** (p. 353), up and over to **Bellagio** (p. 355), one of the most captivating lake towns in the country. Skip over to the western shore to hike up in the scenic hills above **Menaggio** (p. 360). On the opposite shore is **Varenna** (p. 358), an excellent place to have lunch or dinner, especially at **Cavatappi** (p. 360). This is also the side of the lake that has train tracks leading to Milan, and—even better—straight to Bergamo via **Lecco** (p. 326).

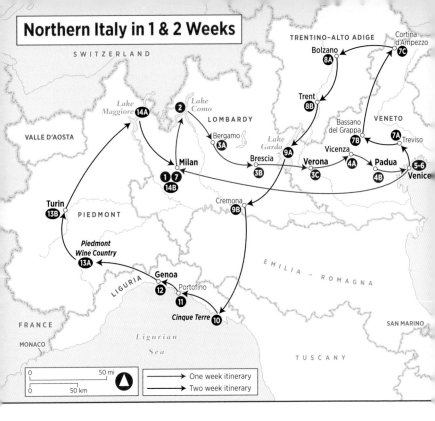

DAY 3: Bergamo, Brescia & Verona ★

Spend the morning exploring Bergamo's Old City, around the stunning **Piazza Vecchia** and **Piazza del Duomo** (p. 328). After a polenta lunch, make a quick stop to see the **Loggia** in Brescia (p. 325) and the city's excellent collection of paintings in the **Pinacoteca Tosio-Matinengo** (p. 325) before heading to Verona for the rest of the afternoon. (Bergamo to Brescia is an hour by train and Brescia to Verona takes half as long.) In Verona, don't miss the slightly hokey but nevertheless magical **House of Juliet** (p. 220) and, if you're there at the right time, an opera inside the city's Roman **Arena** (p. 218). (You'll need to reserve ahead for tickets, and if you have a seat on the floor of the arena, bring some *very* nice clothes so you don't feel out of place.) The performance will be one you'll remember for a lifetime.

DAY 4: Vicenza & Padua ★★

Here are two gems shamefully overlooked by Venice-bound travelers. After a coffee in Verona's **Piazza delle Erbe** (p. 222), head for Vicenza (a 30-min. train ride). Just walking around the city is inspiring enough, as it is a UNESCO World Heritage Site, but take time to see the **Teatro Olimpico** (p. 207) and, if it's open, the **Basilica Palladiana** (p. 208). Two great side trips would be to see the massive outdoor chessboard in Marostica, accessible by a 40-minute bus ride, or, if you are driving, check out the **Villa**

Rotonda (p. 211), on the outskirts of the city. Another 15 minutes on the train will bring you to what will probably be the highlight of the day, Padua's **Scrovegni Chapel** (p. 186) and its frescoes by Giotto. ***Note:*** Padua is so close to Venice (a 25-min. train ride) that budget travelers might plan to book a hotel here, as it will cost a fraction of a night in the lagoon.

DAYS 5 & 6: Venice ★★★

You'll need at least 2 nights in Venice and will wish you had the time and money for 10 more, especially if you come in the off season when the atmosphere is so much more pleasant. (In fact, if you come in July or early Aug, the crowds can really be suffocating. Booking a hotel in advance will be essential.) Try to time your visit with one of the city's many festivals, especially the **Regata Storica** (p. 164). Pick and choose your itinerary from chapter 4, but be sure to spend some time in lesser-visited quarters, such as **Cannaregio** (p. 97) and its **Jewish Ghetto** (p. 160). Don't snub the gondola ride as too touristy; grab a bottle of prosecco and float through the canals at night.

DAY 7: Milan

It's only a 3-hour train ride back to Milan, so you should have lots of time to do the things you missed on the first day. If you've already seen the Scala, why not go for the other end of the cultural spectrum and catch a game at Italy's most revered soccer stadium, **San Siro?** Or if shopping is your priority, don't miss the frequent outdoor markets, listed on p. 288.

FROM TOP: **Bergamo's Piazza Vecchia; the Ponte San Michele in Vicenza.**

The morning fish market in Treviso.

NORTHERN ITALY IN 2 WEEKS

Start with the first 6 days of the previous tour, and then, if you have another week to spend, rent a car in Venice and return westward, dropping it off in Milan. (It will be cheaper than renting it at the beginning and paying an extra week as well as the expense of leaving the car at Venice's parking lot.) With the car, you can check out all the harder-to-reach spots along the way. These include remote roads in the Dolomites and the vineyards near Turin.

DAY 7: Treviso, Bassano del Grappa & Cortina d'Ampezzo

This is a day of driving, with some stunning scenery as the trip progresses. Stop in Treviso to see its lively **fish market** (p. 194) in the morning and work up an appetite for lunch at an inimitable **Toni del Spin** (p. 198). Continue northeast through the region that produces prosecco toward Asolo and Bassano del Grappa, for a great mixture of country life and impressive architecture. Approach Cortina d'Ampezzo in the evening, as the last rays of sun hit off the Dolomites and Cortina's fashionable restaurants and cafes come to life.

DAY 8: Bolzano & Trento

Take a morning drive on one of the most beautiful roads in Italy, the **Great Dolomite Road** (p. 258), which leads through the snowcapped peaks to Bolzano. At the city's archaeological museum, meet Ötzi, the 5,300-year-old **"Ice Man"** (p. 243) found frozen in these mountains in 1991. After lunch, take a side trip to Merano to stretch your legs on a nice walk along its river, and then continue south to Trento for the night. See where the Council of Trent congregated at the **Castello de Buonconsiglio** (p. 235), and have an unforgettable meal at the **Scrigno del Duomo** (p. 239).

DAY 9: Lake Garda & Cremona ★

In the morning, join the windsurfers at **Riva del Garda** (p. 339), then drive slowly down the lake's more interesting western shore visiting the little resort of **Gardone Riviera** (p. 343) on your way to the captivating old city of

Sirmione (p. 340) on the lake's southern edge. Then hop on the A4 highway to Brescia and turn south on the A7 to Cremona. See where **Stradivarius violins** were crafted and be sure to try some of the pumpkin-filled tortellini, one of the best pasta dishes in northern Italy.

DAYS 10 & 11: Cinque Terre & Portofino ★★

The best way to approach the **Cinque Terre** (p. 446) from **Cremona** (p. 323) is to curve onto the A1 to Parma, and from there the A15 to La Spezia. After a morning on the highway, you'll be eager to leave your car behind in either Riomaggiore or Manarola and begin your walk from village to village. (Again, book a hotel ahead of time in high season, as this place has become very popular among American tourists.) Although the extremely winding road between towns is scenic, it is time-consuming and can be downright nauseating. Instead, the next day, hop on the A12 highway for the much shorter route to Portofino, and enjoy a peaceful sunset on the port and perhaps a boat trip along the inlets. Budget travelers might wish to spend the second night in nearby Camogli or Santa Margherita, as Portofino is very expensive.

DAY 12: Genoa ★

After a day of dolphin-watching at sea, younger audiences especially will love Genoa's **aquarium** (p. 416), Europe's largest, which has a slew of activities during the day and even hosts a sleepover for kids at night in front of the shark tank. While the little ones are being entertained, couples can enjoy a candle-lit seafood dinner in the Old Quarter and perhaps a night of symphony at the Teatro Carlo Felice.

FROM TOP: **The northern edge of Lake Garda; the seaside Cinque Terre hiking path.**

DAY 13: Piedmont Wine Country & Turin ★★

South of Alba are the revered vineyards of **Barolo** (p. 395) and **Barbaresco** (p. 395), while just to the west is the town of **Bra** (p. 85), rapidly becoming Italy's culinary capital. After lunch, take a quick drive up to **Turin** (p. 368) to see all that the city has to offer; hint—food is near the top of the list.

DAY 14: Lake Maggiore & Milan ★

Spend a leisurely day strolling the lakeside promenade in lovely **Stresa** (p. 362) and on ferries to the **Borromean Islands** (p. 363). Fortunately, the lake is not far from Turin and extremely close to Malpensa airport, where you can drop off your car.

NORTHERN ITALY FOR GOURMANDS

This 10-day loop includes the area's top winegrowing regions and a sampling of the various local cuisines. Eat and drink your way through the birthplace of chocolate; the home of Italy's finest truffles; the regions that produce Barolo, Amarone, and Soave; and the restaurants that have perfected the recipes for polenta, risotto, and tortelli. There is so much here for gourmands, in fact, that many tasty dishes found on the area's outskirts had to be skipped—the pesto of Genoa and the fondue of the Alps, for example—but it's hard for those simple meals to stack up to the culinary grandeur of northern Italy's heartland.

DAY 1: Milan

Though it's the capital of northern Italy in many senses, and no slouch on the culinary scene, Milan is not hailed for its cuisine in the same way that many other cities around the region are. Instead, the city is best known for its shopping, its culture, and its lively nightlife. Be sure to check out the Pinacoteca di Brera and, of course, the Duomo, before hitting the clothing stores downtown and the cocktail bars of Brera and the Navigli. If you haven't yet reserved tickets to see Leonardo da Vinci's *The Last Supper* (p. 298) or a performance at La Scala (p. 320), this would be a good time to do so in person and save those unforgettable experiences for your last day here. Chances are slim that you will get in to see Leonardo's masterpiece unannounced. For dinner, stop by the **Trattoria Milanese** (p. 314) for the city's famous cutlet and risotto. (***Note:*** It is a universal opinion in Italy that landlocked Milan actually has some of the country's best seafood, because the high prices fetch the best fresh fish. Just don't order it on Monday, the day after the wholesale fish market is closed.)

DAY 2: Turin ★

Did you know that the Torinesi invented solid chocolate? Before them, it had only been consumed as a beverage. But that's not all; this is the capital of a region (Piedmont) with perhaps more claims to both oenological and gastronomic fame than any other in Italy. **C'era Una Volta** (p. 383) and **Ristorante Tre Galline** (p. 385) are two of the most popular eateries, but there are dozens of superb ones from which to choose. Even if you are not a tourist-office kind of traveler, by all means, at least stop by the booth in the Porta Nuova train station to pick up a brochure on the latest culinary

happenings. The city commonly hosts citywide tastings, where restaurants offer special deals and sampling menus. The tourist office also hands out discount passes to such food boutiques as chocolate stores.

DAY 3: Barolo & Barbaresco ★

Anyone serious about Italian wines will already be familiar with these blockbuster names, famous for their rich, full-bodied reds. Bear in mind that the estates around here are not as welcoming to the public as those in, say, Chianti, but a simple drive around the vineyards and a stop in the area's many wine bars is enough to quench any oenophile's thirst. See p. 394.

FROM TOP: **The vineyards of Barolo, in the Piedmont; Alba's white truffles.**

DAYS 4 & 5: Bra, Alba & Asti ★★

In any other kind of tour, this triangle of medieval towns could be skipped, but a gourmand's itinerary of northern Italy without the Langhe, as the area is known, would be like a religious pilgrimage without St. Peter's Basilica. **Asti**'s (p. 389) Moscato grapes produce the country's best-known *spumante,* while **Alba** (p. 392) is ground zero for the legendary white truffle. Not coincidentally, the headquarters for the world's best-known culinary fraternity is based here, in Bra. **Slow Food**—with a culinary school in the city and chapters in Europe, in North America, and across the globe—promotes a doctrine of careful attention to local, quality food. In even-numbered years in Bra, it hosts Salone del Gusto, a sort of culinary trade fair with seminars and tasting booths, while in odd years, the organization holds an international cheese conference, with more varieties than you could sniff in an entire weekend. Check its website (www.slowfood.com) for dates.

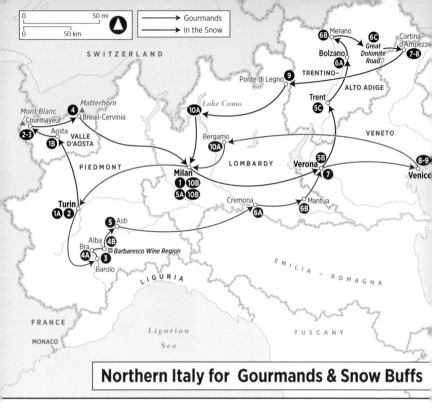

Northern Italy for Gourmands & Snow Buffs

DAY 6: Cremona & Mantua ★★

Hopefully, you've eaten only small, delicate dishes of mushrooms and truffles until this point (however unlikely that is) and have kept an appetite for a great dinner in Mantua. Skip breakfast in Asti and save time in the morning for a side trip to Pavia to pick up a few inexpensive bottles of Oltrepo' Pavese. Stop off in Cremona to see the hometown of **Stradivarius violins** (p. 324) and try some of the area's famous pumpkin-stuffed tortellini. Chances are, you'll like it so much you'll want to order the same thing in Mantua, about an hour away. It is also a specialty there, along with its excellent risotto. Tour the city's marvelous **Palazzo Ducale** (p. 334) and its works by Titian, and then move on to dinner at either the **Trattoria Due Cavallini** (p. 337) or the **Ochina Bianca** (p. 337). Mantua has some of the best dining around for such an unheralded city, and its lovely, quiet streets make for a great postprandial stroll. Either spend the night here or make the brief trip north to Verona for a nightcap at the **Bottega del Vino** (p. 227), boasting one of the most highly respected wine cellars in all of Italy.

DAY 7: Verona & Its Neighboring Vineyards ★★★

The vineyards just north of the city are the home to the whites of Soave and the reds of Valpolicella, including the savored Amarone. The area is so serious about its privacy and guarding its secrets that it doesn't have much tourist infrastructure to speak of. The best place to enjoy the wines is back in the *trattorie* of Verona, either the **Osteria del Duca** (p. 228) or **La Taverna di Via Stella** (p. 228), or in one of the bars on Piazza delle Erbe, perhaps with a well-deserved return trip to the legendary **Bottega del Vino** (p. 227). Even the little touristy restaurants next to the Arena are a memorable experience, especially if there is an opera there that night.

DAYS 8 & 9: Venice ★★

It's easy to get a lousy dinner in Venice, but almost as easy to get a fantastic one. This is your chance for some of the region's freshest seafood and the city's trademark *seppie* (cuttlefish, whose black ink is used to color spaghetti and risotto). It would be uncivilized not to start off in some tiny bar for a glass of the northern Veneto's prosecco (sparkling white wine) or, better, a *spritz* of white wine, soda water, and either Campari or Aperol. Between meals and aperitifs, there should be enough time to see some of the city's famed palaces and take a spin on a **gondola** (p. 100) at night. Don't forget the requisite bottle of prosecco!

DAY 10: Bergamo ★ & Milan

You can't leave northern Italy without having polenta from Bergamo, and there's no better place to do it than at the **Antica Hosteria del Vino Buono** (p. 331). As the name suggests, they have some pretty good wine there, too, not least of which is the locally produced **Franciacorta,** a high-quality sparkling wine made through the same painstaking process used for champagne. Milan is a short drive away, so you'll have time in the afternoon to get that pair of leather pants you had your eye on, or to see the aptly named *The Last Supper* before your flight home.

NORTHERN ITALY IN THE SNOW

The northern border of Italy is a long stretch of snowcapped peaks, teeming with outdoor enthusiasts and offering spectacular Alpine scenery—not to mention some great cheese-loaded food. Most Italians prefer to spend a week in one resort, and indeed most hotels tend to rent out rooms by the week. But it is certainly possible to visit several winter wonderlands in a single trip if you find those hotels that offer a 2- or 3-night stay, and book them well ahead of time. (It's best to try later in the winter, when the snow is better anyway.) This 10-day loop hits the top spots for skiing, snowboarding, and generally soaking in the mountain atmosphere. You will need to rent a car, and if you pick it up and return it at Malpensa airport instead of in Milan, you will save time. Warning: Some mountain roads close after a very heavy snowstorm. In any case, you are required to have tire chains, so book them well ahead of time, with your car.

DAY 1: Turin & Aosta ★

As the 2006 Olympic Games showed, **Turin** (p. 368) is a natural gateway to the Alps and a stunning city in the wintertime. Plus, it's just over an hour's drive from Malpensa airport. Winter sports enthusiasts can check out the multimillion-dollar sports complexes where the ice hockey and skating events were held, but be sure to have an introductory cappuccino at one of the city's centuries-old cafes. Linger over lunch, explore the haunts of Italy's former royalty, and stay until sunset; the city also has a remarkable artists'

Skiing outside Aosta.

lights exhibition, which hangs over each of the major thoroughfares in winter months. It is truly a memorable scene. From Turin, it is only about an hour's drive to **Aosta** (p. 398), in the heart of the Alps and a great place to stay for the night before skiing.

DAYS 2, 3 & 4: Mont Blanc & Cervinia (The Matterhorn) ★★★

Mont Blanc is the pinnacle of the Alps in every sense. It is international, boasting the convergence of France, Italy, and Switzerland; it has great Alpine food and culture at every turn; and it is the highest point in Europe. From **Courmayeur** (p. 399), take the tramway to **Punta Helbronner** (p. 405) and ski/snowboard down the heavenly Vallée Blanche glacier into Chamonix, France. There are buses there for the return trip to Italy, through the tunnel. Guides can take you backcountry skiing just about anywhere you like (weather, crevasses, and avalanche danger permitting). Set aside a day to ski in the shadow of the nearby **Matterhorn** (Monte Cervino to the Italians; p. 400), which is less challenging but just as impressive. Take the cable cars up to Plateau Rosa and wind your way down the slopes to Zermatt, Switzerland, for lunch. At the end of the ski day, don't waste too much time in **Breuil-Cervinia** (p. 400), which is not nearly as cozy and quaint as Courmayeur, and make tracks for Milan for some much better nightlife.

DAY 5: Milan, Verona & Trento ★

This is your big driving day to get to the "other" Alps, the **Dolomites** (p. 232), and Autostrada A4 is far and away the fastest way to go. Take a break from the outdoors, do some shopping in Milan in the morning, and then head out toward Verona for a late lunch and a walk around the home of **Romeo and Juliet** (p. 220). In winter, it will be at its most authentic and almost completely devoid of tourists. The late afternoon, when the sunset starts to reflect off the craggy Dolomite peaks, is the best time to take the scenic A22 highway to **Trento** (p. 232). The city is at the doorstep of the German-speaking part of Italy (which starts just a few more miles farther north) and, especially under a snowfall, is an excellent place to have dinner and spend the evening.

Mont Blanc has snow even when surrounding mountains don't.

DAY 6: Bolzano, Merano & the Great Dolomite Road ★★★

Visit Ötzi, the 5,300-year-old **"Ice Man"** found frozen in the Alps in 1991, who now makes his home in the **South Tyrol Museum of Archaeology** in Bolzano (p. 243). Just 27km (17 miles) away is the magical town of Merano, where snow-scene lovers should take the **Winter Walk** (p. 251) along the Passer River toward the splendid **castle of the counts of Tyrol** (p. 251). Before sunset, start making your way over to Cortina d'Ampezzo along the Great Dolomite Road for perhaps the most amazing mountain drive in Italy. (Remember that this road might be closed after a mighty snowfall, so be prepared to nix Cortina, if necessary, and spend an extra day or two skiing Madonna del Campiglio.)

DAYS 7 & 8: Cortina d'Ampezzo ★★

Keeping to the Winter Olympics theme started in Turin, enjoy one of the older versions in **Cortina** (p. 258), which hosted the games in 1956. Those tired of skiing can always go ice-skating at the old **Olympic rinks** (p. 261), but the slopes are fantastic and have the scenery to match. The town itself is a little pricey at night, but the romantic setting is unmatched anywhere else in the mountains. After making your last turns on the slopes on the second day, head back toward Bolzano on the Great Dolomite Road.

DAYS 9 & 10: Malpensa, Valtellina & Lake Como ★

It is not a long drive along the S42 from Bolzano to Ponte di Legno and its nationally known sled-dog school. Continue on the S42 and turn onto the S39 toward the ski resort of Aprica. From there, the S38 highway leads along the Valtellina valley, where restaurants in the wintertime are almost always serving the inimitable *pizzoccheri* of northern Lombardy: buckwheat pasta mixed with melted Taleggio cheese, potatoes, cabbage, butter, and garlic, a must-have on any ski trip to northern Italy. Soon you'll reach the northern tip of **Lake Como** (p. 349), a peaceful oasis in winter, which is just northwest of Malpensa airport.

VENICE

4

F ew cities in the world are one of a kind, and in that tight fraternity several stand out, perhaps none more than Venice, formerly the Most Serene Republic of Venice. To see for the first time this most improbable cityscape of canals, bridges, gondolas, and stone palaces that seem to float on water is to experience one of life's great pleasures. To see it a second, third, and fourth time is to appreciate Venice's greatness. Tucked away in Italy's northeastern corner at the upper reaches of the Adriatic Sea, it is hard to imagine how Venice parlayed its position into becoming a great maritime power. But then again, this city is full of surprises—the grandeur of Piazza San Marco, the splendid solitude of Cannaregio's canal-side quays, or Rialto's vibrant fish market.

Things to Do After studying **Piazza San Marco,** unquestionably one of the world's great squares both for its beauty and pageantry, see the breathtaking mosaics in **St. Mark's Basilica** and ride the elevator to the top of the **bell tower** for a commanding view of the city. Titian, Giorgione, and Tintoretto feature prominently in the **Accademia Gallery** and in numerous churches, while a rich collection of 20th-century paintings and sculptures can be seen at the **Peggy Guggenheim Collection.** A visit to the outer reaches of Castello, Dorsoduro, and Cannaregio give you a peek at what it's really like to live in this unique city. A **gondola ride** is, perhaps, cliché, but it is also likely to be one of your best Venetian memories.

Relaxation Put on your walking shoes and get lost along the back *calli* (streets), uncrowded *campi* (squares), and hidden *canali* (canals); turn left when the signs to the sights say to go right and in a flash you will encounter the true, living, breathing side of Venice. With nary a car in sight, getting lost has never been this relaxing. Consider coming in winter; while often cold and damp, it just might afford you the memorable experience of walking on planks above the *acqua alta* (high water).

Restaurants & Dining While Venetians, like all Italians, love to linger over a proper meal of primo and secondo (most likely one or both made with fish), this city has garnered fame with its *cicchetti,* tapaslike snacks that are eaten standing at *bacari* (wine bars) and washed down with a glass of *ombra* (wine). *Bacari* are everywhere, but one of the best spots to find them is on the **San Polo** side of the Rialto bridge, where they are frequented by those working in the nearby fish market.

Nightlife & Entertainment There are a few pubs around town and even a dance club, but for the best nightlife, grab a gelato (or a bottle of wine and a

FACING PAGE: **Gondolas stacked up in a Venice canal.**

The Rialto Bridge at night.

few glasses) and head to Piazza San Marco, where you can listen to the music emanating from the cafes for free. Or better yet, seek out one of the numerous *campi* (squares) sprinkled around the city. Alternatively, dress up for an opera at **La Fenice.**

GETTING THERE

BY PLANE You can fly into Venice from North America via Rome or Milan with **Alitalia** or a number of other airlines, or by connecting through a major European city with European carriers. No-frills carrier **easyJet** (www.easy jet.com) flies direct from London much cheaper than the major airlines, as does **Ryanair** (www.ryanair.com), though the latter sometimes uses the airport in nearby Treviso (a 1-hr. bus ride to Venice).

Flights land at the **Aeroporto Marco Polo,** 7km (4¼ miles) north of the city on the mainland (✆ 041-260-9260; www.veniceairport.it). There are two bus alternatives: The **ATVO airport shuttle bus** (✆ 0421-594-671; www.atvo.it) connects with Piazzale Roma not far from Venice's Santa Lucia train station (and the closest point to Venice's attractions accessible by car or bus). Buses leave for/from the airport about every 30 minutes, cost 5€, and make the trip in about 20 minutes. The less expensive local public **ACTV bus no. 5** (✆ 041-2424) costs 2€, takes 30 to 45 minutes, and runs between two and four times an hour depending on the time of day. Buy tickets for either at the newsstand just inside the terminal from the signposted bus stop. With either bus, you'll have to walk to or from the final stop at Piazzale Roma to the nearby *vaporetto* (water bus) stop for the final connection to your hotel. It's rare to see porters around who'll help with luggage, so pack light.

A **land taxi** from the airport to the Piazzale Roma (where you get the *vaporetto*) will run about 40€.

The most fashionable and traditional way to arrive in Piazza San Marco is by sea. For 15€, 13€ if you buy online, the **Cooperative San Marco/ Alilaguna** (✆ 041-240-1701; www.alilaguna.it) operates a large *mo-toscafo* (shuttle boat) service from the airport with stops at Murano and the Lido before arriving after about 1 hour and 15 minutes in Piazza San Marco.

This *Linea Blu* (the blue line) runs almost every 30 minutes from about 6am to midnight. The *Linea Arancio* (orange line) has the same frequency, costs the same and takes the same amount of time to arrive at San Marco, but gets there through the Grand Canal, which is much more spectacular and offers the possibility to get off at one of the stops along the Grand Canal. This might be convenient to your hotel and could save you having to take another means of transportation. If you arrive at Piazza San Marco and your hotel isn't in the area, you'll have to make a connection at the *vaporetto* launches. (Your hotel can help you with the specifics if you booked before you left home.)

A **private water taxi** (20–30 min. to/from the airport) is convenient but costly—there is a fixed 110€ fee to arrive in the city, for up to four passengers with one bag each (10€ more for each extra person up to a maximum of 12). It's worth considering if you're pressed for time, have an early flight, are carrying a lot of luggage (a Venice no-no), or can split the cost with a friend or two. It may be able to drop you off at the front (or side) door of your hotel or as close as it can maneuver given your hotel's location (check with the hotel before arriving). Your taxi captain should be able to tell you before boarding just how close he can get you. Try the **Corsorzio Motoscafi Venezia** (©041-522-2303; www.motoscafivenezia.it) or Venezia Taxi (©041-723-112; www.veneziataxi.it).

BY TRAIN Trains from Rome (3¾ hr.), Milan (2½ hr.), Florence (2 hr.), and all over Europe arrive at the **Stazione Venezia Santa Lucia** (©041-721-253; www.trenitalia.com). To get there, all must pass through (though not necessarily stop at) a station marked Venezia-Mestre. Don't be confused: Mestre is a charmless industrial city that's the last stop on the mainland. Occasionally trains end in Mestre, in which case you have to catch one of the frequent 10-minute shuttles connecting with Venice; it's inconvenient, so when you book your ticket, confirm that the final destination is Venezia Santa Lucia.

On exiting, you'll find the Grand Canal immediately in front of you, a sight that makes for a heart-stopping first impression. You'll find the docks for a number of *vaporetti* lines (the city's public ferries or "water buses") to your left and right. Head to the booths to your left, near the bridge, to catch either of the two lines plying the Grand Canal: the no. 2 express, which stops only at the San Marcuola, Rialto Bridge, San Tomà, San Samuele, and Accademia before hitting San Marco (26 min. total); and the no. 1, which makes 13 stops before arriving at San Marco (a 33-min. trip). Both leave every 10 minutes or so, but in the mornings before 9am and the evenings after 8pm the no. 2 sometimes stops short at Rialto, meaning you'll have to disembark and hop on the next no. 1 or 2 that comes along to continue to San Marco.

Note: The *vaporetti* go in two directions from the train station: left down the Grand Canal toward San Marco—which is the (relatively) fast and scenic way—and right, which also eventually gets you to San Marco (at the San Zaccaria stop) if you are on the 2, but takes more than twice as long because it goes the long way around Dorsoduro (and serves mainly commuters). If you get the no. 1 going to the right from the train station, it will go only one more stop before it hits its terminus at Piazzale Roma.

BY BUS Though rail travel is more convenient and commonplace, Venice is serviced by long-distance buses from all over mainland Italy and some international cities. The final destination is Piazzale Roma, where you'll need to pick up *vaporetto* no. 1 or no. 2 (as described above) to connect you with stops in the heart of Venice and along the Grand Canal.

BY CAR The only wheels you'll see in Venice are those attached to luggage. Venice is a city of canals and narrow alleys. **No cars are allowed,** or more to the point, no cars could drive through the narrow streets and over the footbridges—even the police, firemen, and ambulance services use boats. Arriving in Venice by car is problematic and expensive—and downright exasperating if it's high season and the parking facilities are full (they often are). You can drive across the Ponte della Libertà from Mestre to Venice, but you can go no farther than Piazzale Roma at the Venice end, where many garages eagerly await your euros. The rates vary with, for example, the public **ASM garage** (© 041-272-7111; www.asmvenezia.it) charging 25€ for a 24-hour period, while private outfit **Garage San Marco** (© 041-523-2213; www.garagesanmarco.it) costs 30€ for 24 hours. Some garages also have hourly rates.

Vaporetti lines 1 and 2, described above, both stop at Piazzale Roma before continuing down the Grand Canal to the train station and, eventually, Piazza San Marco.

ORIENTATION
Visitor Information

TOURIST OFFICES The main office is on Fondamenta San Lorenzo, five minutes from Piazza San Marco (© 041-529-8711; www.turismovenezia.it; *vaporetto:* San Zaccaria). It's open daily from 10am to 6pm. During peak season, a small info booth with erratic hours operates in the arrivals hall at

The Grand Canal is Venice's main thoroughfare.

VENICE BY THE numbers

Central Venice is divided by the city's longest (4km/2½ miles) and widest (30–70m/98–230 ft.) waterway, the Grand Canal. Its 118 islands are separated by approximately 170 canals and connected by some 430 footbridges, mostly stone with iron balustrades added in the 19th century.

Only four bridges cross the Grand Canal: the **Ponte degli Scalzi,** just outside and to the left of the train station; the elegant white marble **Ponte Rialto** (the most recognizable bridge in Venice and, for centuries, the only one over the Grand Canal), connecting the districts of San Marco and San Polo; the wooden **Ponte Accademia,** connecting the Campo Santo Stefano area of the San Marco neighborhood with the Accademia museum across the way in Dorsoduro; and, since late 2008, the futuristic **Ponte della Costituzione** (also known as the Calatrava bridge, after famed Spanish architect Santiago Calatrava, who designed it), which you will see around the corner to your right when you exit the train station.

the Marco Polo Airport. You might be better off going to private agencies that often offer help more willingly than the official tourist offices, including booking hotels for a small fee. **Venezia Si** (✆ **041-522-2264**) has a few offices around town, including one inside the train station on your left just before you exit. It is open Monday to Friday 8am to 7pm, and Saturday and Sunday 9am to 1pm and 2 to 5:30pm.

The tourist office's *LEO Bussola* brochure is useful for museum hours and events, but their map helps you find only *vaporetto* lines and stops. (It's well worth buying a street map at a news kiosk; see "Getting Around," below.) More useful is the info-packed monthly *Un Ospite di Venezia* (www. unospitedivenezia.it); most hotels have copies. Also keep an eye out for the ubiquitous posters around town with exhibit and concert schedules. The classical concerts held mostly in churches are touristy but fun and are advertised by an army of costumed touts handing out leaflets on highly trafficked streets.

WEBSITES   The city's official tourist-board site is **www.turismovenezia.it**; the official site of the city government (also full of good resources) is **www.comune. venezia.it**. A good privately maintained site is **www.meetingvenice.it**.

City Layout

Keep in mind as you wander seemingly hopelessly among the *calli* (streets) and *campi* (squares) that the city wasn't built to make sense to those on foot but rather to those plying its canals. No matter how good your map and sense of direction, time after time you'll get lost. Just view it as an opportunity to stumble across Venice's most intriguing corners and vignettes.

Venice lies 4km (2½ miles) from terra firma, connected to the mainland burg of Mestre by the Ponte della Libertà, which leads to Piazzale Roma. Snaking through the city like an inverted S is the **Grand Canal (Canale Grande),** the wide main artery of aquatic Venice.

The city is divided into six *sestieri* ("sixths," or districts or wards): **Cannaregio, Castello, San Marco, San Polo, Santa Croce,** and **Dorsoduro.** In addition to the six *sestieri* that cluster around the Grand Canal there are a host of other islands in the Venice lagoon. Opposite Piazza San Marco and Dorsoduro is **La Giudecca,** a tranquil, mostly residential and working-class place that is administratively part of Dorsoduro and offers great views of Piazza San Marco.

The **Lido di Venezia** is the city's sandy beach; it's a popular summer destination and holds a concentration of seasonal hotels. **San Michele,** located just off of the Cannaregio and Castello *sestieri,* is the cemetery island where such celebrities as Stravinsky and Diaghilev are buried.

Murano, Burano, and **Torcello** are popular destinations northeast of the city and easily accessible by *vaporetto.* Since the 13th century, Murano has exported its glass products worldwide; it's an interesting trip, but if your scope is a glass chandelier or something similar, you can do just as well in "downtown" Venice's myriad glass stores. Fishing village Burano is dotted with colorful houses and is famous for its lace, an art now practiced by very few island women. Torcello is the most remote and least populated. The 40-minute boat ride is worthwhile for history and art buffs, who'll be awestruck by the Byzantine mosaics of the cathedral (some of Europe's finest outside Ravenna). The cathedral's foundation dates to the 7th century, making this the oldest Venetian monument in existence.

The industrial city of **Mestre,** on the mainland, is the gateway to Venice, and while it holds no reason for exploration, in a pinch its host of inexpensive hotels is worth consideration when Venice's are full.

Neighborhoods in Brief

Based on a tradition dating from the 12th century, for tax-related purposes, the city has officially been divided into six *sestieri* that have basically been the same since 1711. The Grand Canal neatly divides them into three on each bank.

SAN MARCO The central *sestiere* shares the side of the Grand Canal with Castello and Cannaregio, anchored by the magnificent Piazza San Marco and St. Mark's Basilica to the south and the Rialto Bridge to the north; it's the most visited (and, as a result, the most expensive) of the *sestieri.* It's the commercial, religious, and political heart of the city and has been for more than a millennium. It is also its musical heart, home to the legendary La Fenice Opera House; devastated by a fire in 1996, it was reopened in 2005 after an extensive restoration. Although you'll find glimpses and snippets of the real Venice here, ever-rising rents have nudged resident Venetians to look for housing in the outer neighborhoods: You'll be hard-pressed to find a grocery store or dry cleaner here. But if you're looking for Murano glass

A statue of Bartolomeo Colleoni in Campo SS. Giovanni e Paolo.

trinkets and mediocre restaurants, you'll find an embarrassment of choices. This area is a mecca of first-class hotels—but we'll give you some suggestions for staying here in the heart of Venice without going broke.

CASTELLO This quarter, whose tony canal-side esplanade Riva degli Schiavoni follows the Bacino di San Marco (St. Mark's Basin), is lined with deluxe hotels. It begins just east of Piazza San Marco, skirting Venice's most congested area north and east of Piazza San Marco (Riva degli Schiavoni can sometimes get so busy as to seem like Times Square on New Year's Eve), but if you head farther east in the direction of the Arsenale or inland away from the *bacino,* the people traffic thins out, despite the presence of such major sights as Campo SS. Giovanni e Paolo and the Scuola di San Giorgio.

CANNAREGIO Sharing the same side of the Grand Canal with San Marco and Castello, Cannaregio stretches north and east from the train station to include the Jewish Ghetto and into the canal-hugging vicinity of the Ca' d'Oro and the Rialto Bridge. Its outer reaches are quiet, unspoiled, and residential ("*What* high-season tourist crowds?" you may wonder); one-quarter of Venice's

> ### A Note on Addresses
>
> Within each *sestiere* is a most original system of numbering the *palazzi,* using one continuous string of 6,000 or so numbers. The format for addresses in this chapter is the official mailing address: the *sestiere* name followed by the building number in that district, followed by the name of the street or *campo* on which you'll find that address—for example, San Marco 1471 (Salizada San Moisè) means the mailing address is San Marco 1471, and you'll find it in the San Marco district on Salizada San Moisè. Be aware that San Marco 1471 may not necessarily be found close to San Marco 1475 and that many buildings aren't numbered at all.

ever-shrinking population of 65,000 lives here. Most of the city's one-star hotels are clustered about the train station—not a dangerous neighborhood but not one known for its charm, either. The tourist shop–lined Lista di Spagna, which starts just to the left as you leave the train station, morphs into Strada Nova and provides an uninterrupted thoroughfare to the Rialto bridge.

SAN POLO This mixed-bag *sestiere* of residential corners and tourist sights stretches northwest of the Rialto Bridge to the church of Santa Maria dei Frari, which houses one of Titian's masterpieces, and the Scuola di San Rocco. The hub of activity at the foot of the bridge is due in large part to the Rialto market that has taken place here for centuries—some of the city's

FROM TOP: **The Calatrava Bridge spans Santa Croce and Cannaregio; a sculpture peering down off the Rialto Bridge.**

best restaurants have flourished in the area for generations, alongside some of its worst tourist traps. The spacious Campo San Polo is the main piazza of Venice's smallest *sestiere*.

SANTA CROCE North and northwest of the San Polo district and across the Grand Canal from the train station, Santa Croce stretches all the way to Piazzale Roma. Its eastern section is generally one of the least-visited areas of Venice—making it all the more desirable for curious visitors. Less lively than San Polo, it is as authentic and feels light-years away from San Marco. The quiet and lovely Campo San Giacomo dell'Orio is its heart.

DORSODURO You'll find the residential area of Dorsoduro on the opposite side of the Accademia Bridge from San Marco. Known for the Accademia and Peggy Guggenheim museums, it is the largest of the *sestieri* and has been known as an artists' haven (hence the tireless comparison with New York's Greenwich Village—a far cry) until recent escalations of rents forced much of the community to relocate elsewhere. Good neighborhood restaurants, a charming gondola boatyard, the lively Campo Santa Margherita, and the sunny quay called le Zattere (a favorite promenade and gelato stop) all add to the character and color that make this one of the city's most-visited areas.

LA GIUDECCA Located opposite the Piazza San Marco and Dorsoduro, La Giudecca is a tranquil working-class residential area where you'll find a youth hostel and a handful of hotels (including the deluxe Cipriani, one of Europe's finest).

LIDO DI VENEZIA This slim, 11km-long (6¾-mile) island, the only spot in the Venetian lagoon where cars circulate, is the city's beach and separates the lagoon from the open sea. The landmark hotels here serve as a base for the annual Venice Film Festival.

Getting Around

Aside from on boats, the only way to explore Venice is by walking—and by getting lost repeatedly. You'll navigate many twisting streets whose names change constantly and don't appear on any map, and streets that may very well simply end in a blind alley or spill abruptly into a canal. You'll also cross dozens of footbridges. Treat getting bewilderingly lost in Venice as part of the fun, and budget more time than you'd think necessary to get wherever you're going.

STREET MAPS & SIGNAGE The free map offered by the tourist office and most hotels has good intentions, but it doesn't even show—much less name or index—all the *calli* (streets) and pathways of Venice. For that, pick up a more detailed map (ask for a *pianta della città* at news kiosks—especially those at the train station and around San Marco) or most bookstores. The best (and most expensive) is the highly detailed Touring Club Italiano map, available in a variety of forms (folding or spiral-bound) and scales. Almost as good, and easier to carry, is the simple and cheap 1:6,500 folding map put out by Storti Edizioni (its cover is white-edged with pink, which fades to blue at the bottom).

Still, Venice's confusing layout confounds even the best maps and navigators. You're often better off just stopping every couple of blocks and asking a local to point you in the right direction (always know the name of the *campo*/square or major sight closest to the address you're looking for, and ask for that).

As you wander, look for the ubiquitous yellow signs (well, *usually* yellow) whose destinations and arrows direct you toward five major landmarks: **Ferrovia** (the train station), **Piazzale Roma** (the parking garage), **Rialto** (one of the four bridges over the Grand Canal), **San Marco** (the city's main square), and the **Accademia** (the southernmost Grand Canal bridge).

BY BOAT The various *sestieri* are linked by a comprehensive *vaporetto* (water bus/ferry) system of about a dozen lines operated by the **Azienda del Consorzio Trasporti Veneziano (ACTV),** Calle Fuseri 1810, near the northwest corner of Piazza San Marco (✆ **041-528-7886;** www.actv.it). Transit maps are available at the tourist office and most ACTV stations. It's easier to get around on foot, as the *vaporetti* principally serve the Grand Canal, the out-skirts, and the outer islands. The crisscross network of small canals is the province of delivery vessels, gondolas, and private boats.

A ticket valid for 1 hour of travel on a *vaporetto* is a steep 6.50€, while the 24-hour ticket is 18€. Most lines run every 10 to 15 minutes from 7am to midnight, and then hourly until morning. Most *vaporetto* docks (the only

---

CRUISING THE canals

A leisurely cruise along the **Grand Canal ★★★** from Piazza San Marco to the Ferrovia—or the reverse—is one of Venice's must-dos (p. 148). It's the world's most unusual Main Street, a watery boulevard whose *palazzi* have been converted into condos. Lower water-lapped floors are now deserted, but the higher floors are still coveted by the city's titled families, who have inhabited these glorious residences for centuries; others have become the summertime dream homes of privileged expats, drawn here as irresistibly as the romantic Venetians-by-adoption who pre-ceded them—Richard Wagner, Robert Browning, Lord Byron, and (more recently, Woody Allen).

As much a symbol of Venice as the winged lion, the **gondola ★★★** is one of Europe's great traditions, incredibly and inexplicably expensive but truly as romantic as it looks (detractors who write it off as too touristy have most likely never tried it). The official, fixed rate is 80€ for a 40-minute tour (100€ 7pm–8am), with up to six passengers, and 40€ for every additional 20 minutes (50€ at night). That's not a typo: 150€ an hour for an evening cruise. *Note:* Though the price is fixed by the city, a good negotiator at the right time of day (when there is not too much business) can sometimes grab a small discount. And at these ridiculously inflated prices, there is no need to tip the gondolier.

Aim for late afternoon before sun-down, when the light does its magic on the canal reflections (and bring a bottle of prosecco and glasses). If the gondola price is too high, ask visitors at your hotel or others lingering about at the gondola stations if they'd like to share it. Though the price is "fixed," before set-ting off establish with the gondolier the cost, time, and route (back canals are preferable to the trafficked and often choppy Grand Canal). They're regulated by the **Ente Gondola** (✆ **041-528-5075;** www.gondolavenezia.it), so call if you have any questions or complaints.

And what of the serenading gondo-lier immortalized in film? Frankly, you're better off without. But if warbling is de rigueur for you, here's the scoop. An ensemble of accordion player and tenor is so expensive that it's shared among several gondolas traveling together. A number of travel agents around town book the evening serenades for around 35€ per person.

There are 12 gondola stations around Venice, including Piazzale Roma, the train station, the Rialto Bridge, and Piazza San Marco. There are also a number of smaller stations, with *gondolieri* in striped shirts standing alongside their sleek 11m (36-ft.) black wonders looking for passengers. They all speak enough English to communi-cate the necessary details.

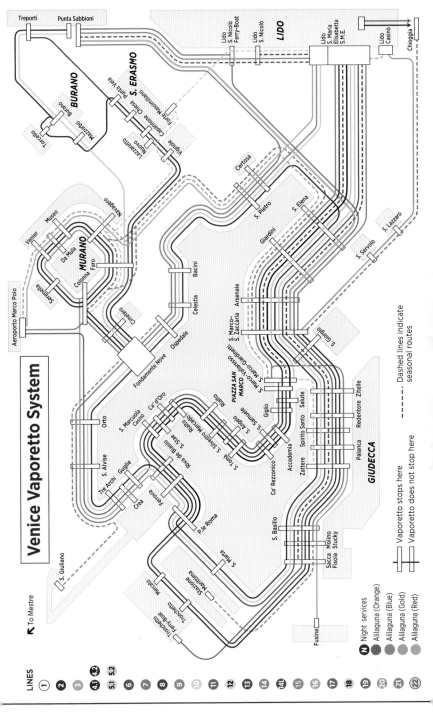

Venice Vaporetto System

↖ To Mestre

Dashed lines indicate seasonal routes

Vaporetto stops here
Vaporetto does not stop here

N Night services
Alilaguna (Orange)
Alilaguna (Blue)
Alilaguna (Gold)
Alilaguna (Red)

LINES
① ② ③ 4.1 4.2 5.1 5.2 ⑥ ⑦ ⑧ ⑨ ⑩ ⑪ ⑫ ⑬ ⑭ 14.1 ⑮ ⑯ ⑰ 18 ⑲ ⑳ 21 22

If, after a few days in Rome and Florence, you were just getting the hang of matching your map with the reality of your new surroundings, you can put aside any short-term success upon your arrival in Venice. Even the Italians (non-Venetian ones) look befuddled when trying to decipher street names and signs (given that you can ever find any).

Venice's colorful thousand-year history as a once-powerful maritime republic helped mold the local dialect, which absorbed nuances and vocabulary from far-flung outposts in the East and from the flourishing communities of foreign merchants who, for centuries, lived and traded in the city. Venetian dialect has in turn left its mark on the vernacular of many languages, including English that has inherited such Venetian words as *gondola* (naturally), *ciao, ghetto, lido,* and *arsenal.*

Venetian dialect is still widely used among the locals and its sing-song tone can be a joy to listen to. For those who know some Italian, try following the conversation between two *gondolieri* to get an idea of how difficult Venetian can be to understand. For the Venice-bound traveler just trying to make sense of Venetian addresses, the following will give you the basics. (**Note:** Spellings can vary slight in Venetian so, for example, *salizada* is sometimes spelled *salizzada.*)

ca' The abbreviated use of the word *casa* is used for the noble *palazzi,* once private residences and now museums, lining the Grand Canal: Ca' d'Oro, Ca' Pesaro, and Ca' Rezzonico. There is only one *palazzo,* the Palazzo Ducale, the former doge's residence. (The doge, or "duke," was elected for life.) However, as time went on, some great houses gradually also began to be called *"palazzi,"* so today you'll also encounter the Palazzo Grassi or the Palazzo Labia.

calle Taken from the Spanish (though pronounced as if Italian, *ca-*lay), this is the most commonplace word for "street," known as *via* or *strada* elsewhere in Italy. There are numerous variations. **Ruga,** from the French word *rue,* is the name given to a few important *calle* near San Marco and the Rialto bridge that are flanked with stores. A **ramo** (literally "branch") is the offshoot of a street and is often used

place you can buy tickets) have timetables posted. Note that not all docks sell tickets after dark. If you haven't bought a pass or extra tickets beforehand, you'll have to settle up with the conductor onboard (you'll have to find him—he won't come looking for you) for an extra .50€ per ticket or risk a stiff fine, no excuses accepted. Also available are 48-hour tickets (28€) and 72-hour tickets (33€). If you're planning to stay in Venice a while, it makes sense to pick up a Venice Card (see "Venice Discounts," on p. 105), with which you can buy 1-hour *vaporetto* tickets for 1.20€. Tickets must be validated in the yellow machines before getting on the *vaporetto.*

Just three bridges spanned the Grand Canal until 2008 when a fourth was added connecting the train station with Piazzale Roma. To fill in the gaps, *traghetti* skiffs (oversize gondolas rowed by two standing *gondolieri*) cross the Grand Canal at eight intermediate points. You'll find a station at the end of any street named Calle del Traghetto on your map and indicated by a yellow sign with the black gondola symbol. The fare is .50€, which you interchangeably with *calle*. **Salizada** (the Venetian dialect equivalent of the Italian word for paved, *selciato*) once meant a street paved in stone, implying that all other, less important *calli* were just dirt-packed or brick-paved alleyways. A **stretto** is a narrow passageway.

campo Elsewhere in Italy, it's *piazza*. In Venice, the only piazza is the Piazza San Marco (and its two bordering *piazzette*); all other squares are *campi* or the diminutive, *campielli*. Translated as "field" or "meadow," these were once small, unpaved grazing spots for the

odd chicken or cow. Almost every one of Venice's *campi* carries the name of the church that dominates it (or once did), and most have wells, no longer used, in the center.

canale There are three wide, principal canals: the Grand Canal (affectionately called "il Canalazzo," the Canal), the Canale della Giudecca, and the Canale di Cannaregio. Each of the other 160-odd smaller canals is called a *rio*. A *rio terrà* is a filled-in canal—wide and straight—now used as a street. A *piscina* is a filled-in basin, now acting as a *campo* or piazza.

fondamenta Referring to the foundations of the houses lining a canal, this is a walkway along the side of a *rio* (small canal). Promenades along the Grand Canal near the Piazza San Marco and the Rialto are called *riva*, as in the Riva del Vin or Riva del Carbon, where cargo such as wine and coal were once unloaded.

sottoportego An alley that ducks under a building. (At left is a mural painted on the ceiling of a *sottoportego*.)

hand to the gondolier when boarding. Most Venetians cross standing up. For the experience, try the Santa Sofia crossing that connects the Ca' d'Oro and the Pescheria fish market, opposite each other on the Grand Canal just north of the Rialto Bridge—the gondoliers expertly dodge water traffic at this point of the canal, where it's the busiest and most heart-stopping.

BY WATER TAXI *Taxi acquei* (water taxis) charge high prices and aren't for visitors watching their euros. The meter starts at a hefty 15€ and clicks at 2€ per minute. Each bag over 50cm long (20 in.) costs 3€, plus there's a 10€ supplement for service from 10pm to 7am and a 10€ surcharge on Sundays and holidays (these last two charges, however, can't be applied simultaneously). If they have to come get you, tack on another 8€. Those rates cover up to two people; if any more squeeze in, it's another 1.50€ per extra passenger (maximum 20 people). Taking a taxi from the train station to Piazza San Marco or any of the hotels in the area will put you back about 65€ for two people, while there is a fixed 100€ fee (for up to four people) to go or come from the airport. Note that only taxi boats with a yellow strip are the official taxis sanctioned by the city.

Six water-taxi stations serve key points in the city: the **Ferrovia, Piazzale Roma,** the **Rialto Bridge, Piazza San Marco,** the **Lido,** and **Marco Polo Airport. Radio Taxi** (☏**041-723-112** or 041-522-2303) will come pick you up anywhere in the city.

BY GONDOLA If you come all the way to Venice and don't indulge in a gondola ride you might still be kicking yourself long after you have returned home. Yes, it's touristy, and, yes, it's expensive (see the "Cruising the Canals" box, on p. 100), but only those with a heart of stone will be unmoved by the quintessential Venetian experience. Do not initiate your trip, however, until you have agreed upon a price and synchronized watches. Oh, and don't ask them to sing.

4 [FastFACTS] VENICE

Acqua Alta During the tidal *acqua alta* (high water) floods, the lagoon rises until it engulfs the city, leaving up to 1.5 to 1.8m (5–6 ft.) of water in the lowest-lying streets (Piazza San Marco, as the lowest point in the city, goes first). Significant *acqua alta* can begin as early as late September or October, but usually takes place November to March. As many as 50 a year have been recorded since they first started in the late 1700s. The waters usually recede after just a few hours. Walkways are set up around town, but wet feet are a given. The complex system of hydraulic dams being constructed out in the lagoon to cut off the highest of these high tides (a controversial project due to its environmental impact) is well underway but won't be operational for years. ***Tip:*** If you are curious to see Acqua Alta

(and it is indeed a wonderful spectacle), but aren't in Venice at the right time, you can still get lucky as very minor occurrences can happen all year round. So if you happen to see big puddles forming in Piazza San Marco in the middle of a dry July day, you'll know what's up.

American Express Unfortunately, American Express closed its Venice office in 2009, leaving offices only in Milan and Rome.

Bookstores See p. 168.

Business Hours Standard hours for shops are Monday to Saturday 9am to 12:30pm and 3 to 7:30pm. In winter, shops are closed on Monday morning, while in summer it's usually Saturday afternoon. Most grocers are closed on Wednesday afternoon year-round. In Venice, just about everything is closed on Sunday,

though tourist shops in the tourist spots such as the San Marco area are permitted to stay open during high season. Restaurants are required to close at least 1 day a week, called *il giorno di riposo,* though the particular day varies from one trattoria to another. Many are open for Sunday lunch but close for Sunday dinner. Restaurants that specialize in fish and seafood also typically close Monday, when the fish market is closed. Restaurants will close for holidays, translated as *chiuso per ferie,* sometime in July or August, frequently over Christmas, and sometime in January before the Carnevale rush.

Climate May, June, September, and early October are the best months to visit with respect to weather (but also the most crowded). July and August are hot—at times,

VENICE discounts

The **Museum Pass** grants one admission to all the city-run museums over a 6-month period. That includes the museums of St. Mark's Square: Palazzo Ducale, Museo Correr, Museo Archeologico Nazionale, and the Biblioteca Nazionale Marciana—as well as the Museo di Palazzo Mocenigo (Costume Museum), the Ca' Rezzonico, the Ca' Pesaro, the Museo del Vetro (Glass Museum) on Murano, and the Museo del Merletto (Lace Museum) on Burano. The Museum Pass is available at any of the participating museums and costs 18€ for adults, 12€ for students under 29. There is also a **San Marco Museum Pass** that lets you into the museums of St. Mark's plus one of the other museums. It costs 14€, and 8€ for students.

The **Venice Card** is the Museum Pass on steroids, with a juiced up price to match: 40€, 30€ for those 6 to 29. It includes, among other things and in addition to everything the Museum Pass offers, discounts on temporary exhibits, more museums and (no kidding) two entrances to the municipal public toilets. You can pick one up at any of the Hellovenezia (www.hellovenezia.com) offices around town (there's one in the train station as well as at the Rialto and Santa Zaccaria *vaporetto* stops) or at the tourist information offices.

Venice, so delicate it cannot handle the hordes of visitors it receives every year, has been toying with the idea of charging admission to get into the very city itself. Slightly calmer heads seem to have prevailed, though, and instead we have **Venice Connected** (www.veniceconnected.it), which started in 2009 and gives discounts if you buy tickets through the website before arriv-

ing. You can get tickets for everything from transportation to museums, but you must do it for a particular day that is at least 4 days in the future. In return, the city gets, at least in theory, a better idea of how many people will be in town on a given day.

Also, for tourists between the ages of 14 and 29, there is the **Rolling Venice** card, which is something akin to the Venice Connected discounts for students. It's valid until the end of the year in which you buy it, costs just 4€, and entitles the bearer to significant (20%–30%) discounts at participating restaurants, and a similar discount on *traghetto* tickets. Holders of the Rolling Venice card also get discounts in museums, stores, language courses, hotels, and bars across the city (it comes with a thick booklet listing everywhere that you're entitled to get discounts). The card can be acquired at the same places as the Venice Card (see above).

unbearably so. April and late October/early November are hit-or-miss; it can be glorious, rainy, cool, or damp, and only marginally less crowded. Also see "Acqua Alta," above.

Consulates The **U.K. Consulate** in Venice is on the mainland in Mestre, at Piazzale Donatori di

Sangue 2 (☎ **041-505-5990**); it's open Monday to Friday 10am to 1pm. The **U.S., Australia, Canada,** and **New Zealand** have consulates in Milan (p. 293); all also maintain embassies in Rome.

Crime Be aware of petty crime like pickpocketing on the crowded *vaporetti*,

particularly the tourist routes, where passengers are more intent on the passing scenery than on watching their bags. Venice's deserted back streets are virtually crime-free, though occasional tales of theft have circulated. Generally speaking, Venice is one of Italy's safest cities.

Drugstores Venice's pharmacies take turns staying open all night. To find out which one is on call in your area, ask at your hotel or check the rotational duty signs posted outside all pharmacies.

Emergencies The best number to call in Italy (and the rest of Europe) with a **general emergency** is ✆ **112;** this connects you to the military-trained **Carabinieri** who will transfer your call as needed; for the **police,** dial ✆ **113;** for a medical emergency and to call an **ambulance,** the number is ✆ **118;** for the **fire department,** call ✆ **115.** All are free calls.

Holidays Venice's patron saint, San Marco (St. Mark), is honored on April 25, which also happens to be a national holiday, Liberation Day, celebrating the end of World War II. For a list of official state holidays, see the "Holidays" section on p. 70.

Hospitals The **Ospedale Civile Santi Giovanni e Paolo** (✆ **041-529-4111**), on Campo Santi Giovanni e Paolo, has English-speaking staff and provides emergency service 24 hours a day (*vaporetto:* San Toma).

Internet Venetian Navigator, Castello 5300 on Calle Casselleria between San Marco and Campo Santa Maria Formosa (✆ **041-277-1056;** www. venetiannavigator.com; *vaporetto:* San Marco,

Zaccaria, Rialto), is open daily 10am to 2:30pm and 4:30 to 8:30pm, and charges 5€ for 30 minutes or 7€ per hour (10% discount with a Rolling Venice card). Venetian Navigator has another location near the Rialto bridge, at San Marco 5239 on Calle Stagneri. **Sala Giochi SS Apostoli** (✆ **041-099-3684**), which is open daily 9:30am to 11pm, is in Campo SS Apostoli, right at the base of the bridge that leads towards Rialto and San Marco. Checking Facebook, e-mail, or sending a few tweets costs 3€ for 30 minutes and 5€ for an hour, though from 9:30 to 10:30am and 6 to 7pm you can surf for free, if you buy a drink. You can also pay for Wi-Fi access (1.50€ for half an hour and 2.50€ for an hour) and there are phones for making cheap international calls.

Laundry The laundry service most convenient to San Marco is **Gabriella** (✆ **041-522-1758**), San Marco 985 on Rio Terrà Colonne (off Calle dei Fabbri), where they wash and dry your clothes within an hour or two for 15€ per load. They are open Monday to Friday 8am to 12:30pm.

Lost & Found The central **Ufficio Oggetti Rinvenuti** (✆ **041-274-8225**) is in the annex to the City Hall (Municipio), at San Marco 4134, on Calle Piscopia o Loredan, just off

Riva del Carbon on the Grand Canal, near the Rialto Bridge (on the same side of the canal as the Rialto *vaporetto* station). Look for *scala* (stairway) C; the lost-and-found office is in the Economato section on the *mezzanino* level, one flight up. The office is ostensibly open Monday to Friday from 9am to 1pm.

There's also an **Ufficio Oggetti Smarriti** at the airport (✆ **041-260-9260**). The train station no longer has a lost-and-found, so if you lose something on the train or in the station, definitely talk to the police (they have a small office next to Track 1), but they are likely to direct you to the central Ufficio Oggetti Rinvenuti in the city hall annex.

Luggage Storage The *deposito bagagli* in the train station (✆ **041-785-531**) is located to the left of the station as you disembark from your train and head towards the exit. It's open daily from 6am to 11:50pm and charges 4€ for each bag for the first 5 hours, and then 60¢ for each additional hour through the 12th hour. Then it's 20¢ an hour.

Post Office Venice's **Posta Centrale** is at San Marco 5554, 30124 Venezia, on the San Marco side of the Rialto Bridge at Rialto Fontego dei Tedeschi (✆ **041-271-7111** or 041-528-5813; *vaporetto:* Rialto). This office sells *francobolli* (stamps) at Window 12 Monday to Saturday 8:30am to 6:30pm (for parcels, 8:10am–1:30pm). If you're at Piazza San Marco and need postal services, walk through Sottoportego San Geminian, the center portal at the opposite end of the piazza from the basilica on Calle Larga dell'Ascensione. Its open Monday to Friday 8:30am to 2pm and Saturday 8:30am to 1pm. You can buy stamps at any *tabacchi* (tobacconists). The limited mailboxes seen around town are red.

Telephones See "Fast Facts: Northern Italy," p. 475. The area code for Venice is ✆ 041.

WHERE TO STAY

Few cities boast as long a high season as that of Venice, beginning with the Easter period. May, June, and September are the best months weather-wise and, therefore, the most crowded. July and August are hot (few of the one- and two-star hotels offer air-conditioning; when they do it usually costs extra). Like everything else, hotels are more expensive here than in any other Italian city, with no apparent upgrade in amenities. The least special of those below are clean and functional; at best, they're charming and thoroughly enjoyable, with the serenade of a passing gondolier thrown in for good measure. Some may even provide you with your best stay in all of Europe.

It's highly advisable to reserve in advance, even in the off season. If you haven't booked, come as early as you can on your arrival day, definitely before noon. There is a **travel agency in the train station** that will book rooms for you, but the lines are often long, especially in the morning.

Another alternative to reserve upon your arrival is through the **A.V.A.** (Venetian Hoteliers Association), ✆**041-522-2264,** or online at www.veneziasi.it. Simply state the price range you want to book, and they'll confirm a hotel while you wait. There are offices at the train station, in Piazzale Roma garages, and in the airport.

The rates below were compiled in late 2011. You can expect an annual increase of anywhere from 2% to 10%, depending on the category, but you might be hit with an increase of as much as 20% if the hotel you pick has been redone recently.

Elevators, light, and space are often in short supply in Venice hotels, characteristics that are a little easier to accept when you remember this is a city built on water. Venice hotels often have tiny bathrooms and the rooms themselves are generally dark and smaller than you'd expect to find in a similar hotel in another city. And that's not all . . . canal views aren't half as prevalent as they should be—and when you have them there's a chance you'll open the window onto a view of a nearby building you could almost touch. This doesn't mean that a welcoming family-run hotel in an atmospheric neighborhood can't offer a memorable stay—just don't expect the amenities of the Danieli or Grand Canal vistas.

SEASONAL CONSIDERATIONS Most hotels observe high- and low-season rates and the high-end hotels generally adapt their prices to availability. In the prices listed below, **single figures represent rack rates,** because the price varies too widely depending on availability, and you can usually get a room for much less, even in high season; when a range is listed, they represent low- and high-season rates unless otherwise noted. Of course, you will almost always get a deal when reserving through the hotel website ahead of time. Even where it's not indicated in the listings, be sure to ask when you

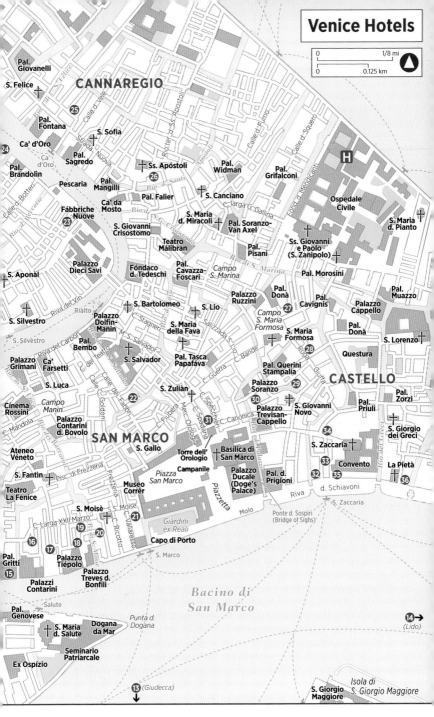

Venice Hotels

CANNAREGIO

Pal. Giovanelli
S. Felice
25
Pal. Fontana
S. Sofia
24
Ca' d'Oro
Pal. Sagredo
Pal. Brandolin
Pescaria
Ss. Apóstoli
26
Pal. Mangilli
Ca' da Mosto
Pal. Falier
S. Canciano
Pal. Widman
Pal. Grifalconi
Ospedale Civile
S. Maria d. Pianto
Fábbriche Nuove
23
S. Giovanni Crisóstomo
S. Maria d. Miracoli
Pal. Soranzo-Van Axel
Ss. Giovanni e Paolo (S. Zanipolo)
S. Aponàl
Palazzo Dieci Savi
Fóndaco d. Tedeschi
Teatro Málibran
Pal. Cavazza-Foscari
Pal. Pisani
Campo S. Marina
Pal. Morosini
S. Silvestro
Riva del Vin
S. Bartolomeo
Rialto
Palazzo Dolfin-Manin
S. Lio
Palazzo Ruzzini
Pal. Donà
27
Pal. Cavignis
Pal. Muazzo
Palazzo Cappello
S. Silvèstro
Riva del Carbon
Pal. Bembo
Ca' Farsetti
S. Salvador
S. Maria della Fava
Campo S. Maria Formosa
S. Maria Formosa
Pal. Donà
S. Lorenzo
Palazzo Grimani
S. Luca
Pal. Tasca Papafáva
28
Questura
Cinema Rossini
Campo Manin
22
S. Zuliàn
Pal. Querini Stampalia
29
Palazzo Soranzo
CASTELLO
Pal. Zorzi
Palazzo Contarini d. Bovolo
SAN MARCO
S. Gallo
31
30
Palazzo Trevisan-Cappello
S. Giovanni Novo
Pal. Priuli
Ateneo Véneto
Torre dell' Orologio
34
S. Giorgio dei Greci
S. Fantin
Campanile
Basilica di San Marco
S. Zaccaria
Teatro La Fenice
Museo Corrèr
Piazza San Marco
Palazzo Ducale (Doge's Palace)
Pal. d. Prigioni
33
Convento
35
La Pietà
36
S. Moisè
21
Piazzetta
32
Riva d. Schiavoni
C. Larga XXII Marzo
19
20
Giardini ex Reali
Molo
Ponte d. Sospiri (Bridge of Sighs)
S. Zaccaria
16
18
Capo di Porto
S. Marco
14
(Lido)
Pal. Gritti
17
Palazzo Tiépolo
15
Palazzi Contarini
Palazzo Treves d. Bonfili
Pal. Genovese
Salute
S. Maria d. Salute
Dogana da Mar
Punta d. Dogàna
Bacino di San Marco
Seminario Patriarcale
Ex Ospízio
13
(Giudecca)
S. Giorgio Maggiore
Isola di S. Giorgio Maggiore

0   1/8 mi
0   0.125 km

book or when you arrive at a hotel whether off-season prices are in effect. Check the site for special offers. High season in Venice is about March 15 to November 5, with a lull in July and August (when hotel discounts are often offered). Some small hotels close November or December until Carnevale, opening for about 2 weeks around Christmas and New Year's at high-season rates.

In San Marco

VERY EXPENSIVE

Hotel Bauer/Bauer il Palazzo ★ Don't let the modern lobby throw you. This inn, just a few blocks from Piazza San Marco, is one of the top deluxe hotels in town and the only one not owned by a large chain. That means Francesca Bortolotto Possati, the chairman, chief executive, and sole owner of the Bauer Hotel Group, and her attentive staff are more likely to give you personal attention. The hotel is split into two parts: the rather disappointing (especially at these prices) 1950s Hotel Bauer, with its standardized rooms and terrace on a side canal, and the Bauer il Palazzo. This 19th-century palace on the Grand Canal behind the modern wing enjoys views of Santa Maria della Salute across the way. The higher the price, the classier the accommodations, with patterned chipped-stone floors, elaborate stuccoed walls and ceilings, engraved mirrors, frescoed bedroom ceilings, and marble bathrooms.

San Marco 1459 (Campo San Moisè), 30124 Venezia. www.bauervenezia.com. ✆ **041-520-7022.** Fax 041-520-7557. 191 units (82 in the Palazzo branch). At Hotel Bauer: 750€ superior; 850€ deluxe double; 1,050€ junior suite; 1,200€ suite. At Bauer Il Palazzo: 950€ double; 1,200€ deluxe suite; 1,500€ double with panoramic view; 1,800€ junior suite with panoramic view; 2,300€ executive suite with panoramic view; 2,600€ Grand Canal suite with panoramic view. Rates include buffet breakfast. AE, DC, MC, V. *Vaporetto:* San Marco–Vallaresso (walk straight up Calle di Ca' Vallaresso then left on Salita San Moisè into the *campo;* the hotel's on the left). **Amenities:** 2 Venetian/Mediterranean restaurants; 2 bars; babysitting; concierge; executive-level rooms (the Palazzo suites); fitness center; Jacuzzi; room service; sauna; smoke-free rooms; spa. *In room:* A/C, TV, VCR (on request in Palazzo), fax (in suites), hair dryer, minibar, Wi-Fi.

Hotel Gritti Palace ★★★ Although there are arguably more chichi hotels along the *bacino* off St. Mark's Square, if you're going for luxury status and the classiest hotel on the Grand Canal, the Gritti has been *it* for decades. It was the 16th-century palace of Doge Andrea Gritti, whose portrait graces one of the antiques-filled lounges, and everyone who is anyone has stayed here over the centuries, from international royalty to captains of industry, literary giants, and rock stars. Rooms have inlaid antique furnishings, gilt mirrors, ornate built-in dressers hand-painted in 18th-century Venetian style, tented curtains over the tall windows, and real box-spring beds set into curtained nooks. Many rooms have connecting doors so that families can share. Three of the suites on the *piano nobile* overlook the Grand Canal from small stone balconies; three more suites overlook the *campo.* Three junior suites open onto a side canal, with walk-in closets and one-and-a-half bathrooms.

San Marco 2467 (Campo del Traghetto/Campo Santa Maria del Giglio), 30124 Venezia. www. hotelgrittipalacevenice.com. ✆ **041-794-611.** Fax 041-520-0942. 90 units. 950€ double deluxe; 1,295€ double with Grand Canal view; 2,300€ junior suite; 2,950€ suite with *campo* (square) view; 4,500€ presidential suite with canal view. AE, DC, MC, V. *Vaporetto:* Santa Maria del Giglio (the hotel is right there). **Amenities:** Venetian/Mediterranean/international restaurant; bar;

babysitting; concierge; room service; smoke-free rooms; courtesy water taxi (free hourly boat to the Hotel Excelsior on the Lido in summer); Wi-Fi. *In room:* A/C, TV w/pay movies, VCR (in suites), fax (in suites), hair dryer, minibar.

Westin Europa & Regina, Venice ★ Hidden down a tiny side alley just 2 minutes from Piazza San Marco, this hotel's Tiepolo and Regina wings sport eclectic early-20th-century European furnishings and modern fabrics. The Europa wing is decorated in traditional Venetian style. There's a cozy bar with tables right on the Grand Canal, elegant salons, and professional service. The restaurant, La Cusina, is excellent (see the full review on p. 129). Room rates vary greatly with season and view (Grand Canal rooms are priciest). This is one of three luxury Starwood properties in Venice, the other two being the Gritti Palace and the Danieli, both of which are listed separately.

San Marco 2159 (off Calle Larga XXII Marzo), 30124 Venezia. www.westineuropareginavenice. com. ✆ **041-240-0001.** Fax 041-523-1533. 192 units. 925€ double; 1,230€ double with canal view; 2,158€ suite; 2,250€ suite with partial canal view; 2,775€ suite with canal view or panorama. AE, DC, MC, V. *Vaporetto:* San Marco (head west out of the southwest corner of Piazza San Marco down Salizada San Moisè; cross the bridge to continue straight on Calle Larga XXII Marzo; you'll see hotel signs directing you down the alleyways to the left). **Amenities:** La Cusina restaurant (p. 129); terrace bar on the Grand Canal; babysitting; concierge; exercise room; room service; sauna; smoke-free rooms; courtesy water taxi (free hourly boat to Hotel Excelsior on the Lido during summer); tennis court; watersports equipment/rentals. *In room:* A/C, TV w/pay movies, fax (on request), hair dryer, minibar, Wi-Fi.

EXPENSIVE

Hotel Concordia ★ The big selling point here: It's the only hotel in Venice with rooms overlooking St. Mark's (technically, the Piazza San Marco, though what you see are the pinnacles and domes on the side of the cathedral). All rooms are nonsmoking, done in 18th-century Venetian period style with ornate little writing desks, gilt mirrors, and Murano chandeliers. Others are done in a slightly scuffed Empire style, with a daybed in the little sitting area. Bathrooms are red marble and though all rooms are perfectly nice, the Concordia really is all about those precious 20 rooms overlooking the side of the Basilica di San Marco. You have to tackle 27 steps before reaching the reception area and its elevator. If you ask, the hotel will provide you with a coupon for 10% off your bill at a parking garage in Piazzale Roma.

San Marco 367 (Calle Larga San Marco), 30124 Venezia. www.hotelconcordia.it. ✆ **041-520-6866.** Fax 041-520-6775. 53 units. 510€ double; 550€ junior suite; 630€ suite. Rates include buffet breakfast. Extra bed 50€. AE, DC, MC, V. *Vaporetto:* San Marco-Giardinetti (walk to the right getting off the *vaporetto,* and then left into Piazza San Marco; cross in front of the basilica and go straight up the Mercerie 1 brief block to take a right on Calle Larga San Marco). **Amenities:** Italian/regional restaurant; bar; babysitting; concierge; room service. *In room:* A/C, TV, hair dryer, minibar, Wi-Fi.

Luna Hotel Baglioni ★★ Just off Piazza San Marco on the street leading down to Harry's Bar, this luxury hotel may be Venice's oldest inn, converted into a hotel from a convent in the 1200s. "Superior" rooms are situated on dreary air-shafts but are otherwise very nice, midsize, and with more modern styling than the pricier-category rooms. The "deluxe" rooms are richly carpeted, with ornate stucco around the wall fabrics, Murano chandeliers and sconces, watercolors and prints, and double sinks with golden fixtures set in the marble bathrooms.

Many sprout small balconies with a partial view of the little Royal Gardens at the Grand Canal. Junior suites are very large, with half-testers and huge bathrooms, though only no. 505 has the views of the Bacino San Marco (into which the Grand Canal empties). The elegant breakfast room is covered with remarkable 18th-century frescoes and gilt-edged paintings.

San Marco 1243 (Calle di Ca' Vallaresso), 30124 Venezia. www.baglionihotels.com. ✆ **041-528-9840.** Fax 041-528-7160. 115 units. 651€ superior double; 690€ superior double with view; 735€ deluxe double; 870€ junior suite; 1,470€ suite; 1,600€ suite with lagoon view; 1,750€ Gran Lagoon suite; 2,050 Giorgione suite on 2 floors. Buffet breakfast 40€ (sometimes included in room rate). AE, DC, MC, V. *Vaporetto:* San Marco–Vallaresso (it's on the street leading straight up from the *vaporetto* stop). **Amenities:** Italian/international restaurant; piano bar (music 2–3 times a week); babysitting; concierge; room service; smoke-free rooms. *In room:* A/C, TV, fax (in suites), hair dryer, minibar, Wi-Fi.

MODERATE

Antica Locanda al Gambero ★★ Midway along a main strip connecting Piazza San Marco and the Rialto bridge, this was once a budget hotel, but after a full renovation, it now caters to a slightly better-heeled crowd. Surrounded by striped bedspreads and curtains, you can slumber in one of the 14 canal-side rooms (no. 203 also has a small balcony). Rooms on the first two floors have higher ceilings, though upstairs rooms are more newly renovated. The entire hotel is nonsmoking. By Venice standards, Gambero has all the comforts of a midscale hotel at moderate prices. Guests receive a 10% discount in the lively ground-floor Bistrot de Venise (p. 129).

San Marco 4687 (on Calle dei Fabbri), 30124 Venezia. www.locandaalgambero.com. ✆ **041-522-4384** or 041-520-1420. Fax 041-520-0431. 30 units. 250€ double; 275€ triple. Rates include continental breakfast. MC, V. *Vaporetto:* Rialto (turn right along canal, cross small footbridge over Rio San Salvador, and turn left onto Calle Bembo, which becomes Calle dei Fabbri; hotel is about 5 blocks ahead on left). **Amenities:** Restaurant (Le Bistrot de Venise, p. 129); bar (in restaurant); concierge. *In room:* A/C, TV, hair dryer, minibar, Wi-Fi.

Hotel Do Pozzi ★ 🍴 Duck off bustling Calle Larga XXII Marzo just 150m (500 ft.) from St. Mark's Square, and you'll find a hidden little *campiello* whose namesake "two wells" flank the round tables where hotel guests take breakfast in warm weather. The quietest rooms overlook this tiny square from flower-fringed windows. The guest rooms, though a bit worn and in need of a makeover, have embroidered fabrics, a few 18th-century Venetian-style pieces, Murano chandeliers, wood floors, and glass mirrors on the closet doors to make the cozy quarters seem roomier. Room nos. 20 and 40 get slivers of Grand Canal views down a short street; no. 47 opens onto the noisy shopping of Calle Larga XXII Marzo, but it comes with frescoed ceilings and a small sitting room. Guests receive a 10% discount off meals at the hotel restaurant, Da Raffaele.

San Marco 2373 (off Calle Larga XXII Marzo), 30124 Venezia. www.hoteldopozzi.it. ✆ **041-520-7855.** Fax 041-522-9413. 30 units, plus 6 in Dépendance Favaro. 98€–280€ double. Rates include breakfast. Extra bed 40€–55€. AE, DC, MC, V. *Vaporetto:* Santa Maria del Giglio (walk straight up from the *vaporetto* stop and turn right out of the *campo,* cross the bridge, follow the street that goes to the left and then the right before opening onto the broad Calle Larga XXII Marzo; take the 1st right down a narrow alley to the hotel). **Amenities:** Venetian/Italian restaurant; babysitting; concierge; room service; smoke-free rooms. *In room:* A/C, TV, hair dryer, minibar, Wi-Fi is said to be coming.

Hotel Flora ★ The name of this small, charming hotel refers to its greatest attribute: a jewel-like patio garden immediately beyond the welcoming lobby. A delightful place to have breakfast, afternoon tea, or an aperitif, the garden is enclosed by climbing vines and ivy-covered walls, with an antique well, potted flowers, and blooming plants that create a cool green enclave. Seamlessly run by two generations of the highly professional Romanelli family and their friendly staff, the Flora is ideally located on a tony shopping street close to Piazza San Marco. Despite rooms that can vary greatly (in size and furnishings) and small bathrooms, it is forever full of loyal devotees and romance-seekers. On the top floor, room no. 47 looks onto what is allegedly the *palazzo* of Desdemona (of Shakespeare's tragedy *Othello*), with the dome of La Salute church beyond.

San Marco 2283a (off Calle Larga XXII Marzo, near Campo San Moisè), 30124 Venezia. www. hotelflora.it. ☏ **041-520-5844.** Fax 041-522-8217. 43 units. 275€ double; 330€ superior double. Rates include buffet breakfast. AE, DC, MC, V. *Vaporetto:* San Marco–Vallaresso (walk down Calle Vallaresso and turn left onto Calle Larga XXII Marzo; after crossing the San Moisè Bridge, you'll see a sign on the left side of street for the hotel, which is located down a narrow passageway). **Amenities:** Bar; babysitting; concierge; small health club; room service. *In room:* A/C, TV, hair dryer, Wi-Fi.

Hotel Violino d'Oro ★★ ✦ This small boutique hotel at a tiny *campiello* with a marble fountainhead on the main shopping drag from San Marco to the Accademia may be relatively new, but the style is ever-popular 18th-century Venetian. The rooms, bathed in rich colors, are compact but graced with nice touches such as gold finishings on the marble-top desks, modest stuccoes and Murano chandeliers on the ceilings, and very firm beds. Six doubles even overlook Rio San Moisè canal, but you'll pay extra for the privilege. The low-season rates are incredible, and even high-season rates are (for Venice) not too bad for this location, level of comfort and style. The entire hotel is nonsmoking.

San Marco 2091 (Calle Larga XXII Marzo), 30124 Venezia. www.violinodoro.com. ☏ **041-277-0841.** Fax 041-277-1001. 26 units. 300€ double; 325€ deluxe double; 410€ deluxe double with view. Ask about bargain rates during low season. Rates include buffet breakfast. AE, DC, MC, V. *Vaporetto:* San Marco–Vallaresso (walk straight up Calle di Ca' Vallaresso, left on Salizada San Moisè; cross the wide footbridge; the hotel is just across the little *campiello* on the left). **Amenities:** Bar; concierge; room service. *In room:* A/C, TV, hair dryer, minibar, Wi-Fi.

INEXPENSIVE

Hotel ai do Mori ★ ☺ ✦ Sure, nobody is going to confuse this with luxury accommodations, but you'll struggle to get this quality at this price just steps from San Marco. The more accessible lower-floor rooms (there's no elevator, and the hotel begins on the second floor) are slightly larger and offer rooftop views, but the top-floor rooms boast views of San Marco's cupolas and the Torre dell'Orologio, whose two bronze Moors (in Venetian dialect, the hotel's name means "at the two moors") ring the bells every hour (the large double-paned windows help to ensure quiet). Every room but two has a private bathroom, and all have wood beams on the ceilings. Room nos. 4 (a small double) and 5 (a triple) share a bathroom and a small hallway and can be turned into a family suite. If noise bothers you, be sure to ask for a courtyard room.

San Marco 658 (on Calle Larga San Marco), 30124 Venezia. www.hotelaidomori.com. ☏ **041-520-4817** or 041-528-9293. Fax 041-520-5328. 11 units. 40€–150€ double; 180€–245€ family suite (up to 5 people). Rates include breakfast. MC, V. *Vaporetto:* San Marco (exit Piazza San

Marco beneath Torre dell'Orologio; make the first right and hotel is on left after about 75m/250 ft.). **Amenities:** Bar; concierge; smoke-free rooms. *In room:* A/C, TV, hair dryer, Wi-Fi (though spotty coverage).

Hotel Locanda Fiorita ★★ 🍴 This pretty little hotel is located in a red *palazzo* that retains the flair of its renovation in 18th-century Venetian style. The wisteria vine partially covering the facade is at its glorious best in May and June, but the Fiorita is appealing year-round, as much for its simply furnished rooms boasting new bathrooms as for its location on a *campiello* off the grand Campo Santo Stefano. Room nos. 1 and 10 have little terraces beneath the wisteria pergola and overlook the *campiello;* they can't be guaranteed on reserving, so ask when you arrive. Each of the two rooms with shared bathrooms has its own private facilities down the hall. Right next door is **Bloom B&B** (✆ **340-149-8872;** fax 041-522-8043; www.bloom-venice.com), the Fiorita's more modern, and more expensive (250€ double) annex.

San Marco 3457a (on Campiello Novo), 30124 Venezia. www.locandafiorita.com. ✆ **041-523-4754.** Fax 041-522-8043. 10 units. 170€ double. Rates include continental breakfast. AE, DC, MC, V. *Vaporetto:* Sant'Angelo (walk to the tall brick building, and turn right around its side; cross a small bridge as you turn left down Calle del Pestrin; a bit farther down on your right is a small square 8 stairs above street level; hotel is in the Campiello). **Amenities:** Babysitting; concierge; room service; smoke-free rooms. *In room:* A/C, TV, hair dryer, Wi-Fi.

In Castello

VERY EXPENSIVE

Hotel Danieli ★★★ Doge Dandolo built his glorious Venetian Gothic palace three doors down from the Palazzo Ducale in the 14th century, and it's been one of the most sumptuous hotels in Venice since 1822. Like the Gritti Palace (both hotels are owned by Starwood, as is the Westin Hotel Europa & Regina), it has been host to innumerable kings, celebrities, and other noted guests as far back as Dickens. The tone of this palatial hotel is set by the astounding four-story lobby of balustraded open balconies and stairwells, Venice's Oriental-tinged Gothic arches, and palm fronds. It's ornate throughout, and the rooms vary in decor, size, and style but are all opulently done. Rooms in the original structure have the most atmosphere but are smaller than the accommodations in the 19th-century wing. Either is far preferable to the 1940s wing next door where the rooms lack that genteel, vintage touch.

Castello 4196 (Riva degli Schiavoni), 30122 Venezia. www.danielihotelvenice.com. ✆ **041-522-6480.** Fax 041-520-0208. 231 units. 300€–870€ double; 505€–1,105€ double with lagoon view; 1,800€–3,090€ suite with lagoon view. Buffet breakfast 52€. AE, DC, MC, V. *Vaporetto:* San Zaccaria (the hotel's right at the *vaporetto* launch). **Amenities:** Roof terrace Italian restaurant; 2 bars (1 w/piano music); babysitting; bikes; children's center; concierge; exercise room; golf course; room service; sauna; smoke-free rooms; tennis court; watersports equipment/rentals. *In room:* A/C, TV w/pay movies, fax (in suite), hair dryer (in most), minibar, Wi-Fi.

EXPENSIVE

Hotel Metropole ★★ Vivaldi lived here from 1704 to 1738, when it was the chapter house of the La Pietà church next door, and he was its violin and concert master. The owner has tried to outfit his hotel as a Victorian-style home, packed with quirky collections of curios (fans, purses, bottle openers, crucifixes, cigarette cases), and its public salons are tucked with cozy bars and sitting niches.

Accommodations vary widely in true Romantic style; you may find such details as Murano glass lamps and chandeliers, inlaid wood furnishings, and Romantic-era watercolors and prints. Rooms overlook the Bacino San Marco, the side canal where water taxis pull up, or the courtyard housing the lovely garden restaurant enlivened by nightly keyboard music. You get free car parking if you let them know you need it before 8pm the day you arrive.

Castello 4149 (Riva degli Schiavoni), 30122 Venezia. www.hotelmetropole.com. ☎ **041-520-5044.** Fax 041-522-3679. 67 units. 225–500€ double; 338–750€ junior suite; 383–1,150€ suite. Buffet breakfast 20€ (sometimes included). AE, DC, MC, V. *Vaporetto:* San Zaccaria (walk right along Riva degli Schiavoni over 2 footbridges; the hotel is next to La Pietà church). **Amenities:** Venetian/Italian restaurant; bar; babysitting; concierge; room service; smoke-free rooms. *In room:* A/C, TV, hair dryer, minibar, Wi-Fi.

Londra Palace ★★ This 19th-century neo-Gothic palace is one of the best values on the prime real estate of the Riva degli Schiavoni. Tchaikovsky wrote his Fourth Symphony in room no. 108. With 100 windows overlooking the San Marco basin, from the "deluxe" rooms you can enjoy people-watching as well as distant vistas of the lagoon. Quieter, cheaper "superior" rooms look out on the inner courtyard. The restaurant, Do Leoni, is one of the best hotel dining rooms in town. The lobby and ground-floor salons were redesigned by the same architect who does Versace boutiques.

Castello 4171 (Riva degli Schiavoni), 30122 Venezia. www.londrapalace.com. ☎ **041-520-0533.** Fax 041-522-5032. 53 units. 230€–450€ standard double; 320€–560€ deluxe double with lagoon view; 410€–670€ junior suite. Rates include buffet breakfast. Extra bed 65€. AE, DC, MC, V. *Vaporetto:* San Zaccaria (on the canal right at the San Zaccaria *vaporetto* stop). **Amenities:** Venetian/international restaurant; bar; babysitting; concierge; golf (on Lido, special rate); room service; tennis (on Lido, special rate). *In room:* A/C, TV, hair dryer, minibar, Wi-Fi.

MODERATE

Hotel Al Piave ★★ ✦ The Puppin family's tasteful hotel is a steal: This level of attention, coupled with the sophisticated *buon gusto* in decor and spirit, is rare in this price category. You'll find orthopedic mattresses under ribbon candy–print or floral spreads, immaculate white-lace curtains, stained-glass windows, new bathrooms, and even (in a few rooms) tiny terraces. The family suites—with two bedrooms, minibars, and shared bathrooms—are particularly good deals, as are the small but stylishly rustic apartments with kitchenettes and washing machines (in the two smaller ones). Reserve far in advance.

Castello 4838-40 (on Ruga Giuffa), 30122 Venezia. www.hotelalpiave.com. ☎ **041-528-5174.** Fax 041-523-8512. 13 units. 125€–180€ double; 145€–235€ superior double; 190€–300€ family suite for 3; 260€–390€ family suite for 4 or 5. Rates include continental breakfast. AE, DC, MC, V. Closed Jan 7 to Carnevale. *Vaporetto:* Rialto (head southeast to the Campo Santa Maria Formosa, which is equidistant from Piazza San Marco and the Rialto Bridge; Ruga Giuffa is the road leaving the southeast corner of the campo). **Amenities:** Babysitting; concierge; smoke-free rooms; Wi-Fi. *In room:* A/C, TV, fridge (family suite), hair dryer, minibar.

Hotel Campiello ★ At this gem on a tiny *campiello*, the atmosphere is airy and bright, and the relaxed hospitality and quality service are provided by the Bianchini sisters, Monica and Nicoletta. Most rooms are done in authentic 18th-century and Art Nouveau antiques with inlaid armoires and bas-reliefs on the headboards. The building's original 15th-century marble-mosaic pavement is still evident, a vestige of the days when the hotel was a convent under the patronage of the nearby San Zaccaria.

Castello 4647 (on Campiello del Vin), 30122 Venezia. www.hcampiello.it. ☎**041-520-5764.** Fax 041-520-5798. 16 units. 100€–250€ double; 120€–270€ triple; 140€–300€ quad; 170€–350€ suite. Ask about discounts in off season. Rates include buffet breakfast. AE, DC, MC, V. *Vaporetto:* San Zaccaria (head down the road that flanks the left side of the Hotel Savoia e Jolanda). **Amenities:** Bar; babysitting; concierge; room service; smoke-free rooms. *In room:* A/C, TV, hair dryer.

Hotel Fontana ★ Three generations of Stainers have been behind the front desk here since 1968 (for the 30 years prior to that, the Fontana was a convent for German nuns), and their warmth seems to pour out of the lobby's leaded-glass windows. The four-story hotel offers a *pensione*-like family atmosphere coupled with a crisp, professional operation. Rooms have lovely antique furnishings but a decided lack of wattage in the overhead lights; the two best on the upper floor have private terraces. The hotel installed an elevator in 2009 that whisks you up to the top for beautiful views of San Zaccaria's 15th-century facade.

Castello 4701 (on Campo San Provolo), 30122 Venezia. www.hotelfontana.it. ☎**041-522-0579.** Fax 041-523-1040. 15 units. 220€ double; 230€ double with balcony; 250€ triple; 300€ quad. Rates discounted as much as 50% in the off season. Rates include buffet breakfast. AE, DC, MC, V. *Vaporetto:* San Zaccaria (head down the road that flanks the left side of Hotel Savoia e Jolanda until you reach Campo San Provolo). **Amenities:** Concierge; room service; smoke-free rooms. *In room:* TV, hair dryer (on request).

Locanda Casa Verardo ★★★ 🏨 In 2000, Daniela and Francesco took over this one-star *pensione* and transformed it into a fine three-star hotel (and more than doubled its size), while still maintaining the feel of a Venetian *palazzo* romantically faded by time. The wood-paneled lobby is anchored by an ancient stone well. The rooms are done in chipped-stone floors, Murano chandeliers, and eclectic furnishings, from imposing armoires and 17th-century reproductions to pseudo Deco and modern functional; three have small terraces. The best accommodations come with stucco wall decorations and scraps of old ceiling frescoes—and tops are the six overlooking a little canal. The airy main hall doubles as a breakfast room.

Castello 4765 (at foot of Ponte Storto), 30122 Venezia. www.casaverardo.it. ☎**041-528-6138** or 041-528-6127. Fax 041-523-2765. 23 units. 90€–250€ double; 125€–340€ deluxe double; 150€–390€ junior suite for 3–4. Rates include buffet breakfast. AE, MC, V. *Vaporetto:* San Zaccaria (walk straight ahead on Calle delle Rasse to Campo SS. Filippo e Giacomo; continue straight through the small *campo* to take Calle Chiesa to cross the 1st small bridge, Ponte Storto, to find the hotel on the left). **Amenities:** Bar; babysitting; concierge; room service; smoke-free rooms. *In room:* A/C, TV, hair dryer (on request), minibar, Wi-Fi.

INEXPENSIVE

Foresteria Valdese (Palazzo Cavagnis) ★★ 🍃 Those lucky enough to get a room at this weathered, though elegant, 16th-century *palazzo* will find simple yet charming accommodations. Affiliated with Italy's Waldesian and Methodist churches, the *palazzo* often fills the large dormitory-style rooms with visiting church groups, though everyone is warmly welcomed, and you'll find an international and inter-religious mix here. Most of the plainly furnished rooms in this once-noble residence open onto a balcony overlooking a quiet canal. The 18th-century frescoes that grace the high ceilings in some doubles (including corner room no. 10) and two of the dorms are by the same artist who worked on the Correr Civic Museum. The reception is open daily from 9am to 1pm and 6 to 8pm. The hotel is nonsmoking. Sheets and towels are provided, but you have to make your own bed. You get the lower end of the price range listed below if you stay more than 1 night.

Castello 5170 (at the end of Calle Lunga Santa Maria Formosa), 30122 Venezia. www. foresteriavenezia.it. © **041-528-6797.** Fax 041-241-6238. 6 units with private bathroom and TV (2–4 beds); 3 dorms (with 8, 11, or 16 beds), all with shared bathroom; 2 mini-apts (sleeping 2) with minikitchen and private bathroom. 95€–115€ double; 120€–140€ double with canal view; 25€–33€ dorm bed. Rates include buffet breakfast. DC, MC, V (but pay 3.5% more to use credit cards). Closed 2 weeks in Nov. *Vaporetto:* Rialto (head southeast to the Campo Santa Maria Formosa, which is equidistant from Piazza San Marco and the Rialto Bridge; look for the Bar all'Orologio where Calle Lunga Santa Maria Formosa begins). *In room:* TV (except in dorms), kitchenette (in apts), no phone.

In Cannaregio

Expect most (but not all) of the least expensive suggestions to be in or near the train-station neighborhood, an area full of trinket shops and budget hotels. It's comparatively charmless (though safe), and in the high season it's wall-to-wall with tourists who window-shop their way to Piazza San Marco, a half-hour to 45-minute stroll away. *Vaporetto* connections from the train station are convenient.

MODERATE

Giardino dei Melograni ★★★ 🎁 In a building once used as a rest home for Venice's elderly Jews, the city's Jewish community offers you simple, spotless accommodations, a welcoming staff, and a perfect setting right on Campo del Ghetto Nuovo. Rooms in this non-smoking, kosher building, where gentiles are just as warmly greeted as Jews, face either the *campo,* where you can watch the kids play in the afternoon, or a pleasant canal. The kosher breakfast is served in a room overlooking the *campo* and there is a private tree-shaded courtyard that invites relaxation; or if you are not the relaxing type and have to catch up on e-mail, the free Wi-Fi reaches out here. **Note:** For religious reasons, payment cannot be made on Saturday, so if that is your checkout day, be sure to settle accounts early.

Cannaregio 4587 (Campo del Ghetto Nuovo), 30131 Venezia. www.pardesrimonim.net. ©/fax **041-822-6131.** 14 units. 120€–140€ standard double; 180€–210€ larger rooms that sleep 4. Rates include kosher breakfast. AE, MC, V. *Vaporetto:* Guglie or San Marcuola (from either of the 2 *vaporetto* stops, or if walking from the train station, locate the Ponte delle Guglie; walking away from the Grand Canal along the Fondamenta di Cannaregio, take the 2nd right at the corner where the Gam Gam restaurant is located; this is the entrance to the Calle del Ghetto Vecchio that leads to the Campo del Ghetto Nuovo). **Amenities:** Wi-Fi. *In room:* A/C, TV, hair dryer (on request), minibar.

Hotel Giorgione ★★ 🎁 Original columns, huge wood beams, and prints of Giorgione's most famous paintings decorate the salons off the reception area of this 16th-century *palazzo,* which is minutes away from the Rialto bridge. The best rooms overlook the private brick courtyard, a shaded breakfast nook with a small, decorative pool, a hushed oasis save for the splashing of the fountain. "Standard" rooms are carpeted, with an early-19th-century style. In "superior" rooms, some beds have a small canopy curtain at the head, others are slightly lofted above the sitting area and flanked by twisting columns; some furnishings are 18th-century Venetian reproductions refreshingly done in brighter modern hues (in fact, each room follows its own, overwhelmingly strict, color scheme). Suites, with midsize sitting rooms and bedrooms, are done in a vaguely romantic style—matching embroidered fabrics, half-testers, and the like. No. 105 has a great private flower-fringed terrace.

Cannaregio 4587 (Campo SS. Apostoli), 30131 Venezia. ☎ **041-522-5810.** Fax 041-523-9092. 76 units. 170€–285€ standard double; 190€–340€ superior double; 245€–370€ junior suite; 250€–390€ suite. Rates include buffet breakfast. AE, DC, MC, V. *Vaporetto:* Ca' d'Oro (walk straight up Calle Ca' d'Oro and turn right onto broad Strada Nuova, which ends in Campo SS Apostoli). **Amenities:** Bar (from 6pm); babysitting; concierge; room service; smoke-free rooms; Wi-Fi. *In room:* A/C, TV, hair dryer, minibar.

INEXPENSIVE

Albergo Santa Lucia Bordered by roses, oleander, and ivy, the flagstone patio/terrace of this contemporary building is a lovely place to enjoy breakfast, with coffee and tea brought to the table in sterling silver pots. The kindly owner, Emilia Gonzato, her son Gianangelo, and his wife, Alessandra, oversee everything with pride, and it shows. The large rooms are simple but bright and clean, with modular furnishings and a print or pastel to brighten things up.

Cannaregio 358 (on Calle della Misericordia), 30121 Venezia. www.hotelslucia.com. ☎ **041-715-180.** Fax 041-710-610. 18 units, 12 with private bathroom. 50€–90€ double with shared bathroom; 70€–115€ double with private bathroom; 90€–145€ triple with private bathroom. Rates include continental breakfast. AE, DC, MC, V. Generally closed Dec 15–Feb 15. *Vaporetto:* Ferrovia (exit the train station, turn left onto Lista di Spagna, and take the 2nd left onto Calle della Misericordia). **Amenities:** Concierge; Internet; room service. *In room:* A/C, TV, hair dryer (on request), Wi-Fi.

Hotel Adua It's not going to be mistaken for luxury accommodations, but it's cheap (for Venice), conveniently located near the station, clean, and very well run. Owned since 1976 by the Adua family, this slightly rundown hotel has largish rooms with contemporary wood furnishings. At an independent *palazzo* across the street and another one next door to the hotel, there are nine refurbished rooms that cost a little less (all have a TV and air-conditioning, but most have to share a bathroom).

Cannaregio 233A (on Lista di Spagna), 30121 Venezia. www.aduahotel.com. ☎ **041-716-184.** Fax 041-244-0162. 22 units, including 9 in 2 annexes. 45€–90€ double with shared bathroom; 70€–140€ double with private bathroom. AE, DC, MC, V. *Vaporetto:* Ferrovia (exit train station and turn left onto Lista di Spagna). **Amenities:** Bar; Wi-Fi. *In room:* A/C, TV, hair dryer.

Hotel Bernardi-Semenzato ★★★ ☺ ✦ Don't be misled by the weather-worn exterior of this *palazzo;* inside, there are exposed hand-hewn ceiling beams, air-conditioned rooms outfitted with antique-style headboard/spread sets, and bright modern bathrooms. The enthusiastic, young English-speaking owners, Maria Teresa and Leonardo Pepoli, offer three-star style at one-star rates. The *dépendance* (annex), 3 blocks away, offers you the chance to feel as if you've rented an aristocratic apartment, with parquet floors and Murano chandeliers—room no. 5 is on a corner with a beam ceiling and fireplace, no. 6 (a family-perfect two-room suite) looks out on the confluence of two canals, and no. 2 overlooks the lovely garden of a *palazzo* next door. The Pepolis also opened yet another annex nearby consisting of just four rooms, all done in Venetian style,

Where to Stay

VENICE

including one large family suite (two guest rooms, one of which can sleep four, with a common bathroom).

Cannaregio 4366 (on Calle de l'Oca), 30121 Venezia. www.hotelbernardi.com. ℭ **041-522-7257.** Fax 041-522-2424. Hotel: 18 units, 11 with private bathroom. Main annex 7 units (www.locandaleo. it). New annex 6 units. *Frommer's* readers take 8% off these official rates: 75€ double with shared bathroom; 110€ double with private bathroom; 95€ triple with shared bathroom; 125€ triple with private bathroom; 110€ quad with shared bathroom; 155€ quad with private bathroom. Rates include breakfast. AE, DC, MC, V. *Vaporetto:* Ca' d'Oro (walk straight ahead to Strada Nova, turn right toward Campo SS. Apostoli; in the *campo,* turn to your left and take the 1st side street on your left, which is Calle de l'Oca). **Amenities:** Babysitting (on request); concierge; room service; Wi-Fi. *In room:* A/C, TV, hair dryer.

Hotel San Geremia ★★ 🏨 If this gem of a two-star hotel had an elevator and was in San Marco, it would cost twice as much and still be worth it. Consider yourself lucky to get one of the tastefully renovated rooms—ideally, one of the seven overlooking the *campo* (better yet, one of three top-floor rooms with small terraces). The rooms have blond-wood paneling with built-in headboards and closets, or whitewashed walls with deep-green or burnished rattan headboards and matching chairs. The small bathrooms offer hair dryers and heated towel racks, and rooms with shared bathrooms have been renovated. Everything is overseen by an English-speaking staff and the owner/manager Claudio, who'll give you helpful tips and free passes to the casino.

Cannaregio 290A (on Campo San Geremia), 30121 Venezia. www.hotelsangeremia.com. ℭ **041-716-245.** Fax 041-524-2342. 20 units, 14 with private bathroom. 60€–75€ double with shared bathroom; 80€–100€ double with private bathroom. Rates do not include breakfast. AE, DC, MC, V. Closed the week of Christmas. *Vaporetto:* Ferrovia (exit the train station, turn left onto Lista di Spagna, and continue for a few minutes to Campo San Geremia). **Amenities:** Babysitting; concierge; room service. *In room:* TV, hair dryer, Wi-Fi.

In San Polo

MODERATE

Ca' Angeli ★★★ ☺ 🏨 Brothers Giorgio and Matteo Wulten, from Dutch stock that came to Venice many generations ago, run this little gem right on the Grand Canal with a care and tenderness that is hard to find in Venice. The doubles are reasonably sized and most allow plenty of light to shine in on the paisley bedspreads and curtains. The bathrooms are modern, but everything else in this non-smoking hotel is antique. Room 5 is the smallest double, but it more than makes up for it with a phenomenal terrace. Room 1, the junior suite, is the only one with a view of the Grand Canal, but everybody else can enjoy the view at breakfast while eating organic products in a wonderfully cheerful room with red carpets, chairs, and curtains that will get your day off in splendid fashion. The apartment sleeps five and is ideal for a family.

San Polo 1434 (on Calle del Traghetto della Madoneta), 30125 Venezia. www.caangeli.it. ℭ **041-523-2480.** Fax 041-241-7077. 7 units. 85€–195€ double; 95€–245€ small double with big terrace; 195–395€ junior suite with Grand Canal view; 215€–395€ apartment for up to 5. Rates include buffet breakfast with certified organic products. MC, V. *Vaporetto:* San Silvestro (leaving the stop at your back go straight ahead to Campo Sant'Aponal; take the middle left, Calle di Mezzo, and follow it for a few minutes to Calle de Forno [if you end up in Campo San Polo you have gone too far], which turns into Calle del Traghetto della Madoneta; the building is at the end on your right). *In room:* A/C, TV, hair dryer, minibar, Wi-Fi.

INEXPENSIVE

Pensione Guerrato ★★★ ☺ 🍴 The Guerrato is as reliable and clean a budget hotel as you're likely to find at these rates. Brothers-in-law Roberto and Piero own this former *pensione* in a 13th-century convent and manage to keep it almost always booked (mostly with Americans). The firm mattresses, good modern bathrooms, and flea-market finds (hand-carved antique or Deco headboards and armoires) show their determination to run a top-notch budget hotel in pricey Venice. The Guerrato is in the Rialto's heart, so think of 7am noise before requesting a room overlooking the marketplace (with a peek down the block to the Grand Canal and Ca' d'Oro). Piero and Roberto have also renovated the building's top floor (great views; no elevator, 70 steps) to create five more rooms—with air-conditioning (for which you will pay 10€).

San Polo 240A (on Calle Drio or Dietro la Scimia, near the Rialto Market), 30125 Venezia. www.pensioneguerrato.it. ✆ **041-522-7131.** Fax 041-528-5927. 20 units, 95€ double with shared bathroom; 140€ double with private bathroom; 120€ triple with shared bathroom; 155€ triple with private bathroom; 185€ quad with private bathroom. Pay in cash, get 10% off. Rates include buffet breakfast. AE, MC, V. Closed Dec 22–26 and Jan 8–early Feb. *Vaporetto:* Rialto (from the north side of the Ponte Rialto, walk straight ahead through the stalls and market vendors until the corner with the UniCredit Banca; go 1 more short block and turn right; the hotel is halfway down the narrow street). **Amenities:** Babysitting; concierge; smoke-free rooms, Wi-Fi. *In room:* A/C (top floor only), hair dryer.

In Santa Croce

EXPENSIVE

Hotel San Cassiano Ca' Favretto ★★ Call this place a moderate splurge choice, which gets two stars for its location and views. About half the rooms look across the Grand Canal to the gorgeous Ca' d'Oro (accounting for the highest rates listed below) and tend to be larger than the others, most of which open onto a side canal. Built into a 16th-century palace, the hotel is steeped in dusty old-world elegance, with Murano chandeliers (but no elevator). The rooms are outfitted in modest, dark-wood 1970s-style faux antiques. The breakfast room is done in 18th-century-style pastels and stuccoes—get to breakfast early to snag one of the two tiny tables on the wide balcony overlooking the Grand Canal. There's also a wood-beam bar and TV lounge with a canal-view window and a few small tables on the private boat launch where you can sip an *aperitivo* in the evening.

Santa Croce 2232 (Calle della Rosa), 30135 Venezia. www.sancassiano.it. ✆ **041-524-1768.** Fax 041-721-033. 35 units. 310€ double; 335€ superior double; 400 double with Grand Canal view. Rates include breakfast. AE, DC, MC, V. *Vaporetto:* San Stae (turn left to cross in front of the church, take the bridge over the side canal and turn right; then turn left, cross another canal, turn right, and then left again; cross yet another canal and turn right, then immediately left and then left again toward the Grand Canal and the hotel). **Amenities:** Bar; babysitting; concierge; room service; smoke-free rooms. *In room:* A/C, TV, hair dryer, minibar, Wi-Fi.

MODERATE

Hotel Ai Due Fanali ★★ 🏨 Ai Due Fanali's 16th-century altar-turned-reception-desk is an immediate clue to this hotel's impeccable taste and pursuit of aesthetic perfection. In a quiet square that's a 10-minute walk from the train station, Signora Marina Stae and her daughter Stefania have turned a part of the 14th-century *scuola* of the San Simeon Profeta church into this lovely hotel.

Guest rooms boast headboards painted by local artisans, high-quality bed linens, chrome and gold bathroom fixtures, and good, fluffy towels. Breakfast is served on a panoramic terrace. Prices drop considerably from November 8 through March 30 with the exception of Christmas week and Carnevale. Ask about the four classy waterfront apartments with views (and kitchenettes), near Vivaldi's Church (La Pietà) east of Piazza San Marco, which sleep four to five people.

Santa Croce 946 (Campo San Simeon Profeta), 30125 Venezia. www.aiduefanali.com. ✆ **041-718-490.** Fax 041-718-344. 20 units. 95€–230€ double; 185€–380€ apt. (minimum 3-day stay). Rates include breakfast, though not at apts. AE, MC, V. Closed most of Jan. *Vaporetto:* Ferrovia (cross the bridge over the Grand Canal; once you are to the other side of the canal, continue straight taking the 2nd left, which will have you cross a bridge before coming to Campo San Simeon Profeta). **Amenities** (at hotel only): Bar; concierge; room service. *In room:* A/C, TV, hair dryer, minibar, Wi-Fi.

INEXPENSIVE

Hotel Falier ★ 🦟 Owned by the same fellow who put the lovely Hotel American Dinesen (see below) on Venice's map of moderately priced lodgings, the Falier is his savvy interpretation of less expensive accommodations, particularly worth booking when half-price low-season rates apply. With standard-size rooms (and modern bathrooms) attractively decorated with white lace curtains and flowered bedspreads, this is a reliable value even towards the upper part of the price range. The old-world lobby has potted ferns, Doric columns, and marble floors. While some may feel the need to be closer to Piazza San Marco, the Falier is much closer to the real Venice. The hotel is in a lively area lined with stores and bars between the large Campo Santa Margherita, one of the city's most character-filled *piazze,* and the much-visited Frari Church.

Santa Croce 130 (Salizada San Pantalon), 30135 Venezia. www.hotelfalier.com. ✆ **041-710-882** or 041-711-005. Fax 041-520-6554. 19 units. 50€–210€ double. Rates include continental breakfast. AE, MC, V. *Vaporetto:* Ferrovia. (If you've packed lightly, the walk from the train station is easy, easier yet from the Piazzale Roma. From the train station, cross the Scalzi Bridge, turn right along the Grand Canal until you get to the first footbridge, then left before crossing the bridge and continue along the little canal until you turn left on Fondamenta Minotti, which becomes Salizada San Pantalon.) **Amenities:** Concierge. *In room:* A/C, TV, hair dryer, Wi-Fi.

In Dorsoduro

MODERATE

Hotel American Dinesen ★★ Despite its decidedly unromantic name (did you travel transatlantic for this?), this hotel has both style and substance. One of the nicest of Venice's moderate hotels, it has the perfect combination of old-fashioned charm and utility. This three-story hotel located near the Peggy Guggenheim Collection offers a dignified lobby and breakfast room dressed with lovely Oriental carpets and marble floors, polished woods, leaded-glass windows and French doors. The best choices are the larger corner rooms and those over-looking a quiet canal; some have small terraces. Every room is outfitted with traditional Venetian-style furnishings that usually include hand-painted furniture and Murano glass chandeliers. If it's late spring, don't miss a drink on the second-floor terrace beneath a wisteria arbor dripping with plump violet blossoms.

San Vio 628 (on Fond. Bragadin), 30123 Venezia. www.hotelamerican.com. ✆ **041-520-4733.** Fax 041-520-4048. 30 units. 80€–310€ double; 100€–370€ double with canal view; 140€–460€

junior suite. Rates include buffet breakfast. AE, MC, V. *Vaporetto:* Accademia (veer left around the Galleria dell'Accademia museum, taking the 1st left turn, and walk straight ahead until you cross the 1st small footbridge; turn right to follow the Fondamenta Bragadin that runs alongside the Rio di San Vio canal; the hotel is on your left). **Amenities:** Bar; babysitting; concierge; room service; smoke-free rooms. *In room:* A/C, TV, hair dryer, minibar, Wi-Fi.

Pensione Accademia ★★ The outdoor landscaping (a flowering patio on the small Rio San Trovaso and a grassy formal rose garden behind) and interior details (original pavement, wood-beam and decoratively painted ceilings) of this *pensione* create the impression that you're a guest in an aristocratic Venetian home from another era. The 17th-century villa is fitted with period antiques in first-floor "superior" rooms, and the atmosphere is decidedly old-fashioned and elegant (Katharine Hepburn's character lived here in the 1955 classic *Summertime*). Formally and appropriately called the Villa Maravege (Villa of Wonders), it was built as a patrician villa in the 1600s and used as the Russian consulate until the 1930s. The best rooms overlook the breakfast garden, which is snuggled into the confluence of two canals. In good weather breakfast is served in the front garden.

Dorsoduro 1058 (Fondamenta Bollani, west of the Accademia Bridge), 30123 Venezia. www.pensioneaccademia.it. © **041-521-0188.** Fax 041-523-9152. 27 units. 135€–260€ double; 170€–320€ superior double; 200€–350€ junior suite. Rates include buffet breakfast. AE, DC, MC, V. *Vaporetto:* Accademia (step off the *vaporetto* and turn right down Calle Gambara, which doglegs 1st left and then right; it becomes Calle Corfu, which ends at a side canal; walk left for a few meters to cross over the bridge, and then head to the right back up toward the Grand Canal and the hotel). **Amenities:** Bar; babysitting; concierge; room service; Wi-Fi. *In room:* A/C, TV, hair dryer, minibar.

Pensione La Calcina ★ British author John Ruskin stayed here in 1877 (you can request his room, no. 2, but good luck getting it), and this hotel on the sunny Zattere in the southern Dorsoduro has remained close to the heart of writers, artists, and assorted bohemians. Half the unfussy but luminous rooms overlook the Giudecca Canal in the direction of Palladio's 16th-century Redentore. Do your best to avoid the side rooms that overlook a very narrow canal and feel a bit claustrophobic. The outdoor floating terrace and the rooftop terrace are glorious places to begin or end the day. There are also three suites and two apartments.

Dorsoduro 780 (on Zattere ai Gesuati), 30123 Venezia. www.lacalcina.com. © **041-520-6466.** Fax 041-522-7045. 29 units. 110€–240€ double without view; 150€–310€ double with Giudecca canal view. Rates include buffet breakfast. AE, DC, MC, V. *Vaporetto:* Zattere (follow le Zattere east; hotel is on water before 1st bridge). **Amenities:** Restaurant; bar; concierge; room service. *In room:* A/C, TV, hair dryer, minibar, Wi-Fi.

INEXPENSIVE

Hotel Galleria ★★ ✦ If you've always dreamed of reconciling your somewhat limited resources with a burning desire to fling open your hotel window and find the Grand Canal in front of you, this 17th-century *palazzo* is for you. But reserve way in advance because this quality-to-price ratio is extremely difficult to find on the canal. Owners Luciano Benedetti and Stefano Franceschini overhauled the hotel in 2004, keeping a sumptuous, 18th-century look in public spaces while giving a cozier feel to the new bedrooms. Six guest rooms overlook the canal; others have views that include the Ponte Accademia over an open-air bar/cafe (which can be annoying to anyone hoping to sleep before the bar closes). Breakfast, with oven-fresh bread, is served in your room.

Dorsoduro 878A (at foot of Accademia Bridge), 30123 Venezia. www.hotelgalleria.it. ☎ **041-523-2489.** Fax 041-520-4172. 9 units, 6 with bathroom. 80€–125€ double with shared bathroom; 90€–155€ double with private bathroom; 150€–235€ triple. Rates include continental breakfast. AE, DC, MC, V. *Vaporetto:* Accademia (with Accademia Bridge behind you, hotel is just to your left, next to Totem II Canale gallery). **Amenities:** Babysitting; concierge; room service. *In room:* Hair dryer.

On Giudecca

You don't stay on Giudecca—the only one of Venice's main islands you must access by boat—for the atmosphere, the sights, or the hotel scene (though it does host the official IYH Hostel, an utterly average hostel that's terribly inconvenient, especially with its curfew). You come for only two reasons: the Cipriani and the new Palladio Hotel and Spa.

VERY EXPENSIVE

Hotel Cipriani ★★★ Long regarded as Venice's top hotel, the elegant Cipriani is set into a string of Renaissance-era buildings on 1.2 hectares (3 acres) at the tip of Giudecca. Although by staying here you give up a central location and easy access to central Venice's sights, shops, and restaurants (it's a 10-min. boat ride to Piazza San Marco), that's the whole point. The hotel was opened in 1959 by Giuseppe Cipriani, who founded Harry's Bar and Torcello's Locanda Cipriani, and was such a good buddy to Ernest Hemingway that he appeared in one of the master's novels *(Across the River and into the Trees)*. Room decor varies greatly, from full-bore 18th-century Venetian to discreetly contemporary, but all are among Venice's most stylish accommodations. The 15th-century Palazzo Vendramin annex, connected via a garden, is for guests who desire more privacy (not unusual, given their celebrity guest list) and a private butler.

Giudecca 10, 30133 Venezia. www.hotelcipriani.com. ☎ **041-520-7744.** Fax 041-520-3930. 95 units. Hotel Cipriani: 930€ double with garden view; 1,100€ double with lagoon view; 1,350€ double with lagoon view and balcony; 2,150€ junior suite with lagoon view and balcony; 2,840€ suite with lagoon view. Rates include American breakfast. AE, DC, MC, V. Closed Nov 2–Apr 11. *Vaporetto:* Zitelle. **Amenities:** 3 restaurants (excellent Italian Cipriani w/lagoon views, bar eatery, poolside lunch); 3 bars; babysitting; courtesy boat (back and forth to Piazza San Marco 24 hr.); concierge; docking facilities; golf course; exercise room; Olympic-size outdoor pool; room service; sauna; spa; indoor tennis courts. *In room:* A/C, TV/VCR (free movies), fax (on request), hair dryer, kitchenette (only in junior suites and suites of the Palazzo Vendramin), minibar, Wi-Fi.

Palladio Hotel & Spa ★★ Francesca Bortolotto Possati, owner of the Hotel Bauer/Bauer il Palazzo (p. 110), opened the Palladio in 2006 in what was a crumbling 16th-century convent designed by Andrea Palladio. There are few other places in Venice—the only one that comes to mind is the Cipriani next door—where you can relax as completely as you can here and yet quickly be in the midst of it all. Venice can seem a long way off, but with a free, solar-powered shuttle boat continually running back and forth between the Hotel Bauer and the Palladio, you are just minutes away from San Marco. All rooms are spacious. Those with the garden views are relaxing, but as long as you are splurging, you may want to opt for a lagoon-view room, where you will be afforded stunning views of the bell tower in Piazza San Marco.

Giudecca 33, 30133 Venezia www.palladiohotelspa.com. ☎ **041-520-7022.** Fax 041-520-7557. 50 units (13 are suites). 775€ double; 950€ double with lagoon view; 1,100€ junior suite; 1,400€ junior suite with lagoon view; 1,300€ suite; 1,650€ suite with lagoon view. Continental breakfast

25€. AE, DC, MC, V. Closed Nov–Apr. *Vaporetto:* Zitelle. **Amenities:** Venetian/Mediterranean restaurant; bar; babysitting; courtesy boat (back and forth to the Hotel Bauer); concierge; Jacuzzi; room service; sauna; smoke-free rooms; spa w/massage and facial. *In room:* A/C, TV, hair dryer, minibar, Wi-Fi.

On the Lido

The Lido offers an entirely different Venice experience. The city is relatively close at hand, but you're really here to stay at an Italian beach resort and day-trip into the city for sightseeing. Although there are a few lower-end, moderately priced hotels here, they are entirely beside the point of the Lido and its jet-set reputation.

If you are looking for a more reasonable option—and one that's open year-round—check out the modern **Hotel Belvedere,** Piazzale Santa Maria Elisabetta 4 (ⓒ **041-526-0115;** fax 041-526-1486; www.belvedere-venezia. com). It's right across from the *vaporetto* stop, has been in the same family for nearly 150 years, and sports a pretty good restaurant and a free beach cabana. It charges 80€ to 319€ for a double.

VERY EXPENSIVE

Hotel Excelsior ★★★ The Excelsior is the first place most celebs phone for film festival or Biennale accommodations. The hotel was the first successful attempt to turn the grassy wilds between the Lido's fishing villages into a bathing resort. Its core was built a century ago in a faux-Moorish style, with horseshoe arches peeking out all over; lots of huge, ornate salons and banquet halls; and a fountain-studded Arabian-style garden. As a purpose-built hotel, the rooms were cut quite large, with nice big bathrooms. Standard rooms keep the Moorish look going, with latticework doors, richly patterned wall fabrics, flamboyant bentwood headboards, and tented ceilings. Even if you don't have a sea view from your balcony, you might overlook the gorgeous garden or the private boat launch. A modern bar spills onto a large terrace overlooking the beach.

Lungarno Marconi 41, 30126 Venezia Lido. www.hotelexcelsiorvenezia.com. ⓒ **041-526-0201.** Fax 041-526-7276. 197 units. 920€ double; 1,020€ double with sea or lagoon view; 2,100€ junior suite; 3,500€ sea-view suite. Rates include buffet breakfast. AE, DC, MC, V. Closed mid-Oct to mid-Mar. *Vaporetto:* Lido, then bus A. **Amenities:** 3 restaurants (Venetian/international terrace restaurant for dinner, lunch restaurants poolside and at beach); 2 bars; babysitting; bikes; courtesy boat (from airport and from central Venice); children's program; concierge; executive-level rooms; exercise room; special rates at nearby golf course; outdoor pool; room service; smoke-free rooms; outdoor lighted tennis courts; watersports equipment/rentals. *In room:* A/C, TV w/ pay movies, hair dryer, minibar, Wi-Fi.

WHERE TO EAT

Eating cheaply in Venice is not easy, though it's by no means impossible. So plan well and don't rely on the serendipity that may serve you in other cities. If you've bought a Rolling Venice card, ask for the guide listing dozens of restaurants offering 10% to 30% discounts for cardholders. Bear in mind that, compared with Rome and other points south, Venice is a city of early meals: You should be seated by 7:30 to 8:30pm. Most kitchens close at 10 or 10:30pm, even though the restaurant may stay open until 11:30pm or midnight.

While most restaurants in Italy include a cover charge (*co-perto*) that usually runs 1.50€ to 3€, in Venice they tend to instead tack on 10% to 12% to the bill for "taxes and service." Some places in Venice will very annoyingly charge you the cover and still add on 12%. A menu should state clearly what extras the restaurant charges (sometimes you'll find it in miniscule print at the bottom) and if it doesn't, take your business elsewhere.

BUDGET DINING Pizza is the fuel of Naples while bruschetta and *crostini* (small, open-face sandwiches) are the rustic soul food of Florence. In Venice it's *tramezzini*—small, triangular white-bread half-sandwiches filled with everything from thinly sliced meats and tuna salad to cheeses and vegetables; and *cicchetti* (tapaslike finger foods, such as calamari rings, speared fried olives, potato croquettes, or grilled polenta squares), traditionally washed down with a small glass of wine, or *ombra*. Venice offers countless neighborhood bars called *bacari* and cafes where you can stand or sit with a *tramezzino*, a selection of *cicchetti*, a *panino*, or a *toast* (grilled ham and cheese sandwich). All of the above will cost approximately 3€ to 6€ if you stand at the bar, as much as double when seated. Bar food is displayed on the countertop or in glass counters and usually sells out by late afternoon, so though it can make a great lunch, don't rely on it for a light dinner. A concentration of popular, well-stocked bars can be found along the Mercerie shopping strip that connects Piazza San Marco with the Rialto Bridge, the always lively Campo San Luca (look for **Bar Torino, Bar Black Jack,** or the character-filled **Leon Bianco** wine bar), and Campo Santa Margherita. Avoid the tired-looking pizza (revitalized only marginally by microwaves) you'll find in most bars; informal sit-down neighborhood pizzerias everywhere offer savory and far fresher renditions for a minimum of 6€, plus your drink and cover charge—the perfect lunch or light dinner.

CULINARY DELIGHTS Venice has a distinguished culinary history, much of it based on its geographical position on the sea and, to a lesser degree, its historical ties with the Far East. You'll see things on Venetian menus you won't see elsewhere, together with local versions of time-tested Italian favorites. For first courses, both pasta and risotto (more liquid in Veneto than usual) are commonly prepared with fish or seafood: Risotto *al nero di seppia* or *alle seppioline* (tinted black by the ink of cuttlefish, also called *risotto nero* or black risotto) or *spaghetti alle vongole* (with clams; clams without their shells are not a good sign) are two commonly found specialties. Both appear with *frutti di mare,* "fruit of the sea," which is mixed shellfish. *Bigoli,* a sort of thick spaghetti that's perfect for catching lots of sauce, is a Venetian staple as is creamy polenta, often served with *gamberetti* (small shrimp) or tiny

Venice Restaurants

0 ——— 1/8 mi
0 ——— 0.125 km

CANNAREGIO

Pal. Giovanelli
S. Felice
Pal. Fontana
Ca' d'Oro
Pal. Sagredo
S. Sofia
Ss. Apóstoli
Pal. Widman
Pal. Grifalconi
H
Ospedale Civile
S. Maria d. Pianto
Pal. Brandolin
Pescaria
Pal. Mangilli
Ca' da Mosto
Pal. Falier
S. Canciano
S. Maria d. Miracoli
Pal. Soranzo-Van Axel
Ss. Giovanni e Paolo (S. Zanipolo)
Fábbriche Nuove
S. Giovanni Crisostomo
Teatro Málibran
Pal. Pisani
Pal. Morosini
S. Aponàl
Palazzo Dieci Savi
Fóndaco d. Tedeschi
Pal. Cavazza-Foscari
Campo S. Marina
Palazzo Ruzzini
Pal. Donà
Pal. Cavignis
Pal. Muazzo
Palazzo Cappello
S. Silvestro
S. Bartolomeo
S. Lio
Campo S. Maria Formosa
Pal. Donà
S. Lorenzo
S. Silvestro
Riva del Vin
Rialto
Palazzo Dolfin-Manin
S. Maria della Fava
S. Maria Formosa
Pal. Bembo
Pal. Tasca Papafáva
Pal. Querini Stampalia
Questura
Palazzo Grimani
Ca' Farsetti
S. Salvador
S. Zulian
Palazzo Soranzo
CASTELLO
S. Luca
Cinema Rossini
Campo Manin
Palazzo Contarini d. Bovolo
SAN MARCO
S. Gallo
Torre dell' Orologio
Basilica di San Marco
S. Giovanni Novo
Pal. Trevisan-Cappello
Pal. Priuli
Pal. Zorzi
Ateneo Véneto
S. Fantin
Museo Corrèr
Campanile
Piazza San Marco
Palazzo Ducale (Doge's Palace)
Pal. d. Prigioni
S. Zaccaria
Convento
S. Giorgio dei Greci
La Pietà
Teatro La Fenice
S. Moisè
Piazzetta
C. Larga XXII Marzo
Giardini ex Reali
Molo
Riva d. Schiavoni
Ponte d. Sospiri (Bridge of Sighs)
S. Zaccaria
Capo di Porto
S. Marco
Palazzo Tiépolo
Palazzo Treves d. Bonfili
Pal. ritti
Palazzi Contarini
Pal. Genovese
Salute
S. Maria d. Salute
Dogana da Mar
Punta d. Dogàna
Bacino di San Marco
Seminario Patriarcale
Ex Ospízio
Isola di S. Giorgio Maggiore
S. Giorgio Maggiore

11
12
13
14
15
16
17
18
19
20
21
22
23
24
25
26
27
28
29

127

Venice's famed Fish Market.

shrimp called *schie,* or as an accompaniment to *fegato alla veneziana* (calf's liver cooked with onions and white wine). Some of the fish and seafood dishes they do particularly well include *branzino* (a kind of sea bass), *rombo* (turbot or brill), *moeche* (small soft-shelled crab) or *granseola* (crab), and *sarde in saor* (sardines in a sauce of onion, vinegar, pine nuts, and raisins).

From a host of good local wines, try the dry white Tocai and pinot from the Friuli region to the northeast of Venice and the light, sparkling prosecco that Venetians consume almost like a soft drink (it is the base of Venice's famous Bellini drink made with white peach purée). Popular local red wines include Bardolino, Valpolicella, and Soave, all of which come from Veneto, the region of which Venice is the capital. International grapes, above all cabernet franc and merlot, are also grown extensively in Veneto and make their way into many local wines. *Grappa,* the local firewater, is an acquired taste and is often offered in many variations. Neighborhood *bacari* wine bars provide the chance to taste the fruits of leading wine producers in the grape-rich regions of Veneto and neighboring Friuli.

In San Marco
VERY EXPENSIVE

Antico Martini ★★ INTERNATIONAL/VENETIAN One of Venice's top restaurants started out in 1720 as a cafe, and the Baldi family, since 1921, has retained its airy, clubby atmosphere, especially at the outdoor tables in summer-time. Venetian specialties such as *risotto di frutti di mare* and *fegato alla Veneziana* are prepared perfectly here, but the food, reputation, and location across from the opera house all come at a stiff price. If you want to dine as if you were at a classic Italian wedding, then try the tasting menu, which comes with both a fish and meat secondo broken up by a lemon sorbet. The price of the tasting menu might not even seem that expensive when you consider you probably won't have to dine for the next 24 hours.

Campo San Fantin (on the square occupied by La Fenice opera house). ⓒ **041-522-4121.** www. anticomartini.com. Reservations required. Primi 19€–32€; secondi 25€–45€; fixed-price tasting menu 115€. AE, DC, MC, V. Daily noon–midnight. *Vaporetto:* Santa Maria del Giglio (walk straight up from the *vaporetto* stop and turn right out of the *campo,* cross the bridge, follow the street that goes to the left and then the right before opening onto the broad Calle Larga XXII Marzo; turn left up Calle delle Veste into Campo San Fantin).

La Cusina ★★ MODERN VENETIAN Excepting the Cipriani, La Cusina is the only hotel restaurant in Venice that deserves singling out on its own. The service is stellar, and the seating is in that most sought-after of spots: a terrace right on the Grand Canal overlooking floodlit Santa Maria della Salute across the water. On the often-changed menu you may find ravioli stuffed with sea bass in a light cream sauce with wild fennel, *maltalgiati* noodles in a duck and truffle ragù, or rabbit saddle with sun-dried tomatoes and grilled leeks.

San Marco 2159 (in the Westin Hotel Europa & Regina off Calle Larga XXII Marzo). ⓒ **041-240-0001.** Reservations highly recommended. Primi 23€–28€; secondi 38€–46€. AE, DC, MC, V. Daily 7–10:30am, 12–2:30pm, and 7:30–10pm. *Vaporetto:* San Marco (head out of the southwest corner of Piazza San Marco down Salizada San Moisè; cross the bridge to continue straight on Calle XXII Marzo; you'll see hotel signs directing you down the alleyways to the left).

Le Bistrot de Venise ★★ FRENCH/VENETIAN At this popular meeting spot for Venetians, you can enjoy a simple and reasonably priced steak and salad, or you can go all out for a five-course dinner that, with a decent wine and the taxes, will cost about 120€ a person. Eel flourish in the rivers that empty into the Venetian lagoon and they are often on the Bistrot's ever-changing menu, including roasted with bay leaves, breadcrumbs, cinnamon, and black pepper. If that is not enough to get your mouth watering (or perhaps slimy fish are not your thing), you can pick one of the other unique dishes made from historic 15th-century Venetian recipes. The faint of heart can always fall back on more typical Venetian favorites.

San Marco 4687 (on Calle dei Fabbri), below the Albergo al Gambero. ⓒ **041-523-6651.** www. bistrotdevenise.com. Reservations not necessary. Primi 19€–26€; secondi 28€–38€; classic Venetian tasting menu 48€; historical 5-course Venetian menu 80€. AE, MC, V. Daily noon–1am. Usually closes Dec. 21–25. *Vaporetto:* Rialto (turn right along canal, cross small footbridge over Rio San Salvador, turn left onto Calle Bembo, which becomes Calle dei Fabbri; Bistrot is about 5 blocks ahead).

Ristorante Quadri ★ VENETIAN Dine by candlelight with a view across St. Mark's Square. That's the selling point of this restaurant, which is almost kitschily romantic—a single red rose, silver dish lids removed with a flourish, threadbare velvet benches, pop ballads by Andrea Bocelli, silk wall coverings, and painted wood ceilings, all in dusty rose shades. The cooking is good, if generally uninspired, and service can be a little sour. But the place has history: In 1725, Giorgio Quadri, from Corfu, and his wife bought this spot and started serving a dark, caffeinated Turkish drink. As Quadri became popular, Austrian officers made it their hangout while Italians preferred the Florian across the way. Definitely call a few days in advance to get one of the few tables next to a window so you can get that view; otherwise, it's really not worth the prices.

Piazza San Marco 120. ⓒ **041-522-2105** or 041-528-9299. www.quadrivenice.com. Reservations highly recommended. Primi 17€–26€; secondi 24€–52€. AE, DC, MC, V. Tues–Sun noon–2:30pm and 7–10:30pm. *Vaporetto:* San Marco (it's on the north side of the square).

Vini da Arturo ★★ 🎁 VENETIAN This narrow dining room has long been one of Venice's hidden gems (and it is, indeed, very hard to find), even if prices have skyrocketed over the past several years. Aside from the friendly service (the owner usually sits and chats with the last few diners at the end of the evening) and first-rate cooking, this place sells itself on being perhaps the only restaurant in Venice with no seafood. Primi are limited and often targeted toward vegetarians—spaghetti with tomatoes and artichokes, or *alla siciliana* with mozzarella, eggplant, and tomatoes—but they are perfectly prepared. Mostly it is known for its meats, such as *straccetti di filetto alla rucola* (beef strips tossed with arugula), *filetto al pepe verde* (steak in a green-peppercorn sauce), and veal scaloppine. It has fewer than 10 tables, so book ahead, and remember to bring lots of cash, as credit cards aren't accepted here.

San Marco 3656A (Calle degli Assassini). ☎ **041-528-6974.** Reservations highly recommended. Primi 13€–20€; secondi 25€–38€. No credit cards. Mon–Sat noon–3pm and 7–10:30pm. Closed for a week in Aug. *Vaporetto:* Sant'Angelo, Rialto (restaurant is btw. Campo Sant'Angelo and Campo Manin).

EXPENSIVE

A Beccafico ★★★ SICILIAN You might wonder why you should have Sicilian food in the heart of Venice . . . until you take your first bite of eggplant-laced *pasta alla norma* at this pleasant restaurant on Campo Santo Stefano. If eggplant is your thing, don't miss the *caponata,* a sort of thick vegetable spread of fried eggplant, pine nuts, and raisins that is served warm and spread over a piece of bread. The portions are not huge, in fact the signature dish, *sarde a beccafico,* comes with just two large, rolled sardines stuffed with breadcrumbs, pine nuts, and currants. But they are superb and, anyway, you'll want room to try a dessert (special mention goes to the tiramisu and the lemon sorbet served in a carved-out half lemon). As an added bonus, the waiters are all smiles, something of a rarity in Venice, and the limoncello is on the house.

San Marco 2801 (in Campo Santo Stefano). ☎ **041-527-4879.** www.abeccafico.com. Reservations recommended. Primi 13€–17€; secondi 20€–22€. AE, MC, V. Daily noon–3:30pm and 7–11pm. *Vaporetto:* Accademia (cross bridge to San Marco side and walk straight ahead to Campo Santo Stefano; the restaurant is on your right and towards the backend of the *campo*).

Trattoria da Fiore ★★ TRATTORIA/VENETIAN Don't confuse this laid-back trattoria with the expensive Osteria da Fiore near the Frari church. Start with the house specialty, the *pennette alla Fiore* for two (with olive oil, garlic, and seven in-season vegetables), and you may be happy to call it a night. Or try the *frittura mista,* over a dozen varieties of fresh fish and seafood. The Bar Fiore next door is a great place to snack or make a light lunch out of *cicchetti* (Wed–Mon 10:30am–10:30pm).

San Marco 3461 (on Calle delle Botteghe, off Campo Santo Stefano). ☎ **041-523-5310.** Reservations recommended. Primi 12€–19€; secondi 14€–25€. AE, MC, V. Wed–Mon noon–3pm and 7–10pm. Closed 2 weeks in Jan and 2 weeks in Aug. *Vaporetto:* Accademia (cross bridge to San Marco side and walk straight ahead to Campo Santo Stefano; as you are about to exit the *campo* at northern end, take a left at Bar/Gelateria Paolin onto Calle delle Botteghe; also close to Sant'Angelo *vaporetto* stop).

MODERATE

Osteria alle Botteghe ITALIAN Casual, easy on the palate, not too hard on the wallet (by Venetian standards), and even easy to find (again, for Venice), this is a decent choice for pizza, a light snack, or an elaborate meal. You can have stand-up *cicchetti* and sandwiches at the bar or window-side counter, while more serious diners head to the tables in back to enjoy the pizzas, pastas, or the glass counter–enclosed buffet of prepared dishes like eggplant *parmigiana,* lasagna, and fresh-cooked vegetables in season, reheated when you order.

San Marco 3454 (on Calle delle Botteghe, off Campo Santo Stefano). ℭ **041-522-8181.** Reservations not necessary. Pizza and primi 7€–12€; secondi 10€–24€; *menù turistico* 17€. DC, MC, V. Mon–Sat 11am–11pm (and Sun in high season). *Vaporetto:* Accademia (cross bridge to San Marco side and walk straight ahead to Campo Santo Stefano; as you are about to exit the *campo* at northern end, take a left at Bar/Gelateria Paolin onto Calle delle Botteghe; also close to Sant'Angelo *vaporetto* stop).

Ristorante Teatro Goldoni FAST FOOD/INTERNATIONAL/ITALIAN Bright and modern (though it has been here for over 50 years), this showcase of Venetian-style fast food tries to be everything: bar, cafe, *rosticceria,* and *tavola calda* (hot foods deli) on the ground floor and a pizzeria upstairs. A variety of sandwiches and pastries beckons from a downstairs display counter, and another offers prepared foods (eggplant *parmigiana,* roast chicken, *pasta e fagioli,* lasagna) that'll be reheated when ordered; there are also a dozen pasta choices. A number of combination salads are a welcome concession to the American set and are freshest and most varied for lunch. This won't be your most memorable meal in Venice, but you won't walk away hungry or broke.

San Marco 4747 (at the corner of Calle dei Fabbri). ℭ **041-522-2446.** Reservations not accepted. Pizza and primi 7.50€–15€; secondi 9€–18€; *menù turistico* with meat 18€, with fish 22€. AE, DC, V. Daily 9am–midnight. *Vaporetto:* Rialto (walk from San Marco side of bridge to Campo San Bartolomeo and exit to your right in direction of Campo San Luca).

Vino Vino ★★★ 🍴 ITALIAN/WINE BAR Vino Vino is an informal wine-bar near the La Fenice opera house serving simple, well-prepared food, but its biggest pull is the impressive selection of local and European wines sold by the bottle or glass. The Venetian specialties are written on a chalkboard but are also usually displayed at the glass counter. After placing your order, settle into one of about a dozen wooden tables squeezed into two storefront-style rooms. Credit the high-quality food to the fact that Vino Vino shares a kitchen (and an owner) with the eminent and expensive Antico Martini restaurant (p. 128) a few doors down. It's also a great spot for a leisurely self-styled wine tasting (around 4€ per glass), with *cicchetti* bar food. At dinner, the food often runs out around 10:30pm, so don't come too late.

San Marco 2007 (at Ponte delle Veste near La Fenice). ℭ **041-241-7688.** Reservations not accepted. Primi 8€–15€; secondi 12€–18€. AE, DC, MC, V. Daily 11:30am–11:30pm. *Vaporetto:* Santa Maria del Giglio (walk straight up from the *vaporetto* stop and turn right out of the *campo,* cross the bridge, follow the street that goes to the left and then the right before opening onto the broad Calle Larga XXII Marzo; turn left up Calle delle Veste to the 1st bridge).

INEXPENSIVE

Rosticceria San Bartolomeo ★ ☺ DELI/ITALIAN With long hours and a central location, this refurbished old-timer is Venice's most popular *rosticceria,* so the continuous turnover guarantees fresh food. With a dozen pasta dishes and as many fish, seafood, and meat entrees, this place can satisfy most any culinary desire. Because the ready-made food is displayed under a glass counter, you (and the kids) will know exactly what you're ordering, and that is sure to help avoid long, little faces. There's no *coperto* (cover charge) if you take your meal standing up or seated at the stools in the aroma-filled ground-floor eating area. If you prefer to linger, head to the dining hall upstairs, though it costs more and, frankly, for the money you can do much better elsewhere than this institutional setting.

San Marco 5424 (on Calle della Bissa). ✆ **041-522-3569.** Pizza and primi 6.50€–10€; secondi 10€–18€; *menù turistico* 10€–24€. Prices are about 20%–30% higher upstairs, and there is a discount if you order to take away. AE, MC, V. Daily 9:30am–10pm (Mon until 3:30pm). *Vaporetto:* Rialto (with bridge at your back on San Marco side of canal, walk straight ahead to Campo San Bartolomeo; take underpass slightly to your left marked SOTTOPORTEGO DELLA BISSA; you'll come across the *rosticceria* at 1st corner on your right; look for GISLON [its old name] above the entrance).

In Castello

VERY EXPENSIVE

Al Covo ★★★ SEAFOOD/VENETIAN For years, this lovely restaurant has been deservedly popular with American food writers, putting it on the short list of every food-loving American tourist. There are nights when you hear nothing but English spoken here. But this slightly unpleasant fact has never compromised the dining at this warm and welcoming spot, where the preparation of super-fresh fish and a wide selection of moderately priced wines is as commendable today—perhaps more so—as it was in its days of pre-trendiness. Much of the tourist-friendly atmosphere can be credited to Diane Rankin, the co-owner and dessert whiz who hails from Texas. She will eagerly talk you through a wondrous fish-studded menu. Her husband, Cesare Benelli, is known for his infallible talent in the kitchen. Together they share an admirable dedication to their charming gem of a restaurant—the quality of an evening here is tough to top in this town.

Castello 3968 (Campiello della Pescheria, east of Chiesa della Pietà in the Arsenale neighborhood). ✆ **041-522-3812.** www.ristorantealcovo.com. Reservations required. Primi 18€–24€; secondi 28€–36€; menu with choice of any combination of 1 primo, 1 secondo, and 1 dessert 54€. MC, V. Fri–Tues 12:45–2pm and 7:30–11pm (closed Mon and Tues at lunch). Closed usually 1 week in Jan. and 1 week in Aug. *Vaporetto:* Arsenale (walk a short way back in the direction of Piazza San Marco, crossing over the 1st bridge and taking the 2nd right onto Calle della Pescheria; otherwise, it is an enjoyable 20-min. stroll along the waterfront Riva degli Schiavoni from Piazza San Marco, past the Chiesa della Pietà; take the 3rd left after the Hotel Metropole).

EXPENSIVE

Osteria alle Testiere ★★ ITALIAN/VENETIAN The limited seating for just 24 savvy (and lucky) patrons at butcher paper–covered tables, the relaxed young staff, and the upbeat tavernlike atmosphere belie the seriousness of this informal *osteria.* This is a guaranteed choice if you are a foodie curious to experience the increasingly interesting Venetian culinary scene without going broke. Start with the carefully chosen wine list; any of the 90 labels can be ordered by the half-bottle. The delicious homemade *gnocchetti ai calamaretti* (with baby squid) makes a frequent appearance, as does the traditional specialty *scampi alla busara,* in a "secret" recipe some of whose identifiable ingredients include tomato, cinnamon, and a dash of hot pepper. Cheese is not a fundamental part of Venetian cuisine, but Alle Testiere has an exceptional cheese platter.

Castello 5801 (on Calle del Mondo Novo off Salizada San Lio). ✆ **041-522-7220.** www.osteri alletestiere.it. Reservations required for each of 2 seatings. Primi 19€; secondi 25€, and many types of fish sold by weight. MC, V. Mon–Sat 2 seatings at 7 and 9:15pm. *Vaporetto:* Equidistant from either the Rialto or San Marco stops. Find the store-lined Salizada San Lio (west of the Campo Santa Maria Formosa), and from there ask for the Calle del Mondo Novo).

Trattoria Corte Sconta ★★ SEAFOOD/VENETIAN The bare, simple decor doesn't hint at the trendiness of this out-of-the-way trattoria, nor at the high quality of its strictly seafood cuisine. The emphasis is on freshness here; they put the shrimp live on the grill. Seafood fans will want to make reservations here on their very first night to hang with the foodies, artists, and writers who patronize this hidden jewel. There's seafood-studded spaghetti, risotti with scampi, and a great *frittura mista all'Adriatico* (mixed Adriatic seafood fry). In nice weather, you can dine under a canopy of grapevines in the courtyard.

Castello 3886 (Calle del Pestrin). ✆ **041-522-7024.** Reservations recommended. Primi 16€– 20€; secondi 22€–28€. MC, V. Tues–Sat 11:30am–3:30pm and 7–11:30pm. Closed Jan 7–Feb 7 and July 15–Aug 15. *Vaporetto:* Arsenale (walk west along Riva degli Schiavoni and over the footbridge; turn right up Calle del Forno, and then as it crosses Calle Crosera, veer right up Calle del Pestrin).

MODERATE

Pizzeria/Trattoria al Vecio Canton ☺ ITALIAN/PIZZA Good pizza can be hard to find in Venice, quite literally. Tucked away in a northeast corner behind Piazza San Marco on a well-trafficked route connecting it with Campo Santa Maria Formosa, the Canton's wood-paneled tavernalike atmosphere and great pizzas are worth the time you'll spend looking for the place. There is a full trattoria menu as well, with a number of pasta and *contorni* (side dishes) of vegetables providing a palatable alternative.

Castello 4738a (at the corner of Ruga Giuffa). ✆ **041-528-5176.** Reservations not accepted. Primi and pizza 6€–11€; secondi 12€–20€. AE, DC, MC. Wed–Mon noon–2:30pm and 7–10:30pm. *Vaporetto:* San Zaccaria (head down the road that flanks the left side of the Hotel Savoia e Jolanda until you reach Campo San Provolo; follow Salizada San Provolo out of the north side of the *campo,* cross the 1st footbridge on your left, and you'll find the pizzeria on the 1st corner on the left).

Trattoria alla Rivetta ★★ SEAFOOD/VENETIAN Lively and frequented by a few gondoliers as well as visitors drawn to its bonhomie and bustling popularity, this is one of the safer bets for genuine Venetian cuisine and company in the touristy San Marco area. All sorts of fish—the specialty—decorate the window of this brightly lit restaurants 10 minutes east of Piazza San Marco. Another good indicator: There's usually a short wait, even in the off season. Beware, the tables are tight and the service can be rushed, so if you want to linger while enjoying a bit of privacy, you best go elsewhere.

Castello 4625 (on Salizada San Provolo). ✆ **041-528-7302.** Reservations recommended. Primi 10€–14€; secondi 12€–18€. AE, MC, V. Tues–Sun noon–2:30pm and 7–10pm. *Vaporetto:* San Zaccaria (with your back to water and facing Hotel Savoia e Jolanda, walk straight ahead to Campo SS. Filippo e Giacomo; trattoria is tucked away next to a bridge off the right side of *campo*).

In Cannaregio
EXPENSIVE
Fiaschetteria Toscana ★★ VENETIAN One hundred years ago, this was a Tuscan wine outlet and community center, so the Busatto family couldn't very

well change the name even if their cuisine is strictly traditional Venetian and fish based. Albino heads up the dining room, wife Mariuccia makes desserts, and son Stefano mans the kitchen. They care about quality here, draping choice San Daniele prosciutto over slices of ripe melon or figs, stuffing ravioli with seafood and coating it with a light parsley sauce, or tossing zucchini flowers with the scampi and homemade *tagliolini*. The *frittura della serenissima* mixes a fry of seafood, sole, zucchini, artichokes, shrimp, baby squid, and octopus.

Cannaregio 5719 (Salizada San Giovanni). ℂ **041-528-5281.** www.fiaschetteriatoscana.it. Reservations recommended. Primi 14€–20€; secondi 14€–35€. AE, DC, MC, V. Closed 1 week in Aug and Dec 8-22. Thurs–Mon 12:30–2:30pm; Wed–Mon 7:30–10:30pm. *Vaporetto:* Rialto (from the *vaporetto* launch, walk left to the bridge, and then right down Salita Pio X to Campo San Bartolomeo; hang a left, past the post office and over a bridge, and the street becomes Salizada San Giovanni).

MODERATE

Osteria L'Orto dei Mori ★★ VENETIAN In this wonderful corner of Venice where the tourists thin out to the point that you can almost forget you are in a sort of Disneyland, you can sample a cuisine that perfectly blends Sicily and Venice while sitting at a table in a splendid, intimate *campo*. The simple, modern decor almost seems a gambit by the two owners, one Venetian and one Sicilian, to get you to concentrate on the food. For those in need of a break from pasta and rice, there are the scrumptious crepe filled with scampi, radicchio and ricotta held together by a thin piece of bacon. The turbot cooked in foil is moist and light, a good thing as you must save space for dessert; the ricotta-and-pear mousse mixed with a hint of red wine will have you calculating if you can manage another meal here before you go back to the mainland.

Cannaregio 3386 (Fondamenta dei Mori at Campo dei Mori). ℂ **041-524-3677.** www.osteria ortodeimori.com. Reservations recommended. Primi 13€–14€; secondi 18€–23€. AE, MC, V. Wed–Mon 12:30–3:30pm and 7–midnight (July–Aug closed for lunch Mon–Fri). *Vaporetto:* Madonna dell'Orto (from the *vaporetto* launch, walk through the campo to the canal and turn right; take the 1st bridge to your left, walk down the street and turn left at the canal onto Fondamenta dei Mori; go straight until you hit Campo dei Mori).

Ostaria da Rioba ★★ VENETIAN Located along a pleasant canal, this place oozes Venice. It offers various local favorites on the menu, such as numerous preparations of cod with polenta and fresh squid ink pasta. Weather permitting, insist on sitting outside, if at all possible, though the simple yet classic decor inside the restaurant will make for a pleasant dining experience as well. If you are outside, beware that about 30m (90 ft.) away there is a bar that often features loud live music.

Cannaregio 2553 (Fondamenta della Misericordia). ℂ **041-524-4379.** Reservations highly recommended. Primi 9€–14€; secondi 19€–25€. MC, V. Tues–Sun 11am–3pm and 6–10pm. *Vaporetto:* San Marcuola (go around the church that's right at the stop, then go straight about 5 blocks until you get to the 1st bridge; cross and turn right on Fondamenta della Misericordia).

INEXPENSIVE

Ai Tre Spiedi ★★ ☺ VENETIAN Once upon a time, Venetians brought their visiting friends here to make a *bella figura* (good impression) without breaking the bank, and then swore them to secrecy. Well, the secret is out, and the prices have surely crept up, roughly coinciding with a change in ownership in 2006. Still, it is a very pleasant setting and the meal is just as appetizing as ever in this small, casually elegant trattoria with great, fresh fish. (When a restaurant is filled exclusively with French tourists, you know the cuisine can't be bad.) Try the traditional *bisato in umido con polenta* (braised eel), or, for a less daring but excellent choice, you can't go wrong with the grilled *orata* (John Dory). This is going to be one of the most reasonable choices for an authentic Venetian dinner of fresh fish; careful ordering needn't mean much of a splurge, either.

Cannaregio 5906 (on Salizada San Cazian). © **041-520-8035.** Reservations not accepted. Primi 7€–10€; secondi 11€–20€; *menù turistico* 13€–17€. AE, MC, V. Tues–Sat noon–3pm and 7–10pm; Sun 7–10pm. Closed July 20–Aug 10. *Vaporetto:* Rialto (on San Marco side of bridge, walk straight ahead to Campo San Bartolomeo and take a left, passing a post office, Coin department store, and the San Crisostomo church; cross 1st bridge after church, turn right at shoe store onto Salizada San Cazian).

In San Polo

MODERATE

Da Sandro ★ ☺ ITALIAN/PIZZERIA Sandro offers dozens of varieties of pizza (his specialty), as well as a full trattoria menu of simple pastas and entrees that will appeal to the kids if they can't stomach another pizza (as unlikely as that is). If you're looking for a 15€ pizza-and-beer meal where you can sit outside, this is a reliably good spot on the main drag linking the Rialto to Campo San Polo. Although Italians consider it sacrilegious, you won't raise any eyebrows if you order a pasta and pizza and pass on the meat or fish: This city has seen it all. There's communal seating at a few wooden picnic tables placed outdoors, with just a handful of small tables stuffed into the two dining rooms—which, unusually, are on opposite sides of the street. You can also get a takeaway pizza and have it in nearby Campo San Polo.

San Polo 1473 (Campiello dei Meloni). © **041-523-4894.** Reservations not necessary. Primi and pizza 8€–10€; secondi 11€–22€. AE, MC, V. Sat–Thurs 11:30am–11:30pm. *Vaporetto:* San Silvestro (with your back to Grand Canal, walk straight to store-lined Ruga Vecchia San Giovanni and take a left; head toward Campo San Polo until you come on Campiello dei Meloni).

Do Spade ★ VENETIAN From 1415 until just a few years ago, workers, fishmongers, and shoppers from the nearby Mercato della Pescheria flocked to this spot, once a colorful wine bar, with bonhomie galore. After a change of ownership in 2007 it became an upscale restaurant, but the rich and elaborate menu was out of place in this spot in Venice, and in 2008 there was another change in management and a return to the place's modest roots, with it being reborn as a friendly place to get exceptional renditions of local favorites at a fair price. The *cicchetti* are tasty and loads can be piled onto a single plate to make a full meal.

San Polo 860 (on Sottoportego do Spade). © **041-521-0574.** Reservations not necessary. Primi 10€–17€; secondi 11€–18€. No credit cards. Daily 10am–3pm and 6–10pm. *Vaporetto:* Rialto or San Silvestro (at San Polo side of Rialto Bridge, walk away from bridge and through open-air market until you come to an intersection with a pharmacy and Cassa di Risparmio di Venezia bank on 2 corners; take a left here and then take 2nd right onto Sottoportego do Spade).

INEXPENSIVE

Cantina do Mori ★★★ ✦ WINE BAR Since 1462, this has been the local watering hole of choice in the market area; legend even pegs Casanova as a habitué. *Tramezzini* (sandwiches; the roast pork with radicchio is incredible) and *cicchetti* (side dishes) take center stage here at what is one of the best of the few remaining old-time *bacari*. For the *ombra*, you've got an embarrassment of choice. Venetians stop in to snack and socialize before and after meals, but if you don't mind standing (there are no tables), this is the perfect choice for a light lunch. Though the *cicchetti* are cheap at about 1.50€ a pop, you are going to need quite a few to fill up, so beware that the cost can add up quickly. The best value are the small, 1€ *tramezzini;* four of these plus two *cicchetti* and a glass of wine will leave you satisfied and only about 12€ will be missing from your wallet as you head out the door.

San Polo 429 (entrances on Calle Galiazza and Calle Do Mori). ℂ **041-522-5401.** *Tramezzini* and *cicchetti* 1€–1.50€ per piece. No credit cards. Mon–Sat 8:30am–8pm (Wed until 2pm; June–Aug closed daily 2–4:30pm). *Vaporetto:* Rialto (cross Rialto Bridge to San Polo side, walk to end of market stalls, turn left on Ruga Vecchia San Giovanni and then immediately right, and look for small wooden cantina sign on right).

In Santa Croce

INEXPENSIVE

Al Bacco Felice ★ ★ 🍴 ITALIAN This is the place in town if you are looking for great Italian standbys like *spaghetti alla carbonara* or *spaghetti all'amatriciana.* While not incredible, the food is very good, and you'll be hard pressed to find a better price-to-quality ratio in town. There is also fresh fish, including a mixed grill; and for those in need of a pizza, you won't be disappointed by the more than 50 choices. While Al Bacco Felice is just steps from the train station and Piazzale Roma, in this wonderfully quiet corner of town you will feel miles from the hustle and bustle.

Santa Croce 197E (on Corte dei Amai). ℂ **041-528-7794.** Primi and pizza 4.70€–15€; secondi 8€–20€. MC, V. Daily noon–3:30pm and 6:15–11pm. *Vaporetto:* Piazzale Roma (you can walk here in 10 min. from the train station; otherwise, from the Piazzale Roma *vaporetto* stop keep the Grand Canal on your left and head towards the train station, passing a park on your right; cross the small canal at the end of the park and immediately turn right onto Fondamenta Tolentini; when you get to Campo Tolentini turn left onto Corte dei Amai).

Pizzeria ae Oche ★ ★ ☺ PIZZERIA This American-style tavern restaurant with wood beams and booths decorated with classic 1950s Coca-Cola signs and the like serves up good pizza at honest prices. You have your pick of two dozen beers to accompany the good-size pizza, and don't sweat the carbs, because the walk to and from this slightly peripherally located hangout (with outside eating during warm weather) will burn a few calories. There are 85 imaginative pizzas on the menu, including ten tomato-sauce-free "white" variety *(pizza bianca).* If you think a pizza is only good if it has tomato sauce, the Bricola with mozzarella, brie, speck, and rucola will set you straight. The clientele is a mixed bag of young and old, students and not, Venetians and visitors. (The price is right, but it is worth noting that a 12% service charge is automatically added to the bill as is a 1.60€ cover charge.)

Santa Croce 1552 (on Calle del Tintor south of Campo San Giacomo dell'Orio). ℂ **041-524-1161.** www.aeoche.com. Reservations recommended Fri–Sat. Primi and pizza 4.70€–9.50€; secondi 9€–17€. MC, V. Tues–Sun noon–midnight (daily in summer). *Vaporetto:* Equidistant from Rio San Biasio and San Stae (you can walk here in 15 min. from the train station; otherwise, find your way to the Campo San Giacomo dell'Orio and exit the *campo* in the southeast corner on to the well-traveled Calle del Tintor.)

In Dorsoduro

EXPENSIVE

Osteria Enoteca Ai Artisti ★★ VENETIAN Adding a touch of Trentino and Naples to traditional Venetian cuisine, Chef Francesca, who shops herself for the raw materials that end up on your plate, turns out memorable dishes that are always fresh and never disappoint. The tagliatelle with zucchini flowers and small prawns reaches near perfection as do most of the fish dishes, including the grilled sea bass and the John Dory with tomatoes and pine nuts. In nice weather ask for a seat outside on the lovely canal that's a five-minute walk from the Accademia bridge.

Dorsoduro 1169A (on Fondamenta della Toletta). ✆ **041-523-8944.** www.enotecaartisti.com. Reservations recommended. Pizza 13€–15€; secondi 19€–22€. AE, DC, MC, V. Mon–Sat noon–4-pm and 7–10pm. *Vaporetto:* Accademia (walk to right around Accademia and take a right onto Calle Gambara; when this street ends at small Rio di San Trovaso, turn left onto Fondamenta Priuli; take the 1st bridge over the canal and onto a road that will quickly lead into Fondamenta della Toletta).

MODERATE

Taverna San Trovaso ★ ☺ VENETIAN Wine bottles line the wood-paneled walls, and low vaulted brick ceilings augment the sense of character in this canal-side tavern, always packed with locals and visitors. The *menù turistico* (a fixed-priced tourist menu that's usually a good deal) includes wine, a *frittura mista* (assortment of fried seafood), and dessert. The gnocchi are homemade; the local specialty of calf's liver and onions is great, and the simply grilled fish is the taverna's claim to fame. There is also a variety of pizzas as well as a few very recognizable Italian dishes, such as lasagne Bolognese, that will appeal to the younger members of your dinner party.

Dorsoduro 1016 (on Fondamenta Priuli). ✆ **041-520-3703.** www.tavernasantrovaso.it. Reservations recommended. Pizza and primi 7€–9€; secondi 9.50€–18€. AE, DC, MC, V. Tues–Sun noon–2:45pm and 7pm–midnight. *Vaporetto:* Accademia (walk to right around Accademia and take a right onto Calle Gambara; when this street ends at small Rio di San Trovaso, turn left onto Fondamenta Priuli).

Trattoria ai Cugnai ★★ 🍴 VENETIAN The unassuming storefront of this longtime favorite does little to announce that herein lies some of the neighborhood's best dining. The owners serve classic *cucina veneziana*, like the reliably good *spaghetti alle vongole veraci* (with clams) or *fegato alla veneziana* (liver). The homemade gnocchi and lasagna would meet most any Italian grandmother's approval (you won't go wrong with any of the menu's *fatta in casa* choices of daily homemade specialties, either). Equidistant from the Accademia and the Guggenheim, Ai Cugnai is the perfect place to recharge after an art overload.

Dorsoduro 857 (on Calle Nuova Sant'Agnese). ✆ **041-528-9238.** Reservations not necessary. Primi 9€–16€; secondi 14€–20€. AE, MC, V. Tues–Sun 12:30–3pm and 7–10:30pm. *Vaporetto:* Accademia (head east of bridge and Accademia in direction of Guggenheim Collection; restaurant will be on your right, off the straight street connecting the 2 museums).

Picnicking

You don't have to eat in a fancy restaurant to enjoy good food in Venice. Prepare a picnic, and while you eat alfresco, you can observe the life in the city's *campi* or the aquatic parade on its main thoroughfare, the Grand Canal. Plus, shopping for your food can be an interesting experience as you will probably have to do it in the small *alimentari* (food shops), as supermarkets are scarce.

MERCATO RIALTO Venice's principal open-air market is a sight to see, even for nonshoppers. It has two parts, beginning with the produce section, whose many stalls, alternating with those of souvenir vendors, unfold north on the San Polo side of the Rialto Bridge (behind these stalls are a few permanent food stores that sell delicious cheese, cold cuts, and bread selections). The vendors are here Monday to Saturday 7am to 1pm, with some staying on in the afternoon.

At the market's farthest point, you'll find the covered **fish market,** with its carnival atmosphere, picturesquely located on the Grand Canal opposite the magnificent Ca' d'Oro and still redolent of the days when it was one of the Mediterranean's great fish bazaars. The area is filled with a number of small *bacari* bars frequented by market vendors and shoppers, where you can join in and ask for your morning's first glass of prosecco with a *cicchetto* pick-me-up. The fish merchants take Monday off and work mornings only.

CAMPO SANTA MARGHERITA On this spacious *campo,* Tuesday through Saturday from 8:30am to 1pm, a number of open-air stalls set up shop, selling fresh fruit and vegetables. This market, coupled with several shops around the *campo,* should ensure you meet all your picnic needs. There's even a conventional supermarket, one of the few in all of Venice, just off the *campo* in the direction of the quasi-adjacent *campo* San Barnaba, at no. 3019. San Barnaba is where you'll find Venice's heavily photographed **floating market** operating from a boat moored just off San Barnaba at the Ponte dei Pugni. This market is open daily from 8am to 1pm and 3:30 to 7:30pm, except Wednesday afternoon and Sunday. If you can't be bothered piecing together the picnic, you can also pick up panini, *tramezzini,* and drinks at any number of nearby bars.

THE BEST PICNIC SPOTS Alas, to picnic in Venice means you won't have much in the way of green space (if you are really desperate for green, you can walk half an hour past San Marco along the water, or take a *vaporetto,* to the Giardini Pubblici, Venice's only green park, but don't expect anything great). A much more enjoyable alternative is to find some of the larger *campi* that have park benches, and in some cases even a tree or two to shade them, such as Campo San Giacomo dell'Orio (in the quiet *sestiere* of Santa Croce). The two most central are **Campo Santa Margherita** (*sestiere* of Dorsoduro) and **Campo San Polo** (*sestiere* of San Polo).

For a picnic with a view, scout out the **Punta della Dogana (Customs House)** near La Salute Church for a prime viewing site at the mouth of the Grand Canal. It's located almost directly across from the Piazza San Marco and the Palazzo Ducale. Pull up on a piece of the embankment here and watch the flutter of water activity against a canvaslike backdrop deserving of the Accademia Museum. In this same area, another superb spot is the small **Campo San Vio** near the Guggenheim, which is directly on the Grand Canal (not many *campi* are) and even boasts two benches as well as the possibility to sit on an untrafficked small bridge. *Note:* It is not by accident that benches in Venice are about as hard to find as that perfect plate of *bigoli*—cafe and bar owners regularly petition the city to limit the number of benches thereby obligating more tourists to stop in for an overpriced cold drink.

In the **patch of sun on the marble steps** leading down to the water of the Grand Canal, at the southern foot of the Rialto Bridge on the San Polo side you won't find a bench, but there is no better ringside seat for viewing the Canalazzo's passing parade. If you don't mind sitting on the ground and the tide is not too high this spot will afford you a memorable picnic.

To go a bit farther afield, you can take the LN *vaporetto* out to Burano and then the T for the 5-minute ride to the near-deserted island of **Torcello.** If you bring a basketful of bread, cheese, and wine you can do your best to reenact the romantic scene between Katharine Hepburn and Rossano Brazzi from the 1955 film *Summertime.*

EXPLORING VENICE

Venice is notorious for changing and extending the opening hours of its museums and, to a lesser degree, its churches. Before you begin your exploration of Venice's sights, ask at the tourist office for the season's list of museum and church hours. During the peak months, you can enjoy extended museum hours—some places stay open until 7 or even 10pm. Unfortunately, these hours are not released until approximately Easter of every year. Even then, little is done to publicize the information, so you'll have to do your own research.

In Piazza San Marco

Basilica di San Marco (St. Mark's Basilica) ★★★ With Venice's wealth growing in the 9th century thanks to its central role in world trade, the city decided that if it wanted to continue its march towards becoming a power to be reckoned with it needed a more important patron saint than the Greek St. Theodore that had been adopted. The city's rise had been rather recent and it had no connection to any of the big saints, so two enterprising Venetian merchants created one. Legend has it that in 828 these two merchants smuggled the remains of St. Mark the Evangelist from Egypt by packing them in pickled pork to bypass the scrutiny of Muslim guards. With the saint's relics in hand, Venice had the link it needed and St. Mark quickly replaced St. Theodore as the city's patron saint. The Venetians built a small chapel to house the relics, one thing led to another, and pretty soon there was the cathedral that you see today.

Venice for centuries was Europe's principal gateway between the East and the West, so not surprisingly the architectural style for the sumptuous Byzantine Basilica di San Marco, replete with five mosquelike bulbed domes, was borrowed from Constantinople. Through the centuries (the original church was consecrated in the 9th c. though much of what you see was constructed in the 11th c.), wealthy Venetian merchants and politicians alike vied with one another in donating gifts to expand and embellish this church, the saint's final resting place and, with the adjacent Palazzo Ducale, a symbol of Venetian wealth and power. Exotic and mysterious, it is unlike any other Roman Catholic church.

And so it is that the Basilica di San Marco earned its name as the Chiesa d'Oro (Golden Church), with a cavernous interior exquisitely gilded with Byzantine mosaics added over some 7 centuries and covering every inch of both ceiling and pavement. For a closer look at many of the most remarkable ceiling

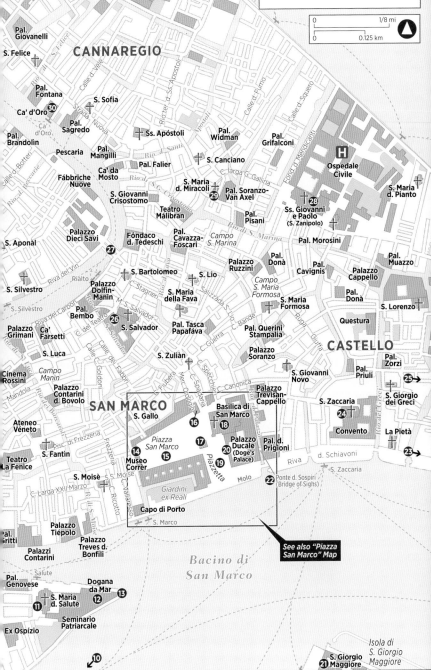

Venice Attractions

0 — 1/8 mi
0 — 0.125 km

CANNAREGIO

Pal. Giovanelli

S. Felice

Pal. Fontana

Ca' d'Oro **30**

Pal. Sagredo

Pal. Brandolin

Pescaria

Pal. Mangilli

Ca' da Mosto

Fábbriche Nuove

S. Sofia

Ss. Apóstoli

Pal. Falier

S. Canciano

Pal. Widman

Pal. Grifalconi

S. Giovanni Crisostomo

S. Maria d. Miracoli **29**

Pal. Soranzo-Van Axel

Teatro Málibran

Pal. Pisani

Ospedale Civile **H**

S. Maria d. Pianto

Ss. Giovanni e Paolo (S. Zanipolo) **28**

S. Aponàl

Fòndaco d. Tedeschi

Palazzo Dieci Savi **27**

Pal. Cavazza-Foscari

Campo S. Marina

Rio di S. Marina

Pal. Donà

Pal. Morosini

Pal. Muazzo

S. Silvestro

S. Bartolomeo

S. Lio

Palazzo Ruzzini

Pal. Cavignis

Palazzo Cappello

Rialto

Palazzo Dolfin-Manin

S. Maria della Fava

Campo S. Maria Formosa

S. Maria Formosa

Pal. Donà

S. Lorenzo

Pal. Bembo **26**

Palazzo Grimani

Ca' Farsetti

S. Salvador

Pal. Tasca Papafáva

Pal. Querini Stampalia

Questura

CASTELLO

S. Luca

S. Zuliàn

Palazzo Soranzo

Pal. Zorzi

Cinema Rossini

Campo Manin

Palazzo Contarini d. Bovolo

S. Giovanni Novo

Pal. Priuli

S. Giorgio dei Greci **25**

Ateneo Véneto

SAN MARCO

S. Gallo

Palazzo Trevisan-Cappello

S. Zaccaria

Convento **24**

La Pietà

Basilica di San Marco **18**

S. Giorgio dei Greci

Teatro La Fenice

S. Fantin

16

Piazza San Marco

17

Palazzo Ducale (Doge's Palace) **20**

Pal. d. Prigioni

S. Moisè

Museo Corrèr **14**

15

19

Piazzetta

23

C-Larga XXII Marzo

Giardini ex Reali

Molo

d. Schiavoni

S. Zaccaria

Ponte d. Sospiri (Bridge of Sighs) **22**

Capo di Porto

S. Marco

Pal. Tiépolo

Palazzi Contarini

Palazzo Treves d. Bonfili

See also "Piazza San Marco" Map

Pal. Gritti

Pal. Genovese

S. Maria d. Salute **11**

Dogana da Mar

12

13

Bacino di San Marco

Seminario Patriarcale

Ex Ospizio

10

S. Giorgio Maggiore **21**

Isola di S. Giorgio Maggiore

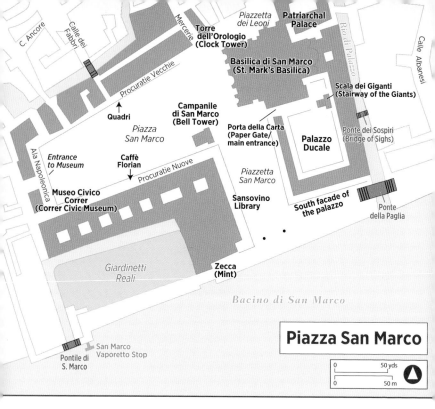

Piazza San Marco

0	50 yds
0	50 m

mosaics and a better view of the Oriental carpet–like patterns of the pavement mosaics, pay the admission to go upstairs to the **Galleria** (the entrance to this and the Museo Marciano is in the atrium at the principal entrance); this was originally the women's gallery, or *matroneum*. It is also the only way to access the outside Loggia dei Cavalli (see below). Here you can mingle with the celebrated *Triumphal Quadriga* of four gilded bronze horses dating from the 2nd or 3rd c. A.D; the restored originals have been moved inside to the small museum. (The term quadriga actually refers to a car or chariot pulled by four horses though in this case there are only the horses.) The horses were brought to Venice from Constantinople in 1204 along with lots of other booty from the Fourth Crusade. For centuries these were symbols of the unrivaled Serene Republic and are the only quadriga to have survived from the classical era. Not to be outdone by loot-ing-prone Venetians, Napoleon carted the horses off to Paris in 1798, though they were returned to Venice in 1815 after the fall of the French Empire.

A visit to the outdoor **Loggia dei Cavalli** is an unexpected high-light, providing a panoramic view of the piazza and what Napoleon

> ### Church Tours
>
> Check with a tourist office for free tours being offered (erratically and usually dur-ing high season) in some of the churches, particularly the Basilica di San Marco and the Frari.

The Triumphal Quadriga, atop the Basilica di San Marco.

called "the most beautiful salon in the world" upon his arrival in Venice in 1797. The 500-year-old **Torre dell'Orologio (Clock Tower)** stands to your right; to your left is the **Campanile (Bell Tower)** and, beyond, the glistening waters of the open lagoon and Palladio's **Chiesa di San Giorgio** on its own island. It is any amateur photographer's dream.

The church's greatest treasure is the magnificent altarpiece known as the **Pala d'Oro (Golden Altarpiece)**, a Gothic masterpiece encrusted with close to 2,000 precious gems and 255 enameled panels. It was created in the 10th century and embellished by master Venetian and Byzantine artisans between the 12th and 14th centuries. It is located behind the main altar, whose green marble canopy on alabaster columns covers the tomb of St. Mark (skeptics contend that his remains burned in a fire in 976 that destroyed the original church). Also worth a visit is the **Tesoro (Treasury),** with a collection of the Crusaders' plunder from Constantinople and other icons and relics amassed by the church over the years. Much of the Venetian booty has been incorporated into the interior and exterior of the basilica in the form of marble, columns, capitals, and statuary. Second to the Pala d'Oro in importance is the 10th-century *Madonna di Nicopeia,* a bejeweled icon taken from Constantinople and exhibited in its own chapel to the left of the main altar.

In July and August (with much less certainty the rest of the year), church-affiliated volunteers give free tours Monday to Saturday, leaving four or five times daily (not all tours are in English), beginning at 10:30am; groups gather in the atrium, where you'll find posters with schedules.

San Marco, Piazza San Marco. $\mathcal{C}$ **041-522-5697.** www.basilicasanmarco.it. Basilica, free admission; Museo Marciano (St. Mark's Museum, also called La Galleria, includes Loggia dei Cavalli) 4€, Pala d'Oro 2€, Tesoro (Treasury) 3€. Basilica, Tesoro, and Pala d'Oro: Summer Mon–Sat 9:45am–5pm, Sun 2–4pm; in winter, closes an hour earlier. Museo Marciano: Summer daily 9:45am–4:45pm. *Vaporetto:* San Marco.

Basilica di San Marco

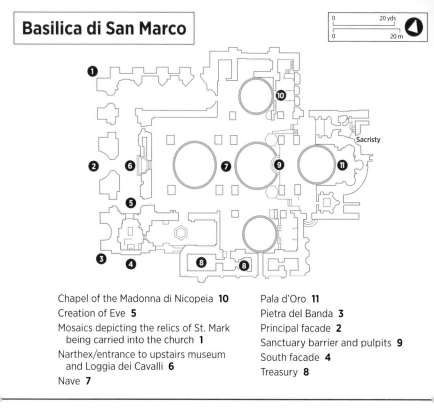

0	20 yds
0	20 m

Chapel of the Madonna di Nicopeia **10**

Creation of Eve **5**

Mosaics depicting the relics of St. Mark being carried into the church **1**

Narthex/entrance to upstairs museum and Loggia dei Cavalli **6**

Nave **7**

Pala d'Oro **11**

Pietra del Banda **3**

Principal facade **2**

Sanctuary barrier and pulpits **9**

South facade **4**

Treasury **8**

Campanile di San Marco (Bell Tower) ★★★ An elevator will whisk you to the top of this 97m (318-ft.) bell tower where you get a breathtaking view of St. Mark's cupolas. It is the highest structure in the city, offering a pigeon's-eye view that includes the lagoon, its neighboring islands, and the red rooftops and church domes and bell towers of Venice—and, oddly, not a single canal. On a clear day, you may even see the outline of the distant snowcapped Dolomite Mountains.

Originally built in the 9th century, the bell tower was then rebuilt in the 12th, 14th, and 16th centuries, when the pretty marble loggia at its base was added by Jacopo Sansovino. It collapsed unexpectedly in 1902, miraculously hurting no one except a cat. It was rebuilt exactly as before, using most of the same materials, even rescuing one of the five historical bells that it still uses today (each bell was rung for a different purpose, such as war, the death of a doge, religious holidays, and so on).

Know Before You Go . . .

The guards at the cathedral's entrance are serious about forbidding entry to anyone in inappropriate attire—shorts, sleeveless shirts (and shirts too short to hide your bellybutton), and skirts above the knee. With masses of people descending on the cathedral every day, your best bet for avoiding the long lines is to come early in the morning. Although the basilica is open Sunday morning for anyone wishing to attend Mass, you cannot enter merely to gawk as a tourist.

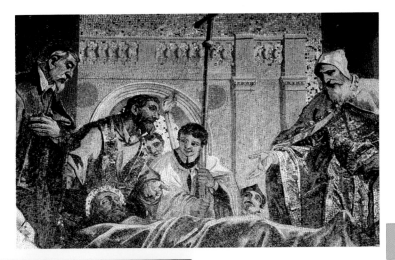

FROM TOP: **San Marco's detailed and extensive mosaics; the Campanile watches over the Piazza San Marco.**

San Marco, Piazza San Marco. ✆ **041-522-4064.** Admission 8€. Easter to June 9am–5pm daily; July–Sept 9am–9pm daily; Oct 9am–7pm daily; Nov–Easter 9:30am–3:45pm daily. *Vaporetto:* San Marco.

Museo Civico Correr (Correr Civic Museum) ★ This museum, which you enter through an arcade at the west end of Piazza San Marco opposite the basilica, is no match for the Accademia but does include some interesting paintings of Venetian life and a fine collection of artifacts—such as coins, costumes, the doges' ceremonial robes and hats, and an incredible pair of 38cm (15-in.) platform shoes—that give an interesting feel for aspects of the day-to-day life in La Serenissima in its heyday. Bequeathed to the city by the aristocratic Correr family in 1830, the museum's biggest draw is its collection of paintings from the 13th to 18th centuries. Vittorio Carpaccio's *Le Cortigiane (The Courtesans),* in room no. 15 on the upper floor, is one of the museum's most famous paintings, as are the star-attraction paintings by the Bellini family, father Jacopo and sons Gentile and Giovanni. There are also some fine pieces from the great Italian neoclassical sculptor Antonio Canova. For a lesson in just how little this city has changed in the last several hundred years, head to room no. 22 and its anonymous 17th-century bird's-eye view of Venice. Most of the rooms have a sign with a few paragraphs in English explaining the significance of the contents.

San Marco, west end of Piazza San Marco. ✆ **041-240-5211.** www.museiciviciveneziani.it. Admission only on San Marco cumulative ticket (see "Venice Discounts," p. 105). Daily 10am–7pm (Nov–Mar until 5pm). *Vaporetto:* San Marco.

Palazzo Ducale and Ponte dei Sospiri (Ducal Palace and Bridge of Sighs) ★★★ The pink- and-white marble Gothic-Renaissance Palazzo Ducale, residence and government center of the doges who ruled Venice for more than 1,000 years, stands between the Basilica di San Marco and St. Mark's Basin. A symbol of prosperity and power, it was destroyed by a succession of fires and was built and rebuilt in 1340 and 1424 in its present form. Forever being expanded, it slowly grew to be one of Italy's greatest civic structures. A 15th-century **Porta della Carta (Paper Gate),** the entrance adjacent to the basilica where the doges' official proclamations and decrees were posted, opens onto a splendid inner courtyard with a double row of Renaissance arches.

Ahead you'll see Jacopo Sansovino's enormous **Scala dei Giganti (Stairway of the Giants),** scene of the doges' lavish inaugurations and never used by mere mortals, which

The eerie Ponte dei Sospiri, or Bridge of Sighs.

leads to the wood-paneled courts and elaborate meeting rooms of the interior. The walls and ceilings of the principal rooms were richly decorated by the Venetian masters, including Veronese, Titian, Carpaccio, and Tintoretto, to illustrate the history of the puissant Venetian Republic while at the same time impressing visiting diplomats and emissaries from the far-flung corners of the maritime republic with the uncontested prosperity and power it had attained.

If you want to understand something of this magnificent palace, the fascinating history of the 1,000-year-old maritime republic, and the intrigue of the government that ruled it, take the **Secret Itineraries tour ★★★** (see "An Insider's Look at the Palazzo Ducale," below). Failing that, at least shell out for the infrared audio-guide tour (at entrance: 6€) to help make sense of it all. Unless you can tag along with an English-speaking tour group, you may otherwise miss out on the importance of much of what you're seeing.

The first room you'll come to is the spacious **Sala delle Quattro Porte (Hall of the Four Doors),** whose ceiling is by Tintoretto. The **Sala del Anticollegio** (adjacent to the College Chamber and with a ceiling by Tintoretto), the next main room, is where foreign ambassadors waited to be received by this committee of 25 members. It is covered in works by Tintoretto, and Veronese's *Rape of Europe,* considered one of the *palazzo's* finest. It steals some of the thunder of Tintoretto's *Three Graces* and *Bacchus and Ariadne*—the latter considered one of his best by some critics. A right turn from this room leads into one of the most impressive of the spectacular interior rooms, the richly adorned **Sala del Senato (Senate Chamber),** with Tintoretto's ceiling painting, *The Triumph* *of Venice.* Here laws were passed by the Senate, a select group of 200 chosen from the Great Council. The latter was originally an elected body, but in the 13th century it became an aristocratic stronghold that could number as many as 1,700. After passing again through the Sala delle Quattro Porte, you'll come to the Veronese-decorated **Stanza del Consiglio dei Dieci (Room of the Council of Ten,** the republic's dreaded security police), of particular historical interest. It was in this room that justice was dispensed and decapitations ordered. Formed in the 14th century to deal with emergency situations, the Ten were considered more powerful than the Senate and feared by all. Just outside the adjacent chamber, in the **Sala della Bussola (The Compass Chamber),** notice the **Bocca dei Leoni ("lion's mouth"),** a slit in the wall into which secret denunciations and accusations of enemies of the state were placed for quick action by the much-feared Council.

The main sight on the next level down—indeed, in the entire palace—is the **Sala del Maggior Consiglio (Great Council Hall).** This enormous space is animated by Tintoretto's huge *Paradiso* at the far end of the hall above the doge's seat (the painter was in his 70s when he undertook the project with the help of his son). Measuring 7×23m (23×75 ft.), it is said to be the world's largest oil painting; together with Veronese's gorgeous *Il Trionfo di Venezia (The Triumph of Venice)* in the oval panel on the ceiling, it affirms the power emanating from the council sessions held here. Tintoretto also did the portraits of the 76 doges encircling the top of this chamber; note that the picture of the Doge Marin Falier, who was convicted of treason and beheaded in 1355, has been blacked out—Venice has never forgiven him. Although elected for life since sometime in the 7th century, over time *il doge* became nothing but a figurehead (they were never allowed to meet with foreign ambassadors alone); the power rested in the Great Council. Exit the Great Council Hall via the tiny doorway on the opposite

AN insider's LOOK AT THE PALAZZO DUCALE

The **Itinerari Segreti (Secret Itineraries)** ★★★ guided tours of the Palazzo Ducale are a must-see for any visit to Venice lasting more than a day. The tours offer an unparalleled look into the world of Venetian politics over the centuries and are the only way to access the otherwise restricted quarters and hidden passageways of this enormous palace, such as the doges' private chambers and the torture chambers where prisoners were interrogated. The story of Giacomo Casanova's imprisonment in, and famous escape from, the palace's prisons is the tour highlight (though a few of the less-inspired guides harp on this aspect a bit too much). It is highly advisable to reserve in advance, by phone (toll free within Italy ℰ **848-082-000,** or from abroad 041-4273-0892) or in person at the ticket desk. Tours often sell out at least a few days ahead, especially from spring through fall. Tours in English are daily at 9:55, 10:45, and 11:35am and cost 18€ for adults, 12€ for children ages 6 to 14 and students ages 15 to 29. There are also tours in Italian at 9:30 and 11:10am and French at 10:20am and noon. The tour lasts about 75 minutes.

side of Tintoretto's *Paradiso* to find the enclosed **Ponte dei Sospiri (Bridge of Sighs)**, which connects the Ducal Palace with the grim **Palazzo delle Prigioni (Prisons).** The bridge took its current name only in the 19th century, when visiting northern European poets romantically envisioned the prisoners' final breath of resignation upon viewing the outside world one last time before being locked in their fetid cells awaiting the quick justice of the Council of Ten. Some attribute the name to Casanova, who, following his arrest in 1755 (he was accused of being a Freemason and spreading antireligious propaganda), crossed this very bridge. One of the rare few to escape, something he achieved 15 months after his imprisonment began, he returned to Venice 20 years later. Some of the stone cells still have the original graffiti of past prisoners, many of them locked up interminably for petty crimes.

San Marco, Piazza San Marco. ℰ **041-271-5911.** Admission only on San Marco cumulative ticket (see "Venice Discounts," p. 105). For Itinerari Segreti guided tour in English, see "An Insider's Look at the Palazzo Ducale" box, below. Daily 8:30am–7pm (Nov–Mar until 5pm). *Vaporetto:* San Marco.

Torre dell'Orologio (Clock Tower) As you enter the magnificent Piazza San Marco, it is one of the first things you see, standing on the north side, next to and towering above the Procuratie Vecchie (the ancient administration buildings for the republic). The Renaissance tower was built in 1496, and the clock mechanism of that same period still keeps perfect time. A lengthy restoration that finished in 2005 has helped keep the rest of the structure in top shape. The two bronze figures, known as "Moors" because of the dark color of the bronze, pivot to strike the hour. The tower is the entryway to the ancient Mercerie (from the word for "merchandise"), the principal souklike retail street of both high-end boutiques and trinket shops that zigzags its way to the Rialto Bridge. Guided tours are required and are included in the price of entrance.

San Marco, Piazza San Marco. Admission 12€, 7€ for children ages 6–14 and students ages 15–29; the ticket also gets you into the Museo Correr, the Museo Archeologico Nazionale, and the Biblioteca Nazionale Marciana (but not Palazzo Ducale, as you get with the San Marco Museum Pass, see "Venice Discounts," p. 105). Daily 10am–3:30pm; tours in English Mon–Wed at 10 and 11am and Thurs–Sun 2 and 3pm. There are also tours in Italian and French. *Vaporetto:* San Marco.

Top Attractions Beyond San Marco

Collezione Peggy Guggenheim (Peggy Guggenheim Collection)★★★
The eccentric and eclectic American expatriate Peggy Guggenheim assembled this compilation of painting and sculpture, considered to be one of the most comprehensive and important collections of modern art in the world. She did an excellent job of it, with particular strengths in cubism, European abstraction, surrealism, and abstract expressionism since about 1910. Max Ernst was one of her early favorites (she even married him), as was Jackson Pollock.

Among the major works here are Magritte's *Empire of Light,* Picasso's *La Baignade,* Kandinsky's *Landscape with Church (with Red Spot),* and Pollock's *Alchemy.* The museum, one of Venice's most-visited attractions, is also home to Ernst's disturbing *The Antipope* and *Attirement of the Bride,* Giacometti's unique figures, Brancusi's fluid sculptures, and numerous works by Braque, Dalí, Léger, Mondrian, Chagall, and Miró.

Directly on the Grand Canal, the elegant 18th-century Palazzo Venier dei Leoni was purchased by Peggy Guggenheim in 1949 and was her home in Venice until her death in 1979. The graves of her canine companions share the lovely interior garden with several prominent works of the Nasher Sculpture Garden, while the canal-side patio watched over by Marino Marini's *Angel of the Citadel* invites you to linger and watch the canal life. An interesting book shop and a cafe/ bistro are located in a separate wing across the inside courtyard where temporary exhibits are often housed.

Don't be shy about speaking English with the young staff working here on internship; most of them are American. Sunday from 3 to 4pm is "Kids Day" with children between 4 and 10 given the chance to take part in a workshop where they create artworks inspired by the museum's collection (make sure your kid doesn't draw inspiration from one of the aforementioned Ernst paintings).

Dorsoduro 701 (on Calle San Cristoforo). ✆ **041-240-5411.** www.guggenheim-venice.it. Admission 12€ adults, 10€ 65 and over and those who present a train ticket to Venice on one of Italy's fast trains (Frecciarossa, Frecciargento, or Frecciabianca) dated no more than 3 days previous, 7€ students 26 and under and children ages 10–18. Wed–Mon 10am–6pm. *Vaporetto:* Accademia (walk around left side of Accademia, take 1st left, and walk straight ahead following signs—you'll cross a canal and then walk alongside another, until turning left to the museum).

Galleria dell'Accademia (Academy Gallery) ★★★ The glory that was Venice lives on in the Accademia, the definitive treasure house of Venetian painting and one of Europe's great museums. Exhibited chronologically from the 13th through the 18th centuries, the collection features no one hallmark masterpiece in this collection; rather, this is an outstanding and comprehensive showcase of works by all the great master painters of Venice, the largest such collection in the world.

It includes Paolo and Lorenzo Veneziano from the 14th century; Gentile and Giovanni Bellini (and Giovanni's brother-in-law Andrea Mantegna from Padua) and Vittore Carpaccio from the 15th century; Giorgione (whose *Tempest* is one

Marino Marini's *The Angel of the City*, at the Peggy Guggenheim Collection.

of the gallery's most famous highlights), Tintoretto, Veronese (see his *Feast in the House of Levi* here), and Titian from the 16th century; and, from the 17th and 18th centuries, Canaletto, Piazzetta, Longhi, and Tiepolo, among others.

Most of all, the works open a window to the Venice of 500 years ago. Indeed, the canvases reveal how little Venice has changed over the centuries. Housed in a deconsecrated church and its adjoining *scuola,* the church's confraternity hall, it is Venice's principal picture gallery, and one of the most important in Italy. Because of fire regulations, admission is limited, and lines can be daunting (check for extended evening hours in peak months), but put up with the wait and don't miss it.

Dorsoduro, at foot of Accademia Bridge. © **041-520-0345.** www.gallerieaccademia.org. Admission 6.50€ adults, 3.25€ EU citizens 19–25 and free for EU citizens 18 and under, free for children 12 and under. Paying 1€ more a ticket, you can reserve tickets by phone or online, thereby saving yourself from potential lines. Daily 8:15am–7:15pm (Mon until 2pm). *Vaporetto:* Accademia.

Grand Canal (Canale Grande) ★★★ A leisurely cruise along the "Canalazzo"

from Piazza San Marco to the Ferrovia (train station), or the reverse, is one of Venice's (and life's) must-do experiences. Hop on the **no. 1** *vaporetto* in the late afternoon (try to get one of the coveted outdoor seats in the prow), when the weather-worn colors of the former homes of Venice's merchant elite are warmed by the soft light and reflected in the canal's rippling waters, and the busy traffic of delivery boats, *vaporetti,* and gondolas that fills the city's main thoroughfare has eased somewhat. The sheer number and opulence of the 200-odd *palazzi,* churches, and imposing republican buildings dating from the 14th to the 18th centuries is enough to make any boat-going visitor's head swim. Many of the largest canal-side buildings are now converted into imposing international banks, government or university buildings, art galleries, and consulates. The *vaporetto*'s Ferrovia (train station) stop is the obvious place to start or conclude a Grand Canal tour (the other being Piazza San Marco) though if you go one stop farther up the canal away from San Marco to Piazzale Roma you get to pass under the Ponte della Costituzione (see "Venice's Newest Bridge," below).

Best stations to start/end a tour of the Grand Canal are Ferrovia (train station) or Piazzale Roma on the northwest side of the canal and Piazza San Marco in the southeast. Tickets 6.50€.

Punta della Dogana ★★★ 📷 The eastern tip *(punta)* of Dorsoduro is cov-

ered by the triangular 15th-century (restructured with a new facade in 1676–82) customs house that once controlled all boats entering the Grand Canal. It's topped by a statue of Fortune holding aloft a golden ball. Now it makes for remarkable, sweeping views across the *bacino* San Marco, from the last leg of the Grand Canal past Piazzetta San Marco and the Ducal Palace, over the nearby isle of San Giorgio Maggiore, La Giudecca, and out into the lagoon itself.

Fondamenta Dogana alla Salute. *Vaporetto:* Salute.

Scuola Grande di San Rocco (Confraternity of St. Roch) ★★★ Jacopo

Robusti (1518–94), called Tintoretto because his father was a dyer (his name being the diminutive of *tintore,* which means dyer), was a devout, unworldly man who traveled only once beyond Venice. His epic canvases are filled with phantasmagoric light and intense, mystical spirituality. This museum is a dazzling monument to his work—it holds the largest collection of his images anywhere. The series of the more than 50 dark and dramatic works took the artist more than 20 years to complete, making this the richest of the many confraternity guilds or *scuole* that once flourished in Venice.

The Galleria dell'Accademia.

A statue of Fortune tops the Punta della Dogana.

Begin upstairs in the Sala dell'Albergo, where the most notable of the enormous, powerful canvases is the moving *La Crocifissione (The Crucifixion)*. In the center of the gilt ceiling of the great hall, also upstairs, is *Il Serpente di Bronzo (The Bronze Snake)*. Among the eight huge, sweeping paintings downstairs—each depicting a scene from the New Testament—*La Strage degli Innocenti (The Slaughter of the Innocents)* is the most noteworthy, so full of dramatic urgency and energy that the figures seem almost to tumble out of the frame. As you enter the room, it's on the opposite wall at the far end of the room.

There's a useful guide to the paintings posted inside on the wall just before the entrance to the museum. There are a few Tiepolos among the paintings, as well as a solitary work by Titian. The works on or near the staircase are not by Tintoretto.

San Polo 3058 (on Campo San Rocco adjacent to Campo dei Frari). ℂ **041-523-4864.** www.scuolagrandesanrocco.it. Admission 8€ adults (price includes audio guide), 6€ ages 18–26, 18 and under free. Daily 9:30am–5:30pm. *Vaporetto:* San Tomà (walk straight ahead on Calle del Traghetto and turn right and immediately left across Campo San Tomà; walk as straight ahead as you can, on Ramo Mandoler, Calle Larga Prima, and Salizada San Rocco, which leads into the *campo* of the same name—look for crimson sign behind Frari Church).

📎 For Church Fans

The **Associazione Chiese di Venezia** (ℂ **041-275-0462;** www.chorusvenezia.org) now curates most of Venice's top churches. A visit to one of the association's churches costs 3€; most are open Monday to Saturday 10am to 5pm and Sunday 1 to 5pm. The churches are closed Sundays in July and August. If you plan to visit more than three churches, buy the 10€ ticket (valid for 1 year), which allows you to visit a host of churches (listed on the website). The association also has audio guides available at some of the churches for 1€.

The ornate facade of the Chiesa di San Salvador.

In San Marco

Chiesa di San Salvador ★ The interior is classic Renaissance, built by Giorgio Spavento, Tullio Lombardo, and Sansovino between 1508 and 1534; the facade is 1663 baroque. It includes a pair of sculptures (*Charity and Hope*) by an elderly Jacopo Sansovino, who may also have designed the third altar, which supports one of the church's treasures, Titian's *Annunciation* (1556). Titian also painted the *Transfiguration* (1560) on the high altar. Ask the sacristan to lower the painting so that you can see the ornate 14th-century silver reredos (ornamental partition) hidden behind. In the right transept rests Bernardino Contino's tomb for Caterina Cornaro (d. 1510), the one-time queen of Cyprus who abdicated her throne to Venice and ended up with Asolo (p. 198) as a consolation prize.

Campo San Salvador (just south from the Rialto Bridge on Via 2 Aprile). ✆ **041-523-6717** or 041-270-2464. Free admission. Daily 9am–noon and 3–6pm. *Vaporetto:* Rialto.

Rialto Bridge ★★ This graceful arch over the Grand Canal is lined with over-priced boutiques and is teeming with tourists and overflow from the daily market along Riga degli Orefici on the San Polo side. Until the 19th century, it was the only bridge across the Grand Canal, originally built as a pontoon bridge at the canal's narrowest point. Wooden versions of the bridge followed; the 1444 one was the first to include shops, interrupted by a drawbridge in the center. In 1592, this graceful stone span was finished to the designs of Antonio da Ponte (whose last name fittingly enough means bridge), who beat out Sansovino, Palladio, and Michelangelo, with his plans that called for a single, vast, 28m-wide (92-ft.) arch in the center to allow trading ships to pass.

Ponte del Rialto.

In Castello

Chiesa di San Zaccaria (Church of St. Zachary) ★ Behind (east of) St. Mark's Basilica is a 9th-century Gothic church with its original 13th-century campanile and a splendid Renaissance facade designed by the Venetian architect Mario Codussi in the late 15th century. Of the interior's many artworks is the important *Madonna Enthroned with Four Saints,* painted by Giovanni Bellini in 1505. Art historians have long held this as one of Bellini's finer Madonnas. Ask the sacristan to see the Sisters' Choir, with works by Tintoretto, Titian, Il Vecchio, Anthony Van Dyck, and Bassano. The paintings aren't labeled, but the sacristan will point out the names of the artists. In the fan vaults of the Chapel of San Tarasio are the faded ceiling frescoes of the Florentine-born artist Andrea del Castagno, who was the first to bring the spirit of the Renaissance to Venice.

Castello, Campo San Zaccaria. ℂ **041-522-1257.** Free admission. Mon–Sat 10am–noon; daily 4–6pm. *Vaporetto:* San Zaccaria.

Museo Storico Navale and Arsenale (Naval History Museum and the Arsenal) ★★ The Naval History Museum's most fascinating exhibit is its collection of model ships. It was once common practice for vessels to be built not from blueprints, but from the precise scale models that you see here. The prize of the collection is a model of the legendary *Bucintoro,* the lavish ceremonial barge of the doges. Another section of the museum contains an array of historic vessels. Walk along the canal as it branches off from the museum to the Ships' Pavilion, where the historic vessels are displayed.

Occupying one-fifth of the city's total acreage, the arsenal was once the very source of the republic's maritime power. It is now used as a military zone and is closed to the curious. The marble-columned Renaissance gate, with the republic's winged lion above, is flanked by four ancient lions, booty brought at various times from Greece and points farther east. It was founded in 1104, and at the height of Venice's power in the 15th century, it employed 16,000 workers who turned out merchant and wartime galley after galley on an early version of massive assembly lines at speeds and in volume unknown until modern times.

The Arsenale is guarded by lions, symbol of Venice.

Castello 2148 (Campo San Biasio). ✆ **041-520-0276.** Admission 3€. Mon–Fri 8:45am–1:30pm; Sat closes at 1pm. *Vaporetto:* Arsenale.

Scuola di San Giorgio degli Schiavoni ★ At the St. Antonin Bridge (Fondamenta dei Furlani) is the second-most-important guild house to visit in Venice. The Schiavoni were an important and wealthy trading colony of Dalmatian merchants who built their own *scuola,* or confraternity (the coast of Dalmatia—the former Yugoslavia—was once ruled by the Greeks, hence the *scuola*'s alternative name of San Giorgio dei Greci).

Between 1502 and 1509, Vittore Carpaccio (himself of Dalmatian descent) painted a pictorial cycle of nine masterpieces illustrating episodes from the lives of St. George (patron saint of the *scuola*) and St. Jerome, the patron saint of Dalmatia. These appealing pictures freeze in time moments in the lives of the saints: St. George charges his ferocious dragon on a field littered with half-eaten bodies and skulls (a horror story with a happy ending); St. Jerome leads his lion into a monastery, frightening the friars; St. Augustine has just taken up his pen to reply to a letter from St. Jerome when he and his little dog are transfixed by a miraculous light and a voice telling them of St. Jerome's death.

Castello 3259, Calle Furlani. ✆ **041-522-8828.** Admission 5€. Tues–Sun 9am–noon; Tues–Sat 3–6pm. *Vaporetto:* San Zaccaria.

SS. Giovanni e Paolo ★ This massive Gothic church was built by the Dominican order from the 13th to the 15th century and, together with the Frari Church in San Polo, is second in size only to the Basilica di San Marco. An unofficial Pantheon where 25 doges are buried (a number of tombs are part of the unfinished facade), the church, commonly known as Zanipolo in Venetian dialect, is also home to a number of artistic treasures.

Visit the **Cappella del Rosario** ★ through a glass door off the left transept to see the three restored ceiling canvases by Paolo Veronese, particularly *The Assumption of the Madonna.* The brilliantly colored *Polyptych of St. Vincent Ferrer* (ca. 1465), attributed to a young Giovanni Bellini, is in the right aisle. You'll also see the foot of St. Catherine of Siena encased in glass.

Anchoring the large and impressive *campo,* a popular crossroads for this area of Castello, is the **statue of Bartolomeo Colleoni** ★★, the Renaissance condottiere who defended Venice's interests at the height of its power and until his death in 1475. The 15th-century work is by the Florentine Andrea Verrocchio; it is considered one of the world's great equestrian monuments and Verrocchio's best.

Castello 6363 (on Campo Santi Giovanni e Paolo). ✆ **041-523-7510** or 041-235-5913. Admission 3€. Mon–Sat 8:30am–12:30pm and 3:30–7pm. *Vaporetto:* Rialto.

In Dorsoduro

The **Accademia,** the **Peggy Guggenheim museums,** and the **Punta della Dogana** are the top sights in this neighborhood and, as such, are both covered under "Top Attractions Beyond San Marco" (p. 148).

Ca' Rezzonico (Museo del Settecento Veneziano; Museum of 18th-Century Venice) ★★ This museum offers an intriguing look into what living in a grand Venetian home was like in the final years of the Venetian Republic.

Begun by Baldassare Longhena, 17th-century architect of La Salute Church, the Rezzonico home is a sumptuous backdrop for this collection of period paintings (most important, works by Venetian artists Tiepolo and Guardi, and a special room dedicated to dozens of works by Longhi), furniture, tapestries, and artifacts. This museum is one of the best windows into the sometimes-frivolous life of Venice of some 200 years ago, as seen through the tastes and fashions of the wealthy Rezzonico family of merchants—the lavishly frescoed ballroom alone will evoke the lifestyle of the idle Venetian rich. The English poet Robert Browning, after the death of his wife, Elizabeth Barrett Browning, made this his last home and died here in 1889.

> ### Back to Scuola
>
> Founded in the Middle Ages, the Venetian *scuole* (schools) were guilds that brought together merchants and craftspeople from certain trades (for example, the dyers of Scuola dei Carmini), as well as those who shared similar religious devotions (Scuola Grande di San Rocco). The guilds were social clubs, credit unions, and sources of spiritual guidance. Many commissioned elaborate headquarters and hired the best artists of the day to decorate them. The *scuole* that remain in Venice today house some of the city's finest art treasures.

Dorsoduro (on the Grand Canal on Fondamenta Rezzonico). ✆ **041-241-0100.** Admission 8€ adults, 5.50€ children 6-14 and students 30 and under, or free with Museum Pass cumulative ticket (see "Venice Discounts," p. 105). Wed-Mon 10am-6pm (Nov-Mar until 5pm). *Vaporetto:* Ca' Rezzonico (walk straight ahead to Campo San Barnaba, turn right at the piazza and go over 1 bridge; then take an immediate right for the museum entrance).

I Gesuati (Santa Maria del Rosario) ★

Built from 1724 to 1736 to mirror the Redentore across the wide Canale della Giudecca, the Jesuits' church counters the Palladian sobriety of the Redentore with rococo flair. The interior is graced by airy 1737–39 ceiling frescoes (some of the first in Venice) by Giambattista Tiepolo. Tiepolo also did the *Virgin in Glory with Saints Rosa, Catherine of Siena,* and *Agnes of Montepulciano* on the first altar on the right. The third altar has a Tintoretto *Crucifixion.*

Fondamenta Zattere ai Gesuati. ✆ **041-275-0462.** www.chorusvenezia.org. Admission 3€ adults, free for children 5 and under, or 9€ on cumulative ticket (see "For Church Fans," above). Mon-Sat 10am-5pm; Sun 1-5pm. *Vaporetto:* Zattere.

San Sebastiano

Way out in the boondocks of Dorsoduro rises a 16th-century church for Paolo Veronese fans. Veronese, who lived nearby, scattered it with paintings from 1555 to 1570 and is buried in the majolica-floored chapel, left of the high altar. The colorful Renaissance master provided the ceiling with paintings on the *Story of Esther,* the choir with a bevy of St. Sebastian–themed works, the organ with painted panels, the sacristy's ceiling with his earliest commissions, the nun's choir with St. Sebastian frescoes, and the third altar on the left with a *Madonna with Saints.* Titian makes a guest appearance with a late *St. Nicholas* (1563) on the first altar on the right.

Fondamenta di San Sebastiano. ✆ **041-275-0462.** 3€ or 9€ on cumulative ticket (see "For Church Fans," above). Mon-Sat 10am-5pm. *Vaporetto:* San Basilio.

Santa Maria della Salute (Church of the Virgin Mary of Good Health) ★

Generally referred to as "La Salute," this crown jewel of 17th-century baroque architecture proudly reigns at a commercially and aesthetically important point, almost directly across from the Piazza San Marco, where the Grand Canal empties into the lagoon.

The first stone was laid in 1631 after the Senate decided to honor the Virgin Mary of Good Health for delivering Venice from a plague. They accepted the revolutionary plans of a young, relatively unknown architect, Baldassare Longhena (who would go on to design, among other projects, the Ca' Rezzonico). He dedicated the next 50 years of his life to overseeing its progress (he would die 1 year after its inauguration but 5 years before its completion).

The octagonal Salute is recognized for its exuberant exterior of volutes, scrolls, and more than 125 statues and its rather sober interior that is livened up in the sacristy where you will find a number of important ceiling paintings and portraits of the Evangelists and church doctors by Titian. On the right wall of the sacristy, which you have to pay to enter, is Tintoretto's *Marriage at Cana*, often considered one of his best paintings.

Dorsoduro (on Campo della Salute). ℰ **041-522-5558.** Free admission to church; sacristy 2.50€. Daily 9am–noon and 3–5:30pm. *Vaporetto:* Salute.

Squero di San Trovaso ★★ 🎁 One of the most interesting (and photographed) sights you'll see in Venice is this small *squero* (boatyard), which first opened in the 17th century. Just north of the Zattere (the wide, sunny walkway that runs alongside the Giudecca Canal in Dorsoduro), the boatyard lies next to the Church of San Trovaso on the narrow Rio San Trovaso (not far from the Accademia Bridge). It is surrounded by Tyrolean-looking wooden structures (a true rarity in this city of stone built on water) that are home to the multigenerational owners and original

FROM TOP: **The dome of La Salute; the workshops on Squero di San Trovaso.**

THE ART OF THE gondola

Putting together one of the sleek black boats is a fascinatingly exact science that is still done in the revered traditional manner at boatyards such as the **Squero di San Trovaso** (see above). The boats have been painted black since a 16th-century sumptuary law—one of many passed by the local legislators as excess and extravagance spiraled out of control. Whether regarding boats or baubles, laws were passed to restrict the gaudy outlandishness that, at the time, was commonly used to "outdo the Joneses."

Propelled by the strength of a single *gondoliere,* these boats, unique to Venice, have no modern equipment. They move with no great speed but with unrivaled grace. The right side of the gondola is lower because the *gondoliere* always stands in the back of the boat on the left. Although the San Trovaso *squero,* or boatyard, is the city's oldest and one of only three remaining (the other two are immeasurably more difficult to find), its predominant focus is on maintenance and repair. They will occasionally build a new gondola (which takes some 40–45 working days), carefully crafting it from the seven types of wood—mahogany, cherry, fir, walnut, oak, elm, and lime—necessary to give the shallow and asymmetrical boat its various characteristics. After all the pieces are put together, the painting, the *ferro* (the iron symbol of the city affixed to the bow), and the wood-carving that secures the oar are commissioned out to various local artisans.

Although some 10,000 of these elegant boats floated on the canals of Venice in the 16th century, today there are only 350. But the job of *gondoliere* remains a coveted profession, passed down from father to son over the centuries.

workshops for traditional Venetian boats (see "The Art of the Gondola," above). Aware that they have become a tourist site themselves, the gondoliers don't mind if you watch them at work from across the narrow Rio di San Trovaso, but don't try to invite yourself in. ***Tip:*** It's the perfect midway photo op after a visit to the Gallerie dell'Accademia and a trip to Gelateria Nico (Zattere 922), whose chocolate *gianduiotto* is every bit as decadent as Venice just before the fall of the republic.

Dorsoduro 1097 (on the Rio San Trovaso, southwest of the Accademia Gallery). No phone. Free admission. *Vaporetto:* Zattere.

In San Polo & Santa Croce

Ca' Pesaro Tired of Venice's one-two punch of baroque and Byzantine? Check out the two museums housed in this late Renaissance *palazzo* on the Grand Canal. The first collection is the **Museo d'Arte Moderna (Museum of Modern Art),** which houses works—most of them bought during Venice's own Biennale over the years—by the likes of Chagall, Kandinsky, Klimt, Miró, Henry Moore, Umberto Boccioni, Morandi, and Filippo De Pisis.

Up on the top level is the **Museo d'Arte Orientale,** a collection of mostly Japanese artifacts, but also Chinese, Javanese, Siamese (Thai), Cambodian, and Indonesian pieces. Rumors that this collection may eventually move, perhaps to the Palazzo Marcello, have persisted for several years, but for the moment nothing has happened.

Santa Croce 2076 (Fondamenta Ca' Pesaro). ℰ **041-721-127.** Admission 8€, 5.50€ for ages 6–14 and students 30 and under. Tues–Sun 10am–6pm (Nov–Mar until 5pm). *Vaporetto:* San Stae.

Santa Maria Gloriosa dei Frari (Church of the Frari) ★★ Known simply as "i Frari," this immense 13th- to 14th-century Gothic church is easily found around the corner from the Scuola Grande di San Rocco—make sure you visit both when you're in this area. Built by the Franciscans (*frari* is a dialectal distortion of *frati,* or "brothers"), it is the largest church in Venice after the Basilica of San Marco. The Frari has long been considered something of a memorial to the ancient glories of Venice. Since St. Francis and the order he founded

A statue above the door of Santa Maria Gloriosa dei Frari.

emphasized prayer and poverty, it is not surprising that the church is austere both inside and out. Yet it houses a number of important works, including two Titian masterpieces. The more striking is his *Assumption of the Virgin* over the main altar, painted when the artist was only in his late 20s. His *Virgin of the Pesaro Family* is in the left nave; for this work commissioned by one of Venice's most powerful families, Titian's wife posed for the figure of Mary (and then died soon afterward in childbirth).

The church's other masterwork is Giovanni Bellini's important triptych on wood, the *Madonna and Child,* displayed in the sacristy; it is one of his finest portraits of the Madonna. There is also an almost primitive-looking woodcarving by Donatello of St. John the Baptist. There is also a grandiose funerary monument to Canova (d. 1822), though the Italian sculptor who led the revival of classicism is buried in his hometown of Possango in Veneto. Canova had designed the monument, which was later realized by his pupils, to be the tomb of Titian, who is also buried in the church though in a more sober setting.

Free tours in English are sometimes offered by church volunteers during the high-season months; check at the church.

San Polo 3072 (on Campo dei Frari). ℰ **041-522-2637.** Admission 3€ or 9€ on cumulative ticket (see "For Church Fans," p. 151). Mon–Sat 9am–6pm; Sun 1–6pm. *Vaporetto:* San Tomà (walk straight ahead on Calle del Traghetto; then turn right and left across Campo San Tomà; walk as straight ahead as you can, on Ramo Mandoler, then Calle Larga Prima, and turn right when you reach beginning of Salizada San Rocco).

In Cannaregio

Ca' d'Oro (Galleria Giorgio Franchetti) ★★ The 15th-century Ca' d'Oro is one of the best preserved and most impressive of the hundreds of *palazzi* lining the Grand Canal. After the Palazzo Ducale, it's the city's finest example of Venetian Gothic architecture. Its name, the Golden Palace, refers to the gilt-covered facade that faded long ago and is now pink and white. Inside, the beam ceilings and ornate trappings provide a backdrop for the collection of former owner Baron Franchetti, who bequeathed his home and artworks to the city during World War I.

The core collection, expanded over the years, now includes sculptures, furniture, 16th-century Flemish tapestries, an impressive collection of bronzes (12th–16th c.), and a gallery whose most important canvases are Andrea Mantegna's *San Sebastiano* and Titian's *Venus at the Mirror,* as well as lesser paintings by Tintoretto, Carpaccio, Van Dyck, Giorgione, and Jan Steen. For a delightful break, step out onto the *palazzo*'s loggia, overlooking the Grand Canal, for a view up and down the waterway and across to the Pescheria, a timeless vignette of an unchanged city. Off the loggia is a small but worthy ceramics collection, open daily 10am to noon.

Cannaregio btw. 3931 and 3932 (on Calle Ca' d'Oro north of Rialto Bridge). ℂ **041-520-0345.** www.cadoro.org. Admission 6.50€, 6€ for ages 6–14 and students 30 and under. Mon 8:15am–2pm; Tues–Sun 8:15am–7:15pm. *Vaporetto:* Ca' d'Oro.

Chiesa Santa Maria dei Miracoli ★ Hidden in a quiet corner of the residential section of Cannaregio northeast of the Rialto Bridge, the small and exceedingly attractive 15th-century Miracoli has one side of its precious polychrome-marbled facade running alongside a canal, creating colorful and shimmering reflections. The architect, Pietro Lombardo, a local artisan whose background in monuments and tombs is obvious, would go on to become one of the founding fathers of the Venetian Renaissance.

The less romantic are inclined to compare it to a large tomb with a dome, but the untold couples who have made this perfectly proportioned jewel-like church their choice for weddings will dispel such insensitivity. The small square in front is the perfect place for gondolas to drop off and pick up the newly betrothed. The inside is intricately decorated with early Renaissance marble reliefs,

The small Campo Santa Maria Nova abutts Santa Maria dei Miracoli.

its pastel palette of pink, gray, and white marble making an elegant venue for all those weddings. In the 1470s, an image of the Virgin Mary was responsible for a series of miracles (including bringing back to life someone who spent half an hour at the bottom of the Giudecca Canal) that led pilgrims to leave gifts and, eventually, enough donations to have this church built. Look for the icon now displayed over the main altar.

Cannaregio, Rio d. Miracoli. No phone. Admission 3€ or 9€ on cumulative ticket (see "For Church Fans," earlier). Mon–Sat 10am–5pm; Sun 3–5pm. *Vaporetto:* Rialto (located midway btw. the Rialto Bridge and the Campo SS. Giovanni e Paolo).

Il Ghetto (the Jewish Ghetto) ★★ Venice's relationship with its longtime Jewish community fluctuated over time from acceptance to borderline tolerance, attitudes often influenced by the fear that Jewish moneylenders and merchants would infiltrate other sectors of the republic's commerce under a government that thrived on secrecy and control. In 1516, 700 Jews were forced to move to this then-remote northwestern corner of Venice, to an abandoned site of a 14th-century foundry (*ghetto* is old Venetian dialect for "foundry," a word that would soon be used throughout Europe and the world to depict an area where isolated minority groups lived).

This *ghetto* neighborhood was totally surrounded by water. Its two access points were controlled at night and early morning by heavy gates manned by Christian guards (paid for by the Jews), both protecting and segregating its inhabitants. Within a century, the community grew to more than 5,000, representing many languages and cultures. Although the original Ghetto Nuovo (New Ghetto) was expanded to include the Ghetto Vecchio (Old Ghetto) and later the Ghetto Nuovissimo (Newest Ghetto), land was limited and quarters always cramped. The fact that the "New Ghetto" preceded the "Old Ghetto," which was in turn was followed by the "Newest Ghetto" can be confusing, but remember that *ghetto* meant "foundry," and when the Jews moved into the area occupied by its ruins, they first occupied the newer part of the former foundry and then the older part and then still later the newest part). In 1797, when Napoleon rolled into town, the *ghetto* as an institution was disbanded and Jews were free to move elsewhere. Still, it remains the center of Venice's ever-diminishing community of Jewish families; although accounts vary widely, it's said that anywhere from 500 to 2,000 Jews live in all of Venice and Mestre.

Aside from its historic interest, this is also one of the less touristy neighborhoods in Venice (though it has become something of a nightspot) and makes for a pleasant and scenic place to stroll.

Venice's first kosher restaurant, **Gam Gam,** opened in 1996 on Fondamenta di Cannaregio 1122 (𝄐**041-523-1495**), near the entrance to the Jewish Ghetto and close to the Guglie *vaporetto*

The Jews of Venice

Jews began settling in Venice in great numbers in the 16th century, and the republic soon came to value their services as moneylenders, physicians, and traders. For centuries, the Jewish population was forced to live on an island that now encompasses the Campo Ghetto Nuovo, and drawbridges were raised to enforce a nighttime curfew. By the end of the 17th century, as many as 5,000 Jews lived in the Ghetto's cramped confines. Today the city's Jewish population is comprised of only about 500 people, few of whom live in the Ghetto.

The Jewish Ghetto is still alive and well today.

stop. Owned and run by Orthodox Jews from New York, it serves lunch and dinner Sunday through Friday, with an early Friday closing after lunch.

Cannaregio (Campo del Ghetto Nuovo). *Vaporetto:* Guglie or San Marcuola (from either of the 2 *vaporetto* stops, or if walking from the train station, locate the Ponte delle Guglie; walking away from the Grand Canal along the Fondamenta di Cannaregio, take the 2nd right at the corner where Gam Gam is located; this is the entrance to the Calle del Ghetto Vecchio that leads to the Campo del Ghetto Nuovo).

Museo Communità Ebraica (Jewish Museum of Venice) ★ The only way to visit any of the area's five 16th-century synagogues is through one of the Museo Communità Ebraica's frequent organized tours conducted in English. Your guide will elaborate on the commercial and political climate of those times, the unique "skyscraper" architecture (overcrowding resulted in many buildings having as many as seven low-ceiling stories, several more than most Venetian buildings), and the daily lifestyle of the Jewish community until the arrival of Napoleon in 1797. You'll get to visit historic temples dedicated to the rites of all three major Jewish groups who called Venice home: Italian (Scola Italiana), Sephardic (Scola Levantina), and Ashkenazi (Scola Canton).

Cannaregio 2902B (on Campo del Ghetto Nuovo). ✆ **041-715-359.** www.museoebraico.it. Museum 3€ adults, 2€ children; museum and synagogue tour 8.50€ adults, 7€ children. Museum Sun–Fri 10am–7pm (Oct–May until 6pm); synagogue tours hourly 10:30am–5:30pm (Oct–May last tour 4:30). Closed on Jewish holidays. *Vaporetto:* Guglie.

On Giudecca & San Giorgio

Chiesa di San Giorgio Maggiore ★★ 📷 This church sits on the little island of San Giorgio Maggiore across from Piazza San Marco. It is one of the masterpieces of Andrea Palladio, the great Renaissance architect from nearby Vicenza. Most known for his country villas built for Venice's wealthy merchant families, Palladio was commissioned to build two churches (the other is the Redentore on the neighboring Giudecca island), beginning with San Giorgio, designed in 1565 and completed in 1610. To impose a classical facade on the traditional church structure, Palladio designed two interlocking facades, with repeating triangles, rectangles, and columns that are harmoniously proportioned. Founded as early as the 10th century, the interior of the church was reinterpreted by Palladio with whitewashed surfaces, stark but majestic, and unadorned but harmonious space. The main altar is flanked by two epic paintings by an elderly Tintoretto, *The Fall of Manna,* to the left, and the more noteworthy *Last Supper,* to the right, famous for its chiaroscuro. Through the doorway to the right of the choir leading to the Cappella dei Morti (Chapel of the Dead), you will find Tintoretto's *Deposition.*

San Giorgio Maggiore as seen from the Venetian lagoon.

To the left of the choir is an elevator that you can take to the top of the campanile—for a charge of 3€—to experience an unforgettable view of the island, the lagoon, and the Palazzo Ducale and Piazza San Marco across the way.

A handful of remaining Benedic-tine monks gather for Sunday Mass at 11am, sung in Gregorian chant.

On the island of San Giorgio Maggiore, across St. Mark's Basin from Piazzetta San Marco. ℂ **041-522-7827.** Free admission. Mon–Sat 9:30am–12:30pm; daily 2–6pm. *Vaporetto:* Take the Giudecca-bound *vaporetto* (no. 82) on Riva degli Schiavoni and get off at the 1st stop, the island of San Giorgio Maggiore.

Il Redentore ★ Perhaps the masterpiece among Palladio's churches, Il Redentore was commissioned by Venice to give thanks for being delivered from the great plague (1575–77), which claimed over a quarter of the population (some 46,000 people). The doge established a tradition of visiting this church by crossing a long pontoon bridge made up of boats from the Dorsoduro's Zattere on the third Sunday of each July, a tradition that survived the demise of the doges and remains one of Venice's most popular festivals (p. 165).

The interior is done in grand, austere, painstakingly classical Palladian style. The artworks tend to be workshop pieces (from the studios or schools, but not the actual brushes, of Tintoretto and Veronese), but there is a fine *Baptism of Christ* by Veronese himself in the sacristy, which also contains Alvise Vivarini's

Adoration and *Angels* alongside works by Jacopo da Bassano and Palma il Giovane, who also did the *Deposition* over the right aisle's third chapel.

Campo del Redentore, La Giudecca. ℂ **041-523-1415.** Admission 3€ or 9€ on cumulative ticket (see "For Church Fans," p. 151). Mon–Sat 10am–5pm; Sun 1–5pm. *Vaporetto:* Redentore.

Especially for Kids

It goes without saying that a **gondola ride** will be the thrill of a lifetime for any child or adult. If that's too expensive, consider the convenient and far less expensive alternative: a **ride on the no. 1 *vaporetto*.** They offer two entirely different experiences: The gondola gives you the chance to see Venice through the back door (and ride past Marco Polo's house); the *vaporetto* provides a utilitarian—but no less gorgeous—journey down Venice's aquatic Main Street, the Grand Canal. Look

The lion represents Mark, patron saint of Venice.

for the ambulance boat, the garbage boat, the firefighters' boat, the funeral boat, even the Coca-Cola delivery boat. Best sightings are the special gondolas filled with flowers and rowed by *gondolieri* in livery delivering a happy bride and groom from the church.

Judging from the squeals of delight, **feeding the pigeons in Piazza San Marco** (purchase a bag of corn and you'll be draped in pigeons in a nanosecond) could be the epitome of your child's visit to Venice, and it's the ultimate photo op. Be sure your child won't be startled by all the fluttering and flapping.

A jaunt to the neighboring **island of Murano** can be as educational as it is recreational—follow the signs to any *fornace* (kiln), where a glass-blowing performance of the island's thousand-year-old art is free entertainment. But be ready for the guaranteed sales pitch that follows.

Before you leave town, take the elevator to the **top of the Campanile di San Marco** (the highest structure in the city) for a pigeon's-eye view of Venice's rooftops and church cupolas, or get up close and personal with the four bronze horses on the facade of the Basilica San Marco. The view from its **outdoor loggia** is something you and your children won't forget.

Some children enjoy the **Museo Storico Navale (Naval History Museum)** and **Arsenale (Arsenal)** with its ship models and old vessels, and the many historic artifacts in the **Museo Civico Correr (Correr Civic Museum),** tangible vestiges of a time when Venice was a world unto itself.

The **winged lion,** said to have been a kind of good luck mascot to St. Mark, patron saint of Venice, was the very symbol of the Serene Republic and to this day appears on everything from cafe napkins to T-shirts. Who can spot the most flying lions? They appear on facades, atop columns, over doorways, as pavement mosaics, on government stamps, and on the local flag.

4

VENICE | Exploring Venice

FESTIVALS & SPECIAL EVENTS

Venice's most special event is the yearly pre-Lenten **Carnevale ★★★**, a 2-week theatrical resuscitation of the 18th-century bacchanalia that drew tourists during the final heyday of the Most Serene Republic. Most of today's Carnevale-related events, masked balls, and costumes evoke that time. Many of the concerts around town are free, when baroque to samba to gospel to Dixieland jazz music fills the *campi* and byways; check with the tourist office for a list of events. Carnevale builds for 10 days until the big blowout, **Shrove Tuesday** (Fat Tuesday), when fireworks illuminate the Grand Canal, and Piazza San Marco is turned into a giant open-air ballroom for the masses. Book your hotel months ahead, especially for the 2 weekends prior to Shrove Tuesday. See "Carnevale a Venezia," below, for more info.

The **Voga Longa ★★** (literally "long row"), a 30km (20-mile) rowing "race" from San Marco to Burano and back again, has been enthusiastically embraced since its inception in 1975, following the city's effort to keep alive the centuries-old heritage of the regatta. It takes place on a Sunday in mid- to late-May; for exact dates, consult the tourist office or www.vogalonga.com. It's a colorful event and a great excuse to party, plus every local seems to have a relative or next-door neighbor competing.

Stupendous fireworks light the night sky during the **Festa del Redentore ★**, on the third Saturday and Sunday in July. This celebration, which marks the July 1577 lifting of a plague that had killed more than a quarter of the city's population, including the great painter Titian, is centered on the Palladio-designed Chiesa del Redentore (Church of the Redeemer) on the island of Giudecca. For the occasion, a bridge of boats across the Giudecca Canal links the church with the banks of Le Zattere in Dorsoduro, and hundreds of boats of all shapes and sizes fill the area. It's one big, floating *festa* until night descends and an awesome half-hour *spettacolo* of fireworks fills the sky.

The **Venice International Film Festival ★★**, in late August and early September, is the most respected celebration of celluloid in Europe after Cannes. Films from all over the world are shown in the Palazzo del Cinema on the Lido as well as at various venues—and occasionally in some of the *campi*. Ticket prices vary, but those for the less-sought-after films are usually modest.

Venice hosts the latest in modern and contemporary painting and sculpture from dozens of countries during the prestigious **Biennale d'Arte ★★★** (✆ **041-521-8711;** www.labiennale.org), one of the world's top international modern art shows. It fills the pavilions of the public gardens at the east end of Castello and in the Arsenale as well as in other spaces around the city from late May to October every odd-numbered year. In the past, awards have gone to Jackson Pollock, Henri Matisse, Alexander Calder, and Federico Fellini, among others. Tickets cost 20€, 16€ for those 65 and over, and 12€ for students and all those 26 and under.

The **Regata Storica ★★** that takes place on the Grand Canal on the first Sunday in September is an extravagant seagoing parade in historic costume as well as a genuine regatta. Just about every seaworthy gondola, richly decked out for the occasion and piloted by *gondolieri* in colorful livery, participates in the opening cavalcade. The aquatic parade is followed by three regattas along the Grand Canal. You can buy grandstand tickets through the tourist office or come early, very early, and find a piece of embankment near the Rialto Bridge for the best seats in town.

Carnevale marionettes for sale in a Venice shop.

Other notable events include **Festa della Salute ★** on November 21, when a pontoon bridge is erected across the Grand Canal to connect the churches of La Salute and Santa Maria del Giglio, commemorating delivery from another plague in 1630. The **Festa della Sensa,** on the Sunday following Ascension Day in May, reenacts the ancient ceremony when the doge would wed Venice to the sea. April 25 is a local holiday, the **feast day of Saint Mark,** beloved patron saint of Venice and of the ancient republic. A special High Mass is celebrated in the Basilica of San Marco, and Venetians exchange roses with those they love.

Finally, the ultimate anomaly: Venice's annual **Maratona (Marathon),** starting at Villa Pisani on the mainland and ending up along the Zattere for a finish at the Basilica di Santa Maria della Salute on the tip of Dorsoduro. It's usually held the last or second-to-last Sunday of October.

SHOPPING

A mix of low-end trinket stores and middle-market-to-upscale boutiques line the narrow zigzagging **Mercerie** running north between Piazza San Marco and the Rialto Bridge. More expensive clothing and gift boutiques make for great window-shopping on **Calle Larga XXII Marzo,** the wide street that begins west of Piazza San Marco and wends its way to the expansive Campo Santo Stefano near the Accademia. The narrow **Frezzaria,** just west of Piazza San Marco and running north-south, offers a grab bag of bars, souvenir shops, and tony clothing stores.

In a city that for centuries has thrived almost exclusively on tourism, remember this: **Where you buy cheap, you get cheap.** There are few bargains to be had; the nonproduce part of the Rialto Market is as good as it gets, where you'll find cheap T-shirts, glow-in-the-dark plastic gondolas, and tawdry glass trinkets. Venetians, centuries-old merchants, aren't known for bargaining. You'll stand a better chance of getting a bargain if you pay in cash or buy more than one item.

Venice is uniquely famous for local crafts that have been produced here for centuries and are hard to get elsewhere: the **glassware** from Murano, the

carnevale A VENEZIA

Venetians once more are taking to the open *piazze* and streets for the pre-Lenten holiday of Carnevale. The festival traditionally was the celebration preceding Lent, the period of penitence and abstinence prior to Easter; its name is derived from the Latin *carnem levare,* meaning "to take meat away."

Today Carnevale lasts no more than 5 to 10 days and culminates in the Friday to Tuesday before Ash Wednesday. In the 18th-century heyday of Carnevale in La Serenissima Republic, well-heeled revelers came from all over Europe to take part in festivities that began months prior to Lent and reached a raucous climax at midnight on Shrove Tuesday. As the Venetian economy declined and its colonies and trading posts fell to other powers, the Republic of Venice in its swan song turned to fantasy and escapism. The faster its decline, the longer, and more licentious, became its anything-goes merrymaking. Masks became ubiquitous, affording anonymity and the pardoning of a thousand sins. Masks permitted the fishmonger to attend the ball and dance with the baroness, the properly married to carry on as if they were not. The doges condemned it and the popes denounced it, but nothing could dampen the Venetian Carnevale spirit until Napoleon arrived in 1797 and put an end to the festivities.

Resuscitated in 1980 by local tourism powers to fill the empty winter months when tourism comes to a screeching halt, Carnevale is calmer nowadays, though just barely. The born-again festival got off to a shaky start, met at first with indifference and skepticism, but in the years since has grown in popularity and been embraced by the locals. In the 1980s, Carnevale attracted an onslaught of what was seemingly the entire student population of Europe, backpacking young people who slept in the *piazze* and train station. Politicians and city officials adopted a middle-of-the-road policy that helped establish

Carnevale's image as neither a backpacker's free-for-all outdoor party nor a continuation of the exclusive private balls in the Grand Canal *palazzi* available to a very few.

Carnevale is now a harlequin patchwork of musical and cultural events, many of them free of charge, which appeals to all ages, tastes, nationalities, and budgets. At any given moment, musical events are staged in some of the city's dozens of *piazze*—from reggae and zydeco to jazz and baroque. Special art exhibits are mounted at museums and galleries. The recent involvement of international corporate commercial sponsors has met with a mixed reception, although it seems to be the direction of the future.

The various masked balls around town are often private; those where (exorbitantly priced) tickets are available are sumptuous, with candlelit banquets calling for extravagant costumes you can rent by the day from special shops. If you can score tickets, splurge some 350€ per person on the **Ballo del Doge (Doge's Ball; ℭ 041-241-3802)**. They throw a real jet-set party (accessible to all) in the 16th-century Palazzo Pisani-Moretta on the Grand Canal (btw. the Rialto and the Foscari), outfitted with Tiepolo frescoes and all the other accouterments of 18th-century Venetian style. Different ballrooms feature minuets, waltzes, baroque chamber orchestras—there's even a modern disco (acoustically self-contained). Those not invited to any ball will be just as happy having their face painted and watching the ongoing street theater from a ringside cafe. There's a **daily market**

of Carnevale masks and costumes on Campo Santo Stefano (10am–10pm).

Carnevale is not for those who dislike crowds. Indeed, the crowds are what it's all about. All of Venice becomes a stage. Whether you spend months creating an extravagant costume or grab one from the countless stands set up about the town, Carnevale is about giving in to the spontaneity of magic and surprise around every corner, the mystery behind every mask. Masks and costumes are everywhere, though you won't see anything along the lines of Teletubbies or Zorro. Emphasis is on the historical, for Venice's Carnevale is the chance to relive the glory days of the 1700s when Venetian life was at its most extravagant. Groups travel in coordinated getups that range from a contemporary passel of Felliniesque clowns to the court of the Sun King in all its wigged-out, over-the-top, drag-queen glory. There are the three musketeers riding the *vaporetto;* your

waiter appears dressed as a nun; sitting alone on the church steps is a Romeo waiting for his Juliet; late at night, crossing a small, deserted *campo,* a young, laughing couple appears out of a gray mist in a cloud of crinoline and sparkles, and then disappears down a small alley. The places to be seen in costume (only appropriate costumes need apply) are the historical cafes lining the Piazza San Marco, the **Florian** being the unquestioned command post. Don't expect a window seat unless your costume is straight off the stage of the local opera house.

The city is the perfect venue; Hollywood could not create a more evocative location. This is a celebration of history, art, theater, and drama that one would expect to find in Italy, the land that gave us the Renaissance and Zeffirelli—and Venice, an ancient and wealthy republic that gave us Casanova and Vivaldi. Venice and Carnevale were made for each other.

delicate lace from Burano, and the *cartapesta* (papier-mâché) Carnevale masks you'll find in endless *botteghe* (shops), where you can watch artisans paint amid their wares.

Now here's the bad news: There's such an overwhelming sea of cheap glass gewgaws that buying Venetian glass can become something of a turnoff (shipping and insurance costs make most things unaffordable; the alternative is to hand-carry anything fragile). There are so few women left on Burano willing to spend countless tedious hours keeping alive the art of lace-making that the few pieces you'll see not produced by machine in Hong Kong are sold at stratospheric prices; ditto the truly high-quality glass (though trinkets can be cheap and fun). Still, exceptions are to be found in all of the above, and when you find them you'll know. A discerning eye can cut through the dreck to find some lovely mementos.

Venice Shopping Strategies

There are two rules of thumb for shopping in Venice: If you have the good fortune of continuing on to Florence or Rome, shop for clothing, leather goods, and accessories with prudence in Venice, because most items are more expensive here. If, however, you happen on something that strikes you, consider it twice on the spot (not back at your hotel), and then buy it. In this web of alleys, you may never find that shop again.

Antiques

The interesting **Mercatino dell'Antiquariato (Antiques Fair)** takes place three times annually in the charming Campo San Maurizio between Piazza San Marco and Campo Santo Stefano. Dates change yearly for the 3-day weekend market but generally fall the first weekend of April, mid-September, and the weekend before Christmas. More than 100 vendors sell everything from the sublime piece of Murano glass to quirky dust collectors. Early birds might find reasonably priced finds such as Murano candy dishes from the 1950s, Venetian-pearl glass beads older still, vintage Italian posters advertising Campari-sponsored regattas, or antique postcards of Venice that could be from the 1930s or the 1830s—things change so little here. Those for whom price is less an issue might pick up antique lace by the yard or a singular museum-quality piece of hand-blown glass from a local master.

Books

Libreria Studium, San Marco 337 (✆041-522-2382), on Calle della Canonica on the northern flank of the Basilica di San Marco, carries lots of travel guides and maps as well as books in English. Another centrally located bookstore is the **Libreria Sansovino** in the Bacino Orseolo 84 (✆041-522-2623), just off the northwest corner of the Piazza San Marco, carrying a good selection of books about Venetian art, history, and literature. If you are in Dorsoduro, you can go to **Libreria Toletta** (✆041-523-2034) on Calle della Toletta between Campo San Barnaba and the Accademia bridge.

For art books and other colorful hardbacks on history and Italian sights to hold down your coffee table at 40% to 50% off, head to **Libreria Bertoni,** San Marco 3637B (Calle della Mandola; ✆041-522-9583), and San Marco 4718 (Calle dei Fabbri; ✆041-522-4615).

Crafts

The **Murano Art Shop,** at San Marco 1232 (on the store-lined Frezzaria, parallel to the western border of, and close to, the Piazza San Marco; ✆041-523-3851), is a cultural experience. At this small shop, every inch of wall space is draped with the whimsical crafts of the city's most creative artisans. Fusing the timeless with the contemporary—with a nod to the magic and romance of Venice's past—the store offers a dramatic, evolving, and expensive collection of masks, puppets, music boxes, and costume jewelry.

When it seems as if every gift-store window is awash with collectible bisque-faced dolls in elaborate pinafores and headdresses, head to **Bambole di Trilly,** at Castello 4974 (Fondamenta dell'Osmarin, off the Campo San Provolo on your way east out of Piazza San Marco in the direction of the Church of San Zaccaria; ✆041-521-2579), where the hand-sewn wardrobes of rich Venetian fabrics and painstakingly painted faces are particularly exquisite. The perfect souvenir starts at about 20€ in this well-stocked workspace north of Campo San Zaccaria.

Foodstuffs

Food lovers will find charmingly packaged food products for themselves or friends at the well-known pasta manufacturer **Giacomo Rizzo,** near the major Coin department store, northeast of the Rialto Bridge at Cannaregio 5778 at Calle San Giovanni Crisostomo (✆041-522-2824). You'll find pasta made in the shape of gondolas, colorful carnival hats, and dozens of other imaginatively shaped possibilities (colored and flavored with squash, beet, and spinach).

For those with a sweet tooth, there's **Fuori Menu,** between Campo Santo Stefano and Campo San Maurizio (San Marco 2769 at Ponte San Maurizio; ✆041-522-9109), where the selection of traditional cookies are already prepackaged for traveling—delicate *baicoli,* cornmeal raisin *zaleti,* and the S-shaped *buranelli.* Or for something different that you are either going to love or hate—this tends to be an acquired taste that takes several trips to Venice to appreciate—try the *pan fragola,* a pink hard bread with strawberry essence and candied fruit. For the less adventurous, there is also an ample selection of decent pizza by the slice.

Glass

If you're going to go all out, look no further than **Venini,** Piazzetta dei Leoni 314 near the base of the clock tower in Piazza San Marco (✆041-522-4045), since 1921 one of the most respected and innovative glassmakers in all of Venice. Their products are more works of art than merely blown glass. So renowned are they for their quality, Versace's own line of glass objects d'art are done by Venini. Their **workshop** on Murano is at Fondamenta Vetrai 50 (✆041-273-7211). Cheap they are not, but no one else has such a lovely or original representation of hand-blown Murano glassware.

For the glass-inclined, there is also the spacious emporium of items at **Marco Polo** (San Marco 1644; ✆041-522-9295), just west of the Piazza San Marco on the Frezzaria. The front half of the first floor offers a variety of small gift ideas (candy dishes, glass-topped medicine boxes, paperweights).

Glass beads are called "Venetian pearls," and an abundance of exquisite antique and reproduced baubles are the draw at **Anticlea,** at Castello 4719A (a bit off Campo San Provolo going north on Calle San Provolo; ✆041-528-

6946). Once used for trading in Venice's far-flung colonies, they now fill the coffers of this small shop east of Piazza San Marco, sold singly or already strung. The open-air stall of **Susie and Andrea** (Riva degli Schiavoni, near Pensione Wildner just east of the Danieli; just ask) has handcrafted beads that are new, well made and strung, and moderately priced. The stall operates from February through November.

Jewelry

Meneghetti, San Marco 5173 (Campo San Bartolomeo; ✆ 041-523-7683), carries gold and silver jewelry by many top international designers including Chimento, which makes its wares in nearby Vicenza.

Tiny **Antichità Zaggia,** Dorsoduro 1195 (Calle de la Toletta west of the Accademia bridge; ✆ 041-522-2115), specializes in genuine antique jewelry (and glassware) of the highest quality and beautiful designs.

Leather & Shoes

One usually thinks of Florence when thinking of Italian leather goods. But the plethora of mediocre-to-refined shoe stores in Venice is testimony to the tradition of small shoe factories along the nearby Brenta canal that supply most of Italy, and much of the world, with made-in-Italy footwear. Venice has plenty of fine shoe stores (doesn't every Italian city?), but one original shop that deserves singling out for sheer oddness is **Atelier Segalin di Daniela Ghezzo,** San Marco 4365 (Calle dei Fuseri a few bridges away from the northwest corner of Piazza San Marco; ✆ 041-522-2115). The fantastical footwear in an acid trip of colors and shapes, some of which are intended for Carnevale costumes, makes it worth stopping by even if you aren't in the market for a 1,000-euro pair of curly toe shoes.

Linens & Lace

Frette, San Marco 2070A (Calle Larga XXII Marzo; ✆ 041-522-4914; www. frette.com), is a long-respected place to head for classy linens, bedclothes, and silk jammies. They'll even do custom work for you.

For hand-tatted lace from the only school still teaching it in Venice, ride out to Burano to visit the **Scuola dei Merletti,** Piazza B. Galuppi (✆ 041-730-034), founded in 1872, closed in 1972, and reopened in 1981. (The Scuola dei Merletti and its accompanying museum reopened in 2011 following a complete overhaul of the exhibition space.)

Masks

A shortage of mask *botteghe* (shops) in Venice is not a problem; the challenge is ferreting out the few exceptionally talented artists producing one-of-a-kind theatrical pieces. You will certainly get original at the tiny **La Bottega dei Mascareri,** San Polo 80 (with the Rialto Bridge at your back, it's quickly on your right amid the tourist booths pushed up against the church; ✆ 041-522-3857), where the charming Boldrin brothers' least elaborate masks begin at about 15€ though you can quickly get up towards 100€. Anyone who thinks a mask is a mask is a mask should come here first for a look-see.

Not only does **Il Canovaccio,** Castello 5369–70 (Calle delle Bande near Campo Santa Maria Formosa; ✆ 041-521-0393), produce high-quality artisan work, but it's undeniably cool. Rolling Stone guitarist Ron Wood has shopped here, and the shop provided the masks and costumes for the orgy scene in Stanley Kubrick's *Eyes Wide Shut.*

At **Rugadoro,** San Polo 1062 (Ruga Vecchia San Giovanni near the Rialto markets; ✆ **041-520-5487**), Sarah Zanarella takes a new twist by covering parts of her masks with antique fabrics. If your Venetian shopping list includes a mask, it's worth coming by here to see these creations, which start at 22€.

Paper Products

Biblos, San Marco 2087 (Calle Larga XXII Marzo; ✆ **041-521-0714**), carries leather-bound blank books and journals, marbleized paper, enamel pill boxes, watercolor etchings, and fountain pens. At nearby **Il Prato,** San Marco 2456 (Calle delle Ostreghe, the continuation of Calle Larga XXII Marzo; ✆ **041-523-1148**), you'll find top-end examples of photo albums, pencil holders, and many other handmade items covered in the typical Venetian paper.

Wine

For a broad selection of wines from Veneto and across Italy at truly decent prices, head to **Bottiglieria Colonna,** Castello 5595 (Calle della Fava; ✆ **041-528-5137**), which will put together gift packets of wines in packs of six, and also handles liqueurs from around the world. There's a more down-to-earth cantina called **Nave de Oro,** Cannaregio 5786B (Salizada San Lio west of Campo Santa Maria Formosa; ✆ **041-522-3056**), where locals bring empty bottles to have them filled with a variety of Veneto table wines at low, low prices—2€ to 3.10€ per liter. Join the fun by bringing any sort of container, even a used water bottle.

VENICE AFTER DARK

Visit one of the tourist information centers for current English-language schedules of the month's special events. The monthly *Ospite di Venezia* is distributed free or online at **www.unospitedivenezia.it** and is extremely helpful but usually available only in the more expensive hotels. If you're looking for serious nocturnal action, you're in the wrong town. Your best bet is to sit in the moonlit Piazza San Marco and listen to the cafes' outdoor orchestras, with the illuminated basilica before you—the perfect opera set.

For just plain hanging out at most any time of day, popular spots that serve as meeting points include **Campo San Bartolomeo,** at the foot of the Rialto Bridge (though it is a zoo here in high season), and nearby **Campo San Luca.** In less busy times you'll see Venetians of all ages milling about engaged in animated conversation, particularly from 5pm until dinnertime. In late-night hours, for low prices and low pretension, the absolute best place to go is **Campo Santa Margherita,** a huge open *campo* about halfway between the train station and the Accademia bridge. Look for the popular **Green Pub** (no. 3053; closed Thurs), **Baretto Rosso** (no. 2963; closed Sun), and **Bar Salus** (no. 3112). **Campo Santo Stefano** on the San Marco side of the Accademia bridge with its cafes has a more formal flair that puts it somewhere between, both figuratively and geographically, Campo Santa Margherita and Piazza San Marco.

The Performing Arts

Venice has a long and rich tradition of classical music, and there's always a concert going on somewhere. Several churches regularly host classical music

The elaborate La Fenice theater is as much a destination as it is a venue.

concerts (with an emphasis on the baroque) by local and international artists. This was, after all, the home of Vivaldi. One of the more popular spots to hear the music of Vivaldi and his contemporaries is **Chiesa Santa Maria della Pietà** (the "Vivaldi Church"; www.vivaldichurch.it), between Campo Santo Stefano and the Accademia bridge. The most popular venue for hearing Vivaldi's works, concerts are held on weekends at 8:30pm; check the website for specific dates and tickets. A number of other churches and confraternities (such as San Stae, the Scuola di San Giovanni Evangelista, and the Scuola di San Rocco) host concerts. People dressed in period costumes stand around in heavily trafficked spots near San Marco and Rialto passing out brochures advertising the classical music concerts, so you'll have no trouble finding up-to-date information.

The city still remembers well when the famous **Teatro La Fenice ★★★** (San Marco 1965, on Campo San Fantin; ✆ **041-2424** or 041-786-511; www. teatrolafenice.it) went up in flames in January 1996. Carpenters and artisans rebuilt the theater, which originally opened in 1836, according to archival designs; and in December 2003 La Fenice (which appropriately means "the Phoenix") arose from the ashes as Ricardo Muti conducted the Orchestra and Chorus of La Fenice in an inaugural concert in a completely renovated hall. Its performances now follow a regular schedule.

Cafes

Venice is a quiet town in the evening and offers very little in the way of nightlife. For tourists and locals alike, Venetian nightlife mainly centers on the many cafe/ bars in one of the world's most remarkable *piazze:* Piazza San Marco. It is also the most expensive and touristed place to linger over a Campari or anything else for that matter, but it's a splurge that should not be dismissed too readily. For those on a particularly tight budget, you can hang out near the cafes and listen to the sometimes quite surprisingly good live classical music (you won't be alone).

The nostalgic 18th-century **Caffè Florian ★★** (San Marco 56A–59A; ✆ **041-241-7286;** closed Wed in winter), on the south side of the piazza, is the most famous and most theatrical inside. Have a Bellini (prosecco and fresh peach nectar) at the bar for half what you'd pay at an indoor table; alfresco seating is even more expensive when the band plays, but it's worth every cent. It's said that when Casanova escaped from the prisons in the Doge's Palace, he stopped here for a coffee before fleeing Venice.

On the opposite side of the square at San Marco 133–134 is the old-world **Caffè Lavena** (✆ **041-522-4070;** closed Tues in winter), and at no. 120 is **Caffè Quadri** ★ (✆ **041-522-2105;** www.caffequadri.it; closed Mon in winter), the first to introduce coffee to Venice, with a restaurant upstairs that sports Piazza San Marco views. See p. 129 for more on Quadri's restaurant. At all spots, a cappuccino, tea, or Coca-Cola at a table will set you back about 8€. But no one will rush you, and if the sun is warm and the orchestras are playing, there's no more beautiful public open-air salon in the world. Around the corner (no. 11) and in front of the pink-and-white marble Palazzo Ducale is the best deal, **Caffè Chioggia** ★★★ (✆ **041-528-5011;** closed Sun). Come here at midnight and watch the Moors strike the hour atop the Clock Tower from your outside table, while the quartet or pianist plays everything from quality jazz to pop until the wee hours.

One of the most atmospheric and hidden places to have a *spritz* (soda water, white wine, and your choice of Campari or Aperol) is **Taverna del Campiello Remer** (Cannaregio 5701; ✆ **349-336-5168**), in the courtyard of the same name, right on the Grand Canal close to the Rialto bridge. The nightly live music—feel free to get up and sing, if you're any good—along with the expertly staffed bar, extensive wine list, and big portions of prosciutto and melon, are a recipe for a romantic night out, especially in this magically restored cantina. It generally stays open until at least 1am (closed Wed).

If the weather is chilly or inclement, or for no other reason than to revel in the history and drama of Venice's grand-dame hotel, dress up and stroll into the landmark lobby of the Danieli hotel and **Bar Dandolo** (Castello 4196 on Riva degli Schiavoni, east of Piazza San Marco; ✆ **041-522-6480**). Tea or coffee costs 8€, a lot, perhaps, if you consider that for the same price you can buy 8 coffees at a bar, but for this fee you can sit forever while enjoying the former residential *palazzo* of a 15th-century doge. A pianist plays from 7 to 9pm and from 10pm to 12:30am. Drinks are far more expensive; ask for the price list before ordering.

Clubs, *Birrerie* & *Gelaterie*

Although Venice boasts an old and prominent university, dance clubs barely enjoy their 15 minutes of popularity before changing hands or closing down (some are open only in the summer months). Young Venetians tend to go to the Lido or mainland Mestre. Evenings are better spent lingering over a late dinner, having a pint in a *birrerie,* or nursing a glass of prosecco in one of Piazza San Marco's or Campo Santa Margherita's overpriced outdoor cafes. (**Note:** Most bars are open Mon–Sat 8pm–midnight.)

As if Campo Santa Margherita didn't already have enough going for it, it is also home to **Il Doge** (no. 3058, at the end of the campo going toward San Barnaba), one of the city's best **gelato** sources. Not to be outdone, Campo Santo Stefano has excellent gelato at **Bar/Gelateria Paolin** (no. 2962; closed Fri). Another good choice is **Gelateria Nico** on the Zattere in Dorsoduro 922, and then there is always **Grom** in Campo San Barnaba and on the Strada Nova near Ca' d'Oro. (To see somebody wax poetic about this ice cream chain, see p. 318.)

For occasional evenings of live music, cabaret, or just a relaxed late-night hangout, consider the ever-popular **Le Bistrot de Venise** (p. 129).

The **Devil's Forest Pub** ★, San Marco 5185, on Calle Stagneri (☎ **041-520-0623;** www.devilsforest.com), offers the outsider an authentic chance to take in the convivial atmosphere and find out where Venetians hang out—despite the fact that the atmosphere is more British than Italian. It's popular for lunch with the neighborhood merchants and shop owners, and ideal for relaxed socializing over a beer and a host of games like backgammon, chess, and Trivial Pursuit. It's open daily 10am to 1am.

Bacaro Jazz ★★, San Marco 5546, just north of Campo San Bartolomeo on the San Marco side of the Rialto Bridge (☎ **041-528-5249**), is a happening cocktail bar (the Bellinis are great) with restaurant seating in the back. It's a mix of jazzy music (often a bit too loud), rough plank walls, industrial-steel tables, and a corrugated aluminum ceiling. It's open Thursday to Tuesday 11am to 2am (happy hour 4–7pm) and with food available until closing time this might be the only place in town where you can get seafood risotto well after midnight. They do play to the tourists here so you will find that purely American creation Fettuccine Alfredo (don't believe anybody who tells you there is any part of Italy that would claim this dish as part of their regional cuisine).

With its walls full of Irish paraphernalia confirming its credentials as the only real Irish pub in town, the **Inishark Irish Pub** ★, at Castello 5787 (Calle Mondo Novo just off Salizada San Lio, near Santa Maria Formosa; ☎ **041-523-5300;** closed Mon), is a big draw for young locals as well as tourists. There is an enormous flatscreen television where they show soccer matches and other sporting events, and they throw in free Wi-Fi. A Guinness and some Internet surfing anybody?

Good food at reasonable prices would be enough to regularly pack **Paradiso Perduto** ★★, Cannaregio 2540, on Fondamenta della Misericordia (☎ **041-720-581**), but its biggest draw is the live jazz performed on a small stage several nights a week. Popular with Americans and other foreigners living in Venice, this bar was once largely devoid of tourists, primarily because of its hard-to-find location, but the word is out. The good selection of well-prepared pizzas and pastas goes for under 10€; arrive early for a table. It's open Thursday to Tuesday 7pm to 1 or sometimes 2am.

The party spills well out from the plate-glass windows of **Bar Torino,** San Marco 459 (Campo San Luca; ☎ **041-522-3914**), a bar that has brought this square to life after dark with live jazz many nights, unusual beer from Lapland, and good panini. It's open Tuesday to Sunday 7am to 2am.

In 1932, famed restaurateur and hotelier Giuseppe Cipriani opened **Harry's Bar** ★★ right at the San Marco–Vallaresso *vaporetto* stop, San Marco 1323 (Calle Vallaresso; ☎ **041-528-5777**). This has been a preferred retreat for everyone from Hemingway—when he didn't want a bloody mary, he mixed his own drink: 15 parts gin, 1 part dry vermouth—to Woody Allen. Regulars prefer the elegant front room to the upstairs dining room (the cooking is decent, and they invented carpaccio, a dish of thinly sliced raw beef now served throughout Italy). Harry's is most famous for inventing the Bellini, a mix of champagne and peach puree. Prices—for both drinks and the fancy cuisine—are rather extravagant.

If you really need that disco fix, you're best off at **Piccolo Mondo** ★, Dorsoduro 1056, turn right onto Calle Corfu as you come off the Accademia bridge into Dorsoduro (☎ **041-520-0371;** www.piccolomondo.biz). Billed as a disco/pub, it serves sandwiches during lunch to the sounds of America's latest dance music, offers a happy hour in the late afternoon in winter, and often features live music. But the only reason you'd want to come is if you want to dance (summer only); the club is frequented mostly by curious foreigners and the young to not-so-young Venetians who seek them out. It's open daily from 10pm to 4am in summer, and 10am to 4pm and 5 to 8pm in winter.

The Casino

From May to October, **Casino Municipale di Venezia,** located at Palazzo Vendramin Calergi, Cannaregio 2040 (Fondamenta Vendramin; ☏**041-529-7111;** www.casinovenezia.it), moves to its nondescript summer location on the Lido, where a visit is not as strongly recommended as during the winter months, when it is housed in this handsome 15th-century *palazzo* on the Grand Canal. Venice's tradition of gambling goes back to the glory days of the republic and lives on in this august Renaissance palace built by Mauro Codussi. This is one of only four casinos on Italian territory. Though not of the caliber of Monte Carlo, what a remarkable setting it is! Richard Wagner lived and died in a wing of this *palazzo* in 1883.

Check with your hotel before setting forth; some offer free passes for their guests. Otherwise, if you're not a gambler or a curiosity seeker, it may not be worth the admission of 5€ to get in. *Tip:* If you pay a higher 10€ admission fee, the casino will provide you with a 10€ credit for gambling, so your admission could actually be free—and perhaps, if you're lucky, better than free. *Note:* A passport and jacket are required for entrance (you can rent the jacket there, the passport you have to bring yourself), and the casino is open daily from 3:30pm (11am for the slots) to 2:30am (Fri–Sat until 3am).

EXPLORING VENICE'S ISLANDS

Venice shares its lagoon with three other principal islands: Murano, Burano, and Torcello. Guided tours of the three are operated by a dozen agencies with docks on Riva degli Schiavoni/Piazzetta San Marco (all interchangeable). The 3- and 4-hour tours run 20€ to 35€, usually include a visit to a Murano glass factory (you can easily do that on your own, with less of a hard sell), and leave daily around 9:30am and 2:30pm (times change; check in advance).

You can also visit the islands on your own conveniently and easily using the *vaporetti.* Line nos. 5, 13, 18, 41, 42, A, B, and LN make the journey to Murano from Fondamente Nove (on the north side of Castello), and line LN continues on to Burano from where there is a boat that makes the short trip to Torcello. The islands are small and easy to navigate, but check the schedule for the next island-to-island departure (usually hourly) and your return so that you don't spend most of your day waiting for connections.

Murano & Its Glass

The island of **Murano ★★** has long been famous throughout the world for the products of its glass factories, but there's little here in variety or prices that you won't find in Venice. A visit to the **Museo del Vetro (Museum of Glass),** Fondamenta Giustinian 8 (☏**041-739-586**), will put the island's centuries-old legacy into perspective and is recommended for those considering major buys. Hours are Thursday to Tuesday 10am to 6pm (Nov–Mar to 5pm), and admission is 6€ for adults and 3.50€ children 6 to 14 and students 30 and under, or free with the cumulative Museum Pass (see "Venice Discounts," on p. 105).

Dozens of *fornaci* (kilns) offer free shows of mouth-blown glassmaking almost invariably hitched to a hard-sell ("No obligation! Really!") tour of the factory outlet. These retail showrooms of delicate glassware can be enlightening or boring, depending on your frame of mind. Almost all the places ship, often doubling the price. On the other hand, these pieces are instant heirlooms.

Murano also has two worthy churches: **San Pietro Martire ★**, with its altarpieces by Tintoretto, Veronese, and Giovanni Bellini, and the ancient **Santa Maria e Donato ★**, with an intricate Byzantine exterior apse and a 6th-century pulpit and columns inside resting on a fantastic 12th-century inlaid floor.

Burano & Its Lace

Lace is the claim to fame of tiny, colorful **Burano ★★★**, a craft kept alive for centuries by the wives of fishermen waiting for their husbands to return from sea. It's worth a trip if you have time to stroll the back streets of the island, whose canals are lined with the brightly colored simple homes of the *buranesi* fisherman. The local government continues its attempt to keep its centuries-old lace legacy alive with subsidized classes.

Visit the **Museo del Merletto (Museum of Lace Making),** Piazza Galuppi (✆ **041-730-034**), to understand why something so exquisite should not be left to fade into extinction. It's open Tuesday to Sunday 10am to 6pm (Nov–Mar to 5pm), and admission is 5€ adults and 3.50€ children 6 to 14 and students 29 and under, or free with the cumulative Museum Pass (see "Venice Discounts," on p. 105).

Torcello & Its Cathedral

Nearby **Torcello ★★** is perhaps the most charming of the islands. It was the first of the lagoon islands to be called home by the mainland population fleeing

Quiet, colorful Burano.

Attila and his Huns (from here they eventually moved to join the growing area around where there is now the Rialto Bridge), but today it consists of little more than one long canal leading from the *vaporetto* landing past sad-sack vineyards to a clump of buildings at its center.

Torcello boasts the oldest Venetian monument, the **Cattedrale di Torcello (Santa Maria Assunta)** ★★★, whose foundation dates from the 7th century (© **041-270-2464**). It's famous for its outstanding 11th- to 12-century Byzantine mosaics—a *Madonna and Child* in the apse and *Last Judgment* on the west wall—rivaling those of Ravenna's and St. Mark's basilicas. The cathedral is open daily 10:30am to 6pm (Nov–Feb to 5pm), and admission is 5€. You can climb the bell tower for a panorama for 3€. Also of interest is the adjacent **11th-century church** dedicated to St. Fosca and a **small archaeological museum;** the church's hours are the same as the cathedral's, and the museum is open Tuesday to Sunday 10am to 5:30pm (Nov–Feb to 5pm). Museum admission is 3€. A combined ticket for all three sights is 8€.

Peaceful Torcello is uninhabited except for a handful of families and is a favorite picnic spot (you'll have to bring the food from Venice—there are no stores on the island and only one bar/trattoria and one rather expensive restaurant, the Cipriani, of Hemingway fame). Once the tour groups have left, it offers a very special moment of solitude and escape when St. Mark's bottleneck becomes oppressive.

The Lido & Its Beaches

Although a convenient 15-minute *vaporetto* ride away from San Marco, Venice's **Lido beaches** are not much to write home about. For bathing and sun-worshipping there are much nicer beaches nearby—in Jesolo, to the north, for example. But the parade of wealthy Italian and foreign tourists (plus a good number of Venetian families with children) who frequent this coastal area throughout summer is an interesting sight indeed, although you'll find many of them at the elitist beaches affiliated with such deluxe hotels as the legendary Excelsior and the Des Bains.

There are two beach areas at the Lido. **Bucintoro** is at the opposite end of Gran Viale Santa Maria Elisabetta (referred to as the Gran Viale) from the *vaporetto* station Santa Elisabetta. It's a 10-minute stroll; walk straight ahead along Gran Viale to reach the beach. **San Nicolò,** about 1.5km (1 mile) away, can be reached by bus B. You'll have to pay 1€ per person (standard procedure at Italy's beaches) for use of the cabins and umbrella rental. Alternatively, you can patronize the more crowded and noisier **public beach,** Zona A at the end of Gran Viale. Keep in mind that if you stay at any of the hotels on the Lido, most of them have some kind of agreement with the different *bagni* (beach establishments).

The Lido's limited sports amenities, such as golf and tennis, are affiliated with its deluxe five-star hotels. Although there is car traffic, the Lido's wide, shaded boulevards are your best bet for jogging while you're visiting Venice. A number of bike-rental places along the Gran Viale rent bicycles for 5€ to 10€ an hour. *Vaporetto* line nos. 1, 2, 51, 52, and LN cross the lagoon to the Lido from the San Zaccaria–Danieli stop near San Marco.

VENETO

5

For centuries the Venetian Republic ruled most of the northeastern region called Veneto, but many of those inland cities had been around for centuries when the city of Venice was officially founded with the election of its first doge in A.D. 726. As ancient Roman strongholds, these cities had already lived through a glorious period. Verona has even been called "Little Rome" for its wealth of Roman sites and magnificent ancient amphitheater.

Until Napoleon arrived in 1797—whereupon he donated Venice to Austria (where it would remain until 1866) and broke up the regional power structure—Veneto shared in the bounty of the Serene Republic, its countryside a mixture of vineyards, fields, and summer villas. Many of the Palladian villas that dot the hills of Veneto were extravagant second homes of wealthy Venetian merchants whose urban *palazzi* lined Venice's Grand Canal. Veneto also boasts buildings that show the Byzantine-Oriental influence so prominent in Venice's Gothic architecture, some adorned with frescoes by Giotto, and later by the Venetian masters Tiepolo, Veronese, Titian, and Tintoretto. Columns topped by the winged-lion mascot of St. Mark and representing the Serene Republic—a symbol of those distant, often glorious times—still stand in the main squares of Veneto's three great city centers: Padua, Vicenza, and Verona.

Indeed, the first architectural movement to sweep through the entire Western world has its roots in Veneto. The geometric and classical form of the

FACING PAGE: **Giotto's frescoes line the Cappella degli Scrovegni;** ABOVE: **Villa Malcontenta looks over the Brenta Canal.**

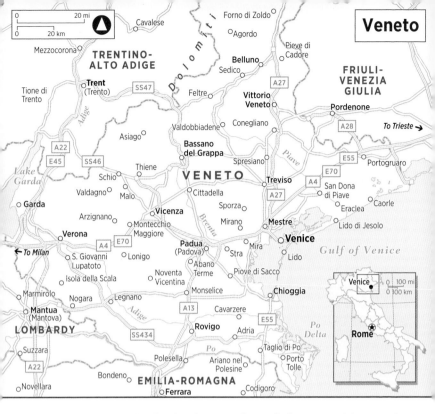

Veneto

High Renaissance that local architect Andrea Palladio practiced became the model for the rest of the world's Renaissance builders—from England's Inigo Jones to Thomas Jefferson's Monticello. Throughout Veneto you'll find a wealth of Venetian Renaissance *palazzi*, frescoed churches, and basilicas, which makes a tour through the region a rewarding and fascinating trip.

Veneto even had a hold on those who knew of its enchantments only from afar. Shakespeare may have never set foot in these parts, but "fair Verona" and the surrounding area so fascinated him that he chose to set some of his best works (*Romeo and Juliet, Two Gentlemen of Verona*) there.

Geographically, Veneto is a region of great diversity. It abuts the Adriatic Sea to the east and shares Lake Garda with Lombardy to the west. Its northern boundaries reach up to the pale, pink-tinged mountain range of the regal Dolomites that separate Italy from the Austrian Tyrol. The southern boundary is the mighty Po River, its relentlessly flat alluvial plains punctuated by the Berici Mountains south of Vicenza and the Euganean Hills near Padua. But Veneto is really defined by the valleys flowing down from the Dolomites and Alps in the north: The Adige, Brenta, Piave, and other rivers make fertile Veneto's middle hills, rich with the vineyards, fruit orchards, and small-scale farms that create the agricultural wealth that has been Veneto's sustenance.

Veneto's three major cities, **Padua, Vicenza,** and **Verona,** hold the most historical and artistic interest in the region, and they are all accessible by public transportation. Trains between these cities run on the Milan-Venice line and, hence, are inexpensive, frequent, and user-friendly. In fact, the distances between the cities are so small that you could very well stay put in Venice and tool into Verona—the most distant of the three—for an easy day trip. But this would be a great shame, as each of the cities warrants a slow exploration.

Enjoy Veneto in the late afternoon and early evening hours when the daytrippers have gone; sip an *aperitivo* or take a leisurely *passeggiata* along streets lined with tiny boutiques. End your day with a moderately priced meal of home-cooked regional specialties in a characteristic wine tavern amid much bonhomie and brio, followed by a good night's rest in a small, friendly hotel located just off the postcard-perfect main square.

Spend time in the region's lesser-explored cities and small towns such as **Treviso, Bassano del Grappa,** and **Asolo.** All offer a host of excursions into the real countryside, where you need only a car or the slightest sense of adventure to jump on a local bus and enjoy the back roads and backwaters of Veneto. Top it off with a leisurely cruise down the Brenta Canal to return to Venice.

PADUA (PADOVA)

42km (26 miles) W of Venice, 81km (50 miles) E of Verona, 32km (20 miles) E of Vicenza, 234km (145 miles) E of Milan

Padua (Padova) founded its university in 1222, and the city was long the academic heartbeat of the powerful Venetian Republic—and far before that, an ancient Roman stronghold—and for this reason one of the most important medieval and Renaissance cities in Italy. Dante and Copernicus studied here, and

Statues line the canal in Padua.

Petrarch and Galileo taught here. When you wander the narrow, cobbled, arcaded side streets in the timeless neighborhoods surrounding the "Bo" (named after a 15th-c. inn that once stood on the present-day site of the university), you will be transported back to those earlier times.

Padua is a vital city, with a young university population that gets about by bicycle and keeps the city's *piazze* and cafes alive. The historic hub of town still evokes the days when the city and its university flourished in the late Middle Ages and the Renaissance as a center of learning and art, although you'll have to visit during the scholastic year to witness it: Padua in summer is something of a ghost town.

Most visitors bypass Padua in their rush to Venice. During peak season, when Venice's hotels are full, some travelers stay here but see little except for the train station. You can spend a few hours or a few days in Padua, depending on your schedule. Its most important sights for those with limited time are

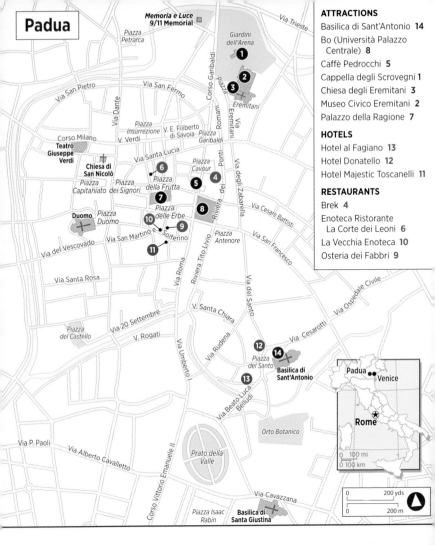

Padua

Memoria e Luce
9/11 Memorial

Piazza
Petrarca

Giardini
dell'Arena

Via Trieste

Corso Garibaldi

Via San Pietro

Via San Fermo

Eremitani

Via Dante

Piazza
Insurrezione
V. Verdi

V. E. Filiberto
di Savoia

Piazza
Garibaldi

Via degli Zabarella

Corso Milano

Teatro
Giuseppe
Verdi

Via Santa Lucia

Chiesa di
San Nicolò

Piazza
Cavour

Piazza
Capitaniato

Piazza
dei Signori

Piazza
della Frutta

Via Cesare Battisti

Duomo

Piazza
Duomo

Piazza
delle Erbe

Via San Martino

Solferino

Piazza
Antenore

Via San Francesco

Via del Vescovado

Via Roma

Riviera Tito Livio

Via Santa Rosa

Via Santa Chiara

Via del Santo

Via Ospedale Civile

Piazza
del Castello

Via 20 Settembre

V. Rogati

Via Umberto I

Via Rudena

Via Cesarotti

Piazza
del Santo

Basilica di
Sant'Antonio

Via P. Paoli

Via Alberto Cavalletto

Via Beato Luca Belludi

Orto Botanico

Prato della
Valle

Corso Vittorio Emanuele II

Via Cavazzana

Piazza Isaac
Rabin

Basilica di
Santa Giustina

Padua
Venice

Rome

0   100 mi
0   100 km

0   200 yds
0   200 m

Giotto's magnificent **frescoes** in the Scrovegni Chapel (fully restored between 1999 and 2001) and the revered pilgrimage site of the eight-domed **Basilica of Sant'Antonio di Padova,** whose important **equestrian statue** by Donatello stands in the piazza before it.

Festivals & Markets The beloved Sant'Antonio is celebrated with a **feast day** on June 13, when his relics are carried about town in an elaborate procession joined in by the thousands of pilgrims who come from all over the world.

The **outdoor markets** (Mon–Sat) in the twin Piazza delle Erbe (for fresh produce) and Piazza della Frutta (dry goods) that flank the enormous Palazzo della Ragione are some of Italy's best. The third Sunday of every month sees the area of the Prato della Valle inundated by more than 200 antiques and collectibles dealers, one of the largest **antiques and collectibles fairs** in the region. Only early birds will beat the large number of local dealers to the worm.

Antiques lovers with a car might want to visit Italy's second-largest **Mercato dell'Antiquariato** at the 18th-century Villa Contarini (in Piazzola sul Brenta, a lovely 30-min. drive that can be combined with visiting some of the other Palladian and Palladian-inspired country villas along the Brenta Canal; see "Day Trips from Padua," p. 192), held the last Sunday of every month. There, an estimated 350 vendors hawk their wares; the villa is open for visits during those hours.

Essentials

GETTING THERE By Train The main train station is at Piazza Stazione (✆ **049-875-1800;** www.ferroviedellostato.it), in the northern part of town, just outside the 16th-century walls. Padua is well connected by frequent train service to points directly west and east: Verona (1 hr.), Venice (30 min.), Vicenza (25 min.), and Milan (2½ hr.).

By Bus The main **APS bus station** is located east of the Scrovegni Chapel and the Arena Gardens area on Via Rismondo 28 ✆ **049-824-1111;** www.apsholding.it/mobilita). Frequent bus service to Venice and Verona costs approximately the same as train tickets, though tourists and locals alike seem to use this station principally for the smaller outlying cities such as Bassano del Grappa.

By Car Padua is located directly on the principal Autostrada A4 that links Venice with Milan. All the points of interest listed below are located in the city's historic center, which is closed to traffic. When booking at your hotel, ask about the closest parking lot. Hotels usually have an agreement with their neighborhood parking lot and pass those savings along to hotel guests.

5

VENETO

Padua (Padova)

Produce for sale in the Piazza delle Erbe.

VISITOR INFORMATION The **tourist office** is in the train station (✆ 049-875-2077; fax 049-875-5008; www.padovanet.it or www.turismopadova.it). April to October, it's open Monday to Saturday 9am to 7pm and Sunday 9am to noon; November to March, hours are Monday to Saturday 9:30am to 6pm and Sunday 9am to noon. From the train station, bus nos. 3 and 8 head downtown (as do nos. 12 and 18 Mon–Sat and no. 32 Sun). There's another **office** on Piazza del Santo (✆ 049-875-3087). It's open April to October 9am to 1:30pm and 3 to 6pm. A third office can be found behind the Caffè Pedrocchi (✆ 049-876-7927). You can also visit the **APT office** at Riviera Mugnai 8 (✆ 049-876-7911) for information.

> ## Cumulative Tickets
>
> If you plan on taking in all the sights of Padua during a short visit—or even if you plan on visiting the Scrovegni Chapel and only one other sight—a **PadovaCard** is a worthwhile investment. In addition to free use of the city's buses and free parking in some areas, the 15€ card gets you admission to the Cappella degli Scrovegni (you must call to make reservations), Musei Civici Eremitani, the Palazzo della Ragione, and other sites in Padua and the province as well as a seat in Caffè Pedrocchi. The card is valid for 48 hours and can be shared by both an adult and a child younger than 12. You'll find the card for sale at tourist offices and at sites at which you can use the card. A 72-hour card costs 20€. See www.padovacard.it.

CITY LAYOUT Pick up a map from the tourist office and plan your attack. The train station marks the city's northernmost point, and the Prato della Valle and Basilica di Sant'Antonio mark the southernmost. The following sites of interest can be organized into three clusters and are all within walking distance of one other: The Cappella degli Scrovegni (also called the Arena Chapel) and the adjacent Museo Civico are across a small piazza from the Eremitani Church; the Caffè Pedrocchi can be found near the Palazzo della Ragione in the Piazza Cavour area (the Piazza della Frutta sits to the north and Piazza delle Erbe just to the south of the *palazzo,* with the Piazza dei Signori bringing up the west); and the Basilica di Sant'Antonio caps the southern end of town, with the enormous Piazza Prato della Valle just beyond.

GETTING AROUND Hotels, restaurants, and major points of interest all fall inside the historic center and can be reached on foot. Public buses service many of the center's streets, which are otherwise limited to foot traffic (pick up a bus map from the tourist office). Single tickets cost 1€ and are valid for 75 minutes; a family ticket is 2€. March through October, a **sightseeing bus** runs about every hour, with a midday break (9:50 and 11am, noon, 2:45, 4, 5, and 6pm); it departs from in front of the Basilica di Sant'Antonio, costs 15€, and includes a small discount at museums. Look for the red double-decker buses.

What to See & Do

Basilica di Sant'Antonio ★★ This enormous basilica's imposing interior is richly decorated, filled with tombs, works of art, and inlaid checkerboard marble flooring. It's all there to honor one man, Padua's patron Saint Anthony. Simply and commonly referred to as "il Santo," Anthony was born in Lisbon in 1195

The interior courtyard of the Palazzo del Bo.

and died just outside of Padua in 1231. Work began on the church almost immediately but was not completed until 1307. Its eight domes bring to mind the Byzantine influence found in Venice's St. Mark's Basilica. A pair of octagonal, minaret-like bell towers enhances its Eastern appearance. Donatello's seven **bronze statues** and towering central *Crucifixion* (1444–48) that adorn the main altar are the basilica's artistic highlights. A series of nine bronze bas-reliefs of scenes from the saint's life are some of the finest works by 16th-century northern Italian sculptors.

The faithful could care less about the architecture and art; they flock here year-round to caress the **tomb ★** holding the saint's body (off the left aisle) and pray for his help in finding what they've lost. The tomb is always covered with flowers, photographs, and handwritten personal petitions left by devout pilgrims from every corner of the globe.

In his lifetime, St. Anthony was known for his eloquent preaching, so interpret as you will the saint's perfectly (some say miraculously) preserved **tongue, vocal chords,** and **jawbone** on display in the Cappella del Tesoro in the back of the church, directly behind the main altar. These treasured relics are carried through town in a traditional procession every June 13 to celebrate the feast day of il Santo. You'll also see one of his original tattered tunics dating from 1231.

In front of the basilica across the large piazza, standing out amid the smattering of stalls selling St. Anthony–emblazoned everything, is Donatello's famous *Gattamelata* **equestrian statue ★★**. The first of its size to be cast in Italy since Roman antiquity, it

The peaceful cloisters of the Basilica di Sant'Antonio.

is important for its detail, proportion, and powerful contrast between rider (the inconsequential Venetian condottiere Erasmo da Narni, nicknamed the "Spotted Cat") and horse. It was a seminal work that influenced Renaissance sculpture and casting and restored the lost art of equestrian statuary.

Piazza del Santo (east of Prato della Valle). ✆ **049-878-9722.** www.santantonio.org. Free admission. Summer daily 6:20am–7:45pm; winter daily 6:20am–7pm. Bus: 3, 8, 12, 18, 32, or 43.

Bo (Università Palazzo Centrale) Galileo's battered desk and podium, from which he taught from 1592 to 1610, are still on display in Italy's second-oldest university (after Bologna). His name joins a legendary honor roll of students and professors—Petrarch, Dante, the poet Tasso, and Copernicus—who came here from all over Europe. The University of Padua was founded in 1222 and grew to become one of the most famous and ambitious learning centers in Europe, reaching its zenith in the 16th and 17th centuries. Today a number of buildings are spread about town, but the Palazzo del Bo (named after the "Bo," or Ox, Inn—a favorite student hangout that stood on this spot in the 15th c.) is the university's main seat. The perfectly preserved **Teatro Anatomico ★**, where professors did autopsies on cadavers, gives a vivid picture of how students learned the intricacies of the human body centuries ago. Built in 1594, it was here that William Harvey most probably developed his theory of the circulation of blood while earning his degree in 1602.

Via VIII Febbraio (south of Piazza Cavour). ✆ **049-827-5111.** www.unipd.it. Admission 5€ adults, 2€ students, by guided tour only, some in English. Ask at tourist office for status of an ongoing renovation and visitor hours. Bus: 3, 8, 12, 16, 18, or 22.

Caffè Pedrocchi ★★ The Pedrocchi is a historic landmark, as beloved by the Padovans as "their" own St. Anthony (who actually hailed from Lisbon). When it first opened in 1831, it was the largest cafe in Europe. Famous literary and political characters and local luminaries made this their command post—French-born Henri Beyle, better known as Stendhal, had it in mind when he wrote, "The best Italian cafe is almost as good as the Parisian ones." Countless others were less reserved, calling it arguably the most beautiful coffeehouse in the world. Heavily damaged during World War II, it has been completely rebuilt in its original neoclassical, 19th-century stage-set splendor, and, after a laborious renovation it is again the social heartbeat of the city.

It has the nicest restrooms in town, for the use of cafe patrons. They're worth the cost of a coffee. In warm weather, Pedrocchi opens wide its doors (and, hence, its curious description as a "doorless cafe") onto the pedestrian piazza. As is always the case, drinks cost less when you're standing at the bar, but then you will have missed the *dolce far niente* (sweetness of doing nothing) experience for which Pedrocchi has always been known. A cappuccino, tea, beer, or glass of prosecco will cost 3€ at your table (half that price at the bar), and there is also a seasonally changing menu with excellent salads. Pedrocchi often hosts live music in the evenings.

Via VIII Febbraio 15 (at Piazza Cavour). ✆ **049-878-1231.** www.caffepedrocchi.it. AE, DC, MC, V. Historical salon upstairs: Daily 9:30am–12:30pm and 3:30–8pm. Bar: Sun–Wed 9am–9pm, Thurs–Sat 9am–midnight. Closed 2 weeks in mid-Aug. Bus: 3, 8, 12, 16, 18, or 22.

Cappella degli Scrovegni (Scrovegni Chapel or Arena Chapel) ★★★ This is the one uncontested must-see during your stay in Padua, so be prepared for lengthy lines in high season, a wait made even longer by the small numbers of

Examining the frescoes of the Scrovegni Chapel.

controlled groups (25 people maximum) allowed to enter the chapel at any one time. Scandalously brief 15-minute visits are the limit imposed during peak periods; check when buying your ticket so you can plan accordingly. Another 15 minutes are spent in a separate room beforehand, watching a mandatory but decent documentary on the frescoes, in order to give the air temperature in the chapel a chance to stabilize in between visits. Art lovers armed with binoculars behold the scene in awe—the recently renovated cycle of **vibrant frescoes** by Giotto that revolutionized 14th-century painting is considered among the most important art leading up to the Renaissance. While some experts have questioned whether the famed frescoes in Assisi are entirely by Giotto, here there is no equivocation: These are the master's works. Cobalt blue is the dominant color; the illustrations are like an easy-to-understand medieval comic-strip, but here they take on an unprecedented degree of realism and emotion.

This cycle is even larger, more complete, and better preserved than the famed St. Francis frescoes in Assisi. Giotto worked from 1303 to 1306 to completely cover the ceiling and walls with 38 scenes illustrating the lives of the Virgin and of Christ from floor to ceiling. With your back to the front door, the three bands that cover the walls are: top right, *Life of Joachim;* top left, *Life of the Virgin;* right center, *The Childhood of Christ;* left center, *Christ's Public Life;* right bottom, *The Passion of Christ* (the third panel of Judas kissing Christ is the best known of the entire cycle); left bottom, *Christ's Death and Resurrection.* Above the entrance is the fresco of the *Last Judgment:* Christ, as judge, sits in the center, surrounded by the angels and apostles. Below him, to the right, are the blessed, while to the left, Giotto created a terrible hell in which devils and humans are condemned to eternal punishment.

Note: If you want to be assured that you will have more time in the chapel, consider visiting between 7 and 9:30pm on the 11€ "Double Turn" ticket, which allows you 30 minutes in the chapel.

Piazza Eremitani 8 (off Corso Garibaldi). ☎ **049-201-0020** for required reservations (call-center lines open Mon–Fri 9am–7pm, Sat 9am–6pm). www.cappelladegliscrovegni.it. For reservations:

musei.comune@padovanet.it. Admission, which includes entrance to the Museo Civico Eremitani and others in the civic museum complex (see below) 13€ adults (includes a 1€ reservation fee), or only 8€ on Mon, as the Museo Eremitani is closed; 6€ ages 6–17; free for children 6 and under (although admission still requires a reservation); free with purchase of PadovaCard (see "Cumulative Tickets," above). Daily 9am–7pm (Mar–Nov until 10pm). Entrance through the Museo Eremitani. Bus: 3, 8, 10, 12, 32, or 42.

Chiesa degli Eremitani (Church of the Hermits) ★ Padua's worst tragedy was the complete destruction of this church by Allied bombs in 1944; some art historians consider it the country's greatest artistic wartime loss. It has been remarkably restored to its original early-13th-century Romanesque style, but the magnificent frescoes by the 23-year-old Andrea Mantegna could not be salvaged, except for a corner of the Ovetari Chapel. Here you'll find enough fragments left in the rubble of the frescoes he painted from 1454 to 1457 to understand the loss of what was considered one of the great artistic treasures of Italy. Mantegna was born in Padua (1431–1506) and studied under the Florentine master Donatello, who lived here while completing his commissions for the Basilica di Sant'Antonio, as well as the famous equestrian statue that now stands in the piazza before it. Classical music concerts occasionally are held in the church.

Piazza Eremitani (off Corso Garibaldi). ✆ **049-875-6410** or 049-876-1855. Free admission. Daily 8:30am–12:30pm and 4:30–7pm. Bus: 3, 8, 10, 12, 32, or 42.

Museo Civico Eremitani ★ These centuries-old cloisters that were once home to the monks (*eremitani* means "hermits") who officiated in the adjacent Scrovegni Chapel have been renovated to provide an airy display space as the city's civic museum. Its collection begins on the ground floor with the Archaeological Museum's division of Egyptian, Roman, and Etruscan artifacts. The upstairs collection represents an impressive panorama of minor works from major Venetian artists from the early 15th century to the 19th century: You'll find works by Titian, Tiepolo, and Tintoretto, whose *Crucifixion* is the museum's finest work. Special mention is given to Giotto's unusual wooden crucifix and Bellini's *Portrait of a Young Senator.*

Piazza Eremitani 8 (off Corso Garibaldi and adjacent to the Cappella Scrovegni). ✆ **049-820-4551** or 049-820-4551. http://padovacultura.padovanet.it/musei. Admission is a joint ticket with the Cappella Scrovegni 13€ adults, 8€ ages 6–17, free for children 6 and under (although admission to the Scrovegni Chapel still requires a reservation); free with purchase of PadovaCard (see "Cumulative Tickets," above). Tues–Sun 9am–7pm. Bus: 3, 8, 10, 11, 12, 32, or 42.

Palazzo della Ragione (Law Courts) ★ Located just south of the historic Caffè Pedrocchi, and a necessary destination for those meandering about the historic center of town, the picturesque open-air markets of **Piazza delle Erbe (Square of the Herbs)** ★★ and **Piazza della Frutta (Square of Fruit)** frame this massive 13th-century *palazzo* and have stood as the town's political and commercial nucleus for centuries.

Before being distracted by the color, smells, and cacophony of the sprawling outdoor fruit and vegetable market stalls, turn your attention to the magnificent Palazzo della Ragione, whose interior is as impressive as its exterior. Food shops by the dozen fill its ground floor, and stand-up bars and outdoor cafes make this lunchtime central. The two-story loggia-lined "Palace of Reason" is topped with a distinctive sloped roof that resembles the inverted hull of a ship, the largest of its kind in the world. It was built in 1219 as the seat of Padua's parliament and was used as an assembly hall, courthouse, and administrative center to celebrate Padua's newly won independence as a republican city. Considered a masterpiece of civil medieval architecture, it was heavily damaged by a fire in 1420 that destroyed, among other things, an elaborate cycle of frescoes by Giotto and his students that adorned **il Salone (the Great Hall).** The hall, 81m (266 ft.) long, was almost immediately rebuilt and today is the prime draw, for both its floor-to-ceiling 15th-century frescoes—commissioned immediately after the fire—and a large wooden sculpture of a horse attributed to Donatello (although many art historians don't agree). The 15th-century frescoes are similar in style and astrological theme to those that had been painted by Giotto, and comprise one of the very few complete zodiac cycles to survive until modern times. In 2011, the building was completely reopened to the public after a 10-year, 1-million-euro restoration.

On the far (west) side of the adjoining piazzas' canvas-topped stalls, flanking the Palazzo della Ragione, is the **Piazza dei Signori,** most noteworthy for the 15th-century clock tower that dominates it, the first of its kind in Italy.

Piazza delle Erbe/Piazza della Frutta. © **049-820-5006.** http://padovacultura.padovanet.it/musei. Admission to *palazzo* 4€ adults, 2€ children (8€ adults and 5€ children when there are exhibitions in the *palazzo*). Tues–Sun 9am–7pm (winter until 6pm). Bus: 3, 5, 6, 8, 9, 10, 11, 12, 13, 15, 18, 22, or 42.

Where to Stay

When making reservations, note that low season is considered December and January, and July and August. Inquire about discounts if you'll be in Padua at this time of year.

Hotel al Fagiano ★ Although small, this family-run hotel is a great value for your money. Located just a few steps off the expansive Piazza del Santo (its most appealing asset), it doesn't exactly ooze coziness and charm, but given the less-than-encouraging hotel situation in town, the Fagiano's clean, bright, eclectic rooms are still a standout choice. Bathrooms have been updated and include such niceties as hair dryers and bright lighting. Also, you rarely find air-conditioning and TVs at these rates. Don't confuse this Fagiano with the Hotel Buenos Aires, formerly known as the Fagiano and just a block away.

Via Locatelli 45 (west of Piazza del Santo), 35123 Padova. www.alfagiano.com. © **049-875-0073.** Fax 049-875-3396. 40 units. 90€ double. AE, DC, MC, V. Private parking 10€. From train station: Bus no. 8, 12, 18, or 22. Pets stay free. **Amenities:** Bar; bikes; concierge; Wi-Fi. *In room:* A/C, TV, hair dryer.

Hotel Donatello ★ This is a modern hotel in an old building, flush with amenities and enjoying a great location right at the Basilica di Sant'Antonio. More than half the rooms overlook the basilica, though those on the inner courtyard are quieter. Guest quarters vary as the owners slowly refresh and update a few each year. Some feature plush modular furnishings, some retro-Empire style. Some of the older bathrooms have tubs with hand-held shower nozzles, but most are modernized. Apartments sleeping three to four come with two bedrooms and a common bathroom.

Via del Santo 102–104, 35123 Padova. www.hoteldonatello.net. ✆ **049-875-0634.** Fax 049-875-0829. 44 units. 198€ double; 231€ triple; 312€ apt for 4. Breakfast 13€. AE, DC, MC, V. Free parking in garage by reservation. Small pets accepted. **Amenities:** International restaurant; bar; concierge; room service. *In room:* A/C, Satellite TV w/pay movies, minibar, safe.

Hotel Majestic Toscanelli ★★ A four-star hotel this nice would cost a great deal more in nearby Venice, which is why the Toscanelli often finds itself with guests who make this their home base while they visit neighboring cities and the surrounding area. The hotel has old-world charm, with rooms tastefully done in classic decor with coordinated pastel themes, burnished cherrywood furniture, and large, bright bathrooms with white ceramic and marble tiles. Off the lobby, a bright and attractive breakfast room serves a good buffet breakfast. This quiet, historic neighborhood, with porticoed alleyways lined with antiques shops and wine bars, is entirely closed to traffic. From here it's an easy walk to the Via Roma and the Piazza delle Erbe.

Via dell'Arco 2 (2 blocks west of Via Roma and south of the Piazza delle Erbe), 35122 Padova. www.toscanelli.com. ✆ **049-663-244.** Fax 049-876-0025. 34 units. 139€–192€ double; 169€–227€ junior suite; 189€–290€ suite. Rates include buffet breakfast. Rates discounted mid-July to Aug. AE, DC, MC, V. Valet garage parking 19€. Pets 10€. **Amenities:** Bar; babysitting; concierge; room service; on-site spa. *In room:* A/C, satellite TV, hair dryer, kitchenette (in 2 units), minibar, Wi-Fi.

Where to Eat

Brek ✦ CAFETERIA/ITALIAN Brek is self-service *all'italiana*, a homegrown northern Italian chain of upscale cafeterias that make concessions to the time-pressed modern world without sacrificing old-world quality. Put your language problems and calorie-counting aside and help yourself to pastas, made fresh while you wait, which are topped with your choice of sauce. It's buffet-style, and mostly priced by weight. There's a counter just for omelets made express, another for entrees and pizza. The dessert cart groans under an array of cheeses, fresh fruits, fruit salads, tarts, and cobblers. Join the thoroughly local eat-on-the-run lunch crowd from the university and surrounding shops, and save your day's budget for dinner.

Piazza Cavour 20. ✆ **049-875-3788.** www.brek.it. Reservations not accepted. Primi and pizza 5€–10€; secondi 5€–10€. AE, DC, MC, V. Daily 11:30am–3pm and 6:30–10pm.

Enoteca Ristorante La Corte dei Leoni ★ 🏛 PADOVAN/WINE BAR After a heady wander among the sights, sounds, and smells of Padua's open-air marketplace, head for a respite at this wine bar. A stylishly minimal decor in the cream-and-rose-petal interior is attractive, but the outdoor courtyard where centuries-old horse stables have been converted for modern-day grazers is the warm-weather draw—especially when the restaurant hosts its monthly jazz concerts in summer. Only a handful of dishes are offered—and the menu changes seasonally—but each is excellently prepared, such as *cavatelli* in a white ragú. Lunch is a fixed menu: 8.50€ for a first course (plus water and coffee), 9.50€ to substitute a second course, 11€ for both.

Via Pietro d'Abano 1 (on a side street just north of the Piazza della Frutta). ℰ **049-875-0083.** www.cortedeileoni.it. Reservations suggested. Lunch prices (fixed menu only): 8.50€–11€. Dinner prices: Primi 8€–10€; secondi 15€–20€. AE, DC, MC, V. Tues–Sun 11:30am–2:30pm; Tues–Sat 6:30pm–midnight. Closed 1 week in Aug and most of Jan.

La Vecchia Enoteca ★★ PADOVAN The sophistication of Veneto's prodigious viticulture is shown off here in an appropriately refined venue. Cozy, in a rustic and elegant kind of way, La Vecchia Enoteca is for that special evening of white linen and smooth service when you'd like the full-blown experience of Padovan cuisine and award-deserving wines. Prices are contained enough to encourage diners to leave caution at the door and indulge in a delicious menu and commendable selection of regional and Italian wines. The menu showcases the bounty-rich Veneto: The traditional polenta and risotto change with the season, as does the light, homemade gnocchi. Meat possibilities are numerous and tempting, while the influence of the Adriatic appears in such entrees as the favored *branzino in crosta di patate,* sea bass roasted in a light potato crust.

Via San Martino e Solferino 32 (just south of Piazza delle Erbe). ℰ **049-875-28-56.** Reservations recommended. Primi 12€–18€; secondi 20€–22€. MC, V. Tues–Sat 12:30–2:30pm; Mon–Sat 7:30–10:30pm. Closed 3 weeks in Aug.

Osteria Dei Fabbri ★ PADOVAN Simple, well-prepared food is the draw here. This rustic, old-fashioned *osteria* (tavern) is a lively spot where intellectual types share tables with Zegna-suited bankers, and students stop by for a tipple or to find a quiet corner in which to pore over the newspaper (a pastime not encouraged during hours when meals are served). There's always at least one homemade pasta choice to start with, and *osso buco,* the specialty of the house, is especially memorable when accompanied by any of the local (and excellent) Venetian wines available by the bottle or glass. The *seppia al nero* (squid in its own ink) served on polenta is faithful to its Veneto roots but maybe just a little too rich for the uninitiated. If you don't come here for dinner, consider stopping by for the *dopo cena* (after-dinner drink) to top off your day in Padua.

Via dei Fabbri 13 (on a side street south of Piazza delle Erbe). ℰ **049-650-336.** www.osteria deifabbri.it. Reservations recommended. Primi 8.50€–11€; secondi 12€–17€. AE, DC, MC, V. Mon–Sat 12:30–3pm and 7:30–10:30pm. Closed Dec 25–Jan 4.

Padua After Dark

The classical music season usually runs from October to April at different venues around town. The historic **Teatro Verdi,** at Via dei Livello 32 (ℰ **049-877-7011** or 049-877-70213; www.teatrostabileveneto.it), is the most impressive location. Programs are available at the tourist office. Look for posters advertising performances by the world-class Solisti Veneti, who are Padovans but spend most of the year traveling abroad.

As a university city, Padua has a large, very visible student population. You can network with the student crowd at any of the popular cafes along Via Cavour, or in the *osterie,* wine bars, and beer dives in the porticoed medieval side streets encircling the Palazzo della Ragione (the area around the Bo) and its bookend Piazza delle Erbe and Piazza della Frutta. In the summer, the toned-down nightlife is to be found mostly around Prato della Valle.

Day Trips from Padua

The **Colli Euganei (Euganean Hills)** are at the center of a small but renowned wine industry located southwest of Padua. You can pick up a *Strada dei Vini* wine route map from the tourist office. It also leads you to the small city of **Terme di Abano** (12km/7½ miles south of Padua), famous as a center for radioactive springs and mud treatments unique to this volcanic range.

THE FORGOTTEN RIVIERA: THE BRENTA CANAL

The navigable **Brenta Canal ★★** links Padua with Venice in the east. Ambitiously called "the Forgotten Riviera" because of the dozens of historic summertime villas built here by Venice's aristocracy and wealthy merchants, it can be visited by car or by boat—you can even stay in a few of the villas (see "Where to Stay on the Brenta," below). Only one was designed by 16th-century master architect Palladio (the Villa Foscari), but many are Palladian-inspired (see "Vicenza," p. 206, for background on Palladio and how to visit his villas). The best way to see the villas is on a cruise down the Brenta (see below). Call the **Brenta Canal tourist office** at ✆ **041-424-973** for more information.

More than 30 villas can be viewed from the boats (some just partially or at a great distance), but only three are visited. The important 18th-century **Villa Pisani ★★** (✆ **0425-920-016;** www.villapisani.com) in Stra was commissioned by the family of a Venetian doge and is famous for its ballroom frescoes by Tiepolo and its extensive gardens. The hedge maze here—something to engage youngsters bored with having to tour all these frescoed mansions—sprouts a tower at the center so that you can get a bird's-eye view of the trip back out; during the crowded summer season, a young man stands up here calling out instructions to maze-goers to hurry them along so the next group can get in. The villa is open Tuesday to Sunday 9am to noon and 1:30 to 6pm (Oct–Easter until 4pm only). Admission is 10€ for the villa, park and gardens. It's free for seniors older than 60 and children 18 and under.

The other two biggies are in Mira, and fair warning: Both keep erratic hours (see notes after each). The 18th-century **Villa Valmarana ★★** (✆ **044-321-803**) is dramatically set amid weeping willows; it's open Tuesday to Sunday (Dec–Feb open only on weekends) and costs 8€, free for children 12 and under. The **Villa Foscari** (also known as Villa Malcontenta, "The Unhappy Woman"; ✆ **041-547-0012** or 041-520-3966; www.lamalcontenta.com) is one of Palladio's finest works. It's open May to October Tuesday to Saturday 9am to noon and costs 10€.

TOURING THE CANAL There are a number of companies willing to take you up the river for anywhere between 50€ and 95€. The tourism office promotes two of them: **I Battelli del Brenta,** Via Porciglia 34 (✆ **049-876-0233;** fax 049-876-3410; www.battellidelbrenta.it), and **Delta Tour,** Via Toscana 2 (✆ **049-870-0232;** www.deltatour.it). Other companies come in and out of the market. For more info on plying the rivers, canals, and other watery byways of the region, check out the local river-craft consortium's website at www.padovanavigazione.it.

I Battelli del Brenta embarks in Padua from the Scalinata del Portello Wednesday, Friday, Saturday, and Sunday at 8:30am, arriving in Venice at 7pm; from Venice's Zattere ai Gesuati, they leave Tuesday, Thursday, and Saturday at 8:30am, finishing in Padua at 7pm. Full-day cruises cost about

85€, including lunch and entrance to all of the above-mentioned villas, while a half-day cruise, at 51€, includes a visit to the Villa Pasani.

Delta Tour greets passengers at the Villa Pisani Tuesday to Friday at 8:30am, visits each of the estates along with a tour guide, and finishes up at Fusina on the coast south of Venice. The 70€ fee includes a fish lunch, the tour guide's services, and entrance to the villas.

If you want to do the tour yourself, the largest concentration of country villas can be found between Stra and Mira. Bus schedules make that option nearly impossible, and a car tour does require some planning, as visiting hours and days differ from villa to villa and season to season. See the tourist office about a map.

WHERE TO STAY ON THE BRENTA

Villa Ducale ★★ This hotel occupies an 1884 villa built atop an older structure amid a lovely park of gravel paths, fountains, and flowering bushes under the shade of exotic palms, magnolias, and pines. Rooms feature marvelous inlaid wood floors, Persian rugs, and Murano chandeliers hanging from high, frescoed ceilings. Wrought-iron bedsteads are surrounded by (mostly) antiques, and the marble bathrooms feature antique brass fittings. "Standard" rooms are smaller (some almost cramped—but those cost less), with simpler parquet floors and smaller bathrooms. "King" rooms are larger and overlook the park from balconies or a small terrace. The breakfast room/restaurant is intimate—in fact, the Ducale has a generally classier setting in its public areas than the Margherita (see below), but the Margherita tends to have classier rooms.

Riviera Martiri della Libertà 75, 30031 Dolo (Venezia). www.villaducale.it. ℂ/fax **041-560-8020.** 11 units. 90€–180€ standard double; 125€–210€ "king" double with park view. Rates include breakfast. AE, DC, MC, V. Free parking. Pets 30€. **Amenities:** Seafood restaurant; bar; babysitting, bikes; concierge; Internet (8€ per hour); room service. *In room:* A/C, TV, hair dryer, minibar.

Villa Margherita ★★★ This 17th-century villa, expanded in the 19th century, once served as guest quarters for the noble Contarini family of Venice. Today it is run with refined gusto by the Dal Corso family, who provide fresh fruit and flowers in your room and a highly polished professional courtesy. All rooms overlook the large, pine-shaded lawn and are soundproofed against the noise of passing cars. "Standard" rooms, on the smaller side of medium size, have rugs scattered over wood floors. "Deluxe" rooms are larger (except for no. 218, which is a cozy lovers' nook with a spacious terrace), with more interesting antiques and richer fabrics, and are more frequently blessed with balconies. "Junior suites" are larger still and feature double sinks. The salons downstairs are appropriately furnished in the manner of a rich country villa, with chessboards fronting fireplaces and plush armchairs.

The Dal Corsos also run Brenta hotel in Mira, about 5

○ A Perfect Picnic Spot

The secondary road S11 runs alongside the canal in spots; it departs from the canal here and there but remains the best roadway for viewing the villas as it skirts the little canal-side villages. If you take a right-branching street through any of the towns, you'll come upon grassy verges leading down to the water—a perfect spot for a picnic (though you might want to bring bug repellent).

minutes away. **Villa Franceschi** (Via Don Minzoni 28, Mira Porte, Venezia; ✆ **041-426-6531;** fax 041-560-8996; www.villafranceschi.com), in the late-16th-century Villa Palladiana, features 33 guest rooms (mostly junior suites), lush gardens, a swimming pool, and an on-site restaurant. Superior doubles run 280€ to 320€, and junior suites cost 390€.

Via Nazionale 416–417 (on the Venice side of Mira), 30034 Mira (Venezia). www.villa-margherita. com. ✆/fax **041-426-5838.** 19 units. 220€ standard double; 240€ deluxe double; 258€ junior suite. Rates often discounted off season and in slower periods. Rates include breakfast. AE, DC, MC, V. Parking free. Public bus stop with half-hourly service to Venice, 15km (9¼ miles) away, is a 5-min. walk. **Amenities:** Frescoed Venetian/fish restaurant across the street; bar; bikes; concierge; room service; smoke-free rooms. *In room:* A/C, TV, hair dryer, minibar.

TREVISO

25km (16 miles) N of Mestre/Venice, 50km (31 miles) NE of Padua

Treviso is a bustling, prosperous small city and center in northern Veneto. It seems to have changed little from its early days as a medieval market town and staunch ally to Venice. Much of the city had to be rebuilt after severe World War II damage, but it was done well. Treviso's medieval *palazzi* and houses with painted facades, churches frescoed by Giotto's follower Tomaso da Modena (1325–79), and pleasant streets cut across by pretty canals together make for a lovely, genuine-Italy break from the tourist beat of Padua-Vicenza-Verona.

Festivals & Markets Treviso leads up to the **Feast of the Assumption** with a week of street theater, dance, music competitions, and other performances (Aug 6–14). The daily **fish market ★★**, on the islets in the Cagnan canal, is a picturesque slice of old Treviso (mornings are best). Treviso hosts an **antiques fair** the fourth Sunday of each month (except July) on Borgo Cavour (✆ **0422-419-195**).

Enjoying a *caffè* in the Piazza dei Signori.

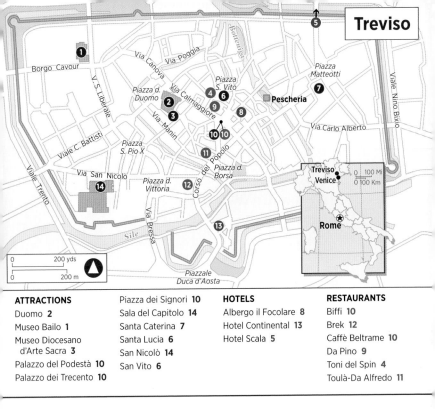

Treviso

ATTRACTIONS		HOTELS	RESTAURANTS
Duomo **2**	Piazza dei Signori **10**	Albergo il Focolare **8**	Biffi **10**
Museo Bailo **1**	Sala del Capitolo **14**	Hotel Continental **13**	Brek **12**
Museo Diocesano	Santa Caterina **7**	Hotel Scala **5**	Caffè Beltrame **10**
d'Arte Sacra **3**	Santa Lucia **6**		Da Pino **9**
Palazzo del Podestà **10**	San Nicolò **14**		Toni del Spin **4**
Palazzo dei Trecento **10**	San Vito **6**		Toulà-Da Alfredo **11**

Essentials

GETTING THERE By Train There are trains two to four times an hour from Venice (25–35 min.). Fifteen runs daily (10 on Sun) come from Vicenza (40–80 min.).

   By Bus Ten buses (☎ **0422-577-311**) run daily from Asolo (55 min.).

   By Car From Venice, the quick way is Autostrada A27 to the Treviso Sud exit, but the more direct route is the SS13 (though that can be slow going at rush hour and midday). From Padua, take Autostrada A4 past Venice to the A27. When booking at your hotel, ask about the closest parking lot.

VISITOR INFORMATION The **tourist office** is just behind the main Piazza dei Signori at Piazza Monte di Pietà 8 (☎ **0422-547-632;** fax 0422-419-092; www.provincia.treviso.it) and is open daily from 9am to 12:30pm, plus Tuesday to Friday 2:30 to 6:30pm and Saturday and Sunday 3:30 to 6pm. There's also a provincial **tourist office** at Via Turazza 7a (☎ **0422-541-052;** fax 0422-540-366; www.trevisotour.org), though it's mostly administrative.

What to See & Do

The center of town is **Piazza dei Signori,** lined with arcades that run under the retro-medieval **Palazzo del Podestà,** rebuilt in the 1870s with a tall clock tower, and spread into a loggia under the 13th-century brick council hall **Palazzo dei Trecento.**

The green copper domes of Treviso's Duomo.

Just beyond this square, on Piazza San Vito, sits a pair of medieval churches: **Santa Lucia,** with Tomaso da Modena frescoes in the first alcove on the right, and **San Vito,** with its rather faded Byzantine-style frescoes from the 12th or 13th century. Both are open daily 9am to noon and 4 to 6pm.

The overbearing facade of the **Duomo ★** is from 1836, but it's flanked by Romanesque lions that, coupled with the seven green copper domes, speak to the cathedral's 12th-century origins in the Venetian-Byzantine style. The second pilaster features a late-1400s relief of the *Visitation,* by Lorenzo Bregno. The chapel altarpiece at the end of the right aisle is an unusually bright and open *Annunciation,* by Titian (chapel founder Broccardo Malchiostro was painted in later, crouching behind the classical building to peep at the scene). The crypt contains a forest of columns and fragments of 14th-century frescoes and mosaics. It's open Monday to Saturday 7:30am to noon and 3:30 to 7pm, Sunday 7:30am to 1pm and 3:30 to 8pm.

Via Canoniche, next to the cathedral, runs past an ancient paleo-Christian mosaic of the 4th century to a Gothic priory housing the **Museo Diocesano d'Arte Sacra** (✆ **0422-416-707**). Inside are 13th-century frescoes, a Tomaso da Modena that used to decorate the bishop's palace, and plenty of medieval sculpture along with vestments and holy silverware—though frankly, if admission wasn't free, it wouldn't be worth it. It's open Monday to Thursday 9am to noon, Saturday 9am to noon and 3 to 6pm.

More interesting is the **Museo Bailo,** Borgo Cavour 24 (✆ **0422-580-567**), previously the Museo Civico, which holds the civic museum's remarkable collection of ancient bronze relics—including swords and ritualistic disks from the 5th century B.C., alongside Roman remains—as well as the city's collection of lesser-known works by the likes of Titian, Tiepolo, and Tintoretto. On the other side of town, across the wide Cagnan canals, whose islands host a daily fish market (see above), stands a (deconsecrated) church that's now well worth seeking out. The highlight of **Santa Caterina** (✆ **0422-591-337**) is its frescoes by Tomaso da Modena, including a Madonna and (detached from a now-destroyed church and kept here) a series on the life of St. Ursula. Admission is 3€ for adults, 2€ for students, and 1€ for kids under 10; it's open every Tuesday to Sunday from 9am to 12:30pm and 2:30 to 6pm.

Down in the southwest corner of town, the big brick 13th- to 14th-century Dominican church of **San Nicolò** ★ houses some good Gothic frescoes. Tomaso da Modena decorated the huge round columns with a series of saints; Antonio da Treviso did the absolutely gargantuan St. Christopher—his .9m-long (3-ft.) feet strolling over biting fish—in 1410. On the right side of the apse, the tomb of Agostino d'Onigo from 1500 has courtly *Pages* frescoed by Lorenzo Lotto, who also did the altarpiece of the *Incredulity of St. Thomas with Apostles* in the chapel right of the altar. The late-14th-century Sienese School frescoes lining the walls include an *Adoration of the Magi,* complete with camels. San Nicolò is open daily 8am to 12:30pm and 3:30 to 7pm. Next door to the (unused) front door of the church is the entrance to the adjoining seminary's **Sala del Capitolo,** Piazzetta Benedetto XI 2 (✆ **0422-3247**), frescoed in 1352 by Tomaso da Modena with 40 Dominicans busily studying and copying out manuscripts at their desks. It's open daily 8am to 6pm; admission is free (ring the bell if the door is shut).

Where to Stay

Treviso doesn't have much of a hotel industry. If the places below are full, consider a lovely option about a 10-minute drive north of the town walls: the **Hotel Scala** ★, Viale Felissent (✆ **0422-307-600;** fax 0422-305-048; www.hotelscala.it), a suburban villa with 20 comfortable bedrooms—all with air-conditioning, TV, telephone, and minibar—and a good restaurant. Doubles go for 85€ to 95€, including breakfast.

Albergo il Focolare ★ This simple hotel sits smack in the center of town, on a little street off the main drag a half-block from the Palazzo Podestà. Three of the largest rooms come with three beds: No. 29 has a small sitting area, no. 30 sits in the narrow end of the buildings with windows on three sides overlooking a canal, and the similar no. 34 lies directly above no. 30 on the top floor, so its windows have views over two canals. This won't be the quietest place you'll ever sleep, but it's clean.

Piazza Ancilotto 4, 31100 Treviso. www.albergoilfocolare.net. ✆/fax **0422-56-601.** 14 units. 100€–120€ double. Breakfast included. Pets allowed. AE, DC, MC, V. **Amenities:** Room service. *In room:* A/C, TV, hair dryer.

Hotel Continental The Continental is a large, well-worn hotel 3 blocks from the train station at the city walls, a 10-minute walk from the central piazza. The modular furnishings are a bit faded, but there are parquet floors and some nice old touches such as ornate wood entablatures, chandeliers, or mirrored closet doors silk-screened with Oriental prints. A few rooms have small vestibule sitting areas, and corner units are larger and tend to be more nicely furnished. There is, however, a bit of street noise from the busy road below, and while some bathrooms are new, others are aging, and many have shower nozzles you have to hold and no shower curtains.

Via Roma 16, 31100 Treviso. ✆ **0422-411-216.** Fax 0422-55-054. 80 units. 90€–205€ double; 115€–256€ triple. Rates include breakfast. AE, DC, MC, V. Parking 15€. Pets allowed. **Amenities:** Nearby restaurant; bar; babysitting; concierge; room service. *In room:* A/C, TV, hair dryer.

Where to Eat

In addition to the choices below, you can get classy, made-to-order cafeteria fare at the Treviso branch of the excellent **Brek** chain, Corso del Popolo 25 (✆**0422-590-012**), open daily. For pizza and people-watching, **Da Pino,** Piazza dei Signori 23 (✆**0422-56-426**), has tables set under the high, wood-coffered arcade of the main square; it's closed Tuesday.

○ Cappuccino on the Piazza

Of the two spots for drinks and snacks at tables set under the loggia overlooking the main Piazza dei Signori, **Caffè Beltrame**, no. 27 (✆ **0422-540-789**), has a better position at the corner of the loggia, while **Biffi**, no. 28 (✆ **0422-540-784**), serves better beer and sandwiches.

Toni del Spin ★★ 🛎 VENETIAN Blackboards with the daily list of dishes hang from the rough crossbeams beneath high, sloping wood ceilings of this legendary eatery. The kitchen prepares a carefully considered mix of simple but intriguing dishes such as *gazbacho andaluz* (cold tomato vegetable soup), *coniglio alle olive* (rabbit with olives), and of course, the ubiquitous *fegato alla veneziana* (Venetian-style liver). The house wine is good, and they charge decent prices on a select list of regional bottles—they even run a wine shop across the street.

Via Inferiore 7. (✆ **0422-543-829**. www.ristorantetonidelspin.com. Reservations not necessary. Primi 6€–8€; secondi 8€–14€. AE, MC, V. Tues–Sat 12:30–2:30pm; Mon–Sat 7:30–10:30pm. Closed 3 weeks in July and 1 week in Aug.

Toulà-Da Alfredo ★ NORTHERN ITALIAN/TREVISANO This chain of up-market northern-cuisine restaurants, founded at the ski resort of Cortina about 2 hours north of Treviso in the Dolomites, is set in a modern series of rooms with odd murals and a ceiling *trompe l'oeil* frescoed with vines. The cuisine is refined yet traditional, and extremely pricey. The specialties often revolve around Treviso's signature roughage: a classic risotto with radicchio, for example, braised radicchio or a radicchio *crespella* pastry.

Via Collalto 26. (✆ **0422-540-275**. www.toula.it. Reservations recommended. Primi 11€–26€; secondi 21€–34€. AE, DC, MC, V. Tues–Sun 12:30–2:30pm; Tues–Sat 7:30–11pm. Closed Aug 2–25. Bus: 1 or 7.

ASOLO

73km (45 miles) N of Padua, 52km (32 miles) NE of Treviso, 16km (10 miles) E of Bassano del Grappa

Known as the "Town of a Hundred Horizons" because of its panoramic views, this nub of a medieval hill town (though it was founded during the twilight of Imperial Rome) has become the secret hideaway for true Veneto aficionados. It's a required stop for folks interested in meandering the backcountry or driving the wine roads, and it's a great place for those on bike tours to take a midday break.

Asolo was the Renaissance-era home of Caterina Cornaro of Venice, who was awarded the realm of Asolo for her help in (unsuccessfully) keeping the Turks out of Cyprus. Much of the 15th-century charm you see today is a result of her 12-year presence and patronage in the town. Other VIP residents were the English poet Robert Browning and Italy's early-20th-century grande dame of the stage, Eleonora Duse.

The panoramic view of and from Asolo.

Festivals & Markets There's an **antiques market** the second Sunday of each month, with a special books and prints edition the third Sunday in October. The local **folk festival** is in honor of San Gottardo on May 5, with a market, procession, and the sale of traditional terra-cotta shepherd flutes. Asolo holds a **Palio race** the third Sunday of September, pitting the town's six *contrade* (neighborhoods) against each other to pull up the hill a Roman-style chariot bearing a local damsel dressed as Caterina Cornaro. There's also a **Festival of Chamber Music** in August and September.

Essentials

GETTING THERE By Train Because the nearest train station is in Cornuda, a 17-minute bus ride away, buses are a better bet. There are a dozen trains into Cornuda daily from Padua (40–60 min.). From Treviso there are only three direct trains (30 min.), at 8:23am, 12:33pm, and 5:28pm, but you can get one of 20 or so daily trains to Montebelluno (20–30 min.) and change to one of 14 trains on to Cornuda (a bit over 10 min.), though the wait may be anywhere from a few minutes to over an hour.

    By Bus A dozen **buses** (✆ 0423-493-464) run daily from Bassano del Grappa (25 min.), and about 10 daily from Treviso (✆ 0422-577-311; 55 min.). Buses stop at Asolo's Ca' Vescovo station on the main highway down in the valley, from which frequent shuttles climb the long hill into the Old Town.

    By Car From Padua, take SS47 north to Bassano di Grappa, and then drive east to Asolo on SS248. From Treviso, take the SS348 to Montebelluno, and then the SS248 west.

VISITOR INFORMATION The genuinely helpful **tourist office** is at Piazza Garibaldi 73 (✆ 0423-529-046; fax 0423-524-137). Another can be found at Piazza Gabrielle d'Annunzio 3 (✆ 0423-55-045; www.asolo.it or www. comune.asolo.tv.it; hours vary, so call ahead).

What to See & Do

Though the area's top sight is the **Villa Barbaro,** outside town (see below), Asolo has a few diversions beyond merely strolling its streets and enjoying its "hundred horizons." Asolo was the seat of a bishopric until 969 and remained a countryside escape for rich Venetians thereafter, so it's no surprise that its cathedral, rebuilt in the 18th century, contains several artistic treasures. They apparently had a thing for paintings of the Assumption. There's one by Lorenzo Lotto (1506; on the left aisle), another by Jacopo "da Ponte" Bassano (1549; next to the last on the left aisle), and a bad 19th-century copy of a Titian version on the high altar. Breaking the theme is Lazzaro Bastiani's stiffly formal *St. Jerome* (1488), which features a pretty countryside in the background.

On the main square, the frescoed **Loggia del Capitano** houses a small museum that contains memorials to Robert Browning (whose son is buried in the local cemetery) and to Caterina Cornaro. Caterina was the queen of Cyprus until her husband died and she abdicated. She sought refuge in the Republic of Venice, which gave her Asolo to rule from 1489 to her death in 1510. Her home was the medieval **Castello,** begun in the late 6th century (there's nothing special to see there now; it just has a cafe tucked against the inside of the old castle's towering wall), which became known as the "Queen's Palace."

Where to Stay

Hotel Duse ✦ The Hotel Duse, named for Italian actress Eleonora Duse, offers a perfect location at decent prices. This small, relatively inexpensive (for Asolo) hotel occupies a 16th-century house right on the corner of the main square. The rooms are tight but nicely furnished with a few art prints on the walls. Top-floor rooms have sloping plank ceilings and a cozy feel.

Via R. Browning 190, 31011 Asolo. www.hotelduse.com. ✆ **0423-55-241.** 14 units. 100€–120€ double; 120€–140€ junior suite. Extra bed 26€. Breakfast 8€. MC, V. Nearby parking 4€. **Amenities:** Golf (nearby); room service. *In room:* A/C, TV, Internet.

Hotel Villa Cipriani ★★ One of the town's beautiful 16th-century villas, once owned by Robert and Elizabeth Barrett Browning, was turned into the area's most sought-after deluxe hotel in 1962 by Giuseppe Cipriani (owner of Venice's Harry's Bar). It retains that private villa feel; its main building wraps around a lovely garden centered on a rose-trimmed well, with an 11-room annex and views spilling down a terraced park and slopes of olive trees. "Superior" rooms—with worn Oriental carpets on parquet floors; stylish, subdued furnishings; and hand-painted Vietri tiles in the bathrooms—are slightly smaller than "Deluxe" accommodations, which often feature beam ceilings, brass chandeliers, painted antiques mixed with discreetly modern TV chests, and a small sitting area of overstuffed easy chairs. Room nos. 101 and 102 enjoy large private terraces with valley views.

Via Canova 298. www.villaciprianiasolo. com. ✆ **0423-523-411.** Fax 0423-952-095. 31 units. 319€ double; 379€ superior double; 438€ deluxe double. Extra bed

Impressions

I assure you that, even though I have knowledge of and have seen with my own eyes the most beautiful panoramas in Italy and elsewhere, I have found nothing quite like the view one can enjoy from the tower of the Queen's Palace.

—**Robert Browning**

The Palladian Villa Barbaro.

80€. Continental breakfast 20€; buffet breakfast 35€. AE, DC, MC, V. Parking 17€. **Amenities:** Restaurant; elegant bar; babysitting; bikes; concierge; exercise room; golf (nearby); room service; Wi-Fi. *In room:* A/C, TV, hair dryer, minibar.

Where to Eat

Hosteria Ca' Derton ★★ VENETIAN This haven of fine dining sits in a 17th-century *palazzo* on a quiet *piazzetta* just off the busy main square. The menu changes with the season and gives a nod to local culinary traditions and the freshest of ingredients to create such dishes as *bigoli al torchio con ragù d'anatra* (fat strands of handmade spaghetti in a duck ragù), *lasagnetta con zucchine e gamberoni* (delicate pasta casserole with zucchini and jumbo shrimp), or simple *tagliata di manzo* (steak perfumed with rosemary). The location is more than easy on the eyes, if the bill is a little tough on the wallet.

Piazza d'Annunzio 11. *☎* **0423-529-648.** Reservations recommended. Primi 6€–9€; secondi 13€–18€. AE, DC, MC, V. Tues–Sun 12:30–2pm; Tues–Sat 7:30–9:45pm.

A Villa Outside Town

The **Villa Barbaro** ★★ (*☎* **0423-923-004;** www.villadimaser.it), also called Villa di Maser, is one of Palladio's most celebrated. It lies down in the valley, east of Asolo outside the hamlet of Maser. Probably the most famous of the Palladian villas (after Vicenza's Villa Rotonda), not to mention one of the most beautiful, the 1560 Barbaro is a standout for its gorgeous frescoes by Veronese (which La Rotonda lacks). It's privately owned by some very, very lucky folks who make you wear giant slippers to shuffle around and admire the frescoes on the ground floor. The hours change almost monthly: March, July, and August, it's open Tuesday, Thursday, and Saturday 10am to 6pm and Sunday 11am–6pm;

> ## A Glass of Wine
>
> The best place in town to duck in for a glass of wine with the locals is **Antica Osteria Al Bacaro,** Via R. Browning 165 (*☎* **0423-55-150**), where townsfolk have gathered since 1892. Enjoy the breathtaking views from the lovely terrace bar for the cost of an iced tea or cocktail.

April, May, June, September, and October, add Wednesday and Friday 10am to 6pm; November to February, Saturday and Sunday 2:30 to 5pm; closed December 24 to January 6. Admission is 6€.

At least 10 to 15 daily **buses** (✆ **0422-577-311**) between Bassano (30 min.) and Treviso (50 min.), with stops at Asolo (15–20 min.), also stop in Maser. If you're coming by car from Asolo, drive down to the main road and turn left; turn left again when you see a pretty church squatting in the middle of the road.

BASSANO DEL GRAPPA

35km (22 miles) NE of Vicenza, 43km (27 miles) N of Padua, 16km (10 miles) W of Asolo, 47km (29 miles) W of Treviso

This picturesque town on the Brenta River is renowned for its centuries-old production of handcrafted ceramics and of grappa, Italy's national firewater of choice (see box below). Its Palladian covered wooden bridge is a highlight of the small *centro storico*. The city's arcaded homes, whose facades are painted in the traditional manner, and small squares make this a lovely break from the larger towns described in this chapter.

Festivals In June, Bassano invites **international street musicians** to perform in a festival. Bassano's annual **Opera Estate Festival ★** takes place from early July through August, with alfresco performances of opera, concerts, a mini–jazz fest, and dance (ballet, modern, and folk). For information, contact the tourist office (Largo Corona d'Italia 35; ✆ **0424-524-214;** fax 0424-525-138; www. comune.bassano.vi.it).

Essentials

GETTING THERE By Bus To get here from Vicenza, you can take one of two dozen daily **FTV buses** (✆ **0424-30-850;** www.ftv.vi.it) that make the 1-hour trip. Frequent buses from Padua take half the time, making fewer stops. There are also a dozen **buses** (✆ **0423-493-464** or 0423-529-966) daily from nearby Asolo (25 min.).

By Car From Asolo, head west on the SS248; from Vicenza, north on the SS248; from Padua, north on the SS47. From Treviso, the more scenic route follows the SS348 northwest to Montebelluno, where you pick up the smaller SS248 west; the faster route is west along the SS53 toward Vicenza, turning north onto the SS47 at Cittadella.

VISITOR INFORMATION For information, call the **tourist office,** Lgo. Corona d'Italia 35 (✆ **0424-524-351;** fax 0424-525-301; www.comune.bassano. vi.it). It's open daily from 9am to 1pm and Monday to Saturday from 2 to 6pm.

What to See & Do

Bassano's historic center is just a half-dozen or so blocks in either direction; its medieval buildings and baroque *palazzi* snuggle along the Brenta River. Andrea Palladio designed Bassano's lovely symbol, the wooden **Ponte degli Alpini ★★** covered bridge, in 1569, and every time floods or disaster have struck, it has been rebuilt precisely along the original plan.

The stars of the **Museo Civico ★**, Piazza Garibaldi (✆ **0424-522-235** or 0424-523-336), are the Bassano family. Patriarch Jacopo was clearly the most talented, evident in his early *Flight into Egypt* and faded frescoes from local house facades to later works such as *St. John the Baptist* (1558) and *Pentecost* (1559), which are looser and show the influence of Titian. His sons Leandro and Francesco il Giovane (responsible for the nice *Lamentation*) had less success, as did their less talented sibling, Gerolano, who stayed in Bassano to run the family workshop. Admission—which also covers the ceramics museum (see below)—is 9€ for adults and 7€ for children 18 and under or seniors 60 and older. It's open Tuesday to Saturday from 9:30am to 6:30pm and Sunday from 3:30 to 6:30pm.

Palazzo Sturm (1765–66), overlooking the Brenta River on Via Schiavonetti, retains some original frescoes and stuccoes, and houses a ceramics museum heavy on 18th- and 19th-century porcelains, with a contemporary collection downstairs. Admission is 4€ adults, 3€ children, or else on the cumulative ticket with the Museo Civico, above. Its hours are also the same.

Where to Stay

Bonotto Hotel Belvedere ★ It looks modern out front, but this has been Bassano's premier hotel since the 15th century. The Belvedere sits on the busy main road skirting the walls of the historic center, 4 blocks from the central Piazza Garibaldi, but the windows' double set of double panes cuts out most noise. Standard rooms in the 1985 wing have modular '80s-style units in baby blue or wood veneer and mirrors to make the midsize rooms feel larger. Superior accommodations are larger, with sturdy dark-wood furnishings and Jacuzzi tubs. Junior suites are spruced up with 17th- and 18th-century Venetian-style antiques and double sinks, though some are done in a modern but still classy style, with embroidered sofas. There's an excellent restaurant on site as well.

Should the Belvedere be full, they may put you up in their modern, 66-room **Hotel Palladio,** around the corner at Via Gramsci 2 (🕾**0424-523-777;** fax 0424-524-050). There, a double runs from 138€ to 160€.

Bassano del Grappa overlooks the Brenta Canal.

Piazzale Giardino 14, 36061 Bassano del Grappa (VI). www.bonotto.it. ✆ **0424-529-845.** Fax 0424-529-849. 87 units. 180€ standard ("Silver") double; 212€ superior ("Gold") double; 280€ junior suite. Rates include breakfast. AE, DC, MC, V. Parking 10€ in garage. **Amenities:** Restaurant; bar; babysitting; free bikes; concierge; exercise room and sauna at sister Hotel Palladio around the corner; discount at golf course in nearby Asolo; room service. *In room:* A/C, TV w/pay movies, hair dryer, Internet, minibar.

Hotel Al Castello ★ ✦ This is the best semibudget option in town, its rooms situated above a neighborhood bar in a goldenrod building against a tower of the half-ruined castle, just 3 blocks from the Ponte degli Alpini. Accommodations are medium to largish, with wood floors, box showers, thick beams, and a touch of class in the wood furnishings. Among the thoughtful touches are heated towel racks in the freshly tiled bathrooms. Room no. 10 is the best, with a small flower-bedecked balcony.

Piazza Terraglio 19, 36061 Bassano del Grappa (VI). www.hotelalcastello.it. ✆/fax **0424-228-665.** 11 units. 40€–60€ single; 70€–100€ double. Breakfast 6€. AE, DC, MC, V. Free parking. **Amenities:** Bar. *In room:* A/C, TV.

Villa Palma ★★ 🏨 Don't be put off by the industrial zone you drive through to get to this 1680 countryside villa 5km (3 miles) outside Bassano. Once inside the gates, it's a quiet walled retreat of birdsong, manicured garden lawns, and pine trees onto which the marble-floor bar opens. Regular rooms are midsize with rattan furnishings, chipped stone floors, thick carpets, and doubled sinks (in most). Junior suites are larger, with elegant period-style furnishings, silk wall coverings, and Murano chandeliers. The most requested suite, no. 39, has a Jacuzzi; no. 53 lacks the Jacuzzi but enjoys long garden vistas. Even singles come with extra-wide *francesina* beds.

Via Chemin Palma 30, 36065 Mussolente (5km/3 miles from Bassano off the road to Asolo/Montebelluno). ✆ **0424-577-407.** Fax 0424-87-687. 21 units. 100€ double; 180€ junior suite. Rates include breakfast. AE, DC, MC, V. Free parking. **Amenities:** Elegant Veneto restaurant; bar; concierge; heated indoor pool at nearby sports center; room service. *In room:* A/C, TV, hair dryer, minibar, Wi-Fi.

Where to Eat

Bassano has long been known for its white asparagus, green peas, and blend of Venetian and mountain cuisines. Unfortunately, few of Bassano's current crop of restaurants live up to its traditions. Along with the excellent restaurant at Bonotto Hotel Belvedere (see above), here are the best of what you will find.

Al Sole VENETIAN This is one of the more refined restaurants in town, serving elegant dishes of seasonal fresh ingredients such as *bigoli al sugo d'anatra* (thick homemade pasta in a duck ragù), *risotto agli asparagi bianchi* (risotto with the tender local white asparagus), or *baccalà con polenta* (salt cod served with creamy polenta). Your best luck with asparagus dishes will be in the spring while it's still in season.

Via Vittorelli 41–43. ✆ **0424-523-206.** Reservations recommended. Primi 6.50€–10€; secondi 10€–17€. AE, DC, MC, V. Tues–Sun noon–2:30pm and 7:30–10pm.

Birreria Ottone ★ AUSTRIAN/ITALIAN This popular 1870 beer hall inhabits a 13th-century *palazzo,* which lent its stone walls to the elegant dining room. Bassano friends and families gather here sometimes just to drink in good company, sometimes for a full meal of grub that runs the gamut from traditional Italian

ITALIAN firewater

As best as we can figure, **grappa** was invented by 11th-century Italian monks fiddling with the leftovers of the winemaking process: grape pulp, seeds, stems, and juices. Distilled and purified, the resulting after-dinner liqueur can range from clear to amber (which is usually aged), *morbido* ("soft" and smooth) to *duro* ("hard" and quite harsh to the uninitiated).

This Italian firewater was long known as *aqua vitae,* the "water of life," for its purported medicinal and restorative properties. Over the ages, it was believed to do everything from reviving the vital spirits, warming the belly (undoubtedly), relaxing the brain, sharpening the intellect, and clearing the vision to removing bodily impurities, repairing memory, prolonging life, and even curing the plague. The only benefit now touted—aside from inflicting raging intoxication—is its role as the ultimate *digestivo,* capable of helping settle your stomach after a huge Italian meal.

Nowadays, grappa is distilled from Piedmont in the west to Friuli in the east and as far south as Tuscany. You'll find bottles in all shapes and sizes; some seem to be sold more as works of glass blowers' art than for the liqueur inside. There are labels hailing from renowned grappa distilleries, high-grade *aqua vitae* produced by vineyards (which have often raised the bar on grappa quality by forgoing the winemaking process entirely, distilling the stuff from whole grapes rather than just the scraps), and homemade hooch made in copper stills that are wheeled from farm to farm.

The most renowned producer in Bassano is **Nardini,** Ponte Vecchio 2 (✆ **0424-227-741;** www.nardini.it), run by the same family since 1779. It is the leader in grappa production, responsible for 25% of the Italian market, and its wood-beam *taverna* at the base of the Ponte degli Alpini is on the register of Italy's Historic Locales. Most people order a Rosso, the house version of Campari and soda, using Nardini's own "Rosso" hair-tonic liqueur. Walk out onto the bridge a bit to look back at the building's wall to see the bullet marks in the plaster from French rifles giving chase to the Archduke of Austria on May 3, 1889.

Just up the street sits **Poli** (✆ **0424-524-426;** www.poligrappa.com), founded in 1898 at nearby Schiavon, where its production is still centered. This Bassano sales outlet is a slick operation, with less atmosphere than Nardini, but it does incorporate a small but very informative grappa museum. It's all in Italian, but if you recall the basics of distillation from high-school science (or your college dorm), it all makes sense—and the elegant glass and copper machinery is beautiful in its own way. Plus, tastings here are free.

dishes and local Veneto specialties to the best of Tyrolean and Austrian cuisines. Via Matteotti 48–50. ✆ **0424-522-206.** Reservations suggested Fri–Sat. Primi 6€–7€; secondi 7.50€–15€. AE, DC, MC, V. Wed–Mon noon–3pm; Wed–Sun 7–11:30pm. Closed 2nd week of Aug.

A Side Trip to Marostica

The delightful medieval-walled village of Marostica, 30km (20 miles) north of Vicenza (7km/4¼ miles west of Bassano), comes alive every other September (in even years only): The entire town dresses up to commemorate a true centuries-old chess game between two knights vying for the hand of Lionora, daughter of a 15th-century local lord. The chivalric **Partita a Scacchi ★★★** is reenacted on the main piazza with real people as the pieces, dressed in elaborate Renaissance costume, preceded by a flag-throwing procession. The whole town takes part, and the torch-lit nighttime setting is gorgeous.

Performances are repeated over the course of the second weekend of September. A few of the worst seats are usually available each day of performance, but it's best to purchase tickets months in advance, costing anywhere from 10€ to 80€ depending on the section. **Tourist information** is at Piazza Castello 1 (☏ **0424-72-127;** fax 0424-72-800; www.marosticascacchi.it). Marostica's engaging **Sagra del Ciliege (Cherry Festival)** takes place in June. You can get here on one of two-dozen daily buses from Vicenza in 40 minutes. Dozens of local buses do the short run daily from Bassano to Marostica. By car, head west on S248.

VICENZA

32km (20 miles) W of Padua, 74km (46 miles) W of Venice, 51km (32 miles) E of Verona, 204km (126 miles) E of Milan

Vicenza pays heartfelt homage to Andrea di Pietro della Gondola (born in Padua in 1508, died in Maser in 1580). He came to Vicenza at the age of 16 and lived out his life and dreams here under the name Palladio at a time when Vicenza was under the sway of the still-powerful Venice Republic. Palladio was the most important architect of the High Renaissance, one whose living monuments have inspired and influenced architecture in the Western world over the centuries to this very day.

Vicenza and its surroundings are a mecca for the architecture lover, a living museum of Palladian and Palladian-inspired monuments—and, consequently,

A public park, Giardini Salvi, adjacent to Vicenza's Piazza Castello.

Vicenza was designated a UNESCO World Heritage Site in 1994. But even if you've never heard of Palladio, you'll find an evening stroll through illuminated *piazze* and boutique-lined streets plenty enjoyable. Plan on taking home a wealth of knowledge about architecture—a day in Vicenza is worth a semester back in school.

Today Vicenza is one of the wealthiest cities in Italy, thanks in part to the recent burgeoning of the local computer-component industry (Federico Faggin, inventor of the silicon chip, was born here). It is also the center of the country's gold-manufacturing industry (one-third of Italy's gold is made here, and each year three prestigious international gold fairs make finding a hotel in these parts impossible), and is one of Europe's largest producers of textiles. The average Vicentino is well off, and it shows.

Festivals The well-established summertime series of **Concerti in Villa ★** ((✆ 0444-399-104)) takes place in June and July; a few concerts are held outdoors at Vicenza's famed Villa la Rotonda; for others, you will need a car. The tourist office will have the schedule and availability of seats; tickets usually cost around 10€ to 20€. The stage of the delightful **Teatro Olimpico** (✆ **347-492-5005;** www.olimpico.vicenza.it) often hosts plays in September and October, and opera and classical music festivals throughout the warmer months. In 2011, the calendar included works by Mozart, Rossini, Brahms and Dvorzak. Tickets for those events usually range from 20€ to 50€ for adults.

Essentials

GETTING THERE **By Train** The **train station** is in Piazza Stazione, also called Campo Marzio (✆ **0444-326-707;** www.ferroviedellostato.it), at the southern end of Viale Roma. There's frequent service (2–3 per hour) connecting Vicenza with Venice (52–67 min.), Padua (20 min.), and Verona (30 min.).

By Bus The **FTV bus station** (✆ **0444-223-111;** www.ftv.vi.it) is located on Viale Milano, just to the west (left) of the train station. Buses leave frequently for all the major cities in Veneto and to Milan; prices are comparable to train travel.

By Car Vicenza is on Autostrada A4, linking Venice to Milan. Coming from Venice (about 1 hr.), you'll bypass Padua before arriving in Vicenza.

VISITOR INFORMATION The main **tourist information office** is at Piazza Matteotti 12 (© **0444-320-854;** fax 0444-327-072; www.vicenzae.org), next to the Teatro Olimpico. The office is open daily from 9am to 1pm and Monday to Saturday from 2 to 6pm. A second office can be found at Piazza dei Signori 8 (© **0444-544-122;** fax 0444-325-001), and it is open daily 10am to 2pm and 2:30 to 6:30pm.

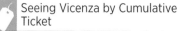

> ## Seeing Vicenza by Cumulative Ticket
>
> The Card Musei—also awkwardly known as the "Vicenza Citta' Bellissima" card—costs 8€ for adults, 6€ for students, and includes admission to the **Teatro Olimpico, Museo Civico, Museo Naturalistico Archeologico,** and the **Galleria di Palazzo Leoni.** Children 14 and under get into every museum for free. For more information, see www.vicenzae.org.

CITY LAYOUT The city's layout is quite straightforward and easy to navigate on foot. The train station lies at its southernmost point. From here, head straight ahead on Viale Roma; it ends at a turnabout with gated gardens beyond. Head right (east) into the *centro storico,* marked by the **Piazza Castello,** from which the main thoroughfare, the **Corso Palladio,** starts. Lined with shops, offices, and banks, the arrow-straight Corso cuts through town, running southwest (from Piazza Castello) to northeast (Piazza Matteotti), site of the Teatro Olimpico. Along the Corso, you'll find urban *palazzi* by Palladio and his students; midway, the **Piazza dei Signori** (and its Basilica Palladiana) will be found on your right (south). Perpendicular to the Corso is the important **Contrà Porti,** a lovely *palazzo*-studded street, on your left (north).

GETTING AROUND There is limited traffic (for taxis, buses, and residents) once you enter the Piazza del Castello and the *centro storico.* Everything of interest can be easily reached on foot; pick up a map at the tourist office. Even the two villas just outside town (see "Villas & a Basilica Nearby," below) can be reached by foot (not suggested in the heat of high season) or bike, as well as by bus or car.

What to See & Do
PIAZZA DEI SIGNORI

South of Corso Palladio on the site of the ancient Roman Forum and still the town hub, this central square is your first introduction to the city and local boy wonder Palladio.

The magnificent, bigger-than-life **Basilica Palladiana ★★** is not a church at all and was only partially designed by Palladio. Beneath it stood the Gothic-style Palazzo della Ragione (Law Courts and Assembly Hall) that Palladio was commissioned to convert to a High Renaissance style befitting a flourishing late-16th-century city under Venice's benevolent patronage. It was Palladio's first public work and secured his favor and reputation with the local authorities. He created two superimposed galleries, the lower with Doric pillars, and the upper with Ionic. The roof was destroyed by World War II bombing but has since been rebuilt in its original style. It's open Tuesday to Saturday from 9:30am to noon and from 2 to 7pm; Sunday from 9:30am to 12:30pm and from 2 to 7pm (Oct–Easter it's closed Sun afternoon). Admission is free. *Note:* As of this writing, the Basilica Palladiana is in the final stages of a massive 15-million-euro overhaul to

Palladio stands outside the Basilica Palladiana.

its roof and other structures, which is slated to be finished by 2012—art exhibits and other cultural events will celebrate the grand reopening throughout the fall and into the winter of 2013.

The 12th-century **Torre Bissara** (or **Torre di Piazza**) bell tower belonged to the original church and stands near two columns in the piazza's east end (the Piazza Blade), one topped by the winged lion of Venice's Serene Republic, the other by the *Redentore* (Redeemer). Also of note in the piazza is the Loggia del Capitaniato (1570), begun but never finished according to plans by Palladio, except for the four massive redbrick columns. Behind the basilica (to the south) is the **Piazza delle Erbe ★**, site of the daily produce market.

CORSO ANDREA PALLADIO

This is Vicenza's main street, and what a grand one it is, lined with the magnificent *palazzi* of Palladio and his students (and *their* students, who, centuries later, were still influenced by Palladio's work). It has since been converted into cafes, swank shops, and imposing banks. The first one of note, starting from its southwest cap near the Piazza Castello, is the **Palazzo Valmarana**, at no. 16, begun by Palladio in 1566. On the right (behind which stands the Piazza dei Signori and the Basilica Palladiana) is the **Palazzo del Comunale**, the Town Hall built in 1592 by Scamozzi (1552–1616), a native of Vicenza and Palladio's protégé and star pupil. This is said to be Scamozzi's greatest work.

Heading northeast from the Corso Palladio, take a left onto the Contrà Porti, the second most important street for its Palladian and Gothic *palazzi*. The two designed by Palladio are the **Palazzo Barbarano Porto,** at no. 11, and (opposite) **Palazzo Thiene,** at no.12 (now the headquarters of a bank). **Gothic** *palazzi* of particular note can be found at nos. 6 to 10, 14, 16, 17, and 19. Parallel, on Corso Fogazzaro, look for no. 16, **Palazzo Valmarana,** perhaps the most eccentric of Palladio's works.

Returning to Corso Palladio, look for no. 145/147, the pre-Palladian **Ca d'Oro (Golden Palace),** named for the gold leaf used in the frescoes that once covered its facade. The simple **16th-century** *palazzo* at no. 163 was Palladio's home.

Before reaching the Piazza Matteotti and the end of the Corso Palladio, you'll see signs for the **Church of Santa Corona ★**, set back on the left on the Via Santa Corona 2 (daily 8:30am–noon and 2:30–6pm). An unremarkable 13th-century Gothic church, it shelters two masterpieces (and Vicenza's most important church paintings) that make this worth a visit: Giovanni Bellini's *Baptism of Christ* (fifth altar on left) and Veronese's *Adoration of the Magi* (third chapel on right). This is Vicenza's most interesting church, far more so than the cavernous Duomo southwest of the Piazza dei Signori, but worth seeking out only if you've got the extra time. At the end of the Corso Palladio at its northeastern end is Palladio's world-renowned **Teatro Olimpico** and, across the street, the **Museo Civico** in the Palazzo Chiericati.

Teatro Olimpico & Museo Civico ★★★ The splendid Teatro Olimpico was Palladio's greatest urban work, and one of his last. He began the project in 1580, the year of his death, at the age of 72; it would be completed 5 years later by his student Vicenzo Scamozzi. It was the first covered theater in Europe, inspired by the theaters of antiquity. The seating area, in the shape of a half-moon, as in the old arenas, seats 1,000. The stage seems much deeper than its actual 4.2m (14 ft.), thanks to the permanent stage "curtain" and Scamozzi's clever use of *trompe l'oeil*. The stage scene represents the ancient streets of Thebes, while the faux clouds and sky covering the dome further the impression of being in an outdoor Roman amphitheater. Drama, music, and dance performances are still held here year-round; check with the tourist office.

Across the Piazza Matteotti is another Palladian magnum opus, the **Palazzo Chiericati,** which houses the **Museo Civico (Municipal Museum).** Looking more like one of the country villas for which Palladio was equally famous, this major work is considered one of his finest and is visited as much for its two-tiered, statue-topped facade as for the collection of Venetian paintings it houses on the first floor. Venetian masters you'll recognize include Tiepolo, Tintoretto, and Veronese, while the lesser known include works from the Vicenzan (founded by Bartolomeo Montagna) and Bassano schools of painting.

Vicenza's hub, the Corso Andrea Palladio.

Piazza Matteotti (at Corso Palladio). ☎ **0444-222-800.** www.museicivicivicenza.it. Admission is 8€ with cumulative ticket (see "Seeing Vicenza by Cumulative Ticket," above); it is not possible to buy a ticket just for the Teatro Olimpico or Palazzo Chiericati. Apr–Sept Tues–Sun 9am–7pm; Oct–Mar Tues–Sun 9am–5pm. Bus: 1, 2, 5, or 7.

OUTSIDE VICENZA

To reach the two important villas in the immediate environs of Vicenza, southeast of the train station, you can walk, bike, or take the no. 8 bus. First stop by the tourist office for a map, and check on visiting hours, which tend to change from year to year. The following two villas are generally open from mid-March to early November.

The **Villa Rotonda ★★★** (☎ **0444-321-793;** fax 0444-879-1380), alternatively referred to as Villa Capra Valmarana after its owners, is considered one of the most perfect buildings ever constructed and has been added to the World Heritage List by UNESCO; it is a particularly important must-do excursion for students and lovers of architecture. Most authorities refer to it as Palladio's finest work. Inspired by ancient Greek and Roman designs, Palladio began this perfectly proportioned square building, topped by a dome, in 1567; Scamozzi completed it between 1580 and 1592, after Palladio's death. It is worth a visit if only to view it from the outside (in fact, you can really see much of it from the gate). Admission to the grounds for viewing is 4€; admission to visit the lavishly decorated interior is 8€. The grounds are generally open from about March 15 to November 4, Tuesday to Sunday 10am to noon and 3 to 6pm; the interior is open only Wednesday during the same hours. The villa is private, like many others around Vicenza, and can be closed for a day or week on short notice, so it's always a good idea to call before going, if possible.

From here, it is only a 10-minute walk to the **Villa Valmarana ★★** (☎ **0444-543-976**), also called *ai Nani* (dwarves) after the statues that line the garden wall. Built in the 17th century by Mattoni, an admirer and follower of Palladio, it is an almost commonplace structure whose reason to visit is an interior covered with remarkable 18th-century frescoes by Giambattista Tiepolo and his son Giandomenico. Admission is 8€, and the villa is open mornings as follows: March 15 to November 5 Wednesday, Thursday, Saturday, and Sunday 10am to noon. It's open afternoons Tuesday to Sunday as follows: March 15 through April, 2:30 to 5:30pm; May through September, 3 to 6pm; and October to November 5, 2 to 5pm. These hours are fungible, so it's a good idea to check with the tourist information office.

Also in this area is the **Santuario di Monte Berico ★** (☎ **0444-559-411**), built in 1668 by a Bolognese architect. If you've already visited the Villa Rotonda, you will understand where the architect got his inspiration. The interior's most important work is in a chapel to the right of the main altar, *Lamentation,* by Bortolomeo Montagna (1500), one of Veneto's most famous artists. The terrace in front of the church affords beautiful views of Vicenza, the Monti Berici, and the distinct outline of the nearby Alps. The basilica is

A Model for Monticello

Villa Rotonda may seem vaguely familiar, for it is the model that inspired Thomas Jefferson's home Monticello, the Chiswick House near London, myriad plantation homes in America's Deep South, and countless other noble homes and government buildings in the United States and Europe.

In addition to visiting the two villas located in the immediate outskirts of Vicenza, a tour of the dozens of country *ville venete* farther afield is the most compelling outing from Vicenza. Guided tours of the villas have become less frequent, although the city's authorized tour guides (see "Organized Tours") offer select visits of a few of the more important ones. Many of the villas are still privately owned, and each has its own hours and restrictions (not all the villas can be visited; others permit visits only to the grounds but not the interiors, and so forth). The tourist office can help you plan your trip around these restrictions, and it also has maps and a host of varied itineraries outlining the most important villas, many of which are UNESCO-protected sites (though not all of them 16th-c. Palladian designs). Public transportation for these visits is close to nonexistent. If you do have access to a car, ask about the summer concert series in June and July, Concerti in Villa (see "Festivals," above), which draws first-class talent in the classical music world.

open in summer months Monday to Saturday from 6am to 12:30pm and 2:30 to 6:30pm, Sunday 6am to 8pm (it closes earlier in winter months); admission is free.

Organized Tours

Each summer brings a different sort of guided tour of the city by the local tourism authorities, often free of charge—but only if you buy the Card Musei (see "Seeing Vicenza by Cumulative Ticket," above). Saturday walking tours start at 12€. Check with the tourist office upon your arrival, or in advance by visiting its website (see "Visitor Information," above). Architecture buffs may want to splurge for an accredited multilingual tour guide through **Guide Turistiche Autorizzate** (*©* **348-677-1271;** www.vicenzatourguide.it). Rates are 105€ for a half-day, for up to 30 people.

Where to Stay

Unlike the tourism-magnet Verona, Vicenza can be very quiet in high season, August, or winter months when trade fairs are not in town; some hotels close without notice for a few weeks if there's little demand. Make sure you call in advance; the number of hotels in the city is limited.

Due Mori ★ Due Mori's history as the oldest family-run hotel in Vicenza and its convenient location on a quiet side street just west of the sprawling Piazza dei Signori make this the (deservedly) most popular spot in town for the budget-minded. Which is to say: Book early. In a modernized shell of a centuries-old *palazzo*, tasteful and authentic 19th-century pieces distinguish otherwise plain rooms whose amenities are kept at a minimum—but, then, so are the prices. This is as good as it gets in the very center of Palladio's hometown.

Via Do Rode 24 (1 block west of Piazza dei Signori), 36100 Vicenza. www.hotelduemori.com. *©* **0444-321-886.** Fax 0444-326-127. 30 units, 27 with private bathroom. 60€ double with shared bathroom, 85€ double with private bathroom. Breakfast 7€. AE, MC, V. Free parking. Pets allowed. **Amenities:** Bar; Wi-Fi. *In room:* Hair dryer (on request).

5

VENETO Vicenza

Hotel Giardini Revamped in 2011, this hotel maintains the welcoming charm emblematic of Italian hospitality, yet boasts a sleek, modern ambience that is temping to international tourists and business travelers. What the rooms lack in spaciousness is compensated for by their clean, quiet, and stylish nature. The staff is attentive and friendly, adding a sense of warmth to the elegant decor gracing the lobby, communal areas, and guest rooms. In a location that can't be beat—it's situated in the center of the city—visitors can take advantage of the city's nightlife and shopping.

Viale Giuriolo (next to Piazza Matteotti and the Teatro Olimpico), 36100 Vicenza. www.hotel giardini.com. ✆ **0444-326-458.** Fax 0444-326-458. 18 units. 120€–180€ double; 130€–180€ suite. Rates include breakfast. AE, DC, MC, V. Parking 20€. Bus from station: 1, 2, 5, or 7. **Amenities:** Bar. *In room:* A/C, satellite TV, hair dryer, minibar.

Where to Eat

Antica Casa della Malvasia ★ VICENTINO This ever-lively, tavernlike *osteria* sits on a quiet, characteristic side street that links the principal Corso Palladio with the Piazza dei Signori. Service comes with a smile and is informal, the cooking homemade and regional. The food is reliably good, but it's just an excuse to accompany the selection of wines (80), whiskeys (100), grappas (150), and teas (over 150). No wonder this place always buzzes. Even if you don't eat here, at least stop in for a late-night toddy, Vicentino style—it's a favorite spot for locals and visitors alike, and there's often live music on Tuesday and Thursday evenings.

Contrà delle Morette 5 (off Corso Palladio). ✆ **0444-543-704.** Reservations suggested during high season. Primi 5€–8€; secondi 7€–13€. Weekday lunch special primi 4€; secondi 6€. AE, MC, V. Tues–Sun noon–3pm and 7pm–midnight (sometimes later).

Gran Caffè Garibaldi CAFE If it's a lovely day, set up camp here in the shade of a table with an umbrella overlooking Vicenza's grand piazza. The most historically significant cafe in town is as impressive inside as you would imagine. The upstairs restaurant is expensive for what it offers, but the outside terrace gives you the chance to sit and gaze upon the wonders of the basilica, yet another Palladian masterpiece, while sipping a drink or having an ice cream. The cuisine is nothing to write a postcard to Grandma about, but the front-row seats on the beautiful Piazza dei Signori are.

Piazza dei Signori 5. ✆ **0444-542-455.** Reservations not necessary. Primi 8.50€; secondi 15€. MC, V. Wed–Mon noon–2:30pm and 7–10:30pm.

Righetti 🍴 ITALIAN/VICENTINO For a self-service operation, this place is a triple surprise: The diners are all local (and loyal); the food is reliably good, of the home-cooked, generous-portions kind; and the interior is rustic, welcoming, and pleasant, considering its inexpensive profile. But it's the opportunity to sit outdoors in the quiet, traffic-free Piazza Duomo that's the biggest draw. First stake out a table by setting your place, and then order your food at the counter (prepared fresh on the spot); when you're finished eating, just tell the cashier what you had and he'll add up the bill. There are three or four first courses to choose from (Tues and Fri are risotto days) and as many entrees. Evenings offer the option of grilled meats (which makes eating indoors in the cold winter months more enjoyable), though this is the perfect relaxed place to revel in a simple lunch of pasta and a vegetable side, opting for a more special dinner venue.

Piazza Duomo 3–4. ✆ **0444-543-135.** Reservations not necessary. Primi 4.50€; secondi 5€–8€. No credit cards. Mon–Fri noon–2:30pm and 7–10pm.

Trattoria Tre Visi ★★ ITALIAN/VICENTINO Operating, from the early 1600s until 1997, around the corner from the current address, this Vicentino institution is now located on an important *palazzo*-studded street in a setting somewhat less dramatic than the previous 15th-century *palazzo.* The menu has stayed unchanged, however, and this is good: Ignore items that concede to foreign requests and concentrate on the regional dishes they know how to prepare best. Almost all the pasta is made fresh daily, including the house specialty, *bigoli con anitra,* fat, spaghetti-like pasta served with duck ragú. The region's signature dish is *baccalà alla Vicentina,* a tender salt codfish simmered in a stew of onions, herbs, anchovies, garlic, and *parmigiano* for 8 hours before arriving at your table in perfection. Ask your waiter for help in selecting from Veneto's wide spectrum of very fine wines: It will enhance your bill but also the memories you'll bring home.

Corso Palladio 25 (near Piazza Castello). *©* **0444-324-868.** Reservations suggested. Primi 10€– 15€; secondi 16€–21€. AE, DC, MC, V. Tues–Sun 12:30–2:30pm; Tues–Sat 7:30–10pm. Closed July.

VERONA

114km (71 miles) W of Venice, 80km (50 miles) W of Padua, 61km (38 miles) W of Vicenza, 157km (97 miles) E of Milan

Suspend all disbelief regarding the real-life existence of Romeo and Juliet, and your stay in Verona can be magical. After Venice, this is Veneto's most-visited city, and for good reason: Verona contains the best of Italy packed into a convenient size—illustrious wines, elegant shopping, romantic alleyways, and even the backdrop of a Roman amphitheater (the best preserved one in the world). It is as though the entire city is a stage and the inhabitants merely players—well dressed and sophisticated players, a remnant from Verona's era of nobility.

Things to Do This storied scenery of everyone's favorite star-crossed lovers is still the embodiment of all that is amorous, and so its activities revolve around pampering the one you love: shopping for silk scarves on **Via Mazzini,** strolling through the picturesque **Piazza delle Erbe,** munching on decadent chocolates. Put yourselves in the mood in the morning by scrawling your initials at **Juliet's house** and finish off the day with a night at the **opera.**

Relaxation This doesn't mean you won't want to pack in as many church visits as you can—this is Italy, after all—and so the easiest way to unwind from that whirlwind is by wine tasting at a vineyard and perusing the wine shops downtown. The countryside just north of the city is home to **Masi** and other famous producers of the Valpolicella fruit, and the *enoteche* and stores in alleyways throughout the city carry all of their labels, including vintages long forgotten back home.

Restaurants & Dining At the very least, this will be a good education for when the dinner hour rolls around. Oddly, for a city known for its noble roots, Verona's best-known dish is probably the simplest—pasta with beans *(pasta e fagioli)*— and restaurateurs are not ashamed to plate specialties from nearby Venice and Vicenza. And although all of its cuisine is brought to life by horseradish and *salsa verde,* it is the city's precious wine that steals the spotlight at dinner, either in the recipe itself or above the spoon and to the right. For a bit of both, linger over a *filetto di manzo al Amarone* at the **Antica Bottega del Vino** and let the grape work its magic.

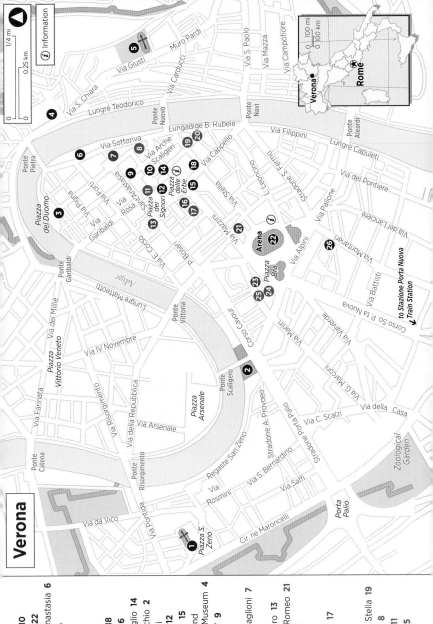

Verona

0 — 0.25 km
0 — 1/4 mi

ⓘ Information

Rome

ATTRACTIONS

Arche Scaligere **10**
Arena di Verona **22**
Basilica di Sant'Anastasia **6**
Basilica San Zeno Maggiore **1**
The Duomo **3**
Giardino Giusti **5**
"Juliet's House" **18**
"Juliet's Tomb" **26**
Loggia del Consiglio **14**
Museo Castelvecchio **2**
Piazza dei Signori (Piazza Dante) **12**
Piazza delle Erbe **15**
Roman Theater and Archaeological Museum **4**
"Romeo's House" **9**

HOTELS

Due Torri Hotel Baglioni **7**
Hotel Aurora **16**
Hotel Gabbia d'Oro **13**
Hotel Giulietta e Romeo **21**
Hotel Torcolo **23**

RESTAURANTS

Bottega del Vino **17**
Brek **24**
Il Desco **20**
La Taverna di Via Stella **19**
Osteria del Duca **8**
Pizzeria Impero **11**
Pizzeria Liston **25**

215

Nightlife A postprandial around the streets in pleasant weather offers little doubt about where you'll find the best shows in town: at either of the ancient monuments, the **Teatro Romano** and the **Arena.** The former regularly hosts Shakespeare (of course, the drama that made Verona famous would not be left out) and the latter is home to magnificent concerts and operatic performances—just be sure to buy your tickets months in advance!

Festivals & Markets The Teatro Romano is known for its **Festival Shakespeariano (Shakespeare Festival)** ★ June through August, which celebrated its 63rd anniversary in 2011. Festival performances usually begin in late May with jazz concerts, while performances of the Bard's plays generally kick off toward the end of June. In July and August, there are a number of ballets (occasionally, Prokofiev's *Romeo and Juliet*) and modern-dance performances. Check the schedule (℗ **045-807-7500** or 045-806-6485; www.estateteatraleveronese. it; or the tourist office). Last-minute tickets go on sale at the Teatro Romano box office at 8:15pm (most performances start at 9pm). Tickets are in the neighborhood of 20€ for the less comfortable general admission seats, and around 35€ for the reserved ones.

During Verona's summer-long festival of the arts, see what's happening in the Piazza dei Signori, where frequent **free concerts** (jazz, tango, classical) keep everyone out until the wee hours. And for something truly unique, check out **Sognando Shakespeare (Dreaming Shakespeare).** Follow this *teatro itinerante* (traveling theater) of young, talented actors in costume as they wander about the medieval corners of Verona from site to site, reciting *Romeo e Giulietta* (in Italian only) *in situ,* as Shakespeare would have loved it to be. For information about performances July through September, call ℗ **045-800-0065.**

Other important events are the famous 4-day **Fieracavalli (horse fair),** in early November, and the important 5-day **VinItaly wine fair** (that overlaps with the Olive Oil Fair) in mid-April. (Verona's schedule of fairs is long and varied; while few may be of interest to those outside the trades involved, their frequency can create problems for tourists in regard to hotel availability.) The Piazza San Zeno hosts a **traveling antiques market** the third Saturday of every month; come early.

The History of Verona

Verona reached a cultural and artistic zenith during the 13th and 14th centuries under the puissant, often cruel, and sometimes quirky della Scala, or Scaligeri, dynasty that took up rule in the late 1200s. In 1405, it surrendered to Venice, which remained in charge until the invasion of Napoleon in 1797. During the time of Venetian rule, Verona became a prestigious urban capital and controlled much of Veneto and as far south as Tuscany. You'll see the emblem of the *scala* (ladder) around town, heraldic symbol of the Scaligeri dynasty. The city has a locked-in-time character that recalls its medieval and Renaissance heyday, and the magnificent medieval *palazzi,* towers, churches, and stagelike *piazze* you see today are picture-perfect testimony to its centuries-old influence and wealth.

ART THOU truly ROMEO?

Though the city has plenty else to recommend it as a sightseeing capital of Veneto, the local tourism economy is underpinned by hordes of bus groups, Shakespearian pilgrims, and hopeless romantics. They come to wander the streets where Capulets and Montagues once fought, Romeo pined, and Juliet sighed from her (completely false) balcony.

Wealthy Veronese families called Capuleti and Montecchi did exist. Did they feud? Probably. That often was the way with local clans vying for city power in the Middle Ages. But did their two houses, so alike in dignity, ever harbor secret, star-crossed lovers? Did Romeo and Juliet really exist?

The story is based in an ancient legend; the core tragic elements go back at least to the Greeks. To trace the Shakespeare version: The basic story was put into novella form (based on a medieval Sienese version) in 1476 and then subsequently retold in 1524 by Veneto-born Luigi da Porto. He chose to set it in Verona in the years 1302 to 1304 during the reign of the Scaligeri, and renamed the young couple Romeo and Giulietta. The popular *storia d'amore* was translated into English, at which point Shakespeare obviously got hold of it and worked his magic.

With the genius of Shakespeare's pen, the story turned into theatrical gold. Translated into dozens of languages and performed around the world (check out the number of Asian and eastern European tourists who flock to Juliet's House), this universal and timeless tale of pure love has forever since been set in the tempestuous days of this medieval city—notwithstanding that version with Leo DiCaprio.

That said, Zeffirelli chose to film his classic 1968 interpretation in the tiny Tuscan town of Pienza, south of Siena. And, of course, the story emigrated to the New World and took up in the mean streets of New York as *West Side Story.*

Essentials

GETTING THERE By Train Verona is easily accessed on the west-east Milan-Venice line, as well as on the north-south Brennero-Rome line. At least 30 trains daily run east from Venice (1½–2 hr.). Even more arrive from Milan (1½–2 hr.). Trains also connect Verona with Vicenza (30–50 min.), Padua (35–50 min.), and Bologna (⅔–2 hr.).

The **Stazione Porta Nuova train station** (© 045-534-221) is located rather far south of the Piazza Brà (and Arena) area and is serviced by at least half a dozen local bus lines. The bus network within the historic center is limited, so if you have luggage, you'll probably want a taxi to get to your hotel.

To get downtown from the train station, walk straight out to the bus island marked MARCIAPIEDE F (parallel to the station) to catch minibus no. 72 or 73 (tickets on sale at the newsstand in the station or the AMT booth on MARCIAPIEDE A). Get off on Via Stella at Via Cappello for the center. Alternatively, over half the buses from the station stop at Piazza Brà, so just peruse the posted route signs.

By Bus The bus station, **A.P.T.** (Azienda Provinciale Trasporti), is at Piazza XXV Aprile (℃ **045-805-7911;** www.aptv.it), across from the train station. Buses leave from here for all regional destinations, including Largo di Garda. Although there is bus service to Vicenza, Padua, and Venice (only the summertime departures for Venice are direct; in other months, there's a change), it is generally easier to travel by train.

By Car The Serenissima autostrada (A4) links Venice and Milan; the exit for downtown Verona is Verona Sud. Coming from the north or south, use the A22 autostrada, taking exit Verona Nord.

VISITOR INFORMATION A **central tourist office** is at Via degli Alpini 9, adjacent to the Arena off Piazza Brà (℃ **045-806-8680;** fax 045-801-0682), open Monday to Saturday 9am to 7pm and Sunday 10am to 4pm. A **small office** at the train station (℃ **045-800-0861**) is open Monday to Saturday

---

NESSUN dorma—NONE SHALL SLEEP!

Verona's renowned **opera season** ★★★ begins in late June and extends through August in Verona's Arena, the ancient amphitheater. Be prepared for gala dresses, much pomp, and a late bedtime—the shows begin just after 9pm and the fat lady sings at midnight.

The tradition began in 1913 with a staging of *Aïda* to commemorate the 100th anniversary of Verdi's birth, and *Aïda* in all of its extravagant glory has been performed yearly ever since. Expect to see other Verdi works such as *Nabucco, La Traviata,* and *Rigoletto,* as well as other big-name crowd pleasers. (The 2012 season, which begins on June 22 with *Don Giovanni,* will also feature *Aïda, Carmen, Romeo and Juliet, Tosca,* and *Turandot.*)

Those seated on the least expensive, unreserved stone steps costing 21€ to 28€ enjoy fresh air, excellent acoustics, and a view over the Arena's top to the city and surrounding hills beyond. The rub is that Jose Carreras will only appear to be an inch high, and if it's a sunny day, the stones will have stored up enough heat to keep a small town humming for days. Numbered seats below cost from about 70€ to 190€ (there are slightly reduced prices for those 27 and under and 65 and over). All tickets are subject to an advance

booking fee that varies depending on how much you spend and is 7.50€ for a purchase of up to 150€ and 12€ for a purchase of up to 250€—worth it, unless you're willing to tough it out by lining up at 4 or 5pm for the 6pm opening of the gates for unreserved seating (and the show doesn't even start until 9:15pm).

The **box office** is located on Via Dietro Anfiteatro 6b; credit card purchase accepted by phone or online (℃ **045-800-5151;** www.arena.it). You pick up tickets the night of the performance. If you hope to find tickets upon arrival, remember that *Aïda* is everyone's most requested performance; weekend performances are usually sold out. As a last resort, be nice to your hotel manager—everyone has a connection. And even on the most coveted nights (weekend performances by top names), scalpers abound. If you want to plan early, tickets generally go on sale at the beginning of October for the season that begins the following June.

9am to 7pm and Sunday 9am to 3pm. Visit their website at www.tourism.verona.it.

GUIDED TOURS An air-conditioned *bus turistico,* called "Romeo," departs thrice daily for a 1½-hour Giro Turistico tour of the city's historic center every day except Monday from June until September 28. The cost is 15€ for adults and 7.50€ for children 17 and under for a recorded spiel in four languages; you can buy your ticket on the bus. It leaves from the Gran Guardia in the Piazza Brà at 10am, 11:30am, 1pm, and 3:30pm (an evening tour leaves Sat and Sun at 9pm). The 3:30pm Saturday tour has a real, live tour guide that ups the cost to 20€. (I think you'll do just as well with this guidebook, however.)

The Piazza Brà is the center of Verona.

CITY LAYOUT The city lies alongside the banks of an S-shaped curve in the Adige River. As far as the average visitor is concerned, everything of interest—with the exception of the Teatro Romano—is found in the *centro storico* on the south side of the river's loop; there's no site that cannot be easily and enjoyably reached by foot.

    The massive ancient Roman amphitheater, the **Arena,** sits at the southern end of the city's hub in the airy cafe-ringed **Piazza Brà.** The piazza is linked by the popular **Via Mazzini** pedestrian thoroughfare to the **Piazza delle Erbe** and its adjacent **Piazza dei Signori.** The grid of pedestrian-only streets between is lined with shops and cafes that make up the principal strolling and window-shopping destinations in town.

    Slightly out of this loop (though still an easy walk) is the **Basilica San Zeno Maggiore,** west of the Arena, and **Juliet's Tomb,** southeast of the Arena (only die-hard Juliet fans will appreciate the trek here). Both the **train station** and the **Fiera di Verona conference center** are located in the southern part of town beyond the Porta Nuova.

GETTING AROUND Verona lends itself to walking and strolling, and most sites are concentrated within a few history-steeped blocks of each other. Venture off the store-lined treadmill and seek out the narrow, cobblestoned side streets that are evocative of eras past. Little to no traffic is permitted in town, so upon arrival, stash your car in a parking area suggested by your hotel (where they'll most likely have a special arrangement), and let your feet do the transporting.

What to See & Do
TOP ATTRACTIONS
If you're in town the **first Sunday** of any month, note that entrance is free for the following sites: Castelvecchio Museum, the Roman Theater, and Juliet's Tomb.

Because there are so many churches in Verona, an admission has been imposed in an attempt to cover custodian charges and offer longer hours.

Arena di Verona ★★★ The best-preserved Roman amphitheater in the world and the best known in Italy after Rome's Colosseum, the elliptical Arena was built in a slightly pinkish marble in the 1st century A.D. and stands in the very middle of town, with the Piazza Brà on its southern flank. Built to accommodate more than 20,000 people (outdone by Rome's contender that could seat more than twice that), it is in remarkable shape today (despite a 12th-c. earthquake that left only four arches of the outer ring standing), beloved testimony to the pride and wealth of Verona and its populace.

Its acoustics (astoundingly good for an open-air venue) have survived the millennia and make it one of the most fascinating venues for live performances today, conducted without microphones. If you're in town during the summer opera performances in July and August, do everything possible to procure a ticket (see "*Nessun Dorma*—None Shall Sleep," above) for any of the outdoor evening performances. Even opera-challenged audience members will take home the memory of a lifetime. Other events, such as orchestral concerts, are staged here whenever the weather permits. Check with the tourist office for more information.

The cluster of outdoor cafes and *trattorie*/pizzerias on the western side of the Piazza Brà line a wide marble esplanade called Il Liston; they stay open long after the opera performances end. Enjoy some serious post-opera people-watching here.

Piazza Brà. 🕐 **045-800-3204.** www.arena.it. Admission 6€, 4€ for students, 1€ for children 8–14. Mon 1:30–7:30pm; Tues–Sun 8:30am–7:30pm (last admission 45 min. before close); July–Aug summer opera season Tues–Sun 9am–3:30pm (and sometimes a little later).

Casa di Giulietta (Juliet's House) ★★ There is no proof that a Capuleti (Capulet) family ever lived here (or, if they did, that a young girl named Juliet ever existed), and it wasn't until 1905 that the city bought what was an abandoned, overgrown garden and decided its future. Rumor is that this was once actually a whorehouse.

So powerful is the legend of Juliet that over half a million tourists flock here every year to visit the simple courtyard and home that are considerably less affluent-looking than the sumptuous Franco Zeffirelli version as you may remember it (the movie was filmed in Tuscany). Many are those who leave behind layer upon layer of graffiti along the lines of "*Valentina, ti amo!*" or who engage in the peculiar tradition (whose origin no one can seem to explain) of rubbing the right breast (now buffed to a bright gold) of the 20th-century bronze statue of a forever nubile Juliet.

The curious might want to fork over the entrance fee to see the spartan interior of the 13th-century home, restored in 1996. Ceramics and furniture on display are authentic to the era but did not belong to Juliet's family—if

Verona by Cumulative Ticket

The **VeronaCard**, a *biglietto cumulativo* (cumulative ticket), will help you visit several of the city's sites for just one fee. Two versions of the card are available. The 15€ card, valid for 2 days, allows you to ride the city's buses and enter its museums, monuments, and churches. The 20€ card offers the same places but allows you 5 consecutive days rather than 1. You'll find the VeronaCard for sale at the sites below, or call 🕐 **045-807-7774.**

Juliet's famous balcony.

there ever was a Juliet at all. No one is willing to confirm (or deny) that the balcony was added to the *palazzo* as recently as 1928 (though that doesn't stop many a young lass from posing on it, staring dreamily at the sky).

La Tomba di Giulietta (Juliet's Tomb; ✆ **045-800-0361)** is about a 15-minute walk south of here (near the Adige River on Via delle Pontiere 5; admission 4.50€ adults, 3€ students and seniors 65 and over, 1€ children 8 to 14, and free the first Sun of each month; Mon 1:30–7:30pm, Tues–Sun 9am–7pm; last admission is 45 min. before closing). The would-be site of the star-crossed lovers' suicide is found within the graceful medieval cloisters of the Capuchin monastery of San Francesco al Corso. Die-hard romantics may find this tomb, with its surely posed "sarcophagus," rather more evocative than the crowded scene at Juliet's House and worth the trip. Others will find it overrated and shouldn't bother. The adjacent church is where their secret marriage was said to have taken place. A small museum of frescoes is also adjacent.

Via Cappello 23 (southeast of Piazza delle Erbe). ✆ **045-803-4303.** Admission (to building only; courtyard is free) 6€ adults, 4.50€ children. Mon 1:30–7:30pm; Tues–Sun 8:30am–7:30pm. (Last admission 45 min. before closing.)

Museo Castelvecchio ★★ A 5-minute walk west of the Arena on the Via Roma and nestled on the banks of the swift-flowing Adige River, the "Old Castle" is a crenelated fairy tale of brick towers and turrets, protecting the bridge behind it. It was commissioned in 1354 by the Scaligeri warlord Cangrande II to serve the dual role of residential palace and military stronghold. The ground-floor rooms, displaying statues and carvings of the Middle Ages, lead to alleyways, vaulted halls, multileveled floors, and stairs, all as architecturally arresting as the Venetian masterworks from the 14th to 18th centuries—notably those by Tintoretto, Tiepolo, Veronese, Bellini, and the Verona-born Pisanello—found throughout. Don't miss the large courtyard with the equestrian statue of the warlord Cangrande I, with a peculiar dragon's head affixed to his back (actually his helmet, removed from his head and resting behind him).

Corso Castelvecchio 2 (at Via Roma, on the Adige River). ✆ **045-806-2611.** www.comune. verona.it/Castelvecchio/cvsito. Admission 6€, 4.50€ children 8–14. Free 1st Sun of each month. Mon 1:45–7:30pm; Tues–Sun 8:30am–7:30pm (last admission 45 min. before closing).

Piazza dei Signori (Piazza Dante) ★ To reach the Piazza dei Signori from the Piazza delle Erbe, exit under the Arco della Costa (see "Liar, Liar," below). The perfect antidote to the color and bustle of the Piazza delle Erbe, the serene and elegant Piazza dei Signori is a slightly somber square, one of Verona's innermost chambers of calm. Its center is anchored by a large 19th-century statue of the "divine poet" Dante, who found political exile from Florence in Verona as a guest of Cangrande I and his Scaligeri family (in appreciation, Dante wrote of his patron in his poem *Paradiso*).

If entering from the archway, you'll be facing the Scaligeri's 13th-century crenelated residence. Left of that, behind Dante's back, is the Loggia del Consiglio (Portico of the Counsel), a 15th-century masterpiece of Venetian Renaissance style. Opposite that and facing Dante is the 12th-century Romanesque Palazzo della Ragione, whose courtyard and fine Gothic staircase should be visited. This piazza is Verona's finest microcosm, a balanced and refined assemblage of historical architecture. Secure an outdoor table at the square's legendary command post, the Antico Caffè Dante, and take it all in over a late-afternoon Campari and soda.

Piazza dei Signori, adjacent to Piazza delle Erbe.

Piazza delle Erbe ★★ This bustling marketplace—the *palazzi*-flanked Square of the Herbs—sits on the site of the Roman Forum where chariot races once took place. The herbs, spices, coffee beans, and bolts of silks and damasks that came through Verona after landing in Venice from faraway Cathay have given way to the fresh and aromatic produce of one of Italy's wealthiest agricultural regions— offset by the presence of T-shirt and french-fry vendors, as the piazza has become something of a tourist trap. But the perfume of fennel and vegetables fresh from the earth still assaults your senses in the early morning, mixing with the cacophony of vendors touting plump tomatoes, dozens of different variations of salad greens, and fruits that can't possibly taste as good as they look, but do. Add to this the canary lady, the farmer's son who has brought in a half a dozen puppies to unload, and the furtive pickpocket who can spot a tourist at 50 paces—and you have one of Italy's loveliest little outdoor markets. Take a rest on one of the steps leading up to the small 14th-century fountain in the piazza's center and a Roman statue dubbed *The Virgin of Verona.*

Btw. Via Mazzini and Corso Porta Borsari. Open-air produce and flower market Mon–Sat 8am–7pm.

MORE ATTRACTIONS

Arche Scaligeri (Scaligeri Tombs)/Torre dei Lamberti ★ Exit the Piazza dei Signori opposite the **Arch of the Rib** (p. 223), and immediately on your right, at the corner of Via delle Arche Scaligeri, are some of the most elaborate Gothic funerary monuments in Italy—the raised outdoor tombs of the canine-obsessed Scaligeri family (seen behind the original decorative grillwork), powerful and often ruthless rulers of Verona.

The most important are those by the peculiar names of Mastino I (Mastiff the First, founder of the dynasty, date of death unknown), Mastino II (Mastiff the Second, d. 1351), and Cansignorio (Head Dog, d. 1375). The most interesting is found over the side door of the family's private chapel, Santa Maria Antica—the tomb of Cangrande I (Big Dog, d. 1329), with *cani* (dogs) holding up a *scala* (ladder), both elements that figure in the Scaligeri coat of arms. That's Cangrande I—patron of the arts and protector of Dante—and his steed you see above (the original can be seen in the Museo Castelvecchio). Recently restored, these tombs are considered one of the country's greatest medieval monuments. Entry is only to the neighboring **Torre dei Lamberti;** the tomb area itself is closed to visitors. The view from atop the 83m (272-ft.) tower is the best in the city and takes in all the vibrant colors of the surrounding landscape.

Around the corner, on Via delle Arche Scaligeri 2, is the alleged 13th-century home of Juliet's significant other, **Romeo Montecchi** (Montague, in Shakespearian), which incorporates the popular Osteria del Duca (see "Where to Eat," below).

Liar, Liar

You'll be able to spot the **Arco della Costa (Arch of the Rib)** by the enormous whalebone hanging overhead. It was placed here 1,000 years ago when it was said to have been unearthed during excavations on this spot, indicating this area was once underwater. Local legend goes that the rib will fall on the first person to pass beneath it who has never told a lie—thus explaining the nonchalance with which every Veronese passes under it.

Via della Costa 1. ✆ **045-927-3027.** Admission 6€, 4.50 students and seniors 65 and over, 1€ children 8–14. Mon 1:45–7:30pm; Tues–Sun 9:30am–7:30pm (last admission 30 min. before closing).

Basilica di Sant'Anastasia Built between 1290 and 1481, this is Verona's largest church, considered the city's finest example of Gothic architecture, even though the facade remains unfinished. A lovely 14th-century campanile bell tower is adorned with frescoes and sculptures. The church's interior is typically Gothic in design, highlighted by two famous *gobbi* (hunchbacks) that support the holy-water fonts, an impressive patterned pavement, and 16 side chapels containing a number of noteworthy paintings and frescoes from the 15th and 16th centuries.

Most important is Verona-born Pisanello's **St. George Freeing the Princess of Trebisonda** (1433). This is considered one of his best paintings and is of the armed-knight-and-damsel-in-distress genre—with the large white rump of St. George's steed as one of its focal points. Also worth scouting out are the earlier 14th-century frescoes by the Giotto-inspired Altichiero in the Cavalli Chapel next door.

Piazza Sant'Anastasia at Corso Sant'Anastasia. ✆ **045-592-813.** www.chieseverona.it. Admission 2.50€. Mar–Oct Mon–Sat 9am–6pm, Sun 1–6pm; Nov–Feb Tues–Sat 10am–4pm, Sun 1–4pm.

Basilica San Zeno Maggiore ★★ This is one of the finest examples of Romanesque architecture in northern Italy, built between the 9th and 12th centuries. Slightly out of the old city's hub but still easily reached by foot, San Zeno (as it's often referred to), dedicated to the city's patron saint, is Verona's most visited church. Spend a moment outside to appreciate the fine, sober facade, highlighted by the immense 12th-century rose window, the **Ruota della Fortuna (Wheel of Fortune).**

This pales in importance compared to the **facade** ★★ below—two pillars supported by marble lions and massive doors whose 48 bronze panels were sculpted from the 9th to the 11th centuries and are believed to have been some of the first castings in bronze since Roman antiquity. They are among the city's most cherished artistic treasures and are worth the trip here even if the church is closed. Not as sophisticated as those that would adorn the Baptistery doors of Florence's Duomo in the centuries to come, these are like a naive illustration from a children's book and were meant to educate the illiterate masses with scenes from the Old and New Testaments and the life of San Zeno. They are complemented by the stone bas-reliefs found on either side of the doors, the 12th-century work of Niccolo, who was also responsible for the Duomo's portal. The 14th-century **tower** on the left belonged to the former abbey, while the free-standing slender **campanile** on the right was begun in 1045.

The massive **interior** ★ is filled with 12th- to 14th-century frescoes and crowned by the nave's ceiling, designed as a wooden ship's keel. But the interior's singular highlight is the famous triptych of the *Madonna and Child*

Enthroned with Saints, by Andrea Mantegna (1459), behind the main altar. Napoleon absconded with the beautiful centerpiece—a showcase for the Padua-born Mantegna's sophisticated sense of perspective and architectural detail—which was eventually returned to Verona, although two side panels stayed behind in the Louvre and in Tours. Look in the small apse to the left of the altar for the colored marble statue of a smiling San Zeno, much loved by the local Veronesi, in an act of blessing.

Piazza San Zeno. ℃ **045-592-813.** www.chieseverona.it. Admission 2.50€. Mar–Oct Mon–Sat 8am–6pm, Sun 1–6pm; Nov–Feb Tues–Sat 10am–1pm and 1:20–4pm, Sun 1–5pm.

Teatro Romano (Roman Theater) and the Museo Archeologico (Archaeological Museum) ★ The oldest extant Roman monument in Verona dates from the time of Augustus, when the Arena was built and Verona was a strong Roman outpost at the crossroads of the Empire's ancient north-south, east-west highways. There is something almost surreal about attending an open-air performance of Shakespeare's *Two Gentlemen of Verona* or *Romeo and Juliet* here—even if you can't understand a word (see "Festivals & Markets," earlier in this section). Classical music, ballet, and jazz performances are also given here, with evocative views of the city beyond. A small archaeological museum (same hours as the site itself) housed in a lovely old monastery is included in the ticket price. On Sunday (only), the promenade is open to the public.

Via Rigaste Redentore (over the Ponte Pietra bridge behind the Duomo, on the north banks of the river Adige). ℃ **045-800-0360.** www.estateteatraleveronese.it. Admission 4€; free 1st Sun of each month. Mon 1:30–6:45pm; Tues–Sun 8:30am–6:45pm; during theater season 9am–3pm.

The Duomo ★ Begun in the 12th century and not finished until the 17th century, the city's main church still boasts its original main doors and portal, magnificently covered with low reliefs in the Lombard Romanesque style that are attributed to Niccolo, whose work can be seen at the Basilica of San Zeno Maggiore. The church was built upon the ruins of an even more ancient paleo-Christian church dating from the late Roman Empire. Visit the **Cappella Nichesola,** the first chapel on the left, where Titian's serene but boldly colorful *Assumption of the Virgin* is the cathedral's principal treasure, with an architectural frame by Sansovino (who also designed the choir). Also of interest is the semicircular screen that separates the altar from the rest of the church, attributed to Sanmicheli. To its right rises the 14th-century tomb of Saint Agatha.

The excavations of Sant'Elena church, also in the Duomo complex, reveal a bit of 6th-century mosaic floor; the Baptistery contains a Romanesque font carved with scenes from the Nativity cycle.

Don't leave the area without walking behind the Duomo to the river: Here you'll find the 13th-century Torre di Alberto della Scala tower and nearby Ponte della Pietra bridge, the oldest Roman monument in Verona (1st c. B.C.; rebuilt

5

VENETO | Verona

Ancient ruins at Verona's Teatro Romano.

in the 14th c.). There has been a crossing at this point of the river since Verona's days as a 1st-century Roman stronghold when the Teatro Romano was built on the river's northern banks and the Arena at its hub.

Piazza Duomo (at Via del Duomo). ☎ **045-592-813.** www.chieseverona.it. Single admission 2.50€. Mar–Oct Mon–Sat 10am–5:30pm, Sun 1:30–5:30pm; Nov–Feb Tue–Sat 10am–1pm and 1:30–4pm, Sun 1–5pm.

Gardens

Close to the Castel San Pietro is the well-known, multitiered **Giardino Giusti** gardens (☎**045-803-4029**), whose formal 16th-century layout and geometrical designs of terraces, fountains, statuary, and staircases inspired, among many, Mozart and Goethe. The gardens are open daily from 9am to dusk; admission is 6€.

Shopping

Unlike in Venice, most of the people walking Verona's boutique-lined pedestrian streets are locals, not tourists. Come to Verona to spend some time doing what the locals do, shopping and stopping in any of the myriad cafes and *pasticcerie*. Shopping is mostly for the Veronesi, and upscale clothing and accessories boutiques line the two most fashionable shopping streets, **Via Mazzini** (connecting the Arena and the Piazza delle Erbe) and **Via Cappello,** heading southeast from the piazza and past Juliet's House. There's also **Corso Borsari** to check out, and **Corso Sant'Anastasia** (heading west and east, respectively, out of the Piazza delle Erbe), the latter having a concentration of interesting antiques stores.

Where to Stay

Although the following prices reflect peak-season rates, expect inflated prices during the July/August opera season or when one of the major trade fairs is in town. With this exception, low season is November through mid-March. The **C.A.V.** (Cooperativa Albergatori Veronesi), at Via Patuzzi 5, is an organization of dozens of hotels that will help you with bookings for a fee determined by your choice of hotel category (☎**045-800-9844;** fax 045-800-9372; www.verona booking.com).

Due Torri Hotel ★★ Verona's top hotel occupies a 14th-century *palazzo* that was reopened in the 1950s. It's where rock stars and opera singers stay when they play in town, picking up where Mozart, Goethe, and Garibaldi left off—perhaps because they're among the few who can afford it. The airy lobby looks like a stage set, with original 1370s columns and carvings and contemporary frescoes of medieval scenes, the ceilings set with oil paintings. The room furnishings range from Louis XIV to Biedermeier, and even standard rooms are luxurious, with patterned wall coverings, Murano chandeliers, and large, marble-sheathed bathrooms with double sinks. Windows are double-paned, so even on the piazza things are quiet. The hotel is in the narrow end of Verona formed by the tight river bend, so many rooms, especially on the third floor, and the rooftop terrace have great views to the hills beyond.

Piazza Sant'Anastasia 4-37121 Verona. http://hotelduetorri.duetorrihotels.com. ✆ **045-595-044.** Fax 045-800-4130. 90 units. 280€–595€ double; 535€–900€ junior suite. Discounts with online booking. Rates include breakfast. AE, DC, MC, V. Valet parking 30€. Small pets allowed. **Amenities:** Veronese/international restaurant; bar; babysitting; concierge; Wi-Fi. *In room:* A/C, TV, hair dryer, Internet, minibar.

Hotel Aurora ★ It used to be location, location, location that had loyal guests returning to the Aurora. But after a refurbishing of all guest rooms and en suite bathrooms, it is the decor that brings them in as well. Six doubles are blessed with views of one of the world's great squares, the Piazza delle Erbe and the white-umbrella stalls that make up the daily marketplace. Consider yourself lucky if you snag the top-floor double (there is an elevator!) with a small balcony. There's another terrace, overlooking the *mercato* (market), for the guests' use on the second floor, just above the breakfast room where the hotel's free daily ample buffet is served.

Piazza delle Erbe 2 (southwest side of the piazza), 37121 Verona. www.hotelaurora.biz. ✆ **045-597-834.** Fax 045-801-0860. 19 units, 16 (including all doubles) with private bathroom. 160€ double. Rates include buffet breakfast. AE, DC, MC, V. Parking 10€. Bus: 72 or 73. **Amenities:** Bar; concierge; room service. *In room:* A/C, satellite TV, hair dryer.

Hotel Gabbia d'Oro ★★ One wall dates to 1320 at this cozy hotel of stone-trimmed doorways, rustic beams, and smart liveried service around the corner from the main piazza, but most of the *palazzo* is 18th century. The atmosphere hovers between medieval and eclectic, vaguely 19th-century Victorian romantic. It's all a bit put on—falsified fresco fragments, half-testers, and collectibles in little glass cases on wall brackets—but the result is more or less effective. Most rooms are terribly snug, but artfully placed mirrors help open up the space. Careful touches abound, from comfy couches in the sitting areas to extra-large shower heads and stone reliefs set in the tubs. A few rooms have small "Romeo-o-Romeo" balconies. The lovely winter garden is half-enclosed and half-open for nice weather.

Corso Porta Borsari 4A, 37121 Verona. www.hotelgabbiadoro.it. ✆ **045-800-3060.** Fax 045-590-293. 27 units. 220€–380€ double; 285€–530€ junior suite. Breakfast included, except during opera season (June 29–Sept 2), when it's 23€. AE, DC, MC, V. Valet parking 30€. Pets allowed. Bus: 72 or 73. **Amenities:** Bar; babysitting; bikes; concierge; room service. *In room:* A/C, TV, hair dryer, Internet, minibar.

Hotel Giulietta e Romeo ★★ A block from the Arena is this handsomely refurbished *palazzo*-hotel recommended for its upscale ambience, cordial can-do staff, and location in the heart of the *centro storico*. Brightly lit rooms are warmed by burnished cherrywood furnishings, and the large marble-tiled bathrooms are those you imagine finding in tony first-class hotels. The hotel takes its name seriously; there are two small marble balconies, à la Juliet, on the facade, but their views are unremarkable. The hotel is located on a narrow side street that is quiet and convenient to everything.

Vicolo Tre Marchetti 3 (south of Via Mazzini, 1 block east of the Arena), 37121 Verona. **℃ 045-800-3554.** Fax 045-801-0862. 30 units. 105€–230€ double; 125€–230€ triple. Rates include buffet breakfast. Mention Frommer's when booking and show book upon arrival for a 10% discount. Add approximately 30% to all above rates during the opera season and major trade fairs. AE, DC, MC, V. Parking 19€. Pets accepted upon request. From train station: Buses going to Piazza Brà. **Amenities:** Bar; babysitting; bikes; concierge; room service. *In room:* A/C, Satellite TV, hair dryer, minibar, Wi-Fi.

Hotel Torcolo ★ Lifelong friends Signoras Silvia and Diana are much of the reason behind the deserving success of this small, comfortable hotel just 1 block off the lively Piazza Brà. Each guest room is individually done. Room no. 31 is a country-style sunny top-floor room (the hotel has an elevator) with exposed ceiling beams; nos. 16 (a triple), 18, 21, and 34 are done with original Liberty-style furnishings. They truly care about your comfort here: Rooms are equipped with orthopedic mattresses on stiff springs, double-paned windows (though it's quiet already), extra air-conditioners on the top floor, and extra-wide single beds. They even keep different typical national travel tastes in consideration: They accept pets in a nod to Swiss travel habits, have a few rooms with tubs for Japanese, and offer some softer beds for the French. You can take the rather expensive breakfast outdoors on the small patio if the weather is pleasant, in a breakfast nook, or in your room.

Vicolo Listone 3 (just 1 block off the Piazza Brà), 37121 Verona. www.hoteltorcolo.it. **℃ 045-800-7512.** Fax 045-800-4058. 19 units. 70€–132€ double; 155€ double during the opera season. Discounted pricing Apr–May. MC, V. Nearby parking garage 12€ (20€ during opera season). Closed around Dec and Jan holidays. From train station: Buses to Piazza Brà. Pets allowed. **Amenities:** Babysitting; concierge; room service. *In room:* A/C, TV, hair dryer, minibar.

Where to Eat

Bottega del Vino ★ VERONESE/WINE BAR Oenophiles can push an evening's meal here into the stratosphere if they succumb to the wine cellar's unmatched 80,000-bottle selection, the largest in Verona. This atmospheric *bottega* first opened in 1890, and the old-timers who spend hours in animated conversation seem to have been here since then. The ambience and conviviality are reason enough to come by for a tipple at the well-known bar, where five-dozen good-to-excellent wines are for sale by the glass for 3.50€ to 12€. There's no mistaking Verona's prominence in the wine industry here. At mealtimes, the regulars head home and the next shift arrives: Journalists and local merchants fill the few wooden tables ordering simple but excellent dishes where Veneto's wines have infiltrated the kitchen, such as the *risotto al Amarone*, sauced with Verona's most dignified red.

Via Scudo di Francia 3 (off Via Mazzini), Verona. **℃ 045-800-4535.** www.bottegavini.it. Reservations necessary for dinner. Primi 11€–15€; secondi 16€–28€. AE, DC, MC, V. Wed–Mon noon–3pm (bar 10:30am–3pm) and 7pm–midnight (bar 6pm–midnight).

Brek ✦ CAFETERIA/PIZZERIA The Veronesi (and Italians in general; Brek is part of a northern Italian restaurant chain) are forever dismissing this place as a mediocre tourist spot. But then who are all these Italian-speaking, local-looking patrons with their trays piled high, cutting in line at the pizza station and clamoring for all the best tables outside with a brilliant view of the sun-kissed Arena? This strip of the Piazza Brà is lined with pleasant alfresco alternatives such as the more serious Olivo and Tre Corone, but Brek is an informal, inexpensive preference for a casual lunch where you can splurge (a lot) and walk away satisfied and solvent. Yes, this is fast-food *alla Veronese*—but do the Italians ever really go wrong in the culinary department? Inside, it's a food fest, with various pastas and fresh vegetables made up as you wait and some self-service where fruit salads and mixed green salads are displayed.

Piazza Brà 20. © **045-800-4561.** www.brek.it. Reservations not accepted. Primi and pizzas 3.50€–6€; secondi 4.20€–11€. AE, MC, V. Daily 11:30am–3pm and 6:30–10pm.

Il Desco ★ VERONESE Il Desco offers highly creative cuisine made with a variety of the best ingredients Veneto has to offer, with warm fresh-baked rolls and odd *amuse-bouches* such as olive-oil gelato with a tomato coulis. They tend to serve all meat dishes—from venison with pearl onions to salmon on a bed of lentils—extremely rare, so order it *ben cotto* (well done) if you want it cooked beyond merely flame-kissed. Some examples of the kitchen's rich creations include papardelle with sea snails, pork ravioli soup with shrimp, and stuffed pigeon and salt cod. Desserts are stupendous. Though the service is refined and the food of the highest quality, the inflated prices keep me from recommending it beyond a single star.

Via Dietro San Sebastiano 7. © **045-595-358.** www.ildesco.com. Reservations highly recommended. Primi 26€–32€; secondi 40€–45€; AE, DC, MC, V. Tues–Sat 12:40–2pm and 7:40–10:30pm (also Mon July–Aug and Dec). Closed 15 days in June and 15 days btw. Dec and Jan.

La Taverna di Via Stella 🎁 VERONESE Opened in 1999 by the Vantini brothers and their two friends, this taverna already has the feel of a popular neighborhood *osteria* that has been around for much longer, likely because all of the antique furniture was recouped from older taverns in the area. The small wooden tables are packed in tightly to seat the locals (the whole fire squad stopped in one time I visited), who come for huge portions of Veronese cuisine. To go with the 180 labels in the wine cellar, try *bigoli al torchio* with shredded duck, *coniglio alla veronese con pesto* (rabbit served in a crushed-basil-and-garlic pesto), or *pastise de' caval con polenta* (horse goulash with polenta).

Via Stella 5C. © **045-800-8008.** Reservations recommended. Primi 7.50€–9€; secondi 9€–15€; fixed-price menu 22€. AE, DC, MC, V. Tues–Sun noon–3pm and 7–11pm.

Osteria del Duca ★★ VERONESE There are no written records to confirm that this 13th-century *palazzo* was once owned by the Montecchi (Montague) family, and, thankfully, the discreet management never considered calling this place the Ristorante Romeo. But here you are, nonetheless, dining in what is believed to be Romeo's house, a characteristic medieval *palazzo,* and enjoying one of the nicest meals in town amid a spirited and friendly neighborhood ambience. You might find *penne con pomodoro e melanzane* (fresh tomato sauce with eggplant) or a perfectly grilled chop or filet with rosemary-roasted potatoes. It will be simple, it will be delicious, you'll probably make friends with the people sitting next to you, and you will always remember your meal at Romeo's Restaurant. If you don't have an adventurous palate, avoid anything on the menu that has *cavallo* or *asino* in it, unless you want to sample horsemeat, a local specialty, or donkey.

Via Arche Scaligeri 2 (east of Piazza dei Signori). ℭ **045-594-474.** Reservations not accepted. Primi 5€–7€; secondi 9€–12€; *menù turistico* 15€. MC, V. Mon–Sat 12:30–2:30pm and 7–10:30pm.

Pizzeria Impero ☺ PIZZERIA/TRATTORIA Location is not everything, but to sit with a pleasant lunch or moonlit dinner in this most elegant piazza will be one of those Verona memories that stays with you. Impero makes an okay pizza—especially for undiscerning tourist tastes—but any of the two dozen or so varieties will taste pretty heavenly if you're sharing an outdoor table with your Romeo or Juliet.

If Impero is full and the Arena area is more convenient to your day's itinerary, try the well-known and always busy **Pizzeria Liston,** a block off Piazza Brà at Via Dietro Listone 19 (ℭ **045-803-4003**), which also serves a full trattoria menu (all major credit cards accepted; closed Wed). Its pizzas are said to be better, but its side-street setting—even with outdoor tables—doesn't quite match that of the Impero.

Piazza dei Signori 8. ℭ **045-803-0160.** Reservations not accepted. Primi and pizzas 6€–9€; secondi 7€–16€. DC, MC, V. Summer daily noon–1am; winter Thurs–Tues noon–3:30pm and 7pm–midnight.

Cafes, Pastry Shops & Wine Bars

When all is said and done in Verona, one of the most important things to consider is where you'll stop to sip, recharge, socialize, nibble, and revel in this handsome town.

CAFES & PASTRY SHOPS Verona's grande dame of the local cafe society is the **Antico Caffè Dante ★**, in the beautiful Piazza dei Signori (no phone). Verona's oldest cafe, it is rather formal indoors (read: expensive) where meals are served. But it's most recommended for those who want to soak up the million-dollar view of one of Verona's loveliest ancient squares from the outdoor tables smack in the middle of it all. During the Arena summer season, this is the traditional après-opera spot to complete—and contemplate—the evening's experience. It's open daily from 9am to 4am.

The oldest of the cafe/bars lining Verona's market square is **Caffè Filippini,** at Piazza delle Erbe 26 (ℭ **045-800-4549**). Renovations have left little of yesteryear's character or charm, but centuries-old habits die hard: It's still the command post of choice whether indoors or (preferably) out, a lovely spot to take in the cacophony and colorful chaos of the market. It's open daily from 8am to 1am (closed Wed in winter).

An old-world temple of caffeine, **Caffè Tubino,** Corso Porta Borsari 15/D, 1 block west of the Piazza delle Erbe (ℭ **045-803-2296**), is stocked with packaged blends of Tubino-brand teas and coffees displayed on racks lining parallel walls in a small space made even smaller by the imposing crystal chandelier. The brand is well known, is nicely packaged, and makes a great gift. It's open daily from 7am to 11pm. On the same street is **Pasticceria Bar Flego,** Corso Porta Borsari 9 (ℭ **045-803-2471**), a beloved institution with eight tiny tables. Accompany a frothy cappuccino with an unbridled sampling of their deservedly famous bite-size pastries by the piece at 1€ each. *Zaletti* are a regional specialty, traditional cookies made with corn flour, raisins, and pine nuts—much better tried than described! It's closed on Monday.

One of Verona's oldest and most patronized *pasticcerie* is **Cordioli,** a stroll from Juliet's House on Via Cappello 39 (📞 **045-800-3055**). There are no tables and it's often crowded at the bar, but with coffee this good and pastries this fresh, it's obvious why the crowds come. Verona's perfect souvenir? How about homemade *baci di Giulietta* (Juliet's kisses, vanilla meringues) and *sospiri di Romeo* (Romeo's sighs, chocolate hazelnut cookies)? It's closed Sunday afternoon and Wednesday.

WINE BARS Verona is the epicenter of the region's important viticulture, but the old-time wine bars are decreasing in number and atmosphere. Recapture the spirit of yesteryear at **Carro Armato,** in a 14th-century *palazzo* at Vicolo Gatto 2A/Vicolo San Piero Martire (1 block south of Piazza Sant'Anastasia; 📞 **045-803-0175**), a great choice when you want to sit and sample some of 30 or so regional wines by the glass (2€–5€) and make an informal meal out of fresh, inexpensive bar food. Oldsters linger during the day playing cards or reading the paper at long wooden tables, while a younger crowd fills the place in the evening. A small but good selection of cheeses and cold cuts or sausages might be enough to take the edge off, but there is always an entree or two and a fresh vegetable side dish. It's open Monday to Friday from 10am to 2pm and 5pm to 2am, Saturday and Sunday 10am to 2am without a lunch break.

The wonderful old wine bar **Enoteca dal Zovo,** on Vicolo San Marco in Foro 7/5 (off Corso Porta Borsari near Caffè Tubino; 📞 **045-803-4369**), is run by Oreste, who knows everyone in town, and they all stop by for his excellent selection of Veneto wines averaging 2€ a glass; or you can go for broke and start with the very best at 4€. Oreste's *simpatica* American-born wife, Beverly, can give you a crash course. Salami, olives, and finger foods will help keep you vertical, as the few stools are always occupied by senior gentlemen who are as much a part of the fixtures as the hundreds of dusty bottles of wines and grappa that line the walls. It's open Tuesday to Sunday from 9am to 8pm.

Side Trips from Verona

The ancient Greeks called Italy *Enotria*—the land of wines. It produces more wine than anywhere else, so the annual **VinItaly ★★** wine fair held every April in Verona is an understandably prestigious event, drawing vintners from around the world. Veneto produces more DOC (Denominazione di Origine Controllata, zones of controlled name and origin) wines than anywhere else in Italy, particularly the Veronese trio of Bardolino and Valpolicella (reds) and soave (white).

The costly, dry Valpolicello wine known as Amarone comes from the vineyards outside Verona. **Masi ★** is one of the most respected producers, one of many in the Verona hills, whose *cantine* are open to the public for wine-tasting stops. Visit Verona's tourist information office for a listing of wine estates open to the public. No organized tours are available, and you'll need your own wheels, but oenologically minded visitors will want to taste some of Italy's finest wines at the point of their origin.

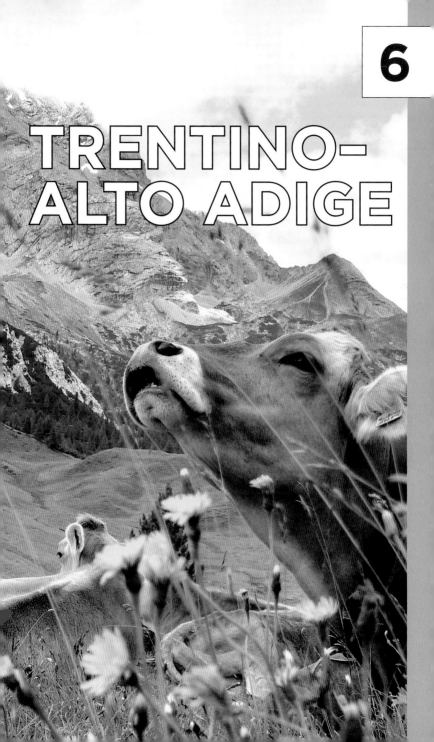

TRENTINO–ALTO ADIGE

M ountains dominate much of this region, which stretches north along the Adige River valley from the intersection of Lombardy and Veneto. The soaring landscape of the Alps and the Dolomites (Dolomiti) presides over a different Italy, one that often doesn't seem very Italian at all.

Most of the Dolomites and Trentino–Alto Adige (which is made up of two regions: Trentino, where most people are Italian-speaking; and Alto Adige/Südtirol/South Tyrol, where most people are German-speaking) belonged to Austria until it was handed over to Italy at the end of World War I. In fact, many residents, especially in and around Bolzano, Merano, and Brixen, still prefer the ways of the north to those of the south. They eat Austrian food, go about life with Teutonic crispness, and, most noticeably, tend to avoid speaking Italian in favor of their native German-based dialect. Some villages even speak Ladin, a vestigial Latin dialect related to Switzerland's Romansch. And they live amid mountain landscapes that are more suggestive of Austria than of Italy.

The eastern Alps that cut into the region are gentle and beautiful. A little farther to the east rise the Dolomites—dramatically craggy peaks that are really coral formations that only recently (in geological terms) reared up from ancient seabeds. Throughout Trentino–Alto Adige, towering peaks, highland meadows, and lush valleys provide a paradise for hikers, skiers, and rock climbers. Set amid these natural spectacles are pretty, interesting towns and castles to explore and a hybrid Teutonic-Latin culture to enjoy.

TRENT (TRENTO)

230km (143 miles) NW of Milan, 101km (63 miles) N of Verona, 57km (35 miles) S of Bolzano

Surrounded by mountains, this beautiful little city, founded by the Romans on the banks of the Adige River, definitely has an Alpine flair. It spent most of its history, from the 10th century though 1813, as a German-Austrian bishopric ruled by powerful princely bishops from their seat in the Castello del Buonconsiglio. In fact, the town's status as an Italian city at the crossroads of the Teutonic and Latin worlds, along with the bishop's dual role as subject both to the pope and to the German emperor, made Trent the ideal compromise site for the Council of Trent called in the 16th century to address the Protestant Reformation (see "Europe Divided," below).

PREVIOUS PAGE: Relaxing in the rugged South Tyrolean landscape outside Bressanone.

> **Trentino–Alto Adige on the Web**
>
> In addition to the city websites listed under each town throughout this chapter, the Trentino province around Trent maintains its own site at www.provincia.tn.it. The South Tyrol is also represented by private sites such as www.sudtirol.com and www.suedtirol.info, while the Dolomites can be researched at various sites claiming to be "the official" one (all are loaded with good information, at any rate); the most reputable site is www.dolomiti.it.

Trentino–Alto Adige

Napoleon's imperial sweep through Italy sent the last prince-bishop packing in 1796, and by 1813, Trent came under a century of direct Austrian rule. Austria's hegemony was constantly challenged by the local pro-Italian *Irredentist* movement, which was delighted when the treaties ending World War I landed Trent on the Italian side of the border in 1918.

And indeed, unlike other towns up here in the far north, which tend to lean heavily on their Austrian heritage, Trent is essentially Italian. The *piazze* are broad and sunny, the palaces are ocher-colored and tile-roofed, Italian is the lingua franca, and pasta is still a staple on menus. With its pleasant streets and the remnants of its most famous event, the 16th-century Council of Trent, Trent is a nice place to stay for a night or to visit en route to Bolzano (discussed later) and other places in the Trentino–Alto Adige.

Festivals & Markets In May and June, churches around the city are the evocative settings of performances of the ***Festivale di Musica Sacra* (Festival of Sacred Music).** Its final performances coincide with **Festive Vigiliane,** a medieval pageant for which townspeople turn up in the Piazza del Duomo appropriately decked out. Call the tourist office (*©*0461-839-000) for performance dates.

An ambitious program aptly named **Superfestival** stages musical performances, historic dramas, and reenactments of medieval and Renaissance legends in castles surrounding Trent; it runs late June through September.

A small daily **food market** covers the paving stones of Piazza Alessandro Vittorio every day from 8am to 1pm. A **larger market,** this one with clothing, crafts, and bric-a-brac as well, is held Thursday 8am to 1pm in Piazza Arogno near the Duomo; this same piazza hosts a **flea market** the third Sunday of every month.

Essentials

GETTING THERE By Train Strategically located on a main north-south rail line between Italy and Austria, Trent is served by some 21 trains a day to and from Verona (55–69 min.), a major transfer point for trains to Milan, Florence, Rome, Venice, Trieste, and all points south. There are about

EUROPE divided

As you amble around this lovely town, you'll quickly learn that much of what is notable about it is in some way connected with the historic 16th-century **Council of Trent,** in which the Catholic church closed ranks against the **Reformation,** the waves of Protestant reform coming from the north.

In late medieval Europe, power was consolidated through an intricate network wherein the secular princes, answerable to the Holy Roman Emperor, intersected with an overlying ecclesiastical structure of churches and monasteries, answering to the pope. Therefore, the Protestant revolutions of the 16th century being fired in the north by Martin Luther and other reformers—who were distressed by the corruption on the part of the official church and its pope in regard to worldly interests—were seen as much more than a mere argument over style of worship: They threatened Europe's entire power base.

Germanic Holy Roman Emperor Charles V—who had brought that office to the heights of its power, ruling or controlling much of Europe—recognized this threat, both to Catholicism and to his domain. But he spent so much of his time and effort fighting wars with France and others that, despite holding his own diets to stamp out Luther's ideas, Protestantism kept growing in Germany. Charles eventually pressured the pope into instituting a great council to refute the reformers, and the Vatican called the council in 1536. But it took

another 9 years to settle on Trent as the ideal compromise location in which to hold it.

Far from taking Protestant complaints to heart, the council took a hard line, becoming more of a defensive strategy session. The Vatican dug in its heels and its doctrine, reorganizing church structure and policies to *tighten* control rather than loosen it. This became the Counter-Reformation, which, while not quite reaching the terrifying extremes of the Spanish Inquisition, brought the yardstick of conservatism down hard on the knuckles of Catholic Europe.

Still, it was all too late to stem the tide of Protestantism—and a general progressive slide away from the remnants of feudal power structures. The Germanic countries, soon to be followed by England, increasingly turned their backs on the Vatican. Charles V was the last German emperor to be crowned by the pope. The Papal States and the continent's secular kingdoms drifted apart, and the old power system gradually unraveled as Europe groped its way toward the system of nation-states we know today.

two-dozen trains a day from Bolzano (32–49 min.). To reach the center of town from the train station, follow the Via Pozzo through several name changes until it reaches the Piazza del Duomo as Via Cavour.

By Bus Trentino Trasporti (☏ **0461-821-000;** www.ttesercizio.it), which leaves from a terminal next to the train station, is the major link to outlying mountain towns. There's also hourly service to and from Riva del Garda on Lago di Garda (1 hr., 40 min.; p. 346).

By Car Autostrada A22 connects Trent with Verona in about an hour; from Verona, you can connect with the A4 for Milan (total trip time btw. Milan and Trent is about 2½ hr.), and with the A22 to Modena and, from there, the A1 for Florence and Rome. (Trent is a drive of about 3½ hr. from Florence and about 6½ hr. from Rome.) A22 also runs north to Bolzano, a little more than half an hour away; the slower S12 also connects Trent and Bolzano, and from it you can get on the scenic Strada di Vino.

VISITOR INFORMATION The local **tourist office,** near the Duomo at Via Manci 2 (☏ **0461-216-000;** fax 0461-232-426; www.apt.trento.it), is open daily 9am to 7pm.

What to See & Do

Castello del Buonconsiglio ★ Many Council of Trent sessions were held in this bishop's palace/fortress on the north edge of town, which you can reach by walking north from the Duomo along Via Belenzani, and then east on Via Roma

---

Trent on Two Wheels

The city offers bikes to those who sign up for the **TrentoCard,** which also offers discounts for municipal museums and transportation. A 1-day card costs 10€, and a 2-day card costs 15€. Pick one up at the tourist office, which sometimes offers guided cycling tours on weekend mornings in warmer months. Call ☏ **0461-216-000** to see if there is one planned and to reserve a space.

The manicured gardens of the Castello del Buonconsiglio.

(though it's a bit of a trek from the rest of the center and the train station)—both streets, especially the former, are lined with the palaces, many with faded frescoes on their facades, built to house the church officials who came to Trent to attend the council sessions. The mazelike *castello* incorporates the 13th-century Castelvecchio, surrounded by medieval fortifications, and the elegant Magno Palazzo, a palace built for a prince-bishop in the 15th century.

Among the many small collections contained within the vast complex is the Museo Provincale d'Arte, where the pride of the collection is the **Ciclo dei Mesi (Cycle of the Months)** ★★, an enchanting fresco cycle painted around 1400. It presents a detailed look at life at court and in the countryside, showing amusements among the lords and ladies and much hard work among the peasants. It's housed in the Torre dell'Aquila, or Eagle's Tower; for admission, ask the guards at the Loggia del Romanino, an atrium named for the Renaissance artist who frescoed it.

You can also visit the cell where native son Cesare Battiste was held in 1916 for his part in the *Irredentist* movement, which sought to return Trent and other parts of the region to Italy—which, indeed, came to pass with the Treaty of Versailles in 1919, but not before Battiste was hanged in the moat that surrounds the Castelvecchio.

Via Bernardo Clesio 3. ✆ **0461-233-770** or 0461-492-840. www.buonconsiglio.it. Admission 8€ adults, 5€ children. Apr–Sept Tues–Sun 10am–6pm; Oct–Mar Tues–Sun 9:30am–5pm. Bus: 5, 7, 10, or B.

Duomo The outcomes of many Council of Trent sessions were announced in this 13th- to 16th-century cathedral, delightfully situated on the wide expanse of the cafe-filled Piazza Duomo. This square, with a statue of Neptune at its center, is referred to as the city's *salotto* (sitting room), so popular is it as a place to pass the time. The decrees that came out of the council were read in the Duomo's Chapel of the Crucifix, beneath an enormous 15th-century cross. Beneath the altar of the main church is the crypt-cum-basilica Paleocristiana, a 6th-century church later used as a crypt for the city's powerful prince-bishops. A few scraps of mosaic and carvings remain.

Piazza Duomo. ✆ **0461-234-419.** Admission to the crypt 1€, or free with the Museo Diocesano ticket (see below). Mon–Sat 9:30am–12:30pm and 2:30–6pm; crypt 10am–noon and 2:30–6pm. Bus: A.

Museo Diocesano Tridentino The cathedral's museum is housed in the adjoining, heavily fortified palace of these bishops. The museum displays some fascinating paintings of council sessions that serve almost as news photos of the proceedings (one provides a seating plan for delegates), as well as 16th-century tapestries and statuary, objects from the Duomo's treasury, and a collection of medieval and Renaissance paintings. The latter often showcase local Saint Vigilio, Trent's 4th-century bishop and a literal iconoclast whose destruction of a Saturn idol earned him his martyrdom as enraged pagans beat him to death with their wooden shoes. By the Renaissance, these nail-studded sandals had inexplicably become the *zoccolo,* a silken slipper, which the hapless saint is always holding up in paintings as the symbol of his martyrdom.

Piazza Duomo 18. ✆ **0461-234-419.** www.museodiocesanotridentino.it. Admission (includes Duomo's crypt; see above) 4€ adults, 1€ ages 12–18, 8€ family. Wed–Mon 9:30am–12:30pm and 2:30–5:30pm (June–Sept to 6pm). Bus: A.

A painting in the Museo Diocesano Tridentino of a Council of Trent session.

Santa Maria Maggiore The pretty little church is a set piece of Lombard Renaissance architecture, designed and decorated almost entirely in the second quarter of the 16th century. Inside is an organ gallery ornately carved by Vincenzo Grandi in 1534. The church hosted several Council of Trent sessions, including the last ones.

Piazza Santa Maria Maggiore (btw. Via Rosimini and Via Cavour). ℂ **0461-239-888.** Free admission. Mon–Sat 9:30am–12:15pm and 3:30–7:30pm. Bus: NP.

Where to Stay

Trent, despite its history, has a pretty sorry hotel crop, with most of the nicer joints outside the center and focused mainly on conference centers and corporate rates. If you want a bit more class and a full complement of amenities in your hotel, you might check out the **Grand Hotel Trento,** Via Alfieri 1–3 (ℂ **0461-271-000;** fax 0461-271-001; www.grandhoteltrento.com), a large and elegant but somewhat bland business-oriented hotel near the bus and train station, a few blocks from the Duomo. Doubles go for between 110€ and 165€; prices depend on availability. All major credit cards are accepted. The hotels listed below are located in the *centro storico,* much of which is closed to traffic.

Accademia Hotel ★ This sim-ple but nice hotel is the best choice in the center, though prices are a bit steep. It's set in a restored medieval house on an alley about a

Getting a Lift out of Town

For a breezy view of Trent and a heart-thumping aerial ride as well, take the **cable car** from Ponte di San Lorenzo near the train station up to Sardagna, a village on one of the mountainsides that encloses the city. You may want to provision yourself at the market and enjoy a picnic on one of the grassy meadows nearby. The cable car (ℂ **0461-822-075**) runs daily every 30 minutes from 7am to 10:30pm (7:30pm on weekends), and the fare is 1€ each way.

block from the Duomo and Piazza Santa Maria Maggiore (whose bell tower some rooms overlook). The reception area's whitewashed vaulted ceilings and stone doorjambs don't really carry over into the rooms, which are a bit spartan, if well equipped with modular or rattan furnishings, sometimes under nice sloping ceilings. The one drawback to its central location is its proximity to the church bells.

Vicolo Colico 4–6, 38100 Trento (off Via Cavour). www.accademiahotel.it. © **0461-233-600.** Fax 0461-230-174. 50 units. 150€–165€ double; 180€–195€ triple; 200€–220€ junior suite. Rates include buffet breakfast. AE, DC, MC, V. **Amenities:** Restaurant; woodsy *enoteca* (wine bar); bikes; concierge; room service. *In room:* A/C, TV, hair dryer, minibar, Wi-Fi.

Hotel Aquila D'Oro ★ This centuries-old *palazzo* has some of the nicest rooms in Trent, with a spalike focus on health and fitness in an ancient location right around the corner from Piazza Duomo. Each of the doubles has either a Roman sauna or a therapeutic shower known as a "water paradise," as well as either stationary bikes or treadmills. Decor throughout is stylishly contemporary, with a nice smattering of Oriental carpets, vaulted ceilings, and other interesting and cozy architectural touches in public rooms.

Via Belenzani 76, 38100 Trento. www.aquiladoro.it. ©/fax **0461-986-282.** 19 units. 90€–250€ double (prices vary greatly depending on the individual room you choose). Rates include buffet breakfast. AE, DC, MC, V. **Amenities:** Bar; concierge; room service; smoke-free rooms. *In room:* A/C, TV, hair dryer, minibar, Wi-Fi.

Hotel Garni (aka Hotel Venezia) This old hotel is very basic. It is rather less charming than its next-door neighbor, Aquila D'Oro (see above), and its "amenities" consist entirely of toilet paper and one towel, but it's cheap. Marked by 1950s-style furnishings, the simple, high-ceiling rooms are a bit dowdy but offer solid, old-fashioned comfort (unfortunately, some beds still bear the sags left by generations of travelers). Its selling point: The rooms in the front come with stunning views over the Piazza Duomo. For the reception, walk around the corner to the "unofficial" entrance, on Piazza Duomo, to find someone to check you in. **Note:** Though the hotel's official name is now Hotel Garni, the name painted on the side of the building still says HOTEL VENEZIA (because it's a historic landmark, they can't change the outside!).

Via Belenzani 70/Piazza Duomo 45, 38100 Trento. www.hotelveneziatn.it. ©/fax **0461-234-559.** 50 units, 28 with private bathroom. 59€ double without private bathroom; 76€ double with private bathroom; 92€ triple with private bathroom. Rates include continental breakfast. MC, V. Free parking 200m (650 ft.) from hotel. **Amenities:** Wi-Fi. *In room:* Hair dryer, no phone.

Where to Eat

It's almost a requirement to stroll down Trent's Renaissance streets with a gelato from **Torre Verde-Gelateria Zanella,** on Via Suffragio 6 (© **0461-232-039**). Many flavors are made from fresh, local fruits in season, while others make no such attempt at wholesomeness and incorporate the richest chocolate and cream.

Birreria Pedavena BEER HALL/PIZZA This hip beer hall and cafe draws a big crowd for coffee and pastries in the morning and keeps serving a huge mix of pastas, *Würstel* (sausages), and its own beer all day. You will probably be happiest if you order simply, maybe a plate of *Würstel* or goulash. Additionally, it keeps some of the latest hours in town, making Pedavena something of a late-evening spot in a town where the nightlife is scarce. There is a separate room for smokers.

Piazza Fiera 13 at Via Santa Croce. ℂ **0461-986-255.** www.birreriapedavena.com. Primi 5€–7€; secondi 6€–12€; pizza 6€–8€. MC, V. Mon and Wed–Thurs 9am–12:30am; Fri–Sat 9am–1am; Sun 9am–midnight. Sometimes closed in July.

La Cantinota ITALIAN With its white tablecloths, excellent service, and reasonably priced menu, La Cantinota may be the most popular restaurant in Trent. The fare includes Italian and Tyrolean dishes and is truly inspired, making use of fresh local ingredients: wonderful homemade gnocchi, *strangola preti* (spinach dumplings coated in melted butter), rich risottos with porcini mushrooms, and venison with polenta. The adjoining piano bar is popular with local talent who tend to intersperse Frank Sinatra renditions with yodeling.

Via San Marco 24. ℂ **0461-238-527.** www.cantinota.editarea.com. Reservations recommended. Primi 6.50€–8€; secondi 11€–13€. Tasting menus 25€–30€. AE, MC, V. Fri–Wed noon–3pm and 7–11pm (piano bar 10:30pm–2am).

Scrigno del Duomo ★★ ITALIAN/WINE BAR This stylish wine bar and restaurant offers creative cooking in a stellar location. From the front courtyard, with tables set under the frescoed facade, you can peek through the gate at the fountain splashing away on Trent's main piazza while sipping on a glass from the huge wine list and nibbling on intricate twists on Northern Italian classics: a pigeon carpaccio or sea bream in a wild thyme sauce. Dishes change constantly with the seasons and chef's whims but usually include pasta or gnocchi with some combination of lake fish and zucchini, and its signature cheek of beef, stewed in merlot with cream of celery sauce and candied baby carrots.

Piazza Duomo 29. ℂ **0461-220-030.** www.scrignodelduomo.com. Reservations recommended. Primi 6€–8€; secondi 9€–15€; tasting menu 47€ without wine. MC, V. Daily 11am–2:30pm and 6pm–midnight.

The Southern Trentino

Castello di Avio The first historical mention of the spectacular **Castello Sabbionara** (ℂ**0464-684-453**), at the town of Avio, 21km (13 miles) south of Rovereto, is from the 13th century, though the castle dates back at least to the 11th century. It was built on the ever-shifting battle line between the dominions of Austrian emperors and the Venetian Republic—so it's no surprise that, during a 13th-century period of Venetian control when the castle was enlarged, the Casa delle Guardie (Guard's House) was frescoed with marvelous medieval battle scenes featuring the castle in the background. Local folklore whispers that public executions were once carried out inside the imposing Picadòra tower, which defends the north side. A more pleasant part of the house is the beautifully

The Guard's House of the Castello di Avio.

frescoed Room of Love on the top floor. The castle is open February to December 17, Tuesday to Sunday 10am to 1pm and 2 to 6pm (Oct–Dec 17 to 5pm); admission 5€ adults, 2.50€ children ages 6 to 10.

Rovereto   There are two main reasons to visit this noble, medieval town 24km (15 miles) south of Trent. One is simply to stroll through its winding streets and elegant, quiet piazza, both of which lie in the shadow of the 15th-century **Castello di Rovereto** (✆ **0464-438-100**). This Venetian-built castle reminds its visitors that this is as far north as Venice got (by 1418) in its long battle with Austrian powers over control of the Tyrol. By 1487, the Austrian factions had control again, but Italian hopes, and the native pro-Italy *Irrendentisti,* never truly disappeared. This brings us to the other reason to visit: to pay homage to the thousands of mostly Italian and Austrian soldiers who died in the surrounding hills during some of the fiercest fighting of World War I.

These soldiers are commemorated mainly by two sites: the daily sunset ringing of the world's largest peal bell, the **Campana dei Caduti,** or Bell of the Fallen (✆ **0464-434-412;** daily 9am–6:30pm; 3€ adults, 2€ ages 6–18), which perches atop the hillside near a neoclassical rotunda temple to the casualties of war, and the **Museo Storico Italiano della Guerra** (✆ **0464-438-100**). The latter occupies part of the castle, at Via Castelbarco 7, and displays photographs, weaponry, and other memorabilia associated with this and other battles. The museum hours are Tuesday to Sunday 10am to 8pm. Admission is 7€ adults, 2€ ages 6 to 18.

Another reason to come to Rovereto is to attend one of its much-heralded cultural events: The **Rovereto Festival,** in early September, features dance performances and a major exhibition of contemporary art; and the late-September **Festival Internazionale Mozart** (✆ **0464-439-988**) features world-renowned performances of the composer's work.

Rovereto is less than half an hour south of Trent via A22. About two buses an hour make the 45-minute trip; contact **Trentino Trasporti** (✆ **0461-821-000;** www.ttspa.it) for more information. The **APT tourist office,** at a park on the Leno River at Corso Rosmini 6A (✆ **0464-430-363;** fax 0464-435-528; www.visitrovereto.it), is open Monday to Friday 8:30am to 12:15pm and 2:30 to 6pm, and Saturday (summer only) 8:30am to 12:15pm.

En Route to Bolzano: The Strada di Vino

Some of Italy's finest wines are produced on the vines that cloak the hillsides between Trent and Bolzano. (These local wines include many pinot grigios and pinot noirs, and Vernatsch, the most common red of the region.) If you are traveling by car between the two cities, you can make the trip on the well-marked **Strada di Vino** or **Weinstrasse** (Wine Road; www.weinstrasse.com). Leave Trent on S12; 15km (9¼ miles) north, you will come to the main turnoff for the village of Lavis; take this turnoff, and from here, easy-to-follow yellow signs will lead you along a series of twisting roads past vineyards and around Lago di Caldaro to Bolzano. Many of the vineyards have tasting rooms open to the public and sometimes offer cheese, sandwiches, and other refreshment as well.

The **Vini Josef Hofstätter** cantina, on Piazza Municipio 5 in Termeno (✆ **0471-860-161**), welcomes drop-ins for free tastings, but for most vineyards you must book ahead (keep in mind that most are closed from around noon–2pm). The Hofstätter vineyard (www.hofstatter.com), for example, accepts reservations for 60-minute tours or 90-minute tours and tastings for 10€ and 15€ per person, respectively. Also check out **Georg Baron Widmann,** Via im Feld 1 in Cortaccia (© **0471-880-092**); **Alois Lageder** in Magrè (© **0471-809-500;** www.aloislageder.eu); and **Castel Schwanburg** in Nalles (© **0471-678-622**). There's the small **Südtiroler Weinmuseum** in the Caldaro village outside Termeno at Goldgasse 1 (© **0471-963-168**), open Monday to Saturday 9:30am to noon and 2 to 6pm, Sunday 10am to noon. If you don't have your own wheels, the tourist offices in Trent and Bolzano can provide lists of local tour companies that lead wine tours.

BOLZANO

154km (95 miles) N of Verona, 118km (73 miles) S of Innsbruck, 57km (35 miles) NE of Trent

Without even crossing a border, by heading north from Trent into the Alto Adige region, you'll find yourself in a place that doesn't resemble Italy at all. During its long history, this pretty town at the confluence of the Talvera and Isarco rivers has been ruled by the bishops of Trent, the counts of Tyrol, and the Habsburgs, to name but a few of its lords. Bolzano (**Bozen** in German) has been part of Italy only since the end of World War I. As you explore the narrow streets and broad *platzen* (*piazze* in Italian) and stroll through the parks that line the town's two rivers, you get the sense that, with its gabled, Tyrolean-style houses and preference for Germanic dialect, the city is still more Teutonic than Italian.

Bolzano's foundation dates back to the Iron Age—evidenced by the famous **Ice Man** cooling his 5,000-year-old heels in the excellent local archaeology museum. But Bolzano didn't really pick up steam until the Middle Ages, when its situation at a river confluence just south of an Alpine pass made it an important small market town.

Festivals & Markets Bolzano celebrates spring with **weekend concerts** throughout April and May in Piazza Walther, and adds a **flower show,** with more music, around the first of May. The city's most serious musical event is the **Concorso Internazionale Piantistico F. Busoni,** an international piano competition held the last 2 weeks of August. The **Festival del Teatro di Strada** draws wandering musicians, mimes, puppeteers, and other performers to the streets of the Old City in October. One of the more colorful events in the region is the **Bartolomeo Horse Fair,** which brings together the region's most beautiful equines on the Renon plateau, which can be reached by funicular (see "Cable Cars," on p. 245).

One of the most enjoyable walks in the Old City takes you through the stalls of the **fruit-and-vegetable market** in Piazza delle Erbe, which operates Monday through Saturday from 8am to 7pm. From November 28 to December 23, the city hosts a much-attended **Mercatino di Natale (Christkindlmarkt,** or **Christmas Market**), in which handmade ornaments, wooden toys, and other seasonal crafts, along with Christmas pastries and mulled wine, are sold from booths in a festively decorated Piazza Walther.

A **flea market** fills the Passeggiata del Talvera along the River Talvera (follow Via Museo from the center of town) the first Saturday of the month (except July–Aug), opening at 8am and closing at 5pm.

Essentials

GETTING THERE By Train Bolzano is on the north-south rail line that links Verona with Innsbruck, Austria, via the Brenner Pass. There are some 17 trains daily from Verona (1½–1¾ hr.) and 25 trains a day from Trent (32–45 min.). Hourly train service links Bolzano with Merano (38 min.).

By Bus Bolzano is the hub of the excellent **SAD bus** network, serving even the most remote mountain villages (✆ **0471-450-111;** www.sad.it). There are hourly buses to and from Merano (1 hr.) and Bressanone (1 hr.). Two daily morning buses (currently departing at 9:15 and 11:10am) make the trip to Cortina, with a change in Dobbiaco (about 4 hr.). The extremely helpful staff at the bus station, the round building a block up from the train station and on the left, will help you make sense of the routing.

By Car Autostrada A22 connects Bolzano with Trent in a little over half an hour and with Verona (where you can connect with the A4 for Milan and Rome) in a little over an hour; and, farther south, Modena (where you can connect with the A1 for Florence and Rome); A22 runs north to Innsbruck. Avoid parking in the criminally expensive public garages; most hotels have arrangements for considerably less.

By Plane Bolzano's dinky **airport** (✆ **0471-254-070;** www.abd-airport.it), on the south side of the Isarco River, a few minutes' taxi ride from the center, is the Dolomite's official airport and has daily flights from Rome and Frankfurt, as well as service from Vienna.

VISITOR INFORMATION The **city tourist office,** near the Duomo at Piazza Walther 8 (✆ **0471-307-000;** fax 0471-980-128; www.bolzano-bozen. it), dispenses a wealth of information on Bolzano and the South Tyrol. It's open Monday to Friday from 9am to 6:30pm and on Saturday from 9am to 12:30pm.

A Stroll Around Bolzano

With its two rivers, surrounding hills, expansive greens, and medieval center, Bolzano is an extremely appealing city that seems to effortlessly meld urban sophistication with an appreciation for nature. The compact medieval Old City is still the heart of town, and, at its center, is **Piazza Walther,** honoring a 12th-century wandering minstrel. The piazza captures the mood of its lighthearted historical associations with a fringe of cafe tables to one side and the brightly tiled roof and lacy spire of the **Duomo** on the other. The interior of this 12th- to 14th-century edifice is far plainer, enlivened somewhat by much-faded frescoes and an intricately carved pulpit (✆ **0471-978-676;** Mon–Fri 9:45am–noon and 2–5pm, Sat 9:45am–noon; Sun for services only).

A far more enticing church is the **Chiesa dei Domenicani** (✆ **0471-973-133**), just

The spire of Bolzano's Duomo.

An extensive selection of produce at Bolzano's fresh market.

a few steps west of the Duomo. Inside the 13th-century church are two sets of frescoes, the city's greatest artistic treasures. One from the 15th century, on the walls of the cloisters, depicts court life. The other, in the Capella di San Giovanni (under the arch behind the altar and to the right), is a 14th-century religious cycle attributed to the school of Giotto, including the *Triumph of Death.* In these rich frescoes, you can see the beginnings of the use of such elements as perspective and foreshortening, suggesting the influence of the early Renaissance. It's open Monday to Saturday 9:30am to 6pm, Sunday for services only.

There is one more church to see in Bolzano, but before you reach it, you will be distracted by the considerable worldly pleasures this city offers. If you walk north from Piazza Walther, you will soon come to the lively clamor of **Piazza dell'Erbe,** actually one long, wide street that winds past a statue of Neptune through the Old Town and is so called because it has hosted the city's **fruit-and-produce market** for centuries. At the north end is Bolzano's atmospheric main shopping street, **Via dei Portici,** also closed to traffic and lined with 15th-century houses whose porticoes overhang the sidewalk to create a cozy effect that is definitely more northern European than Italian.

The **Chiesa dei Francescani** (© 0471-977-293) is across Via dei Portici on Via Francescani. Inside there's a sumptuously carved **altar** ★ from 1500, one of the Gothic masterpieces of the Trentino–Alto Adige. The 14th-century cloisters are charming—intimate, frescoed on one side, gracefully vaulted, and beautifully planted—and are open Monday to Saturday 10am to noon and 2:30 to 6pm, Sunday for services only.

Bolzano's most popular attraction by far is the thoroughly modernized **South Tyrol Museum of Archaeology ★★★,** Via Museo at Via Cassa di Risparmio (© 0471-320-100; www.iceman.it), better known as Ötzi's House, as it was remodeled in 1998 to house the famed 5,300-year-old "Ice Man." This mummy made headlines in 1991 when a pair of German hikers discovered him sticking out of a melting glacier high in the Tyrol mountains—though whether he was of Alpine origin or merely trying to cross the Alps is still being debated. His equipment and one of his last meals seem to have come from lower-altitude valleys, nearer Verona.

Forensic analysis brought the surprise revelation that, apparently, he was shot in the shoulder with an arrow shortly before he died. Further research, published in 2003 (and based on blood samples, microscopic fibers, and re-creations of wound placements—real *CSI* kinda stuff) revealed that the Ice Man was killed in a battle or skirmish of some sort—shot in the back, although probably killed by a blow to the head, and then carried off by a companion who must have removed the arrow for him.

Along with the mummy were preserved remnants of clothing (including shoes and a bearskin hat), a flint dagger, a copper ax, and a quiver with flint-tipped arrows he was in the process of making. The museum is open Tuesday to Sunday 10am to 6pm, and daily in December, July, and August. Admission is 9€ adults, 7€ students 27 and under and seniors 65 and over. The highly recommended audio guides are an extra 2€, while a guided tour for groups up to 15 people is 38€ per guide.

Across the **River Talvera** (follow Via Museo west across the Ponte Talvera) lies the pleasant confines of **Gries ★**, once an outlying village and now a quaint, leafy neighborhood. It grew up around the Abbazia dei Benedettini di Gries, a Benedictine abbey (not usually open to the public) that is prettily surrounded by vineyards and gardens. Just beyond is the **Vecchia Parrochiale di Gries,** the village's parish church, whose treasures include a 12th-century crucifix and an elaborately carved 15th-century altar (✆ **0471-283-089;** Mon–Fri 10:30am–noon and 2:30–4pm; closed Nov–Mar).

If you wish to continue walking or biking, Gries contains one end of the **Passeggiata del Guncina,** a beautifully maintained 8km-long (5-mile) trail that leads through parklike forests planted with many botanical specimens to a belvedere and a waterfall before dumping you back into town. You wind up at the northerly end of the park stretched along the north bank of the Talvera River.

CASTLES Of the many castles that surround Bolzano, the closest to the center is the **Castel Mareccio,** just a short walk along the River Talvera (from the Piazza delle Erbe, follow the Via Museo west to the Ponte Talvera and, from there, the Lungo Talvera Bozen north for less than .5km/¼ mile). Though it is now used as a convention center and its five towers rise from a residential neighborhood of recent vintage, this 13th-century fortress is a stunning sight, all the more so because it is surrounded by a generous swath of vineyards that have been saved from urban encroachment and backed by forested hills. You can step inside for a glimpse at the stone-walled medieval interior and enjoy a beverage at the bar; the castle is open to the public Wednesday through Monday 9am to 6pm (hours vary when conferences are in session; ✆ **0471-976-615**).

A longer walk of about 2km (1¼ mile, or take the free bus from Piazza Walther, which goes back and forth only btw. the piazza and the castle) leads out of town north to the **Castel Roncolo ★★** (✆ **800-210-003** or 0471-329-808; www.roncolo.info), beautifully ensconced high above the town and beneath a massive, foreboding cliff face. The interior of this 13th-century castle is decorated with faded but fascinating frescoes from the 14th and 15th centuries that depict secular scenes from the story of *Tristan and Isolde* and other tales of romantic love and chivalry. These painted scenes are remarkably moving in their almost primitive craftsmanship that nonetheless reveals a certain worldliness. Admission is 8€ adults, 5.50€ students and seniors 60 and over; hour-long guided tours in English cost an extra 3€ per person (minimum six people). The castle is open Tuesday to Sunday 10am to 6pm (July–Sept to 8pm). To get here, follow the Via Castel Roncolo north from the Chiesa dei Francescani; you will pass one side of the Castel Mareccio, at which point signposts will lead you along Via Beatro Arrigo and Via San Antonio for a gradual uphill climb to Castel Roncolo.

CABLE CARS Several **cable cars** will whisk you right from the center of Bolzano into the surrounding mountains. The most dramatic ride takes you from a terminal near the train station 900m (3,000 ft.) up to the **Altopiano del Renon** (www.renon.com), a pasture-covered plateau that provides dizzying views down to Bolzano and up to higher Dolomite peaks. The ride deposits you in SopraBolzano (aka Oberbozen), where you can sip a beer, enjoy the view, and then venture farther by footpath or an electric tram into a bizarre landscape of spindly rock spires—worn needle-thin by erosion, each seeming to balance a boulder on the top—that surrounds the village of Collabo. The cable car (✆**0471-978-479**) makes the ascent in 15 minutes and operates daily from a terminus about 450m (1,500 ft.) east of the train station on Via Renon; it operates hourly from 7am to 8pm. Costs are 2.50€ from Bolzano to Soprabolzano and 2.50€ for the tram between SopraBozen and Collabo.

The **Funivia di San Genesio** takes you up a forested hillside to the pretty village of San Genesio Atesino, surrounded by woods and mountain peaks. Cable cars (✆**0471-978-436**) leave hourly from 7am to 7pm (Sun from 8am) from a terminus on Via Sarentino on the northern outskirts of Bolzano (take bus no. 12 or 14). The trip takes 15 minutes, and the round-trip fare is 3.20€. San Genesio's little **tourist office,** at Schrann 7 (✆**0471-354-196;** fax 0471-354-085; www.jenesien.net), is open Monday to Friday 9am to 1pm (July–Oct also 4–6pm). It can set you up with one of the horseback-riding schools that offer rides across the high Alpine meadows for about 20€; call ahead.

Where to Stay

Hotel Feichter This charming little inn is one of the few hotels in the Old City itself and, for the location and atmosphere it provides, is one of the city's better lodging values. On the main floor, there's a restaurant that resembles a *Weinstube* (tavern). The rooms may not be full of mountain ambience (and the bathrooms are cramped), but they contain serviceable, modern, comfortable furnishings. The extremely firm beds are equipped with that wonderful local luxury: thick down comforters. There's also a narrow courtyard set with picnic tables and shaded by a grape arbor.

Via Grappoli 15, 39100 Bolzano. www.hotelfeichter.it. ✆ **0471-978-768.** Fax 0471-974-803. 49 units. 85€ double; 105€ triple. Rates include breakfast. MC, V. Parking 5€ in garage (10 spots). Closed 3 weeks in Feb. **Amenities:** Tyrolean restaurant; bar; concierge. *In room:* TV, hair dryer (on request).

Hotel Greif ★★★ The boutique hotel has a motto, "very personal," and it shines through—from the laptop PC with free Internet access in every room to an extraordinary attention to detail (the silver umbrellas ranked by the doors match the burnished steel and glass of the entryway). Each überstylish, modern room is unique, featuring an original work by a Tyrolean artist (each key chain is a tiny catalog for that room's artist). Most accommodations are spacious, some with lofted bedrooms, others with Jacuzzi tubs and views over the main square. The furnishings are a mix of modern and late-19th-century antiques, including gorgeous inlaid wood dressers and desks. Room no. 211 is like a musician's studio apartment, with deep sloping ceilings, dormer windows onto Piazza Walther, and even a baby grand.

Piazza Walther, 39100 Bolzano. www.greif.it. © **0471-318-000.** Fax 0471-318-148. 33 units. 172€–193€ comfort double; 210€–233€ superior double; 243€–270€ deluxe double; 287€–317€ junior suite; 360€ junior suite with sauna and grand piano. Buffet breakfast 20€ extra. AE, DC, MC, V. Parking 17€. **Amenities:** Restaurant; bar (at Parkhotel Laurin, see below); babysitting; children's center at Laurin; concierge; golf (nearby); pool at Laurin; room service. *In room:* A/C, TV, hair dryer, laptop w/Internet connection, minibar, free movies.

Hotel Regina ☺ For pleasant and affordable lodgings in Bolzano, you need look no farther than this modern hotel across the street from the train station—a decent location, as you're still only 3 blocks from the main square, but the rate disparity below reflects the noisiness of the busy main street out front. *Families take note:* The bright rooms are unusually large, and there are several quads and one mansard quintuplet on hand. Although accommodations are quite plain, they're nicely decorated with streamlined Scandinavian furnishings, and all offer a free crib if necessary.

Via Renon 1, 39100 Bolzano. www.hotelreginabz.it. © **0471-972-195** or 0471-974-099. Fax 0471-978-944. 40 units. 90€–130€ double; 110€–155€ triple; 130€–175€ quad. Rates include breakfast. MC, V. Free on-street parking. **Amenities:** Bar; concierge. *In room:* A/C, TV, hair dryer, Internet.

Parkhotel Laurin ★ This early-20th-century Liberty-style edifice takes up an entire city block just a few hundred meters from both the train station and Piazza Walther. Though it's full of modern comforts, the quirky old structure gives it character and style (and plenty of windows). Rooms are spacious. About half the "superior" rooms overlook the garden, while the others face downtown. Suites are like mini-apartments with a hall off of which open the bedroom, a tiny sitting room (often with a balcony), and the bathroom (in brown marble with double sinks and separate tub and shower stalls); one even has its own sauna. The hotel's real selling point is its large, landscaped garden of flower-lined and tree-shaded gravel paths.

Via Laurin 4, 39100 Bolzano. www.laurin.it. © **0471-311-000.** Fax 0471-311-148. 96 units. 128€–152€ standard double; 194€–216€ superior double; 275€–306€ junior suite. Breakfast included. AE, DC, MC, V. Parking 13€. **Amenities:** Italian restaurant; period bar; babysitting; children's center and small playground; outdoor heated pool; room service (5€ service fee). *In room:* A/C, TV, hair dryer, Internet, minibar.

Stadt Hotel Città ★★ This modernized old hotel, with an attractive arcaded facade typical of this city's distinctive architecture, commands a sunny corner of Bolzano's main piazza. Its location and the sleek new feel of the hotel are good reasons to gravitate here, especially if you are partial to waterbeds, which some superior doubles have. The large and bright guest rooms have been done in a contemporary style; top-floor rooms are cozier. The best rooms overlook the square and the Duomo; Mussolini stayed in one of them (no. 303), a suite with a corner balcony. The ground-floor bar and cafe, which opens to the square, is a popular gathering spot.

Piazza Walther 21, 39100 Bolzano. www.hotelcitta.info. © **0471-975-221.** Fax 0471-976-688. 102 units. 136€–180€ double; 160€–220€ waterbed double; 220€–350€ family apt for up to 5. Rates include breakfast. AE, DC, MC, V. Parking 13€ in garage. **Amenities:** Mediterranean/Tyrolean restaurant; bar under the arcades of Piazza Walther; babysitting; concierge; room service; large sauna/baths complex in basement w/Turkish baths and huge whirlpool tub; smoke-free rooms. *In room:* A/C, TV, hair dryer, Wi-Fi.

Mountain Hotels En Route to Bressanone

High on the eastern wall of the Adige valley, halfway up the Siusi Alps above the road from Bolzano to Bressanone, lies the **Schlern plateau** (Sciliar in Italian). Its summertime meadows and forest trails for hiking and mountain biking, modestly decent winter skiing, half-ruined castles, colorful folk festivals, and cute Tyrolean villages draw a small clutch of devoted vacationers. It's also got some great hotel deals in a perfect Tyrol setting that gets you away from it all, but is still just a half-hour from the large towns down in the valley.

Cavallino d'Oro/Goldenes Rössl ★★ This 15th-century inn right on the main square of its little village does an excellent job of marrying traditional and cozy Tyrolean style with modern comforts—the parquet-floored lounge has a picture window overlooking the Alps in the backyard right next to a widescreen TV with 300 channels. The nicest rooms have four-poster beds with carved wood canopies, and all have new widescreen TVs. Room no. 24 is simply huge, featuring a four-poster bed and a small terrace. All rooms on the back have balconies with mountain vistas, while rooms on the front overlook the cobblestone main square and fountain. Off the excellent restaurant, with its mountain views, is a wood-paneled *Stuben* (beer nook) that's 18th century right down to the filament bulbs. Guests receive a warm, friendly reception from the owners, the Urthalers, who love Frommer's (they made a 32-state U.S. odyssey using Frommer's guides).

Piazza Kraus, 39040 Castelrotto/Kastelruth (Bolzano). www.cavallino.it. © **0471-706-337.** Fax 0471-707-172. 20 units. 102€–150€ double. Add 10€ per person for half-board. AE, DC, MC, V. Free parking. Closed Nov. **Amenities:** Fine restaurant; old-fashioned tavern w/food; babysitting; bikes; children's center nearby; concierge; room service; sauna; tanning bed. *In room:* TV, hair dryer.

Romantik Hotel Turm ★★ At the very top of this medieval hamlet and modest mountain resort lies the Turm, a series of buildings dating in part to the 13th century that have served time as a tribunal, a prison, and an *osteria*. During blizzards, the whole village would come to the *osteria* and shut themselves in together to feast, play cards, and wait out the storm. This tradition gave rise to its role as an inn, which stands today as a collection of three towers and a *wagenhaus*, sort of like an upscale garage, the most prized property today. Stefan Pramstrahler has gradually morphed this communal tradition into the modern concept of a "wellness" retreat to accompany the luxurious suites. Choose from hay baths (apparently a long-standing tradition), a massage on a heated stone bed, or a candlelight bath for two in the emperor's tub.

39050 Fié allo Sciliar/Völs am Schlern (Bolzano). www.hotelturm.it. © **0471-725-014.** Fax 0471-725-474. 35 units. 170€–280€ double without balcony; 226€–310€ double with balcony; 250€–335€ suite in the main tower; 270€–360€ deluxe suite. Half-board add 30€ per person. MC, V. Free parking. **Amenities:** Tyrolean restaurant; *Stube* bar; babysitting (book ahead); 3 free bikes; concierge; Jacuzzi; 2 pools (indoor and outdoor heated); room service; sauna; tennis courts (in town); extensive "wellness" center. *In room:* TV, hair dryer, minibar.

Where to Eat

Some of the least expensive (and tasty) meals in town are supplied by the vendors who dispense a wide assortment of *Würstel* from carts in the Kornplatz and Piazza dell'Erbe.

Batzenhäusl TYROLEAN The two floors of dining rooms here are charming and cozy, with dark carved Tyrolean benches, hardwood floors, and heavily beamed ceilings; downstairs is primarily a *Weinstube*, a tavernlike room where you are welcome to linger over a beer and a plate of cheese. On both floors, you can also order from a menu that, like those in many other restaurants in town, is typically Tyrolean, which means mostly Austrian with some Italian touches. While an excellent minestrone is sometimes available, this is also the place to sample *Leberknödelsuppe,* a thick broth with a liver dumpling floating in it. Pork loin, roast beef with potatoes, and other heavy northern fare dominate the entrée choices.

Via Andreas Hofer/Andreas Hoferstrasse 30. ✆ **0471-050-950.** Reservations not accepted. Primi 4.50€–6.50€; secondi 10€–13€. No credit cards. Wed–Mon 6:30pm–2am (Sun to 1am).

Cavallino Bianco TYROLEAN This atmospheric *Stube* (beer hall) is darkly paneled and decorated with carved wooden furniture to create a cozy, typically Tyrolean atmosphere. The restaurant opens early to operate as a cafe, dispensing coffee and pastries for breakfast, and remains open well into the night, sending out hearty lunches and dinners of local fare with only a slight Italian influence. Fried Camembert, herrings, and assorted salami are among the dozens of appetizers, while a pasta dish (and there are many to choose from) is likely to followed by a main course of Wiener schnitzel or *Würstel.*

Via dei Bottai/Bindergasse 6. ✆ **0471-973-267.** Reservations not accepted. Primi 3.50€–8€; secondi 4€–15€. No credit cards. Mon–Fri 8am–1am; Sat 8am–3pm.

Ristorante Hostaria Argentieri SEAFOOD You'll feel like you've come back to Italy when you step into this attractive cream-colored, tile-floored room. There are several risottos and a grilled steak on the menu, but most of the offerings are fishy—unusual and much in demand up here in the Dolomiti. You can start with tasty *tagliolini al salmone* or *bigoli alla veneta* (homemade pasta with anchovies and capers), followed by grilled *branzino, rombo,* or *trancio di spada* (swordfish steak). In good weather, you can dine on a tiny terrace in front of the restaurant, facing an attractive cobblestone street that is indeed Tyrolean in character.

Via Argentieri 14. ✆ **0471-981-718.** Reservations highly recommended. Primi and secondi 12€–20€. DC, MC, V. Mon–Sat noon–2:30pm and 7–10:30pm.

Scheune PIZZA/TYROLEAN This welcoming and cozy *Bierhalle* (beer hall) has remarkable rough-hewn beams; the log-cabin looks of the place are genuine—its name is Tyrolean dialect for "hayloft," and the interior was lifted, intact, from an abandoned hayloft high up in the mountains. A cherry tree is planted in the middle of the bar, where Warsteiner beer flows from the taps. The tables in back wrap around a big, square, rustic room-heating stove. Along with the 20-odd pasta dishes and typical Tyrolean fare, such as goulash and Wiener schnitzel, they have added decent pizzas.

Weintraubengasse 9. ✆ **0471-978-838.** Reservations not accepted. Primi 6€–8€; secondi 7€–15€; DC, MC, V. Daily 11am–11pm. Closed last 2 weeks of June.

Vogele TYROLEAN If you ask someone in Bolzano where to eat, there's a very good chance you will be sent to this attractive, always busy *Weinstube* and restaurant in the center of the Old City just off Piazza Erbe. (Its original name translated to "The Eagle," but the locals always referred to it as the *"vogele,"* or the "little bird.") Like many such places in Bolzano, it is open continuously all day and night, and some of the patrons seem to stop by for every meal and for coffee and a beer in between. One of the two long cross-vaulted rooms is set up as a cafe, and the other as a dining room (or you can eat under the arcade out front). Both have traditional, woody Tyrolean furnishings, and wherever you sit you can order from the long appetizer menu: maybe a platter of *speck* (ham) or *affumicato della casa* (smoked meats). First and second courses include many traditional favorites; a wonderful *zuppa di vino* (a soup with a white wine and cream base) or different kinds of *canederli* (dumplings that here are laced with liver, bacon, or ham) are the ways to begin, followed by a *stinco di maiale* (roast pork shank) or other roast meat dish.

Via Goethe 3. ℂ **0471-973-938.** Primi 4€–8€; secondi 8.50€–17€. MC, V. Mon–Fri 9am–midnight; Sat 9am–3pm.

Bars & Cafes

Nightlife in Bolzano is certainly not its greatest draw, but what life there is mostly centers around the long curve of Piazza delle Erbe. There you'll find a few other wine bars, pubs, *Stube,* and tiny live-music venues in addition to the following establishments.

The glitzy but down-to-earth **Rise Club** (ℂ **0471-502-298**), on the southern edge of town, is filled with a mixed-age dance crowd at night and provides a welcome alternative to the many *Weinstuben* around the center with deejays and parties. On weekend evenings, the elegant **Laurin Bar,** in the Parkhotel Laurin (ℂ **0471-311-000;** see above), turns its Art Nouveau lobby—a sumptuous room overlooking the hotel's private park—into a jazz club. An enthusiastic crowd shows up, making this one of the most popular places in town.

In Bolzano, you won't find a more distinctive locale in which to bend your elbow than **Fishbanke,** at Via Dr. Streiter 26A (ℂ **0471-971-714**); in fact, a stop at this outdoor wine bar run by a gregarious artist is mandatory, and a unique experience in an otherwise homogenous field of beer halls and taverns. Wine, beer, and a few snacks (cheese and bruschetta) are served on the well-worn stone slabs of Bolzano's centuries-old former fish market, an unusual experience that attracts a friendly crowd of regulars who are always pleased to welcome strangers into their midst.

MERANO

86km (53 miles) N of Trent, 28km (17 miles) NW of Bolzano

This well-heeled resort (**Meran** in German), tucked into a valley half an hour west of Bolzano, sports Europe's northernmost palm trees—the product of a mild microclimate ensuring that summers are never too hot or humid and that winter temperatures remain above freezing even when the surrounding slopes fill with snow.

Austrian nobility and, in their wake, bourgeois vacationers from all over the Continent, have been descending on Merano since the 19th century for their famous grape cure (see "Taking the Cure," below). But the town flourished long before that. In fact, the counts of Venosta were lords of what would become Austria through much of the 13th and 14th centuries; the name "Tyrol" came from the Castel Tirolo, just above Merano, from which they ruled. The capital of the territories that passed from the house of Venosta to the Habsburgs was moved from Merano to Innsbruck until 1420.

With its handsome shop-lined streets, riverside promenades, and easy access to mountainous wilderness, Merano is a nice place to visit for a day or two of relaxation or hiking.

Festivals & Markets The Piazza del Duomo is the scene of Merano's civic life. A morning **fruit-and-produce market** is held here from 8am to 1pm Monday to Saturday. From late November through Christmas, the piazza fills with stalls selling carved ornaments and other seasonal paraphernalia during the town's **Christkindlmarkt (Christmas Market).** From late August through September, the town hosts **Settimane Musicali Meranesi (Music Weeks Merano)** in several concert halls and churches around town (✆ 0473-221-447; www.meranofestival.com). On the second Sunday of October, enthusiasts of the grape take over the square for a **wine festival,** honoring the wines and grape juice yielded by local vineyards.

Essentials

GETTING THERE **By Train** Hourly train service links Merano with Bolzano (40 min.).

By Bus SAD buses (✆ 0471-450-111 in Italy; www.sad.it) arrive and depart from the train station and stop in the center of town, connecting Merano with Bolzano hourly (1 hr.) and with villages throughout the region.

By Car Route S38, a pretty road that cuts through vineyards and mountain meadows, links Merano and Bolzano in less than half an hour.

VISITOR INFORMATION The **tourist office,** Corso Libertà/Freiheistrasse 45 (✆ 0473-272-000; fax 0473-235-524; www.meran.eu), is open March through September, Monday to Friday 9am to 6:30pm, Saturday 9:30am to 6pm, and Sunday 10am to 12:30pm; October through February, Monday to Friday 9am to 12:30pm and 2:30 to 6:30pm, Saturday 9:30am to 12:30pm.

A good source of information on hiking the region is the local office of the **Club Alpino Italiano,** at Via K. Wolf 15 (✆ 0473-448-944; www.cai.it). It's open Monday to Friday from 9am to 1pm, plus Thursday from 7 to 8:30pm.

What to See & Do

The charming Old Town, a vestige of Merano's noble past, clusters around the **Piazza del Duomo,** where the namesake 14th-century cathedral has a crenelated facade and heavy buttresses that make it look almost like a castle. Nearby, just to the west on Via Galilei, is a dollhouse-size castle—**Castello Principesco** or **Landesfürstliche Burg,** built by the counts of Tyrol in 1470 and still filled with the austere furnishings they installed, along with a collection of armor and musical instruments. The castle (✆ 0473-250-329) is open Tuesday to Saturday 10am to 5pm, Sunday 10am to 1pm (closed Jan–Feb). Admission is 2€ adults, 1.50€ students and seniors 60 and over.

Merano's picturesque main shopping street, **Via Portici** (leading west from Piazza del Duomo), is lined with Tyrolean-style houses whose porticoes extend over the sidewalk. The preferred places to stroll in Merano, though, are along any number of scenic promenades. Two follow the banks of the River Passer: the

 Free Wheels

Late May through September, the town provides free bikes at the main parking lot (near the Terme, across the river from the center), at the tennis center on Via Piave 46 and at the train station. Just leave a 5€ deposit and a driver's license, and return the bike by 7pm.

Taking the Cure

With its mild climate and mineral-rich springs bubbling up from beneath the town, Merano has long enjoyed a reputation as a spa town. To this day, one of Merano's most popular pastimes is taking the cure. You can take a complete treatment (mud bath, mineral wrap, hydrotherapy) at the **Terme di Merano** (*C* **0473-237-724;** www.termemerano. com), in the center of town, across the river at Via Piave 9, or just take a dip in the pool of mineral-rich water. There is a wide range of prices for individual treatments, such as apple aromatherapy and hay baths, but a 2-hour pass for the pool alone costs 12€, 13€ for 3 hours, and 18€ for the day. Add about 6€ for the sauna, but so you're not shocked: No bathing suits are allowed.

Passeggiata d'Inverno (Winter Walk, which faces south) and **Passeggiata d'Estate** (Summer Walk, which faces north).

The top of the Passeggiata is just below **Castel Tirolo ★** (*C* **0473-220-221**), which you can also reach by car or by walking along Via Monte San Zeno for 5km (3 miles) from Merano. Here you can see the throne room from which the counts of Tyrol ruled much of present-day Austria and northern Italy, and a beautifully frescoed Romanesque chapel with a 1330 carved wood crucifix (and enjoy a magnificent view that hasn't changed much since then). The castle is open Easter through November, Tuesday to Sunday 10am to 5pm. Admission is 6€ adults, 3€ students 27 and under; there's no admission fee for children 14 and under. Occasional guided tours are available for a 2€ supplement. To get here without too much hoofing, you can take a half-hourly bus from Merano's train station or center to the village of Tyrol, and then finish the beautiful 15-minute walk along a trail amid grapevines and apple groves.

The National Parks

Merano is the gateway to two national parks. The tourist office in town provides information on them, as does the Club Alpino Italiano (see "Visitor Information," above); both parks also have visitor centers within their boundaries.

PARCO NAZIONALE DELLA STELVIO In this vast 520,000-hectare (1.3-million-acre) wilderness east of Merano, elk and chamois roam the mountainsides, and craggy, snowcapped peaks pierce the sky. A network of trails crisscross almost virgin wilderness, and some of Europe's largest glaciers provide year-round skiing. The official **park office** (*C* **0342-903-030**), in the center of the park, is open March to November daily 9am to 1pm and 4 to 6pm; in winter, call *C* **0342-903-300.** The office dispenses maps and lists of hiking trails and *rifugi* (huts where hikers can overnight) within the park; several buses a day travel from Merano to Silandro, at the park entrance, about 30km (20 miles) east via route S38.

The Passo Della Stelvio, one of the world's great driving roads, in the Parco Nazionale Della Stelvio.

PARCO NAZIONALE DI TESSA This Alpine wonderland surrounds Merano with a pleasant terrain of meadows and gentle, forest-clad slopes. A relatively easy path, the southern route of the Meraner Hohenweg allows even the most inexperienced hikers to cross the park effortlessly (in 2 days, if you wish to follow the entire route) and is conveniently interspersed with restaurants and farmhouses offering rooms. The northern route is much more isolated, difficult, and scenic, with snack bar–equipped *rifugi* conveniently placed every few hours or so along the route. The **park office** in Naturno, about 15km (9¼ miles) west on Route S44 (Via dei Campi 3; ☏ **0473-668-201**), provides a wealth of information on hiking trails, meals, and accommodations. Hourly buses run between Merano and Naturno in about half an hour.

Where to Stay

April, August through October, and the Christmas holidays constitute high season in Merano, when rates are most expensive and rooms are scarce. The two hotels in the center of town are easy enough to find; for the Castel Rundegg and Hotel Castello Schloss Labers, follow the yellow arrows on *alberghi* road signs (Merano has a complicated color-coded, geographical breakdown for all its hotels; just trust me and follow the yellow arrows) until a small brown-on-white sign for the hotels tells you otherwise.

Castel Rundegg ★★ Unlike most Merano castle hotels, the Rundegg is barely outside town, offering the convenience of downtown with the atmosphere of a restored 1152 castle. It bills itself as a "Hotel & Beauty Farm," and many guests come to avail themselves of the spa and its programs, which make good use of the large exercise room, sauna, Turkish steam baths, various body treatments, Jacuzzi, tanning beds, and beauty center. The cross-vaulted reception halls and restaurant stuffed with painted wood statues set the tone of the hotel. Even the standard rooms are large and perfectly nice, with rich tapestries upholstering the 18th-century-style chairs and bed frames, small lofted sitting areas or nooks, and tiled bathrooms with double sinks. Some "deluxe" rooms, such as no. 20, have balconies over the courtyard with views of the mountains; a few even have small private gardens. Room no.15 has views over the valley and the hotel's own large park, where goldfish ponds and small lawns set with sunning chairs highlight the garden paths lined with trees, plants, and flowers.

Via Scena 2 (at the end of Via Cavour), 39012 Merano. www.rundegg.com. ℂ **0473-234-100.** Fax 0473-237-200. 30 units. 240€–330€ double; 330€–380€ suite. Rates include buffet breakfast. Half-board add 30€. Discounts, but with half-pension included, for stays of 3 nights or more. Aug 4–25 and Dec 22–Jan 6 minimum stay 7 nights; Easter minimum stay 5 nights. AE, DC, MC, V. Parking free in lot or 6€ in garage. Bus: 1, 3, or 5. **Amenities:** Mediterranean restaurant; bar; bikes; 9-hole golf course 4km (2½ miles) away; large health club and spa; indoor pool; room service; nearby tennis courts. *In room:* TV, hair dryer, high-speed Internet, minibar.

Garni Domus Mea Simple little bed-and-breakfasts are just about the only alternative to Merano's high-priced lodging, and this pleasant *pensione* in a modern multiuse building is one of the nicer of them. It is well located, on a major street about a 10-minute walk on the other side of Ponte Teatro from the center of town, and the prices never seem to go up. The friendly proprietor keeps the premises immaculately clean and welcoming, with cut flowers and freshly waxed floors. The rooms are basically but nicely furnished with wood dressers and armoires, and some have balconies overlooking the peaks. A small living room sports a TV. Places like this tend to fill up quickly, so be sure to reserve in advance.

Via Piave 8, 39012 Merano. www.domusmea.com. ℂ **0473-236-777.** 13 units. 74€–86€ double. Rates include breakfast. MC, V. Parking free in courtyard or 2.50€ in garage. **Amenities:** Room service. *In room:* TV, hair dryer, high-speed Internet.

Hotel Castello Labers ★ The Stapf-Neubert family turned its pitch-roofed castle (begun in the 11th c.) into a remarkable hotel in 1885. The dark, airy, hunting lodge–style salons, library, and billiards and dining rooms of the former residence have been seamlessly converted to guest use. Upper floors house distinctive and gracious accommodations, many with small terraces, no two of which are alike—in some, cozy conversation nooks are tucked into towers; others are luxurious garretlike arrangements under the eaves, and some are simply commodious, high-ceilinged, and elegantly appointed. The grounds wander down toward the surrounding grapevine-covered hillside, with a pleasant rose garden terrace overlooking the valley below and the peaks that hem it in.

Via Labers 25 (in Maia Alta, 3km/1¾ miles east of town), 39012 Merano. www.castellolabers.it. ℂ **0473-234-484.** Fax 0473-234-146. 36 units, 25 with private bathroom. 160€ small double; 220€ regular double; 260€ double with terrace; 330€ suite. Rates include breakfast. Stays of 3 nights or more include half-pension (meals available a la carte if your stay is fewer than 3 nights). MC, V. Free parking. Closed Nov 9–March. Bus: 1a. **Amenities:** Tyrolean/Italian restaurant; bar; babysitting; billiards room; outdoor heated pool; room service; sauna; smoke-free rooms; tennis court. *In room:* TV, hair dryer, Internet.

Hotel Europa Splendid ★ Conveniently located in the center of town a block off the Passer River, the Europa is an old-fashioned hotel that caters to guests who return year after year. The decor is charmingly faded, with an elegant, Regency-style salon and Tyrolean-style bar downstairs. Many of the rooms have small balconies, and a large, sunny hotel terrace is on the first floor. The rates reflect both season and room type ("standard" rooms suffer from less space, a poorer view, or more noise). Corner rooms (nos. 208, 308, and 408) are choice, with windows on two sides and small balconies.

Corso Liberta 178, 39012 Merano. www.europa-splendid.com. ℂ **0473-232-376.** Fax 0473-230-221. 52 units. 108€–146€ standard double; 120€–158€ comfort double; 132€–170€ deluxe double. Rates include buffet breakfast. AE, DC, MC, V. Parking 9.50€. **Amenities:** Tyrolean/Italian restaurant; bar; concierge; room service. *In room:* TV, hair dryer, minibar.

Where to Eat

Yes, with all the grapes around, this region produces excellent, crisp wines. But be sure to set aside at least one *"Prost!"* (German for "cheers!") for a frosty glass of **Forst,** a rich and slightly bitter golden beer brewed here in Merano.

Caffè Darling CAFE The so-called "Winter Walk" along the banks of the Passer River is lined with cafes, and this one is especially pleasant. There's an awning out front, but the tables stretch much farther along the cobblestones to where they're practically hanging over the river. The interior room has a casual ambience that's not too common in this staid, refined resort area. You'll probably feel comfortable passing some time reading a book here while sipping a beer or a glass of the house grape juice. Pastries and light sandwiches are also available.

Passeggiata d'Inverno 5-9. ✆ **0473-237-221.** Pastries from 1€; sandwiches from 2€. MC, V. Thurs-Tues 7:30am-1am.

Forsterbrau ☺ TYROLEAN This sprawling beer hall and eatery whose name plays homage to the hometown brew offers a sampling of Tyrolean fare and, of course, the local lager. Put it all on one plate with the *piatto Forst,* a spread of roast pork leg, dumplings, mixed sausages and sauerkraut. The staff is helpful with the kids, providing them with colored pencils and a coloring page while the adults examine the ambers and other golden hues in their steins.

Corso della Liberta'. ✆ **0473-236-535.** Antipasti 7€-8€; secondi 12€-20€. MC, V. Tues-Sat 11am-2:30pm and 5:30-9:30pm.

BRESSANONE

40km (25 miles) N of Bolzano, 68km (42 miles) E of Merano

Tucked neatly in the Val d'Isarco between the Eisack and Rienz rivers, and surrounded by orchards and vineyards that climb the lower flanks of the surrounding peaks, Bressanone (**Brixen** in German) is a gem of a Tyrolean town with a hefty past that today's quaint, small-town atmosphere belies. From 1027 to 1803, it was the center of a large ecclesiastical principality, and its bishop-princes ruled over much of the South Tyrol. Their impressive monuments preside over the town's heavily gabled, pastel-colored houses and narrow cobblestone streets.

Festivals & Markets With its cozy, twisting medieval lanes and snug Tyrolean-style houses, Bressanone is especially well suited to Christmas celebrations. The main holiday event is a **Christkindlmarkt (Christmas market)** from late November to Christmas Eve; stalls on and around Piazza Duomo sell hand-carved ornaments, crafts, holiday pastries, and other seasonal merchandise. A **fruit-and-vegetable market** enlivens Piazza Parrocchia near the Duomo Monday through Saturday from 8am to noon and 3 to about 6pm.

Essentials

GETTING THERE By Train Bressanone lies on the same north-south rail line as Bolzano and Verona, making connections between those cities extremely easy, with more than 18 trains a day from Bolzano (25–35 min.). From Trent, trains run almost hourly (1–1¼ hr.).

By Bus STI buses (✆ **0472-801-075** or 800-846-047; www.sii. bz.it) leave from the front of the train station and connect Bressanone and Bolzano (1 hr.) and outlying villages, including several daily (half-hourly in ski season) to Sant'Andrea, a good base for hiking and skiing (see below; 20

min.). Service is augmented by a ski bus that is free for pass holders. There are also two daily buses to Cortina, with a change at Dobbiaco (about 2¾ hr.).

By Car Bressanone is about a half-hour drive north of Bolzano on A22. It's easy to get around Bressanone by foot—the town is compact, and many of its streets are closed to cars. If you arrive by car, you will probably use the large parking lot south of the city on Via Dante (you will pass it as you drive into the city from the autostrada); the center is 5 minutes away up the Via Roma. From the train station, follow Viale Stazione for about 10 minutes to the center.

VISITOR INFORMATION The **tourist office,** at the *centro storico* end of Via Stazione leading from the train station at no. 9 (©**0472-836-401;** fax 0472-836-067; www.brixen.org), is open Monday to Friday 8:30am to 12:30pm and 2:30 to 6pm, Saturday 9am to 12:30pm. The provincial website, **www.provinz.bz.it,** has a section with tourism links.

What to See & Do

The center of town is the **Piazza Duomo,** a long, rectangular tree-shaded square with cafes on one side and the white facade of the Duomo on the other. A baroque renovation to the tall exterior, flanked by two bell towers, has masked much of the cathedral's original 13th-century architecture, which you'll see more of in the interior and in the crypt. The heavily frescoed cloisters (entered through a door to the right of the main one) are especially charming, even though the view of Judgment Day they portray is gloomy. The cathedral is open daily 6am to noon and 3 to 6pm; there are guided tours (in Italian and German) Monday through Saturday at 10:30am and 3pm.

Just south of the Piazza del Duomo, on the adjoining Piazza Vescovile, stands the **palace of the prince-bishops,** whose power over the region—and the fragility of that power—is made clear by the surrounding moat and fortifying walls. The massive 14th-century palace now houses the **Museo Diocesano,** where more than 70 rooms display wooden statuary, somewhat unremarkable Renaissance paintings by local artists, and what is considered to be the museum's treasure and the objects most likely to capture your attention—an extensive and enchanting collection of antique Nativity scenes, filling eight rooms and one of the largest such assemblages anywhere. The museum (©**0472-830-505;** www.dioezesanmuseum.bz.it) is open March 15 to October 31, Tuesday through Sunday 10am to 5pm; the Nativity-scene galleries are open only December and January, Tuesday through Sunday from 2 to 5pm (closed Dec 24–25); admission, including the Nativity scenes, is 7€. Note that frequent exhibits often double the admission price.

Where to Stay

Goldene Krone Vital Stadthotel Everything about this amiable hotel at the edge of the old city suggests solid comfort, from the homey, wood-paneled lounge to the *Weinstube*-style bar to the breakfast room and restaurant, where booth tables are lit by pretty shaded lamps. There are two categories of guest rooms, hence the range of prices. Those in the lower range are pleasant enough, with streamlined modern furnishings, and many have terraces. The more expensive rooms are really quite special, though, and well worth the extra money. They're actually suites, with separate sitting and sleeping areas, equipped, respectively, with roomy couches and armchairs and king-size beds. The bathrooms are grand, with double sinks and large tubs equipped with Jacuzzi jets.

Hitting the Slopes

Bressanone's major playground is Monte Plose, and the gateway to ski slopes and hiking trails alike is the outlying village of **Sant'Andrea** (see "By Bus," above). Skiing here is not as glamorous as it is in better-known resorts like Cortina, but it is excellent and much less expensive. A whole laundry list of prices can be found at **www.dolomitisuperski.com**, but a 1-day pass at Plose and the Valle Isarco costs 30€ to 38€ for an adult, 22€ to 26€ for juniors, and gives access to nine lifts. One of them is the **Sant'Andrea cable car** (☎ **0472-200-433**), which costs 10€ round-trip for adults and 8€ for children ages 8 to 14. The cable car runs from July through September weekdays 9am to noon and 1 to 6pm, Saturday and Sunday 9am to 6pm; and December through May daily 9am to 4:30pm. (Winter schedules vary considerably with snow conditions; a summer ascent will take you to a network of Alpine trails near the stop at Valcroce.) The tourist board in Bressanone provides maps and information on skiing, mountain refuges, and other details you need to know to enjoy this mountain wilderness.

Via Fienili 4, 39042 Bressanone. www.goldenekrone.com. ☎ **0472-835-154.** Fax 0472-835-014. 35 units. 144€–186€ double. Rates include breakfast. Half-board 25€ more per person. MC, V. Free parking. Closed Jan 6–Feb 6. **Amenities:** Italian/Tyrolean restaurant; bar; babysitting; free bikes; children's program; concierge; gym; room service. *In room:* TV, hair dryer, Internet, minibar.

Hotel Angerer Like many of the other well-heeled resorts in this part of the world, downtown Bressanone offers few inexpensive beds. So it's well worth a taxi ride across the river, in the direction of the skiing, to find better value. That's where the Angerer resides, a typical chalet with all the right amenities for a reasonable price, and a great location for those who are looking for a mixture of city and slopes. The rooms offer an Alpine feel—pinewood surroundings, firm beds, and cool mountain air—and spacious bathrooms. The sauna and heated pool are good therapy for ski-worn muscles, and the selection of beers at the hotel's tavern doesn't hurt, either.

Via Plose, 48, 39042 Bressanone. www.hotel-angerer.com. ☎ **0472-833-279.** Fax 0472-834-004. 28 units. 80€–96€ double. Rates include breakfast. Half-board 12€ more per person. MC, V. Closed early Jan to mid-Feb. **Amenities:** Tavern; concierge; indoor/outdoor pool; room service; sauna. *In room:* TV, hair dryer.

Hotel Elephant One of the Tyrol's oldest and most famous inns (also sometimes spelled Hotel Elefant) is named for a 16th-century guest—an elephant accompanying Archduke Maximilian of Austria on the long trek from Genoa to Vienna, where the beast was to become part of the royal menagerie. During its 2-week stay, the pachyderm attracted onlookers from miles around, and the innkeeper renamed his establishment and commissioned a delightful elephant-themed fresco that still graces the front of the building. Today's hotel matches its provenance with excellent service and extraordinary environs that include dark-paneled hallways and grand staircases. The distinctive old rooms are furnished with heavy Tyrolean antiques and tasteful modern pieces. The buffet breakfast emphasizes delicious Austrian pastries.

Via Rio Bianco 4, 39042 Bressanone. www.hotelelephant.com. ☎ **0472-832-750.** Fax 0472-836-579. 44 units. 140€–224€ comfort double; 192€–246€ deluxe double; 212€–282€ junior suite. Half- and full-pension available. Ask about discounted rates for stays of more than 3 nights. Breakfast 13€. AE, DC, MC, V. Parking 6€. Closed Jan 7–Feb 28 and Nov 5–30. **Amenities:** Tyrolean restaurant; bar; babysitting; bikes; concierge; small exercise room; outdoor heated pool; room service; 2 saunas; tennis courts. *In room:* TV, hair dryer, Internet, minibar.

Where to Eat

Caffè Duomo CAFE These minimalist walls hold a contemporary version of the woody taverns that prevail in this part of the world (there are still little nooks off to one side for intimate conversation). No attempt is made at serious cuisine here, but there is a nice selection of panini made with local hams and mountain cheeses, and sumptuous cakes and pastries. The coffee is excellent, and the wine-and-beer list extensive.

Piazza Parocchia 3. *©* **0472-838-277.** Reservations not accepted. Sandwiches and snacks from 3€. No credit cards. Mon–Fri 8am–8pm; Sat 12:30–8pm.

Fink TYROLEAN It only seems right that Bressanone's charmingly arcaded main street should have a restaurant that looks like this, with paneling hung with antlers and oil paintings, while dishing out typical fare. Fink offers many mountain-style dishes that you are likely to encounter only within a close radius of Bressanone, including a *piatto alla Val d'Isarco,* a platter of locally cured hams and salamis, and a *zuppa di vino,* a traditional Tyrolean soup made with white wine and, here, crusty pieces of cinnamon toast. The *miale gratinato,* a pork roast topped with a cheese sauce, is surprisingly light and absolutely delicious, as are the local cheeses served for dessert. If in doubt about what to order, just ask—the English-speaking staff is extremely gracious.

Via Portici Minori 4. *©* **0472-834-883.** Reservations not necessary. Primi 5€–10€; secondi 7€–16€. AE, DC, MC, V. Thurs–Tues noon–2:30pm; Thurs–Mon 7–10pm. Closed July 1–14.

Oste Scuro/Finsterwirt TYROLEAN/WINE BAR What may be Bressanone's temple of gastronomy occupies a welcoming series of intimate candlelit rooms above the Finsterwirt *Weinstube* (wine bar). This is a favorite of the Germany-born reigning pope, who last stopped by here in 2008. A *terrina di formaggio di capra fresco* is a concoction of creamy cheese atop a bed of lightly sautéed spinach and greens; even if you have found the region's steady diet of *canederli* (dumplings) heavy, try them here, where they are light and infused with fresh wild mushrooms. The kitchen excels at meat dishes, including an herb-infused veal roast. For dessert, fresh, seasonal berries top off a meal, and the strudels are done to perfection. A lovely rear garden, candlelit at night, is open throughout the summer and well into chillier days when people from more southerly climes wouldn't think of sitting outdoors.

Vicolo Duomo 3. *©* **0472-835-343.** www.finsterwirt.com. Reservations recommended. Primi 9€–11€; secondi 15€–18€. AE, DC, MC, V. Tues–Sun noon–2pm; Tues–Sat 7–9pm. Closed Jan 11–Feb 2 and June 21–July 5.

En Route to Cortina: The Great Dolomite Road

The **Grande Strada delle Dolomiti,** the scenic route between Bolzano (follow signs to Eggental/Val d'Ega) and Cortina going east, S241 and S48, is 110km (68 miles) of stunning views. The road curves around some of the highest peaks in the Dolomites, including 3,000m-tall (9,800-ft.) **Marmolda,** and goes through a scattering of mountain villages and ski resorts before dropping out of a high pass into Cortina. Some tour buses follow this route (the tourist offices in Bolzano and Cortina can provide a list of tour operators; check with the bus station in Bolzano), as do two daily buses of the **STI network** July through September (check with the bus station in Bolzano or call ✆ **0471-450-111;** www.sii.bz.it). You may want to rent a car, if only for a day, to make the spectacular round-trip, one of Europe's most scenic drives (allow at least 2½ hr. each way over the twists and turns of the passes). Keep in mind that the Grande Strada delle Dolomiti is often closed to vehicles because of heavy snow in the winter months, and you will often need chains on your tires between November and April.

CORTINA D'AMPEZZO

133km (82 miles) E of Bolzano, 166km (103 miles) N of Venice

Technically, Cortina d'Ampezzo is part of Veneto, not Alto Adige, but it is grouped here alongside other Dolomite landmarks because of its Teutonic flavor.

Italy's best-known mountain resort, put on the international map when it hosted the 1956 Winter Olympics, is often associated with wealth and sophistication. Long before the Olympics, though, Cortina was attracting European Alpine enthusiasts, who began coming here for stays in the town's first hotels as early as the 1860s. In 1902, Cortina hosted its first ski competitions, and in 1909, the completion of the first road in and out of the town, the magnificent Strada di Dolomiti (built by the Austro-Hungarian military), opened the slopes to more skiers.

Even without its 145km (90 miles) of ski runs and 50 cable cars and chairlifts that make the slopes easily accessible, Cortina would be one of Europe's most appealing Alpine towns. The surrounding Dolomite peaks are simply stunning. Eighteen of them rise more than 3,000m (9,800 ft.), ringing Cortina in an amphitheater of craggy stone. In full light the peaks are a soft bluish gray, and when they catch the rising and setting sun, they take on a welcoming rosy glow.

Italy's best-known mountain resort, Cortina d'Ampezzo.

A Cortina cable car.

True to its reputation for glamour, Cortina can be expensive (especially in Aug and the high-ski-season months of Jan–Mar). Many well-to-do Italians have houses here, and a sense of privilege prevails. What's often forgotten, though, is that for all of the town's fame, strict zoning has put a damper on development; as a result, Cortina is still a mountain town of white timbered houses, built aside a rushing stream and surrounded by forests, meadows, and, of course, stunning Dolomite peaks.

Festivals & Markets The **Piazza Italia** near the bus station doubles as Cortina's marketplace. Stalls sell produce, mountain cheeses, clothing, housewares, and other items on Tuesday and Friday mornings from 8:30am to 1pm. While chic Cortina concerns itself mostly with secular pursuits, the town turns out for a solemn religious procession down the main street, Corso Italia, on **Good Friday.**

Essentials

GETTING THERE By Train The closest train station to Cortina is the one at **Calalzo di Cadore,** 30km (20 miles) south. From Calalzo, 30 daily buses connect with Cortina. There are 10 trains a day to Calalzo from Venice, but only two are direct (2½ hr; with connections, allow 3–4 hr.). There are also six daily direct runs from Padua (3 hr.).

By Bus Frequent **STI bus service** provides the only public transportation in and out of Cortina (℃ **800-846-047** in Italy; www.sii.bz.it). There are two daily buses each from Bolzano (about 4 hr.), stopping in Bressanone (about 2¾ hr.), that head to Cortina, but with a change in Dobbiaco. There is also one daily bus to and from Venice (℃ **035-237-641;** 4½ hr.) and a daily bus to and from Milan (℃ **02-801-161;** 6½ hr.). The bus station in Cortina is located in the former train station on Via Marconi.

By Car The spectacularly scenic Grande Strada delle Dolomiti (see above) links Bolzano and Cortina, while S51 heads south toward Venice, connecting south of Belluno to Autostrada A27, for a total trip time of about 3 hours between Cortina and Venice.

VISITOR INFORMATION The **APT tourist office,** Piazetta San Francesco 8 (☎ **0436-3231;** fax 0436-3235; www.cortina.dolomiti.com or www.dolomiti.com), is open daily 9am to 12:30pm and 4 to 7pm. In addition to a list of accommodations, the English-speaking staff will provide a wealth of information on ski slopes, hiking trails, and bus schedules.

What to See & Do

The primary activity in Cortina appears to be walking up and down the main street, the pedestrian-only **Corso Italia,** in the most fashionable skiwear money can buy. Most of the buildings are pleasingly low-scale and Alpine in design, and at the town center is the pretty 18th-century church of **Santi Filippo e Giacomo,** with a charming bell tower eclipsed in height only by the majestic peaks. It is on these peaks that most visitors set their sights, enjoying an array of outdoor activities on the slopes.

EXPLORING PEAKS Skiers and nonskiers alike will enjoy the eye-popping scenery on a trip up the surrounding mountainsides on the cable car systems that leave right from town. The most spectacular trip is the ascent on the **Freccia nel Cielo (Arrow in the Sky),** which departs from a terminus near the Stadio Olimpico del Ghiacchio (Olympic Ice-Skating Stadium), about a 10-minute walk north and west of the town center. It has three segments. The top station is at **Cima Tofana,** at 3,163m (10,375 ft.); the round-trip is 26€. It is a little less expensive (21€)—and just as satisfying, if mountain scenery and not high-Alpine skiing is your quest—to make the trip only as far as **Ra Valles,** the second stop, at 2,550m (8,364 ft.). The views over glaciers and the stony peaks are magnificent, and a bar serves sandwiches and other refreshments on an outdoor terrace. Or, for 12€, you could take the tramway as far as **Col Druscie,** whose views are still nothing to sneeze at, and there is a decent restaurant there as well. The cable car runs from mid-July to late September and mid-December to May 1, with departures every 20 minutes from 9am to 4 or 5pm, depending on the time of sunset; call ☎ **0436-5052** for information.

The **Funivia Faloria** (☎ **0436-2517**) arrives and departs from a terminus on the other side of town, about a 10-minute walk southeast of the town center. The ride is a little less dramatic than the one on the longer Freccia nel Cielo. Even so, the ascent over forests and meadows and then up a sheer cliff to the 2,100m-high (6,900-ft.) ski station at Faloria is not without thrills, and the view from the terrace bar at Faloria, down to Cortina and to the curtain of high peaks to the north, is one you won't soon forget. Like the Freccia nel Cielo, the Funivia Faloria runs from mid-July to late September and mid-December to May 1, with departures every 20 minutes from 9am to 4 or 5pm, depending on the time of sunset; round-trip fare is 16€.

Another trip for cable car enthusiasts is the one from the top of **Passo Falzarego,** 25km (16 miles) west of Cortina, to Lagazoul, a little skiing and hiking station at the 2,550m (8,364-ft.) level. In summer, you can follow a network of trails at the top and scamper for miles across the dramatic, rocky terrain, and as an eerie alternative to the cable car, you can make the climb up or down through a series of tunnels dug into the cliff during World War I battles. If you are not driving, five buses a day make the 35-minute trip between Cortina and the cable car stop at the top of the Passo Falzarego; the fare is 1.50€ each way. It runs from mid-July to late September and mid-December to May 1, with departures every 30 minutes; round-trip fare is 12€; call ✆ **0436-867-301** for information.

DOWNHILL SKIING Cortina is Italy's leading ski resort, and it lives up to its reputation with eight exceptional ski areas that are easily accessible from town. Two of the best, **Tofana-Promedes** and **Faloria-Tondi,** are accessible by cable cars that lift off from the edges of town (see "Exploring Peaks," above), as are the novice slopes at **Mietres.** You can enjoy these facilities fairly economically with one of the comprehensive Dolomiti Superski passes that provide unlimited skiing (including all chairlift and gondola fees, as well as free shuttle bus service to and from Cortina and the ski areas) at all eight of Cortina's ski areas and those at 10 outlying resorts. You can get passes for any number of days, up to 21. A few sample prices: During high season, December 21 to January 6 and February 1 to March 13, the cost is 35€ for 1 day, and 188€ for 7 days. For more information, contact the **tourist office** or **Dolomiti Superski,** Via Marconi 15b, 32043 Cortina (✆ **0436-866-525** or 0471-867-448; www.dolomitisuperski.com).

For **lessons,** contact the **Scuola di Sci Cortina,** Corso Italia (✆ **0436-2911;** www.scuolascicortina.com). Prices start at about 35€ per hour in low season, 50€ per hour in the holiday season, though cheaper weeklong rates are available.

You can **rent skis** at many outlets throughout town, including stands at the lower and upper stations of the Freccia nel Cielo cable car and other funiculars; rentals average 15€ to 25€ per day.

HIKING & ROCK CLIMBING In this mountainous terrain, these two activities are often synonymous. The tourist office can provide maps of hiking trails throughout the surrounding region. For high-altitude hiking, canyoning, and rock climbing, you may want to join one of the excursions led by **Gruppo Guide Alpine Cortina,** Corso Italia 69A (✆ **0463-868-505;** www.guidecortina.com), open daily 8am to noon and 4 to 8pm. A 3-day climbing course, for example, is 270€.

ICE-SKATING At the **Stadio Olimpico del Ghiaccio,** just to the northwest of the town center on Via del Stadio (✆ **0436-866-342**), you can practice turns on the two recently refurbished rinks where Olympians tried for the gold in the 1956 games. Admission plus skate rental is 7€.

MOUNTAIN BIKING The roads and tracks leading up to the peaks provide arduous biking terrain; cyclists from all over the world come to Cortina to practice for events. If you want to test your mettle, rent a bike from the **Mountain Bike Center,** Corso Italia 294 (✆ **347-128-1607**). Rentals are 30€ for a day and half-price in the off season, for which there are no set dates but roughly correspond to spring and fall. (No one rides here in the winter.) The staff will try to point you in the direction of routes that match your abilities.

Where to Stay

Cortina is booked solid during the high season: August, Christmas, and late January through March. You should reserve well in advance. Rates are lowest in late spring and early fall. It's closed down tight in June. Keep in mind that many innkeepers prefer to give rooms to guests who will stay several days or longer and will take meals at the hotel.

The breathtaking Dolomite Mountains.

Hotel Bellaria The Majoni family owns this pleasant hotel a short walk from the center on the northern edge of town, and they choose to keep prices down for the benefit of the patrons who come here year after year. (In ski season, the hotel generally rents out doubles by the week.) They provide some of Cortina's most reasonably priced accommodations, and they house their guests in handsome, sunny rooms that overlook the mountains and have fresh Alpine-style pine furnishings, firm new beds, and crisp fabrics. All of the bathrooms are fitted with heated towel racks. Downstairs there's a lovely paneled lounge, a dining room, a pleasant terrace in front of the house, and a lawn out back.

Corso Italia 266, 32043 Cortina d'Ampezzo. www.hbellaria.it. © **0436-2505.** Fax 0436-5755. 22 units. 90€–160€ double; in winter, half-board and long stays may be required: weekly rates 500€–610€. DC, MC, V. Free parking. Closed 1 month in fall or spring. **Amenities:** Tyrolean/Italian restaurant; bar; babysitting; concierge; room service; smoke-free rooms. *In room:* TV, hair dryer.

Hotel Menardi One of the oldest and most charming hostelries in Cortina successfully combines the luxury and service of a fine hotel with the homelike comfort of a mountain inn. The Menardi family, who converted their farmhouse into a guesthouse in the 1920s, has beautifully appointed the public rooms with antiques and comfortable furnishings. Rooms in the rear of the house are especially quiet and pleasant, looking across the hotel's spacious lawns to the forests and peaks; some newer (but still panel-and-pine Alpine) rooms are located in an annex next door; many have large balconies with picnic tables. Most guests take half-board, but it is also possible to make bed-and-breakfast arrangements when the hotel is not fully booked. A pretty foot trail leads from the back lawn into town in 15 minutes.

Via Majon 110, 32043 Cortina d'Ampezzo. www.hotelmenardi.it. © **0436-2400.** Fax 0436-862-183. 49 units. 100€–220€ double; 190€–260€ in winter, including requisite half-board. Rates include breakfast. Add 20€–23€ per person for half-board; add 30€–32€ per person for full board. DC, MC, V. Free parking outside or 8€ in garage. Closed Apr 10–June 15 and Sept 21–Dec 20. **Amenities:** International/Tyrolean restaurant; bar; bikes; children's playground; concierge; golf course (9 holes, 3km/1¾ miles away); room service; smoke-free rooms. *In room:* TV, hair dryer, minibar, Wi-Fi.

Hotel Montana ★ Right in the center of town, this hotel occupies a tall, pretty Alpine-style house and is run by the amiable Adriano and Roberta Lorenzi, who provide some of the resort's nicest lodgings for the price. Guest rooms are pleasant and cozy, with old-style armoires, hardwood floors, and down quilts on the beds, and many open onto balconies overlooking the peaks. Most of the doubles are quite large, and many are beautifully paneled and have separate sitting areas. Half the rooms here are singles, making this an ideal spot for solo travelers. Breakfast is served in a pleasant room where guests tend to linger through much of the morning.

Corso Italia 94, 32043 Cortina d'Ampezzo. www.cortina-hotel.com. ✆ **0436-862-126.** Fax 0436-868-211. 30 units. In winter 620€–1,160€ double per week; in summer 88€–175€ double per night. Rates include breakfast. AE, DC, MC, V. Free parking. Closed Nov and June. **Amenities:** Babysitting; bikes; concierge; room service. *In room:* Satellite TV, hair dryer, high-speed Internet.

Miramonti Majestic Grand Hotel The top deluxe spot in town since 1893, this enormous golden-age beauty of a hotel is set just outside and above the village, backed up against the pine forests with sweeping views of the cut-glass peaks. The decor, if uninspired, is perfectly pleasant, where 19th century meets modern, classy lines, and rooms contain a full complement of amenities. Public spaces devoted to après-ski fun include a piano bar, a billiards room, and even a small cinema, and it calls a (separately managed) golf course its next-door neighbor.

Loc. Peziè 103, 32043 Cortina d'Ampezzo. www.miramontimajestic.it. ✆ **0436-4201.** Fax 0436-867-019. 105 units. 255€–440€ superior double with half-board. (Even in off-season, a 3-day minimum is often required.) AE, DC, MC, V. Parking 43€ in garage. Closed Apr–June and Sept–Nov. **Amenities:** Regional/international restaurant; piano bar; babysitting; free bikes; children's center; exercise room; indoor heated pool; sauna; tennis courts (lighted at night). *In room:* TV, hair dryer, Internet.

Villa Nevada On a grassy hillside overlooking the town, valley, and mountains, the Villa Nevada is a low-slung Alpine building that has the appearance of a private home. The same ambience prevails inside, where an attractive paneled lounge is grouped around a hearth and opens to a sunny terrace. The guest rooms are bright and afford wonderful views over the Alpine landscape; they are rustically furnished with dark-stained pine pieces and thick rugs or carpeting, and all have large balconies. Located on the road to the outlying settlement of Ronco, the center of Cortina is a pleasant 20-minute walk downhill, but it could be a long uphill trek home.

Via Ronco 64, 32043 Cortina d'Ampezzo. www.villanevadacortina.com. ✆ **0436-4778.** Fax 0436-4853. 11 units. In winter 700€–1,000€ double per week; in summer 560€–790€ double per week. Rates include buffet breakfast. No credit cards. Free parking. Closed first Sun Oct–Dec 1 and after Easter to mid-June. **Amenities:** Bar; room service. *In room:* TV, hair dryer.

Where to Eat

Inexpensive meals are hard to come by in Cortina—even pizzerias are few and far between. For a low-cost meal, you might want to equip yourself for a picnic at **La Piazzetta,** Corso Italia 53, with a mouthwatering assortment of salamis, cheeses, breads, and other fare.

Al Camin ALPINE If you follow the Via Alverà along the Ru Bigontina, a rushing mountain stream, about 10 minutes east from the center of town, you'll come to this charming restaurant, rustic in appearance, but the cuisine is anything but unrefined. Next to a large stone fireplace you can enjoy *kenederli* (these dumplings flavored with liver are known as *canederli* outside Cortina) *in brodo* or *al formaggio,* as well as dishes that you may not encounter elsewhere, like *radicchio di prato,* a mountain green that appears in early spring and is served dressed with hot lard; and, in winter *formaggio fuso con funghi e polenta,* a lush combination of creamy melted mountain cheese and wild mushrooms served over polenta. The wine list is extensive.

Via Alverà 99. ✆ **0436-862-01.** www.alcamincortina.dolomiti.org. Reservations recommended. Primi 6€–9.50€; secondi 7€–18€. MC, V. Tues–Sun noon–3pm and 7–11:30pm.

Caffè Royal CAFE The Corso Italia, Cortina's pedestrians-only main street, is the center of the town's social life. This cafe is one of several that occupy the ground floor of large hotels along the street, and it is one of the more pleasant. As soon as it's even remotely possible to sit outdoors, tables are set out front on a sunny terrace. At other times, patrons are welcome to sit for hours over coffee, pastries, or light fare such as sandwiches in a pleasant room off the lobby of this hotel of the same name.

Corso Italia. ✆ **0436-867-045.** Reservations not accepted. Sandwiches and snacks from 2€. MC, V. Wed–Mon 8am–9pm.

La Tavernetta ALPINE A former barn, just steps from the Olympic ice-skating stadium, has been delightfully converted to a very stylish yet reasonably priced restaurant. The menu relies on local ingredients and typical dishes of the Alto Adige, and the rustic environs inspire you to eat heartily. You might want to begin with a dish of *gnocchi di spinachi* (filled with spinach and topped with a rich wild-game sauce), and then a robust *stinco di vitello con patate* (veal shank served with creamy potato) or *cervo in salsa di mirtilli* (venison with a sauce of myrtle berries with polenta).

Via del Stadio 27 a/b. ✆ **0436-867-494.** Reservations recommended. Primi 6.50€–12€; secondi 11€–20€. AE, MC, V. Thurs–Tues noon–2:30pm and 7:30–11pm.

Ospitale ALPINE A trip out to this high-gabled house (about 8km/5 miles north of Cortina on the road to the village and lake of Dobbiaco) is a favorite outing for residents of Cortina. There, the Alvera family prepares pasta dishes with whatever vegetables are in season, such as *casunziei rossi,* a short, local pasta mixed with beets, and gnocchi made from squash and stuffed with ricotta.

Locale Ospitale. ✆ **0436-4585.** Reservations recommended. Primi 5€–7€; secondi 8€–15€. AE, MC. Tues–Sun noon–2:30pm and 7–10pm.

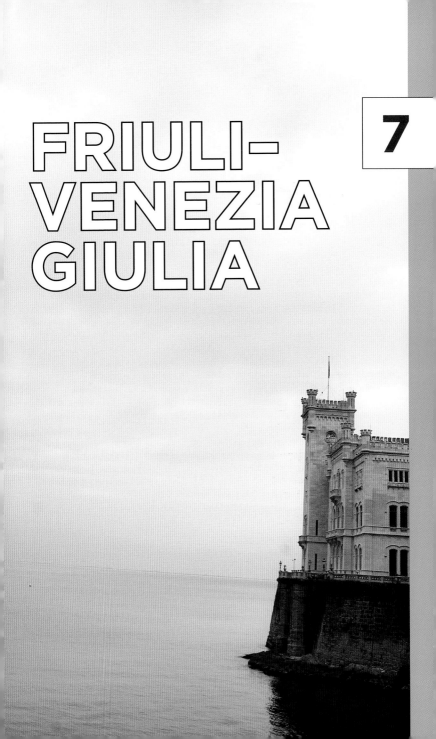

FRIULI-VENEZIA GIULIA

7

Trieste's Friuli–Venezia Giulia region is a sliver of coastline across the Adriatic Sea from Venice. Any glance at a map will show you that it would probably be part of Slovenia today were it not for the border juggling that followed World War I. Though primarily known for the shipping industry and naval yards around the Habsburgs' old port city of Trieste, this region was actually a major center of both ancient Rome and the Dark Ages' Lombards.

The Friuli–Venezia Giulia region comprises Venezia Giulia, of which Trieste is the capital, and the much larger Friuli, with Udine as its capital. There's an interesting inverse proportion between the size of the Friuli–Venezia Giulia's most interesting centers and each one's era of domination over local affairs. Rule by the sprawling free port and current capital of Trieste dates back only through Austro-Hungarian control and the 16th century. The midsize city of **Udine** held the patriarchy and regional power from the 13th century, until it came under Venetian control in the 15th century. Udine had wrested that patriarchal seat, and control of it, from what is today the oversize town of **Cividale,** where, in the early Middle Ages, the Lombards inaugurated their ruling system of duchies. Even the sleepy backwater town of **Aquileia,** with its ruins and early Christian mosaics, once held a position of power as the fourth-most-important city of the Roman Empire.

Almost every town in the region has a museum or two devoted to the Risorgimento (Italy's unification) and/or World War I. Well worth a visit to help understand the history of this region (a history, unfortunately, rarely explained in English), these museums trace the Italian national movement from its mid-19th-century beginnings through the intense fighting that took place in Friuli's mountains to the border disputes involving the line separating Italy from Yugoslavia. Even then, these disputes were not always happily resolved. The Treaty of Paris plopped the national boundary right through the town of **Gorizia.** It wasn't until later compromises in the 1970s that the line was finally moved over so that only Gorizia's eastern suburbs, just beyond the medieval Castello's hill, remained Slovenian (called Nova Gorica).

TRIESTE

158km (98 miles) E of Venice, 68km (42 miles) SE of Udine, 408km (253 miles) E of Milan

Trieste faces west, toward the rest of Italy, to which it is connected only by a strip just a few miles wide. For many of its traditions—from the Slavic dialects you are likely to hear in the streets to the appearance of goulash and Viennese pastries on its menus—this handsome city of medieval, neoclassical, and modern buildings turns to other parts of Europe and is rightly considered a Habsburgian Adriatic port, tied more to Vienna than to Venice.

PREVIOUS PAGE: **Lonely Miramare Castle overlooks the Adriatic.**

Friuli–Venezia Giulia

Already a thriving port by the time it was absorbed into the Roman Empire in the 2nd century A.D., Trieste competed with Venice for control of the seas from the 9th through the 15th centuries. For several centuries, it thrived under the Habsburgs; in the late 18th century, Maria Theresa, and later her heirs and successors, gave the city its grandiose neoclassical look. Trieste was the chief seaport of the Austro-Hungarian Empire until the conclusion of World War I, when Trieste became part of Italy. At the end of World War II, Allied forces and Yugoslavia jointly occupied Trieste, which became a free city issuing its own stamps and currency until 1954, when it was given back to Italy.

You're likely to notice that Trieste is still very much a seagoing city. The traditional *passeggiata* here means a stroll along the waterfront to enjoy a sea breeze and watch the sun set over the Adriatic.

In the cafes that remain (fewer now than before World War I), you can experience the city's history as one of Europe's intellectual centers. James Joyce arrived in 1904 and stayed for more than a decade, teaching English and writing *A Portrait of the Artist as a Young Man, Dubliners,* and at least part of *Ulysses;* the poet Rainer Maria Rilke lived nearby; Sigmund Freud spent time here; and the city was home to Italo Svevo, one of Italy's greatest 20th-century novelists, and to Umberto Saba, one of its greatest 20th-century poets.

Festivals & Markets The city celebrates summer with a **series of concerts and films,** many free and held in the outdoor theater in the Castello di San Giusto. If you are going to be in Trieste at this time, ask the tourist office for a copy of *Eventi Luglio-Agosto*. The **International Operetta Festival** presents three or four noted masterworks (and a new piece or two) in June and July in the Teatro Lirico Giuseppe Verdi (✆ **040-672-2500;** www.teatroverdi-trieste. com). The **Barcolana Autumn Cup,** held in the Golfo di Trieste on the second Sunday in October, is the largest sailing regatta in Southern Europe. For more information, call ✆ **040-411-664,** or visit www.barcolana.it.

An **antiques market** fills the streets of the Old City the third Sunday of every month, while early November brings an important **antiques fair,** especially noted for Liberty (plus its Austrian cousin Jungendstil) and Biedermeier pieces, to the conference center of the Stazione Maritima (✆ **040-304-888**). Trieste's two **food markets** provide colorful surroundings and a chance to eye the local cuisine. The covered market, at the corner of Via Carducci and Via della Majolica, is open Monday from 8am to 2pm and Tuesday through Saturday from 8am to 7pm. The open-air market is on Ponte Ponterosso, alongside the canal that cuts into the center of the city from the harbor, and it operates Tuesday through Saturday from 8am to 5:30pm.

Essentials

GETTING THERE By Train Trains arrive at and depart from **Stazione Centrale** on Piazza della Libertà (✆ **040-412-695**), northwest of the historic center. There are, on average, two trains an hour to and from Venice (2½–3 hr.), where you can make connections to Milan and other Italian cities. There are also twice-hourly connections to and from Udine (1–1½ hr.). Two trains a day connect Trieste to Budapest, Hungary (11 hr.), three daily to Ljubljana, Slovenia (3 hr.).

By Bus The **bus station** is on Corso Cavour, to the left of the train station (✆ **800-915-303;** www.saf.ud.it). Frequent buses (28 a day) link Trieste and Udine (1½ hr.), and many other towns throughout the region. There's also one bus Monday to Saturday (check for the schedule, as it often changes) to Ljubljana, Slovenia (2¾ hr.).

By Car Trieste is a 2-hour trip from Venice along Autostrada A4.

Trieste's Canal Grande cuts through the downtown.

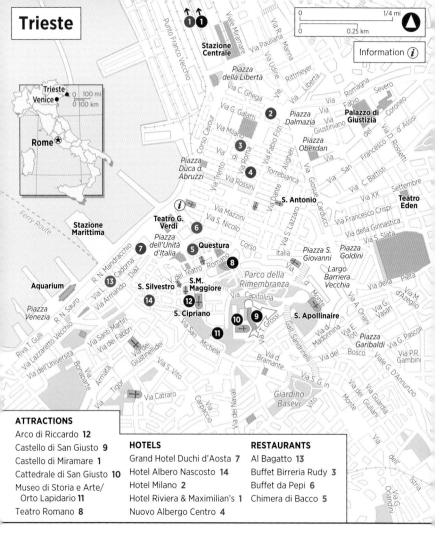

Trieste

Trieste
Venice

Rome

Punto Franco Vecchio

Viale Miramare

Viale Pauliana

Stazione Centrale

Piazza della Libertà

Via C. Ghega

Via Udine

Rittmeyer

Via Libertà

Romagna

Severo

Coroneo

Via G. Galatti

Via Milano

Corso Cavour

Via di Roma

Via Trento

Via Rossini

Piazza Dalmazia

Via Fabio Filzi

Via Giustiniano

Palazzo di Giustizia

Via del

Via d. Rossetti

Via d. Assisi

Piazza Oberdan

Piazza Duca d. Abruzzi

Torrebianca

Via Dante Alighieri

Via San Francesco

Via C. Battisti

Settembre

Via XX

Teatro Eden

Via Mazzini

Via S. Nicolo

S. Antonio

Via S. Lazzaro

Via Giosue Carducci

Via Francesco Crispi

Via della Ginnastica

Via S. Slata

Ferry Route

Stazione Marittima

Teatro G. Verdi

Piazza dell'Unità d'Italia

Via del Teatro Romano

Corso Italia

Questura

Piazza S. Giovanni

Piazza Goldini

Largo Barriera Vecchia

Via della Pietà

R. N. Mandracchio

Cadorna

Diaz

Aquarium

R. N. Sauro

Via Armando

Via Santi Martiri

Via dei Fabbri

S. Silvestro

S.M. Maggiore

S. Cipriano

Parco della Rimembranza

Via Capitolina

Via T. Grossi

Via G. Oberti

Via A. Oriani

Via G. Vasari

Via M. d'Azeglio

Via G. Pascoli

Via P.R. Gambini

Piazza Venezia

Via Lazzaretto Vecchio

Via dell'Università

Bonaparte

Tigor

Via Armata

Via San Michele

Via dei Giustinelli der

Via S. Vito

Via Catraro

Carpaccio

Via dei Navali

Via d Bramante

Via S. G. in Monte

S. Apollinaire

Via E. Madonnina

Via E. Toti

Piazza Garibaldi

Via del Bosco

Viale G. D'Annunzio

Giardino Basevi

Via d. Giuliani

Viale Guardia

Via G. Orlandini

Via Istria

ATTRACTIONS
Arco di Riccardo **12**
Castello di San Giusto **9**
Castello di Miramare **1**
Cattedrale di San Giusto **10**
Museo di Storia e Arte/ Orto Lapidario **11**
Teatro Romano **8**

HOTELS
Grand Hotel Duchi d'Aosta **7**
Hotel Albero Nascosto **14**
Hotel Milano **2**
Hotel Riviera & Maximilian's **1**
Nuovo Albergo Centro **4**

RESTAURANTS
Al Bagatto **13**
Buffet Birreria Rudy **3**
Buffet da Pepi **6**
Chimera di Bacco **5**

VISITOR INFORMATION The **tourist office** is at Piazza dell'Unità d'Italia 4B near the waterfront (© **040-347-8312;** fax 040-437-8320; www.turismo fvg.it; Mon–Sat 9am–7pm, Sun 9am–1pm).

CITY LAYOUT The **center** of Trieste, which is snuggled between the hills and the sea, is compact and easy to get around on foot. The bus and train stations are at the northern end of the center, on the **Piazza della Libertà.** From there, follow the harbor south for about 10 minutes along Corso Cavour (you'll soon cross Trieste's Canal Grande) and its continuation, Riva III Novembre, to the **Piazza dell'Unità d'Italia.** This dramatic space— with Habsburg-commissioned, neoclassical buildings on three sides, the sea on one side, and a fountain in its center—is the heart of old Trieste and the present-day city as well. **Via Carducci,** Trieste's main shopping street, cuts through the center of the orderly 19th-century city. It begins in Piazza

Oberdan (a few blocks east of the train station on Via Ghega) and cuts a straight swath south to Piazza Goldoni; from there the Corso Italia leads west to Piazza dell'Unità d'Italia and the sea.

GETTING AROUND Central Trieste is easily navigable on foot, but the footsore can use the extensive network of **TT buses and trams** (✆ **040-425-001** or 800-016-675 in Italy; www.triestetrasporti.it) that runs throughout the city. You can purchase tickets at any *tabacchi* (tobacconist) for 1.10€ for 60 minutes (valid for 4 hr. on Sun) or 3.60€ for a day pass. One foot-saving route is the no. 24 line from the train station to the hilltop Castello di San Giusto and its adjoining cluster of remarkable buildings (see below), or call a **taxi** at ✆ **040-307-730.**

What to See & Do

The oldest part of Trieste climbs the **Colle Capitolino (Capitoline Hill),** just behind the grandiose **Piazza dell'Unità d'Italia ★**. This is where many of the city's most interesting museums and monuments (including Roman remains) are located. A good way to approach the hill is to leave the southeastern end of Piazza dell'Unità d'Italia and step into Piazza Cavana.

In contrast to the assemblage of 18th- and 19th-century buildings on the main piazza, this part of Trieste, a warren of tiny streets climbing the hillside away from the sea, is medieval. From Piazza Cavana, follow Via Felice Veneziano to Piazza Barbacan, where you take a left to duck under the 1st-century-A.D. **Arco di Riccardo,** and then turn right up Via Cattedrale, and follow that for about 10 minutes up the flanks of the Colle Capitolino to the **Cattedrale di San Giusto** (see below). Just above that is the **Castello di San Giusto** (see below), from which Trieste and the Adriatic unfold in an unforgettable view at your feet.

For a quicker descent, you can take the 265-step **Scala dei Giganti (Steps of the Giants)** back down the hill to Piazza Goldoni and Via Carducci, Trieste's main shopping street.

Trieste's expansive Piazza dell'Unità d'Italia.

Castello di San Giusto ★ The tall walls of this bastion, built between 1470 and 1630, rise just behind the cathedral. Within the walls are an open-air theater, the **Cortile delle Milizie,** where a summer film-and-concert festival is held (see "Festivals & Markets," above), and a museum. But the walls themselves steal the show. A walk along them affords views over Trieste and the Adriatic, making this a popular spot just before its sunset closing time. The **Civic Museum** provides an interesting, if not profound, experience—among a series of period rooms is a "Venetian chamber" filled with antique chests, 17th-century Flemish tapestries, and other furnishings—as does the **Appartamento del Capitano,** the residence of the castle's 18th-century commander. A collection of antique weaponry is housed in the rooms of the castle watch.

Piazza Cattedrale, Colle Capitolino. ✆ **040-309-362.** www.triestecultura.it. Castle ramparts 1€; Civico Museo del Castello 4€. Castle daily 9am–7pm (Oct–Mar until 5pm). Museum Tues–Sun 9am–1pm. Bus: 24.

Cattedrale di San Giusto ★ This hilltop basilica is one of several remarkable buildings atop the Capitoline Hill, which is littered with Roman ruins, evidence of the city's long history as an important port. In fact, the cathedral's squat, 14th-century **campanile** rises from the ruins of a 1st-century-A.D. Roman temple. Pleasingly asymmetrical, the cathedral is dedicated to Saint Just, Trieste's patron. It incorporates two 5th-century Romanesque basilicas, one already dedicated to San Giusto, the other to Santa Maria Assunta. You'll see what remains of both as you step inside: The two right aisles belong to the original San Giusto, the two left aisles to Santa Maria Assunta, and in the center is the 14th-century nave that was added to bring them together. The apse mosaics at the ends of the aisles are from the 13th century; those in the main apse date from 1932.

Piazza Cattedrale 3, Colle Capitolino. ✆ **040-302-874** or 040-309-666. Free admission. Daily 8:30am–noon and 4–7pm. Bus: 24.

Museo di Storia e Arte/Orto Lapidario The Museum of Art and History is Trieste's archaeological collection, and it includes prehistoric finds, exquisite Greek pieces (including some fine vases and a 4th-century-B.C. silver Rhyton, a chalice shaped as a deer's head, from Taranto), and remnants of the city's Roman past. Most of the Roman architectural fragments, though, are scattered about

---

Trieste Walking Tours

If you don't have a friend to show you the sights of Trieste, make a new one at the tourist office: a local tour guide. The tourism office offers walking tours between April and December, including a comprehensive 2-hour tour of the historic center. For literary buffs, there is a 2-hour walking tour that shows you where James Joyce walked, ate, and drank coffee, as well as the surroundings that inspired local writers Italo Svevo and Umberto Saba.

All tours start at 10am at the tourist office in Piazza dell'Unità d'Italia. Admission is 4€ for each of the tours, or free with an FVG Card—see below. (Historic center tour: daily from Apr to mid-Oct and Sat, Sun, and holidays for the rest of the year. James Joyce tour: usually two Sat a month Apr–Sept. Food tour: usually two Sat a month Apr–Oct.) See the tourist office or check www.turismofvg.it for details.

the **Orto Lapidario (Lapidary Garden).** A few rooms of the museum house a growing Egyptian collection, including a female mummy.

Another outdoor remnant of Roman Trieste lies near the bottom of the Colle Capitolino. On Via Teatro Romano, you'll find the **Teatro Romano (Roman Theater),** built in the 2nd century A.D. Only partially unearthed, the ruins can be glimpsed for free through a fence; let your imagination take you to the days when 6,000 spectators packed in for gladiatorial contests.

Piazza Cattedrale 1. ☎ **040-310-500.** www.triestecultura.it. Admission: Museum 3.60€ adults, 2.60€ students 25 and under and seniors 65 and older; Orto Lapidario 4€ adults, 3€ students and seniors. Tues–Sun 9am–1pm (Wed until 7pm). Bus: 24.

Nearby Sights

Castello di Miramare ★★ This vision of gleaming white turrets looms over the coast north of the city, 7km (4¼ miles) from the center. Archduke Maximilian, brother of Austrian Emperor Franz Joseph, built this castle in the late 1850s when he was sent to Trieste to command the Austrian Navy. The interior reflects the somewhat insipid royal taste of the day, with room after room of gilt and velvet. Far more romantic are the adjoining gardens, where oaks, firs, and cypresses sway in sea breezes. Alluring, too, is the legend that those who sleep in the castle will meet a violent end, a belief to which history has given some credence—Maximilian went to Mexico in 1864 to assume the brief role of emperor and was shot there in 1867; Archduke Ferdinand spent the night here before journeying to Sarajevo, where he was assassinated on the eve of World War I; and a later owner, Duke Amadeo of Austria, was also assassinated in 1938.

For sheer theatrics in such a theatrical setting, you can attend one of the campy sound-and-light shows in July and August. They depict Maximilian's final days in Mexico and are staged Tuesday, Thursday, and Sunday at 9:30 and 10:45pm; tickets begin at 10€.

Via Miramare, Grignano. ☎ **040-224-143.** www.castello miramare.it. Castle 6€ adults, 4€ E.U. citizens ages 18–24, free for E.U. children 17 and under and seniors 65 and older; grounds free. English-language tours available for 21€ for 1–10 people. Castle: Daily 9am–7pm (last admission 30 min. before closing). Grounds: Apr–Sept daily 8am–7pm; Mar and Oct daily 8am–6pm; Nov–Feb daily 8am–5pm. Oct–Mar entrance to the Castello after 5pm is from Viale dei Lecci only. Bus: 36 (catch at train station). Parking .50€ per hour, or free along road and walk 5 min.

Grotta Gigante The "Gigantic Cave" lives up to its name: 114m high, 924m long, and 65m wide (374 ft.×3,031 ft.×213 ft.), this single-chamber cave is the world's largest underground cavern open to the public. *Warning:* The requisite guided tours descend and ascend about 500 stairs total. Tours are in Italian, though if your group is mixed, they may play English and German recordings. The cave is about 15km (9¼ miles) north of the city near Opicina. An exciting way to get here is via the rickety tram that climbs into the hills from Piazza Oberdan (just west of the train station) and ends at Opicina, where you

Remains of a cave bear (*Ursus spelaeus*) in the Grotta Gigante.

> ### Cumulative Tickets
>
> **The region of Friuli–Venezia Giulia offers a cumulative ticket called the FVG Card, which includes admission to all regional museums and guided tours; discounts on natural parks, boat rides, and ski lifts; and free transport on Udine city buses and trams. It costs 15€ for 48 hours, 20€ for 72 hours, and 29€ for a week. See www. turismofvg.it for more information.**

can catch the no. 42 bus to the cave. The tram runs every 20 minutes from 7:30am to 8pm daily, and the fare is 1.10€.

Opicina. ✆ **040-327-312.** www.grotta gigante.it. Admission 11€ adults, 9€ students 26 and under and seniors 65 and over, 8€ children ages 6–16. Tues–Sun tours every hour Nov–Feb 10am–noon and 2–4pm, Mar and Oct 10am–4pm; tours every half-hour Apr–Sept 10am–6pm. Bus: 42.

Where to Stay

The **C.A.T.** (✆ **040-630-286;** www.cat-trieste.com) office inside the train station will help you find a room if the choices below are full. Also, if you stay at one of their associate hotels (all of the ones listed below except the Hotel Riviera & Maximilian's and the Grand Hotel Duchi d'Aosta), you get a special shopping card good for a reduced price at most museums in town (and a reduction on the audio guide at Castello Miramare), plus 10% off at more than three dozen shops and restaurants.

Grand Hotel Duchi d'Aosta ★ This is Trieste's best hotel, installed in one of the neoclassical buildings right on Piazza dell'Unità d'Italia. It is business oriented and modernized—with snappy service, a thermal pool, and Jacuzzi box showers in the marble bathrooms—but retains plenty of class in the stylish wood furnishings and old-world charm of its reception and Harry's Grill, which has tables on the square.

Piazza dell'Unità d'Italia 2, 34121 Trieste. www.grandhotelduchidaosta.com. ✆ **040-760-0011.** Fax 040-366-092. 53 units. 160€–330€ double. Breakfast 20€. AE, DC, MC, V. Parking 21€ in nearby garage. **Amenities:** International restaurant; bar; babysitting; concierge; indoor pool; room service; smoke-free rooms. *In room:* A/C, TV w/pay movies, hair dryer, minibar, free Wi-Fi.

Hotel Albero Nascosto ★ 🏠 The "hidden tree" hotel is a secluded gem in the historic center by the seafront. For the price, the rooms are very well equipped (compact apartments, really), with ample bathrooms and a kitchenette in most units. The recently restored rooms have a sleek but charming feel, with hardwood floors, exposed beams, and modern art gracing the walls, with sophisticated touches such as stocked bookshelves. Beyond its convenient but quiet location and excellent wine bar/tavern downstairs, the most compelling reason to stay at the Albero Nascosto may be the friendly and genteel staff.

Via Felice Venezian 18, 34124 Trieste. www.alberonascosto.it. ✆ **040-300-188.** Fax 040-303-733. 10 units. 75€–115€ single; 95€–165€ double; 115€–170€ triple. Rates include breakfast. AE, DC, MC, V. No parking. **Amenities:** Wine bar; concierge. *In room:* A/C (in some rooms), TV, hair dryer, kitchenette, minibar, Wi-Fi.

Hotel Milano Quiet and geared to business travelers as well as foreigners, this modern hotel is near the train station but within an easy walk to most of the sights in the city center. There's a spacious lounge and bar on the ground floor, as well as a breakfast room where a generous buffet (the only meal served) is laid out in the morning. Its greatest asset is its convenient location.

Via Ghega 17, 34132 Trieste. www.hotel-milano.com. ✆ **040-369-680.** Fax 040-369-727. 44 units. 140€ double; 170€ triple. Rates include breakfast. AE, DC, MC, V. Parking 12€ in garage.

Amenities: Bar; concierge; room service. *In room:* A/C (in some rooms), TV, hair dryer, minibar, Wi-Fi (3€ for 1 hr., 5€ for 2 hr.).

Hotel Riviera & Maximilian's ★★ This seaside retreat has been steadily expanded since it opened in 1910. Rooms in the older half have parquet floors, blue-tiled bathrooms, and carved wood furnishings with modern prints, and many neighboring doubles can be connected to make suites. Number 101 is a family suite, though it is one of only three rooms without a sea view. In the new half, rooms have balconies that are shaded by umbrella pines, cypress, and palms, and are cooled by Adriatic breezes. Rooms on the first floor have terraces opening directly onto the garden; those on the side have less of a sea view but more greenery.

The Maximilian's separate residence is made up of 12 apartments, rented by the week. They have stylish, modern furnishings in burnished steel and light wood tones, minimalist and low to the ground for a vaguely Japanese-industrial look. In the single-bedroom apartments and in one of the bedrooms in the two- or three-room units, the bed folds away and an end table unfolds into a large desk. The kitchenettes are slipped behind pocket doors, so the rooms can be sold as doubles as well. The hotel's catwalk leads from the panoramic terrace with umbrella-shaded tables to an elevator tower down to two private beaches (the second, which includes the pools, is a 5-min. walk along the coast).

Strada Costiera 22 (just north of Castello Miramare, 8km/5 miles from Trieste's center), 34010 Trieste. www.hotelrivieraemaximilian.com. ✆ **040-224-551.** Fax 040-224-300. 70 units. 140€–240€ double; 420€–1,250€ 1-room apt for 2 guests per week; 665€–2,100€ 2-room apt for 2 guests per week. Rates include breakfast. AE, DC, MC, V. Free parking. **Amenities:** International/Italian terrace restaurant; beach buffet in summer; bar; babysitting; children's center at beach; concierge; golf course; 2 outdoor pools (1 for adults, 1 for kids); room service; smoke-free rooms; nearby tennis courts; watersports equipment/rentals. *In room:* A/C, TV w/pay movies, hair dryer, kitchenette (in apts), minibar, Wi-Fi.

Nuovo Albergo Centro ✦ This clean *pensione* is very livable, while still maintaining low prices and simple comforts, including free wireless Internet access in each room, a solid breakfast, and bike rental for 10€ a day. It occupies two floors of a large building about midway between the train station and the Piazza dell'Unità d'Italia, and it is less than a 10-minute walk from either. Rooms have firm beds, modular furnishings, and parquet floors. Two of them have balconies: room 214, with a private bathroom, and 109, without.

Via Roma 13, 34132 Trieste. www.hotelcentrotrieste.it. ✆ **040-347-8790.** Fax 040-347-5258. 24 units, 16 with private bathroom. 45€–60€ double with shared bathroom; 60€–80€ double with private bathroom. Rates include buffet breakfast. AE, DC, MC, V. Parking 15€ in garage. **Amenities:** Bikes; concierge; smoke-free rooms. *In room:* TV, hair dryer, Wi-Fi.

Where to Eat

Al Bagatto ★★ SEAFOOD The best fish restaurant in Trieste occupies simply decorated quarters, overseen by a staff that seems to have been working the perpetually crowded dining room for decades. The emphasis is clearly on the freshest fish in simple but tasty preparations. *Tartara di branzino* is a fine example, a sea bass tartare with fresh ricotta. It would be a shame, though, to come this far and not join most of the other diners in ordering the house's *frittura mista,* a delicately fried sampling of the sea creatures that were fresh at the market that morning.

Via Felice Venezian 2/Via Cadorna. ✆ **040-301-771.** www.albagatto.it. Reservations required. Primi 15€–20€; secondi 20€–30€. AE, DC, MC, V. Mon–Sat noon–2:30pm and 7pm–midnight. Closed Aug 15–30 and Dec 15–31.

Buffet Birreria Rudy AUSTRIAN/TRIESTINO Just because Trieste is currently part of Italy doesn't mean you can't indulge in the cuisines of its former identities. This small Austrian/Bavarian *Bierhalle* serves Spaten beer on tap and sausages, wurst, and goulash alongside pastas, soups, and boiled meats. If you can't choose between a primo or a secondo, get both at once; the gnocchi with goulash is memorable. Otherwise, stand at the bar and choose nibblers from behind the glass—roasted peppers, fried zucchini, rice croquettes, frankfurters in pastry—or grab a straw-bottomed chair at the little tables under Bavarian banners and pick from the chalkboard menu.

Via Valdirivo 32. ✆ **040-639-428.** www.buffetrudyspaten.it. Reservations not accepted. Primi 4€–5€; secondi 9€–10€. AE, DC, MC, V. Mon–Sat 11am–midnight.

Buffet da Pepi ★ TRIESTINO Trieste has many such *tavola caldi* (hot-foods delis) like this one, though none compare to century-old Pepi, a much-beloved institution. You can get a panino of cold cuts or splurge on a 10€ platter of the house specialty, many varieties of pork: spicy *cotechini* (pork sausages), *porchetta* (roast pork), *bollito di maiale* (a Trieste dish of boiled pork), and prosciutto, all served with *crauti* (sauerkraut) and other vegetables.

Via della Cassa di Risparmio 3 (near Piazza della Borsa, 1 block from the water and 2 blocks north of Piazza dell'Unità d'Italia). ✆ **040-366-858.** Reservations not accepted. Sandwiches and dishes 4€–11€. AE, DC, MC, V. Mon–Sat 9am–9pm. Closed July 15–Aug 7.

Chimera di Bacco ★ MODERN TRIESTINO Cuisine in Italy is changing to reflect more modern and refined tastes, and Chimera di Bacco leads that charge in Trieste on a little alleyway behind city hall. The clean and modern decor reflects the minimalist but elegant dishes, which range from *triestino* favorites such as *la jota,* a stew of cabbage, potatoes, and beans, to a delicate boneless rabbit done with a Madeira sauce and Croatian prosciutto. You won't find a wide selection of fish dishes here, but rather a heavy emphasis on the best cuts of meat in an intricate presentation. A good selection of local wines paves the way to a romantic evening and a culinary treat.

Via del Pane 2. ✆ **040-364-023.** Reservations not necessary. Primi 7€–9€; secondi 13€–19€. DC, MC, V. Mon–Sat noon–3pm and 6–11pm.

Coffee & Gelato

Coffee is one of Trieste's most important products—Illy and many other major Italian brands are located here (in fact, an Illy family member has even served as the city's mayor). More to the point for travelers, drinking coffee is a local pastime, and Trieste's exquisite blends can be enjoyed in any number of august cafes.

Caffè degli Specchi, at Piazza dell'Unità d'Italia 7 (✆ **040-365-777;** www.caffespecchi.it), enjoys a marvelous position on the city's main seafront piazza, making its terrace a prime spot to linger. In bad weather, a series of elegant rooms fill with shoppers and businesspeople. The pastries are excellent, as is the coffee. James Joyce spent much of his 12 years in Trieste at **Caffè-Pasticceria Pirona ★**, at the east end of Via Carducci at Largo Barriera Vecchia 12 (✆ **040-636-046**). It was here that he allegedly wrote part of *Ulysses*. With its photographs of old Trieste and gilded mirrors, the premises bear the mark of one of

Europe's great remaining literary cafes. **Caffè San Marco ★★**, at Via Battisti 18 (✆ **040-371-373**), is one of Trieste's most elegant cafes; it dates from 1914, with a Liberty-style (as Art Nouveau is called in Italy) interior. A pianist puts the final touches on the ultimate cafe experience.

Gelateria Zampolli, at Via Ghega 10 (✆ **040-364-868**), is reputed to be the best gelateria in Trieste. It's located near Stazione Centrale and the city center, serving more than 50 flavors made on the premises daily. Another Zampolli, owned by a different member of the same family, is located on Piazza Cavana 6 (✆ **040-306-003**), just south of Piazza dell'Unità d'Italia.

An Ancient Diversion En Route to Gorizia

Aquileia ★★ is one of those perfect Italian sites. This tiny village of just over 3,000 souls was once a major Roman city and early Christian stronghold, with a rich heritage that has left it littered with ruins and some of the best paleo-Christian mosaics in Europe. The Roman colony was founded in 181 B.C. and witnessed such momentous ancient events as Emperor Augustus's meeting with King Herod of Judea in A.D. 10, the murders of would-be Emperor Maximinus (by his own army) and Emperor Constantine II (by his brother), and the sacks of Attila the Hun in 452.

Remains of the **Roman colony ★** are open sites (open 8:30am to an hour before sunset; free admission), some still being excavated, that lie scattered north of the current town. Just to the north of the main Piazza Capitolo, behind the tourist office, are a set of Roman houses and Christian oratories with excellent floor mosaics. From here, walk right (east) a bit to turn north up Via Sacra alongside the river, which leads to the remains of the Roman harbor. Turn left on Via Gemina then left again on Via Giulia Augusta to pass, on the right, a stretch of ancient road and, on the left, a row of standing columns marking one edge of the **Forum ★** (among the items displayed here, look for the Gorgon's head). The road forks at the **Grande Mausoleo,** a 1st-century-A.D. tomb hauled here from the edge of town. The right fork (Via XXIV Maggio) will lead you past the remaining scraps of the amphitheater and baths (still being excavated).

The left fork (really straight on down Via Giulio Augusto) takes you in a few blocks to Via Roma and the **Museo Archeologico ★** (✆ **0431-91-016** or 0431-91-035), which houses some nice statuary, mosaics, bronzes, and glassware, plus the excellently preserved hull of a Roman ship. Admission to the museum is 4€ for adults, 2€ for E.U. citizens ages 18 to 25, and free for those 18 and under and 65 and older; it's open Monday 8:30am to 2pm, Tuesday to Sunday 8:30am to 7:30pm (June–Sept open to 11pm on Sat). The last admission is half an hour before closing.

Christianity is also ancient in Aquileia. A major church council called here in 381 was attended by such towering early theologians as saints Jerome and Ambrose. The fabulously mosaic-filled **Basilica ★★** on Piazza Capitolo (✆ **0431-919-719**) is precisely as old as the official church in Italy, founded in 313, the same year Emperor Constantine declared Christianity to be the state religion. In the early 20th century, the church's original 4th-century **mosaic floor ★★★** was uncovered to reveal a colorful cornucopia of early Christian iconography mixed with pagan symbols and portraits of 4th-century congregants spreading over 700 sq. m (7,500 sq. ft.). The basilica was substantially rebuilt in the early 11th century, when the now-faded apse frescoes were painted. In the chapel, to the left of the altar, is a **bas-relief ★**, from 1170, of Christ with St. Peter and the freshly martyred St. Thomas of Canterbury. Later frescoes also

The mosaic floor of Aquileia's Basilica.

litter the church, including some lovely 12th-century Byzantine ones in the **main crypt ★★**.

The **Cripta Affreschi ★★** is entered next to the medieval reconstruction of the Holy Sepulcher at the entrance end of the basilica's left aisle. The mosaics here hail from three eras: Augustan ones from a Roman house (just to the left), an early-4th-century floor laid at the same time as the Basilica's (this was once a neighboring church), and later-4th-century ones as well. Admission to the Basilica is free, though the Cripta charges a fee. Both are open daily November to March 9am to 5pm (Sat and Sun until 6pm), and April to October 9am to 7pm. Admission is 3€ for adults and free for children 10 and under.

Aquileia lies on local road 352 (take the Palmanova exit from the A4) some 11km (6¾ miles) inland from Grado, a low-key Venice Lido–like semi-island resort where Aquileia's population, and fortunes, moved to escape Dark Ages barbarian raids by the likes of Huns and Lombards. The easiest way here without your own wheels is the bus from Udine to Grado, though you can also catch a bus from the Cervignano del Friuli train station 8km (5 miles) to the north on the Trieste-Venice line.

Aquileia's **tourist office** is on the main Piazza Capitolo (© **0431-91-087** or 0431-919-491; www.aquileia.net).

UDINE

71km (44 miles) NW of Trieste, 127km (79 miles) NE of Venice

Surrounded by the green, rolling plains of the Friuli, Udine is a delightful small city with a vibrant air, captivating medieval squares and Gothic and Renaissance monuments, and some stunning artworks by the rococo painter Tiepolo. A possession of the Venetian Republic from the 14th century, Udine has enjoyed great prosperity as a major trading center and a crossroads for trade across the Alps, just to the north. The late 18th century saw an Austrian takeover, the 19th century witnessed unification with Italy, and the 20th century brought intense World War II bombings. Through it all, the city's landmarks and distinct character (reflecting Italian, Nordic, and central European influences) have remained intact.

Festivals & Markets **Udine d'Estate** is the city's major festival, running from July to mid-September, with concerts and theatrical performances in churches and on Udine's beautiful *piazze*. An **outdoor food market** fills the atmospheric Piazza Matteotti daily from 8am to 1pm.

Essentials

GETTING THERE **By Train** About two trains an hour arrive at Udine's station on Viale Europa Unità from both Venice (1¾–2 hr.) and Trieste (1–1½ hr.).

By Bus The bus station is 1 block east of the train station on Viale Europa Unità. There is extensive service to other cities and towns in Friuli–Venezia Giulia, but little outside it, provided by **SAF** (© **800-915-303;** www.saf.ud.it). Hourly buses (more frequent btw. 7–9am and 4–7pm) make the hour-long trip to and from Trieste.

By Car Udine is an easy 2-hour drive northeast of Venice, first east on the A4, then north on the A23. From Trieste, it's a trip of a little under an hour west on the A4 and then north on A23. If you are driving from Cortina d'Ampezzo or another Dolomite resort, you will drop down from the mountains toward Belluno on SS51 as if you were going to Venice, but at Vittorio Veneto head east on the state roads toward Pordenone and then Udine. Allow about 3 hours for the drive.

VISITOR INFORMATION The **tourist office** is at Piazza I Maggio 7 (the other side of the Castello from Piazza della Libertà; © **0432-295-972;** fax 0432-504-743; www.turismo.fvg.it) and is open Monday to Saturday 9am to 1pm and 3 to 6pm.

CITY LAYOUT Much of the center of Udine is closed to traffic and surrounded by ring roads. The train and bus stations are at the southern end of this ring network, on Viale Europa Unità. From there it is about a 15-minute walk into the center, following Via Aquileia and its continuation, Via Veneto, to Piazza della Libertà. Bus no. 1 makes the trip from the train station to the center (1€).

What to See & Do

In Udine's center, handsome streets open every few blocks or so onto another stunning piazza and sometimes even cross little streams. The effect is like walking from one stage set to another. The heart of the city is the elegant **Piazza della Libertà ★★**, which bears the telltale marks of the Venetian presence in Udine: On one side is the **Loggia del Lionello,** the town hall, built in the mid–15th century in Venetian style with a pink-and-white-striped facade. Across the piazza is the Renaissance **Porticcato di San Giovanni ★★**, with a long portico supported by slender columns and, rising above it, a Venice-inspired clock tower emblazoned with the Venetian lion and topped with two Moors who strike the hours.

The great Renaissance architect Palladio designed the **Arco Bollani,** located to one side of the clock tower. Pass through it and make the short climb through verdant gardens to the somber 16th-century **Castello ★★**, which rises above the Piazza della Libertà on a hillock. Many Udinese come up here just to admire the view over the town and countryside, but you can also venture into the castle and visit the **Musei Civici.** While many of the galleries house an eclectic collection that includes coins, ancient pottery, and old photographs of Udine, the real treasures can be found in the **Galleria d'Arte Antica ★**. Here you'll get a taste of the work of Giambattista Tiepolo, who came to Udine from Venice in 1726, when he was 30 and already regarded as a master of a rococo style that was the last great burst of Italian painting. His *Consilium in Arena* is pure Tiepolo, a swirl of lush skies and plump putti. The museum (© **0432-271-591**) is open Tuesday to Sunday 10:30am to 7pm (Oct–Apr until 5pm); admission is 5€ and 3€ for those 18 and under and 65 and over, respectively.

Many visitors come to Udine just to enjoy the Tiepolos that grace many of its buildings. To follow in their footsteps, descend again to Piazza della Libertà and follow Via Veneto south for a block or so to Piazza Duomo. The **Cathedral** ★ (daily 7am–noon and 4–8pm) dominates the square with its 14th-century Gothic facade, but the interior is theatrically baroque. The first, second, and fourth altars in the right nave are adorned with Tiepolo paintings; in the fourth chapel, his airy version of *Christ's Ascension* imparts lightness and a sense of exhilaration at leaving Earth (Tiepolo also did the frescoes here).

Tiepolo also frescoed the **Oratorio della Purità** ★ across the piazza (✆ **0432-506-830**). In *Fall of the Angels,* the plummeting cherubs look like children who have just been scolded. An *Assumption,* appropriately adorning the ceiling, is so light that it seems to draw the viewer right off the floor. To enter the oratory, rustle up a sacristan in the Duomo (but not on Sun), or try ringing the bell (mornings only).

Udine's largest collection of the artist's works adorns the **Palazzo Patriarcale** or **Palazzo Arcivescovile** ★★ (✆ **0432-25-003**), just north of the Duomo on Piazza Patriarcato. This palace was once home to Udine's patriarchal bishops. One of the last (before the position was dissolved) was Dionisio Delfino (1699–1734), from a wealthy and influential Veneto family (they produced several Udine patriarchs; look for their "three dolphins on a blue field" coat of arms all over the *palazzo*). Delfino was the guy who brought Tiepolo to Udine to paint the second floor's airy frescoes, which depict Old Testament scenes full of familiar biblical characters wearing fashionable 18th-century clothing. The most impressive room is the narrow **Galleria degli Ospiti,** though the balustraded **Biblioteca (library)** and double-decker **Sala del Trono (Throne Room)** are also notable. The Sala del Trono is plastered with portraits of the patriarchs, many redone by Tiepolo. Dionisio is the one on the bottom at the far left of the window wall. The *palazzo* (which also houses the Duomo's Museo Diocesano on the first floor containing Friuliana-School wood statues spanning

the 13th to 18th c.) is open Wednesday to Sunday 10am to noon and 3:30 to 6:30pm. Admission is 5€ for adults and 3€ for children 10 and under.

One more museum here deserves a visit, the **Galleria d'Arte Moderna** ★ (✆ **0432-295-891**), on the other side of the city on Piazza Diacono (from Piazza della Libertà, follow Via Mazzini and Via Anton Morro north to the edge of the old center). Here you will be shaken out of the reverie induced by Tiepolo's airy views of miracles and the afterlife—the galleries are filled with the works of 20th-century powerhouses such as Picasso and Giorgio de Chirico, as well as 1970s works by the likes of Lichtenstein and De Kooning. It's open Wednesday to Monday 10:30am to 7pm (Oct–Apr until 5pm). Admission is 5€ for adults, 2.50€ for those younger than 18 and older than 65.

A view of Udine from the hill.

Where to Stay

Astoria Hotel Italia This is a classy business hotel, smack in the center of town, that, unfortunately, charges expense-account rates. The rooms are smallish but not cramped, with firm enough beds and a mix of furnishings from cherry-veneer mod and 1980s vintage floral-print-on-black to restructured 18th- and 19th-century antiques. Oddly, the bathrooms are old-fashioned (some outright old and in need of renovation), with nowhere to hang the shower nozzle.

Piazza XX Settembre 24, 33100 Udine. www.hotelastoria.udine.it. ✆ **0432-505-091.** Fax 0432-509-070. 75 units. 120€–218€ double; 138€–250€ superior double; 168€–290€ suite. Rates include breakfast. AE, DC, MC, V. Parking 16€ in garage. **Amenities:** Highly refined restaurant; bar; babysitting; concierge; room service. *In room:* A/C, TV, hair dryer, minibar, free Wi-Fi.

Hotel Clocchiatti ★★ The Clocchiatti family provides both homey, cozy accommodation in a Liberty-style 19th-century villa and a sleek, futuristic feel in its annex next door, each offering peace and quiet on the outskirts of town. The historic villa setting means guest quarters vary widely in size, shape, and decor, though all enjoy rich fabrics and carpets. One of the nicest is suite no. 102, large and on a corner, with floor-to-ceiling windows and a sofa that can be replaced by a double or twin beds for families. In the minimalist and modern annex, called Next, all rooms give out onto a leafy courtyard, except for the "Japanese Room," which has a secluded gravel patio with an Asian feel.

Via Cividale 29, 33100 Udine. www.hotelclocchiatti.it. ✆/fax **0432-505-047.** 14 units. 140€–180€ double; 180€–200€ junior suite. Rates include breakfast. AE, DC, MC, V. Parking free in small lot. Closed 2 weeks around Christmas. **Amenities:** Bar; bikes; concierge; room service. *In room:* A/C, TV, hair dryer, minibar, Wi-Fi (2€ for 3 hr., 3€ for 12 hr.).

Hotel Europa The blocks in front of Udine's train station make up a pleasant residential neighborhood where many of the city's hotels are clustered. The Europa is one of the nicest, with the exception of a sometimes-rude staff. The guest rooms are handsomely outfitted with sleek wood cabinetry and headboards, thick carpeting, and some nice touches that include brass wall lamps and framed reproductions. The quietest rooms are those in the back, facing a sunny courtyard, but double-glazing on the front-room windows keeps noise there to a minimum as well.

Viale Europa Unità 47, 33100 Udine. www.hoteleuropa.ud.it. ✆ **0432-508-731** or 0432-294-446. Fax 0432-512-654. 48 units. 68€–92€ double; 89€–110€ triple. Breakfast included. AE, DC, MC, V. Parking 10€ (sometimes included for stays of more than 1 day). **Amenities:** Regional restaurant next door; bar; concierge; room service. *In room:* A/C, TV, hair dryer, minibar, Wi-Fi.

Where to Eat

Al Vecchio Stallo ★★ TRATTORIA In the 1920s, this served as a post station, offering refreshments and fresh horses to mounted mail carriers. Today it has been transformed into a full-fledged *osteria,* serving simple, filling, cheap traditional dishes, along with lots of local wine. Things haven't changed much, though a token national Italian dish such as *penne amatriciana* is often added to the daily menu. Those in the know, however, recommend that you stick to local specialties like *orzo e fagioli* (barley and bean soup), *frico con polenta* (cheese melted over potatoes), *nervetti con cipolla* (cow leg tendons and veins tossed with onions—I think you have to be from Udine to appreciate them), or the ever-popular *polpettone con pure* (slices of giant meatball with mashed potatoes). Service is brisk but jocular.

Via Viola 7 (off Viale Marco Volpe, near Piazza XXVI Luglio). © **0432-21-296.** Reservations recommended. Primi 6€–11€; secondi 8€–12€. No credit cards. Mon–Tues and Thurs–Sat 11am–3pm and 6pm–midnight.

Caffè Bistrot CAFE This welcoming cafe faces Udine's oldest square, which is surrounded by tall old houses with porticos and which is the site of a colorful morning produce market. You can take in these atmospheric surroundings from a table on the terrace, though the interior rooms, which spread across two floors, are inviting. Students, businesspeople, and neighborhood residents alike sit for hours chatting and reading while they sip cups of coffee or one of the excellent local wines served by the glass. The delicious homemade pastries make this a popular breakfast spot. Sandwiches and a few other dishes, including an *insalata caprese* (with mozzarella, basil, and tomato) and crepes filled with ham and cheese, are also served throughout the day and night (after dark, in fact, this cafe often becomes a focal point of Old City nightlife; on some nights, a DJ spins records while students dance on the flagstones of the raised square).

Piazza Matteotti. No phone. Reservations not accepted. Sandwiches and snacks from 2.50€. MC, V. Tues–Fri 7:45am–2am; Sat 9am–2am.

Ristorante-Pizzeria Al Portici ★ PIZZERIA Udine has a large and energetic population of students, and they seem to spend much of their time in this large trattoria with red-checked tablecloths. The pizza oven turns out the most popular fare, but you can also dip into some of the city's simple, casual cuisine here, such as *cialzons*—as gnocchi are called here—which are often stuffed with smoked ricotta cheese, and *brovada* (a poor man's dish of turnips and pork sausage). Given the establishment's long open hours, you can stop by any time during the day for a coffee or beer, or a glass of some of the excellent Friuli wines.

Via Veneto 8. © **0432-508-975.** Reservations not accepted. Primi 5€–9€; secondi 7€–18€; pizza 5€–10€. MC, V. Wed–Mon 9am–1am.

A Day Trip to Cividale del Friuli

When the Lombards founded their first Italian duchy in the Dark Ages, it was centered on this pretty little city, so the entire region became known as Friuli after a corrupt elision of this Roman colony's original name, Forum Iulii (Caesar had modestly founded it as "Julius' Forum"). It later produced a few Lombard "Kings of Italy" from the 8th to 10th centuries, and until the Middle Ages, it was the seat of the local patriarch, after which its fortunes fell off. These days it's a largely medieval town perched on the lip of an impressive river gorge, where some of the best Lombard-era stone carving in Italy is preserved.

VISITOR INFORMATION The **tourist office,** Corso Paolino d'Aquileia 10 (©**0432-731-398** or 0432-731-461; fax 0432-731-398; www.comune. cividale-del-friuli.ud.it), is open Monday to Friday 9am to 1pm and 3 to 7pm.

A STROLL THROUGH TOWN

From the train station, turn left on Viale Libertà to Via C. Alberto, where you can take a right and follow it (it becomes Corso Mazzini) into the heart of town. After Piazza Duomo, the road becomes Corso Paolino d'Aquileia, and then you cross the Ponte del Diavolo over the deep and seriously impressive limestone gorge carved by the Natisone River.

The current **Duomo** (backtrack from the bridge to the central Piazza Duomo) is largely of the 16th and 17th centuries, though its bare interior does house a fantastic silver altarpiece set with gold-backed enameled scenes from the 12th century. A small series of rooms opens on the right aisle, with detached frescoes and several gorgeously carved stone relief panels, including a cobbled-together 8th-century baptistery, an 11th-century throne for the patriarch, and the **altar of the Duke of Ratchis ★★** (A.D. 744–49), duke of the Friuli and king of Italy, featuring gibbon-armed angels surrounding a beardless Christ, with side panels of the *Visitation* and *Adoration of the Magi.* The cathedral is open daily 9am to noon and 3 to 7pm (Nov–Mar to 6pm, closed on Sun mornings).

Around the corner on Piazza Duomo sits the **Palazzo dei Provveditori Veneti,** designed by Andrea Palladio (but construction began only after his death, in 1581; the building was finished in 1596). It now houses the **Museo Archeologico Nazionale ★** (© 0432-700-700), whose treasures include ancient bronzes (look for the fragment of a toga-wearing man from the early 1st c. A.D.), a Roman mosaic of Oceanus, and numerous early medieval pieces. Among the latter, standouts include the 6th-century Treasure of Duke Gisulfo (gold accouterments and a gem-studded cross, all found in his sarcophagus), and the Pace of Duke Ursus, an A.D. 800 ivory crucifixion scene surrounded by a silver frame. Admission is 2€, free for children 18 and under and seniors 65 and over. It's open Tuesday to Sunday 8:30am to 7:30pm, Monday 9am to 1:30pm.

Medieval streets behind the Palazzo dei Provveditori Veneti lead under the Romanesque Porta Patriarchale to Piazzetta San Biagio and the entrance to Cividale's top sight, the **Tempietto Longobardo ★★★** (© 0432-700-867). The Lombards carved this cliff-side church directly into the limestone in the 8th century, decorating it with saintly high-relief statues and stuccoes. The stalls date to the 14th century. Admission is 4€ for adults, 3€ for seniors 65 and over and 1.50€ for students. It's open daily 9:30am to 12:30pm and 3 to 6:30pm (Oct–Mar until 5pm).

For kicks, ask the guy at **Bar all'Ippogeo,** on Corso Paolino d'Aquileia at the corner with Via Monastero (on Mon, when the bar is closed, ask at the tourist office), for the *chiave all'Ippogeo Celtico* ("key to the Celtic Tomb"), an artificial grotto of uncertain date with a few highly worn carvings at Via Monastero 6 (© 0432-701-211). It's free, but an espresso or Campari at the bar when you return the key never hurts!

WHERE TO EAT

For a quick bite or a sampler platter of meats and cheese near the Tempietto Longobardo, pop into the **Osteria Bar Al Tempietto,** Via Michele della Torre 2 (© 0432-731-071; www.altempietto.it).

Osteria d'Italia/Enoteca de Feo ★★ MODERN ITALIAN This wood-paneled modern joint has old-fashioned values. There's a wine-tasting bar down below and just five tables in the lofted dining nook (three more are squirreled away in the basement). Because this place is *vino* driven, you can order a dozen red and white wines by the glass for 2€ to 6€ each. The music is jazz, the service professional, and the food impeccable. Start off with a "salad" of prosciutto from San Daniele, *caprino* (soft goat cheese), and figs before moving on to a primo such as a *zuppa di orzo* (pasta soup with potatoes, asparagus, and summer vegetables) or *cannoli di crespelle alla ricotta di bufala* (pasta crepes stuffed with buffalo-milk ricotta). Secondi are hearty and come with side dishes: steak alongside oven-roasted potatoes, or sea bass filets with steamed veggies.

Via Adelaide Ristori 29. © **0432-701-425.** Reservations recommended. Primi 8€–10€; secondi 9€–16€. AE, DC, MC, V. Tues–Sun 11am–3pm and 5pm–midnight.

8

MILAN & LOMBARDY

T here's a lot more to Italy's most prosperous region than the factories that fuel its economy. Many of the attractions here are urban—in addition to Milan, a string of Renaissance cities dots the Lombardy plains, from Pavia to Mantua. To the north the region bumps up against Switzerland, craggy mountains and romantic lakes (see chapter 9, "The Lakes"), and to the south Lombardy spreads out in fertile farmlands fed by the Po and other rivers.

The Lombards, originally one of the Germanic barbarian hordes who crossed the Alps during Rome's decline and ended up staying to settle down, have been ruled over the centuries by feudal dynasties, the Spanish, the Austrians, and the French. They tend to be more Continental than their neighbors to the south, faster talking, and more fast-paced as well.

MILAN (MILANO)

552km (342 miles) NW of Rome, 288km (179 miles) NW of Florence, 257km (159 miles) W of Venice, 140km (87 miles) NE of Turin, 142km (88 miles) N of Genoa

While it's unlikely to knock you over with its beauty, Milan is wonderful place to visit for both its big-ticket items—Leonardo's *The Last Supper,* Michelangelo's final sculpture, the Duomo—and its hidden treasures. That aloofness you feel when you enter Milan for the first time is a facade, and once you break through you'll realize a trip to Northern Italy without a stop in Milan is like *Risotto alla Milanese* without the saffron.

Things to Do The vastness of the Duomo and its *piazza* create a stunning contrast to the little, sinuous Medieval streets that make navigating the center of Milan a constant challenge. A spin through town should include a stop at *The Last Supper,* the essence of Milan, but just a smidgen of an art scene that is continually renewing itself, most recently with the opening of the Museo dell'Novecento dedicated to the 20th century.

Shopping A city that gave us Prada, Armani, and Versace could only be a shopper's paradise. But Milan is not only about the famous fashion brands that populate Via Montenapoleone and the surrounding streets; this is also a haven for fashionistas on a budget. And while you will find most Italian brands cost less in Milan than back home, you are also likely to notice subtle differences in styles and colors in what is on the shelves.

Restaurants & Dining One of Milan's many contradictions is that it sets one of the finest (and most expensive) tables in Italy and yet you can also dine like a local for under 10€ during *aperitivo* hour. Pasta is everywhere here, just as it is in the rest of Italy, but your meal is just as likely to include polenta or risotto, both of which are served in variations that can sometimes stand in for an entire meal.

PREVIOUS PAGE: **The intricate spires of Milan's Duomo.**

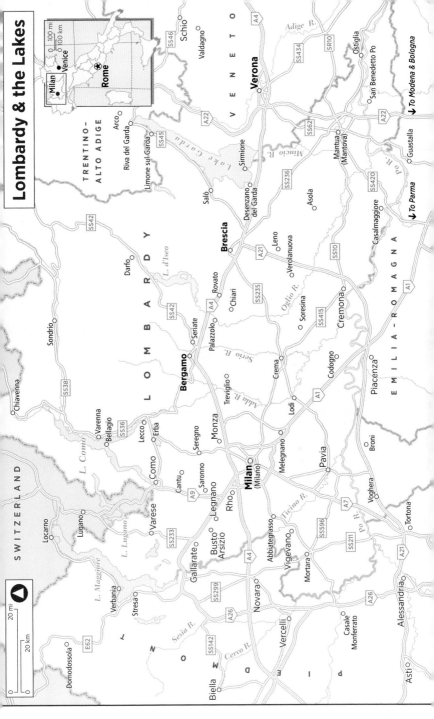

Lombardy & the Lakes

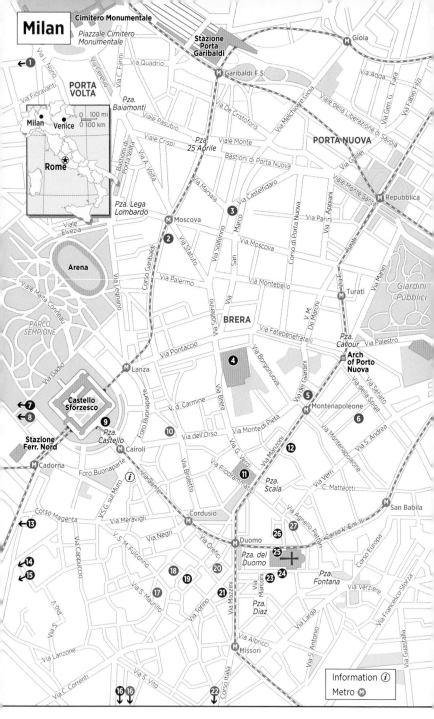

Milan

Cimitero Monumentale

Piazzale Cimitero Monumentale

PORTA VOLTA

Milan · Venice
Rome
0 100 mi
0 100 km

Stazione Porta Garibaldi

Gioia

Garibaldi F.S.

Via Quadrio

Via C. Farini

Via Fioravanti

Via Nono

Via Cereso

Pza. Baiamonti

Viale Pasubio

Via De Cristoforis

Via Adda

Viale della Liberazione di Savoia

Via Gen. G. Fara

Via Fabio Filzi

PORTA NUOVA

Viale Crispi

Pza. 25 Aprile

Viale Monte

Bastioni di Porta Nuova

Via Galieri

Viale Monte Santo

Bastioni di Porta Volta

Via A. Volta

Via Marsala

Via Castelfidaro

Via Parini

Via Appiani

Repubblica

Pza. Lega Lombardo

❸

Moscova

Via Solferino

Via San Marco

Via Moscova

Corso di Porta Nuova

Viale Elvezia

❷

Via Statuto

Via San

Via Montebello

Arena

Corso Garibaldi

Via Palermo

Via Legnano

Giardini Pubblici

PARCO SEMPIONE

Via Solferino

BRERA

Via Fatebenefratelli

Turati

Viale Malta Conneda

Via Pontaccio

Via Borgonuova

V. M. De Marchi

Via Gadio

❹

Pza. Cavour

Via Palestro

Lanza

Via Brera

Via dei Giardini

Arch of Porto Nuova

Via Senato

Via della Spiga

❼
❽

Castello Sforzesco

Foro Buonaparte

V. d. Carmine

❺

Montenapoleone

❻

Stazione Ferr. Nord

❾

Pza. Castello

❿

Via dell'Orso

Via Monte di Pietà

Via S. Andrea

Cadorna

Cairoli

Via G. Verdi

Via Fiodrammatici

Via Manzoni

⓬

Via Montenapoleone

Via Verri

Foro Buonaparte

ⓘ

Via Dante

⓫

Pza. Scala

C. Matteotti

Corso Magenta

V.S.G. sul Muro

Cordusio

San Babila

❶❸

Via Meravigli

Via Negri

Via Orefici

⓱

Corso V. Em. II

Via Capuccio

V. S. M. Fulcorino

Duomo

⓴❷

❷❼

❷❻

Corso Europa

❶❹
❶❺

⓲

⓳

Pza. del Duomo

❷❺

❷❹

Pza. Fontana

Via S. Maurilio

⓱

Via Torino

❷❶

❷❸

Via Marconi

Pza. Diaz

Via Verziere

Via A. Old

Via S.

Via Mazzini

Via Larga

Via S. Antonio

Via Lanzone

Missori

Via Albrici

Via Francesco Sforza

Via C. Correnti

Via S. Vito

❶❻ ❶❻

❷❷

Corso Italia

Via Guastalla

Information ⓘ
Metro Ⓜ

286

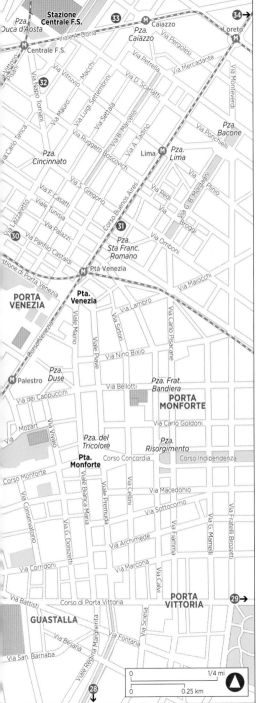

ATTRACTIONS

Basilica di San Lorenzo Maggiore **16**
Basilica di Sant'Ambrogio **14**
Castello Sforzesco **9**
Chiesa Santa Maria Presso San Satiro **21**
Duomo & Baptistery **25**
Duomo Museum **24**
Galleria Vittorio Emanuele II **26**
Leonardo da Vinci National Museum
 of Science and Technology **15**
Museo del Novecento **23**
Museo Poldi-Pezzoli **12**
Museo Teatrale alla Scala **11**
Pinacoteca Ambrosiana **19**
Pinacoteca di Brera **4**
Santa Maria delle Grazie/
 The Last Supper **13**
Teatro alla Scala **11**
Triennale Design Museum **7**

HOTELS

Antica Locanda Solferino **3**
Ariosto Hotel **8**
Art Hotel Navigli **22**
Carlyle Brera Hotel **2**
Doria Grand Hotel **33**
Four Seasons Hotel Milano **6**
Grand Hotel et de Milan **5**
Hotel Aliseo **22**
Hotel Aurora **31**
Hotel Berna **32**
Hotel Gran Duca di York **18**
Hotel XXII Marzo **29**
Ripa del Naviglio **22**

RESTAURANTS

Acquasala **16**
Al Pont de Ferr **16**
Da Abele **34**
Da Claudio **10**
Dongiò **28**
Joia **30**
Kiosk **16**
La Crêperie **16**
La Rosa dei Venti **1**
Luini Panzerotti **27**
Peck **20**
Piadineria Carletto **16**
Pizzeria Naturale **16**
Trattoria Milanese **17**

Nightlife & Entertainment Whether it's a beer and a stroll along the canals in the Navigli neighborhood or the pumping music of a dance club behind a nondescript door somewhere around town, Milan has it in spades. This is also home to La Scala, one of the world's premier opera houses.

Festivals & Markets Though it's overshadowed by the goings-on in Venice, Milan's pre-Lenten **Carnevale** is a reasonably big deal in the city, with costumed parades and an easygoing good time, much of it focusing around Piazza del Duomo beginning a week or so before Ash Wednesday. Milan's biggest holiday, however, is December 7, the **feast of its patron saint,** Sant'Ambrogio (St. Ambrose). Those who don't leave the city for their sacrosanct day off can most likely be found milling about the *o bei o bei* **outdoor fair** (usually held in Piazza Castello or Piazza Sant'Ambrogio) that runs for several days around December 7.

Just before the city shuts down in August, the city council stages a series of June and July **dance, theater, and music events** in theaters and open-air venues around the city; call © **02-7740-4343** for more information.

In a city as well dressed as Milan, it only stands to reason that some great-looking cast-offs are bound to turn up at **street markets.** Milan's largest street market is the one held on Viale Papiniano in the Ticinese/Navigli district (Metro: Sant'Agostino) on Tuesday mornings from 8am to 2pm and on Saturday from 9am to 7:30pm; some stalls sell designer seconds as well as barely used high-fashion ware, though most offer basic staples like underwear and belts, usually cheaper than in department stores.

There's an **antiques market** on Via Fiori Chiari in the Brera district (Metro: Moscova) the third Saturday of each month, from 9am to about 7:30pm, but not in August, and another the last Sunday of each month on the quays along the Naviglio Grande in the Navigli district, from 9am to about 7:30pm (Metro: Porta Genova).

Each Saturday morning there's a large **flea market,** with everything from books to clothing to appliances, where Via Valenza meets Alzaia Naviglio Grande (when coming down Via Valenza, just before the bridge go down the driveway on the right and into the parking lot; Metro: Porta Genova). An even bigger flea market is held on Sundays at the San Donato Metro stop.

The city's largest **food market** is at Piazza Wagner, just outside the city center due west of the church of Santa Maria delle Grazie (follow Corso Magenta and its extension, Corso Vercelli, to Piazza Piemonte; the market is 1 block north; Metro: Piazza Wagner). It's held Monday through Saturday from 8am to 1pm and Tuesday through Saturday from 4 to 7:30pm; the displays of mouthwatering foodstuffs fill an indoor market space and stalls that surround it.

Stopping by **Eataly** (p. 306) in the Coin department store that dominates Piazza Cinque Giornate, a 15-minute walk east of the Duomo, is something of an obligation for all foodies. The **top floor of the Rinascente department store** in Piazza Duomo, with its mozzarella bar and fine selection of packaged Italian goodies, is another haven for food connoisseurs (as an added bonus, you get a close-up view of the Duomo).

Essentials

GETTING THERE By Plane Both of Milan's major airports are operated by **SEA** (© **02-232-323;** www.seamilano.eu).

Milan Malpensa, 45km (28 miles) northwest of the center, is Milan's major international airport and an important hub for southern Europe.

Conveniently, a 40-minute express train heads half-hourly to Cadorna train station, which is just as central as Stazione Centrale. There are also buses that will take you to Centrale in 50 minutes without traffic. The train, known as **Malpensa Express** (☏ 800-500-005), costs 11€, while two bus companies run a combined five times per hour (**Malpensa Shuttle** at ☏ 02-6749-3083, or **Autostradale** at ☏ 02-7200-1304), and cost 7.50€ (see "Getting There," in the "Planning Your Trip" chapter, p. 458, for more information on the bus service). By taxi, the trip into town costs a wallet-stripping 85€, but it's the best choice when you are running late and it's not rush hour, or else after midnight, when it is indeed the only choice.

Milan Linate, only 8km (5 miles) east of the center, handles some European flights and many domestic flights. **Starfly** (☏ 02-5858-7237) makes the 30-minute trip from 6am to midnight from Linate to Milan's Stazione Centrale for 4€. City bus no. 73 leaves every 10 minutes for the San Babila Metro stop downtown (1€ for a regular bus ticket bought from any newsagent inside the airport, 1.50€ onboard and you must have exact change) and takes about 25 minutes. The express no. 73X is faster though there is only one an hour. The trip into town by taxi costs about 15€.

Malpensa Shuttle buses also connect Malpensa and Linate about every 2 hours from 9:30am to 4:30pm daily. The trip takes 1 hour and costs 13€.

Budget-minded flyers should consider a third option, **Orio Al Serio** (www.sacbo.it) airport. Located just outside Bergamo and about an hour from Milan, Orio al Serio is a hub for discount airline Ryanair and a number of other budget airlines. Direct buses run to and from Stazione Centrale several times an hour.

By Train Milan is one of Europe's busiest rail hubs. Trains arrive and depart about every half-hour to and from Venice (2½ hr.), Florence (1¾ hr.), and Rome (3 hr.). **Stazione Centrale,** a vast structure of Fascist-era design, is about a half-hour walk northeast of the center, with easy connections to Piazza del Duomo by Metro, tram, and bus. The station stop on the Metro is Centrale F.S.; it is only 10 minutes (and 1€) away from the Duomo stop, in the heart of the city. If you want to see something of the city en route, take the no. 1 tram from the station to Piazza del Duomo. If you walk, follow Via Pisani through the district of high-rise office buildings to the equally cheerless Piazza della Repubblica, and from there continue south on the much more interesting Via Turati and Via Manzoni to Piazza del Duomo.

Chances are, you will arrive at Stazione Centrale, but some trains serve Milan's other train stations: **Cadorna** (with service to and from Como and Malpensa airport, for example), **Stazione Lambrate** (with service to and from Bergamo and other points east), and **Porta Garibaldi** (with service to and from Lecco and other points north). Conveniently, all three of these stations, along with Stazione Centrale, are on the same subway line: Linea 2, the green one.

A tip: Lines at Centrale's ticket windows can be epic, so save time and stress by using one of the many automatic ticket machines (p. 464) that take both cash and credit cards.

By Bus Given Milan's excellent rail links with other cities in Lombardy and throughout Italy, it's usually unnecessary to travel by long-distance buses, which tend to take longer, unless you are going to certain destinations such as the ski resorts in Valle d'Aosta. If you choose to travel by intercity bus, you'll likely arrive at and depart from the Lampugnano bus terminal (Metro: Lampugnano) though a few lines originate in Piazza Castello (Metro: Cairoli). Autostradale (✆ 02-7200-1304; www.autostradale.it), which operates many of the most popular bus lines, has ticket offices in front of the Castello Sforzesco on Piazza Castello, open daily 8:30am to 6pm, and on Via Paleocapa

Bus Tours

CitySightseeing Milano (✆ 02-867-131; www.milano.city-sightseeing.it) has two 90-minute bus tours of Milan's major sights. The double decker, open-top buses leave every 45 minutes from in front of the Castello, daily 9:30am to 5:30pm, though you can start your tour at any of the 15 stops around town. For 20€ you have 2 days in which you can take both tours, getting on and off as often as you like. Commentary is available in eight languages including English.

1 flanking the Cadorna train station, open daily 7am to 7pm, where you are much more likely not to have to wait. Savda (**0165-367-011;** www.savda.it) runs three daily buses (more in the winter) to and from the hard-to-reach-by-train Aosta (2½ hr.).

By Car Milan is well served by Italy's superhighway (autostrada) system. The A1 links Milan with Florence and Rome (Florence is a little over 3 hr. away by car, Rome is a little under 6 hr.), and the A4 connects Milan with Verona and Venice to the east and Turin to the west (Venice is about 2½ hr. from Milan by car; Turin is a little over 1 hr.). Driving and parking in Milan are not experiences to be relished, and a fee must be paid to enter the central part of the city where you will find many one-way streets and others closed to all traffic except trams, buses, and taxis. Many hotels make parking arrangements for guests; ask when you reserve a room.

VISITOR INFORMATION The main **Azienda di Promozione Turistica (APT) tourist office** is at Piazza Castello 1, on the south side of the square where it meets via Beltrami (✆ 02-7740-4343; www.visitamilano.it). Hours are Monday to Friday from 9am to 6pm, Saturday 9am to 1:30pm and 2 to 6pm, Sunday from 9am to 1:30pm and 2 to 5pm. There is also an office in **Stazione Centrale** (✆ 02-7740-4318), in front of tracks 13 and 14 with the same hours.

These offices issue free maps, museum guides, hotel and restaurant listings, and a wealth of other useful information, including the free and excellent **Milano Mese,** which lists everything that is going on about town. The free monthly events brochure *Hello Milano* (www.hellomilano.it) and expatriate monthly *EasyMilano* (www.easymilano.it) each have listings of museum exhibitions, performances, and other events.

CITY LAYOUT Milan is best imagined as a series of concentric circles radiating from the Piazza del Duomo at the center. Within the inner circle, once enclosed by the medieval city walls, are most of the churches, museums, and shops that will consume your visiting hours. Within the next circle, once enclosed by the so-called Spanish walls built in the 15th century, you will find some of the more outlying sites such as Parco Sempione and the church housing *The Last Supper.*

Strolling through Brera.

The city's major neighborhoods encircle the hub of all the circles, **Piazza del Duomo.** Looking west from the Duomo, you can see the imposing **Castello Sforzesco** at one end of the well-heeled Magenta neighborhood. You can walk to the Castello in about 15 minutes by following first Piazza dei Mercanti or Via Orefici to Piazza Cordusio and, from there, Via Dante. The other major tourist draw in Magenta is the church of **Santa Maria delle Grazie;** to reach it, you'll leave Via Dante at Via Meravigli, which becomes Corso Magenta and leads to the church (total walking time from Piazza del Duomo to the church is about 25 min.).

Heading north from the Piazza del Duomo, walk through the glass-enclosed shopping center (the world's first), the **Galleria Vittorio Emanuele II.** As you emerge from the northern end of the Galleria, you'll find yourself in **Piazza della Scala** and in front of Milan's famous **opera house.** A 5-minute walk northeast along Via Manzoni takes you to Via Montenapoleone and the city's **high-fashion shopping district,** the epicenter of Italian design. A walk of about 10 minutes north of Piazza della Scala along Via Verdi, which then becomes Via Brera, brings you into the atmospheric **Brera neighborhood**—once home to the city's brothels, though it has gentrified

Cruising the Canals

Milan's *navigli,* or canals, are a focal point of the preparation for **Expo 2015,** but you can already start exploring these canals. **Navigli Lombardi** (℅ **02-9227-3118;** www.naviglilombardi. it) offers **canal tours** that bring visitors around Milan's historic canals and offer a new perspective on the historic Navigli neighborhood. Tour boats leave seven times a day from the top of the

Naviglio Grande where it meets the Darsena, Milan's old port that connects the Naviglio Grande with the Naviglio Pavese. Cruises are 55 minutes long and cost 12€ for adults, 10€ for seniors 65 and over and children 12 and under; children 5 and under ride free. There are four departures Friday through Sunday between 3 and 6:10pm, and three morning departures Saturday and Sunday.

over the last 3 or 4 decades—where cobblestone streets and old *palazzi* surround the city's major art collection, the **Pinacoteca di Brera.**

Another neighborhood to set your sights on is **Ticinese/Navigli,** usually referred to by the last word in that combination, which translates as "canals." Beyond the central city and due south of Piazza del Duomo, the Navigli's old quays follow what remains of an elaborate canal system, designed in part by Leonardo da Vinci, that once laced through the city. The charm of these waterways has not been lost on well-heeled young Milanese who have moved en masse into refurbished buildings that were once the haunts of the working classes. Bars, restaurants, shops, and galleries have populated the ground floors, making this a great neighborhood to head for at any time of day. Come to the Navigli for a stroll and a boat ride (see "Cruising the Canals" box) during the day, come back for an *aperitivo* and then stay for dinner and the nightlife (it's also the only bit of town that remains lively through Aug). You can walk to the Navigli in about 30 minutes from Piazza del Duomo by following Via Torino southwest to Corso di Porta Ticinese, alternatively you can take any number of trams or hop on the Metro to Porta Genova.

GETTING AROUND An extensive mix of **metros, trams,** and **buses** makes it very easy to move around Milan on public transportation. The Metro closes at midnight (Sat at 1am); buses and trams run all night. Tickets good for a combination of Metro-trams-buses for 1¼ hr. cost 1€. You can also purchase a carnet of 10 tickets for 9.20€ as well as a ticket good for unlimited travel for 1 day (3€) or 2 days (5.50€). Tickets are available at Metro stations and at newsstands. Stamp your ticket when you board a bus or tram—you can be slapped with a hefty fine if you don't. For information about Milan public transportation, visit the ATM information office in the Duomo Metro stop, open Monday through Saturday 7:45am to 7:15pm (✆ **800-808-181;** www.atm.it).

[Fast**FACTS**] MILAN

American Express The office is a few blocks from the Duomo, at Via Larga 4, on the corner with Via dell'Orso (✆ **02-721-041**), and is open Monday to Friday from 9am to 5:30pm (Metro: Duomo). Card members can arrange cash advances, receive mail (the postal code is 20121), and wire money.

Bookstores Milan has two English-language bookshops. The **American**

Bookstore, between the Duomo and Castello Sforzesco at Via Camperio 16, at the corner with Via Dante (✆ **02-878-920**), is open Monday 1 to 7pm, Tuesday to Saturday 10am to 7pm (Metro: Cordusio). The **English Bookshop,** Via Ariosto at Via Mascheroni 12 (✆ **02-469-4468**), is open Monday to Saturday 9am to 8pm. **Rizzoli,** the glamorous outlet of one of Italy's leading publishers,

in the Galleria Vittorio Emanuele (✆ **02-8646-1071**), also has some English-language titles, as well as a sumptuous collection of art and photo books; it's open daily 9am to 9pm (opens Sun at 10am, closes Sun–Mon at 8pm). There are several other big bookstores in and around Piazza del Duomo that also have a few English-language titles. English-language newspapers and magazines can be found at newsstands in Stazione Centrale and around Piazza del Duomo as well as at many other newsstands near tourist spots.

Consulates The **U.S. Consulate** is at Via Principe Amedeo 2/10 (℃ **02-2903-5333**); it's open Monday through Friday from 8:30am to noon for emergencies, otherwise only by appointment (Metro: Turati). The **Canadian Consulate** is at Via Vittor Pisani 19 (℃ **02-67-581**), open Monday through Friday from 8:30am to 12:30pm and 1:30 to 4pm. The **British Consulate,** Via San Paolo 7 (℃ **02-723-001**), is open Monday to Friday from 9:30am to 12:30pm and 2:30 to 4:30pm (Metro: Duomo). The **Australian Consulate,** at Via Borgogna 2 (℃ **02-777-041**), is open Monday to Thursday 9am to noon and 2 to 4pm (Metro: San Babila). And the **New Zealand Consulate,** at Via Terraggio 17 (℃ **02-7217-0001**), is open Monday to Friday from 8:30am to 12:30pm (Metro: Cadorna or Sant'Ambrogio).

Crime For police emergencies, dial ℃ **113** (a free call); you can reach the English-speaking staff of the tourist police at ℃ **02-863-701.** There is a police station in Stazione Centrale; and the main station, the **Questura,** is just west of the Giardini Pubblici, at Via Fatebenefratelli 11

(℃ **02-62-261;** Metro: Turati). Milan is generally safe, though public parks and the area in front of and to the west of Stazione Centrale are better avoided at night.

Drugstores Pharmacies rotate 24-hour shifts; dial ℃ **192** to find pharmacies that are open around the clock on a given day, or look for signs posted in most pharmacies announcing which shop is keeping a 24-hour schedule. The **Farmacia Stazione Centrale** (℃ **02-669-0735**), in the train station, is open 24 hours daily and some of the staff speak English.

Emergencies The best number to call in Italy with a **general emergency** is ℃ **112,** which connects you to the military-trained **Carabinieri** who will transfer your call as needed; for the **police,** dial ℃ **113;** for a **medical emergency** and to call an ambulance, the number is ℃ **118;** for the **fire department,** call ℃ **115.** All are free calls.

Holidays Milan's patron saint, Sant'Ambrogio (St. Ambrose), is honored on December 7. For a list of official state holidays, see the "Holidays" section on p. 70.

Hospitals The **Ospedale Maggiore Policlinico** (℃ **02-55-031**) is centrally located a 5-minute walk southeast of the Duomo at Via Francesco Sforza 35 (Metro: Duomo or Missori).

Some of the medical personnel speak English.

Internet As you exit the front of the Centrale train station, on your left is **Grazia Internet Café** (Piazza Duca D'Aosta 14; ℃ **02-670-0543**), with some 50 PCs and the possibility to pay for Wi-Fi access, open Monday to Friday 8am to midnight and Saturday and Sunday 9am to midnight. **Fnac** (℃ **02-869-541**), on Via Torino about a 10-minute walk south of the Duomo, is open Monday to Saturday 9:30am to 8pm and Sunday 11am to 8pm. **Secure Money Transfer** in the Duomo Metro station (℃ **02-3652-1721**) sells Internet access Monday to Friday 8am to 8pm, Saturday 9am to 7pm, and Sunday 9am to 5pm.

Laundry Self-service laundromats are sprinkled all over the city; one chain is **Lav@sciuga** (www.lavasciuga.net), which has several locations in Milan.

Lost & Found The lost-baggage number for **Malpensa** and **Linate** airports is ℃ **02-7485-2200.** The English-speaking staff at these offices handles luggage that has gone astray on most airlines serving the airports, though a few airlines maintain their own lost-baggage services. The **lost and found at Stazione Centrale** is open daily from 8am to 4pm.

Luggage Storage The luggage storage office in Stazione Centrale is on the ground floor near the ticket windows and is open daily from 6am to 11:50pm; the fee is 4€ per piece of baggage for the first 5 hours. It is an additional .60€ per hour for the next 7 hours and then an additional .20€ per hour after that.

Post Office The main post office, **Poste e Telecommunicazioni,** is just west of Piazza del Duomo at Via Cordusio 4 (☎ **02-7248-2126;** Metro: Cordusio). Windows are open Monday to Friday 8am to 7pm and Saturday 8:30am to 1:50pm. Most branch offices are open Monday to Saturday 8:30am to 1:30pm and some until 7pm. There is a post office in Stazione Centrale, open Monday through Friday 8am to 5:30pm and Saturday 8:15am to 3:30pm.

Taxis It is often difficult to flag down a taxi in Milan (though don't let that stop you from trying; if the light on the roof is on, it means the driver is free to pick up passengers), so your best bet is to go to the nearest taxi stand, usually located near major *piazze* and major Metro stops. There is a large taxi stand in Piazza del Duomo and another in Piazza della Scala. Or call a **radio taxi** at ☎ **02-4040,** 02-6767, 02-8585, 02-5353, or 02-8383 (the desk staff at many hotels will be happy to do this for you, even if you are not a guest). Cab meters start at 3.10€ and add a nighttime surcharge of 3.10€ and a Sunday surcharge of 1.55€. **Note:** When you call a taxi, the meter starts as soon as the car gets the call and begins towards your pick-up spot.

Telephones See "Fast Facts: Northern Italy," p. 468. The area code for Milan is ☎ **02.**

Travel Services For budget travel, including low-cost flights, contact **Zani Viaggi,** Foro Bonaparte 76 near the castle (☎ **02-867-131**), open Monday through Friday from 9am to 7pm (Sat unitl 5pm). Students and those 25 and under should try **CTS (Centro Turistico Studentesco),** Corso di Porta Nuova 46 (☎ **02-2901-4553**), open Monday through Friday from 9am to 7pm and Saturday 10am to 1pm. This is the most centrally located CTS, but there are five others sprinkled around town including one on Corso di Porta Ticinese 100 near the Navigli.

What to See & Do
THE TOP SIGHTS
Castello Sforzesco ★★ Though it's been clumsily restored many times, most recently at the end of the 19th century, this fortresslike castle continues to evoke Milan's two most powerful medieval and Renaissance families, the Visconti and the Sforza. The Visconti built the castle in the 14th century, and the Sforza, who married into the Visconti clan and eclipsed them in power, reconstructed it in 1450. The most influential residents were Ludovico il Moro and Beatrice d'Este (he of the Sforza and she of the famous Este family of Ferrara). After ill-advisedly calling the French into Italy at the end of the 15th century, Ludovico died in the dungeons of a château in the Loire valley—but not before the couple made the Castello and Milan one of Italy's great centers of the Renaissance. It was they who commissioned the works by Bramante and Leonardo da Vinci, and these splendors can be viewed on a stroll through the miles of rooms that surround the Castello's enormous courtyards.

The rooms house a dozen city-administered museums known collectively as the Musei del Castello Sforzesco. They include a *pinacoteca* with works by Bellini, Correggio, and Magenta, and the extensive holdings of the Museo d'Arte

Bus trips organized by **Zani Viaggi** are tailored to all sorts of appetites, especially those that Milan cultivates so well, namely fashion and soccer. Excursions to the Serravalle outlet village (about 90 min. outside town); FoxTown (just across the border in Switzerland, about 1 hr. drive); and the Meazza stadium, also known as San Siro (home to Inter and AC Milan), leave from Foro Bonaparte 76, in front of the Castello.

The shopping trip to Serravalle departs daily at 10am and costs 20€ round-trip, with return buses leaving Serravalle at 5pm. There is a daily bus to FoxTown (20€) at 2pm, with a return at 7pm. The 3-hour trip to Meazza stadium (28€) leaves Thursday at 10:30am, though it is sometimes cancelled if there are not enough people signed up. For more info, call ☎ **02-867-131** or visit www. zaniviaggi.it.

Antica, filled with prehistoric finds from Lombardy, and the last work of 89-year-old Michelangelo, his unfinished *Pietà Rondanini* ★★. There is also a small Egyptian museum (with the title being used a bit liberally by the city as there is really just one room).

Piazza Castello. ☎ **02-8846-3700.** Free admission to the castle courtyards daily 7am–6pm (summer until 7pm). Musei del Castello Sforzesco Tues–Sun 9am–5:30pm. Admission 6€ (there is some talk of reducing the entrance fee and cancelling the fee altogether for the Pietà Rondanini). Metro: Cairoli, Cadorna, or Lanza.

Duomo ★★★ When Milanese think something is taking too long, they refer to it as *la fabbrica del duomo*—the making of the Duomo, a reference to the 6 centuries it took to complete the magnificent Gothic cathedral that rises from the center of the city (the last of the bronze doors was put up only in 1960). The last of Italy's great Gothic structures—begun by the ruling Visconti family in 1386—the Duomo is one the largest churches in the world (all agree that St.

Castello Sforzesco lies at the foot of Piazza Castello.

Ornate Gothic embellishments on the Duomo.

Peter's in Rome is the biggest, but after that there is some discussion, though it seems likely Milan's Duomo is in fourth place behind Seville's cathedral, and Brazil's Basilica of the National Shrine of Our Lady of Aparecida). There are numerous flying buttresses, 135 marble spires, a stunning triangular facade, and 2,000 statues adorning the massive but airy, almost fanciful exterior. Looking at the facade from directly in front of the Duomo can be overwhelming as you feel almost oppressed by the seemingly flat structure. To get a more telling perspective of both the facade and the entire church, view the Duomo from the far-end of the piazza where Via Mercanti starts. Another interesting perspective is from the courtyard in front of Palazzo Reale.

The cavernous **interior,** lit by brilliant stained-glass windows, seats 40,000 but is unusually Spartan and serene, divided into five aisles by a sea of 52 columns. The poet Shelley used to sit and read Dante here amid monuments that include a gruesomely graphic statue of **St. Bartholomew Flayed ★** and the tombs of Giacomo de Medici, two Visconti, and many cardinals and archbishops. Another British visitor, Alfred, Lord Tennyson, rhapsodized about the **view** of the Alps from the **roof ★★★** (elevators on the church's exterior northeast corner; stairs on the exterior north side), where you get to wander amid the Gothic pinnacles, saintly statues, and flying buttresses. You are joined high above Milan by the spire-top gold statue of the *Madonnina* (the little Madonna), the city's beloved protectress.

Back on terra firma, the **crypt** contains the remains of San Carlo Borromeo, one of the early cardinals of Milan. A far more interesting descent is the one down the staircase to the right of the main entrance to the **Battistero Paleocristiano,** the ruins of a 4th-century baptistery believed to be where Saint Ambrose baptized Saint Augustine.

The Duomo houses many of its treasures across the piazza from the right transept in the *Museo del Duomo*—closed for restoration in 2009 without a definite reopening date. Among the legions of statuary saints is a gem of a painting by Jacopo Tintoretto, *Christ at the Temple,* and some riveting displays chronicling the construction of the cathedral.

Though the scaffolding from its most recent restoration is down, visitors may still encounter some restoration work as the Duomo is always being touched up. The most recent restoration, completed in 2009, brought luster back to the

---

Temporary but Great

Milan gets many first-rate temporary exhibits on everything from contemporary Chinese art to retrospectives on Edward Hopper, the Impressionists, Caravaggio, and Canaletto. Most of these are held at the Palazzo Reale on the south side of Piazza Duomo. While hanging out in the piazza, mosey over to see if any of the exhibits suit your fancy, and if nothing else take a walk through the beautiful courtyard. Palazzo Reale, which dates back almost 1,000 years and housed first the city government in the Middle Ages and then various royals in the centuries that followed, suffered serious damage in an Allied bombardment in 1943 that partially destroyed the complex. Prices for the exhibits vary as do the opening hours, which are usually Monday 2:30 to 7:30pm and Tuesday through Sunday 9:30am to 7:30pm (Thurs and Sat until 10:30pm).

church's white marble. Other restoration projects will continue on the sides and interior of the Duomo in a never-ending bid to keep the building looking its best.

Piazza del Duomo. ✆ **02-7202-2656.** Duomo: free admission; roof: 6€ by stairs, 10€ with elevator; crypt: 2€; baptistery: 4€; museum: before its closing, admission was 6€ adults, 3€ children 17 and under and seniors 65 and over. Duomo: daily 8:30am–6:45pm; roof: daily 9am–5:45pm (Apr–Sept until 10pm); crypt: daily 9am–noon and 2:30–6pm; baptistery: Tues–Sun 10am–noon and 3–5pm; museum: before its closing, Tues–Sun 9:30am–12:30pm and 3–6pm. Metro: Duomo.

Galleria Vittorio Emanuele II ★★★ Milan's late-19th-century version of a mall is this wonderful steel-and-glass-covered, cross-shaped arcade. The elegant Galleria is the prototype of the enclosed shopping malls that were to become the hallmark of 20th-century consumerism. It's safe to say that none of the imitators have come close to matching the Galleria for style and flair. The designer of this urban marvel, Giuseppe Mengoni, didn't live to see the Milanese embrace his creation: He tripped and fell from a girder a few days before the Galleria opened in 1878. His shopping mall par excellence provides a lovely route between the Duomo and La Scala and is a fine locale for watching the flocks of well-dressed Milanese—you'll understand why the Galleria is called *Il Salotto di Milano* (Milan's drawing room).

Just off Piazza del Duomo and Piazza della Scala. Metro: Duomo.

Pinacoteca di Brera ★★★ This 17th-century *palazzo* houses one of Italy's best collections of medieval and Renaissance art; and with its works spanning 6 centuries it's inarguably the world's finest assembly of northern Italian painting. The concentration of so many masterpieces here is the work of Napoleon, who used the *palazzo* as the repository for the art he confiscated from public and private holdings throughout northern Italy; fittingly, a bronze likeness of the emperor greets you upon entering the courtyard. Upon entering the museum, be sure to look through the large glass door to the left that affords a wide open view of a room in the incredible Biblioteca Nazionale Braidense, one of Italy's largest public libraries. If you want to see more of this library that looks like it belongs in a Medieval monastery, before heading up the stairs to the museum, keep walking straight down a corridor until you see a staircase on the left that goes to the library (the librarians will usually let you have a look around even if you are not there to check out a book).

Three of Italy's greatest masterpieces hang in the Pinacoteca di Brera: Andrea Mantegna's amazingly foreshortened **Dead Christ ★★★**, Raphael's **Betrothal of the Virgin ★★★**, and Piero della Francesca's **Madonna with Saints ★★** (the *Montefeltro Altarpiece*). It is an indication of this museum's ability to overwhelm visitors that the last two absolute masterpieces hang near each other in a room dedicated to works by Tuscan and Umbrian painters. Other pieces not to miss include Jacopo Tintoretto's **Finding of the Body of St. Mark ★**, in which the dead saint eerily confronts appropriately startled grave robbers who come upon his corpse; Caravaggio's **Supper at Emmaus ★★**; and Francesco Hayez's **The Kiss ★★★**, probably Italy's most famous 19th-century painting, which, surprisingly enough, depicts a young couple kissing, though it actually represents the alliance between France (the woman dressed in blue) and Italy (the man in the red, white, and green of the Italian flag) that defeated the Austrians who at the time occupied a large swath of northern Italy. The final rooms include a few works by Canaletto including his *View of the Grand Canal* and several late 19th century paintings by Giovanni Segantini. Before exiting into the gift shop you are met by the enormous *Fiumana,* Giuseppe Pellizza da Volpedo's preparatory work for his masterpiece *The Fourth Estate,* which hangs in the Museo dell'Novecento (p. 301). Via Brera 28. ✆ **02-7226-3264.** www.brera. beniculturali.it. Admission 9€; 6.50€ EU citizens 18–25; free for EU citizens 17 and under and 65 and over; free after 7pm on the last Tues of every month when the museum closes at 11pm (this praxis has been renewed the last few years, but it is not a given it will continue). Tues–Sun 8:30am–7:15pm. Metro: Lanza or Montenapoleone. Tram: 1, 4, 8, 12, 14, or 27.

Santa Maria delle Grazie/The Last Supper ★★★ The *Cenacolo Vinciano,* Leonardo da Vinci's *The Last Supper,* is perhaps Milan's biggest draws and one of the most famous pieces of

Santa Maria delle Grazie in spring.

art in the world. From 1495 to 1497, Leonardo painted this poignant portrayal of confusion and betrayal for the far wall of the refectory when this was a Dominican convent. Aldous Huxley called this fresco the "saddest work of art in the world," a comment in part on the deterioration that set in even before the paint had dried on the moisture-ridden walls. (It probably didn't help that the monks cooked their meals here.) The fresco got a lot of well-intentioned but poorly executed "touching up" in the 18th and 19th centuries, though a lengthy restoration completed in 1999 has done away with these centuries of overpainting, as well as tried to undo the damage wrought by the clumsy patching and damage inflicted when Napoleon's troops used the wall for target practice, and from when Allied bombing during World War II tore off the room's roof, leaving the fresco relatively untouched, but exposed to the elements for 3 years.

In short, *The Last Supper* is a mere shadow of the work the artist intended it to be, but the work, which captures the moment when Christ told his Apostles that one of them would betray him, remains amazingly powerful and evocative.

A Last-Minute Invitation to *The Last Supper*

The Last Supper is seemingly on every tourist's itinerary of Milan, as well it should be. And with only 25 people allowed in at a time, not surprisingly it can be difficult to get a ticket if you don't book well in advance. If you can't get a reservation, in a pinch you can take an Autostradale (✆ **02-3391-0794;** www.autostradale.it) guided 3-hour bus and walking tour of Milan's top attractions that guarantees admission to *The*

Last Supper as part of the package. The tours cost 55€ and leave at 9:30am every day except Monday (also Wed 1pm and Fri–Sat 2:15pm) from near the taxi stand in Piazza Duomo. **Zani Viaggi** (✆ **02-867-131;** www.zaniviaggi.it) has a similar tour with guaranteed admission to *The Last Supper* that costs 60€ and leaves from Foro Buonaparte in front of the castle Tuesday to Sunday at 9:30am and 2:30pm.

Only 25 people are allowed to view the fresco at one time, and they must pass through a series of devices that remove pollutants from clothing. Accordingly, lines are long and tickets usually sell out days, if not weeks (and sometimes months), in advance so reserve early either online or over the phone (see below).

Often overlooked are the other treasures of the late-15th-century church itself, foremost among them the fine dome and other architectural innovations by one of the great architects of the High Renaissance, Donato Bramante (one of the first architects of St. Peter's in Rome). To one side of the apse, decorated in marble and terra cotta, is a lovely cloister.

Piazza Santa Maria delle Grazie. *The Last Supper:* ✆ **02-9280-0360.** www.cenacolovinciano. org. Admission 6.50€ plus a booking fee of 1.50€; 3.25€ plus 1.50€ booking fee for EU citizens 18 to 25; EU citizens 17 and under and 65 and over pay only the booking fee. Tues–Sun 8:15am–6:30pm. Church: ✆ **02-467-6111.** Free admission. Mon–Sat 7:30am–noon and 3–7pm; Sun 7:20am–12:15pm and 3:30–9pm (may close earlier in winter). Metro: Cadorna or Conciliazione.

MORE SIGHTS

Basilica di San Lorenzo Maggiore ★ The oldest church in Milan attests to the days when the city was the capital of the Western Roman Empire. This 4th-century, early-Christian structure has been rebuilt and altered many times over the centuries (its dome, the highest in Milan, is a 16th-c. embellishment and the facade is from the 19th c.), but it still retains the flavor of its roots in its octagonal floor plan and a few surviving remnants. These include 5th-century mosaics in the Cappella di Sant'Aquilino, which you enter from the atrium. A sarcophagus in the chapel is said to enshrine the remains of Galla Placidia, sister of Honorius, last emperor of Rome and wife of Ataulf, king of the Visigoths. Ironically, her mausoleum is one of the mosaic masterworks of Ravenna, and she is most likely buried in Rome, where she died. You'll be rewarded with a glimpse at even earlier history if you follow the stairs from behind the altar to a cryptlike room that contains what remains of a Roman amphitheater.

Roman columns from the 4th century line the Basilica di San Lorenzo Maggiore.

In the piazza in front of the church stand the **Columns of San Lorenzo** ★★, 16 monumental Corinthian columns that were part of a Roman temple that probably stood in what is now Piazza Santa Maria Beltrade near the top of Via Torino and were set up here in the 4th century when the San Lorenzo Maggiore was being built.

Corso di Porta Ticinese 🕾 **02-8940-4129.** www.sanlorenzomaggiore.com. Church: Free admission. Cappella di Sant'Aquilino: 2€ adults, 1€ children. Daily 7:30am–12:30pm and 2:30–6:30pm. Bus: 94. Metro: Missori. Tram: 3.

Basilica di Sant'Ambrogio ★★ From the basilica that he constructed on this site in the 4th century A.D.—when he was bishop of Milan and the city, in turn, was briefly capital of the Western Roman Empire—Saint Ambrose had a profound effect on the development of the early church. Little remains of Ambrose's church, but the 11th-century structure built in its place, and renovated many times since, is remarkable. It has a striking atrium, lined with columned porticos and opening on the side to the brick facade, with two ranks of loggias and, on either side, a bell tower. This church set the standard for Lombard Romanesque architecture that you'll see imitated many times on your travels through Lombardy, and elsewhere as well; the imitation has continued through the centuries, including with the University of California Los Angeles' Royce Hall built in the 1920s.

On your wanderings through the three-aisle nave you'll come upon a gold altar from Charlemagne's days in Milan, and, in the right aisle, the all-too-scant remains of a Tiepolo fresco cycle, most of it blown into oblivion by World War II bombs. The little that remains of the original church is the Sacello di San Vittore in Ciel d'Oro, a little chapel in which the cupola glows with 5th-century mosaics of saints (enter from the right aisle). The skeletal remains of Ambrose himself are on view in the crypt. As you leave the main church from the left aisle, you'll see another work of the great architect Bramante—his late-15th century Portico della Canonica, lined with elegant columns, some of which are sculpted to resemble tree trunks.

Piazza Sant'Ambrogio 15. 🕾 **02-8645-0895.** www.basilicasantambrogio.it. Church: Free admission. Sacello di San Vittore: 2€. Mon–Sat 10am–noon and 2:30–6pm; Sun 3–5pm. Bus: 50, 58, or 94. Metro: Sant'Ambrogio.

Chiesa Santa Maria Presso San Satiro ★ Part of what makes this charming little structure, just south of Piazza del Duomo, so exquisite is what it doesn't have—space. Stymied by not being able to expand the T-shaped apse to classical Renaissance, cross-shaped proportions, the architect Bramante created a marvelous relief behind the high altar. The effect of the *trompe l'oeil* columns and arches is not entirely convincing, but it is nonetheless magical. Another gem lies to the rear of the left transept: the Cappella della Pietà, so called for

---

📎 Milan on Two Wheels

The city began a bike-sharing program at the end of 2008 that, though directed at locals and commuters, is also a fun way for tourists to see more of the city. For 2.50€ a day and 6€ a week, you can buy a pass that gives you unlimited use of the bikes for 30-minute increments (then you pay .50€ for each half hour after that, up to a maximum of 2 hr.). You pick up a bike in one of the many racks around town and leave it at another. Buy your pass online or at the **ATM** offices at the Centrale, Cadorna, Garibaldi, Duomo, Loreto, or Romolo Metro stops from 7:45am to 7:15pm (🕾 **800-80-8181;** www.bikemi.com).

the 15th-century terra-cotta *Pietà* it now houses; the Cappella was built in the 9th century to honor Saint Satyrus (Satiro in Italian), Saint Ambrose's brother. While this little-visited complex is now eclipsed by other, more famous Milan churches, it was an important pilgrimage site in the 13th and 14th centuries, after news spread through Christendom that an image of the Madonna here shed blood when stabbed.

Via Torino (at Via Speronari). Free admission. Daily 9am–noon and 2:30–6pm. Metro: Duomo or Missori.

La Triennale di Milano Design Museum ★ Opened in 2007, this museum dedicated to design was long overdue for a city that has meant so much to the world of avant-garde chairs, couches, teapots, lamps, and every other imaginable household item. There is a permanent collection (in name only as it is changed every year or two) dedicated to Italian industrial design that will interest even those convinced that a fork is a fork no matter how and by whom it is designed. There are also always temporary exhibits, sometimes as many as six on at the same time, which are usually dedicated to photography or some particular aspect of design such as the contribution of a particular country or person. To fuel up before or after a visit, there is a very pleasant cafe with a view onto Parco Sempione and an ever-changing selection of chairs that have made an impact on the design world through the ages.

Viale Alemagna 6. © **02-724-341.** www.triennaledesignmuseum.it. Admission 8€ adults, 6.50€ students 25 and under and seniors 65 and over; temporary exhibits range from free to 8€. Tues–Sun 10:30am–8:30pm (Thurs–Fri until 11pm). Bus: 61. Metro: Cadorna.

Museo del Novecento (Museum of 20th-Century Art) ★★ Milan's newest museum, which opened in late 2010, is proof that Italy's contribution to art did not stop in the 17th century and is worth a visit even for those who find 20th century abstract paintings too much trouble to try to understand. You'll find a few pieces by some of the international greats, including Picasso and Kandinsky, but the focus here is on Italian artists and their effect on the artistic movements of the last century. Most interesting is Futurism and the work of Umberto Boccioni, who has his works presented in the first rooms. The futurists' manifesto said, "everything is in movement, everything runs, everything passes quickly" and nowhere is that philosophy more evident than in Boccioni's *Elasticity* and perhaps even more so in his sculpture *Unique Forms of Continuity in Space,* a preview of which you can get on the back of the Italian .20€ coin. There is a room farther along dedicated to De Chirico, but in general the museum peters out as you move up to the higher floors. From the top floor you get a commanding view of the Duomo and the piazza, and you can pull up a chair and enjoy a free hour of Wi-Fi if you have a smart phone or computer in tow. Watching the hundreds of people scurrying about in the piazza might be all you need to be sold on the Futurist manifesto.

Tip: The undisputed star of the museum's collection is Giuseppe Pellizza da Volpedo's *The Fourth Estate,* which you can see for free. If you don't want to visit the rest of the museum, at least come for this massive homage to striking workers. When you enter the main door of the museum, rather than buy a ticket at the desk on the right, head straight up the circular staircase on the left and after a few curves you get to Volpedo's masterpiece, which was not well-received when unveiled 1901, but later became a symbol of oppressed workers around the world.

FROM LEFT: Milan's statue of Leonardo's horse, re-created from the master's original sketches and models; listening to an audio tour of the Museo Poldi-Pezzoli.

Farther up the ramp is the entrance to the museum's collections.

Piazza Duomo 12 (palazzo dell'Argenario). © **02-7634-0809.** www.museodelnovecento. org. Admission 5€ adults, 3€ students and seniors 65 and over, free for everybody Fri after 3:30pm. Tues–Sun 9:30am–7:30pm (Thurs and Sat until 10:30pm), Mon 2:30–7:30pm. Metro: Duomo.

Museo Nazionale della Scienza e della Tecnologia Leonardo da Vinci (Leonardo da Vinci National Museum of Science and Technology) ★ ☺

The heart and soul of this engaging museum are the **working scale models ★★** of Leonardo's submarines, airplanes, and other engineering feats that, for the most part, the master only ever invented on paper (each exhibit includes a reproduction of his drawings and a model of his creations). This former Benedictine monastery and its beautiful cloisters are also filled with planes, trains, carriages, sewing machines, typewriters, optical devices, and other exhibits, including some enchanting re-creations of workshops, all of which makes up one of the world's leading mechanical and scientific collections.

Via San Vittore 21. © **02-485-551.** www.museoscienza.org. Admission 10€ adults, 7€ 25 and under and adults (up to 2 per group) accompanied by at least 2 children 14 and under, 4€ 65 and older. Tues–Sun 10am–5:30pm (Sat–Sun until 7pm). Metro: Sant'Ambrogio.

Museo Poldi-Pezzoli ★ The pleasant effect of seeing the Bellinis, Botticellis, and Tiepolos amid these salons is reminiscent of a visit to other private collections, such as the Frick Collection in New York City and the Isabella Stewart Gardner Museum in Boston. This stunning treasure trove leans a bit toward Venetian painters (such as Francesco Guardi's elegantly moody *Grey Lagoon*), but also ventures widely throughout Italian painting and into the northern and Flemish schools. It was amassed by 19th-century collector Giacomo Poldi-Pezzoli, who donated his villa and its treasures to the city in 1881. Antonio Pollaiuolo's *Portrait of a Young Woman* is often likened to the *Mona Lisa,* in that it is a haunting image you will recognize immediately. The collections also include porcelain, watches, jewels, and many of the *palazzo*'s original furnishings. For those not convinced this museum is a must see, it could become a golden option for a rainy Monday when most of the other museums in town are closed.

Via Manzoni 12. ✆ **02-794-889.** www.museopoldipezzoli.it. Admission 9€ adults, 6€ for ages 11–18 and seniors over 60. Weds–Mon 10am–6pm. Metro: Duomo or Montenapoleone. Tram: 1 or 2.

Pinacoteca Ambrosiana ★★ This exquisite collection focuses on treasures from the 15th through 17th centuries: An *Adoration* by Titian, Raphael's cartoon for his *School of Athens* in the Vatican, Botticelli's *Madonna and Angels,* Caravaggio's *Basket of Fruit* (his only still life), and other stunning works hang in a series of intimate rooms. Notable (or infamous) among the paintings is *Portrait of a Musician,* attributed to Leonardo but, according to many scholars, of dubious provenance; if it is indeed a Leonardo, it would be the only portrait of his to hang in an Italian museum. The adjoining Biblioteca Ambrosiana—open (except for special exhibitions) only to scholars—houses a wealth of Renaissance literaria, including the letters of Lucrezia Borgia and a strand of her hair. The most notable holdings, though, are Leonardo's *Codice Atlantico,* 1,750 drawings and jottings the master did between 1478 and 1519. These and the library's other volumes, including a rich collection of medieval manuscripts, are frequently put on view to the public; at these times, a fee of 10€ allows entrance to both the library and the art gallery.

Piazza Pio XI 2. ✆ **02-806-921.** www.ambrosiana.eu. Admission 8€ adults, 5€ children. Tues–Sun 10am–6pm. Metro: Cordusio or Duomo.

Shopping

The best fashion gazing is to be done along four adjoining streets north of the Duomo known collectively as the **Quadrilatero d'Oro (Golden Quadrilateral): Via Montenapoleone, Della Spiga, Via Borgospesso,** and **Via Sant'Andrea,** lined with Milan's most expensive high-fashion emporia. From Piazza della Scala, follow Via Manzoni a few blocks north or take the Metro to Via Montenapoleone. The main artery of this shopping heartland is Via Montenapoleone, lined with the most chichi boutiques and most elegant fashion

Via Montenapoleone showcases all of Milan's hottest labels.

outlets, with parallel Via della Spiga (the nicer of the two to walk down as it is closed to traffic) running a close second.

For more Milanese shopping, the less economically crippling type, cruise bustling Corso Buenos Aires (northeast of the center and just east of Stazione Centrale), home to a little bit of everything, from shops that hand-sew men's dress shirts to CD megastores. As it crosses Piazza Oberdan/Piazza Venezia heading south, it becomes Corso Venezia and the stores move up the scale very quickly. Corso Vercelli between the Wagner and Conciliazione Metro stops is another popular shopping street.

HIGH FASHION: CLOTHING, ACCESSORIES & SHOES

Milan is home to the flagship stores of a litany of designers: Armani, Prada, Krizia, Versace, Ermenegildo Zegna, Missoni, Moschino, Mila Schön, and Trussardi.

While high fashion, chillingly expensive boutiques, and designer labels all come down to personal taste, one store deserves a visit whether you're into his übertrendy designs or not: The Grand Central of Italian fashion is the flagship **Armani Megastore,** Via Manzoni 31, near La Scala (☎ **02-7231-8600;** Metro: Montenapoleone). This flagship store (and offices) covers close to 1,000 sq. m (11,000 sq. ft.) and sells everything Giorgio Armani—high-fashion creations, Emporio Armani, Armani Jeans, the Armani Casa selection of home furnishings, and sparkling iPhone and iPad covers—and also houses flower, book, and art shops as well as a high-tech Sony electronics boutique/play center in the basement, an Emporio Café, and a branch of New York's Nobu sushi bar. An Armani hotel being built on the top floors is scheduled to open in 2012.

Of course, other major labels also have Milan addresses. Here are some of the most popular; unless otherwise noted, the shops are quite close to both the Montenapoleone and San Babila Metro stops. **Dolce e Gabbana** carries women's wear at Via della Spiga no. 26 (☎ **02-7600-1155;** www.dolcegabbana. it); accessories can be found nearby at no. 2 (☎ **02-799-950**), while menswear is at Corso Venezia 15 (☎ **02-7600-4091;** Metro: Palestro). **Etro** has its lines of clothing for men and women, along with accessories, at Via Montenapoleone 5 (☎ **02-7600-5450;** www.etro.it), with a discount outlet at Via Spartaco 3 (Bus: 84, Tram: 9).

Ermenegildo Zegna began as a textile house in 1910 (they still weave their own fabrics) and, since the late 1960s, has turned to making elegant, ready-to-wear men's suits that look custom tailored, sold in Milan at Via Montenapoleone 27/A (☎ **02-7600-6437;** www.zegna.com).

Though in recent years it has finally started to go out of fashion for many, a fur coat has long, long been, and continues in some circles to still be, de rigueur for Italian women heading out for an evening. Without a doubt, one of Italy's top purveyors of furs is **Fendi,** Via Sant'Andrea 16 (☎ **02-7602-1617;** www.fendi.com).

The firm that shod Hollywood's stars during its later golden era, **Ferragamo** has an outlet for men's shoes at Via Montenapoleone 20 (☎ **02-7600-6660;** www.ferragamo.com), and for women's shoes at Via Montenapoleone 3 (☎ **02-7600-0054**).

Gianfranco Ferré sells men's and women's wear as well as accessories at Via Sant'Andrea 15 (☎ **02-794-864;** www.gianfrancoferre.com); Ferré Milano, another line of Ferré clothes and accessories, can be found at Via della Spiga 6 (☎ **02-783-050**). Florentine leather specialist **Gucci** has a store selling bags, accessories, and clothing for men and women at Via Montenapoleone 7 (☎ **02-771-271**).

Krizia, Via della Spiga 23 (☎ 02-7600-8429; www.krizia.it), and **Laura Biagiotti,** Via Borgospesso 19 (☎ 02-799-659; www.laurabiagiotti.it), are devoted exclusively to women's wear.

Mila Schön's elegant clothing for women and men is displayed along with accessories, perfumes, and linens, at Corso Venezia 18 (☎ 02-8969-2891; www.milaschon.com; Metro: Palestro). **Miu Miu** carries women's wear and shoes at Via Sant'Andrea 21 (☎ 02-7600-1799; www.miumiu.com). **Missoni**'s colorful sweaters for men and women can be found at Via Montenapoleone 8, enter at Via Sant'Andrea on the corner of Via Bagutta (☎ 02-7600-3555; www.missoni.com). **Moschino** has men's women's wear at Via della Spiga 6 (☎ 02-7600-4320), and women's wear at Via Sant'Andrea 12 (☎ 02-7600-0832; www.moschino.com).

Prada has five stores in the Montenapoleone area selling its minimalist red-stripe fashions, none of them cheap. There's a bit of everything (men's and women's wear, accessories, and jewelry) in the high-profile boutique at the crossing of the Galleria Vittorio Emanuele II (☎ 02-876-979; www.prada.com; Metro: Duomo); menswear, shoes, and accessories at Via Montenapoleone 6 (☎ 02-7602-0273); women's wear and accessories at Via Montenapoleone 8 (☎ 02-777-1771); women's bags, shoes, and accessories at Via della Spiga 18 (☎ 02-780-465); and a mix of stuff for both sexes at Corso Venezia 3 (☎ 02-7600-1426).

Trussardi sells men's and women's wear as well as accessories at Via Sant'Andrea 5 (☎ 02-781-878; www.trussardi.com). **Valentino** wear for men and women is kept at Via Montenapoleone 20 (☎ 02-7602-0285; www.valentino.com). **Versace** carries its men's and women's wear and accessories in its shop at Via Montenapoleone 11 (☎ 02-7600-8528; www.versace.com).

DESIGNER DISCOUNTS

If your fashion sense is greater than your credit line, don't despair: Even the most expensive clothing of the Armani ilk is usually less expensive in Italy than it is abroad, and citywide *saldi* (sales) run from early January into early February and again in late June and July.

Inspired by the window displays in the **Quadrilatero,** you can scour the racks of shops elsewhere for designer seconds, last year's fashions, imitations, and

---

○ Cooking Like a Pro

While not on the top of the must-do list of most tourists, a 3-hour cooking course with Congusto (☎ 02-6347-1266; www.congusto.it) may well afford you your take-home memory from a trip to Milan. In an intimate setting with a maximum of 12 students, you will first be schooled by professional chefs in the finer points of cooking. A large chunk of your time will be spent with hands on cooking in a sleek kitchen and, of course, at the end of it all you eat what you make. Congusto, which has been teaching people to cook since 2003, welcomes English speakers to its varied courses that include southern Italian cuisine, Milanese, vegetarian finger foods, Italian desserts, and quick menus. Classes, which are held in late morning as well as in the evening, start at 70€ and for those who will be hanging out in Milan for a while there are "masters courses" that last from 4 to 12 sessions.

other bargains. The best place to begin is **Il Salvagente,** off Corso XXII Marzo at Via Fratelli Bronzetti 16 (© **02-7611-0328;** bus: 60 or 73, tram: 12 or 27), where you can browse through an enormous collection of designer clothing for men, women, and children (mostly smaller sizes) at wholesale prices. **DMagazine,** Via Montenapoleone 26 (© **02-7600-6027;** Metro: Montenapoleone), may sit on the boutique-lined main shopping drag, but its merchandise is pure discount overstock from big labels such as Armani, Prada, and Fendi.

Another haven for fashionistas looking for slightly eccentric designer clothes on a budget is the **Ticinese/Navigli** neighborhood. Women can shop at **Anna Fabiano** on Corso di Porta Ticinese 40 (© **02-5811-2348** or 5830-6111; Metro: Sant'Ambrogio). Fabiano, who learned her tricks while designing for Fiorucci, favors linear cuts and mixing different types of fabrics to create an original style with a 1960s feel. Another Navigli stop is **Mauro Leone,** on Corso di Porta Ticinese 60 and 103 (© **02-8942-9167;** www.mauroleone. com), where you will find all types of well-priced, Italian-made women's shoes. **Biffi,** on Corso Genova 5/6 (© **02-831-1601;** www.biffi.com; Bus: 94, Metro: Sant'Ambrogio), attracts fashion-conscious hordes of both sexes in search of designer labels and the store's own designs.

Some of the best Milanese fashion deals can be found in stores that are tucked into some of the less trodden and more atmospheric medieval alleys of the city center. On one of those streets, you will find **Donatella Pellini,** at Via Morigi 9 (© **02-7201-0199**), selling her own line of beautiful costume jewelry that looks like the real deal. In the Morigi shop, she sells her romantic and minimalist creations made with glass and synthetic resin; for more flamboyant costume jewelry, visit Pellini's shops on Via Manzoni 20 (© **02-7600-8084**) and on Corso Magenta 11 (© **02-7201-0569**).

If you are fond of colors and not afraid to wear them, visit the two tiny **Gallo** shops on Via Manzoni 16/b (© **02-783-602**) and Via Durini 26 (© **02-7600-2023**), where you'll find their signature multicolored striped socks, along with multicolored scarves, gloves, and T-shirts. The socks won't seem cheap compared with what you buy at Target, but a pair will give you an affordable piece of Milan fashion to bring home—even if you couldn't afford that Armani suit or Prada bag you had your eye on.

For designer shoes at a discount to go with the new socks, there is **Rufus,** Via Vitruvio 35 (© **02-204-9648;** Metro: Centrale or Lima), which carries men's and women's styles from lots of labels for under 100€.

HOUSEWARES

The top name in Italian houseware design since 1921 has been **Alessi,** which has hired the likes of Michael Graves, Philippe Starck, Frank Ghery, and Ettore Sottsass to design the latest in teakettles, bottle openers, and other housewares since the late 1980s. They maintain a main showroom at Corso Matteotti 9 (© **02-795-726;** Metro: San Babila) and a sales outlet at Via Montenapoleone 19 (© **02-7602-1199;** www.alessi.com; Metro: Montenapoleone). You can also pick up Alessi stuff at the **Rinascente** department store next to the Duomo (© **02-88-521;** Metro: Duomo), Milan's less-over-the-top response to London's Harrods, or at **Coin,** a slightly lower-end department store at Piazza Cinque Giornate (© **02-5519-2083**).

The 1980s saw a renaissance of Italian industrial design when design team **Memphis,** led by Sottsass, virtually reinvented the art form, recruiting the best and brightest architects and designers to turn their talents to lighting fixtures,

MILAN IN style

Everyone knows Milan to be a fashion hub, with visitors flocking to Armani super-stores and Dolce & Gabbana boutiques while ticking off the **fashion shows** (www.cameramoda.it) on their calendars: late September and late February for women's apparel, January and June for men's apparel.

What many foreigners forget, though, is that Milan does not just draw the line for clothing. It also dreams up some of the sexiest cars, couches, and kitchenware that Italy has to offer.

You know that **Alfa Romeo,** while built in Turin, is designed in Milan by just taking a look at the logo: It sports the city's red cross on the left, taken from its Crusaders' tunics, and the serpent favored by the ruling Visconti family on the right. The names of Alfa's models should also give some indication of which city rules the roost: the Milano, the Visconti, the Monza, and so forth. (Chevrolet and GM would later borrow some of these model names, though unfortunately not the designs themselves.)

For just about any other type of household mechanical device, if it looks good, chances are it was also designed in Lombardy or Piedmont. For example, **Pininfarina, Alessi,** and the **Memphis Group** are all from Turin, Milan, or somewhere in between.

Alessi, founded on the shores of Lake Orta, counted within its stable of architects such leading lights as Philippe Starck and Ettore Sottsass. But in 1980, the latter went on to form the Memphis Group, poaching some of the other top talent from his former employer as well. The event that launched the start-up group to fame was the 1981 edition of the Salone del Mobile, an annual furniture design show that draws industry leaders and tourists from around the globe.

The **Salone del Mobile** (www.cosmit.it) is nothing like what a casual customer would expect out of a furniture show. Held in mid-April, it brings a lot more than just the latest designs in kitchens, living rooms, bathrooms, and lighting fixtures. It is essentially a contemporary art museum, complete with installation art and spectacles that fascinate even the least design-conscious observer. Most of all, it is the top excuse for Milan to throw parties that regular people actually have a chance of attending.

If you're not here in April, not to worry—the latest models tend to make their way into galleries and design stores around the city right away, making for a nice, city-wide tour of the latest living-room curves. Start off at **Galleria Post Design,** Via della Moscova 27 (✆ 02-655-4731; www.memphis-milano.it), which is the flagship store of the Memphis movement. Admire a multicolored bookshelf that could double as contemporary sculpture, and an assortment of rugs, lamps, and more. Even more avant-garde is **Dilmos,** Piazza San Marco 1 (✆ 02-2900-2437; www.dilmos.com), which almost crosses the line as a museum space rather than a retail store.

If, on the other hand, you're just looking to pick up a sleek, spider-shaped juicer or a stainless-steel toothpick holder, check out the flagship **Alessi** store, Via Manzoni 14/16 (✆ 02-795-726; www.alessi.com). If you happen to be driving around Lake Maggiore (or you're staying at Stresa and it's raining), it might be worth stopping in for a few bargains at Alessi's **factory outlet** in Crusinallo, Via Privata Alessi (✆ 0323-868-611). Your kitchen counter will thank you.

kitchen appliances, office supplies, even furnishings. Italian style has stayed at the very top of the designer housewares market (sharing popularity space with Scandinavian furniture) ever since. Part of the Memphis credo was to create the new modern and then bow out before they became establishment (they self-destructed in 1988). You can still find their influential designs in many houseware shops and in the showroom **Post Design** at Via della Moscova 27 (✆ **02-655-4731;** Metro: Turati or Moscova).

LINENS

For Milanese high-fashion linen including tablecloths, towels, robes, and bedding, you can't do better than **Frette,** which supplies to the world's top hotels. The store at Via Montenapoleone 21 (✆ **02-783-950;** Metro: Montenapoleone) carries the luxury line while Via Manzoni 11 (✆ **02-864-433;** Metro: Montenapoleone), Corso Buenos Aires 82 (✆ **02-2940-1072;** Metro: Lima), and Via Belfiore 16 (✆ **02-498-9756;** Metro: Conciliazione) is the place to go for cheaper offerings.

The elegant swirling paisleys of **Etro,** Via Montenapoleone 5 (✆ **02-7600-5049;** www.etro.it; Metro: Montenapoleone), have been decorating the walls, furniture covers, and accessories in some of Italy's richest and aristocratic homes since 1969. They've since expanded into full lines of clothing and leather goods, as well as perfumes and accessories (the latter are available at the branch on the corner of Via P. Verri and Via Bigli; ✆ **02-7600-5450;** Metro: San Babila).

Bassetti Outlet, Via Procaccini 32 (✆ **02-3450-125;** Bus: 37, Tram: 12 or 14), is a discount outlet of the august Bassetti line of high-quality linen, and the huge space offers the luxurious towels and sheets at good prices. There is another outlet at Via Botta 7A (✆ **02-5518-3191;** Metro: Porta Romana), or you can visit the regular (nondiscount) store at Corso Buenos Aires 52 (✆ **02-2940-0048;** Metro: Lima).

Where to Stay

While you can pay more for a hotel room in Milan than you would almost anywhere else in Europe, there are also some decent accommodations at reasonable prices in good locations. It's difficult to find rooms in any price category when fashion shows and trade fairs are in full swing (the worst periods are the second half of Feb and Sept, when the woman's fashion shows are on, as well as mid-Apr, when the city is overrun by those attending the Salone del Mobile). All hotels (from the one-stars on up) raise their prices at these times and the upper end of the price range in the listings below is reserved for these periods. The lowest prices will be found in August, and to a lesser extent July, and the weekends tend to cost less than during the week. Remember that Milan is relatively small so unless you chose a hotel way out in the boondocks, you'll be reasonably close to everything.

NEAR THE DUOMO
Very Expensive
Four Seasons Hotel Milano ★★★ Milan's top five-star deluxe hotel, a converted 15th-century convent with a soothing courtyard, lies just off Via Montenapoleone, the city's swankiest shopping boulevard. Standard rooms, confusingly called "superior," are on the street (protected from noise by effective double-paned windows), with queen-size beds. Rooms are spacious, with thick

rugs or parquet, designer chairs in comfy sitting areas, large marble-sheathed bathrooms with heated floors, and walk-in closets. "Executive" suites have a mid-size sitting area and can be connected to deluxe doubles to form a family suite. Five bi-level suites on the ground floor of the cloisters have vaulted ceilings and overlook a neighbor's quiet grassy garden.

Via Gesù 8, 20121 Milan. www.fourseasons.com/milan. ✆ **800-819-5053** in the U.S. and Canada, or 02-77-088 in Italy. Fax 02-7708-5000. 118 units. 520€–600€ superior double; 640€–710€ deluxe double; 640€–800€ junior suite; 1,350€–1,500€ executive suite; 9,300€ Royal Suite. (Prices do not include taxes and service charges.) AE, DC, MC, V. Valet parking 51€. Bus: 54, 64, 65, or 73. Metro: Montenapoleone. **Amenities:** 2 restaurants (elegant restaurant under celebrity chef, casual restaurant open lunch and dinner); bar; babysitting; bikes; children's program and kids' menu; concierge; executive-level rooms; small exercise room; room service; smoke-free rooms. *In room:* A/C, TV/VCR, hair dryer, kitchenette (in Royal suite), minibar, Wi-Fi.

Grand Hotel et de Milan ★★★ Perhaps Milan's most intimate luxury hotel, the Grand Hotel et De Milan balances family management with refined service in an 1863 building. It's positioned near La Scala (3 blocks away) and the shopping of Via Montenapoleone just across the street. The bathrooms are done in marble; rooms feature king-size beds and heavy curtains, chipped stone floors, elegant upholstered furnishings, and muted skylight domes. "Deluxe" rooms are larger than "classic" ones and have genuine antiques. The suites genuinely feel like small apartments rather than hotel rooms, with their homelike arrangement of antiques and piped-in opera (perhaps something by Maria Callas, once a regular guest). The presidential Giuseppe Verdi Suite is preserved with the same furnishings as when the composer spent his last 30 years here (he even died in this room), including the desk upon which he composed many operas.

Via Manzoni 29, 20121 Milan. www.grandhoteletdemilan.it. ✆ **02-723-141.** Fax 02-8646-0861. 95 units. 455€ classic double; 535€ deluxe double; 645€ junior suite; 900€–1,175€ suite. Breakfast 35€. AE, DC, MC, V. Garage parking 43€. Metro: Montenapoleone. **Amenities:** 2 Italian/Milanese restaurants; bar; babysitting; bikes; concierge; large exercise room; room service. *In room:* A/C, TV w/pay movies, hair dryer, minibar, Wi-Fi.

Moderate

Hotel Gran Duca di York ★ Scholars studying at the nearby Biblioteca Ambrosiana used this phenomenally placed *palazzo* in the 19th century. A restructuring completed in 2009 has greatly improved the hotel's look and the rooms are now sleek and simple yet inviting and comfortable. The windows on the rooms facing the street do not keep out all the traffic noise (which isn't constant, but is noticeable). The beds are hard, but if that takes away from your sleep you can always head to the minibar where the drinks are compliments of the hotel. The location, just off the main pedestrian drag leading from the Duomo to Castello Sforzesco, is tough to beat.

Via Moneta 1A, 20123 Milan. www.ducadiyork.com. ✆ **02-874-863.** Fax 02-869-0344. 33 units. 135€–240€ double. Rates include breakfast. AE, MC, V. Parking in nearby garage 30€. Metro: Cordusio. **Amenities:** Bar; babysitting; concierge; room service. *In room:* A/C, TV, hair dryer, minibar, Wi-Fi.

Inexpensive

Hotel Aliseo A 10-minute walk south of the Duomo, this *pensione* offers good quality for the price, add the stellar location and this becomes an attractive budget option. The management is friendly, and rooms are furnished with pleasant modern pieces and decent beds. Five of the rooms have en suite bathrooms while the remaining seven share the three squeaky-clean common facilities in the hallway. Rooms on the street side open to small balconies but are noisier than those overlooking the courtyard. One of the bathrooms is equipped with a washing machine, and guests can do a load for 10€. As it is one of the few good-priced alternatives remaining in the city center, the Aliseo books up quickly.

Corso Italia 6, 21023 Milan. www.hotelaliseo.it. ✆ **02-8645-0156.** 12 units. 50€–75€ double with shared bathroom; 75€–110€ double with bathroom; 80€–110€ triple with shared bathroom; 100€–130€ triple with bathroom. Continental breakfast included. MC, V. Bus: 54. Metro: Duomo. Tram: 12, 15, 16, 24 or 27. **Amenities:** Concierge; computer in lobby with Internet connection. *In room:* TV, hair dryer.

IN MAGENTA & BRERA
Expensive

Antica Locanda Solferino ★★ Italian film great Marcello Mastroianni preferred to stay here on his trips to Milan as did many other cinema stars. The rooms have more character than they do modern comforts, but, to the loyal guests, the eclectic smattering of country antiques and Art Nouveau pieces more than compensates for the absence of minibars. Nor do the repeat customers seem to mind that some of the bathrooms are minuscule (though modern). The rooms on the tiny courtyard are quieter, but those on the street have plant-filled balconies (the best is no. 10 on the corner, if you don't mind a tub rather than a shower). The management also rents two apartments in the neighborhood, each with a living room, a bedroom, and a Jacuzzi, with the decorations straight out of the 1960s.

Via Castelfidardo 2, 20121 Milan. www.anticalocandasolferino.it. ✆ **02-657-0129.** Fax 02-657-1361. 11 units. 180€–400€ double. Rates include in-room breakfast delivered with your newspaper of choice. Extra bed 50€. AE, DC, MC, V. Parking 30€ in nearby garage. Closed 2–3 weeks in mid-Aug. Bus: 37 or 43. Metro: Moscova or Repubblica. Tram: 9 or 33. **Amenities:** Concierge. *In room:* A/C (2 rooms), TV, hair dryer, Wi-Fi.

Moderate

Ariosto Hotel ★★ Tucked away in a residential neighborhood of apartment houses and old villas near the Santa Maria delle Grazie church, the Ariosto is a refreshingly quiet retreat—all the more so because many of the newly refurbished rooms face a private garden, and some open onto balconies overlooking it. All rooms are decorated with wood-and-wicker furnishings, shiny parquet floors, and hand-painted wallpaper. Most of the doubles are decently sized (though singles tend to be narrow) with separate dressing areas off the tile or stone bathrooms, a few of which are equipped with Jacuzzis.

Via Ariosto 22, 20145 Milan. www.hotelariosto.com. ✆ **02-481-7844.** Fax 02-498-0516. 49 units. 85€–290€ double; 100€–310€ triple. Rates include breakfast. AE, DC, MC, V. Parking 25€ in garage. Closed 3 weeks in Aug. Metro: Conciliazione. Tram: 19. **Amenities:** Restaurant (Italian); bar; bikes; concierge; room service; smoke-free rooms. *In room:* A/C, TV w/pay movies, hair dryer, minibar, Wi-Fi.

Carlyle Brera Hotel ★ This sleek hotel located in the heart of Brera gives great value for what it costs. All rooms have parquet floors that, combined with the light-wood paneling found on some of the walls, create a minimalist look more common to hotels in a higher price range. Superior rooms are more spacious than a classic double, but other than that they are about the same. No matter what room you pick, you have a choice of eight types of pillows—no kidding.

Corso Garibaldi 84, 20121 Milan. www.hotelcarlyle.com. ℂ **02-2900-3888.** Fax 02-2900-3993. 97 units. 115€–305€ double. Rates include breakfast. AE, DC, MC, V. Parking 35€ in garage next to hotel. Bus: 94, Metro: Moscova. Tram: 2, 12, 14. **Amenities:** Restaurant (Italian); bar; room service; smoke-free rooms. *In room:* A/C, TV w/pay movies, hair dryer, minibar, Wi-Fi.

EAST OF THE DUOMO
Inexpensive
Hotel XXII Marzo ★★ 🦌 This clean and friendly family-run hotel is a pleasant 20-minute walk (or 10-min. tram ride) from the Duomo along a bustling street making it a good option if you don't have to be right in the center and you are okay with simple. The beds in the tile-floored rooms are old, though not overly soft, and the bathrooms tight, but if you are feeling cramped you can sit out in the little park in front of the hotel and watch the local fauna do their thing. If size is key and you want to be sure not to get one of the smaller rooms, you can pay 10€ more and book a triple for double occupancy.

Piazza Santa Maria del Suffragio 3 (just off Corso XXII Marzo near Piazza Cinque Giornate), 20129 Milan. www.hotel22marzo.com. ℂ/fax **02-7010-7064.** 15 units. 65€–170€ double. Rates include breakfast. AE, MC, V. Bus: 73. Tram: 12 or 27. **Amenities:** Bar. *In room:* A/C, TV, Wi-Fi.

NEAR STAZIONE CENTRALE & CORSO BUENOS AIRES
Expensive
Doria Grand Hotel ★ This luxury hotel offers enormously discounted prices on weekends, most of August, and the Christmas/New Year's holiday. Located about halfway between the main train station and Piazzale Loreto, it is far more comfortable and stylish than most hotels in its luxury class. The good-size rooms are exquisitely appointed with handsome wood, marble-topped furniture, and rich fabric wall coverings. The beautiful marble bathrooms are equipped with generous-size tubs, vanities, and a good selection of toiletries. A sumptuous buffet breakfast is served in a stylish room (where they also serve 30€ fixed-price menus at mealtimes), and Thursday and Friday evenings the piano bar becomes a jazz club.

Viale Andrea Doria 22, 20124 Milan. www.doriagrandhotel.it. ℂ **02-6741-1411.** Fax 02-669-6669. 124 units. 100€–300€ double. Rates include buffet breakfast. AE, DC, MC, V. Parking 30€ in garage. Bus 90, 91, or 92. Metro: Loreto or Caiazzo. Tram: 1. Amenities: Restaurant; cafe; babysitting; concierge; room service; smoke-free rooms. *In room:* A/C, TV w/pay movies, hair dryer, minibar, Wi-Fi.

Moderate
Hotel Berna ★★ The breakfast, which is up to the standards of most luxury hotels, coupled with friendly service and lots of little freebees such as hot and cold non-alcoholic drinks (both in the minibar and in the lobby) make staying here a very positive experience. Most standard doubles are small, but the furnishings are relatively new and light pastel colors are used for curtains, walls, and bedding making the spaces seems airy enough. High ceilings also help. Comfortable mattresses and good sound-proofing ensure that you will get a good night's sleep here.

Via Napo Torriani 18, 20124 Milan. www.hotelberna.com. ℂ **02-6773-1800.** Fax 02-669-3892. 106 units and 16 across the street in Berna Tower. 109€–179€ double. Rates include breakfast. MC, V. Parking 18€ in hotel garage or free on street. Metro: Centrale. Tram: 1 or 5. **Amenities:** Bar. *In room:* A/C, TV, hair dryer, Wi-Fi.

Inexpensive

Hotel Aurora 🗡 This 16-room hotel one flight up in a building on lively Corso Buenos Aires has only one star, but it's clean, the rooms are decently sized, and though the bathrooms are small, they're in excellent condition. Rooms 110, 111, and 114 overlook the main street, yet the incredibly insulating windows block out just about all the noise, making these rooms desirable as they allow you to pop your head outside and watch the action down below. Donato Casella, the gregarious owner of the Hotel Aurora since 1987, lived for more than a decade in New York City and he's always ready to use his near-perfect English to tell you about his latest trip to the Big Apple. Sometimes a voucher for breakfast at a bar downstairs is thrown in with the room; if not, you're better off taking care of your hunger needs on your own rather than paying the 5€.

Corso Buenos Aires 18, 20124 Milan. www.hotelauroramilano.com. © **02-204-7960.** Fax 02-204-9285. 16 units. 65€–150€ double. MC, V. Parking 24€ per day in nearby garage. Metro: Porta Venezia. Tram: 5 or 33. **Amenities:** Bar. *In room:* A/C, TV, hair dryer, Wi-Fi.

TICINESE/NAVIGLI

Moderate

Art Hotel Navigli ★ With its location just steps from the Naviglio Grande, this hotel is slightly removed from most of the tourist sites, but it more than makes up for that with its vicinity to the trendy shops and booming nightlife found up and down the canal. While the facade is shockingly nondescript, inside you will find a slightly artsy air (the hotel desperately tries to live up to its name) that includes fanciful carpets, modern art on the wall and a minimalist edge to the furniture that rejuvenates without being overwhelming. Most of the rooms are large and come with marble-countered bathrooms, and a few also have a small terrace. There is a miniature garden with a few tables and umbrellas that offer a chance to unwind after running around town.

Via Angelo Fumagalli 4, 20143 Milan. www.arthotelnavigli.com. © **02-8941-0530.** Fax 02-5811-5066. 103 units. 115€–215€ double. Rates include breakfast. AE, DC, MC, V. Parking 20€ in hotel garage or free on the street. Bus: 74. Metro: Porta Genova. Tram: 2. **Amenities:** Bar; smoke-free rooms. *In room:* A/C, TV w/pay movies, hair dryer, minibar, Wi-Fi.

Ripa del Naviglio ★★ 🏠 Located right above the Naviglio Grande, this splendid B&B has been open since late 2009 with the owners living on the floor above the three good-sized guest rooms. Two rooms look out onto the canal and on clear days have a view of Monte Rosa straddling the Swiss border while the third one, which is a little bigger and can be set up with a third bed, overlooks the inner courtyard. The rooms are spotless, have large showers, and are tastefully decorated, including interesting paintings by the owner's brother. Weather permitting, you can breakfast out on the balcony in front of the entrance. The price is pretty much fixed at 110€ except for the week of the Salone del Mobile in mid-April.

Ripa di Porta Ticinese 71, 20143 Milan. www.ripadelnaviglio.it. © **02-8969-3343.** 3 units. 110€–140€ double. Rates include breakfast. AE, MC, V. Parking in nearby garage 20€ or free on the street. *In room:* A/C, TV, hair dryer, Wi-Fi.

Where to Eat

Like all self-respecting Italians, the Milanese love their long, drawn-out sit-down meal, but this is also the financial capital with several large universities so in addition to the exceptional world-class dining options, you'll find many pizzerias

There are many opportunities to eat well, and cheaply, while you're powering through the sites in and around Piazza Duomo. **Luini Panzerotti** (see separate entry) should be tried at least once on every trip to Milan. **Piadineria Bottega Artigianale** on Via dell'Unione 4 just off Via Torino is a chain where you can get a good *piadina* (a thin tortilla-like piece of bread that gets filled with anything you might find in a sandwich) though a better one, and perhaps the best in Milan, can be had in the Navigli neighborhood at **Piadineria Carletto** (p. 316). **Princi** at Via Speronari, 6 (with stores also at Piazza XXV Aprile 5, Largo La Foppa 2, and Via Ponte Vetero 10, all of which are in or near Brera) sells tasty pizza by-the-slice all day and warm dishes at lunch time. The **Billa** supermarket right next to the FNAC at the intersection of Via Torino and Via della Palla is a great place to go if you need a drink or sandwich and want to save a few euros from what you'd pay at a bar. If you want to eat light fin anticipation of a big dinner, there's always the gelato option at **Grom** on Via Santa Margherita 16 near La Scala (p. 318).

and other low-cost eateries where you can grab a sandwich or other light fare on the run.

Tip: From late spring to late summer Milan is home to legions of mosquitos, particularly around the canals. Dusk is when they come to feed and unless you have something in your blood that keeps them away, make sure your dinner or *aperitivo all'aperto* in the Ticinese/Navigli neighborhood is accompanied by the proper precautions (bug spray or clothing that leaves no exposed skin).

NEAR THE DUOMO

Luini Panzerotti ★★ LIGHT FARE At this stand-up counter near the Galleria, a Milan institution since 1949, you'll have to elbow your way through a throng of well-dressed patrons to purchase the house specialty: *panzerotto,* a pocket of pizza crust stuffed with all sorts of ingredients, including the basic cheese-and-tomato, that is either fried or baked.

Via Santa Radegonda 16. ℰ **02-8646-1917.** www.luini.it. Reservations not accepted. Panzerotto 2.30€–2.50€. No credit cards. Mon 10am–5pm; Tues–Sat 10am–8pm. Closed Aug. Metro: Duomo.

Peck ★★ ITALIAN Milan's most famous food emporium offers a wonderful selection of roast veal, risottos, *porchetta,* salads, cheeses, pastries, and other fare from its exquisite larder in this cafe upstairs from its **shop ★★★,** which is itself worth a visit. If you want the experience of consuming Peck food on the premises while keeping costs to a minimum, the cafe has sandwiches for 8.50€.

Via Spadari 9. ℰ **02-802-3161.** www.peck.it. Reservations not accepted. Primi 14€–18€; secondi 15€. AE, DC, MC, V. Mon–Sat 9:15am–7:30pm. Closed Jan 1–10 and July 1–20. Metro: Duomo.

MAGENTA

Da Claudio ★★ RAW BAR One of Milan's idiosyncrasies is that it is a landlocked city and yet it has the freshest fish in the country. There is an explanation: The best catch is trucked up here from the shore every night to chase those bankers' euros. A fun place to enjoy Milan's maritime bounty without dispensing a fortune is at this Brera fish market, which becomes a popular raw bar at night. Almost everyone goes for the mixed plate, which includes some combination of raw tuna, sea bass, salmon, red snapper, sturgeon, shrimp, prawns, and cod. Order a plate and enjoy it while sitting on one of the bar stools next to young professional who have just gotten off work. All plates come with a complimentary glass of prosecco and another dozen wines can be sampled by the glass (the Falanghina marries perfectly with the raw fish).

Via Cusani 1. ☎ **02-80-56-857.** www.pescheriadaclaudio.it. Reservations not accepted. Mixed raw plate 11€–14€; 3 oysters 10€. AE, MC, V. Mon–Sat 11am–9:30pm (Mon until 8pm). Metro: Lanza or Cordusio.

Trattoria Milanese ★★★ MILANESE Giuseppe and Antonella Villa preside with a watchful eye over the centuries-old premises (a restaurant since 1933), tucked into a narrow lane in one of the oldest sections of Milan, just west of the Duomo. In the three-beamed dining room, Milanese families and other patrons share the long, crowded tables. Giuseppe, in the kitchen, prepares what many patrons consider to be some of the city's best traditional fare. The *risotto alla Milanese*, with saffron and beef marrow is unforgettable, as is the minestrone that's served hot in the winter and at room temperature in the summer. The *cotoletta alla Milanese*, breaded and fried in butter, is made with the choicest veal chops and is served with the bone. Polenta with rich Gorgonzola cheese is one of the few nonmeat second courses.

A TASTE OF bitter LOVE

For some people, the allure is the signature salt shaker–shaped, neon red bottle, often neatly lined up on windowsills in restaurants and bars. Others know it for its placement in vintage Art Deco posters. For many people, it's simply a bitter alcoholic concoction that tastes like cough medicine. But for many Milanese, it's the reward at the end of a hard day at work and the beginning of a night on the town.

Love it or hate it, **Campari** is the soul of Milan and is at the heart of all its signature cocktails. Campari is a bitter alcoholic drink that was invented in 1860 in Novara, a city in the Piedmont region. Today, Campari is manufactured in Piedmont at the home of its sweeter friend, Cinzano. (The vermouth company was purchased by Campari Group in the 1990s. The group is now headquartered just outside Milan in Sesto San Giovanni, though all the drinks are manufactured near Turin.)

Together, Campari, vermouth, and a splash of seltzer make up the *americano,* a drink that is usually served in street-side cafes with an orange slice on its rim. Its cousin, the *negroni,* skips the seltzer in favor of gin and is also usually served with orange garnishes though the fruit is often dropped at swankier night spots as the night goes on. A *negroni sbagliato* uses sparkling wine, often prosecco, instead of gin. A *Campari orange,* half Campari and half OJ, is a less-alcoholic option that will help you keep coherent later into the night.

What gives Campari its unique bitter and tangy essence? Local lore says that the secret blend of herbs is guarded by the manufacturing director and one other undisclosed custodian. One thing that is known, and frankly should have remained a secret, is the ingredient behind its almost fluorescent red hue: the squashed skeletons of South American insects. *Negroni,* anyone?

Via Santa Marta 11. ℂ **02-8645-1991.** Reservations required. Primi 12€–16€; secondi 16€–25€. AE, DC, MC, V. Wed–Mon noon–3pm and 7–11:30pm. Metro: Cordusio.

NEAR STAZIONE CENTRALE & CORSO BUENOS AIRES

Da Abele ★ MILANESE This friendly trattoria specializes in risotto, you will never find pasta on the constantly changing menu, and it caters to local residents (hence its evening-only hours—they schedule reservations only before 8:30pm; afterward it's first-come, first-served). There are always three types of risotto on the menu, some quite adventurous such as with duck and berries, though it's anybody's guess which three will be there when you stop by. If risotto is your thing then you can't go wrong, and there are also good salads. The amiable staff doesn't mind if you venture no farther into the menu, but if you do, you'll find succulent roast meats. Da Abele is tucked away in a pleasant enclave of shops and apartment houses east of Stazione Centrale and north of the Corso Buenos Aires shopping strip (a few blocks north of Piazzale Loreto).

Via Temperanza 5. ℂ **02-261-3855.** Reservations recommended. Primi 9€; secondi 12€–15€. MC, V. Tues–Sun 8–11:30pm. Closed July 25–Sept 1. Metro: Pasteur.

Joia ★★ VEGETARIAN Some will no doubt welcome the respite from northern Italy's often heavy cuisine offered by Joia, which in 1996 became Europe's first vegetarian restaurant to be awarded a Michelin star. The refined atmosphere, created by the use of blond-wood and neutral tones, is the perfect setting for the innovative vegetarian creations of Swiss chef Pietro Leemann, a star in his profession. He uses only organic products and everything is always incredibly fresh, which you'd have to expect at these prices. The menu changes with the seasons and dishes come and go so a return visit always offers surprises. Primi, such as au gratin green ravioli filled with a mix of chickpeas and celery and served over a bed of string beans, can be ordered as a main course. There's an abundant assortment of cheeses and, as befits a place with a Michelin star, an impressive wine list.

Via P. Castaldi 18. ℂ **02-2952-2124.** www.joia.it. Reservations highly recommended. Primi 22€–25€; secondi 30€; tasting menu 65€–80€. AE, DC, MC, V. Mon–Fri noon–2:30pm and 7:30–11:30pm. Closed Aug. Metro: Repubblica or Porta Venezia.

IN THE NAVIGLI

Acquasala ★★★ 🍴 APULIAN Southern Puglia in the far southeastern corner of Italy, in the heel of the boot, is home to wonderful sea, beautiful baroque buildings, and most importantly if you are not going to make it there on this trip to Italy, mouth-watering food. Acquasala has brought one of that winning troika to the outer reaches of the string of bars and restaurants on the Naviglio Grande. In a break from the heavier Milanese food, here you'll find dishes that are lighter in everything but taste, including *orecchiette con cima di rape* (small ear-shaped pasta topped with rape) and *orecchiette con pomodorini freschi, rucola e caciori-cotta* (with fresh tomatoes, arugula, and aged ricotta). The service is very friendly and they start you off with some bruschetta and salami on the house. When they bring the paper bag, don't bring that home, it's filled with Apulian bread and taralli, an addictive twisted cracker that's a local specialty.

Ripa di Porta Ticinese 71 (on the Naviglio Grande). ℂ **02-8942-3983.** Reservations recommended. Primi 8€–12€; secondi 9€–15€. Tues–Sun 12:30–2:30pm and 7:30–11:30pm. AE, MC, V. Metro: Porta Genova. Tram: 2.

Al Pont de Ferr ★ ITALIAN This is one of the culinary high points of the dozens of restaurants around the Navigli, with tables set out on the cobblestones overlooking the canal in the summer. Unfortunately, the price has skyrocketed in the last few years and what used to be a true find has become a place with very good food with prices that come in somewhere between fair and slightly too high for what you get. In keeping with the theme of going up market, dishes have turned away from local traditions and now are mostly curious inventions that almost always turn out to be mouth-wateringly good. How about ravioli filled with smoked bacon, capers, lemon, and milk? (Yes, you read that right.) You down these in one big bite—no cutting, or else your plate starts resembling the Venetian lagoon. Secondi are just as inventive, and with the small portions here you almost certainly have to get one to follow your primo.

Ripa di Porta Ticinese 55 (on the Naviglio Grande). © **02-8940-6277.** Reservations highly recommended. Primi 12€–17€; secondi 27€ (prices cheaper at lunchtime). Daily 12:30–2:30pm and 8–11pm. AE, MC, V. Metro: Porta Genova.

Kiosk ★★ SEAFOOD This stand on Piazza XXIV Maggio offers wonderfully tasty fried fish that isn't greasy and won't make your stomach churn as you walk the nearby canals. You point, the guy weighs, you pay, and then you dig in either standing while watching the traffic, sitting at one of the few tables set up on the side of the stand, or, and this is the best option, you take your loot across the street where you eat while staring at the *darsena* (a bustling port until the 1960s). The fish on offer usually includes calamari (rings and tentacles are separated, convenient for those grossed out by the latter), shrimp, crab, and cod. There's also a bit of grilled fish on offer. The fresh fish on sale at the same stand will put to rest any questions you have regarding the quality of what you're eating.

Piazza XXIV Maggio (on the southwest side of the square close to the beginning of the Naviglio Pavese). © **02-8940-2224.** Reservations not accepted. Serving 5€–10€. Tues–Sat noon–7:30pm (summer Thurs–Sat until midnight, Sun until 9pm). Tram: 3 or 9.

Piadineria Carletto ★★ ITALIAN This small place right on busy Piazza XXIV Maggio, with no tables and only a few bar stools where you can sit, makes what are most probably Milan's best *piadine,* thin tortilla-like pieces of bread that get folded over and filled with anything you might find in a sandwich. The *piadina,* the actual bread, is made in front of you, standard practice in the Romagna region of central Italy from where the *piadina* hails, but all but impossible to find in Milan. The very friendly owners, Alessandro and his American wife Laurie, are here on the weekends at lunch and can advise which of the many choices is right for you. The classic is squacquerone (a delicious, fresh creamy cheese) with arugula, but some of the inventive combinations are also terrific such as with sausage, squacquerone, and porcini mushrooms. Like the Italian panino, these are not drowned in sauce.

Piazza XXIV Maggio 1/10 (on the northeast side of the square just down the street from McDonald's). © **02-8977-2938.** Reservations not accepted. Piadina 4€–8€. Mon–Fri noon–1am, Sat noon–2am, Sun 1–11pm. Tram: 3 or 9.

Pizzeria Naturale ★★ ☺ ITALIAN/PIZZA There are many good places in Milan to get a pizza (see "Pizza Galore," below), but this one adds a good location with a great space and efficient service. Some of the products used are organic (including beers). The restaurant is located in a large open space flooded with light and decorated with tall columns of wine bottles. There is also seating out front and on a large terrace in the back. The pizzeria is located on the Naviglio Grande at the far end of the area where all the bars and restaurants are. There is another Pizzeria Naturale—the pizza is just as good, but the space much tighter and slightly less appealing—at Via De Amicis 24, about halfway between the canals and the Duomo. Via Ripa di Porta Ticinese 79. ☎ **02-8942-0299.** Reservations recommended Fri–Sat. Pizza 5€–12€. MC, V. Daily noon–3pm and 6–11pm. Metro: Porta Genova. Tram: 2.

ELSEWHERE

La Rosa dei Venti ★★ ITALIAN/SEAFOOD Fresh fish and pasta coupled with warm service, which includes a complimentary glass of prosecco and a bruschetta, are the hallmarks of this unassuming restaurant that's a 15-minute walk from the beginning of Corso Sempione. Fabrizio, who waits on the tables with his wife, and Matteo, the cook, opened in 2001 and have been gaining return customers ever since. The perfect way to begin this culinary bliss is with the "La Rosa dei Venti" starter, which has five miniportions including a lightly breaded and fried shrimp covered in sesame seeds, a small stuff squid, and a tepid octopus salad. The *spaghetti chitarra alla carbonara di mare,* which revisits the old standby by substituting fish for the bacon, will leave you wondering why you never thought of doing this at home. Matteo has Celiac disease and will cook up a special gluten-free meal if you call ahead.

Via Piero della Francesca 34. ☎ **02-347-338.** www.ristorantelarosadeiventi.it. Reservations highly recommended. Primi 15€–20€; secondi 20€–35€. AE, MC, V. Tues–Sun 12:30am–2:30pm and 7–11pm (Sat closed at lunchtime). Bus: 43 or 57. Tram: 1 or 19 (also, trams 12 and 14 stop about 4 blocks away).

Dongiò ★★ SOUTHERN ITALIAN The red-hot chili pepper is native to the Americas, but few places in the world have learned to work with the plant better than the Calabrians in the toe of the Italian boot; and few restaurants besides Dongiò have brought such wonderful Calabrian cuisine to Northern Italy. All the pasta is made in-house and is coupled with Calabrian specialties, including sausage, sweet Tropea onions, *pancetta,* aged ricotta, and *n'duja,* a spicy, spreadable salami. For a mouthwatering taste of how these ingredients can be meshed into a primo approaching perfection, try the *Spaghettoni alla Tamarro,* thick spaghetti topped with a red sauce that includes *n'duja* and a dash of the aged ricotta that has been worked into a cream. *N'duja* makes it onto the antipasto menu, and if you still haven't had enough of this most signature of Calabrian specialties, for your *secondo* you can get a large slice of grilled *Caciocavallo Silano* cheese filled with *n'duja.*

Via Bernardino Corio 3 (near Porta Romana) ☎ **02-551-1372.** Reservations highly recommended. Primi 8.50€; secondi 10€–18€. MC, V. Mon–Fri 12:30–3pm and 7:30–11pm; Sat 7:30–11pm. Metro: Porta Romana.

> ### 🖊 Pizza Galore
>
> In addition to Pizzeria Naturale, there are many other options for a terrific pizza that you will be talking about long after you've finished that last wedge. If you can accept a long wait (sometimes even if you have reserved) and dodgy service, then **Da Maruzzella** (☎ **02-2952-5729**) at Piazza Oberdan 3, at the beginning of Corso Buenos Aires, is THE spot for excellent pizza. **I Capatosta** (☎ **02-8941-5910**), on the Naviglio Grande at Alzaia Naviglio Grande 56 (not far from Pizzeria Naturale), also makes tasty pizza. Two more options, **Fratelli la Bufala** and **Rossopomodoro,** are mentioned under "Pubs & Bars" below.

La Crêperie CREPERIE About a 15-minute walk southeast of Piazza Duomo, this busy creperie is an ideal stop for a light lunch or a snack while visiting the nearby church of Sant'Ambrogio or Museo Nazionale di Scienza e di Tecnica. The far-ranging offerings include meal-like crepes such as *prosciutto e formaggio* (ham and cheese) or more dessertlike options (Nutella features prominently in many of these). Italians split foods like crepes into two categories: *dolci* (sweet) and *salati* (salty). A *dolci* crepe might have Nutella in it, a *salati*, ham and cheese. La Crêperie has 14 salty crepes and 16 sweet ones, or else you can mix and match to create one all your own.

Via C. Correnti 21. ✆ **02-839-5913.** Reservations not accepted. Crepes 3€–4€. No credit cards. Mon–Sat noon–3pm and 6–9pm (Thurs until midnight, Fri–Sun until 1am). Metro: Sant'Ambrogio.

CAFES & GELATO

Bar Zucca/Caffè Miani, at the Duomo end of the Galleria Vittorio Emanuele II (✆ **02-8646-4435;** www.caffemiani.it; Metro: Duomo), is a Milan institution that is said to have been a favorite watering hole of Giuseppe Verdi and Arturo Toscanini following performances at La Scala. While Milan does not have the same tradition of wonderful old cafes that you find seemingly on every street in the center of Turin, Bar Zucca, with its more than 140 years of history, does Milan proud. It was here that Campari (p. 314) was introduced to the world and it is here that you should find time to have a Campari drink while lingering at the tables in the Galleria or in one of the Art Nouveau rooms inside. After ponying up for the drink here, you can head out to cheaper haunts to continue your evening (see "Pubs & Bars," below).

For gelato, perhaps the best in the city can be found at **Grom,** Via Santa Margherita 16 (✆ **02-8058-1041;** www.grom.it), right by La Scala; Corso di Porta Ticinese 51, near the San Lorenzo church; Corso Buenos Aires 13, perfectly placed for a break from your shopping spree; Corso XXII Marzo 5, a few steps from the Coin department store (see "Housewares," p. 306); and Via A. da Giussano 1, just off the line of stores on Corso Vercelli. Even the most ardent opponent of chain stores (Grom is selling its *Fragola, Nocciola,* and *Cioccolato* all over Italy as well as in New York, Malibu, Paris, Tokyo, and Osaka) will be hard pressed not to admit that Grom is the exception to the rule that teaches us to steer clear of standardization. If there is better gelato somewhere in northern Italy, please do let me know. The lines are often out the door, literally, and the price is slightly higher than most other gelato shops, but as you dig in it will become abundantly clear why. Look out for the flavor of the month, which is almost always worth a try.

Strollers in the atmospheric Brera neighborhood will want to make sure they pass by **Gelateria Toldo,** Via Ponte Vetero 9 (✆ **02-8646-0863;** Metro: Cordusio or Lanza), where the gelato is wonderfully creamy and many of the *sorbetto* selections are so fruity and fresh, they seem healthy. Going north on Via Ponte Vetero you get to Corso Garibaldi, one of the nicest streets on Milan to stroll, where at number 55 you will find some more mouth-watering gelato at **Gelateria Garibaldi Créme,** run by a husband-and-wife team (he makes the gelato in the back and she mans the scooper), as well as surprisingly tasty soya-based sorbets, especially the cinnamon.

The **Pasticceria Confetteria Cova,** Via Montenapoleone 8 (✆ **02-600-0578;** Metro: Montenapoleone), is nearing its 200th year in refined surroundings near the similarly atmospheric Museo Poldi-Pezzoli. It's usually filled with

The prime spot for a *passeggiata* (stroll) is the Piazza Duomo and the adjoining Galleria, Corso Vittorio Emanuele II, Via Mercanti, and Via Dante, but many of the neighborhoods that fan out from the center are ideal for wandering and looking into the life of the Milanese. The **Quadrilatero d'Oro** (the city's center for high fashion), just north of the Piazza Duomo on and around Via Montenapoleone, is known for window shopping and trendy cafes and bars; **Magenta** is an old residential quarter, filled with some of the city's most venerable

churches, west of Piazza Duomo (follow Via Orefici and its extension, Via Dante, toward the Castello Sforzesco, pictured below left); **Brera,** a once-seedy section that is now gentrified, is filled with bars and restaurants along the streets clustered around the Pinacoteca di Brera (follow Via Brera from the Teatro alla Scala and be sure to walk around pedestrian-only Via Fiori Chiari and then eventually head north on Corso Garibaldi); and Via Torino heads southwest from Piazza Duomo to Corso di Porta Ticinese and the popular **Navigli** neighborhood where you can walk along the remaining *navigli* (canals) that once laced the city, the former warehouse entrances along them now house funky shops and galleries as well as hopping and unpretentious bars, *birrerie* (pubs), restaurants, and small clubs (to arrive directly at Navigli, take the Metro to Porta Genova). **Parco Sempione,** the large park behind the castle, is another ideal spot for a stroll and can provide respite on a hot day. A proper stroll in Milan is always accompanied by a stop at a cafe or gelateria (see above).

shoppers making the rounds in this high-fashion district. You can enjoy a quick coffee and a brioche standing at the long bar, or take a seat in one of the elegant adjoining rooms as you dig into one of their many sweets. You can also buy goodies to bring home.

The **Pasticceria Marchesi,** Via Santa Maria alla Porta 13 (✆ **02-862-770;** Metro: Cordusio), is a historic pastry shop with an adjoining tearoom dating back to the first half of the 19th century. Because it's not far from Santa Maria delle Grazie, you can enjoy the old-world ambience and a cup of coffee (or one of the many teas and herbal infusions) as you dash off postcards of *The Last Supper.* You'll want to accompany your beverage with elegant pastries, perhaps a slice of the *panettone* (cake with raisins and candied citron) that's a hallmark of Milan. No one prepares it better than Marchesi. If your budget is tight, it's still worth coming here for a coffee or cappuccino standing at the bar.

Milan After Dark

On Wednesday and Thursday, Milan's newspapers tend to devote a lot of ink to club schedules and cultural events. If you don't trust your command of Italian to plan your nightlife, check out the tourist office in Piazza Castello—there are usually piles of fliers lying about that announce upcoming events. The tourist office also keeps visitors up-to-date with *Milano Mese,* a periodical it distributes for free with schedules of events, as well as listings of bars, clubs, and restaurants.

THE PERFORMING ARTS On the other side of the Galleria from the Duomo is Italy's premier opera house, **Teatro Alla Scala ★★**, Piazza

Scala (© 02-887-91), known to everyone as "La Scala." The calendar of events and online ticket office can be found at www.teatroallascala.org. Tickets go on sale about 3 months before a performance and sell out quickly for popular performances. Tickets can also be had the day of a performance; check the ticket office at the Duomo Metro stop for details on availability. Purchase tickets online (all major credit cards accepted) or at about a dozen travel agencies around the city, and at various travel agencies throughout the country. For a complete list, visit the website.

The adjacent museum, **Il Museo Teatrale Alla Scala** (© 02-8879-7473), pays tribute to the leading Italian lights in opera and ballet, often hosting exhibits of costumes worn at La Scala performances long ago. Also of note for scholars is a library of more than 40,000 musical works. The museum and library are open daily from 9am to 12:30pm and from 1:30 to 5:30pm. Entrance is 5€.

MOVIES In Italy, English-language films are almost always dubbed into Italian, providing English speakers with an opportunity to bone up on their Italian but taking some of the fun out of a night at the movies. Fortunately, there are a few theaters that screen English-language films in the original version 1 night a week. These three theaters take turns showing the same film on different nights of the week (the film changes every week): **Anteo,** Via Milazzo 9 (© 02-659-7732; Metro: Moscova), on Monday; **Arcobaleno,** Viale Tunisia 11 (© 02-2940-6054; Metro: Porta Venezia), on Tuesday; and **Mexico,** Via Savona 57 (© 02-4895-1802; Metro: Porta Genova), on Thursday.

PUBS & BARS One of the most storied Brera hangouts is **Bar Jamaica,** Via Brera 32 (© 02-876723; Metro: Lanza), an old-school bar where Mussolini once sat to work on his newspaper articles, and now arty locals and literati tolerate the company of better-heeled partygoers at the outdoor tables.

A publike atmosphere, induced in part by Guinness on tap and a very crowded *aperitivo* hour (see "How the Milanese Unwind," p. 321), prevails at Liberty-style **Bar Magenta,** Via Carducci 13, at Corso Magenta (© 02-805-3808; Metro: Cadorna), in the neighborhood from which it takes its name; it's open Tuesday to Sunday 9am to 2am and has good panini.

En route to the Navigli, you can't help noticing the huge crowd of 20-somethings milling around outside the Basilica di San Lorenzo, maybe kicking around a soccer ball through the crowd, usually with cocktails and beers in hand. Chances are those drinks came from **Luca's Bar,** Corso Porta

Ticinese 51 (✆ **02-5810-0405;** bus: 94, Metro: Sant'Ambrogio, tram: 3; just under the arch by the basilica), or **Martin Café** (✆ **02-837-3721**) next door, right on the piazza. Both places close at 2am and between them offer up a choice of about 15 beers on tap and in bottles costing 3€ to 5€ and cocktails at 4€ to 6€. Once you have a drink in hand you can search for a place to sit on the benches in the piazza or take up a spot on the pavement. If your stomach starts growlign after a few drinks, there are two good joints nearby that sell takeout pizza that you can bring back to the piazza: **Fratelli la Bufala** right on the square (✆ **02-837-6529**), and **Rossopomodoro** around the corner at Via Molino delle Armi 48 (✆ **02-8940-1333**).

The **Naviglio Pavese** also attracts a young crowd. Follow the left side of the canal as you leave the city center at your back and you will immediately come to a succession of bars, many of which have tables outside along the canal. The crowd that frequents the more picturesque **Naviglio Grande** is mixed and you'll find everybody from young revelers to families with young children. If you have only one night out in Milan this is probably where you will want to spend it (you can always pop over to the Naviglio Pavese for a look). The left side of the canal as you leave the center is filled mostly with bars and in the summer months is closed to traffic. The right side, which is closed to traffic year-round, has mostly restaurants, all of which put tables out weather permitting. Several foot bridges let you cross over. This is a great area for an evening stroll even if you don't plan to drink or eat.

JAZZ CLUBS While Milan's jazz-club scene is limited, the two choices you have are excellent. **Le Scimmie,** which has its own bar-boat moored in the Naviglio Pavese canal, is in the Navigli at Via Ascanio Sforza 49 (✆ **02-8940-2874;** www.scimmie.it; Metro: Porta Genova or Romolo, tram: 3) and operates Monday to Saturday, with shows starting between 10 and 10:30pm. **Blue Note,** an offshoot of the famous New York club, is at Via Borsieri 37 (✆ **02-6901-6888;** www.bluenotemilano.com; Metro: Garibaldi or Zara), just north of the Porta Garibaldi train station and gets the biggest names in jazz. Shows, which last about 75 minutes, are Monday through Saturday and usually start at 9pm and 11pm (Jun–Aug usually

HOW THE MILANESE unwind

From about 6pm the Milanese begin to flood the bars around town for the time-honored *aperitivo.* You pay for your drink and then get as many trips to the buffet table as your stomach can manage. The food on offer varies from a few sad pieces of dry sliced deli meats to extensive spreads of pasta, rice, vegetables, fruit, and everything else imaginable. Most places with a good spread charge about 8€ for a drink during the *aperitivo* time (the price drops once the food is taken away). Come by 7pm if you want to chow down because when the food runs out that's it. For a vast selection of *aperitivo* places, walk the left side of the Naviglio Grande until you find your favorite. **¡Mas!,** at no. 11, with a pseudo-Spanish theme, consistently has one of the best selections of food. Nurse your drink and you can have an abundant, and excellent, dinner for under 10€; by the third go at the buffet your stomach will be crying *no mas.*

closed). You can buy tickets in person at the club, online, or by calling Monday through Friday 2 to 7pm.

MUSIC & DANCE CLUBS The dance scene changes all the time in Milan, but at whatever club is popular (or in business) at the moment, expect to pay a cover of 10€ to 15€—sometimes more for big-name live acts. **Tocqueville** (☎ 333-827-6676), which is open Tuesday through Sunday and gets a young crowd moving to dance music. For something a little funkier, try **Plastic,** Viale Umbria 120 (☎ 02-733-996; bus: 92, tram: 12, 27), where the people are a bit more colorful and the music more alternative. It's open Friday to Sunday.

> **Note:** There are no specific club hours in Milan. Opening and closing times vary with the seasons and the crowds, with openings anywhere from 7 to 11pm and closings anywhere from 1am to dawn.

GAY CLUBS **Rhabar,** Via Alzaia Naviglio Grande 150 (☎ 393-904-5796 or 393-971-9561), caters to women and is open Wednesday to Sunday 7pm to 2am. Wednesday is singles night, Thursday karaoke. Big crowds come on the weekend. Take the no. 2 tram to the San Cristoforo stop, cross the foot bridge and turn left keeping the canal on your left.

The two most popular bars in the center of town are the pseudo-1960s **Mono Bar,** Via Lecco 6 (☎ 339-481-0264), open daily 6:30pm to 1am (Fri–Sat to 2am); and **Lelephant,** Via Melzo 22 (☎ 02-2951-8768), which attracts a mostly young and gay-friendly crowd and is open Tuesday to Sunday 6:30pm to 2am. Both are near the Porta Venezia Metro stop.

For a slightly older crowd there is **Company Club** (☎ 02-282-9481), near the Cimiano Metro stop. Fashionistas into cocktails and dancing should check out the centrally located **G-Lounge,** Via Larga 8 (☎ 02-805-3042), on Thursday nights. **Magazzini Generali,** a popular dance club at Via Pietrasanta 16 (☎ 02-539-3948; www.magazzinigenerali.it), attracts a young gay and lesbian crowd on Saturday nights (in June and July, the party moves to an outdoor pool, Piscine Saini, at Via Corelli 136).

Day Trips from Milan
PAVIA & THE CERTOSA

At one time, the quiet and remarkably well-preserved little city of **Pavia,** 35km (22 miles) south of Milan, was more powerful than Milan. It was the capital of the Lombard Kingdom in Italy (most of what is now modern day Italy except for Sicily and Sardinia) in the 7th and 8th centuries, and by the early Renaissance, the Viscontis and later the Sforzas, the two families who so influenced the history of Milan and all of Lombardy, were wielding their power here. It was the Viscontis who built the city's imposing **Castello,** made Pavia one of Europe's great centers of learning (when they founded the university) in 1361, began construction on the **Duomo** (with the third-largest dome in Italy) in 1488, and founded the city's most important monument and the one that brings most visitors to Pavia, the Certosa.

The **Certosa** ★★★ is 8km (5 miles) north of Pavia. One of the most unusual buildings in Lombardy, if not in all of Italy, this religious compound was commissioned by Gian Galeazzo Visconti in 1396 as a Carthusian monastery and a burial chapel for his family—officially as thanks for curing his second sickly wife (the first died) and granting him children and heirs. It was completed by the Sforzas. The facade of colored marbles, the frescoed interior, and the riot of

The Certosa's marble facade.

funerary sculpture is evidence that this brood of often-tyrannical despots were also dedicated builders with grand schemes and large coffers. The finest and most acclaimed statuary monument here, that of Ludovico il Moro (buried in France, where he died a prisoner of war) and Beatrice d'Este (buried in Milan's Santa Maria delle Grazie), sits in the left transept of the massive church, beneath lapis lazuli–rich frescoes by Bergognone. Its presence here is a twist of fate—the monks at Milan's Chiesa di Santa Maria delle Grazie (which houses *The Last Supper*) sold the tomb to the Certosa to raise funds. In the right transept is the 15th-century tomb of Gian Galeazzo Visconti.

Across from the tomb is the entrance to the enormous cloister, lined with the monks' cells, each of which is actually a two-story cottage with its own garden plot. Most are now inhabited by a small community of Cistercian monks. It is possible to visit their refectory and an adjoining shop, where they sell their Chartreuse liqueur and herbal soaps and scents.

Admission to the Certosa (© **0382-925-613**) is free; May to August, it's open Tuesday to Sunday 9 to 11:30am and 2:30 to 6pm (Nov–Feb to 4:30pm; Mar and Oct to 5pm; Apr and Sept to 5:30pm).

GETTING THERE Hourly trains from **Milan** stop at the station near the Certosa, just before the main Pavia station (30 min.). **Note:** There are many trains that go to Pavia without stopping at the Certosa. To reach the Certosa from Pavia, take one of the half-hourly buses from the Autocorriere station (next to the train station); the trip takes about 15 minutes. By car, the Certosa is about half an hour south of Milan via Autostrada A7 (follow exit signs).

VISITOR INFORMATION The **tourist office** is near the main university building at Piazza Italia 5 (© **0382-596-022**); it's open Monday to Thursday from 9:15am to noon and 2:45 to 4:30pm, Friday 9:15am to noon.

CREMONA

Violins have been drawing visitors to this little city on the river Po, 92km (57 miles) southeast of Milan, since the 17th century, when fine string instruments began emerging from the workshops of Nicolò Amati and his more famous protégé, Antonio Stradivari. The tradition continues: Cremona's Scuola di Luteria (Violin School) is world renowned.

Cremona's charms extend far beyond the musical. Its central **Piazza del Commune** ★★ is one of the largest and most beautiful town squares in Italy, fronted by remarkable structures. Among these is the 12th-century **Duomo** (✆ **0372-26-707**), clad in pink marble and overshadowed by Italy's second-tallest campanile (the tallest, by just a few meters, being a 20th-c. brick construction in Udine). Inside, the Duomo is covered with 16th-century frescoes (free admission; daily 7:30am–noon and 3:30–7pm).

FROM TOP: The arcade of the Palazzo del Comune; the anatomy of a violin at the Museo Stradivariano.

The **Palazzo del Comune** rises gracefully above a Gothic arcade and is embellished with terra-cotta panels. Its **Raccolta dei Violini** ★ displays a small collection of 17th- and 18th-century violins by Amati, the Guarneri, and one Stradivari (✆ **0372-22-138**). The **Museo Stradivariano** ★, in the Museo Civico alongside an unimportant *pinacoteca* collection of paintings at Via Palestro 17 (✆ **0372-461-886**), displays the finest violins ever made, including those by Amati, Stradivari, and Guarneri.

Admission to the Museo Civico is 7€, including the Stradivarius museum, and it's open Tuesday to Saturday 9am to 6pm, Sunday 10am to 6pm. Admission to the Raccolta dei Violini is 6€; it's open Monday to Saturday 9am to 5pm. The instruments are regularly bowed most mornings by local musicians to keep their coveted tones intact. These "concerts" are open to the public, though for this honor, you must call the Comune at ✆ **0372-22-138** a few weeks ahead of time to book a seat for an extra 2€.

GETTING THERE Trains arrive almost hourly from **Milan** (65 min.). Hourly trains to **Brescia** (50 min.) also make it possible to combine an excursion from Milan to Cremona and Brescia (see below). If you are traveling by car, you can make the trip to Cremona by following A1 from Milan to Piacenza and A21 from Piacenza to Cremona.

VISITOR INFORMATION The **tourist office** is near the Duomo at Piazza del Comune 5 (©**0372-23-233;** www.cremonaturismo.it); hours are daily 9:30am to 1pm and 2 to 5pm (closed Sun afternoon in summer).

BRESCIA

Ringed by industrialized suburbs, Brescia (97km/60 miles east of Milan) doesn't readily beckon travelers to stop. Those who do, however, have the pleasure of wandering through a centuries-old town center where Roman ruins, not one but two duomos, and medieval *palazzi* line winding streets and gracious *piazze*.

The center of Brescia is Piazza Paolo VI, better known as Piazza del Duomo after its two duomos—the 17th- to 19th-century Duomo Nuovo (New Duomo), which is pretty bland, and the much more charming (on the outside, though it's nearly bare inside) 11th- to 12th-century **Duomo Vecchio (Old Duomo) ★**, also called Rotonda, for its shape. Year round, the New Duomo is open Monday to Saturday 7:30am to noon and 4 to 7:30pm, and Sunday 8am to 1pm and 4 to 7:30pm. April to September, the Old Duomo is open Wednesday to Monday 9am to noon and 3 to 7pm; October to March, hours are Saturday and Sunday 9am to noon and 3 to 6pm. Next to the New Duomo rises the Broletto, Brescia's medieval town hall.

Brescia's Roman past emerges if you leave the piazza on Via dei Musei and follow it to the **Capitolino ★**, a temple erected in A.D. 73. Jog up Vicolo del Fontanone to its right to see the remains of the **Teatro Romano (Roman Theater).** A few blocks farther down the street is the **Monasterio di Santa Giulia ★★**, at Via dei Musei 1B (©**030-297-7834;** www.bresciamusei.com), where Charlemagne's ex-wife, Ermengarde, spent her last days. Admission is 8€ for adults, 4€ for those 14 to 18 or 65 and over. The monastery incorporates several churches and museums, together housing a rich collection of prehistoric, Roman, and medieval objects (lots of them high-quality pieces). It is divided into two itineraries, a history of the monastery and a history of the city, called the **Museo della Città.** Everything is well documented and explained in Italian and English. It's open Tuesday to Sunday June to September 10am to 6pm and October to May 9:30am to 5:30pm. Special exhibits raise the prices a tad and lengthen the hours. *Note:* Brescia's exceptional painting collection, the **Pinacoteca Tosio-Matinengo ★★**, was closed for remodeling in 2009 and wasn't scheduled to reopen until early 2013. Many of the most important paintings have been temporarily moved to the museum at the Monasterio di Santa Giulia.

If you leave Piazza del Duomo from the other direction, through the archways into Piazza Loggia, you come upon Brescia's most enchanting building, the Renaissance **Loggia ★★**, a two-story colonnade festooned with reliefs and statues, and dating to the turn of the 16th century (the bottom half) and the mid-1550s through 1570s (the top half). As beautiful and renowned as the Loggia is, oddly enough, we don't know who designed it, though great names such as Jacopo Sansovino and Andrea Palladio have been suggested. The Torre dell'Orologio, on the opposite side of the square, resembles the campanile on Piazza San Marco in Venice, bespeaking the days when Brescia was a Venetian stronghold.

GETTING THERE Trains arrive from Milan about every half-hour (45–65 min.). Brescia is linked to Milan by the A4, which continues east to Verona and Venice; the trip from Milan to Brescia takes a little more than an hour.

VISITOR INFORMATION There's a **tourist info office** at Piazza Loggia 6 (☎ **030-240-0357**), open Monday to Saturday 9:30am to 6:30pm, and Sunday 10am to 6pm. There is another tourist office on Via dei Musei in front of the entrance to the Santa Giulia Monastery (☎ **030-374-9916**), open Monday to Saturday 9am to noon and 2 to 4:30pm (summer closed Sat). You can get more details at www.bresciaholiday.com.

BERGAMO

47km (29 miles) NE of Milan, 52km (32 miles) NW of Brescia

Bergamo is two cities. **Città Bassa,** the lower, a mostly 19th- and 20th-century city, concerns itself with everyday business. **Città Alta,** a beautiful medieval/Renaissance town perched on a green hill, concerns itself these days with entertaining the visitors who come to admire its *piazze, palazzi,* and churches; enjoy the lovely vistas from its belvederes; and soak in the hushed beauty that inspired Italian poet Gabriele d'Annunzio to call old Bergamo "a city of muteness." The distinct characters of the two parts of this city go back to its founding as a Roman settlement, when the town was on the hill and farms and suburban villas dotted the plains below.

Festivals & Markets Bergamo is a cultured city, and its celebrations include the May-to-June **Festival Pianistico** (which it shares with Brescia), one of the world's major piano competitions. In September, the city celebrates its native composer, Gaetano Donizetti, with **performances of his works,** most of them at the Teatro Donizetti in the Città Bassa (see below).

Essentials

GETTING THERE **By Train** Trains arrive from and depart for Milan hourly (50 min.); service to and from Brescia is even more frequent, with half-hourly service during peak early-morning and early-evening travel times (50 min.). Given the frequency of train service, you can easily make a daylong sightseeing loop from Milan, arriving in Bergamo in the morning, moving on to Brescia in the afternoon, and returning to Milan from there. If you're coming from or going to nearby Lake Como, there's hourly service between Bergamo and Lecco, on the southeast end of the lake (40 min.).

 By Bus An extensive bus network links Bergamo with many other towns in Lombardy. There are five to six buses a day to and from Como (2 hr.) run by **SPT** (☎ **031-247-247;** www.sptlinea.it). Service to and from Milan by **Autostradale** (☎ **02-7200-1304;** www.autostradale.it) runs every half-hour (1 hr. trip time). The bus station is next to the train station on Piazza Marconi.

 By Car Bergamo is linked directly to Milan via the A4, which continues east to Brescia, Verona, and Venice. The trip between Milan and Bergamo takes a little under an hour without traffic, but this is reputed to be the busiest stretch of autostrada in all of Italy so traffic is always a possibility. Parking in or near the Città Alta, most of which is closed to traffic, can be difficult. There is a parking lot on the northern end of the Città Alta near Porta Garibaldi (1.50€ per hour) and street parking along Viale delle Mura, which loops around the flanks of the walls of the Città Alta.

VISITOR INFORMATION The **Città Bassa tourist office** (☎ **035-210-204;** www.turismo.provincia.bergamo.it) is right next to the train and bus stations at Viale Papa Giovanni XXIII 57; it's open daily 9am to 12:30pm and 2 to 5:30pm. The **Città Alta office** is at Via Gombito 13 (℃ **035-232-730**), right off Via Colleoni, and is open daily the same hours. If you are planning to travel farther afield and into the hills, ask either tourist office for the trail map of the Bergamo province.

CITY LAYOUT   Piazza Vecchia, the Colleoni Chapel, and most of the other sights that bring visitors to Bergamo are in the **Città Alta**—the exception is the Accademia Carrara, which is in the Città Bassa but on the flanks of the hillside, so within easy walking distance of the upper-town sights. **Via Colleoni** cuts a swath through the medieval heart of the Città Alta, beginning at **Piazza Vecchia.** To reach this lovely square from the funicular station at **Piazza Mercato delle Scarpi,** walk along **Via Gombito** for about 5 minutes. Most of the Città Alta is closed to traffic, but it's compact and easy to navigate on foot. Down below, the main square known as the **Sentierone** is the center of the **Città Bassa.** It's about a 5-minute walk from the train station north along **Viale Papa Giovanni XXIII.**

GETTING AROUND   Bergamo has an extensive **bus system** that runs through the Città Bassa and to points outside the walls of the Città Alta; tickets are 1€ and are available from newsstands and tobacco shops. With the exception of the trip from the train or bus stations up to the Città Alta, you probably won't have much need of public transit, as most of the sights are within an easy walk of one another.

To reach the Città Alta from the train station, take bus no. 1 or 1A and make the free transfer to the **Funicolare Bergamo Alta,** connecting the upper and lower cities and running every 7 minutes from 6:30am to 12:30am. You can make the walk to the funicular station in about 20 minutes (and see something of the new city en route) by following Viale Papa Giovanni XXIII and its continuations Viale Roma and Viale Vittorio Emanuele II.

If you're feeling hearty, a footpath next to the funicular winds up to Città Alta; the steep climb up (made easier by intermittent staircases) takes about 30 minutes. Bus no. 1A also continues up and around the Città Alta walls to end just outside Porta San Vigilio, and is more convenient to hotels San Lorenzo and Gourmet.

Exploring the Città Bassa

Most visitors scurry through Bergamo's lower, newer town on their way to the Città Alta, but you may want to pause long enough to enjoy a coffee along the **Sentierone,** the elongated piazza/street at the center of town. This spacious square graciously combines a mishmash of architectural styles (including 16th-c. porticos on one side, the Mussolini-era Palazzo di Giustizia and two imitation Doric temples on another). Locals sit in its gardens, lounge in its cafes, and attend classical concerts at the **Teatro Donizetti.** This 19th-century theater is the center of Bergamo's lively culture scene, with a fall opera season and a winter-to-spring season of dramatic performances; for details, check with the tourist office or call the theater at ℃ **035-416-0611** (http://teatro.gaetano-donizetti.com).

The main draw for most visitors down here, though, is the **Galleria dell'Accademia Carrara ★★**, Piazza Carrara 82a (℃ **035-270-413;** www. accademiacarrara.bergamo.it). The city's exquisite art gallery is one of the finest in northern Italy, founded in 1795 when Napoleon's troops were busy rounding up the art treasures of their newly occupied northern Italian states. Many of these works ended up in Bergamo under the stewardship of Count Giacomo Carrara. The collection came into its own after World War I, when a young Bernard Berenson, the 20th century's most noted art connoisseur, took stock of what was here and classified the immense holdings, making sure "every Lotto [was] a Lotto." Lorenzo Lotto (1480–1556) was a Venetian who fled the stupefying society of his native city and spent 1513 to 1525 in Bergamo perfecting his highly emotive portraits. His works take their place in the salons of this neoclassical palace alongside a staggering inventory with paintings by Bellini, Canaletto, Carpaccio, Guardi, Mantegna, and Tiepolo. Most of these masterworks are in the 17 third-floor galleries.

It's easy to become overwhelmed here, but among the paintings you may want to view first is Lotto's **Portrait of Lucina Brembrati,** in which you'll see the immense sensitivity with which the artist was able to imbue his subjects. Look carefully at the moon in the upper-left corner—it has the letters ci painted into it, a playful anagram of the sitter's first name; in Italian, *moon* is *luna,* and this one has a ci in the middle. Botticelli's much-reproduced **Portrait of Giuliano de Medici** hangs nearby, as does Raphael's sensual **St. Sebastian.** You can visit the Accademia on foot from the Città Alta by following Via Porta Dipinta halfway down the hill to the Porto Sant'Agostino and then a terraced, ramplike staircase to the doors of the museum. From the Città Bassa, the museum is about a 10-minute walk from the Sentierone—from the east end of the square, take a left on Largo Belotti, then a right on Via Giuseppe Verdi; follow that for several blocks to Via Pignolo where you turn left and then take the first right, Via Tomaso, which takes you to Piazza Carrara (the route is well signposted). Admission is 5€, 3€ for those 11 and under or 60 and over. It's open June to September Tuesday to Sunday 10am to 9pm, Saturday until 11pm. From October to May the museum is open Tuesday to Friday 9:30am to 5:30pm and Saturday and Sunday 10am to 6pm. **Note:** The museum is closed for restoration until mid-2012, though many of the works are visible at the Palazzo della Ragione (see below) in the Città Alta in the meantime.

Across the street is the **Galleria d'Arte Moderna e Contemporanea** (✆ **035-270-272;** www.gamec.it), containing works by such 20th-century masters as Boccioni, De Chirico, Morandi, and Kandinsky. Admission is free, and it's open Tuesday to Sunday 10am to 1pm and 3 to 7pm.

Exploring the Città Alta

The higher, older part of Bergamo owes its stone *palazzi,* proud monuments, and what remains of its extensive fortified walls to more than 3 centuries of Venetian rule, beginning in 1428, when soldiers of the Republic wrestled control of the city out of the hands of the Milan-based Visconti. The Venetians left their mark elegantly in the town's theatrically adjoining squares, **Piazza Vecchia** and **Piazza del Duomo,** which together create what French writer Stendhal went so far as to call the "most beautiful place on earth."

On Piazza Vecchia, you'll see traces of the Venetian presence in the 12th-century **Palazzo della Ragione (Courts of Justice),** which has been embellished with a graceful ground-floor arcade and the Lion of Saint Mark, symbol of the Venetian Republic, above a 16th-century balcony reached by a covered staircase (the bells atop its adjoining tower, the **Torre Civico,** sound the hours). The recently restored halls often host traveling art exhibits. Venice's Sansovino Library provided the inspiration for the **Biblioteca Civica (Public Library)** across the square. Piazza del Duomo, reached through one of the archways of the Palazzo

The dome of Bergamo's Duomo.

della Ragione, is filled with an overpowering collection of religious structures that include the **Duomo** and the much more enticing **Cappella Colleoni** (see below), the **Baptistery,** and the **Basilica di Santa Maria Maggiore** (see below).

Bergamasco strongman Colleoni (see the Cappella Colleoni entry, below) lent his name to the upper town's delightful main street, cobblestoned and so narrow you can just about touch the buildings on either side when standing in the center. If you follow it to its far northwestern end, you'll emerge into **Largo Colle Aperto,** refreshingly green and open to the Città Bassa.

For better views and a short excursion into the countryside, board the **Funicolare San Vigilio** for the ascent up the San Vigilio hill; the funicular runs daily every 12 minutes or so between 7am and midnight and costs 1€. The strategic importance of these heights was not lost on Bergamo's medieval residents, who erected a summit-top **Castello** (© **035-236-284**), now mostly in ruin. Its keep, still surrounded by the old walls, is a park in which every bench affords a far-reaching view. It's open daily April to September 9am to 8pm, October and March 10am to 6pm, and November to February 10am to 4pm. When you head back down to the Città Alta, either by foot or with the funicular, instead of following Via Colleoni back into the center of the town, you can turn onto Viale delle Mura and follow the 16th-century bastions for about .8km (½ mile) to the Porta Sant'Agostino on the other side of the town.

Basilica di Santa Maria Maggiore ★ Behind the plain marble facade and a portico whose columns rise out of the backs of lions lies an overly baroque gilt-covered interior hung with Renaissance tapestries. **Gaetano Donizetti,** the wildly popular composer of frothy operas, who was born in Bergamo in 1797 (see Museo Donizettiano, below) and returned here to die in 1848, is entombed in a **marble sarcophagus** that's as excessive as the rest of the church's decor. The finest works are the **choir stalls,** with rich wood inlays depicting landscapes and biblical scenes; they're the creation of Lorenzo Lotto. The stalls are usually kept under cloth to protect the sensitive hardwoods from light and pollutants, but they're unveiled for Lent. The octagonal **Baptistery** in the piazza outside the church was originally inside but removed, reconstructed, and much embellished in the 19th century.

Piazza del Duomo. © **035-223-327.** Free admission. May–Sept Mon–Sat 9am–12:30pm and 2:30–6pm, Sun 9am–1pm and 3–6pm (Oct–Apr closed at 5pm).

Cappella Colleoni ★★★ Barto-lomeo Colleoni was a Bergamasco *condottiere* (captain) who fought for Venice to maintain the Venetian stronghold on the city. In return for his labors, the much-honored soldier was given Bergamo to rule for the republic. If you've already visited Venice, you may have seen Signore Colleoni astride the Verrocchio equestrian bronze in Campo Santi Giovanni e Paolo. He rests for eternity here in Bergamo in this elaborate funerary chapel designed

Relief sculptures on the Cappella Colleoni.

by Amadeo, the great sculptor from nearby Pavia (where he completed his most famous work, the Certosa; see p. 322). The pink-and-white marble exterior, laced with finely sculpted columns and loggias, is airy and almost whimsical; inside, the soldier and his favorite daughter, Medea, lie beneath a ceiling frescoed by Tiepolo and are surrounded by reliefs and statuary. As in Venice, Colleoni appears on horseback atop his marble tomb.

Piazza del Duomo. ✆ **035-210-061.** Free admission. Apr–Oct daily 9:30am–12:30pm and 2–6pm; Nov–Mar Tues–Sun 9:30am–12:30pm and 2–4:30pm.

Museo Donizettiano This charming little museum commemorates Gaetano Donizetti, who was born in Bergamo in 1797 and became one of Italy's most acclaimed composers of opera. Fans can swoon over his sheet music, piano, and other memorabilia and see the deathbed where he succumbed to syphilis in 1848. Thus inspired, you can make the pilgrimage to the humble house where he claimed to have been born in a cellar, the **Casa Natale di Gaetano Donizetti,** Via B. Canale 14 (✆**035-399-432**), a rural street that descends the hillside from the Porta Sant'Alessandro on the northwestern edge of the city. It's open Saturday and Sunday only 11am to 6:30pm (donations requested).

Via Arena 9. ✆ **035-247-116.** www.bergamoestoria.it/museo_donizettiano.aspx. Admission 3€. June–Sept daily 9:30am–1pm and 2–5:30pm; Oct–May Tues–Sun 9:30am–1pm, Sat–Sun 2–5:30pm. Bus: 1 or 1A.

Where to Stay

The charms of staying in the Città Alta are no secret. Rooms tend to fill up quickly, especially in summer and on weekends. Reserve well in advance.

Agnello d'Oro ★★ 🍴 In keeping with its location a few steps from Piazza Vecchia, the Agnello d'Oro looks like it's right out of an old tourist brochure extolling the quaint charms of Italy. The tall, narrow, ocher-colored building, with flower boxes at its tall windows, overlooks a small piazzetta where a fountain splashes next to potted greenery. The wood-paneled lounge and intimate dining room add to the charm quotient, which declines somewhat as you ascend in a tiny elevator to the rooms. These lean more toward serviceable comfort than to luxury, but warm color schemes and old prints compensate for the lack of space and amenities; the bathrooms are roomy and have been modernized. Front rooms have balconies overlooking the piazza. This is the most popular spot in the Città Alta (even though the friendliness level of the staff can vary wildly), so reserve early.

Via Gombito 22, 24129 Bergamo Alta. www.agnellodoro.it. ✆ **035-249-883.** Fax 035-235-612. 20 units. 93€ double. Continental breakfast 6€. AE, DC, MC, V. **Amenities:** Concierge, free Wi-Fi. *In room:* TV, hair dryer.

Il Gourmet ★ This pleasant hotel offers the best of both worlds—it's only steps away from the Città Alta (a few hundred feet outside the Porta Sant'Agostino on the road leading up to the Castello) but on a rural hillside, giving it the air of a country retreat. The villa-style building is set behind walls in a lush garden and enjoys wonderful views. A wide terrace on two sides makes the most of these views. Many of the very large, bright rooms look across the hillside to the heavily developed valley. They have plain, wood-paneled furniture, a fashion geared more to solid comfort than to style, and king-size beds. They also rent a large two-floor suite with a sitting area and kitchen downstairs. There's a very good restaurant on the premises—hence the name—with indoor and outdoor tables and midrange prices on Bergamasco and Lombard cuisine.

Via San Vigilio 1, 24129 Bergamo. www.gourmet-bg.it. ✆/fax **035-437-3004.** 11 units. 100€– 130€ double; 110€–150€ triple; 180€–230€ apt. with 2 double rooms. Continental breakfast 10€. AE, DC, MC, V. Closed Dec 27–Jan 7. **Amenities:** International/Bergamasco restaurant; bar; room service. *In room:* A/C, TV, hair dryer, minibar.

Where to Eat

Your gambols through the Città Alta can be nicely interspersed with fortifying stops at the city's many pastry shops and stand-up eateries. **Forno Tresoldi,** Via Colleoni 13, sells yummy pizzas and focaccia by the slice topped with cheese, salami, and vegetables (from 2€). It's open Tuesday to Sunday from 8am to 1:30pm and 4 to 10pm.

Al Donizetti ★ WINE BAR This charming restaurant faces the upper city's old covered market, whose sole purpose these days is to look medieval and romantic. In good weather, tables are set out under the market's arcaded loggia, and meals are also served in the two small vaulted-ceiling dining rooms. The bulk of the menu is devoted to various kinds of salami, ham, and cheeses, though many dishes also rely on fresh vegetables—perhaps a light zucchini flan or *radicchio con gorgonzola* (the bitter chicory is lightly grilled and the creamy cheese added at the last minute). There are also the tried-and-true battle horses of northern Italian cuisine, such as polenta with braised pork. More than 700 wines are available, including dozens by the glass, and the staff will help you choose the right one.

Via Gombito 17A. ✆ **035-242-661.** www.donizetti.it. Reservations not necessary. Panini from 4€; salads and platters of cheese and/or meats 12€–17€. MC, V. Daily 11am–1am.

Antica Hosteria del Vino Buono ★★ NORTHERN ITALIAN The new ownership of this restaurant (formerly a wine bar) near the top of the funicular takes its food and wine seriously. It's a pleasure to dine in the handsome surroundings of brick, refinished in 2006 to give an older feel. For an introduction to food from the region, try one of the several tasting menus. Polenta figures prominently, including with wild mushrooms. Polenta *taragna* uses buckwheat and cornmeal as its base and here they fill it with Taleggio cheese. The main courses lean toward meat. A dish like roast quail or rabbit should be accompanied by a Valcalepio Rosso, a medium-strength red from local vineyards. The house wine, a local cabernet, is more economical, perhaps a little young but perfectly drinkable.

Piazza Mercato Delle Scarpe 25. ☏ **035-247-993.** Reservations recommended. Primi 8€; secondi 11€; *menù turistico* 23€, wine included. AE, DC, MC, V. Tues–Sun noon–2:30pm and 7–10:30pm (Tues closed for lunch).

Taverna del Colleoni & Dell'Angelo ★ NORTHERN ITALIAN Pierangelo Cornaro and chef Odorico Pinato run one of Bergamo's top restaurants, and possibly its priciest. It's right on the main square in a Renaissance *palazzo*—in summer the best tables are outside on the piazza; otherwise, you're in a refined medieval-looking space of high vaulted ceilings. The ingredients used here are fresh and the recipes inspired by local tradition, but the menu is a more creative *cucina nuova* (nouvelle portions, nouvelle prices). The best part of the menu is the back page, where they list some of their more typical dishes, such as *cannoli di farro al ragù di cinghiale, salsa di zucca e patate* (pasta tubes made of spelt flour stuffed with wild boar and served under a pumpkin-potato sauce).

Piazza Vecchia 7. ☏ **035-232-596.** Reservations recommended. Primi 16€–21€; secondi 27€–32€; "gourmand" menu 63€, excluding wine. AE, DC, MC, V. Tues–Sun noon–2:30pm and 7:30–10:30pm.

Cafes

Caffè del Tasso ★, Piazza Vecchia 3, is a prime piece of real estate on the main square of the Città Alta. It began life as a tailor's shop 500 years ago, but it's been a cafe and bar since 1581. Legend has it that Garibaldi's Red Shirts used to gather here (Bergamo was a stronghold of Italian independence, which explains why an edict from the 1850s on the wall of this cafe prohibits rebellion).

While the location of **Caffè della Funicolare** in the Piazza Mercato delle Scarpe, in the upper terminal of the funicular that climbs the hill from the Città Bassa to the Città Alta, doesn't suggest a memorable dining experience, the station dates from 1887 and has enough Belle Époque flourishes and curlicues to make the surroundings interesting. Plus, the dining room and terrace look straight down the hill to the town and valley, providing some of the best tables with a view (accompanied by low-cost fare) in the upper town. Stop in for a coffee, 1 of the 50 kinds of beer on tap, a sandwich, or a salad.

MANTUA (MANTOVA)

158km (98 miles) E of Milan, 62km (38 miles) N of Parma, 150km (93 miles) SW of Venice

One of Lombardy's finest cities is in the farthest reaches of the region, making it a logical addition to a trip to Venice or Parma as well as to Milan. Like its neighboring cities in Emilia-Romagna, Mantua owes its past greatness and its beautiful Renaissance monuments to one family, in this case the Gonzagas, who rose from peasant origins to conquer the city in 1328 and ruled benevolently until 1707. The Gonzagas were avid collectors of art and ruled through the greatest centuries of Italian art, and you'll encounter the treasures they collected in the massive Palazzo Ducale that dominates much of the town center; in their refreshing suburban retreat, the Palazzo Te; and in the churches and *piazze* that grew up around their court.

One of Mantua's greatest charms is its location—on a meandering river, the Mincio, which widens here to envelop the city in a necklace of romantic lakes. Often shrouded in mist and surrounded by flat plains, Mantua, which has been recognized as a UNESCO World Heritage Site since 2008 for its excellence as an example of Renaissance town planning, can seem almost melancholy. But the Palazzo Ducale, the Galleria Museo Palazzo Valenti Gonzaga, and other monuments have been restored since the 1930s, and what will probably strike you more is what a remarkable gem of a city Mantua is.

Festivals & Markets Mantua fights the post-summer blues with a **literature festival** the second weekend of September.

Year-round, Piazza delle Erbe is the scene of a bustling **food market** Monday through Saturday from 8am to 1pm. On Thursday mornings, a **bigger market,** filled with clothing, housewares, and more food, spills through Piazza Magenta and adjoining streets.

Essentials

GETTING THERE **By Train** Ten trains daily arrive from Milan (2 hr.). There are hourly runs from Verona, with connections to Venice (30–40 min.).

By Car The speediest connections from Milan are via the *autostrade,* the A4 to Verona, and the A22 from Verona to Mantua (the trip takes about 2 hr.). From Mantua, it's an easy drive south to Parma on the SS420, or you can reach Modena on the A22 and then connect to the A1 to Bologna.

VISITOR INFORMATION The **tourist office** is at Piazza Mantegna 6 (© **0376-432-432;** www.turismo.mantova.it), open daily from 9am to 5pm (Apr–Sept to 6pm).

CITY LAYOUT Mantua is tucked onto a point of land surrounded on three sides by the **Mincio River,** which widens here into a series of lakes, named prosaically **Lago Superiore, Lago di Mezzo,** and **Lago Inferiore.** Most of the sights are within an easy walk of one another within the compact center, which is only a 10-minute walk from the lakeside train station. Follow **Via Solferino e San Martino** to **Via Marangoni,** turn right, and follow that to **Piazza Cavallotti,** where a left turn on **Corso Umberto I** will bring you to **Piazza delle Erbe,** the first of the gracious *piazze* that flow through the city center to the palace of the Gonzagas. You can also make the trip on the no. 2 bus, which leaves from the front of the station.

Exploring the City

As you wander around, you'll notice that Mantua's squares are handsomely proportioned spaces surrounded by medieval and Renaissance churches and *palazzi.* The *piazze* open one into another, creating the wonderful illusion that walkers in the city are strolling through a series of opera sets.

The southernmost of these squares, and the place to begin your explorations, is **Piazza delle Erbe (Square of the Herbs)** ★, so named for the produce-and-food market that has been held here for centuries (see "Festivals & Markets," above). Mantua's civic might is clustered here in a series of late-medieval and early Renaissance structures that include the **Palazzo della Ragione (Courts of Justice)** and **Palazzo del Podestà (Mayor's Palace)** from the 12th and 13th centuries, and the **Torre dell'Orologio,** topped with a 14th-century astrological clock. Also on this square is Mantua's earliest religious structure, the **Rotunda di San Lorenzo** ★, a miniature round church from the 11th century (summer daily 10am–noon and 2:30–4:30pm, winter daily 11am–noon, though hours may vary; free admission). The city's Renaissance masterpiece, **Basilica di Sant'Andrea** (see below), is off to one side on Piazza Mantegna.

In the adjoining **Piazza Broletto** (just north as you work your way through the Old City), the statue of Virgil commemorates the poet who was born near here in 70 B.C. and celebrated Mantua's river Mincio in his *Bucolics*. The next square, **Piazza Sordello,** is huge, rectangular, and lined with well-restored medieval *palazzi*. Most notable, though, is the massive hulk of the **Palazzo Ducale** (see below) that forms one wall of the piazza. To enjoy Mantua's soulful lakeside vistas, follow Via Accademia through Piazza Arche and the Lungolago Gonzaga.

The Rotunda di San Lorenzo dates to the 11th century.

Basilica di Sant'Andrea ★ A graceful Renaissance facade fronts this 15th-century church by Leon Battista Alberti, with an 18th-century dome by Juvarra. The simple arches seem to float beneath the classic pediment, and the unadorned elegance forms a sharp contrast to other Lombardy monuments, such as the Duomo in Milan, the Cappella Colleoni in Bergamo, and the Certosa in Pavia. Inside, the classically proportioned vast space is centered on a single aisle. The Gonzaga court painter Mantegna is buried in the first chapel on the left. The crypt houses a reliquary containing the blood of Christ (allegedly brought here by Longinus, the Roman soldier who thrust his spear into Jesus' side), which is carried through town on March 18, the feast of Mantua's patron, Sant'Anselmo.

Piazza Mantegna. Free admission. Daily 7:30am–noon and 3–7pm.

Galleria Museo Palazzo Valenti Gonzaga After a restoration that lasted 2 decades, this 16th-century palace, which is still inhabited today, reopened its doors to visitors in 2008. The palace retains much of its former splendor, and visitors can wander through the public spaces, which are the *piano nobile* and the rooftop garden (the other floors are inhabited). This palace offers insight into how Mantuan noble families lived throughout the centuries; it is also home to a wonderfully restored cycle of 17th-century frescoes by Frans Geffels, which will appeal to fans of Flemish painting and subjects.

Via Pietro Frattini 7. ✆ **0376-364-524** or 348-441-9954. www.valentigonzaga.com. Admission 8€ adults; 6€ seniors 65 and over; free for children 12 and under. Sat–Sun only with hourly guided tours 10 to noon and 3–6pm; Mon–Fri only with a previous reservation. Reservations and tickets at Piazza Mantegna 9/a right off Piazza Broletto.

Palazzo d'Arco Mantua's aristocratic D'Arco family lived in this elegant Renaissance *palazzo* until 1973, when the last member of the family donated it to the city. Though most of the extant *palazzo* is neoclassical (1780s), the gardens shelter a wing from the 15th century; the highlight of the rooms is the Sala dello Zodiaco, brilliantly frescoed with astrological signs by Giovanni Falconetto in 1520.

Piazza d'Arco 4. ✆ **0376-322-242.** Admission 5€. Tues–Fri 10am–1pm and 2:30–5:30pm, Sat–Sun 9:30am–1pm and 2:30–6pm.

Palazzo Ducale ★★ Behind the walls of this massive fortress/palace lies the history of the Gonzagas, Mantua's most powerful family, and what remains of the treasure trove they amassed in a rule that began in 1328 and lasted into the early

18th century. Between their skills as warriors and their penchant for marrying into wealthier and more cultured houses, they managed to acquire power, money, and the services of some of the top artists of the time including Pisanello, Titian, and, most notably, Andrea Mantegna, their court painter, who spent most of his career working for his Mantua patrons.

The most fortunate of these unions was that of Francesco Gonzaga to Isabelle d'Este in 1490. This well-bred daughter of Ferrara's Este clan commissioned many of the art-filled frescoed apartments you see today, including the Camera degli Sposi in Isabella's apartments—the masterpiece, and only remaining fresco cycle, of Mantegna. It took the artist 9 years to complete the cycle, and in it, he included many of the visitors to the court; it's a fascinating account of late-15th-century court life. Mantegna's *trompe l'oeil* oculus in the center of the ceiling is an icon of Renaissance art and a masterpiece of foreshortening.

Most of Mantegna's works for the palace, though, have been carted off to other collections; his famous *Parnassus,* which he painted for an intimate room known as the *studiolo,* is now in the Louvre, as are works that Perugino and Correggio painted for the same room.

The Gonzagas expanded their palace by incorporating any structure that lay within reach, including the Duomo and the Castello di San Giorgio (1396–1406). As a result, it's now a small city of 500 rooms connected by a labyrinth of corridors, ramps, courtyards, and staircases, filled with Renaissance frescoes and ancient Roman sculptures. The frescoes in the Sala del Pisanello feature Arthurian legends (mostly Tristan and Isolde) painted by Pisanello between 1436 and 1444. They were discovered beneath layers of plaster only in 1969. The Sale degli Arazzi (Tapestry Rooms) are hung with copies—woven at the same time but by a different Flemish workshop—of the Vatican's tapestries designed by Raphael and his students.

The Palazzo Ducale from across Lago di Mezzo.

Other highlights include the Galleria degli Specchi (Hall of Mirrors); the low-ceiling Appartamento dei Nani (Apartments of the Dwarfs), where a replica of the Holy Staircase in the Vatican is built to miniature scale (in keeping with noble custom of the time, dwarfs were part of Isabella's court); and the Galleria dei Mesi (Hall of the Months). Some of the mostly delightful chambers in the vast complex make up the Appartamento Estivale (Summer Apartment), which looks over a courtyard where hanging gardens provide the greenery.

Piazza Sordello. ✆ **0376-382-150.** www.mantovaducale.beniculturali.it. Admission 6.50€, 3.25€ ages 18–25, free for those 17 and under. Tues–Sun 8:15am–7:15pm (last entrance at 6:20pm).

Palazzo Te ★ Federico Gonzaga, the pleasure-loving refined son of Isabella d'Este, built this splendid Mannerist palace as a retreat from court life. As you enter the courtyard, you'll see that the purpose of this palace was to amuse— the keystone of the monumental archway is designed to look like it's falling out of place. Throughout the whimsical interior, sexually frank frescoes by Giulio Romano (who left a scandal behind him in Rome over his licentious engravings) depict *Psyche* and other erotically charged subject matter and make unsubtle reference to one of Frederico's favorite pastimes (horses and astrology, Federico's other passions, also figure prominently). The greatest and most playful achievement here, though, has to do with power: In the **Sala dei Giganti (Room of the Giants) ★★**, Titan is overthrown by the gods in a dizzying play of architectural proportion that gives the illusion that the ceiling is falling. The Palazzo Te is the home of the Museo Civico, whose permanent collections on the upper floor include the Gonzaga family's coins, medallion, and other displays of its wealth and power, alongside more recently donated works of art.

The *palazzo* is a 20-minute walk from the center of town along Via Mazzini. En route, at Via Acerbi 47, sits **Casa di Mantegna,** the house and studio of Andrea Mantegna. Admission is free and it's open Tuesday to Sunday 10am to 12:30pm and 3 to 6pm (✆ **0376-360-506;** hours may vary).

Viale Te. ✆ **0376-323-266.** www.palazzote.it. Admission 8€ adults, 5€ seniors 60 and over, 2.50€ ages 12–18 and university students, and free for children 12 and under. Mon 1–6pm, Tues–Sun 9am–6pm.

Where to Stay

The tourist office can provide a complete list of what's available in the city and in farmhouses in the surrounding countryside, though they won't make the calls to reserve for you. Rates at the farmhouses tend to run about 35€ to 40€ per person. Because several of the properties are within a few kilometers of town, you can reach them without too much trouble by bike or combination bus ride and trek.

Broletto ★★ This atmospheric old hotel is in the center of the Old City, only a few steps from the lake, the *castello,* Piazza Sordello, and Piazza delle Erbe making it the perfect base to start a late-night stroll. The rooms have contemporary furnishings that are vaguely rustic in design, with orthopedic bed frames. Bright corner room no. 16 has balconies and windows on two sides. The most alluring features of the decor, though, are the massive beams on the ceilings and other architectural details from the *palazzo*'s 16th-century origins.

Via Accademia 1, 46100 Mantova. www.hotelbroletto.com. ✆ **0376-326-784.** Fax 0376-221-297. 16 units. 95€–130€ double. Rates include continental breakfast. AE, DC, MC, V. Closed Dec 23–28. **Amenities:** Babysitting; concierge. *In room:* A/C, TV, hair dryer, minibar, Wi-Fi.

EXPLORING THE TOWN

In addition to its attractive, albeit tourist-shop-ridden Old Town, Sirmione has many lakeside promenades, pleasant beaches, and even some open countryside where olive trees sway in the breeze. Anything you'll want to see can be reached easily on foot, though an open-air tram makes the short run out to the Roman ruins from the northern edge of the Old Town (but not btw. 12:30 and 2:30pm).

The moated and turreted **Castello Scaligero** (© **030-916-468**) marks the only landside entrance to the Old Town. Built in the 13th century by the della Scala family, who ruled Verona and many of the lands surrounding the lake, the castle warrants a visit mainly for the views from its towers. It's open Tuesday to Sunday 9am to 7pm. Admission is 4€.

From the castle, Via Vittorio Emanuele leads through the center of the town and emerges after a few blocks into the greener, garden-lined lanes that wind through the tip of the peninsula to the **Grotte di Catullo** (© **030-916-157**). Whether or not these extensive ruins at the northern tip of the peninsula were really, as they're alleged to have been, the villa and baths of the pleasure-loving Roman poet Catullus is open to debate. Even so, their presence here, on a hilltop fragrant with wild rosemary and pines, demonstrates that Sirmione has been a deservedly popular retreat for millennia, and you can wander through the evocative remains while enjoying wonderful lake views. March to October 14, the ruins are open Tuesday to Saturday 8:30am to 7pm and Sunday 9:30am to 6pm; admission is 4€ for adults, 2€ for those 18 to 25, and free for children 17 and under and seniors 65 and over.

If you want to enjoy the clean waters of the lake, the place to head is the small **Lido delle Bionde,** near the castle off Via Dante. In summer, the beach concession rents lounge chairs with umbrellas for 10€ per day, as well as kayaks and pedal boats for 8€ per hour.

WHERE TO STAY

Sirmione has many pleasant, moderately priced hotels, all of which book up quickly in July and August, when they also charge higher rates (reflected in the higher end of the rates below). You aren't allowed to drive into the Old Town until a guard at the entrance near the castle confirms that you have a hotel reservation. The tourist office will help you find a room in your price range on the day you arrive, but they won't book ahead of time.

Corte Regina ★ This attractive older hotel is housed in a stone building on a narrow side street leading to the lake and a beach. While it doesn't have the same lakeside views the Grifone enjoys (see below), the Corte Regina, with its pleasant accommodations and friendly ambience, is a valid alternative if that hotel is full. Outside there's

The crenellated walls of Castello Scaligero.

a sunny terrace. Upstairs the large tile-floored rooms have contemporary furnishings and bathrooms with box showers.

Via Antiche Mura 11, 25019 Sirmione (BS). www.corteregina.it. ℭ **030-916-147.** Fax 030-919-6470. 14 units. 80€–110€ double; 130€–160€ family suite for 4. Rates include breakfast. AE, DC, MC, V. Free parking nearby or 10€ in garage. Closed Jan–Mar. **Amenities:** Fish restaurant; bar; babysitting; room service; Internet. *In room:* A/C, TV, hair dryer, minibar.

Eden ★ The American poet Ezra Pound once lived in this pink-stucco lakeside hotel, located on a quiet side street leading to the lake in the center of town. Despite its long history as a lakeside retreat, the Eden has been modernized with taste and an eye to comfort. You can see the lake from most of the attractive rooms, which are decorated with contemporary furnishings. The mirrored walls enhance the light and lake views. The bathrooms are large and many have big tubs. The marble lobby opens to a delightful shaded terrace and a swimming pier that juts into the lake.

Piazza Carducci 17/18, 25019 Sirmione (BS). www.hoteledenonline.it. ℭ **030-916-481.** Fax 030-916-483. 33 units. 100€–160€ double; 140€–190€ double with balcony and lake view. Rates include breakfast. AE, DC, MC, V. Free parking nearby or 10€ in garage. Closed Nov–Easter. **Amenities:** Bar; babysitting; concierge; room service; tennis courts nearby. *In room:* A/C, TV, hair dryer, minibar.

Grifone ★★ ☕ One of Sirmione's best-value lodgings is also one of its most romantic—the vine-clad stone building next to the castle enjoys a prime piece of lake property. You can enjoy this setting from a shady patio off the lobby, from a small beach, or from any of the guest rooms with a view. Brother and sister Nicola and Christina Marcolini oversee the hotel and adjoining restaurant, carrying on several generations of a family business. The rooms are simple but pleasant, with tile floors and plain furnishings; top-floor rooms (nos. 36–42) have small balconies from which to survey the views. The tidy bathrooms have stall showers or curtainless tubs. The Grifone books up quickly, often with return guests, so reserve well in advance.

Via Bocchio 4, 25019 Sirmione (BS). ℭ **030-916-014.** Fax 030-916-548. 16 units. 70€–100€ double. MC, V. Free parking. Closed late Oct–Easter. **Amenities:** International restaurant; bar. *In room:* Hair dryer (on request).

Hotel Speranza This modest hotel occupies the upper floors of an old building that arches across Sirmione's main street, providing a prime location near the castle and only a few steps in either direction from the lake. The emphasis here is on clean efficiency rather than luxury: Public rooms consist of a tiny lobby and breakfast room, and the bare-bones rooms are perfectly serviceable. In fact, the modern furnishings set against parquet floors and stark white walls make for a fairly chic look. Bathrooms are modernized (save for the flat waffle towels on heated racks) and have box showers.

Via Castello 6, 25019 Sirmione (BS). http://hotelspateranza.sitonline.it. ℭ **030-916-116.** Fax 030-916-403. 13 units. 90€–105€ double. Rates include breakfast. AE, DC, MC, V. Free parking in square with permit, available from hotel. Closed mid-Nov to late Feb. **Amenities:** Concierge. *In room:* A/C, TV.

Olivi ★★ This pleasant modern hotel offers the chance to live the high life at rates that won't break the bank. It's not directly on the lake, which you can see from most rooms and the sunny terrace, but instead commands a hilltop position near the Roman ruins amid pines and olive groves. The rooms are stunningly decorated in varying schemes of bold, handsome pastels and earth tones. There are separate dressing areas off the bathrooms, and most have balconies. There's a pool in the garden and an artificial river streams past the terrace and windows of the lobby and breakfast room.

Via San Pietro 5, 25019 Sirmione (BS). www.hotelolivi.it. ✆ **030-990-5365.** Fax 030-916-472. 58 units. 145€–202€ standard double; 173€–228€ "quality" double with balcony and lake view. Rates include breakfast. AE, MC, V. Free parking on grounds. Closed Jan. **Amenities:** 3 restaurants; 2 bars; babysitting; concierge; pool; room service. *In room:* A/C, TV, hair dryer, minibar, Wi-Fi.

WHERE TO EAT

In addition to the choices below, you can get a quick pizza with a lake view from the terrace at **L'Arcimboldo,** Via Vittorio Emanuele 71 (✆ **030-916-409;** closed Tues).

Osteria Al Torcol ★★ ITALIAN Fresh food, well-priced wine, and good service come together in what is almost certain to be your best meal in the area. The menu changes with the seasons though thanks to its popularity you're likely always to find the counterintuitive yet delicious *tagliolini* (fresh egg noodles) with pistachios and shrimp. Unless you have something particular against noodles, eggs, pistachios or shrimp, this dish must be ordered by somebody in your group so everybody can have a taste. The fish, both from the lake and the Mediterranean, is always grilled just right and on nice days you can enjoy it out on the patio under the trees. You won't have the views available at so many of the other mediocre (at best) restaurants that populate the lake front, but you'll be glad you came all the same.

Via San Salvatore 30. ✆ **030-990-4605.** Reservations highly recommended. Primi 12€–15€; secondi 15€–25€. MC, V. May–Sept daily 12:30–3pm and 7:30–10:30pm; Oct–Jan open only Sat–Sun; Feb–Apr open only in evening.

Ristorante Pace ITALIAN For the total experience at this elegant and scrumptious restaurant you can arrive directly from the lake by boat. Once there, ask for, or better yet reserve, a table with a lake view from which you can see the sunset. The prices are a bit above the norm for Sirmione, but after your first spoon full of fish soup or the first bite of a perfectly grilled steak you will know the extra euros have been well spent. There is also seating in an inner area immersed in flowers and trees from where the adventurous can try the frog risotto.

Piazza Porto Valentino 5. ✆ **030-990-5877.** Reservations recommended. Primi 16€–24€; secondi 22€–26€. AE, MC, V. Daily 12:30–2:30pm and 7:30–10:30pm. In winter, closed 1 day a week, usually Mon.

Gardone Riviera

The little resort of Gardone Riviera, 47km (29 miles) south of Riva del Garda on the western shore of the lake, has two interesting attractions. Once Italy's most famous soldier/poet, Gabriele d'Annunzio is today remembered at **Il Vittoriale** (✆ **0365-296-511;** www.vittoriale.it), a hillside estate that is one of Lago di Garda's major sites, not for his lackluster verse, but more for his adventures and grand lifestyle. He bought the estate in 1921 and died here in 1936. The claustrophobic rooms of this ornately and bizarrely decorated villa are filled with bric-a-brac and artifacts from the poet's colorful life, including many mementos of his long affair with actress Eleonora Duse. Elsewhere on the grounds, which

The ochre Il Vittoriale.

cascade down the hillside in a series of luxuriant gardens, are the patrol boat D'Annunzio commanded in World War I, a museum containing his biplane and photos, and his pompous hilltop tomb.

Admission to the grounds only is 8€ for adults and 6€ for children ages 7 to 18 and seniors 65 and older; you pay 5€ adults, 3€ kids and seniors additional to tour the villa, which you can visit only via a 25-minute guided tour (in Italian; even if your Italian doesn't go much beyond pasta, pizza and gelato, it's worth taking the tour to look inside the villa). April to September the grounds are open daily 8:30am to 8pm, and the villa is open Tuesday to Sunday 9:30am to 7pm; October to March the grounds are open daily 9am to 5pm, the villa Tuesday to Sunday 9am to 1pm and 2 to 5pm. The villa also hosts a July-to-August season of concerts and plays; call ✆ **0365-20-072** (www.teatrodelvittoriale.it) for more information.

Just down the hill on Via Roma is the **Giardino Botanico Hruska** (✆ **0365-20-347**), a small but delightful bower planted a hundred years ago by the Swiss naturalist Arturo Hruska (a dentist whose clientele included European royalty). More than 2,000 species of exotic flora from around the world continue to thrive in the balmy microclimate around the lake here. Admission is 6€. March 15 to October 15, the garden is open daily from 9:30am to 6:30pm.

GETTING THERE   For ferry connections with Riva del Garda and Sirmione, see those sections elsewhere in this chapter. You can also bus here from Riva del Garda in 65 minutes. From Sirmione, you have to transfer at Desenzano del Garda for one of six daily runs (1 hr. total). Hourly buses also make the 1-hour trip to and from Brescia, and two buses a day make the 3-hour trip to and from Milan.

VISITOR INFORMATION   Gardone's **tourist office** is at Corso Repubblica 8 (✆ **0365-20-347**). Hours April to October daily 10am to 12:30pm and 3 to 6:30pm; November to March Monday to Wednesday and Friday 9am to 12:30pm and 3 to 6pm, and Thursday 9am to 12:30pm.

WHERE TO STAY & EAT

Grand Hotel Fasano ★★ Terraces and balconies overlook a palm- and willow-shaded garden right on the lake, where guests can take breakfast or dinner and swim off the small pier. The terraces above the gardens host the awning-shaded, fan-cooled restaurant and bar, which feature live piano music several times a week. Rooms at either end of the villa are larger, those in the long connecting wing smaller but with larger terraces. "Classic" rooms are fitted with simple, homey furnishings but are very comfy, featuring modern bathrooms and paintings of putti. "Superior" rooms are larger, with small, curtained-off terrace/sitting areas. Accommodations in the separate Villa Principe, set amid the trees at one end of the property, are slightly more exclusive, with larger rooms but similar furnishings.

25083 Gardone Riviera (BS). www.ghf.it. © **0365-290-220.** Fax 0365-290-221. 63 units in main hotel, 12 in Villa Principe. 110€–130€ standard double without lake view; 120€–145€ superior double without lake view; 130€–165€ standard double with lake view; 155€–205€ superior double with lake view; 185€–230€ deluxe double with lake view; 340€–435€ suite. Rates include breakfast. Half-board available for stays of at least 3 nights. MC, V. Free parking. **Amenities:** 4 restaurants; bar; babysitting; bikes; concierge; fitness center; nearby golf course; outdoor heated pool; room service; outdoor tennis courts; watersports equipment/rentals. *In room:* A/C, TV, hair dryer, minibar, Wi-Fi (in some rooms, otherwise cable Internet).

Villa Fiordaliso ★★ This gorgeous villa, built in 1903, is a mix of neoclassical and Liberty style, has hosted several famous guests, including poet Gabriele d'Annunzio, from 1921 to 1923, and Mussolini's mistress, Claretta Petacci, in 1944. The dictator visited his lover frequently at the villa, which has been a hotel since 1990. All rooms have lake views except the "Mimosa," which overlooks the garden from a small terrace. The "Gardenia" and the "Magnolia" below it have windows on three sides (lake view, garden view, and a view overlooking the road). The exquisite restaurant (closed Tues at lunch and Mon all day) has a Michelin star. In warm weather, meals are served on a broad terrace where the lake laps almost to the tables; in winter you dine in a series of rooms with inlaid wood floors and decorated ceilings.

Via Zanardelli 150, 25083 Gardone Riviera (BS). www.villafiordaliso.it. © **0365-20-158.** Fax 0365-290-011. 7 units. 350€–500€ double; 700€ Claretta suite. Rates include continental breakfast. AE, DC, MC, V. Free parking. Closed Nov–Feb. Children 12 and under are not allowed. **Amenities:** Michelin star restaurant; bar; concierge; room service; watersports equipment/rentals. *In room:* A/C, TV, hair dryer, minibar, Wi-Fi.

Riva Del Garda

The northernmost town on the lake is not just a resort, but a real, prosperous Italian town, with medieval towers, a nice smattering of Renaissance churches and *palazzi*, and narrow cobblestone streets where everyday business proceeds in its alluring way.

Festivals & Markets Riva del Garda becomes a cultural oasis in July, when the town hosts an **international festival of classical music.**

ESSENTIALS

GETTING THERE By Train See "Getting There," under Sirmione, p. 340, for connections to Desenzano del Garda, from which you must take a bus (see below).

By Bus Six buses a day link Riva del Garda and Desenzano del Garda on the southern end of the lake, about a 2-hour trip. You can also travel between Sirmione and Riva del Garda by bus, though except for a 4:30pm direct run, you must transfer at Peschiera (2 hr.). From Limone sul Garda, there are 11 trips daily (18 min.). Twenty-five daily buses connect Riva del Garda and Trent (1⅔ hr.). From Verona there are 16 a day (2 hr.), and from Brescia five daily (2 hr.).

By Boat Navigazione Laghi (see "Sirmione," p. 340, for more information) runs the boats. Fifteen ferries and four hydrofoils per day connect Riva del Garda with Limone sul Garda (35–45 min. by ferry, 30 min. by hydrofoil). Two ferries and four hydrofoils per day connect Riva del Garda with Gardone (2¾ hr. by ferry; 1 hr., 20 min. by hydrofoil), Sirmione (almost 4 hr. by ferry, 2¼ hr. by hydrofoil), and Desenzano del Garda (4¼ hr. by ferry, 2½ hr. by hydrofoil). Schedules vary with the season, with very limited service in the winter.

By Car The fastest link between Riva del Garda and points north and south is via the A22, which shoots up the east side of the lake (exit at Mori, 13km/8 miles east of Riva del Garda). A far more scenic drive is along the western shore, on the beautiful corniche between Riva del Garda and Salò that hugs cliffs and passes through mile after mile of tunnel. Depending on the route, by car Riva del Garda is about an hour from Verona and about 45 minutes from Sirmione.

VISITOR INFORMATION The **tourist office,** which supplies information on hotels, restaurants, and activities in the area, is near the lakefront at Largo Medaglie d'Oro 5 (☎ **0464-554-444;** www.visittrentino.it). Mid-April to mid-September, it's open daily 9am to 7pm; mid-September to mid-April, hours are daily 9am to 6pm, though they can vary.

EXPLORING THE TOWN

Riva del Garda's Old Town is pleasant enough, though the only historic attractions of note are the 13th-century **Torre d'Apponale** (a picturesque medieval tower on the main square, which is sometimes open for climbing) and, nearby, the moated lakeside castle, **La Rocca.** Part of the castle interior now houses an unassuming collection of local arts and crafts (☎ **0464-573-869**). It's open Tuesday to Sunday 10am to 12:30pm and 1:30 to 6pm; admission is 2€, free for children 12 and under and seniors 65 and over. The castle also occasionally hosts concerts and minor traveling exhibits.

The main attraction here is the **lake,** which Riva del Garda takes advantage of with a waterside promenade stretching for several miles past parks and pebbly beaches. The water is warm enough for swimming May to October, and air currents fanned by the mountains make Garda popular for windsurfing year-round.

WATER & LAND SPORTS A convenient point of embarkation for a lake outing is the beach next to the castle, where you can rent rowboats or pedal boats for about 8.50€ per hour (buy 2 hr., get a 3rd free); from March to October, the concession is open daily 8am to 8pm.

For a more adventurous outing, check out the **sailing** and **windsurfing** at **Sailing Du Lac,** Viale Rovereto 44 (☎ **0464-552-453;** www.sailingdulac.com), where you can rent windsurf equipment for 45€ per day, 39€ for a half-day, or 19€ for an hour. Multiday and weekly packages, as well as lessons, are also available.

Riva del Garda butts up against Lake Garda.

You can rent **bikes** from **Superbike Girelli,** Viale Damiano Chiesa 15 (☎ **0464-556-602**), for 12€ to 14€ per day for a mountain bike; or from **Cicli Pederzolli,** Viale dei Tigli 24 (☎ **0464-551-830**), which charges 9€ per day for a city bike and 14€ for a mountain bike.

WHERE TO STAY

Hotel Sole ★★ Despite the very reasonable prices, this is one of the finest places in town to lodge and offers a wonderful location right on the lake at the main square. The lobby is filled with rare Persian carpets and abstract art. The rooms, reached via a sweeping circular staircase, are warm and luxurious with tasteful furnishings and marble-trimmed bathrooms. The best rooms have balconies facing the lake. Lakeview rooms are outfitted in antique style while those overlooking the square and town are modern. The rooftop solarium and sauna are perfect for relaxing after a hard day on the lake.

Piazza III Novembre 35, 38066 Riva del Garda (TN). www.hotelsole.net. ☎ **0464-552-686.** Fax 0464-552-811. 81 units. 78€–150€ double without lake view; 102€–176€ double with lake view. Add 15€ per person for half-board and 25€ for full board. AE, DC, MC, V. Parking on street 5€, in garage 10€. Closed Nov to 2 weeks before Easter (except at Christmastime and during frequent trade fairs). **Amenities:** International restaurant; bar; free bikes; concierge; small exercise room; room service; sauna. *In room:* A/C (in some rooms), TV, hair dryer, minibar, Wi-Fi.

Montanara It ain't fancy, but it's real cheap. The Montanara is squirreled away above its cheap trattoria in a quiet part of the Old Town. The wood-floor, midsize rooms occupy three stories of an old *palazzo* and are exceedingly basic—not to mention a bit down at the heels—but are kept immaculate, with a picture or two framed on the whitewashed walls for relief from the spartan environs. Rooms with shared bathrooms at least have a sink. The two top-floor accommodations are the best for their general brightness and high ceilings.

Via Montanara 18–20, 38066 Riva del Garda (BS). ☎/fax **0464-554-857.** 9 units, 6 with private bathroom. 48€ double with shared bathroom; 50€ double with private bathroom; 74€ triple with private bathroom. Rates include breakfast. MC, V. Parking on street 5€, in garage 10€. Closed Nov–Easter. **Amenities:** Restaurant; bar. *In room:* No phone.

WHERE TO EAT

Birreria Spaten ITALIAN This noisy indoor beer garden occupies the ground floor of an old *palazzo* and features a wide-ranging mix of food from the surrounding regions (Trentino, Lombardy, or from the other side of the Alps). Many of the German and Austrian visitors who favor Riva del Garda opt for the schnitzel-sauerkraut-sauerbraten fare, but you can also enjoy decent pasta dishes, a pizza, or a simply grilled lake trout. If you can't decide, the *Piatto Spaten* is an ample 16€ sampler of their Tyrolean specialties, including wurstel, *canederli* (a

Limone sul Garda's chief export.

giant bread dumpling), a ham steak, and sauerkraut. The restaurant will reopen in April 2012 following a complete internal renovation and though the cuisine will remain the same, expect prices to be a bit higher as the owners seek to earn back some of their investment.

Via Maffei 7. ℂ **0464-553-670.** Primi and pizza 6€–10€; secondi 7.50€–16€. MC, V. Thurs–Tues noon–2:30pm and 6–11pm. Closed Nov–Mar.

Limone sul Garda

Limone sul Garda is a pretty resort wedged between the lake and mountains just 10km (6¼ miles) south of Riva del Garda. For ferry connections with Riva del Garda and Sirmione, see their earlier sections. Despite the onslaught of tourists who come down through the mountains from Austria and Germany, it's a pleasant place to spend some time and offers more moderately priced lakeside hotels than those found in Riva del Garda. Romans planted lemon groves here (hence the name) and lemon trees continue to thrive on every available parcel of land.

There's an **IAT tourist info office** at Via IV Novembre 29 (ℂ **0365-918-987**). From April to September, it's open daily 8am to 10pm; October to March, hours are daily 8am to 8pm (Dec–Jan closed on the weekends). Also try the private website **www.limone.com**. *Note:* You'll find that most of the resorts in Limone, including Le Palme listed below, require a 3-night minimum stay, especially in high season.

WHERE TO STAY

Le Palme ★★ This gracious hotel is one of the most pleasant places to stay on Garda. It's on the lake at one end of Limone sul Garda's narrow main street and surrounded by *palme* (palm trees). Downstairs, a bar and reasonably priced restaurant flow onto a flowery terrace right on the lake. Upstairs, the large, pleasant rooms are furnished in Venetian-style antiques (some genuine, others reproduction), and all but a few face the lake; the three best have small balconies over the water (if your room doesn't have a balcony,

Two-Wheeling Limone

Rent a mountain bike in Limone sul Garda at **Tombola Rent**, Via L. Einaudi 1B (ℂ **0365-954-051**; www.tombolarent.it). Rates are 11€ for 5 hours, 17€ for a full day (9am–7pm). They also rent scooters (for two people) starting at 27€ for 3 hours, 37€ for 5 hours, and 50€ for a full day.

you can enjoy the lake from the downstairs terrace or rooftop solarium). A small beach is just a few steps down the road, and the hotel has a small pool amid lemon-shaded terraces. There's also a larger pool available at its sibling hotel, the hillside Splendid Palace, where they'll be happy to reserve a room for you if Le Palme is full.

Via Porto 36, 25010 Limone sul Garda (BS). www.sunhotels.it. *✆* **0365-954-681** or 0365-954-612. Fax 0365-954-681. 28 units. 80€–152€ double. Rates include breakfast. Add 16€ per person for half-board. MC, V. Free private parking. Closed Nov–Easter. **Amenities:** International/Italian restaurant; bar; children's games; concierge; pool; room service; tennis courts nearby. *In room:* A/C, TV, hair dryer, Wi-Fi.

WHERE TO EAT

Ristorante Gemma ITALIAN In a town where many restaurants cater to tourists with bland fish and chips and bratwurst, Gemma remains an authentic, family-style trattoria. It also enjoys a pretty lakeside location, and the waves lap right up against the dining terrace. This is the best place in town for grilled lake trout, which can be accompanied by handmade spaghetti with seafood.

Piazza Garibaldi 12. *✆* **0365-954-014.** www.ristorantegemma.it. Primi 7€–10€; secondi 9€–20€. MC, V. Thurs–Tues 11:30am–2:30pm and 6:30–10:30pm. Closed mid-Oct to Mar.

LAKE COMO (LAGO DI COMO)

Como (town): 65km (40 miles) NE of Milan; Menaggio: 35km (22 miles) NE of Como and 85km (53 miles) N of Milan; Varenna: 50km (31 miles) NE of Como and 80km (50 miles) NE of Milan

The first sight of the dramatic expanse of azure-hued **Lake Como ★★★**, ringed by gardens and forests and backed by the snowcapped Alps, is likely to evoke strong emotions. Romance, soulfulness, even gentle melancholy—these are the stirrings that over the centuries the lake has inspired in poets (Lord Byron), novelists (Stendhal), composers (Verdi and Rossini), and plenty of other visitors, too—be they deposed queens, such as Caroline of Brunswick, whom George IV of England exiled here for her adulterous ways, well-heeled modern travelers who glide up and down these waters in the ubiquitous lake steamers, or, these days, the rich and über-famous (George Clooney owns a villa here).

Less than an hour from Milan by train or car, Como's verdant shores provide a wonderful respite from modern life. Tellingly, Lake Como served as a backdrop for the romantic scenes in *Star Wars II: Attack of the Clones*—one of the very few settings in the film that was *not* created entirely by computer programs. It seems even George Lucas realized Como is better than any digital creation he can come up with.

Como

The largest and southernmost town on the lake isn't likely to charm you immediately, but the historic center is lovely if you take the time to stroll it and pop into its little churches. Long a center of silk making, Como still bustles today with commerce and industry. You'll probably want to stay in one of the more peaceful settings farther up the lake, but Como amply rewards a day's visit with some fine Renaissance churches and palaces, a nice lakefront promenade, and the chance to take a funicular for a bird's eye view of the lake.

Lake Como

SWITZERLAND

Domaso
Gravedona
Dongo
Piona
Colico
Delebio
SS38
Adda R.
Musso
Pianello
Dervio
Lake Como
Bellano
Menaggio
Varenna
Cadenabbia
Tremezzo
Bellagio
Lenno
SS340
Lierna
Lezzeno
Limonta
Argegno
Lake Lecco
Brienno
SS583
Nesso
Mandello
Laglio
Careno
SS36
Urio
Pognara Lario
Onno
Moltrasio
Cernobbio
Torno
Lecco
Tavernola
Blevio
Malgrate
L. Garlate
Como
Erba
SS639
A9
L. Annone
SS35
SS342
L. Alserio
L. Pusiano
SP72

Lake Lugano

SWITZ.

0 ___ 5 mi
0 ___ 5 km

Milan
0 ___ 100 mi
0 ___ 100 km
Rome

ESSENTIALS

GETTING THERE By Train One to three trains hourly connect Milan and Como's Stazione San Giovanni on Piazzale San Gottardo (regional from Milan's Piazza Garibaldi station, 55–60 min.; high-speed from Milan's Stazione Centrale station, 40 min.). There are also twice-hourly trains from Milan's Cadorna station to the more convenient Como Lago station right on the shorefront at Piazza Giacomo Matteotti. These trains take an hour.

VISITOR INFORMATION The **regional tourist office** dispenses a wealth of information on hotels, restaurants, and campgrounds around the lake from its offices at Piazza Cavour 17 (© **031-269-712;** www.lakecomo.org). It's open daily 9am to 1pm and 2 to 5pm. There is also a **city tourist office** in a little trailer along Via Maestri Comacini around the right side of the

Lake Como as seen from Villa Carlotta.

cathedral (☎ **031-264-215**). It's open Tuesday to Friday 10am to 12:30pm and 2:30 to 6pm, Saturday and Sunday 10am to 1pm and 2 to 6pm.

EXPLORING COMO

Part Gothic and part Renaissance, the **Piazza del Duomo,** in the center of town just off the lake, is festooned with exuberant masonry and sculpture. The main entrance is flanked by statues of Como natives Pliny the Elder and Pliny the Younger (the former wrote a 37-volume encyclopedia in the 1st century A.D. and the latter produced, among other things, a famous account of the eruption of Vesuvius that buried Pompei in A.D. 79). Inside, beneath an 18th-century dome by Juvarra—the architect who designed much of Turin—is a lavish interior hung with mostly 16th-century paintings and tapestries, with lots of helpful leaflets in English to explain the major works of art. It's open daily 7:30am to noon and 3 to 7pm. The black-and-white-striped 13th-century **Broletto (Town Hall)** abuts the Duomo's left flank, and adjoining it is the **Torre del Comune.** As a study in contrasts, the starkly modernist and aptly named **Casa del Fascio,** built in 1936 as the seat of the region's Fascist government, rises just behind the Duomo.

Como's main street, **Corso Vittorio Emanuele II,** cuts through the medieval quarter, where wood-beamed houses line narrow streets. Just 2 blocks south of the Duomo, the five-sided, 12th-century **San Fedele** stands above a charming square of the same name; parts of the church, including the altar, date from the 6th century. It's open daily 8am to noon and 3:30 to 7pm. To see Como's most alluring church, though, it's necessary to venture into the dull outlying neighborhood southwest of the center, where, just off Viale Roosevelt, you'll come to the five-aisle heavily frescoed **Basilica di Sant'Abbondio,** a Romanesque masterpiece from the 11th century with great 14th-century frescoes (bring coins; you'll need to pay .50€ to illuminate them). It's open daily 8am to 6pm.

With Northern Italy offering so much, you are likely to wish you had another day, week, or even month to do everything you have set your sights on. With that in mind, here is a suggestion for **the perfect day trip to Lake Como from Milan.** Get an early train to Como and spend a few hours taking in the city, including a lakeshore walk to Villa Olmo and perhaps a trip up to Brunate on the funicular, especially if it is a clear day. Then grab a ferry (only take the hydrofoil, in which you will be forced to be inside for the whole trip, if you are in a real rush) to Bellagio where you can stroll the town and enjoy a late lunch. As the afternoon fades into early evening, get another ferry for the short trip to Varenna on the eastern shore. With gelato in hand, walk along Varenna's lovely lakeside before popping into a small trattoria for dinner (you are on vacation so gelato before dinner is allowed, but if you are a fundamentalist on these matters do dinner first then the walk/gelato). With appetite satiated and legs tired, head up the steps to Varenna's train station for the last run back to Milan (usually at 10:20pm, arriving at 11:35pm, but be sure to check as schedules change).

Lakeside life revolves around Piazza Cavour and the adjoining Giardini Pubblici, where the circular **Tempio Voltiano** (✆ 031-574-705) houses memorabilia on the life and experiments of native son and electricity pioneer Alessandro Volta. Admission is 3€. It is open Tuesday to Sunday 10am to noon and 3 to 6pm (Oct–Mar 2–4pm). For picturesque views of the lake, there is a **short, pleasant walk** up the western shore to the neoclassical Villa Olmo where interesting art exhibitions are often held.

For a quick retreat and stunning views of the lake, and on clear days the Alps, take the **funicular** (✆ 031-303-608; www.funicolarecomo.it) for a 7-minute ride up to Brunate (it leaves from the Lungo Lario Trieste every 15 min. or so, in summer every half-hour), a tiny town that sits right above Como. Brunate is the starting point for many hiking trails including one that takes you all the way to Bellagio.

WHERE TO STAY

With Como's fame has come a paucity of decent moderately priced hotels. Fortunately, there are still a few options and for those ready to splash out, really splash out, nearby Cernobbio is home to one of the top hotels in Italy.

Hotel Metropole Suisse ★ This massive 1892 hotel closes one side of Como's main square overlooking the lake. Accommodations vary; some rooms are carpeted and have nice contemporary furnishings; others are older, with wood floors, brass beds, and embroidered upholstery. Almost all rooms overlook the lake at least partially—some full-on (the best with small balconies), some askance over the cafes ringing the piazza, and others beyond the tree-lined promenade leading to the city park. The corner bar/lounge has picture windows for lake views, and the restaurant (under separate management) has tables out on the piazza.

Piazza Cavour 19, 22100 Como. www.hotelmetropolesuisse.com. ✆ 031-269-444. Fax 031-300-808. 71 units. 128€–198€ double; 160€–246€ junior suite. Rates include buffet breakfast. AE, DC, MC, V. Parking 16€. **Amenities:** International restaurant; bar; babysitting; concierge; nearby golf course; room service; sauna; smoke-free rooms; free Wi-Fi. *In room:* A/C, TV w/pay movies, hair dryer, minibar.

9

Le Stanze del Lago ★★ 🏖 The *stanze* (rooms in Italian) are actually five small apartments that are in tiptop shape and kept immaculately clean. Opened in 2009 by Luca and his wife Barbara, the apartments all have a bedroom with a double bed and a living room with a pullout couch, table, and a small kitchen area off to the side. La Stanza sui Tetti and La Stanza del Faro have sloped ceilings that give a cozy feel to the apartments while La Stanza dell'Elba and La Stanza del Duomo have exposed-brick walls for a more rustic setting. The location is as central as you can get, right above the Ristorante Sociale (see review below), which offers discounts to guests at Le Stanze, and a few steps from both the Duomo and the Como Lago train station.

Via Rodari 6, 22100 Como. www.lestanzedellago.com. ✆ **339-544-6515** or 339-837-4590. 5 units. 80€–100€ for 2 people; 90€–110€ for 3–4 people. AE, DC, MC, V. **Amenities:** Wi-Fi. *In room:* A/C, TV, kitchenette.

WHERE TO EAT
Ristorante Sociale 🏖 ITALIAN/TRATTORIA This trattoria, located on an unassuming street behind the Duomo, is where locals go after a play or a concert at the nearby Teatro Sociale to enjoy one of the lake's best-priced meals. You'll find well-done standbys such as risotto *alla milanese* and beef stew with polenta, but also nice alternatives including stuffed vegetables, risotto with radicchio, and a refreshing chicken, tomato, basil, and pineapple salad that only appears on the menu in the summer months. You can choose between three distinct dining environments: The ground floor has vaulted brick ceilings that recall an osteria of yesteryear; go a flight up and you find a more refined atmosphere with a painted frieze circling the room; and weather permitting you can dine in a pleasant, though cramped, courtyard that comes complete with a view of the lake (well, painted onto one of the walls).

Via Rodari 6. ✆ **031-264-042.** www.ristorantesociale.it. Reservations not necessary. Primi 6€– 15€; secondi 8.50€–19€. AE, MC, V. Wed–Mon noon–2pm and 7:30–10:30pm.

A TOP HOTEL IN NEARBY CERNOBBIO
Villa d'Este ★★★ One of the most exclusive hotels in the world, this Renaissance villa is set amid 4 hectares (10 acres) of meticulously landscaped lakeside gardens. It has hosted everyone from Mark Twain to Joseph Heller, Clark Gable to Mel Gibson, Carreras to Madonna. Guests can arrive by helicopter or private boat (something which, incidentally, you can rent for yourself when you arrive). No expense is spared, from the marble in the spacious bathrooms and the genuine antique prints and oil paintings lining the halls and rooms, to the Como silk brocades covering the antiques and the Empire furnishings that actually date back to Napoleon's stay here when it was still a private villa. No two rooms

> ### Lake Como on the Big Screen
>
> Picturesque Lake Como has been featured in several films. Parts of *Star Wars Episode II: Attack of the Clones* (2002) were filmed at a villa in Lake Como, including the scene in which Anakin Skywalker and Padmé secretly marry. *Ocean's Twelve* (2004) also featured Lake Como as home to infamous thief and rival to Daniel Ocean, The Night Fox. In *Casino Royale* (2006), James Bond spends some time recuperating at a hospital in Lake Como after being tortured; this is also where he starts to fall in love with Vesper Lynd, a Bond girl.

are alike, but all are fit for royalty. The main pool floats on the lake while indoor you'll find another pool as well as tennis and squash courts.

Via Regina 40, 22012 Cernobbio, Lago di Como. www.villadeste.it. ✆ **031-3481.** Fax 031-348-873. 152 units. 490€–810€ double; 835€–1,750€ junior suite. Rates include buffet breakfast (or continental breakfast served in your room). AE, DC, MC, V. Free parking. Closed mid-Nov to Feb. **Amenities:** 3 restaurants (a formal, jacket-and-tie international restaurant; casual dinner-only grill in Queen's Pavilion; Japanese dinner restaurant); 2 bars (1 elegant w/music, the other pool-side); babysitting; free bikes; concierge; exercise room; 7 18-hole golf courses (14km/8¾ miles away); Jacuzzi; 2 heated pools (indoor and outdoor); room service; sauna; spa; 2 tennis courts (indoor and lighted outdoor); watersports equipment/rentals. *In room:* A/C, TV w/pay movies, hair dryer, minibar, VCR (on request), Wi-Fi.

Bellagio & the Central Lake Region

By far the loveliest spot on the lake (and where travelers should definitely set their sights) is the section known as the Centro Lago. Three towns—**Bellagio, Varenna,** and **Menaggio**—sit across the water from one another on three different shorelines.

ESSENTIALS

GETTING THERE & GETTING AROUND By Train The closest train station to Bellagio is in Varenna, with trains hourly to and from Milan (about 70 min.). Alternatively you can train to Como (see above)—from where you can continue by bus or boat. If you're planning to leave the central part of the lake after dinner, the 10:20pm train from Varenna to Milan (with an hour stopover in Lecco) will be your last chance to do so. *Tip:* The ticket window at Varenna's station is rarely, if ever, open, and the automatic ticket machine has been broken for the better part of a decade. Get on without a ticket and find the ticket collector, who will have you pay a regular-price ticket without tacking on the large onboard acquisition fee.

By Boat From Como, boats arriving at the Centro Lago towns stop first at Bellagio: by ferry 2 hours, by hydrofoil 35 to 45 minutes. They continue on to Menaggio (by ferry another 15 min., by hydrofoil another 5 min.). About half the boats then stop in Varenna as well (plus there are about two dozen short-haul ferries each from Bellagio and Menaggio to Varenna; by ferry 10 min.; by hydrofoil 5 min.). You can also get day passes good for just the central lake or for the whole lake.

Many of the ferries carry cars for an additional fee. Schedules vary with the season, but from Easter through September a ferry or hydrofoil makes the trip from Como to Bellagio and other towns along the lake at least hourly. For more information, contact **Navigazione Laghi** (✆ **800-551-801** or 031-579-211; www.navlaghi.it); the office is on the lakefront in Como on Lungo Lario Trieste.

By Bus One to three **SPT buses** (✆ **031-247-247;** www.sptlinea.it) per hour travel from Como to Bellagio (a little more than 1 hr.). Hourly buses to Menaggio take a little more than an hour. Buses leave Como from the bus station in Piazza Matteotti next to the Como Lago train station. Buses to Menaggio and other towns on the western edge of the lake also stop at the San Giovanni train station; get bus tickets at the bar inside the train station.

By Car Bellagio is connected to Como by a picturesque lakeshore road, SS583, which can be very crowded in summer. The A9 links Como with Milan in about an hour. To reach Menaggio from Como, follow route SS340 along the western shore of the lake. For Varenna, follow SS342 from Como to Nibionno, a speck of a town where you transfer to the SS36, which runs north through Lecco and then along the lake's eastern shore.

BELLAGIO

Bellagio ★★★ is at the tip of the peninsula at a point where the lake forks into three distinct basins: One long leg sweeps north into the Alps, Como is at the southern end of the western leg, and Lecco is at the southern end of the eastern leg. Boats from Bellagio make it easy to visit the nearby shores of the Centro Lago—not that you'll be in a great hurry to leave the steep narrow streets, lakeside piazza, and beautiful gardens.

FESTIVALS & MARKETS A pleasant way to spend a summer evening in Bellagio is at one of the concerts held in the Chiesa dei Cappuccini, on the grounds of the Rockefeller Foundation in June and July. Bellagio's outdoor market fills the waterfront every third Wednesday of the month.

VISITOR INFORMATION The **IAT tourist office** is at Piazza Mazzini on the lakefront (✆ **031-950-204**). It's open April to October Monday to Saturday 9am to 12:30pm and 1 to 6pm, Sunday 10am to 2pm; November to March Monday, Tuesday, Thursday 9am to 12:30pm and 2:30 to 5pm, Wednesday 9am to 1pm, Friday and Saturday 9am to 7pm, Sunday 3 to 6pm. There is also a Bellagio city tourist office at Piazza della Chiesa 14 (✆ **031-951-555;** www.bellagiolakecomo.com). Its hours are Monday 9:30am to 1pm, Tuesday to Sunday 9:30 to 11am and 2 to 4pm (Wed and Sun closed at 3:30pm).

Exploring the Town

Bellagio, nestled amid cypress groves and verdant gardens, features earth-toned old buildings climbing from the lakefront promenade along stepped cobbled

The red tile roofs of Bellagio.

lanes. While Bellagio is a popular retreat for everyone from Milanese out for a day of relaxation to British and Americans who come to relax for a week or two, the town has, for the most part, managed to keep its dignity despite the crush of tourists that arrive in the summer months.

One of Bellagio's famed gardens surrounds the **Villa Melzi** built by Francesco Melzi, a friend of Napoleon and an official of his Republic. The villa was the retreat of Franz Liszt and is now the home of a family that allows the public to stroll through their acres of manicured lawns and fountains and to visit a pavilion where a collection of Egyptian sculpture is on display. It's open from late March through October daily 9:30am to 6:30pm; admission is 6€ (for information on guided tours: ✆ **339-457-3838;** daniela@giardinidivillamelzi.it).

Bellagio's other famous gardens are those of the **Villa Serbelloni,** occupying land once owned by Pliny the Younger and now in the hands of the Rockefeller Foundation. You can visit the gardens on twice-daily guided tours (reserve ahead), about 1½ hours long, in Italian and English (tours require 6 people minimum, 20 people maximum). From April to October, tours are Tuesday to Sunday at 11am and 4pm and cost 6.50€; for more information and to book a spot on the tour, call ✆ **031-951-555.** You meet at the little tower on the back side of Piazza della Chiesa, a steep block and a half up from the port.

Where to Stay

For a wider selection of moderately priced hotels, you'd do best to head across the lake from Bellagio to Menaggio or Varenna (see below).

Giardinetto ✦ The best lodging deal is at this little hotel at the top of town, reached from the lakefront by Bellagio's narrow-stepped streets. A snug lobby with a big fireplace opens to a gravelly grapevine-covered terrace, where you're welcome to bring your own food for an alfresco meal. Most of the rooms are quite large and bright, with big windows (those on the upper floors provide nice views from balconies over the town and lake beyond, especially nos. 18–20) and furnishings like solid old armoires and, in the better rooms, box-spring-and-mattress beds rather than cots. Some rooms are on the airshaft, however, and others come with no window whatsoever so make sure you ask what you are getting. All in all, this hotel is basic but comfortable enough.

Piazza della Chiesa, 22021 Bellagio. giardinetto@aol.it. ✆ **031-950-168.** 13 units, 11 with private bathroom. 65€–70€ double. Breakfast 6€. No credit cards. Parking 10€ in nearby garage. Closed Nov– Apr. *In room:* Hair dryer.

Grand Hotel Villa Serbelloni ★★ A grandiose 1850s villa lies at the core of this luxury hotel whose vast grounds expand from Bellagio's central square along the lake and up into the wooded hills. The tone is set by the high-ceilinged salons, frescoed with *grotteschi* (fanciful stucco ornamentation) and blessed with lake views and live music on some evenings. Rooms vary widely in decor, with stucco ceilings in some, walnut furnishings in others, and oil paintings on the walls of most. Room categories boil down mostly to size, though almost all lakeview rooms are deluxe (though not all deluxe rooms have the view), executive, or suite. They also run a health and beauty center with a large exercise room and full-body treatments. In the back of the property, over the spa, is the **Residence Ulivo,** a series of apartments recommended separately below.

Via Roma/Piazza Mazzini, 22021 Bellagio. www.villaserbelloni.com. ☎ **031-950-216.** Fax 031-951-529. 83 units. 375€–475€ classic double; 510€–610€ deluxe double; 750€–825€ executive double; 970€–1,100€ senior suite. Half-board available. Rates include breakfast. AE, DC, MC, V. Free parking. Closed mid-Nov to Mar. **Amenities:** 2 Italian/international restaurants (1 jacket-and-tie terrace restaurant, 1 informal nautical-looking dinner-only restaurant); bar; babysitting; children's playground; concierge; exercise room; nearby golf course (in Menaggio); 2 heated pools (indoor and outdoor); room service; sauna; spa; outdoor tennis courts; watersports equipment/rentals; Wi-Fi. *In room:* A/C, TV, hair dryer, minibar.

Hotel Du Lac ★★ The Leoni family has been providing old-fashioned comfort at this 150-year-old hotel overlooking the lake from the main piazza for half a century. Downstairs, a bar spills onto the arcaded sidewalk in front and there are a series of pleasant sitting rooms. Meals are served in a nicely appointed dining room with panoramic views of the lake, and in the guest rooms, each of which is unique; cushy armchairs and a nice smattering of antiques and reproductions lend a great amount of charm. Many of the smallish rooms have balconies or terraces, and there's a rooftop sun terrace with sweeping lake views. Guests have free access to a sports center nearby with a pool, tennis courts, and children's play area.

Piazza Mazzini 32, 22021 Bellagio. www.bellagiohoteldulac.com. ☎ **031-950-320.** Fax 031-951-624. 39 units. 150€–200€ double; 210€–240€ superior double with lake view. Rates include buffet breakfast. Half-board available. MC, V. Parking 10€ in nearby garage. Closed early Nov–Easter. **Amenities:** Restaurant (Italian/international); bar; babysitting; concierge. *In room:* A/C, TV, hair dryer, minibar, Wi-Fi.

An Apartment Stay

Residence Ulivo ★★ 🦋 For those looking for less grandiose and expensive accommodations than those the Villa Serbelloni (see above) while still enjoying all the hotel's amenities—including its lovely lakeside pool, private beach, fitness club with sauna, game room, and frescoed salons—there are these stylish apartments in a building on the hotel grounds above the lake. All have sitting areas and either separate bedrooms or alcove sleeping areas, and are nicely decorated with terra-cotta floors and attractive rattan furniture. All have large kitchenettes; the best have partial views of the lake (no. 10 gets the best vistas, while no. 8 is larger and has some partial views, including from the bedroom). Although rentals are officially by the week, shorter stays can be arranged when space is available. Even when the main hotel is closed (mid-Nov to Mar), the Residence stays open.

Via Roma/Piazza Mazzini, 22021 Bellagio. www.residence-bellagio.com. ☎ **031-956-434.** Fax 031-951-529. 13 apts. Weekly rates for 2 people: 959€–1,330€ small apt; 1,148€–1,470€ medium apt; 1,540€–1,925€ large apt. Extra bed 105€–140€. Buffet breakfast in main hotel (walk down a path to get there) 22€. AE, DC, MC, V. Free parking. **Amenities:** Italian/international restaurant; bar; babysitting; children's playground; concierge; exercise room; nearby golf course (in Menaggio); 2 heated pools (indoor and outdoor); room service; sauna; spa; outdoor tennis courts; watersports equipment/rentals. *In room:* A/C, TV, kitchenette, Internet.

Where to Eat

Bar Café Rossi ★★ LIGHT FARE One of the nicest of Bellagio's pleasant lakefront cafes is tucked under the arcades of the town's main square. You can dine at one of the few outside tables or in the delightful Art Nouveau dining room, with intricate tile work, carved wood cabinets, and stucco ceilings. Wine and the excellent house coffee are available all day, but a nice selection of pastries and sandwiches makes this a good stop for breakfast or lunch.

Piazza Mazzini 22/24. ✆ **031-950-196.** Sandwiches 8€. AE, DC, MC, V. Apr–Oct daily 7:30am–midnight; Nov–Mar Fri–Wed 7:30am–10:30pm.

La Grotta ★ 🍴 ITALIAN/PIZZERIA Tucked away on a stepped street just off lakefront Piazza Mazzini, this cozy restaurant consists of a series of vaulted-ceiling dining rooms. The service is extremely friendly, and the wide-ranging menu includes the famous *pizzoccheri,* the sinfully rich buckwheat pasta with melted cheese, butter, and cabbage from Valtellina just north of here. For something lighter, you won't go wrong with the fish specials, especially the lake trout, or the delectable pizzas that are the best for miles around.

Salita Cernaia 14. ✆ **031-951-152.** Reservations not necessary. Primi and pizza 6€–11€; secondi 7€–15€. AE, MC, V (credit cards accepted only for bills of more than 25€). Daily noon–3pm and 7–11:30pm (Oct–June closed Mon).

Ristorante Barchetta ★★ SEAFOOD One of Bellagio's best restaurants specializes in fresh lake fish and other seafood. In all but the coldest weather, food is served on a bamboo-enclosed heated terrace. There is also a bar on the terrace. Most of the pastas don't use seafood but are innovative variations on traditional recipes, such as *ravioli caprino* (filled with goat cheese, topped with pear sauce) and savory risotto with hazelnuts and pistachios. For a main course, however, you should try one of the delicious preparations of local perch or angler fish; the meat entrees, including baby lamb chops with rosemary, are also good. You can enjoy a pasta dish, as well as a meat and a fish dish, on one of the set menus.

Salita Mella 13. ✆ **031-951-389.** Reservations highly recommended. Primi 10€–20€; secondi 16€–25€; tasting menu (for 2 only) 45€ per person, not including wine. AE, DC, MC, V. Thurs–Mon noon–2:30pm and 7–10:30pm. Closed Nov–Mar.

VARENNA

You can happily spend some time clambering up and down the steep steps that substitute for streets in this charming village (on the eastern shore of the lake, about 10 min. by ferry from Bellagio) that, until not too long ago, made its living by fishing. The main attractions, though, are outside town.

The hilltop ruins of the **Castello di Vezio** (✆ **348-824-2504;** www. castellodivezio.it) are about a 20-minute walk above the town on a gradually ascending path. The main reason for a visit is to enjoy the stunning views of the lake, its shoreline villages, and the backdrop of mountains at the northern end. The castle is open daily from 10am. April through June and September, it closes at 6pm (Sat–Sun at 7pm); July and August, it closes at 7pm (Sat–Sun at 8pm); March and October, it closes at 5pm (Sat–Sun at 6pm). The castle is closed November to February, and closes when there is bad weather. Admission is 1€.

The **gardens of the Villa Monastero** (✆ 0341-295-450) are more easily accessible, at the southern edge of town along Via 4 Novembre, and you can reach them by following the series of lakeside promenades through the Old Town from the ferry landing. This villa and the terraced gardens that rise up from the lakeshore were once a not-so-spartan monastery—until it was dissolved in the late 17th century when the nuns in residence began bearing living proof that they were on too-friendly terms with the priests across the way. If you find it hard to tear yourself from the bowers of citrus trees and rhododendrons clinging to terraces, you'll find equally enchanting surroundings in the adjoining gardens of the **Villa Cipressi** (✆ 0341-830-113).

Both gardens are open daily March to October: Villa Monastero 10am to 7pm and Villa Cipressi 9am to 7pm. Admission is 3.50€ for adults, and 2€ for children under 10 and seniors over 60 to just one garden. It is 6€ adults and 3€ kids and seniors to visit both.

In season, **ferries** make the 10-minute run between Bellagio and Varenna about every half-hour (see "By Boat," earlier). There's a tiny **tourist office** at Piazza Venini, 1 (✆ 0341-830-367; www.varennaitaly.com), open Saturday and Sunday 10am to 12:30pm and 3:30 to 6:30pm (Aug also open Mon–Fri).

Where to Stay

Albergo Milano ★★ ✐ A friendly Italian-Swiss couple took over this old house hanging over Varenna's lakefront in 2002 and turned it into one of the

A statue watches over Villa Monastero and Lake Como.

most pleasant retreats by the lake. All rooms are non-smoking and have balconies or terraces from which to enjoy the views—nos. 1 and 2 open onto a wide terrace, and nos. 5 and 6 both have full-on lake vistas; the other half overlook the neighbor's pretty garden with partial lake views. In summer, breakfast is served on the outdoor terrace. There are also three nearby annexes that enjoy all the services of the main hotel including breakfast. The **Casa Gialla** is a two-bedroom apartment with views of a quiet alley that accommodates up to five guests. The **Casa Rossa** offers five rooms in an adjacent building with either a balcony or terrace and great lake views. **Casa 3Archi** can sleep up to four in a bedroom and large living room.

Via XX Settembre 29, 23829 Varenna. www. varenna.net. ✆ **0341-830-298.** Fax 0341-830-061. 8 units. 115€–145€ double with lateral lake view and balcony; 150€–160€ double with full lake view and balcony; 160€–170€ double with full lake view and terrace. Rates include buffet breakfast. 3-course dinner 35€ upon request (restaurant closed Tues and Sun). MC, V. Free parking on the street or 14€ in nearby garage. Closed mid-Nov through Mar. **Amenities:** Restaurant; bar; concierge; room service; Wi-Fi. *In room:* Hair dryer (on request), Wi-Fi (Casa Gialla and Casa 3Archi don't have any Internet connection, but guests can connect in lobby of the hotel).

Where to Eat

Cavatappi ★★ 🎁 ITALIAN With five tables placed in a rustic setting of stone walls and copper pots hanging over the fireplace, this is the type of simple, homey restaurant where you expect to eat well. And eat well you will whether it's the lake fish that has just been brought up from Varenna's tiny port, risotto cooked with smoked cheese and red wine, or the beef filet and lamb ribs that will remind you that when the raw materials are right the preparation is almost a formality. A place that calls itself *cavatappi* (corkscrews) is obliged to have an excellent wine list so no surprise there (a 2000 Sassicaia with the beef?). With space tight, the restaurant is not always so child friendly, especially if you're expecting to have junior sleep in the stroller parked by your table while you eat.

Via XX Settembre 10. 🕻 **0341-815-349.** www.ilcavatappiwine-food.it. Reservations highly recommended. Primi 10–12€; secondi 12€–20€. MC, V. Thurs–Tues 12:30–2:30pm and 7:30–10pm.

MENAGGIO

This lively resort town hugs the western shore of the lake, across from Bellagio on its peninsula and Varenna on the distant shore. Hikers should stop in at the **tourist office** on Piazza Garibaldi 8 (🕻/fax **0344-32-924;** www.menaggio. com), open daily 9am to 12:30pm and 2:30 to 6pm (Nov–Mar closed Wed and Sun). The very helpful staff distributes a booklet, ***Hiking in the Area around Menaggio,*** with descriptions of more than a dozen walks, with maps and instructions on what buses to take to trail heads. The town's **bus stop** is at Piazza

---

chords & CANVAS

In 2008, Bellagio held an exhibition of watercolor paintings that met with such success that the town made the festival an annual tradition. This weeklong exhibition showcases the works of watercolor painters from around the world. It is held at the end of April or early May (contact the tourist office for the exact dates) and closes out with a competition to see who has created the most beautiful painting.

Across the lake, Menaggio began a guitar festival in 2007 that has become a yearly event. Held the last weekend of August, the festival is 3 days of free concerts held in churches and a temporary tent pavilion. The festival has already begun to attract well-known international musicians, but lesser-known guitarists also perform in the local bars during the festival. There are also workshops where different playing styles are discussed and demonstrated. Menaggio recently instituted a shuttle service that makes the run on the state road to and from nearby Tremezzo and Cadenabbia late into the evening, giving those lodged farther down the lake a chance to enjoy an evening in Menaggio when public buses are no longer operating, without having to spring for a taxi to get back (4€ one-way, 6€ round-trip).

Villa Carlotta's perfect gardens.

Garibaldi (Sun on Via Mazzini); tickets are sold at Bar Centrale or the newsstand on Via Calvi at the piazza.

The major nearby attraction is **Villa Carlotta** (*℄0344-40-405;* www.villa carlotta.it), located about 2.5km (1½ miles) south of town. Begun in 1643, this is the most famous villa on the lake. After a succession of owners, including Prussian royalty who lavished their funds and attention on the gardens, the villa is now in the hands of the Italian government. It's filled with romantic paintings, statues by Canova and his imitators, and Empire furnishings, but the gardens are the main attraction, with azaleas, orchids, banana trees, cacti, palms, and forests of ferns spreading in all directions. You can take the no. C10 bus from Menaggio or walk along the lake (about 30–45 min.). The nearest ferry landing is at Cadenabbia. The villa and gardens are open daily April to October from 9am to 6:30pm, and in March from 9am to 4pm. Admission is 8.50€ for adults and 4.50€ for seniors 65 and over and students.

WATERSPORTS The lido, at the north end of town, has a good **beach,** as well as a **pool,** and is open late June to mid-September daily 9am to 7pm. The tourist office has information on water-skiing and other activities. Also ask at the hostel (see below) about boat and bike rentals, which are available to nonguests during slow periods.

Where to Stay & Eat

Albergo-Ristorante Il Vapore ★ This very pleasant small restaurant/hotel faces a quiet square just off the lakefront. The rooms are comfortable, with rather nice modern furnishings (plus antiques in a few), though the bathrooms are cramped. Six rooms open onto partial lake views: nos. 21 and 22 from tall windows, nos. 25 and 26 from small terraces, and nos. 28 and 29 (the biggest room, with windows on two sides for a breeze) from tiny balconies. Meals of local specialties from the nearby mountain valleys are normally served beneath the wisteria-shaded arbor of the entryway or in an attractive pale-blue dining room with paintings by local artists. It's best to call ahead in winter to make sure they are open.

Piazza Grossi 3, 22017 Menaggio. www.hotelvapore.it. *℄* **0344-32-229.** Fax 0304-34-850. 10 units. 55€ double without lake view; 60€ double with lake view. Breakfast 7€. No credit cards. **Amenities:** Restaurant; bar. *In room:* No phone.

Menaggio Youth Hostel ♦ This youth hostel is easily accessible by boat from Bellagio and other towns on the Centro Lago and is frequented about evenly by frugal adults and backpacking students. The dorms are relatively cozy, with no more than six beds per room. Most of the rooms, admittedly a little run-down, have a view of the lake—nos. 3, 4, and 5 on the first floor even share a balcony. Everyone enjoys the view from the large, sunny communal terrace. The hostel serves a 12€ dinner that even attracts locals. (You're expected to set your own table on the porch, retrieve each course as it's called, and wash your own dishes.) Saturday night there is a barbecue with meat, polenta, and couscous.

Via IV Novembre 86 (on the south edge of town), 22017 Menaggio (CO). www.menaggiohostel. com. ✆/fax **0344-32-356.** 35 beds. 17€ per person in dorm; 68€ triple with bathroom; 74€ family room with private bathroom (up to 4 people). Rates include breakfast. No credit cards. Closed 1st weekend in Nov to Mar 15. Office open 8am–2pm and 5pm–midnight. **Amenities:** Restaurant; bar; private beach; bike, kayak, and rowboat rental. *In room:* No phone, Wi-Fi.

LAKE MAGGIORE (LAGO MAGGIORE) & THE BORROMEAN ISLANDS

Stresa: 90km (56 miles) NW of Milan

Anyone who reads Hemingway will know this lake, its views of the Alps, and its forested shores from *A Farewell to Arms.* That's just the sort of place Lake Maggiore is—a pleasure ground that's steeped in associations with famous figures (Flaubert, Wagner, Goethe, and many of Europe's other great minds seem to have been inspired by the deep, moody waters) and not-so-famous wealthy visitors. Fortunately, you need not be famous or wealthy to enjoy Maggiore, the top bit of which is in Switzerland.

Stresa

The major town on the lake is a pretty, festive little place, with a long lake-front promenade, a lively and attractive commercial center, and a bevy of restaurants and hotels that range from the expensively splendid to the affordably comfortable.

Festivals & Markets May to September, Stresa draws visitors from around the world for its **Settimane Musicali,** or Festival of Musical Weeks, a major gathering of classical musicians. The festival has an information office at Via Carducci 38 (✆ **0323-31-095;** www.stresafestival.eu).

ESSENTIALS

GETTING THERE By Train Stresa is linked with Milan by 20 trains a day (regional: 55 min.–75 min.).

By Boat Boats arrive and depart from Piazza Marconi, connecting Stresa with the Borromean Islands (Isole Borromee) and with many other lakeside spots; most boats on the lake are operated by **Navigazione Laghi** (✆ **800-551-801** or 0322-233-200; www.navlaghi.it).

By Car A8 runs between Milan and Sesto Calende, near the southern end of the lake; from there, Route SS33 follows the western shore to Stresa. The trip takes a little over an hour.

VISITOR INFORMATION The **tourist office** is at the ferry dock (✆/fax **0323-31-308**) and is open daily 10am to 12:30pm and 3 to 6:30pm (Nov–Feb closed Sun). You can also get info from private websites (try www.lago maggiore.it). For hiking information, ask for the booklet *Percorsi Verdi.*

Terraced houses on Isola Bella.

Exploring Stresa & the Islands

STRESA

Strolling and relaxing are the main activities in Stresa. The action (that is to say the strolling and relaxing) takes place mostly at the lakeside promenade, running from the center of town north past the grand lakeside hotels, including the Iles des Borromées, where Hemingway set *A Farewell to Arms.* Sooner or later, though, most visitors climb into a boat for the short ride to the Borromean Islands.

BORROMEAN ISLANDS (ISOLE BORROMEE)

These three islands, named for the Borromeo family that has owned them since the 12th century, float just off Stresa and entice visitors with their stunning beauty. Note that Isola Bella and Isola Superiore have villages you can hang out in for free while Isola Madre consists solely of the admission-charging gardens.

Public **ferries** leave for the islands every half-hour from Stresa's Piazza Marconi; a 12€ **three-island pass** is the most economical way to visit them—and if you buy your admission tickets for the *isole* sights at the Stresa ferry office along with your ferry tickets, you'll save 1€ off each—though the generally grumpy ticket agents will not advise you of this; you have to ask. Buy tickets only from the public Navigazione Laghi (see "Getting There by Boat," above), in the big building with triple arches. Private boats also make the trip out to the island—at obscene rates; you'll see other ticket booths as well as hucksters dressed as sailors trying to lure you aboard (for large groups, the prices can be reasonable, but do your negotiating on the dock before you get on the boat). For more information, visit www.borromeoturismo.it.

ISOLA BELLA Isola Bella (5 min. from Stresa) remains true to its name, with splendid 17th-century gardens that ascend from the shore in 10 luxuriantly planted terraces. The Borromeo *palazzo* provides a chance to explore opulently decorated rooms, including one where Napoleon and Josephine once slept. It's open daily late March to mid-October, 9am to 5:30pm. Admission is 13€ for adults and 5.50€ for children ages 6 to 15. Audio tours help make sense of it all for 3.50€ each or 5€ to rent two sets of headphones. For more details, call ☏**0323-30-556.**

ISOLA SUPERIORE Most of Isola Superiore, also known as Isola Pescatori (10 min. from Stresa), is occupied by a not-so-quaint fishing village in which everyone of the tall houses on this tiny strip of land seems to harbor a souvenir shop or pizza stand, and there are hordes of visitors to keep them busy. If you come when the crowds are absent, the visit is certainly worthwhile.

ISOLA MADRE The largest and most peaceful of the islands is Isola Madre (30 min. from Stresa), every inch of which is covered with the exquisite flora and exotic colorful birds of the 3.2-hectare (8-acre) **Orto Botanico** (☎ **0323-31-261**). The map they hand out at the entrance/ticket booth details all the flora; you're on your own to identify the various peacocks, game fowl, exotic birds, funky chickens, and other feathered creatures that strut, flit, and roost amid the lawns around the central villa (1518–85), filled with Borromeo family memorabilia and some interesting old puppet-show stages. The botanical garden is open late March through mid-October daily 9am to 5:30pm; admission is 11€ for adults and 5.50€ for children ages 6 to 15. A joint 1-day ticket for the Isola Bella palazzo and the Isola Madre gardens costs 18€ for adults and 8€ for children.

HIKING & BIKING IN THE AREA

The forested slopes above Stresa are prime hiking and mountain biking terrain. To reach a network of trails, take the **cable car** (☎ **0323-30-295;** www.stresa-mottarone.it) from near the lakefront at the north end of town up **Monte Mottarone;** it runs every 20 minutes from roughly 8am to 5:30pm (hours vary with the season). It costs 11€ one-way to take the cable car along with a bike, which you can rent at the station for 25€ for a half-day or 30€ for a full day. A round-trip ticket without a bike costs 14€ for adults and 8.50€ for children ages 4 to 12. The **Alpinia botanical garden** halfway up is open April to October daily from 9:30am to 6pm. A round-trip ticket to Monte Mottarone gives you the right to jump off at the intermediate stop and gives free entry into the garden. If you don't want to venture too far from the lake, there's a nice **beach** near the station.

WHERE TO STAY

Very Expensive

Grand Hôtel et des Iles Borromées ★★★ This was a favorite of Ernest Hemingway, who set part of *A Farewell to Arms* here. The elegance to the decor—gilded stuccoes, mosaics lining the hall runners, giant Murano chandeliers—takes you back to the spirit and style of the 1860s when the hotel was built. The Liberty facade is surrounded by perfectly manicured gardens of palms, flowers, ponds, and fountains. Rooms come in various types. "Alla Stresa" means 19th-century-style furnishings in intricately inlaid wood; large, comfy beds; and marble bathrooms. "Al Impero" rooms are done in Empire style, with gilded Napoleon-type

> ### 📎 Budgeting Your Time
>
> To squeeze as much of Stresa's sights as you can into a day, note that the ferry back from the Isole Borromee stops first at the Mottarone cable-car area before chugging down the coast to the center of Stresa and the main docks. You can hop off at this first stop to either ride the cable car up the mountain or simply walk back into Stresa itself along a pretty lakeside promenade, past crumbling villas and impromptu sculpture gardens, in about 20 minutes.

Piedmont & Valle d'Aosta

of Italian unification, Turin has transformed itself from a former industrial power into a vibrant city full of museums, enticing cafes, beautiful squares, and a riverside park that is perfect for relaxing after a day of heavy touring. Those who take the time to look around the historic center will find an elegant and sophisticated city with the charm of a place that, for all its Francophile leanings, is quintessentially Italian and perhaps the most pleasant big city in northern Italy.

Festivals & Markets Dance, opera, theater, and musical performances (mostly classical) are on the agenda all year long, but September is the month to really enjoy classical music—more than 60 classical concerts are held on stages around the city during the month-long **Settembre Musica** festival (© **011-442-4787;** www.mitosettembremusica.it), which is hosted together with Milan.

Bric-a-brac of all kinds, be it household utensils, books, or used clothing, fills the stalls of the **Mercato del Balon,** held every Saturday at Piazza della Repubblica. **Gran Balon** fills the piazza the second Sunday of every month and is a larger affair, with some genuine antiques and artworks included in the mix. **Mercato della Crocetta,** at Largo Cassini, sells clothing at very low prices. For a look at the bounty of the surrounding farmlands, wander through the extensive **outdoor food market** at Porta Palazzo, open Monday through Friday from 8:30am to 1:30pm and all day Saturday until 6:30pm.

Essentials

GETTING THERE By Plane Domestic and international flights land at the **Caselle International Airport** (✆ 011-567-6361; www.aeroportoditorino. it), about 15km (10 miles) north of Turin. Buses run between the airport and the city's main train stations, Porta Nuova and Porta Susa. The trip takes about 40 minutes. A **taxi** from the airport takes about 30 minutes and costs around 35€.

   By Train Turin's main train station is **Stazione di Porta Nuova** (www.trenitalia.com), just south of the center on Piazza Carlo Felice, which marks the intersection of two of Turin's major thoroughfares, Corso Vittorio Emanuele and Via Roma. Porta Nuova was completely redone a few years ago making it a nice enough place to mingle before you catch a train or, alternatively, there is a nice park in front of the station (May–Sept 8am–11pm and until 7pm the rest of the year). From Porta Nuova, there are two dozen trains a day to and from Milan—the trip takes 1 hour each way on the fastest trains; otherwise, it can take as long as 2 hours (some trains to and from Milan also stop at Turin's other station, Stazione di Porta Susa). There are two direct trains a day to and from Venice (4½ hr.); otherwise with a change in Milan it actually takes less time if you take the fast trains on both legs (4 hr.). There are 15 trains a day to and from Genoa (2 hr.), and 15 trains a day to and from Rome (4½ hr.). **Stazione di Porta Susa,** west of the center on Piazza XVIII Dicembre, connects Turin with many outlying Piedmont towns; it is also the terminus for TGV service to and from Paris, with two trains a day making the trip in just under 6 hours.

   By Bus Turin's main bus terminal is **Autostazione Terminal Bus,** Corso Vittorio Emanuele II 131 (near Stazione di Porta Susa; www. autostazionetorino.it). The ticket office is open daily from 9am to 1pm and 3 to 7pm. Buses connect Turin and Courmayeur (2½ hr.), Aosta (2 hr.), Milan (2 hr.), Chamonix (3½ hr.), and many smaller towns in Piedmont.

   By Car Turin is at the hub of an extensive network of autostrade. A4 connects Turin with Milan, about an hour and a half; A6 connects Turin with the Ligurian coast (and, from there, with Genoa via A10, with a total travel time between the two cities of about 1½ hr.); A5 connects Turin with Aosta (about 1½ hr.); and A21 connects Turin with Asti and Piacenza, where you can connect with the A1 for Florence (about 4 hr. from Turin) and Rome (about 6½ hr. from Turin).

VISITOR INFORMATION There is a **tourist office** at **Piazza Castello** (✆ 011-535-181; fax 011-530-070; www.turismotorino.org) that's open daily from 9am to 7pm. There's also an office in **Stazione Porta Nuova** with the same hours. If you're coming to Turin on the weekend, check in with the tourist office's website, as you may be able to take advantage of a **"Torino Weekend"**

Turin

Piazza della Repubblica

1

Via del Carmine

Piazza Savoia

2

Via della Corte d'Appello

N. 4 Marzo

Pza. San Giovanni

5 **4** **6**

Giardino Reali

Via Garibaldi

3

Pza. XVIII Dicembre

Autostazione Terminal Bus

Piazza Arbarello

Stazione di Porta Susa

Via Cernaia

Via Pietro Micca (i) **7**

Pza. Castello

Via S. Teresa

Piazza Solferino

8 **9**

Pza. San Carlo

Via Maria

Via Princ. Amedeo

10

Via Po

Via Giuseppe Verdi

11

Via Rossini

Pza. Carlo Emanuele II

Via Carlo Alberto

Via Giovanni Giolitti

15

Pza. Bodoni

Pza. Accademia Albertina

Pza. Cavour

Aiuola Balbo

Vittoria **16**

Pza. Vittorio Veneto

Largo Vitt. Eman. II

12

Pza. Carlo Felice

13 **14**

(i)

Stazione di Porta Nuova

18 **19**

Corso Vittorio Emanuele II

Via Frat Calandra

Ponte Vitt. Eman. I

17

Gran Madre di Dio

20

21

Via Berthollet

Ponte Umberto I

Museo d. Montagna

Corso Guglielmo Marconi

Parco del Valentino

Viale Virgilio

Via Madama Cristina

Castello del Valentino

Corso Raffaello

Via Caluso

Via Madama d'Azeglio

Parco del Valentino

Corso Moncalieri

22 **Torino Esposizioni**

Po River

Corso Cairoli

0 — 1/4 mi
0 — 0.25 km

ATTRACTIONS
Basilica di Superga **17**
Cattedrale di San Giovanni
Battista/The Shroud of Turin **5**
GAM (Galleria Civica d'Arte
Moderna e Contemporanea) **12**
Mole Antonelliana & Museo
Nazionale del Cinema **11**
Museo dell'Automobile **22**
Museo di Arte Orientale **2**
Museo Egizio & Galleria Sabauda **8**
Museo Nazionale del
Risorgimento Italiano **9**
Palazzina di Caccia di Stupinigi **22**
Palazzo Madama/
Museo Civico di Arte Antica **7**
Palazzo Reale & Armeria Reale **6**

HOTELS
Hotel Bellavista **21**
Hotel Bologna **13**
Hotel Due Mondi **18**
Hotel Mobledor **10**
NH Santo Stefano **4**
Victoria Hotel **15**

RESTAURANTS
C'era Una Volta **19**
Cianci **3**
Pastificio De Felippis **14**
Porto di Savona **16**
Ristorante Tre Galline **1**
Trattoria Salentina **20**

Turin

Rome

0 — 100 mi
0 — 100 km

deal, which offers 2 nights in a hotel plus two Torino+Piemonte Cards (see below), from 84€ to 195€ per person depending on the hotel chosen.

GETTING AROUND   It's easy to get around central Turin **by foot.** There's also a vast network of GTT trams and buses as well as one metro line (© **800-019-152** in Italy, or 011-57-641; www.comune.torino.it/gtt). Tickets on public transportation are available at newsstands for 1€ and are valid for 70 minutes. With the **Torino+Piemonte Card** (see "What to See & Do," below), you can ride the city's public transportation for free for 48 hours. Longer periods are available as well.

CITY LAYOUT   You will get a sense of Turin's refined air as soon as you step off the train into the mannerly 19th-century Stazione di Porta Nuova. The stately arcaded Via Roma, lined with shops and cafes, proceeds from the front of the station through a series of *piazze* toward the Piazza Castello and the center of the city, about a 15-minute walk.

Directly in front of the station, the circular **Piazza Carlo Felice** is ringed with outdoor cafes and built around a garden. Walking farther along the street will lead you into the **Piazza San Carlo,** one of the most beautiful squares in all of northern Italy and home to two historic cafes as well as the twin churches of San Carlo and Santa Cristina. At the end of Via Roma, the **Piazza Castello** is dominated by the **Palazzo Madama,** so named for its 17th-century inhabitant Christine Marie. Just off the piazza is the **Palazzo Reale,** residence of the Savoys from 1646 to 1865, whose gardens now provide a pleasant respite from traffic and paving stones.

From here, a walk east toward the river along Via Po takes you through Turin's university district to one of Italy's largest squares, the much-elongated Piazza Vittorio Veneto and, at the end of this elegant expanse, the Po River. Two enjoyable streets to stroll that are closed to traffic are Via Garibaldi from Piazza Castello to Piazza Statuto and Via La Grange from Piazza Castello to Corso Vittorio Emanuele II.

[Fast FACTS] TURIN

Bookstores Libreria Internazionale Luxemburg, Via C. Battisti 7 (☏ 011-561-3896), has a large selection of British books and a helpful English-speaking staff; it is open Monday through Saturday from 8am to 7:30pm, and Sunday from 10am to 1pm and 3 to 7pm. Another good bet for books in English is the chain **Feltrinelli,** Piazza Castello 19 (☏ 011-541-627), and inside Stazione Porta Nuova (☏ 011-563-981). Turin has many stores specializing in rare books and old prints, and many of these shops sell their wares from the secondhand-book stalls along the Via Po, which runs between Piazza Castello and the river.

Crime Turin is a relatively safe city, but use the same precautions you would exercise in any large city. Specifically, avoid the riverside streets along the Po after the revelers have gone home. In an **emergency,** call ☏ 113; this is a free call. The **central police station** is near Stazione di Porta Susa at Corso Vinzaglio 10 (☏ 011-558-81).

Drugstores A convenient late-night pharmacy is **Farmacia Boniscontro,** Corso Vittorio Emanuele 66 (☏ 011-538-271); it is open most of the day and night, closing only between 12:30 and 3pm.

Emergencies The general emergency number is ☏ 113; for an ambulance, dial ☏ 118. Both are free calls.

Holidays Turin's patron saint, San Giovanni Battista (Saint John the Baptist), is honored on June 24. For a list of official state holidays, see the "Holidays" section, on p. 70.

Hospitals The **Ospedale Maggiore di San Giovanni Battista,** Via Cavour 31 at Piazza Cavour (☏ 011-633-1633), offers a variety of medical services.

Internet For Internet access, **1PC4YOU,** at Via Verdi 20/G (☏ 011-026-8001), is open Monday through Friday 9am to 9pm, Saturday 10am to 8pm, and Sunday 2 to 8pm. Or try the **FNAC superstore,** on Via Roma 56 (☏ 011-551-6711), which is open daily 9:30am to 8pm.

Laundry **Lav@sciuga,** a laundromat/Internet point with seven locations across the city (☎ **335-750-7813;** www.lava sciuga.torino.it), charges 7€ for a wash-and-dry of a small load. They're open daily from 8am to 10pm. The nearest location to the train station is Via San Anselmo 9.

Luggage Storage Luggage storage is available at the Porta Nuova train station at the head of track 1: 4€ per bag for the first 5 hours, .60€ for each successive hour up to the 12th hour, and .20€ per hour after that. The office is open daily from 6:30am to 10pm.

Post Office Turin's main post office is just west of Piazza San Carlo at Via Alfieri 10 (☎ **011-506-011**); it is open Monday through Friday from 8:30am to 7pm and Saturday from 8:30am to 1pm. The postal code for Turin is 10100.

Taxis You can find taxis at cabstands; especially convenient in the central city are the stands in front of the train stations and around Piazza San Carlo and Piazza Castello. To call a taxi, dial ☎ **011-5737,** 011-5730, or 011-3399.

Telephone See "Fast Facts: Northern Italy," p. 468. The area code for Turin is ☎ 011

What to See & Do

The tourist office sells an extremely worthwhile **Torino+Piemonte Card** for 22€, valid for one adult plus one child 12 and under. The card grants you 48 hours of free public transport within Turin; access to more than 180 museums, monuments, castles, royal residences, and the like; and discounts on car rentals, ski lifts, theme parks, concerts, and sporting events. The card is also available in 3-, 5-, and 7-day versions. You can purchase the card at the tourist offices in Piazza Castello and Stazione Porta Nuova; visit www.turismotorino.org for more information.

In March 2011, **Turin's Automobile Museum** opened after a 4-year face-lift that turned the already appealing museum into a true gem. Even the biggest car-skeptics are likely to find something interesting that will make them happy they took the small detour from downtown. For history buffs, the **Museo Nazionale del Risorgimento Italiano,** which chronicles the country's 19th-century push towards independence from foreign occupiers, has recently reopened after a 5-year renovation.

Since hosting the Winter Olympics in 2006, Turin has done a stellar job of converting its Olympic venues into long-lasting structures that continue to be used. The **Palasport Olimpico (Olympic Arena),** designed by Japanese architect Arata Isozaki, was used for ice hockey competitions during the 2006 Olympics, but since then it has hosted performances by Bruce Springsteen, R.E.M., the Harlem Globetrotters, Depeche Mode, and many of the events in the Settembre Musica festival (see "Festivals & Markets," p. 369). Check the **Olympic Park** website (www. torinolympicpark.org) for a list of upcoming events.

Piazzo San Carlo, the perfect spot for a *caffè.*

Cattedrale di San Giovanni Battista ★

When the controversial **Shroud of Turin (Sacra Sindone)** is put on display, it is in this otherwise uninspiring 15th-century church, one of the few pieces of Renaissance architecture in baroque-dominated Turin. When the shroud is not out for viewing, the church's main draw is the **Cappella della Santa Sindone,** the only problem being that the chapel has been closed since a 1997 fire (one of many the shroud has miraculously survived over the centuries) and there is little chance it will open anytime soon. While the only piece of the chapel that is visible is the black marble that somberly covers the part facing the inside of the church, the faithful still come in droves to venerate the shroud and its chapel.

The subtle Shroud of Turin, top left.

The shroud, of course, is allegedly the one in which the body of Christ was wrapped when taken from the cross—and to which his image was miraculously affixed. The image is of a man 1.7m tall (5 ft., 7 in.), with bloodstains consistent with a crown of thorns, a cut in the ribcage, cuts in the wrists and ankles, and scourge marks on the back from flagellation. Recent carbon dating suggests that the shroud was manufactured sometime around the 13th or 14th century, but the mystery remains, at least in part, because no one can explain how the haunting image appeared on the cloth. Also, additional radio carbon dating has suggested that, since the shroud has been exposed to fire (thus affecting carbon readings), it could indeed date from around the time of the death of Christ. Regardless of scientific skepticism, the shroud continues to entice hordes of the faithful.

Around the corner at the **Museo della Sindone (Holy Shroud Museum),** Via San Domenico 28 (© **011-436-5832;** www.sindone.org), open daily from 9am to noon and 3 to 7pm, you can find out more than you ever wanted to know about the shroud; admission is 6€ for adults and 5€ for those 12 and under or 65 and over and students 25 and under. Technically the shroud is put on display only in Jubilee years, though it tends to pop up every 10 years more or less for special occasions. Otherwise, you'll have to content yourself with a series of dramatically backlit photos of the relic near the entrance to the cathedral, and another in the church of San Lorenzo. The museum houses a plethora of information (including photos, X-rays, and history) relating to the shroud.

In front of the cathedral stand two landmarks of Roman Turin—

A Rare Glimpse: The Shroud of Turin

The Shroud of Turin—the garment that Christ was allegedly wrapped in when he was taken from the cross—is put on display about once a decade at the Cattedrale di San Giovanni Battista. The last viewing was in 2010.

the remains of a theater and the **Porta Palatina,** a Roman-era city gate, flanked by twin 16-sided towers.

Piazza San Giovanni Battista. ☏ **011-436-1540.** Free admission. Mon–Sat 7:15am–12:30pm and 3–7pm (Sun open 8am). Bus: 11, 12, 19, 27, 50, 51, or 57. Tram: 3, 4, 7, or 16.

Galleria Sabauda ★ The Savoys' magnificent collection of European paintings fills the salons of the **Galleria Sabauda** on the floors above the Museo Egizio. The Savoys' royal taste ran heavily to painters of the Flemish and Dutch schools, and the works by Van Dyck, van Eyck, Rembrandt, Rubens, and Van der Weyden, among others, make up one of Italy's largest collections of northern European paintings. In fact, two of Europe's most prized Flemish masterpieces are here, Jan van Eyck's *Stigmata of St. Francis* and Hans Memling's *Passion of Christ.* If the Baroque extravagance of Rubens is your thing, be sure to search out *Saint Sebastian and the Angel.* Italian artists are also well represented; one of the first canvases you see upon entering the gallery is Fra'Angelico's sublime *Virgin and Child,* and in the room dedicated to artists from Veneto you'll find Veronese's huge *The Meal at the House of Simon,* the same scene that the artist did as a fresco in the Villa Barbaro (p. 201). The galleria is scheduled to be moved to Palazzo Reale (p. 379) in 2014 where it will find more space to display its 1,200 works.

Via Accademia delle Scienze 6. ☏ **011-547-440.** www.museitorino.it/galleriasabauda. Admission 4€ adults, 2€ for E.U. citizens ages 18–25, free for those 18 and under and 65 and older. Tues and Fri–Sun 8:30am–2pm; Wed–Thurs 2–7:30pm. Bus: 11, 12, 27, 55, 56, or 57. Tram: 13 or 15.

GAM (Galleria Civica d'Arte Moderna e Contemporanea) ★ Turin's modern-art museum is one of the most important in Italy. It was founded in 1863, so its collections actually start with late-18th- and 19th-century neoclassical and Romantic works by Piemontese and other artists (Canova, Massimo d'Azeglio, Francesco Hayez)—in fact, the modern building itself makes a sharp point about our notions about art and its relevance with a glowing sign on the roof: ALL ART HAS BEEN CONTEMPORARY. The collections are largely arranged chronologically, with rooms focusing on specific movements or periods. Of the more than 600 works on display, you'll see art by Modigliani, Giorgio de Chirico, Gino Severini, Otto Dix, Max Ernst, Paul Klee, and Andy Warhol. On the first Friday of each month, you can take a free guided tour of the museum. Call for times.

Via Magenta 31. ☏ **011-442-9518.** www.gamtorino.it. Admission 7.50€ adults, 6€ ages 10–18 and seniors 65 and over; free 1st Tues of the month. Tues–Sun 10am–6pm. Bus: 5, 52, 55, 64, or 68. Tram: 7 or 9. Metro: Re Umberto or Vinzaglio.

Mole Antonelliana & Museo Nazionale del Cinema (National Film Museum) ★★ Turin's most peculiar building—in fact, one of the strangest structures anywhere—comprises a squat brick base, which supports several layers of pseudo-Greek temples piled one atop the other, topped in turn by a steep conelike roof and a needlelike spire, all of it rising 167m (548 ft.) above the streets of the city center. Begun in 1863 and designed as a synagogue, the Mole, now a monument to Italian unification and architectural hubris, is home to Italy's **National Film Museum.**

The museum's first section tracks the development of moving pictures, from shadow puppets to kinescopes. The rest is more of a tribute to film than a true museum, offering clips and stills to illustrate some of the major aspects of movie production, from *The Empire Strikes Back* storyboards to the creepy steady-cam work in *The Shining.* Of memorabilia, masks from the original *Planet*

of the Apes, Satyricon, and *Star Wars* hang together near *Lawrence of Arabia*'s robe, *Chaplin*'s bowler, and *What Ever Happened to Baby Jane*'s dress. Most of the clips (all in Italian-dubbed versions), as well as posters and other memorabilia, are heavily weighted toward American movies, with exceptions mainly for the major players of European/international cinema like Fellini, Bertolucci, Truffaut, and Wim Wenders.

FROM TOP: **Mole Antonelliana's distinct architecture is immediately recognizable; an exhibit at the Museo dell'Automobile.**

Even if you skip the museum, you can (and should) still ascend to an observation platform at the top, an experience that affords a stunning view of Turin and the surrounding countryside backed by the Alps.

Via Montebello 20. ✆ **011-813-8560.** www.museocinema.it. Museum admission 7€; 5€ students 25 and under, and seniors 65 and over; 2€ children 6–18; free for children 5 and under. Observation platform 5€; 3.50€ students 25 and under, seniors 65 and over, and children 6–18; free for children 5 and under. Admission to both 9€, 7€ students 25 and under and seniors 65 and over, 4.50€ children 6–18, free for children 5 and under. Tues–Sun 9am–8pm (Sat until 11pm). Bus: 18, 55, 56, 61, or 68. Tram: 13, 15, or 16.

Museo dell'Automobile (Automobile Museum) ★ This shiny collection of mostly Italian automobiles—housed in a purpose-built, light-filled exhibition hall of classic 1960s design that reopened in 2011 after a 4-year makeover—draws car buffs from all over the world. Not too surprisingly, a century's worth of output from Fiat, which is headquartered less than a mile away, and the brands it owns are well represented. The collection includes most of the cars that have done Italy proud over the years, including Lancias, Alfa Romeos, and Ferraris that can top 160 miles an hour, but you will also find the automobiles of many other manufacturers including a Ford Model T from 1916 and a Trabant, the signature car of the former German Democratic Republic. With unexpected exhibits, including a mock apartment filled with things made from car parts, the curator has gone out of his way to make the museum engaging for those who prefer to walk or bike. In a nod to the undeniably heavy environmental impact of the car industry, another peculiar exhibit shows a few burned-out cars in a desolate, black landscape strewn with tires and dead trees.

Corso Unità d'Italia 40. ℂ **011-677-666.** www.museoauto.it. Admission 7€ adults, 5€ children 15 and under and seniors 65 and over. Mon 10am–2pm; Tues 2–7pm; Wed–Sun 10am–7pm (Fri–Sat until 9pm). Bus: 1, 18, 34, 35, 55, or 74. Metro: Lingotto.

Museo di Arte Orientale (MAO; Oriental Art Museum) ★ While you probably came to Italy dead set on seeing your favorite Botticelli, Raphael, or Caravaggio, you might want to set aside time for some non-Italian art and stop in at the MAO, which opened in December 2008 and catapulted Turin into the position as the premier place in the country to see Iranian porcelain, Chinese bronze art from 4,000 years ago, and Indian terracotta. The MAO has works from across Asia, including separate collections dedicated to Southeast Asia, China, India, Japan, the Himalayas, and Gandahara (an ancient kingdom located in what is now northwestern Pakistan and eastern Afghanistan). There is also an Islamic art gallery. The 1,500 pieces spread across the various galleries of the museum's 18th century Palazzo Mazzonis can be a bit much to take in on one visit, so you'd do well to choose a few areas to concentrate on.

Via San Domenico 11. ℂ **011-443-6927.** www.maotorino.it. Admission 7.50€ adults, 6€ ages 18–25 and seniors 65 and over, free for children 18 and under; free 1st Tues of the month if it's not a national holiday. Tues–Sun 10am–6pm. Bus: 11, 12, 27, 51, or 57. Tram: 4.

Museo Egizio (Egyptian Museum) ★★★ ☺ Turin's magnificent **Egyptian collection** is one of the world's largest. In fact, this was the world's first Egyptian museum, thanks to the Savoys, who amassed artifacts through most of their reign

A detail from the Museo Egizio's *Book of the Dead.*

(the museum continued to mount collecting expeditions throughout the early 20th c.). The most captivating exhibits are in Area 2 on the ground floor. These include the **Rock Temple of Ellessiya,** from the 15th-century B.C., which the Egyptian government presented to the museum in 1966 in gratitude for Italian efforts to save monuments threatened by the Aswan Dam. The two rooms nearby are staggering in the size and drama of the objects they house, most notably two sphinxes and a massive, richly painted statue of Ramses II. Smaller objects—mummies, funerary objects, and a papyrus *Book of the Dead*—fill the galleries on the next floor including palm leaf sandals found in the tomb of Queen Nefertari and what are thought to be her knees. Nothing beats a 4,000-year-old mummy to cheer up kids who are tired of touring (well, maybe a gelato would work even better).

Via Accademia delle Scienze 6. ✆ **011-561-7776.** www.museoegizio.it. Admission 7.50€ adults, 3.50€ ages 18–25, free for children 18 and under and seniors 65 and over 65. DC, MC, V. Tues–Sun 8:30am–7:30pm. Bus: 11, 12, 27, 55, 56, or 57. Tram: 13 or 15.

Museo Nazionale del Risorgimento Italiano (National Museum of the Risorgimento) An important slice of modern Italian history has been played out in Turin, and much of that in this *palazzo* that was home to the first king of a unified Italy, Vittorio Emanuele II, and the seat of its first parliament, in 1861. While any self-respecting town in Italy has a museum of the Risorgimento, the movement that launched Italian unification, this one is the best. Documents, paintings, and other paraphernalia recount the heady days when Vittorio Emanuele banded with Garibaldi and his Red Shirts to oust the Bourbons from Sicily and the Austrians from the north to create a unified Italy. The plaques that sum up each room are in English, and they will finally reveal to you the people behind the names of half the major streets and *piazze* in Italy—including Mazzini, Vittorio Emanuele II, Massimo d'Azeglio, Cavour, and Garibaldi. The last rooms house a fascinating collection that chronicles Italian Fascism and the resistance against it. Following a 5-year revamping, the museum reopened in March 2011, just in time to celebrate the 150th anniversary of Italy's unification.

Via Accademia delle Scienze 5. ✆ **011-562-1147.** www.museorisorgimentotorino.it. Admission 7€ adults; 5€ students 25 and under, and seniors 65 and over; 4€ high school students; 2€ middle and elementary school students; children 5 and under free. Tues–Sun 9am–7pm. Bus: 11, 12, 27, 55, 56, or 57. Tram: 13 or 15.

Palazzo Madama—Museo Civico di Arte Antica (Civic Museum of Ancient Art) ★ Don't be misled by the baroque facade, added by architect Filippo Juvarra in the 18th century. If you walk around the exterior of the *palazzo* (named for its most popular resident, Christine Marie of France, the daughter of French king Henry IV and Marie de' Medici), you'll discover that the massive structure incorporates a medieval castle, a Roman gate, and several Renaissance additions. Juvarra also added a monumental marble staircase to the interior, most of which is given over to the far-reaching collections of the Museo Civico di Arte Antica. The holdings focus on the medieval and Renaissance periods, shown off against the castle's unaltered, stony medieval interior. One of Italy's largest collections of ceramics is here, as well as some stunning canvases, including Antonello da Messina's *Portrait of a Man.*

In the Palazzo Madama, Piazza Castello. ✆ **011-443-3501.** www.palazzomadamatorino.it. Admission 7.50€ adults, 6€ youths 18–25 and seniors 65 and over. Tues–Sat 10am–6pm; Sun 10am–8pm. Bus: 11, 12, 27, 51, 55, 56, or 57. Tram: 4, 13, 15.

Arcaded sidewalks line Turin.

Palazzo Reale (Royal Palace) & Armeria Reale (Royal Armory) ★ The residence of the House of Savoy, begun in 1645 and designed by the Francophile Amedeo di Castellamonte, reflects the ornately baroque tastes of European ruling families of the time—a fact that will not be lost on you as you pass from one opulently decorated, heavily gilded room to the next. (The Savoys had a keener eye for paintings than for decor, and most of the canvases they collected are in the nearby Galleria Sabauda.) Most notable here are some of the tapestries, including the Gobelins depicting the life of Don Quixote, in the Sala delle Virtù (Hall of Virtues), and the collection of Chinese and Japanese vases in the Sala dell'Alcova. One of the quirkier architectural innovations, though not open to the public, is an antidote to several monumental staircases, a manually driven elevator from the 18th century.

One wing houses the **Armeria Reale,** one of the most important arms and armor collections in Europe, especially of weapons from the 16th and 17th centuries. Behind the palace, and offering a refreshing change from its frippery, are the **Giardini Reali (Royal Gardens),** laid out by Le Nôtre, more famous for Paris's Tuileries park and the gardens at Versailles.

Piazzetta Reale Palazzo: ℂ **011-436-1455.** Admission 6.50€ adults, 3.25€ ages 18–25, free for children 18 and under and seniors 65 and over. Tues–Sun 8:30am–7:30pm. Armeria: ℂ **011-543-889.** Admission 4€, 2€ ages 18–25, free for children under 18 and seniors over 65. Tues–Sun 8:30am–7:30pm. Bus: 11, 12, 27, 51, or 57. Tram: 4.

Piazze & Parks

Piazza San Carlo, Turin's most beautiful square, is the city's outdoor living room, surrounded by arcaded sidewalks that house the tables of the cafes for which Turin is famous (see "Cafes & Delicacy Shops," later). In the center is an equestrian statue of Duke Emanuele Filiberto of Savoy, and facing each other at the southern end of the piazza is a pair of 17th-century churches, San Carlo and Santa Cristina. The overall effect is one of elegant harmony.

At almost any time of day you will see the Torinesi out enjoying their beloved **Parco del Valentino,** a park flanking the Po river that is about 3 blocks wide and 1.6km (1 mile) long. The park is slightly displaced from the downtown area, but it is worth a visit because walking along the river immersed in green as you watch the rowers speed up and down the water is something that will remain with you for a long time. And for those who are up for a longish walk, in about 45-minutes by foot, and flanking the river the entire time, you can go from the top of the park (at the Umberto I bridge) to the Automobile Museum (p. 376).

Walking south in the park you will pass by the **Castello del Valentino,** a royal residence, begun in the 16th century but completed in the 17th century for Turin's beloved Marie Christine ("Madama Reale," wife of Savoy king Vittorio Amedeo) as a summer residence. It's a sign of Madama's Francophile leanings that, with its sloping roofs and forecourt, the castle resembles a French château. Used as a school of veterinary medicine, a military barracks, and currently as a university facility, the *castello* is continually undergoing renovations, and much of it, including many frescoed salons, is open to the public only on special occasions.

A little farther on, but still in the park, you will come to the **Borgo e Rocca Medioevale** (☏ 011-443-1701)—a faithful reconstruction of a medieval village (daily 9am–7pm, until 8pm in summer) built for Turin's 1884 world exposition—where you will find shops, taverns, houses, churches, and even a castle. The walk through the village is free, and pleasant enough, but since Piedmont and the rest of northern Italy are home to hundreds of bona fide medieval villages, in the case of the Rocca, it's hard to find a good reason to pony up 5€ for a look around a make-believe castle (Tues–Sun 10am–6pm).

Nearby Attractions

Basilica di Superga ★★ As thanksgiving to the Virgin Mary for Turin's deliverance from the French siege of 1706, Vittorio Amedeo II commissioned Juvarra, the Sicilian architect who did his greatest work in Turin, to build this baroque basilica on a hill high above the city. The exterior, with a beautiful neoclassical porch and lofty drum dome, is more interesting than the gloomy interior, a circular chamber beneath the dome with six chapels. The church serves as a

The Basilica di Superga, built high above the city.

pantheon for the House of Savoy, whose tombs are scattered about, many in the Crypt of Kings beneath the main chapel. The building also includes some royal apartments. The name "Superga," however, in the Italian memory will forever be associated with a plane crash there in 1949 that killed the members of the Torino soccer club, the reigning champions, who were flying home from Portugal. A small museum there about the "Grande Torino" squad is a fitting tribute to players who have become almost patron saints of the city. The trip up to the hilltop on a narrow railway through a verdant park is a favorite Torinese outing.

Strada della Basilica di Superga 73, about 6.5km (4 miles) northeast of the town center in Parco Naturale della Collina di Superga. © **011-899-7456.** www.basilicadisuperga.com. Free admission. Daily 9am–noon and 3–6pm (Nov–Mar until 5pm). Grande Torino Museum admission 2€. Reached by rack railway (4€ round-trip) with a terminus at Stazione Sassi on Piazza Gustavo Modena (follow Corso Casale on east side of the River Po). Bus: 61 from side of Vittorio Emanuele I bridge opposite Piazza Vittorio Veneto to Stazione Sassi.

Palazzina di Caccia di Stupinigi ★ The other great work of the architect Juvarra (besides the Basilica di Superga) is this sumptuous, lavishly decorated hunting lodge that the Savoys commissioned in 1729. The main part of the lodge, to which the members of the House of Savoy retired for hunts in the royal forests that still surround it, is shaped like a Saint Andrew's cross (the lower arms extended and curved back inward like giant pincers), fanning out from a circular, domed pavilion topped with a large bronze stag. The lavish interior is filled with furniture, paintings, and bric-a-brac assembled from the many Savoy residences, technically comprising a **Museo d'Arte e Ammobiliamento (Museum of Art and Furniture).** Stroll through the acres of excessively decorated apartments to understand why Napoleon chose this for his brief residency in the region. Outstanding among the many, many frescoes are the scenes of a deer hunt in the King's Apartment and the triumph of Diana in the grand salon. The elegant gardens and surrounding forests provide lovely terrain for a jaunt.

Piazza Principe Amedeo 7, Stupingi-Nichelino, 8.5km (5¼ miles) southwest of the city center. © **011-358-1220.** Admission 6.20€ adults, 5.15€ children 6–14. Tues–Sun 10am–6pm (late Oct to late Mar until 5pm). Bus: 63 from Porta Nuova train station to Piazza Caio Mario; change to bus 41.

Reggia di Venaria Reale ★ Built in the mid-17th century on a design by Amedeo di Castellamonte, who had previously worked on Turin's Palazzo Reale (p. 379), this massive complex and surrounding park is Turin's answer to Versailles. The UNESCO heritage site reopened in 2011 following a royal makeover that brought the palace back to life after decades of work. The Savoys used Venaria as a hunting lodge, and what a lodge it was with two picturesque internal courtyards and impressive royal gardens. But it is the Venaria's stately rooms, the most noteworthy of which is the *Salone di Diana*, that will likely remain in your memory long after you've left.

Piazza della Repubblica, Venaria Reale, 10km (6¼ miles) northwest of the city center. © **011-499-2333.** www.lavenaria.it. Admission 12€ adults, 8€ children 18 and under and seniors 65 and over, under 12 free. Tues–Fri 9am–6pm, Sat 9am–9:30pm, Sun 9am–8pm; shorter hours Nov–Apr. Royal gardens: Admission 4€ adults (5€ Sun and holidays), 3€ children 18 and under and seniors 65 and over (4€ Sun and holidays), under 12 free. Tues–Sun 9am–8pm (closed Oct, Mar at 7pm; Nov, Feb 6pm; Dec, Jan 5pm). Bus: 11 from Piazza Repubblica or 72 from northwest corner of downtown. There is also the Venaria Express bus that takes 40 minutes and runs Tues–Sun with stops downtown near Stazione Porta Nuova, on XX Settembre at corner of Via Bertola and at Stazione Porta Susa.

Where to Stay

EXPENSIVE

NH Santo Stefano ★ Just a few steps from the cathedral and Piazza Castello, this is perhaps the best located of Turin's high-end hotels. A stunning wooden staircase circles above the lobby giving a medieval air to this very modern hotel. Most rooms are big, all are comfortable and sleek, and because the hotel opened just in time for the 2006 Olympics, everything is relatively new. All fifth-floor rooms and half of the fourth-floor rooms have sloped ceilings that give the rooms a homey feel. The impressive breakfast can be consumed in the courtyard in good weather.

Via Porta Palatina 19, 10122 Torino. www.nh-hotels.com. 🕿 **011-522-3311.** Fax 011-522-3313. 125 units. 160€–245€ double; 185€–265€ superior double. Rates include breakfast. AE, MC, V. Parking 20€ in garage. **Amenities:** Bar; concierge; room service; spa (not included in room rate); Wi-Fi. *In room:* A/C, TV, hair dryer, Internet, minibar.

Victoria Hotel ★★ Step through the doors of this somewhat plain-looking building between the Via Roma and the river, and you'll think you're in an English country house. That's the whole idea, and the Anglophile decor works splendidly. The lobby is decorated as a country-house drawing room, with floral sofas, deep armchairs, and a view onto a garden; the room doubles as a bar and is a pleasant place to enjoy a drink before setting out for one of the nearby restaurants. The glass-enclosed breakfast room, where a sumptuous buffet is served, resembles a conservatory. "Deluxe" accommodations, each with its own distinctive look, are oversized and furnished with carefully chosen antiques and such flourishes as canopied beds, richly covered divans, and marble bathrooms. Room 309 has the price of a standard double, but you also get a large terrace, while room 408, a suite, has a Jacuzzi in the room.

Via Nino Costa 4, 10123 Turin. www.hotelvictoria-torino.com. 🕿 **011-561-1909.** Fax 011-561-1806. 106 units. 155€–245€ standard double; 180€–280€ deluxe double; 260€–325€ suite. Rates include breakfast. AE, MC, V. Parking 22€ at hotel (you must reserve a space) or 20€ in nearby garage. **Amenities:** Bar; bikes; concierge; pool; room service; smoke-free rooms; spa w/hot tub, sauna, and massage and facial services. *In room:* A/C, TV, hair dryer, minibar, Wi-Fi.

MODERATE

Hotel Bologna ★ 🗡 Just across the street from the Porta Nuova train station (under the arcade to the left), this is a good option for affordable comfort. Each of the 45 rooms, spread over several floors of a gracious 18th-century apartment house, is different from the next. Some are quite grand, incorporating frescoes, fireplaces, and other original details (no. 52 hasn't changed since five-time Italian Prime Minister Giovanni Giolitti stayed here at the turn of the 20th century, while 68 has a splendid painted ceiling). Other rooms have been renovated in sleek modern style, with laminated, built-in cabinetry and neutral carpeting. Still others fall in between, with well-maintained 1970s-style furnishings and linoleum flooring. Whatever the vintage, all the rooms are spotlessly clean and nicely maintained. It's key to ask for an internal room if the street traffic is going to bother you.

Corso Vittorio Emanuele II 60, 10121 Turin. www.hotelbolognasrl.it. 🕿/fax **011-562-0193.** 45 units. 75€–100€ double. Rates include breakfast. MC, V. Free parking (call ahead for a space). **Amenities:** Bar; concierge; room service. *In room:* A/C (in some), TV, hair dryer, minibar, Wi-Fi.

Hotel Due Mondi This modern hotel in a residential neighborhood 2 blocks east of Porta Nuova train station has comfortable beds, modern units, and has been somewhat remodeled in recent years. Rooms are a wee bit cramped but retain some nice touches, such as faded remnants of frescoes on some ceilings. The hotel is worthwhile only near the low end of the wide fork in room rates (the highest prices are only applied during trade fairs).

Via Saluzzo 3, 10125 Torino. www.hotelduemondi.it. © **011-650-5084** or 011-669-8981. Fax 011-669-9383. 42 units. 65€–190€ double. Rates include breakfast. AE, MC, V. Parking 15€ in hotel garage. **Amenities:** Italian restaurant; bar; concierge; room service; smoke-free rooms. *In room:* A/C, TV w/pay movies, hair dryer, minibar, Wi-Fi.

INEXPENSIVE

Hotel Bellavista What will strike you first about this *pensione,* which occupies the sixth floor of an apartment house on a quiet street not far from Hotel Due Mondi, is just how pleasant the surroundings are—step off the elevator and you will find yourself in a sun-filled corridor that's a garden of houseplants and opens onto a wide terrace. There's also a pleasant bar area. Rooms are airy and comfortable but a little less inspiring in decor, with banal, functional modern furnishings. Most, though, afford pleasant views over the surrounding rooftops—the best outlooks in the house are across the river toward the hills. What most rooms don't have is a private bathroom, though the several communal ones are well placed so most rooms are only a few steps away from a facility.

Via Galliari 15, 10125 Turin. www.bellavista-torino.it. © **011-669-8139.** Fax 011-668-7989. 18 units. 40€–50€ double; 60€–70€ triple. Rates include breakfast. AE, MC, V. Free parking. **Amenities:** Bar; smoke-free rooms. *In room:* TV.

Hotel Mobledor Located just steps from the Mole, the Mobledor is quiet, unassuming, and ideal for those interested in only a nice, clean place to spend the night. The rooms are simple but tastefully decorated like the guest room of your grandmother's cottage, with plants and framed prints. There are showers and sinks in every room, but you have to share a bathroom, and you will have to push two single beds together to make a "double".

Via Accademia Albertina 1, 10123 Turin. www.hotelmobledor.it. © **011-888-445.** Fax 011-812-5805. 10 units. 60€ double. No credit cards. Parking 20€ in nearby garage. *In room:* A/C, TV.

Where to Eat

One of the great pleasures of being in Piedmont is sampling the region's unique cuisine. Two pastas you will encounter on menus are *agnolotti* (a type of ravioli often stuffed with an infusion of cheese and meat) and *tajarin,* a flat egg noodle that is often topped with porcini mushrooms. While the Piemontesi love their grilled meat and game, there are enough vegetables in the local diet to make a meatless meal pretty easy to have; one of the favorite preparations is *bagna cauda* (hot dip), in which raw vegetables are dipped into a heated preparation of oil, anchovies, and garlic. If you have a sweet tooth, you will quickly discover that Turin and outlying towns can amply satisfy cravings for sweets, largely with pastries. Additionally, with wines as good as Piedmont produces (see "Visiting the Wine Villages," p. 394), even a carafe of the house red is likely to be memorable.

C'era Una Volta ★★★ PIEMONTESE A large, old-fashioned dining room filled with heavy, old tables and chairs and dark credenzas greets you as you enter "Once Upon a Time." While this is a quintessentially Torinese establishment that is committed to the heritage of the region's cuisine, you will also likely find some variations such as buttery spinach dumplings, and tagliatelle with fava beans. For secondo, if you are ready to turn your back on the usual Piemontese standbys (all done perfectly), you won't go wrong with the succulent grilled lamb chops or the local Toma cheese served with speck (smoked ham) and orange marmalade. The menu, which changes monthly and is based on the availability of ingredients, almost always has one or two fish dishes, though you're much better off opting for the meat, cheese, and vegetables. You can accompany your meal with a fine Barolo or any other of the cellar's 300 local labels.

Corso Vittorio Emanuele II 41. © **011-655-498.** www.ristoranteceraunavolta.it. Reservations recommended. Primi 7.50€–9.50€; secondi 14€–17€; tasting menu 26€–28€. AE, MC, V. Mon–Sat 8–11pm (sometimes they will open if you call to reserve for Sun or for lunch during the week). Closed Aug.

Cianci ★★ 🎁 PIEMONTESE/TRATTORIA If you're disappointed at not having meet a Torinese who invites you home for dinner, come to this friendly trattoria where the experience will be as close to a home cooked meal as you are going to get at a restaurant. Marco, Gianni, and Danilo, who opened Cianci in 2010, are constantly changing the menu, which you will find displayed on a big chalkboard near the entrance to the restaurant. There is usually at least one Piemontese standby among the primi (often tajarin in some incarnation) and secondi (here it's anybody's guess, though if rabbit is on the menu that's always a good bet). The cheap prices are accompanied by an offering of Piemontese wine (the heavier ones like Barolo are only available in the winter) and the possibility to sit out in an enchanting little square if the weather permits.

Largo IV Marzo 9B. © **338-876-7003.** Reservations recommended. Primi 5€; secondi 6€. MC, V. Mon–Sun noon–3pm and 7:30–11pm. Bus: 11, 12, 27, 51, or 57. Tram: 4.

Pastificcio De Felippis ★★ 🎁 ITALIAN This is pasta at its freshest. Since 1872, De Felippis has been making fresh pasta that the Torinesi take home, throw in boiling water, and serve up on special occasions. In 2007, they set out some tables on Via La Grange, which had just been closed to traffic, and started boiling the water themselves. All sauces, whether the pesto, fish, or ragù are subtle because here it is all about the pasta and the idea is to make sure an overly aggressive sauce doesn't steal the show. There are a few secondi on the menu, but your best bet is to come here for a light lunch, order only a pasta (and perhaps one of the sumptuous desserts—vanilla crème brûlée anybody?) and then save space for a large dinner. If you do go for dessert, avoid the *mattone,* the aptly named "brick," which is their interpretation of tiramisu.

Via La Grange 39. © **011-542-137.** www.pastificiodefilippis.com. Reservations recommended. Primi 9€–10€; secondi 9€–12€. MC, V. Mon–Sun noon–3pm and 7:30–11pm. Bus: 11, 12, 27, 51, or 57. Tram: 4.

Porto di Savona ★★ 🍴 PIEMONTESE/TRATTORIA What might be the most popular trattoria in Turin has been tucked under the arcades along the city's largest piazza since 1863, when Turin was briefly the capital of the just-unified Italy. Seating is family style, at long tables that crowd a series of rooms beneath old photos and mementos, and the typically Piemontese fare never fails to please (all the more so on Sun, when many other restaurants in central Turin are closed). Gnocchi are made fresh daily and you can usually also find hand-made *tajarin,* a flat egg noodle. If you haven't yet had agnolotti (meat-filled pasta ringlets) in Turin, your dinner at Porto di Savona will be the chance to rectify your critical oversight. This is also the place to close your eyes and try the *fritto misto piemontese* (fried beef innards); love it or not, you'll have a good story to tell when you're back home.

Piazza Vittorio Veneto 2. www.foodandcompany.com/food&company.html. ☎ **011-817-3500.** Reservations recommended. Primi 7€–8.50€; secondi 8.50€–20€. MC, V. Daily 12:30–2:30pm and 7:30–10:30pm. Bus: 53, 55, 56, or 61. Tram: 13 or 15.

Ristorante Tre Galline ★ PIEMONTESE As one of Turin's most popular eateries for more than 3 centuries, this bright wood-paneled restaurant has friendly, professional service and a good-value tasting menu. The *salumi* are hand-carved at your table for an appetizer, and the ever-changing menu mixes Torinese and Piemontese specialties with slightly creative dishes that use local ingredients. While two of their better creations include *agnolotti* in ragù and rabbit cooked in apple vinegar, the restaurant is probably best known for its *bollito misto* (boiled meat) that is served from a cart that periodically appears between the tables. Same idea as the dessert cart only you are picking out the piece of boiled meat you want, served with various sauces. The formidable *fritto misto piemontese* is only served in the winter.

Via Gian Francesco Bellezia 37. ☎ **011-436-6553.** www.3galline.it. Reservations highly recommended. Primi 13€–15€; secondi 20€–25€; tasting menu 50€, not including wine. AE, MC, V. Tues–Sat 12:30–2:15pm and 7:45–11pm; Mon 12:30–2:15pm. Bus: 3, 4, 16, or 57.

Trattoria Salentina ★ 🍴 APULIAN/TRATTORIA At a certain point, you'll need something lighter than Piemontese cuisine can offer. That's okay—it happens to everybody who comes to Turin and when it does, Trattoria Salentina with its southern Puglia cuisine is a good bet. The down-homey get-up of the trattoria (copper pots hanging from a yellow wall with a slightly ridiculous fresco) matches the food. Apulian specialties such as *orecchiette con rape* and *ciceri e tria* (egg pasta cooked in a broth of tomatoes, celery, garlic, onion, carrot, and chickpeas and topped with a little bit of crunchy, fried pasta), are near perfect, not surprising since the trattoria is run by a family from Salento (the heel of the Italian boot). Fridays and Saturdays, there's a *fritto misto* (large pieces of fried fish) that's crispy yet light enough that you'll still have space for a homemade dessert.

Via Galliari 10bis/A. ☎ **011-427-0532.** Reservations not accepted. Primi 4€–6€; secondi 5€–9€. Mon–Sat noon–2:30pm and 7–11:30pm (Sat closed for lunch). Bus: 1, 34, 35, 52, 67, or 68. Tram: 7 or 9.

Cafes & Delicacy Shops

Cafe sitting is a centuries-old tradition in sophisticated Turin. Via Roma and the *piazze* it widens into are lined with gracious salons that have been serving coffee to Torinese for centuries. Below are some of the city's classic cafes. While espresso and pastries are the mainstays of the menu at all of them, most also serve chocolates—including the mix of chocolate and hazelnuts known as *gianduiotti*—that are among the city's major contributions to culinary culture.

Keep in mind that as is the case all across Italy, in the fancier cafes the price of getting your drink served at a table can be three times what you will pay standing at the bar (in Caffè Torino, for example, a cappuccino costs 1.60€ at the bar and 5.50€ at a table, while in Caffè San Carlo the difference is 1.40€ versus 4.50€). The same goes for pastries and sandwiches that can be consumed standing up or at a table.

Turin has a sizable sweet tooth, satisfied by any number of pastry and candy shops. One of the best chocolatiers in all of northern Italy is **Guido Gobino ★**, Via Lagrange 1/A (☎ **011-566-0707**), open daily 10am to 8 pm (Mon opens at 3pm). If Guido Gobino is not the best, that title very well might go to **Guido Castagna ★**, Via Maria Vittoria, 27/C (☎ **011-1988-6585**), open Tuesday through Saturday 10:30am to 7:30pm and Monday 3:30 to 7:30pm (June and July closed Mon, and 2–3pm other days). Walk into Guido Castagna and you are likely to think you've stumbled into a jewelry shop—such is the presentation and veneration afforded the chocolate. A wide variety of chocolates and other sweets, including sumptuous meringues, have been dispensed since 1836 at **Fratelli Stratta,** Piazza San Carlo 191 (☎ **011-547-920;** www.stratta1836.it), open Monday through Friday 8am to 8pm, Saturday 9am to 8pm, and Sunday 10am to 7pm.

The surrounding region is known not only for its wines but also for vermouth—the famed **Cinzano,** for instance, is produced south of the city in the town of Santa Vittoria d'Alba. Come evening, a glass of vermouth is the preferred drink at many of the city's cafes. **Paissa,** at Piazza San Carlo 196 (☎ **011-562-8462**), open Monday through Saturday 9am to 7:30pm, is the place to purchase local vermouths.

Caffè Confetteria al Bicerin ★ CAFE What claims to be Turin's oldest cafe, open since 1763 and still sporting the original 18th-century counter as well as marble-topped tables, is famous for its illustrious clientele, which has included Nietzsche, Dumas, and Puccini, as well as its signature drink—the Bicerin (local dialect for "small glass"). This calorie bomb combines coffee, hot chocolate, and cream and though it can be had in other cafes around town, if you are going to indulge you might as well have the best.

Piazza della Consolata 5. ☎ **011-436-9325.** www.bicerin.it. Bicherin 5€. MC, V. Thurs–Tues 8:30am–7:30pm.

Caffè Fiorio ★ CAFE Opened in 1780, the Fiorio was also a mainstay on the social circuit for aristocrats and other habitués with too much time on their hands and too many thoughts on their minds (Herman Melville and Mark Twain are said to have stopped by on their trips through Turin). It serves a lunch buffet and some of the best ice cream in town.

Via Po 8. ☎ **011-817-3225.** www.fioriocaffegelateria.com. Sandwiches, pastries, ice cream, and dishes 2.50€–12€. AE, MC, V. Daily 8am–1am (Sun opens 8:30am; Fri–Sat closes 2am).

Caffè-Pasticceria Baratti e Milano CAFE No small part of the pleasure of sitting for a time in this stylish cafe, opened in 1875, is watching a clientele that includes auto executives, elegantly clad shoppers, and visitors to the nearby museums, all sipping espressos and munching on the delicious house pastries.

Piazza Castello 27. ☎ **011-440-7138.** www.barattiemilano.it. Sandwiches and pastries 3€–8€. AE, MC, V. Tues–Sun 8am–8pm.

Caffè San Carlo ★★ CAFE One of the essential stops on any tour of Turin is this classic cafe. The San Carlo opened its doors in 1837 and ever since has been accommodating patrons beneath a huge chandelier of Murano glass in a salon that is a remarkable assemblage of gilt, mirrors, and marble. An adjoining, frescoed tearoom is quieter and only a little less grand.

Piazza San Carlo 156. ☎ **011-532-586.** Sandwiches and pastries 2.50€–12€. AE, DC, MC, V. Daily 8am–midnight (Mon–Tues until 9pm).

Caffè Torino ★★ CAFE The mirrored and frescoed salons in Caffè Torino, opened in 1903, create an unforgettable atmosphere for one of the pastries or chocolates handsomely displayed in the main room. This place is great for a cheap, fast, light meal: At lunch and dinner, plates at the bar are loaded with bite-size sandwiches, pizzas, stuffed olives, fried cheese and veggies, and other goodies—all yours for the gobbling with the purchase of a drink.

Piazza San Carlo 204. ⓒ **011-545-118.** www.caffe-torino.it. Sandwiches and pastries 2€–7€. AE, MC, V. Daily 7:30am–midnight.

Turin After Dark

Turin has a lively classical music and opera scene, and you can get info on these and other cultural events at the **Vetrina Infocultura** office at Piazza Castello 161, at the beginning of Corso Garibaldi (ⓒ **011-535-181**), open daily 9am to 7pm. This office also doubles as one of the two tourist offices in town. Aside from the city's much-attended summer festivals (see "Festivals & Markets," p. 369), there are regular classical concerts by the National Symphonic Orchestra at **Auditorium della RAI,** Via Rossini 15 (ⓒ **011-810-4653;** www.orchestra sinfonica.rai.it). Other concerts, dance performances, and operas are staged at the city's venerable **Teatro Regio** (ⓒ **011-881-5241;** www.teatroregio.torino. it), in the center of the city on Piazza Castello. If instead you are looking for an after-dinner drink in a hip yet relaxed atmosphere filled with Torinesi young and old, there is **La Drogheria** at Piazza Vittorio Veneto 18 (ⓒ **812-2414**), open daily until 2am (Fri–Sat until 3am).

Day Trips from Turin

SACRA DI SAN MICHELE ★★★

Perched high atop Monte Pirchiriano—part of it projecting over the precipice on an elaborate support system that was one of the engineering feats of the Middle Ages—this dramatically situated **abbey** (ⓒ **011-939-130;** www.sacradisan michele.com) dedicated to Saint Michael provides views and an astonishing look at medieval religious life. It may well remind you of Mont Saint-Michel monastery in France (Mont Saint-Michel, off the Normandy coast of France, was one of the 176 religious institutions that once fell under the jurisdiction of Italy's San Michele, which today is all but forgotten). But with its dizzying views and scary drops, it just as easily may remind you of the abbey in the novel and film *The Name of the Rose* (author Umberto Eco based his fictional abbey on this one). It was started in 983, but the extant church dates to the abbey's 12th-century heyday. A vast staircase hewn out of rock and clinging to the abbey's buttresses (known as *Scalone dei Morti* [Stairs of Death] because monks' corpses were once laid out here) leads to the massive carved doorway depicting the signs of the zodiac and the drafty Gothic and Romanesque church, decorated only with scraps of 16th-century frescoes by Secondo del Bosco. Another stairway leads down to three tiny chapels, carved into the rock, that contain tombs of some of the earliest members of the House of Savoy.

On Saturday evenings (and some Fridays) from March to December, the atmospheric church hosts **concerts** of everything from chant and liturgical music to Renaissance chamber pieces, gospel, and traditional Celtic airs; check the website for schedules.

The abbey is outside Avigliana, 15km (9¼ miles) west of Turin's ring road. Admission is 5€ adults, 4€ children 6 to 14 and seniors 65 and over. It's open Tuesday to Saturday 9:30am to 12:30pm and 2:30 to 5pm; Sunday 9:30am to noon and 2:40 to 5pm (mid-Mar to mid-Oct open an hour later; July–Sept open Mon).

GETTING THERE Take one of 20 trains a day from Turin to Avigliana (30 min.); from there, it's a 1½-hour trek up to the abbey from the Sant'Ambrogio station, or else you can get a taxi to take you the 13km (8 miles) from Avigliana train station. On Sundays from May to September, there is a shuttle that runs back and forth between the Avigliana train station and the abbey, but it sometimes gets cancelled so check with the tourist office in Turin if you are counting on it. By car, follow the A32 from Turin's western ring highway toward Bardonecchia/Frejus. Get off at the Avigliana Est exit and follow the brown signs to Sacra di San Michele; the trip takes about an hour.

Crumbling ruins on Monte Pirchiriano, at the Sacra di San Michele.

SAVIGLIANO & SALUZZO

Savigliano ★★ is one of those towns everyone dreams of stumbling upon in Italy—it's filled with Renaissance riches, but it's still undiscovered. The town center is the broad expanse of the Piazza Santa Rosa, surrounded by arcades, overlooked by a medieval tower, and lined with many of the town's grand palaces, which once housed summering members of the Savoy clan. Unfortunately, these and another fine collection of *palazzi* along the Via Jerusalem are closed to the public, so you'll have to settle for a gander at their gorgeous facades.

The pride of **Saluzzo** ★ is its sleepy upper town, huddled beneath its Castello di Manta. Along the warren of narrow lanes, you'll find the 13th-century Chiesa di San Giovanni and the Casa Cavassa, which is worth a look not for the musty civic museum it houses, but for its porticoed courtyard.

GETTING THERE Savigliano is 54km (33 miles) south of Turin, from which there are two to four trains per hour (35–50 min.). From there, hourly trains make the 13-minute run to Saluzzo. Saluzzo is also connected with Turin by 15 buses a day. The most direct driving route to Savigliano from Turin follows Autostrada A6 for 34km (21 miles) south to the exit near Bra. From the exit, follow S231 west for 9.5km (6 miles). Saluzzo is another 13km (8 miles) west on S231. If you are making the sweep through the wine country via Asti and Alba (see below), you can continue west from Alba for 34km (21 miles) on S231 to Savigliano.

THE PIEDMONT WINE COUNTRY

Asti: 60km (37 miles) SE of Turin, 127km (79 miles) SW of Milan; Alba: 60km (37 miles) S of Turin, 155km (96 miles) SW of Milan

South of Turin, the Po valley rises into the rolling Langhe and Roero hills, flanked by orchards and vineyards. You'll recognize the region's place names from the labels of its first-rate wines, among them **Asti Spumanti, Barbaresco,** and **Barolo.** Tasting these vintages at the source is one reason to visit the wine country, of course; another is to stroll through the medieval and Renaissance towns that rise from the vineyards and the picturesque villages that crown many a hilltop. And vines are not all that flourish in the fertile soil—truffles top the list of the region's gastronomic delights, which also include down-home country fare like rabbit and game dishes, excellent cheeses, and plump fruit.

Asti

The Asti of sparkling-wine fame is a bustling city more concerned with everyday business than with entertaining visitors, but there are many treasures to be found in the history-drenched Old Town—medieval towers (120 of them still stand), Renaissance palaces, and broad *piazze* provide the perfect setting in which to sample the town's famous product.

Festivals & Markets In late June and early July, Asti stages **Astiteatro** (✆ 0141-399-111), a theater festival with performances that incorporate dance and music. September, though, is the town's busy cultural month, with townsfolk and horses alike donning medieval garb for its famous **Palio** on the third Sunday (see the "Horses & Donkeys" box, above). Local wine producers converge on the

---

HORSES & donkeys

Asti and Alba, bitter rivals through much of the Middle Ages, each celebrate the autumn harvest with equine celebrations that are horses of a very different color.

The **Palio** (✆ 0141-399-482; www.palio. asti.it), Asti's annual horse race, is run the third Sunday of September. Like the similar but more famous horse race that the Tuscan city of Siena mounts, Asti's Palio begins with a medieval pageant through the town and ends with a wild bareback ride around the Campo del Palio. The race coincides with Asti's other great revel, the **Douja d'Or** (www. doujador.it), a weeklong fair-cum-bacchanal celebrating the grape.

On the first Sunday of October, Alba pulls a spoof on Asti with the **Palio degli Asini (Race of the Asses; ✆ 0173-362-806)**. The event, which coincides with Alba's annual truffle fair, is not as speedy as Asti's slicker horseback Palio, but it's a lot more fun. Good-natured as the event is, though, it is rooted in some of the darkest days of Alba's history. In the 13th century, Asti, then one of the most powerful republics of northern Italy, besieged Alba and burned the surrounding vineyards. Then, to add insult to injury, the victors held their *palio* in Alba, just to put the humbled citizenry further in its place. Alba then staged a *palio* with asses, a not-so-subtle hint of what they thought of their victors and their pompous pageantry.

town the 2 weeks before the Palio for the **Douja d'Or** (www.doujador.it), an exhibition of local vintages accompanied by tastings; this is the perfect way to sample the products of the many wineries in the hills surrounding Asti and nearby Alba. On the second Sunday of September, surrounding villages mount feasts (almost always accompanied by a communal meal) known collectively as the **Pjasan.**

Being the agricultural center that it is, Asti has two **food markets.** The larger is held Wednesdays and Saturdays 7:30am to 1pm in the **Campo del Palio,** with stalls selling every foodstuff imaginable—seeds, herbs, flowers, farm implements, and no end of other merchandise—and spilling over to the Piazza della Libertà and Piazza Alfieri. Meanwhile, Asti's covered food market, the **Mercato Coperto,** is also located in this vicinity, on Piazza della Libertà, and is open Monday through Wednesday and Friday 8am to 1pm and 3:30 to 7:30pm, Thursday 8:30am to 1pm, and Saturday 8am to 7:30pm. There's also a small **antiques fair** on the fourth Sunday of every month except August.

ESSENTIALS

GETTING THERE By Train One to four trains an hour link Asti with **Turin** (30–60 min.). There are 14 trains daily between Asti and Alba, some of which require that you change trains at Nizza Monferrato or occasionally at Castagnole delle Lanze (35 min.–1 hr.).

By Bus From Turin, **Arfea** (☏ 0144-322-023; www.arfea.com) runs two buses per day, one morning and one mid-afternoon, on the hour-long ride to Asti. **Giachino** (☏ 0141-937-510; www.giachino.it) makes the hour-long trip to and from Alba, about once per hour.

By Car Asti, 60km (37 miles) east of Turin, can be reached from Turin in less than an hour via Autostrada 21.

VISITOR INFORMATION The **APT tourist office** is near the train station at Piazza Alfieri 34 (☏ 0141-530-357). Hours are Monday to Saturday 9am to 1pm and 2:30 to 6:30pm, and Sunday 9am to 1pm. Among the office's offerings is a *Carta del Vini,* an annotated map that will point you to surrounding vineyards that provide wine tastings.

EXPLORING THE TOWN

If you take the train to Asti, you will step right into the heart of the action—the town's lively clothing-and-food **markets** occupy three adjoining *piazze* just to the north of the station (Campo del Palio, Piazza Libertà, and Piazza Alfieri). If you're arriving by car, you're most likely to find parking in one of the lots in this area as well.

Walk through the *piazze* to **Corso Alfieri;** the town's Renaissance palaces are located on or just off this major thoroughfare, usually closed to traffic. This street and Asti's grandest piazza are named for the town's most famous native son, the 18th-century poet Vittorio Alfieri. His home, on the Corso at 375, houses a small, memento-filled museum.

Second to none in Asti is San Secondo, the town's patron saint. He was imprisoned at the western end of Corso Alfieri in the **Torre Rossa**—much of which dates to the 1st century (probably part of a Roman gate) with two levels tacked on in the 11th century—then beheaded on the spot just south of Corso Alfieri, where the **Collegiata di San Secondo** (☏ 0141-530-066) now stands. Not only does this Romanesque-Gothic structure have the honor of housing the saint's remains in its eerie crypt, but it is also the permanent home of the coveted Palio Astigiano, the banner awarded to the horseman who wins the town's annual Palio (see the "Horses & Donkeys" box, above; Secondo is the patron saint of this event). The church is open daily from 10:45am to noon and 3:30 to 5:30pm (Sun morning for Mass only).

Asti's "other" church is its 14th-century, redbrick **Cattedrale** (✆ **0141-592-924**), which you can reach by walking through Piazza Cairoli, at the western end of Corso Alfieri, into the nearby Piazza Cattedrale. Every inch of this brick church's cavernous interior is festooned with frescoes by late-18th-century artists, including Gandolfino d'Asti; trompe l'oeil vines climb many of the columns. The cathedral is open daily from 8:30am to noon and 3 to 5:30pm.

The most notable feature of the church of **San Pietro in Consavia** (✆ **0141-353-072**), at the eastern end of Corso Alfieri, is its round, 10th-century baptistery; the 15th-century interior and adjoining cloisters house a one-room paleontology collection (Tues–Sun 10am–1pm and 4–7pm; Nov–Mar until 6pm).

WHERE TO STAY

Hotel Aleramo ★ Located just around the corner from Hotel Rainero, this slightly more up-scale option offers spotless rooms, comfortable beds and a designer feel. Rooms vary considerably in their getup so if that's important, make sure you ask what room you are getting. The "Japanese room" is predictably minimalist in black and white. There are also "orange," "yellow," and "blue" rooms as well as a "gold and silver room" with a slightly psychedelic floral pattern on the wall behind the headboard.

Via Filiberto 13, 14100 Asti. www.aleramo.it. ✆ **0141-595-661.** Fax 0141-30-039. 42 units. 120€–140€ double; 160€ triple. Rates include breakfast. AE, DC, MC, V. Parking in garage 14€. **Amenities:** Room service. *In room:* A/C, TV, hair dryer, minibar, Wi-Fi.

Hotel Rainero ★ ☺ The Rainero, which has been run by the same family for three generations and was being restructured in 2012, enjoys a wonderful location just west of the Campo del Palio. Not only is this setting convenient, but since many of the surrounding streets are closed to traffic, the neighborhood is quiet. Room nos. 309 to 311 have terraces (views only of surrounding modern buildings), and nos. 153 and 155 have balconies looking onto a cobbled street; there's also a large roof terrace. Room 158 is large enough to be a quad and has a table and chairs on the walkway out front. Large room no. 161 gets one of those plant-filled courtyards all to itself.

Via Cavour 85, 14100 Asti. www.hotelrainero.com. ✆ **0141-353-866.** Fax 0141-594-985. 55 units. 85€–110€ double; 140€–150€ suite. Breakfast 8€. AE, DC, MC, V. Parking in lot in front of hotel 10€. Closed 1st week of Jan. **Amenities:** Bar; room service, Wi-Fi (fee). *In room:* A/C, TV, hair dryer, minibar.

WHERE TO EAT

Campanarò ★ PIEMONTESE For years Duilio Moiso ran a popular restaurant in a medieval *palazzo,* but when that lease ran out in 2003 he moved over here, a few steps from Piazza Alfieri, where he is still serving up fantastic Piemontese food though in a less suggestive setting. Delicious local dishes you'll find on the ever-changing menu may include *agnolotti* in ragù, *taglierini* with truffles, *cinghiale* (stewed wild boar), *stracotta alla Barbera* (strip beef cooked in red wine), or *coniglio al vino bianco* (rabbit cooked in white wine). All the pasta is made on site and the extensive wine list is well priced.

Via Secondo Arò 30. ✆ **0141-33252.** Reservations recommended. Primi 9€–13€; secondi 10€–15€. AE, MC, V. Thurs–Tues noon–3pm and 7:30–10pm (Sat closed at lunch).

Il Convivio ★★ PIEMONTESE The no-nonsense decor reflects the fact that the main business at this restaurant located on a small street just south of the Collegiata di San Secondo is to serve perfectly prepared food and accompany it with the region's best, but not necessarily most expensive, wines (these are dispensed from an extensive cellar that you can visit). Only a few starters, pasta dishes, and main courses are prepared daily. You'll always find wonderful fresh-made pastas such as *taglierini* in a light vegetable sauce, a soup incorporating vegetables bought that morning from Asti's markets, and serious meat dishes, such as a masterful *osso buco di vitello, brasato di cinghiale,* or *coniglio* sautéed with olives and white wine. Desserts, including a heavenly *panna cotta al cioc-colato,* are as memorable as the rest of the dining experience.

Via G. B. Giuliani 4-6. ✆ **0141-594-188.** Reservations recommended. Primi 8€–11€; secondi 10€–13€. AE, DC, MC, V. Mon–Sat noon–2:30pm and 8–10pm. Closed last 2 weeks of Aug and Dec 24–Jan 6.

Alba

Alba retains a medieval flavor that's as mellow as the wines it produces. It's a pleasure to walk along the Via Vittorio Emanuele and the narrow streets of the Old Town, visit the 14th-century Duomo, and peer into shop windows with lav-ish displays of Alba's wines; its other famous product, truffles; and its less noble, but enticing, *nocciolata,* a decadent concoction of nuts and chocolate.

Festivals & Markets October is Alba's big month. Its annual **truffle festival** is held the first week, and this, in turn, climaxes in the **Palio degli Asini** (see "Horses & Donkeys" box, above). On Saturday and Sunday mornings, from the second weekend in October through December, Alba hosts a **truffles market,** where you may well be tempted to part with your hard-earned cash for one of the fragrant specimens (the price of which depends on how much the local truffle hunters have managed to dig up; in particularly lean years it can top 1,500€ per pound).

ESSENTIALS

GETTING THERE By Train Only one direct train (in the evening, after 6pm) runs between Turin and Alba (1 hr.); otherwise, there's one per hour requiring a change either in Bra or Cavallermaggiore (1¼–2 hr.). There are 11 trains daily between Alba and Asti (30–60 min.).

The truffle market in Alba.

By Bus Alba's Autostazione bus terminal (✆ **0175-478-811;** www.atibus.it) is on Piazza Medford. Hourly GTT (✆ **800-019-152;** www.comune.torino.it/gtt) buses make the trip between Alba and Turin in about 1¾ hours.

By Car The most direct way to reach Alba from Turin is to follow Autostrada A6 for 35km (22 miles) south to the exit near Bra, and from the Autostrada exit S231, go east for 24km (15 miles) to Alba. If you want to work Alba into a trip to Asti, take A21 to Asti and, from there, follow S231 southwest for 30km (19 miles) to Alba.

Alba's **tourist offices,** which also serves the surrounding area, is near the Duomo at Piazza Risorgimento 19 (✆**0173-35-833;** fax 0173-363-878; www.langheroero.it) and is open daily 9am to 6:30pm (Sat–Sun from 10am).

EXPLORING THE TOWN

Alba's two major sights face the brick expanse of **Piazza Risorgimento,** at the northern end of its major thoroughfare, **Corso Vittorio Emanuele.** The 14th-century brick **Duomo** is flanked by a 13th-century bell tower. Most of the interior and paintings hail from the late 19th century, save the two late baroque lateral chapels and the **elaborately carved and inlaid choir stalls** ★ from 1512.

The town's two art treasures hang in the council chamber of the **Palazzo Comunale** across the square (go through the door on the right and up to the top of the stairs)—an early-16th-century portrait of the Virgin by Alba's greatest painter, Macrino d'Alba, and *Concertino,* by Mattia Preti, a follower of Caravaggio. It's open only during city office hours, Tuesday through Friday 8:15am to 12:15pm, Saturday 8:15am to noon.

From here, stroll the shopping promenade **Corso Vittorio** a few blocks to enjoy the low-key pace in the traffic-free heart of the town.

WHERE TO STAY

Hotel Savona ★ The simple yet spacious rooms in this hotel facing a shady piazza at the south edge of the Old Town have a slick, modern look. The rooms are pleasantly decorated in pastel shades and have contemporary furnishings and shiny new bathrooms, most with bathtubs and many with Jacuzzis. Many rooms open onto small terraces; the quietest face an interior courtyard. If you are looking for a thrill, the hotel sells package deals that include the use of a Vespa, the perfect way to explore the surrounding wine villages (2 nights for two people with the use of a Vespa for a day will cost you 310€). And if you have come to town to spend on shoes and shirts rather than truffles and Barolo, the hotel can hook you up with a personal shopper.

Via Roma 1 (just off Piazza Savona), 12051 Alba (CN). www.hotelsavona.com. ✆**0173-440-440.** Fax 0173-364-312. 90 units. 105€–127€ double. Rates include breakfast. AE, DC, MC, V. Parking 6€ in courtyard. **Amenities:** Restaurant (local cuisine); bar; concierge; room service. *In room:* A/C, TV w/pay movies, hair dryer, minibar, Wi-Fi.

WHERE TO EAT

Enoclub ★ PIEMONTESE The evocatively chic brick-vaulted basement here is devoted to fine wine coupled with solid, slightly refined Piemontese cooking. The nice variety of rich pasta dishes includes *tajarin* (Piedmont's answer to tagliatelle) topped with a rich lamb sauce, and *fettuccine di farro* (noodles made from barley rather than wheat) tossed with pesto and served with potatoes and beans. Because this is Piedmont, the secondi are meaty: veal steak with aromatic herbs, rabbit cooked in red wine, and duck breast in a black-olive paste.

Up on the ground floor is the busy **Umberto Notte** bar (open evenings only), one of Alba's few late-night scenes, dispensing wines by the glass, from 3€. This is a fine place to sample the produce of the local vineyards as well as wines from all over the world.

Piazza Savona 4. ✆**0173-33-994.** Reservations not necessary. Primi 10€–15€; secondi 11€–17€; tasting menu 40€. AE, MC, V. Tues–Sun noon–2:30pm and 7:30pm–midnight. Closed Aug.

La Libera ★★ PIEMONTESE The simple and wonderful *carne cruda* (raw veal) is something of a synthesis of this place, simple and wonderful. The chef, Marco Forneris, humbly says "it's not hard to make good food in Piedmont because the raw materials are excellent." Perhaps, but he has a special touch that makes this stylish *osteria* in the center of town as close to a must-visit as you are going to get for any place in Piedmont. Here you'll find slight variations on local cuisine, and you can watch it being prepared through the large window that sits between the dining room and kitchen. The *antipasto misto*—which often includes *insaltina di tacchino* (a salad of fresh greens and roast turkey breast), *vitello tonato* (the traditionally warm-weather dish of veal and tuna sauce), and *fiori di zucca* (zucchini flowers stuffed with a trout mousse)—will get you started right. As for primi, the *agnolotti* (pasta stuffed with cabbage and rice) are hard to beat.

Via E. Pertinace 24a. ☎ **0173-293-155.** www.lalibera.com. Reservations recommended. Primi 9€–14€; secondi 13€–24€. AE, DC, MC, V. Tues–Sat noon–2pm; Mon–Sat 8–10pm. Closed 2 weeks in late Feb/early Mar and last 2 weeks of Aug.

Visiting the Wine Villages

Just to the south of Alba lie some of the region's, and Italy's, most enchanting wine villages. As you set out to explore the wine country, consider three words: **Rent a car.** While it's quite easy to reach some of the major towns by train or bus from Turin, setting out from those centers for smaller places can be difficult (there are some buses, but they are scarce and with your own wheels you'll see in a day what will take 3 days with public transport). In Turin, contact **Avis,** Via Lessona Michele 30 (☎ **011-774-1962;** www.avis.com), or **Hertz,** at Corso Turati 37 (☎ **011-502-080;** www.hertz.it). Before you head out on the labyrinth of small country roads, outfit yourself with a good map and a list of vineyards from the tourist office in Alba or Asti.

THE WINES While the wines of Chianti and other Tuscan regions are on the top of the list for many oenologically minded travelers, the wines of Piedmont are often less heralded among non-Italians, and unjustifiably so. Most are of exceptional quality and usually made with grapes grown only in the Piedmont and often on tiny family plots, making the region a lovely patchwork of vineyards and small farms. Below are some wines you are likely to encounter repeatedly as you explore the area.

Barolo is called the king of reds (and is considered one of Italy's top three wines, the others being Tuscany's Brunello and Sassicaia), the richest and heartiest of the Piedmont wines, and the one most likely to accompany game or meat. **Barbaresco,** like Barolo, is made exclusively from the Nebbiolo grape though it is less tannic and often more approachable. **Barbera d'Alba** is smooth and rich, the product of many of the delightful villages south of Alba. **Dolcetto** is dry, fruity, and mellow (not sweet, as its name leads many to assume). **Nebbiolo d'Alba** is rich, full, and dry (though remember that the best Nebbiolo grapes are used to make Barbaresco and Barolo).

Spumanti is the sparkling wine that has put Asti on the map for many travelers, and **Moscato d'Asti** is a floral dessert wine. You can taste and purchase these wines at cantinas and *enoteche* in almost all towns and villages throughout the region; several are noted below.

THE REGION The central road through the region and running between Alba and Asti is S231, a heavily trafficked and unattractive highway that links

Vineyards outside La Morra.

many of the region's towns and cities; turn off this road whenever possible to explore the region's more rustic backwaters.

One of the loveliest drives takes you south of Alba to a string of wine villages in what are known as the **Langhe hills** (from Corso Europa, a ring road that encircles the Old City in Alba, follow signs out of town for Barolo). After 8km (5 miles), you'll come to the turnoff for **Grinzane di Cavour,** a hilltop village built around a castle housing an *enoteca* (© **0173-262-159**), open daily 9am to 7pm, where you can enjoy a fine sampling of local wines from their more than 300 labels.

Continuing south another 4km (2½ miles), you'll come to the turn-off to **La Morra,** another hilltop village that affords stunning views over the rolling, vineyard-clad countryside from its central Piazza Castello (with parking). It has places to eat (see below) and to taste the local wines. The **Cantina Comunale di La Morra** (© **0173-509-204**), on the Piazza del Municipio, operates both as the local tourist office and as a representative for local growers, selling and offering tastings of Barolo, Nebbiolo, Barbara, and Dolcetto. You can also procure a map of hikes in the local countryside, many of which take you through the vineyards to the doors of local growers. It's open Wednesday to Monday 10am to 12:30pm and 2:30 to 6:30pm.

Barolo, a romantic place dominated by its 12th-century castle (about 5km/3 miles from La Morra), is directly across the valley from La Morra and enticingly in view from miles around. Here, too, are a number of restaurants (see our top choice, La Cantinetta, below) and shops selling the village's rich red wines. Among these outlets is the **Castello Falletti ★** (© **0173-56-277;** www.baroloworld.it), which houses a small wine bar, *enoteca* (where you can taste), and tourist office in its cavernous cellars. A tasting of three of Barolo's wines (all from the same year but different zones, so you can more accurately compare labels) costs 5€. It's open Friday to Wednesday 10am to 12:30pm and 3 to 6pm, and 10am to 4:30pm in February, November, and December (closed Jan).

Tiny **Novello** is a hilltop village about 15km (9¼ miles) south of Alba and located about 3km (1¾ miles) away from Barolo on well-signposted roads. It crowns the adjoining hilltop, offering some pleasant accommodations and stunning views.

WHERE TO STAY

See "Visiting the Wine Villages," above, for information on how to get to the towns where the following hotels and restaurants are located.

Barbabuc ★ This charming and intimate hotel, which wraps around a garden, lies behind the centuries-old facade of a house near the village square and is managed by the same private tourism consortium that owns the castle in nearby Barolo. Walls of glass brick and open terraces fill the premises with air and light. Guest rooms are placed on different levels of a central staircase, ensuring privacy, and are simply furnished in a tasteful mix of contemporary Italian pieces and country antiques on terrazzo floors. A few have third beds or hide-a-beds for families. A roof terrace offers countryside views over the surrounding houses; downstairs you'll find a handsome bar area and sitting room that opens to the pretty garden, an *enoteca* where local wines can be tasted, and an intimate little dining room where a lavish buffet breakfast is served. The entire hotel is smoke-free.

Via Giordano 35, 12060 Novello. www.barbabuc.it. ✆ **0173-731-298.** Fax 0173-744-500. 8 units. 90€ double; 110€ triple. Rates include buffet breakfast. AE, DC, MC, V. Free parking. Closed Jan. **Amenities:** Bar; bikes; concierge; golf courses nearby; room service. *In room:* TV (in some), hair dryer, Wi-Fi.

La Cascina del Monastero ★★ 🏠 The main business at this delightful farm complex, just minutes away from La Morra toward Barolo (4km/2½ miles), is bottling wine and harvesting fruit. But Giuseppe and Velda di Grasso have converted part of the oldest and most character-filled building into a bed-and-breakfast. Guests can relax on a large covered terrace, furnished with wicker couches and armchairs, or on the grassy shores of a pond. A sumptuous breakfast of fresh cakes, yogurt, cheese, and salami is served in a vast brick-walled reception hall. The guest rooms, reached by a series of exterior brick staircases, have been smartly done with exposed timbers, golden-hued tile floors, and attractive antique bureaus, armoires, and brass beds. Bathrooms are sparkling and quite luxurious, with state-of-the-art stall showers and luxuriously deep basins.

Cascina Luciani 112A, Frazione Annunziata 12064 La Morra (CN). www.cascinadelmonastero.it. ✆/fax **0173-509-245.** 10 units. 100€–120€ double; 110€–130€ apt. Rates include breakfast. No credit cards. Free parking. Closed Jan and sometimes Feb. **Amenities:** Bike rental; small children's playground; small exercise room; outdoor pool; room service; sauna; Wi-Fi. *In room:* Hair dryer, kitchenette, minibar, no phone.

WHERE TO EAT

La Cantinetta PIEMONTESE Brothers Maurilio and Paolo Chiappetto do a fine job of introducing guests to the pleasures of the Piemontese table in their cozy dining room grouped around an open hearth (in nice weather, book ahead for a table out on the tiny back terrace). The menu changes daily and, if you are lucky, will include: a wonderful country pâté; powerful *bagna cauda*; subtle ravioli in a truffle sauce; thick slabs of roast veal; and salad made with wild herbs. If you're not lucky, that's okay too because no matter what comes out of the kitchen here it's a good bet you won't be disappointed. The wonderful house wines come from the vines that run right up to the back door of this delightful restaurant (a bar/*enoteca* is located up front).

Via Roma 33, Barolo. ✆ **0173-56-198.** Reservations recommended. Primi 10€; secondi 12–15€; tasting menu 37€, not including wine. AE, DC, MC, V. Fri–Wed 12:15–3pm; Fri–Tues 7:30–11pm. Closed Feb.

Ristorante Belvedere PIEMONTESE The view from the baronial main room, built around a large brick hearth and perched high above vineyards that roll away in all directions, is in itself a pleasure and draws many diners here. When tour buses arrive to fill the back rooms and downstairs, service can turn brusque. But while the Belvedere is no longer the welcoming rustic retreat it once was, its moves toward refinement (classy table settings, complimentary Spumanti and *crostini* while you consider the menu, for example) have been pulled off well, and the kitchen maintains the high standards that have made it one of the region's most popular restaurants. A wonderful salad of truffles and Parmesan cheese, and homemade ravioli in a mushroom sauce, are among the house specialties, which include many other pastas and risottos. The wine list is 83 pages long and has a table of contents, and the prices are surprisingly decent.

Piazza Castello 5, La Morra. ✆ **0173-50-190.** www.belvederelamorra.it. Reservations recommended. Primi 12€; secondi 18€–25€; fixed-price menu 45€, not including wine. AE, DC, MC, V. Tues–Sun 12:30–2pm; Tues–Sat 7:30–9pm. Closed Jan–Feb.

AOSTA & VALLE D'AOSTA

Aosta: 113km (70 miles) N of Turin, 184km (114 miles) NW of Milan; Courmayeur-Entrèves: 35km (22 miles) W of Aosta, 148km (92 miles) NW of Turin

Skiers, hikers, and outdoor enthusiasts, eager to enjoy one of Italy's favorite Alpine playgrounds, flock to this tiny mountainous region 1 hour by car north of Turin (and 2 hr. by train). At its best, **Valle d'Aosta** fulfills its promise: snowcapped peaks, among them the Matterhorn (Monte Cervino in Italian) and Mont Blanc (Monte Bianco), as well as verdant pastures, thick forests, waterfalls cascading into mountain streams, and romantic castles clinging to wooded hillsides.

Also plentiful in Valle d'Aosta are crowds—especially in August, when the region welcomes hordes of vacationing Italians, and January through March, the height of the winter ski season—and one too many overdeveloped tourist centers to accommodate them. You're best off coming at one of the nonpeak times, when you can enjoy the valley's beauty in relative peace and quiet.

A waterfall in Parco Nazionale del Gran Paradiso.

Whenever you happen to find yourself in Valle d'Aosta, three must-sees are the town of **Aosta** itself, with its Roman and medieval monuments set dramatically against the backdrop of the Alps (and a fine place to begin a tour of the surrounding mountains and valleys), and the natural wonders of **Parco Nazionale del Gran Paradiso.** The third, more dramatic to-do is the thrilling cable-car ride from fashionable ski resort **Courmayeur-Entrèves** over the shoulder of **Mont Blanc** to France. While much of Valle d'Aosta is accessible by train or bus, you'll probably want a car to ease your exploration of the quieter reaches of the region.

Of course, recreation, not sightseeing, is what draws many people to Valle d'Aosta. Some of the best **downhill skiing,** accompanied by the best facilities, is on the runs at Courmayeur, Breuil-Cervinia (the town on the Italian side of the Matterhorn), and at the large Monte Rosa ski area that is centered around the towns of Champoluc and Gressoney. Valle D'Aosta also offers excellent **cross-country skiing** and **hiking** (see the "Into the Great Outdoors" box, below).

Festivals & Markets Aosta celebrates its patron saint and warm winter days and nights with the **Fiera Sant'Orso** on the last 2 days of January. During the festival, the locals dance, drink vast quantities of mulled wine, and peruse the local crafts pieces, such as lovely woodcarvings and woven blankets, which vendors from throughout Valle d'Aosta offer for sale. Aosta's other major event is the **Bataille de Reines (Battle of the Queens).** The queens in question are cows, and these mainstays of the local economy lock horns; the main event is held the third Sunday in October, and preliminary heats take place throughout the spring and summer. Aosta's **weekly market** day is Tuesday, when stalls selling food, clothes, crafts, and household items fill the Piazza Cavalieri di Vittorio Veneto.

Aosta

GETTING THERE By Train Aosta is served by 20 trains a day to and from **Turin** (2 hr., with a change in Chivasso or Ivrea); there are 10 trains a day to and from **Milan** (3½–4 hr., with a change in Chivasso, and sometimes another in Ivrea).

By Bus Aosta's bus station, across the piazza and a bit to the right from the train station, handles about eight buses (only one or two direct; most change in Ivrea) to and from **Turin** daily; the trip takes 3 hours (2 hr. on the direct). Three daily buses run between Aosta and **Milan** (2½ hr.). Buses also connect Aosta with other popular spots in the valley, among them **Courmayeur,** where you can connect to the Palud cable car (see "Mont Blanc by Cable Car," p. 405) and **Cogne,** a major gateway to the Parco Nazionale del Gran Paradiso (see below). For information, call ✆ **0165-262-027.**

By Car Autostrada A5 from Turin shoots up the length of Valle d'Aosta en route to France and Switzerland via the Mont Blanc tunnel; there are numerous exits in the valley. The trip from Turin to Aosta normally takes about an hour and a half, but traffic can be heavy in high season, especially on Friday nights going into the valley and Sunday nights come back towards Turin and Milan.

VISITOR INFORMATION The **tourist office** in Aosta, Piazza Chanoux 2 (✆ **0165-236-627;** www.regione.vda.it/turismo), dispenses a wealth of info on hotels, restaurants, and sights throughout the region, along with listings of campgrounds, maps of hiking trails, information about ski-lift tickets and special discounted ski packages, outlets for bike rentals, and rafting trips. It's open daily 9am to 8pm from mid-June to the end of September and from December 26 to January 6. The rest of the year the office closes at 6:30pm.

EXPLORING THE TOWN

This mountain town, surrounded by snowcapped peaks, not only is pleasant but has soul—the product of a history that goes back to Roman times. While you're not going to find much in the line of pristine Alpine quaintness here in Valle d'Aosta's busy tourist and economic center, you can spend some enjoyable time strolling past Roman ruins and medieval bell towers while checking out the chic shops that sell everything from Armani suits to locally made Fontina cheese.

The "Rome of the Alps" sits majestically within its preserved walls, and the monuments of the empire make it easy to envision the days when Aosta was one of Rome's most important trading and military outposts. Two Roman gates arch gracefully across the Via San Anselmo, Aosta's main thoroughfare: the **Porta Pretoria,** the western entrance to the Roman town, and the **Arco di Augusto** (sometimes called Arco Romano), the eastern entrance, built in A.D. 25 to commemorate a Roman victory over the Celts. A **Roman bridge** spans the River Buthier while just a few steps north of the Porta Pretoria, you'll find the facade of the **Teatro Romano (Roman Theater)** and the ruins of the **amphitheater,** which once accommodated 20,000 spectators. The ruins of the **forum** are in an adjacent park. The theater and forum are open daily, in summer from 9:30am to noon and 2:30 to 6:30pm, in winter from 9:30am to noon and 2 to 4:30pm; admission is free. Architectural fragments from these monuments and a sizable collection of vessels and other objects unearthed during excavations are displayed in Aosta's **Archaeological Museum,** at Piazza Roncas 12 (✆ **0165-275-902**); it's open daily from 9am to 7pm, and admission is free.

Behind the banal 19th-century facade of Aosta's **Duomo,** Piazza Giovanni XXIII (✆ **0165-40-251**), lie two remarkable treasures: an ivory diptych, from A.D. 406, that depicts the Roman emperor Honorius, which is housed along with other precious objects in the treasury; and 12th-century mosaics on the floor of the choir and before the altar. Heavy-handed restorations cloud the fact that the church actually dates from the 10th century. It's open daily from 7am to noon and 3 to 7pm (Apr–Sept until 8pm).

INTO THE GREAT outdoors

Recreation is what draws most people to Valle d'Aosta. You'll find some of the best **downhill skiing** and facilities on the runs at **Courmayeur, Breuil-Cervinia,** and in the **Monte Rosa** ski area that centers around the towns of Champoluc and Gressoney. Multiday passes, providing access to lifts and slopes of the entire valley, run 120€ for 3 days and 158€ for 4 days, with per-day rates sliding down a scale to 14 days at 434€. For more info, call ✆ **0165-238-871** or visit www.skivallee.it. Ski season starts in early December and runs through April, if the snow holds out.

One money-saving option is to take one of the *settimane bianche* **(white-week) packages** that include room and board and unlimited skiing, and are available at resorts throughout Valle d'Aosta. You can expect to pay at least 500€ at Courmayeur, and slightly less at Cogne or one of the other less-fashionable resorts. Over the Christmas and New Year's vacation period, prices practically double and hotels often sell out well before Thanksgiving. A popular option is to rent a chalet in the area: The tourist board (www.regione.vda.it) is a good resource to start looking for availabilities (or for real-estate agents who specialize in short-term lets) and more information on weeklong packages.

Cross-country skiing is superb around Cogne in the Parco Nazionale del Gran Paradiso, where there are more than 50km (30 miles) of trails. Valle d'Aosta is also some of Italy's best **hiking** terrain. For information about hiking in the Parco Nazionale del Gran Paradiso, ask at the tourist offices of Aosta and especially Cogne.

The **Collegiata dei Santi Pietro e Orso,** at the eastern edge of the Old City off Via San Anselmo 9 (☎ **0165-262-026**), is a hodgepodge from the 6th through the 18th centuries. This 11th-century church, built over a 6th-century predecessor, has been periodically enhanced with architectural embellishments representing every stylistic period from the Gothic through the baroque. In a room above the nave (the door on the left aisle marked AFFRESCHI OTTONIANI; search out the sacristan or ring the bell), the remains of an 11th-century fresco cycle recount the life of Christ and the Apostles on the bits of medieval church wall above the 15th-century vaults. The frescoes are open daily 8:30am to 6:30pm (Oct–Mar until 4:30pm). The 12th-century cloisters are a fascinating display of Romanesque storytelling—40 columns are capped with carved capitals depicting scenes from the Bible and the life of Aosta's own Saint Orso.

SIDE TRIPS FROM AOSTA

CASTELLO DI FENIS (CASTLE OF FENIS) Built by the Challants, viscounts of Aosta throughout much of the Middle Ages, this castle (☎ **0165-764-263**), near the town of Fenis, is the most impressive and best preserved of the many castles perched on the hillsides above Valle d'Aosta. From it, you can enjoy some fine views of the Alps and the valley below. One of the most appealing parts of a visit to Fenis is catching a glimpse into everyday life in a medieval castle—you can climb up to wooden loggias overlooking the courtyard and visit the cavernous kitchens. Alas, you cannot scamper among the ramparts, turrets, towers, and dungeons, thanks to an Italian safety law.

March through June and September, the castle is open daily 9am to 7pm; July and August, hours are daily 9am to 8pm; October through February, hours are Wednesday through Sunday 10am to noon and 1:30 to 5pm (Sun to 6pm). Requisite half-hour guided tours (Italian only) leave every 30 minutes. Come early; tours tend to fill up quickly in summer, and you can't book them in advance. Admission is 5€ for adults and 3.50€ for students, 17 and under free. The castle is 30km (20 miles) east of Aosta on route S26; there are 13 buses a day (only one, at 6:20am, on Sun from Aosta; the ride takes 30 min.).

BREUIL-CERVINIA & THE MATTERHORN You don't come to Breuil-Cervinia to see the town, a banal collection of tourist facilities—the sight to see, and you can't miss it, is the **Matterhorn** (**Monte Cervino** in Italian) ★. Its distinctive profile looms majestically above the valley, beckoning year-round skiers and those who simply want to savor a refreshing Alpine experience by ascending to its glaciers via cable car to the Plateau Rosa (26€ round-trip; closed Sept 10 to mid-Oct). An excellent trail also ascends from **Breuil-Cervinia** up the flank of the mountain. After a moderately strenuous uphill trek of 90 minutes, you come to a gorgeous mountain lake, **Lac du Goillet** ★, and from there, it's another 90 minutes to the **Colle Superiore delle Cime Bianche** ★, a plateau with heart-stopping views.

The **tourist office,** Via Rey 17 (☎ **0166-949-136;** www.breuil-cervinia .net or www.cervinia.it), can provide information on other hikes, ski packages, and serious ascents to the top of the Matterhorn. Breuil-Cervinia is 54km (33 miles) northeast of Aosta via routes A5 and S406. **From Aosta,** you can take one of the Turin-bound trains, get off at Chatillon (20 min.), and continue from there on one of the seven daily buses to Breuil-Cervinia (1 hr.).

PILA It's well worth the trip up the winding road about 15km (10 miles) south from Aosta to this resort, at 1,782m (5,845 ft.). Aside from getting an eagle's-eye view of the valleys rolling away in all directions at your feet—and access to over a dozen trails around and to the tops of the surrounding mountains—you will glimpse the peaks of Europe's two most spectacular mountains, Mont Blanc on the far left and the Matterhorn peeking up to the far right. Directly in front of you, the Gran Combin rises over Aosta to 4,271m (14,009 ft.). The little information office in back of the Pila gondola station (✆**0165-521-148;** fax 0165-521-437; www.pila.it) has a good hiking map and is open daily in July, August and December 8 through April 25 from 9am to 12:30pm and 2 to 5pm (mid-July to mid-Aug until 6pm).

A gondola runs to Pila in 20 minutes (3€ one way and 5€ round-trip) from Aosta, July through September and during the ski season daily from 8am to 5pm. It leaves from a large parking lot southwest of the train station (shortcut: Take the *sottopassaggio* passage under the tracks at the station to Via Paravera, turn right then take your first left). To drive, follow Via Ponte Suaz—next to the train station—south out of town.

PARCO NAZIONALE DEL GRAN PARADISO ★ The little town of Cogne is the most convenient gateway to one of Europe's finest parcels of unspoiled nature, the former hunting grounds of King Vittorio Emanuele that now make up this vast and lovely national park. The park encompasses five valleys and a total of 3,626 sq. km (1,414 sq. miles) of forests and pastureland where many Alpine beasts roam wild, including the ibex (a long-horned goat) and the chamois (a small antelope), both of which have hovered near extinction in recent years.

Humans can roam these wilds via a vast network of well-marked trails. Among the few places where the hand of man intrudes ever so gently on nature are a few scattered hamlets within the park borders and in the **Giardino Alpino Paradiso** (✆**0165-74-147**), a stunning collection of

HIGH mountain UNIVERSITY

In the mountains that straddle Aosta's eastern border, you can take courses that prepare you to conquer the highest peaks in the world. At the base of Monte Rosa, the second-tallest massif in the Alps after Mont Blanc, Silvio Mondinelli, one of Italy's greatest living mountain climbers, will teach you all he has learned in 50 years of trekking. The school, **High Mountain University** (✆ **0163-922-970;** www.himu.eu), is based in Alagna Valsesia, a mountain hamlet just across the border in Piedmont. The first courses were held in the summer of 2009, and the cost for a daylong class is about 150€.

Mondinelli (who goes by "Gnaro," which means "baby" in the dialect of the town where he was born) is convinced that the lessons that are learned in the mountains can also benefit people in their everyday lives. "This is a school that, among other things, will teach people how to better confront life and function as part of a team," said Mondinelli, who is one of a dozen people to have scaled the world's fourteen 8,000m (26,247 ft.) peaks without supplemental oxygen.

rare Alpine fauna near the village of Valnontey, just 1.5km (1 mile) south of Cogne. It's open mid-June through mid-September daily 10am to 6:30pm (June and Sept until 5:30pm); admission is 3€ for adults and 1.50€ for ages 7 to 19 and those 71 and over.

VISITOR INFORMATION Cogne also offers some downhill skiing, but it is better regarded for its many cross-country skiing trails. The **tourist office** in Cogne, Via Bourgeois (✆ **0165-74-040;** www.cogne.org), provides a wealth of information on hiking and skiing trails and other outdoor activities in the park and elsewhere in the region; it's open daily July to September 15 from 9am to 7pm and the rest of the year from 9am to 1pm and 3 to 6pm. You can also get info on the national park at www.pngp.it. Cogne is about 30km (20 miles) south of Aosta via S35 and S507; there are seven buses a day to and from Aosta.

Hiking through the Parco Nazionale del Gran Paradiso.

WHERE TO STAY

Many hotels in Valle d'Aosta require that guests take their meals on the premises and stay 3 nights or more. However, outside of busy tourist times, hotels often have rooms to spare and are willing to be a little more flexible with their policies. Rates vary almost month by month; in general, expect to pay the most for a room in August and at Christmas and Easter, and the least for a room in the fall. For the best rates, check with the local tourist boards for information on *settimane bianche* (white week) packages, all-inclusive deals that include room, board, and ski passes.

Belle Epoque ✦ Simple, very simple, but also cheap and well located in a quiet corner of the historic center. The stucco exterior has a cozy Alpine look to it, but the same can't be said of the somewhat stark interior. What is appealing about this hotel is the family-run atmosphere and the price. There is no elevator so you'll be taking the stairs to the spartan but clean rooms. A trattoria occupies most of the ground floor where you can arrange a half-board deal. Skip the breakfast and spend your money much more wisely in town, whether for a banana in the supermarket or a cappuccino and pastry at a bar.

Via d'Avise 18, 11100 Aosta. www.hotelbellepoqueaosta.it. ✆ **0165-262-276.** Fax 0165-261-196. 14 units, 11 with private bathroom. 46€–54€ double with shared bathroom; 50€–66€ double with private bathroom. Breakfast 6.50€. AE, MC, V. Free parking. **Amenities:** Restaurant; bar; room service. *In room:* A/C.

Milleluci ★★★ 🎒 From its noticeably cooler perch on a hillside just above the town, this chaletlike hotel in a breezy garden offers pleasant views. Current owner Cristina's great-grandmother converted the family farm into a hotel 50 years ago, and it's been handed down from mother to daughter ever since. Downstairs, a large wood-beamed sitting area is grouped around an attractive hearth (always ablaze in winter) and bar. The spacious rooms (larger on the second floor; cozy on the first) sport some nice touches like traditional wood furnishings, beamed ceilings, canopied beds (in suites and in one double), rich fabrics, terrazzo floors, and handsome prints. The stupendous buffet breakfast alone would be reason to stay: all homemade cakes, freshly whipped cream, *frittata* wedges (eggs from their own chickens, veggies from the garden), Alpine cheeses, and more. In nice weather, you can take breakfast on the wraparound terrace overlooking the town.

In Roppoz (off Via Porossan 1km/½ mile northeast of Arco di Augusto), 11100 Aosta. www.hotel milleluci.com. © **0165-23-5278.** Fax 0165-235-284. 31 units. 150€ double without balcony; 160€–250€ double with balcony. Rates include breakfast. AE, DC, MC, V. Free parking. **Amenities:** Babysitting; children's playground; concierge; Jacuzzi; outdoor heated pool; room service; sauna; smoke-free rooms. *In room:* TV/VCR, hair dryer, minibar, Wi-Fi.

Roma Tucked into a cul-de-sac near the Porta Pretoria, this place is not going to win you over with its charm, but it's clean and the location is superb (in the dead center of Aosta not far from the train station and the cable car to Pila). The paneled lobby and adjoining bar are pleasant places to relax and, with their plaid carpet and furnishings, are a little cozier than the nondescript guest rooms upstairs.

Via Torino 7, 11100 Aosta. www.hotelroma-aosta.it. © **0165-41-000.** Fax 0165-32-404. 38 units. 87€–96€ double; 117€–129€ triple. Rates include breakfast. AE, DC, MC, V. Limited free parking. **Amenities:** Bar; room service; Wi-Fi. *In room:* TV, hair dryer.

WHERE TO EAT

This is the land of mountain food—hams and salamis are laced with herbs from Alpine meadows; creamy cornmeal polenta accompanies meals; a rich beef stew, *carbonada,* warms winter nights; and buttery Fontina is the cheese of choice.

Caffè Nazionale CAFE This lovely fixture on Aosta's main square dates from 1886, and little has changed since then. For an almost sacred experience, try taking your coffee and pastry in the frescoed room that was once a chapel of the dukes of Aosta. It is said that Ava Gardner had romantic trysts here.

Piazza Chanoux 9. © **0165-262-158.** Reservations not accepted. Pastries from 3€. AE, DC, MC, V. Tues–Sun 8am–2am.

Grotta Azzurra PIZZA/SOUTHERN ITALIAN The best pizzeria in town also serves, as its name suggests, a bounty of fare from southern climes, along the likes of spaghetti with clam sauce. The Neapolitan owners serve up a wide selection of fresh fish, which makes this somewhat worn-looking trattoria popular with a local clientele. The pizzas emerge from a wood-burning oven and are often topped with Fontina and other rich local cheeses and salamis. If you are spending more than a few days in Valle d'Aosta you will be clamoring for a place like this where you can escape, ever so briefly, from the clutches of the heavy mountain fare.

Via Croix de Ville 97. © **0165-262-474.** Reservations not necessary. Primi 6€–12€; secondi 7€–16€; pizza 4.50€–9.50€. Thurs–Tues (daily in summer) 12:15–2:30pm and 6–10:30pm. Closed 3 weeks in July.

Osteria da Nando VALDOSTAN The focus here is on hearty local cuisine: dishes such as *fonduta* (a creamy fondue made mostly with Fontina), *crepes à la Valdostana* (filled and topped with melted cheese), and *carbonada con polenta* (beef stew dished over polenta). Germana Scarpa has been running Osteria da Nando since 1957 and every night she still manages to give it a personal, family touch. Her son Corrado looks after guests and will suggest which of the many

Valle d'Aosta wines on the list will pair best with what you're eating. And, if you must, you can get a pretty decent pizza. Dessert is not to be missed, especially the licorice and cinnamon panna cotta. Via Sant'Anselmo 99. ℰ**0165-44-455.** www.osteriada nando.it. Reservations not accepted. Primi 7€–13€; secondi 10€–20€; pizza 5€–9€. AE, DC, MC, V. Tues–Sun noon–3pm and 7:15–10pm. Usually closed 15 days in late June/early July.

Courmayeur-Entreves

The one-time mountain hamlet of **Courmayeur** is now Valle d'Aosta's resort extraordinaire, a collection of traditional stone buildings, pseudo-Alpine chalets, and large hotels catering to a well-heeled international crowd of skiers. Even if you don't ski, you can happily while away the time sipping a grog while regarding the craggy bulk of Mont Blanc (Monte Bianco on this side of the border), which

Heading up into the Dolomites by cable car.

looms over this end of Valle d'Aosta and forms the snowy barrier between Italy and France. The Mont Blanc tunnel—scene of a devastating fire in 1999—makes it possible to zip into France in just 20 minutes.

Entrèves, 3km (2 miles) north of Courmayeur, is the sort of place that the latter probably once was: a pleasant collection of stone houses and farm buildings surrounded by pastureland. Quaint as the village is in appearance, at its soul it is a worldly enclave with some nice hotels and restaurants catering to skiers and outdoor enthusiasts who prefer to spend time in the mountains in surroundings that are a little quieter than Courmayeur.

ESSENTIALS

GETTING THERE By Bus About a dozen daily buses connect Courmayeur with Aosta (1 hr.). At least hourly buses (more in summer; ℰ**0165-841-305**) run between Courmayeur's Piazzale Monte Bianco and Entrèves and La Palud (10 min.), just above Entrèves.

By Car Autostrada A5 from Turin to the Mont Blanc tunnel passes Courmayeur; the trip from Aosta to Courmayeur on this much-used route takes less than half an hour (lots of time in tunnels; for scenery, take the parallel S26, about 1 hr.), and total travel time from Turin is less than 2 hours.

VISITOR INFORMATION The **tourist office** in Courmayeur, Piazzale Monte Bianco 8 (ℰ**0165-842-060;** www.regione.vda.it/turismo), provides information on hiking, skiing, and other outdoor activities in the region, as well as hotel and restaurant listings. Mid-June through September, the office is open daily 9am to 7pm; October through mid-June, 9am to 1pm and 2 to 6pm.

WHERE TO STAY

Edelweiss ★ In winter, the pine-paneled salons and cozy rooms of this chalet-style hotel near the center of town attract a friendly international set of skiers, and in summer, many Italian families spend a month or two here at a time. The Roveyaz family extends a hearty welcome to all and provides modern mountain-style accommodations. Many rooms open onto terraces overlooking the mountains, and the nicest rooms are those on the top floor, tucked under the eaves.

MONT BLANC BY cable car

One of Valle d'Aosta's best experiences is to ride the series of cable cars from La Palud, just above Entrèves, across Mont Blanc to several ski stations in Italy and France and down into Chamonix, France. You make the trip in stages—first past two intermediate stops to the last aerie on Italian soil, **Punta Helbronner** (20 min. each way; 35€ round-trip or 96€ for a family pass valid for two adults and two children ages 6–11). At 3,300m (10,800 ft.), this ice-clad lookout provides stunning views of the Mont Blanc glaciers and the Matterhorn and other peaks looming in the distance. In summer, you may want to hop off before you get to Punta Helbronner at **Pavillon Frety** (14€ round-trip) and tour a pleasant botanic garden, Giardino Alpino Saussurea (📞 **333-446-2959;** www.saussurea.net), open daily from the end of June through September; admission is 2.50€, or 1.50€ with your cable car ticket.

For sheer drama, continue from Punta Helbronner to **Aiguille du Midi ★★★** in France in a tiny gondola to experience the dramatic sensation of dangling more than 2,300m (7,500 ft.) in midair as you cruise above the Géant Glacier and the Vallée Blanche (30 min. each way; tack on another 20€ round-trip). From Aiguille du Midi, you can descend over more glaciers and dramatic valleys on the French flank of Mont Blanc to the resort town of **Chamonix** (50 min. each way; 50€). If you go all the way to Chamonix, the best way to return to Italy is to hop on a bus back through the tunnel, for a final 12€ per person. Buses take 45 minutes and leave Chamonix at 8:45 and 10:10am, and at 1:30, 3, 4, and 5:45pm.

Hours for these cable cars vary wildly, and service can be sporadic, depending on weather conditions (winds often close the gondola between Helbronner and Aiguille du Midi; this is, after all, the tallest mountain in western Europe), but in general, they run every 20 minutes from 7:20am (8:20am in fall and spring) to 12:30pm and 2 to 5:30pm (July 22–Aug 27 all day long; closed

Nov 2–Dec 10). The last downward run is 5:30pm in summer and 4:30pm in winter. The Helbronner–Aiguille du Midi gondola is open only May through September. **Note:** Children 5 and under travel free, while those ages 6 to 11 get 50% off the prices above, and seniors 66 and older get a 10% discount. Hourly buses make the 10-minute run from Courmayeur to the cable car terminus at La Palud. For more info, call 📞 **0165-89-925** (www.montebianco.com). For a report of weather at the top and on the other side, dial 📞 **0165-89-961.**

A cheaper but far less dramatic way to cross over just one flank of Mont Blanc (but missing out on that thrilling 2.5km/1½-mile dangle in the air while you cross a massive glacier field into France) is on the Courmayeur Monte Blanc Funivia, which leaves from a terminus in Entrèves and ascends to the Val Veny. The round-trip fare is 14€, with 20% off for those 66 and older and free for children shorter than 1.3m (4 ft., 4 in.). Cars depart every 20 minutes from 9am to 12:50pm and 2:15 to 5:40pm; closed from late August/early September to late December.

Basic, nonfussy meals are served in the cheerful main-floor dining room; you can arrange a half-board deal if you wish. The hotel also has a small exercise room for those who haven't done enough hiking or skiing during the day.

Via Marconi 42, 11013 Courmayeur. www.albergoedelweiss.it. 📞 **0165-841-590.** Fax 0165-841-618. 30 units. Summer 80€–140€ double per person, per day; winter 310€–420€ double per person, per week. Rates include breakfast. MC, V. Free parking. Closed Oct-Nov and May-June. **Amenities:** Regional restaurant; bar; a few free bikes; exercise room; sauna; smoke-free rooms. *In room:* TV, hair dryer, Wi-Fi (fee).

La Grange ★★ What may well be the most charming hotel in Valle d'Aosta occupies a converted barn in the bucolic village of Entrèves and is ably managed by

Bruna Berthold. None of the rooms are the same and all are decorated with a pleasing smattering of antiques and rustic furnishings; some have balconies overlooking Mont Blanc, which, quite literally, looms over the property. The stucco-walled, stone-floor lobby is a fine place to relax, with couches built around a corner hearth and a little bar area. A lavish buffet breakfast is served in a prettily paneled room off the lobby, and the hotel also has an exercise room and a much-used sauna. The price-to-quality ratio of La Grange is outstanding if you don't come from about July 20 to August 20, when the prices, while still reasonable, are at their maximum.

Strada La Brenva 1, Entrèves. www.lagrange-it.com. ✆ **0165-869-733**, or 335-646-3533 in the off season. Fax 0165-869-744. 22 units. 80€–150€ double; 100€–180€ triple; 150€–230€ suite; there are discounts for stays of 3–5 days that don't include Fri-Sun. Rates include American breakfast. AE, DC, MC, V. Free parking. Closed May–June and Oct–Nov. **Amenities:** Bar; babysitting; bikes; concierge; exercise room; room service; sauna. *In room:* TV, hair dryer, minibar.

WHERE TO EAT

La Maison de Filippo ★★★ VALDOSTAN The atmosphere at this popular and cheerful restaurant in Entrèves is delightfully country Alpine, and the offerings are so generous you may not be able to eat again for a week. Daily menus vary but often include an antipasto of mountain hams and salamis, a selection of pastas filled with wild mushrooms and topped with Fontina and other local cheeses, and a sampling of fresh trout and game in season. Service is casual and friendly, and in summer you can choose between a table in the delightfully barn-like structure or one on the flowery terrace.

Loc. Entrèves. ✆ **0165-869-797**. www.lamaison.com. Reservations required. Fixed-price menu 48€ not including wine. MC, V. Wed–Mon 12:30-2:30pm and 7:30-10:30pm. Closed June and Nov.

Ristorante La Palud SEAFOOD/VALDOSTAN A table in front of the hearth in this cozy restaurant is just the place to enjoy the local specialties including creamy *polenta concia* (with Fontina cheese and butter folded in) and *cervo* (venison) in season. There is a selection of mountain cheeses for dessert, and the wine list borrows heavily from neighboring Piedmont but also includes some local vintages. On Fridays, you can enjoy a wide selection of fresh fish brought up from Liguria and you can always opt for one of the more than 200 types of pizza prepared in the wood-burning oven.

Strada la Palud 17, Courmayeur. ✆ **0165-89-169**. www.lapalud.it. Reservations recommended. Primi 7€–10€; secondi 8:50€–21€; fixed-price menus 18€–25€ (the more expensive one includes wine). AE, MC, V. Thurs–Tues noon–3:30pm and 7:30-10:30pm.

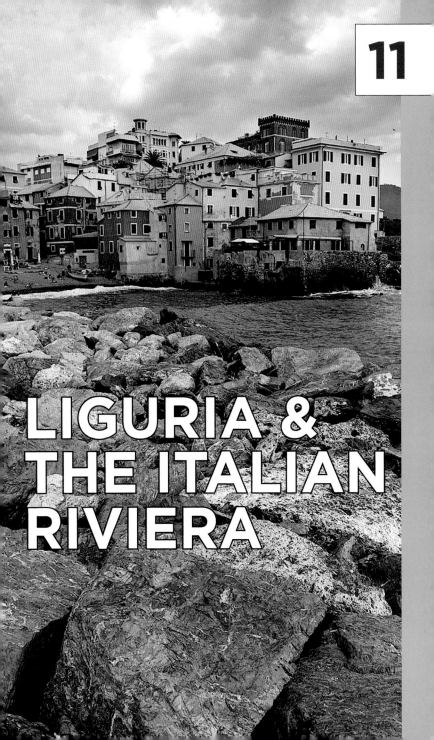

LIGURIA & THE ITALIAN RIVIERA

From the top of Tuscany to the French border, along the Ligurian Sea, Italy follows a crescent-shape strip of seacoast and mountains that make up the region of Liguria. The pleasures of this region are no secret. Ever since the 19th century, world-weary travelers have been heading for Liguria's resorts to enjoy balmy weather (ensured by the protective barrier of the Ligurian Alps) and turquoise seas. Beyond the beach, the stones and tiles of fishing villages, small resort towns, and proud old port cities bake in the sun, and hillsides are fragrant with the scent of bougainvillea and pines.

Liguria is really two coasts. First, the beachier stretch west of Genoa known as the **Riviera di Ponente (Setting Sun),** is studded with fashionable resorts, many of which, like San Remo, have seen their heydays fade but continue to entice visitors with palm-fringed promenades and gentle ways.

The rockier, more colorful fishing-village-filled stretch to the southeast of Genoa, known as the **Riviera di Levante (Rising Sun),** extends past the posh harbor of Portofino to the remote hamlets of the Cinque Terre.

The province's capital, Genoa, is Italy's busiest port, an ancient center of commerce, and one of history's great maritime powers. However, though it is one of Italy's most historic places, it is also one of the country's least-visited large cities. But don't judge the area by its capital: Genoa's gritty feel and its brusque and clamorous elements are a world apart from the easygoing and charming seaside villages and resorts that populate the region as a whole.

GENOA

142km (88 miles) S of Milan, 501km (311 miles) NW of Rome, 194km (120 miles) E of Nice

With its dizzying mix of the old and the new, **Genoa (Genova)** is as multilayered as the hills it clings to. It was and is, first and foremost, a port city: an important maritime center for the Roman Empire, boyhood home of Christopher Columbus (whose much-restored house still stands near a section of the medieval walls), and, fueled by seafaring commerce that stretched to the Middle East, one of the largest and wealthiest cities of Renaissance Europe.

Genoa began as a port of the ancient Ligurian people at least by the 6th century B.C. and by the early Middle Ages had become a formidable maritime power, conquering the surrounding coast and the mighty outlying islands of Corsica and Sardinia. Genoa established colonies throughout North Africa and the Middle East, and made massive gains during the Crusades. With bigger success came new, bigger rivals, and Genoa locked commercial and military horns with Venice, which eventually took the upper hand in the late 14th century. Genoa increasingly fell under the control of outsiders and though self government returned for

PREVIOUS PAGE: **The port town of Genoa.**

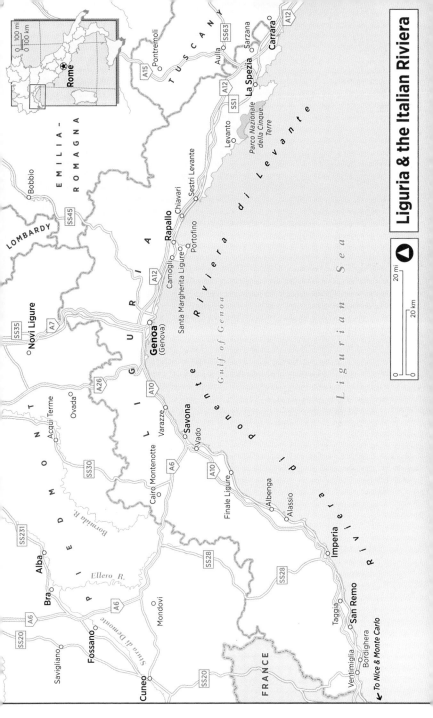

Liguria & the Italian Riviera

Christopher Columbus's boyhood home.

a while in the 16th century, by then sea trade was rapidly shifting to Spain and eventually to its American colonies, a trend exemplified by Genoa's most famous native son, Columbus, who had to travel to Spain to find the financial backing for his voyage of exploration across the Atlantic.

It's easy to capture glimpses of Genoa's former glory days on the narrow lanes and dank alleys of the portside Old Town, where treasure-filled palaces and fine marble churches stand next to laundry-draped tenements and brothels. In fact, some of the life within the old medieval walls doesn't seem to have changed since the days when Genovese ships set sail to launch raids on the Venetians, crusaders embarked for the Holy Land, and Giuseppe Garibaldi shipped out to invade Sicily in the 19th-century struggle to unify Italy. The other Genoa, the modern city that stretches for miles along the coast and climbs the hills, is a city of international business, peaceful parks, and breezy belvederes from which you can enjoy fine views of this colorful metropolis and the sea that continues to define its identity.

Once a Port, Always a Port

Though Genoa has almost completely cleaned up its historic center, and popular restaurants and wine bars have taken over previously shady piazze, be aware that prostitutes and other unsavory characters still exist in a few of the darker alleyways, all night *and* all day long. Don't let this deter you as the city is very safe and if you stumble into a questionable alleyway during the day all that will happen is that you get propositioned (if you are a man) or get an askance glance (if you are a woman). After dark it's better not to stray from

the Old Town's main streets where there is lots of foot traffic well into the night. The seediness is concentrated off Via della Maddalena going towards Via Garibaldi and on the small alleys west of Via Lomellini. A succession of mayors, who have their office in city hall right on Via Garibaldi a short block from where the propositioning takes place, have decided rather blatant prostitution is not a problem and some locals will tell you it is part of their neighborhood's folklore. This is, after all, and has been for centuries one of Europe's busiest ports.

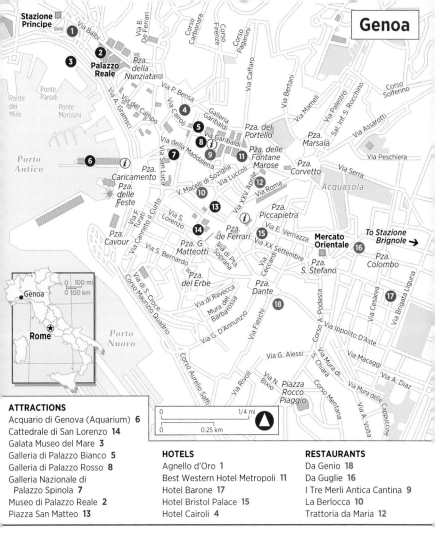

Genoa

ATTRACTIONS

Acquario di Genova (Aquarium) 6
Cattedrale di San Lorenzo 14
Galata Museo del Mare 3
Galleria di Palazzo Bianco 5
Galleria di Palazzo Rosso 8
Galleria Nazionale di
  Palazzo Spinola 7
Museo di Palazzo Reale 2
Piazza San Matteo 13

HOTELS

Agnello d'Oro 1
Best Western Hotel Metropoli 11
Hotel Barone 17
Hotel Bristol Palace 15
Hotel Cairoli 4

RESTAURANTS

Da Genio 18
Da Guglie 16
I Tre Merli Antica Cantina 9
La Berlocca 10
Trattoria da Maria 12

Festivals & Markets In June, an ancient tradition continues when Genoa takes to the sea in the **Regata delle Antiche Repubbliche Marinare** (not to be confused with Venice's own **Regata Storica;** see p. 164), competing against crews from its ancient maritime rivals, Amalfi, Pisa, and Venice, who host the event in turn. Another spectacular—though more modern—regatta takes place every April, the Millevele, or "thousand sails," when Genoa's bay is carpeted with the mainsails and spinnakers of nautical enthusiasts from around the world.

Genoa adds a touch of culture to the summer season with an **International Ballet Festival** that attracts a stellar list of performers from around the world. Performances are held in the beautiful gardens of Villa Gropallo in outlying Nervi, a late-19th-century resort with lush parks and a lively seaside promenade. Contact the tourist office in Genoa for schedules and ticket information, as well as for the summer concerts staged at different venues, many of them outdoors, around the city.

The **Mercato Orientale,** Genoa's sprawling indoor food market, evokes the days when ships brought back spices and other commodities from the ends of the earth. Still a boisterous affair and an excellent place to stock up on olives, herbs, fresh fruit, and other Ligurian products, it is held Monday through Saturday 7:30am to 1pm and 3:30 to 7:30pm, with entrances on Via XX Settembre and Via Galata (about halfway btw. Piazza de Ferrari at the edge of the Old Town and Stazione Brignole). The district just north of the market (especially Via San Vin-cenzo and Via Colombo) is a gourmand's dream, with many bakeries, *pasticcerie* (pastry shops), and stores selling pasta and cheese, wine, olive oil, and other foodstuffs.

To enjoy what is probably the most delectable food court you have ever come across, take the elevators up to **Eataly ★★**, open daily 10am to 10pm, in the building right in front of the massive white Bigo (p. 421) in the Porto Antico. This is the same outfit that can be found on 5th Avenue in New York City as well as in Milan (p. 306) and a few other Italian cities. There are five separate places to order food—including delicious pizza, salads, grilled meat, and fresh mozzarella—that you take to one of the tables and enjoy in an informal setting. You can also buy food in what is essentially a market of all the best Italian products and take it outside to eat on the benches facing the port. If you need a jar of pesto to bring home, this is a good place to get it, and if you need a cold drink, buying it up here will cost you a third of what you pay at the fast food joint downstairs. Even if you aren't going to eat, come up to have a look and enjoy the great free view of the harbor.

Essentials

GETTING THERE By Plane Flights to and from most European capitals serve **Cristoforo Colombo International Airport,** just 6.5km (4 miles) west of the city center (© 010-60-151; www.airport.genova.it). **Volabus** (© 010-558-2414 or 800-085-311 toll free from within Italy; www.amt.genova.it) connects the airport with the Principe and Brignole train stations, with buses running the 30-minute trip once or twice an hour from 5am to 10pm; buy tickets (6€, includes a transfer to or from the city transportation network) on the bus. The nearest airports handling overseas flights are at Nice, 188km (117 miles) west just over the border with France, and Milan, 136km (85 miles) to the north; both cities are well connected to Genoa by highways and train service.

By Train Genoa has two major train stations, **Stazione Principe** (designated on timetables as Genova P.P.), near the Old Town and the port on Piazza Acquaverde, and **Stazione Brignole** (designated on timetables as Genova BR.), in the modern city on Piazza Verdi. Many trains, especially those on long-distance lines, service both stations; however, some stop only at one, making it essential that you know the station at which your train is scheduled to arrive and from which it will depart. Trains (free, as they don't check tickets btw. the downtown stations) connect the two stations in 5 minutes and run about every 15 minutes. The city buses nos. 36 and 37 also run between the two train stations, leaving from the front of each station about every 15 minutes; the trip can take anywhere from 10 to 20 minutes depending on traffic.

Genoa is the hub for trains serving the Italian Riviera, with trains arriving and departing for Ventimiglia on the French border about every half-hour, and **La Spezia,** at the eastern edge of Liguria, even more frequently, as often as every 15 minutes during peak times between 7am and 7pm (regional: 1½ hr.; high-speed: 1¼ hr.). The regional trains make local stops at almost all the coastal resorts while the faster trains stop at only a few of the towns (for towns covered in this chapter, see individual listings for connections with Genoa). Lots of trains connect Genoa with major Italian cities: **Milan** (one to two per hour; regional: 2 hr.; high-speed: 1½ hr.), **Rome** (hourly; 5–6 hr.), **Turin** (one per hour; regional: 2¼ min.; high-speed: 1¾ hr.), **Florence** (hourly but always with a change, usually at Pisa; 3 hr.), **Pisa** (hourly; regional: 3 hr.; high-speed: 1½–2 hr.).

By Bus An extensive bus network connects Genoa with other parts of Liguria, as well as with other Italian and European cities, from the main bus station next to Stazione Principe. While it is easiest to reach seaside resorts by the trains that run up and down the coast, buses link to many small towns in the region's hilly hinterlands. For tickets and information, contact **PESCI,** Piazza della Vittoria 94r (✆ 010-564-936).

By Car Genoa is linked to other parts of Italy and to France by a convenient network of highways. The A10 follows the coast and passes through numerous tunnels to link Genoa with France to the west (the border is about 90 minutes away and Nice is another half hour) while the A12, with even more tunnels, goes to Pisa, about 2 hours to the southeast. The A7 links Genoa with Milan, about an hour and a half to the north. Genoa has lots of parking around the port and the edges of the Old Town, so you can usually find a spot easily, but it can be pricy (1.60€–2€ an hour) though in some lots you don't pay for the overnight hours.

By Ferry Genoa is linked to several other major Mediterranean ports, including Barcelona, as well as Sardinia and Sicily by ferry service (www.traghettitalia.it). Most boats leave and depart from the Stazione Marittima (✆ 010-089-8300), which is on a waterfront roadway, Via Marina D'Italia, about a 5-minute walk south of Stazione Principe. For service to and from the **Riviera Levante,** check with **Tigullio** (✆ 0185-284-670; www.traghettiportofino.it); there's almost hourly service from 9am to 5pm daily in July and August.

VISITOR INFORMATION The **main tourist office** is on **Via Garibaldi 12r** across from the beautiful city hall (✆ 010-557-2903; www.genovaturismo.it), open daily 9am to 6:30pm. There are branches also in **Piazza de Ferrari** (✆ 010-806-6122), open daily 9am to 1pm and 2:30 to 6:30pm; **Piazza Caricamento** near the aquarium (✆ 010-557-4200), open daily 9:30am to 6:30pm; **Cristoforo Colombo airport** (✆ 010-601-5247), open daily 9am to 1pm and 1:30 to 5:30pm.

CITY LAYOUT Genoa extends for miles along the coast, with neighborhoods and suburbs tucked into valleys and climbing the city's many hills. Most sights of interest are in the **Old Town,** a fascinating jumble of old *palazzi,* laundry-festooned tenements, cramped squares, and tiny lanes and alleyways clustered on the eastern side of the old port. The city's two train stations are located on either side of the Old Town. As confusing as Genoa's topography is, wherever you are in the Old Town, you are only a short walk or bus or taxi ride from one of these two stations. **Stazione Principe** is the closest, just to the west; from **Piazza Acquaverde,** in front of the station, follow **Via Balbi** through **Piazza della Nunziata** and **Via Bensa** to **Via Cairoli,** which runs into

Via Garibaldi (the walk will take about 15 min.). **Via Garibaldi,** lined with a succession of majestic *palazzi,* forms the northern flank of the Old Town and is the best place to begin your explorations. Many of the city's most important museums and other major monuments are on and around this street, and from here you can descend into the warren of little lanes, known as **caruggi,** that lead through the cluttered heart of the city and down to the port.

From **Stazione Brignole,** walk straight across the broad, open space to Piazza della Vittoria/Via Luigi Cadorna and turn right to follow broad **Via XX Settembre,** one of the city's major shopping avenues, due west for about 15 or 20 minutes to **Piazza de Ferrari,** which is on the eastern edge of the Old Town. From here, **Via San Lorenzo,** accessed by exiting the southwest corner of the square, will lead you past Genoa's cathedral and to the port. To reach Via Garibaldi, go north from Piazza de Ferrari on **Via XXV Aprile** to **Piazza delle Fontane Marose.** This busy square marks the eastern end of Via Garibaldi.

GETTING AROUND Given Genoa's labyrinth of small streets (many of which cannot be negotiated by car or bus), the only way to get around much of the city is on foot. This, however, can be a navigational feat that requires a good map. Sometimes the tourist office gives out terrific maps and other times they are a bit basic. Consider purchasing a more detailed map—preferably one with a good street index and a section showing the Old Town in detail— at a newsstand. Genovese are usually happy to direct visitors, but given the geography with which they are dealing, their instructions can be complicated. Also be aware of Genoa's unusual street numbering system: Addresses in red (marked with an *r* both below and in any literature you might pick up) generally indicate a commercial establishment; those in black are offices or residences. So two buildings on the same street can have the same number, one in black, one in red.

By Bus Bus tickets (1.50€) are available at newsstands and at ticket booths, *tabacchi* (tobacconists, marked by a brown and white т sign), and at the train stations; look for the symbol **AMT** (✆ **010-558-2414;** www.amt. genova.it). Otherwise, they cost 2.50€ on board. You must stamp your ticket when you board. Bus tickets can also be used on the funiculars and public elevators that climb the city's steep hills surrounding the ancient core of the town (see "Public Transportation Has Never Been This Fun" box, p. 421). Tickets good for 24 hours cost 4.50€ or 9€ for four people (two people travel for free). You can also buy a pack of 10 single tickets for 14€.

By Taxi Metered taxis, which you can find at cabstands, are a convenient and safe way to get around Genoa at night if you are tired of navigating mazelike streets or trying to decipher the city's elaborate bus system. For instance, you may well want to consider taking a taxi from a restaurant in the Old Town to your hotel or to one of the train stations (especially Stazione Brignole, which is a bit farther). Cabstands at Piazza della Nunziata, Piazza Fontane Marose, and Piazza de Ferrari are especially convenient to the Old Town, or call a **radio taxi** at ✆ **010-5966.**

By Subway The city's nascent subway system is still a work in progress, as there are still only seven stops on a single line between Piazza De Ferrari and a suburb to the northwest called Certosa (there are convenient stops in between at Stazione Principe and at Dinegro close to the ferry port). The tickets are the same those used for the bus.

[FastFACTS] GENOA

Bookstores Genoa's best source for English-language books and other media is **Feltrinelli,** Via Ceccardi, 16, near Piazza De Ferrari, just off of Via XX Settembre (✆ **010-573-331;** www.lafeltrinelli.it).

Crime Genoa is a relatively safe city, but some of the very small alleyways of the Old Town near the port can be sketchy at night, and even during the day they can sometimes make you feel unsafe. Violent crime in the city center is extremely rare, but use caution, good sense, and take the same precautions you would exercise in any large city (wait for other people, preferably locals, before entering little-trafficked alleyways and avoid any streets that make you feel uneasy. In an **emergency,** call ✆ **113;** this is a free call. There is a **police station** on the cusp of the Old Town and the port at Via Balbi 38/B (✆ **010-254-871**).

Drugstores Pharmacies keep extended hours on a rotating basis; dial ✆ **192** to learn which ones are open late in a particular week. Several that are usually open overnight are **Pescetto,** Via Balbi 185r

(✆ **010-246-2697**), across from Stazione Principe; **Ghersi,** Corte Lambruschini 16 (✆ **010-541-661**); and **Europa,** Corso Europa 676 (✆ **010-397-615**).

Emergencies The general emergency number is ✆ **113;** for an ambulance, dial ✆ **118.** Both are free calls.

Holidays Genoa's patron saint, San Giovanni Battista (Saint John the Baptist), is the same as Turin's and is honored on June 24. For a list of official state holidays, see p. 70.

Hospitals The **Ospedale San Martino,** Largo Rosanna Benzi 10 (✆ **010-5551**), offers a variety of medical services.

Internet Fnac, Via XX Settembre 46r (✆ **010-290-111**) charges 2€ for 30 minutes and 3€ per hour, and stays open daily 9:30am to 8pm (Sun open 10am). **Khairan Phone Center** on the other side of town at Via Balbi 148r near Stazione Principe is open daily 9am to midnight and charges 1€ an hour.

Laundry There is a self-service laundromat, **Lavanderia Self-Service,** at Via Gramsci 181R (✆ **340-235-1492**), open Monday

to Saturday 9am to 6pm. Small washing machines and driers are 3.50€ per load, large ones 6€.

Luggage Storage The luggage storage office in Stazione Principe is along track 11 and is open daily 7am to 11pm; the fee is 4€ per piece of baggage for the first 5 hours. It is an additional .60€ per hour for the next 7 hours and then an additional .20€ per hour after that. In Stazione Brignole the storage office is on the ground floor; it has the same hours and prices as its sister station.

Post Office Genoa's main post office is at **Piazza Dante 4** (✆ **010-591-762**). This office is open Monday through Saturday 8:10am to 7:40pm, while the other offices around town—including those at the two train stations and the airport—have shorter hours.

Telephone The area code for Genoa is ✆ **010.**

Travel Services CTS, Via Colombo 21R (✆ **010-564-366**), specializes in budget travel. It's open Monday to Friday 9:30am to 6:30pm.

Seeing the Sights

Acquario di Genova (Aquarium of Genoa) ★★★ ☺ Europe's largest aquarium is Genoa's biggest draw and a must-see for travelers with children. The structure alone is remarkable, resembling a ship and built alongside a pier in the old harbor (the aquarium is about a 15-min. walk from Stazione Principe and about 10 min. from Via Garibaldi). Inside, more than 50 aquatic displays re-create Red Sea coral reefs, pools in the tropical rainforests of the Amazon River basin, and other marine ecosystems.

Relief panels by Pisaro at the Museo Sant'Agostino.

These environments provide a pleasant home for sharks, seals, dolphins, penguins, piranhas, and just about every other known kind of creature that has lived in the sea, lakes, or near a major river. Look out for the tiny orange frogs from Madagascar the size of a thumbnail—you may find it hard to draw your gaze away from these tiny colorful creatures. During the day, playful seals and dolphins like to blow trick bubbles to entertain you, and there are small rays in a shallow pool that you can pet. All the descriptions are posted in English. There's also a 3-D film on ocean life (ask for a sheet with the narration in English).

Ponte Spinola (at the port). ✆ **010-234-5678.** www.acquariodigenova.it. Admission 18€ adults, 16€ for seniors 65 and over, 12€ children 4–12. Mon–Fri 9:30am–7:30pm; Sat–Sun 9:30am–8:30pm; July–Aug daily until 10:30pm. Bus: 1, 2, 3, 4, 5, 6, 7, 8, 12, 13, 14, or 15. Metro: Darsena.

Cattedrale di San Lorenzo ★ The austerity of this black-and-white-striped 12th-century structure is enlivened ever so slightly by the fanciful French Gothic carvings around the portal and the presence of two stone lions. A later addition is the bell tower, completed in the 16th century. In the frescoed interior, chapels house two of Genoa's most notable curiosities: Beyond the first pilaster on the right is a shell fired through the roof from a British ship offshore during World War II that never exploded, and in the Cappella di San Giovanni (left aisle), a 13th-century crypt contains what crusaders returning from the Holy Land claimed to be relics of John the Baptist. Fabled tableware of doubtful provenance appears to be a quirk of the adjoining treasury: the plate upon which Saint John's head was supposedly served to Salome, a bowl allegedly used at the Last Supper, and a bowl thought at one time to be the Holy Grail. The less fabled but nonetheless magnificent gold and bejeweled objects here reflect Genoa's medieval prominence as a maritime power. Entrance to the treasury is only by guided tour and

A Cumulative Ticket

Admission to Genoa's major **palaces and art galleries** is grouped together on the **Card Musei** (12€ for 1 day, 16€ for 2; 14€ and 20€ respectively also gets you unlimited use of the city's public transport), which includes entrance to the principal palaces, the Museo Sant'Agostino, San Lorenzo, the Galleria Nazionale di Palazzo Spinola, the Museo di Palazzo Reale, and a handful of other museums around town, plus a discount on admission to the aquarium and movie theaters. Pick one up at any city museum, the airport tourist office, and a handful of bookstores downtown (www.genova-turismo.it).

The Palazzo Bianco houses the city's most famous works of art.

though they are in Italian, it's interesting to see what is inside even if the extent of your Italian is gelato, pizza, and pasta al pesto.

Piazza San Lorenzo. ☏ **010-254-1250.** Admission to cathedral free; treasury 5.50€ adults, 4.50€ seniors 61 and over and students. Cathedral: Mon–Sat 9am–noon and 3–6pm. Treasury: By half-hour guided tour only (ask when you get there) Mon–Sat 9am–noon and 3–6pm. Bus: 1, 7, 8, 17, 18, 19, or 20.

Galata Museo del Mare (Museum of the Seas) ★★ ☺ Genoa's glory, past and present, has always been linked to the sea. For a taste of the sea's continued importance today, it is enough to take a walk around the port to see the massive cruise ships and smaller ferries; you can get a glimpse of the cargo docks, though most of those are farther up the coast. To appreciate what the sea has meant to Genoa in past centuries there is no better place than this appealing four-floor museum. The first section is dedicated to the port and includes 17th-century paintings that show you what was happening here all those years ago. Naturally, there is a large room dedicated to Christopher Columbus.

One of the best exhibits, and sure to get a few wows from the kids, is a full-scale reproduction of a Genovese galley, the attack ship the Genoa republic built in large numbers both to conquer far off corners of the Mediterranean, but also to protect their maritime trade. You'll see lots of props and panels, all with English translations, that describe the trials and tribulations of being a rower on one of these galleys and you can't help but walk away pleased to have your job, whatever it may be. There is also an interesting section dedicated to the overseas trip taken by the mass of Italians who from 1892 to 1914 left Genoa, having arrived from all corners of the country, for the United States via New York's Ellis Island.

Ponte Parodi (at the port). ☏ **010-234-5655.** www.galatamuseodelmare.it. Admission 11€ adults, 9€ for seniors 65 and over, 6€ children 4–12. Mar–Oct daily 10am–7pm; Nov–Feb Tues–Fri 10am–6pm, Sat–Sun 10am–7:30pm (last entry 90 minutes before closing). Bus: 1, 2, 3, 4, 5, 6, 7, 8, 12, 13, 14, or 15. Metro: Darsena (it's a 10-minute walk to the aquarium or else you can hop on the 1€ shuttle).

Galleria di Palazzo Bianco (White Palace) ★★ One of Genoa's finest palaces, built of white stone by the powerful Grimaldi family in the 16th century and reopened to the public in 2004 after an extensive renovation, it houses the city's most notable collection of art. The paintings reflect the fine eye of Maria Brignole-Sale De Ferrari, the duchess of Galliera, who donated the palace and her art to the city in 1884, 4 years before her death. Her preference for painters of the northern schools, whom the affluent Genovese imported to decorate their palaces and paint their portraits, is obvious. Van Dyck and Rubens, both of whom came to Genoa in the early 17th century, are represented here as they are in the city's other major collections. One of the museum's most notable holdings is *Portrait of a Lady,* by Lucas Cranach the Elder. The collection also has works by other masters (Filippino Lippi, Veronese, and Caravaggio). Some local artists are also present such as Bernardo Strozzi, whose early-17th-century school made Genoa an important force in the baroque movement. Its small rooftop terrace offers (for a fee) superb 360-degree views of the city.

Via Garibaldi 11. ✆ **010-557-2193.** Admission 8€ adults, 6€ for seniors 65 and over, free for EU citizens 18 and under; includes entrance to Palazzo Rosso and Palazzo Tursi. Tues–Thurs 9am–7pm; Fri 10am–11pm; Sat–Sun 10am–7pm. Bus: 18, 19, 20, 30, 35, 37, 39, 40, 41, or 42.

Galleria di Palazzo Rosso (Red Palace) This extraordinary 17th-century palace houses a magnificent collection of art, as does its neighbor, the Galleria di Palazzo Bianco (see above). Many of the works—including vibrant frescoes—were commissioned or acquired by the Brignole-Sale, an aristocratic family who once lived in this red-stone palace. Van Dyck painted two members of the clan, Pauline and Anton Giulio Brignole-Sale, and their full-length portraits are among the masterpieces in the second-floor portrait galleries, whose ceilings were frescoed by Gregorio de Ferrari and Domenico Piola. *La Cuoca,* widely considered to be the finest work of Genovese master Bernardo Strozzi, and works by many other Italian and European masters—Gudio Reni, Dürer, Titian, Guercino, and Veronese among them—hang in the first-floor galleries.

Via Garibaldi 18. ✆ **010-557-4972.** Admission 8€ adults, 6€ for those 65 and over, free for EU citizens 18 and under; includes entrance to Palazzo Bianco and Palazzo Tursi. Tues–Thurs 9am–7pm; Fri 10am–11pm; Sat–Sun 10am–7pm. Bus: 18, 19, 20, 30, 35, 37, 39, 40, 41, or 42.

Galleria Nazionale di Palazzo Spinola ★ Another prominent Genovese family, the Spinolas, donated their palace and magnificent art collection to the city only recently, in 1958. One of the pleasures of viewing these works is seeing them amid the frescoed splendor in which the city's merchant/banking families once lived. As in Genoa's other art collections, you will find masterworks that range far beyond native artists like Strozzi and De Ferrari. In fact, perhaps the most memorable painting here is *Ecce Homo,* by the Sicilian master Antonello da Messina. Guido Reni and Luca Giordano are also well represented, as are Van Dyck (including his fragmentary *Portrait of Ansaldo Pallavicino* and four of

---

Some Antiques with Those Frescos?

To see what very well might be the most beautiful inside of a shop anywhere, stop in at **Galleria Imperiale** (✆ **010-251-0086**) at Campetto 8 near Piazza San Matteo, where the vaulted ceilings are covered in 16th-century frescos by Luca Cambiaso, whose work can also be seen in Palazzo Bianco (p. 417). Even if you aren't thinking of shipping home a 7,000€ antique table, this is worth a stop. Open Monday to Saturday 9am to 12:30pm and 3:30 to 7:30pm.

the *Evangelists*) and other painters of the Dutch and Flemish schools, whom Genoa's wealthy burghers were so fond of importing to paint their portraits.

Piazza Pellicceria 1. ℂ **010-270-5300.** www.palazzospinola.it. Admission 4€ adults, 2€ for those 18–25; free for those 18 and under or 65 and over, or pay 12€ for a Card Musei cumulative ticket (see box below). Tues–Sat 8:30am–7:30pm; Sun 1:30–7:30pm. Bus: 1, 3, 7, 8, 18, 20, or 34.

Museo di Palazzo Reale (Royal Palace) The Royal Palace takes its name from its 19th- to early-20th-century tenants, the Royal House of Savoy, who greatly altered the 17th-century palace built for the Balbi family. The Savoys endowed the already rich surroundings with ostentatious frippery, most in evidence in the **hall of mirrors ★**, the ballroom, and the throne room. The rooms are filled with the dusty accouterments of the Italian royalty who once lived here (or at least used it as a home when they occasionally passed through) and a lot of paintings by relative nobodies interspersed with a few by Tintoretto, Luca Giordano (in the crushed velvet throne room), and Van Dyck. The English placards explaining each room will help you identify them. Even if you don't visit the museum, come by during opening hours to see (for free) what a regal Genovese **courtyard ★** of an old palace looks like.

Via Balbi 10. ℂ **010-271-0236.** www.palazzorealegenova.it. Admission 4€ adults, 2€ ages 18–25, free for those 18 and under or 65 and over, or pay 12€ for a Card Musei cumulative ticket (see box below). Tues–Wed 9am–1:30pm; Thurs–Sun 9am–7pm. Bus: 20, 30, 32, 34, or 35.

Historic Squares, Streets & the Porto Antico

PIAZZA DANTE Though most of this square just south of Piazza de Ferrari is made of 1930s office buildings, one end is bounded by the twin round towers of the reconstructed **Porta Soprana ★★**, a town gate built in 1155. The main draw, though, is the small **house** (rebuilt in the 18th c.), still standing a bit incongruously in a tidy little park below the gate, said to have belonged to **Christopher Columbus's father,** who was a weaver and gatekeeper (whether young Christopher lived here is open to debate). To get there, take bus no. 14, 35, 42, 44, or 46.

PIAZZA SAN MATTEO ★★ This beautiful little square 2 blocks off the northwest edge of Piazza de Ferrari is the domain of the city's most acclaimed family, the seagoing Dorias, who ruled Genoa until the end of the 18th century. The church they built on the piazza in the 12th century, **San Matteo,** contains the crypt of the Dorias's most illustrious son, Andrea, and the cloisters are lined with centuries-old plaques heralding the family's many accomplishments, which included drawing up Genoa's constitution in 1529. The church

Genoa's Old Town alleys.

is open Monday to Saturday 8am to noon and 4 to 5pm, and Sunday 4 to 5pm. The **Doria palaces** surround the church in a stunning array of loggias and black-and-white-striped marble facades denoting the homes of honored citizens—Andrea's is at **no. 17.** To get there, take bus no. 18, 19, 20, 30, 32, 33, 35, 37, 40, or 41.

VIA GARIBALDI ★★   Many of Genoa's museums and other sights are clustered on and around this street, one of the most beautiful in Italy, where Genoa's wealthy families built palaces in the 16th and 17th centuries. Aside from the art collections housed in the **Galleria di Palazzo Bianco** and **Galleria di Palazzo Rosso** (see above), the street contains a wealth of other treasures. The **Palazzo Podesta,** at no. 7, hides one of the city's most beautiful fountains in its courtyard, and the **Palazzo Tursi,** at no. 9, now housing municipal offices, proudly displays artifacts of famous locals: letters written by Christopher Columbus and the violin of Nicolo Paganini (which is still played on special occasions). Visitors are allowed free entry to the buildings when the offices are open: Monday through Friday 8:30am to noon and 1 to 4pm. To get there, take bus no. 19, 20, 30, 32, 33, 35, 36, 41, or 42.

Tours, Vistas & Whale-Watching

The Genoese for centuries have provided large boats to take passengers somewhere else. More recently, they have become proud purveyors of their own city's sights, both by sea and by land.

The **Consorzio Liguria Via Mare** (② **010-265-712;** www.liguriaviamare.it or www.whalewatchliguria.it, which also gives information in English) offers a range of cruises that depart from the Porto Antico, near the aquarium, and go to Portofino, Camogli, and Alassio, as well as nighttime harbor cruises and whale-watching expeditions. For the whale watches, led by marine biologists from the World Wildlife Fund, you must check the schedule closely, as they usually run

---

walk **LIKE A GENOVESE**

To **wander the squares and streets** of Genoa's **Old Town** is to get the essence of this incredible city. Via Garibaldi, Piazza Dante, and Piazza San Matteo (listed separately) are the absolute highlights, but your walk should take in a much larger swath of the historic center. One might start in **Piazza Banchi** near Piazza Caricamento at the port and follow **Via San Luca, Via Fossatello** (with a detour up Via Lomellini), and **Via del Campo,** one long shop-lined stretch, to the 12th-century **Porta dei Vacca** gate, once the western edge of town. You can continue along **Via di Prè,** cut up to **Via Balbi,** and follow that to **Via Garibaldi.**

Following **Via Macelli di Soziglia,** which connects Via Garibaldi to Piazza Banchi, will bring you by many historic shops. Going a few blocks south from Piazza Banchi will bring you to the wide **Via San Lorenzo,** which goes by the cathedral, **Piazza Matteotti** (home to the Palazzo Ducale), and eventually up to Piazza de Ferrari (where you see another side of Palazzo Ducale) and Piazza Dante. Save time to explore the characteristic neighborhood south of Via San Lorenzo.

Add in a stroll along the Porto Antico from the Museo del Mare to the Bigo and the aquarium, with detours along the piers jutting out into the port.

Much like Lisbon, Portugal, through the years Genoa has sought to dominate its hilly geography through a combination of elevators, funiculars, and cog railways. Whether you care about getting splendid views of the city or not, it can be great fun to take these innovative modes of public transportation, some of which date back more than a century.

The **Ferrovia Principe-Granarolo,** a cog railway dating back to 1901, leaves from Via Legaccio, just behind the Piazza Principe railway station, and ascends 300m (980 ft.) to Porto Granarolo, one of the gates in the city's 17th-century walls. At the top there's a belvedere. *Note:* The railway closed in early 2011 for a complete restructuring that is slated to take at least a year. The **Funicolare Zecca-Righi,** the first piece of which opened in 1895, takes 12 minutes and five intermediate stops to bring you from Largo della Zecca (once home to Genoa's mint or *zecca*) near Via Garibaldi to the Righi neighborhood from where you get a terrific view of the city. The **Funicolare Sant'Anna,** which came into service in 1891, making it the oldest funicular or public elevator in town, will take you from Piazza del Portello just above Via Garibaldi up to Via Bertani/Corso Magenta for another great view. Incredibly, this funicular used to work thanks to a counterbalanced system that made use of water. The conductor in the top carriage would take note of the number of people in the carriages at the top and the bottom of the funicular and would then add water to a tank in the top carriage. The extra weight of the water would make the top carriage descend and in the process it would pull up the other carriage. *Note:* Sant'Anna, which is now run on electricity, is closed until early 2012 for obligatory repairs that must be made every 20 years.

You have your pick of 11 *ascensori* (public elevators), though the one not to miss is the **Ascensore di Castelletto Levante,** which connects Piazza del Portello with Belvedere Montaldo. The upper station, built in 1910, is a spectacular display of Art Nouveau architecture from where you can view the city and the surrounding hillside. The **Ascensore di Castelletto Ponente** also reaches the Beledevere Montaldo though any romanticism is lost as you have to access it from a traffic tunnel that connects Piazza del Portello with Largo della Zecca.

To ride the Ferrovia Principe-Granarolo and the Zecca-Righi funicular you need a regular bus ticket that costs 1.50€ each way. The Sant'Anna Funicular and all the elevators cost .80€, or 2.80€ for four tickets. Your best bet though is to get a 24-hour public transport ticket for 4.50€ (see p. 414 for information on special deals) and take as many as you can manage. The funiculars generally run every 15 minutes and the elevators are continually going up and down.

only on Saturdays in July, August, and September, plus an occasional midweek cruise. Tickets are 32€ per adult, 18€ for ages 3 to 12, and last 6 to 7 hours. Reservations are required.

From April through October, open-top tour buses leave every day on the half-hour (11am–5:30pm) from in front of the aquarium, and every 90 minutes in the off season. Tickets are 20€ per adult, 5€ for children 4 to 12. Commentary is available in English.

Another alternative to get a new perspective on the city is the elevator that lifts visitors to the top of **Il Bigo,** the modern, mastlike tower designed by Italian architect Renzo Piano to commemorate the Columbus quincentennial celebrations in 1992. This has become one of the centerpieces of the port and one of Genoa's signature landmarks—just don't try it after having had too much to drink for lunch as the constant rotation may go to your head. The observation platform provides an eagle's-eye view of one of Europe's busiest ports for 4€ for adults, 3€ for children ages 4 to 12. It's open Monday 2 to 6pm and Tuesday to Sunday 10am to 6pm (June–Aug until 11pm; Jan–Feb and Nov–Dec only on weekends 10am–5pm). Genoa also offers many cheaper (or free if you are willing to do the steep climbs) ways to get great vistas; see box below.

Where to Stay

Despite the draw of the aquarium and its intriguing Old Town, Genoa is still geared more to business than to tourism, and as a result, decent inexpensive rooms are scarce. On the other hand, just about the only time the town is booked solid is during its annual boat show, the world's largest, in October. It is best to avoid hotels in the heart of the Old Town, especially around the harbor, as many are a little sketchy. The upper end of the price range given in most cases is applied only the week of the boat show and the maximum the rest of the year is considerably lower, sometimes as much as 25%.

VERY EXPENSIVE

Hotel Bristol Palace ★ The majestic oval staircase and stained-glass dome of this historic late-19th-century *palazzo* set the tone for this oasis of comfort and calm in chaotic Genoa. It sits on the main shopping street one block off Genoa's main central piazza, halfway between the train station and the tangle of alleys that make up the center, but it is impressively quiet for the location. The recently renovated and soundproofed rooms have modern bathrooms, but still retain their period furnishings and classic air. A few choice rooms along the front of the hotel are larger, some with marvelous inlaid wood floors and Art Deco furnishings. The range for doubles below reflects a lower rate for most weekends.

Via XX Settembre 35, 16121 Genova. www.hotelbristolpalace.com. ✆ **010-592-541.** Fax 010-561-756. 133 units. 109€–450€ double; 199€–800€ junior suite. Buffet breakfast included. AE, DC, MC, V. Parking in garage 25€. **Amenities:** Restaurant; bar; babysitting; bikes; concierge; room service; smoke-free rooms. *In room:* A/C, TV w/pay movies, hair dryer, minibar, Wi-Fi.

EXPENSIVE

Best Western Hotel Metropoli ★★ Facing a lovely square, just around the corner from Via Garibaldi, the recently restored Metropoli brings modern amenities combined with a gracious ambience to the Old Town. No small part of the appeal of staying here is that many of the surrounding streets are open only to pedestrians, so you can step out of the hotel and avoid the onrush of traffic that plagues much of central Genoa. Guest rooms have somewhat banal and businesslike contemporary furnishings, but with double-pane windows and pleasing pastel fabrics, they provide an oasis of calm. Refurbished bathrooms are equipped with hair dryers, heated towel racks, and double sinks with lots of marble counter space.

Piazza delle Fontane Marose, 16123 Genova. www.hotelmetropoli.it. ✆ **010-246-8888.** Fax 010-246-8686. 48 units. 93€–246€ double; 99€–260€ triple. Rates include buffet breakfast. AE, DC, MC, V. Parking 20€ in nearby garage. **Amenities:** Bar; room service; smoke-free rooms. *In room:* A/C, TV, hair dryer, minibar, Wi-Fi.

MODERATE

Agnello d'Oro ★ ☺ This converted convent enjoys a wonderful location a few short blocks from Stazione Principe on the edge of the Old Town, which can be viewed from a nice terrace. A few of the lower-floor rooms retain the building's original 16th-century character, with high (rooms numbered in teens) or vaulted (rooms numbered under 10) ceilings. Those upstairs have been completely renovated in crisp modern style, with warm-hued tile floors and mostly modular furnishings; though many have only curtainless tubs with hand-held nozzles. Some top-floor rooms come with the added charm of balconies and views over the Old Town and harbor (best from no. 56). There is also a three-bedroom, two-bathroom apartment that can sleep up to six and is perfect for those travelling with a few kids. The friendly proprietor dispenses wine, sightseeing tips, and breakfast in the cozy little bar off the lobby.

Via Monachette 6 (off Via Balbi), 16126 Genova. www.hotelagnellodoro.it. ☎ **010-246-2084.** Fax 010-246-2327. 20 units. 70€–120€ double; 140€ for 4 people in 3-bedroom apt., 2 more people can be added for 20€ each. Rates include breakfast. AE, DC, MC, V. Private parking 15€–25€. **Amenities:** Restaurant; bar; concierge; room service; smoke-free rooms, Wi-Fi. *In room:* A/C, TV, hair dryer (in some), minibar.

INEXPENSIVE

Hotel Barone Near Stazione Brignole, this family-run *pensione* occupies the high-ceilinged large rooms of what was once a grand apartment. And it offers unusually pleasant accommodations at very reasonable rates—a rarity in Genoa. Marco, the young proprietor, gives a gracious welcome; self-service espresso is available around the clock. The rooms are indeed baronial in size (some can be set up with extra beds for families) and are reached by elegant halls hung with gilt mirrors and paintings. While the eclectic furnishings are a bit less grand, many retain lovely touches, like a stuccoed ceiling here (in most, actually) or a chandelier there. The beds are firm and comfortable, the linens are fresh, and the TVs get satellite channels. The shared facilities are spotless. All the bathroomless accommodations have a shower in the room, but you must share the hall toilets.

Via XX Settembre 2 (3rd floor), 16121 Genova. ☎/fax **010-587-578.** www.hotelbaronegenova.it. 12 units, 1 with private bathroom. 55€–65€ double with shared bathroom; 65€–80€ double with private bathroom. AE, DC, MC, V. Free parking in public lot nearby. Bus: 41. **Amenities:** Bar, Wi-Fi. *In room:* TV, hair dryer (on request), Wi-Fi (in some, otherwise in common area).

Hotel Cairoli ★★ Renovated in 2006, this pleasant family-run hotel on the third floor of an old building has an excellent location on the street that continues west from Via Garibaldi. The small rooms are extremely pleasant, with tasteful modern furnishings and tidy little bathrooms; double-pane glass keeps street noise to a minimum. The friendly management gives it the homey feel of an upscale youth hostel, leaving a little basket of snacks in your room. In good weather, you can relax on a terrace covered with potted plants (no. 9 opens onto it). They also have a small weight room, in case you feel the need to work off all that *trofie* (rolled gnocchi). The cost of a double usually maxes out at 105€, and the top price listed below is only during the boat show and a few other days a year.

Via Cairoli 14, 16124 Genova. www.hotelcairoligenova.com. ☎ **010-246-1524.** Fax 010-246-7512. 12 units. 75€–160€ double. Rates include breakfast. AE, DC, MC, V. Parking 15€ in nearby garage. Bus: 18, 19, 20, 30, 34, 35, 37, 39, 40, 41, or 100. **Amenities:** Bar; concierge; small exercise room; room service; smoke-free rooms. *In room:* A/C, TV, hair dryer, minibar, Wi-Fi.

Where to Eat

Also don't miss out on the good food at the wine bar **I Tre Merli,** recommended under "Genoa After Dark," below.

Da Genio ★ GENOVESE Handily situated near Piazza Dante in the Old Town, Da Genio is wonderfully animated. The works of local artists brighten the cozy dining rooms, which are almost always full of Genovese businesspeople and families who have been coming here for years. The assorted antipasti provide a nice introduction to local cuisine, with such specialties as stuffed sardines and *torte di verdure* (vegetable pies). From there you can move on to some of the standbys the kitchen does so well, such as *spaghetti al sugo di pesce* (topped with a fish sauce) or an amazingly fresh *insalata di mare* (seafood salad). Another valid option is to follow the antipasti with Liguria's single most popular and famous traditional dish, *trenette al pesto.* The wine list includes a nice selection from Ligurian vineyards.

Salita San Leonardo 61r. ℰ **010-588-463.** Reservations recommended. Primi 7€–11€; secondi 8.50€–14€. AE, MC, V. Mon–Sat 12:30–3pm and 7:30–10pm. Closed Aug.

Da Guglie LIGURIAN The busy kitchen here, with its open hearth, occupies a good part of this simple restaurant, which serves this neighborhood near Stazione Brignole with takeout fare from a counter and accommodates diners in a bare-bones little room off to one side. There's no attempt at all to provide a decorative ambience. The specials of the day (which often include octopus and other seafood) are displayed in the window; tell the cooks behind the counter what you want and they will bring it over when it's ready. Don't be shy about asking for a sampling of the reasonably priced dishes, because you could happily eat your way through all the greatest hits of Genovese cuisine here. You can accompany the warm *farinata* and the other dishes with Ligurian wines served by the glass or carafe.

Via San Vincenzo 64r. ℰ **010-565-765.** Reservations not necessary. Primi 5€–10€; secondi 6€–13€. No credit cards. Daily noon–10pm.

La Berlocca GENOVESE Enrico Reboscio has turned this old pie and *farinata* shop, located between Via Garibaldi and the port, into an oasis of good food. Service can be a bit slow in the two tiny rooms of small, sturdy wooden tables under stuccoed ceilings, but the seasonal Ligurian menu marrying sea and garden is delicious. That coupling is nowhere more on display than with the *buridda,* a traditional dish of salted cod, tomatoes, and other vegetables. If you were thinking of trying this particular, yet tasty, dish this is as fine a place as any to do it. Otherwise you will find many other traditional Genovese favorites. There's a good wine selection, too.

Via dei Macelli di Soziglia 47r. ℰ **010-247-4162.** Reservations recommended. Primi 7€–16€; secondi 12€–18€. AE, DC, MC, V. Tues–Sat noon–3pm and 7–11pm; Sun for lunch only with reservation. Closed last week of July to 3rd week of Aug.

Trattoria da Maria ★★ 🍴 LIGURIAN Think simple, think good, think simple again, and you have all you really need to know about this Genovese institution. The cooking and the close-knit ambience of the two-floor restaurant on the cusp of the Old Town near Piazza delle Fontane Marose draw a crowd of neighborhood residents, students, businesspeople, and tourists of all nationalities. This unlikely mix sits side-by-side at long tables covered with red- or blue-checked

Fast . . . And Oh So Good

All over Genoa you'll find shops selling **focaccia**, Liguria's answer to pizza, a sort of thick flatbread often stuffed or topped with cheese, herbs, olives, onions, vegetables, or prosciutto. Many of these *focaccerie* will also be selling *farinata*, a crepe made from chickpea flour that usually emerges from the oven in the shape of a big round pizza. Just point and make a hand gesture to show how much you want. Prices are by weight and in most cases a piece of either will cost about 1.50€ to 3€. Most focaccia, especially if it has cheese, and all *farinata* are better warm so if the piece you are getting looks like it has been there a while ask for it to be warmed up.

A favorite place for focaccia and *farinata,* and so close to Stazione Principe that you can stop in as soon as you step off the train, is **La Focacceria di** **Teobaldo** ★, Via Balbi 115r, open daily 8am to 8pm. **Focacceria di Via Lomellini** ★, on Via Lomellini 57/59 in the heart of the Old Town and open Monday to Saturday 8am to 7:30pm, has great *focaccia di Recco,* sometimes also called *focaccia al formaggio,* a super-thin focaccia filled with cheese that is the specialty of the nearby town of Recco. **Focaccia & Co.,** Piazza Macelli di Soziglia 91r, open Monday to Saturday 7am to 7:30pm, is across from Fratelli Klainguti (see below) so you can try some of the many focaccia offerings, all terrific, then take a few steps and continue with some sweets. If you are down at the Porto Antico and realize you need a focaccia fix, as happens often once you have tried this delicacy for the first time, **Il Localino** at Via Turati 8r, open Monday to Saturday 9am to 7pm, is your quickest road to bliss.

---

tablecloths while the staff hurries about shouting orders up and down the shaft of a dumbwaiter. The stupendously cheap menu—which is listed on sheets of paper on the shiny pale green walls—has such simple main courses as a filet of fish sautéed in white wine, or grilled sausages. The pasta with pesto is simply delicious. The *pansotti,* small ravioli covered with a walnut-cream sauce, are also tasty.

Vico Testadoro 14r (just off Via XXV Aprile). ✆ **010-581-080.** Reservations not necessary. Primi 5€–7€; secondi 5€–9€. MC, V. Sun and Tues–Fri 11:45am–2:15pm and 7–9:15pm; Mon 11:45am–2:45pm.

PASTRY & GELATO

Fratelli Klainguti ★★, on Piazza Soziglia 98r–100r (✆ **010-860-2628**), is considered by most to be Genoa's best bakery, as well as its oldest—it was founded in 1828 by a Swiss family. One satisfied customer was the composer Giuseppe Verdi, who said the house's Falstaff (a sweet brioche) was better than his. This and a stupefying assortment of other pastries and chocolates, as well as light snacks (including panini), are served in a pretty rococo-style room or in the piazza out front. It's open Monday to Saturday 7am to 8pm.

For gelato in the Old Town, a good bet is **Excelsa** on Via San Luca 88r right in the midst of the busy shop-lined street and open Monday to Saturday noon to 7:30pm. **Gelateria Balbi,** Via Balbi 165r, is very close to Stazione Principe and excels in rich cream flavors; it's open Monday to Saturday noon to 8pm. And then there is always **Grom** on Via San Lorenzo 53r near the cathedral as well as at Via San Vincenzo 81 near Stazione Brignole (p. 412). Grom is open daily 11am to 11pm (Fri–Sat until midnight).

RECE · CAROLO · FELICI · DVCE · NOSTRO
GENVENSIS · SATAGENTE · HECTORE · IENNEO · REGIO · GVBERNATORE · CON
TOT · INSIGNIBVS · MONVMENTIS · INSTRVCTAE · THEATRVM · SPECTABILI
MDCCCXXVII

Teatro Carlo Felice, flanked by a statue of Giuseppe Garibaldi.

Genoa After Dark

The Old Town, some parts of which are sketchy in broad daylight, is especially unseemly at night. Confine late-hour prowls in this area to the well-trafficked streets such as Via San Lorenzo and Via Garibaldi. On the edges of the Old Town, good places to walk at night are around the waterfront, Piazza Fontane Marose, Piazza de Ferrari, and Piazza delle Erbe, where many bars and clubs are located.

If you are looking for a nice walk to burn off some of your dinner, you could do some or all of a loop that starts in Piazza Caricamento at the waterfront. From there you take Via San Lorenzo (conveniently passing by Grom, where you can get dessert; see above) up to Piazza De Ferrari, then follow Via XXV Aprile up to Piazza Fontane Marose from where you can pass onto Via Garibaldi. Follow the continuation of Via Garibaldi (Via Cairoli and then Via Bensa) into Piazza della Nunziata where you can turn left onto Via delle Fontane, which will take you back to the waterfront.

PERFORMING ARTS Genoa has two major venues for culture: the restored **Teatro Carlo Felice,** Piazza de Ferrari (☎ 010-589-329; www.carlofelice. it), which is home to Genoa's opera company and also hosts visiting companies; and the modern **Teatro Stabile di Genova** (☎ 010-53-421; www. teatrostabilegenova.it), on Piazza Borgo Pila near Stazione Brignole, which hosts concerts, dance, and other cultural programs.

BARS & CLUBS If you've had it with Ligurian white wine and really need a Guinness, **Brittania,** at Vico Casana (just off Piazza De Ferrari), serves pints Monday to Saturday from 11am to the wee hours (☎ 010-247-4532). The pub closes for a month every year either in July or August.

New Yorkers will recognize the name and chic ambience in **I Tre Merli Antica Cantina,** at Vico Dietro il Coro della Maddalena 26r (☎ 010-247-4095; www.itremerli.it), which does a brisk business in Manhattan with four restaurants. Here in Genoa, I Tre Merli operates a couple of *enoteche* (wine bars), and this one, located on a narrow street just off Via Garibaldi, is delightful, even if the surrounding alleyways are sometimes seedy. A dark stone floor and walls of brick and stone provide a cozy setting, augmented by "refined country"–style tables and chairs. You can sample the wide selection of wines from throughout Italy by the glass, and there is a full bar. The half-dozen each of primi and secondi are refined Ligurian and, along with the cheese and salami platters, make this a good spot for a late-night meal; it's open Tuesday to Sunday 7pm to 1am. I Tre Merli also has an *enoteca* in Camogli.

Le Courbusier, Via San Donato 36 (✆ **010-246-8652**), opens early and closes late. This coffeehouse-cum-bar, in the Old Town just west of Piazza delle Erbe, is especially popular with students. They are perpetually busy, dispensing excellent coffee and sandwiches (from 4.50€), as well as beer, wine, and spirits.

Quick Escapes

Two seaside retreats within the city limits are Boccadasse and, a little farther out, Nervi, both to the east of the city center and easily reached by public transportation. Take bus no. 41 from Stazione Principe or Piazza de Ferrari to Boccadasse (the trip takes 20–30 min., depending on traffic, and costs the same as a regular city bus ticket: 1€) and bus no. 17, or one of the frequent trains from Stazione Brignole to Nervi (the train trip takes only 15 min.).

Once a quaint fishing village, **Boccadasse** has long since given way to some urban development. Even so, this bustling seaside community is still a pleasant corner of the city. Fishing boats and nets litter the shore, and the rocky seaside is lined with tall, colorful Ligurian houses, whose bottom floors now accommodate gelaterie, focaccerie, and simple restaurants with outdoor terraces.

Nervi was a fashionable resort a century ago, and it's still easy to see why. A 1.5km-long (1-mile) seaside promenade affords stunning views of the sea, and elegant villas are surrounded by a lush profusion of flora. One of the most pleasant retreats in Genoa is Nervi's Parco Villa Grimaldi, where more than 2,000 varieties of roses bloom. Each July, Nervi hosts Genoa's International Ballet Festival (see "Festivals & Markets," earlier in this section).

THE RIVIERA DI PONENTE

San Remo: 140km (87 miles) W of Genoa, 56km (35 miles) E of Nice; Bordighera: 152km (94 miles) W of Genoa, 12km (7½ miles) W of San Remo, 44km (27 miles) E of Nice

San Remo

Gone are the days when Tchaikovsky and the Russian empress Maria Alexandrovna joined a well-heeled mix of titled Continental and British gentry in strolling along San Remo's palm-lined avenues. They left behind an onion-domed Orthodox church, a few grand hotels, and a casino, but **San Remo** is a different sort of town these days. It's still the most cosmopolitan stop on the Riviera di Ponente, as the stretch of coast west of Genoa is called, and caters mostly to sun-seeking Italian families in the summer and Milanesi who come down in the winter months to get away from the fog and chilly temperatures of their city.

In addition to the gentle ambience of days gone by, San Remo offers its visitors a long stretch of beach and a hilltop Old Town known as La Pigna. For cosmopolitan pleasures, the casino attracts a well-attired clientele willing to try their luck.

San Remo is an excellent base from which to explore the rocky coast and Ligurian hills. So is Bordighera, a quieter resort just up the coast. With excellent train and bus connections, both are within easy reach of a full itinerary of fascinating stops, including Giardini Hanbury, one of Europe's most exquisite gardens; the fascinating prehistoric remains at Balzi Rossi; and Dolceacqua, perhaps the most enticing of all the inland Ligurian villages.

Festivals August 15, the **Feast of the Assumption,** is celebrated with special flair in San Remo, with the festival of Nostra Signora della Costa (Our Lady of the Coast). The Virgin Mary allegedly saved a local sailor from drowning, and she is honored with fireworks and a procession in medieval garb to her shrine on a hillside high above the town.

> ### A Day at the Beach
>
> Plunging into the Ligurian Sea in San Remo means spending some money. The pebbly beach below the Passeggiata dell'Imperatrice is lined with beach stations, where many visitors choose to spend their days: easy to do, since most provide showers, snack bars, and, of course, beach chairs, lounges, and umbrellas. Expect to spend up to 15€ for a basic lounge, but more like 20€ for a more elaborate sun-bed arrangement with umbrella. *Note:* As is standard at most European resort towns without "public" sections of beach (which are usually not very nice anyway), you cannot go onto the beach without paying for at least a lounge chair.

Since the 1950s, the **Sanremo Festival** (in late Feb or early Mar) has been Italy's—and one of Europe's—premier music fests. It's sort of an Italian version of the Grammy Awards, only spread out over several days with far more live performances—by Italian pop stars, international headliners, and plenty of up-and-coming singers, songwriters, and bands. "Volare" was Sanremo's first-ever Best Recording, and today if you peruse the CD collections of most Italian households, you'll find at least a few of the yearly compilation albums the festival puts out. The festival has spawned many other contests/celebrations of film and music (international folk to *musica lirica*) throughout the year, but this is the big one, booking hotels up and down the coast months in advance. Call the tourist office if you want to try to score tickets.

ESSENTIALS

GETTING THERE By Train There are trains hourly to and from **Genoa** (1¾–2½ hr.). Two to three trains per hour connect with **Bordighera** (8 min.). Trains from Genoa continue west for another 20 minutes to **Ventimiglia** on the French border. Some trains continue on into France, otherwise you can cross the border on one of the twice-hourly trains to **Nice,** 50 minutes west.

By Bus Riviera Trasporti buses (*✆* **0183-7001;** www.riviera trasporti.it) run every 15 minutes between San Remo and **Bordighera** (20 min.). Almost as many buses continue on to **Ventimiglia** (40 min. from San Remo).

By Car The fastest driving route in and out of San Remo is Autostrada A10, which follows the coast from the French border (20 min. away) to Genoa (about 45 min. away). The slower coast road, SS1, cuts right through the center of town and is the best option if you are not going very far (Bordighera and Ventimiglia are reached more quickly on the SS1, traffic permitting).

San Remo's seaside Corso Imperatrice.

VISITOR INFORMATION The **APT tourist board** is at Largo Nuvoloni 1 (*©*0184-590-523; www.turismoinliguria.it), at the corner with Corso Imperatrice/Corso Matteotti (cross the street from the old train station and go to the left a few hundred feet). It's open Monday to Saturday 8am to 7pm and Sunday 9am to 1pm. In addition to a wealth of information on San Remo, the office dispenses information on towns up and down the nearby coast, known as the Riviera dei Fiori.

STROLLING AROUND TOWN

San Remo's underground railway station, buried into the coastal hills much like its counterpart in nearby Monaco, is sleek and clean, but there are a few disadvantages. For one thing, the walk from the tracks to the exit is formidable (*Note:* Leave plenty of time to catch a train), and the walk from there to the center of town is also considerably longer than from the old station, which sits downtown, just by the coast. This leads to the final problem: Even today, more than a decade after the inauguration of the new station, some locals might give you directions to a hotel, restaurant, and such, referring to the "train station," when, in fact, they mean the former station.

To get downtown from the new train station, walk straight out of the exit, cross Corso Cavallotti, and continue downhill until you reach Corso Trento e Trieste. Take a right on that road, which hugs the shore and leads to the old port.

To the right of the old station are the beginnings of Via Roma and Corso Matteotti, San Remo's two main thoroughfares. Corso Matteotti will lead you past the **casino** (see below) and into the heart of the lively business district. Continue on that until it runs into Piazza Colombo and the flower market. If, instead, you turn left (north) on Via Feraldi about midway down Corso Matteotti, you will find yourself in the charming older precincts of town. Continue through Piazza degli Eroi Sanremesi to Piazza Mercato, where Via Montà leads into the old medieval quarter, **La Pigna.** The hill on which this fascinating district is located resembles a pine cone in its conical shape, hence the name. Aside from a few restaurants, La Pigna is a residential quarter, with tall old houses that overshadow the narrow lanes that twist and turn up the hillside to the park-enclosed ruins of a **castle** at the top.

VISITING THE CASINO

San Remo's white palace of a casino (*©*0184-5951), set intimidatingly atop a long flight of steps across from the old train station and enclosed on three sides by Corso degli Inglesi, is the hub of the local nightlife scene. You can't step foot inside without being properly attired (jacket for gents Oct–June) and showing your passport. You must be 18 or older to enter. There are poker tables starting at 2€ games, but there are more serious tables that attract high rollers from the length of the Riviera. Gaming rooms are open daily 2:30pm to 3am (weekends to 4am). Things are more relaxed in the rooms set aside for slot machines, where there is no dress code. They are open Sunday to Friday 10am to 3am.

WHERE TO STAY
Very Expensive
Royal Hotel ★★★ Since 1872, the Bertolini family's Royal Hotel has been the preferred retreat of jet-setters as well as the first place rock stars call for a suite during the music festival. The terraces of palms and flowers of its 1.6-hectare (4-acre) park leading up to its edifice from the main road blend seamlessly with the verdant public gardens next door, and the stucco-ceilinged bars and salons, framed by granite ionic columns, promise a cushy, elegant stay. The rooms have rugs on the polished parquet, comfortable beds, spacious bathrooms, and are exceedingly comfortable. The shared door of neighboring corner rooms can be opened to make family suites. The best accommodations, obviously, are those that enjoy the sea view from small terraces or small balconies. It wouldn't be "royal" if it didn't have a private beach across the road.

Corso Imperatrice 80, 18038 San Remo. www.royalhotelsanremo.com. ℭ **0184-5391.** Fax 0184-661-445. 136 units. 275€–475€ double; 375€–560€ junior suite. Add 40€ for half-pension. Rates include breakfast. AE, DC, MC, V. Parking 10€, or 20€ in garage. Closed early Oct to mid-Dec. **Amenities:** 3 Italian/international restaurants (elegant dining room, terrace dining in summer, poolside lunch restaurant Apr–Oct); 2 bars (1 at pool); babysitting; bikes; children's center (high season); concierge; nearby golf course; exercise room; minigolf; park; large outdoor heated salt-water pool; room service; outdoor tennis court; watersports equipment/rentals. *In room:* A/C, TV, hair dryer, minibar, Wi-Fi.

Moderate
Hotel Miramare Continental Palace ★ 🏊 The Miramare is a Liberty-style villa of sedate, faded elegance, and the only hotel on the shore side of the main road, but it is a 15-minute walk from the center. You really come for the setting, not the rooms, which are a bit small, with modular furnishings and sea views. The hotel is set in a 1-hectare (2½-acre) park of flower-fringed palms and a mighty baobab tree. A private pathway leads right onto the beach, and next door is an indoor lap swimming pool that's heated in winter and open to the public.

Corso Matuzia 9, 18038 San Remo. www.miramaresanremo.it. ℭ **0184-667-601.** Fax 0184-667-655. 59 units. 120€–230€ double. For half-board, add 20€ per person; for full board, add 40€. Rates include breakfast. AE, DC, MC, V. Free parking. **Amenities:** Italian/international/regional restaurant; bar; babysitting; concierge; nearby golf course; indoor heated seawater pool; room service; smoke-free rooms. *In room:* TV, hair dryer, minibar, Wi-Fi.

Hotel Villa Maria ★★ It's fairly easy to imagine San Remo's late-19th-/early-20th-century heyday in this charming hotel incorporating three villas on a flowery hillside above the casino. The promenade

---

Is Board Necessary?

Many hotels offer room-and-board rates that include breakfast, lunch, and dinner (full board), or breakfast and one of these other two meals (half-board or half-pension). Only in the busy late July and early August beach season do many require you to take these meals, however. If you can procure a room without the meal plan, do so—San Remo has many excellent restaurants, and this is not a place where you have to spend a lot for a good meal.

is only a short walk downhill, yet the hubbub of the resort seems miles away from this leafy residential district. A series of elegant salons and dining rooms with parquet floors, richly paneled ceilings, and crystal chandeliers spread across the ground floor, and many of these public rooms open to a nicely planted terrace. The bedrooms, too, retain the grandeur of the original dwellings, with silk-covered armchairs and antique beds; many have balconies facing the sea. Since rooms vary considerably in size and decor, ask to look around before you settle on one that strikes your fancy.

Corso Nuvoloni 30, 18038 San Remo. www.villamariahotel.it. © **0184-531-422.** Fax 0184-531-425. 38 units, 36 with private bathroom. 70€–140€ double. For half-board (required Easter, Christmas, and Aug 1–15), add 30€ per person. Rates include continental breakfast. AE, DC, MC, V. Free parking. **Amenities:** Restaurant (international); concierge; room service; smoke-free rooms. *In room:* TV, hair dryer.

Inexpensive

Hotel Sole Mare ★ Don't let the location on a drab side street near the train station put you off. This cheerful *pensione* on the upper floors of an apartment building is a delight and offers guests a friendly welcome, along with some of the best-value lodgings in the resort area. A lounge, bar area, and dining room are spacious and flooded with light, and have gleaming white-tile floors and open onto a wide terrace. The large guest rooms are also cheerful and equipped with the trappings of much more expensive hotels—pleasant modern furnishings and soothing pastel fabrics and small but modern well-lit bathrooms—and almost all enjoy sea views, about half from wide balconies.

Via Carli 23, 18038 San Remo. www.solemarehotel.com. © **0184-577-105.** Fax 0184-532-778. 21 units. 70€–136€ double. Half-board 45€–75€ per person; full board 50€–80€ per person. Rates include breakfast. AE, DC, MC, V. Parking 7€ in nearby garage. **Amenities:** Restaurant (international); bar; babysitting; concierge; room service. *In room:* A/C, TV, hair dryer, minibar, Wi-Fi.

WHERE TO EAT

Ristorante da Giannino ★ LIGURIAN With Anna in the kitchen and Giuseppe in the modern dining room, the Gasparini family runs one of the top (but also priciest) restaurants in town. In the summer months, it moves from its Corso Cavallotti address, near the train station, to an open space by a pool just a few dozen meters away on Via Anselmi. The menu is well balanced between surf and turf, and you can follow a *risotto* or *linguine ai frutti di mare* (rice or noodles richly studded with seafood) with *coniglio alle erbe* (rabbit roasted with fresh herbs), or catch of the day grilled or served under a cream sauce spiced with whole green peppercorns.

Corso Cavallotti 76 (in summer months, Via Anselmi 6). © **0184-504-014.** Reservations recommended. Primi 18€–27€; secondi 23€–30€; tasting menu 60€, not including wine. AE, DC, MC, V. Tues–Sat noon–2:30pm; Mon–Sat 7:30–10pm.

Ristorante L'Airone ★ LIGURIAN/PIZZA With its pale gold walls and green-hued tables and chairs, this delightful, friendly restaurant in a pedestrian-only section of the city center looks as though it's been transported over the border from Provence. The food, though, is definitely Ligurian. There is a wide selection of pasta, including *spaghetti con le vongole,* which comes smothered in clams. For the secondi you are better off with the fish, perhaps a *grigliata mista* (mixed grilled fish) or grilled sole, rather than the meats that tend to disappoint. You can also get a pretty good light-crusted pizza (always available in the evening though at lunch time only on Tuesday and Saturday). In good weather, meals are served in a small garden out back covered by a reed-thatched tent—and there are some tables on the piazza outside (which, admittedly, is nothing special).

Piazza Eroi Sanremesi 12. ✆ **0184-541-055.** www.ristorantelairone.it. Reservations not necessary. Primi 6€–14€; secondi 7€–17€; pizza 5€–10€; *menù turistico* 13€, not including wine; *menù degustazione* 31€, not including wine. DC, MC, V. Sat–Wed noon–2:30pm and 7:30–11:30pm (Fri only in the evening).

THE CAFE & BAR SCENE

Agorà Cafè, on Piazza San Siro (no phone), which faces San Remo's cathedral, makes no claim other than to be a comfortable watering hole, a function it performs very well. For footsore travelers, the terrace out front, facing the pretty stone piazza and cathedral of San Siro, is a welcome oasis. Sandwiches and other light fare are served late into the night, when an after-dinner crowd tends to make this one of the livelier spots in town. It's closed Monday.

Wanderings through the center of town should include a stop at **Enoteca Bacchus ★★** (Via Roma 65; ✆ **0184-530-990**), a handsome wine bar open Monday to Saturday 10am to 9pm. Wine is served by the glass at a sit-down bar or at one of the small tables, and you can accompany your libations with fresh focaccia, cheeses, vegetable tarts, and even such substantial fare as *buridda,* a dish of salted cod, tomatoes, and other vegetables. If you find any particularly interesting wine, you can buy a bottle to take away.

THE RIVIERA DI LEVANTE

Camogli: 26km (16 miles) E of Genoa; Santa Margherita Ligure: 31km (19 miles) E of Genoa; Portofino: 38km (24 miles) E of Genoa; Rapallo: 37km (23 miles) E of Genoa

The coast east of Genoa, the **Riviera di Levante (Shore of the Rising Sun),** is more ruggedly beautiful than the Riviera Ponente, less developed, and hugged by mountains that plunge into the sea. Four of the coast's most appealing towns are within a few kilometers of one another, clinging to the shores of the Monte Portofino Promontory just east of Genoa: Camogli, Santa Margherita Ligure, Rapallo, and little Portofino.

Camogli

Camogli remains delightfully unspoiled, an authentic Ligurian fishing port with tall houses in various pastel colors facing the harbor and a nice swath of beach. Given also its excellent accommodations and eateries, Camogli is a lovely place to base yourself while exploring the Riviera Levante. This is also a restful retreat from which you can explore Genoa, which is only about 30 minutes away. One interpretation of Camogli's name is that it derived from "Ca de Mogge," or "House of the Wives" in the local dialect, and was named for the women who held down the fort while their husbands went to sea. Another possibility is that it comes from "Ca a Muggi," or "clustered houses," which will seem the perfect name when you are out swimming in the sea and turn to look up at the town's wonderful agglomeration of colorful buildings. Other interpretations of the name abound.

Festivals & Markets Camogli throws a well-attended annual party, the **Sagra del Pesce ★★,** on the second Sunday of May, where the town fries up thousands of sardines in a 3.6m-diameter (12-ft.) pan and passes them around for free—a practice that is accompanied by an annual outcry in the press about health concerns and even accusations that frozen fish is used.

The first Sunday of August, Camogli stages the lovely **Festa della Stella Maris.** A procession of boats sails to Punta Chiappa, a point of land about 1.5km (1 mile) down the coast, and releases 10,000 burning candles. Meanwhile, the same number of candles is set afloat from the Camogli beach. If currents are favorable, the burning candles will come together at sea, signifying a year of unity for couples who watch the spectacle.

ESSENTIALS

GETTING THERE By Train One to three trains per hour ply the coastline, connecting Camogli with **Genoa** (30–45 min.), **Santa Margherita** (5 min.), and **Monterosso** (50–60 min.) and other Cinque Terre towns.

By Bus There is at least one Tigullio (✆ **0185-373-239;** www.tigullio trasporti.it) bus an hour, often more, from **Santa Margherita;** since the bus must go around and not under the Monte Portofino Promontory, the trip takes quite a bit longer than the train—about half an hour.

By Boat In summer, boats operated by Golfo Paradiso (✆ **0185-772-091;** www.golfoparadiso.it) sail from Camogli to **Portofino.**

By Car The fastest route into the region is Autostrada A12 from Genoa; exit at Recco for Camogli (the trip takes less than half an hour). Route SS1 along the coast from Genoa is much slower but more scenic. In the summer months, parking in Camogli can be a real challenge.

VISITOR INFORMATION The **tourist office** is across from the train station at Via XX Settembre 33 (✆/fax **0185-771-066;** www.prolococamogli.it or www.portofinocoast.it). It's open Monday to Saturday 9am to 12:30pm and 3 to 7pm (Mar–Oct it closes at noon and 6:30pm, respectively), Sunday 9am to 12:30pm.

EXPLORING THE TOWN

Camogli is clustered around its delightful waterfront, from which the town ascends via steep, staircased lanes to Via XX Settembre, one of the few streets in

Camogli's beach is picture perfect.

the town proper to accommodate cars (this is where the train station, tourist office, and many shops and other businesses are located). Adding to the charm of this setting is the fact that the oldest part of Camogli juts into the harbor on a little point (once an island) where ancient houses cling to the little **Castello Dragone** (now closed to the public) and the **Basilica di Santa Maria Assunta** (*℗* **0185-770-130**), an originally 12th-century structure that has been much altered through the ages and now has an overwhelming baroque interior that's open daily 7:30am to noon and 3:30 to 7pm. Most visitors, though, are drawn to the pleasant **seaside promenade** ★ that runs the length of the town. You can swim from the pebbly beach below, and should you feel your towel doesn't provide enough comfort, rent a lounge from one of the few beach stations for about 15€.

WHERE TO STAY

Albergo Augusta *♨* This is an acceptable alternative if La Camogliese (below) is full, and, more than a fallback, it's pleasant and convenient, with a handy location a short walk up a steep staircase from the harbor. The couple and their son who run this *pensione* also operate the ground-floor trattoria, which serves as a sitting room for the hotel guests and makes it easy to enjoy a cup of coffee or glass of wine. The clean guest rooms are extremely plain, with functional furnishings and drab decor, but most are large and have good-size bathrooms. You also get 15 minutes of free Internet access (in the reception area) per day. Ask for a room in front—those in back face the train tracks.

Via Schiaffino 100, 16032 Camogli. www.htlaugusta.com. *℗* **0185-770-592.** 14 units. 55€–110€ double; 90€–135€ triple. AE, DC, MC, V. Parking 12€. **Amenities:** Restaurant (local cuisine); bar; room service. *In room:* A/C, TV, Internet.

Hotel Cenobio dei Dogi ★★ This oasis sits just above the sea at the end of town and against the forested flank of Monte Portofino. The oldest part of the hotel incorporates an aristocratic villa dating from 1565. Converted to a hotel in 1956, the premises now include several wings that wrap graciously around a garden on one side and a series of terraces facing the sea on the other. There's a pool and a private beach as well as a lovely lounge area and a glass-enclosed breakfast room that hangs over the sea (the view from here is by itself almost worth whatever you happen to pay for a room). The guest rooms, 44 of which face the sea, vary considerably in size and shape, but all are furnished with a tasteful mix of reproduction writing desks, contemporary glass-top tables, and island-style furnishings (bent bamboo headboards and the like).

Via Cuneo 34, 16032 Camogli. www.cenobio.it. *℗* **0185-7241.** Fax 0185-772-796. 105 units. 160€–230€ standard double with garden view; 220€–320€ standard double with sea view; 190€–270€ superior double with garden view; 300€–430€ superior double with sea view. Rates include buffet breakfast. AE, DC, MC, V. Free parking. **Amenities:** 2 Ligurian/international restaurants (1 at beach, which is only open in the summer); 2 bars; babysitting; concierge; nearby golf course; outdoor saltwater pool; outdoor lighted tennis courts; watersports equipment/rentals. *In room:* A/C, TV, hair dryer, minibar, Wi-Fi.

La Camogliese ★★ Genovese and Milanese come out to spend the weekend in this friendly, attractive little hotel near the waterfront, and they appreciate it for the same simple charms that will appeal to travelers from farther afield. (In fact, given the hotel's popularity, it's fundamental to reserve well in advance, especially on weekends and in the summer.) The large, bright rooms are decorated in modern furnishings that include comfortable beds. Some have balconies, and although the house isn't right on the waterfront, it faces a little river and is close enough to the beach that a slight twist of the head usually affords a view of the sea (best from rooms 3 and 16B). Rooms 4, 5, 14, 18, and 23 have balconies with side views of the sea. Bathrooms are small but adequate.

Via Garibaldi 55, 16032 Camogli. www.lacamogliese.it. © **0185-771-402.** Fax 0185-774-024. 21 units. 80€–115€ double. Rates include breakfast. AE, DC, MC, V. Parking 15€, call ahead to alert them. **Amenities:** Babysitting; concierge; exercise room; outdoor pool; room service. *In room:* TV, hair dryer, Internet.

WHERE TO EAT

Bar Primula CAFE/LIGHT FARE If you need a light meal (a pasta dish and seafood plate or two are usually available, along with sandwiches, salads, omelets, and pizza), this is the most convenient spot, but many people come in simply for a cup of espresso and dessert, which presents a difficult choice between the delicious ice cream and pastries.

Via Garibaldi 140. © **0185-770-351.** Reservations not accepted. Salads and other light fare, including pizza 9€–15€. AE, MC, V. Daily 9am–1am.

Lo Strufugio ★★ SEAFOOD What you give up in the view—the place is on the main drag up above the seaside promenade—you more than make up with the food. The intimate setting (there are only five tables), personal service, and an open kitchen create an enticing atmosphere that makes you happy even before your food arrives. And when it does, you'll soon be wondering if you can squeeze in another trip here before leaving town. The menu changes often, but if *gnocchi con gamberi, zucchine e bottarga* (gnocchi topped with tiny shrimp, zucchini, and shaved fish roe) is there your choice is made. The fried fresh anchovies are light, fluffy, and never enough, so don't share. Little or no English is spoken here and the menu is only in Italian, so bring your dictionary and be ready to interpret hand gestures.

Via della Repubblica 64. © **0185-771-553.** Reservations highly recommended. Primi 9€–18€; secondi 12€–24€. MC, V. Sun 12:30–2:30pm and Wed–Sun 5:30–10pm.

Focaccia by the Seaside

It might be the perfect seaside setting or perhaps there is something in the water, no matter the reason, Camogli has some of the best focaccia in all of Liguria. Along Via Garibaldi, the promenade above the beach, there are many *focaccerie* to choose from and though it is hard to go wrong with any of them, one stands out. At **Revello** (© **0185-770-777**) on Via Garibaldi 183 (the part closest to the church) Tino is carrying on the tradition passed down by his uncle, who first began pulling focaccia out of the oven here in 1964.

It's likely they haven't messed up a batch once since then. Revello, which is open Wednesday to Monday 10am to 6pm (summer until 7pm), has a few benches outside where you can enjoy your loot while watching the kids play soccer in the little square overlooking the beach. **O'Becco** next door also makes some mean focaccia—special mention goes to the one with fresh anchovies, parsley, garlic, and olive oil—and **U Caruggiu** at the other end of Via Garibaldi has Kamut focaccia on the weekends.

Ristorante La Camogliese SEAFOOD You probably won't be surprised to find that the menu at this bright seaside spot, perched over the beach on stilts, leans heavily to seafood. In fact, when the weather is pleasant and the windows that surround the dining room are open, you feel you are at sea. That's the real draw of this place, as the service here is shaky, and there are better dishes to be had on this coast. That said, the hearty fish soup for two is quite good, and you can never go wrong with a lightly fried swordfish steak.

Via Garibaldi 78. ℭ **0185-771-086.** Reservations recommended. Primi 9€–14€; secondi 10€–15€. AE, DC, MC, V. Daily 12:30–2:30pm and 7:30–10:30pm (Oct–June closed Wed).

A HOTEL BETWEEN CAMOGLI & SANTA MARGHERITA LIGURE

Hotel Portofino Kulm ★★ This grand old hotel, slung in a skyscraping hammock of greenery in the midst of the Tigullio's parkland halfway between Camogli and Santa Margherita Ligure, was opened in 1908 but for decades stood derelict until Camogli's Cenobio dei Dogi overhauled it to reopen in 2000. The long vistas sweep across the forest down to the Riviera north of the promontory toward Genoa in one direction, and in the other over Santa Margherita down the coast toward the Cinque Terre. Many balconies and rooftop terraces take full advantage of the panoramas. The modest-size, carpeted rooms come with wrought-iron bedsteads, stylish furnishings, marble bathrooms, and queen-size beds. The best ones come with those sea views from balconies. Four rooms are in a separate structure a smidgen higher up the driveway, with even better views. Sometimes the hotel offers special deals if you stay more than 2 nights.

Viale Bernardo Gaggini 23 (6km/3¾ miles from Camogli on the over-mountain road to Santa Margherita Ligure), 16030 Ruta di Camogli, Portofino Vetta (GE). www.portofinokulm.it. ℭ **0185-7361.** Fax 0185-776-622. 77 units. 140€–180€ double with park view; 160€–200€ double with sea view; 180€–220€ double with sea view and terrace. Rates include breakfast. AE, DC, MC, V. Free parking. **Amenities:** International/Ligurian restaurant; bar; babysitting; bikes; concierge; tiny exercise room; Jacuzzi; indoor heated pool; room service; sauna. *In room:* A/C, TV, hair dryer, minibar, Wi-Fi.

Santa Margherita Ligure

Santa Margherita had one brief moment in the spotlight, at the beginning of the 20th century when it was an internationally renowned retreat. Fortunately, the seaside town didn't let fame spoil its charm, and now that it's no longer as well known a destination as its glitzy neighbor Portofino, it might be the Mediterranean retreat of your dreams. A palm-lined harbor, a decent beach, and a friendly ambience make Santa Margherita a fine place to settle down for a few days of sun and relaxation.

Festivals & Markets Santa Margherita's winters are delightfully mild, but even so, the town rushes to usher in spring with a **Festa di Primavera,** held on moveable dates in February. Like the Sagra del Pesce in neighboring Camogli, this festival also features food—in this case, fritters are prepared on the beach and served around roaring bonfires. One of the more interesting daily spectacles in town is the **fish market** on Lungomare Marconi from 8am to 12:30pm. On Friday, Corso Matteotti, Santa Margherita's major street for food shopping, becomes an open-air **food market.**

ESSENTIALS

GETTING THERE **By Train** One to three trains per hour connect Santa Margherita with **Genoa** (25–30 min.), **Camogli** (5 min.), Rapallo (3 min.), and **Monterosso** (40–55 min.) of the Cinque Terre.

By Bus There is at least one Tigullio (℡ **0185-373-239;** www.tigullio trasporti.it) bus an hour to **Camogli** (30–35 min.) and to **Rapallo** (10 min.), leaving from Piazza Vittorio Veneto. Buses also follow the stunningly beautiful coast road to **Portofino,** leaving every 20 minutes from the train station and Piazza Vittorio Veneto (25 min.).

By Boat Tigullio ferries (℡ **0185-284-670;** www.traghettiportofino. it) make hourly trips to **Portofino** (15 min.) and **Rapallo** (15 min.). In summer, there is a boat several days a week to the Cinque Terre. Hours of service vary considerably with season; schedules are posted on the docks at Piazza Martiri della Libertà.

By Car The fastest route into the region is A12 Autostrada from Genoa; the trip takes about half an hour. Route SS1 along the coast from Genoa is much slower but more scenic.

VISITOR INFORMATION The **tourist office** is near the harbor at Via XXV Aprile 2B (℡ **0185-287-485;** www.turismoinliguria.it). Summer hours are daily 9:30am to 12:30pm and 2:30 to 8pm; winter hours are Monday to Saturday 9am to 12:30pm and 2:30 to 5:30pm.

EXPLORING THE TOWN

Life in Santa Margherita centers on its palm-fringed **waterfront,** a pleasant string of marinas, docks for pleasure and fishing boats, and pebbly beaches, in some spots with imported sand of passable quality. Landlubbers congregate in the cafes that spill out into the town's two seaside squares, Piazza Martiri della Libertà and Piazza Vittorio Veneto.

The train station is on a hill above the waterfront, and a staircase in front of the entrance will lead you down into the heart of town. Santa Margherita's one landmark of note is its namesake **Basilica di Santa Margherita,** just off the seafront on Piazza Caprera. The church is open daily 7:30am to noon and 2:30 to 7pm and is well worth a visit to view the extravagant, gilded, chandeliered interior.

WHERE TO STAY

Annabella The nice proprietors manage to accommodate groups of just about any size in this old apartment that's been converted to a very basic, yet clean and attractive *pensione* with comfortable old modular furniture and whitewashed walls. Some of the rooms sleep up to four, and one family-style arrangement includes a large room with a double bed and a tiny room outfitted with bunk beds for children. None of the rooms have private bathrooms, but the four shared facilities are ample and hot water is plentiful.

Via Costasecca 10, 16038 Santa Margherita Ligure (GE). ℡ **0185-286-531.** 11 units, none with private bathroom. 60€–85€ double; 85€–100€ triple. No credit cards. Parking on the street nearby. *In room:* No phone.

Grand Hotel Miramare ★★ This was one of the first grand hotels on this coast, converted in 1903 from a massive private villa a 10-minute walk from the town center along the road to Portofino. Rooms are enlivened by some modest stucco decorations on the walls and ceilings, from which hang chandeliers over parquet floors scattered with Persian rugs and slightly funky walnut and veneer furnishings. The first-floor suite where Marconi stayed when conducting his radio experiments has been kept in 19th-century style, while fifth-floor suites are more modernized. A very steep, pretty park rises behind the hotel, from which a trail leads over the headland to Portofino (it also makes for a pleasant view, especially if you don't get a room with that preferred sea vista). There's a small, private pebble beach/beach terrace across the busy road.

Via Milite Ignoto 30, 16038 Santa Margherita Ligure (GE). www.grandhotelmiramare.it. ℂ **0185-287-013.** Fax 0185-284-651. 84 units. 255€–397€ double with park view; 305€–458€ double with sea view; AE, DC, MC, V. Parking 25€. **Amenities:** 2 restaurants (1 poolside lunch buffet; 1 international/regional); 2 bars (piano bar inside, pool bar); babysitting; concierge; nearby exercise room; nearby golf course; outdoor heated saltwater pool; room service; nearby sauna; nearby outdoor lighted tennis courts; watersports equipment/rentals. *In room:* A/C, TV, hair dryer, minibar, Wi-Fi.

Hotel Metropole ★★ ☺ This popular hotel is just above the port and a 5-minute stroll from the center. Accommodations are split between the main, modern building and the far-preferable Villa Porticciolo, a dusty red villa right on the beach; the rooms are smaller in the latter, but they're graced with 19th-century stuccoes, and the sea laps practically right up against the building. Six rooms up on the far end of the garden have large terraces. All other guest rooms have large balconies. The fourth floor is made up of junior suites and one double with sloped ceilings. Two suites on the lower floor of the main building open onto small private gardens. Several rooms can be joined to make family suites and there's day care at the beach, with a separate area of sand just for the kiddies. The small private beach includes a curving sunbathing terrace and a private boat launch.

Via Pagana 2, 16038 Santa Margherita Ligure (GE). www.metropole.it. ℂ **0185-286-134.** Fax 0185-283-495. 59 units. 100€–242€ double; 136€–286€ double with half-board; 156€–306€ double with full board. Rates include buffet breakfast. AE, DC, MC, V. Parking 12€ outside or 18€ in private garage. **Amenities:** 2 restaurants (1 international/regional dining room; 1 beachside lunch restaurant); bar; babysitting; children's center (in summer); private beach; small exercise room; nearby golf course; swimming pool; sauna; watersports equipment/rentals. *In room:* A/C, TV, hair dryer, Internet, minibar, Wi-Fi.

Nuova Riviera ★ 🌶 The Sabini family acts as if its sunny, early-20th-century Liberty-style villa in a quiet neighborhood behind the town center was a private home and guests were old friends. Every room is different, and though eclectically furnished with pieces that look like they may have passed through a couple of generations of the family, most rooms retain the high-ceilinged elegance of days gone by and have a great deal more character than you're used to finding in rooms at this end of the budget scale. The best rooms have expansive bay windows. Modular furnishings are mixed with antiques, the beds are springy (very springy), and a few rooms get balconies. Ask for an internal room as scooters cruise the street in front of the hotel at all hours. They also rent out rooms in another nearby structure (70€–125€ for two people with a 3-night minimum, no breakfast).

Via Belvedere 10–2, 16038 Santa Margherita Ligure (GE). www.nuovariviera.com. ℂ/fax **0185-287-403.** 9 units. 85€–130€ double. Rates include breakfast. MC, V. **Amenities:** Restaurant (local cuisine, winter only); bar; smoke-free rooms. *In room:* TV, hair dryer, no phone.

WHERE TO EAT

Trattoria Baicin ★ LIGURIAN The husband-and-wife owners, Piero and Carmela, make everything fresh daily, from fish soup to gnocchi, and still manage to find time to greet diners at the door of their cheerful trattoria just a few steps off the harbor. You can get a glimpse of the sea if you choose to sit at one of the tables out front, and the owner/cooks are most happy preparing fish, which they buy fresh every morning at the market just around the corner. The sole, simply grilled, is especially good here, and the *fritto misto di pesce* constitutes a memorable feast. You must begin a meal with one of the fresh pastas made that morning. The fixed-price menus are good value and give you a nice sampling of what's on offer.

Via Algeria 9. ✆ **0185-286-763.** Reservations recommended for outdoor seating. Primi 5€–8€; secondi 9€–16€; fixed-price menus 20€–22€. AE, DC, MC, V. Tues–Sun noon–3pm and 7–10:30pm. Closed Jan.

Trattoria da Pezzi ⚑ GENOVESE/LIGURIAN The two whitewashed, tile-floored rooms of this cozy little restaurant in the center of town near the market are usually filled with local workers and businesspeople who invite newcomers to share a table when no other place is available. Service is minimal—the chef puts what he's prepared for the day on a table near the front door, you tell him what you want, and one of the staff brings it to the table when it's ready. Focaccia, *farinata,* and other Genovese specialties are usually on hand, as are at least one kind of soup (the minestrone is excellent), a chicken dish, and grilled fresh fish.

Via Cavour 21. ✆ **0185-285-303.** Reservations not accepted. Primi 6€–8.50€; secondi 6€–10€. MC, V. Sun–Fri 11:45am–2:15pm and 6–9:15pm. Closed the 2nd week of Sept and mid-Dec to mid-Jan.

Portofino

Portofino is almost too beautiful for its own good—in almost any season, you'll be rubbing elbows on Portofino's harborside quays with day-tripping mobs who join Italian industrialists, international celebrities, and a lot of rich-but-not-so-famous folks who consider this little town to be the epicenter of the good life. If you make an appearance in the late afternoon when the crowds have thinned out a bit, you are sure to experience what remains so appealing about this enchanting place—its untouchable beauty.

ESSENTIALS

GETTING THERE By Train Get off in Santa Margherita (see above) and catch the bus.

By Bus The **Tigullio** bus (✆**0185-373-239;** www.tigullio trasporti.it) leaves from the train station and Piazza Vittorio Veneto in **Santa Margherita** every 20 minutes and follows one of Italy's most beautiful coastal roads (25 min.). In Santa Margherita, you can change for a bus to **Rapallo** (another 15 min.).

By Boat The best way to arrive in Portofino is on your private yacht. If you have left it at home for this visit to Italy, the next best thing is to sail in on one of the Golfo Paradiso ferries (✆**0185-772-091;** www.golfo paradiso.it) from **Camogli,** or on one of the Tigullio ferries (✆**0185-284-670;** www.traghettiportofino.it) from **Santa Margherita** or **Rapallo.**

By Car On a summer visit, you may encounter crowds even before you get into town, since traffic on the corniche from Santa Margherita, just a few kilometers down the coast of the promontory, can move at a snail's pace. In fact, given limited parking space in Portofino, visitors must pay obscene rates to use the town garage. You would do well to leave your car in Santa Margherita and take the bus or boat.

Old and new collide in Portofino's harbor.

VISITOR INFORMATION Portofino's **tourist office** is at Via Roma 35 (✆ **0185-269-024;** www.turismoinliguria.it). Summer hours are Tuesday to Saturday 10am to 1pm and 2 to 6pm, Sunday 9:30am to 12:30pm and 3:30 to 6:30pm; winter hours are Tuesday to Saturday 9:30am to 1:30pm and 2 to 5pm.

AN excursion TO SAN FRUTTUOSO

Much of the **Monte Portofino Promontory** can be approached only on foot or by boat (see below), making it a prime destination for hikers. If you want to combine some excellent exercise with the pleasure of glimpsing magnificent views of the sea through a lush forest, arm yourself with a map from the tourist offices in Camogli, Santa Margherita Ligure, Portofino, or Rapallo and set out. You can explore the upper reaches of the promontory or aim for the **Abbazia di San Fruttuoso** (✆ **0185-772-703**), a medieval abbey (pictured at right) that is surrounded by a tiny six-house hamlet and two pebbly beaches. It is about 2½ hours away from Camogli and Portofino by a not-too-strenuous inland hike, or 3½ hours away by a cliff-hugging, up-and-down trail. En route, you can clamor down well-posted paths to visit San Rocco, San Niccolò, and Punta Chiappa, a string of fishing hamlets on the shore of the promontory.

Once you reach San Fruttuoso, you may well want to relax on the pebbly beach and enjoy a beverage or meal at one of the seaside bars. You can tour the stark interior of the abbey for 6€. It is open June to mid-September daily 10am to 5:45pm; in May Tuesday to Sunday 10am to 5:45pm; March, April, and October Tuesday to Sunday 10am to 3:30pm; and November to February Saturday and Sunday 10am to 3:30pm. Note, though, that despite these official hours, the abbey tends to close whenever the last boat leaves (see below). The abbey is just a plain, evocatively simple medieval monastic complex with a stellar setting on the coast. There's nothing really to "see" except how the

EXPLORING THE TOWN & SEA

The one thing that won't break the bank in Portofino is the scenery. Begin with a stroll around the stunningly beautiful **harbor,** which is lined with expensive boutiques, eateries, and colorful houses set along the quay and steep green hills rising behind them. One of the most scenic walks takes you uphill for about 10 minutes along a well-signposted path from the west side of town just behind the harbor to the **Chiesa di San Giorgio** (✆0185-269-337), built on the site of a sanctuary Roman soldiers dedicated to the Persian god Mithras. It's open daily 9am to 7pm.

From there, continue uphill for a few minutes more to Portofino's 15th-century **Castello Brown** (✆0185-267-101; www.castellobrown.it), which has a lush garden and offers great views of the town and harbor below. It costs 5€ (includes access to special exhibitions when they are going on) and is open daily 10am to 7pm from March to October, and the rest of the year on Saturday and Sunday from 10am to 5pm.

For more lovely views on this stretch of coast and plenty of open sea, go even higher up through lovely pine forests to the *faro* (lighthouse).

From Portofino, you can also set out for a longer hike on the paths that cross the **Monte Portofino Promontory** to the Abbazia di San Fruttuoso (see the box "An Excursion to San Fruttuoso," below), a walk of about 2½ hours from Portofino. The tourist office provides maps.

monks lived. Should you happen to have your scuba or snorkeling gear along, you can take the plunge to visit Christ of the Depths, a statue of Jesus erected 15m (49 ft.) beneath the surface to honor sailors lost at sea.

You can also visit San Fruttuoso with one of the **boats** that run almost every hour during the summer months from Camogli. A round-trip costs 13€ (10€ one-way if you then plan to head southward from the abbey) and takes about 30 minutes. For more information, contact Golfo Paradiso (✆ **0185-772-091;** www.golfoparadiso.it). *Note:* You can also reach it by hourly (in summer) Tigullio boats (✆ **0185-284-670;** www. traghettiportofino.it) from Portofino (20 min.; 11€ roundtrip), Santa Margherita (35 min.; 15€ roundtrip), and Rapallo (50 min.; 15€ roundtrip). Bear in mind that the seas are often too choppy to take passengers to San Fruttuoso, because docking there can be tricky. In that case, there are private boats you can take—smaller, rubber crafts capable of bad-weather landings—though they are expensive: From Portofino, you will likely be charged 100€ for up to 12 people.

There's not much else to see in town, but most people are here to spend time on the water. If you're yachtless, one alternative is to take a dolphin-spotting cruise with **Delfini Metropolitani** (✆ **010-234-5666;** www.incomingliguria. it). A 2-day tour, hotel accommodations in Genoa included, costs about 140€ per person, or 70€ for children 4 to 12 years old.

WHERE TO STAY

Hotel Eden ★ Osta Ferruccio runs this cozy *pensione* in the heart of the tiny town, a long block up from the harbor. There are no views of the sea here, though those over the town's rooftops are pleasant enough. The most sought-after room is no. 7, which comes with a small terrace. The bathrooms are tight but well equipped and there's a lovely small garden where Ligurian dishes are served in summer. While not exactly cheap, in Portofino this qualifies as a budget hotel and it's one of the few of any category that's open year-round.

Vico Dritto 18, 16034 Portofino (GE). www.hoteledenportofino.com. ✆ **0185-269-091.** Fax 0185-269-047. 12 units. 140€–290€ double. Rates include breakfast. AE, DC, MC, V. Parking 20€ in nearby lot. **Amenities:** Restaurant (Ligurian); bar; babysitting; concierge. *In room:* A/C, TV, hair dryer, Wi-Fi.

Hotel Nazionale ★★ ✦ It may be set smack in the middle of Portofino's harborfront square, amid some of the priciest real estate in Italy, but the Nazionale costs only one-third to one-half the price of its pricier neighbors. Decoration of the smallish to midsize rooms is minimal, but the pieces are a masterful mix of modern and antique, which adds to the relaxing elegance of the place. Several of the rooms are lofted suites with the bedroom upstairs. Only five rooms, all junior suites, enjoy views of the harbor.

Via Roma 8, 16034 Portofino (GE). www.nazionaleportofino.com. ✆ **0185-269-575.** Fax 0185-269-138. 12 units. 200€–275€ double without sea view; 300€–375€ junior suite with sea view. Rates include breakfast. MC, V. Parking 20€ in nearby lot. Closed mid-Dec to Mar. **Amenities:** Restaurant (Italian); bar; concierge; room service. *In room:* A/C, TV, hair dryer, minibar, Wi-Fi.

Hotel Splendido/Splendido Mare ★★ This 19th-century villa grafted onto the remains of a 16th-century monastery has been a hotel since 1901 and, since the early 1950s, one of those fabled retreats of the international rich and famous, of rock stars and Oscar winners. It's perched in a panoramic position atop the headland just before the last curve of the road into town (yes, it's a good 10-min. walk to Portofino harbor—and an uphill haul back—but there's a regular shuttle). The spacious junior suites come with parquet floors, king-size beds, and antique-style furnishings that hide the high-tech entertainment centers. Some come with a small terrace, and a few are set into the very private next-door building fronted by a grape arbor. A series of olive-lined, rosemary-scented paths wrap around the panoramic pool terrace and stretch along the hillside to various little lookouts. Though the Splendido closes down in winter, its sister, Splendido Mare (eight doubles and eight suites on Portofino's harborfront *piazzetta*), stays open year-round.

Salita Baratta 16, 16034 Portofino (GE). www.hotelsplendido.com. ✆ **800-237-1236** toll free in the U.S. and Canada, or 0185-267-801 in Italy. Fax 0185-267-806. 80 units (of which 16 at Splendido Mare). At Hotel Splendido (all rates include half-board): 975€–1,545€ double (separate rates for garden view, sea view, and balcony overlooking the sea); 1,565€–2,455€ junior suite; 2,165€–4,365€ suite. At Splendido Mare: 620€–750€ double with village view; 760€–960€ double with sea view; 1,130€–1,640€ junior suite. Half-board supplement at Splendido Mare 79€

per person. Rates include full American breakfast. A 10% VAT charge is added to all room rates. AE, DC, MC, V. Parking 21€ in garage. Closed Nov 12–Feb 28. **Amenities:** 2 restaurants (regional cuisine in an indoor/outdoor terrace dining room; poolside lunch buffet); bar (piano bar in the evening); babysitting; bikes; concierge; exercise room; nearby golf course; outdoor heated sea-water pool; room service; sauna; spa; outdoor tennis courts; watersports equipment/rentals. *In room:* A/C, TV w/free movies, hair dryer, kitchenette (in some), minibar, VCR, Wi-Fi.

WHERE TO EAT

Portofino's charms come at a steep price. Its few hotels are expensive enough to put them in the "trip of a lifetime" category, and the harborside restaurants can take a serious chunk out of a vacation budget as well. An alternative is to enjoy a light snack at a bar or one of the many shops selling focaccia, and wait to dine in Santa Margherita or one of the other nearby towns.

La Gritta American Bar CAFE/BAR This very attractive, very friendly place is far enough along the harborside quay to be a little less hectic than other establishments. Most patrons stop in for a (pricey) cocktail, coffee, or other libation (the floating terrace out front is perfect for a drink at sunset), but light fare, such as omelets and salads of tomatoes and mozzarella, are also available to provide a light and relatively affordable meal.

Calata Marconi 20. ✆ **0185-269-126.** Reservations not necessary. Salads and other light fare from about 10€. AE, MC, V. Fri–Wed noon–1am. Closed Nov.

Ristorante Puny ★★ LIGURIAN The gregarious owners make this a Portofino landmark, and also a difficult place to score a table in the summer. Right on the *piazzetta*, its tables enjoy views of the boats bobbing in the harbor and yachts having size contests beyond. Definitely book ahead to drink in those views and dig into *risotto al curry e gamberi* (curried rice embedded with tiny shrimp); *penne al puny* (pasta quills in a sauce of tomatoes, *pancetta* bacon, and mushrooms); fresh fish *al verde* (in a green sauce of parsley, lemon, and white wine) or *al sale* (baked under a thick salt crust); or *carne all'uccelletto* (diced veal sautéed in butter then cooked in white wine with bay leaves).

Piazza Martiri dell'Olivetta 5. ✆ **0185-269-037.** Reservations highly recommended. Primi 11€–20€; secondi 14€–25€; AE, MC, V. Wed, Thurs, Sat, Sun 12:30–3:30pm and Wed–Fri 7:30–11pm.

Rapallo

When you step out of Rapallo's busy train station, you may be put off by the traffic, the blocks of banal apartment houses, and the runaway development that in some places has given the resort the look of any other busy town. Keep walking, though, because at its heart, Rapallo remains a gracious old seaside playground and port, and it's easy to see what drew the likes of Ezra Pound, Max Beerbohm, and D. H. Lawrence to take up residence here. Most of the town follows the sweep of a pretty harbor guarded by a medieval castle, and the gracious seafront promenade is cheerfully busy day and night, mostly with families.

Festivals & Markets Rapallo is at its most exuberant July 1 to 3, when it celebrates the **Madonna di Montallegro,** whose hilltop sanctuary, the Santuario di Montallegro, crowns the town (see below). A famous icon of the Virgin is carried through the streets, and a huge fireworks display culminates in the burning of the castle (a mock event, of course). Piazza IV Novembre/Via Gramsci is the site of a lively outdoor **food market** on Thursday mornings.

ESSENTIALS

GETTING THERE **By Train** More than 30 trains a day connect Rapallo and **Genoa** (30–40 min.). The same trains connect Rapallo with **Camogli** (10 min.), **Santa Margherita** (3 min.), and **Monterosso** (35–50 min.) at the north end of the Cinque Terre.

By Bus At least one bus an hour runs between Rapallo and **Santa Margherita** (about 15 min.).

By Boat **Tigullio** ferries (✆0185-284-670; www.traghettiportofino. it) make hourly trips to **Portofino** (30 min.) via **Santa Margherita** (15 min.). In summer, there is a boat several days a week to the Cinque Terre. Hours of service vary considerably with season; schedules are posted on the docks.

By Car Autostrada A12 connects Rapallo with Genoa and takes about half an hour. Route SS1 along the coast from Genoa is much slower but more scenic.

VISITOR INFORMATION The **tourist office** is at Lungomare Vittorio Veneto 7 (✆0185-230-346; www.turismoinliguria.it) and is open Monday 9am to 2pm, Tuesday to Saturday 8am to 2pm and 3:30 to 6pm, Sunday 9:30am to 12:30pm and 3:30 to 6:30pm. The hours are reduced in the winter.

EXPLORING THE TOWN

From the train station, it's a walk of only about 5 minutes to the **waterfront** (follow Corso Italia to Piazza Canessa and the adjoining Piazza Cavour, and from there, Via Cairoli to the harborside Piazza IV Novembre). Dominating this perfect half-circle of a harbor is a **castle** built on a rocky outcropping reached by a causeway; it is open only for special exhibitions, but the boulders around its base are usually teeming with sunbathers. Nearby, two other buildings reflect the fact

that Rapallo enjoyed a long and prosperous existence before it became known as a retreat for pleasure seekers. The **Cathedral of Santi Gervasio e Protasio,** on Via Mazzini, was founded in the 6th century, and the leper house of **San Lorenzo** across the street dates from the Middle Ages. You can go inside the church but not the leper house.

For striking views over the town and surrounding seacoast, make the ascent to the **Santuario di Montallegro** (✆0185-239-000). You can take a bus from the train station (1€) or an aerial *funivia* (cableway) from Via Castagneto on the eastern side of town. The *funivia* (✆0185-52-341) operates daily every 30 minutes from 9am to 12:30pm and 2 to 6pm (winter until 4:45pm); the trip takes 7 minutes and costs 5.50€ one-way or 8€ round-trip. Inside this 16th-century church are interesting frescoes and a curious Byzantine icon of the Virgin that allegedly flew here on its own from Dalmatia. The views over the sea and surrounding valleys are the main reason to come up here, though, and they are even grander from the summit of Monte Rosa, a short uphill hike away.

Frescoes of the Santuario di Montallegro.

WHERE TO STAY

Hotel Riviera ★★ 🏆 The Gambero family has run this small hotel, which occupies an old villa on the waterfront, since 1935, and it is now in the capable hands of Claudio and Silvana. The guest rooms have hardwood floors, with matching handsome wood desks and shelving units. Double-pane windows keep noise from the seaside avenue out front to a minimum, and bathrooms feature top-of-the-line fixtures. Many of the fine old touches remain, including small balconies off many of the rooms with vistas over the harbor. Three of the suites are perfect for families, consisting of two separate bedrooms and a shared bathroom off a hall, while the fourth is a single large corner room with three balconies, one off the double-sink bathroom. A sunny terrace overlooking the sea extends from the restaurant/breakfast room, where a generous buffet is served every morning and reasonable fixed-price menus (as well as a la carte) at mealtimes.

Piazza IV Novembre 2, 16035 Rapallo (GE). www.hotelrivierarapallo.com. ☎ **0185-50-248.** Fax 0185-65-668. 20 units. 100€–154€ double; 140€–170€ double with sea view; 155€–194€ suite. Rates include breakfast. AE, MC, V. Free parking. Closed Nov–Dec 23. **Amenities:** Restaurant; bar; babysitting; bikes; concierge; nearby golf course; room service; tennis courts. *In room:* A/C, TV, hair dryer, minibar, Wi-Fi.

Hotel Rosa Bianca ★ 🏨 This small, lovely hotel is quiet, unassuming, and exceedingly personable, with friendly management and a perfect location right at the end of the main road at the port. It has great views over the harbor and restaurant-lined promenade, all the way to the castle. Most rooms are small and could do with some redecorating, but they are nevertheless pleasant and have beds with genuine box springs. Most of the corner rooms have little semicircular balconies and are flooded with light. The hotel is across and down a bit from the Riviera (see above), but enjoys better views.

Lungomare Vittorio Veneto 42, 16035 Rapallo (GE). www.hotelrosabianca.it. ☎ **0185-50-390.** Fax 0185-65-035. 18 units. 119€–145€ double; 130€–180€ suite. Rates include buffet breakfast. AE, DC, MC, V. Parking 15€. **Amenities:** Bar; babysitting; concierge; room service; smoke-free rooms. *In room:* A/C, TV, hair dryer, minibar, Wi-Fi (in some; otherwise in lobby).

WHERE TO EAT

O Bansin 🏆 LIGURIAN This colorful and boisterous restaurant has been a Rapallo institution since 1907, and even though the new young owners have moved it a few blocks away from the marketplace and spruced it up a bit, they've kept the original respect for simplicity, low prices, and traditional Ligurian cuisine. Minestrone, *pasta al pesto* or *al Bansin* (with tomatoes, pesto, and cream), *polpette in umido* (stewed meatballs served with peas), and *sardine alla piastra* (roast sardines) are served without pomp and circumstance at communal tables in a plain interior room or, when warm enough, on the covered, semi-open deck out back. The service is as warm and friendly as the environs.

Via Venezia 105. ☎ **0185-231-119.** www.obansin.weebly.com. Reservations recommended in summer. Primi 7€–9€; secondi 8€–18€; fixed-price menu at lunch (Mon–Sat) 10€, including wine. AE, DC, MC, V. Tues–Sat 12:15–2pm and 7:15–10pm; Sun–Mon 12:15–2pm. Closed Oct 8–20.

Ristorante Elite SEAFOOD This popular seafood restaurant is just up a busy avenue from the harbor, and the pleasant room, hung with paintings of local scenes, is a little less formal (and less overpriced) than the many seafood restaurants on the waterfront. The kitchen long ago won the approval of locals, who come here for the fresh fish of the day, which can follow such starters as seafood salad, a *risotto gamberetti e asparagi* (risotto with small prawns and fresh asparagus), or a *zuppa di pesce* (a hearty fish soup). Fresh fish can also be enjoyed on the fixed-price menus, veritable feasts that also include hot and cold seafood appetizers and a pasta course.

Via Milite Ignoto 19. ✆ **0185-50-551.** www.eliteristorante.it. Reservations recommended in summer. Primi 6€–11€; secondi 8€–22€; fixed-price chef's menu 21€–32€, not including wine. AE, DC, MC, V. Thurs–Tues (summer daily) noon–2:30pm and 7:30–10pm. Closed Nov.

THE CINQUE TERRE

Monterosso, the northernmost town of the Cinque Terre, 93km (58 miles) E of Genoa

Olive groves and vineyards clinging to hillsides, proud villages perched above the sea, hidden coves nestled at the foot of dramatic cliffs—the **Cinque Terre** is about as beautiful a coastline as you're likely to find in Europe. What's best about the Cinque Terre (named for the five neighboring towns of Monterosso, Vernazza, Corniglia, Manarola, and Riomaggiore) is what are *not* here—automobiles, large-scale development, or much else by way of 20th- and 21st-century interference. The pastimes in the Cinque Terre don't get much more elaborate than **walking** ★★★ from one lovely village to another along trails that afford spectacular vistas, plunging into the Mediterranean, or basking in the sun on your own waterside boulder, and indulging in the tasty local food and wine.

Not too surprisingly, these charms have not gone unnoticed, and American tourists especially have been coming here in increasing numbers. In summer (weekends are worst), you are likely to find yourself in a long procession of like-minded, English-speaking trekkers making their way down the coast or elbow to elbow with day-trippers from an excursion boat. Even so, the Cinque Terre manages to escape the hubbub that afflicts so many coastlines, and even a short stay here is likely to reward you with one of the most memorable seaside visits of a lifetime.

Essentials

GETTING THERE By Train You often cannot coast directly into the Cinque Terre towns, as they are served only by local train runs. Coming from Florence or Rome you will likely have to change trains in nearby **La Spezia** (one or two per hour; 8 min.) at the coast's south tip or in **Pisa** (about six daily; 1¼ hr.). There are one or two direct trains per hour from **Genoa** to La Spezia (1 hr., 40 min.); many more from Genoa require a change in Levanto or Sestri Levante, both a bit farther north up the coast from Monterosso.

By Car The fastest route is via Autostrada A12 from Genoa, getting off at the Corrodano exit for Monterosso. The trip from Genoa to Corrodano takes less than an hour, while the much shorter 15km (9¼-mile) trip from Corrodano to Monterosso (via Levanto) is made along a narrow road and can take about half that amount of time. Coming from the south or Florence, get off Autostrada A12 at La Spezia and follow CINQUE TERRE signs.

By Boat Navigazione Golfo dei Poeti (✆ **0187-732-987;** www. navigazionegolfodeipoeti.it) runs erratic service from the **Riviera Levante towns,** as well as from **Genoa,** mid-June to mid-September, though these tend to be day cruises stopping for anywhere from 1 to 3 hours in Vernazza (see description below) before returning (though you can usually talk them into not picking you up again for a day or three).

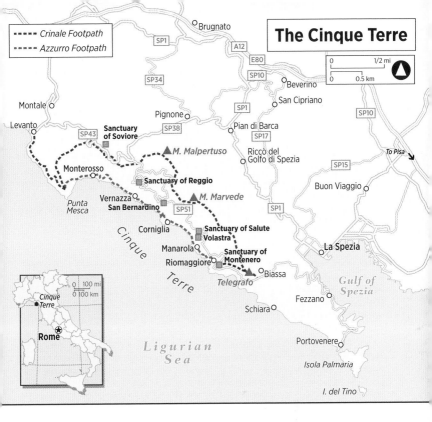

The Cinque Terre

Crinale Footpath

Azzurro Footpath

Brugnato

SP1

A12

E80

SP10

Beverino

SP34

San Cipriano

Pignone

SP1

Montale

Pian di Barca

Levanto

SP43

Sanctuary of Soviore

SP38

Riccò del Golfo di Spezia

SP17

To Pisa

M. Malpertuso

SP10

Monterosso

Sanctuary of Reggio

SP15

Buon Viaggio

Punta Mesca

Vernazza

San Bernardino

M. Marvede

SP51

SP1

Corniglia

Sanctuary of Salute Volastra

La Spezia

Manarola

Riomaggiore

Sanctuary of Montenero

Telegrafo

Biassa

Cinque

Terre

Gulf of Spezia

Cinque Terre

Fezzano

Rome

Schiara

Portovenere

Ligurian Sea

Isola Palmaria

I. del Tino

GETTING AROUND **By Foot** The best way to see the Cinque Terre is to devote a whole day and hoof it along the trails. See "Exploring the Cinque Terre," below, for details.

By Train Local trains make frequent runs (two to three per hour) between the five towns; some stop only in Monterosso and Riomaggiore, so check the posted *Partenze* schedule at the station first to be sure you're catching a local. One-way tickets between any two towns are available, including one version that is good for 6 hours of travel in one direction, meaning you can use it to town-hop—or you can buy a day ticket good for unlimited trips.

By Car A narrow, one-lane coast road hugs the mountainside above the towns, but all the centers are closed to cars. Parking is difficult and, where available, expensive.

Riomaggiore and Manarola both have small **public parking facilities** just above their towns and minibuses to carry you and your luggage down. The

Trains link the towns of the Cinque Terre.

cheapest option is the big open dirt lot right on the seafront in Monterosso. The priciest is the garage in Riomaggiore.

By Boat From the port in Monterosso, **Navigazione Golfo dei Poeti** (✆ **0187-732-987;** www.navigazionegolfodeipoeti.it) makes 8 to 10 trips a day between Monterosso and Riomaggiore (a 25-min. trip), all stopping in Vernazza and half of them stopping in Manarola as well.

VISITOR INFORMATION The **tourist office** for the Cinque Terre is underneath the train station of Monterosso, Via Fegina 38 (✆ **0187-817-506;** www.turismoinliguria.it). It's open Easter to the end of September daily 9am to 5pm; hours are reduced the rest of the year. Even when it's closed, you will usually find posted outside the office a handy display of phone numbers and other useful info, from hotels to ferries.

Useful websites for the region include www.cinqueterre.it, www.parconazionale5terre.it, and www.turismoinliguria.it.

Exploring the Cinque Terre

Aside from swimming and soaking in the atmosphere of unspoiled fishing villages, the most popular activity in the Cinque Terre is **hiking from one village to the next** ★★★ along centuries-old goat paths. Trails plunge through vineyards and groves of olive and lemon trees and hug seaside cliffs, affording heart-stopping views of the coast and the romantic little villages looming ahead in the distance. The well-signposted walks from village to village range in difficulty and length, but as a loose rule, they get longer and steeper—and more rewarding—the farther north you go. Depending on your pace, and not including eventual stops for focaccia and *sciacchetrà,* the local sweet wine, you can make the trip between Monterosso, at the northern end of the Cinque Terre, and Riomaggiore, at the southern end, in about 4½ hours. You should decide whether you want to walk north to south or south to north. Walking south means tackling the hardest trail first, which you may prefer, because you'll get it out of the way and things will get easier as the day goes on and you start to tire. Heading north, the trail gets progressively harder between each town, so perhaps you might like this if you want to walk just until you get tired and then hop the train.

The walk from **Monterosso to Vernazza** is the most arduous and takes 1½ hours, on a trail that makes several steep ascents and descents (on the portion outside Monterosso, you'll pass beneath funicular-like cars that transport grapes down the steep hillsides). The leg from **Vernazza to Corniglia** is also demanding and takes another 1½ hours, plunging into some dense forests and involving some lengthy ascents, but is probably the prettiest and most rewarding stretch. Part of the path between **Corniglia and Manarola,** about 45 minutes apart, follows a level grade above a long stretch of beach, tempting you to break stride and take a dip. From **Manarola to Riomaggiore,** it's easy going for about half an hour along a partially paved path known as the Via dell'Amore, so named for its romantic vistas (great to do at sunset).

Because all the villages are linked by rail, you can hike as many portions of the itinerary as you wish and take the train to your next destination. Trails also cut through the forested, hilly terrain inland from the coast, much of which is protected as a nature preserve. The tourist office in Monterosso can provide maps.

BEACHES The only sandy beach in the Cinque Terre is the crowded strand in **Monterosso,** on much of which you will be asked to pay about 20€ per day for two chairs and an umbrella.

Hiking the Cinque Terre outside Monterosso.

Guvano Beach is a long, isolated, pebbly strand that stretches just north of Corniglia and is popular with nudists (almost entirely men, many of whom are happy it's almost entirely men). You can clamber down to it from the Vernazza-Corniglia path, but the drop is steep and treacherous. A weird alternative route takes you through an unused train tunnel that you enter near the north end of Corniglia's train station. You must ring the bell at the gated entrance and wait for a custodian to arrive to unburden you of 2.50€, good for passage through the dank, dimly lit 1.5km-long (1-mile) gallery that emerges onto the beach at the far end.

There's also a long, rocky beach to the south of **Corniglia,** and it is easily accessible by some quick downhill scrambles from the Corniglia to Manarola path. **Riomaggiore** has a tiny crescent-shaped pebble beach reached by a series of stone steps on the south side of the harbor. Everywhere else, you'll be swimming off piers or rocks.

Monterosso

The Cinque Terre's largest village seems incredibly busy compared to its sleepier neighbors, but it's not without its charms. Monterosso is actually two towns—a bustling, character-filled Old Town built behind the harbor, as well as a relaxed resort that stretches along the Cinque Terre's only **sand beach** and is home to the train station and the tiny regional tourist office (upon exiting the station, turn left and head through the tunnel for the Old Town; turn right for the newer town and Il Gigante restaurant; see below).

The region's most famous art treasure is here: Housed in the **Convento dei Cappuccini,** perched on a hillock in the center of the Old Town, is a *crucifixion* by Anthony Van Dyck, the Flemish master who worked for a time in nearby Genoa (you can visit the convent daily 9am–noon and 4–7pm). While you will find the most conveniences in citified Monterosso, you'll have a more rustic experience if you stay in one of the other four villages.

WHERE TO STAY

Aside from the traditional options below, you might try your luck at booking one of the rooms at **A Ca du Gigante** (Via IV Novembre; ✆**0187-817-401;** www.ilgigantecinqueterre.it; 80€–180€ for a double with breakfast included).

Hotel La Colonnina ★★ 🏷 This friendly family-run gem is perfectly located in the heart of town just a few minutes from the beach. Sloped ceilings, marble bathrooms, small desks, and comfy chairs all make these large rooms seem as though they should be located in a much more expensive hotel. Some rooms come with a terrace, but even if you don't get one, all are welcome on the rooftop terrace that has a great view of the sea. The relatively rich buffet breakfast has mostly local items, some of which are organic. There is also a beautiful garden where you can relax and recoup after a day on the trails.

Via Zuecca 6, 19016 Monterosso al Mare (SP). www.lacolonninacinqueterre.it. ✆**0187-817-439.** Fax 0187-817-788. 21 units. 120€–143€ double. Rates include buffet breakfast. MC, V. Parking 9€ in nearby public lot. Closed early Nov to Easter. **Amenities:** Wi-Fi. *In room:* A/C, TV, hair dryer.

Hotel Pasquale ★★ 🏷 The Pasquale gives you spectacular views for the money, and the family who runs it will make you feel extremely welcome. It's built into a cliff face—some of which shows through the walls inside—right at the port of the Old Town, so all rooms overlook the beach and sea. The green tile floors support simple beds and basic, built-in units. Rooms are midsize, but bathrooms are cramped. Families will appreciate quad no. 3, with its two separate bedrooms. Note that this room is also right next to the train tracks, though most of the noise can be held at bay by keeping the window closed. The owners of the Pasquale also run Hotel Villa Steno in Monterosso, another excellent option with doubles from 120€ to 200€ (✆**0187-817-354;** www.villasteno.com).

Via Fegina 4, 19016 Monterosso al Mare (SP). www.hotelpasquale.it. ✆**0187-817-477.** Fax 0187-817-056. 16 units. 155€–200€ double; 185€–240€ triple. Rates include breakfast. AE, MC, V. Parking 9€ in nearby public lot. Closed Dec 6–26. **Amenities:** Bar; concierge; room service. *In room:* A/C, TV, hair dryer, minibar, Wi-Fi.

WHERE TO EAT

All the towns in the Cinque Terre have little shops like **Enoteca Internazionale ★★** on Via Roma 62 in Monterosso, where you can taste and purchase the local wines by the bottle, or simply enjoy a glass of Cinque Terre DOC (starting at about 3€) or *sciacchetrà* (3.50€) on the premises. The selection here, in the bustling part of old Monterosso, also includes olive oil pressed just down the street and jars of homemade pesto.

Focacceria Il Frantoio LIGHT FARE Many patrons say this bustling shop, with a takeout counter and a few tables where you can dine on the premises, serves some of the best focaccia in Liguria. That's quite a claim, but suffice it to say that the freshly baked bread (especially when topped with fresh vegetables) is heavenly and provides one of the best fast meals around.

Via Gioberti 1 (off Via Roma). ✆**0187-818-333.** Reservations not accepted. Pizza and focaccia from 1.50€. No credit cards. Fri–Wed 9am–2pm and 4–7pm. Closed Oct–Mar.

Ristorante Miky ★ ☺ SEAFOOD The first thing to strike you at this friendly and elegant restaurant is the giant scallop shells, loaded with *trenette alla pescatrice* (homemade pasta with mixed shellfish) that waiters carry out to hungry patrons. The shells are actually made of dough, and in fact, all of the dishes are served in pottery or some other sort of creative presentation. Adding to the charm is the restaurant's position right on the beach, set in a blooming garden. The specialty here is *pesce al sale,* which is your choice of seafood covered in coarse salt and slowly cooked in a wood-burning oven (the salt is removed before the fish is served).

Via Fegina 104. ℂ **0187-817-608.** Reservations recommended. Primi 8€–15€; secondi 10€–20€. AE, DC, MC, V. Daily noon–3pm and 7:30pm to late. Closed Tues in winter.

NIGHTLIFE

Monterosso's nightlife centers on the Old Town. There is a **free outdoor dance club** Saturday nights in summer at one end of the bocce ball court between the elevated railroad tracks and the beach. Under the railroad tracks and in town itself, you'll find **Fast,** Via Roma 13 (ℂ**0187-817-164**), a pub plastered with movie posters and serving the cheapest beer in town.

Vernazza

It's hard not to fall in love with this pretty village. Tall houses cluster around a natural harbor (where you can swim among the fishing boats) and beneath a **castle** built high atop a rocky promontory that juts into the sea (this castle, which is nothing special, is open Mar–Oct daily 10am–6:30pm; admission 2€). The center of town is waterside **Piazza Marconi,** itself a sea of cafe tables. The only Vernazza drawback is that too much good press has turned it into the Cinque Terre's ghetto of American tourists, especially in summer.

WHERE TO STAY

Besides the Barbara (see below), you can rent one of **Trattoria Gianni Franzi**'s 23 rooms spread across two buildings; some come with a bathroom, some with excellent views up the coast, all with a steep climb up the streets of the town and then up the stairs within the building. No matter what room you get, it's worth the money. Rates are 65€ for a double with a shared bathroom, 80€ for a double with a shared bathroom and a sea view, 100€ for a double with a private bathroom and a sea view, and 140€ for a triple with all the luxuries. Call ℂ**0187-821-003** or fax 0187-812-228 to book, or when you arrive in town, stop by the trattoria's harborside bar at Piazza Marconi 5 (closed Wed, except during the busy summer months; if you arrive on a Wed when the trattoria is closed, there is usually somebody there in the afternoon to take care of new arrivals, otherwise you can call ℂ **393-900-8155**). They're closed January 10 to March 10.

Albergo Barbara ♦ This is an exceedingly basic, but clean and cheap *pensione* in a stellar location at the center of the tiny harbor piazza with views over the fishing boats and Mediterranean. The *pensione* is on the two upper floors of a tall old house on the waterfront and you have to climb 63 steps to get there, and many of the rooms are reached by an additional climb up a spiral staircase. These efforts are rewarded by an eagle's-eye view of Vernazza's harbor from five of the rooms, and a partial view in others. Accommodations, though barebones, are not without charm—there's a pleasant smattering of homey furniture and cool tile floors. **Note:** The top floor can get especially hot in the summer, and the walls are thin so you might hear your neighbors. If no one answers the buzzer, inquire at the **Taverna del Capitano** restaurant across the square.

Piazza Marconi 30, 19018 Vernazza. www.albergobarbara.it. ℂ **0187-812-398.** 9 units. 55€ small double upstairs with shared bathroom; 65€ double with private bathroom down the corridor; 70€ double with private bathroom; 110€ large double with private bathroom and sea view. No credit cards. Closed early Dec to early Feb. *In room:* No phone, Wi-Fi.

WHERE TO EAT

Ristorante Gambero Rosso ★ LIGURIAN/SEAFOOD Enjoying the home-made pasta, fresh fish, and aromatic herbs on the terrace at this restaurant on the harbor is a pleasurable experience (though across the square at Taverna del Capitano, you can do it for cheaper and get better food to boot). At Gambero Rosso you can explore some hard-to-find dishes such as *acciughe* (fresh, local anchovies) baked with onions and potatoes, and *ravioli di pesce* (a delicate fish ravioli). Though the terrace is one of the main draws here—another being the *paccheri alla gambero rosso* (large, flattened tubular pasta served with tomato sauce and fish)—the stone-walled, stone-floored, timber-ceilinged dining room is a pleasant alternative when you can't eat outside. Gambero Rosso's owners also rent out four apartments (✆ **335-269-436;** www.toninobasso.com).

Piazza Marconi 7. ✆ **0187-812-265.** www.ristorantegamberorosso.net. Reservations recommended. Primi 10€–16€; secondi 16€–25€; AE, DC, MC, V. Tues–Sun 12:30–4pm and 7:15–10:30pm (summer sometimes open Mon). Closed Dec 15–Mar 1.

Taverna del Capitano ★★ LIGURIAN You'd have trouble finding a more pleasant way to take in the scene on Vernazza's lively harborside square than to do so while enjoying the seafood risotto and *muscoli ripieni* (*muscoli* is the Ligurian word for mussels, known as *cozze* elsewhere in Italy; here they are stuffed with fresh herbs). This place has been open since 1966, so they were serving their tasty cuisine way before Cinque Terre made it onto the tourist circuit. The service could use the some polishing, but then again that's pretty much the case for most of the places around here when you come during the summer crush. Dish for dish this place beats Gambero Rosso across the square and it's also cheaper. The owners also rent out three rooms (70€–90€ for a double with private bathroom), ask at the restaurant for details.

Piazza Marconi 21/24. ✆ **0187-812-201.** www.tavernavernazza.com. Reservations recommended. Primi 8€–12€; secondi 10€–20€. AE, DC, MC, V. Wed–Mon noon–3pm and 7–10:30pm. Closed mid-Nov to end-Dec.

Corniglia

The quietest village in the Cinque Terre is isolated by its position midway down the coast, its hilltop location high above the open sea, and its hard-to-access harbor. Whether you arrive by boat, train, or the trail from the south, you'll have to climb more than 300 steps to reach the village proper (arriving by trail from the north is the only way to avoid these stairs), which is an enticing maze of little walkways overshadowed by tall houses.

Once there, though, the views over the surrounding vineyards and up and down the coastline are stupendous—for the best outlook, walk to the end of the narrow main street to a belvedere that is perched between the sea and sky. Corniglia is the village most likely to offer a glimpse into life in the Cinque Terre the way it was decades ago.

WHERE TO STAY

Da Cecio ★★ 🏠 Elia and her son Carmelo rent out the second floor of their old stone house in the countryside just 2 minutes outside Corniglia (on the road to Vernazza) and offer what is one of the Cinque Terre's most pleasant inns. The rooms are big, bright, and stylish, with dark-wood veneer headboards and furnishings. Most feature great views over the sea, the olive groves, and the hilltop

Corniglia, perched atop a cliff.

town (nos. 2 and 6 are on a corner with vistas out both windows). Bathrooms are on the small side. The sun-drenched rooftop deck or flowery terrace downstairs (which, at mealtimes, serves as an outdoor dining room for the restaurant; see below) is the perfect place to idle away an afternoon. If no rooms are available, one of the proprietors will take you down to their four pleasant rooms in the village. The church bell rings right near the annex so bring some earplugs.

Via Serra 58, 19010 Corniglia. www.cecio5terre.com. © **0187-812-043.** Fax 0187-812-138. 12 units (4 are in a nearby building). 60€ double; 80€ triple. Breakfast 5€. MC, V. Closed Nov. **Amenities:** Ligurian restaurant (see review below); bar. *In room:* Hair dryer, no phone.

WHERE TO EAT

Osteria a Cantina de Mananan ★★ LIGURIAN The trek up to hilltop Corniglia is worth it anyway, but include a meal at this tiny restaurant carved into the stone cellars of an ancient house and you have a perfect combination. Agostino and Marianne, the husband-and-wife owners and chefs, draw on age-old local recipes and use only the freshest ingredients in their preparations. The results, posted on a blackboard in the one handsome vaulted room furnished with granite tables, are wonderful. Fresh vegetables from gardens just outside the village are grilled and mixed with herbs and smoked mozzarella as a simple appetizer. This can be followed by any of the hand-rolled pastas topped with homemade pesto or porcini. You can continue in this nonmeat direction with a plate of mussels, grilled fish, or fresh anchovies stuffed with herbs, but the few meat dishes on the menu are also excellent—especially the *coniglio* (rabbit) roasted in a white sauce.

Via Fieschi 117, Corniglia. © **0187-821-166.** Reservations recommended. Primi 8€–10€; secondi 9€–15€. No credit cards. Wed–Mon 12:30–2:30pm and 7:30–9:30pm. Closed Nov, Mon–Fri in December, and part of Jan–Feb.

Ristorante Cecio ★ LIGURIAN Like the inn upstairs, the stone-walled, wood-beamed dining room and flower-filled terrace overlooking olive groves provide extremely pleasant surroundings. The family-run kitchen serves up a nice selection of simple, homemade fare such as fresh pasta with pesto or walnut sauce or *alla scogliera,* topped with fresh clams and mussels. Meat and fish are grilled over an open hearth. Outside of peak mealtimes, you can sit on the terrace and enjoy the view over a beer or glass of the house wine.

Via Serra 58, Corniglia. ℂ **0187-812-043.** www.cecio5terre.com. Reservations recommended. Primi 7.50€–15€; secondi 8€–20€. MC, V. Thurs–Tues (summer daily) noon–3:30pm and 7–11pm. Closed Nov.

Manarola

Not as busy as nearby Riomaggiore or as quaint as its neighbor Corniglia, Manarola is a near-vertical cluster of tall houses that seems to rise piggyback up the hills on either side of the harbor. In fact, in a region with no shortage of heart-stopping views, one of the most amazing sights is the descent into the town of Manarola on the path from Corniglia: From this perspective, the hill-climbing houses seem to merge into one another to form a row of skyscrapers. Despite these urban associations, Manarola is a delightfully rural village where fishing and winemaking are big business. The region's major **wine cooperative,** Cooperativa Agricoltura di Riomaggiore, Manarola, Corniglia, Vernazza e Monterosso, made up of 300 local producers, is here; call ℂ **0187-920-435** for information about tours of its modern (est. 1982) facilities.

WHERE TO STAY

Manarola's **Ostello Cinque Terre** (ℂ **0187-920-215;** fax 0187-920-218; www.cinqueterre.net/ostello) offers cheap accommodations: 20€ to 25€ for beds in six-bed dorm rooms, 55€ to 70€ for a room with two single beds and private bathroom, or 126€ to 156€ for six-bed family rooms with private bathroom. The hostel, which is in the center of town near the church, offers services such as kayak, bike, and snorkel rental; Internet access; and cheap laundry. It's closed January 6 to February 15 and November 4 to December 6. Especially in high season, you must book a week in advance.

Marina Piccola ★★ Many of the rooms in this cozy inn on Manarola's harbor have a sea view and the decor in the whole establishment is a cut above that of most inns in the region. The charming rooms have old prints, faded floor tiles, and light pine-veneer furnishings. Rooms in the other building (the next one up the hill, containing the hotel lobby) are done in more of a country style, with nicer heavy wooden furnishings, flower-edged wallpaper, and fancy scrolled headboards. Service can occasionally be a bit rude and in the busy summer months you might be required to take half-board.

Via Birolli 120, 19010 Manarola. www.hotelmarinapiccola.com. ℂ **0187-762-065.** Fax 0187-762-291. 13 units. 120€ double. Half-board 90€ per person in double. Rates include breakfast. AE, DC, MC, V. Closed Nov. **Amenities:** Restaurant (local cuisine); bar. *In room:* A/C, TV.

WHERE TO EAT

Aristide ★ LIGURIAN In this old house up the hill from the harbor (just below the train station), diners are accommodated on a couple of levels of small rooms, as well as on a covered terrace across the street. Many of Aristide's patrons live in the Cinque Terre or take the train here from nearby La Spezia, because this long-standing trattoria is known for its heaping platters of grilled fish, *gamberoni* (jumbo prawns), and *frittura di mare* (a selection of fried seafood). The *antipasto di mare* includes a nice selection of octopus, clams, sardines, and other local catches and serves well as a lighter meal. The house's white wine is from the hills above the town, and if the owner is in a good mood, he may come around after your dinner to offer a complimentary glass of *sciacchetrà*, the local dessert wine.

Via Discovolo 290. ⓒ **0187-920-000.** Reservations recommended. Primi 8€–12€; secondi 8€–20€; fixed-price fish menu 40€, including wine. AE, DC, MC, V. Tues–Sun noon–2:30 and 7–9pm.

Riomaggiore

Riomaggiore clings to the vestiges of the Cinque Terre's rustic ways while making some concessions to the modern world. The old fishing quarter has expanded in recent years, and Riomaggiore now has some sections of new houses and apartment blocks. This blend of the old and new works well—Riomaggiore is bustling and prosperous and makes the most of a lovely setting, with houses clinging to the hills that drop into the sea on either side of town. Many of the lanes end in seaside belvederes.

From the parking garage, follow the main drag down; from the train station, exit and turn right to head through the tunnel for the main part of town (or, from the station, take off left up the brick stairs to walk the Via dell'Amore to Manarola).

That tunnel and the main drag meet at the base of an elevated terrace that holds the train tracks. From here, a staircase leads down to a tiny fishing harbor, off the left of which heads a rambling path that, after a few hundred meters, leads to a pleasant little **beach** of large pebbles.

WHERE TO STAY

There are lots of folks renting out rooms illegally in the Cinque Terre, especially in Monterosso and Riomaggiore. These rooms are fine—usually—and the price is right; it's just that they don't have the permits to do this, the properties are not inspected by the proper authorities, and of course it's all under the table so they don't pay taxes. It's a bit of a crapshoot if you rent one of these unpermitted rooms though it should be kept as an option if you arrive late in the day in the summer.

One person renting out rooms who has gone to the trouble of filing the paperwork with the authorities and submitting his rooms to oversight, meaning you'll be assured a certain guarantee of quality, is Mario Franceschetti. His rental room business, called **Mar Mar,** is run out of Via Malborghetto 8 (turn left when you come out of the tunnel from the train station; ⓒ/fax **0187-920-932;** www.5terre-marmar.com). Mario's very helpful business partner, Amy, is Californian and can be found in the office most days except Wednesday from 11am to 1:30pm. A bed in a coed dorm costs 15€ to 22€; double rooms cost 60€ to 80€. There are also eight apartments that sleep two to six people (65€–90€ for a double; 80€–120€ for the larger apartments with price depending on how many are in the room). Some of the rental units come with TV and private bathroom, and some have kitchenettes. Mar Mar's office is open daily from 9am to 5pm.

Hotel Villa Argentina The only full-fledged hotel in Riomaggiore is in the newer section of town, on a hillside about a 5-minute walk (up a lot of stairs) from the center. This location affords astonishing views, which you can enjoy from most of the guest rooms, and provides a nice retreat from the tourist-crowded main street and harbor. A breezy, arbor-shaded terrace and a bar area decorated by local artists off the lobby are the places to relax. And while the blandly furnished, tile-floored rooms upstairs will not overwhelm you with their character, they are large and pleasant, with ceiling fans and balconies (except room nos. 4–6 and 10) featuring views over the town to the sea. The hoteliers also offer apartments accommodating two to six people.

Via de Gaspari 187, 19017 Riomaggiore (SP). www.hotelvillargentina.com. © **0187-920-213.** Fax 0187-760-531. 15 units. 94€–139€ double; 40€–60€ per person in apts. Rates include breakfast. MC, V. Parking 10€. **Amenities:** Bar; concierge; room service; nearby sauna; watersports equipment/rentals, Wi-Fi. *In room:* TV, hair dryer, no phone.

Locanda Ca' dei Duxi This is one of the more established outfits in the center, constantly expanding their little hospitality empire and offering more hotel-style amenities than most rental rooms around, spread across two *locande* (the original six-room 18th-c. building and a five-room inn across the street, which opened in summer 2001), three rental rooms, and several apartments. All of the midsize rooms are simple, with new modular furnishings, tile floors, and firm wood-slat beds. On the top floor, room nos. 5 and 6 have exposed beams and a bit of castle view.

Via Colombo 36/Via Pecunia 19, 19017 Riomaggiore (SP). www.duxi.it. © **0187-920-036** or 338-841-8175. Fax 0187-920-036. 16 units, plus 3 in-house apts. 60€–130€. Rates include breakfast. AE, DC, MC, V. Parking 7€. **Amenities:** Room service. *In room:* A/C, TV, hair dryer (on request), minibar.

WHERE TO EAT

La Lanterna ★ LIGURIAN/SEAFOOD From a table on the terrace here, perched only a few meters above Riomaggiore's snug harbor, you can hear the waves lap against the rocks and watch the local fishermen mend their nets. Seafood, of course, dominates the menu, with many Ligurian dishes, such as *spaghetti allo scoglio* (spaghetti with mussels and shrimp in a white-wine sauce) or *spaghetti ai ricci di mare* (with sea urchins). The antipasto of shrimp, smoked tuna, and grilled swordfish is excellent and can suffice as an entree; you should, however, make room for one of the house specialties, *chiche*—homemade gnocchi filled with seafood and topped with a spicy tomato sauce.

Riomaggiore. © **0187-920-589.** Reservations highly recommended. Primi 8.50€–11€; secondi 10€–22€. AE, DC, MC, V. Daily 11am–midnight. Closed Nov.

PLANNING YOUR TRIP
TO NORTHERN ITALY

ith so much on offer in the way of historical treasures, epicurean pleasures, and tempting outdoor resorts, the hardest part of planning a trip to northern Italy will be deciding where to spend your time.

As with any trip, a little preparation is essential before you start your journey to northern Italy. This chapter provides a variety of planning tools, including information on how to get there, tips on accommodations, and the inside track regarding local resources.

Getting around northern Italy is a breeze (minus the city and highway traffic and the occasional jam-packed train), and getting to and from the region couldn't be easier with a nice selection of local airports and a well-served international airport in Milan.

For certain things—including getting a nice hotel room in Milan, especially during the spring and fall fashion weeks and the design trade show in April—it is key to plan ahead. Many mountain resorts fill up months prior to the first snowfall, and the choicest spots on the Riviera (especially the Cinque Terre) are snapped up before it starts getting hot. As for Venice, it's a general mob scene in any month not containing an *R* and during any of its spectacular festivals.

If you do your homework on special events, pick the right place for the right season, and pack for a variety of climates, preparing for a trip to northern Italy should be pleasant and uncomplicated.

GETTING THERE
By Plane

If you're flying across an ocean, you'll most likely fly into Milan's **Malpensa Airport** (**MXP;** ✆ **02-232-323;** www.seamilano.eu), 45km (28 miles) from downtown.

From **Malpensa** terminal 1, you have the choice of a 50-minute train ride with **Trenitalia** to Stazione Centrale (leaves hourly and costs 7€), the city's main train station, or a 30-minute trip with **Malpensa Express** that costs 11€ and heads half-hourly to Cadorna train station (also in central Milan, but towards the western side of town). From Cadorna, a short metro or taxi ride will bring you to Stazione Centrale from which trains depart for all corners of northern Italy. There are also two bus companies calling in at both Terminal 1 and Terminal 2 that make the 50-minute run to the east side of Stazione Centrale and that between them have a departure about every 10 minutes. In both cases, you can buy the tickets on the bus for no extra charge. **Malpensa Shuttle** costs 7.50€ as does **Autostradale** though the latter also has a three-tickets-for-the-price-of-two deal (you don't have to use all three tickets at the same time so you can save one or two for your trip back to Malpensa). A **taxi** to the city center has a fixed price of 85€.

For flights to Milan from within Europe, you might also fly into the ridiculously convenient **Linate Airport** (**LIN;** ✆ **02-7485-2200;** www.sea milano.eu), about 8km (5 miles) east of the city. From **Linate, Starfly** shuttles

PREVIOUS PAGE: **Scooter is the only way to get around Italy.**

(**☎ 02-5858-7237**) make the 30-minute trip from 6am to midnight to Milan's Stazione Centrale for 4€. **City bus no. 73** leaves every 10 minutes for the San Babila Metro stop downtown (1€ for a regular bus ticket bought from any news-agent inside the airport, 1.50€ onboard and you must have exact change) and takes about 25 minutes. The **express no. 73X** is faster though there is only one an hour. The trip into town by **taxi** costs about 15€.

FLYING DIRECTLY TO GENOA, BERGAMO, OR VENICE

Budget carriers within Europe fly to a number of northern Italian cities; three of the most popular are Genoa's **Cristoforo Colombo Airport** (www.airport. genova.it), Bergamo's **Orio al Serio** (www.sacbo.it), and Venice's **Marco Polo Airport** (www.veniceairport.it).

In Venice, **ATVO** buses (www.atvo.it) run every 30 minutes between Piazzale Roma and the airport for 5€, and also run more frequently to the busy train station in nearby Mestre. Bergamo's airport is easily reached from Milan with a shuttle that leaves every 30 minutes from Stazione Centrale, takes about an hour and costs 9.90€. Genoa's airport is very close to the downtown, taking 20 minutes on the bus (4€) that runs to the Stazione Principe.

By Car

If you're planning to rent a car, you'll get the **best rental rate** if you book your car from home instead of renting direct in Italy—in fact, if you decide to rent once you've arrived, it's worth it to call home to have someone arrange it all from there. You must be 25 or older to rent from most agencies (although some accept ages 21 and up).

The legalities and contractual obligations of renting a car in Italy (where ac-cident and theft rates are very high) are more complicated than those in almost any other country in Europe. You must have nerves of steel, a sense of humor, and a valid driver's license or International Driver's Permit. Insurance on all vehi-cles is compulsory, though what kind and how much is up to you and your credit card company: Ask the right questions and check with your credit card company before leaving home.

Note: If you're planning to rent a car in Italy during high season, you should book well in advance. It's not at all unusual to arrive at the airport in Milan in June and July to find that every last agent is all out of cars, perhaps for a week. Although the 19% IVA value-added tax is unavoidable, you can do away with the government airport tax of 10% by picking up your car at an office in town.

The main *autostrada,* or super highway, that runs the length of the Po val-ley from Turin to Trieste is the A4. From Milan, follow the signs for the *tangen-ziale,* or beltway, which will eventually lead to the exit to your highway of choice. Getting onto the *tangenziale,* however, can be tricky so insist on specific, detailed directions from the car rental agencies and make use of a co-pilot who knows how to use a map.

Northern Italy is rather compact. Genoa to Milan, for example, is 130km (81 miles) on a highway where people regularly drive in excess of 130kmph (81mph). But don't think it will take you only an hour to drive from Milan to Genoa as you have to budget for the potentially slow-going from downtown to the *tangenziale* and then the highway. Milan to Verona is about 160km (100 miles), and Verona to Venice is another 121km (75 miles). Coast to coast, then, is only 4 hours, even at North American driving speeds (if traffic isn't bad). The first part of the A4 heading east from Milan towards Verona and Venice is the most traveled highway in Europe, so the going can get slow, especially on Friday afternoons leaving the cities and Sunday nights on the way back into town, and rush hour around the cities any day of the week can be epic. Plan to travel mid-week and midday, if possible. See **www.autostrade.it** for live traffic updates.

Tolls can also get expensive, costing about 1€ for every 16km (10 miles), which means that it would cost about 15€ for a trip from Milan to Venice. Add in the gasoline and the car rental, and it's often cheaper to take the train from city to city, even with two people.

For more information on driving in Italy, from road rules to gasoline, see "Getting Around," below.

By Train

Traveling to northern Italy by train is the best option if you're looking to visit the major sites without the hassle of renting and driving a car. Most towns in northern Italy have their own train stations; the major train hubs are in Milan, Genoa, Turin, and Verona. The travel times and the price of the trains vary considerably depending on what type of train you are traveling on.

Along the major east-west train line in northern Italy, from Turin to Milan it will take you an hour (32€ second class) on the nicest and fastest train and 2 hours (9.55€) on the sometimes slightly grimy local. Milan to Verona ranges in price from 9€ and 19€. Verona and Padua are 40 to 90 minutes apart by train, and the trip costs 5€ to 16€. The train continues east to Venice; from Padua, it will take 25 to 50 minutes to get to Venice and will cost 3€ to 15€. The fastest connection onto Trieste from Venice costs 18€ and takes about an hour and a half.

The major north-south train lines in northern Italy are Milan-Genoa (1½ hr. and 18€ on the fastest train) and Trento-Verona (1 hr. and 6€). Otherwise, apart from the main artery that runs from Milan to Rome and quicker lines along the coasts, north-south routes can be pretty slow going because they rely on the regional trains that stop at every minor hamlet.

For more information about train travel in Italy, see "Getting Around," below.

GETTING AROUND
By Plane

The only flight within northern Italy that is vaguely worth considering is Milan-Trieste, which takes an hour. Though Alitalia has a pretty good lock on the route, you can sometimes find cheap deals so it might be worth considering starting your trip in Milan, working your way with the train or a car slowly east all the way to Trieste and then taking a flight back to Milan where you will probably have your international flight back home.

By Car

Much of northern Italy is accessible by public transportation, but to explore vineyards, ski resorts, and smaller towns on the lakes, a car will save you tons of time.

Driving in Italy can be nerve-racking—for both the winding roads and the Italian penchant for always driving as if they absolutely had to be home 10 minutes ago. Both rental-car and gas prices are as high as they get in all of Europe.

Before leaving home, you can apply for an **International Driving Permit** from the American Automobile Association (AAA; ✆ 800/622-7070 or 650/294-7400; www.aaa.com). In Canada, the permit is available from the Canadian Automobile Association (CAA; ✆ 416/221-4300; www.caa.ca). In the U.K., contact the British Automobile Association (AA; ✆ 08706/000-371; www.theaa.com). Technically, you need this permit and your actual driver's license to drive in Italy, though in practice your license itself often suffices.

Italy's equivalent of AAA is the **Automobile Club d'Italia (ACI),** a branch of the Touring Club Italiano. They're the people who respond when you place an emergency call to ✆ 803-116 for road breakdowns, though they do charge for this service if you're not a member. You may join at the border as you're driving into Italy or at one of the club's regional offices (in Milan, Viale Sarca 189, ✆ 02-643-2142) or online at **www.aci.it**.

DRIVING RULES Italian drivers aren't maniacs; they only appear to be. Well, some actually are maniacs and with those the best you can do is just get out of their way. Spend any time on an Italian highway and you will have the experience of somebody driving up insanely close to you from behind while flashing their headlights. The first time this happens, it will cause an immediate hot sweat and will make the heart of even the most stoic of drivers miss a beat. Take a deep breath and don't panic, this is the rather aggressive signal for you to move to the right so he can pass and until you do he will stay mind-bogglingly close to you. On a two-lane road, the idiot passing someone in the opposing traffic who has swerved into your lane expects you to veer obligingly over into the shoulder so three lanes of traffic can fit—he would do the same for you. Many Italians seem to think that using their blinkers is optional, so be aware that the car in front of you could be turning at any time.

Autostrade are toll highways, denoted by green signs and a number prefaced with an *A*, like the A1 from Milan to Rome. A few aren't numbered and are simply called *raccordo,* a connecting road between two cities (such as Florence-Siena and Florence-Pisa). **Strade statali** (singular is *strada statale*) are state roads, usually without a center divider and two lanes wide (though sometimes they can be a divided four-way highway), indicated by blue signs. Their route numbers are prefaced with an *SS,* as in the SS11 from Milan to Venice. On signs, however, these official route numbers are used infrequently. Usually, you'll just see blue signs listing destinations by name with arrows pointing off in the appropriate directions. Even if it's just a few kilometers down on the road, often the town you're looking for won't be mentioned on the sign at the appropriate turnoff. It's impossible to predict which of all the towns that lie along a road will be the ones chosen to list on a particular sign. Sometimes the sign gives only the first minuscule village that lies past the turnoff, at other times it lists the first major town down that road, and some signs mention only the major city the road eventually leads to, even if it's hundreds of kilometers away. It pays to study the map before coming to an intersection. The *strade statali* can be frustratingly slow due to traffic, traffic lights, and the fact that they cross through countless towns so when possible opt to pay for the *autostrade.*

The **speed limit** on roads in built-up areas around towns and cities is 50kmph (31 mph). On rural roads it's 90kmph (56 mph) and on the highway its 130kmph (81 mph). Italians have an astounding disregard for these limits, mostly because they're enforced only if the offense is egregious. However, police can ticket you and collect the fine on the spot. The blood-alcohol limit in Italy is 0.05%, often achieved with just two drinks; driving above the limit can result in a fine, driving ban, or imprisonment. Safety belts are obligatory in both the front and the back seats

As far as **parcheggio** (parking) is concerned, on streets, white lines indicate free public spaces, blue lines are pay public spaces, and yellow lines mean only residents are allowed to park. Meters don't line the sidewalk; rather, there's one machine on the block where you punch in how long you want to park. The machine spits out a ticket that you leave on your dashboard. Sometimes streets will have an attendant who'll come around and give you your time ticket (pay him or her when you get ready to leave). If you park in an area marked PARCHEGGIO DISCO ORARIO, root around in your rental car's glove compartment for a cardboard parking disc (or buy one at a gas station). With this device, you dial up the hour of your arrival and display it on your dashboard. You're allowed *un'ora* (1 hr.) or *due ore* (2 hr.), according to the sign. **Parking lots** have ticket dispensers, but booths are not usually manned as you exit. Take your ticket with you when you park; when you return to the lot to get your car and leave, first visit the office or automated payment machine to exchange your ticket for a paid receipt that you then use to get through the automated exit.

ROAD SIGNS Here's a brief rundown of the road signs you'll most frequently encounter. A **speed limit** sign is a black number inside a red circle on a white background. The **end of a speed zone** is just black and white, with a black slash through the number. A red circle with a white background, a black arrow pointing down, and a red arrow pointing up means **yield to oncoming traffic,** while a point-down red-and-white triangle means **yield ahead.** Many city centers are closed to traffic and a simple white circle with a red border, or the words *zona pedonale* or *zona traffico limitato,* denotes a **pedestrian zone** (you can drive through only to drop off baggage at your hotel); a white arrow on a blue background is used for Italy's many **one-way streets;** a mostly red circle with a horizontal white slash means **do not enter.** Any image in black on a white background surrounded by a red circle means that image is **not allowed** (for instance, if the image is two cars next to each other, it means no passing; a motorcycle means no Harleys permitted, and so on). A circular sign in blue with a red circle-slash means **no parking.**

Gasoline (gas or petrol), *benzina,* can be found in pull-in gas stations along major roads and on the outskirts of town, as well as in 24-hour stations along the *autostrade.* Almost all stations are closed for the *riposo* and on Sundays (except for those on the *autostrade*), but the majority have a pump fitted with a machine that accepts cash so if you have bills in your wallet you can fill up at any time of day. Gasoline is very expensive in Italy and even a small rental car guzzles 40€ to 60€ for a fill-up. Unleaded gas is *senza piombo.*

By Train

Italy, especially the northern half, has one of the best train systems in Europe and you'll find most destinations connected. The vast majority of lines are run by the state-owned **Ferrovie dello Stato,** or **FS** (✆ **892-021** for info and to buy tickets; www.trenitalia.com).

The speed, cleanliness, and overall quality of **Italian trains** varies enormously. *Prima classe* (first class) is usually only a shade better than *seconda classe* (second class) and the only real benefits of first class come if you're traveling overnight (in which case you'll often have four berths per compartment rather than six), or the train is overcrowded and there are seats available only in first class.

The **Frecciarossa** is the nicest of the nice and the fastest of the fast (Italy's bullet train) while the **Frecciabianca** uses the same hardware, but is a bit slower. They are both also generically called **Eurostar (ES)** and are up to the standard of the best trains in northern Europe, zipping between Italy's biggest cities including on the Milan-Naples line with stops in Bologna, Florence, and Rome (there are also trains doing Milan-Rome nonstop). The Eurostar also runs on the Milan-Venice line—with stops at Verona, Vicenza, and Padua along the way—and does Milan-Turin in an impressive 63 minutes (a trip that takes almost 2 hours on the slower trains). Speed and cleanliness come at a price with tickets for the Eurostar trains costing as much as three times the cheapest regional train. With the Eurostar you must make a reservation for a particular train when you buy a ticket.

Intercity (IC) trains are a step down from the Eurostar, both in speed and comfort, but are an extremely valid option and are unlikely to provide any shocks. The slower *Regionale* (R) and *Regionale Veloce* (RV) make many stops and can sometimes be on the grimy side of things, but they are also ridiculously cheap (a Milan-Turin second-class ticket will put you back only 9.55€ compared with 32€ on the Eurostar). **Espresso** trains are the cheap option if you are traveling long distances, though in terms of comfort and speed you'll be somewhere between a *Regionale* and *Intercity.*

Few visitors are prepared for how **crowded** Italian trains can sometimes get, though you can count your blessings that, with the increase in automobile travel, they're not as crowded as they were in times gone by. An Italian train is full only when the corridors are packed solid and there are more than eight people sitting on their luggage in the little vestibules by the doors. Overcrowding is often a problem on Friday evenings, weekends, and holidays, especially in and out of big cities, or just after a strike. In summer, the crowding escalates, and any train going toward a beach in August all but bulges like an overstuffed sausage.

When buying a **regular ticket,** ask for either *andata* (one-way) or *andata e ritorno* (round-trip). If the train you plan to take is an ES or IC, ask for the ticket *con supplemento rapido* (with speed supplement) to avoid on-train penalty charges. The best way to avoid presenting yourself on the train with the wrong ticket is to tell the person at the ticket window exactly what train you are going to take, for example, "the 11:30am train for Venice."

If you don't have a ticket with a reservation for a particular seat on a specific train, then you must **validate you ticket by stamping it in the little yellow box** on the platform before boarding the train. If you board a train without the correct ticket, or without having validated your ticket, you'll have to pay a hefty fine on top of the ticket or supplement, which the conductor will sell you. If you knowingly board a train without a ticket or realize once onboard that you have the wrong type of ticket, your best bet is to search out the conductor who is likely to be more forgiving because you found him and have as such made it clear you weren't trying to ride for free.

Schedules for all trains leaving a given station are printed on yellow posters tacked up on the station wall (the equivalent white poster lists all the arrivals). These are good for getting general information, but you must keep your eye on the electronic boards/television screens throughout the stations that are updated with delays and track *(binario)* changes. You can also get official schedules (and more train information, also in English) and buy tickets at **www.trenitalia.com**.

In the big cities (especially Milan) and the tourist destinations (above all Venice), the lines can be dreadfully long. There is a solution though: **automatic ticket machines.** They are easy to navigate, allow you to follow instructions in English, accept cash and credit cards, and can save your life by cutting down on the stress that comes with waiting on an interminably slow line as you see the minutes tick away until your train is set to leave.

With ticket in hand, the next step is **finding your track.** This is easy at small towns, but can become a challenge in big cities, especially Milan where there are more than two-dozen tracks and trains leaving every few minutes. All trains to Venice and Milan terminate there so all you have to do is look on the electronic boards for those cities, but if you are traveling from Milan to Verona, for example, you must know the terminus station, which might be Verona, but also could be Venice, Trieste, or even Munich in Germany. This information is easily consultable on the aforementioned yellow posters or you can ask the conductors who stand at the head of trains coming close to departure time.

Stations tend to be well run, with luggage storage facilities at all but the smallest and usually a good bar attached that serves surprisingly palatable food. If you pull into a dinky town with a shed-size station, find the nearest bar or *tabacchi,* and the man behind the counter will most likely sell you tickets.

SPECIAL PASSES & DISCOUNTS To buy the **Eurail Italy Pass,** available only outside Italy and priced in U.S. dollars, contact **Rail Europe** (www.rail europe.com). You have 2 months in which to use the train a set number of days; the base number of days is 3, and you can add up to 7 more. For adults, the first-class pass costs $278, second class is $227. Additional days cost roughly $30 more for first class, $25 for second class. For youth tickets (25 and under), a 3-day pass is $183 and additional days about $20 each. Saver passes are available for groups of two to five people traveling together at all times, and amount to a savings of about $40 off each adult pass.

There are also Italy-Greece, Italy-Spain, and Italy-France combinations, in addition to a **rail-and-drive pass.** This is valid for 2 months, during which you can use 3 rail days and 2 car days (and add more car or rail days cheaply). Prices start at $361 for second-class tickets and an economy car with unlimited miles from Hertz.

When it comes to regular tickets, if you're **25 or under,** you can buy a 40€ **Carta Verde (Green Card)** at any Italian train station that gets you a 10% discount for domestic trips and 25% on international connections for 1 year. Present it each time you buy a ticket. A similar deal is available for anyone **61 and over** with the **Carta d'Argento (Silver Card):** 15% off domestic and 25% off international, for 30€ (the Carta d'Argento is free for those 76 and over). Children 11 and under ride half-price while kids 3 and under don't pay (though they don't have the right to their own seat).

By Bus

Although trains are quicker and easier, you can get just about anywhere through a network of dozens of local, provincial, and regional bus lines (see below), but in northern Italy you'll mainly be using buses in the cities. **Schedules** in cities are posted in a little box on the pole of the large orange or yellow signs that demarcate the stops. Keep in mind that in smaller towns, buses exist mainly to shuttle workers and schoolchildren, so the most runs are on weekdays, early in the morning, and usually again in midafternoon.

In a big city, the **bus station** for trips between cities is usually near the main train station while a small town's **bus stop** is usually either in the main square on the edge of town or the bend in the road just outside the main city gate. You should always try to find the local ticket vendor—if there's no office, it's invariably the nearest newsstand or *tabacchi* (signaled by a sign with a white T), or occasionally a bar—but you can usually also buy tickets on the bus. You can also flag down a bus as it passes on a country road, but try to find an official stop (a small sign tacked onto a telephone pole). Tell the driver where you're going and ask him courteously if he'll let you know when you need to get off. When he says *"È la prossima fermata,"* that means yours is the next stop. *"Posso scendere?"* (Poh-so *shen*-dair-ay?) is "Can I get off?"

NORTHERN ITALY BUS LINES Unlike in central Italy and the South, buses in northern Italy have limited appeal, as nearly every town is easily reached by train. Popular destinations for buses include hard-to-reach ski areas in the Alps and Dolomites, isolated towns in Veneto, and the Lakes Region (although it is a much prettier ride by boat).

Autostradale, with an office in Piazza Castello, Milan (✆ **02-7200-1304;** www.autostradale.it), offers regular service to Aosta and to the Dolomite ski resorts of Madonna del Campiglio and Cortina d'Ampezzo. To move around the Dolomites, you can catch a bus from the unfortunately acronymed **SAD** company (✆ **0471-450-111;** www.sad.it). To get to the Alpine resorts from Aosta, look for **SAVDA** buses (✆ **0165-367-011;** www.savda.it).

The Lakes Region is also best navigated by bus if you find the ferry too expensive or the schedule inconvenient. For towns on the west side of Lake Garda, contact **Trasporti Brescia** (✆ **030-44-061**) in Brescia and **APT** (✆ **045-805-7811**) in Verona for towns on the east side of the lake. For Lake Como, look for the blue **SPT** buses (✆ **031-247-247**) in the center of any of the towns.

In Veneto, neither Bassano del Grappa nor Asolo is reachable by train. To get to Bassano, and then on to Asolo, you'll need to catch an **FTV** bus (✆ **0444-223-115;** www.ftv.vi.it) in Vicenza.

TIPS ON ACCOMMODATIONS

The cheap, family-run *pensione* with the shared bathroom and personal attention does still exist in Italy, but it is increasingly hard to find. Not to fear though, in the past decade the country's stock of accommodations has increased and improved to the point that in most spots you are likely to visit you will have a wide array of choices.

Hotels are **rated** by regional boards on a system of one to five stars. Prices aren't directly tied to the star system, but for the most part, the more stars a hotel has, the more expensive it'll be—but a four-star in a small town may be cheaper than a two-star in Venice. The number of stars awarded a hotel is based strictly on the amenities offered and not how clean, comfortable, or friendly a place is, or whether it's a good value for the money overall.

A few of the four- and five-star hotels have their own private **garages,** but most city inns have an agreement with a local garage. In many small towns, a garage is unnecessary because public parking, both free and pay, is widely available and never too far from your hotel. Parking costs and procedures are indicated under each hotel, and the rates quoted are per day (overnight). It should go without saying that there are no garages in Venice, as there are no cars.

The **high season** throughout most of northern Italy runs from May to early September—peaking June through August—and from December 24 to January 6. You can almost always bargain for a cheaper rate if you're traveling in the shoulder season (early spring and late fall) or winter off season (not including Christmas). The reviews usually quote a range of prices; if there is only one figure, it represents the maximum. Prices vary so wildly, depending entirely on availability, that sometimes the only dependable figure is the highest the hotel is allowed to charge. The moral of the story: If it seems like availability is high, you should be getting a discount from the prices you see here.

Most hotels include **breakfast** automatically in the room rate. With very few exceptions, which include most high-end accommodations, Italian hotel breakfasts tend to consist of a *brioche* (croissant) and coffee/cappuccino, occasionally with juice and fresh fruit as well. It's rarely worth the 5€ to 15€ charged for it, since you can get the same breakfast—and freshly made instead of packaged—for around 3€ at the bar down the block. It's always worth asking what kind of breakfast is offered and for your room quote without breakfast: *prezzo senza colazione* (*pretz*-zoh *sen*-zah coal-lat-zee-*oh*-nay).

Agriturismo (Farm Stays)

The *agriturismo* movement has exploded in recent years. Though Tuscany is at the forefront, northern Italy also highlights this rural movement. *Agriturismi* are working farms or agricultural estates that offer accommodations to visitors who want to stay out in the countryside. An operation can call itself *agriturismo* only if it offers fewer than 30 beds total, and the agricultural component of the property brings in a larger economic share of profits than the hospitality part—in other words, the property has to remain a farm and not become just a rural hotel. That's why you'll almost always be offered homemade sausages, home-pressed olive oil, and so on, either because they've been doing it that way for years or because these country barons essentially have been required to become farmers by law.

Agriturismi are generally a crapshoot. The types of accommodations can vary dramatically. Most, though, are miniapartments, often rented out with a minimum stay of 3 days. Sometimes you're invited to eat big country dinners at the table with the family; other times you cook for yourself. Rates can vary from 60€ for two per day to 250€ and beyond—as much as a board-rated four-star hotel in town. A few choice *agriturismi* are included throughout this book.

There are three independent national organizations that together represent almost all *agriturismi*.

Go to the website of **Terranostra** (www.terranostra.it) and click on *"Cerchi un agriturismo?"* then from there you can switch to English. The site lets you refine your search by region (there are almost 150 listed for Lombardy), price, services, and products produced at the farm.

At the site of **Turismo Verde** (www.turismoverde.it), click on *"Scegli il tuo Agriturismo,"* and choose from a list of regions and then provinces (for example, click on Liguria and then La Spezia for something in or near Cinque Terre); this will give you a list of local *agriturismi*. Another useful website is **Agriturist** (www.agriturist.it), which is easy to navigate and offers its text in English. You can find hundreds upon hundreds of individual properties via a search engine.

Villa Rentals

Each summer, thousands of visitors rent an old farmhouse, or "villa," a marketing term used to inspire romantic images of manicured gardens, a Renaissance mansion, and rolling green hills, but in reality this term guarantees no more than four walls and most of a roof.

Actually, finding your countryside Eden isn't that simple, and if you want to ensure a romantic and memorable experience, brace yourself for a lot of research and legwork. Occasionally, you can go through the property owners themselves, but the vast majority of villas are rented out via agencies (see below).

Shop around for a trustworthy agent or representative. Often several outfits will list the same property but charge radically different prices. At some, you sign away any right to refunds if the place doesn't live up to your expectations. Make sure the agency is willing to work with you to find the right property. Always ask to see lots of photos: Get the exterior from several angles to make sure the railroad doesn't pass by the back door, as well as pictures of the bedrooms, kitchen, and bathrooms, and photos of the views out each side of the house.

Ask to see a floor plan to make sure access to the bathroom isn't through a bedroom. Find out if this is the only villa on the property—some people who rent the villa for the isolation find themselves living in a small enclave of foreigners all sharing the same small area. Ask whether the villa is purely a rental unit or if the owners live there during winter but let it out during summer. Renting a lived-in place offers pretty good insurance that the lights, plumbing, heat, and so on will all be working.

One of the best agencies to call is **Rentvillas.com,** 700 E. Main St., Ventura, CA 93001 (✆ **800/726-6702** or 805/641-1650; fax 805/641-1630; www.rentvillas.com). It has almost 1,000 villas and apartments on offer in Italy and its agents are very helpful in tracking down the perfect place to suit your needs. Marjorie Shaw's **Insider's Italy** (✆ **914/470-1612;** fax 914/470-1612; www.insidersitaly.com), is a small, upscale outfit run by a very personable agent who's thoroughly familiar with all of her properties and with Italy in general.

The **Parker Company Ltd.,** Seaport Landing, 152 Lynnway, Lynn, MA 01902 (✆ **800/280-2811** or 781/596-8282; fax 781/596-3125; www.theparkercompany.com), handles overseas villa rentals and offers several properties in northern Italy.

For some top properties, call **Cottages to Castles,** Tuscany House, 10 Tonbridge Rd., Maidstone, Kent ME16 8RP, U.K. (✆ **0044/1622-775-217;** www.cottagestocastles.com).

House-Swapping

House-swapping is becoming a more popular and viable means of travel; you stay in their place, they stay in yours, and you both get a more authentic and personal view of a destination—the opposite of the escapist retreat many hotels offer. Try **HomeLink International** (www.homelink.org), the largest and oldest home-swapping organization, founded in 1952, with more than 13,000 listings worldwide ($119 to list a house for a year). **InterVac.com** ($100 for over 10,000 listings) is also reliable. **Craigslist.org** also has an extensive list of housing swap options in Italy, as many Italians are eager to find a cheap vacation alternative in American cities. As with any transaction on Craigslist, do some serious due diligence so you know you are dealing with a reputable person.

Villas and Apartments Abroad, Ltd., 183 Madison Ave., Ste. 1111, New York, NY 10017 (*©* **212/213-6435;** fax 212/213-8252; www.vaanyc.com) has a select few offerings in northern Italy including in Venice, Lake Como, and around Portofino.

Homelidays (www.homelidays.com) is an excellent choice for everything from villas to apartments by the sea and chalets in the Dolomites. You deal directly with the owner and the listings contain copious amounts of information, photos, and testimonials from people who have stayed before you.

[FastFACTS] NORTHERN ITALY

Area Codes The **country code** for Italy is **39. City codes** (for example, Milan's is 02, Venice's is 041) are incorporated into the numbers themselves. Therefore, you must dial the entire number, *including the initial zero,* when calling from *anywhere* outside or inside Italy and even within the same town. To call Milan from the States, you must dial **011-39-02,** then the local phone number. Phone numbers in Italy can range anywhere from 6 to 12 digits in length.

Business Hours General open hours for **stores, offices,** and **churches** are from 9:30am to noon or 1pm and again from 3 or 3:30pm to 7:30 or 8pm. The early afternoon shutdown is the *riposo,* the Italian siesta (in the downtown area of large cities stores don't close for the *riposo*). Most stores close all day Sunday and many also on Monday (morning only or all day). Some shops, especially grocery stores, also close Thursday afternoons. Some services and business offices are open to the public only in the morning. Traditionally, **museums** are closed Monday, and though some of the biggest stay open all day long, many close for *riposo* or are only open in the morning (9am–2pm is popular). Some churches open earlier in the morning, but the largest often stay open all day. **Banks** tend to be open Monday through Friday 8:30am to 1:30pm and 2:45 to 4:15pm.

Car Rental See "By Car," p. 459.

Cellphones See "Mobile Phones," p. 471.

Customs Italy's *Guardia di Finanza* is in charge of checking what people bring into and out of Italy. Foreign visitors can bring along most items for personal use duty-free, including merchandise up to $800. If you are planning to mail items to Italy, you can mail only merchandise costing up to $200. For information on what you're allowed to bring home, contact your country's customs agency.

Disabled Travelers In Italy, a few of the top museums and churches have installed ramps at their entrances, and some hotels have converted first-floor rooms into accessible units by widening the doors and bathrooms. Other than that, don't expect to find much of northern Italy—or really any part of Italy—easy to tackle. Builders in the Middle Ages and the Renaissance didn't have wheelchairs or mobility impairments in mind when they built narrow doorways and spiral staircases, and preservation laws keep modern Italians from being able to do much about this.

Many buses and trains can cause problems as well, with high, narrow doors and steep steps at entrances (notably, the Malpensa Express train from the airport to Milan is wheelchair accessible). For those with disabilities who can make it on to public transportation, there are usually seats reserved for them and Italians are quick to give up their place for somebody who looks like they need it more than them.

Accessible Italy (☎ **378-0549-9411;** www.accessibleitaly.com) provides travelers with information on accessible tourist sites and places to rent wheelchairs, and also sells organized "Accessible Tours" around Italy.

Drinking Laws People of any age can legally consume alcohol, but a person must be 16 years old in order to be served alcohol in a restaurant or a bar. Similarly, laws in other countries that exist in order to stamp out public drunkenness simply aren't as necessary in Italy, where binge-drinking is unusual. Noise is the primary concern to city officials, and so bars generally close at 2am at the latest, though alcohol is commonly served in clubs after that. Supermarkets generally carry beer, wine, and sometimes spirits.

Driving Rules See "Getting Around," p. 461.

Electricity Italy operates on a 220 volts AC (50 cycles) system, as opposed to the United States' 110 volts AC (60 cycles) system. You'll need a simple adapter plug to make the American flat pegs fit the Italian round holes and, unless your appliance is dual-voltage (as some hair dryers, travel irons, and almost all laptops are), an electrical currency converter. You can pick up the hardware at electronics stores, travel specialty stores, luggage shops, and airports.

Embassies & Consulates The **Australian Embassy** is in Rome at Via Antonio Bosio 5 (☎ **06-852-721;** www.italy.embassy.gov.au). Australia's consulate in Milan is at Via Borgogna 2 (☎ **02-777-041**), open Monday through Thursday 9am to noon and 2 to 4pm.

The **Canadian** Embassy is in Rome at Via Zara 30 (☎ **06-854-443-937;** www.canada international.gc.ca/italy-italie). The Canadian consulate in Milan is at Via Vittor Pisani 19 (☎ **02-67-581**), open Monday through Friday 8:30am to 12:30pm and 1:30 to 4pm.

The **New Zealand Embassy** is in Rome at Via Clittuno (☎ **06-853-7501;** www.nzembassy. com/italy). New Zealand's Milan consulate is at Via Terragio 17 (☎ **02-7217-0001;** fax 02-4801-2577), open Monday through Friday 8:30am to 12:30pm and 1:30 to 5pm.

The **U.K. Embassy** is in Rome at Via XX Settembre 80a (☎ **06-4220-0001;** fax 06-4220-2334; http://ukinitaly.fco.gov.uk/it). The **U.K. consulate in Milan** is at Via San Paolo 7 (☎ **02-723-001;** fax 02-869-2405). It's open Monday to Friday 9:30am to 12:30pm and 2:30 to 4:30pm.

The **U.S. Embassy** is in Rome at Via Vittorio Veneto 121 (☎ **06-46-741;** fax 06-488-2672 or 06-4674-2217; http://italy.usembassy.gov). The **U.S. consulate in Milan**—for passport and consular services but *not* for visas—is at Via Principe Amadeo 2/10 (☎ **02-2903-5333;** fax 02-2903-5273; http://milan.usconsulate.gov); it's open for drop-ins Monday through Friday 8:30am to noon for emergencies, otherwise only by appointment.

Emergencies The best number to call in Italy (and the rest of Europe) with a **general emergency** is ☎ 112, which connects you to the military-trained **Carabinieri** who will transfer your call as needed; for the **police,** dial ☎ 113; for a **medical emergency** and to call an **ambulance,** the number is ☎ 118; for the **fire department,** call ☎ 115. If your car breaks down, dial ☎ **116** for **roadside aid** courtesy of the Automotive Club of Italy. All are free calls.

Family Travel Italy is a family-oriented society, and kids have free rein just about anywhere they go. A crying baby at a dinner table is greeted with a knowing smile rather than with a stern look. Children under a certain age almost always receive discounts, and maybe a special treat from the waiter.

Female Travelers Women feel remarkably welcome in Italy—sometimes a bit too welcome, actually. It seems every young Italian male is out to prove himself the most irresistible lover on the planet; remember, this is the land of Romeo and Casanova, so they have a lot to live up to. And with most every Italian woman playing the especially hard-to-get Juliet, well, you see what's coming next for foreign women.

It should be noted that, culturally, northern Italy feels a lot more like its Austrian and Swiss neighbors in the sense that the divide between the sexes is not quite as deep, a lot more egalitarian, and perhaps less chivalrous than, say, Sicily, but naturally attractive women everywhere will, er, attract attention.

The attention is mostly kept to verbal flirtation (but should there be inappropriate touching, immediately speak up and report it to police). These men want to conquer you with their charm, not their muscles. Rape is much rarer in Italy than in the United States, but it does happen (mostly by non-Italian men, if you believe the newspapers). Use common sense: Don't walk through poorly lit city parks alone late at night, especially in Milan, Turin, and Genoa.

Gasoline See "By Car," p. 459.

Health There are no special health risks you'll encounter in Italy. If you do need medical attention, Northern Italy has good **hospitals** (see below), and the country's public health care system is generally well regarded.

While Italy offers universal health care to its citizens and those of other European Union countries, others should be prepared to pay medical bills up front. Before leaving home, find out what medical services your **health insurance** covers. *Note:* Even if you don't have insurance, you will be treated in an emergency room.

Pharmacies offer essentially the same range of generic drugs available in the United States, plus a lot of them that haven't been approved yet by the U.S. Food and Drug Administration. **Pharmacies** are ubiquitous (look for the green cross) and serve almost like miniclinics, where pharmacists diagnose and treat minor ailments, like flu symptoms and general aches and pains, with over-the-counter drugs. Carry the generic name of prescription medicines, in case a local pharmacist is unfamiliar with the brand name. Pharmacies in cities take turns doing the night shift; normally there is a list posted at the entrance of each pharmacy informing customers which pharmacy is open each night of the week.

Holidays Banks, government offices, post offices, and many stores, restaurants, and museums in Italy are closed on the following legal national holidays: January 1 (New Year's Day), January 6 (Epiphany), Easter Sunday and the following Monday (called *pasquetta,* or Little Easter), April 25 (Liberation Day), May 1 (Labor Day), June 2 (Republic Day), August 15 (Feast of the Assumption), November 1 (All Saints' Day), December 8 (Immaculate Conception), and December 25 and December 26 (Santo Stefano).

For more information, see "Holidays," p. 70.

Hospitals In Milan, the **Ospedale Maggiore Policlinico** (✆ **02-5503-3103;** www. policlinico.mi.it) is centrally located a 5-minute walk southeast of the Duomo at Via Francesco Sforza 35 (Metro: Duomo or Missori). In Venice, the **Ospedale Civile Santi Giovanni e Paolo** (✆ **041-785111**), on Campo Santi Giovanni e Paolo, has English-speaking staff and provides emergency service 24 hours a day (*vaporetto:* San Toma).

Insurance Italy may be one of the safer places you can travel in the world, but accidents and setbacks can and do happen, from lost luggage to car crashes. For information on traveler's insurance, trip cancellation insurance, and medical insurance while traveling, please visit www.frommers.com/tips.

Internet Access Internet cafes are in healthy supply in most Italian cities though don't expect to find them in smaller towns. If you are traveling with your own computer or smart phone, you will find wireless access in many hotels in the bigger cities of northern Italy, especially Milan, but if this is key for your stay make sure you ask before booking and certainly don't expect to find a connection in a rural *agriturismo* (disconnecting is part of their appeal). In a pinch, hostels, local libraries, and often pubs will have some sort of terminal for access. Several spots around Milan are covered with free Wi-Fi access provided by the city, but at these and any other Wi-Fi spots around Italy, anti-terrorism laws make it obligatory to register for an access code before you can log on. Milan's two airports offer wireless Internet access for a fee.

Language Italians may not be quite as polished with their English as some of their European counterparts, but they've been hosting Anglophones for a long time, and English is a regular part of any business day. In very rural parts, slow and clear speech, a little gesticulating, and a smile will go a long way. In Venice, you will probably be the 20th English-speaking tourist they've spoken with that day. Italians love it when foreigners speak their language, no matter how pathetically, so you can earn lots of good will and smiles by familiarizing yourself with the "Useful Terms" (p. 478).

Legal Aid Your embassy or consulate can provide a list of foreign attorneys, should you encounter legal problems in Italy. In criminal cases, if you cannot afford an attorney, the local court will provide one for you.

LGBT Travelers Italy as a whole and northern Italy in particular, is gay-friendly. Homosexuality is legal, and the age of consent is 16. Luckily, Italians are already more affectionate and physical than Americans in their general friendships, and even straight men occasionally walk down the street with their arms around each other—however, kissing anywhere other than on the cheeks at greetings and goodbyes will certainly draw attention. As you might expect, smaller towns tend to be less permissive than cities. Milan has the largest and most visible homosexual population, and during fashion week especially, gay travelers will feel particularly at home.

Italy's national association and support network for gays and lesbians is **ARCI-Gay/ ARCI-Lesbica.** The national website is **www.arcigay.it**, and most cities have a local office (though not Venice). In **Trieste,** it is found at Via Pondares 8 (✆ **040-630-606**); in **Verona,** Via Nichesola 9 (✆ **045-973-003**); in **Milan,** Via Bezzecca 3 (✆ **02-5412-2225;** www.arcigaymilano.org); in **Genoa,** Via Mezzagalera 3 (✆ **010-565-971;** http:// nuke.arcigaygenova.it); and in **Turin,** Via Fratelli Faà di Bruno 2 (✆ **333-713-8813;** www.arcigaytorino.it).

Mail Sending a postcard or letter up to 20 grams, or a little less than an ounce, costs 0.75€ to other European countries, 1.60€ to North America, and a whopping 2€ to Australia and New Zealand.

Medical Requirements There are no special medical requirements for entering Italy. For more information on staying healthy while over there, see "Health" above.

Mobile Phones GSM (Global System for Mobile Communications), is a cellphone technology used by most of the world's countries that makes it possible to turn on a phone with a contract in Australia, Ireland, the U.K., Pakistan, or almost every other corner of the world and have it work in Italy without missing a beat. (In the U.S., some service providers use a different technology than GSM, and phones used with those networks won't work in Italy.)

Any phone that works in the U.K., Ireland, Australia, or New Zealand will work in Italy, where coverage is excellent just about everywhere, but if you are coming from the U.S. or Canada you might need a multiband phone. In some cases you might have to activate "international roaming" on your account so check with your service provider at home before leaving.

Using your cellphone in a different country can be very expensive so another option, once you arrive, is to buy an Italian SIM card (the fingernail-size removable plastic card found in all GSM phones that is encoded with your phone number and account information). This is not difficult and an especially good idea if you will be in Italy for more than a few weeks. You can **buy a SIM card** at one of the many cellphone shops you will see around every city (the biggest service providers are TIM, Vodafone, Wind, and 3). If you have an Italian SIM card in your phone, local calls may be as low as .10€ per minute, and incoming calls are free. *Note:* Some cellphones are "locked" and will only work with the SIM card provided by the service provider back home so check to see that you have an unlocked phone.

Buying a phone is another option, and in the bigger cities in northern Italy you shouldn't have too much trouble finding one that won't put you back more than about 40€. Another, usually more expensive, option is to **rent a phone** from kiosks at airports, car-rental agencies, or in a number of places in Milan.

Money & Costs Frommer's lists exact prices in the local currency. The currency conversions quoted below were correct at press time. However, rates fluctuate, so before departing, consult a currency exchange website, such as **www.oanda.com/convert/classic**, to check up-to-the-minute rates.

THE VALUE OF THE EURO VS. OTHER POPULAR CURRENCIES

	Aus$	Can$	NZ$	UK£	US$
1	A$1.36	C$1.41	NZ$1.70	£0.88	$1.45

Like many other European countries, Italy uses the euro as its currency. Euro coins are issued in denominations of .01€, .02€, .05€, .10€, .20€, and .50€, as well as 1€ and 2€; bills come in denominations of 5€, 10€, 20€, 50€, 100€, 200€, and 500€.

The aggressive evolution of international computerized banking and consolidated ATM networks has led to the triumph of plastic throughout the Italian peninsula—even if cold cash is still the most trusted currency, especially in smaller towns or cheaper mom-and-pop joints, where credit cards may not be accepted. Traveler's checks, while still the safest way to carry money, are going the way of the dinosaur.

You'll get the best rate if you **exchange money** at a bank or one of its ATMs. The rates at "Cambio/change/wechsel" exchange booths are invariably less favorable but still a good deal better than what you'd get exchanging money at a hotel or shop (a last-resort tactic only). The bill-to-bill changers you'll see in some touristy places exist solely to rip you off.

Vaporetto ticket (from/to anywhere in the city)	6.50€
Double room at Hotel Cipriani with lagoon view (very expensive)	1,100.00€
Double room at Pensione Accademia (moderate)	260.00€
Double room at Hotel Bernardi-Semenzato (inexpensive)	110.00€
Continental breakfast (cappuccino and croissant standing at a bar)	3.00€
Lunch for one at Cantina Do Mori with glass of wine (inexpensive)	12.00€
Dinner for one, with table wine, at Fiaschetteria Toscana (expensive)	70.00€
Dinner for one, with table wine, at Osteria da Robia (moderate)	45.00€
Dinner for one, with table wine, at Trattoria alla Rivetta (inexpensive)	25.00€
Glass of wine standing at a bar	2.00€–7.00€
Coca-Cola (standing/sitting in a bar)	3.00€/4.50€
Cup of espresso (standing/sitting in a bar)	0.80€/2.50€
Admission to the Accademia	6.50€

The easiest and best way to get cash away from home is from an ATM (automated teller machine), referred to in Italy as a *bancomat.* ATMs are very prevalent in the cities of northern Italy and while every town usually has one, it's good practice to fuel up on cash in urban centers before traveling to smaller towns.

Be sure to confirm with your bank that your card is valid for international withdrawal and that you have a four-digit PIN. (Some ATMs in Italy will not accept any other number of digits.) Also, be sure you know your daily withdrawal limit before you depart. *Note:* Many banks impose a fee every time you use a card at another bank's ATM, and that fee can be higher for international transactions (up to $5 or more) than for domestic ones (where they're rarely more than $2). In addition, the bank from which you withdraw cash may charge its own fee, although this is not common practice in Italy.

If at the ATM you get a message saying your card isn't valid for international transactions, don't panic: It's most likely the bank just can't make the phone connection to check it (occasionally this can be a citywide epidemic) or else simply doesn't have the cash. Try another ATM or another town.

Credit cards are widely accepted in northern Italy, especially in hotels and larger establishments. However, it is always a good idea to carry some cash, as small businesses may accept only cash or may claim that their credit card machine is broken to avoid paying fees to the credit card companies.

Visa and **MasterCard** are almost universally accepted at hotels, plus most restaurants and shops; the majority of them also accept **American Express. Diners Club** is gaining some ground.

Finally, be sure to let your bank know that you'll be traveling abroad to avoid having your card blocked after a few days of big purchases far from home. *Note:* Many banks assess a 1% to 3% "transaction fee" on **all** charges you incur abroad (whether you're using the local currency or your native currency).

Multicultural Travelers Many Italians are still grappling with the new reality that theirs is no longer the homogenous society that it was for centuries. You will see non-white immigrants everywhere you travel in northern Italy, with the exception of mountain villages. But because most of the immigrants that you, and most Italians, will meet are working as street vendors and not bankers means that travelers with darker skin may feel—correctly at times—as if they're being looked at or in some way singled out.

Pockets of outright racism do exist in Italy, especially in Veneto and the Northeast in general. There African and South Asian workers fill the need for low-paid labor and, according to outfits like the Northern League, are responsible for all crime that occurs. Skinhead violence is extremely rare, but you might expect the occasional slur from a soccer hooligan and maybe some sideways glances from a few provincial old men.

Newspapers & Magazines The *International Herald Tribune* (published by the *New York Times* and with news catering to Americans abroad) and *USA Today* are available at just about every newsstand, even in smaller towns. You can find the *Wall Street Journal Europe,* European editions of *Time* and *Newsweek,* the *Economist,* and most of the major European newspapers and magazines at the larger kiosks in the bigger cities.

Sports daily *La Gazzetta dello Sport* is Italy's best-selling newspaper while *Corriere della Sera* is the best selling general-interest daily. Both are based in Milan and can be found on any newsstand across northern Italy.

Parking See "By Car," p. 460.

Passports Anyone traveling to Italy from outside the 25 Schengen Agreement countries (which essentially comprises all of western Europe except the U.K. and Ireland) will need a passport to enter. You're required to present a passport at hotel desks in Italy. Citizens of the United States, Canada, the U.K., Australia, and New Zealand are allowed to stay in Italy for 90 days; after that period, they are required to have a visa.

See www.frommers.com/tips for information on how to obtain a passport. See "Embassies & Consulates," above, for whom to contact if you lose yours while traveling in Italy. For other information, please contact the following agencies:

For Residents of Australia Contact the **Australian Passport Information Service** at ✆ **131-232,** or visit the government website at www.passports.gov.au.

For Residents of Canada Contact the central **Passport Office,** Department of Foreign Affairs and International Trade, Ottawa, ON K1A 0G3 (✆ **800/567-6868;** www.ppt. gc.ca).

For Residents of Ireland Contact the **Passport Office,** Setanta Centre, Molesworth Street, Dublin 2 (✆ **01/671-1633;** www.foreignaffairs.gov.ie).

For Residents of New Zealand Contact the **Passports Office** at ✆ **0800/225-050** in New Zealand or 04/474-8100, or log on to www.passports.govt.nz.

For Residents of the United Kingdom Visit your nearest passport office, major post office, or travel agency, or contact the **United Kingdom Passport Service** at ✆ **0870/521-0410,** or search its website at www.homeoffice.gov.uk/agencies-public-bodies/ips.

For Residents of the United States Call the **National Passport Information Center** toll-free number (✆ **877/487-2778**) for automated information or visit http://travel. state.gov/passport.

Petrol See "By Car," p. 459.

Police For emergencies, call ✆ **113.** Italy has several different police forces, but there are only two you'll most likely ever need to deal with. The first is the *polizia,* whose city headquarters is called the *questura,* which is the place to go for help with lost and stolen property or petty crimes. The *carabinieri* (✆ **112**) normally only concern themselves with more serious crimes or problems.

Safety Italy is a remarkably safe country. The worst threats you'll likely face are the pickpockets that sometimes frequent touristy areas and public buses; keep your hands on your camera at all times and your valuables in an under-the-clothes money belt. Don't leave anything valuable in your rental car overnight, and leave nothing visible in it at any time to avoid tempting a would-be thief. If you are robbed, you can fill out paperwork at the nearest police station, but this is mostly for insurance purposes and perhaps to get a new passport issued—don't expect them to actually spend any resources hunting down the perpetrator.

In general, avoid public parks at night and public squares in the wee hours of the morning. The square in front of Milan's main train station is pretty dodgy after hours and travelers—especially women—should avoid Genoa's port area after dark. Other than that, there is a remarkable sense of security in this wealthy corner of the world.

Senior Travel Seniors and older people are treated with a great deal of respect and deference throughout Italy, but there are few specific programs, associations, or concessions made for them. The one exception is on admission prices for museums and sights, where those ages 60 or 65 and older will often get in at a reduced rate or even free. There are also special train passes and reductions on bus tickets and the like in many towns (see "Getting Around," p. 460). As a senior in Italy, you're *un anziano* (*una anziana* if you're a woman), or "elderly"—it's a term of respect, and you should let people know you're one if you think a discount may be in order.

Single Travelers On package vacations, single travelers are often hit with a "single supplement" to the base price. To avoid it, you can agree to room with other single travelers on your tour.

Smoking Smoking has been eradicated from restaurants, bars, and most hotels in Italy. Naturally, many smokers remain, and they tend to take the outside tables at bars and restaurants. Be aware that if you are keen for an outdoor table, you are essentially choosing a seat in the smoking section, and requesting that your neighbor not smoke may not be politely received.

Student Travelers Formed in 1949, the **International Student Travel Confederation** (**ISTC;** www.istc.org) seeks to make travel around the world more affordable for students. The website gives comprehensive travel services information and details on how to get an **International Student Identity Card (ISIC),** which qualifies students for substantial savings on rail passes, plane tickets, entrance fees, and more. It also provides students with basic health and life insurance and a 24-hour help line. The card is valid for one year. You can apply for the card online or in person at **STA Travel** (✆ **800/781-4040** in North America; www.statravel.com), the biggest student travel agency in the world; check out the website to locate STA Travel offices worldwide. If you're no longer a student but are still 25 and under, you can get an **International Youth Travel Card (IYTC)** from the same agency, which entitles you to some discounts. **Travel CUTS** (✆ **800/592-2887;** www.travelcuts.com) offers similar services to Canadians and U.S. residents alike. Irish students can turn to **USIT** (✆ **01/602-1904;** www.usit.ie), an Ireland-based specialist in student, youth, and independent travel.

In northern Italy, students will find many university cities that offer ample student discounts and inexpensive youth hostels. Padua is home to one of Italy's oldest universities, founded in 1222, and today it is still a thriving student city with a young university population that keeps the city's *piazze* and cafes alive.

Taxes There's no sales tax added onto the price tag of your purchases, but there is a 19% value-added tax (in Italy: IVA) automatically included in just about everything. For major purchases, you can get this refunded. Some four- and five-star hotels don't include the 13% luxury tax in their quoted prices. Ask when making your reservation.

Telephones To call Italy: (1) Dial the international access code: 011 from the U.S.; 00 from the U.K., Ireland, or New Zealand; or 0011 from Australia. (2) Dial the country code 39. (3) Dial the city code (for Milan: 02) and then the number. (Do not drop the initial 0 as you might in other European countries.) Even when calling within Italy, you always need to dial the city code first.

To make international calls: To make international calls from Italy, first dial 00 and then the country code (U.S. or Canada 1, U.K. 44, Ireland 353, Australia 61, New Zealand 64). Next, dial the area code and number. For example, if you wanted to call the British Embassy in Washington, D.C., you would dial 00-1-202-588-6500.

For directory assistance: Each cellphone carrier has its own directory assistance number, which is listed automatically in the address book of your SIM card. For Telecom Italia, and its mobile carrier, TIM, the directory assistance number is ✆ **1254.**

For operator assistance: For operator assistance in making either a domestic or an international call from a Telecom Italia land line, call ✆ **187.**

Toll-free numbers: Numbers in Italy beginning with 800 or 877, and a few others beginning with 8, are toll-free, but calling a 1-800 number in the States from Italy is not toll-free. In fact, it costs the same as an overseas call.

Throughout Italy you'll find public telephones that accept **Telecom Italia phone cards** *(scheda telefonica),* which you can purchase at tobacco shops in various denominations. With the ubiquity of cell phones, public phones are going the way of the Stegosaurus so actually finding one in which to use your phone card can be a challenge.

You can also buy phone cards with special fixed rates to the United States, Canada, Australia, and other countries *(una carta telefonica prepagata per chiamare gli Stati Uniti, Canada . . .)* that can be used from any phone. The rates on these phone cards, which can be found at newsstands and tobacconists, are heavily discounted from what you would pay from a land line and far less expensive than calling abroad from a cellphone.

Time Italy is in the same Western European time zone as Paris, Brussels, and Berlin—that is, GMT plus 1 hour.

Tipping In **hotels,** a service charge is usually included in your bill. In family-run operations, additional tips are unnecessary and sometimes considered rude. In fancier places with a hired staff, however, you may want to leave a .50€ daily tip for the maid, pay the bellhop or porter 1€ per bag, and tip a helpful concierge 2€ for his or her troubles. In **restaurants,** a 1€ to 3€ service charge is automatically added to the bill and in some tourist areas, especially Venice, another 10% to 15% is tacked on (except in the most unscrupulous of places, this will be noted on the menu somewhere; to be sure you can ask, *è incluso il servizio?*). It is not necessary to leave any extra money on the table though it is not uncommon to leave up to 5€, especially for good service. At **bars and cafes,** you can leave something very small on the counter for the barman (maybe

1€ if you have had several drinks), though it is hardly expected; there is no need to leave anything extra if you sit at a table, as they are probably already charging you double or triple the price you'd have paid standing at the bar. It is not necessary to tip **taxi** drivers, though it is common to round up the bill to the nearest euro or 2.

Toilets Aside from train stations, where they cost about .50€ to use, and gas/petrol stations, where they are free (with perhaps a basket seeking donations), public toilets are few and far between in northern Italy. Standard procedure is to enter a cafe, make sure the bathroom is not *fuori servizio* (out of order), and then order a cup of coffee before bolting to the facilities. In Venice, the price of using a toilet is a little steeper: about 1.50€ in the major squares and parking garages, and they usually close at 8pm. It is advisable to always make use of the facilities in the hotel, restaurant, and bar before a long walk around town.

VAT See "Taxes" earlier in this section.

Visas Travelers from Australia, Canada, New Zealand, the U.S., and the U.K. can visit Italy for up to 90 days without a visa, though they need a valid passport. Visits of more than 90 days may require a visa, but the requirements vary depending on the purpose of your visit.

For more information on visas to visit or stay in Italy, go to the Foreign Ministry's English-language page at **www.esteri.it/visti**.

Visitor Information In Milan, the main **Azienda di Promozione Turistica (APT) office** is at Piazza Castello, 1 on the south side of the square where it meets via Beltrami (℡ **02-7740-4343;** www.visitamilano.it). Hours are Monday to Friday 9am to 6pm, Saturday 9am to 1:30pm and 2 to 6pm, Sunday 9am to 1:30pm and 2 to 5pm. There is also an office in **Stazione Centrale** (℡ **02-7740-4318**), in front of tracks 13 and 14 with the same hours.

In Venice, the main tourist office is on Fondamenta San Lorenzo, 5 minutes from Piazza San Marco (℡ **041-529-8711;** www.turismovenezia.it); it's open daily 10am to 6pm. There is also a small, private tourist office in Venice's train station.

See "Visitor Information," in each of the chapters, for more information.

Water Though Italians take mineral water with their meals, tap water is safe everywhere. Unsafe sources, for example on trains, will be marked ACQUA NON POTABILE. The water from fountains in public parks is not only potable, it's often the best water you've ever tasted.

Wi-Fi See "Internet Access," earlier in this section.

USEFUL TERMS & PHRASES

THE BASICS

USEFUL ENGLISH-ITALIAN PHRASES

English	Italian	Pronunciation
Thank you	**Grazie**	*graht*-tzee-yey
You're welcome	**Prego**	*prey*-go
Please	**Per favore**	*pehr* fah-*vohr*-eh
Yes	**Si**	see
No	**No**	noh
Good morning or Good day	**Buongiorno**	bwohn-*djor*-noh
Good evening	**Buona sera**	*bwohn*-ah *say*-rah
Good night	**Buona notte**	*bwohn*-ah *noht*-tay
It's a pleasure to meet you.	**Piacere di conoscerla.**	pyah-*cheh*-reh dee *koh*-noh-shehr-lah
My name is ____.	**Mi chiamo ____.**	mee *kyah*-moh
And yours?	**E lei?**	eh lay
Do you speak English?	**Parla inglese?**	*pahr*-lah een-*gleh*-seh
How are you?	**Come sta?**	*koh*-may *stah*
Very well	**Molto bene**	*mohl*-toh *behn*-ney
Goodbye	**Arrivederci**	ahr-ree-vah-*dehr*-chee
Excuse me (to get attention)	**Scusi**	*skoo*-zee
Excuse me (to get past someone)	**Permesso**	pehr-*mehs*-soh

GETTING AROUND

English	Italian	Pronunciation
Where is . . . ?	**Dov'è . . . ?**	doh-*vey*
the station	**la stazione**	lah stat-tzee-*oh*-neh
a hotel	**un albergo**	oon ahl-*behr*-goh
a restaurant	**un ristorante**	oon reest-ohr-*ahnt*-eh
the bathroom	**il bagno**	eel *bahn*-nyoh
I am looking for . . .	**Cerco . . .**	*chehr*-koh
a porter	**un facchino**	oon fahk-*kee*-noh
the check-in counter	**il check-in**	eel check-in
the ticket counter	**la biglietteria**	lah beel-lyeht-teh-*ree*-ah
arrivals	**l'area arrivi**	*lah*-reh-ah ahr-*ree*-vee
departures	**l'area partenze**	*lah*-reh-ah pahr-*tehn*-tseh
gate number	**l'uscita numero**	loo-*shee*-tah *noo*-meh-roh
the waiting area	**l'area d'attesa**	*lah*-reh-ah daht-*teh*-zah
the men's restroom	**la toilette uomini**	lah twa-*leht woh*-mee-nee
the women's restroom	**la toilette donne**	lah twa-*leht dohn*-neh
the police station	**la stazione di polizia**	lah stah-*tsyoh*-neh dee poh-lee-*tsee*-ah
a security guard	**una guardia di sicurezza**	*ooh*-nah *gwahr*-dyah dee see-koo-*ret*-sah
the smoking area	**l'area fumatori**	*lah*-reh-ah foo-mah-*toh*-ree
the information booth	**l'ufficio informazioni**	loof-*fee*-choh een-*fohr*-mah-*tsyoh*-nee
a public telephone	**un telefono pubblico**	oon teh-*leh*-foh-noh *poob*-blee-koh
an ATM/cashpoint	**un bancomat**	oon *bahn*-koh-maht
baggage claim	**il ritiro bagagli**	eel ree-*tee*-roh bah-*gahl*-lyee
a luggage cart	**un carrello portabagagli**	oon kahr-*rehl*-loh *pohr*-tah-bah-*gahl*-lyee
a currency exchange	**un cambiavalute**	oon *kahm*-byah-vah-*loo*-teh
a cafe	**un caffè**	oon kahf-*feh*
a restaurant	**un ristorante**	oon ree-stoh-*rahn*-teh
a bar	**un bar**	oon bar
a bookstore	**una libreria**	*oo*-nah lee-breh-*ree*-ah
a duty-free shop	**un duty-free**	oon duty-free
To the left	**A sinistra**	ah see-*nees*-tra
To the right	**A destra**	ah *dehy*-stra
Straight ahead	**Avanti (or sempre diritto)**	ahv-*vahn*-tee (*sehm*-pray dee-*reet*-toh)

DINING

English	Italian	Pronunciation
Breakfast	**Prima colazione**	*pree*-mah coh-laht-tzee-*ohn*-ay
Lunch	**Pranzo**	*prahn*-zoh
Dinner	**Cena**	*chay*-nah
How much is it?	**Quanto costa?**	*kwan*-toh *coh*-sta
The check, please	**Il conto, per favore**	eel *kon*-toh *pehr* fah-*vohr*-eh

A MATTER OF TIME

English	Italian	Pronunciation
When?	**Quando?**	*kwan*-doh
Yesterday	**Ieri**	ee-*yehr*-ree
Today	**Oggi**	*oh*-jee
Tomorrow	**Domani**	doh-*mah*-nee
What time is it?	**Che ore sono?**	kay *or*-ay *soh*-noh
It's one o'clock.	**È l'una.**	*eh loo*-nah
It's two o'clock.	**Sono le due.**	*soh*-noh leh *doo*-eh
It's two thirty.	**Sono le due e mezzo.**	*soh*-noh leh *doo*-eh eh *mehd*-dzoh
It's noon.	**È mezzogiorno.**	*eh* mehd-dzoh-*johr*-noh
It's midnight.	**È mezzanotte.**	*eh* mehd-dzah-*noht*-teh
It's early.	**È presto.**	*eh prehs*-toh
It's late.	**È tardi.**	*eh tahr*-dee
in the morning	**al mattino**	ahl maht-*tee*-noh
in the afternoon	**al pomeriggio**	ahl poh-meh-*reed*-joh
at night	**di notte**	dee *noht*-the

DAYS OF THE WEEK

English	Italian	Pronunciation
Monday	**Lunedì**	loo-nay-*dee*
Tuesday	**Martedì**	mart-ay-*dee*
Wednesday	**Mercoledì**	mehr-cohl-ay-*dee*
Thursday	**Giovedì**	joh-vay-*dee*
Friday	**Venerdì**	ven-nehr-*dee*
Saturday	**Sabato**	*sah*-bah-toh
Sunday	**Domenica**	doh-*mehn*-nee-kah

MONTHS & SEASONS

English	Italian	Pronunciation
January	**gennaio**	jehn-*nah*-yoh
February	**febbraio**	fehb-*brah*-yoh
March	**marzo**	*mahr*-tso
April	**aprile**	ah-*pree*-leh
May	**maggio**	*mahd*-joh
June	**giugno**	*jewn*-nyo
July	**luglio**	*lool*-lyo
August	**agosto**	ah-*gohs*-toh
September	**settembre**	seht-*tehm*-breh
October	**ottobre**	oht-*toh*-breh
November	**novembre**	noh-*vehm*-breh
December	**dicembre**	dee-*chehm*-breh
spring	**la primavera**	lah pree-mah-*veh*-rah
summer	**l'estate**	lehs-*tah*-teh
autumn	**l'autunno**	low-*toon*-noh
winter	**l'inverno**	leen-*vehr*-noh

NUMBERS

English	Italian	Pronunciation
1	**uno**	*oo*-noh
2	**due**	*doo*-ay
3	**tre**	tray
4	**quattro**	*kwah*-troh
5	**cinque**	*cheen*-kway
6	**sei**	say
7	**sette**	*set*-tay
8	**otto**	*oh*-toh
9	**nove**	*noh*-vay
10	**dieci**	dee-*ay*-chee
11	**undici**	*oon*-dee-chee
20	**venti**	*vehn*-tee
21	**ventuno**	vehn-*toon*-oh
22	**venti due**	*vehn*-tee *doo*-ay
30	**trenta**	*trayn*-tah
40	**quaranta**	kwah-*rahn*-tah
50	**cinquanta**	cheen-*kwan*-tah
60	**sessanta**	sehs-*sahn*-tah
70	**settanta**	seht-*tahn*-tah
80	**ottanta**	oht-*tahn*-tah

English	Italian	Pronunciation
90	**novanta**	noh-*vahnt*-tah
100	**cento**	*chen*-toh
1,000	**mille**	*mee*-lay
5,000	**cinquemila**	*cheen*-kway *mee*-lah
10,000	**diecimila**	dee-ay-chee-*mee*-lah

A SHOPPER'S PHRASE FINDER

English	Italian	Pronunciation
Can you please tell me . . .	**Può dirmi per favore . . .**	*pwoh deer*-mee pehr fah-*voh*-reh
how to get to a mall	**come si arriva ad un centro commerciale**	*koh*-meh see ahr-*ree*-vah ahd oon *chehn*-troh kohm-mehr-*chah*-leh
the best place for shopping	**il posto migliore per fare compere**	eel *pohs*-toh meel-*lyoh*-reh pehr *fah*-reh *kohm*-peh-reh
how to get downtown	come si arriva in centro	*koh*-meh see ahr-*ree*-vah een *chehn*-troh
Where can I find a . . .	**Dove trovo . . .**	*doh*-veh *troh*-voh
antiques shop	**un negozio di antichità**	oon neh-*goh*-tsyoh dee ahn-tee-kee-*tah*
bookstore	**una libreria**	*oo*-nah lee-breh-*ree*-ah
cigar shop	**un tabaccaio**	oon tah-bahk-*kah*-yoh
clothing store for men/women/children	**un negozio di abbigliamento per uomo/donna/bambini**	oon neh-*goh*-tsyoh dee ahb-beel-lyah-*mehn*-toh pehr *woh*-moh/*dohn*-nah/bahm-*bee*-nee
designer fashion shop	**una boutique di moda firmata**	*oo*-nah boutique dee *moh*-dah feer-*mah*-tah
jewelry store	**una gioielleria**	*oo*-nah joh-yehl-leh-*ree*-ah
shoe store	**un negozio di scarpe**	oon neh-*goh*-tsyoh dee *skahr*-peh
souvenir shop	**un negozio di souvenir**	oon neh-*goh*-tsyoh dee souvenir
stationery store	**una cartoleria**	*oo*-nah kahr-toh-leh-*ree*-ah
toy store	**un negozio di giocattoli**	oon neh-*goh*-tsyoh dee joh-*kaht*-toh-lee
vintage clothing store	**un negozio di abiti usati**	oon neh-*goh*-tsyoh dee *ah*-bee-tee oo-*zah*-tee
flea market	**un mercatino delle pulci**	oon mehrkah-*tee*-noh *dehl*-leh *pool*-chee
I'm looking for a size . . .	**Cerco una taglia . . .**	*chehr*-koh *oo*-nah *tahl*-lyah
extra-small	**molto piccola**	*mohl*-toh *peek*-koh-lah
small	**piccola**	*peek*-koh-lah
medium	**media**	*meh*-dyah
large	**grande**	*grahn*-deh
extra-large	**molto grande**	*mohl*-toh *grahn*-deh
I'm looking for . . .	**Cerco . . .**	*chehr*-koh
cashmere	**qualcosa in cashmere**	kwahl-*koh*-zah een cashmere

English	Italian	Pronunciation
a coat	**una giacca**	*oo*-nah *jahk*-kah
cotton pants	**dei pantaloni di cotone**	day pahn-tah-*loh*-nee dee koh-*toh*-neh
a hat	**un cappello/berretto**	oon kahp-*pehl*-loh/behr-*reht*-toh
a silk blouse	**una camicia di seta**	oo-nah kah-*mee*-chah dee *seh*-tah
socks	**dei calzini**	day kahl-*tsee*-nee
sunglasses	**degli occhiali da sole**	*dehl*-lyee *ohk*-kyah-lee dah *soh*-leh
sweaters	**delle maglie**	*dehl*-leh *mahl*-lyeh
a swimsuit	**un costume da bagno**	oon kohs-*too*-meh dah *bahn*-nyoh
underwear	**della biancheria intima**	*dehl*-lah byahn-keh-*ree*-ah een-tee-mah
May I try it on?	**Posso provarlo?**	*pohs*-soh proh-*vahr*-loh
Where can I try this on?	**Dove posso provarlo?**	*doh*-veh *pohs*-soh proh-*vahr*-loh
This is . . .	**Questo è . . .**	*kwehs*-toh *eh*
too tight	**troppo stretto**	*trohp*-poh *streht*-toh
too loose	**troppo largo**	*trohp*-poh *lahr*-goh
too long	**troppo lungo**	*trohp*-poh *loon*-goh
too short	**troppo corto**	*trohp*-poh *kohr*-toh
This fits great!	**È perfetto!**	*eh* pehr-*feht*-toh
Thanks, I'll take it.	**Grazie, lo prendo.**	*grah*-tsyeh loh *prehn*-doh
Do you have that in . . .	**Ce l'ha in . . .**	cheh *lah* een
a smaller/larger size	**una taglia più piccola/grande**	oo-nah *tahl*-lya *pyoo* peek-*koh*-lah/*grahn*-deh
a different color	**un altro colore**	oon *ahl*-troh koh-*loh*-reh
How much is it?	**Quanto costa?**	*kwahn*-toh *kohs*-tah
Is there a craft/artisan market?	**C'è un mercato di artigianato?**	ch-*eh* oon mehr-*kah*-toh dee ahr-tee-jah-*nah*-toh
That's beautiful. May I look at it?	**Che bello. Posso vederlo?**	keh *behl*-loh *pohs*-soh veh-*dehr*-loh
When is the farmers' market open?	Quando apre il mercato di frutta e verdura?	*kwahn*-doh *ah*-preh eel mehr-*kah*-toh dee *froot*-tah eh vehr-*doo*-rah
Is that open every day of the week?	**È aperto tutti i giorni della settimana?**	eh ah-*pehr*-toh *toot*-tee ee *johr*-nee *dehl*-lah seht-tee-*mah*-nah
How much does that cost?	**Quanto costa?**	*kwahn*-toh *kohs*-tah
That's too expensive.	**È troppo caro.**	eh *trohp*-poh *kah*-roh
How much for two?	**Quanto per due?**	*kwahn*-toh pehr *doo*-eh
Do I get a discount if I buy two or more?	**Mi fa lo sconto se ne compro due o più?**	mee fah loh *skohn*-toh seh neh *kohm*-proh *doo*-eh oh *pyoo*
Do I get a discount if I pay in cash?	**Mi fa lo sconto se pago in contanti?**	mee fah loh *skohn*-toh she *pah*-goh een kohn-*tahn*-tee
No thanks. Maybe I'll come back.	**No grazie. Magari torno.**	noh *grah*-tsyeh mah-*gah*-ree *tohr*-noh
Would you take euros?	**Vanno bene euro?**	*vahn*-noh *beh*-neh *eh*-oo-roh

English	Italian	Pronunciation
That's a deal!	**Affare fatto!**	ahf-*fah*-reh *faht*-toh
Do you have a less expensive one?	**Ne ha uno meno caro?**	neh ah oo-noh *meh*-no *kah*-roh
Is there VAT tax?	**C'è l'IVA?**	ch-*eh lee*-vah
May I have the VAT forms? (Europe only)	**Posso avere un modulo per il rimborso dell'IVA?**	*pohs*-soh ah-*veh*-reh oon *moh*-doo-loh pehr eel reem-*bohr*-soh dehl-*lee*-vah
Is there a _____ nearby?	**C'è _____ qui vicino?**	ch-*eh* _____ kwee vee-*chee*-noh
bookstore	**una libreria**	*oo*-nah lee-breh-*ree*-ah
newsstand	**un'edicola**	oon-eh-*dee*-koh-lah
Do you have _____ in English?	**Avete _____ in inglese?**	ah-*veh*-teh _____ een een-*gleh*-seh
books	**libri**	*lee*-bree
books about local history	**libri di storia locale**	*lee*-bree dee *stoh*-ryah loh-*kah*-leh
magazines	**riviste**	ree-*vees*-teh
maps	**cartine**	kahr-*tee*-neh
newspapers	**giornali**	johr-*nah*-lee
picture books	**libri illustrati**	*lee*-bree eel-loos-*trah*-tee
travel guides	**guide turistiche**	*gwee*-deh too-*rees*-tee-keh
Can I play this in the U.S.?	**Funziona questo negli Stati Uniti?**	foon-*tsyoh*-nah *kwehs*-toh *nehl*-lyee *stah*-tee oo-*nee*-tee
Will this game work on my game console in the U.S.?	**Questo gioco funziona su una console americana?**	*kwehs*-toh *joh*-koh foon-*tsyoh*-nah soo *oo*-nah kohn-*sohl* ah-meh-ree-*kah*-nah
Do you have this in a U.S. market format?	**C'è questo in formato americano?**	ch-*eh kwehs*-toh een fohr-*mah*-toh ah-meh-ree-*kah*-noh
Can you convert this to a U.S. market format?	**Si può convertire questo in formato americano?**	see *pwoh* kohn-vehr-*tee*-reh *kwehs*-toh een fohr-*mah*-toh ah-meh-ree-*kah*-noh
Will this work with a 110V AC adaptor?	**Questo funziona con un adattatore da 110 volt?**	*kwehs*-toh foon-*tsyoh*-nah kohn oon ah-daht-tah-*toh*-reh dah *chehn*-toh-*dyeh*-chee volt
Do you have an adaptor plug for 110 to 220 volts?	**Avete un adattatore da 110 a 220 volt?**	Ah-*veh*-teh oon ah-daht-tah-*toh*-reh dah *chehn*-toh-*dyeh*-chee ah doo-eh-*chehn*-toh-*vehn*-tee volt
Do you sell electronic adaptors here?	**Vendete adattatori per sistemi elettronici?**	vehn-*deh*-teh ah-daht-tah-*toh*-ree pehr sees-*teh*-mee eh-leht-*troh*-nee-chee
Is it safe to use my laptop with this adaptor?	**Posso usare il computer portatile con questo adattatore?**	*pohs*-soh oo-*zah*-reh eel computer pohr-*tah*-tee-leh kohn *kwehs*-toh ah-daht-tah-*toh*-reh
If it doesn't work, may I return it?	**Se non funziona, posso portarlo indietro?**	seh nohn foon-*tsyoh*-nah *pohs*-soh pohr-*tahr*-loh een-*dyeh*-troh
May I try it here in the store?	**Posso provarlo qui in negozio?**	*pohs*-soh proh-*vahr*-loh kwee een neh-*goh*-tsyoh

ARCHITECTURAL TERMS

Ambon A pulpit, either serpentine or simple in form, erected in an Italian church.

Apse The half-rounded extension behind the main altar of a church; Christian tradition dictates that it be placed at the eastern end of an Italian church, the side closest to Jerusalem.

Atrium A courtyard, open to the sky, in an ancient Roman house; the term also applies to the courtyard nearest the entrance of an early Christian church.

Baldachin (also ciborium) A columned stone canopy, usually placed above the altar of a church; also spelled *baldaquin* in English.

Baptistery A separate building or a separate area in a church where the rite of baptism is held.

Basilica Any rectangular public building, usually divided into three aisles by rows of columns. In ancient Rome, this architectural form was frequently used for places of public assembly and law courts; later, Roman Christians adapted the form for many of their early churches.

Caldarium The steam room of a Roman bath.

Campanile A bell tower, often detached, of a church.

Capital The top of a column, often carved and usually categorized into one of three orders: Doric, Ionic, or Corinthian.

Castrum A carefully planned Roman military camp, whose rectangular form, straight streets, and systems of fortified gates became standardized throughout the empire; modern cities that began as Roman camps and still more or less maintain their original forms include Chester (England), Barcelona (Spain), and such Italian cities as Lucca, Aosta, Como, Brescia, Florence, and Ancona.

Cavea The curved row of seats in a classical theater; the most prevalent shape was that of a semicircle.

Cella The sanctuary, or most sacred interior section, of a Roman pagan temple.

Chancel Section of a church containing the altar.

Cornice The decorative flange defining the uppermost part of a classical or neoclassical facade.

Cortile Courtyard or cloisters ringed with a gallery of arches or lintels set atop columns.

Crypt A church's main burial place, usually below the choir.

Cupola A dome.

Duomo Cathedral.

Forum The main square and principal gathering place of any Roman town, usually adorned with the city's most important temples and civic buildings.

Grotesques Carved and painted faces, deliberately ugly, used by everyone from the Etruscans to the architects of the Renaissance; they're especially amusing when set into fountains.

Hypogeum Subterranean burial chambers, usually of pre-Christian origins.

Loggia Roofed balcony or gallery.

Lozenge An elongated four-sided figure that, along with stripes, was one of the distinctive signs of the architecture of Pisa.

Narthex The anteroom, or enclosed porch, of a Christian church.

Nave The largest and longest section of a church, usually devoted to sheltering or seating worshipers and often divided by aisles.

Palazzo A palace or other important building.

Piano Nobile The main floor of a palazzo (sometimes the second floor).

Pietra Dura Richly ornate assemblage of semiprecious stones mounted on a flat decorative surface, perfected during the 1600s in Florence.

Pieve A parish church.

Portico A porch, usually crafted from wood or stone.

Pulvin A four-sided stone that serves as a substitute for the capital of a column, often decoratively carved, sometimes into biblical scenes.

Putti Plaster cherubs whose chubby forms often decorate the interiors of baroque chapels and churches.

Stucco Colored plaster composed of sand, powdered marble, water, and lime, either molded into statuary or applied in a thin concretelike layer to the exterior of a building.

Telamon Structural column carved into a standing male form; female versions are called *caryatids*.

Thermae Roman baths.

Transenna Stone (usually marble) screen separating the altar area from the rest of an early Christian church.

Travertine The stone from which ancient and Renaissance Rome was built, it's known for its hardness, light coloring, and tendency to be pitted or flecked with black.

Tympanum The half-rounded space above the portal of a church, whose semicircular space usually showcases a sculpture.

MENU TERMS

Abbacchio Roast haunch or shoulder of lamb baked and served in a casserole and sometimes flavored with anchovies.

Agnolotti A crescent-shaped pasta shell stuffed with a mix of chopped meat, spices, vegetables, and cheese; when prepared in rectangular versions, the same combination of ingredients is identified as ravioli.

Amaretti Crunchy, sweet almond-flavored macaroons.

Anguilla alla veneziana Eel cooked in a sauce made from tuna and lemon.

Antipasti Succulent tidbits served at the beginning of a meal (before the pasta), whose ingredients might include slices of cured meats, seafood (especially shellfish), and cooked and seasoned vegetables.

Aragosta Lobster.

Arrosto Roasted meat.

Baccalà Dried and salted codfish.

Bagna cauda Hot and well-seasoned sauce, heavily flavored with anchovies, designed for dipping raw vegetables; literally translated as "hot bath."

Bistecca alla fiorentina Florentine-style steaks, coated before grilling with olive oil, pepper, lemon juice, salt, and parsley.

Bocconcini Veal layered with ham and cheese, and then fried.

Bollito misto Assorted boiled meats served on a single platter.

Braciola Pork chop.

Bresaola Air-dried spiced beef.

Bruschetta Toasted bread, heavily slathered with olive oil and garlic and often topped with tomatoes.

Bucatini Thick, hollow spaghetti.

Busecca alla milanese Tripe (beef stomach) flavored with herbs and vegetables.

Cacciucco alla livornese Seafood stew.

Calzone Pizza dough rolled with the chef's choice of sausage, tomatoes, cheese, and so on, and then baked into a kind of savory turnover.

Cannelloni Tubular dough stuffed with meat, cheese, or vegetables and then baked in a creamy white sauce.

Cappellacci alla ferrarese Pasta stuffed with pumpkin.

Cappelletti Small ravioli ("little hats") stuffed with meat or cheese.

Carciofi Artichokes.

Carpaccio Thin slices of raw cured beef, sometimes in a piquant sauce.

Cassata alla siciliana A richly caloric dessert that combines layers of sponge cake, sweetened ricotta cheese, and candied fruit, bound together with chocolate butter-cream icing.

Cervello al burro nero Brains in black-butter sauce.

Cima alla genovese Baked filet of veal rolled into a tube-shaped package containing eggs, mushrooms, and sausage.

Coppa Cured morsels of pork filet encased in sausage skins, served in slices.

Costoletta alla milanese Veal cutlet dredged in bread crumbs, fried, and sometimes flavored with cheese.

Cozze Mussels.

Fagioli White beans.

Fave Fava beans.

Fegato alla veneziana Thinly sliced calves' liver fried with salt, pepper, and onions.

Focaccia Similar to pizza and eaten both *semplice* (with nothing on top but a bit of salt) as well as garnished with everything you can think of.

Fontina Rich cow's-milk cheese.

Frittata Italian omelet.

Fritto misto A deep-fried medley of whatever small fish, shellfish, and squid are available (with the exception of Piedmont where a fritto misto is traditionally a mix of fried beef innards).

Fusilli Spiral-shaped pasta.

Gelato (produzione propria) Ice cream (homemade).

Gnocchi Dumplings usually made from potatoes *(gnocchi di patate)* or from semolina *(gnocchi alla romana),* often stuffed with combinations of cheese, spinach, vegetables, or whatever combinations strike the chef's fancy.

Gorgonzola One of the most famous blue-veined cheeses of Europe—strong, creamy, and aromatic.

Grana Padano Hard cheese similar to Parmesan, but less flavorful, less aged (and less expensive).

Granita Flavored ice, usually with lemon or coffee.

Insalata di frutti di mare Seafood salad (usually including shrimp and squid) garnished with pickles, lemon, olives, and spices.

Involtini Thinly sliced beef, veal, or pork, rolled, stuffed (can be roasted, baked, sometimes fried).

Minestrone A rich and savory vegetable soup usually sprinkled with grated parmigiano and studded with noodles.

Mortadella Mild pork sausage, fashioned into large cylinders and served sliced; the original lunchmeat bologna (because its most famous center of production is Bologna).

Mozzarella A nonfermented cheese, made from the fresh milk of a buffalo (or, if unavailable, from a cow), boiled, and then kneaded into a rounded ball, served fresh.

Mozzarella con pomodori (also caprese) Fresh tomatoes with fresh mozzarella, basil, pepper, and olive oil.

Nervetti A northern Italian antipasto made from chewy pieces of calves' foot or shin.

Osso buco Beef or veal knuckle slowly braised until the cartilage is tender and then served with a highly flavored sauce.

Pancetta Herb-flavored pork belly, rolled into a cylinder and sliced—the Italian bacon.

Panettone Sweet yellow-colored bread with candied fruits that is eaten around Christmas time.

Panna Heavy cream.

Pansotti Pasta stuffed with greens, herbs, and cheeses, usually served with a walnut sauce.

Pappardelle alle lepre Super-wide fettuccine with wild hare sauce.

Parmigiano Parmesan, a hard, aged yellow cheese usually grated over pastas and soups but also eaten alone; the official name is Parmigiano-Reggiano.

Peperoni Green, yellow, or red sweet peppers (not to be confused with pepperoni).

Pesce al cartoccio Fish baked in a parchment envelope with onions, parsley, and herbs.

Pesto A flavorful green sauce made from basil leaves, Parmesan and pecorino cheese, garlic, and pine nuts.

Piccata di vitello al Marsala Thin escalope of veal braised in a pungent sauce flavored with Marsala wine.

Piselli al prosciutto Peas with strips of ham.

Pizza Specific varieties include *capricciosa* (its ingredients can vary widely, depending on the chef's culinary vision and the ingredients at hand), *margherita* (with tomato sauce, mozzarella, fresh basil, and memories of the first queen of Italy, Marguerite di Savoia, in whose honor it was first made by a Neapolitan chef), *napoletana* (with capers, tomatoes, oregano, mozzarella, and the distinctive taste of anchovies), *quattro stagioni* (translated as "four seasons" because the pizza is divided into four distinct areas, each with a differing set of toppings), and *siciliana* (with black olives, capers, and mozzarella).

Pizzaiola A process in which something (usually a beefsteak) is covered in a tomato-and-oregano sauce.

Polenta Thick porridge or mush made from cornmeal flour.

Polenta e coniglio Rabbit stew served with polenta.

Pollo alla cacciatora Chicken with tomatoes and mushrooms cooked in wine.

Pollo alla diavola Highly spiced grilled chicken.

Ragù Meat sauce.

Ricotta A soft bland cheese made from cow's or sheep's milk.

Do's & Don'ts

Italians measure foodstuffs by the kilogram or smaller 100g unit (**ettogrammo** abbreviated to *etto,* equivalent to just under 4 oz.). **Pizzerie al taglio** (pizza slice shops) generally run on this system, but hand gestures can suffice. A good server poises the knife, then asks for approval before cutting. **Più** (*pyoo*) is "more," **meno** (*meh-noh*) "less." **Basta** (*bahs-tah*) means "enough." To express "half" of something, say **mezzo** (*mehd-*zoh).

Risotto Italian rice dish that comes in many varieties.

Risotto alla milanese Risotto made with saffron.

Salsa verde "Green sauce," made from capers, anchovies, lemon juice and/or vinegar, and parsley.

Saltimbocca Veal scallop layered with prosciutto and sage; its name literally translates as "jump in your mouth," a reference to its tart and savory flavor.

Salvia Sage.

Scaloppina alla Valdostana Escalope of veal stuffed with cheese and ham.

Scaloppine Thin slices of veal coated in flour and sautéed in butter.

Semifreddo A frozen dessert; usually ice cream with sponge cake.

Seppia Cuttlefish (a kind of squid); its black ink is used for flavoring in certain sauces for pasta and also in risotto dishes.

Sogliola Sole.

Spaghetti A long, round, thin pasta, variously served: *alla bolognese* (with ground meat, mushrooms, peppers, and so on), *alla carbonara* (with bacon, black pepper, and eggs), *al pomodoro* (with tomato sauce), *al sugo/ragù* (with meat sauce), and *alle vongole* (with clam sauce).

Spiedini Pieces of meat grilled on a skewer over an open flame.

Strozzapreti Small nuggets of pasta, usually served with sauce; the name is literally translated as "priest-choker."

Stufato Beef braised in white wine with vegetables.

Tagliatelle Flat egg noodles.

Tonno Tuna.

Tortelli Pasta dumplings stuffed with ricotta and greens.

Tortellini Rings of dough stuffed with minced and seasoned meat, and served either in soups or as a full-fledged pasta covered with sauce.

Trenette Thin noodles served with pesto sauce and potatoes.

Trippe alla fiorentina Beef tripe (stomach).

Vermicelli Very thin spaghetti.

Vitello tonnato Cold sliced veal covered with tuna-fish sauce.

Zabaglione/zabaione Egg yolks whipped into the consistency of a custard, flavored with Marsala, and served warm as a dessert.

Zampone Pigs' feet stuffed with spicy seasoned port, boiled and sliced.

Zuccotto A liqueur-soaked sponge cake, molded into a dome and layered with chocolate, nuts, and whipped cream.

Zuppa inglese Sponge cake or lady fingers soaked in liqueur and covered in custard and chocolate cream.

INDEX

See also Accommodations and Restaurant indexes, below.

Accommodations

Restaurants

PHOTO CREDITS

Studies in Theology and Sexuality, 5

The Good News of the Body

of the

Sexual Theology and Feminism

Edited by Lisa Isherwood

Sheffield
Academic Press

Published by Sheffield Academic Press Ltd
Mansion House
19 Kingfield Road
Sheffield S11 9AS
England

Printed on acid-free paper in Great Britain
by Bookcraft Ltd
Midsomer Norton, Bath

British Library Cataloguing in Publication Data

A catalogue record for this book is available
from the British Library

♠

ISBN   1-84127-129-2 cl
1-84127-130-6 pbk

CONTENTS

CONTRIBUTORS

Marcella Althaus-Reid, Lecturer, University of Edinburgh, Edinburgh

Beverley Clack, Senior Lecturer, Roehampton Institute of Higher Education, London

Lisa Isherwood, Senior Lecturer, College of St Mark and St John, Plymouth

Grace Jantzen, John Rylands Professor, University of Manchester, Manchester

Melissa Raphael, Senior Lecturer, Cheltenham and Gloucester College of Higher Education, Cheltenham

Lallene Rector, Lecturer, Garrett Evangelical Seminary, Evanston, Illinois

Rosemary Radford Ruether, Georgina Harkness Professor, Garrett Evangelical Seminary, Evanston, Illinois

Elizabeth Stuart, Professor of Christian Theology, King Alfred's College, Winchester

Adrian Thatcher, Professor of Applied Theology, College of St Mark and St John, Plymouth

Alison Webster, Social Responsibility Officer, Worcester

Foreplay: Stirrings Around the Hetero-patriarchal
Narrative of our Time[*]

'Are we having sex yet?' was the vexed question that many a Catholic adolescent asked themselves, but rarely each other, as they tiptoed through those confusing years of raging hormones, heaving flesh and moral absolutes. What exactly was allowed and how many Hail Mary's would be required to rectify transgression was a matter of great importance during my Catholic influenced upbringing. Perhaps it is this background that makes me ponder this question at all. Although what constitutes sex in our society and who decides is a rather more complex question than in my youth. This is graphically illustrated by the conviction with which the President of the United States assured us he had not had sex with 'that woman'. I feel sure that in his own mind, and the minds of many men, he had not. However, in the innocent days of my youth it was father who decided and who made everything alright in the end—for the not *so* bad. He defined the edges of one's sexual world and there were times we were glad of it because it took away our responsibility and placed us in a framework of life that offered us security and showed us how things should be and what our place was. Nevertheless, it also made us unhappy and confused because it did not speak to us in the way our bodies did. Now there's the catch: it was not our story but it told our lives. It told them in large part before we even lived them. Had we had the words we would have understood this to be an early implanting of the patriarchal narrative that cites authority and excludes autonomy. We would have understood that our embodiment was to be bent to conform to absolutes and male normative patterns. However, we did not and so we tried to live within the rules that others set. We did not see the whole picture and so we missed the significance

[*]   I am using the word in its patriarchal context, that is by assuming that the real thing comes next, this is just a warm-up!

of our piece of the jigsaw, we just thought that we were either good or bad, we had no idea that other thoughts were possible and good at the same time. Does this sound familiar?

Over the centuries, Catholicism has generated libraries of books dedicated to the appropriate penances for various acts of intimacy. A Vatican committee even debated for eight years whether a marriage is considered consummated if a condom is used. The consensus seems to be that ejaculation into and not within a vagina makes a woman a wife. Here we find a hint of the power of the hetero-patriarchal narrative, it is the penis and the 'divine fluid' (according to Aquinas) that flows from it that has the power to transform a female from girl to woman to wife. Indeed, under British law even into adulterer since it is only the act of penetration that constitutes adultery. It has been said that women are wholly defined in relation to men, although I would like to redefine this and say rather, in relation to penises, since we are not defined in relation to those men whose penises have no interest in us, namely gay men. Gay men themselves suffer 'penis definition' since those who receive one are lower down the male contempt list then those who insert one. This is a powerful organ indeed, or so the story goes! All real women are dying for one, all good Christian women refuse one until after marriage and all real men know how to use one for power and influence in the world. The penis decides if a woman is a wife, frigid, lesbian, a tease, adulteress or whether a man is a faggott. The lack of one means that women can not be priested in the Catholic Church. The penis is used in war to emphasize victory and to humiliate the loser. Evidence is emerging of rape being used as a means of cultural genocide in Bosnia. While in Pristina boxes of condoms were found in police stations next to knuckle dusters, what are we to understand by this? It seems that the message is clear: the penis can terrorise, torture and kill. This is a strange but powerful narrative.

It is a narrative that penetrates most areas of life. Even Freud told women that it is their lack of castration anxiety that makes them immoral and dysfunctional human beings. It is only a penis and fear of losing it that can incline persons to moral virtue. Certainly the Church Fathers shared the view that it was only possession of a penis that made a person truly moral. Women, on the other hand, due to their different anatomy, are sexually insatiable and therefore prone to witchcraft (isn't the logic wonderful?). It was this insatiable desire for a penis that led women to reduce men to animals who had lost their reason and their spiritual enlightenment, or caused women to castrate men with a glance and store the removed organs in birds' nests—presumably for later use! Modern day Freudians assure us that our desire for a penis, hence why witches cut them off, is to do with the power they represent rather than the joy they bring. (We know we have to be men if we are to be taken seriously.) This is an even more chilling statement since it describes a narrative that is in no small measure correct, that those with a penis do, in fact, have power even in these liberated times.

This is sadly true in relation to women's bodies. We have been led to believe that the sexual revolution has freed us, but are we simply free to live out the hetero-patriarchal narrative more fully? Has our desire been taken seriously or have our bodies just been made more accessible? Certainly Sheila Jeffreys concludes that the sexual revolution is nothing but an anticlimax for women, there is no more freedom or pleasure to be found and therefore no more embodied empowerment.[1] Do we then, in fact have the freedom to write a new script? I fear that a script is even difficult to think under the weight of our present circumstances. There is very little language that we can use that is not imbued with phallocentric meaning.[2] Indeed, the picture is much worse if we are to believe Elisabeth Grosz who suggests that the dominance of the penis in the world in which we live and the sexual discourses we are shaped by makes women's sexual organs appear to be an absence.[3] This in turn signifies a lack of autonomy, because the female body is always imaged as lacking and therefore in some sense unworthy. If this is to be reversed then women have to challenge the discourses that claim to explain and analyse the body, such as biology, sociology and psychology. Further, we have to reframe the terms in which the female body is socially represented. No easy task when our knowledge and our language are situated in other bodies than our own.

If sex in our society is to do with the penis and the power it has to define, then women have a further question to answer: 'Who are we when we are having sex?'. If we are passive receivers are we even in a position to claim agency to answer that question? Missionary position

---

1. Sheila Jeffreys, *Anticlimax: A Feminist Perspective on the Sexual Revolution* (London: Women's Press, 1990).

2. See, for example, Luce Irigaray, *This Sex Which is Not One* (Ithaca, NY: Cornell University Press, 1985).

3. Elisabeth Grosz, *Volatile Bodies: Toward a Corporeal Feminism* (Bloomington: Indiana University Press, 1994), p. x.

sex gives us a clear picture of our place in society and it is no accident
that the stricter the Christian observance the more this position is insisted upon. For example, it is the only legal position in the Bible Belt
states in America, since it reinforces in an embodied way unequal complimentarity implicit in the Genesis narrative. This implicit inequality is
drawn out by the rabbis when telling us of Lillith, the first wife of
Adam. They claim that it was her refusal to adopt the missionary
position that led to her being cast into the wilderness and a new model
made. Her reasoning was sound, she was an equal partner in creation
and was not to be pinned almost immobile on the receiving end of
sexual power. She argued for equality, side by side and face to face.
This did not find favour with Adam, who feared he would become im-
potent, or with God, and so she was banished. The new wife, while
coming from the side of Adam, was to know her place, under him.
While Christians have not had the Lillith story to inform them they
have taken the post-lapsarian curse uttered by God as a directive.
Woman will desire her husband and he will rule over her (Gen. 3.16).
This, it is argued, is best illustrated through missionary position sex.
The position most likely to emphasize duty, not pleasure, since it is the
least likely to enable women's orgasm.

Are we women, then, purveyors of a grand narrative that we had no
part in shaping or are we a threat that needs controlling and taming, the
shrew who will rip the balls off patriarchy if given half a chance?
Perhaps we are the outlaw dyke who as yet has no narrative to call her
own let alone a meta one—God forbid! Or are we the small child who
has no words to describe what is happening to her...she is confused
because daddy is telling her it should feel good, but it doesn't...and she
is silent.

Are we having sex yet? Language has not yet been found that can
give voice to an answer and embolden the writing of a new script. So
we have to find a language, a way to move us to the deeply felt but the
not yet actualized. Women have first to hear their bodies without the
deadening silencer of the patriarchal script intervening and reversing
reality for the sake of normality and life as it really is. Reflection on
these lived experiences will allow women to see most clearly since it is
the same bodies which have borne the weight of the metanarrative until
each sinew screams or is deadened by the crushing weight of it. Even
the language of the body is hard to hear as it has been silenced by generations of theology, philosophy and latterly sexology—male experts

declaring the reality of women's bodies, placing a deep distrust not only in the male psyche but also that of women. The 'easy answers' that Father had to hand are now at best looking suspicious and at worst they make no connection with the complex labyrinth of feeling and empowerment that *is* the reality of a woman's body. Why was Father so keen to give advice that made one feel like an alien in one's own skin? To conclude that he was simply finding fulfillment for his own chained desires is too easy an answer and one that does not take seriously enough the question of his own bondage.

It is important to me to find answers that spring from and reflect my own religious tradition, one that is rooted in incarnational theology. Indeed, it is necessary that a religion that throbs with incarnational redemption should at last release its followers from the prison of their own skins that the traditions have made. It seems that incarnational theology speaks of a world that experiences *metanoia*, is turned round, through the skin. God herself took flesh in order that this process might become embedded in fleshy reality. How then is it that we have imagined that disembodied spiritual perfection is the way to make of this earth a heaven, the incarnate dwelling-place of the divine? What has gone wrong is not the subject of this book. Here authors try to imagine other ways. [4]

However, if the body is as important in the process of redemption as the Christian faith has said it is then our task is to declare the good news of the body. After all, the man Jesus, while being declared divine, was also portrayed as a very earthy man. A man who made strong political statements through the powerful symbolism of touch and feeding. He touched the most untouchable in a society, not unlike our own, which had very entrenched ideas about insiders and outsiders and through so doing challenged the status quo and gave strength and healing to those as oppressed by the system as by their illness. In both the feeding of the thousands and the symbolic actions of the last meal he shared Jesus made embodied political points. When all share there is enough for all and when that sharing is a sign of radical equality it becomes a subversive symbol in a world where some are more equal than others. Once the eucharist is stripped of the comfortable metaphysics that have grown around it, and the sanitized host is replaced by

---

4. See Lisa Isherwood and Elisabeth Stuart, *Introducing Body Theology* (Introductions in Feminist Theology, 2; Sheffield: Sheffield Academic Press, 1998), for more on this.

the equal sharing of life-sustaining 'real' bread placed in the empty bellies of 80 per cent of the world's population, then the power of embodied action (incarnation) is made manifest.

It seems that flesh, which was once important in the finding and living of the divine has been swamped by the Word and made silent or is now seen as rebellious. The Church Fathers who were so concerned with church order were right to be concerned about the body and control over it. In seeking to develop and sustain a hierarchical structure they did well to recognize that once bodies are controlled then societies can be tightly regulated. Bodies know more deeply than minds alone and so once people are taught to doubt their body knowing and see their embodiment as something to be overcome the ground work is laid for tight control. It is this denial of the body that has ultimately led to the genocidal reality of advanced capitalism among other atrocities. However, once the body is placed at the centre of theological reflection, rather than the disembodied Word, then the starving and battered bodies of oppressed people demand that new ways are found. Their flesh becomes word, bodies become the incarnational starting point for liberating/redemptive praxis.[5]

How would this look if women's bodies were the incarnational starting point for sexual/body politics? Bodies free, integrated and celebratory of the divine power that courses through the veins and pulsates in every cell. Free from the patriarchal rhetoric that allows only half truths. Free to subvert cultures and religions and speak a new language—of exploration and joy, not breeding and control.

The Book

This collection of essays attempts to provide some ways forward in body/sexual politics. It does not touch other equally important areas such as employment, capitalism and so on. It is, of course, even with a limited brief, a very partial answer, since there are many missing from this book who, in the ideal world, should be here. There is no Womanist voice (the authors both had to withdraw at the last moment), no Muslim, Hindu, Buddhist voice and no voice from the furthest margin of all, that of sado-masochism (although Alison Webster does touch on the subject). At best then, this collection is a start, one thread in the

---

5.   See more of this argument in Lisa Isherwood, *Liberating Christ* (Cleveland, OH: Pilgrim Press, 1999).

quilt. Thankfully feminist theology illuminates the fact that the time is over of 'definitive' works that tie up all the theological ends and provide authoritative guidance in all matters. The theological landscape is shifting and varied and very hard to pin down as this volume shows through its omissions as well as its inclusions.

In 'Sex and Body Politics' I attempt to frame the problem through an examination of some of the vast array of material available on the subject of the body. Unfortunately, it appears that the academic theory is underpinned by the lived experience of women and it is this that provides the resource for feminist theological reflection. During the course of compiling this book I was reminded that I 'tell horror stories' when discussing my work. On reflection, this is not because I am a particularly gruesome or depressed person but because much of the reality of women's lives reads like a horror story. This is very different from dwelling on victims and I hope it is clear that women are not innocent victims, we are simply situated differently in a patriarchal world. As this is one that values all that we naturally are not, there is bound to be tension and pain. My article attempts to highlight some of the tensions and to suggest ways ahead. In 'Sex in the Catholic Tradition' Rosemary Ruether traces the relationship that the Catholic Church has with sexuality and shows that it is far more complex than many would suppose. She advocates a new *ars erotica*, an unrestrained celebration of sexuality which would bring together the three aspects of Christian love: eros, philia and agape. The church, she thinks, should teach young people, perhaps through the medium of ritual not just dogma, to delight in their sexuality and understand it as a process. In other words it is unreasonable to suppose that people can be virgins one day and married for the rest of their lives the next. Here is a voice of sanity amidst the hysterical babble of catholic sexual teaching. In 'Refresh me with Apples for I am Faint with Love' Melissa Raphael takes us on a wonderful journey through Jewish sexual and mystical teaching. She warns us not to be fooled by the Jewish call for sexual pleasure as on examination this is seen in male terms. She believes that liberation of Jewish women as subjects of their own sexual experience and the liberation of God as divine subject are a single process. Raphael calls us to celebrate the Jewish mystical traditions, the understanding of shekinah restored to God and the world through sexual union, a union that involves covenanted love and a seeing and knowing of the other as the portrait of God.

Lallene Rector begins the section on women's power with a sobering look at how we are at times compliant in our own oppression, how we are in bondage to wrong relation. By exploring the work of Benjamin, Chodorow and others she shows how social patterns of child-rearing lead to male domination. Issues of separation, self-assertion and recognizing the other are all key early years matters and we often foster patterns that do not lead to the best outcomes. The problem for women is difficulty in experiencing their own subjectivity, including sexual subjectivity, which often leads to women 'giving it all away', that is being passive receivers of whatever relationships throw at them. Just in case we were all concluding that such problems do not occur for lesbians Alison Webster sounds a note of caution. Her article looks at the ways in which power has been understood to date in lesbian and feminist analyses of lesbian sexuality and she examines how this is worked out in terms of difference. She is concerned to avoid any glorifying of lesbian relationships but also keen to show that the differences when worked on and understood as a hard won process have much to offer in the arena of sexual politics. Webster looks at SM and butch/femme role-playing as she guides the reader to an awareness of how power works and how it may be reimaged. In 'Human Sexuality and the Concept of the Goddess' Beverley Clack reminds us that images of the divine are not 'drawn from nowhere' and along with Lacan considers that they have sprung from male reflections on their bodies. She sets out to reflect upon the female body and asserts that this will give us a different, and probably more cosmos friendly, image of the divine. Clack is not advocating an essentialist and polarized view of men and women but is rather challenging the entire picture and appealing for a more fluid approach to our understanding of sexuality, bodies, the world and the divine. Is it a tall order? All it takes is a change of mind.

In the third section Adrian Thatcher looks at the views of feminists and popes on contraception and I examine the possibilities for erotic celibacy as a form of resistance to patriarchy. Thatcher is amazed to find that feminists at times reach the same conclusions as popes but, of course, for very different reasons and via very different routes. He argues that contraception has done nothing to destabilize the 'coital imperative' that can be shown to be harmful to women's health. Indeed, it has 'normalized and routinized' intercourse and therefore made women more available and potentially less empowered. Thatcher acknowledges the massive benefits of available contraception but questions whether this simply increases the exercise of male 'power' on the female body. In 'Erotic Celibacy' I continue the theme of sexual alternatives with an examination of the power of celibacy for women. A look at the history of celibacy shows that there were often very different understandings held by women who lived it. Rather than fleeing from the flesh and the things of the world they were claiming their equality in Christ, which required a withdrawal from patriarchal society. By an examination of feminist Christology and body politics I ask what celibacy might look like today and wonder whether it does provide an erotic empowered space for women.

In section four Elizabeth Stuart considers how disabled bodies have 'queered the pitch' of much theology of embodiment, Grace Jantzen examines pleasure and death in modernity and Marcella Althaus-Reid ponders excessive sex and the crisis of theological representation. Stuart points out that the oppression of disability is not only to do with societal construction of disability but also to do with the pain and limitations of such conditions. Just by changing society we will not overcome the reality. Society tends to de-sex the disabled and so overlook some of the central questions, such as sexual surrogacy, understandings of masculinity and femininity with bodies that do not fit the stereotypes as well as the use of pornography and the part of care workers in the sex lives of the disabled. Stuart examines all these and comes up with thought-provoking reflections. Grace Jantzen takes us back in time to the work of John Donne, who claimed that sex was for pleasure at a time (the early part of the seventeenth century) when the church was declaring it was purely for procreation. Donne's writings show with particular clarity the interplay of religion, culture and gender and it is with reference to them that Jantzen makes her case. She argues that sexual pleasure does not come alone; it is part of the package of secular modernity. As such there are things within it that benefit women and others that do not such as the identification of sex and violence, individualism, economic oppression and a symbolic linkage of sex and death. Marcella Althaus-Reid considers issues of women and divine representation in cultural contexts. She opens with an identification of God as the prostitute Madame Edwarda of the novel of the same name by Georges Bataille. This identification comes from excess orthopraxis, that is, not from generations of rational reflection on the nature of the divine but from an anguished search for meaning. The answer to this is grounded at the margins of poverty and sexuality. Althaus-Reid calls for a theology from mistresses and battered lovers, from lesbian families and prostitutes and declares this to be the only way to move beyond the 'internalized oppression of androcentric theology'. Finally I wonder where all this had led us and how safe sex can be for women in a patriarchal world.

There are many more perceptions of the problems and different situating of the politics of the body than are represented here.[6] This collection, then, has modest claims. It looks from a predominantly, but not exclusively, Christian perspective at sex, religion and issues of visibility and liberating praxis. Its aim is to promote discussion and reflection and to so infuriate people that more will be written on the subject by way of reply. In bringing together the authors that it does this book acts as a place of detonation, not of leadership. It gives a voice, if only a whisper, to women's flesh and some of our sexual realities.

6.   This can be seen more clearly through the work of the Good Sex Project which is looking at the question of women and sexuality from a multi-faith, multi-cultural perspective. Both Grace Jantzen and Mary Hunt are involved in this project.

Part I

WOMEN, SEX AND ESTABLISHED RELIGIONS

SEX AND BODY POLITICS: ISSUES FOR FEMINIST THEOLOGY

Lisa Isherwood

Christians of most denominations can be pushed to exclaim that sex is natural and God given when they are being closely questioned about the perceived tension between the divine and human sexuality. Even at first glance this is not as open a statement as we may think, since it is usually quickly revisited with a number of defining remarks. Sex is only alright in marriage or between two people of the opposite sex and so on. However, these riders are not the subject of this article. Rather what interests me is the inaccuracy of the statement itself. Sex is not a natural matter, it is a highly constructed reality reflecting the power structures of the society in which it resides. It could hardly be any other way, since bodies through which it is both experienced and practised are like sponges which absorb meaning, and 'highly political' meaning at that.[1] Political in the sense that the body is used to regulate and shape society, indeed the body can be used as 'a model for any bounded system'.[2] In this way then, sex is not God given although God has assumed a very significant part in the sex lives of believers. For believers it is God who 'decides' what is blessed and what is cursed in terms of sexual expression and it is the patriarchal God who has sanctioned hierarchical monogamous heterosexuality as the most legitimate form of activity, or so the story goes.

The interplay between religion and society is a complex matter and it is difficult to measure the exact influence of one upon the other. However, it is not too contentious to claim that there is a relationship even in these secular days. I wish to argue that the patriarchal structures that

1. Anthony Synnott, *The Body Social: Symbolism, Self and Society* (London: Routledge, 1997), p. 1.
2. Mary Douglas quoted in Simon J. Williams and Gillian Bendelow, *The Lived Body: Sociological Themes, Embodied Issues* (London: Routledge, 1998), p. 27.

underpin both society and religion feed upon each other and produce patterns of relating that seem to be free and liberated but are in reality narrow and constraining. As a liberation theologian I find this unacceptable and therefore wish to look at the ways in which religion can purge itself of patriarchal assumptions and requirements and issue a radical and transgressive challenge to society. I believe that the challenge can begin with the body and sexuality, since it is in our most intimate space that we can be colonized or liberated. Our bodies and our sexuality are most our own but at the same time are the most taken away by all the edifices of patriarchy, medicine, religion, the law, psychologists, sexologists—the list is endless. Here is a good place to start the revolution!

However, the reality, and therefore the starting point, is that theology, rooted as it is in a mildly erotic sado-masochistic Mills & Boon perception of the post-lapsarian primal pair,[3] has been slow to catch up with the insights of sociology and psychology in the area of sexuality. It prefers to keep its eyes focused on an unequal model of complimentarity, a wayward woman, a seductive snake and the dire consequences. These ingredients when passed through the ages and the lenses of Greek metaphysics, parousial anxiety and patriarchy make a powerful cocktail in the normalizing and divinizing of neurosis, fear and a will to power exercised on and through the female body.

This body becomes the 'other' and bears all the weight of guilt and distrust that men are unable to carry themselves. At times in Christian history the female body becomes the demonic body and everything about it seems charged with evil and corruption. While we have discarded a great deal of our mediaeval past we still resonate with vestiges of our heritage, the female body is still something to be possessed by others, capitalist advertisers if not demons, and is still the cause of the fall of man. Our Christian past lingers on and we still see as natural much of the constructed reality emanating from that mindset. I wish to argue that religions should be powerful forces in freeing us from the bodily constraints that they largely helped to construct and have continued unquestioningly to believe. The circle must be broken.

Feminist theology is not the first to see the body as central in our construction of reality. The Greeks conceived of citizens, cities and the cosmos as built on the same principles. Indeed, from Plato to Hobbes

---

3. By this I mean that we are meant to be unquestioning and happy with the secondary status of the woman whose fulfilment is *her man*.

and through Adam Smith to Luce Irigaray the body has been seen as a means of diagnosis of social and political life. Therefore I am not alone when, as a feminist theologian, I begin with the reality of women's lived experience and ask in what ways the female body is a theatre on which patriarchy is enacted and how those same bodies may become sites of resistance to patriarchy. My starting point is an understanding of the body 'as is' rather than with a theological overlay. This, of course, is no easy matter, despite the popularity of the body in sociological research. The body is everywhere yet agreement about what it is can be hard to come by. That is, beyond a general consensus that it is 'the primordial basis of our being in the world and the discursive product of disciplinary technologies of power/knowledge'.[4] There is very little that is natural about it beyond its fleshy mass and we have to catch it early to even assume that this has no cultural significance. Of course, there is a positive side to this, which is that it cannot be assumed that all future definitions of the body will be patriarchal.

There is not even agreement over how many bodies we have, Mary Douglas declaring we have two while Nancy Scheper-Hughes and Margaret Lock prefer to think of three (Csordas 1997). For Douglas, we have both our physical and our social body; they are, of course, related but the former is often seen through the lense of the latter. Scheper-Hughes and Lock favour three: the individual, which is the lived experience of the body as self; the social, which is a representational use of the body as a symbol of nature; and the political, which involves the regulation and control of the body.[5] It is very clear that what is at stake in the struggle for control over the body is power in social relations. Against this background I wonder if it is helpful to add yet another body to those that make us up, that of the divine body. I do not wish to imply any kind of dualism or metaphysics when I suggest this, since as a feminist theologian I have a far more materialist starting point.[6] This body is the transgressive signifier of radical equality. The body that attempts to subvert the weight of patriarchy upon it through enactment of counter cultural actions. To put it another way, living in the world but not chained by its narrow definitions and hierarchical power sys-

---

4.   Williams and Bendelow, *The Lived Body*, p. 2.

5.   J. Csordas, *Embodiment and Experience: The Existential Ground of Culture and Self* (Cambridge: Cambridge University Press, 1997), pp. 25-27.

6.   See Lisa Isherwood, *Liberating Christ* (Cleveland, OH: Pilgrim Press, 1999), for more on this.

tems, it has a broader vision. The divine body is the grounded, acting, stubborn objection to life as it is. It is this body that theology and religion should be attempting to empower rather than create competing definitions and restrictions for the physical body through emphasis on the virtual reality of the spiritual body. Much of the oppression of the subject is carried out because there seems to be no place to go, no place to stand that is other than the crushing reality of the present. The divine body gives space for the creativity of rebellion to find itself while remaining rooted in life and not fleeing from practical solutions to a place where we can bear it now and it will be better in the end. I acknowledge that many who have held fast to the idea of the spiritual body have also been involved in very practical solutions to crushing problems of oppression but they are in the minority. What happened to the rest?

I have some sympathy with those who advocate a reinvention of the 'old feminist' discourses of the 1960s and 1970s with its categories of oppressor and oppressed. This is not because I wish to place hostility at the heart of the discourse but rather because standing against institutions and technologies makes the struggle that much harder. Where are they located, how do we hit them where it hurts? Of course, I have no desire to make women victims or saints as the oppressed. However, there seems to be a place for naming as oppressive people as well as institutions. Both can be dealt with by the divine body as it charts its transgressive course, naming as false oppressions and oppressors simply by living. This may be an unpopular statement in these postmodern times when values are diverse, but even feminists need to call things wrong. The difference is perhaps that there are broader definitions and shifting boundaries. The difficulty of leaving this in the realm of discourse is beautifully illuminated by the response of one of the prostitutes in the Brock and Thistlethwaite study.[7] When asked what she thought of the draft of the book which used 'discourse' as a central theme her response was, 'it's sex honey, it ain't discourse'.[8] That woman does not have the privilege of using her body as a site of discourse nor does she experience the reality of her life as discourse; it is sex acted out upon her with all the cultural force that her client and society requires.

Location is an important concept for Donna Haraway, who insists

---

7. Rita Brock and Susan Brooks Thistlethwaite, *Casting Stones: Prostitution and Liberation in Asia and the United States* (Minneapolis: Fortress Press, 1996).

8. Brock and Thistlethwaite, *Casting Stones*, p. 228.

that personal or social bodies are not natural in the sense of existing outside human labour. For her the alternative to an essentialized and naturalized body is not relativism but location. In other words, we are all positioned in non-equivalent locations in webs of interconnection.[9] This makes us aware of what we do not know and the partial nature of many of our connections and much of our knowledge. While I have no desire to descend into essentialism I am not convinced that location alone solves the problem. After all the fact remains that we are located as females in a patriarchal society and while that does differ from culture to culture and situation to situation there are certain constants. However, even if that were not the case an understanding of experience as more than my privatized world necessitates that I take the situations of other women seriously when assessing patriarchy. Starting with experience will relativize, and to some degree trivialize, if we do not grasp that the edge of our skin is not the end of our experience. As a woman what happens beyond it, to other women, affects me, as a woman. The prostitute in *Casting Stones* is a reminder that none of us is free until we are all free. While sex not discourse *is* the order of the day there is no comfort in knowing that it can at times simply be relocated—to the body of a prostitute rather than being enacted on a wife or girlfriend. While sex, understood as the enactment of unequal gender roles, remains foundational, discourse and location remain very thin veils indeed. The personal is political in that what happens to one, can and may, happen to all.

It is not just feminists who are declaring that the personal is political. Sociologists of the body also understand that our bodies are at once private and at the same time under societal control.[10] This is obvious with such things as the Vaccination Act or the Contagious Diseases Act but becomes more complex when we move further into what we consider to be a very private world, that of our sex lives. People *are* judged by their bodies and what they do with them even if those acts are in private. The truth and power of this reality is strongly felt by those who dare to digress in any way. Our bodies influence how our life is lived and we are not as free as we think we are. Synnott shows that even the food we eat and the way we eat it is genderized, a steak or a light salad,

9. Donna Haraway, *Simians, Cyborgs and Women: The Reinvention of Nature* (New York: Routledge, 1991), p. 20.

10. Anthony Synnott, *The Body Social: Symbolism, Self and Society* (London: Routledge, 1997), p. 33.

a pint or a white wine do we gobble or nibble, gulp or sip? Women are not supposed to show their hunger publicly and so we have commercials that show women barely tasting things. However, when women are shown to be enjoying food it is often linked with sexuality, the Flake advert and recent Magnum posters being the most prominent examples. (Synnott has a very extensive list and a very sound case which is backed up by a glance around one's neighbourhood.) Feminist theorists have argued that the real issue here is not food at all but controlling the female body in a public space, which links with control of women in the workplace. What is at stake here is female hunger for power and this has to be controlled in a patriarchal society and is done by control of the body in public space.[11] Of course, this is done through what appear to be trivial routines and rules of etiquette and in this way the control is put beyond consciousness. However, the body knows and it is not unusual to find epidemics of eating disorders particularly at times of cultural backlash, as women either attempt to make their bodies fit the space available or attempt to take more. Synnott suggests that we even dance in different ways, allowing our bodies to take more or less space and making forceful or refined movements. For Synnott, ballroom dancing epitomizes the sexual relations of the genders, 'the male fittingly "leads" the female who walks backwards into the future. She is entirely dependent on the male's vision of the path ahead' and, of course, she is tottering on high heels and therefore very destabilized.[12] It would seem that the body is more than a set of biological givens; it is a battle ground where women are constantly driven along the way or wrong-footed.

Feminists have argued over the years that the battle rages most intensely in the arena of sex, the actions involved as well as the rhetoric about it. Put simply, research such as that of Shere Hite shows that the vast majority of women do not favour penetration as a form of sexual activity.[13] Despite this, penetration is still considered to 'be sex' with all other activities relegated to 'foreplay'. The simple question, which leads to a complex answer, is who decides this and why? The answer

11. Susan Bardo, 'The Body and the Reproduction of Femininity: A Feminist Approach to Foucault', in Alison Jaggar and Susan Bardo (eds.), *Gender/Body/Knowledge: Feminist Reconstruction of Being and Knowing* (New York: Rutgers University Press, 1992), pp. 13-31 (22).

12. Synnott, *The Body Social*, p. 66

13. See for example Shere Hite, *The Hite Reports: Sexuality, Love and Emotion* (London: Bloomsbury, 1993).

acknowledges that actions carry meanings far beyond themselves and that the meanings are commonly held. The common language associated with intercourse gives a clue as to the symbolic power it is thought to have. A woman is fucked, poked, given one, screwed, had, taken: the list is endless and the words do not describe an act filled with mutuality and empowerment. From this we see that intercourse takes place in the context of power relations, whatever the intentions of the individuals. Andrea Dworkin is eloquent on this subject, insisting that intercourse depersonalizes women into a function.[14] She says that 'physically the woman in intercourse is a space inhabited, a literal territory occupied'.[15] This becomes the bedrock of the language that develops around the act and it is a language that women do not speak. Giving women the power to refuse the language and the act in favour of more diffuse and tender sensualities is acknowledging that women are equal as persons, not that they are free to dominate. Sadly, we are nowhere near this as a culture. Dworkin draws attention to the double standards involved with physical activity: the penetration of females makes them real women while the penetration of men is a criminal offence in many countries. She asks why and concludes that penetration symbolizes power and men are not to endure the same subordination that they so easily inflict on women. Man will be undermined by this action carried out on his body but empowered if he carries it out on others.[16] What are we to conclude then— that women learn their place through penetration and the cultural weight it carries? Many will not agree with Dworkin but the question still remains as to why penetration carries such a power to define.

Despite the volumes of academic writing on the subject of power inequality in sexual relationships it is still tempting to assert that the young women of today are daughters of feminist mothers and are not playing the same old tune. They are into 'girl power', knowing their own minds and their own desires in a way that would have been unthinkable for the majority of their grandmothers. It's a nice thought but it does not appear to be true. The recent publication of the findings of the WRAP (Women, Risk and AIDS) and MRAP (Men, Risk and AIDS) projects[17] makes very depressing reading. Their research was

14. Andrea Dworkin, *Intercourse* (New York: Free Press Paperbacks, 1987).
15. Dworkin, *Intercourse*, p. 133.
16. Dworkin, *Intercourse*, p. 155.
17. Janet Holland, Caroline Ramazanoglu, Sue Sharpe and Rachel Thomson,

carried out over nine years, involved young people from the age of 16 to 21 and focused on Manchester and London. It covered a range of class, ethnic and educational backgrounds and aimed to see if heterosexual relations were becoming more equal. Have women, after generations of trying, become subjects in the heterosexual discourse? The answer, is no.

The researchers were themselves struck by the 'discrepancies between expectations and experience; between intention and practice; between different discourses of femininity' and they found that

> young women's ability to choose safer sex practices, or to refuse unsafe (or any other) sexual activity, not as an issue of free choice between equals, but as one of negotiation within structurally unequal social relationships.[18]

The title of the book, *The Male in the Head*, gives a clue to just how difficult this negotiation can be. The authors conclude that heterosexuality is not just male dominated and male defined but rather it is masculinity. Young women are taught not just about sex but about their place in heterosexuality[19] and of course this is a place which is most pleasing to men and fits with their status as 'other' in the discourse of masculinity. The authors suggest that masculinity and femininity are not two opposites within the heterosexual framework but are rather locations within the same male-dominated framework, they both reproduce male dominance. Therefore, female desires that may lead to resistance are viewed as unruly forces that have to be kept under control, by violence if necessary.[20] Indeed, female desire does not seem to play a large part in the sex education of girls either at home or in school. The young women questioned reported being told a great deal about their reproductive capacity in conjunction with warnings about men who are 'only after one thing'. The latter serving to express a strong message of female passivity and the strength of male desire and their dominance. Physical pleasure and the clitoris were totally absent from both formal and home based conversations about sex. Young men, on the other hand, were being told how good sex is and how real men are 'knowing

The Male in the Head: Young People, Heterosexuality and Power (London: The Tufnell Press, 1998).

18. Holland, *et al.*, *The Male in the Head*, pp. 5-6.
19. Holland, *et al.*, *The Male in the Head*, p. 54.
20. Holland, *et al.*, *The Male in the Head*, p. 11.

agents in pursuit of sexual pleasure'.[21] Young men felt that they had to express desire and young women that they had to satisfy it.

These two approaches need not be mutually exclusive but once again the research showed that they tend to be. Of course, beginning with the idea that intercourse is something enacted on women by men and that this implicitly holds power is not the best place to start in search of a discourse of mutuality but unfortunately this does seem to be the starting point. Further, it was found that girls tend to distance themselves from the ways in which boys talk about sex and this means that they do not have a language of their own. They do have a language to do with relationships, but not to do with sex and this places them in limbo— desire without language to express it is not the best place from which to find embodied empowerment. Instead young women learn 'the boundaries of feminine identity and the social mechanisms of sexual reputation'.[22] Heterosexuality, then, is more than a set of sexual practices; it actually grounds and embodies a range of gender relations (these also include gay and lesbian relations; see Alison Webster's article) which in turn underpin patriarchal society. Making the power of heterosexuality visible is very difficult because it is assumed that the world works this way. It seems that religions can have a very active role to play in this arena by questioning the naturalness of these unequal power relations rather than in supporting them through embarrased conformity and anti-pleasure/procreative diatribes.

The researchers did find that young women were having sex with some pleasure but this notion was gender defined. They note that 'young women are drawn into their own disempowerment through their conception of what sexual encounters are about'.[23] Sadly they are understood as his orgasm and her part in it. Many of the women felt that if they made their desires known this could lead to the end of the relationship or it could reinforce the man's idea of control. The language used was that of gift and pleasing with nothing about desire and pleasure. Often women reported that their pleasure was in giving the man what he wanted. Some women reported having to curb their desire as men found it too threatening. This is not unlike women friends of mine who report that men like the idea of a sexually assertive female but find the reality too unnerving and either control it in the moment or use it as

21. Holland, *et al.*, *The Male in the Head*, p. 7.
22. Holland, *et al.*, *The Male in the Head*, p. 68.
23. Holland, *et al.*, *The Male in the Head*, p. 9.

a weapon in the armoury of relationship, usually misunderstanding the pleasure as something they have given her all on their own and therefore as a means of control. In some cases the women are simply cast aside as nymphomaniacs and whores.

The project findings are no more encouraging when it comes to who defines what sex is. Many of the women enjoyed non-penetrative sex the most but gave in to male definitions of this as merely foreplay and consented to penetration which they enjoyed much less. Further, the question of consent was found to be a tricky one. In some cases women consented for fear of violence and in others because they believed they were responsible for male arousal and therefore responsible for satisfying it in the way the man wanted. The latter being an example of the power of the cultural construction of male desire as a driving need. All reported that they received, in one way or another, undue pressure to have penetrative sex. This was not the end of the story. Once they had agreed to 'sex' they had to be mindful of how much pleasure they could show without falling into the nymphomaniac trap. Most said that they faked orgasms and generally suggested more pleasure than they were actually experiencing. This makes the Hite Report seem rather optimistic, as she declared that it was only 69 per cent of men who were uninformed and unaware of their partners' sexual pleasure. The vast majority reported that the male orgasm signalled the end of sex for them both and most agreed that sex was judged as good or bad according to closeness not physical pleasure. A small number of women in the study did report actively asserting their desire and this was found to link with questioning the way they understood (were willing to play out) femininity. The report suggests that while women are capable of expressing their desires and receiving satisfaction within certain relationships, this is not really a form of empowered embodiment that they can carry with them to other relationships, it really does depend on the man. In other circumstances the way that those same women would ask for physical satisfaction could place them on the receiving end of violence.

Of course, it is not only physical pleasure that young women have trouble negotiating within hetero-patriarchy, it is also their health. The study found that young women had great difficulty, despite their wishes, in getting partners to use condoms. Once again it was found to be an area of gender related power games: the girl who carries them is a slag and the one who insists on their use is a kill-joy. Men were more amenable to using condoms if they thought of the girl as a 'slag' as they wished to protect themselves from disease. However, they felt that once there was trust in a relationship they should not have to bother. Women often gave in under those circumstances as they felt a condom might diminish their partner's pleasure.[24] Men, on the other hand, had no idea how a condom affected the pleasure of their partner. Even when women know that they may be placing their lives at risk through AIDS/HIV the male in the head dictates the sexual patterning. This is a frightening reality.

The study seems to suggest that women's sexuality is disembodied. Indeed it shows that women

> are under pressure to construct their bodies into a model of femininity which is both inscribed on the surface, through such skills as dress, make-up and dietary regimes, and disembodied, in the sense of detachment from their sensuality and alienation from their material bodies.[25]

The result being that women are made into passive and fragmented sexual objects, both of which are necessary if they are to be eroticized in cultures that see sexual relations as power relations. Women are encouraged to gain control over the surfaces of their bodies but to give away all control in social relations, intercourse and pleasure. It is a grim picture and while young women are aware of what they see as double standards in the sexual arena they are, for the most part, resigned to acceptance. In reality they have very little choice.

This is the stuff of feminist theological reflection. How do we grasp liberation, mutuality and our divine essence from the many layered oppressions that are as intimate to us as our own thoughts and our body touching? To speak of women's experience as liberative in the light of the WRAP study is indeed a leap of faith since it is asserting that there is enough in their body knowing for women to find and hold as their own in order to resist the dominant discourse. The question remains as to whether there are sufficient theological and religious resources to aid women in this struggle or whether sexual relations as lived are rooted in original religious suspicions of, and desires to control, the female body which are far from purged. It goes without saying that we can no longer hold on to ideas of the insatiable witch, but what of the virgin? Can Christians who are looking for women's embodied empowerment still proclaim that Jesus was born of a virgin? The answer is surely no in the

24. Holland, *et al.*, *The Male in the Head*, pp. 40-41.
25. Holland, *et al.*, *The Male in the Head*, p. 109.

traditional sense, that is the young pure woman who answers the request/command of a disembodied deity submissively and humbly. What difference is there between this and the young women of the WRAP study? Both are not really part of the discourse but end up satisfying male desire, be it for sex or a son. Can feminist theology salvage anything of worth from this pillar of Christian belief? Some Latin American feminists claim they can see in the virgin a powerful symbol of single motherhood and the self contained sexual power that often accompanies such a life.[26] For them the virginity of the mother of Jesus is not a biological fact but rather shows that she is a person who has grown to wholeness through well-fought-for autonomy. She did not lead a derived life, that is, she is not merely someone's wife or mother but a person in her own right. Further, the fact that the story excludes any male fathering is seen as a sign that the patriarchal order of fathers is overthrown. In this way the virgin acts as a symbol of resistance to patriarchal values and lifestyles.[27] This is further borne out by the words of the Magnificat where Mary is shown to be on the side of those who are the underdogs within a patriarchal society. This virgin is never a victim and sounds more like the virgins that Marilyn Frye envisages than the Pope would hold as a role model for all women.[28] Frye declares that all women should be virgins, that is they should never be conquered by men but always renewed and self-contained in their own bodily strength. These virgins fuck with gender as they never play it the way that hetero-patriarchy wishes and they never become the property of others, not even in their most intimate moments. They overcome the unequal power relations that are at the heart of heterosexual relating and they declare themselves as fresh, untouched and as creatively maid-enlike as ever. They are undomesticated and wild, delighting in their sexuality and remaking all the rules. Is this the model of the virgin that churches should be encouraged to promote if women are to find embodied empowerment? It is a start.

Patriarchy as a system of domination goes right to the heart of our being and social relating, it even attacks desire. That is it 'reduces it to

26. Chung Hyun Kyung, *Struggle to be the Sun Again: Introducing Asian Women's Theology* (London: SCM Press, 1991), pp. 74-84.

27. Chung Hyun Kyung, *Struggle to be the Sun Again*, p. 77.

28. See Marilyn Frye, *Willful Virgins: Essays in Feminism* (California: The Crossing Press, 1976).

sex and then defines sex in the politicised terms of gender'.[29] The roots
of our desire are therefore steeped in patriarchy and while the churches
tell us to control desire they say nothing about its hierarchical nature.
The bodies of women seem to suggest another approach, that of releasing desire. The WRAP study showed that when women are removed
from their own desire, disembodied, they become fragmented and alien-
ated people within their own skins. The release of desire in that arena
would lead to a reintegration and not the choas that churches often warn
against when talking of unchained desire. Carter Heyward argues that
when we give up *dunamis* or erotic power, which is our birthright, we
become disheartened people who are not truly capable of changing
anything.[30] However, if as Jesus did, we claim that right we begin to
live from a level of mutuality and connectedness that is truly revolutionary and world changing. We are filled with passion/desire which is
body based and justice seeking. We can overthrow worldly principali-
ties/patriarchies! The churches then should be helping us to awaken to
our desires, our passion, and the best way to do this is through our
bodies. Theology must celebrate the body and religious practice should
become more embodied and sensual—sensuous sacramentality becoming the order of the day, a riot of smell, colour and most importantly,
touch. A celebration of all our senses and a connection with the organic
sensuality of the earth and each other. We need to be awakened and this
is unlikely to happen with a piece of dry wafer and warnings about the
sins of the flesh. Incarnation demands more engagement.

Once we locate ourselves in our divine bodies we are faced with the
challenge to find alternatives to the way things are, to engage in an
obstinate way with the patriarchal world and declare another set of
values. Of course, this location while in our bodies is an enactment that
goes far beyond the edges of the skin. It is a counter cultural enactment
for and with others, our protest is not just about those things which
oppress us, our redemption is tied up with that of all. There is a sense in
which we may assert that the grounded reality of our lives also gives us
a transcendent quality, it is the radical nature of our incarnation that

29. Muriel Dimien, 'Power, Sexuality and Intimacy', in Jaggar and Bardo
(eds.), *Gender/Body/Knowledge*, pp. 37-42 (38).

30. See Carter Heyward, *The Redemption Of God: A Theology of Mutual
Relation* (New York: University of America Press, 1982) and *idem*, *Touching our
Strength: The Erotic as Power and the Love of God* (San Francisco: HarperSan-
Francisco, 1989).

moves us into a place that may be called transcendent. This does not imply a moving beyond but rather broadening of vision and joining in the struggle with those we do not know and cannot see. In this way the divine body is a symbol of co-creation and co-redemption, it is through us, with us, in us by the power of our divine humanity that we change the world. We change it through the powerful enactment of embodied alternatives. This is the meaning of incarnation. What would the church look like if women's bodies were taken seriously enough to be placed at the centre of such a revolution? It would be a place of diversity celebrated and bodies glorified, a place that had many locations and in each brought solace, not through platitudes and charity, but radical alternatives. It would be a church embracing each divine incarnation placed in front of it with awe, respect and commitment to the fulfilment of that promise, whatever the price.

As a start to what seems a very grand vision theology and religion should have as a priority the honouring and fostering of the autonomy of women. It was no other than Kant who declared that where there is no autonomy there is no personhood and we have seen through the WRAP report that the personhood of young women is diminished through lack of sexual autonomy. Naturally this applies to matters such as contraception and abortion but it goes much deeper, to a place that may in fact make such choices less pressing. It is time that Christianity honoured women's sexual power not only as procreators but as embodied and powerful persons. As people who may claim their desires and in so doing bring forth new ways of being and knowing. The female self under male domination is riddled with false and contained desire and one role the churches should play is to help remove the demons of patriarchy. The male in the head must go and so the patriarch in the sky must also be challenged. Taking seriously women's empowerment means removing all obstacles, even *the* divine image itself. Hierarchy cannot give life to radical equality. Daphne Hampson has rightly pointed out that Christianity is heteronomous while feminism encourages autonomy, there can be no half-way house on this.[31] As the WRAP study so graphically illustrated qualified autonomy is no autonomy at all. The young women in that study in theory are free and have choice; in reality they live within a system that limits choice, and indeed it does more, it encourages compliance. Christianity is just such a system and

31. Daphne Hampson, *Swallowing a Fishbone? Feminist Theologians Debate Christianity* (London: SPCK, 1996).

so cannot create an environment in which autonomous people will flourish and bloom. This is not in the interests of women.

Christianity has often imaged itself as a pilgrim and resurrection community and so it should not be too difficult for such a community to understand its role as that of 'nomadic subjects' dislocating the grip of patriarchy.[32] The nomadic subject is one whose identity is coherent and mobile. The nomadic consciousness aims to 'rethink the unity of the subject' and has no confidence that this process will be aided by the systems from which the subject sprang.[33] It is the nomadic, transitory and transgressive nature of the nomad that allows for connections across a wide range of people and ideas. Braidotti believes that the nomad can dramatically change the nature of gender construction. Is it really such a large step from the Christian pilgrim to the transgressive nomad? It really is not if we shift our gaze from the Christ of Caesar and Greek metaphysics to the early Jesus movement. This is a shift from absolutes and conquest to wanderings and living as though the expected kingdom were here. In other words, transgressive living, crossing boundaries, seeking radical equality and questioning authority and received wisdom. Doing things differently. If Christianity is to be a positive force in the arena of body politics Christ the nomad needs to replace Christ the Lord and believers need to rip up their cosy preconceived ideas and stereotypes and follow.

The culturally constructed and gendered nature of lived experience presents feminist theology with many challenges. At the same time the work of feminist sociologists and psychologists present us with major opportunities to explore new ways of being and knowing. As each layer of patriarchal construction is uncovered theologians have the chance to reimage the divine discourse based on the reawakened knowledge of female power. This is both exciting and frightening. The edges of our constructed worlds are being shaken and we are left to embrace the fullness of our own incarnation.

---

32. Rosi Braidotti, *Nomadic Subjects: Embodiment and Sexual Difference in Contemporary Society* (New York: Columbia University Press, 1994).

33. Braidotti, *Nomadic Subjects*, pp. 31-32.

SEX IN THE CATHOLIC TRADITION

Rosemary Radford Ruether

Roman Catholic Christianity is sometimes presented as suffering from a solely negative view of sexuality, rooted in hostility to women. This view is sometimes contrasted with robust and positive views of sexuality in the 'pagan' and the Jewish worlds, although the negative Catholic views are sometimes also blamed on Platonism, supposedly in contrast to the positive Jewish views. These negative views are seen as having been overcome either by Protestantism which embraced sexuality as good and/or modern 'enlightened' views, allowing modern Europeans to embrace sex as innocent and happy pleasure.[1]

The reality of this historical trajectory is, predictably, much more complex. Neither Judaism nor the Greek and Roman cultures viewed sex as unambiguously good. The near impeachment of American President Bill Clinton for stand-up sex with White House intern Monica Lewinsky in the corridor of the Oval Office testifies to the extreme ambiguity with which recreational sexual pleasure is still regarded, at least in US American public culture.

Western European and North American cultures operate out of a deep split personality toward sexuality. I call this split the 'puritan-prurient syndrome'.[2] On the level of super-ego sex is distained, feared and treated as an obscene subject. On the 'id' level convert sexuality takes place in all sorts of places outside of marriage, often in exploitative and violent ways that are implicitly, if not explicitly misogynist. Women are

---

1. For a good evaluation of the complexity of this heritage see the introductory essay in Adrian Thatcher and Elizabeth Stuart, *Christian Perspectives on Sexuality and Gender* (Grand Rapids, MI: Eerdmans, 1996), pp. ix-xiv.

2. As far as I know this term is my own construction. For my earlier development of this split, see Rosemary R. Ruether, 'The Personalization of Sexuality', in Eugene C. Bianchi and Rosemary Radford Ruether (eds.), *From Machismo to Mutuality: Woman-Man Liberation* (New York: Paulist Press, 1976), pp. 70-86.

seen both as creatures to be put on a pedestal as 'beyond' sexual feelings and as sexual objects to be used and discarded. If women themselves become agents of their own sexual activity, making their own
decisions about both when and how to enjoy sex and how to limit its
reproductive effects on their bodies, they are seen as disgraceful sinners
who must be punished and forced to submit to male definitions of their
sexual roles.

Western Europe and North America are by no means unique in this
ambiguity toward sex. Sex is seen as a volatile force in most cultures, to
be variously used, repressed and channeled, and this combination of use
and repression is entangled with ambiguous views of women as desired
virgin, honored mother and despised whore. It is not ambiguity, but the
particular configurations of the ambiguity that differ somewhat from
culture to culture. Western European and North American cultures have
been shaped by their roots in Catholic and Protestant Christianities,
both in their overt puritanism and their covert revolts against religious
constraints. In this essay I propose to review something of the teaching
on sexuality in the Latin Catholic tradition that have shaped this situation.

These teachings emerged from early Christian asceticism, but they
are not a straight-line development. Early Christian asceticism had elements of a counter-cultural, subversive movement against the dominant
patterns of family and society. In the new Christian 'family' class and
ethnic lines were leveled, and women emancipated to preach alongside
men. In Christ the 'orders' of a fallen creation were overcome: there
was no more divison of male and female, Jew and Greek, slave and
free.[3]

Very early, however, within the first two generations of the Christian
movement whose traditions are part of the New Testament, a reaction
against the radical implications of this idea of the Church as a new
egalitarian family arose, that sought to reinstate patriarchal hierarchy
within the Christian movement and to model an emerging clerical hierarchy after it. Wives obey your husbands, slaves your masters, children
your parents thunder the patriarchal Paulinists of the New Testament.
Equality of women with men, slaves with masters, ethnic groups with
each other is spiritualized in a way that reaffirms patriarchal social hierarchy. Those liberated by Christ will now voluntarily obey their fathers,

---

3.   See Rosemary R. Ruether, *Women and Redemption: A Theological History*
(St. Paul, MN: Fortress Press, 1998), pp. 13-30.

husbands and masters as the Lord, and will thereby earn their reward in heaven.[4]

In the second and early third centuries radical movements, such as Marcionism, Montanism and Valentinianism, that equated Christianity with rejection of sex and marriage, in a way that emancipated women from social subjugation and allowed them prophetic leadership in the church, continued to flourish. But the Church fathers who shaped the church that became dominant set their face against such views. Gradually there emerged victorious a complex synthesis of patriarchy and celibacy.

In this synthesis celibacy for men was identified with male clerical hierarchy over the laity. Male church authority sought (not always successfully) to strip female celibacy of its subversive potential as liberating women for new roles of public power and to confine nuns to strict monastic enclosure, enforced by obedience to male clerical superiors. Marriage was affirmed for the laity, although as a spiritually inferior choice to celibacy. Within that state of life women's subordination was doubly affirmed, to their husbands and to clerical authorities, while their sexual and reproductive roles were linked to sin and death.

Sexual renunciation was still linked with higher holiness for Christians of the late Patristic and medieval eras, but its subversive potential as leveling class and gender hierarchy was curbed and incorporated into a new status hierarchy that included the dominance of a celibate clergy over a married laity. Yet sexual renunication itself continued to carry a radical vision in late Patristic asceticism, a promise of overcoming not only sin, but of dissolving the limits of finitude governed by the rule of the cosmos that held the body hostage to death.

As Peter Brown has shown, in his masterful work on sexual renunciation in early Christianity,[5] Christians came to focus much more insistently on the body and the repression of its needs for food, sleep and sexual urges than pagan ascetics, because it had a more radical vision of its potential for transformation. Males of the pagan classical world

4.   See Col. 3.11, 18-24, where ethnic and class divisions (but not gender) are seen as overcome, but this is followed by a reaffirmation of patriarchal hierarchy. On this passage, see Ruether, *Women and Redemption*, pp. 39-40. Also Elizabeth Schüssler Fiorenza, *In Memory of Her: A Feminist Theological Reconstruction of Christian Origins* (New York: Crossroad, 1983), pp. 266-70.

5.   Peter Brown, *The Body and Society: Men, Women and Sexual Renunciation in Early Christianity* (New York: Columbia University Press, 1988).

looked on the body as an inferior, not unlike the inferiority of slaves and women. The philosopher, as respectable *paterfamilias*, should discipline these inferiors to serve the patriarchal household, kinship group and civic society. But they should also give them their due.

There was a place for the delights of marriage and the table, although excesses should be curbed. Well-tempered sexual intercourse to produce well-formed, legitimate children was a responsibility of every householder, and the prime purpose of women's existence. But in due time the philosophically-inclined should reduce these pleasures to the minimum, even letting sexual intercourse go altogether, in preparation for that separation of soul from body in which the intellect would soar free to the stars unencumbered by mortal clay.

Christians entertained a more unthinkable notion, the resurrected body. Far from doffing the body at death to live an immortal life of the soul alone, the Christian expected the body to be transformed, losing its urges to sex, food and sleep that signaled its fall into mortality. This immortalized body, the companion of the soul, would be exalted with it into a new redeemed world of the 'new creation'. The urges of the body must be more severely suppressed to anticipate this transformation in which the body's finitude would be discarded in a redemptive transmutation.

For ancient Christianity the incarnation of the Logos of God in the body meant something different from a modern Christian use of that doctrine to claim an embrace of mortal physicality.[6] For Patristic thought the incarnation of God into the human body meant that the immortal, unchangeable substance of God has descended into mortal flesh in order to transmute it into an immortalized form, free from death and decay. God became human to make us divine was the ancient Christian understanding of incarnation, not to celebrate but to overcome the frailties of the flesh that tied it to corruptibilty and death.[7]

Many of the forms of Christianity of the second century sought to live out that vision as one that was already transforming daily life by a

6.   Modern theologians who celebrate the theme of 'incarnation' as central to Christian doctrine assume it means an embrace of finite, material embodiment and thus contradicts the Christian history of negation of such embodiment, failing to see how the early Christian reading of incarnation in fact promoted this repression: see Sallie McFague, *The Body of God: An Ecological Theology* (Minneapolis: Fortress Press, 1993), pp. 163-64.

7.   For example, Athanasius, *On the Incarnation of the Word*.

deep renunciation of all the ways the finite body reproduced itself through temporal processes. By such practices as sexual continence, fasting and vigils Christians anticipated the definitive transformation of the bodily in a redeemed cosmos whose imminent arrival they expected, and their repressed bodies became a sign that they had already shifted their allegiance from the present world to the world to come.

Renunciation of sex was seen as a key expression of world renunciation, not necessarily because sex was the most urgent need of the body. Indeed emaciated people lose sexual urges. For many monks, hunger, the cravings of the belly, were more insistent bodily demands and less easy to control.[8] But sex tied the person to marriage and family, to the pride and avarice of the kinship group that desired to reproduce the large houses, the great landholdings with its crowds of slaves and clients, the demand for power and status in the civil and imperial world. Through sex and marriage 'the world' as a social system of power and possessions was reproduced. To renounce marriage was to renounce that 'world' in all its social, economic and political implications.

Some of this radical vision of liberation through asceticism lingers in Eastern Church Fathers, such as Gregory of Nyssa, writing in the last quarter of the fourth century. For him, sex, physical procreation, the temporal corruptibility of the body, were no part of the original intention of God for creation. Humans were created with spiritual bodies and would have reproduced by some 'angelic' means if they had not fallen. Maleness and femaleness were there only potentially, in view of the fallen state to come.[9]

With the fall from God, the body took on 'coats of skin', the attributes of corruptible finitude.[10] Physical sex for procreation then became necessary in order to compensate for the loss of the original immortality of the spiritual body. Gregory sees the reascent of the embodied self from the fallen state as a long process of reawakened communion with God, reflected in the inner spiritual nature of the mind or soul. It is the

8. On the relation of famine and fasting in Egyptian monasticism, see Brown, *Body and Society*, pp. 218-20.

9. Gregory of Nyssa, 'On the Making of Man', *NPNF*, V, pp. 387-427.

10. On the interpretation of 'coats of skin' in Gen. 3.7 (Septuagint: *dermatinous chitonas*) see Gregory of Nyssa, 'On the Making of Man'. For the same idea in Gregory Nazianzus, see Rosemary Ruether, *Gregory of Nazianzus: Rhetor and Philosopher* (Oxford: Clarendon Press, 1969), pp. 135-36.

attachment to temporal needs, pride, avarice, bondage to sexual pleasure, that are to be given up through the disciplines of ascetic renunciation and contemplative thought.

Thereby the self also frees itself from the anxieties associated with
these needs: the fears that wealth, once accumulated, will be taken
away; the attachment to a spouse and the pride of progeny dashed by
early death. Virginity, for Gregory, is this inner spiritual process of
freeing the self from greed and fear associated with attachment to
transient material things. Marriage and sex are one expression of this
attachment, but not the most insistent of them. Gregory, himself married in his youth, can envision a chaste wedlock gradually given up for
higher philosophical pleasures.[11]

Gregory's focus is the deeper process of self-transmutation of body/
soul by which the Christian anticipates a final transformation in which
the material body is changed into the spiritual body of the resurrection.
Then the body will lose its temporal accretions or 'coats of skin' that tie
it to eating, evacuation, procreation, sleeping and decay and become the
immortalized body that can share in the endless ascent of the soul to
fuller and fuller communion with God, going on 'from glory to glory'.

By the late fourth century the monastic movement had gained ascendency in Eastern and Western Christianity, and there was the beginning
of the effort to insist that the clergy remain celibate, although this
would have indifferent success in Latin Christianity until it was forcibly
enforced by the twelfth-century reforms. Then the problem was dealt
with by defining clerical marriage as concubinage and the offspring of
such unions as bastards who could not enter the clergy or inherit church
property.[12]

In the fourth-century Latin world hostility grew to the ascendency of
the monastic class, and their denigration of marriage. Two Christian
writers, Helvidius and Jovinian, sought to mediate this conflict by
defining marriage and celibacy as equally holy. Mary was seen by these
writers as epitomizing the holiness of both states of life, having lived
before marriage and borne her first son in the virginal state, while
assuming sexual relations and bearing further children to Joseph thereafter. The enthusiasts for celibacy were declared to be bordering on

11. Gregory of Nyssa, *De Virginitate*, PG 46, cols. 318-416.

12. For the history of the enforcement on clerical celibacy and the twelfth-
century debates, see Anne Llewellyn Barstow, *Married Priests and the Reforming
Papacy: The Eleventh Century Debates* (Toronto: Edwin Mellen Press, 1982).

Manichaeanism, the belief that matter and the body are evil and reproduction is to be shunned.[13]

These efforts to give equal status to marriage and celibacy were
vehemently attacked by St Jerome who declared that Mary has never
departed from the virgin state, the brothers of Jesus of the New Testament being cousins, not children of Mary. In his exaltation of the superiority of virginity and sexual continence over the debasement of sex,
Jerome's rhetoric threatened to erase any difference between sex within
marriage and prostitution.

Augustine sought to repair the negative impression created by
Jerome's intemperate defense of the superiority of virginity and continent widowhood to marriage. In his treatise 'On the Good of Marriage',
he sought a more measured approach. He defended marriage as imbued
with three 'goods': progeny, fidelity and sacrament. These purposes of
marriage give the good benefits of producing children and channeling
the sexual urge into faithful wedlock, thus guarding against the worse
evil of fornication. In addition, marriage symbolizes the union of Christ
and the Church, and thus expresses the sacramental bond of Christian
community.[14]

Augustine would gradually back away from his earlier Origenist view
of original creation, rejecting the common Eastern Christian view that
there would have been no sexual differentiation and reproduction in
Paradise.[15] In Augustine's later exegesis of Genesis 1 he would come to
accept the view that sexual reproduction would have taken place in the
original creation. Gender differentiation, marriage, sexual coupling for
reproduction were all part of God's original plan, not things added only
after or with a view to the Fall.[16]

Yet Augustine would also limit these affirmation in ways that made
marital sex distinctly third rate, bordering on sinfulness. In Augustine's

13. The treatises of Helvidius and Jovinian are lost and are known only through
Jerome's polemics against them: see Jerome's 'On the Perpetual Virginity of Mary,
Against Helvidius'; and 'Adversus Jovinius', *PL* 23, cols. 211-336.

14. Augustine, *De Bono Conjugali*, *PL* 15, cols. 373-94.

15. Augustine, *De Genesi Contra Manichaeos* and *De Genesi ad litteram
imperfectus liber*, *PL* 34, cols. 173-245.

16. Augustine, *The Literal Meaning of Genesis*; *The City of God* 14.10, 22-26.
For the evolution of Augustine's anthropology, see Elizabeth Clark, ' "Adam's Only
Companion": Augustine and the Early Christian Debate on Marriage', *Recherches
Augustiniennes* 21 (1986), pp. 139-62.

view, although there would have been physical sex and reproduction in God's original plan, this sex would have been devoid of the hot pleasure of male sexual ejaculation. Concupiscence, Augustine believed, had come about only through the Fall, and expressed the loss of control of mind over body, the division in the self which expressed division from God. Thus in our present fallen state, sex, even in marriage, carried with it sin. Through it the original sin of Adam was passed on to the next generation.[17]

Thus Augustine's view of sex, even in chaste marriage, was distinctly ambiguous. Although the end, children, was good and continued to be blessed by God, reproduction could not take place without sinful 'lust'. The sexual act was itself the means of generating sinful offspring, who could only become children of God through baptism. This sinful act of sex was allowed for the good end of reproduction (hence forgiven) and yet still sinful in its objective nature and consequences.

Paradisal sex also differed from present fallen sex in other ways. Women would not have been 'deflowered' by it, but would have retained their 'virginal integrity', like Mary, in both the sexual act and parturition, suffering no labor pains, a view that suggests something less than fully embodied sexual 'penetration' and childbirth. This view would be expanded to claim that women would not have menstruated; women's monthly bleeding was an expression of their 'cursed' fallen state.[18]

Moreover Augustine, like Jerome, is convinced that marital sex and procreation are no longer commmanded by God, although still allowed in the Christian era. In creating humanity, God blessed reproduction in order to produce a certain number of humans from which the elect would be drawn. The Patriarchs of the Old Testament were even allowed multiple wives in order to hasten this process by which the generations of humanity were born to the time of Christ.[19]

But with the birth of Christ, the new era of the virginal has dawned in

17. Augustine, *De Peccatorim Meritis et Remissione* 1.29; *De Gratia Christi et de Peccato Originali* 1.27; 2.41-44; *De Nuptiis et Concupisceutia* 1, 13, 22; *Contra Julianum* 3.7; 5.14.

18. Augustine, *Civ. Dei* 14.26. For the medieval belief that loss of virginity and menstruation would not have occurred before the Fall, see Charles T. Wood, 'The Doctor's Dilemma: Sin, Salvation and the Menstrual Cycle in Medieval Thought', *Speculum* 56 (1981), pp. 710-27.

19. Augustine, *De Bono Conjugali* 17-20; *De Nuptiis et Concupisceutia* 1, 9-10.

human history, anticipating the culmination of this present world and the dawn of the New Creation, when marriage will be no longer necessary. It is virgins who represent this redeemed era. To be fully dedicated to Christ is to put aside reproductive sex.[20] Thus Augustine suggests that marriage is in some sense sub-Christian. Although still retaining its 'goods' from its creational mandate, it is essentially flawed by the Fall and will have no place in the age to come, which Christian life should mirror and anticipate.

These views of Augustine would be passed on to the Medieval Latin Church as orthodoxy. Sex outside of marriage was totally sinful, but sex even within marriage was degrading and to be hedged around with severe restrictions. No contraception was allowed, since sex was allowable only for its main 'good', procreation. But women should submit to the sexual demands of their husbands, even if pregnant or if their husbands were violent or suffered from leprosy, in order to avoid the far worse possibility that their husbands might seek sexual gratification elsewhere.[21] The definition of sex in marriage as 'remedy of concupiscence' defined wives as a kind of sink for their husbands' sexual urges, regardless of the personal or physical effects on their wives.

Repression of sex even within marriage was seen as contributing to holiness, if both partners agreed to it. Moreover the medieval church advocated periodic abstinence from sex, on holy days and special seasons of the year. It reinforced these recommendations by implanting the suspicion that children born defective were the result of sex during forbidden seasons or engaged in with too much ardor (a theory that may have accelerated the tendency to abandon deformed children).[22] Thus

20. Augustine, *De Nuptiis et Concupisceutia* 1.14-15; *De Bono Conjugali* 13; *De Bono Viduitatis* 8.11; *De Sancta Virginitate* 9.16; also Jerome, *Adversus Jovinius* 1.36.

21. See Eleanor McLaughlin, 'Equality of Souls, Inequality of Sexes: Women in Medieval Theology', in Rosemary Ruether and Eleanor McLaughlin (eds.), *Religion and Sexism: Images of Women in the Jewish and Christian Traditions* (New York: Simon and Schuster, 1974), pp. 225-26, citing Thomas Aquinas, *Summa Theologica*, Suppl. 64.1, ad. 4.

22. See Jo Ann McNamara, 'Chaste Marriage and Clerical Celibacy', in Vern L. Bullough and James Brundage (eds.), *Sexual Practices and the Medieval Church* (Buffalo, NY: Prometheus Books, 1982), pp. 23-33; also John Boswell, *The Kindness of Strangers: The Abandonment of Children in Western Europe from Late Antiquity to the Renaissance* (New York: Pantheon, 1988), for the suggestion that the

the celibate clergy injected into its teaching on marital sexuality its anti-sexual hostility and attempted to imbue the 'work' of the marital bed with feelings of shame, guilt and degradation. These attitudes lingered in official Catholic teachings and in the psychology of many married Catholics until the mid-twentieth century.

The medieval church developed no spirituality for the married laity, but only offered to them the option of sexual continence if they would be truly holy.[23] Unlike the Greco-Roman culture that allowed the married to see the procreative fire in their bodies as an expression of the same divine energy that sustained the cosmos,[24] Christians were taught to see only shame in their sexual coupling, separating them from God.

The degrading of married sexuality in the light of anti-sexual purity also shaped a mystical spirituality for men and women built on sexual sublimation. The man taught to abhor attraction for real women could meditate on vivid visions of being joined in marriage with a beautiful young virgin Mary.[25] Christian women, warned against all sexual feelings that lurk in their own bodies and those of men, could yet be admired as saints when they had visions of being espoused to Christ as celestial lover, and of birthing and suckling the baby Jesus.[26] The powerful urges for a sexuality united to affective love for spouse and children, rigorously repressed on the physical level, reappear as vivid spiritual visions, but in a way that despised rather than rehabilitated their negated physical counterparts.

The sixteenth-century Reformers revolted against this system of male celibate clericalism triumphant over sex and marriage. But the Protes-

---

belief that deformed children were caused by parental sin was an impetus for parents to abandon such children.

23. See Barstow, *Married Priests*, pp. 181-83.

24. Cicero, *De natura deorum* 2.10.28: Brown, *Body and Society*, pp. 27-28.

25. See David Herlihy, *Medieval Households* (Cambridge, MA: Harvard University Press, 1985), pp. 118-20.

26. For the fusion of mysticism and erotic courtly love, see particularly Mechthild of Magdeburg, *The Flowing Light of Godhead* (trans. Christine Mesch Galvani; New York: Garland Books, 1991). For discussion see Ruether, *Women and Redemption*, pp. 97-104; also Barbara Newman, *From Virile Woman to Woman Christ: Studies in Medieval Religion and Literature* (Philadelphia, PA: University of Pennsylvania, 1995), pp. 137-67. For mystical visions of suckling the infant Jesus in Marie d'Oignies, and bridal mysticism in Hadewijch of Brabant, see Elizabeth A. Petroff, *Medieval Women's Visionary Literature* (Oxford: Oxford University Press, 1986), pp. 182, 196-97.

tant Reformation would only revise rather than deeply transform the Augustinian presuppositions about nature, sin, sex and gender on which it was based. In his writings on marriage, Luther insisted that marriage is the vocation to which all humans are called by God. The Catholic exaltation of celibacy is a violation of God's commandment to marry and its blessings in the order of creation.[27]

Not only are all humans called to marriage as their creational vocation and duty, but all humans have sinned. Following Augustine, Luther saw sin as corrupting sex into lust, but he also rejected the ascetic belief that the urges of lust could be transcended through transforming grace and spiritual discipline. Celibacy denies the divinely-given remedy for lust through marriage and so leads celibates to a worse sinfulness of unmarried promiscuity, not to a higher holiness. For Luther, all are called to marry, both to obey God's command in creation and to avoid the greater evil of fornication.

Both Protestant and Catholic leaders agreed on the Augustinian teaching that women were created subordinate to men and have incurred the greater sin through their priority in disobedience that caused the Fall.[28] For Protestants women are all to marry and to be subjugated to their husbands. For Catholics most should marry and some may choose the higher vocation of celibacy, but both choices carry the demand to submit to male authority, whether that of husbands for wives or clergy for nuns. Both are to lead silent, subordinate lives and play no public leadership roles in church or society.

Yet the Reformation was fought in highly sexualized language. The Protestants accused Catholic celibates, priests and nuns, of practicing secret fornication under the robes of higher holiness. Catholics, in turn, impuned the virtues of Protestant clerical marriage, implying that Luther and his confreres violated their vows of celibacy to marry because of an incapacity to contain their lustful urges. Catholic teachings on the counter-Reformation reaffirmed traditional teaching that priests are to be

---

27. Martin Luther, 'A Sermon on the Estate of Marriage' (1519), in James Atkinson (ed.), *Luther's Works* (Philadelphia, PA: Fortress Press, 1966), XLIV, pp. 3-14 and 'The Estate of Marriage' (1522) (ed. Warther Brandt; Philadelphia, PA: Muhlenberg Press, 1962), XLV, pp. 11-50.

28. On Luther and Calvin's continuation of the Augustinian view of women's subordination in creation, doubled by sin, see Ruether, *Women and Redemption*, pp. 117-26.

celibate and that celibacy expresses a higher holiness than marriage.[29] Marriage, while allowable, should be limited to procreation or at least may never intentionally prevent procreation. Married people should distain sexual pleasure and sublimate their sexual urges through prayer as much as possible, ideally choosing to have no sex at all, either throughout their marriage or after producing children.

This teachings which rejected contraception and the possibility of the goodness of sexual pleasure for its own sake continued to characterize Catholic teachings into the 1950s, reinforced by modern Catholic campaigns against birth control.

The Second Vatican Council in the 1960s gave voice to various movements seeking to revise Catholic teachings and practice in a number of areas, including the question of the sinfulness of contraception within marriage. The effort to revise these teachings on the purposes of sex inevitably involved questioning the traditional Augustinian view that sexual pleasure is inherently disordered and sinful and allowable only within marriage for the purpose of procreation or at least without impeding procreation.

Protestantism, with its renewed Augustinian theology, accepted the teaching that contraception was sinful until the mid-twentieth century. The birth control movement that arose in the 1920s was linked to feminism and socialism and thus was seen as a radical challenge to traditional society. However, by the 1930s the birth control movement had been tamed and transferred to conservative concerns about the overpopulation and the proliferating numbers of poor, ethnic minority groups, at a time when the white middle class of Western Europe and the United States had adopted the two to three child family.[30]

English and American Protestants accommodated to the demand for family-planning in the 1930s to 50s, and Roman Catholicism softened its stance to allow the newly discovered 'rhythm method' of periodic continence. By the 1950s this had become the 'Catholic' method of birth control, jokingly called 'Vatican roulette'. Many Catholic couples

---

29. For the Council of Trent's decrees on celibacy and marriage, see R. Po-Chia Hsia, *The World of Catholic Renewal, 1540–1770* (New York: Cambridge University Press, 1998), pp. 22-25; also J. Waterworth (trans.), *Canons and Decrees of the Council of Trent* (London: C. Dolman, 1948), pp. 193-201.

30. For the birth control movement and Margaret Sanger's shift from radical to conservative politics, see David M. Kennedy, *Birth Control in America: The Career of Margaret Sanger* (New Haven, CT: Yale University Press, 1970).

who faithfully sought to follow Church teachings struggled to manage their marital sexuality under a regime that demanded that they confine sexual activity to the part of the month when women menstruate and often feel less sexually inclined, a method which still resulted in unplanned pregnancies.

By the time the Second Vatican Council was called in 1960 by the new liberal Pope John XXIII, revolt was stirring among a newly articulate Catholic laity ready to testify that the rhythm method did not work and caused inordinate anxiety in marital relations. Moral theologians, such as Charles Curran,[31] were aware of this discontent and recognized the logical incoherence of allowing an elaborate method of avoidance of procreation through manipulation of the woman's monthly cycle, while disallowing contraception as a terrible sin. Clearly the rhythm method sought to separate sex from procreation, but ineffectively. Did its moral acceptability lie in the combination of periodic continence plus ineffectiveness?

During the Vatican Council articles by theologically trained laity and moral theologians criticizing the traditional teachings circulated among the Council Fathers. One such collection was the book endorsed by Bishop Thomas D. Roberts, S.J., *Contraception and Holiness*.[32] Pope Paul VI recognized the danger of a dispute on the Council floor over this volatile issue, and avoided it by forming a Papal Commission on Birth Control to meet separately from the Council. The Council was to include liberal and conservative bishops and moral theologians, but also experts on demography and even married couples! Three married couples drawn from the Catholic Family Movement were included, thus for the first time actually seeking to listen to the experience of married men and women on the issue.[33]

The American leaders of the Catholic Family Movement, Pat and

31. Charles Curran, *Contraception: Authority and Dissent* (New York: Herder and Herder, 1969).

32. *Contraception and Holiness: The Catholic Predicament* (New York: Herder and Herder, 1964). Introduction by Bishop Thomas D. Roberts, S.J..

33. The three couples from the international Catholic Family Movement that were members of the Papal Commission on Birth Control were Pat and Patty Crowley (USA), Dr and Mrs Laurent Potvin (Canada) and Dr and Mrs Charles Rendu (France). For a photo of the three couples at the meeting of the Commission, see Rosemary S. Keller and Rosemary R. Ruether, *In Our Own Voices: Four Centuries of American Women's Religious Writing* (San Francisco, CA: HarperSanFrancisco, 1995), p. 33.

Patty Crowley, collected testimony from couples of their movement about the ineffectiveness and stress of the rhythm method. During the meetings of the Commission some moral theologians and clergy listened to this testimony with surprise and concern. Clearly up until that time such theologians had pontificated about marital sexuality, but had never really listened to those who practiced it.

The result was a volte face in Church teaching. The majority of the Commission voted overwhelmingly for a change in which all medically approved methods of contraception could be used within marriage and within an overall commitment to faithful marital relations and child-bearing. There was no minority report of this commission.[34]

Nevertheless a few bishops and moral theologians who clung to the traditional view were outraged and believed that any change on this teaching would threaten the laity's faith in the Church's capacity to teach inerrantly. One bishop was quoted by Patty Crowley as exclaiming at the end of the Commission, 'What about all those who have been sent to Hell because of disobedience to the Church's teachings?', to which Crowley replied, 'Your excellency, do you think that God has obeyed all your orders?'[35]

While Crowley might take such a divergence between God and church authorities lightly, for some Catholic authorities this was a serious question. Those who objected to the Commission report convinced Pope Paul VI to reject the conclusion of his own Commission, and reaffirm the traditional anti-contraceptive teaching. The Pope did so by issuing the encyclical, *Humanae Vitae* in 1968. The result was a major revolt in the ranks of moral theologians, priests, bishops and most of all the laity. The open questioning of the validity of the encyclical by priests and theologians, such as Charles Curran, were quickly suppressed by Church discipline. But most laity voted with their bodies, by

34. Robert B. Kaiser, *The Politics of Sex and Religion: A Case History of the Development of Doctrine, 1962–1984* (Kansas City, MO: Leaven Press, 1985), and Robert McClory, *Turning Point: The Inside Story of the Papal Birth Control Commission and How Humanae Vitae Changed the Life of Patty Crowley and the Future of the Church* (New York: Crossroad, 1995).

35. This remark was made during an interview with Patty Crowley in her home, Chicago, Illinois, 17 June 1993. For the Crowley's collection of testimonies from CFM couples on the rhythm method and their report on this to the Commission, see John Kotre, *Simple Gifts: The Lives of Pat and Patty Crowley* (Kansas City, MO: Andrews and McMeel, 1979), pp. 98-99.

simply refusing to comply with Catholic teachings on this issue, while no longer regarding it as a sin to be confessed or as a reason to leave the Church.[36]

In the 1970s to 90s most educated Catholics in the Western world have gone their own way on this issue, even while the present Pope, John Paul II, has continually reasserted the unchangeability of the traditional teaching, thus effectively preventing debate on it. The chief victims of the teachings are poorer Catholics, particularly in countries in Africa and Latin America, where the influence of the Catholic Church prevents access to contraception. The newly formed group, Catholics for Contraception, is seeking to shift the focus from abortion by reopening the debate on the Catholic Church's anti-contraceptive teachings.[37]

At international meetings of the United Nations, gathered to shape world policies on population and development, such as that held in Cairo in 1994, the Vatican has stood with conservative Muslims and a handful of Catholic countries, such as Malta, in continuing to oppose contraception, not only for heterosexual couples, but even for the prevention of disease, such as AIDS.[38] For the Vatican, Augustine's views still reign: sex is only for procreation within marriage and it is mortally sinful outside that context, even for married heterosexual couples. Sex is never allowable for the unmarried, and homosexual sex is always disordered and sinful, even if it takes place between faithful, committed couples.

Catholic teachings have thus come to be seen as a major international obstacle to liberalized laws on such topics as contraception, legal abortion, divorce and remarriage and the acceptance of homosexuality as a normal human variant of sexual orientation. Since the Vatican brooks no debate on these issues, most Catholics who have changed their minds on these issues simply absent themselves from public argument to go their own way in good conscience, selectively practicing those

36. Andrew Greeley, *The Communal Catholic: A Personal Manifesto* (New York: Seabury Press, 1976).

37. Literature on Catholics for Contraception is available from 1436 U Street, N.W., suite 301. Washington, D.C. 20009-3997.

38. For literature on the United Nations Conference on Population and Development in Cairo in 1994 and the follow-up meetings in the Hague and New York in 1999, called 'Cairo Plus Five', contract Catholics for Contraception, as above.

aspects of Catholicism which they find meaningful, such as the liturgy and the teachings on social justice.[39]

In the 1970s the American organization of Catholic theologians, the Catholic Theological Society, attempted a major work of revisionist sexual ethics, published under the title *Human Sexuality*.[40] In this work they moved away from the view that sex was moral only within the legal boundaries of marriage between heterosexuals and for the purpose of procreation. They accepted the Papal Commission's view that all medically approved methods of contraception were acceptable, but they went farther. They revised the criteria by which sex is to be judged as moral or immoral.

In the view of these writers, sex is moral to the degree that it is integrated into friendship and takes place in the context and as an expression of the qualities of love, commitment, fidelity and mutual concern for one another. Sex is immoral to the degree that it departs from this context of friendship and lacks qualities of love, commitment, fidelity and mutuality. The difference between moral sex that expresses such moral qualities and immoral sex which does not is a spectrum rather than a fixed legal boundary. Sex is the more immoral to the degree that it is violent, uncommitted, exploitative and lacks mutuality. Sex grows into being more moral to the degree that the couple grows into greater love and friendship, commitment and mutuality.

Thus moral or immoral sex is a question of the moral growth of the couple in their over-all relationship to each other. Such a revisionist view of what makes sex moral or immoral would revolutionize traditional teachings. It would mean that a married heterosexual relationship in which sex is violent, abusive and exploitative, where the man dominates the woman and exerts his demands selfishly without regard to her feelings and needs, is deeply immoral. By contrast an unmarried rela-

39. Conservative Catholics accuse liberal Catholics of being 'cafeteria Catholics', choosing to accept only appeals to them. This implies that conservatives accept all Church teachings with equal authority, but it is evident that they also 'pick and choose', ignoring teachings that stress social justice. For studies of right- and left-wing Catholics, see Mary Jo Weaver and R. Scott Appleby, *Being Right: Conservative Catholics in America* (Bloomington, IN: Indiana University Press, 1995), and the companion volume by the same editors, *What's Left: Liberal Catholics in America* (Bloomington, IN: Indiana University Press, 2000).

40. Anthony Kosnik, *et al.*, *Human Sexuality: New Directions in American Catholic Thought* (New York: Paulist Press, 1977).

tionship which has qualities of love and mutuality, although somewhat defective in commitment, is nevertheless more moral than an abusive relationship within marriage.

The authors of the study also revised the traditional views on homosexuality. Rather than the view that God 'makes' all people heterosexual and allows sex only within procreative marriage, the authors lean to the view that homosexual orientation is normal and hence God-given for some regular percentage of humanity, quoting one study that compared it to left-handedness.[41] Such persons are not to be denied sexual fulfillment, nor is the lack of procreative potential an impediment to the goodness of such sexuality, since most human sexual acts are not procreative, both by nature (periodic and post-menopausal infertility) or by choice.

Homosexual sexuality, like heterosexual sexuality, should strive to develop the qualities of expressing friendship, mutuality and fidelity. Like heterosexual sex and judged by the same standards, homosexual sex should be judged moral or immoral to the extent that it is loving, mutual and faithful or not. Here faithfulness is taken out of its legal definition of marriages recognized by the state, and becomes a moral quality of committed concern and determination to care for the other and not to betray the other in deceitful and double-dealing ways.

This study by the Catholic Theological Society was not accepted as official teaching by the American Catholic bishops, who refused to grant it their imprimatur. Yet it stands as an important expression of what I believe should be the direction of a revised sexual ethic for Christians (and all people) today. As I have noted in the opening of this article, the negative teachings of the church on sexuality as degrading has not resulted in a Western society that is abstemious, but also has not produced a healthy view of sex. Rather what has developed is the 'puritan-prurient' syndrome: sex is distained as beneath respectability and exploited pornographically, both of which privilege men over women.

What is needed for the church, and for moral culture and socialization, is a new *ars erotica*. Such an *ars erotica* would seek to help people develop their capacity for sexual pleasure and enjoyment, while integrating it into deepening friendship, so that sex becomes increasingly an expression of love, commitment and a caring that seeks to be truly mutual. This process of developing the capacity for erotic delight

41. Kosnik, *et al.*, *Human Sexuality*, pp. 58, 204-206, 211-15.

in sexual activity, while integrating it into deepening friendship and care, should be understood as a process of moral growth over many years. It is not a matter of fixed legal boundaries that separate the married from the unmarried, the heterosexual from the homosexual, those who wish to procreate (which may include homosexuals) from those who do not.

The development of such an *ars erotica* should not be an esoteric or pornographic literature. It should become a normal part of culture that is discussed with the young. Youth, males and females, should be taught during puberty (perhaps in new coming-of-age ceremonies, as well as in general socialization) how to develop their capacity for erotic delight, practice contraception so they can responsibly choose when to have a child, and regard their sexual partner as one to be loved and cherished.[42] They should be helped to see this as a process of moral development, not a once-for-all leap from virginity to marriage that can take place overnight at the point where church and state pronounces them 'man and wife'.

The impact of Christian puritanism, Catholic and Protestant, has prevented the emergence of a genuine *ars erotica* in Western culture, and has often resulted in the repression of positive erotic cultures in other societies through the impact of missionaries. Although cultures such as that in India have traditions celebrating the erotic, this was regarded as shameful and shocking by Westerners.[43] Moreover in patriarchal societies such erotic cultures were deformed by lack of mutuality of men and women.

Homosexual relations also have languished under the veil of shame and exploitation by dominant males. An *ars erotica* that includes gay males and lesbians is the product of the modern gay and lesbian liberation movements. Here, too, male voices have often dominated. The female tendency to integrate sex into deepening friendship has often been overshadowed by the male preference for casual relations.[44] Gay

42. Such coming of age ceremonies that include sexual and contraceptive teaching are discussed in my forthcoming book, *Christianity and the Making of the Modern Family* (Boston, MA: Beacon Press, 2000), Chapter 9.

43. On the Indian manual of erotic love, see *Kama Sutra* (Bombay: D.B. Taraporevala Sons, 1963); also Indian erotic art, *Kama Shilpa: A Study of Indian Sculpture Depicting Love in Action* (Bombay: D.B. Taraporevala, 1962).

44. This greater tendency of women to seek integration of sex with friendship and commitment and men to seek casual affairs is probably a combination of social-

people have only begun to ask what deeper friendship and fidelity means for gay relations in a way that is not simply the mimic of heterosexual monogamy with its defective legalism and exclusivism.[45]

Thus Western cultures are a long way from imagining, much less seeking to inculcate through sensitive socialization, a happy celebration of sexual pleasure, connected to deepening friendship, an *ars erotica* that brings together the three loves of *eros*, *philia* and *agape*: sexual delight, friendship and mutual service. The time is long overdue for such cultural development. Let us begin.

ization and physical structure. Women as those who are 'penetrated' by the male sexual act and are vulnerable to both rape and impregnation against their will have a stake in tying sex to relationship, while the male sexual act and male socialization to aggression more easily allow men to externalize the sexual act and see it as 'conquest'. For lesbian women's construction of relationship as committed family, see Kath Weston, *Families We Choose: Lesbians, Gays, Kinship* (New York: Columbia University Press, 1991).

45. For a discussion of fidelity, mutuality and accountability in the context of gay and lesbian relations, see Elizabeth A. Say and Mark R. Kowalewski, *Gays, Lesbians and Family Values* (Cleveland, OH: Pilgrim Press, 1998), pp. 19-46.

'REFRESH ME WITH APPLES, FOR I AM FAINT WITH LOVE' (SONG OF SONGS 2.5): JEWISH FEMINISM, MYSTICAL THEOLOGY AND THE SEXUAL IMAGINARY

Melissa Raphael

The Jewish tradition's discourse on sexual pleasure at once invites and repels a feminist hermeneutic. While the tradition sacralizes sexual pleasure as a religious joy whose intimacy is both a symbol and enactment of the covenantal intimacy with God, and there is manifest concern on the part of the rabbis that sexual pleasure be mutual and tender, it is also discoursed upon from an unremittingly masculine perspective and assumes that the theological meaning of sex is exclusively and normatively heterosexual and marital.[1] The tradition is suspicious of romantic love and the purpose of its discourse on sex is not primarily to enhance its pleasures but to prohibit illicit (that is, non-marital) sexual relationships.[2] Judaism may not attempt to suppress human sexuality but sexual

---

1.   A notable, though non-authoritative, exception to the masculine monopoly on public sexual discourse is where Orthodox women publicly address one another on the pragmatic benefits to women of keeping the laws of menstrual purity (namely a respite from their husband's sexual attentions and pleasure in the *frisson* of sexual separation and reunion). Such intra-female discourse does little or nothing, however, to challenge patriarchal assumptions about, for example, women's sexual passivity or availability. See, e.g., Tehilla Abramov, *The Secret of Jewish Femininity: Insights into the Practice of Taharat HaMishpachah* (Southfield, MI: Targum, 1988).

2.   Lev. 18.2 proscribes all those sexual activities (the practices of 'Egypt') forbidden to men: incest, adultery, bestiality, male homosexuality, and sex with a menstruant. Women are only specifically addressed with the prohibition of bestiality (Lev. 18.23). There is no clear scriptural prohibition of lesbian relationships (though they are condemned twice in the Talmud as 'lewdness' or 'licentiousness'). Lesbianism is not perceived as a strictly legal problem because it entails no waste of male seed and what mattered to the law was, as Ellen Frankel puts it in *The Five Books of Miriam: A Woman's Commentary on the Torah* (New York: HarperSanFrancisco, 1996), p. 177, 'who was *engendering* whom'. In general, though, homo-

desire is nonetheless channeled and socialized within the institution of marriage alone.[3]

The purpose of this essay is not simply to examine how progressive Jewish feminists[4]—heterosexual or lesbian, married or otherwise—can find at least a comfortable and creative space within this discourse, but more significantly to propose that both the liberation of the Jewish woman as the subject of her own sexual experience and the liberation of God as divine subject from Jewish patriarchal discourse are a single process. For a Jewish feminist theology of sexual desire must be just that: a theology of sexual subjects whose sexual fulfillment is not merely culturally contingent upon a feminist political shift. True, the meaning and value of sexual experience is largely contingent on its sexual-political context, but I also want to say that its *a priori* meaning and value is necessarily and primarily theological in character.

This discussion of the relation between the redemption of Jewish female subjecthood, the subjecthood of God and sexual pleasure will not be entirely clear without at least an overview of biblical and rabbinic sexual ethics and the constructions of female sexuality they assume. So I shall begin by outlining how aspects of traditional sexual discourse have been both deplored and welcomed by Jewish feminists, and will follow Judith Plaskow in noting the patriarchal, but nonetheless discursively ambiguous, nature of the tradition's views about sexual relationships. Having done so, I shall turn to the progressive responses to this tradition, arguing that the Jewish feminist response in particular has been insufficiently theological (probably because theological perspectives are in any case hard to come by in the Jewish feminist literature).[5] To shift the focus from the customary legal and sociological

sexuality is prohibited in rabbinic literature as an abomination or error because it is counterfamilial, counterprocreative and has a purely sensual motivation. (See David Novak, 'Some Aspects of Sex, Society, and God in Judaism', in Elliot N. Dorff and Louis E. Newman [eds.], *Contemporary Jewish Ethics and Morality: A Reader* [New York: Oxford University Press, 1995], pp. 271-88 [pp. 227, 275-76]; Rachel Biale, *Women and Jewish Law: An Exploration of Women's Issues in Halakhic Sources* [New York: Schocken Books, 1984], pp. 175, 195.)

3. See Novak, 'Some Aspects of Sex', pp. 272-74.

4. For an account of the varieties of Jewish feminism see Nurit Zaidman, 'Variations of Jewish Feminism: The Traditional, Modern, and Postmodern Approaches', *Modern Judaism* 16 (1996), pp. 47-65.

5. On the whole, Jewish feminists have been little more attentive to theology than the wider Jewish community. That Judith Plaskow's *Standing again at Sinai:*

preoccupations of Jewish feminism, I suggest that a Jewish feminist construal of Jewish mysticism's highly sexualized discourse—far more than progressive Jewish discussions about sexual pleasure which tend to focus on rabbinic injustices or turn to non-Jewish or para-Jewish sources of inspiration—can suggest a new and properly theological imaginary. Within such an imaginary the redemption of the femaleness of God from patriarchal theology and religious practice would encompass, indeed, *produce*, the redemption of Jewish women as agents and subjects of their sexual pleasure.

The Ambiguity of the Tradition

As I have indicated, much in the tradition bodes well for the prospects of a Jewish feminist spirituality of sexual pleasure. In Judaism, sexual love and affection within marriage are a means to human fulfillment[6] (and, as we shall see, in the mystical tradition, to divine fulfillment as well).[7] Biblical and rabbinic Judaism is largely free from asceticism— there is virtually no tradition of vocational celibacy and (marital) sexual relationships are a central element within the divine economy of the holy. Indeed, the rabbinic laws of *onah* schematize the husband's religious obligation to give regular sexual satisfaction to his wife. While he must never force himself upon her, she is entitled to sexual pleasure regardless of whether she is fertile, pregnant or post-menopausal. These laws, framed in proportion to the physical demands of a man's work, are a clear demonstration of the rabbis' appreciation of sexual pleasure as a human good and holy mystery irrespective of its primary purpose as a means to procreation.[8]

Judaism from a Feminist Perspective (New York: HarperSanFrancisco, 1990) is, to date, one of only two full-length works of Jewish feminist theology, is probably because the majority of Jewish feminists (Cynthia Ozick has been influential here) share the wider community's prejudices against theology and regard women's status in Judaism as a principally halakhic (legal) problem and therefore awaiting a sociological rather than theological resolution.

6.   See Maurice Lamm, *The Jewish Way in Love and Marriage* (New York: Jonathan David Publishers, 1991).

7.   As far back as the mid 1970s Rita Gross hinted at a feminist theological construal of kabbalistic mysticism in the opening paragraph of an article reprinted in Sara Plant and Judith Plaskow (eds.), *Womanspirit Rising: A Feminist Reader in Religion* (New York: HarperSanFrancisco, 1992), pp. 167-73 (167).

8.   See esp. *The Holy Letter: A Study in Jewish Sexual Morality* (trans. Sey-

Of course it was rabbis, not women, who framed the laws of *onah* and they have continued to do so according to their own masculine perception of women's sexual needs and on the assumption that men will initiate and take the active role in sex (which women's modesty does not permit her to do) during that period of roughly twelve days in the menstrual cycle in which they have deemed a woman ritually 'clean'. Moreover, the discursive emphasis on sexual tenderness and respect for women does not mean that the Jewish community is in fact free from abuse.[9]

So that while it is true to say that halakhic Judaism is generally non-ascetic and may even feminize what it sees as the proper Jewish moral and spiritual and moral posture in relation to God,[10] this is not to say that its discourse on sex is anything other than patriarchal. Biblical law is unambiguously so, and its severe statutes on adultery and virginity are premised on the protection of male ownership and rights to female sexuality. During the biblical period, the patriarchal family was in a process of consolidation and women were 'given' and 'taken' in marriage (Gen. 11.29; 29.28) for the procreation of (preferably male) offspring. A woman's availability for licit sexual activity was, at this time, her chief contribution to the community.[11]

The primal patriarchal association of male sexual agency and the subjugation of women is evident in the Hebrew Bible's representation of sexual desire as a curse on women, punishing them for Eve's disobedience: 'In pain shall you bear children, yet your urge shall be for your

---

mour J. Cohen; Northvale, NJ: Jason Aronson, 1993): a translation of the thirteenth-century Hebrew mystical text *Iggeret haKodesh*, traditionally attributed to Nahmanides. For useful overviews of halakhic texts on sex within and outside marriage, see e.g., Biale, *Women and Jewish Law*, Chapters 5 and 7; Hannah Rockman, 'Sex, Shmex—As Long As You Love your Wife: A Review of the Laws and Guidelines Regarding Sexual Behaviour among Orthodox Jews', *Sexual and Marital Therapy* 8 (1993), pp. 255-67. Jonathan Magonet (ed.), *Jewish Explorations of Sexuality* (Providence: Berghahn Books, 1995) is also invaluable.

9. See, e.g., Julie Ringold Spitzer, *When Love is not Enough: Spousal Abuse in Rabbinic and Contemporary Judaism* (New York: Women of Reform Judaism, Federation of Temple Sisterhoods, 1995).

10. See Jacob Neusner, *Androgynous Judaism: Masculine and Feminine in the Dual Torah* (Macon, GA: Mercer University Press, 1993).

11. Plaskow, *Standing again at Sinai*, pp. 172-73.

husband and he shall rule over you' (Gen. 3.16).[12] Female sexual desire (at least being acknowledged as a fact) becomes a central prophetic metaphor ('whoring' after foreign gods) for Israel's infidelity to her long-suffering husband, Yahweh. Women in the Hebrew Bible are far from asexual (or witless), but there a number of women like Jael, Judith and even Ruth whose seductiveness has little to do with love, but is more the work of strategy and ulterior motive.

Jacob Neusner's interpretation of the role of female sexuality in shaping the status of women in Mishnaic (early) Judaism has had a considerable influence on the Jewish feminist critique. Using Simone de Beauvoir's notion of the patriarchal construction of female alterity, Neusner argues that women are an anomaly—the Other—in a religious system where men represent the normal. It is women's sexuality that is the essence of their abnormality and constitutes their threat to the sacred order. From puberty to menopause, female sexuality (especially when it is not contained within the usual sexual statuses of wife or daughter) is a source of chaos. For the sake of Israel's defining sacral equilibrium in which all things must remain in their appointed place, women must be controlled: kept in their place or returned to stasis by their sanctification. As subject to the sanctifying order of law, where the male (whether a father or husband) maintains control of a woman's biological and material property, the threat of the disordering female is defused.[13]

And yet simplistic dismissals of Jewish sexual discourse as *only* patriarchal are inadvisable. Jewish patriarchy is neither static nor a blunt instrument.[14] The matter is clouded by questions of religio-evolutionary change,[15] historical reaction,[16] rabbinic multivocality,[17] and the

12. See Frankel, *The Five Books of Miriam*, pp. 8-9; Biale, *Women and Jewish Law*, pp. 122-24.

13. Neusner, *A History of the Mishnaic Law of Women* (Leiden: E.J. Brill, 1980); Neusner, 'Thematic or Systematic Description: The Case of Mishnah's Division of Women', in *Method and Meaning in Ancient Judaism* (Missoula, MT: Scholars Press, 1979).

14. Judith Hauptman's book *Rereading the Rabbis: A Woman's Voice* (Boulder, CO: Westview Press, 1998) makes this admirably clear.

15. In early biblical literature female sexuality poses certain problems and yet there is little anxiety about heterosexual sex as such. However, the upheavals of the postexilic period saw a greater sexual repressiveness accompanying a general pessimism about the human, and in particular, the Jewish condition. Although basic biblical prohibitions remain in force throughout the rabbinic literature, rabbinic law

nature and content of covenantal and mystical Jewish theology itself. David Novak notes that rabbinic Judaism (especially in its banning of polygamy and concubinage) demonstrates a commitment to greater mutuality in marital relationships than is evident in scriptural law. In rabbinic Judaism a woman is not to be married against her will, and, contrary to scriptural law, a father wishing to marry off a girl child must wait until she is mature enough to give her consent. Novak regards 'the entire development of Jewish matrimonial law as the steady emancipation of women from anything even resembling slavery'. In its theology of monogamous marriage '*both* the man and the woman are exclusively sanctified to each other'.[18]

Not surprisingly, then, in her discussion of Jewish attitudes to sexual desire within and outside marriage, Plaskow detects profound ambiguities. On the one hand, there is a broad perception of the human sexual impulse as a God-given, normal and healthy part of a holy (married)

---

elaborated, tightened, dropped or added to biblical law where necessary. Judaism has, then, been subject to gradual change in its sexual ethics (in the tenth century CE, and perhaps wishing to gain greater acceptance of the community by its Christian neighbours, Rabbi Gershom forbade Western Jewry to take more than one wife). Postbiblical law more closely regulated modesty (especially the display of married women's hair, legs, chest and shoulders) and unchaperoned meetings between unmarried men and women were outlawed. Such laws were intended to reduce the possibility of male sexual temptation (Plaskow, *Standing again at Sinai*, pp. 176-77). From the third century the segregation of men and women at religious assemblies gradually became the norm. A woman's voice in prayer—even the sight of her little finger—could occasion desire. See Denise L. Carmody, 'Judaism', in Arvind Sharma (ed.),*Women in World Religions* (Albany, NY: State University of New York Press, 1987), pp. 183-206 (193); pp. 192-200 for a summary of Talmudic misogynistic statements about women.

16. Some (perhaps much) of the traditional Jewish discourse on sex is less derived from theology or from some putative abstract essence of the religion, but rather from a reaction—justified or otherwise—to the Pagan sexual practices of Canaanite religion and later to the sexual mores of an often oppressive Hellenistic culture.

17. Rabbis differ (as they do on other matters) in their attitudes to foreplay and sexual positions: some countenance only the missionary position (see, e.g., *b. Git.* 70a, *b. Nid.* 31b); others are markedly unpuritanical. Nonetheless, as Plaskow points out (*Standing again at Sinai*, p. 183), while the rabbis may be less negative about licit sex than the Church Fathers, they share similar preoccupations with the latter about controlling female temptation to men and containing male sexual desire.

18. Novak, 'Some Aspects of Sex', pp. 278, 280.

life, and on the other, as a chaotic force that requires containment within marriage and the laws of family purity.[19] So that while

> an avowal of a link between sex and spirit is…by no means foreign to Jewish experience… Yet again and again in theology and practice, Judaism turns away from and undermines this acknowledged connection by defining sexuality in terms of patriarchal possession and control.[20]

And yet it seems to me that the ambiguity of the tradition—whether it is, in fact, pro or anti-sex is largely irrelevant. What is surely at issue here is the question of whether the Jewish woman is a sexual subject, and that she *is* one has not been clearly established in traditional Judaism. In Mishnaic Judaism (the bedrock of later Judaism) women are chattels whenever that is necessary to establish the sexual rights of men to the benefits occasioned by women's biological functions, and persons whenever it is not.[21] More broadly, as we have seen, conjugal relations are the obligations of husbands to wives, rather than vice versa and the only laws directly addressed to women are those of the laws of *niddah*.[22] Even here, though, the need to control and order female sexuality was, and in different ways, remains, fully apparent.[23] As Judith Plaskow summarizes, in classical Judaism,

> to speak of sexuality is to speak of women occasionally as fellow people—themselves desirous but subject to social restraint—but mainly as objects, as Others, as dangers to male moderation, as hazards to the balance and moderation that mark the sacred order.[24]

So despite factors which prohibit crudely dismissive judgments, the exclusively male elite control over theology and practice makes a fully relational, mutual Judaism impossible (as does its outlawing of gay and lesbian commitments, inequalities in the conduct of divorce and perpetuation of the view that a woman's sexuality is not her own). There cannot be authentic love between a male subject and a female object

19. *Standing again at Sinai*, p. 179.

20. *Standing again at Sinai*, p. 197.

21. Judith Romney Wegner, *Chattel or Person: The Status of Women in Mishnaic Judaism* (New York: Oxford University Press, 1988), p. 171.

22. Biale, *Women and Jewish Law*, pp. 121-22. See also p. 197.

23. See Johnah Steinberg, 'From a "Pot of Filth" to a "Hedge of Roses" (and Back): Changing Theorizations of Menstruation in Judaism', *Journal of Feminist Studies in Religion* 13 (1997), pp. 5-26.

24. *Standing again at Sinai*, p. 185.

because the subject/object relation produces alienation and injustice. This demands not only a 'radical transformation of the institutional, legal framework within which sexual relations are supposed to take place',[25] but, above all, a consideration of women's subjecthood in relation to God's. In a Jewish religious ideology where female sexuality is a source of religious chaos, distraction and temptation and as a symbol of Paganism's supposedly degenerate worship of goddesses,[26] and where women represent *gashmiut* (physicality) as opposed to the male *ruhniut* (spirituality) and therefore are perceived as unable to transcend their sexuality as can men, female metaphors for God represent a sexualization of God unacceptable to patriarchal theology. It is here, then, that contestation must be taken beyond the realm of legal reform (however radical) and into that of theology.

Progressive Jewish Responses

Critical judgments on Judaism's sexual discourse can be traced back to first wave Jewish feminism. In 1904 Bertha Pappenheim condemned what she perceived to be Judaism's halakhic and mystical focus on reproductivity. She felt that the Jewish view of women as a mere 'sexual receptacle' paid no heed to women's needs or their capacity for spirituality and love. Indeed, Pappenheim regarded the consequent blunting of women's sexual responses as contributing to the prevalence of prostitution among Eastern European Jewish women during this period.[27] And, in our own time, Arthur Waskow is probably right in commenting that: 'few progressive Jews—indeed, rather few Jews of almost any political and religious hue—turn to the traditional Jewish code of sexual behaviour as an authoritative or practical guide to their actual behaviour'.[28] Although a small number of relatively permissive rabbinic authorities are sometimes cited as proof-texts for a progressive orientation, rabbinic sexual legislation as a whole is largely regarded as out-dated by mainstream Jewish communities and all but the most

25. *Standing again at Sinai*, p. 199.

26. *Standing again at Sinai*, p. 170.

27. Naomi Shepherd, *A Price Below Rubies: Jewish Women as Rebels and Radicals* (London: Weidenfeld & Nicolson, 1993), pp. 232-33.

28. 'Down-To-Earth Judaism: Sexuality', in Elliot N. Dorff and Louis E. Newman (eds.), *Contemporary Jewish Ethics and Morality: A Reader* (New York: Oxford University Press, 1995), pp. 289-99 (289).

Orthodox contemporary Jews regard the choice between traditional early marriage or pre-marital celibacy as both inadvisable and unrealistic.

However, while the vast majority of Jews remain committed to the heterosexual marital norm, progressive Jews regret that there is 'almost no public Jewish way of honoring or celebrating sexual relationships other than marriage'[29] and in these circles, alternative rituals are being developed—Rabbi Elizabeth Sarah and her partner Cathy Burnstone, for example, adopted one shared middle name (*Tikvah*, meaning 'hope') during their *Berit Ahavah* (Covenant of Love) ceremony in June 1998.[30] And rejecting conservative sexual ethics, Jews in the progressive *havurot*[31] may contain those whom Arthur Waskow describes as 'fluidly coupled and uncoupled'.[32] This does not mean that Waskow and those like him are advocating promiscuity. Rather, Waskow takes heart from Judaism's ancient sacralization of community, justice and the mundane or earthy as grounding his own and other progressive Jews' bid to reimage God in the light of the physico-spiritual yearning to be whole (*Shalem*). This, he claims, is nourished not by the *legislation* of relationality, but from just and stable loving connections between persons and between persons and the earth. It is in the health or wholeness of persons in connection with all other living things that the presence of God—the Breath of Life—is manifest.[33]

The Jewish feminist movement would be substantially in agreement with Waskow. But in her systematic feminist critique of traditional Judaism, *Standing again at Sinai*, Plaskow (who is one of the relatively few Jewish feminists committed to the Jewish theological project) concentrates most of her space and energies to a (necessary) critique of traditional Jewish constructions of sexuality in the classical rabbinic sources. Having done so, she arrives at her relatively brief constructive

---

29. Waskow, 'Down-To-Earth Judaism', p. 290.

30. Elizabeth Tikvah Sarah, review of Judith Hauptman, *Rereading the Rabbis* in *Hochmah* newsletter no. 14 September 1998/Rosh Ha Shanah 5759, pp. 17-19 (19).

31. *Havurot* are informal study and prayer groups generally comprised of Jews sympathetic to progressive movements such as feminism, the green movement and ethical *kashrut* (dietary law) and who wish to respond justly and creatively to the challenges of modernity.

32. Waskow, 'Down-To-Earth Judaism', p. 291.

33. Waskow, 'Down-To-Earth Judaism', p. 295.

theology of erotic connection having largely relinquished the Jewish theological idiom, drawing as she does not so much on reclaimable images from within her own tradition, but on the (wholly admirable) non-Jewish writings of James Nelson, Audre Lorde, Starhawk and Beverly Harrison. Plaskow makes passing references to the celebration of sexual passion evoked by *Shir Hashirim* (Song of Songs) and female sexual metaphors for God are adverted to as suggesting a sensuality and mutuality that would be characteristic of Jewish feminist sexual ideals, but none of this is pursued in the theological context to which she is committed.[34]

By contrast, I want to see what imaginal resources the tradition itself can yield to feminist theology. In particular, I want to see how kabbalistic myth can function in the sense that John Hick describes: namely in its capacity to evoke an appropriate dispositional response to God (or what he calls 'the Real'). Like Hick, I would not want to assert the literal truth of myth, but am interested rather in its metaphorical dynamics as a means to mythological truth.[35] In other words, that Jewish mysticism has so notably deployed sexual tropes and sexual practices in an attempt to 'penetrate and even describe the mystery of the world as a reflection of the mysteries of the divine life'[36] seems to suggest a means by which Jewish feminist criticism can move beyond a critique of biblical and rabbinic sexual legislation and begin to pose sharp feminist theological questions about the cosmic and ontological (not only social) effects of patriarchal religio-sexual discourse and its alliances with other operations of patriarchal power.

Towards a Mystical Jewish Feminist Sexual Imaginary

It is customary for commentators to note that Jewish mysticism is heterodox in its sexualization of the inner life of God. The most familiar form of Jewish mysticism to do so is that of Lurianic kabbalah whose basic scheme can be outlined as follows.[37] When God emerged from concealment in order to create the universe, the vessels of the

34. *Standing again at Sinai*, pp. 206-207, 210.

35. John Hick, *An Interpretation of Religion: Human Responses to the Transcendent* (Basingstoke: Macmillan Press, 1989), pp. 348-53.

36. Gershom Scholem, *On the Kabbalah and its Symbolism* (trans. Ralph Manheim; New York: Schocken Books, 1996), pp. 1-2.

37. Rabbi Isaac Luria was a leading sixteenth-century Jewish mystic.

lower *sefirot* (or emanations of God) shattered because they could not contain the divine light that filled them. This stream of holy light ran down from world to world until, catastrophically, it reached the 'Other Side'. Here, the 'shells' (*kelipot*) or forces of impurity spilled the light and its sparks fell into the material world. The redemption of the world is brought about when Jews consecrate the world by their goodness, rescuing the scattered or hidden sparks and returning them to God. The fall of Adam corresponds with the breaking of the vessels and is responsible for the exile or separation of the *Shekhinah* from the other *sefirot*. But good deeds will enable the female *Shekhinah*[38] or *Sefirah Malkhut*—the emanation of God closest to humanity—to be reunited with the male *Sefirah Tiferet* (beauty): a sacred marriage restoring the original creative unity of the masculine and feminine within God, peace and harmony to the *sefirot* and enabling the free flow of divine grace to a world fragmented by the shattering of the divine.[39]

Among the Lurianic kabbalists of sixteenth-century Safed, the exile of the *Shekhinah* consists in the separation of masculine and feminine elements in God as a result of human sin. Her exile is a symbol of human guilt, and all religious activity must seek to bring her exile to an end. Each sin deepens the exile of the divine soul and each good deed furthers the homecoming of the banished soul. Thus in Lurianic Kabbalah the exile is not only a punishment for sin or a test of faith, it is also 'a symbolic mission. In the course of its exile Israel must go everywhere, to every corner of the world, for everywhere a spark of the *Shekhinah* is waiting to be found, gathered and restored by a religious act.'[40] Traditions of the exile of the *Shekhinah* can be traced back to the Talmud (*Meg.* 29a): 'In every exile into which the children of Israel went, the *Shekhinah* was with them.' In the Kabbalah, however, it is

38. In the Bible God's presence is referred to as 'God's face'; in rabbinic Judaism, as his *Shekhinah*. In the older Jewish literature, *Shekhinah* is not a separate hypostasis. By the time of the early Kabbalists, *Shekhinah* had become a quasi-independent female aspect within God. Non-kabbalistic rabbinic Jews were offended by this development, but it caught the popular imagination nonetheless (Scholem, *On the Kabbalah*, p. 105).

39. Scholem, *On the Kabbalah*, p. 108. See also Elliot R. Wolfson, 'Woman—the Feminine as Other in Theosophic Kabbalah: Some Philosophical Observations on the Divine Androgyne', in Laurence J. Silberstein and Robert L. Cohen (eds.), *The Other in Jewish Thought and History: Constructions of Jewish Culture and Identity* (New York: New York University Press, 1994), pp. 166-204.

40. Scholem, *On the Kabbalah*, pp. 115-16.

taken to mean that *'a part of God Himself is exiled from God'*.[41] Although the separation of the masculine and feminine principles within God is a 'cosmic calamity', nonetheless, properly conducted, the act of sexual union mirrors the reunion of God and his *Shekhinah*; it represents the harmonious joining of the masculine and feminine in God and is therefore at the very heart of the redemptive process.[42]

Two things seem particularly significant here: first, the kabbalists' practical insistence that every religious act should be performed 'for the sake of the reunion of God and His *Shekhinah*'.[43] And second, the kabbalists' theological recognition of (admittedly heterosexual) union as a symbolic but also actually redemptive participation in the union of male and female aspects within the Godhead. Both of these factors are open to feminist construal. For religious feminism insists that all persons— female and male—have a stake in the redemptive process that is a possibility of their daily lives. Also, religious feminism denies that God's separation from God is a function of God's creativity or immanence, or that it is a result of human sinfulness *per se*. Rather, the separation of God from God is a function of the patriarchal alienation or exile of the femaleness of God from God,[44] of which the alienation of women's sexual subjecthood is a reflection and product. As we have seen, the misogynistic sexual superstition and prudery of rabbinic law[45] is underpinned by its majority view that only men are made in God's likeness, with the female being later formed from the male body.[46] As such

41. Scholem, *On the Kabbalah*, p. 107.

42. Plaskow, *Standing again at Sinai*, p. 188; see also Lawrence Fine, 'The Contemplative Practice of Yihhudim in Lurianic Kabbalah', in Arthur Green (ed.), *Jewish Spirituality from the Sixteenth-Century Revival to the Present* (London: SCM Press, 1989), pp. 83-87.

43. Scholem, *On the Kabbalah*, p. 108. This was a common liturgical formula until the nineteenth century when it was deleted by modernists (*On the Kabbalah*, p. 109).

44. By the 'femaleness of God' I do not mean that God is biologically female but that traits and capacities commonly associated with women can be (critically) attributed to God in feminist theological descriptions of God's relation with the world.

45. During sex, husbands are enjoined to refrain from looking at their wives' genitals (lest they find them off-putting), and sacred texts are to be removed from the room where the couple make love.

46. Judith R. Baskin, 'Rabbinic Judaism and the Creation of Woman', in Miriam

mystical Judaism may intend to presentiate God in the marital relationship but actually, as a heterodox Orthodoxy, does the opposite. Its exile of God from women as a masculine divine other and women as a female other to God, perpetuates the exile of the *Shekhinah*; God is lost to God because it is hard for God to see God's glorious face (for some kabbalists, the very purpose of creation) in an abject/object other.

A feminist version of Lurianic myth might want to say that God has sought and yearned for a sight of her veiled face, hidden from view behind every discursive, cultural and material *mehitzah*.[47] And if Ze'ev Meshel and others are right, God has done so since the loss of God's female consort, Asherah,[48] or perhaps much earlier still. It is told that Abraham Halevi Berukhim would run through the streets of Safed at midnight, weeping and crying out: 'Arise in God's name, for the *Shekhinah* is in exile, the house of our sanctuary is burned, and Israel is in great distress.' This same mystic had a vision of the *Shekhinah* clad in black at the wailing wall, weeping and lamenting.[49] The mystics had a sense that the world was evidence that something had gone cosmically as well as historically amiss. From a feminist perspective it is also possible to see Shekhinah[50] at the wailing wall in black, lamenting because the world is suffering the patriarchal fragmentation and dispersal of God's femaleness: the alienation of God from God. But just as on the Sabbath, the mystics' sexual union intended a sacred marriage celebrating the return of God from exile, so too Jewish women might welcome Shekhinah's return to feminist Judaism, in white and in joy as bride to the masculine, patriarchal God, not merely to complete God, but to restore the shattered God (and therefore women) to wholeness.

Of course it is important to be aware that a feminist sexual symbolic cannot be straightforwardly derived from Jewish mystical sources as these are informed by powerful ascetic elements. Although, within mar-

Peskowitz and Laura Levitt (eds.), *Judaism Since Gender* (London: Routledge, 1997), p. 128.

47. A *mehitzah* is a screen of various type and degree and is erected to segregate women from men on public religious occasions.

48. See Asphodel Long's discussion of Meshel's archeological findings in 'The Goddess in Judaism—an Historical Perspective', in Alix Pirani (ed.), *The Absent Mother: Restoring the Goddess to Judaism and Christianity* (London: Mandala, 1990), pp. 27-65 (41-46).

49. Scholem, *On the Kabbalah*, pp. 149, 140.

50. I cease to italicize 'Shekhinah' when it ceases to be a technical term for an aspect of God, and becomes the immanent God's 'female' name.

riage, sexual union was a mystery and a means to mystical meditation, any perceived abuse of a man's generative powers became a means by which the demonic 'other side' could engender its own progeny. Fear of impurity produced a specifically mystical cult of purity and attendant practices of self-mortification,[51] the urgency of which is in no doubt: impurity left the kabbalistic (male) Jew personally responsible for the continued rupture of God.[52]

And yet, while this ascetic element must be acknowledged, it does not exhaust the self-multiplying meanings of Jewish mystical discourse which, like any other discursive tradition can be counter-read or re-meant in each new context. That is, despite its being a product of the patriarchal worldview, the Jewish mystical symbolic already drives towards an association of redemption with both the (at least notionally) female presence of God and the presence of women in sacred space. For the *Shekhinah* is also the Bride or Queen of the Sabbath and every Jewish woman who welcomes the *Shekhinah* into her space when she lights the sanctifying Sabbath candles is herself both medium and present-ation of the *Shekhinah*.

Just before the Sabbath came in, Kabbalists in sixteenth-century Safed and Jerusalem would go out into the fields in the afternoon, to 'meet the Bride'. At the Sabbath table, a hymn (Prov. 31) was (and still is) sung by husbands to their wives; a hymn that was also a hymn to the *Shekhinah*, and one which was redemptive: it would hurl the demons

---

51. Scholem, *On the Kabbalah*, p. 155. Even marital relations were considered to be endangered by Lilith's attempt to 'infringe on the domain of Eve'. Lilith could entice any man to masturbation and waste of seed. Accordingly, rites were developed to keep her away from the marriage bed. (The Zohar recommends the chanting of sacred verses, the wrapping of man and wife's heads in cloth and then sprinkling the bed with fresh water.) (See Scholem, *On the Kabbalah*, p. 157; Fine, 'The Contemplative Practice of Yihhudim', p. 77. Novak, following R.J.Z. Werblowsky, is rightly unhappy with the 'countersexual' nature of the kabbalistic symbolisation of human sexuality. He is perturbed by its lack of a more embodied sexual theology and its assumption that divine love is essentially self-enclosed. By contrast he sees divine love as 'an act of God's self-transcendence, his recognition of a truly non-divine *other*' ('Some Aspects of Sex', p. 282). Moreover, in their sacramentalization of the sexual act, kabbalists subordinated the actuality of the relationship and of the sexual act to its mystical intentionality ('Some Aspects of Sex', p. 287 n. 101).

52. See Fine, 'The Contemplative Practice of Yihhudim', pp. 72, 74.

back into the abyss.[53] Later that night, sexual union completed the welcome of the *Shekhinah* returned from exile. That mystical Judaism used the myth and ritual of the return of a banished female divinity to overcome evil; to both presentiate God and (in an overtly sexual manner) to reunite a lost part of God to God immediately suggests the contours of a Jewish feminist mythography: one which will maintain a necessary (if somewhat one-sided) conversation with tradition, but also provide a symbolic structure by which to understand and resist the manifold evils of alienation and colonization produced by the patriarchal occlusion of God. Here sexual union is not, of course, the only feminist means to *tikkun* or redemption, but can become a central practical and imaginal process by which a post-patriarchal peace is restored to the intra-human and cosmic realms.

That rabbinic and mystical texts enjoin men to use the Sabbath as a time for marital intercourse suggests, then, a feminist sexual symbolic that includes sexual pleasure but also, in its context of sacred time and space, points towards the restoration of social and ecological peace of which the Sabbath is already a prolepsis. Feminist sexual love becomes one of the most profound functions of the Sabbath as the patriarchal worship of a fragment of God at the expense of the monotheistic whole requires precisely the theological restoration, mending and recreation of knowledges that the Sabbath promises. *Shalom bayit* (the sacramental peace of the household) is the proper context for sexual love and maintaining this has traditionally been the responsibility of women. But men have an equal responsibility for *shalom bayit* and when they refuse to sacralize the rabbinic othering of women and insist on the full humanity of women, the blessings of *shalom bayit* will be manifest. Conversely, where the image of God in women is refused and unnamed then Shekhinah will be unknown—a stranger—to their place.

It seems to me that a Jewish feminist theological sexual imaginary, to *be* Jewishly theological must be covenantal and therefore (at least quasi-) marital in character. And it is because of the inherent relationality within the concept of a covenant that I am happy to figure a sexual theology within a marital mode—here broadly conceived as any intentionally permanent covenant of love between two Jews or between a Jew and non-Jew who both wish to live as Jews, whatever their sexual orientation.

53. Scholem, *On the Kabbalah*, pp. 141-42, 145.

The Orthodox Jewish feminist, Blu Greenberg, notes that the full religious status of women—'the maturation of woman as Jew' rather than damaging marital relationships, could actually 'subtly enhance them in a number of ways'.[54] She does not elaborate here, but it seems to me that it can do far more than that. The Jewish marital ideal of upholding 'a covenant rooted in the covenant between God and his people Israel'[55] promises much for feminist theology when dislodged from its narrow referential frame. Judaism has always insisted that God is present within marriage. Quoting the *aggadic* view that 'it is impossible for man to live without woman; it is impossible for woman to live without man; and it is impossible for both to live without God's presence (*Shekhinah*)', David Novak argues that the presence of God in the marital relationship correlates with the status of the human person as the image of God. It also entails that 'God's love is the primary reality in which human love becomes a participation'.[56] Further, Novak argues that in the covenantal relationship of which finite marital sexual love is a significant form, God's infinite love for his people is manifest: 'If, then, we can love with an undying love, it is only because we have been loved by God.'[57] Novak must be right, but only partially so. Because women cannot know and love God to the full until God's female face is revealed to them as the Holy One in whose image they are made and are known to themselves. In the uncovering and opening of sexual union a woman may be revealed as what she is (and I make no apologies for ontological essentialism): a mirror to God's face. The covenantal act and context of love is therefore epistemically central to the generation of a Jewish feminist theology.

Sexual union, socialized by a feminist covenant of love, is not only a seeing of the other but can also can figure a mystical openness to the unveiled nakedness of God as the one whose truest name may be no more and no less than 'I AM (with you)' (Exod. 3.14). For until now,

---

54. *On Women and Judaism: A View from Tradition* (Philadelphia: The Jewish Publication Society of America, 1981), pp. 55, 53.

55. Novak, 'Some Aspects of Sex', p. 280.

56. Novak, 'Some Aspects of Sex', p. 281.

57. Novak, 'Some Aspects of Sex', p. 288 n. 110. While I sympathize with much of Novak's argument, I cannot accept his implication that only heterosexual marital relationships are covenantal and his dualistic contention that (heterosexual) ecstatic love intends extra-bodily transcendence in the undying love of God ('Some Aspects of Sex', p. 282).

like that of women, the Jewish God's female face/presence (Shekhinah) has been both veiled and masked by patriarchal identities and that veiling has been a sign of her subjection. Now, as in the traditional Ashkenazi *bedeken di kale* ritual before a marriage,[58] feminist celebration of Shekhinah can ritually draw back her veil and cover her again so that, faint with love, she can see God and (in all senses) live; so that she can know God to be the one who women have claimed her to be and cover her once more, her holiness protected from the desecratory gaze.

The restoration of women as subjects made in the image of God is at once, then, the restoration of God's 'female' subjecthood to God: a (re)marriage or new covenant which restores the knowledge—and therefore the presence of—Shekhinah both to God and to the world. The sanctity of a marriage sanctifies its place. The rabbis once described how the *Shekhinah* hovered over the matriarch Sarah's tent as a divine Cloud of Glory. Sarah's Sabbath lights were not extinguished but burned there all week long.[59] So too, the place of Jewish love should be like Sarah's tent: *a chuppah*—a marriage canopy—or even just a shelter under which a new covenant or *ketubah*[60] of relationship between the people Israel and between Israel and God can be drawn up, its text decorated with flowers, illuminated in gold and sealed with love. And just as the *hallah dekel* covering the two Sabbath loaves is a traditional symbol of mutual care within the home,[61] so too should the covers of the marital bed form a canopy or *chuppah* of care stretched out under the stars, over the world.

It should have become apparent that the theological significance of persons coming together *face to face* in the knowing of love is not, or should not be, privatized, even if sexual intimacy is properly private between two lovers. Indeed, the privatization of Jewish women's sexu-

---

58. In *Holocaust Project: From Darkness into Light* (New York: Viking, 1993), p. 16, Judy Chicago describes how she adopted the Hasidic *bedeken* ceremony for her own marriage to Donald Woodman which was officiated over by the feminist rabbi Lynn Gottlieb. Chicago found Woodman's lifting of the veil 'nothing if not erotic': 'When Donald walked over to me I was trembling. When he lifted my veil I beheld him—in his white tuxedo with a white floral wreath on his head—transformed from Donald into *my groom*. He was radiant and I guess I must have been too.'

59. See Frankel, *The Five Books of Miriam*, p. 37.

60. The *ketubah* is the marriage contract without which a husband is forbidden to live with his wife.

61. Angela Wood, *Judaism* (London: B.T. Batsford, 1984), p. 49.

ality has been politically disempowering. The rabbis described women's arousal as hidden, internal and, unlike men's, invisible (*b. Sanh.* 7a). A cognate social ideology of embodiment has entailed that the modesty of a woman's arousal is 'naturally' matched by the modesty of her religious life which is likewise non-public or hidden from view. And it would seem that the codes of modesty were even inflicted upon God in her theological seclusion in the realms of heresy or silence. This means that the restoration of divine and human female agency is an ontological and political act: a restitution of power to the divine and human subject. It is in this light that I understand the Jewish feminist liturgical words:

> I give praise to you, *HaMakom*, the Place of Power. *Shekhinah*, in the darkness of Your Womb we find comfort and protection. *Rakhameima*, Mother of Compassion, in the Darkness of Your Hidden Place we find the Source and the Power.[62]

Figuring the protectiveness and creativity of God-She in the image of the womb has been prevalent in Jewish feminist circles from the inception of the movement, but it may be that female sexual pleasure *as well as reproductivity* can come to share in the revelatory yield of Jewish feminism. After all, there are clear vulval overtones in the well-loved Jewish feminist symbol of the biblical Miriam's legendary well: an underground spring whose eternal living waters (*mayim hayim*) bubble forth to sustain new life and carry refreshment to the (patriarchal) desert on its gentle flow. According to tradition, when Miriam died, the well dried up. But this is not true: Miriam's well may dry up if abused, but its source is ever-renewing. Female sexuality can be experienced as a cup of Miriam (*Kos Miryam*)—a cup which Penina Adelman likens to 'the portable ark in the desert, [which] may be carried everywhere, brimming full of the living waters which sustain the Jewish people'.[63] That is, the sexual symbolic I have only begun to outline may prove to be no mere linguistic conceit, but a way of mapping the female body onto Judaism's whole redemptive imaginary.

To conclude, I have wanted to celebrate the Jewish mystical tradition's perception of the presence of the *Shekhinah* restored to God and to the world in the act of sexual union, here defined as the union of

---

62. Penina V. Adelman, 'A Drink from Miriam's Cup: Invention of Tradition among Jewish Women', *Journal of Feminist Studies in Religion* 2 (1994), pp. 151-66 (165).

63. Adelman, 'A Drink from Miriam's Cup', p. 163.

those who have made between them a covenant of love whose sexual sealing is a form of seeing/knowing which reveals each to the other as a portrait of God. I have wanted to say that Shekhinah, exiled by patriarchal theology and practice, returns and therefore becomes knowable when a woman is undressed by the eyes of love as an image of God so that, in the same moment she becomes visible to God, God's female face is restored to her. God and Israel's relationship has been marred by infidelity; not by Israel's lusting after false gods, but by Israel's infidelity to God-She in their midst. The commandment to love God with all our heart and soul (Deut. 6.4) is at the very heart of Jewish law. But Israel disobeys this commandment when it refuses to love God in God's inclusive oneness. The biblical prophetic call for Israel to repent its infidelity to God must now induce Israel to draw up a new *ketubah* promising to love God and *therefore* love women *as* moral and religious subjects with all the joy and tenderness the tradition itself prescribes.

Part II

SEXUAL THEOLOGY AND WOMEN'S POWER

ARE WE MAKING LOVE YET?
THEOLOGICAL AND PSYCHOLOGICAL PERSPECTIVES ON THE ROLE OF GENDER IDENTITY IN THE EXPERIENCE OF DOMINATION

Lallene J. Rector

All of us are, to some significant degree, in bondage to wrong relation...
(Heyward 1989: 105)

Introduction

Feminist scholars and theologians have long sought an explanation for the realities of male domination, both its origins and its persistence. As a psychotherapist, it is not unusual to hear repeated stories of one or another variation from women struggling to maintain a sense of self within relationship, typically within an intimate heterosexual relationship. While there are more gross and violent kinds of male domination (sexual abuse, domestic violence, rape and so on), the situations frequently reported in psychotherapy are usually experienced as very subtle forms of domination. From the woman's perspective, she feels she is submitting or surrendering her own desires and preferences in deference to her male partner. The case of Ms B. is illustrative. Ms B. is middle-aged, married, and has her own professional life. In addition, there are several other interests which she pursues: a book club, a Bible study group, regular exercise and collecting antiques. Her husband is retired and is also involved in a number of creative activities. She describes him as a wonderful person in many respects, highly regarded in their community, civic minded and generous. He is enviably able to live his life and follow his interests in ways that seem to Ms B. free of the relational constraints she feels. He appears to simply do what he desires as if this was the natural order of the world, without the anxiety of being abandoned by or disconnected from the ones he loves.

While the relationship is quite companionable and mostly amiable, Ms B. complains about her experience of his emotional distance. Of particular difficulty is the struggle to pull herself away from his plans for a given day. If he wants to watch the morning television news, read the newspapers in bed, or go for a bike ride, Ms B. finds that it takes an intentional effort on her part to act independently. Even when she is aware of her own preferences and agenda, she frequently accommodates to his schedule, unbeknownst to him.

Similar dynamics are reported in their sexual relationship. Ms B.'s husband has a chronic problem with impotence and so Ms B. has adapted to this difficulty by having sex when *he* wants to, and in the position that causes *him* the least anxiety. His orgasm virtually always comes first, so that Ms B.'s pleasure is relegated to a rather uninspired effort by an exhausted partner, as a secondary consideration. It should be noted again that none of this has occurred in a context of overt and dramatic domination by her husband, nor accompanied by explicit demands on his part. Women often accommodate male sexual desire and feel dominated by it without much sense that a different choice might be exercised, even though they seem to participate willingly. Or, perhaps they labor under the expectation that self-assertion in a different direction would cause unwanted and sometimes anxiety provoking conflict. Why is this? Is it the way gender roles for men and women are socialized in our culture? Or, is it the idiosyncratic psychopathology of Ms B. and other women like her? Or, some combination of both?

Feminist theologians have been committed to an analysis and deconstruction of patriarchal ideologies regarding them as the primary source of male domination. It is recognized that patriarchy is a complex and insidious phenomenon which necessitates theoretical examination, social and economic intervention, and psychological assessment as at least part of the means of accomplishing a more thorough-going equality of the sexes. This paper seeks to offer a critical consideration of the relationship between gender identity and the experience of domination within the larger context of the social justice agenda of feminist scholars, theologians and psychologists. As a way of setting the theological stage on the issue of male domination, the paper begins with a brief review of Rosemary Radford Ruether's historical and theological assessment of the major claims of feminist theologies, especially through the doctrine of redemption (1996). All feminist theologies call for an end to male domination, and all offer various strategies for the accomplishment of it. In particular, when Ruether, in the name of feminist theologies, calls for a personal conversion and an opening up to one another as one part of the means of redemption, the considerations of female psychology and feminist psychoanalytic theorizing become relevant specifically in their contribution to the consciousness-raising which must undergird other efforts to challenge and change patriarchal ideology and social structures. It is at this juncture that a *psychological* perspective on domination and the role of gender identity becomes useful to the larger project of feminist theologians.

After reviewing Ruether's work, the paper turns to psychological perspectives, first considering the relational feminist approach of Nancy Chodorow (1978, 1979, 1994), and then focusing on the work of Jessica Benjamin (1988). Benjamin's intersubjective theorizing represents one of the more recent psychoanalytic investigations of the phenomenon of domination. Of particular interest and provocation is Benjamin's insistence that the experience of the one dominated, including the ways in which one desires and/or participates willingly in being dominated must also be explored. Feminism has too often ignored this aspect of domination as a contributing factor to its preservation.[1] While there are many feminist psychological perspectives (Butler 1990; Mitchell 1974; Gilligan 1982; Jordan *et al.* 1991 and 1997; Irigaray 1985; Kristeva 1986; 1989), Benjamin's theory deals explicitly and extensively with the issue of domination. The article concludes with a critique of Benjamin and returns to a theological consideration of gender identity as a counter-argument to gender hierarchy. The consideration of values and ethics which underly the feminist vision of gender equality is inescapable. Feminist theology is predicated on such a vision.

Feminist Theological Perspectives

In *Women and Redemption* (1996) Ruether traces the history of controversy within the Christian traditions regarding 'changing paradigms of gender, male and female, in relation to the Christian claim of a universal and inclusive redemption in Christ' (p. 1).[2] She describes a long

---

1. See Ann Ferguson (1989) for a discussion of the various feminist perspectives on what kind of sexual liberation ought to be sought. Some call for the minimal condition of consent (Rubin 1984; Sawicki 1986) criticizing sexual ethics which create a hierarchy of sexual correctness. Others call for a kind of reciprocity, or free choice, which they believe is currently impossible in the structure of sex roles within a patriarchal context (Dworkin and MacKinnon 1985).

2. The limitations of this paper do not allow a fuller representation of Ruether's

history in which men and women believed in the vision of a 'new humanity' that would overcome gender hierarchy. Ruether also follows the development of counter-arguments and theological positions against the claims that women were created second and therefore inferior; that women sinned first; that women are to be relegated to subordinate roles; and that God must therefore be symbolized in masculine terms. Contemporary Christian feminists assume women's equal humanity with men and the right to equally access the benefits and privileges of society. They reject 'any theological or sociobiological justifications of women's subordination as due to some combination of (1) natural inferiority, (2) a divine mandate that women be subordinate in the order of creation, and (3) punishment for their priority in sin' (1996: 7). Further, it is assumed that domination of men over women is sinful; social structures which promote it must be dismantled; and supporting ideological and theological justifications must be deconstructed.

Of particular interest to a psychology of domination is the issue of anthropology (i.e. assumptions about human nature) which Ruether identifies as an ongoing disputed question. What is the relation of human nature to maleness and femaleness? She explains that 'one-nature' anthropology claims one human nature possessed equally by men and women, but tends toward an androcentric bias. A 'two-nature' anthropology claims essential difference between male and female, with women being excluded as active participants in society.

> Feminists have sought to define an enlarged understanding of the human that unites all human qualities in a transformed whole and to define journeys of growth into wholeness for women and men by which each can reclaim those lost parts that have been assigned to the other sex. But questions of how women are different (better?) from men, while at the same time being *equal* and possessing the *same* humanness as a basis for equal rights in society, continue to plague feminist anthropology (Ruether 1996: 10).

Postmodernist feminists question any concept of universal essential humanness, and women of color call for a perspective of infinite particularity in which their specific context and social location define human nature.

work. However, her 1996 volume is to be commended for both its sweeping historical consideration, as well as its careful analysis of the theological and biblical interpretive shifts since the beginning of the early church which have undergirded the more contemporary development of feminist theological perspectives.

Ruether traces at least three significant theological shifts that characterize core perspectives within feminist theology. The first is represented by the thinking of Agrippa von Nettesheim in the sixteenth century, in which women were accorded an original equality with men and in which the subordination of women was regarded as 'sinful domination'. The second shift occurred between the seventeenth and nineteenth centuries in which an alternative undestanding of redemption was considered, that is that redemption is not an other-worldly, future oriented event, but a this-worldly mandate to transform unjust social structures and relations. The social gospel and liberation theologies of the nineteenth and twentieth centuries have extended the this-worldly focus on redemption by emphasizing both personal conversion and social justice dimensions of a revised concept of redemption. In contemporary feminist theology gender hierarchy is regarded as a pivotal justice issue and central to the foundation of patriarchal systems. 'Feminism sees patriarchy as a multilayered system of domination, centered in male control of women but including class and race hierarchy, generational hierarchy, clericalism, and expressed also in war and domination of nature' (1996: 274). Hence, 'redemption means overcoming all forms of patriarchy' (1996: 274).

Redemption then becomes reinterpreted and expressed by Ruether in one form as the need for a personal conversion of consciousness that eschews gender hierarchy (and other dualisms) requiring a more open and equal relationship between self and other. Theologically, this 'new humanity' is based on a sense of original goodness (versus original sinfulness) and communion with the divine.[3] With the introduction of views of human nature, concerns with the relationship between sameness and difference, gender as a category of analysis, and a call for personal transformation, psychological perspectives on domination become not only relevant, but necessary. Even so, it is only a part of the larger redemptive agenda and vision of feminist theologies.

The Psychology of Domination and the Role of Gender

Psychoanalytic theory has in the last 25 years enjoyed a renewed interest in and critique by feminists. Of particular import have been the

---

3. For a Trinitarian perspective which includes a consideration of feminist scholarship, see Volf (1996) on male domination and the issues of sameness and difference in gender identity.

examination of theories of gender acquisition and sexuality and their implications for understanding the phenomenon of male dominance and oppression of women. Psychoanalytic theory in its emphasis on the role of the unconscious and its exploration of human motivation has a unique potential for providing at least part of an explanation for domination. However, it must be noted that a psychoanalytic perspective is limited in that its interests are psychological, and only partly social, with little or no attention to economic and power dynamics.

Although a philosopher rather than a psychologist, Simone de Beauvoir's claims in *The Second Sex* (1952) have strongly influenced relational feminists Nancy Chodorow (1978) and Jessica Benjamin (1988). Beauvoir's observation that women are always defined as Other and valued negatively, while men carry a more universalized and positive human identity suggests that identity is a product of a subject-object opposition and one that is quickly turned into a hierarchical dualism of the superior male over the inferior female.

> ...we find in consciousness itself a fundamental hostility towards every other consciousness; the subject can be posed only in being opposed—he sets himself up as the essential as opposed to the other, the inessential, the object (de Beauvoir 1952: 17).

This defining of masculinity as something opposed to femininity in the form of a subject-object dichotomy was continued in early psychoanalytic theory about gender.

Initially, feminist psychoanalytic considerations (Mitchell 1974) focused on Freud's gender theory and the oedipal phase as the developmental fulcrum of the personality, even though they offered a reinterpretation of penis envy as a symbolic issue rather than a literal desire. Freud theorized that during the oedipal period of development (approximately ages 3–6) the little boy and girl shift from strictly dyadic relational concerns to triadic relational awareness. This brings the experience of desiring the parent of the opposite sex and the wish for an exclusive arrangement with him or her. Competitive feelings for the same-sex parent arise and are accompanied by certain anxieties. These sexual and aggressive impulses constituted for Freud the motivational forces of the human personality (i.e. his view of human nature) and were understood as biologically derived. Hence, sexualization of the emotional oedipal dynamics was expectable. The boy fears castration at the hand of the father as a punishment for his incestuous wishes. He has learned that castration is possible from having seen a little girl's and/or his mother's genitals. Briefly put, castration anxiety leads him to give up his wish for the mother, to reject femininity, and to identify with his powerful father.

The little girl's experience is more complex, at least in the explanation of the development of an heterosexual orientation.[4] When she discovers that she does not have a penis, she immediately wants one and becomes envious and angry at the mother whom she blames for her 'castrated' state. The daughter then turns to father with her desire for a penis. When she realizes he cannot give her a penis, she wants to possess the father's penis, which is then transformed into a wish for a baby from father. In further disappointment and acceptance that this is not possible, the girl develops a feminine identification with the mother and an acceptance of her sexually passive role in relation to men. As noted above, the (conservative) feminist interpretation of the oedipal phase moved away from the literal claim of penis envy to an interpretation of the phallus as a *symbol* of male power. A sense of primary femininity or masculinity constitute gender acquisition and are understood as one of two particularized reactions to male power. Girls are not interested in actually possessing a penis, but they realize that those who do also have access to the outside world and to power.[5] Mother becomes perceived as the powerless and less valuable one.[6]

Nancy Chodorow (1978) offers a different psychoanalytic perspective on gender acquisition and the characteristics of femininity and masculinity, thus paving the road for Benjamin's intersubjective approach.

---

4. Freud realized in his later theorizing (1920; 1924; 1925; 1931; 1933) that the girl's oedipal experience was not a mirror image of the boy's. Unlike the boy, the girl has to shift her erotic interest from the original female object, mother, to a male object, the father. The wish for the penis and its substitute in the wish for a baby was Freud's explanation of heterosexuality in the female.

5. See Irene Fast (1984) for a fascinating reconceptualization of how children of both sexes, at a particular early developmental stage in the acquisition of gender, desire possession of the other's genitals, but not at the expense of retaining their own original endowment. Little boys have a wish to bear children and little girls wish to have a penis. The developmental challenge is to accept the limits of what one does have, with pride, and to value and respect what the other possesses. The theological concept of omnipotence is relevant to this interpretation of gender acquisition, especially during a developmental period in which the child desires to be and have everything.

6. See Joan Lang (1984) for a self psychology developmental interpretation of how women become devalued in this society.

Her perspective is based upon object relations theory which shifts from traditional Freudian perspectives in several significant ways. First, the developmental focus is preoedipal during a period when attachment to the mother is primary.[7] Secondly, object relations theory has a different view of human motivation. Rather than a biological bedrock of sexual and aggressive drives, object relations theory argues that the need for connection with others is the primary driving force of human personality (Fairbairn 1952).[8] And finally, given other gender identity related research (Stoller 1979 and 1985; Lothstein 1988), the preoedipal period (up through ages 2-3), is generally accepted as the developmental period during which a sense of gender is acquired. Children enter the oedipal phase already with a sense a being male or female.

Chodorow's primary thesis (1978) is that it is the virtually exclusive parenting of infants by women that leads to male domination. Negotiation of separation from the mother is integral to the acquisition of gender. She argues that mothers experience their daughters as more like themselves and relate to them out of an experience of identification. She and the daughter share an intimacy that creates permeable interpersonal boundaries, perhaps a greater, or at least more natural capacity for empathy (Jordan *et al.* 1991), and a relational connection orientation to the world. The girl never separates quite as clearly from the mother as the boy does, nor does the boy experience this kind of intimacy with the father. The girl's inability to identify with a more distant father leads her frequently, in adulthood, to desire having children of her own or to nurture other children. This is not only an identification with the mother, but also a way of re-experiencing some of the original attachment to the mother which was modified in her heterosexual development.

The mother experiences the little boy as different from herself and relates to him as 'other'. In order to establish his masculinity, the boy has to separate from mother by identifying with father. Unlike the girl, he is encouraged to separate from mother. He develops firmer interper-

7. The relational feminist orientation in Chodorow and Benjamin assumes that the primary care-taker of most children is still a female figure. Therefore the use of 'mother' in this paper recognizes that sometimes a male may have primary responsibility for infant and toddler care, but that this is still rather unusual in American and other Western societies.

8. John Bowlby's work on attachment, separation, and loss (1969; 1973; 1980) does postulate a biologically derived motivation for attachment, however, the object relations theorists do not usually speak in these terms.

sonal boundaries and a more clearly separate identity from mother. The father's distance (which Chodorow assumes as a matter of course) leads both boys and girls to have a more abstract idea about masculinity. Boys depend on a negative definition of masculinity, that is, what is not feminine. Because this identity is more defensively maintained, Chodorow argues that masculine gender identities are less secure, though boys are more able to assert themselves without getting as caught in relational concerns about the other. Chodorow is positive about the possibility for change. She suggests a significant shift in individual psychology would result from fathers being equally involved in early infant care. Girls would have the experience of difference, thus enabling a more balanced consideration of self in the context of relational concerns. Boys would have an experience of sameness which would provide a potentially greater capacity for emotional intimacy. In summary, Chodorow approaches the phenomenon of male dominance basically as an issue of gender identity acquisition and the parental roles in it.[9]

The Bonds of Love

Jessica Benjamin seeks to outline a psychology of domination based upon the theory of intersubjectivity (1988; 1994; 1998). She asserts that domination is not only a matter of aggression or obedience, but also an extension of 'the bonds of love'. Often, the focus is on the psychology of the one who exercises power, but she emphasizes the two-way process of domination and investigates also the psychology of those who submit to it. Noting that Freud's discussion of authority takes place from the perspective of the man's world, that is father and son, she observes that women are relegated to one of three possibilities: (1) as a temptation to regression; (2) as a prize; or (3) as the third part of an oedipal triangle. Noting Beauvoir's early observations of the opposition of subject and object, and women's 'otherness' for men, Benjamin

9.   In a critique of Chodorow, Iris Young (1990) suggests that gender personality is not a sufficient explanation for how public institutions give men the power to dominate women. 'Description and explanation of male domination still require reference to material relations of dependence and autonomy, access to resources, and material means of coercion, as well as to the structural relation among institutions that reinforce or change these' (p. 53). Young's caveat is well-taken in that feminist psychologists should recognize the perspectival nature of their contributions.

attends to the gender polarity which underlies many common dualisms: master/slave, power/surrender, self/other, independence/dependence, and mother/father.

Benjamin argues there is a basic tension in the human personality between the need for self-assertion and the need for mutual recognition. Her view of human nature, or psychological anthropology, is quite different from Freud's and follows the more general view of object relations theorists, namely that human beings are fundamentally relational beings. Following Stern's (1985) infant observation studies, Benjamin assumes that babies come into the world with emergent selves ready to engage the other. This stands in contrast to Mahler *et al.*'s (1975) notion of the self differentiating out of a merged oneness with the other.[10] The mutuality of need for recognition has not been adequately acknowledged in theory development with regard to the role of the mother's subjectivity. There is a paradox in all of this. Though the child desires recognition from the mother, the child must first recognize the other as a separate person. This capacity begins in infancy and without it, the exchange of recognition is often converted into a dynamic of domination and submission.

> ...domination and submission result from a breakdown of the necessary tension between self-assertion and mutual recognition that allows self and other to meet as sovereign equals (Benjamin 1988: 12).

The need for self-assertion and mutual recognition may conflict at times. For example, the mother needs recognition and pursues the baby. The baby needs space and feels intruded upon. Benjamin calls this the negative cycle of recognition. 'In a negative cycle of recognition, a person feels that aloneness is only possible by obliterating the intrusive other, that attunement is only possible by surrendering to the other' (1988: 28). Benjamin argues that the rigidity or permeability of an individual's boundaries are shaped, at least in part, by the nature of these experiences of early mutuality. The negative cycle of recognition may lead to the development of defensive boundaries in which the other must be kept out, separate and distinct. More positive experiences of attunement lead to the capacity to enter into experiences (e.g. religious,

---

10. In later writing (1995), Benjamin is more explicit about her theoretical preference to live in a both/and tension between contradictory theories rather than choosing one theory over the other in an either/or approach to theoretical commitments.

sexual, creative) in which the boundaries between inside and outside are not so definitely felt.[11] Ms B. seems to struggle, at least in part, with precisely this dynamic.

A common response to managing the conflict between one's own desire, which may differ from the other's, and the desire to remain connected through the experience of attunement is to accommodate to the other's wish, or to one's perception of the other's wish. Winnicott (1960) called this the development of a False Self; Benjamin characterizes the dynamic as an act of submission. Avoiding submission means dealing with the other as an equal. This brings the self face to face with the problem of omnipotence. Different styles of parenting can lead to two possible developmental extremes regarding the fate of omnipotent wishes and fantasies. One arises from an overly permissive parent, who essentially, is self-denying. The child has nothing, no one and no limit to bump up against. While the child's sense of omnipotence is not challenged, nothing is really won in terms of the need for recognition. The child feels abandoned. The other scenario derives from the parent who has little tolerance for the child's attempt to do things independently. Freedom is felt as an impossibility; what is required is compliance. One's own sense of agency is suppressed and omnipotence is attributed to the parent. In neither case has 'the process of recognition begun'.

> Establishing myself…means winning the recognition of the other, and this, in turn, means I must finally acknowledge the other as existing for him self and not just for me (1988: 36).

Experiences of sameness and difference are critical for development and change. Benjamin implicitly critiques Freud in her observation that though there is plentiful evidence of the striving for omnipotent control and hostility to otherness, intersubjective theory (and object relations before it) appeals to a fundamental human motivation to connect with another and to create unities. The dominant-submissive complementary unity forms the basic structure of domination: '…the struggle for recognition requires the self to relinquish its claims to absoluteness' (p. 49).

To summarize thus far, domination and the 'willing' submission to it are phenomena based on a certain view of human nature, that is that the fundamental human motivations are the needs for recognition *and* assertion, or cast somewhat differently, the needs for freedom and commu-

---

11. See Winnicott's concept of the intermediate area of experiencing (1971).

nion.[12] The optimal fulfillment of these needs requires an acknowledgment of the difference between self and other, dependence on the other, and the recognition of the subjectivity of the self, as well as the other. In domination, there is a breakdown of the tension between self and other and a relationship of complementarity usurps one of mutuality: '...the underlying wish to interact with someone truly outside, with an equivalent center of desire, does not emerge' (1988: 73). The experience of domination is constituted by the inability of a subject to experience or acknowledge the other's subjectivity.

Referring back to Hegel's discussion of the dynamics between master and slave (1952), Benjamin describes the dynamics of each according to her categories of the basic needs for recognition and assertion, as well as considering the vicissitudes of omnipotence in both the dominator and the dominated. The master cannot accept dependence on and need of the other, an other who cannot be controlled. The solution is found in the transformation of need into subjugation of the other, attempting to coerce a recognition which heretofore the other has been unwilling to give. Essentially, the master refuses the condition of sustaining a tension between asserting oneself and recognizing the (independence of) other. The maintenance of this tension would constitute true independence. The master assumes omnipotence in the assertion of the self subjugating the other. 'The underlying theme of sadism is the attempt to break through to the other' (1988: 71-72), so that violation becomes the extreme form of assertion. The other is assimilated into the self.

Conversely, Benjamin recognizes that even when people do not submit, per se, fantasies of being dominated may play a significant part in their mental lives. In explaining this phenomenon and the reality of those who do consent to subjugation, she suggests that in a paradoxical way, a person may seek freedom in submission to slavery. This may be expressed in a subtle form of the experience of psychological domination, as in the case of Ms B., or as a part of sadomasochistic sexual enactment.[13] Physical pain substitutes for the psychological pain caused

12. Similar tensions are described in the work of Robert Kegan (1982) in his developmental spiral of inclusion and belonging versus autonomy; in Fairbairn's (1952) concept of the schizoid continuum; and, in Gehrie's (1999) elaboration of forms of relatedness in the interpersonal and intrapsychic management of closeness versus distance.

13. See Erich Fromm (1941). In addition, the concepts of negative selfobject

by the lack of recognition. Submission becomes an extreme form of losing the self in order to gain recognition. With the loss of the self, one hopes to gain access to a more powerful self perceived in the other. Another version of the assimilation of self and other obtains here as well. Omnipotence is projected on to the other with whom one then merges.

The clearest application of the master–slave enactment in the sexual arena is represented in sadomasochism. Benjamin notes that the sado-masochistic fantasy is the most common form of erotic domination. Current psychoanalytic theory regards pain as 'a route to pleasure, only when it involves submission to an idealized figure' (1988: 60-61). Vio-lation of the body, as Benjamin interprets it, represents a struggle, sometimes 'to the death' for recognition. What is intolerable for the masochist is abandonment. 'Submission…is often motivated by the fear of separation and abandonment: masochism reflects the inability to express one's own desire and agency' (1988: 79). What is intolerable for the sadist is the death of the other, therefore thwarting the other's recognition of the self and making one's own self-assertion meaning-less. Basically the masochist desires recognition and discovery, while the sadist attempts to connect to the other who has been experienced as distant.

Gender Polarization of Domination and Subjugation

Benjamin acknowledges the observation that certain personality traits, as well as sexual inclinations have been divided along gender lines since the beginning of psychoanalysis, and well before that. As sug-gested above, Freud describes a dualism in which femininity is linked with passivity, narcissism and masochism, and masculinity with activ-ity, aggression and sadism. Though contemporary feminism criticizes this division of characteristics, it has continued to perpetuate these dualisms in claims that women develop a natural capacity for empathy and emotional connectedness (Jordan, *et al.* 1991); women have their own ethic of caring (Gilligan 1982); and women have their own strug-gle with sin (Saiving 1979). Though there may be some empirical basis

(Gehrie 1996), internalized bad objects (Fairbairn 1952), the false self (Winnicott 1960), and anxious attachment (Bowlby 1969; 1973; 1980) all address the phe-nomenon, from different theoretical vantage points, of a compelling need to remain connected to painful forms of relating.

for these observations, the debate continues about whether or not these are essential differences, or the consequences of socially constructed gender categories. Chodorow and Benjamin are social constructivists in the sense that they believe these characteristics are socialized through the vehicle of gender polarization. In an argument initially similar to Chodorow's, Benjamin suggests that male children develop masculinity, at least in part, by rejecting an original identification with the mother. This often interferes with the boy recognizing mother as a subject, rather than primarily as an other. 'The complement to the male refusal to recognize the other is the female's own acceptance of her lack of subjectivity, her willingness to offer recognition without expecting it in return' (1988: 78). This leads to a male denial of the other and a female denial of the self.[14] The mother's renunciation of her own desire and will leads to her children not perceiving her subjectivity. As suggested above, the male child repudiates his commonality with her, thereby leading to the identification of masochism with the female, and sadism with the male. The girl's lack of having a way to disidentify with the mother leads her to a less developed sense of independence. Benjamin, like Chodorow, locates the significant responsibility for the problem of domination with the gender socialization process and the parents' role in it. There is a failure of vision for the optimal personhood of the mother within psychological theory. 'The possibility of balancing the recognition of the child's needs with the assertion of one's own has scarcely been put forward as an ideal' (1988: 82).

The Problem of Women's Desire and Ideal Love

Benjamin addresses the problem of many women who do not experience their own subjectivity, including their own sexual subjectivity and desire. She characterizes the current situation in which '...even today, femininity continues to be identified with passivity, with being the object of someone else's desire, with having no active desire of one's own' (1988: 87). In the psychology of Freud, the phallus and masculinity are equated with sexual agency and desire. Femininity is acquired through the experience of penis envy, passive love of the father and acceptance of sexual passivity as the object of desire. One solution to

14. This is another psychological perspective on Valerie Saiving's (1979) claim that women struggle with the sin of self-abnegation, and men struggle with the sin of pride.

the problem of sexual objectification and the self-surrender toward which one feels drawn is to leave sexual involvement behind altogether.

> ...many women enter into love relationships with men in order to acquire vicariously something they have not got within themselves. Others try to protect their autonomy by resisting passionate involvement with men: because their sexuality is bound up with the fantasy of sub-mission to an ideal male figure, it undermines their sense of a separate self (1988: 89).

Independence is purchased at the expense of relational loss.[15]

Developmentally, Benjamin understands penis envy to represent the girl's effort to separate from the mother by identifying with the exciting father. However, this attempted solution results in a common dilemma: trying to escape maternal control of the mother by identifying with the father brings the girl up against her fears of paternal intrusion, the 'threatening genital fantasies inspired by the oedipal father' (1988: 97), as well as her own anxieties about the loss of connection with the hold-ing, soothing mother. The difficulty begins with the daughter's attempt to identify with the preoedipal father who is perceived as the exciting, powerful one that desires. The identification is dually motivated, both as a compensation for loss and as a result of becoming conscious of one's own desire and agency. The little girl wants these qualities to be recognized by the father. With this recognition, she can deny her depen-dency on the maternal object. This identification with the preoedipal father constitutes the basis for a new kind of love, identificatory love.

Benjamin regards identificatory love as the prototype of ideal love, one in which the ideal image of the self is sought in the other. Underly-ing both is the desire for recognition, however women's search for identificatory love often leads to submission. The girl begins to express her need for the father as an identification with separation (from mother), and as a representative of the outside world, but the father's need to assert his difference from the feminine may lead him to relate to his daughter as a 'sweet adorable thing, a nascent sex object' (1988: 109). The father withdraws leaving the daughter to return, psychologi-cally, to the mother. Her aspirations for independence are turned in-

---

15. Allison Weir (1996) mistakenly interprets and criticizes Benjamin as defining autonomy negatively, rather than seeing Benjamin's claim that autonomy (independence or assertion) is but one side of the psychological paradox within which human beings experience the fundamental needs of recognition and assertion (Benjamin 1998).

ward, she feels angry at not being recognized, and becomes depressed.

> ...for women, the 'missing father' is the key to their missing desire, and
> its return in the form of masochism... Unprotected by the phallic sign of
> gender difference, unsupported by an alternate relationship, they
> relinquish their entitlement to desire (1988: 107, 109).

Further, the little girl's identificatory love of the father becomes the basis for later heterosexual love. She attempts to *have* what she cannot *be*. Thus, many women are left with a life-long admiration for and idealization of men who possess what they cannot, that is, power and desire, those 'who get away with their sense of omnipotence intact' (1988: 109). This admiration is often expressed in relationships of overt or unconscious submission. The thwarting of identificatory love (with what is exciting and outside) in these early developmental periods is damaging to a general sense of agency, and specifically to a sexual sense of agency. Ideal love, with its inclination toward submission, emerges as a substitute for one's own agency.

Intersubjectivity as the Means of Transformation

Benjamin argues that the gender polarization which now exists makes it impossible to reconcile agency and desire with femininity. The problem of differentiation from an omnipotent mother is not resolved by submitting to an omnipotent father. Omnipotence has to be broken out of altogether. Here, the theory of intersubjectivity provides an alternative position in which a 'sense of self and other evolves through the consciousness that separate minds can share the same feelings and intentions, through mutual recognition' (1988: 125).[16] Gender polarity must be overcome such that a different representation of desire emerges. She criticizes, as do others (Bem 1993), feminists whose sole solution is that of substituting a female organ as the new symbol of desire. It only reinforces a different gender polarity. This is problematic in two ways: first, these symbols derive power from the total gestalt of the parent, so that if the maternal figure is a source of fear, then this supports negative feelings about female organs. Secondly, the symbolic level of the

---

16. Weir (1996) offers an alternative perspective to intersubjectivity and the processes of identification. She prefers an emphasis on the process of internalization and the recognition that subjectivity is primarily a cognitive, rather than an affective achievement.

psyche is already occupied by the phallus, so that an active mother is equated to a phallic woman. Rather, Benjamin appeals to an under-standing of intersubjectivity in which each person appropriates his or her own subjectivity, desire, and the activity which accomplishes it (Benjamin 1998).

Benjamin concludes that mutual recognition lies at the heart of a differentiation that acknowledges both the subjectivity and desire of the self *and* the other. With regard to parenting, she avers,

> Any vision of change must challenge the fundamental structure of het-erosexuality in which the father supplies the missing excitement, 'beats back the maternal power,' and denies the mother's subjectivity because it is too dangerous… As long as the father stands for subjectivity and desire at the level of culture, woman's desire will always have to contend with his monopoly and the devaluation of femininity it implies (1988: 123).[17]

As noted above, Benjamin is careful to point out the role of the cultural representation of desire in the maintenance of current gender arrange-ments. She observes the intractability of these social structures and con-cludes that current parenting styles are not the primary foundation of gender polarization. The images of femininity and masculinity in cul-ture tend to operate nearly as powerfully as the valuation of images pre-sented to children by their parents.[18] Benjamin concludes with an obser-vation commonly made in feminist scholarship (Bartky 1990), namely that the split which constitutes gender polarity is replicated in intellec-tual and social life beyond the psychology of gender acquisition.[19]

17. Young (1990) suggests that female heterosexuality may entail an element of coercion, that is, in a heterosexual society, gender acquisition entails learning what one's desire should be for.

18. Lang's (1984) perspective remains one of the very few within self psychol-ogy which takes seriously the impact of culture upon what parents will mirror and idealize in their children regarding feminine and masculine characteristics. This in turn has direct bearing on the content of and the affective relationship to one's images of God (Rizzuto 1979; Vergote and Tamayo 1981; Rector 1996).

19. While she is sensitive that much of her theorizing has assumed a hetero-sexual, two-parent family constellation, when many children in Western society are raised in other constellations, the cultural images of mother and father, femininity and masculinity still play a significant role in individual psychology and gender acquisition. See Irene Fast (1984) on the relationship between one's own subjective sense of femininity/masculinity and the degree of congruence with the dominant cultural images.

Conclusion

In conclusion, this article has addressed the development and role of gender identity and its relation to the experience of domination. Much has been written about the phenomenon of male domination from feminist philosophical perspectives, feminist theological perspectives, and feminist psychological perspectives. As *feminist* perspectives, per se, there is always an agenda for change and transformation whether it is social, economic, political, theological or psychological, change that at its most general level pertains to a critique of patriarchy and the concomitant negative valuation of women. The social justice agenda of these feminist scholars eventually requires a psychological perspective to assist in understanding what the feminist theologians have called a 'personal conversion' (Ruether 1996).

The focus of this article was delimited to a consideration of relational feminist psychology with particular emphasis on the work of Jessica Benjamin. It was observed that domination is often experienced as a 'bond of love' in which persons participate willingly.[20] Submission and domination both represent a defensive (protective) strategy for dealing with the human inclination toward omnipotence, as well as the basic human needs for recognition and assertion. Benjamin demonstrates how the socialization of gender acquisition and the lack of perception of mother's subjectivity inculcates a gender polarization and hierarchy. The resulting male psychology and sense of masculinity regards the female as object and other, lacking her own subjectivity. He privileges assertion (domination) in his own search for recognition and assumes the omnipotence of his desire. However, his failure to recognize the other as a separate and independent subject results in the failure to receive full recognition that can only come from one who is a separate self.

The female identifies with a mother who does not recognize her own subjectivity and thus learns to privilege recognition of the other (submission) at the expense of her own assertion of self. Without having her own subjectivity recognized by the preoedipal father, the girl develops

---

20. It could still be argued that women who appear to 'willingly' submit are not truly free, at least psychologically, to choose otherwise. And even then, an individual woman would still have to contend with the very significant pressure of the larger cultural images of femininity and masculinity.

an inclination toward ideal love. She loses a sense of her own desire and assumes that the male possesses desire and the capacity for assertion. Projecting her own omnipotence onto the other, she is socialized to care for others and to fear abandonment should she fail to make these accommodations. The case of Ms B. was illustrative.

Finally, Benjamin appeals to an intersubjective perspective that requires an individual to live with the tension of the paradoxical needs for recognition and assertion. She challenges a renewal of mutual recognition, as

> ...not a final redemptive 'end of prehistory'; rather it is a necessary part of the continuing process of individual and social change...if we suffocate our personal longings for recognition, we will suffocate our hope for social transformation as well (1988: 223, 224).

It is within this psychic space that a 'personal conversion' can occur, and where the experience of sexual desire is transformed into an engagement of mutual recognition. The desire for oneness with the other, or momentary loss of self, is often the central desire of erotic union (and religious, mystical experience, as well). For Benjamin, this union is really another form of recognition. Getting pleasure in and with the other is predicated on the mutuality of recognition and the assertion of self. Only then can a shift occur from *having sex* to *making love*.

Bibliography

Bartky, S.L.
  1990   *Femininity and Domination: Studies in the Phenomenology of Oppression* (New York: Routledge).
Beauvoir, S. de
  1972   *The Second Sex* (trans. H.M. Parshley; Harmondsworth: Penguin Books [1952]).
Bem, S.L.
  1993   *The Lenses of Gender: Transforming the Debate on Sexual Inequality* (New Haven: Yale University Press).
Benjamin, J.
  1988   *The Bonds of Love: Psychoanalysis, Feminism, and the Problem of Domination* (New York: Pantheon Books).
  1995   *Like Subjects, Love Objects* (New Haven: Yale University Press).
  1998   *Shadow of the Other: Intersubjectivity and Gender in Psychoanalysis* (New York: Routledge).
Bowlby, J.
  1982   *Attachment*, I (New York: Basic Books, 2nd edn [1969]).

1973   *Separation: Anxiety and Anger*, II (New York: Basic Books).

1980   *Loss: Sadness and Depression*, III (New York: Basic Books).

Butler, J.

1990   *Gender Trouble* (New York: Routledge).

Chodorow, N.J.

1978   *The Reproduction of Mothering* (Berkeley: University of California Press).

1989   *Feminism and Psychoanalytic Theory* (New Haven: Yale University Press).

1994   *Femininities, Masculinities, Sexualities: Freud and Beyond* (Lexington, KY: University Press of Kentucky).

Dworkin, A., and C. MacKinnon

1985   *The Reasons Why* (Cambridge, MA: Harvard Law School).

Fairbairn, R.

1952   *Psychoanalytic Studies of Personality* (London: Tavistock).

Fast, I.

1984   *Gender Identity: A Differentiation Model* (Hillsdale, NJ: The Analytic Press).

Ferguson, A.

1989   *Blood at the Root: Motherhood, Sexuality, and Male Dominance* (London: Pandora Press).

Freud, S.

1920   'The Psychogenesis of a Case of Homosexuality in a Woman', *Standard Edition* 18: 145-72.

1924   'The Dissolution of the Oedipus Complex', *Standard Edition* 19: 173-79.

1925   'Some Psychical Consequences of the Anatomical Differences between the Sexes', *Standard Edition* 19: 248-58.

1931   'Female Sexuality', *Standard Edition* 21: 225-43.

1933   'Femininity', *Standard Edition* 22: 112-35.

1953   'Three Essays on the Theory of Sexuality', *Standard Edition* 7 (London: Howarth Press): 135-43.

Fromm, E.

1976   *Escape from Freedom* (New York: Avon [1941]).

Gehrie, M.J.

1996   'Empathy in Broader Perspective: A Technical Approach to the Consequences of the Negative Selfobject in Early Character Formation', in Arnold Goldberg (ed.), *Basic Ideas Reconsidered: Progress in Self Psychology*, XII (Hillsdale, NJ: The Analytic Press): 159-79.

2000   'Forms of Relatedness: Self Preservation and the Schizoid Continuum', in Arnold Goldberg (ed.), *How Responsive Should We Be: Progress in Self-Psychology*, XVI (Hillsdale, NJ: The Analytic Press): 17-32.

Gilligan, C.

1982   *In a Different Voice* (Cambridge, MA: Harvard University Press).

Hegel, G.W.F.

1979   *The Phenomenology of the Spirit* (trans. A.V. Miller and J.N. Findlay; New York: Oxford University Press [1952]).

Heyward, C.

1989   *Touching our Strength: The Erotic as Power and the Love of God* (San Francisco: Harper & Row, 1989).

Irigaray, L.
    1985a   *The Speculum of the Other Woman* (trans. Gillian C. Gill; Ithaca: Cornell
                University Press).
    1985b   *This Sex Which is Not One* (trans. Catherine Porter with Carolyn Burke;
                Ithaca: Cornell University Press).
Jordan, J.V. *et al.* (eds.)
    1991   *Women's Growth in Connection: Writings from the Stone Center* (New
                York: Guilford Press).
Jordan, J.V. (ed.)
    1997   *Women's Growth in Diversity: More Writings from the Stone Center*
                (New York: Guilford Press).
Kegan, R.
    1982   *The Evolving Self: Problem and Process in Human Development* (Cam-
                bridge, MA: Harvard University Press).
Kristeva, J.
    1989   *Black Sun: Depression and Melancholia* (trans. Leon S. Roudiez; New
                York: Columbia University Press).
    1986   *The Kristeva Reader* (ed. Toril Moi; Oxford: Basil Blackwell).
Lang, J.
    1984   'Notes Toward a Psychology of the Feminine Self', in Paul E. Stepansky
                and Arnold Goldberg (eds.), *Kohut's Legacy: Contributions to Self
                Psychology* (Hillsdale, NJ: The Analytic Press): 51-70.
Lothstein, L.
    1988   'Selfobject Failure and Gender Identity', in Arnold Goldberg (ed.),
                Frontiers in Self Psychology: Progress in Self Psychology (Hillsdale, NJ:
                The Analytic Press), III: 213-35.
Mahler, M., *et al.*
    1975   *The Psychological Birth of the Human Infant* (New York: Basic Books).
Mitchell, J.
    1974   *Psychoanalysis and Feminism* (New York: Pantheon).
Rector, L.J.
    1996   'The Function of Early Selfobject Experiences in Gendered Representa-
                tions of God', in Arnold Goldberg (ed.), *Basic Ideas Reconsidered:
                Progress in Self Psychology* (Hillsdale, NJ: The Analytic Press), XII:
                249-68.
Rizzuto, A.
    1979   *The Birth of the Living God: A Psychoanalytic Study* (Chicago: Univer-
                sity of Chicago).
Rubin, G.
    1984   'Thinking Sex: Notes for a Radical Theory of the Politics of Sexuality', in
                Carol Vance (ed.), *Pleasure and Danger: Exploring Female Sexuality*
                (London: Routledge): 267-319.
Ruether, R.R.
    1996   *Women and Redemption: A Theological History* (Minneapolis: Fortress
                Press).
Saiving, V.
    1979   'The Human Situation: A Feminine View', in J. Plant and J. Plaskow
                (eds.), *Womanspirit Rising* (San Francisco: Harper & Row).

Sawicki, J.

1986   'Foucault and Feminism: Toward a Politics of Difference', *Hypatia* 1.2: 23-36.

Stern, D.

1985   *The Interpersonal World of the Infant* (New York: Basic Books).

Stoller, R.

1979   *Sexual Excitement* (New York: Pantheon).

1985   *Observing the Erotic Imagination* (New Haven: Yale University Press).

Vergote, A., and A. Tamayo

1981   *The Parental Figures and the Representation of God: A Psychological And Cross-Cultural Study* (New York: Mouton Publishers).

Volf, M.

1996   *Exclusion and Embrace: A Theological Exploration of Identity, Otherness, and Reconciliation* (Nashville: Abingdon Press).

Weir, A.

1996   *Sacrificial Logics: Feminist Theory and the Critique of Identity* (New York: Routledge).

Westcott, M.

1986   *The Feminist Legacy of Karen Horney* (New Haven: Yale University Press).

Winnicott, D.

1960   'Ego Distortion in Terms of True and False Self', in *idem, The Maturational Processes and the Facilitating Environment* (New York: International Universities Press): 140-52.

1971   *Playing and Reality* (London: Routledge).

Young, I.M.

1990   'Is Male Gender Identity the Cause of Male Domination?', in *idem, Throwing Like a Girl and other Essays in Philosophy and Social Theory* (Bloomington, IN: Indiana University Press): 36-61.

SAME DIFFERENCE? POWER, EQUALITY AND LESBIAN RELATING

Alison Webster

Age. Race. Money. Class. Ability. Politics. Health. Religion. Appearance. These are just some of the factors that distinguish women from one another—differences that determine the resources we have at our disposal relative to other women. In short, these differentials are about power—structural power and personal power. They form the backdrop against which lesbian relationships are negotiated; they provide the experiential raw material from which lesbian relational lives are created. Yet there has been little systematic discussion of power differences between women in lesbian relationships in lesbian and/or feminist theory.

In her contribution to the anthology of writing from lesbians of African and Asian descent, *Talking Black*, Linda Bellos says, 'Black lesbians can and do oppress others unless we recognise the existence of the power that we do possess. To deny that one has any power because one is oneself the subject of other people's power is damaging and ultimately dangerous.'[1] She continues, 'We have not been very honest about the role of power in the sexual activities we enjoy'.[2] This is true not just of black lesbians, but of lesbians in general. Because we are ourselves subject to the power of others, we have not paid sufficient attention to the dynamics of power that exist between ourselves—not least in our partnerships and sexual relationships.

There are good historical reasons for this. Within feminist thought lesbian relationships have often functioned as a counterpoint to hegemonic and oppressive heterosexuality. For all of us, our relationships constitute the arena in which we live out, in the most intimate and

1. L. Bellos, 'A Vision Back and Forth', in V. Mason-John (ed.), *Talking Black: Lesbians of African and Asian Descent Speak Out* (London: Cassell, 1995), pp. 52-71 (64).
2. Bellos, 'A Vision Back and Forth', p. 67.

personal way, our socially constructed selves. For heterosexual feminists, one-to-one relationships with individual men, including sexual relationships, have been subject to intense exploration and analysis. In such a context the alternative possibility of intimate relationships with women has represented the chance of 'love between equals' in a way that heterosexuality has not (and some would argue never could). In her exploration of heterosexuality, Segal sums up the results of this: '..."lesbian sex" began to be a model for describing what was "good sex", rather than what lesbians actually do...'[3] For lesbians, this has not been altogether helpful. As Segal continues, '...there was no longer any room for feminists to discuss the realities of lesbian desire or the complexities of lesbian relationships'.[4] Healey has also explored this. As she says, 'For some women, the constant reinforcement of the message that women's relationships with women would be based on "caring", "sharing" and "mutual support" did not hide the fact that their relationships were none of those things. Lesbianism became idealised as the perfect sort of relationship where a woman would never have to worry about pain or a broken heart.'[5]

It is my contention in this article that this idealization has reinforced the tendency to over-emphasize gender as a signifier of difference, while failing to give sufficient attention to other differentials, not least the structural ones of race and class. I will begin by outlining some of the ways in which notions of power have been utilized to date in feminist and lesbian analyses of lesbian sexuality and relationships, exploring three broad categories of thinking in this area: the 'lesbian feminist' approach, the 'sex radical' approach and the 'therapeutic' approach, looking in each case at how power is perceived and understood. Please note that I do not perceive these three approaches to be 'identity categories' into which lesbian writers and thinkers may be unambiguously placed. Rather, I see them as clusters of ideas that have developed at different historical moments for the different, context-specific reasons. Nevertheless, I believe that they offer, in different ways, resources for the analysis of power differences between women in lesbian relationships. Having explored these strands of thought, I will then focus on some specific examples of power differences in lesbian relationships in

3. L. Segal, *Straight Sex: The Politics of Pleasure* (London: Virago, 1994), p. 51.

4. Segal, *Straight Sex*, p. 51.

5. E. Healey, *Lesbian Sex Wars* (London: Virago, 1996), p. 76.

order to see what we can glean from them regarding new ways forward in lesbian ethics.

The 'Lesbian Feminist' Approach

An important strand in feminist theory has been that which posits sexuality as a prime site (or, sometimes *the* prime site) of women's oppression. The structural and material social privilege afforded to men is, according to this strand of thought, carried into sexual relationships between individual men and individual women (and girls) such that abuses of power by men are socially sanctioned—or, indeed, are considered not to *be* abuses of power at all. Feminist attention and action has focused, in this approach, upon sexual violence as contextual rather than episodic. As a result, an important plank in the strategy for women's liberation has been escape from situations in which women might be placed in positions of socially-endorsed subjugation to individual men. Turning away from men and towards women in woman-identified separatism, coupled with the theory of lesbianism as a continuum constitute the roots of lesbian feminist thinking.[6] A second important plank in the strategy for women's liberation, however, is the reconstruction of sexuality itself in ways which combat, rather than underscore, the subordination of women. It is in lesbian feminist writings about this task that much is said about 'power'.

Sheila Jeffreys is one of the most prominent proponents of the lesbian feminist approach. At the heart of her project is the transgressive act of the eroticization of equality and mutuality—or, as Jeffreys terms it, the construction of 'homosexual desire'. This involves combating 'heterosexual desire' wherever it is found, including within lesbian relationships. She defines heterosexual desire as: '...sexual desire that eroticises power difference. It originates in the power relationship between the sexes and normally takes the form of eroticising the subordination of women.'[7] Her central claim is that, 'Heterosexuality as an institution is founded upon the ideology of "difference". Though the difference is seen as natural, it is in fact a difference of power'.[8] Janice Raymond, a

6. A. Rich, *Compulsory Heterosexuality and Lesbian Existence* (London: Onlywomen Press, 1981).

7. S. Jeffreys, *Anticlimax: A Feminist Perspective on the Sexual Revolution* (London: Women's Press, 1990), p. 2.

8. Jeffreys, *Anticlimax*, p. 299.

US writer who shares much in common with Jeffreys agrees with her that, 'Hetero-relations can function quite smoothly in the lives of lesbians who merely "commit" lesbian sex acts or in the lives of women who make of lesbianism a lifestyle. Hetero-relations can function, more specifically, in lesbian role-playing, in lesbian S and M, in the lesbian objectification of other women.'[9]

Jeffreys talks very definitely in terms of *material* power. She attacks what she calls 'lesbianandgay theory' for she says it has little time for, '...material power relations, for economics, for power that does not just play around but resides in the hands of particular classes and elites',[10] along with 'post-modern feminism' in which, she says, 'Power becomes, in a Foucauldian sense, something that just floats about constantly reconstituting itself for no real purpose and with no real connection with real human beings'.[11]

There is something of a puzzle here at the heart of the lesbian feminist approach which seems to assert, at one and the same time, that social power relations (especially between men and women) are congealed and unchangeable, but also socially constructed and therefore malleable and open to transformation. The first assertion is evidenced, for instance, in lesbian feminist talk of avoidance: the need to keep oneself pure from the corrupting influence of heteroreality. Jeffreys, for instance, cites with apparent approval the example of, '...lesbians who have chosen to eschew sexual practices altogether on the grounds that dominance and submission are too deeply ingrained in how we feel about sex to be altered'.[12] And Raymond uses the language of 'withdrawal', and of avoidance of 'assimilation' to the values of heteroreality.[13] Lesbian feminist condemnation of forms of sexual expression that are considered to replicate heteroreality are, of course, legendary. Tamsin Wilton expresses her frustration with Jeffreys who, she says, forbids too much while constructing only vague relational values in place of sexual activity: '...so much lesbian sexual activity is forbidden in the revolutionary lesbian-feminist vision of sex—vaginal or anal pen-

---

9. J. Raymond, *A Passion for Friends: Toward a Philosophy of Female Affection* (London: Women's Press, 1986), p. 14.

10. S. Jeffreys, *The Lesbian Heresy: A Feminist Perspective on the Lesbian Sexual Revolution* (London: Women's Press, 1994), p. 98.

11. Jeffreys, *The Lesbian Heresy*, p. 99.

12. Jeffreys, *The Lesbian Heresy*, p. 203.

13. Raymond, *A Passion for Friends*, p. 169.

etration, the use of sex toys, s/m, butch-femme role play, "objectifying" women's bodies...'[14]

Karen Rian, a contributor to the famous volume, *Against Sadomasochism*, voices her optimism about the possibility of changing power imbalances in relationships:

> Although power imbalances are an existing reality, I do not believe they are inevitable or unchangeable. To the extent that we justify expressions of power in intimate relationships, we capitulate, I believe, to the ideologies and social structure which presents personal aggressiveness as a necessary condition of human nature.[15]

She also says,

> While no one is in a position to judge the 'political correctness' of anyone's sexual desires, we can—and must—discuss the political desirability of our goals for sexual relationships. I, for one, cannot accept dominance and submission as a desirable goal for any area of personal relationships, including sexuality. I believe that an appropriate feminist goal is not the expression—or even equalization—of power, but rather the elimination of power dynamics in sexual, and other, relationships[16]

and finally, 'In claiming control over our own lives, it is thus within our power to create our sexuality according to our own interests, and, if we so desire, even to remove sexuality from the realm of power relationships'.[17]

Transposing Rian's reflections to our enquiry, then, it can be seen that according to the lesbian feminist approach, power differences between women in lesbian relationships can and should be eliminated. This is the goal of a feminist reconstruction of sexuality, and it can be achieved through the re-education of our desires. This perspective is prominent in Jeffreys' thought, for she asserts that what we desire and what gives us pleasure is changeable; subject to re-formation by an act of will. If we 'get off' on fantasies or activities that are unethical, we should retrain ourselves to 'get off on' things that are more wholesome. In her words, '...it is this avenue [the eroticization of mutuality and equality] that we should seek to open up while gradually shutting down

14. T. Wilton, *Finger-Licking Good, the Ins and Outs of Lesbian Sex* (London: Cassell, 1996), p. 110.

15. Robin Ruth Linden *et al.* (eds.), *Against Sadomasochism* (Palo Alto, CA: Frog in the Well Press, 1982), p. 47.

16. Linden *et al.* (eds), *Against Sadomasochism*, p. 49.

17. Linden *et al.* (eds), *Against Sadomasochism*, p. 46.

those responses and practices which are not about sexual "pleasure" but the eroticising of our subordination'.[18] Her language is rather more cautious than Rian's, but she nevertheless holds out the possibility of change:

> It may well be true that a lesbian reared under male power can never entirely know what a sexuality constructed in a context of equality might resemble. But I think that the struggle to transform sexuality and pursue homosexual desire by emphasising the areas of our sexual experience we feel comfortable with and limiting those which seem to be in conflict with our visions of a lesbian sexual future is worthwhile.[19]

Criticisms of the lesbian feminist approach are many and varied, but there are specific issues of importance in our exploration of power dynamics within lesbian relationships. In her book *Lesbians Talk Queer Notions*, Cherry Smyth reflects upon her experience of the time when the lesbian feminist approach was at the height of its influence within the lesbian community. She says, 'The silencing of anything but "right on" forms of sexual expression led to a failure to negotiate issues of desire and power, as lesbian feminists propagated the belief that women did not objectify each other sexually and that lust was a gentle wild orchid'.[20] She identifies an important weakness here. Whether by accident or design, the lesbian feminist approach seems to have been adopted by some in a rigid and censorious manner, leading to—at least in some sections of the lesbian community—a culture of fear and recrimination, and to a silencing of those whose experiences did not fit the dominant philosophy of the time. Such silencing, as Smyth points out, was counterproductive in that it inhibited the discussion necessary to assess and evaluate the different possibilities of lesbian existence. Emma Healey has documented what have become known as the 'lesbian sex wars'.[21] Disagreement tended to focus upon specific issues like butch/femme and s/m, which were unambiguously ruled out as recuperative by lesbian feminists for replicating power difference rather than equality.

Perhaps the key criticism lies in the nature of lesbian feminist theory itself. For it proffers a singular and uncompromisingly simple explanation for an extremely complex set of issues: human equality and the role

18. Jeffreys, *Anticlimax*, p. 313.
19. Jeffreys, *The Lesbian Heresy*, p. 204.
20. C. Smyth, *Lesbians Talk Queer Notions* (London: Scarlet Press, 1992), p. 36.
21. Healey, *Lesbian Sex Wars*.

of gender, sexuality and sexual desire within it. In the lesbian feminist approach, gender becomes the over-arching signifier of inequality. All other inequalities are, in effect, collapsed into gender—hence the terminology, 'homosexual' and 'heterosexual' desire. All potential forms of inequality are seen through the lens of gender. Furthermore, specific sexual acts and ways of relating in sexual relationships are given 'objective meanings' over and above the meaning which those undertaking them might *wish* to give them. While this indicates an attempt to take seriously the social structures within which all so-called 'individual' relational activity takes place, it also leads to a rigid notion of power as a stable entity: those with 'more' are readily identifiable, as are those with 'less'. The logical conclusion is that a relationship of equality can only be undertaken by those who are similarly positioned within the social power structures. This does not, I believe, offer analytical tools which are complex or flexible enough to deal with the very many different forms of power that any lesbian may deploy or have deployed against her.

The 'Sex Radical' Approach

Where the lesbian feminist approach assumes the possibility of eliminating power differentials between women, there is another approach, which I shall term the 'sex radical' approach, which assumes its *impossibility*. Criticizing lesbian feminist approaches, Loulan says this: 'The lesbian who subscribes to the androgynous imperative idealizes a relationship that has no differences in power. There is no way to keep a relationship of any sort power-free. The fact that there are two people exchanging energy means they are passing power back and forth.'[22]

But not only does the sex radical approach assume that it is *impossible* to eliminate power difference, it also considers it *undesirable*. For sexual pleasure and desire are considered to be the *product* of such difference. To remove it is to undermine sex itself, and therefore to undermine lesbian relationships. Here we see clearly the influence of psychoanalytic theory, which holds that desire is produced by difference.

Despite their opposition to one another, lesbian feminist and sex radical approaches do share one thing in common in that both could be

---

22. J. Loulan, *The Lesbian Erotic Dance: Butch, Femme, Androgyny and other Rhythms* (Minneapolis: Spinsters Ink, 1990), p. 76.

described as political/ethical projects. Both aim to undermine and overcome heterosexism. It is just that their methodologies are rather different. In the sex radical literature, lesbian desire is considered very much as a powerful force for change, particularly in the writings of Pat Califia:

> ...like Nestle, [Califia] recognises the subversive potential inherent in an active, desiring lesbian sexuality outside male control. Moreover, in opposition to the political-lesbian feminist ideology which mandates an extreme degree of control over sexuality in the interests of the political struggle, Califia proposes integrating the exploration and validation of sexual pleasure into her feminist agenda. Thus, her efforts at giving pleasure to the readers of her erotic fiction are an integral part of her liberationary agenda.[23]

Whereas the lesbian feminist approach deplores the corrupting influences of 'heteroreality' upon lesbian sexuality, the 'sex radical' approach embraces the ambiguities involved and turns them to good use: 'The woman performing the masculine in the context of other lesbians becomes erotic for some lesbians because of internalisations of heterosexuality, but also because of the powerful excess created by the transgression, assumption, and parody of gender'.[24] That 'good use' is, ultimately, the undermining of the assumed naturalness of heterosexuality, and therefore, the subversion of heteroreality:

> The potential subversive qualities of the oft-ignored Femme side, as the womanish woman who falls in love with a woman, involve the most powerful challenge to the hegemony of heterosexuality...she remains the impossible space, in and out of gender, unaccountable...the Femme brings into question the necessary heterosexual orientation of the feminine woman.[25]

To follow through this one illustration then: while the lesbian feminist approach eschews any 'butch/femme' role playing as collusion with heteroreality, its rigid gender constructions and the power imbalances that are built into those constructions, the sex radical argues that it is the adoption of these gender performances within *a lesbian context* which transforms them. In effect, the lesbians have the last laugh. In performing butch/femme, lesbians are not dupes of heterosexism—rather,

23. Wilton, *Finger-Licking Good*, p. 121.
24. J. Roof, *A Lure of Knowledge: Lesbian Sexuality and Theory* (New York: Columbia University Press, 1991), p. 249.
25. Roof, *A Lure of Knowledge*, p. 250.

they are calling into question rigid gender divisions and their 'natural' alignment with sex (male/female).

However, as with the lesbian feminist approach, there is a puzzle and potential contradiction at the heart of 'sex radicalism'. In order to fulfil its politically transformative agenda, it has to allow that power differentials in sexual relationships both affect and are affected by, those in the wider world. But at the same time it has to posit a limit to those effects. Califia, for instance, draws a distinction between how power operates in sexual fantasy, and how it operates in 'real life':

> ...having an S/M fantasy and dealing with second-class status in a male-dominated society are very different things. Women work at low-paying jobs because they must survive and those jobs are often all that is available. An S/M fantasy is a choice made out of a field of possible erotic themes. Saying, 'yes, mistress' to a lover who has you beside yourself with pleasure is not the same thing as saying 'yes, sir' to a boss.[26]

But there are hints, picked up by other analysts, that her theory is not thoroughgoing: '...while practitioners [of S/M] argue that the power dynamics do not overspill into everyday life, when Pat Califia boasts that the nature of her non-monogamous relationship makes her partner "think twice" before using her safe word, this may be seized upon as evidence to the contrary'.[27] Cherry Smyth lets this slip in her defence of a sex radical position:

> lesbians who were pro-sex found themselves accused of being anti-feminist or even fascist, while trying to defend the right to have SM sex, without trashing 'vanilla' sex as dull and unexploratory. The reactionary, divisive dichotomy of good/bad girl silenced doubt and confusion, pressurised women to join one camp or the other. For women involved in SM practices, there was nowhere to express *fears that their power dynamics might be slipping over into other parts of their lives or whatever*, so busy were they defending their right to exist at all.[28]

The vagueness of Smyth's analysis here is symptomatic of the sex radical literature which holds, at one and the same time, that sexual activity and sexual fantasy represent a safely demarcated space, separate from

26. P. Califia, *Sapphistry: The Book of Lesbian Sexuality* (Florida: Naiad Press, 1988), p. 119.

27. E. Creith, *Undressing Lesbian Sex: Popular Images, Private Acts and Public Consequences* (London: Cassell, 1996), p. 74.

28. Smyth, *Lesbians Talk Queer Notions*, p. 38. Italics mine.

the everyday material world, where 'power' and 'difference' can be 'played with' with no socially negative consequences. Yet in order to argue that such activity can be socially transformative—for example through the subversion of heterosexuality—there must be some connection between sex, fantasy, and (for want of a better term) 'real life'. But precisely what this connection constitutes is not satisfactorily explored or spelt out.

The Therapeutic Approach

In contrast to the first two categories, for advocates of our third strand of thought—what I shall call 'the therapeutic approach'—ethics, politics and social transformation figure hardly at all. Except in so far as it is 'good' for lesbian women to have as much information as possible about the possibilities of lesbian sex and sexuality. The genre of the therapeutic approach is the 'how to' book, such as those by Bright and Loulan. Sometimes the paradigm is one of 'healing'; sometimes it is one of 'play'. In both cases the emphasis is individualistic rather than social. The underlying assumption is that sex is just sex, and should be fun and enjoyable. It is something to be undertaken without guilt or shame. Sex and wider social structural power relations can be dislocated from one another. Tamsin Wilton exposes the dangers of this approach when she explores Loulan's approach to physical disability:

> ...a discussion about social responses to impairment, followed by a brief exercise on 'self-love' is of limited use to disabled lesbians trying to find the kind of practical information which they are too often denied. Moreover, to suggest that disabled lesbians should work on 'enhancing your own level of acceptance of your body' and reassuring your inner child is to hand responsibility firmly back to them. At a time when disabled activists promote a social model of disability and insist that the (currently) able-bodied mainstream take responsibility for the exclusionary and oppressive practices which dis-able people with impairments, this self-love approach on its own is reactionary and dis-abling.[29]

There is a marked reluctance in this 'therapeutic' approach to making ethical judgments about anything. The emphasis on 'toys' and 'play' reinforces the message that it would be inappropriate to do so. In the midst of fierce ideological battles within the lesbian community about the use of dildos, for instance—whether or not their deployment consti-

29. Wilton, *Finger-Licking Good*, p. 115.

tutes a collusion with patriachal domination—the approach taken by a popular lesbian sex manual, *Making Out: The Book of Lesbian Sex and Sexuality* is as follows: '...there is no reason why a piece of plastic or rubber used to heighten sexual enjoyment has to be identified with anything beyond itself—any other interpretation is simply a cultural construct. A woman's cunt is her own—just enjoy!'[30]

Interestingly, this 'value-free' approach in sex manuals and popular literature has been taken up in academic circles too. It is argued that because no form of sexuality is inherently less oppressive than any other, and because all relationships, whatever the gender combination/s, are fraught with power dynamics, we should just relax and enjoy them and avoid ethical analysis, which must of necessity involved 'policing'. So says Grosz, for instance:

> It is not only utopian but also naïve to take the moral high ground in proclaiming for oneself the right to judge the transgressive or other status of desire and sexuality: the function of moral evaluations of the sexual terrain can only be one of policing and prohibition, which does not deal with and does not explain the very desire for and energy of transgression.[31]

I detect a fundamental confusion in Grosz's thought between moralism (imposing a strict set of rules on others from a position of relative power), and 'moral evaluation'. I would defend the need for the latter—though I would prefer to call it 'ethical analysis'—not least in order that the former be avoided. Ethical analysis demands that we reflect critically and reflexively on our own lives, and those of others, discerning patterns regarding that which is damaging and that which is life-enhancing. Developing the necessary tools to bring such assessments to lesbian relationships is crucial, particularly in the context of the theme of this essay.

So where does our brief and incomplete survey of various lesbian theories of power in relationships leave us? First, it seems to leave us with several models of power. For instance, when Loulan speaks of 'passing power back and forth' within a relationship,[32] she is using the

30. Z. Schramm-Evans, *Making Out: The Book of Lesbian Sex and Sexuality* (London: Pandora, 1995), p. 89.

31. E. Grosz, *Volatile Bodies: Toward a Corporeal Feminism* (Bloomington: Indiana University Press, 1994), p. 77.

32. Loulan, *The Lesbian Erotic Dance*, p. 76.

word 'power' rather differently from Sheila Jeffreys when she speaks
of, 'material power relations…economics…power that doesn't just play
around but resides in the hands of particular classes and elites'.[33] It
seems that some writers are talking about personal differences between
individuals, while others are talking of structural difference involving
inequality. When we hear, in theories of psychoanalysis, of desire being
brought about by difference, this seems to imply simply 'otherness'
rather than inequality. Perhaps a brief look at lesbian experiential reality may help us at this stage. What kinds of power inequalities do
lesbians negotiate? How do the personal and the structural interrelate?

One form of power difference that has received some attention in the
literature and which is particularly pertinent here, is that of racial difference. What is at stake in inter-racial relationships is well put by Helen
(charles) in this brief excerpt from her article, 'Not Compromising:
Inter-Skin Colour Relations':

> That love is controlled, and not the neutral bond between two individuals
> that the discourse of romance would have us believe, puts into question
> the power relations involved. When one partner belongs to a sub-culture
> and the other to a dominant, does the inter-play between them include
> the sharing or giving up of power? Is it logically possible? Can power be
> used playfully—or will it always end in tears?[34]

Here there is a recognition that, while lesbians-in-relation are individuals—each of us unique—the structural power hierarchies in which we
are embedded, and our position within those, will profoundly affect our
relationships. In other words, we are not merely individuals—our identities are shaped in community; we are corporate beings too. This means
that our histories are important—the histories that are personally known
to us, and those which are not; our individual histories, and those of the
group/s to which we belong.

So negotiating racial difference within lesbian relationships is a complex process. In her essay focusing on White subjectivity and inter-
racial relationships, Kathryn Perry says, 'Romance begins with desire.
It is almost inevitable that the white person who desires a black partner
must step into an arena choked with the lusts of their white ancestors

33. Jeffreys, *The Lesbian Heresy*, p. 98.
34. H. (charles), 'Not Compromising: Inter-Skin Colour Relations', in L. Pearce
and J. Stacey (eds.), *Romance Revisited* (London: Lawrence and Wishart, 1995),
pp. 197-209 (204).

and the history of their violent retributions.'[35] This is undoubtedly the
case, whatever our sexuality. In a lesbian relationship, however, there
are additional issues. When the black woman and the white woman
become lovers, they bring racial histories to the relationship as well as
other people's problems with it. They also relate within the context of a
taboo against intimacy between white and black people. 'Other people's
problems' with lesbian relationships are also, of course, context-specific. The dynamics of homophobia/heterosexism will function differently
within different racial groupings. In Britain, part of the self-understand-
ing of the white majority community is that it is 'less homophobic' than
minority ethnic communities—especially African-Caribbean communities which are portrayed as virulently homophobic. Such inaccurate and
racist stereotyping helps to shore up a white self-image of 'liberality'
which bears no resemblance to reality, and can have unfortunate effects
upon attempts by black and white lesbians in Britain to familiarize ourselves with one another.

Savi Hensman calls our attention to other possible effects of structural racism upon personal relationships:

> In this society, Black people were judged mainly by usefulness, as a
> cheap, mobile and easily discarded source of labour with perhaps some
> novelty value, and by extension became a backdrop for other people's
> fears and fantasies. Without great care, this could spill over into intimate
> relationships.[36]

So in inter-racial relationships, a host of issues arise regarding power
and equality. How far is it possible for an individual to remould herself
and reinvent herself in opposition to her history? What does it mean to
fancy someone of a different racial identity anyhow? Is it simply the
force of individual personality transcending difference, or is it the difference in itself which is attractive? Or a mixture of both? If it is 'difference' in itself that is attractive, does that matter? And how does the
racial identity of the 'desirer' affect the way in which it matters? Is
there an element of seeking the 'exotic other' in inter-racial attractions?
In her article, 'White Girls Are Easy, Black Girls Are Studs', Inge
Blackman quotes various women speaking of desire in the context of

35. Perry, 'The Heart of Whiteness: White Subjectivity and Interracial Relationships', in Pearce and Stacey (eds.), *Romance Revisited*, pp. 171-84 (177).

36. S. Hensman, 'Black Together Under One Banner', in V. Mason-John (ed.),
Talking Black: Lesbians of African and Asian Descent Speak Out (London: Cassell,
1995), pp. 52-71 (45).

racial difference: 'I'm attracted to White women because my White lover is Other to me and that turns me on'[37]; 'In sex the body for me becomes fetishised. I get off on the contrast of colour. I find difference incredibly erotic.'[38] Kathryn Perry raises the question of whether white people in inter-racial relationships are in flight from their own identity, seeking to be subsumed in that of another who's story seems to be more interesting: 'White people may...welcome engulfment in alien culture. Many find their white culture restrictive, cerebral and lifeless. They crave the supposed glamour, vitality, and originality of black culture. They long for a renewal of enthusiasm and vigour, as if to be magically awakened from a spellbound sleep.'[39] Finally, there are a host of issues about *how to live* in a relationship when one partner belongs, as Helen (charles) puts it, to a sub-culture, and the other belongs to a dominant culture: how to cope with differing reactions and expectations from family, friends and political communities; the need for one partner constantly to educate the other about the experience of belonging to a less-powerful sub-culture.

Similar practical level concerns arise when other forms of difference are negotiated in lesbian relationships. Another interesting case-study for our present purposes is that of differentials in age. In her book, *Lesbians Over 60 Speak for Themselves*, Monika Kehoe points out how rarely sexual activity among older people has been recognized as important by both professional and lay people. The idea of same sex sexual activity is therefore anathema, but, 'The incredible idea of homosexual relationships between the young and old is not even suggested, yet 29 of our 100 subjects have had relationships with women more than 10 years younger (some as much as half their age), although the majority did express a preference for those within 10 years of their own age'.[40] Heterosexual culture has a fairly clear value system when it comes to age differences in relationships between adults. When the man is the oldest almost any age difference is permissible, though anything over a quarter of a century may raise an eyebrow. When the woman is the older partner, heterosexual society is rather less free and easy—

37. I. Blackman, 'White Girls Are Easy, Black Girls Are Studs', in Pearce and Stacey (eds.), *Romance Revisited*, pp. 185-96 (186).

38. Blackman, 'White Girls Are Easy, Black Girls Are Studs', p. 188.

39. Perry, 'The Heart of Whiteness', p. 179.

40. M. Kehoe, *Lesbians Over 60 Speak for Themselves* (New York: Harrington Park Press, 1989), p. 43.

anything over 10 years is considered odd. But lesbians have no such tried and tested patterns to fall back upon.

The issues at stake are interesting, however. Which is the 'more powerful'—the older woman or the younger? How does this shift and change with age? It is likely that many of the power differentials that appear to be age-related are more to do with other things that usually correlate with age: financial resources, career successes, expectations of leisure time, demands of other family members (including offspring), health and energy levels, physical attractiveness, and so on. But this whole area is rarely talked about in lesbian literature. An article in the lesbian magazine, *Diva*, came close to opening up some of the serious issues at stake, but drew back from any proper consideration of them:

> I love older women. I admit it. I don't always date older women, but I definitely prefer them. They're more stable and more secure. They don't stress about coming out to their parents because they're either dead or so old that they are taking care of them. Most importantly, though, they are no longer trying to find out who they are. They know.[41]

Age relates, often, to the thorny but crucial power issue of money. Interestingly it is a heterosexual writer, Susie Orbach, who has high-lighted sensitively how deep our feelings about imbalances in material resources can go:

> ...one of the things often underestimated in the pursuit of a rational stance towards money is the ways in which, for all of us, it encodes contradictory ideas and assumptions about desire, power, emotional deprivation, avarice, abundance, sharing or withholding... Where there is an imbalance in income between two women, 'heterosexually' con-structed scenarios impinge, creating complex resentments...in a lesbian relationship, where there are discrepant incomes and resources, both women may encounter the wish to be economically cared for.[42]

There is a huge agenda here which is beyond the scope of this short article, but which needs urgently to be addressed. Differences of race and age involve issues of structural power, but they also incorporate the personal and the individual, and it is the complexity brought about by the combination of these various factors that any analysis of power imbalances between women in lesbian relationships must take account of. For instance, a black woman who has had a loving and stable family

41. V. Stagg Elliot, 'May and December', *Diva* (June 1996).
42. S. Orbach, 'For Richer for Poorer', *The Guardian Weekend* (29 June 1996).

background which has imbued her with robust self-esteem and self-respect will bring very different resources to a relationship than a white woman who has survived sexual abuse in childhood, and for whom building and retaining any level of self-esteem is a constant challenge. There are questions in any relationship of health and well-being, and personal strength. These differences are not so obviously assessed as those of structural inequality, but they are nevertheless crucial. As Inge Blackman puts it,

> Public dialogue between races has been informed by identity politics which is framed by ideas of hierarchy and oppression, socio-economic status, and history. However, lovers operate in a private space where intimate conversations are not publicly studied. Power hierarchies of identity politics are considered to be irrelevant in love affairs between two women even though power relationships are constantly shifting in any lesbian relationship. In a mixed-race relationship the White woman is not always in control, nor the Black woman always powerless. An essential ingredient of loving anyone and having sex with them is that each lover submits to the loved one.[43]

In the Final Analysis

Where does this brief look at power differences in lesbian relationships leave us in terms of our ethical agenda?

First, it leaves us with a conviction that any idealization of lesbian relationships as inherently more egalitarian than heterosexual ones is damaging and unhelpful. As Grosz says,

> Lesbian relationships are no better, nor any worse, than the complexities involved in all sociosexual interrelations. Nor are they in any sense a solution to patriarchal forms of sexuality, because lesbianism and gay male sexuality are, as much as heterosexuality, products of patriarchy. There is no pure sexuality, no inherently transgressive sexual practices.[44]

The idealization of lesbian relating is born of (and leads to) an over-emphasis upon our sameness (as women). Now the time has come to refocus upon women's diversity and differences from one another. Judith Roof talks of the 'polymorphous diversity' within the category lesbian, which is characterized by 'multiple desires, diverse races, classes, ages, educational levels, sexual backgrounds and practices, political

---

43. Blackman, 'White Girls Are Easy, Black Girls Are Studs', p. 195.
44. Grosz, *Volatile Bodies*, p. 77.

consciousness, and physical appearance'.[45] But if we are going to celebrate the diversity of lesbian community, how are we to live with it in
our personal relationships?

Theologian and ethicist, Marie Fortune, has addressed some of these
questions in her book, *Love Does No Harm: Sexual Ethics for the Rest
of Us*. Coming, as it does, out of many years of practical and theological work ameliorating the devastating effects of sexual violence, the
primary concern of her work is the avoidance of abuses of power in
intimate relationships. Fortune suggests the following ethical guideline
as a starting point: 'Is my choice of intimate partner a peer, ie someone
whose power is relatively equal to mine? We must limit our sexual
interaction to our peers. Some people are off limits for our sexual interests.'[46] She concludes her chapter on 'Choosing Peer Relationships' as
follows:

> Seeking a peer relationship in which to find sexual intimacy is the best
> insurance there is for avoiding abuse and for finding trust and fulfillment
> in relationship. Look for a partner who is your equal, who is a grown-up,
> who knows how to take care of him/herself, earns his/her own living,
> and is not threatened by your strengths and capabilities.[47]

The concept of a peer relationship is useful as an explanation of why
sexual contact between children and adults, or between professionals
and clients, is off-limits. It is important to say, at this point, that Fortune
explains in her book that, '...it is possible for women and men to relate
as peers in an intimate relationship *if* they openly acknowledge the
reality of the social, political, and economic context in which they live
and adjust accordingly'.[48] For our current purposes, therefore, we might
extend this guideline about the structural power difference of gender to,
for example, race and age. Yet it seems to me that there is a danger in
positing peer status as a necessary *starting point* for intimate
relationships. What happens, for instance, to those who will never be
able to 'look after themselves'? To those who have not, and may never
have, an independent income? Is there not also a temptation to seek out
relationships with those who are 'like us'—particularly, for instance, in
terms of our racial and class backgrounds, thus missing out on fruitful

45. Roof, *A Lure of Knowledge*, p. 250.
46. M. Fortune, *Love Does No Harm: Sexual Ethics for the Rest of Us* (New
York: Continuum, 1995), p. 75.
47. Fortune, *Love Does No Harm*, p. 84.
48. Fortune, *Love Does No Harm*, p. 81.

interractions which might be possible within what Roof calls a polymorphously diverse lesbian community?

It seems to me that there is a danger of relying too heavily on unproblematized identity categories in order to assess what is a 'peer relationship' and what is not. In order to circumvent this, there is a need for the theoretical formulations of lesbian ethics to catch up with those through which we negotiate the politics of identity. Judith Butler helps us to see how this might be achieved: 'The question of locating "agency" is usually associated with the viability of the "subject", where the "subject" is understood to have some stable existence prior to the cultural field that it negotiates'.[49] She goes on to state that, 'Paradoxically, the reconceptualisation of identity as an *effect*, that is, as *produced* or *generated*, opens up possibilities of "agency" that are insidiously foreclosed by positions that take identity categories as foundational and fixed'.[50] She concludes, 'My argument is that there need not be a "doer behind the deed", but that the "doer" is variably constructed in and through the deed'.[51] In the context of the current discussion, Butler's insights lead us to posit peer status not as the *necessary prerequisite* to a an intimate/sexual relationship—but as the *aim* of our relating in those relationships.

We saw earlier how lesbian feminists argue for the 'eroticization of equality'. But without the insights of Butler regarding identity and subjectivity we are, I believe, in danger of utilizing a deficient model of equality. This model is of equality as static entity which is either 'present' or 'absent' in relationships, according to particular characteristics of those involved. In the light of Butler's insights on subjectivity, agency, 'doer' and 'deed', I would argue for a new conception of *equality as process*. According to the old model, equality is defined in terms of people 'having equal power' as a starting point for relationship. This allows certain assumptions to be made, such as lesbian relationships being inherently more equal than heterosexual ones. The search for an equal relationship is defined in terms of lining up a list of considerations (such as age, race, class, and so on. This is the famous 'embarrassed etc'. referred to by Butler[52] as she demonstrates the impossibility

49. J. Butler, *Gender Trouble: Feminism and the Subversion of Identity* (London: Routledge, 1990), p. 142.

50. Butler, *Gender Trouble*, p. 147 (italics original).

51. Butler, *Gender Trouble*, p. 142.

52. Butler, *Gender Trouble*, p. 143.

of encompassing a situated subject) and making sure they are pretty much all the same.

The alternative model does not constitute a call to abandon all notions of structural power—or to instigate, by default, a notion that no-one has more power than anyone else. Quite the opposite. It could be said to call *more* attention to the realities of the operations of power, for the model of *equality as process* allows for no assumptions. This means that less obvious differences (such as some of those mentioned above to do with personal constitution, self-esteem and upbringing) which are often hidden when equality is based on identity politics, stand more chance of coming to the fore. The importance of difference in general is reconfigured, for there is no longer any reason why it should be either annihilated or avoided as the instigator or site of sexual desire. Rather, the ethical priority is to mitigate the negative effects that spring from the structural social inequalities that attach to particular forms of difference.

And so we emerge with a political and ethical form of lesbian desire that is productive of equality and sexual justice—a process which is itself an ongoing task, achieved by the negotiation of difference. Thus the old adage that desire is produced by difference is replaced by the idea that desire is productive through the utilization of difference, and the mitigation of inequality.

HUMAN SEXUALITY AND THE CONCEPT OF GOD/ESS

Beverley Clack

Introduction

The aim of this article is to consider the way in which reflection upon women's bodies might provide a suitably modern model for the divine. To aid this end, the main concern of this article is with a model of 'Goddess' drawn from reflection on the nature and possibilities of female bodies. While this might be seen as an aberration from the way in which the divine has been habitually conceived,[1] reflection on the ideas of Jacques Lacan suggest that, far from reflecting a 'view from nowhere', the traditional concept of God has itself developed from (male) reflection upon the male body. Consideration of the role/rule of the Phallus in Lacanian thought leads itself to a dilemma for any attempt to ground a concept of the divine in the processes of the human body: in offering a model for the divine which valorizes the properties of female bodies, is an equally engendered model for the divine proffered which itself excludes half the human race? Can the values drawn from the female body be applied to develop a more unifying account of the divine and spirituality than its exclusive predecessors? The intention of this paper is to show that this might, indeed, be the case.

Conceiving the Goddess

In the language of the Goddess, the female body is an important metaphor for the creative powers of the earth body (Christ 1997: 91).

The Goddess has been perceived in recent years as providing a strong symbol for the revaluation and reappropriation of the female body. The potential creativity of the female body has been adopted by thealogians such as Carol Christ as a way of conceiving divinity anew. The power

---

1. Cf. Swinburne 1994: 125-26.

of such a shift in thinking cannot be underestimated: either in its power to move, or, indeed, in its power to shock. Consideration of the different attitudes towards female genitalia reveals something of a discrepancy between the negative views of the Western tradition and the positive value ascribed to women's bodies and sexuality in thealogical thought. Reflection on what should be a fairly straightforward word for female genitalia—'cunt'—reveals something of the disconcerting and despised nature of female biological sexual identity. 'A highly taboo word' completes the dictionary definition.[2] Indeed, 'acceptable' alternatives for female genitalia are hard to find: 'vagina' (too clinical), 'womb' (too medical), 'fanny' (too comical). A plethora of words, devoid of approbation are, by way of contrast, available to describe male genitalia. Moreover, the definition for 'phallus' includes the information that this is 'a symbol of generative power in nature'. How interesting that the place from whence all new human life is born is not similarly defined.

Yet perhaps this linguistic sidetrack tells us something about the dubious status ascribed to female sexuality in the Western tradition. A few examples will suffice to suggest something of the 'problems' which arise when attempting to base a model for the divine upon the female body. A key feature of Western society, itself reflected in the concept of God, involves the prioritizing of cultural 'order' above natural 'chaos'. Similarly, the biblical creation narrative suggests the defeat of primeval chaos in language which resonates with the defeat of the goddess Tiamat by the god Marduk in the Babylonian *Enuma Elish*. The concern with right order is likewise reflected in Western political structures, and in the hierarchical structure of the church which mirrors this. Against such a backdrop, the female body may seem a less than obvious symbol for the divine, given the frequent connection between female sexuality and the chaotic. So, for mediaeval man, the 'vagina dentata' (the womb with teeth) spoke of woman's chaotic power and her (potential) ability to castrate; while, according to classical medical theory, 'hysteria' was a peculiarly female disorder arising from the wandering of the womb.[3]

This identification of the female body with the chaotic pervades even

---

2.   'cunt / kʌnt / n. coarse sl. 1 the female genitals. 2 offens. an unpleasant or stupid person. A highly taboo word. [MEf. Gmc]' (*The Concise Oxford English Dictionary*).

3.   For a fascinating discussion of such theories, see Tuana (1993: Chapter 5).

radical philosophical discourse. Again, one example will suffice. Jean-Paul Sartre's existentialism, adopted and employed in Simone de Beauvoir's feminist thinking, by no means offers a positive view of female sexuality. At one point, Sartre links 'femininity' with nothingness in a graphic allusion, itself reminiscent of other words for female sex organs:

> The obscenity of the feminine sex is that of everything which 'gapes open'. It is *an appeal to being* as all holes are (Sartre 1958: 613).

Female sexuality stands as an affront to the patriarchal desire for order, completeness and integrity; it must be filled by that which the male can offer, the phallus. The womb/cunt is itself a herald of death: its mucous nature reminds the man seeking an immortal legacy or immortality itself of that place from whence he has come and to the state to which he must return. Small surprise, then, that Sartre connects the quality 'slime' with the feminine:

> Slime is the revenge of the In-Itself. A sickly-sweet feminine revenge which will be symbolized on another level by the quality 'sugary' (Sartre 1958: 609).

De Beauvoir's work offers little by the way of recompense for such language. Like Sartre, she views female sexuality with distaste, as something which must be rejected and subjugated if woman is to attain the same potentially transcendent existence as the male:

> The feminine sex organ is mysterious even to the woman herself, concealed, mucous, and humid, as it is; it bleeds each month, it is often sullied with body fluids, it has a secret and perilous life of its own. Woman does not recognize herself in it (de Beauvoir 1972: 406).

The womb is uncontrollable: 'it has a secret and perilous life of its own'. If a woman is to take charge of her life, she must reject the control which her sexuality exerts over her. Note how de Beauvoir's words reiterate the desire for order and control. If woman is to be truly free, according to de Beauvoir, she must reject her sexuality.

Against such a backdrop, it would seem that the desire to develop a female divine is misplaced. Yet recent thealogical writing suggests a very different view of female sexuality. Far from rejecting the apparently chaotic nature of the womb, Goddess women have sought to celebrate it. As Melissa Raphael has noted, menstruation, far from implying a fundamental problem or weakness with the female body, has been seized upon by Goddess women as offering a possible source of creative power (Raphael 1996: 197). Having reclaimed menstruation in this way, it is a relatively small step to move on to claim that the divine incorporates such embodied creativity.

Consideration of the historical development of the Goddess suggests a similar reification of female sexuality and particularly the possibility of bringing about new life. Archaelogical finds from the Neolithic Age of images of women/goddesses[4] suggest a celebration of these powers. Here, female figures are depicted with large breasts, broad hips, rounded belly. Fertility and the ability to birth seem to be the key features alluded to in such images. These features have been seized upon and celebrated by contemporary Goddess women; so Jan Dianne Jansak from an invocation to the Goddess says 'Her body is full and round, as all ripens within Her warm embrace. And we celebrate the rhythms of Her Body' ('We'moon 1994: Gaia Rhythms for Womyn').

This emphasis on sexuality and birthing suggests one of the reasons for resisting the Goddess as a model for the divine. The messy, painful, and sometimes tragic business of procreation and life-giving has not been seen as appropriate for the God of order celebrated in the Western tradition. Better that God should create by his word than through the organic process of birthing! Connected to this objection has been the rather strange idea that a female deity would be gender-specific in a way the (gender-neutral) male God of Western religion is not. So Richard Swinburne explains his continuing use of the male pronoun for God, despite calls for inclusive language, thus:

> The English language, unfortunately, does not today possess a pronoun suitable for persons without seeming to beg questions about gender. As the pronoun 'he' has been used in the past for reference to a person without seeming to beg questions about their gender, and 'she' has never been used in this way, I shall use the pronoun 'he' to refer to any divine individual, without the implication that the individual is male (Swinburne 1994: 125-26).

Swinburne is evidently only talking about the use of language: what would he think of a concept of God/ess drawn specifically from the reproductive functions of one half of the human race? Is this offering a divinity which is gender-specific in a way in which the apparently neutral and neutered Western concept of God is not? Let us for a moment

---

4.   For a discussion of the 'controversy' surrounding such images—are they women or goddesses?—see Christ (1997: 79-80).

consider such claims. The implication seems to be that the concept of God as we have it is asexual, genderless and abstract, despite the use of male pronouns and images in defining this God. Before outlining the potential power of the female body for a radical concept of God, it is worth considering some ideas of the French psychoanalyst Jacques Lacan which prove useful in establishing the gendered (male) nature of the Western God.

Men's Bodies and (the) God

In approaching any discussion of the concept of God, feminist critics have argued that the dominant Western formulation can be shown to embody male values; moreover, that it can be understood as a divinization of the male individual. This, it is claimed, has had a corresponding impact upon male/female relations; famously, Mary Daly has argued that 'if God is male, then the male is God' (Daly 1986: 19). Indeed, if we consider the attributes commonly ascribed to God we find a divinization of the values held in high regard by patriarchal society. Just as power, knowledge, invulnerability and steadfastness are privileged in an androcentric culture, so omnipotence, omniscience, impassibility and immutability are central to the classical concept of God.

While these values might be deemed 'masculine', rather than male, and thus acquire a potentially universal applicability, evidence can be accrued to support the claim that the Western concept of God is ultimately derived from the male body and its experiences. Classically, the concept of God has been defined as a being external to the world, somewhat like an autonomous, rational individual.[5] This notion of God can, interestingly, be paralleled by the very experience which is invariably distanced from the nature of spirituality: sexuality; and in this instance with male sexual experience as an external event, or an achievement. James Nelson, in support of such a theory, writes of how his experience of sex as something which happened externally to himself was reflected in his understanding of God:

> Personally, I know for most of my life I assumed automatically that the proper object of my spiritual life was really 'out there', rather than a mystery dwelling deeply within me. It was something I have to penetrate. My desire was to grasp, to understand, to analyze, and possibly to

---

5.   Cf., for example, Swinburne (1977: 1) for a classic statement of the nature of God.

control and possess... So it was with God, the ultimate mystery. God
appeared more transcendent than immanent, more beyond than within
(Nelson 1988: 35).

If we take seriously such a connection, Christianity, the dominant religion of Western society, becomes particularly problematic from a feminist perspective. As Ruether among others has pointed out, Christianity
raises considerable problems for women, for masculine concepts *and*
the male body are divinized in the person of Christ. Consideration of
the history of the tradition reveals a corresponding problematization of
the female body. For Ruether, exposing this polarization of the male
and female body leads to a crucial question for feminists: 'can a male
saviour save women?' (Ruether 1983: 116). A deity which corresponds
to the normative power of the male body in patriarchal society will have
little to say to a woman's experience of her own body. Against such a
context, the kind of thealogical claims considered in the previous section for a deity that corresponds to women's life-experience provides
not just a religious but also a political challenge.[6]

Alternative solutions have also been advanced. Recent moves by
those espousing a 'radical orthodox' position have sought to resist the
claim that the maleness of Christ presupposes a male conception of
deity. This is potentially an important development for any article suggesting that the female body might proffer a more adequate contemporary account of the divine. In developing the ideas of radical orthodoxy,
the work of Lacan has proved invaluable. It is argued that the maleness
of Christ's body can be accepted, for it is a subversive maleness leading
to a renewed and revitalized concept of God (Ward 1998). Crucial
to this subversive account of the male body is Lacan's work on the
phallus.

God and the Phallus

In a recent paper, Graham Ward argues that the maleness of Christ
should not be problematic for feminists. It is, after all, a subversive
maleness, a maleness that calls into question our habitual understandings of what it means to be embodied. At one point, he makes the
following controversial comment: 'God may have a phallus, but he cer-

---

6.   Cf., for example, Luce Irigaray: 'If she is to become woman, if she is to
accomplish her female subjectivity, woman needs a god who is a figure for the perfection of *her* subjectivity' (1993: 63).

tainly doesn't have a penis' (Ward 1998: 173). This may, at first, seem a contradictory idea (indeed, as I shall argue, even when this phrase is explained in Lacanian terms, it fails to make sense). How can one separate the phallus—the erect, turgid penis—from the penis itself? If we are to understand what lies behind Ward's phrase—and its implications for any concept of God/ess—we need to consider the role of the phallus in the thought of Lacan, for it is undoubtedly Lacan's ideas which lead Ward to this strange conclusion.

At the outset, it is important to be aware that Lacan's central concern lies with culture, not with any 'determining' biological powers. It is this concern that has led to different interpretations of his apparent sexism or lack of it. For some feminists, he is an enemy to be defeated; for others, he simply exposes the phallocentric basis of human culture.[7] At any rate, his interest with the phallus lies not with the biological role of erection, but with the cultural power of this image. As such, when he explores the realm of 'the Symbolic'—what Malcolm Bowie defines as 'a supra-personal structural order' (Bowie 1991: 58)—the phallus becomes the chief signifier for meaning.

This leads us to a further point: if we are to understand the role that the phallus plays within human culture, we must engage with the key category of the symbolic: 'that which makes the Symbolic possible' (Bowie 1991: 108). In Lacan's terms, it is 'The Name-of-the-Father' which ensures the development of a human symbolic order. In applying this term, Lacan draws upon the powers which restrict infantile desire by threatening punishment (castration); it is, if you like, the father who comes between the mother and child to stop a too narrow and confining dualism between the pair developing, thus thrusting the child into the human world of meaning, symbol and law.[8] Against such a context, the phallus becomes 'the signifier which holds all signifieds in thrall' (Bowie 1991: 124); it is the symbol 'through which human desire finds form' (Bowie 1991: 128). At this point, it would seem that the phallus is being distinguished from the penis; to use more traditional language, the phallus operates on a metaphysical rather than a physical level. It represents power, it represents the law to which we are subjected (Mitchell and Rose 1982: 28), and it represents that which humanity

---

7.   For discussion of these different responses, see Grosz (1990: Chapter 6).

8.   Lacan's postulation of the necessity of defeating the mother is mirrored in Erich Neumann's account of why the defeat of the Goddess was necessary for the development of ego and rationality (cf. Neumann 1971).

desires. (Perhaps we can see why Ward will want to link this signifier with God.) But the phallus should not be confused with the all-too-'human' penis. If we consider this dimension of Lacan's thought, some light might be thrown upon Ward's claim: God does not have a penis (that which distinguishes the male from the female) but he does have a phallus (in other words, 'he' embodies the symbol of power, and is that which humans desire).

The controlling power of the phallus over human desire should be explored, for it throws further light upon Ward's assertion. It is the phallus, the emblem of power, that human beings want. And this has to be understood differently for men and women. The male, through his body, is capable of 'having' the phallus; the female, because she lacks that which has come to be linked with the phallus, the penis, can 'be' the phallus (in other words, she can be desired/take the place of the phallus for the male), but she cannot herself possess the phallus. At this point the notion that the phallus can be constructed as a concept distinct from the male body starts to break down. If men and women relate differently to this symbol *because* of their different bodies, how can we possibly be dealing with a neutral term? Only those with a penis can possess the phallus. And if this is the case for human beings, what are we saying about a God who is described as possessing the phallus? If anything, the route taken by Ward entails an even more male/masculine conceptualization of the divine than that offered within the classical Western tradition: at least for defining figures like Aquinas, God is understood as incorporeal (without a body).[9]

If we delve deeper into Lacan's work, focusing on the perceived relationship between men and women, the notion of a neutral phallus becomes even more fragile. 'The other', as it has in so many other Western philosophies,[10] comes to play a key part in Lacan's account of the development of the self. Once again, it is woman who takes on this role. So, in a process described by Bowie:

> The divided subject, haunted by absence and lack, looks to the other not simply to supply his needs but to pay him the compliment of an unconditional *yes* (Bowie 1991: 135).

The mother's role in this development is paramount. She constructs an other/(m)other whose first obligation is to be present. Ultimately, the

---

9. So, 'in no sense is God a body…' (*Summa Theologiae*, 1a, 3 article 1).
10. For a succinct account of this identification see Lloyd (1984).

child will lose this all-present other. Then, this 'pure loss' will become desire. As Lacan puts it, 'desire is neither the appetite for satisfaction, nor the demand for love, but the difference that results from the sub-traction of the first from the second, the very phenomenon of their splitting' (Lacan 1958: 81). In such an economy, one can begin to see why Ward views Lacan's ideas as useful for a realist account of God— God becomes part of the economy of desire. God is the infinitely desirable, in whom we will ultimately find the kind of love demanded by the hungry self.

However, the androcentrism of this account of desire should not be underplayed, as it is by Ward. In developing his notion of desire, woman's role looks sadly familiar. In Lacan's universe, women are less subject than men; they are signifiers of *desire* (shades of the old con-nection made between women and sexuality, perhaps); they seek the phallus they lack; and so on. As Bowie so tellingly says when con-sidering Lacan's attitude towards women, 'scattered sociological obser-vations [are] being passed off as a theory of sexual difference' (Bowie 1991: 143). Indeed, women's very existence and sexuality are forced into an account of desire and sexuality formed purely by male construc-tions of what these concepts/realities mean. So, when Lacan reflects upon woman's experience of *jouissance* (or orgasm) he falls into a binary understanding of sexuality which defines woman's experience as that which is 'not-man's'. His reflections on female *jouissance* begin with a statement that this goes 'beyond the phallus' (Lacan 1972: 145): quite a claim for a writer who argues that the phallus is the prime signi-fier of the symbolic order. He goes on:

> There is a *jouissance* proper to her, to this 'her' which does not exist and which signifies nothing. There is a *jouissance* proper to her and of which she herself may know nothing, except that she experiences it—that much she does know. She knows it of course when it happens. It does not happen to all of them (Lacan 1972: 145).

What, then, is the significance of this experience, which suggests a pas-sivity about the woman experiencing it ominously close to the passivity ascribed to her by Aristotelian biology? Despite the apparent downplay-ing of its significance in this passage and in Lacan's economy of desire, it has been argued that he is offering a radical meaning for female sexuality which undercuts the apparent phallocentrism of his argument. (Will it undercut the similar trend in Ward's theology?) Evidence for such an interpretation comes from his reflections upon Bernini's statue of St Theresa. The clearly sexual nature of her ecstasy forms the basis for the following comment:

> Might not this *jouissance* which one experiences and knows nothing of, be that which puts us on the path of ex-istence? And why not interpret one face of the Other, the God face, as supported by feminine *jouissance*? (Lacan 1972: 147)

Suddenly, a completely different account of the divine is introduced which seems to displace the phallus. There is something mysterious here, something that refutes the clear-cut nature of the role/rule of the phallus. Could Lacan be undercutting the phallocentrism of the Western concept of God with an alternative model, based on the genuine alterity of female sexual experience? It is difficult to say; more so when one starts to unpack some of Lacan's key expositions on the phallus. The focus on the phallus could be simply part of an honest reflection on the nature of Western culture; or it could reflect a patriarchal mind set; or perhaps it reflects both. An example might be helpful here. When reflecting on why the phallus might have become the privileged signifier of human desire, Lacan writes:

> One might say that this signifier is chosen as what stands out as most easily seized upon in the realm of sexual copulation, and also as the most symbolic in the literal (typographical) sense of the term, since it is the equivalent in that relation to the (logical) copula. One might say that by virtue of its turgidity, it is the image of the vital flow as it is transmitted in generation (Lacan 1958: 82).

But this is to suggest the primacy of lineal, externalized ways of thinking/being: the kind of ideas which, remember, Nelson suggests stem from male sexual experience and which helped form the theological concept of God. Male-dominance is presupposed. What if the prime signifier was what was happening in the *female* body? What if the waves and cycles of the womb/vagina/clitoris were what informed our understanding of copulation? What if the *internalized* experience of female sexuality came to inform our structures, our understanding of ourselves, *and* our theology? The extent to which we continue to take male experience and the processes of the male body as normative for our experience of the world is astounding. Witness my own surprise—and delight!—at Christine Battersby's recent attempt to define the nature of the *human* self upon birthing as a normative feature of *human being* (Battersby 1998). It seems strange to move from an experience which only a woman can have to a general claim about human existence; yet the equation 'male = human' is still accepted. Lacan's thought does not seem to offer a move beyond the habitual denigration of female experience. While he may be fascinated by the almost 'other-worldly' power of female *jouissance*, he maintains a purely male-defined account of the sexual, denying the idea that any real significance can be derived from female sexual experience. Like Freud before him, Lacan affirms the normative status of male sexual experience, and like Freud he is just as unhelpful for any attempt to reflect seriously upon women's experience unhampered by patriarchal interpretation.

In such a context, 'woman [is] a foil to the ratiocinative, knowledge-seeking and system-building intelligence that Lacan unself-consciously thinks of as male' (Bowie 1991: 153-54). So while Lacan might envy woman her ecstasy, 'when their transport ceases they have little to do and nothing at all to say' (Bowie 1991: 156). Can adopting such a position have anything positive to offer feminists? Juliet Mitchell, alongside others such as Julia Kristeva, thinks so. Mitchell rejects the charge that Lacan is phallocentric:

> [T]heir [Freud and Lacan's] task is not to produce justice but to explain this difference which to them uses, not the man, but the phallus to which the man has to lay claim as its key term (Mitchell and Rose 1982: 8).

On one level, Mitchell may be correct; however, this justification of Lacan misses the point. First, I am not convinced that any account of the phallus can be distinguished from the man. This may suggest something of the potential problems for the attempt to develop an inclusive model of the divine based upon the Goddess. What would it mean to distinguish the vagina from the woman? Secondly, the phrase which Mitchell employs—'the phallus to which the man has to lay claim'—betrays the male-centredness of this approach. Where are women in all of this striving and desire for achievement? Women do not have to seek affirmation for their femaleness; witness the reality of monthly menstruation. Masculinity, by way of contrast, involves notions of achievement.[11] While reflection on the phallus may suggest something about the nature of masculinity, it has little to say to women or their experience of the world. Finally, and most importantly, from a feminist perspective, what is the point of *describing* reality if one is not prepared to *challenge* the androcentric concepts that have shaped and

11. Miles (1992: Chapter 4).

continue to shape human culture? Mitchell seems too prepared to simply accept the *status quo*.

It is at this point that Ward's redefinition of God proves so unhelpful for women. In seeking a new way of thinking about God which is grounded in the ideas of Lacan, Ward simply reveals the problematic nature of the Western concept of God which itself valorizes the male body. In patriarchal culture, not only does God have a phallus, 'he' is also understood to have a penis.

Human Bodies and the Concept of God/ess

Consideration of Lacan raises significant questions for any theology attempting to define divine power in terms of the phallus. Ward's account of the divine, despite his initial claims, has little to offer women. The attempt to distinguish the phallus from the male body is shown to be a misleading diversion from the attempt to address the androcentrism of the Western concept of God. In Lacan's thought, ideas of 'male' and 'masculine' are—not surprisingly—ultimately blurred. A privileged position is maintained for male sexual experience which necessitates the denigration of female sexuality.

It would seem that, for women at least, the claims of radical orthodoxy will not be radical enough. Yet reflection upon the problems of moving from the male body to an adequate concept of the divine raises an important question for the argument of this article: can any concept of the divine be profitably drawn from the realm of human sexuality? If we accept the gendered nature of concepts of God/ess, and we decide that the female body provides an appropriate locus for the divine, are we locked into espousing mutually exclusive concepts of God and Goddess, or can a model for the divine be developed which affirms *human* sexuality in all its different facets and expressions?

Christine Battersby's account of human personhood suggests a potential way forward. According to Battersby the female body and its ability to birth can be used as a normative concept for developing a notion of humanity as a whole. So, the flexibility of personhood, the possibility of making space within one's self for another individual, and so on, are not qualities which apply exclusively to women.[12] These are features of *human* being; albeit human being as it forms itself in one sex. Basing an

12. As a twist to this point, at the time of writing there are claims that in the future there could be pregnant men (22 February 1999).

account of the self upon such ideas will undoubtedly be wrought with difficulties: is an imaginary being developed which will privilege female experience over male experience? Grace Jantzen's comments on such fears can usefully be applied here: in basing a model for the divine upon the processes of the female body it is unlikely that we will take such ideas to mean that God/ess is literally female (Jantzen 1998: 182). Rather, by using this model we suggest something about the goal of human spirituality: in Jantzen's terms, the desire to become divine.[13] If we take such an approach seriously, we might be able to derive values from the female body—and particularly female sexuality—which can provide an appropriate model for human spirituality. The remainder of this article will suggest that reflection upon female bodily experience can form the basis for a model of the divine applicable to both women and men. Of particular concern is the desire to establish a spirituality which seeks to view the world as in some sense sacred. Seeing the world thus is by no means a viewpoint exclusive to women. Indeed, in developing an eco-friendly spirituality, I intend to draw upon recent developments in the scientific understanding of the world which suggest a ready correspondence between the sense of humanity as an intimate part of the physical world and a holistic spirituality.

Remaking the Self

'We are of the soil and the soil is of us' (Luther Standing Bear).

Any revised account of the divine will have to take seriously contemporary developments in the understanding of the self. What we say of the divine, we in some sense say of ourselves.[14] In recent years the understanding of the autonomous immortal self which has come down to us via Plato and Descartes has come under considerable pressure. The idea that there is a fixed 'I' distinct from the changing world of experience and appearance is difficult to maintain.[15] When Christine

13. For details of what she means by this, see Jantzen (1998).

14. This may mean returning to Feuerbach and his theory of projection (cf. *The Essence of Christianity* [1841]); regardless of the value ascribed to Feuerbach's ideas, it is interesting to note that Ward's radical orthodoxy is itself dependent on accepting Lacan's development of the psychoanalytic account of the self.

15. This is not only the case in the psychoanalytic theories of Freud and Lacan, but has also been challenged in the work of Wittgenstein and, more recently, in Parfit (1984).

Battersby attempts to define human selfhood according to the ability to birth, she is similarly concerned to stress the fluidity of the self. The human self is an individual which, under certain conditions, is able to create within itself space for a new life, a new individual (Battersby 1998: 1-14). For some feminists (notably Daphne Hampson) this notion of a subject in flux is problematic: in challenging the independent self we seem to neglect the fact that it is only in recent years that women have come to see themselves as individuals, rather than as defined through their (often subordinate) relationships. A solution is possible to this apparently intractable problem. We need to accept the importance of women finding their own individuality and autonomy, while recognizing that this does not necessitate accepting the old view of the self and its attendant interpretation of such features which lead to the domination of the physical world.[16] Might it not be possible to have a sense of selfhood and self-fulfilment, while recognizing that we are all selves in flux, constantly changing as we journey through life? When we consider our own pasts, we see that this is obviously the case. While I am not the same as the child I was then (indeed, when remembering events they often seem to have happened to someone else!), I know that the events of my past have framed to a large extent what I am doing now and how I respond in particular situations. There is both difference and continuity.

Jantzen's development of a symbolic of natality takes such reflections a stage further. The process of birthing reveals a primary dependence upon the mother which, given time, results in an independent human being. However, we never lose that initial grounding of our self in relation to others: we are all born into communities, and we all grow and develop in community. In this sense, the radically independent self is an inaccurate myth (Jantzen 1998: 243). In developing an eco-friendly spirituality, such reflections mean that we must recognize our dependence on the physical world itself. Humanity, like every other animal and plant life, is part of an interconnected ecosystem. We cannot survive without each other, and our understanding of the self—and the concept of God which springs from this—should reflect this sense of dependence.

---

16. For a detailed account of this legacy, see Plumwood (1993).

Female Sexuality

This sense of the self in flux, yet grounded in relationship, is reiterated if we consider female orgasm (*jouissance*) *on its own terms*. Mary Pellauer's account of female orgasm suggests the breaking down of boundaries between self and other, self and the world (Pellauer 1994: 149-68).[17] While Lacan might claim that women cannot describe their own *jouissance*, Pellauer is rather effective at highlighting how the experience of female orgasm reveals something about our total relation to the universe and to others; in her words:

> I am most fully embodied in this explosion of nerves and also broken open into the cosmos. I am rent open; I am cleaved/joined not only to my partner, but to everything, everything-as-my-beloved (or vice versa), who has also become me (Pellauer 1994: 155).

Such an account is of particular importance for a world facing an ecological disaster which has arisen precisely through human unwillingness to be identified with the natural world. Rather than distancing ourselves from the things of this world, we need to adapt to our historical situation, throwing ourselves into this world in order to save both the ecosystem and ourselves. Breaking down a too rigid distinction between self and other is important here, and suggests a rather different account of sexual intercourse than that habitually offered by masculinist society. James Nelson has highlighted 'the genitalization of sex' (Nelson 1988: 35) in masculinist thinking: male sexual experience is defined according to specific acts, concerned with taking charge, and so on. This suggests a separate self which engages (somewhat distantly) in these sexual acts. Nelson wants to resist such an account of human sexuality, writing that 'we have had enough of separation' (Nelson 1988: 45). Forming an account of the fluid self may go some way to changing such an idea. At this point a note of caution should be sounded. While arguing for a more flexible account of the self we should not take this to imply that the destruction of all boundaries is necessary for a feminist account of the self. Boundaries are important—for testimony, see survivors of sexual abuse. I am not advocating an abusers' charter. What is needed is a sense of the flexibility of the self, while maintaining the idea that 'I' am an individual always in relationship.

---

17. For development of Pellauer's ideas, see B. Clack (1998).

Women's Bodies and the Goddess

Accepting this account of the self necessitates a different understanding of divinity. If, rather than thinking of the self as a rigid, fixed, change-less entity, we were to consider the fluidity of existence suggested by our experiences of life in this world, the traditional concept of God (as changeless, radically independent and so forth) will seem anachronistic. The Western tradition has not valued ideas of change, linking it, inevi-tably, with suffering, decay and death. Yet such a privileging of change-lessness neglects a key feature of human existence. The nature of women's bodies is such that the radical change which is part of all human existence is much in evidence. Menstruation, pregnancy, meno-pause, all reveal the changing nature of the human body. And it should be emphasized that it is not only women who change: while there is less obvious physical evidence, men's bodies change too. This notion of the changing human body may seem alarming to a culture which fears age-ing and yearns for stability. Yet the positive role that change plays in the life of the earth is becoming more apparent. Rather than change being something to be resisted, geologists are increasingly coming to believe that change is that which makes the world a living and vital place. Without the ever-shifting geological plates on which the con-tinents sit, and the earthquakes and volcanoes which ring them, there would be no recycling of carbon, and consequently no life (Lamb and Sington 1998). Our very place in the universe is maintained by such changing physical conditions. Our human lives are defined by change. Against such a context, the continued prioritizing of changelessness and lineal thinking, itself reified in the concept of God, makes little sense. If we are to truly live in harmony with the forces that created us we need a concept of divinity which does not falsely set us apart from the natural world.

Conclusion

At such a juncture the model of the female divine takes on a radical power of its own. Carol Christ has pointed to the reluctance of scholars to take seriously the notion of the Goddess 'because they have been taught to view the body and sexuality, especially the female body and female sexuality, as being "lower" than the rationality that is associated with divinity and "man's" "higher" nature' (Christ 1997: 78). Perhaps it is only by recourse to such a neglected and challenging image of the divine that a fundamental shift in our understanding of the divine will take place. Traditionally, humans looked to the Goddess for a celebration of human sexuality, fertility and the cyclical nature of things. Our world needs to reflect upon such ideas more than ever. In this sense, the model of the Goddess offers an imaginary which does not simply affirm women's lives: although this in itself is important. It also facilitates a fundamental reappraisal of the relationship between human beings and the rest of this living world. How apt that this necessitates taking seriously the experiences of the sex habitually defined in relation to the natural world: women.[18] Yet in so doing something more radical than a simple polarization of male and female occurs: what we are actually contemplating is a revolution in our understanding of ourselves, our world, and the divine.

Bibliography and Further Reading

Battersby, Christine
    1998   *The Phenomenal Woman* (Cambridge: Polity Press).
Beauvoir, Simone de
    1972   *The Second Sex* (trans. H.M. Parshley; Harmondsworth: Penguin Books [1949]).
Bowie, Malcolm
    1991   *Lacan* (London: Fontana).
Christ, Carol P.
    1997   *Rebirth of the Goddess* (Reading, MA: Addison-Wesley).
Clack, B.
    1998   'Virgins and Vessels', in Wendy Porter, Michael A. Hayes and David Tombs (eds.), *Religion and Sexuality* (Sheffield: Sheffield Academic Press): 193-202.
Daly, Mary
    1986   *Beyond God the Father* (London: Women's Press).
Freud, Sigmund
    1905   'Three Essays on the Theory of Sexuality', in *The Penguin Freud Library*. VII. *On Sexuality* (Harmondsworth: Penguin Books).
    1923   'The Infantile Genital Organization', in *The Penguin Freud Library*. VII. *On Sexuality* (Harmondsworth: Penguin Books).
    1924   'The Dissolution of the Oedipus Complex', in *The Penguin Freud Library*. VII. *On Sexuality* (Harmondsworth: Penguin Books).

18. For discussion of this connection, see Ortner (1995: 36-55).

1925 'Some Psychical Consequences of the Anatomical Distinction Between the Sexes', in *The Penguin Freud Library*. VII. *On Sexuality* (Harmondsworth: Penguin Books).

1931 'Female Sexualty', in *The Penguin Freud Library*. VII. *On Sexuality* (Harmondsworth: Penguin Books).

Grosz, Elizabeth

1990 *Jacques Lacan: A Feminist Introduction* (London: Routledge).

Hampson, Daphne

1996 *After Christianity* (London: SCM Press).

Irigaray, Luce

1993 *Sexes and Genealogies* (trans. G.C. Gill; New York: Columbia University Press [1984]).

Jantzen, Grace

1998 *Becoming Divine* (Manchester: Manchester University Press).

Lacan, Jacques

1958 'The Meaning of the Phallus', in Mitchell and Rose 1982.

1972 'God and the *Jouissance* of Woman', in Mitchell and Rose 1982.

Lamb, Simon, and David Sington

1998 *Earth Story: The Shaping of Our World* (London: BBC Books).

Lloyd, Genevieve

1984 *The Man of Reason* (London: Methuen).

Miles, Rosalind

1992 *The Rites of Man* (London: Paladin).

Mitchell, Juliet, and Jacqueline Rose (eds.)

1982 *Female Sexuality* (London: Macmillan).

Nelson, James

1988 *The Intimate Connection* (Philadelphia: Westminster Press).

Neumann, Erich

1971 *The Origin and History of Consciousness* (trans. R.F.C. Hull; Princeton, NJ: Princeton University Press [1949]).

Parfit, Derek

1984 *Reasons and Persons* (Oxford: Oxford University Press).

Pellauer, Mary D.

1994 'The Moral Significance of Female Orgasm: Toward Sexual Ethics that Celebrates Women's Sexuality', in James Nelson and Sandra Longfellow (eds.), *Sexuality and the Sacred* (London: Mowbray): 149-68.

Plumwood, Val

1993 *Feminism and the Mastery of Nature* (London: Routledge).

Raphael, Melissa

1996 *Thealogy and Embodiment: The Post Patriarchal Reconstruction of Female Sexuality* (Sheffield: Sheffield Academic Press).

Ruether, Rosemary Radford

1983 *Sexism and God-Talk* (London: SCM Press).

Sartre, Jean-Paul

1958 *Being and Nothingness* (trans. H.E. Barnes; London: Methuen [1943]).

Swinburne, Richard

1994 *The Christian God* (Oxford: Clarendon Press).

1997 *The Coherence of Theism* (Oxford: Clarendon Press).

Tuana, Nancy
    1993   *The Less Noble Sex* (Indianapolis: Indiana University Press).
Ward, Graham
    1998   'The Gendered Body of the the Jewish Jesus', in Michael Hayes, Wendy
                   Porter and David Tombs (eds.), *Religion and Sexuality* (Sheffield:
                   Sheffield Academic Press): 170-92.

Part III

CELIBACY AND CONTRACEPTION

A STRANGE CONVERGENCE? POPES AND FEMINISTS ON CONTRACEPTION

Adrian Thatcher

1. *Introduction*

The publication, in 1968, of *Humanae Vitae*, confirmed the official teaching of the Roman Catholic church that no contraceptive practices are lawful within marriage. The journal *Inside the Vatican* defiantly published a special supplement celebrating *Humanae Vitae* 30 years on, declaring Pope Paul VI, the author of the encyclical, a prophet.[1] While the anti-contraceptive arguments of the encyclical and subsequent official endorsements of them are generally rejected by Christians and non-Christians, a set of converging arguments leading to similar conclusions, emerges from an unexpected quarter—a strand of twentieth-century feminism. Many people may find these arguments equally implausible. In this essay I analyse both streams of argument. Some points of convergence are noted, the arguments re-stated, and the conclusion reached that there remains a remarkable wisdom in each of them.

2. *Papal Teaching*

Papal arguments against contraception can be usefully classified into three types. These are that contraception is (1) contrary to natural law; (2) contrary to the 'inseparable connection' between 'procreative' and 'unitive' sexual activity; and (3) an expression of a decadent society, culture, or 'mentality'.[2] In this section each type is described and criticized.

---

1. E.g., John Mallon, 'The Scandal of the Century—Thirty Years of Prophecy Ignored', *Inside the Vatican* (special supplement) (August/September, 1998), p. 3.

2. For a more detailed account of these types of anti-contraceptive argument, see my *Marriage after Modernity: Christian Marriage in Postmodern Times* (STAS, 3; Sheffield: Sheffield Academic Press; New York: New York University Press, 1999), pp. 182-204.

1. *The Natural Law Argument*

Pope Pius XI's principal argument, nearly 40 years before *Humanae Vitae*, was that nothing which is 'intrinsically *against nature* may become conformable to nature and morally good'.[3] Re-stating the traditional position which Vatican II was to modify, he argued that 'since... the conjugal act is destined primarily by nature for the begetting of children, those who in exercising it deliberately frustrate its natural power and purpose, sin against nature, and commit a deed which is shameful and intrinsically vicious'. The use of infertile periods, still incorrectly recognized in 1930, for sexual intercourse was considered a permitted exception. Those 'who, in the married state, use their right [to sexual intercourse] in the proper manner, although on account of natural reasons either of time or of certain defects, new life cannot be brought forth' are not to be 'considered as acting against nature'. The natural law argument, and the exception, were re-emphasized by *Humanae Vitae* in 1968. 'God has wisely arranged that the natural laws and times of fertility so that successive births are naturally spaced...' Based on natural law, the church teaches 'that it is necessary that each conjugal act remain ordained in itself to the procreating of human life'.[4] Since 1930 knowledge of the monthly cycle is much improved, and use of it to achieve or avoid pregnancy is officially sanctioned, and its practice described in several volumes.[5] It is called NFP (Natural Family Planning), and, despite widespread disbelief, provided it is properly taught and carefully implemented, it is effective.[6]

---

3.   *Casti Connubii* (1930), part iv. He was responding to the 1930 Lambeth Conference, which, with several qualifications, approved contraceptive practice within marriage.

4.   *Humanae Vitae*, section 10, in Janet E. Smith, *Why Humanae Vitae Was Right—A Reader* (San Francisco: Ignatius Press, 1993): 327-42. Ralph McInery defends this position in '*Humanae Vitae* and the Principle of Totality'. See Smith, *Why Humanae Vitae Was Right*, p. 332. And see Pontifical Council for the Family, *Preparation for the Sacrament of Marriage* (1994), section 35: *Evangelium Vitae* 97 and *Catechism of the Catholic Church*, nos. 2366-371.

5.   E.g., John F. Kippley and Sheila K. Kippley, *The Art of Natural Family Planning* (Cincinnati: Couple to Couple League, 4th edn, 1997).

6.   It is important to be precise. A secular British source says, 'Natural methods' means the 'sympto-thermal method' which 'combines the temperature method, cervical mucus method and calendar method with some other signs. These signs include the position, softness or firmness of your cervix and whether its entrance is slightly open or tightly closed, ovulation pain and breast discomfort.' If it is used

There are obvious arguments against natural law. First 'the spacing of births' relies on advanced medical knowledge, yet this very knowledge was unknown to earlier generations and brings the very reproductive and contraceptive technologies the Vatican dislikes. Second, as an Anglican report argued in 1958, the spiritual nature of women and men enables them both to stand outside 'nature' while firmly belonging to it.[7] Third, the issue remains whether couples who deliberately abstain from love-making during fertile periods but who make love at other times are practising the 'spacing of births', or NFP, or whether they are practising contraception. This is because not having sex at certain times is not just not doing anything, and so not doing anything wrong. As Gareth Moore points out 'They do not just not have intercourse; they actively avoid intercourse, as part of their plan to avoid children', and this practice, although allowed by *Casti Connubii*, is clearly inconsistent with that encyclical's portentous proscription of 'any use whatsoever of matrimony exercised in such a way that the act is deliberately frustrated in its natural power to generate life'.[8] Fourth, there is a theological problem about the mission of transmitting human life. While God may 'plan' to perpetuate the human race through the uncontracepted love-making of spouses, it does not follow from this rather anthropomorphic depiction of God's intention that *every* act of love-making must be uncontracepted.

2. The 'Unbreakable Connection' between 'Procreative' and 'Unitive' Sexual Activity

Conjugal love is stated in *Humanae Vitae* to be 'a very special form of personal friendship whereby the spouses generously share *everything* with each other'.[9] Granted the totality of 'everything', contraception is then able to be interpreted as a withholding of each partner from the

according to instructions it is '98% effective'. Leaflet 'Contraception: Choosing and Using Natural Methods', Contraceptive Education Service and Family Planning Association, undated (but in circulation in 1997).

7. For a forceful exposition of this point in the nineteenth century, see John Stuart Mill's 'Nature', in *Nature, the Utility of Religion, and Theism* (written 1850–58), text in Alasdair Clayre (ed.), *Nature and Industrialization* (Oxford: Oxford University Press, 1977), pp. 303-12.

8. Gareth Moore, *The Body in Context: Sex and Catholicism* (London: SCM Press, 1992), p. 165.

9. *Humanae Vitae*, section 9, emphasis added.

other, a failure to share the God-given power of fecundity. Conjugal love is required to be 'both *faithful and exclusive* to the end of life'.[10] But the Church's teaching about the operation of this natural law is that 'it is necessary that *each* conjugal act remain ordained in itself to the procreating of human life'.[11] However, the grounds offered for the view that each act must be open to life are based a priori on the doctrine of marriage revised as recently as the Second Vatican Council, and not on natural law at all. Just as marriage has two ends, 'the procreation and education of children' and the 'mutual love of the partners',[12] so sexual intercourse conveys these meanings simultaneously, and inseparably.

Once again there are compelling counter-arguments. First, there has to be a suspicious ring about the centrality of mutual love in the doctrine of marriage. However welcome the emphasis, it is a very late development in Catholicism, occurring first in *Casti Connubii* in 1930. It is an island of innovation in a sea of conservatism. Second, married partners may wish, as an *expression* of mutual love, to separate union from procreation, something 'nature' in any case may be said to achieve for them most of the time. Third, we might reopen the question why all love-making a married couple ever makes must fall under the joint rubrics of mutual self-donation and potential openness to the creation of new life? Why could not the couple cooperate with God in the mission of procreation by *sometimes* being open to new life? This position was adopted by the Lambeth Conferences of 1958 and 1968 and was recommended to Pope Paul VI by the commision whose advice he rejected in *Humanae Vitae*. The dogma of the unbreakable connection when applied to each act of sexual intercourse within marriage has no historical warrant and can impose intolerable strains on marriage.

3. *Moral Deficit Arguments*

According to this type of argument the evil of contraceptive use is either its contribution to a culture of death, or already a consequence of such a culture. Paul VI held contraception would 'justify behavior leading to marital infidelity or to a gradual weakening in the discipline of morals'.[13] A decade or so after *Humanae Vitae*, *Familiaris Consortio*

10. *Humanae Vitae*, section 9 (translator's emphasis).

11. Emphasis added. McInery defends this position in '*Humanae Vitae* and the Principle of Totality', p. 332.

12. *Gaudium et Spes*, section 50.

13. *Humanae Vitae*, section 17.

warned against a 'contraceptive mentality', a term which would appear more frequently in forthcoming Vatican documents. It was associated with 'a corruption of the idea and the experience of freedom, conceived not as a capacity for realizing the truth of God's plan for marriage and the family, but as an autonomous power of self-affirmation, often against others, for one's own selfish well-being'.[14] Contraception, then, is direct evidence of selfishness. The Pontifical Council for the Family document *Preparation for the Sacrament of Marriage* associates the contraceptive mentality with 'widespread, permissive laws' and 'all they imply in terms of contempt for life from the moment of conception to death'.[15] The 'prevailing mentality' is to be sharply rejected. In *Evangelium Vitae* contraception and abortion are linked with a 'culture of death', a 'conspiracy against life',[16] and another negative mentality, hedonism.

> In very many...instances such practices are rooted in a hedonistic mentality unwilling to accept responsibility in matters of sexuality, and they imply a self-centered concept of freedom, which regards procreation as an obstacle to personal fulfilment. The life which could result from a sexual encounter thus becomes an enemy to be avoided at all costs, and abortion follows on from failed contraception.[17]

Investment in both contraception and abortion is evidence of a 'veritable *structure of sin*', a '*war of the powerful against the weak*', and a '*conspiracy against life*'.[18] Alternatively contraception is associated with *consumer* and *anti-life* mentalities, the ultimate reason for which is the absence in people's hearts of God...'[19]

These arguments combine deeply-held convictions held by almost all Christians with highly contentious claims that detract from the extent of agreement which may already exist. One might ask whether the absolutist and increasingly strident position taken over all contraceptive use achieves anything, or is theologically unsustainable. Contraceptives cannot be disinvented; their use, however, is able to be modified, and this appears to be the more urgent problem, confining procreative sex-

---

14. *Familiaris consortio*, 6, 'The Situation of the Family in the World Today'.

15. Pontifical Council For The Family, *Preparation for the Sacrament Of Marriage*, section 49.

16. *Evangelium Vitae* (Dublin, Veritas Pub., undated), p. 22.

17. *Evangelium Vitae*, p. 24.

18. *Evangelium Vitae*, p. 22.

19. *Familiaris consortio*, section 30.

ual activity to marriage. Even if it were true that contraceptives make adultery more likely because they make pregnancy less likely, that claim would sanction an argument to confine contraceptives within marriage, not to eliminate them altogether. Fidelity has always needed to be encouraged whether or not condoms are on sale or wives are on the pill. Again, is it the case that husbands lose respect for their wives because of contraception? If so, is it because they forget the natural fertility of their wives' bodies, and come to see them only as pleasure-giving? Is it obviously true that in marriages where there has been no contraception, husbands' respect for wives was maintained? The so-called rendering of the marital debt was just such an arrangement, and it contributes little to an adequate theology of marriage.

A principled argument exists that in some poor countries it would be better for fewer children to be born. There are also unexamined problems in the depiction of a culture of death, and in the unqualified support for 'life'. Between 1950 and 1990 worldwide child mortality declined by two-thirds from around 300 births to 100 births per thousand, an improvement 'to a greater degree than in the whole of previous world history'.[20] This is a remarkable achievement, but is it not arguably a remarkable contribution to a culture of *life*? The culture of death also seems to be identified narrowly with the practices of contraception, abortion and euthanasia. (It is not extended, for example, to experimentation on animals, or the factory-farming of chickens or calves, or the shooting of migrating birds or wild animals for sport.) Couples who postpone the advent of children in order to establish careers, or to pay off their university tuition fees, or afford the down payment on a house and the enormous interest on a mortgage, may be offended by the suggestion that consumerism drives and ultimately corrupts their intentions.[21]

---

20. Norbert Mette, 'Not a "Century of the Child"—the Situation of Children in the World in the 1990s', in Maureen Junker-Kenny and Norbert Mette (eds.), *Concilium—Little Children Suffer* (1996.2), pp. 5-6. Mette uses the World Bank 1993 annual report as her source.

21. The document *Preparation for the Sacrament of Marriage* (1996), in its description of 'an accentuated deterioration of the family and a certain corrosion of the values of marriage' includes marriage 'usually contracted at a later age'. See Introduction, section 1. The Council has not taken into account that the rising age of marriage is in fact a return to Elizabethan levels.

These arguments do not establish their desired conclusions or disguise that they rest on contested claims to authority. Despite these obvious difficulties, however, they deserve a rereading. Indeed, if they could be deployed to reach rather more modest, positive, conclusions, they might well increase their inductive credibility and engage the interest of a broader range of people. Before attempting a rereading it is time to consider very different arguments against contraception.

3. *Some Feminist Arguments against Contraception*

While moral deficit arguments lament the role of contraception in contributing to promiscuity, selfishness, lack of respect, contempt for life, and so on, some feminist arguments against contraception are based on *the loss of control by women over their own bodies*. Feminists at the turn of the century located men's desire for heterosexual sexual intercourse as a root cause of their sexual and social subjugation.[22] The removal of the fear of pregnancy which the growing availability of the condom was beginning to offer, was also, they noticed, the removal of the principal reason for refusing unwelcome sexual advances from men. The solution was not contracepted sexual intercourse but the complete reformation of sexual relations between men and women.

Francis Swiney, feminist and theosophist who wrote exactly a century ago, before the campaigning of Stella Browne and Marie Stopes for 'birth control' had begun, is one such feminist. While she hated church and religion for their complicity in the male-domination of women, she couched some of her arguments in terms that are remarkably redolent of papal language and teaching. She even proclaimed a doctrine of Natural Law which became the basis for the theosophical society she founded. Two of the rules were 'to hold in reverence and sanctity the creative organs and functions, only exercising them for their natural, ordained and legitimate use', and

> to keep, as far as possible by individual effort, the Temple of the Body
> pure and undefiled; raising sex relations from the physical to the spiritual
> plane, and dedicating the creative life in the body to the highest uses,
> Man regarding Woman as the creatrix of the Race, Woman regarding

22. Sheila Jeffreys, *The Spinster and her Enemies: Feminism and Sexuality 1880–1930* (London: Pandora, 1987), especially Chapters 1 and 2.

Man as the appointed coadjutor in the supreme task of racebuilding, both labouring in Love to produce a perfect work.[23]

The congruence between papal pronouncement against, and feminist deprecation of, illicit or excessive sexual intercourse in the early twentieth century, is extraordinary. Despite intense hostility between these types of thought, each has a doctrine of natural law. Each is worried by sexual immorality. Each thinks there is a purpose to sexual intercourse, and that that purpose is the procreation of children. Swiney's language appears to echo, even if it does not endorse, a divine ordination and legislation of heterosexual sexual relations which excludes pleasure. Continence is the supreme virtue, whether for feminist or catholic. Clear echoes of Pauline teaching resonate within these feminist, anti-religious sentiments, while the assumed relationship between sexuality and spirituality, regarding one as 'higher' than the other, identifies more with contemporary conservative Christianity than with liberation movements, religious or secular.

Swiney and others advocated 'free love', yet this term meant the opposite of the meaning it came to have in the 1960s. Sexual intercourse was 'free' when, and only when, women consented to it, whether in marriage or not. Intercourse they thought, had become an activity too closely associated 'with man's view of woman as simply a sexual function and the notion that he could not survive without a sexual outlet'.[24] Such a view was held responsible for the acceptance of prostitution, child abuse and rape. Lucy Re-Bartlett and other feminists, *with no idea that they were proclaiming longstanding Christian teaching*, held that 'Sex union in the human being should be limited strictly to the actual needs of creation'.[25] A picture of early twentieth-century sexology builds in which regular sexual intercourse is thought necessary for everyone's health. The condom, by greatly reducing the risk of pregnancy, removed the main reason for refusing sexual intercourse. 'Frigidity' was invented to make avoidance of sexual intercourse a pathology, while spinsters, who lacked the obvious benefits available to married women, were accused of channelling their repressed sexual energy into other, more dubious activities, and spinster teachers (it was darkly

23. Francis Swiney, *Man's Necessity* ([pamphlet] Cheltenham: League of Isis, n.d.), cited in Jeffreys, *The Spinster*, pp. 37-38.

24. Jeffreys, *The Spinster*, p. 40.

25. Lucy Re-Bartlett, *The Coming Order* (London: Longmans, 1911), p. 51, cited in Jeffreys, *The Spinster*, p. 51.

alleged) would make girls improperly critical of men. 'Women were required to enjoy sexual intercourse, not just to take part in it'.[26]

The feminist movement, then, was divided about the advantages of contraception, and those feminists who were opposed to it, offered reasons thoroughly consistent with those offered by Roman Catholicism at the end of the same century. Continence, not indulgence, is the answer to the problem of unwanted pregnancy, inside or outside marriage. Several Christian arguments in support of celibacy as a total way of life were open to the feminists, even if they were not in fact known or used. While Helen Wright and Marie Stopes and everyone else in the birth control movement thought they were restoring to women control over their fertility and sexuality, an alternative interpretation of their achievements held that they were 'in many respects undermining the sexual autonomy of women even further'.[27] Margaret Jackson strikingly sums up twentieth-century sexology as an affirmation of the 'coital imperative', which contraception encouraged and enforced. The coital imperative, she argues, legitimized 'male sexual violence and exploitation and undermined both the campaign for an equal moral standard and the construction of a feminist model of sexuality'. After women had secured the vote in the United Kingdom, 'the popular purveyors of the new "facts of life" promote, in the guise of sexual "liberation", a form of heterosexuality and sexual pleasure which eroticized male dominance and female submission, and pathologized all manifestations of female sexual autonomy or resistance, including spinsterhood, lesbianism, and "frigidity" '.[28]

As with papal arguments, there are some fairly obvious criticisms to be made here before the work of restatement begins. First, there appears in the authors just discussed little appreciation of the possibility of mutual pleasure with heterosexual partners through sexual intercourse. While there is undoubtedly a strong experiential element in the fairly obvious dislike of sex with men, at least in the social circumstances in which they wrote, even the *possibility* of sexual relations with men which play a part in mutual fulfilment and happiness seem precluded. Second, the reference to spiritual love, while it seeks to deflect and reconstitute the (male?) desire for genital sex, appears instead to en-

26. In Jeffreys, *The Spinster*, pp. 169, 180-81.

27. Margaret Jackson, *The Real Facts of Life: Feminism and the Politics of Sexuality c1850–1940* (London: Taylor & Francis, 1994), p. 173.

28. Jackson, *The Real Facts of Life*, p. 183.

force the well-known dualism between sexuality and spirituality, so that however spirituality is defined, sexuality is not part of it. Such a view is surely disastrous for both sexuality and spirituality, whether one assumes a religious or a secular stance (and much contemporary theological writing seeks to reintegrate them).[29]

Third, the informal appeal to a version of natural law runs into similar difficulties afflicting more official versions of it. Natural law gives everything a single purpose, one moreover which reason enables the mind to discover unaided. The purpose of sex is 'racebuilding': how we know this is not discussed. Presumably, spirituality is not required? Fourth, sexual intercourse appears to be invested with an inevitable negative symbolic charge. The very act of copulation signifies the passive, subjugated, penetrated state of women under patriarchy. Indeed the inevitability of domination by men over women who enter into sexual relations with them, extends to an argument for lesbian separatism. It becomes apparent that the similarities between papal and feminist criticisms of contraception extend also to fairly obvious criticisms of them. Catholic thought has, until the twentieth century, been squeamish about the admission of sexual pleasure; it has treated spirituality and sexuality irreconcilably; it has defined the purpose of sex on the basis of natural law. It still teaches the subordination of women and upholds the view that celibacy is a more exalted state than marriage.

4. A Rereading of the Arguments

Having criticized both streams of argument, it is now appropriate to appreciate them. It is possible to understand the tradition of natural law, as it applies to sex, in a more imaginative way than was managed by Pius XI. Male and female bodies, whether or not joined together in heterosexual intercourse, provide powerful and regular reminders of their reproductive capacities. These reminders are fundamental to being human, that is, they operate at a level logically prior to historical

---

29. Joan H. Timmermann, *Sexuality and Spiritual Growth* (New York: Crossroad, 1993): Evelyn E. Whitehead and James D. Whitehead, *A Sense of Sexuality: Christian Love and Intimacy* (New York: Crossroad, 1994): James Nelson, *Body Theology* (Louisville, KY: Westminster/John Knox Press, 1992); Elizabeth Stuart and Adrian Thatcher, *People of Passion—What the Churches Teach about Sex* (London: Mowbray, 1997).

change, or social construction, or interaction with culture.[30] If appeals
to 'nature' and 'natural' are directed to our deeply-rooted awareness of
ourselves as sexual, and therefore reproductive beings, then the practice
of contraception by heterosexual couples (whether by barrier or other
methods) may perhaps be seen as 'contrary' to it. If our natural state
propels us towards ovulation, ejaculation, copulation, conception, and
so on, sexual practices which are 'contra-conception' may be thought to
frustrate the outcomes of these activities. Indeed, that is why they are
practised at all. In a cultural context where sexual pleasure and sexual
reproduction have become widely separated and have assumed the
status of a barely challengeable secular dualism, reminders of our natural fecundity are timely.

The expression of heterosexual sexuality cannot be finally separated
from reproductive capacity and so from prospective parenthood. This is
precisely what contraception does. But NFP, medically expounded, and
carefully implemented, is commendable beyond the narrow domain of
official Roman Catholic teaching. Despite Protestant contempt for it,
extending to the medical profession and its dislike of theology, it is at
least as effective as the pill. It works. There is an impressive, theological, pastoral and medical literature about it.[31] The 'sympto-thermal
method' is much more reliable than the older 'rhythm' method. NFP is
very plausibly said to make a couple more aware of their fertility. It
provides a self-knowledge that comes about through heightened body-
awareness, through listening, observing, touching, sensing. Users are
quick to point out that none of the modern paraphernalia of chemicals,
hormones, implants, bits of copper, plastic or rubber, and so on are
needed to make love without making babies. They also avoid the
hazards associated with other forms of contraception. Pill users increase
the likelihood of breast cancer. There is a statistical link between the
pill and cervical cancer. Pill users are more likely to have liver tumors,

30. See Lisa Sowle Cahill, *Sex, Gender and Christian Ethics* (Cambridge: Cambridge University Press, 1996), Chapter 4, ' "The Body"—in Context', for a very
illuminating study.

31. See, e.g., Richard J. Fehring and Robert T. Kampic, *Natural Family Planning Bibliography* (Washington, DC: National Conference of Catholic Bishops,
1995): Hanna Klaus, *Natural Family Planning: A Review* (NFP Center of Washington, DC: 2nd edn, 1995): Kippley and Kippley, *The Art*; John F. Kippley, *Sex and
Marriage Covenant: A Basis for Morality* (Cincinnati, OH: Couple to Couple
League, 1991).

3 to 11 times the risk of developing blood clots; twice as likely to have heart attacks, and 12 times as likely if they smoke. Not to mention scores of possible side effects and the strong possibility that it decreases the desire for sex. NFP requires periodic abstinence from intercourse which may itself challenge the set of modern assumptions about phallo-centric behaviour, the normativity of penetration as standard sexual activity, and the continuous availability of women's bodies.

If the unbreakable connection argument is recast in a slightly different form, this too is able to be appropriated by most married couples who are Christians. The different form? That married life as a whole itself suggests an unbreakable connection between procreation and union. By understanding the couple's union to be the marriage as a whole, and not a state which is repeatedly achieved in every act of intercourse, the link between love-making and baby-making, which contraception breaks, is restored without being required every time a couple makes love. A common strand of moral deficit arguments is that children are to be prevented at all costs. Having a child amounts to a terrible mistake, a liability not a gift of God. Having children with one's partner is a good test for deciding when to have penetrative sex with him. If either unmarried person would not at some time in the future want a child with their present partner, their sexual repertoire should not include penetrative sex. The test of when to start might well be: whether they would be faithful to any children who might result.[32]

A retrospection on the feminist arguments in the previous section shows them too, to be perspicacious. While contraception provides millions of women with more control over reproduction than any generation before, a new generation is growing up which appears to have *less* control over decisions about sexual intimacy. That is because penetrative sexual intercourse has become the routinized, standardized, socially accepted, socially demanded form of sexual practice. The more refined contraception becomes (e.g. the 'morning after pill'), the weaker will be the intention to avoid pregnancy by avoiding intercourse. The intensification of peer-pressure on girls to have penetrative sex at an ever earlier age fatally undermines the resolve to remain chaste. Young males, scarcely pubescent, expect penetrative sex, and young women are under great social pressure to provide it. Contraception normalizes the expectation. Their autonomy *is* undermined. As Sally Cline has pointed out

32. For the detail, see my *Marriage After Modernity*, Chapter 4, 'Cohabitation, Betrothal and the Entry into Marriage'.

modern sexual mores provide a strong argument for women's celibacy. The regularization of sexual intercourse outside committed relationships represents the extension of 'sexual consumerism' into the most intimate areas of our lives.[33]

There is undoubtedly a 'coital imperative' which militates against women's health. As well as the massive social effect on sexual behaviour, there may also be harmful side effects for individual women. While the argument that the purpose of sex must be confined to the propagation of the species will be accepted by very few, the attempt to question the morality of established sexual practices by raising questions about their *telos* is surely appropriate. Some cultural assumptions about sexual intercourse, for example, that it is morally acceptable outside of commitments, or merely for pleasure, are best questioned in this way. The advocacy of continence could hardly be more apt.

Contraception may be seen as a striking product of modernity. It is mass-produced, and over half the world's population now uses it. It has brought with it massive normalization and routinization. Sex education programmes assume intercourse and the need to contracept consequences. By contrast, the strands of argument considered in this paper are pre-modern. They converge in upholding the virtue of chastity. They lead to an understanding of safer sex that is not only learning about how to use a condom, but about learning to value other forms of intimacy that do not inevitably escalate into intercourse.

Contraception has been invaluable for millions of women desiring fewer children and having career aspirations, but it is linked with the expectation that their bodies are always available to their male partners, even if the partner is a passing stranger. Women's health may be better served by the Pope's prescriptions than by the expectations that they should ever be available, sterile, uncomplaining and unaware of the need for radical alternatives such as that offered by the Holy Father. In postmodernity strange alliances are formed. In the case of contraception postmodernity may be said to have arrived.

33. Sally Cline, *Women, Celibacy and Passion* (London: André Deutsch, 1993), p. 1.

EROTIC CELIBACY: CLAIMING EMPOWERED SPACE*

Lisa Isherwood

'[Celibacy] an act of heresy in a society where sex is holy because of its role as a sacred ritual in the dominant-submissive relationship set out for men and women'.[1]

Many women find themselves living celibate lives, although not always from choice. I do not mean that they simply do not have sexual partners but rather that what is on offer in terms of heterosexuality under patriarchy is not appealing. If that is it, then many would rather do without it. Conversely many religious sisters find celibacy is a requirement but no one has really explained what it is. It is not uncommon to find that orders have held many conferences on the meaning of obedience in the modern world but none on celibacy. Why is this? Is it a question that body politics have not entered the religious life or that they have been encouraged to image themselves to be disembodied despite recent rhetoric about sexuality being part of a path to God? This is an increasingly perplexing problem for those sisters who know themselves to be lesbian and have only ever had to deal with a heterosexual definition of sex. As a feminist theologian I am interested in how celibacy becomes reimaged under the weight of feminist Christology, body politics and lived experience.

The history of celibacy within the Christian church has been a varied one, moving from meaning simply unmarried to unmarried and not sexually active. For the most part its significance has been underpinned by an understanding of Christology that owes more to Aristotle than to Jesus of Nazareth. This is a Christology that despite speaking of incarnation is distant and hierarchical, one that divides the self between body and soul and places more value on the things of the spirit. Jesus becomes the eternal word and therefore the guardian of orthodoxy

---

* The theory set out in 'Sex and Body Politics' underpins much of this article.
1. Sally Cline, *Women, Celibacy and Passion* (London: Optima, 1999), p. 152.

rather than the radical rabbi who encourages liberative praxis. This elevated status of Jesus owed much to a belief in his purity of body and later to that of his mother and eventually his grandmother. This desexualized lineage resulting in the super-pure son of God laid the foundations for many Christians to have a very neurotic relationship with their bodies. The Church Fathers, of course, are largely to blame for the antibody theology that Christianity has been burdened with for so long. An exhaustive examination is not necessary here; it is sufficient to say that the body was seen as a snare to trap the soul. While this was true for both sexes, women were viewed as particularly dangerous, as the changing nature of the female body was seen as the furthest away from the unchanging and everlasting spiritual realm.

However, the idea of celibacy goes back further than the Fathers with Paul declaring that he wished all men were like him (that is celibate) but he knows they are not and so encourages them to marry. At first glance this may seem to be a nod in the direction of sexual activity but on closer inspection it appears to be more about protecting his own position. The household in the time of Paul was the power base of society and the means by which he conveyed his message. Therefore, had he encouraged the total dissolution of such an institution he 'would have broken the subtle chain of command by which his own teachings were passed on to each local community through the authority of local householders'.[2] It is certainly true that the upside of such a dissolution would have been a community in which women and slaves, freed from household hierarchy, could realize the equality promised them in the rituals of baptism but it would also have made Christianity a very isolated community. Paul decided to retain the status quo and find support for his mission and so slaves and wives had to stay in their place (1 Cor. 7.17, 21).

The interesting consequence of this selective celibacy was the development of a hierarchy. Only a few could be called by God to be celibate and this in a sense set them apart and above. Celibacy then became a very useful power tool. This does not mean that celibates were from the start raised in status above others, simply that there was a trend. Ignatius of Antioch certainly saw no difference between celibates and others, seeing it merely as a matter of choice. However, this does not mean that Ignatius did not have his own ideas about where power should lie and

2.   Peter Brown, *The Body and Society: Men, Women and Sexual Renunciation in Early Christianity* (London: Faber & Faber, 1989).

how society should be ordered. He thought the church should be 'made up of generous householders, well-disciplined children, submissive wives and reliable slaves... Marriage was to be arranged by the bishop himself... The mystical end of an undivided church was to be achieved by singularly prosonic family arrangements'.[3] It seems, then, that wherever they stood on matters of celibacy there was an understanding that the control of people's sexual arrangements leads to a control of society. Further, they understood that the ways in which sexuality is arranged in a community gives it a distinct character. For example, for Judaism the continuity of the line through marriage and procreation was very important. It was understood as part of God's covenant with Abraham and therefore one of the central components of Jewish self understanding. Christians therefore used their bodies to challenge this notion of continuity since they believed that time was very short. Chastity, then, became a sign of the imminent approach of a new creation, one that would overturn the existing order, including that of birth and death. There is further evidence of a distinctive character being sought in Justin's 'Apology', written in the second century. In it he calls for very strict sexual codes which are based on Jewish law but go further in terms of harshness; he prohibits divorce, is scathing about the remarried and praises celibacy as an act of heroism equivalent to facing death in the arena. He claims that celibacy testifies to the universal nature of Christianity by showing the power of God to overcome the weakness of all humans, namely sexuality. Of course, using sexuality as a place of control was a good move since all the nations that were atttracted to Christianity shared the common desire if not the common practices. Unifying the practice of sexuality was a very powerful way to unify the church. It would be too easy to say that there was only one approach to the control of sexuality but there is evidence of it happening.

While many saw celibacy as a natural state that came with old age and could be cultivated in order to acquire wisdom, others saw it as a necessary virtue if people were to be filled with the spirit. Certainly in the days of martyrdom the indwelling of the spirit was seen as a bonus since it helped one meet a brave and sincere end. Despite this it does seem to be the case that for the majority of celibates in these early years it was a state that came later in life either through the loss of a partner of choice. This is very significant in the case of women who would

3. Brown, *The Body and Society*, pp. 58-59.

have already fulfilled their procreative obligation and therefore be members of a family unit (power structure). These women received praise but it was not always the case for those women who wished to live celibately as a whole life choice.

Orthodox writers did not address the question of women embracing celibacy as a way of life until women themselves had made it a reality. In other words, there seemed to be no idea that women could free themselves from the role of wife and mother, simply that they could embrace celibacy later in life. It is ironic that Anthony, who is honoured as being the founder of monasticism, placed his sister in a community before setting off for the desert. The irony being that until recently scholars have not thought to ask what type of community that might be and therefore whether Anthony was indeed the first to found a monastic way of life! This not only makes us question who indeed founded monasticism, it also changes the way we look at the motivation for women taking to religious life. The tradition tells us that confessors and spiritual advisors encouraged women to enter convents but if they were there before men even thought of 'inventing' them there is a different tale to tell. It is also perhaps worth noting that while Anthony and those who followed lived solitary lives, at the height of the movement it is estimated that some 5000 people lived seperately in the desert, the women lived in communities. (When Jerome visited the desert in 373 CE he complained that it was overcrowded!)

It has been suggested that monasticism and asceticism flourished when they did, at the end of the fourth century, because this was the end of the era of martyrs. People were no longer being persecuted and so they turned to a kind of internal martyrdom, waging war against imaginary demons through starvation and beatings, let alone the isolation of the desert. This does not seem to be the story for women. Their story seems to be far more about flourishing and becoming whole. It is not easy to discover when Christian women actually started living celibate communal lives although there is evidence to suggest that it was as early as the second century CE.[4] This coincides with a trend towards the segregation of women and a reducing of their worlds. This can be seen as early as 100 CE when Clement of Rome wanted house churches to be replaced by temples and all ministerial roles to pass from women to men. In the end there was an order of widows whose role was confined

---

4.　Jo Ann McNamara, *A New Song: Celibate Women in the First Three Christian Centuries* (New York: Harrington Park Press, 1985), p. 78.

to attending women, which still gave women freedom but not as much as previously and not as much as desired.

It was against this background and in the light of the gospel and baptismal promises of equality that women started to look for other ways of living. The message of Jesus appeared to hold out a hope of life beyond the narrow confines that antiquity offered women. The call to turn the existing order upside down and to release the captives was believed by many women to include release from patriarchal marriage and its life-threatening potential. Under Roman law a woman always remained the property of her father, even when married, and he held the power of life and death over her or could take her back into his household at any time. With such a vast empire Romans were in need of manpower and Augustus Caesar even introduced laws to penalize women who did not have enough children. The message of Jesus pointed away from the power of earthly patriarchs and many women saw this as a welcome release. They had expected the Christian community to embody these ideals and were sadly let down. There is evidence that in the early years of the Jesus movement women and men changed the power balance of relationships but this is soon overcome with Paul telling women to once again obey their husbands.[5] The solution to this retrograde step was for many to remove themselves and to live the radical gospel in communities of women. In this way they carried out a social revolution of vast proportions by forcing their societies to recognize their new status and to give them some sort of standing within it.[6] This was a new status that they believed was a part of the coming of the kingdom, a time when all wordly order would be overcome, including gender organization and the attendant power imbalance. Celibacy for these women was a revolt against male definitions and a rejection of sexual stereotyping.

These women seem to have drawn their inspiration from the gospels, including the apocryphal gospels, some of which were probably written by women.[7] Many of these works dwelt on the role of Mary after the crucifixion and many had very positive female role models, women who actively contributed to the development of the church acting beyond stereotypical roles. The apocryphal gospels also reflected upon and refuted some of the anti-woman material that was becoming part of the

5. McNamara, *A New Song*, p. 41.
6. McNamara, *A New Song*, p. 4.
7. McNamara, *A New Song*, p. 78.

growing Christian literature and they reversed the patriarchal mindsets. Further, it was not uncommon for apocryphal material to portray men as the truly fallen ones because they lusted after both the flesh and power. Through these writings and a life of celibacy in community women were finding ways to challenge the structural sin of sexism. The women who formed these celibate groups were in no way heretical. They were simply finding the space in which to develop their autonomy and exercise their talents. Their presence caused problems for the male clergy who even felt they had to debate whether these were still women. Tertullian and the African churches agonized over whether female virgins were allegorical males and if so could they exercise male roles within the church?[8] We see then that there is an understanding, even be it unconscious, that a woman is unequal in power relation to a man. Remove the man and one has to ask if these females are women any more. The body which defines women as 'other' has been renamed, and they become free to be more than women.

These women created a new space for themselves within a society that could not initially understand the concept of celibacy for life, but they never really found equality with men. The clergy had no intention of sharing their power. We therefore witness a power struggle that has continued, in one way or another, from those early times to the present. The clergy trying to gain control over communities of women and the women in turn attempting to retain autonomy gives the present pope many sleepless nights! There are many notable examples of individual women, if not communities, who made very creative space for themselves under the blanket of celibacy. Hildegard of Bingen is a name that springs to mind when thinking of strong women who had influence both within and far outside her community. She was able to develop her own talents within the convent and is recognized as a poet, theologian, musician, gynaecologist and mystic. This is also true of Sor Juana of Mexico who was recognized as possessing the most acute intellect of her day but in order for this to be used she had to enter a convent. However, what is interesting in her case and no doubt that of many others, is that the ability to continue with research and writing was in many ways at the discretion of male clerics. Nevertheless, the fact remains that the convent did allow that space. The tale of Bridgit of Kildare is intructive in that respect. She would not allow a man, not

8.   McNamara, *A New Song*, p. 112.

even a priest, over the threshold of her convent. This was not because of sexual temptation being provided for the sisters but rather because she was aware that female autonomy is easily lost to males. The resulting tradition that the Abbess of Kildare was made a bishop existed until the twelfth century.

A case can be made to suggest that women in the early church communities, and then in convents, paid for autonomy with celibacy. However, I am not claiming that this was complete autonomy or that all the women who embraced celibacy did so with the same intention. For many, celibacy was to do with the purity of Jesus and the sinfulness of the flesh, just as it was for their male counterparts. It is very interesting to see that some Protestant groups understood celibacy to be more to do with sexual equality than the innate sinfulness of the flesh. The Shakers, and Koreshans made links between female power, economic independence, sexual equality and celibacy. The Koreshans thought of marriage as sex slavery for women since they believed that sexual activity was the root of inequality.[9] This was a view also held by the Shakers, who went further, seeing celibacy as a sign of symbolic unity of all creation. The thinking behind this was that a celibate life dissolved the false ties and loyalties of the family and opened people up to relationality beyond such a narrow and controlled arena.

Of course their thinking was underpinned by their theology. The Shakers thought of their founder, Mother Ann Lee, as the female messiah. Believing as they did that God was both male and female they could not consider that a once and for all male messiah could be the whole divine story. The divine glory could only fully shine when balance was found between the sexes, including balance in incarnations. Mother Lee was herself celibate but had not always been having suffered abuse by her father and then being forced into marriage where she bore four children, all of whom died. It is not really surprising that such experiences would lead her to reflect on the oppressive nature of the sexual realities of her day. What is surprising and something to be celebrated is that with such a history of abuse she could declare, and grasp, a way to embodied empowerment for herself and for other women. We know only too well how patterns of abuse make it very difficult for women and men to live in any other way; sexual suffering diminishes self esteem to such an extent that there seems no way out

9.   Sally L. Kitch, *Chaste Liberation: Celibacy and Female Cultural Status* (Chicago: University of Illinois Press, 1989), p. 59.

and so the circle continues. What is also extraordinary is that Mother Lee never described sex itself as evil although she abhorred the consequences of it for women under patriarchy.

The Shakers of the late nineteenth century understood free and equal women to be a major factor in the redemption of man. Frederick Evans made a link between male lust and many social problems such as war, the class system and competitive capitalism. They all sprang from the owning, moulding and dominating pattern of male sexuality. Evans believed that female victimization was a metaphor for all human victimization and therefore female freedom would bring peace and harmony to earth.[10] In this very embodied and practical sense Evans and other Shakers of the day saw women's celibacy as redemptive. This was not only for males, of course, since the women themselves, it was believed, gained a new sense of self and became more self directive. Celibacy would turn the world upside down, acting as an alternate foundation for radical and new ways of being in the social/political world. The power that the Shakers attached to heterosexuality as practised in a patriarchal world is not outstripped by the most radical sociologists of our day—the difference being that they understood the overcoming of such an arrangement to be a divine imperative.

The Shakers and the Koreshans thought that it was the act of intercourse itself that led to gender identities and therefore gender hierarchy and the stratification of nature and culture. The Koreshans believed that celibacy would actually lead to the hermaphrodite being the most common and sanctified human person, as this would mirror the divine condition.[11] This is not quite as encouraging as it sounds since this 'human' person would actually have predominantly male characteristics. However, the insights of the Shakers and Koreshans are an amazing step on the road to the analysis of gender inequality. Further, the movement from perceiving woman as the cause of the fall to an understanding of the male desire to dominate activated and let loose through intercourse as the cause of all human ills, is truly amazing. While the notion of the bisexuality of God and the glorified body of the hermaphrodite are revolutionary ideas in any age.

As a feminist theologian looking at the issue of celibacy at the end of the twentieth century I find a rich heritage to engage with, but alone it does not solve the problems of today. Sex in the twentieth century has

10. Kitch, *Chaste Liberation*, p. 134.
11. Kitch, *Chaste Liberation*, p. 187.

turned into an industry (Frederick Evans had a point) whose advertisers encourage the notion that sex is a recreational pursuit that is surpassed by none. The pornographic industry being perhaps one of those with the largest turn over, some £17 billion per year. However, this is not the whole story pharmaceutical companies that provide oral contraceptives and the remedies for the problems they did not warn women of, such as strokes, heart problems and breast cancer do very well from the 'industry'. Condom manufactureres are laughing all the way to the bank. In addition the leather industry is experiencing a boom as sado-masochism becomes the fastest growing sexual recreation of the middle aged and middle class. If we look globally we see that some economies only barely survive because of the sex tourist trade and horrifying facts are emerging regarding the setting up of such economies. Brock and Thistlethwaite illustrate how the sex industry was planned as a strategy of development in Asia and was backed by the World Bank, the IMF and the United States Aid for International Development fund.[12] Women and children are provided on the cheap in Asia for Western men who often believe they are making life better for those they are abusing. What, if anything, does a theology of celibacy have to say to such figures?

Of course, in order to partake in this sex recreation one has to look the part; the figure, the face, the clothes and so on all have to be just right. This creates a great deal more money for those who propogate the patriarchal myths of youth and beauty. The cosmetics industry is worth $20 billion a year while the diet industry tops that at $30 billion. More worrying yet is the boom of genital cosmetic surgery in the United States. Women are being encouraged to have 'designer genitals', vaginas 'tidied up' in order to give their men more pleasure. One American surgeon was proud to have carried out over 4000 such operations, saying that vaginal orgasm would now be more of a possibility for these women.[13] This is body colonization in the extreme, being physically moulded to increase pleasure for your partner and perhaps for yourself but certainly made to 'fit' the penetrative requirement. No question here that a woman's pleasure can be sought through a more imaginative and explorative range of sexual activities, the knife fixes the 'problem'. All these recreational, sex-as-industry, 'products' place women in danger

12. Rita Brock and Susan Thistlewaite, *Casting Stones: Prostitution and Liberation in Asia and the United States* (Minneapolis: Fortress Press, 1996), p. 114.
13. Cline, *Women, Celibacy and Passion*, p. 138.

and many lose their lives, be it through servicing hard core porn, Western tourists, the diet industry or the surgeon's knife. The jury is still out about the number of deaths from the use of oral contraception but it already looks alarming. How can a theology of celibacy remove such pressures from women's lives?

Celibacy, as we have seen so far, can combine the personal, social and political as well as serving the spiritual and it is my contention that it can still do so. However, it will begin from a different place if feminist Christology is at its heart. A Christology that encourages passionate engagement with the world rather than a suspicion of the flesh and a cautious connection with the world. The works of both Carter Heyward and Rita Brock make a very useful starting point for a christological base to contemporary celibacy. They both speak of Christology as based in the erotic. For Heyward *dunamis* is the raw, dynamic energy with which we are born and which is our divine birth right.[14] It is the energy that allows mutual relation through opening us to others in a spontaneous and whole way. This power can be frightening as it propels us to ever deeper relationality and the exposures of self that come with such a level of being. It is, however, the power that confirms us all as divine/human and as in a process of mutual divinizing. As erotic suggests, this process involves a fully embodied engagement with the world and those in it. However, the emphasis is not on the erotic in the narrow sense of genital sexuality but rather points to a fully alive and embodied connection with all aspects of life. We move towards divinity through choice and activity.

For Brock[15] the use of the term erotic power illustrates that she too is concerned with the material and not just abstract concepts. She also emphasizes that this power does not offer us safety and conventionality, it challenges us to explore the edges to find new redemptive possibilities in a world geared towards objectivity and exploitation. Erotic power is wild and beautiful but it also makes us vulnerable, not only to others but to the knowledge that we are damaged people in need of healing. It is in this knowing and the anger that it generates that the passion for change can be found and it is from this place that the Christ

14. See Carter Heyward, *The Redemption of God: A Theology of Mutual Relation* (New York: University of America Press, 1982).

15. See Rita Brock, *Journeys by Heart: A Christology of Erotic Power* (New York: Crossroad, 1988).

who increases in the sharing emerges and demands alternatives.[16]

Both Heyward and Brock acknowledge that this view of Christology has embodied consequences for those who hold it. Certainly we are all called to action but it goes deeper than that. Brock believes it requires the healing of ourselves, others and the world, while Heyward understands it to require nothing less than a revolution. It is a revolution that begins when we are open to each other and honest in an embodied way. Heyward is explicit in declaring that sex and sexuality have a major part to play in this as they both bring us present to ourselves and to one another. Can we perhaps call her priviledged in the light of a feminist analysis of body politics which understands that women are removed from their bodies to the degree to which they serve patriarchy? She does acknowledge that she operates in a different world, that of lesbian feminism, where even there the pitfalls of lack of relation are only too evident. However, it is her contention that patriarchy is not as engrained and as necessary for survival as within heterosexuality and therefore a head start could be claimed.

Perhaps Christology as envisaged by these two scholars can underpin a revolutionary view of celibacy in the new millenium. It is a Christology that calls us forth through our bodies and not in the absence of them. This calling forth is to be full, embodied and mutually empowering individuals and so offers a challenge to hetero-patriarchy that can be called truly world shattering. The equality that women in the early years of Christianity felt compelled to find in convents away from engaged sexuality can be found through bodies as they challenge the unconscious dance of patriarchy that is the western sexual agenda. How?

I wish to find a definition for celibacy that is in the tradition of our early foremothers in faith if not in line with their understanding of what constitutes sex. Celibacy is a quest for equality that was promised in the incarnate message of Jesus, that is to say, the promise was not spiritual and otherworldly and so the lived reality has to reflect the hope. This was sought through a withdrawal, a removal of the body, from the arena of inequality. Erotic celibacy, on the other hand, holds out the same hope but engages the body which then becomes a place of metanoia, a place where alternate realities are lived and where patriarchy is actively resisted. This means that women need to understand their capacity for pleasure and not be afraid to grasp it. As we saw in 'Sex and Body

16. See Lisa Isherwood, *Liberating Christ* (Cleveland, OH: Pilgrim Press, 1999) for more on these and other feminist Christologies.

Politics', young women begin very early to give away their right to pleasure and so this has to be the starting point in resistance. Sally Cline believes it is no accident that historically, women who masturbate have received very severe treatment by society. It was as late as 1947 that such 'feisty' women were genitally mutilated in Britain. Isaac Baker Brown, the President of London's Medical Society who developed this practice in 1858 claimed that it was a cure for female antisocial behaviour. This behaviour consisted of 'a great disposition for novelties—the patient desiring to escape from home, fond of becoming a nurse in hospitals or other pursuits' while married women showed 'a distaste for marital intercourse'.[17] If we look at this another way we can say that the woman who is a little less passive through her embodied and invigorating relationship with her own body is antisocial because she refuses to play the game according to male rules. It is curious that boys were never castrated for masturbation, although I do acknowledge that some awful devices were produced to control them.

Young girls need to develop a joyful relationship with their own bodies and masturbation then seems to be the place to begin building up the kind of self love and self esteem that will be a critique of patriarchy. This is not the whole story, of course; what I am arguing for is that the natural joy that children have in their bodies be enhanced, not restricted, and that gendered interpretations of their embodied connections be removed from the scene. This is particularly crucial for young girls who need a very strong sense of embodied pleasure if they are to withstand the onslaught of patriarchy. What has to be built up in them is an understanding that their bodies are right, they are as they should be and the responses they are capable of are not disfunctional. Theologies need to endorse this view and not make the body the enemy or at best the worst kept secret in the world. Liturgies can celebrate the joy of awakening sexuality and these too can be sensuous. However, they should not just celebrate the procreative nature of women but rather they should revel in the capacity for pleasure that a woman has and the vast potential that pleasure has to change the world. Can I see this happening? Well, can you?

This encouragement of real self love, acceptance and the self esteem that flows from it is the first step towards women not becoming the 'objects' of male desire. Young women need to understand that they

17. Quoted in Cline, *Women, Celibacy and Passion*, p. 63.

are women and they can be women in whatever way they choose, they are not made into women by the gaze of others. The Aretha Franklin song 'You Make Me Feel Like a Natural Woman' says it all. Women somehow have to be 'naturalized', which in reality is mutilated mentally if not physically, to fit a pattern that is not their own. We have to be encouraged by the weight of society to 'give it all away', society depends on it. We have seen what making us feel like natural born women can involve and so declaring that we know we are women has definite implications also.

Placing women's sexual pleasure at the centre of theological reflection does not lead to the chaos that male theologians have led us to believe it would. It certainly signals the end of the world as they have known it but surely that is to be celebrated! What it does is provide a very strong embodied base for challenging consumerism and poor ecological awareness as well as domestic violence, rape and other acts of female objectification. Challenging the penetrative norm also throws into relief the procreative imperative of which Adrian Thatcher speaks. The whole question of fertility and infertility becomes one that moves beyond producing babies, since the worth of a woman can no longer be judged in that way. Many women, even in these so-called enlightened days feel the pressure/shame of being childless and clinics are making a great deal of money from those feelings. I do not wish to suggest that this is the whole story but it is a large part of it and one that could be changed.

When women no longer understand themselves as consumable goods for the delight of men it will have an effect on the way they consume. Many of the trappings of the mating game can then be discarded, which will have both economic and ecological benefits. This is not to say that attraction will become unimportant but rather that it will be face to face, not image to image. The present rate of consumption cannot be sustained by the planet and while not all consumption is to do with enhancing ourselves, a large amount is. The reduction of this would have major benefits not only on the environment but also in individual lives. Of course, a very real and immmediate ecological improvement will be made if women stop using oral contraceptives. The estrogen contained in these have found their way into the water and are making fish and men infertile. Add to this the reduced medical costs because of the side effects of this bitter pill and the foundations of an argument are laid.

Erotic celibacy, then, is erotic sex that challenges the reality of patri-

archy as engrained upon our bodies. This for the most part means challenging the myth of the power of penetrative sex and the vaginal orgasm
and demanding exquisite pleasure with one or many partners. Gay
theologians are beginning to share experiences of the reality of AIDS in
their communities and one surprising outcome is in relation to the
change in sexual practice. The threat of death has made many gay men
think about alternatives to penetrative sex and this flight of imagination
has brought about an engagement with the body that many could never
have thought possible. Martin Stringer argues that getting away from
purely genital sexuality has released gay men into a sense of playful
intimacy, which in turn releases them from the power-laden agendas of
penetrative sex.[18] This new pleasure seeking has brought many to a new
understanding of mutuality, imagination and selfhood in which they can
unselfconsciously give and receive. Some gay Christians understand
this as a reflection of the self giving love of Christ.

Stringer goes a little further with his examination of this new reality
and likens this kind of sex to sharing a meal.[19] Sharing food with one
person does not exclude us from sharing with others and Stringer
believes that sex can be the same. He sees this kind of sharing as
releasing people from notions of ownership and indeed understands it to
reflect something of Jesus' sharing of his body with all. There seems to
be a lesson here for women who all too easily are understood as the
property of men. However, I am not naive enough to suggest that
women can pursue this end in the same way as gay men who are, after
all, differently situated in the patriarchal hierarchy then women. A
woman seeking a non-penetrative, full bodied erotic experience that
does not imply ownership is in a far more precarious position than a
gay man. Nevertheless, the lived experience is there, which suggests
that sex can become more mutual and empowering when partners get
away from the predetermined performance/act approach and enter into
a more playful exploration of each other's bodies. Of course, the other
great challenge that this presents is to pair bonding, which forms the
base of an advanced capitalist society. When even a socialist government is making marriage preparation part of the school curriculum we
know that sexual arrangements and finance are linked. The family is

18. Martin Stringer, 'Expanding the Boundaries of Sex: An Exploration of
Sexual Ethics after the Second Sexual Revolution', *Theology and Sexuality* 7
(1997), pp. 27-43 (35).

19. Stringer, 'Expanding the Boundaries', p. 41.

both a very viable consumer outlet and a solid producer of workers. It is therefore very important if capitalism is to thrive. Any challenge to this is seen as deeply subversive, so should not Christians who see the globally devastating effects of advanced capitalism be challenging it? As we have seen, Christianity has a tradition of using the body to subvert widely held beliefs and this needs to continue. Instead of herding us into marriage the churches should be issuing a challenge to capital ownership that begins with freedom and ownership of one's own body.

Erotic celibacy challenges women to place our embodied selves on the line as points of resistance to patriarchy. It takes seriously our capacity for pleasure as one element to that challenge and it calls us out to mutually empowering relationships. It does not make us virgins, mothers or whores but it celebrates the power and the beauty of female passion. The way we and others relate with our bodies sets the pattern for relations beyond the edges of our skin. Like our monastic foresisters we live in a world that thrives on inequality but like them some of us still hold the message of equality to be more than a vague half promise. Achieving such equality in the modern world is as much a matter for transgressive sexuality as it is for cloistered withdrawal. The erotic celibate refutes the received wisdom of the hetero-patriarchal sexual narrative and becomes a sexual reminder of radical incarnationalism, of metaphysics lived through the skin.

Part IV

REFLECTIONS FROM THE EDGES

DISRUPTIVE BODIES:
DISABILITY, EMBODIMENT AND SEXUALITY

Elizabeth Stuart

The disabled body queers a great deal of the pitch upon which theologies of sexuality and gender have built themselves. For a start, as Jackie Leach Scully has noted, the disabled body casts a shadow over the effort of these theologies to claim embodiment as good. For however true it might be that disability is a social construction, pain and degeneration constitute a different sort of suffering from that created by a society unable or unwilling to embrace the disabled body and any attempt to theologize positively about them is unconvincing.[1] Having a black skin or gay sexual orientation are not problematic in themselves—the suffering and oppression associated with them is caused by the interpretations of these things by society. Being disabled is to experience a double oppression in the sense that while disability is certainly a social construction and the interpretation of the disabled body by society is oppressive to disabled people, one cannot be liberated from one's own body and if your body is a site of pain a liberatory theology of disability will not be enough.

Secondly, the production and maintenance of gender operates differently around the non-disabled and disabled body in contemporary Europe and North America. Feminism has been slow to recognize this fact or reflect upon it. Disabled people are often subject to a process of de-sexing by society. This is perhaps most clearly symbolized in the common sight of signs indicating toilet facilities 'Men', 'Women', 'Disabled'. This de-sexing is often worked out in various processes of infantilization to which large numbers of disabled people are subjected, processes which include an assumption of asexuality, the explicit denial of sexual needs in group homes and the dressing of adults in child-like

---

1. Jackie Leach Scully, 'When Embodiment Isn't Good', *Theology and Sexuality* 9 (1998), pp. 10-28.

clothes.[2] Disabled men may experience their masculinity in a different way to non-disabled men. If the social construction of masculinity is built upon notions of physical strength and general potency then disabled men are frequently excluded from it and do not necessarily benefit from the normal privileges of masculinity. Issues of 'communication, institutionalisation, dependency, insecurity, invasion, assumption and justification'[3] seem to make disabled men and women more vulnerable to abuse, with around 48 per cent of men and women suffering from some sort of sexual abuse.[4] The deaf and those with learning difficulties are particularly vulnerable. This has to be taken into full account in any theologizing around sexuality and disability. Nevertheless every effort must be made to avoid portraying disabled people as 'natural' victims, which is another strategy widely used to disempower people.

Thirdly, a whole cluster of uncomfortable ethical issues surrounding sexuality and disability present themselves over which there is much disagreement among disabled people themselves. Among these issues are the use of sexual surrogates who are paid and specially trained to have sex with disabled people (sexual surrogacy is understood by its advocates to be a type of therapy), the use of prostitutes and pornography and the part played by care-workers in meeting their clients' sexual needs. These are difficult issues to accommodate in a feminist paradigm which has stressed the ethical primacy of relationships of mutuality and reciprocity. Yet feminist theologies and theologies of sexuality have also generally subscribed to the current Western cultural view that sexual agency is one of the most important and precious elements of mature personhood. When disability is constructed in such a way as to deny disabled people sexual agency or prevent them exercising that agency in ways that the non-disabled take for granted then the feminist ideal becomes problematic. Lastly, the disabled body does not just represent an exception to the general experience of bodiliness whose epistemology must be found a place within a general theory of embodiment as an exception to the norm. Good health is never a permanent state, the chance of experiencing permanent or temporary disablement (physical

2. Tom Shakespeare, Kath Gillespie-Sells and Dominic Davies, *The Sexual Politics of Disability: Untold Desires* (London: Cassell, 1996), pp. 49-82.

3. Shakespeare, Gillespie-Sells and Davies, *The Sexual Politics of Disability*, p. 139.

4. Shakespeare, Gillespie-Sells and Davies, *The Sexual Politics of Disability*, p. 139.

or mental) is high and almost an inevitability as a person gets older. The contrast is not between the abled and disabled but between the temporarily able and the disabled. In truth the human body is only ever temporarily abled and hence reflection on the disabled body should be central to any theorizing on the body.

In this essay I hope to construct a model for Christian theological reflection upon the body and sexuality which centralizes the disabled body. Unlike other contemporary theologies of disability, however, this essay will not adopt the standard methodology of a liberationist approach by beginning with disabled experience and proceeding to offer theological reflection upon it. This has been done more than adequately by theologians such as Nancy Eiesland and Don Saliers[5] and in any case I am becoming increasingly convinced that theological reflection upon experience, while being extremely effective in deconstructing dominant models of theological reflection and empowering and providing a voice to those previously excluded from the theological arena, needs to be part of the process of reconstruction, if that reconstruction is to engage and enrich the whole body of Christ. Engagement with the tradition as the primary matrix of authority is necessary because in a real sense the tradition is all Christians have in common and it constitutes and generates its common language. Only by starting with the tradition and assuming its primacy will the disabled body ever enter into the consciousness of some Christians. Along with the Radical Orthodox school of theology I want to claim that the tradition is far richer than either contemporary Protestantism or Catholicism is willing to acknowledge.[6] Also with the Radical Orthodox school and from the Christian tradition, my starting point is the theological concept of participation which allows for no place where God is not. This not only means that there is no sphere for which theological reflection is inappropriate and that divine illumination is available to any form of knowledge, but also that when talking about bodies, sexuality and so on one is appealing to an eternal source for these things. This is not to deny their materiality but to affirm 'that behind this density resides an even greater

---

5.   Nancy L. Eiesland, *The Disabled God: Toward a Liberatory Theology of Disability* (Nashville, TN: Abingdon Press, 1994); Nancy L. Eiesland and Don E. Saliers (eds.), *Human Disability and the Service of God: Reassessing Religious Practice* (Nashville, TN: Abingdon Press, 1998).

6.   John Milbank, Catherine Pickstock and Graham Ward, *Radical Orthodoxy: A New Theology* (London: Routledge, 1999), p. 2.

density—beyond all contrasts of density and lightness (as beyond all contrasts of definition and limitlessness). This is to say that all there is *only* is because it is more than it is.'[7]

Everywhere and Nowhere? Disability and the Christian Tradition

It is one of the paradoxes of the Christian Scriptures and tradition that disabled people are everywhere and nowhere at the same time. The Gospels are populated by disabled people, it is impossible to read more than a few verses without encountering someone with a paralysis, disease or some other physical impairment, or people possessed by unclean spirits. Unlike women or sexual minorities disabled people are very visible in the Gospels. Yet even as they become visible they are rendered invisible again by the healing touch of Jesus. The disabled appear to be rendered non-disabled. The focus of the stories is either on the authority of Jesus as healer or on the faith of the person being healed. In both cases the consequences are unfortunate from the perspective of the modern disability rights movement because the first gives the impression that physical and mental 'wholeness' are pre-requisites for entrance into the kingdom of God and the second that such wholeness and any healing necessary to achieve it is dependent upon the faith of the person concerned.[8] In the Hebrew Scriptures the book of Leviticus in particular again makes the disabled person very visible because the authors of the book are concerned with the connections between physical state and purity. But:

> Decisions about physical purity/impurity have a strongly visual basis, and deviations from physical norms may be interpreted as signs of God's displeasure... According to these passages (Leviticus 13–14 and 21.16-24), within the religious community physical imperfection can result in some form of exclusion. The exclusion can range from restrictions in privileged access to divine communion to complete and permanent exclusion from the residential community.[9]

In Leviticus, then, disabled people are often made visible for the

---

7. Milbank, Pickstock and Ward, *Radical Orthodoxy*, p. 4.

8. Colleen C. Grant, 'Reinterpreting the Healing Narratives', in Eiesland and Saliers (eds.), *Human Disability and the Service of God*, pp. 72-87.

9. Sarah J. Melcher, 'Visualising the Perfect Cult: The Priestly Rationale for Exclusion', in Eiesland and Saliers (eds.), *Human Disability and the Service of God*, pp. 55-71 (69).

purposes of some kind of exclusion, to highlight the wholeness and purity of an able body.

Pre-Enlightenment discussion of the resurrected body also provided some implicit theological reflection upon the disabled body. Pre-modern Christians simply could not imagine a full resurrected life without a body and a body which had some kind of direct continuity with the earthly body.[10] This strong sense of the somatic dimension of personhood was rendered ambiguous, however, by a deep uneasiness with the change and decay of bodily existence. This led to huge amounts of speculation as to the nature of the resurrected body—its gender, height, weight, age and so on. The overriding consensus seems to have been that the resurrection represented a triumph over the body's orientation towards decay, imperfection and death and hence bodies would be raised, repaired and perfected; certainly by contrast hell was often conceived as a place of eternal dismemberment, mutilation and digestion of the body. In this scheme of things the disabled body functions as a reminder of the fallen, even damned body.

Yet this telling of the Christian tradition is only half the story. Within the New Testament, as within a great deal of ancient literature, the disabled body is often constructed in paradoxical terms, as Simon Horne put it, 'within inability is striking capability'.[11] One of the most common manifestations of this in ancient literature is the blind person who has extraordinary insight. The Gospels pick up on this theme on a number of occasions. The man born blind in John 9 is, as Colleen Grant points out, the only reasonably well rounded disabled character in the Gospels.[12] On the one hand this is a story about healing as a means of inclusion. James Alison has noted that the means of healing through the use of clay suggests that in this healing Jesus is completing the creation of this man.[13] Indeed Alison maintains that Jesus' practice of healing on the Sabbath can be read as a denial that God's work of creation is

10. Caroline Walker Bynum, *The Resurrection of the Body in Western Christianity, 200–1336* (New York: Columbia University Press, 1995).

11. Simon Horne, ' "Those who are blind see": Some New Testament Uses of Impairment, Inability and Paradox', in Eiesland and Saliers (eds.), *Human Disability and the Service of God*, pp. 88-101 (89).

12. Grant, 'Reinterpreting the Healing Narratives', p. 79.

13. James Alison, 'The Man Blind from Birth and the Subversion of Sin: Some Questions about Fundamental Morals', *Theology and Sexuality* 7 (1997), pp. 83-102.

complete and that God rests. And this is what is implied in Jesus' reply
to 'the Jews' in Jn 5.17, 'My Father is still working and I am also working.' The perfection of his creation allows the blind man to be fully
included in the Jewish community. This is symbolized by the fact that
after bathing in the pool of Siloam and receiving his sight he is talked to
rather than about. And yet this inclusion is only temporary because 'the
Jews' cannot cope with the implications of the healing and drive him
out. In the middle of the confusion caused to 'the Jews' by the healing
the man himself gradually comes to understand who Jesus is and this is
really the completion of his humanity. The question which the disciples
ask at the beginning of the story 'Who sinned, this man or his parents,
that he was born blind?' (Jn 9.2) is used to expose a false understanding
of sin: sin is not some fault that prevents inclusion, sin consists of processes of exclusion and active participation in them, it is not identical
with them.

> God has not the slightest difficulty in bringing to a fullness of creation
> the person who is in some way incomplete and recognises this. The
> problem is with those who think they are complete, and that creation is,
> at least in their case finished, and for this reason that goodness consists
> in the maintenance of the established order... The righteous members of
> the group, thinking that they see, become blind precisely by holding on
> to the order which they think they have to defend.[14]

What is particularly interesting about this story is that while it has
parallels with the ancient tradition of the paradox of the impaired, the
parallels are not exact for the man gains insight after he is cured. His
blindness is a symptom of creation not yet complete but so is the spiritual blindness of the Pharisees. The blind man comes to 'see' in both
senses of the word; others do not. This story does not romanticize the
impairment of blindness but it does explicitly deconstruct the stub-
bornly consistent connection between impairment, sin and exclusion
and reconstruct the understanding of sin as exclusion with an explicit
connection established between the maintenance of systems of exclusion and a spiritual blindness, blindness to the continuing creative and
subversive presence of God in the world. Throughout the Gospels those
with physical impairments are portrayed as at least open to, at best
audaciously seeking, this presence—in direct contrast to the able bodied
who consistently fail to grasp what is going on.

14. Alison, 'The Man Blind from Birth and the Subversion of Sin', p. 94.

A less radical rendition of the disabled paradox is found in Luke's account of Paul's conversion. Paul is blinded by his encounter with Christ (Acts 9.1-9). Once again we have the juxtaposition of blindness and faith. And once again the restoration of sight is associated with inclusion and the fulfilment of creation, occurring as it does when Paul receives the Holy Spirit and is baptized. In his letters Paul himself positively delights in the paradox of impairment. In 2 Cor. 12.7-10 he asserts that 'to keep me from being too elated, a thorn was given me in the flesh, a messenger from Satan to torment me, to keep me from being too elated. Three times I appealed to the Lord about this, that it would leave me, but he said to me, "My grace is sufficient for you, for power is made perfect in weakness".' The Greek word translated as 'weakness' here, ἀσθένεια, is associated with illness. Paul uses it in contrast with, δύναμις, translated as 'power', also carrying the meaning of 'ability' or 'capacity'. God's ability is fulfilled in incapacity, which is why Paul can boast in his own weakness, incapacity or impairment, whatever that may be, and it is necessary for Paul so to boast in order that 'the power of Christ may dwell in me'. Horne notes that the word ἐπισκηνώσῃ, translated here as 'may dwell in me', conjures up images of a tent (σκηνή) and an allusion to the tabernacle, the dwelling place of God, which according to Leviticus, is a place from which are excluded priests who suffer from certain illnesses or disabilities (21.16-24).[15] Paul subverts this exclusion: it is in places of weakness, illness and disability that Christ dwells and the power of God can be most clearly encountered. This subversion of notions of incapacity is part of Paul's wider theology of the cross. The scandal of the cross is that this supreme moment of weakness is the moment of salvation.

The Christ/Messiah saves 'in weakness' (2 Cor. 13.4). This subversion is also evident in the emergence from the tomb of the one whom Nancy Eiesland has called 'the disabled God'.[16] Both Luke and John portray the risen body of Christ as an impaired body, Jesus still bears the marks of his crucifixion. If, as the early Church theologians believed, the resurrected body of Christ recapitulated the fallen bodiliness of Adam and manifested true, perfected humanity then perfect humanity seems to include an embracing of the contingency of human life and an 'unself-pitying, painstaking survival'.[17]

---

15. Horne, ' "Those who are blind see" ', p. 95.
16. Eiesland, *The Disabled God*, pp. 89-105.
17. Eiesland, *The Disabled God*, p. 101.

Jesus Christ the disabled God, is not a romanticised notion of 'overcomer' God. Instead here is God as survivor...the image of survivor here evoked is that of a simple, unself-pitying, honest body, for whom the limits of power are palpable but not tragic. The disabled God embodies the ability to see clearly the complexity and the 'mixed blessing' of life and bodies, without living in despair.[18]

The disabled God reveals the full personhood of disabled people and therefore is a crucial symbol and concept in the development of a theology of disability. In the resurrection disabled people are made permanently visible in the image of God. But the subtleties of the resurrection stories should not elude us. The resurrection story is not simply a cheap fairy tale in which everything is all right in the end. It is also more than a story of survival. It is a story of a profound victory which involves both radical continuity and crucial discontinuity. It is a story of victory over death. Jesus who is now alive bears the marks of his death. Death has been resurrected and in the process been neutralized. Death, while a biological inevitability, should no longer have any power over human culture because it is not a theological reality. God does not acknowledge death, it does not disrupt the divine-human relationship and hence it should not cast its shadow over our lives and relationships. Death does not arrest the process of creation. The resurrected body of Jesus, while having a direct continuity with the pre-resurrection body, also demonstrates a radical discontinuity expressed in the inability of his friends to recognize him when he first appears to them. It is a body that certainly eats and drinks but also walks through walls and appears and disappears. What this serves to emphasize is that the body cannot be fully grasped or contained, it is ultimately always a mystery, and there is always more to be revealed. The resurrected body of Jesus participates in the natural and supernatural processes of bodily change and in this process complicates attitudes to the disabled body. On the one hand with the conquering of death the disabled body is redeemed from the symbolics of death and the absence of the divine. This insight is to be found even in the inhospitable part of the tradition. The second century Acts of Paul is clear that the resurrected flesh of all believers bears the marks of suffering and Gregory of Nyssa reflecting on the death of his sister Macrina was clear that she would bear the scars of a healed tumour in the resurrection, for these scars functioned

18. Eiesland, *The Disabled God*, p. 102.

as identity markers.[19] It is also perceivable in the Levitical commandment 'You shall not revile the deaf or put a stumbling block before the
blind; you shall fear your God: I am the Lord.' (19.14) But this does not
rule out the possibilities of a new form of bodiliness in which pain and
suffering is absent and the processes of creation continue disrupting all
our perceived notions of materiality. Therefore the beliefs that the resurrection involves some kind of bodily change and that bodies continue to
bear the scars of human contingency are not necessarily incompatible.
Indeed they are mysteriously connected.

But, perhaps most importantly, 'Jesus Christ, the disabled God, disorders the social-symbolic orders of what it means to be incarnate'.[20] It is
this theological fact, that the body of Jesus disrupts both the symbolic
orders and the material orders which are inextricably bound together,
that seems to me to offer the most effective hermeneutical principle
with which to interpret the Christian Scripture and tradition on the disabled body. Graham Ward offers a fascinating analysis of how the body
of Jesus is displaced in the Gospel accounts of his incarnation, circum-
cision and transfiguration, extended in the Eucharist and transposed in
the ascension.[21] This procession of displacement reveals the instability
of matter and the symbolics of the material, culminating in the final
displacement of the ascension in which the Church becomes the body
of Christ: 'The body of Jesus Christ, the body of God, is permeable,
transcorporeal, transpositional. Within it all other bodies are situated
and given their significance. We are all permeable, transcorporeal and
transpositional.'[22] The Church as the body of Christ (and therefore the
paradigmatic human and eschatological community) shares in the unstable body of Christ. The symbolics and social and cultural constructions of the body are rendered profoundly unstable among the baptized,
which is why St Paul could declare to the Galatians that 'there is no
longer Jew or Greek, there is no longer slave or free, there is no longer
male or female; for you are all one in Christ Jesus' (Gal. 3.28).

We cannot, of course, live beyond social and cultural constructions.
They are ironically part of the processes of creation as human beings
struggle to cooperate with the divine in the bringing of creation to

19. Bynum, *The Resurrection of the Body*, pp. 29, 81-86.
20. Eiesland, *The Disabled God*, pp. 103-104.
21. Graham Ward, 'Bodies: The Displaced Body of Jesus Christ', in Milbank,
Pickstock and Ward (eds.), *Radical Orthodoxy*, pp. 163-81.
22. Ward, 'Bodies: The Displaced Body of Jesus Christ', p. 176.

fulfilment. The problem is that the very sense of 'lack' that propels us towards God and the activity of creation is also the sense that leads us into the temptation of thinking that our constructions are final and complete. Within the body of Christ all cultural and social constructions are redeemed and given back to us as parodies of their former selves. I do not use parody in the conventional sense of sending up something but, following Linda Hutcheon, as 'an extended repetition with critical difference' which has 'a hermeneutical function with both cultural and even ideological implications'.[23] Christians operate within culture, which is in the process of being redeemed. It is hard if not impossible to resist the identities our culture gives to us but the Christian is obliged to live out these identities with 'critical difference', the difference being shaped by the ecclesial self which is 'permeable, transcorporeal and transpositional'. This will often involve a deliberate subversion of identity categories. The Christian performance of maleness and femaleness will therefore be strange (and indeed throughout Christian history has often been very strange),[24] but so will be Christian visions of perfection, beauty and understandings of embodiment and sexuality.

The disabled body, because it participates in the image of the disabled God, functions both as a reminder of the instability of embodiment and is itself caught up in the constant process of unmaking and remaking in which all bodies participate in the body of Christ. Diane DeVires, born without arms and legs, and subjected to all the oppressive attitudes that societal understandings of disability generate, has yet maintained an entirely positive attitude to her body. She has a strong sense of her body as extendable. It does not end with her flesh and bone but also encompasses her wheelchair. DeVires also experiences fluid boundaries between her own body and those of other people. Her close relationship with her sister enables her to experience things such as dancing and walking through her sister's body. DeVires's sense of the fluidity of her own embodiment echoes something of the fluidity of the body of Christ and her identification with the Venus di Milo destabilizes notions of perfection and beauty in much the same way as the disabled God does.[25]

23. Linda Hutcheon, *A Theory of Parody: The Teaching of Twentieth-Century Art Forms* (New York: Methuen, 1985), pp. 2-7.

24. See my *Spitting at Dragons: Towards a Feminist Theology of Sainthood* (London: Mowbray, 1996).

25. Eiesland, *The Disabled God*, pp. 33-40.

Within the Church, then, the disabled body should be valued as one that bears the image of the disabled God and that constantly reminds the body of Christ of the fluidity of all bodies. In other words, the presence of the disabled body is essential to remind the Church of the revelation through which it is constituted and which it is called to bear in its own bodiliness. And by 'presence' I mean here a real presence not a marginal presence. It is scandalous that the Eucharist, which is the place par excellence in which Christian identity is produced and performed in a continuous act of breaking open and pouring out of the body of Christ, should often be a place of exclusion or marginalization for disabled people. Often the bread and wine are distributed in such a way that disabled people are not able to participate in the same way as the majority of those present. In this way the disabled body is problematized rather than centralized. Similarly the exclusion of people with a variety of disabilities from the priesthood and ministry is also a blasphemous denial of the disabled God and the destabilizing of embodiment that takes place in Christ. The celebrant is the one who represents Christ to the people and the people to Christ; it is therefore highly appropriate theologically for that person to be disabled or in some other way (e.g. by being female, gay or transgendered) to represent the slipperiness of the symbolics of the material order in the body of Christ.

Paul, in his development of the concept of the Church as the body of Christ, explicitly draws attention to the subversion of cultural and social constructions that have to take place in the body of Christ:

> the members of the body that seem to be weaker are indispensable, and those members of the body that we think less honourable we clothe with greater honour, and our less respectable members are treated with greater respect... But God has arranged the body, giving the greater honour to the inferior member, that there may be no dissension within the body, but the members may have the same care for one another. If one member suffers, all suffer together with it, if one member is honoured, all rejoice together with it (1 Cor. 12.23-26).

The body of Christ needs to break itself open to make room at its heart for the disabled body. It is called to parody the world in which the disabled body is marginalized, excluded, problematized and infantalized.

Are They Having Sex?: The Disabled Body, Sexuality and Theology

It is ironic that Paul, in making reference to the 'weakest' and 'inferior' members in developing his concept of the Church as Christ's body, was probably making allusion to the body's sexual organs. For the Church has not proved itself sensitive to the sexual needs of disabled people. The procreative principle, which though now radically moderated even with the Roman Catholic Church, nevertheless continues to exercise an influence over the cultural constructions of sexuality in the Western world. We can only comfortably imagine sexual activity among the young and those whose bodies measure up to the ideal projected to us constantly. The elderly and the disabled are therefore desexualized and in the process the Church avoids dealing with some uncomfortable issues that the sexual disabled body raises.

One of the most notable developments in the Church in the twentieth century has been the gradual embracing of the view that sexuality is an essential part of personhood. Even within the Roman Catholic Church marriage has eclipsed the celibate religious life as the ideal Christian state. On the one hand this has been a positive movement, recentering the body and sexual relationships within the matrix of Christian discipleship. But in buying into the modern understanding of desire as having its ultimate end, its *telos*, in heterosexual sexual relations, the Church has misplaced the ancient Christian belief that all desire has its *telos* in God. This has important repercussions. The Church finds itself on the one hand promoting a sexual relationship as a human good but on the other hand, having implicated itself in the project of modern heterosexual marriage, finds itself relegating those who for whatever reason cannot enter into it to a moral no mans land where whatever they do sexually will at best fall short of a God-given ideal, at worst bog them down in a morass of sin. Even if we were to accept this as a theologically and pastorally justified position we might then ask what the Church does to encourage disabled people on the path towards marriage? Generally speaking, the Church seems content to let people find each other through the usual social channels and only then steps in to solemnize the relationship. But what if some people cannot find each other through the usual social channels because those social channels are in various ways inaccessible to them? If there is no part of existence in which God is not and through which God cannot work then it is imperative that the Church should actively work to ensure that such channels are accessible. This will involve the body of Christ concerning itself with accessibility issues in terms of public transport, pubs and clubs, dating agencies and so on. It will address issues of privacy in residential homes. It will campaign for effective sex education for people with learning difficulties. It will endeavour to participate in the deconstruction of cultural notions of perfection, beauty and attractiveness through attention to its own language, imagery and liturgical and pastoral practice. The disabled body challenges the Church to acknowledge its part in promoting what Shakespeare, Gillespie-Sells and Davies refer to as 'fucking ideology', that is, associating 'sex' exclusively with penetrative intercourse.[26] This prevailing attitude desexualizes many disabled people in the eyes of society and in their own eyes. The giving and receiving of love through the exchange of physical pleasure is not dependent upon penetrative intercourse or indeed genital contact. As a sexual body called to engage in a parodic critique of cultural constructions the body of Christ should promote a more diffuse understanding of sexual activity in which the possibilities for the Christian virtues of patience, equality, mutuality, passion and hospitality can be practised with perhaps more success than may be allowed by an exclusively penetrative model of sexual activity, bound up as it undoubtedly is with patriarchal constructions of reality.

But as always the Church becomes really unstuck when it has to deal with those who for whatever reason cannot marry. For the maxim of sex within marriage, celibacy without, does not have any integrity in an ecclesial and cultural context in which sexual agency is regarded as being an essential part of adulthood. To say that those who cannot get married, be it because of sexual orientation or life situation, are called to sexual abstinence and when they fail to live up to this calling they 'fall short' or sin simply does not ring true now that the Church has embraced the modern valorization of sexuality. The current debate on homosexuality within all mainstream Christian denominations is an indication of an implicit awareness at least of this dissonance. Yet that debate is largely and exclusively in official public debate conducted in the context of permanent, stable unions. The Church seems to have little constructive to say to those for whom stable and permanent unions, straight or gay, are an impossibility because of societal attitudes to disability. Traditionally one of the ways in which Christians subversively parodied identities and relationships was by the refusal to enter into sexual relations. The refusal to marry or engage in sexual relations embodied the resurrection state (Mt. 22.30) and therefore another way of existing and relating that casts a long and critical shadow over contem-

26. Shakespeare, Gillespie-Sells and Davies, *The Sexual Politics of Disability*, p. 97.

porary society.[27] For most of Christian history the freely chosen celibate life has been valorized by the Christian community because it provides a consistent critique of society's construction and valorization of sexual relationships. There is an urgent need to restore some of the balance that has been lost in the Church's embrace of modern constructions of sexuality and embodiment at the expense of the single life. Single people can only successfully be caught up in the Christian project of holy parody if though living the 'single' life in fact their experience is of not being single at all. Theologically, in the body of Christ no one is single because all share in the one flesh relationship of Christ with his Church (1 Cor. 6.12-20). All members of the body belong to one another. There should be no loneliness in the body of Christ, no lack of physical affection, companionship, laughter, empathy and friendship. So to be single in such a context is not be single at all. Just as to be 'male' in the body of Christ should not to be male at all, in the sense that there is a deliberate resistance to societal constructions of masculinity and once again the disabled body functions as a medium of grace in representing alternative constructions of gender. Yet also within the body of Christ the kind of mystical connection that exists between Christ and Church and is replicated in the relationship between members of his body must have some parallels with Diane DeVries's experience of a porous relationship between her own embodiment and that of her sister's, enabling her to 'experience through connection what she could not realise independently'.[28] No experience is completely beyond any member of the Church. Just as Christ stands in complete solidarity with humanity and has assumed the totality of human experience, so the Church as his body should be able to bear each other's experience in their bodies both in terms of feeling the pain of another and in sharing in the joy and pleasure that others embody. Such bearing of each other's bodies within the body of Christ is what makes it possible to speak of the Church 'having AIDS' or 'being gay' or 'being disabled'. It is also what makes it possible to speak of the Church as a sexual community in which the single life is an honoured model of discipleship. The single life also serves to remind everyone that the end of desire is not heterosexual or indeed any sexual relationship but God. This theological fact should act

27. Peter Brown, *The Body and Society: Men, Women and Sexual Renunciation in Early Christianity* (London: Faber & Faber; Boston: Columbia University Press, 1988), p. 32.

28. Eiesland, *The Disabled God*, p. 38.

as a brake on the Church's capitulation to the modern valorization of sexual relationships. The presentation in positive terms of a 'single' life is part of the Church's tradition but it has to be presented as an equally valid way of life to the married, not just a fall back position for those who cannot enter into marriage as it is now. And it has to understand such relationships within the context of the symbolic disordering of the experience of embodiment that Christ's body inaugurates. It is this disordering that creates the possibility of a celibate vocation in the body of Christ and it is this disordering of gender that makes any discrimination between heterosexual and homosexual relations within the body of Christ nonsensical. Within the body of Christ gender is subverted in such a way as to render moral distinctions based upon gender as void distinctions based upon other forms of embodiment. The Church's own tradition and indeed its head and saviour force it to face the question: is sexual agency an essential part of adult maturity? It must question the pressure that is put upon all people to buy into this myth and at the same time affirm the potential goodness and source of grace of sexual relationships and ensure that all have equal opportunities to enter into such a relationship if they feel so called; while also being aware of and doing all it can to recognize and prevent possibilities for abuse and violence within sexual relationships. This balancing act the Church as a corporate body has yet to achieve, although individuals and groups within it may have had better success in attaining such a balance.

Difficult ethical issues are raised in the contemporary disability rights movement concerning the use of personal assistants or carers for the fulfilment of sexual needs, both with regard to facilitating sexual relationships in terms of positioning and so on and even more controversially in entering into client–carer sexual relationships. In a cultural context in which sexual agency is so highly valued as a signifier of mature personhood, to facilitate a disabled person's work, social life, personal needs but not their sexual relationships seems unjustifiable, provided that the employment rights of the carer or assistant are guarded. Indeed, the involvement of a third party in facilitating sexual activity might serve to remind both Church and society that sexual activity is never simply a private affair—it always has a public dimension and impacts upon other people. All sexual activity is to some extent facilitated by others in one way or another. A Christian theology grounded in the primacy and normativity of the body of Christ in which members bear one another's bodies and hold the 'weakest' members in the highest honour should have no intrinsic difficulty with a third party facilitating a disabled person's sexual activity as long as the dignity of all parties involved is respected. A direct sexual relationship between a carer/assistant and a disabled person is more problematic. Bearing in mind the shocking levels of abuse in the disabled community, the protection of disabled people from abuse must be a priority. There is also the danger of abuse from the other side, as one disabled man, Stuart, notes,

> I think personally as a disabled man, I don't like what I see when disabled men exploit female personal assistants, first because of the gender oppression which is reinforced, but also lots of disabled men employ sexual pressure upon their personal assistant to have relationships.[29]

Stuart goes on to argue that such relationships reinforce the idea that it is OK for paid carers and assistants to have sex with disabled people whether they consent or not. If an attraction between the two parties develops, then it should immediately cease to be a working relationship. Zebedee, on the other hand argues that 'if an able-bodied person wants to masturbate they do it. In my view, it ought to be taken on by carers if you can't do it yourself.'[30] And there are undoubtedly issues here that cannot just be dismissed. Even though the *Catechism of the Catholic Church* describes masturbation as 'an intrinsically and gravely disordered action'[31] there was a marked shift in Christian attitudes to masturbation in the twentieth century so that even some contemporary Catholic moral theologians acknowledge the grace filled possibilities of masturbation for various groups of people, including the lonely, those who have been abused and need to relearn to love their bodies, for adolescents discovering their bodies for the first time and for partners isolated from each other for some time. [32] A Church of Scotland report on human sexuality noted the need to acknowledge the sexual needs of the elderly and disabled and that this involves understanding that masturbation often gives comfort and relief and therefore should be dealt

29. Shakespeare, Gillespie-Sells and Davies, *The Sexual Politics of Disability*, p. 38.

30. Shakespeare, Gillespie-Sells and Davies, *The Sexual Politics of Disability*, p. 37.

31. *Catechism of the Catholic Church* (London: Geoffrey Chapman, 1994), para. 2352, p. 503.

32. Evelyn Eaton Whitehead and James D. Whitehead, *A Sense of Sexuality: Christian Love and Intimacy* (New York: Crossroad, 1994), pp. 133-37.

with sensitively within an institutional setting.[33] But what has the Church to say to those who are physically unable to masturbate but still crave the comfort and relief it brings? If it is possible for a person to be employed to act as someone's eyes and hands when they do not have the use of their own, is there anything intrinsically wrong with the use of that person to give sexual relief as long as that person is in full agreement? The issue of masturbation is different from a non-masturbatory social-sexual relationship, for it is purely a matter of physical relief and the carer/assistant is acting purely as an extended limb of the disabled person. Might it be possible for Christians who operate within a concept of the body as unstable and with fluid boundaries, while always maintaining the integrity of individual bodies and seeking to protect them from violence and abuse, to imagine a situation in which one person's hand might act in place of another's? This situation is markedly different from the issue of sexual surrogacy which causes tensions with the disabled community itself. Presented as a form of therapy rather than prostitution and largely practiced in the Netherlands, people are especially trained and paid to have sexual relations with disabled people. The idea has come in for a great deal of criticism from disabled people themselves for reinforcing the medical (rather than social) understanding of disability and internalized feelings of inadequacy and inferiority.[34] From a theological point of view the isolation of sexual satisfaction from other bodily needs and desires presents a problem, for the body both individual and corporate is one. Paul's words in 1 Corinthians also need heeding, 'Do you not know that your bodies are members of Christ? Should I therefore take the members of Christ and make them members of a prostitute? Never!' (6.15) To unite a body with that of any kind of sex worker in their capacity as a sex worker is to unite that body and Christ with it with the social conditions that usually drive women and men into prostitution and the exploitation and violence that can characterize the sex worker's life. Christ stands alongside prostitutes as he does all exploited persons but he stands against exploitation. From a theological perspective another person's body cannot be reduced simply to a tool for self gratification; all bodies caught up in the mysterious body of the body of Christ are related and therefore unemotional

---

33. The Board of Social Responsibility of the Church of Scotland, *Report on Human Sexuality* (Edinburgh: Church of Scotland, 1994), para. 7.1.4.

34. Shakespeare, Gillespie-Sells and Davies, *The Sexual Politics of Disability*, pp. 131-34.

sex, sex that is detached from relationship, is a counter sign to the body of Christ.

The use of pornography is also a problematic area for many disabled people. Once again some feel that they have a right to purchase and use pornography for sexual gratification because it is the only form of sexual gratification open to them.[35] A theology informed by feminism will be deeply uncomfortable with the use of pornography[36] by anyone because it involves the sexual exploitation of the powerful by the less powerful, the erotic pleasure lying in the playing out of those power relations. The objectification of a person made in the image and likeness of God and therefore made for relationship not exploitation and objectification is sinful. The disabled body has often been used in this way and problems caused by fetishism among non-disabled people often hamper the formation of relationships.[37] So the body of Christ will oppose the production, sale and use of pornography by anyone. Mindful, however, of the marginalization of disabled people and the part the Church has played in creating and reinforcing that marginalization, members of the body of Christ can never simply take away with one hand without giving with another. The Church has in its deposit a whole body of erotic literature, from the Song of Songs through to the writings of the mediaeval mystics, which celebrates sexual desire and activity in a non-exploitative way and as a unitive, hospitable expression of love that is intricately related to the search for God. The celebration of human bodiliness and sexual desire in such a way as to arouse the body and the spirit is a noble part of Christian tradition and while condemning pornography the Church should be welcoming and encouraging the creation of erotic texts.

35. Shakespeare, Gillespie-Sells and Davies, *The Sexual Politics of Disability*, pp. 122-24.

36. Defining pornography as including 'any sexually explicit material (books, magazines, movies, videos, TV shows, telephone services, live sex acts) produced for the purpose of sexual arousal by eroticising violence, power, humiliation, abuse, dominance, degradation, or mistreatment of any person, male or female, and usually produced for monetary profit. Any sexually explicit material that depicts children is pornography.' (The Office of the General Assembly, The Presbyterian Church [USA], *Pornography: Far from the Song of Songs* [Louisville, KY, 1988], p. 11).

37. Shakespeare, Gillespie-Sells and Davies, *The Sexual Politics of Disability*, pp. 124-31.

Conclusion

Reflection upon the disabled body is essential in any attempt to theologize around sexuality because the disabled body reminds all of us
that embodiment (as our ancestors in faith knew well) is always an
ambiguous experience even when rid of a dualistic interpretation, and
that all bodies, like all aspects of human experience, are in need of
redemption in the ongoing project of creation. Yet the symbol of the
disabled God also confirms the full humanity of disabled people and
their place at the heart of the body of Christ. Centralizing the disabled
body in the body of Christ serves to remind the Church of its call to
participate in the continuing creation of the world through parody of the
necessarily incomplete and transitory cultural constructions of human
identity and the practices that are attached to them. The concept of
participation in a 'permeable, transcorporeal and transpositional' body,
which is something that disabled people may be better able to understand than the temporarily able, offers creative possibilities for the sharing of experience and pleasure as well as pain between disabled and the
temporarily able. The disabled body raises issues around sexuality,
somewhat detached from issues of gender, that challenge the Church to
face its own compliance with an over-romanticized idealization of heterosexual desire produced by modernity and to engage in a parody-
critique not only of modernity's construction of sexuality but of its own
embrace of it.

'CANONIZED FOR LOVE': PLEASURE AND DEATH IN MODERNITY[*]

Grace M. Jantzen

'For God's sake hold your tongue, and let me love…'

So says John Donne in his poem 'The Canonization' to those who would chide him for putting his sexual pleasure ahead of political expediency, honour, or fortune, as he had done by secretly marrying Anne More, the sixteen-year-old niece of his employer, much to the latter's displeasure. Donne, in the early years of the seventeenth century, marks a new step in the genealogy of sex, a step that would prove decisive for the development of sex in secular modernity and in modern feminism. Whereas there were dominant voices in the church that had taught that sex was for procreation only, and that pleasure was suspect if not downright sinful, Donne claims sexual pleasure as a core value. Indeed, in this poem he suggests sexual pleasure as a criterion for sainthood. Whereas canonization—the process by which the church declares someone a saint—had most often been reserved for those who had abstained from sex, Donne in this poem and many others overturns this putative value of virginity. It is not for abstinence that honour will be accorded, but for sexual pleasure and prowess: we will be 'canonized for love' (Hollander and Kermode 1973: 526-27).

But this is to over-simplify. Although it is certainly true that the Catholic Church had emphasized virginity, it must not be forgotten that marriage was a sacrament. In many mediaeval writings, particularly those for monks and nuns, chastity and virginity were taken as a supreme good, and marriage a lesser path. Nevertheless, this emphasis on virginity was directed to those who had renounced marriage or were considering doing so; and side by side with it was an emphasis which

* I am grateful to the John Rylands Trust for their support of this and all my research; and to my colleagues, especially Professors Elaine Graham and Graham Ward, for their perceptive conversations.

should not be overlooked on the lawfulness, validity, and even sacramental nature of marriage. If this were taken seriously, it would mean that sexual pleasure, at least within marriage, could be recognized as a sign and source of divine grace, not a sin or shame. Although this sacramental nature of sex was often lost sight of by those who took the guilty and confused teachings of such Church Fathers as Augustine and Jerome as normative, it was nevertheless firmly embedded in the Catholic faith. And John Donne had been brought up a Catholic (Sabine 1996, 1992).

Now, although the Reformation in Europe and the rise of the Puritans in England had shifted the emphasis from the monastery to the family as the site where sanctity could be pursued, and extolled the merits of child-bearing and even the legitimacy of sex within marriage, it nevertheless rejected the Catholic teaching that marriage was a sacrament. For Puritans, marriage was a legal contract, entered into for the purpose of procreation and the orderly inheritance of property. During the Protectorate the ceremony took place not in church but in a magistrate's office, and the Directory of Public Worship replaced the Bible or Prayer Book in its administration.[1] Although the family was emphasized, family relationships, including the times and manner of sexual relations in marriage, were carefully circumscribed and defined in detail by such writers as William Gouge in his *Of Domesticall Duties* (1626). Sexual relationships outside of marriage, whether same sex or heterosexual, were completely proscribed.

John Donne was a cradle Catholic, born in 1572. After some resistance, during which his manner of life and his sexually explicit poems earned him the reputation of something of a rake, he eventually became a conforming Protestant, and during his marriage to Anne More, took holy orders and finally became Dean of St Paul's. In his early poems, he can be read as defiantly celebrating sexual pleasure; but it has been argued in his relationship with Anne he at least sometimes saw sexuality in sacramental terms, as a means of grace (Sabine 1996; Guibbory 1996). With his turn to Protestantism, however, he becomes more and more uncertain of this, and is filled with fear, guilt and an expectation of punishment expressed in obsession with death. When Anne More dies at the age of 33, bearing their twelfth child, Donne, unusually for

---

1. For an example of one couple to whom this caused distress, see the Memoirs of Lady Halkett in Loftis (ed.), 1979. This was, of course, some twenty years after Donne wrote; but in his writings one can sense the direction of the wind.

the time, pledges to remain single; and his poetry and prose thereafter are filled with agonizing conflict between guilt at the love he had and still has for Anne and his unwillingness to relinquish that love as he feels he must do to please a jealous God.

There is, of course, a huge industry of literary criticism around the writings of Donne, and it would be foolish to present my interpretation as the only possible one. What I do wish to suggest, however, is that if we look at Donne's writings in terms of the question of sexual pleasure as sacrament, then we can see that the transition to secularism taken up by modern feminists is by no means unambiguous for a reclamation of sexual pleasure as a good for women. With the secularism of which English Puritanism was a harbinger, sexual pleasure is no longer sacramental. God is removed from sex; and while modern feminists now claim sexual pleasure as our right and reject the double standards that have hitherto prevailed in the West, this sexual pleasure has been emptied of the divine. Has it therefore lost its power to be transformative? While in no way wanting to return to the guilt and misogyny around sexual pleasure that has characterized much of its genealogy in Western discourse, I wish to suggest that in modernity sexual pleasure comes in a constellation that feminists have been slow to examine; and when we do so, we find some unsavoury elements which should lead us to reconsider the whole symbolic of sexual discourse and its place in the framework of modernity.

What I wish to do in this article, therefore, is to reconsider sexual pleasure in its setting in the Western cultural symbolic, using the work of John Donne to do so. I shall claim that sexual pleasure does not come on its own: it is part of the package of secular modernity in the West. That package includes things that women value and from which, arguably, we benefit: educational and career opportunities, better health care, the vote, religious freedom. But it also includes less welcome dimensions: an identification of sex and violence, a virulent individualism, oppressive economic and symbolic structures, and, above all, an obsessive linkage of sexual pleasure and death. John Donne is by no means the only early modern writer in whose work these aspects emerge. They can be found in his work with particular clarity, however; so I shall use his writings as a focus for the triangulation of religion, culture and gender in modernity. A recognition of some of the aspects that emerge will be a basis for rethinking feminism's reclamation of sexual pleasure.

1. *Whose Pleasure? Whose Death?*

Perchance as torches which must ready be,
Men light and put out, so thou deal'st with me,
Thou cam'st to kindle, goest to come; then I
Will dream that hope again, but else would die.
('The Dream' in Hollander and Kermode 1973: 533).

Donne's poem, one of his early ones, is a poem of a sexual dream from which he wakes unsure of whether the woman with whom he is sleeping is actually inviting him to pleasure or whether he is merely dreaming that she is. In these few lines we have the thick tissue of sexual word play typical of Donne: the allusions to erection and detumescence, always a preoccupation for Donne, are obvious; as of course is the double meaning of 'come'. Here, too, is the common double meaning of 'die': orgasm, the little death, is what Donne wants, and he is determined to have it whether dreaming or awake.

The identification of sexual pleasure and death, common in early modern writers, is particularly acute in Donne, from his early poems when he was 'Jack the Rake' to his later pious meditations and Holy Sonnets. In his poetry and his sermons, his ribald presentations of amorous encounters and his devotional prayers, from first to last Donne makes death central to all his thinking. His most famous sermon, 'Death's Duelle, or, a Consolation to the Soule, against the Dying Life, and Living Death of the Body,' was preached when, as Dean of St Paul's, he himself was dying before the eyes of his listeners. Isaac Walton, in his biography of Donne, tells how after he had preached this sermon he hired a painter to prepare his monument, and posed for him standing on an urn in his winding sheet 'so tied with knots at his head and feet and his hands so placed as dead bodies are usually fitted to be shrouded and put into their coffin or grave' (Walton in Hollander and Kermode 1973: 1017). The painting complete, Donne retired to his bed and stayed there until he expired some weeks later.

It is remarkable how many of Donne's early poems, often celebrating sexual encounters, have the word 'die' in the last line: for example,

Whatever dies, was not mixed equally;
If our two loves be one, or, thou and I
Love so alike that none do slacken, none can die.
('The Good Morrow' in Hollander and Kermode 1973: 525).

The irony, of course, is that the making one of two loves in sexual encounter, consummation, will ensure precisely the 'slackening' and metaphorical death that Donne ostensibly wishes to avoid. If he succeeds in love, he must fail. The same irony is apparent in 'The Dream', already quoted, which also ends with 'die'. Given the sexual meaning, Donne will 'die' whether he chooses to make love or to return to his sexual dream. These examples stand for many more that revolve around sexual pleasure and death; and the regularity with which they are linked together in Donne and many other early modern writers should begin to arouse feminists' suspicions. Just whose pleasure is this, and whose death?

These suspicions would be strengthened by noting that although Donne is supposedly writing about love for a woman, such love does not preclude virulent misogyny, a misogyny already apparent in his youthful writings on such topics as whether it is possible to find virtue in women, or why anyone should think that women have souls (Abrams 1968: 524-25). This glares out again in his poem 'The Relic', which, like the ones already quoted, again links love and death.

> When my grave is broke up again
> Some second guest to entertain,
> (For graves have learned that woman-head
> To be to more than one a bed)
> And he that digs it spies
> A bracelet of bright hair about the bone,
> Will he not let us alone...?
> ('The Relic' in Hollander and Kermode 1973: 544).

That Donne should attribute promiscuity to women in this way is, to say the least, a glaring instance of double standards, given his own reputation at the time. Indeed in his poems of amorous conquest it often seems that the subjectivity of the woman, and her pleasure, is hardly important, so long as he can have sex: I shall return to this hedonistic theme in section four. For the moment the point to note is that along with Donne's urgency to have sexual pleasure, indeed inseparable from it, there is in Donne considerable fear and insecurity, often projected on to women, and often linked with death.

This suggestion that women are blameworthy is intensified in poems like 'Nocturnal upon St Lucy's Day'. In this poem Donne appropriates death to himself as though it were somehow uniquely his, or at least as though he is more closely identified with death than are other people; and moreover that he is so by the greatness of his love.

> For I am every dead thing,
> In whom love wrought new alchemy...
> He ruined me, and I am re-begot
> Of absence, darkness, death; things which are not.
> All others, from all things, draw all that's good,
> Life, soul, form, spirit, whence they being have;
> I, by love's limbeck, am the grave
> Of all, that's nothing.
> ('Nocturnal' in Hollander and Kermode 1973: 536).

The misogyny here is much more subtle than in the previous poem, but it is here nonetheless. Since it is love that enables the alchemist to do his work of ruin, woman must be to blame: if she did not draw such passion from him, Donne would not be the victim of such deadly desire. Maureen Sabine, in her commentary on this poem, suggests that it was written at the death bed of Donne's wife Anne in 1617. If she is right, it makes the case worse, since Donne would then be using her death as an occasion to blame her for his own, an irony not decreased by the fact that she died giving birth to their twelfth child.[2]

It was a commonplace of early modernity, repeated by Donne, that sexual 'spending' shortens a man's life, 'since each such act, they say, diminisheth the length of life a day' ('Farewell to Love' in Hollander and Kermode 1973: 543). In the light of the frequency of women's death in childbirth during this period, the unintended irony only reveals further the extent of male self-absorption and possibly guilt. Yet in Donne, as in many others, it is the woman who brings death, and she brings it through sexual pleasure. She brought it in the first place in Eve, who subjected all humanity to death through her sin. She brings it in her temporality and mutability into which she introduces everyone born from her womb. And she brings it again, a bit at a time, on each occasion of sexual intercouse.

> For that first marriage was our funeral:
> One woman at one blow, then kill'd us all,
> And singly, one by one, they kill us now.
> We do delightfully our selves allow
> To that consumption; and profusely blind,

---

2. This is not Sabine's interpretation. She instead sees in this and other poems an unconventional insistence on the religious value of sexual passion (Sabine 1996).

We kill ourselves, to propagate our kind.
('Anatomy of the World' in Patrides 1985: 331).[3]

'We' are obviously male: there is no comment about what happens to women. The womb, the source of birth, is taken over for a symbolic of death. Jonathan Dollimore observes that

> In his last sermon Donne tells his congregation that the womb is not a place of life but a place of death from which we are delivered into 'the manifold deaths of this world': we come from the mother's womb 'to seek a grave,' and 'we celebrate our own funerals with cries, even at our birth; as though our threescore and ten years of life were spent in our mother's labour, and our circle made up in the first point thereof' (1998: 73-74).

One could argue that it was Donne's absorption with death that framed his fear and fascination with women/sexual pleasure; or one could equally argue that his attitude to women as objects for his gratification ensured his continued entanglement in an obsession with death. Donne unhesitatingly links women and death in his symbolic structure so that the two preoccupations reinforce one another, as they have in the Western symbolic ever since.

Donne's is an extreme case; and one might argue that it is perfectly possible for a feminist to emphasize sexual pleasure without buying into the obsession with death which Donne links with it. While I think that this is true and important, I suggest that it is much less straightforward than it sounds. The symbolic of Western modernity mixes sexual pleasure and death together with other ingredients—violence, dominance, and hedonistic individualism—in such a way that it becomes difficult to emphasize one without the rest, as I shall show in the sections that follow. If feminists wish to claim our sexual pleasure as a good—and we do—then we need also to destabilize the whole death-dealing structure in which it is embedded in modernity, and develop a way of thinking and living in which sexual pleasure is instead embedded in a symbolic of flourishing (cf. Jantzen 1998: Chapter 7).

2. Battering to Save?

It must be granted that for all Donne's use of women as sexual objects, a theme to which I shall return, his early poems seldom valorize overt

---

3. I have silently modernized spelling and punctuation here and elsewhere in quoting Donne.

violence; and in this contrast favourably to those of some of his contemporaries. Seduction and conquest are Donne's themes, but not outright brutality. All the more shocking, then, is his coupling of sex and
violence in what is probably the most famous of all his Holy Sonnets.

> Batter my heart, three-personed God; for you
> As yet but knock, breathe, shine, and seek to mend;
> That I might rise and stand, o'erthrow me, and bend
> Your force, to break, blow, burn, and make me new...
> Take me to you; imprison me, for I
> Except you enthral me, never shall be free,
> Nor ever chaste, except you ravish me.
> (Hollander and Kermode 1973: 552).

If rape is Donne's religious/sexual fantasy in relation to himself, it is
hardly surprising that when he writes about women they will be construed as objects for domination.

What was it that made Donne feel himself so impervious to divine
love that God would have to rape him in order to set him free from his
enthrallment? As already mentioned, in about 1602 Donne had secretly
married Anne More, who was the neice of his employer Sir Thomas
Egerton, the Lord Keeper. The ensuing scandal resulted in Donne being
dismissed from his post, and even briefly imprisoned; and when he was
released he and Anne went to live in the country and seem to have been
in some poverty, especially as their family grew. The marriage is usually presented as a happy one; and as already discussed, it has been
argued that during this time Donne claimed the sacramental power of
sexual pleasure as a means of transformative grace. Yet it is also true
that during this period Donne wrote an extended treatise, *Biothanatos*,
in which he argued for the lawfulness of suicide: this and some of his
poems of the time reveal deep unhappiness and restlessness.

Above all, there is a sense of guilt, a guilt which intensifies as he
reflects on his relationship with Anne, his sexual passion which he can
neither deny nor accept. The internal struggle continued even after she
died: even then he could not renounce his love for her, nor could he
believe that God would countenance such love. In poem after poem he
pleads with God for forgiveness and for divine intervention into his
passion for his (deceased) wife. Donne's God is a jealous God, jealous
and unforgiving of any other love, even Donne's love for his wife,
which must be excised from his heart if he is to escape damnation. In a
sermon, Donne cited with approval St Jerome's condemnation of a man

who felt the sexual passion for his wife that he would have felt for a whore: such passion is adulterous and idolatrous even if the couple are married (*Sermons* 2.345).

Thus in his poems Donne struggles with the guilt of sexual pleasure, a guilt which is sure of punishment and which therefore turns violence upon himself, whether in thoughts of suicide or in his fantasies of divine rape. Many of the Holy Sonnets are meditations on the Final Judgment, and try to arrive at the reassurance that in spite of his continuing guilt (as he saw it), he will not be damned.

> Thou has made me, And shall thy work decay?
> Repair me now, for now mine end doth haste,
> I run to death, and death meets me as fast,
> And all my pleasures are like yesterday,
> I dare not move my dim eyes any way,
> Despair behind, and death before doth cast
> Such terror, and my feeble flesh doth waste
> By sin in it, which it t'wards hell doth weight...
> (Patrides 1985: 434).

By the end of the poem, Donne has managed to convince himself that God will save him. The reassurance soon evaporates, however, and in the next Sonnet he begins again on the same theme of guilt and damnation.

> Oh my black soul! now thou art summoned
> By sickness, death's herald, and champion;
> Thou art like a pilgrim, which abroad hath done
> Treason...
> (Patrides 1985: 436).

It is as though he can never gain adequate reassurance; and he dwells on the terrors of judgment, as well as on bodily decay and dissolution, with a morbid fascination. He shows the same macabre fixation in his Sermons as Dean of St Paul's, still occupied with guilt about his sexual passion even though his wife had died years before.

> If my soul could ask one of those worms which my dead body shall produce, Will you change with me? that worm would say, No; for you are like to live eternally in torment; for my part, I can live no longer, than the putrid moisture of your body will give me leave, and therefore I will not change; nay, would the Devil himself change with a damned soul? I cannot tell...
> (Quoted in Wilson 1983: 13).

The guilt Donne struggled with in relation to his sexual passion was often worked out in his poems in a play on the names of his wife and himself, 'More' and 'Donne/done'. In his 'Hymn to Christ,' written two years after Anne's death, he seems to be trying to bargain with God, offering to sacrifice his home and well-being to God if only God will forgive his sins. He confronts God with the challenge,

> ...as Thou
> Art jealous, Lord, so I am jealous now;
> Thou lov'st not, till from loving more, Thou free
> My soul... (Abrams 1968: 522).

Donne must be set free from his love for his wife before he can love God acceptably: sexual passion has turned into an idol, not a sacrament.

This struggle against his love for 'more' is most pronounced in 'Hymn to God the Father' written a few years later. It begins by asking pardon for the sins in which he was conceived, 'original sin' present in his parents' act of begetting him:

> Wilt thou forgive that sin where I begun,
> Which is my sin, though it were done before?

In the sexual passion that resulted in his conception, his parents sinned, and he, like all human beings, was tainted with this sin. But in his own sexual passion he continues that same sin; and even if God will forgive him for this, it is not enough, because he still feels passion for his wife. The refrain is repeated, playing on the two names:

> When thou hast done, thou hast not done,
> For I have more...
> (Hollander and Kermode 1973: 555).

At last he admits to his 'sin of fear' that at his death he will be condemned; and pleads for God to swear by his Son that this will not be so.

> And having done that, thou hast done,
> I fear no more...

No more what? Damnation, obviously; but given that in the whole poem 'more' plays on his wife's name there is here a recognition of the fear which she—or his feelings for her—aroused in him, from which only death will free him. Achsah Guibbory has argued that in this last stanza Donne might be recognizing that the one really unforgiveable sin is despair (Guibbory 1996: 212); yet even if this is so, Donne still feels it incumbant upon him to surrender his love for Anne as the only way to peace with God. Sexual pleasure, even in marriage, has come to be understood not as a sacrament, a means of grace whereby lives can be touched and transformed, but as an idolatrous sin of the flesh; and Donne's inadequacy is measured in the very fact of his continued love for his wife. This inadequacy, this pleasure, can only be exterminated by ruthless divine battering, a rape which will make him never want sex again.

We have, here, a mixture of guilt, violence and sexual confusion set in religious terms. It is a lethal mixture that reaches far into modernity even while its overt religious framework has largely been dropped. The symbolic of sex and violence ubiquitous in contemporary culture bespeaks harshly repressed feelings of guilt and inadequacy, failure to measure up to internalized expectations. That this violence is then often visited by men on the objects of their passion—that far more women are battered, raped, or killed by their husbands or lovers than by strangers—is therefore all of a piece with the way in which sexual passion is construed in modernity. Feminists need to think long and hard about what, of this mixture, we wish to reclaim, and how we can do so without being sucked into the whole deadly package. Clearly it will not do to simply celebrate our own sexual pleasure free from guilt or condemnation by a jealous God, important though it is to do so. Unless we also address the deeper sources of guilt and anxiety in modernity, its violent manifestations will continue.

3. *Exporting Sex, Exporting Death*

As already noted, guilt and fear about sexual pleasure far too often turn into violence. In Donne's case such violence was largely turned in on himself, especially in fantasies about divine punishment as we have seen. However, there is no reason to suppose that Donne himself was violent to women, even though his symbolic of sexual pleasure and guilt is one in which violence could easily have found a place. Nevertheless, one of the features of Donne's construction of sexual pleasure as it was taken up in modernity is the way in which it is intertwined with the developing discourse and practice of violent colonialism; and this interconnection, I suggest, should again caution feminists against an easy appropriation of the right to sexual pleasure. At whose expense is such pleasure claimed? If women from 'third world' contexts are suspicious of the Western feminism of modernity partly because of its sexual permissiveness, is this because of prudery on their part, or is it perhaps because in terms of both the rhetoric and the practice of sexuality, they have too often paid the cost of Western sexual pleasure? It is a truism to say that seventeenth-century thought regularly sexualized its colonial exploits, with the 'new' lands and native peoples portrayed as feminine, and the colonizing power by implication as male. What is less often noticed is how this rhetoric and practice shaped the symbolic of sexual pleasure for modernity in ways which I believe feminists should ponder before adopting an uncritical acceptance of sexual pleasure as a central human value. Again, Donne's writings focus the shifts in the genealogy of pleasure.

Although English colonizing in North America had begun in the late sixteenth century, it was not until the early seventeenth century that English merchants began to see its economic possibilities and started to offer major financial backing. At the same time, cartography and a great interest in maps was developing, an interest in exotic foreign places but also an identification by English people of the particular space which they themselves inhabited. As if to indicate this claiming of space, the king's body, which had once been prominent in maps, was now placed on its margins. The marginalization was symbolic as well as literal: people were identifying their own places and the places of others they knew; they were also increasingly aware of vast spaces unknown to them which they thought of as empty and passive, waiting to be claimed like a young maiden awaiting a husband.

Donne's early poem, 'Love's Progress', is a witty and sexually explicit description of a female body for purposes of male passion; the various parts of the anatomy are like parts of the world that must be traversed before coming to the 'centric part'. Donne actually offers two separate routes, one longer and the other shorter, as though one could circumnavigate the globe going either west or east and come to the same place in the end. Indeed anyone not making for that end is as 'one that goes to sea for nothing but to make him sick' ('Love's Progress' in Hollander and Kermode 1973: 520). The first and longer way begins with the woman's hair, which 'a forest is of ambushes, of springs, snares, fetters and manacles'. Next comes the brow, where one could be either 'becalmed' or 'shipwrecked'; then the nose like a meridian, cheeks like two hemispheres, the two lips like ambrosial Canary Islands, and so on down the anatomy, each part linked to parts of the world

(India, the Atlantic, and so on) which are treated as obstacles to be overcome in order to reach the goal. As Walter Lim, in his fine book *The Arts of Empire* puts it, 'the treacherous journey across the ocean is inseparable from the destructive nature of feminine beauty and its charms. After having highlighted in detail the treacherous terrain of the female body, the male speaker proceeds to offer a more direct route to "the centric part," beginning this time with the lower extremities' (1998: 69).

When seventeenth-century writers wanted to encourage colonization, they could write about the lands to be possessed as exotic and enticing virgins; when their purpose was to legitimize conquest and violence the rhetoric would be in terms of devilry and witchcraft. Either way, the land and its peoples were characterized as the female Other in relation to male desire for control described in terms of sexual passion. When, for example, Samuel Purchas, chaplain to the archbishop of Canterbury, wanted to foster colonial enterprise in Virginia early in the century, he wrote:

> But look upon Virginia; view her lovely looks (howsoever like a modest Virgin she is now veiled with wild coverts and shady woods, expecting rather ravishment than marriage from her native savages) survey her heavens, elements, situation; her division by arms of bays and rivers into so goodly and well-proportioned limbs and members; her virgin portion being nothing impaired, nay not yet improved, in Nature's best legacies; her neighbouring regions and seas so commodious and obsequious; her opportunities for offence and defence; and in all these you shall see, that she is worth the wooing and loves of the best husband (1625: XIX, 242).

It is a feminization of the land; but the trope only works because it rests upon and reasserts male assumptions about their right to sexual pleasure, a pleasure characterized by possession and mastery.

But what happens when that mastery is challenged? Then it must be violently reasserted, with a very different portrayal of the rebellious but still feminized Other. In 1622, several hundred English colonists in Virginia were killed in an uprising of native Americans who had grievances about English presence and practices. This precipitated still more violent acts by the English. A war of extermination was declared by the governor of the colony. The accompanying rhetoric was a rhetoric which portrayed the native peoples as demonic savages, ruthless, utterly without God and with no spark of human goodness, their godless nature revealed by their nakedness and sexual practices. Donne's friend

Christopher Brooke wrote 'A Poem on the Late Massacre in Virginia' in which he describes Indians as 'the very dregs, garbage, and spawn of the earth' and looks for their utter destruction (Lim 1998: 73).

Whatever Donne thought of Brooke's exhortation to genocide, his own preferred methods were more subtle. In November 1622, as Dean of St Paul's, he preached a sermon to the Virginia company which advocated conversion of the Indians rather than their extermination. He even suggested that God had particularly singled out England for such missionary activity. If his hearers will heed his admonition to preach the gospel, then

> ...you shall have made this island, which is but as the suberbs of the old world, a bridge, a gallery to the new; to join all to that world that shall never grow old, the kingdom of heaven, you shall add persons to this kingdom, and to the kingdom of heaven, and add names to the books of our chronicles, and to the Book of Life (1622: X, 281).

This, coupled with obedience to the divine command to dominate the earth and make it yield its bounty (which in English perspective the Indians were not doing) was to be the motivation for colonization. Though the methods Donne advocated were less harsh than those of some of his contemporaries, the goal, English mastery, was the same, and the mastery could now be carried forward in God's name.

The consequences of these various measures of mastery for native Americans were predictably horrific. But there were consequences, too, for the developing symbolic of sexual pleasure. No longer sacramental, pleasure itself was now increasingly constructed in terms of mastery, a need for control and domination that bespeaks deep-rooted anxiety about identity and fear of difference. If that mastery could be obtained by compliance, well and good; it could even be seen to be godly. But by fair means or foul, sexual pleasure is seen as a right, and on a model of conquest, even as the body is seen as a map to be appropriated and explored.

In Donne's 'Hymn to God my God, in my Sickness' he plays on the analogy of the body as a map. His physicians 'are grown cosmographers, and I their map, who lie flat on this bed'; and he describes himself as sailing west—that is declining—through the hot strait of fever (Hollander and Kermode 1973: 554-55). All the places of the world, the Pacific Sea, Jerusalem, Gibralter, can be scrutinized and evaluated in terms of his immortal destiny. As Walter Lim points out, Donne in this poem once again speaks in the language of a technology of control. The anatomist as cartographer possesses an omniscience that is the attribute of deity. This fantasy of being in control of the world, figured in the activity of scrutinizing a cartographic parchment, cannot ultimately be separated from the economy of desire: of setting forth to bring under control the wide space of the New World and the metonymized body of the woman (1996: 84).

The combination of sexual desire and anxiety in a desacralized world becomes an urgency for dominion and displaced violence.

Again, feminists would prefer to believe that we can claim the right to sexual pleasure while rejecting the ideology and practice of violence and domination with which it has been constructed in modernity. Indeed we might wish to insist that it is precisely in claiming our own pleasure as women that we are subverting the masculinist ideology that must always assume a missionary position. While I want to applaud the importantly disruptive impact of feminism on the symbolic of sexual pleasure, I do not think that we should suppose that all is now well. The colonialism of the seventeenth century continues in new guises, closely linked with Western insistence on the right to sexual pleasure: for example, pharmaceutical companies can test products ranging from contraceptives and drugs against AIDS and to assist new reproductive technologies with far fewer restrictions in 'developing' countries than in the West; and sex tourism is a growth industry in which the rhetoric of sexual pleasure as a private good draws its life from the bodies of women and children in economically deprived countries. Feminists who deplore such injustices need to consider how our claiming of sexual pleasure might collude with it if that claim privatizes pleasure and thus does not take its place within wider concerns for justice. Moreover, we have only to remember the 'determination and resolve' of Western leaders to stamp their will upon the world, by diplomacy if possible but by bombing campaigns if not, and to be conscious of the sexualization and eroticization of the violence of such campaigns, to see that we are far from free of the symbolic of sexual pleasure that packages it with death, violence and mastery.

4. *The Pleasure of her Sex*

All these themes come together in another way when we notice the self-referential nature of the emphasis on sexual pleasure in the modern symbolic, a theme again significantly focused by Donne. I begin this discussion with an early poem, 'To His Mistress Going to Bed' (Hollander and Kermode 1973: 523-24), in which Donne verbally undresses the nameless woman in an extended sexual fantasy wherein he removes her clothes piece by piece. His attention, though ostensibly on her, is actually on himself and his own sexual arousal, for which she serves as a pretext. He lingers over her girdle, her breastplate, her busk and gown; but he does not mention her actual body, let alone her face. Rather, he contrasts her angelic spirit with an evil spirit, not in relation to her but by measuring his own response: 'those set our hairs, but these our flesh upright'; and he concentrates on his own 'roving hands'. The lines that follow equate sexual exploration with the discovery of other worlds, with colonization and dominion, as Donne 'dis-covers' the woman's body:

> O my America, my new found land,
> My kingdom, safeliest when with one man manned,
> My mine of precious stones, my empery,
> How blest am I in this discovering thee!

Is *she* also 'blest', I wonder? Does he care? The poem crystallizes the egocentric shaping of the cultural symbolic, in which new lands, like women, are taken as existing not for themselves or even as having their own name, but for men's exploitation and conquest, where sex and violence are self-reflexive images of one another. Indeed by the end of the poem Donne's absorption with himself is so complete that rather than continuing to undress his mistress he hurriedly strips himself:

> To teach thee, I am naked first, why then
> What needs't thou have more covering than a man?

But the question of need should surely be directed back at Donne. The intensity and culminating urgency of Donne's fantasy leads Thomas Docherty to interpret the poem as 'a study not in sexual relation but rather in auto-eroticism, masturbation, talking to the isolated self' (1986: 81). It is the male, indeed the Phallus, which Docherty points out constitutes 'the stable point of reference, the Self which explores, exploits and determines the boundaries and worth of the Other, here the space of the female body' (1986: 81-82) in a narcissistic attempt to determine its own boundaries and worth. The woman is there, like the land, not for herself but for his sexual pleasure through which he constitutes his self-identity by mastery of her. To the extent that she might have an identity of her own she is feared, obliterated if possible, and symbolically linked with death: *man's* death, which she brings about in sexual terms through his very desire of her.

In poem after poem Donne focuses entirely on himself and his own feelings, using sexual pleasure and women as the means of doing so. Thus for instance in 'The Fever' he writes,

> Oh do not die, for I shall hate
>> All women so when thou art gone,
> That thee I shall not celebrate
>> When I remember, thou wast one.
> (Hollander and Kermode 1973: 529).

The poem carries no account of the beloved, no distress for her, but only for himself; indeed Donne's consolation is that he 'had rather owner be of thee one hour, than all else forever' (530). If that is meant to be a compliment, I wonder how the woman in question felt about such ownership. Again, in 'Song' he writes:

> Sweetest love, I do not go,
>> For weariness of thee,
> Nor in the hope the world can show
>> A fitter love for me;
> But since that I
>> Must die at last, 'tis best
> To use myself in jest
>> Thus by feigned deaths to die.
> (Hollander and Kermode 1973: 528).

Best for whom? For the woman? Even if Donne learns how to die lightheartedly by thus leaving the woman, what could she gain by it? Those are questions Donne never considers in his poem, which can, of course, also be read as his quasi-apology for impotence following the 'little death', indeed each reading contains the other. Even so, however, there is no concern for her fulfilment or how she might feel about it: 'think that we are but turned aside to sleep...'—but does *she* want to sleep? Paavo Rissanen dates this poem about 1611, after 10 years of marriage which Rissanen describes in rosy terms; and he reads this poem as expressing 'genuine tenderness' as Donne takes leave of his wife to go on a trip abroad with Sir Robert Drury (Rissanen 1983: 24). The dating, however, is uncertain; and so, I suggest, is the interpretation.

In Donne's anxieties about his sin and guilt, and his obsession with death, his preoccupation with himself continues unabated, not only through his 'rakish' youth but also in what are usually taken to be devout meditations and semons. In lines that have often been quoted, he writes,

> Who bends not his ear to any bell which upon any occasion rings? But who can remove it from that bell which is passing a piece of himself out of this world? No man is an island, entire of itself; every man is a piece of the continent, a part of the main; if a clod be washed away by the sea, Europe is the less, as well as if a promontory were, as well as if a manor of thy friend's or of thine own were. Any man's death diminishes me, because I am involved in mankind; and therefore never send to know for whom the bell tolls; it tolls for thee ('Meditation XVII' in Hollander and Kermode 1973: 557).

These lines are frequently taken as an indication of our profound connection with one another, against the atomistic individualism whose deep ruts run from the seventeenth century into modernity (cf. Rissanen 1973). I suggest that the opposite interpretation is more plausible. It is apparent that Donne's preoccupation is with himself as an individual at the very centre of this meditation: even other people's deaths are not thought of in terms of themselves, their lives, their relatives, but in relation to how it 'diminishes me'. Donne is not interested in finding out the name or identity of the deceased, but only in appropriating their death for his own spiritual advancement, 'if by this consideration of another's danger, I take mine own into contemplation, and so secure myself...' (557).

The hedonism and narcissistic individualism of modernity has often been remarked; and we can see Donne as helping to create the channel through which it would run to the present time, not least in the claiming of sexual pleasure. This pleasure is now disconnected from religious considerations, and seen in secular terms as the right of women as much as men. But if it thereby becomes an egoistic hedonism, does it lose its transformative power? While feminists rightly reject sexual oppression and double standards, and celebrate the pleasures of sexual passion, my suggestion in this article is that we do not sufficiently consider the ways in which our claiming of sexual rights, whether same sex or heterosexual, is interwoven with selfishness, domination, violence and death in the secular discourses of modernity. Indeed I would argue that feminists have lost more than we have gained in an unproblematized secularism in which sexual pleasure is no longer sacramental, no longer a means of grace and transformation. Of course we cannot go back to a premodern religious faith, nor should we want to. But as we claim our own forms of sexual pleasure in post/modernity, feminists who are still concerned with justice and the transformation of the world need to find ways to destabilize the patriarchal and racist structures of secular modernity, and find new ways to be canonized for love.[4]

Bibliography

Abrams, M.H. *et. al.* (eds.)
> 1968   *The Norton Anthology of English Literature: Major Authors Edition Revised* (New York: W.W. Norton and Co.)

Docherty, Thomas
> 1986   *John Donne, Undone* (London: Methuen).

Dollimore, Jonathan
> 1998   *Death, Desire and Loss in Western Culture* (New York: Routledge; Harmondsworth: Penguin Books).

Donne, John
> 1948   *The Sermons of John Donne* (10 vols.; ed. Evelyn Simpson and George R. Potter; Berkeley: University of California Press).

Gouge, William
> 1626   *Of Domesticall Duties* (London).

Guibbory, Achsah
> 1996   'Fear of "loving more": Death and the Loss of Sacramental Love', in M. Thomas Hester (ed.), *John Donne's 'desire of more': The Subject of Anne More Donne in his Poetry* (Newark: University of Delaware Press; London: Associated University Presses): 204-27.

Hollander, John, and Frank Kermode (eds.)
> 1973   *The Literature of Renaissance England* (New York: Oxford University Press).

Jantzen, Grace M.
> 1998   *Becoming Divine: Towards a Feminist Philosophy of Religion* (Manchester: Manchester University Press; Bloomington, IN: Indiana University Press).

Lim, Walter
> 1998   *The Arts of Empire: The Poetics of Colonialism from Ralegh to Milton* (Newark: University of Delaware Press; London: Associated University Presses).

Loftis, John (ed.)
> 1979   *The Memoirs of Anne, Lady Halkett and Ann, Lady Fanshawe* (Oxford: Clarendon Press).

Patrides, C.A. (ed.)
> 1985   *The Complete English Poems of John Donne* (London: Everyman: J.M. Dent).

4.   I have explored these themes further in 'Good Sex: Beyond Private Pleasure', forthcoming, and in Jantzen (1998).

Purchase, Samuel
1905–1907 'Virginias Verger: Or a Discourse shewing the benefits which may grow to this Kingdome from American English Plantations, and especially those of Virginia and Summer Ilands', in *Hakluytes Posthumous of Purchas His Pilgrimes: Contayning a History of the World in Sea Voyages and Lande Travells by Englishmen and Others*, XIX (20 vols.; Glasgow: James MacLehose and Sons, [1625]).

Rissanen, Paavo
1983 *John Donne's Doctrine of the Church* (Helsinki: The Finnish Society for Missiology and Ecumenics).

Sabine, Maureen
1992 *Feminine Engendered Faith: The Poetry of John Donne and Richard Crashaw* (London: Macmillan)
1996 'No Marriage in Heaven: John Donne, Anne Donne, and the Kingdom Come', in M. Thomas Hester (ed.), *John Donne's 'desire of more': The Subject of Anne More Donne in his Poetry* (Newark: University of Delaware Press; London: Associated University Presses): 228-55.

Wilson, A.N.
1983 *The Life of John Milton* (Oxford: Oxford Univesity Press).

INDECENT EXPOSURES: EXCESSIVE SEX AND THE CRISIS OF THEOLOGICAL REPRESENTATION

Marcella María Althaus-Reid

'What is truth, except for the representation of excess, if we cannot see what exceeds the possibility of seeing or what is intolerable for us to see..?' (Bataille 1981: 28)

As a Note of Protest on Aesthetically Correct Theologies

Are you a blonde summer woman who dresses in pastel colours or are you a winter woman like myself with dark eyes and hair who should dress in black to look her best? As a Third World theologian,[1] colouring fashion style provides me with a metaphor for the aesthetic (theo)logic of the West. In theology, the discourses from the margins have been re-absorbed by the centre in a sort of a 'Colour me beautiful' logic of representation, especially designed with women theologians in mind. In theology, as in fashion design, it has become a question of apparently knowing your colours. It saves you time to know which colour of scarf you should use for a job interview, but also to know which theological discourse is aesthetically correct for you, if poverty is your issue or questions of sexuality and identity. We are all accustomed to somehow expect that a British feminist theologian would not write a book on women in Whitfield,[2] while an Argentinian theologian cannot be preoccupied with sex but only with economics. However, in the same way that a British theologian may not consider what is involved in identity constructions while a woman is queuing for her giro, Third World women theologians may be considering issues of women and divine

---

1.   In this essay I will use the term 'Third World' instead of other terms more in vogue such as 'Two Thirds World', since it has been successfully reappropriated by people in my own Latin American theological discourse.

2.   Whitfield is a deprived area of Dundee, Scotland, where I used to work.

representation in a cultural context sometimes de-sexualized beyond the politics of motherhood and reproduction. We must all try to escape what has become accepted in wider circles of theology, that is, that we must remain using our right colouring in order to be taken seriously in our contributions. It has become clear for me at the moment that the crisis of representation in theology (divine and women's representation) is a welcome crisis brought about by women who refuse to use the right, expected colours according to race, gender, sexuality and culture. What has sex to do with hyperinflation and the external debt? Well, everything. There is a basic patriarchal epistemology, or common frame of assumptions and understanding of life and work behind the social organization of relationships and exchange systems. The marginaliza-tion of sexuality from issue-based theologies from poverty in my continent shows how far we are still from renouncing the masquerade of sexual ideology presented as theology, and that of course this needs to be engaged to our contexts. Mine is the context of urban poverty in Buenos Aires, and although I work and live in Scotland now, it is still part of my identity and form of thinking. This reflection is a piece of diasporic theology, in the hope that all our theology may always be somehow diasporic and scandalous as we engage deeply with *Others*, allowing them to challenge us beyond the comfortable frontiers pro-vided by centuries of representation of God in an androcentric universe. This is part of an excessive task: the exceeding of what limits our mem-ory of the past, our present reality and our visions for the future.

> [*'You see... I am GOD...*]
>
> -I am crazy…
> *- No. That is not true and you should look at me. Look! …Kiss me!*
> -But…in the presence of everybody?
> -Of course!' (Bataille 1981: 44-45)

This dialogue is taken from a novel written by the French philosopher Georges Bataille. It is part of a conversation between a woman–God and a poor man, a sort of mystical seeker. Bataille's genius in this novel has been to present God as a poor and 'sexually explicit' woman, since 'Madame Edwarda' is God incarnated as a prostitute. The woman–God is therefore a metaphor of God incarnated in a context of poverty, violence and sexuality. Theologically this is a very interesting challenge which deserves our consideration. A poor woman prostitute is repre-sented *as* God not from the excess of Orthodoxy (as is usually the case) but from the excess of Orthopraxis. The theological representations of

God usually come from Orthodoxy, that is, from the surplus of theoretical elaboration about God accumulated during centuries of Western Systematic Theology. These of course, are representations taken from the decent constructions of Orthodoxy: God inside the laws and customs of society although occasionally also challenging them from the margins. In this case, however, the image of God comes to us from the margins of the margins of the praxis of theology, if by that we understand searching for God in the midst of sexuality and poverty, which especially for women, always includes a sexual story too, even if it is only the consideration of marriage for the purpose of survival. The argument of Bataille's novel is simple: an anguished person searching for divine meaning in life encounters a prostitute in a brothel (Madame Edwarda) and she reveals herself as God. It is not through her words though, but in the intimacy of his relationship with Madame Edwarda and in the vision of her body ('Look...Kiss me!') that he receives the revelation of her transcendental, yet so bodily grounded divinity. In the story, Madame Edwarda has not only told him the truth but it happens that She is The Truth. And it is in this sordid context of poverty and women and sexuality that God reveals herself as a prostitute to a mystical seeker, by exposing her naked body but also her own anguished suffering as a woman. As Bataille himself recognizes, this is not a representation of a God of rational sense, and, we may add, at least not of a dualistic patriarchal rationality where body and soul are split. This is a God from the margins of poverty and sexuality and a non-dualistic understanding of grounded and 'excessive' theology: one that goes beyond the limits of common-sense representations.

This story, which was written under a pseudonym at the time as it was so scandalous, has never been taken up in Systematic Theology for a serious discussion on issues related to the representation of God. Suppose that following Paul Tillich, we wanted to say that any event or story can be a medium for revelation, and that the final revelation of faith can only be accepted if in it we can recognize the focus of a kind of self-denying transcendental truth (Tillich 1948: 77). As Tillich says, such a revelatory event provides us with the experience of the ultimate which is very near but very remote at the same time. 'Religious symbols are double-edged. They are directed toward the infinite which they symbolise and toward the finite through which they symbolise it' (1948: 63). Therefore, if we want to continue Tillich's thought, we will find that a prostitute is the perfect symbol of faith where economic and

sexual oppression are the boundaries of the incarnation (like being born
in occupied territory from a poor single mother was for Jesus) while the
prostitute's suffering and struggle may direct us toward the revelation
of divine justice at odds with patriarchal justice. The suffering body of
a woman becomes then the space of God, and her sex, the privileged
site of a transcendental meaning which does not exclude hyperinflation
and under-employment, but relates to them.

In French philosophy Luce Irigaray has elaborated a deep reflection
informed by the dialectics of the feminine lips and the epistemological
meaning of the embrace of a woman's sex. However, systematic theologians have not yet become completely aware of the importance of a
reflection based on the dialectic of *the lips of God*; the lips that Madame
Edwarda shows to the divine seeker as a testimony of her divinity,
while asking him to look at and kiss her as in a parallel episode with a
'doubting Thomas'. The reason for that exclusion of women's lips in
theological representations of God seems obvious, though. A theology
which takes seriously Madame Edwarda's metaphor of God would be
considered an *indecent exposure* of God, in a scandalous combination
of sexual persona and poverty. The problem is that this is a metaphor of
an excessive God represented in the excess of poverty and women's
sexuality. A God represented by the excess of sex from the margins
seems to be so deeply destabilizing and theologically threatening that it
makes us dismiss that sheer materiality of the representation of God as
Madame Edwarda almost instinctively.[3] However, that representation of
a woman–God is full of theological promise. For a start, it promises to
dis-cover for us a deeper understanding of the sacred in relation to
feminine sexuality. Second, it confronts us with the fact that the crisis
of theological representations of God, poverty and women are linked to
each other by close ties. Third, it makes obvious that our problem is not
only that as women we do not have a theological language, but on the
contrary, that we may have too much of it. We are not doing theology
from an empty space of symbolic systems but on the contrary, our work
is deeply attached to a theological method of discernment and representation embodied in the ideals of Androcentric Systematic Theology,
with all the traditions of argumentation, representation and inner logic
obeying androcentric forms of economic and sexual production. These

3.   A student from the USA said that she needed to reread one article I wrote on
Christology 'for women who like to do theology without using underwear' to
understand 'why she first felt so offended' (Althaus-Reid 1999: 39-51).

forms of production are basically obsessively sexual. They are based on dualistic epistemologies and sexual constructs of understanding reality. Our challenge as women in theological reflection is therefore, one of renunciation. We need to renounce and become strangers to faith and theology as metaphorical texts, in order to recover in this way the context of our discourses. This is our challenge: one of sexual concreteness in theological reflection, and in the quest for a non-transcendental feminist theology. This obeys the experience that we have as women, recognizing that Androcentric Theology has never been a transcendental theology. Its methods and concern (its whole orthodoxy) come from ideological (and sexually ideological) understandings of reality that have been systematically projected towards a construction of the sacred. This is therefore the reason why theology falls easy prey to 'masquerades', or carnival representations of reality which have been reified by sexual ideologies from the past. If we wanted to find a metaphor for Androcentric Theology, we would find it in the book of Esther from the Hebrew Scriptures, as nobody in that book is what s/he is supposed to be. In the book of Esther people's names are changed and identities are in struggle and disguise. Androcentric theologies cover, reorganize and disorganize bodies while adjudicating them false identities. God is also a case of false identity entrapped in the claim of transcendence, while in reality, one can hardly speak of transience if the concept of God cannot cross the pavement between a heterosexual and a lesbian; or between a prostitute and an Almighty Father. However, the path of sexual theologies has taught us how to dis-cover the face of God in the midst of people's relationships: a method and a model of finding God from below. A transcendental theology done from below, finding its transcendence in finitude, and in the finitude of women's exploitation and desires. Madame Edwarda as a scandalous God, provides us with an exercise of representing God from below in a methodology of indecent exposure at the confluence of women, poverty and sexuality. It is in metaphors like this that we may perhaps find the only chance we have to recover the context and truth of our theological pursuits, carried with that theological sincerity that is the gift of the strong, courageous people who dare to doubt theologically imposed sexual and political ideologies. Paraphrasing La Rochefoucault, we may say that in theology, 'weak people cannot be sincere' (La Rochefoucault quoted in Pla 1966: 12, 19). That level of theological sincerity is usually tested in reflecting in theology and sexuality.

I Saw God in the Street Walking with her Friend

My starting point for this reflection was not originally Bataille's novel. It was more related to that theological sincerity on which we are starting to reflect now. Madame Edwarda came to me as part of theology as a second act, one that we can join only after experience. I came somehow across the prostitute-God of Bataille last year in Buenos Aires on a walk during a hot siesta. I saw her in the poor women of the street who were very probably prostitutes, because I recognized that there is that of God in every woman. I also 'saw her' as if embodied in the pervasive sense of the divine which in my own experience seems to occur in the midst of poverty and the miserable conditions of life among women. It was the Christmas season in the streets of my poor neighbourhood. Prostitutes were walking in pairs in what is called a *zona roja* (red area)[4] of Buenos Aires, that is the legal spaces organized not only for prostitution, but for any other expressions of sexuality at the margins such as transvestism or homosexuality. A space for poor lovers on the margins of heterosexuality to walk hand in hand; for poor old men to go shopping using make up and for women to embrace each other publicly. In many Third World countries such as Argentina, the margins of poverty and the margins of sexuality generally match each other, because marginalization is basically a displaced way of knowledge and an illegal epistemological process in itself. So the sexualities at the margins of heterosexuality are a high form of 'displaced love-knowledge'. There are many forms of knowledge which are systematically marginalized in society as happens, for instance, in economic theory (the understanding of relationships and systems of exchange and production) but this also happens in theology. These epistemologies from the margins have different processes of formation than the hegemonic ones and also different dynamics. Moreover, they are the producers of sometimes subversive sexual knowledge too. It is not difficult to identify distinct forms of sexual knowledge behind different economic theories, such as, for instance, the rigid heterosexuality of hierarchical dualistic theories of society and market production, to which

---

4.   Contrary to the usage of some countries of having a main red light area in their cities, separated from residential zones, the *zonas rojas* of Buenos Aires mingle with family houses, schools and amenities because they are located in poor neighbourhoods.

more ambivalent sexual experiences can be contrasted not only in sexual forms of encounter among people but also in forms of organization and economic exchange. That may be a challenge that bisexual epistemology brings to economic science. However, displaced epistemologies are more than a geography of central/margins dialectics. They have particular forms of representation too, although they may be obscured by the dominant commonsense symbolic systems in power. Usually, those systems of representations from a marginalized way of knowing are perceived as indecent. For example, in Western theology promiscuity has a high negative value which is related to its equal negative value in relationships as part of contractual legal systems placing private ownership rights very high. However, this does not need to be the case among poor people who by definition are excluded from society. Promiscuity among poor women is a fact of life and survival in more than the economic sense: it provides them with a network of emotional support and may link people in chains of solidarity too. Theology may find it indecent and under canonical laws, even illegal. However, promiscuity may just represent another form of a judicial system which is not invalid per se, but displaced by centres of power such as church and state. Prostitution for poor women is a way of life, not necessarily associated with sexual exploitation but with the fact that poor women in many cultures have married and found new partners according to need as a substitute for a job: marriage as a means of economic survival, has traditionally been encouraged among young women who are little more than children.

I was walking and reflecting on these issues when I saw a second-hand volume of *Madame Edwarda* standing in a window shop of that poor street in my neighbourhood. The shop had the promiscuous atmosphere of poverty. Books were piled up among old magazines, some may have been goods exchanged for other goods: a novel for a kettle; a pair of fancy stockings for a basket of plastic cutlery. As we say in Buenos Aires, that shop was a promiscuous place, a place where you could find a Bible and a gas boiler sitting together on the same shelf (*La Biblia y el calefón*). It is extraordinary how poverty, like women, is always visible and concrete; it even smells of poverty. However, it is frequently rendered invisible by discourses in power. President Menem of my country once said, 'Argentina is not a Third World Country' and by that he meant that we are not poor in spite of the evidence of everyday life. In the same way Systematic Theology has a discourse which says that we only have one kind of legal sexual desire, which also needs to be tightly regulated. Unfortunately for us, a radical theology such as Liberation Theology considers that sex and poverty do not mix well. It may be the same in the case of God: God is visible, almost corporeal in God's presence in the concreteness of history but rendered invisible by theology. If the poverty of the women of that neighbourhood needed to be represented to a Western theological discourse, it would not fit the Orientalist representation of poverty which some readers of Third World Theology are sometimes so anxious to find. Poverty is a bodily matter, and a sexual one. So is God amidst the life of poor women: not an Orientalist representation but the acknowledgment of a God at the margin as a Marginal-God. It seems so obvious to say that poor women are sexual beings, struggling with desires and miserable circumstances at the same time. Women's poverty is not a romantic issue for Western theology in the way that it has sometimes been represented. We are all familiar with images of women as poor mothers and devoted Christian women struggling in solidarity from a base of Christian spiritual values in Basic Ecclesial Communities (BECs). Those communities exist, but they constitute a fragment of the reality of poverty that is the reign of the sordid, the violent and the anxious struggle for life of many women in Latin America. There are other communities which do not have the clear boundaries of sacramental BECs, from where other images of Jesus-God[5] can come powerfully. Not only 'Jesus the worker', or 'Jesus the poor incarnated God' is showing resemblance with a native Latin American person. There are harder and tougher images of Christ to be found in the margins; less domesticated images, which are more subversive too. Besides the BECs we have the communities of the boarding houses and *casas ocupadas* (illegally occupied houses) where we can find the solidarity of the people at the margins *with* the values of the margin too. This is why Madame Edwarda is important as a metaphor for God: She is not only a woman-God at the Margin, but a Marginal Woman-God. It is clear that this representation of God may bring to our theological reflections new intuitions and visions if, as we have said

---

5.   The Basic Ecclesial Communities in Latin America have usually represented God as Jesus. The Jesus spirituality is very important for people in these communities. Jesus is their theological text more than the Bible or even church doctrines. However BECs needs to be seen according to specific political and social periods in which they are inserted, as their relevance or irrelevance is clearly dependent on that.

before, we have renounced some at least of the burden of androcentric assumptions in theological representations. It may be that a dialogue with the margins bring us values that may enter into dialogue with, for instance, Liberation Theology, yet unfortunately theology by its very nature easily tends to establish the centrality of its discourse among the margins. The poor, and especially poor women, become theologically coopted. This is somehow unavoidable. After all, theology will always have the tension of centrality in the hegemonic conceptions of God and people. In its best dialogic mood, theological orthodoxy can find ways to negotiate with women, but it will seldom depart from its own 'centrality' or understanding of its non-negotiable theological premises. God can never be seen as a poor prostitute woman. Or the trinity as a community of heterosexual dissidents. Or Jesus as a poor male prostitute, even if the *crux* of prostitution is precisely, the poverty that highlights the reality of sexual oppression. Theological systems may condescend to the Other but they seldom become the Other. It would be suicidal to the hegemonic pattern of androcentric theology to allow a complete redefinition of the theological representation of God. If the Other redefines God as an Other, then a new epistemology based on a displaced form of knowledge becomes a contender for the central hegemonic conception. This goes beyond changing one image for another: Was not the issue of representing God as a man dying on a cross a question of making of God an Other? Historically this may be correct, and although somehow patriarchally outdated as the idea of a God-man may be, symbolically there was something there similar to the idea of a 'Marginal God'. However, religious symbolism also requires renovation, not only of symbols of God, but of the concept which organizes such symbolic representations. Stagnation is bad for theological representations because our historical consciousness develops at a pace that the symbolic of gods does not necessarily match. Therefore, something to look forward to would be a form of theological suicide (or 'letting go') of hegemonic representations of God in theology. That will be something to wait for in hope and not necessarily in fear and women theologians may be the courageous voices encouraging systematic theological (and hierarchical ecclesiastical) suicides.

The crises of representations of women and God in theology are in mutual dependency with each other because women and God depend on theological representation systems working by repetition and exclusion, or what Irigaray calls Pavlovian and Darwinian models of knowledge

(Irigaray 1993: 37). A Darwinian systematic theological model has been built on the pattern of exclusion of *adversaries*. These adversaries are constituted by conceptual frames and reflections which do not fit in either Orthodoxy or Orthopraxis per se. In theology, 'a woman' is a conceptual frame that does not fit in patriarchal divine understanding because she tends to exceed those created patterns by her own sexual identity. However, this is the pattern of God's transcendence too, in that of God which cannot be completely fixed in history because God God-self is always 'more' or excessive. The excess of women in theology is a fact that makes of lesbian, bisexual women, transgendered or hetero-sexual women alike, a threat to established frontiers in theology. It is important to remember that patriarchy claims to define heterosexuality, but heterosexuality is still something to be discussed; patriarchy cannot define sexual reality; it only represents it ideologically, even for women who love men. There are many desires and needs in the life of hetero-sexual women which do not fit properly into what patriarchal society and theology expect. Heterosexual women know that they are 'closeted' heterosexuals too; that the truth of heterosexual women's life also exceeds current definitions of acceptability. A woman, no matter her sexuality, is always more. A woman has a vocation to be more, to be able always to express something else not yet said: she is the 'but' and the 'and also' of theology. Her historic experience is always in contra-diction with idealistic theology and women, and poor women, have the gift of irrupting into theological discourses saying 'but it is not like that', denouncing fraud and lies, and allowing contradictions to live with each other since life in patriarchal society is a contradictory expe-rience of economic and sexual interests.

Back to the 'Madame Edwarda' Question...

Feminist theologies have fought against evolutionary theories in church and academic discourses. They have fought against the pattern of exclu-sion of adversaries in theology, by introducing new themes, issues and perspectives of reflection but generally speaking there are still difficul-ties in avoiding the Pavlovian repetitive, adaptation models of theology. What are the 're-readings' of the Scriptures that we have been doing for such a long time if in the end, they do not dangerously succeed in 'adapting' masculine world views to feminist ones? Of course, I must concede that there are several degrees of subversion in rereading texts, but if they are going to be really subversive, they need to be made sexually explicit too. To provide an escape from the performative, divine comedy art of masculine theology a non-repetitive model of representation needs to be grossly indecent, that is, out of order according to the accustomed heterosexual agency in theology and requires to become an issue demanding our attention whatever our contexts, cultures, sexual and class positions. This brings us to the Madame Edwarda/God image again. Why can God not be represented as a prostitute? Beyond any rhetorical consideration of the point which I have already partly developed elsewhere (Althaus-Reid 1999), the important thing to consider here is the act of indecent questioning as both provocative of the final collapse of Christian hermeneutics and as the beginning of a new form of representation in theology. We are referring here to the suspicion in theological systems of representation which arises when we posit the 'Madame Edwarda question'. What is it in the life and sufferings of a poor prostitute (female or male) that the current theological representation of God cannot cope with? What is the real nature of the excess and overflowing which sexuality, women and poverty bring to theology? Hermeneutically there are some elements to consider here.

1. The 'closedness' or short-circuit of heterosexual representation systems. Their claustrophobic atmosphere admits a limited range of adaptations more than changes.
2. The consequences of what we can call 'excessive sex' in theological representations.
3. The fact that there are still few hermeneutical clues developed in feminist theology strong enough to destabilize the theological androcentric system as we know it.

My claim is that only by indecent exposure can Systematic Theology be shocked enough to allow us to represent God and ourselves in the betweenness or gaps that masculine symbolic systems have. The gap in Godself, the indecency of incompleteness and the subversive promiscuity of meanings which escape hegemonic orders.

1. The Closedness of Heterosexual Representation Systems
It was Drucilla Cornell who, analysing the crisis of ethical feminism considered the closedness or the limitations of systems of meaning, when depending on an understanding of what is thought to be truly representative of reality (Cornell in Benhabib *et al.* 1995: 76). That which is 'truly representative of reality' is of course, a given, a meta-narrative of patriarchal cosmovisions so closed to our understanding of

God. Cornell's main point of argument, which I find profoundly relevant for our own theological enquiry here, is that the construction of women in symbolic systems works by producing fantasies, a machine of illusionary creations. These fantasies are held together by a common glue-like element: the understanding of what is meant by being a woman as a philosophical negation; being a woman is being a 'no-man'. The differences between sexes as established through gender historical traditions are not built so much by qualities related to unlikeness but by what can be called 'a dispensable meaningful material' coming from male symbolization processes. In Marxist terms, a woman fits in systematic theological representation of God and salvation, redemption, sin, grace and so on, as a user of surpluses of male systems of meaning. This is what does not fit in the 'Colour me beautifully' Systematic Theological enquiry as seen for instance, in the sexualization and genderization of Christian virtues. In any culture and beyond their differences, women are allocated with the virtues that do not define masculinity in that culture. Sadly, we may say that as on earth, so it is in Heaven. Why is it so difficult to make a comprehensible theological system of representation of God-woman, as one who truly represents the confluence of many coordinates of oppression, together with a passion for life manifested in lust and sexual voracity as in Madame Edwarda? This is very curious, since Jesus is the God incarnated Messiah who is supposed to make a virtue of precisely that: poverty; obscure sexual family circumstances surrounding his birth; a Jew in a country under foreign occupation; a misfit from his own religious establishment; a childless man and so forth. If we want to represent God by adding more or even new categories of suffering carried by innocent people (such as AIDS) there is no reason why we should not be looking into the extreme forms of women's suffering too. However, the problem needs to be considered from this perspective of women as fitting into the surpluses of male symbolic religious systems. Since the virtues of humanity are male defined, a God-woman definition will make of God a concept worked on dispensable, superfluous heterosexual meanings. God would then become as expendable as women, in relation to the surplus meanings with which we construct God. The feminization of God cannot be accepted not because Jesus was apparently a man (however we want to define maleness in this case, either biologically or gender-wise), and because the chosen disciples were also, apparently, male. The feminization of the sacred is not accepted because it threatens to destabilize the centrality of God, which depends basically on male-centric systems of meaning. If God is a woman she will be a woman from the margins. It becomes clear then, that for women, the crisis of representation of God is linked to the limitations of epistemological, meaningful fixation of borders of sexual and gender constructions.

This happens, for instance, by the process of continuous allocation of sexual hierarchical paradigms to any sexual or gender representation we make in everyday life. In theology this has been shown in different ways. First, by a denial of sexuality: this is the classical 'evolved' understanding that God has no sex, and we need to move forward sexual representations of God as male, because we need to dispense with anthropomorphic representations of God in general. This argument, of course, invalidates any representation of a God-woman by default but this is not the only problem it presents. Basically, the de-sexualization of God ignores that sexual representations are at the core of any meaningful representation system, be it judicial, political or theological. As we have legal systems regulated according to sexual knowledge, as for instance treating people differently and creating different legal expectations according to an understanding of sex as 'value granting powers', we also have the gospels according to sex. Theological virtues come with genitalia included. Salvation may be presented with a Jesus whose penis is exposed on the cross but not with the open lips of Madame Edwarda, even if both were perhaps raped. Rape is a common form of torture, performed on women and men alike. It is not impossible to consider that Jesus may have been raped or sexually humiliated as a political prisoner before his execution. Even Salvation discriminates according to genitalia and sexual functions, as if salvation for women could also be a case of discarded meaning which is not central for male self-identity in relation to the sacred. Christianity and the Christian conception of God come from people who live in a sexed universe. Some languages such as my own native Spanish sexualize objects and gestures of everyday life to infinite degrees. For me, 'to eat' is masculine (*el comer*) and so are all the verbal infinitive forms, although 'food' (*la comida*) is feminine. In the same way 'to pray' (*el orar*) is masculine but prayer is feminine (*la oración*, related to pray but also to other speech forms) while *el rezo* is masculine (related to more specific worship forms of prayer). Even the concepts of the Theology of Liberation such as *el pobre* (the poor—masculine) produce all the 'right' associations of the option for the poor, but to say *la pobre* (the poor—feminine) simply means 'pity on her' or the equivalent in English 'poor soul'. Although sexuality and gender construction in language do not always match our present reality the fact that for many people, even at subconscious levels, there is not a single object or action in the entire universe which is not sexually represented, sexualizes God. Moreover, our concept of God is made of our sexual experience in the world as mediated by heterosexual epistemologies. In this sense, the discourse of 'God the Mother' is part (and an integral one) of the 'God the Father' one. The God-Mother becomes a 'non-Father' theology; a conception of motherhood made from the fantasy land of patriarchy, but also a de-sexualized project since mothers in Christianity are not represented as sexually voracious women or non-heterosexual female lovers.

2. *Excessive Sex*

I may be a Liberation Theologian used to contradicting the 'Colour me beautiful' design patterns expected in my field, but I cannot help questioning why, after we have been working in a hermeneutical circle of suspicion for almost 30 years, the sexual representation of the universe, God included, has not been taken seriously and subjected to theological suspicion, with the exception of my Latin American women theologian colleagues. The limits of the hermeneutical circle have been fixed by sexual assumptions, and any woman theologian who crosses these boundaries is either ignored or her challenges simply fail to become crucial for every Liberationist's orthopraxis. Feminist theologies remain 'a woman's issue', an almost domestic space which has been created for women to say their own things at the margins of the main theological discourses, and as long they do not present a menace to their current thinking. In a sense, all feminist theologians remain as peripheral as Madame Edwarda is peripheral to God's revelation in our lives. Considering the limitations of male systems of representation and the problems that they posit to feminist ethics, Cornell has made some interesting reflections on this issue of 'periphery' using the framework of psychoanalytical Lacanian analysis. Lacan, a rereader of Freud, has, as Cornell rightly points out, a conflictive position in the scope of feminist theory. Lacanian thought in a nutshell, is that women do not have a fixed place in the masculine system of representation; there is an inherent instability in their position because, as Lacan says, it is speech which gives a place for a person in society and women are not included in language. However, Cornell takes this theory as a positive point of departure and perhaps, we may add, even of creative subversion for women (Cornell 1995: 98). Thus, it is only by fully understanding that women cannot be represented in the masculine universe of theo/logical discourses and the 'dereliction of women' brought upon us by the fact that we do not have any means to represent ourselves divinely in a masculine universe (Irigaray 1988: 111), that we can start considering our second point: that the disbalance of theology as a hermeneutical art (or process of interpretation of God and humankind relationship) is usually produced by an excess of sex. This I call the crucial point of 'indecent exposures', that is, the beginning of a process of destabiliza-tion of theological representations of God and spiritual goods such as salvation by expanding the sexual borders of the properly theologically dressed women, thus becoming indecent theologians.

Indecent Exposures may be related, then, to the identification of that condition of excessiveness existing in being a woman. At least, a woman always exceeds, in one way or another by the mere fact of being a woman, any male representation of humanity (*man*kind) and sacred humanity (*man*kind and God) in any culture, notwithstanding the differ-ences. As a Latin American, I may exceed the *Machista* universe in a different way than a friend from Africa, Asia or Europe but the act of 'exceeding' by merely existing as women is what we always seem to have in common, even if we measure the excess in different ways or consider it in different sets of relationships. In the same way, a woman, by her mere existence, also exceeds God and Christianity. A woman by her mere existence exceeds systematic theologies and destabilizes orthodoxies by the fact that she 'hardly fits' there, and, as we have seen in the outstanding research produced in recent years by women theolo-gians from different continents, language, method and interpretation need to be continuously exceeded in order to create space for women. Women exceed theology and current representations of God as an over-flow of their sexuality, as their own bodies seem to exceed them during the monthly rhythms of the menstrual cycle, changing and expanding. This works out theologically by allowing us to discover in the process that unless there is excess in God too, we women cannot be represented. Would it be possible then to consider that sexual dis-orders in theology may bring us closer to a rediscovery of the true face of God in the present time? Could it be possible to exceed the limitations of hetero-sexual performativity in Jesus, God and the history of Salvation? For that we need to consider our last point, which is related to sexual hermeneutical clues in theology.

3. *Interrupting the 'Divine Comedy' of Theology*

Excess is a category usually related to interruption, more than to continuations. Excess transforms an apparent continuation of 'the same' into something of a different character and what exceeds is in reality more than just an issue of quantity but quality too. Systematic theology seems to have been working historically with premises of sexual limitations in tension and conflict with people's sexual and economic lives and realities. We may label as 'divine comedies' these theological discourses which have constructed their characters as detached from their addressees or the people whose lives may be affected by such theological constructions. Women are excellent examples of this, as the construction of women in theology has traditionally been done in detachment from real women's lives. The only possible interruption is therefore the interruption of the excess of sex in what is a closed circuit orthodox theological pattern. This has been done by theologians such as Elizabeth Stuart in Britain or Mary Hunt and Robert Goss in the US, for instance, but this is only a beginning. The challenges of excessive sex are to be seen at two levels: methodological and thematical. Methodologically, the queering, indecent questioning of theology is just at the beginning. What are the consequences of the discourse of the constant embrace of the feminine lips as described by Irigaray in our conception of the Trinity? Can we conceive of a 'Trinity' beyond numerology, and in a plurality self-contained and yet, expectant for the presence of someone else? This model may provide us with a better God-in-community pattern than trying to include the ubiquitous female presence to fit between the Father and the Son, while complicating the countdown of systematic theologians who are afraid of replacing a Trinitarian with a Quaternian model. The two lips are one, yet they are two. A unit and an expectancy. A promise and a self-fulfilment: Was this what the seeker saw in Madame Edwarda when she asked him to look, in order to recognize her as God? By showing some form of obedience to theological sexual principles or virtues, it will be impossible to disorganize the traditional representation of God in theology, which affects us so much in as far its representation is taken from our own sexual identity constructions and reprojected into the sacred.

By using a sexual theological methodology that only allows theology to come as a second act, reality becomes the disorganizing principle for idealistic models so ingrained in our reflections. Madame Edwarda as Woman-God carries the excess of many crosses: sexual abuse and poverty; misery and destitution; but also fierce independence and resolution of self-satisfaction. She is a God who knows and honours her desires, and irrupts scandalously into the life and expectations of others. A God who is a parable of sexuality and poverty, who can show us how one cannot rethink the resolution of the foreign debt if women's oppression continues to be subsumed into general oppression, if modes of thinking about human relations and economics are not finally put together. It was Marx who in his 'Critique of the Gotha Programme' said that although the bourgeois discourse speaks of equality for all, concepts such as 'all members of society and equal rights' were just 'mere phrases' (Marx in Fernbach 1974: 344). In theology, as we know, it is much the same and the current representations of God expose the ideological biases of the several combinations of systems of sexual, racial and class oppression. However, and in the same text, Marx also said that equality in the distribution of labour and wealth presupposes an equal distribution of the instruments of labour. What does it mean to have the tools of labour distributed amongst the workers on a cooperative basis, in the context of theological Orthopraxis? If we like to think about Orthopraxis as a piece of collective work, a promiscuous mixture of life, Scriptures and traditions, the instruments of work that need to be shared are our life experiences as befitting the theological discourse of Systematic Theology.

The 'tools of action and reflection' which need to be claimed as ours are the methods of doing sexual political theology as a second act, giving priority to the most common and scandalous issues of women's lives. A theology from mistresses and of battered lovers; a theology of the family written by lesbians, and a Christology of prostitution are all reflections which are needed if we want to go beyond the point of 'theological illustrations'. They are needed to rethink the Trinity, the Sacraments or the whole concepts of Redemption and Salvation, because these are all relational concepts and require the presence of a cooperative effort, of equal distribution or sharing of our stories and reflections, and of the presence of God in them. Of course, Madame Edwarda need not be our exclusive model of representation of God, but we need to learn to recognize an image of God nearer to our collectively scandalous, indecent lives trying to survive patriarchal society and religion, while finding, (paraphrasing Cornell) God in the 'betweenness' of our lives and in our own margins which are sexual and economic margins of contradiction, and love and some hope. What is required is an Indecent Exposure of God, which may help us to overcome the internalized oppression of Androcentric Theology while encouraging us to develop solidarity at the margins of the margins of constructed sexuality, theology and economy.

Bibliography

Althaus-Reid, Marcella
  1999   'On Wearing Skirts Without Underwear: "Indecent Theology Challenging the Liberation Theology of the *Pueblo*". Poor Women Contesting Christ', *Feminist Theology* 20: 39-51.
Bataille, Georges
  1981   *Madame Edwarda* (Introduction and translation by Salvador Elizondo; Mexico: Lucas).
Cornell, Drucilla
  1995   'What is Ethical Feminism?', in S. Benhabib *et al.*, *Feminist Contentions: A Philosophical Exchange* (London: Routledge).
Fernbach, David (ed.)
  1981   *The First International and After: Political Writings*, III (Harmondsworth: Penguin Books).
Irigaray, Luce
  1993   *Je, tu, nous. Toward a Culture of Difference* (London: Routledge).
Pla, Josep
  1966   *Obra Completa* (Barcelona: Edicions Destino).
Tillich, Paul
  1948   *The Protestant Era* (London: James Nisbet).

Safe Sex: A Feminist Theological Reflection

So how do women have safe sex? It is no longer a matter of condoms, coils and morning after pills. The emphasis on women's control over their own bodies has shifted under the weight of feminist analysis to that of embodied counter culturalism, fucking with gender, erotic celibacy and virgin heterosexuality among other things.[1] All these approaches turn the received wisdom on its head and allow women more space in which to flourish. The embodied voices of women are diverse and do not fit one neat pattern that can be called feminist body politics. The issue of sado-masochism, which has not received the space it deserves in this volume, is just one case in point. While many women claim that the violence involved is against all feminist principles others declare that it is the highest form of mutuality, empowerment and trust. Who is right? Ultimately everyone, since I suspect that both claims are true depending on the people and the circumstances. For me, the subject illustrates the degree to which we cannot take things for granted any more, actions cannot be carried out as though they have innate/divine meaning that will become apparent in the acting. We shape our reality and our embodiment is a central element in that construction. How we act, in each moment, is charged with divine/political meaning and it is the consciousness of that which shapes reality.

There are no doubt voices raised which claim that there is nothing wrong with the way that sexuality is practised and understood in the West. Transgressive sexuality, for these people, is something that sits on the edges of sexual reality carried out by freaks and perverts. This volume is claiming that what is truly obscene and abusive is sex as experienced under patriarchy, because real women are lost in the process and constructed according to a set of values that are not their own.

---

1. These terms refer to a way of practising sexuality that is beyond the boundaries of the patriarchal script.

We live in a world that has numbed us to the obscenity of the surgeon's knife shaping women to fit the accepted norm, yet we cry out about genital mutilation in other countries. Sexism and racism are closely linked. We do not see the pressure to 'be a woman' that frightens many into anorexia and bulimia but instead point to unstable personalities. In a country where 90% of women are on diets (*The Times*, 14 April 2000) we surely have to question the easy option of blaming individuals. As with many things in patriarchy, individual moral weakness is used to hide the devastating reality which is that the system hurts, at times it kills. We ignore the call for equal rights for gay and lesbian people; seeing it as pushing the boundaries just too far, the hetero-patriarchal narrative would sacrifice lives[2] rather than offer dignity of living. The disabled and the mentally ill, if thought of in the light of sexuality, are objects of ridicule, disgust and abuse, while the elderly are simply written off. Where are the voices of the prostitutes and battered wives that Marcella Althaus-Reid longs to hear? Silenced and marginalized, an embarrassment to polite society. There is something deeply wrong with the way we understand sex in our society; too many people are left out of the equation and those who are included are often too moulded. Once we see this we, with Catherine MacKinnon have to declare that 'a good fuck is no excuse for getting fucked'.[3] In other words, however satisfying we may find our own individual sexual encounters they should not be understood in isolation, they make up part of a whole and one that at present is deeply dysfunctional. We all need to be part of the questioning and challenging or once again patriarchy can sideline the real issues through segregating the questioners, they become man haters, outlaw dykes, perverts, anything that can be silenced and ignored. The truth, if heard, is that we are passionate women who wish our capacity for body knowing to be taken seriously in religious and political reflections.

Can we then afford the luxury of safe sex which in our world would be whatever plays by male rules? As we have seen in certain articles in this book sex, even by those rules, is not always safe. We just have to remember the young women of the WRAP study or the prostitute in the Brock book. Ultimately the safest way is the one that at the moment

2.   The number of teenage suicides due to sexual orientation and the blindness of society and religion is on the increase.

3.   Catherine MacKinnon quoted in Gabriele Griffin, *Stirring It: Challenges For Feminists* (London: Taylor and Francis, 1994), p. 178.

may seem the most perilous, that towards self determination and sexual self esteem. Before sex can become the discourse we are all told it is we have to interrupt the male monologue that it really is in the lives of so many women. Indeed, we have to awaken to the fact that this is what it is. So persuasive is the diatribe that many women are numbed to their own body knowing. Lesbians who are smiling with glee at the idea of being free of this patriarchal vice should think again. Where have the sexual models come from? How is power played out in relationships that seem so different yet have still been formed in a patriarchal society? Sheila Jeffreys bemoans the move in lesbian life towards modelling relationships on those of gay men.[4] Her argument has economics as much as sexual politics at its heart. The new wealth found among lesbians has made them targets for the peddlers of consumer sex and the pattern for this is patriarchy at its most rampant. The results are, in her eyes, devastating: women buying women for sex, S/M, racist, violent pornography and power games in personal relationships. She feels there is nothing to be smug about but much to be vigilant over. She claims there is a wholesale rejection of feminism by younger lesbians who regard it as a kill-joy philosophy. Sex is becoming very unsafe in this burgeoning lesbian environment.

The very term 'safe sex' points me to seeing it as transgressive sex. If it is to be really safe for women it has to explode the embodied myths of femininity and masculinity upon which so much inequality rests. This is not to suggest that neutral bodies should or could engage in the dance of desire but rather that people become aware of the constructed way in which they relate. Once this awareness is a reality, then acts of subversion can be consciously embodied. Pushing the edges of who we think we are through passionate engagement with another is one way to expand the liberative space we share. A space that in time will go beyond the boundaries of our own private pleasure and change the way we are in the world. Our sex acts become public as transgressive/redemptive moments for others as well as ourselves.

Religion, sex and culture together make the strong bonds of patriarchy that actually inhibit themselves and us. They are so tightly wound that it seems that unravelling one will affect them all. We are small compared to these edifices but the power of our embodied selves should

4.   Sheila Jeffreys, *The Lesbian Heresy: A Feminist Perspective on the Lesbian Sexual Revolution* (London: Women's Press, 1994).

not be underestimated. We can begin unravelling by becoming present to ourselves, alive to our pasions and transgressive in our actions.

Safe sex involves rooting deep in our passion and finding imaginative and challenging ways of expression. It is holding on to our passion in the face of societal pressure to do otherwise, it is believing in the not yet and embodying it through action in the now. Safe sex is radical incarnation in that it embodies all our eschatological hopes in and between us in acts of vulnerability and passion. It is also redemptive as it ushers in a revolution that turns the existing order on its head.

The Afterglow

So how was it for you? Did the earth move and have the edges of your preconceived mindsets shifted? Are you exploding the patriarchal construction that holds your body tight, by an ecstatic and gloriously empowered embodied release? Can you feel the stirrings of the endless capacity for erotic revolution that lies in a woman's body? Or are you still getting fucked by the hetero-patriarchal meta-narrative of our time...

INDEX OF AUTHORS